SHOTSHELLS AND BALLISTICS

SHOTSHELLS AND BALLISTICS

*Ballistic Data Out to 70 Yards for Shotshells from .410-bore, 28-, 20-, 16-, 12-,
and 10-Gauge for over 1,700 Different Loads and 23 Manufacturers*

by

John Taylor

SAFARI PRESS INC

The trademark Safari Press ® is registered with the U.S. Patent and Trademark Office and in other countries.

Taylor, J.

First Edition

Safari Press Inc.

2003, Long Beach, California

ISBN 1-57157-262-7

Library of Congress Catalog Card Number: 2002110548

10 9 8 7 6 5 4 3 2

Readers wishing to receive the Safari Press catalog, featuring many fine books on big-game hunting, wingshooting, and sporting firearms, should write to Safari Press Inc., P.O. Box 3095, Long Beach, CA 90803, USA. Tel: (714) 894-9080 or visit our Web site at www.safaripress.com.

TABLE OF CONTENTS

See the next page for a detailed table of contents for the ballistics tables.

FOREWORD

He is a big man, and that made the already small 28-gauge pump shotgun look even toy-like in his hands. But it didn't perform like a toy, as John smoked target after target on the challenging sporting clays course. He cycled the slide action repeater so smoothly and quickly, it could have been a semi-automatic. John handled this course with the skill and dexterity of a man who knew his business and loved it.

John Taylor didn't develop this kind of skill by accident. He has a penchant for excellence in all his endeavors. Commitment, hard work, and the quest for knowledge are all qualities I've seen in the years I've known him. John has excelled in music (both in and out of the military service), competition duck calling, shotgunning, hunting, photography, and especially writing.

His music career as a tuba player is extensive. After earning his degree in Music Education from the University of Wisconsin-Plattsville, he studied with some of the finest teachers at the Chicago Symphony Orchestra, The New York Philharmonic, and the Baltimore Symphony. He also performed in many other bands, symphonies, and orchestras, including the North Carolina Symphony, Buffalo Philharmonic, CBC's Quebec Orchestra, and the United States Army Band. John even wrote a book about music, *Song and Wing*, on the famous music teacher, Arnold Jacobs. John's successes are not about luck.

This music background surely helped John succeed in his duck calling competitions. John was the Mason-Dixon Champion Caller from 1976-1978 and competed in the World Duck Calling Championship in Stuttgart, Arkansas, during that same period of time. He was called on frequently to judge national duck and goose calling championships over the years.

John has hunted all over the United States, Canada, Europe, and Africa, pursuing his love of shotgun sports in the quest for game birds and waterfowl of all types. His pursuits have enabled him to evaluate shotshell performance and to write about hunting and shotgunning in nearly every publication available for shotgun hunting and shooting sports; including *Outdoor Life, Sports Afield, Guns and Ammo, Wildfowl, Shooting Sportsman, Double Gun Journal, Sporting Clays, Gun Digest,* and the *American Shotgunner*. He now regularly contributes to *American Rifleman* and *American Hunter*. His other book *Shotgun Encyclopedia* was published by Safari Press in 2001 and is a "must have" reference guide for any avid shotgunner for terminology and shotgun facts.

Of his many accomplishments, shotgunning is still John's real love, and it shows in his projects, his writing, and in his vocation. He has given us many, many articles on our favorite sport and even the *Shotgun Encyclopedia*. Now, most importantly, he gives us a real shotgunners' source book to find how your favorite load performs, or to find a shotshell to meet your specific needs. Load specifications, pellet time of flight, and remaining energy out to 70 yards are parameters you seldom have a chance to see. This book has most of the hard-to-find data (usually available only to industry professionals) in one place, to get us started selecting the right shotshell loads for the job at hand.

Every serious shotgunner can benefit from the valuable information in this latest book, *Shotshells and Ballistics*.

Your friend and compadre in shotgunning,
Mike Jordan
Winchester Ammunition Division,
Olin Industries

FOREWORD

INTRODUCTION

Today the shotgunner is confronted with a seemingly ever-expanding menu of shotshells. Certainly, the major brands—Federal, Remington, and Winchester—are widely distributed and are the norm by which all others are measured. Nowhere in the world are shotshells so well made and so reliable—in terms of both function and downrange ballistics—as they are in the United States. But what happens when the corner gun shop or gun club gets a shipment of shells from a previously unknown maker? Where were these shells made? What are they intended for—game or clays? The questions are numerous, and I hope this book will serve as a handy reference when those uncertainties arise, or when you just want to see what a favorite load will do.

I have assembled the list of manufacturers from discussions I have had with the companies themselves and from the materials—catalogs and monographs—that I have collected at several of the annual SHOT (Shooting, Hunting, and Outdoor Trade) shows. I chose this venue in particular because virtually everyone who makes any hunting or shooting product displays his wares to the trade and media at this show. Attendance is restricted to dealers, wholesalers, and bona fide media personnel. However, the annual National Rifle Association (NRA) convention is open to the association's multimillion membership and, while not as large, attracts many of the same manufacturers, who, like at the SHOT Show, display their products. All of the data in this book, therefore, have been taken from advertised material collected at these various shows. How accurate might these data be? Though it is true that velocity data may be subject to variation, years of testing various loads over my own chronograph have shown me that advertised velocities are quite accurate, given the same parameters of barrel length, diameter, and ambient temperature.

As you read further, you will find chapters on all the facets of shotgunning that pertain to downrange shotshell performance. Whatever the question you might have about patterning, chokes, shot sizes, and all the other ephemera that make shotgunning so fascinating, a check of the appropriate chapter should give you answers or provide directions for your own tests. All too often, shotgunners select a box of shells based on price, tradition, or some other factor not fully supported by the science of shotshells. Armed with deepened knowledge and some tests, the hunter or clay-target aficionado will be able to make a far more informed selection.

Displayed are essential downrange ballistics as generated by E. D. Lowry's excellent shotshell computer program. The former chief ballistician at Winchester-Western, Lowry is one of the great figures in ammunition development. He was there when steel shot became an issue and did some of the most important studies in determining the lethality of steel. But his contributions are not limited to nontoxic ammunition; they also include the development of the Winchester Super-X Double-XX Magnum that showed the importance of buffering lead shot, as well as other developments too numerous to mention. The charts show what pellets do downrange: how fast they fly, how fast they slow, and how hard they hit. It is not possible to provide pattern data for each load, simply because each shotgun barrel is unique unto itself and each load responds differently when shot through each individual barrel-choke combination. When you are confronted by a new shotshell or want to check the performance of an old favorite load, look it up in the performance section and find the table that displays your load's specifications. It's that simple.

Some of the ammunition listed herein is available only in limited areas. Foreign ammo manufacturers often seek distributors in the United States, but often with very limited results. Some shotshells are local to certain geographic areas. For example, shells loaded in Mexico show up frequently along the U.S.-Mexican border, where it is cheaper to import and deliver them than it is some domestic brands, which are manufactured in the Midwest and mid-South. Other companies, such as Estate Cartridge and Polywad, load their own brands but also offer custom loading for other manufacturers. If a sufficiently large order is placed, outfits like Estate and Polywad will produce rounds bearing the customer's logo imprinted on the hull.

One aspect of firearm ownership that can't ever be overlooked is safety. While there is no section in this book dealing with this important factor, each of the shotshell performance charts includes the distance or range at which pellets from a load with that size and type of shot at the listed velocity will pierce human flesh. Be aware that this isn't a definitive range, because damage can occur well beyond that range, especially to unprotected eyes. There is no safe downrange distance, but the data supplied here will show just how far pellets can cause damage. As far as game regulations go, hunting and shooting are often permitted as close as 100 yards to an inhabited structure, and a glance at these charts will indicate that a misdirected shot at that range could injure someone or cause property damage, if only broken windows. So, as much as we enjoy shooting, we still must be aware of potential safety hazards.

Relative recoil is another issue that the data seek to demonstrate. Many currently manufactured shotguns are very light. For example, the popular 12-gauge Remington 870 pump is in the 7¼-pound range. Other pump-action shotguns, like the popular Mossberg 835 UltiMag, are similarly lightweight. In terms of carrying a shotgun all day in the field, these lightweights are a blessing. However, both of the shotguns cited here are chambered for the very potent 3½-inch magnum. Fire one of those heavy loads in one of these light guns, and injury is possible. Turkey hunters shooting one of these light shotguns with their back and shoulder against a tree have suffered broken collarbones or at least deep bruising. In an effort to provide some comparison of the recoil of each load, I show the relative recoil in both velocity (how fast the gun moves to the rear) and force (how hard the gun hits the shoulder). For the sake of comparison, a common or average weight of eight pounds is used for the gun; the sole exception is the 10-gauge, for which a ten-pound shotgun is used as the standard.

In the end, I feel confident that this book will provide insight into how shotshells work, how they perform, what you, the consumer, can expect, where brands unknown to you are made, and how they stack up against a more familiar load.

How to Use This Book

Whenever we fire a shotshell, lots of interconnected phenomena occur. The manner in which shotshells are assembled and the quality of the components used govern how well a selected load performs. At one time, hunters and, to a lesser extent, clay-target shooters paid little attention to downrange ballistics. They bought the same brand and load every time and relied on known results. At the turn of the nineteenth century, even the major ammunition companies would assemble custom loads, some in custom cases, if you ordered sufficient quantities. In late 1911, the Wigeon Duck Club in central California special-ordered ten DHE-grade Parker doubles in three-inch 20-gauge magnum. A photo in Larry L. Baer's *The Parker Gun* (pp. 37-38) shows several Peters three-inch shells along with one of the Wigeon Club's shotguns. By the time World War II had ended, shotshells were made by Winchester-Western, Remington-UMC, Peters, and Federal Cartridge Company. Soon Remington acquired Peters, and the "big three" of ammunition manufacturing were established. Overseas, much the same contraction occurred as a result of the war. Though many British companies still offered cartridges under their proprietary names, many companies dropped their loading rooms and farmed out ammunition production to companies such as Eley, Gamebore, and others.

In Europe the war effectively destroyed many ammunition manufacturers, and as a consequence, many shotshells today are loaded in the Scandinavian countries—Denmark, Norway, and Sweden—which suffered far less wartime devastation. Today, shotshell loading is also carried on in Germany, Italy, France, and Spain.

Canada's only brand was CIL (Canadian Industries Limited). Like Remington in the United States, owned for decades by DuPont, CIL was owned by a chemical company that made paint and other products. CIL always made good, reliable ammunition and was perhaps best known for the very long high-brass heads on its heavy and magnum loads. In the company's last years, CIL placed its target loads in plastic hulls. By virtue of the fact that a skeet-shooting legend, Major B. C. "Barney" Hartman, Royal Canadian Air Force, Retired, was its customer-relations man and professional shooter, CIL's target loads were ranked among the very best. CIL ammunition disappeared in the early 1980s, when the parent company deemed it unprofitable and closed the factory. Today Canada is represented by Kent Cartridge Canada, although its loading is done in England and the United States.

Included in this book are ammunition companies whose products may or may not be encountered on the shelves of your local gun shop. Some companies are icons, others virtually unknown. Within the past few years, more and more foreign-made ammunition has reached these shores, much of it at bargain prices. If what you seek is not represented in these pages, check out the velocity and look for something comparable, and you'll have a good idea of what that ammunition can do. Along with this influx of foreign-produced ammunition have come increased numbers of shotshells heretofore not readily available, such as 2-inch and 2½-inch 12- and 16-gauge shells, and 24-, 32- and 36-gauge shells loaded by Fiocchi and Clever. Fiocchi also loads 9mm Flobert for 9mm-chambered "garden guns." Although the vast majority of shotgunners don't give these unique shells a thought, increasing numbers of shooters have those guns and seek ammunition for them.

When you open this book, you will find a great deal of material, including many charts and other data. If you have a particular manufacturer's load in hand, chances are that it will be found here. However, some may not be. Just as early shotgunners relied on their gun shop to recommend ammunition, that philosophy still prevails today in England and Europe, and with good reason. Local gun shop proprietors know the local conditions and are in a position to authoritatively recommend a particular load for whatever game is being pursued. Consequently, many non-U.S. ammunition manufacturers do not supply velocity data for their loads and are reluctant to release it to the public. In their defense, it is only in the past few years that American ammunition manufacturers have begun printing velocities on their products' boxes and in their catalogs.

In some instances I've taken the liberty to extrapolate velocities using known information such as dram equivalents that produce fairly specific velocities with specific loads. This was done in a judicious manner so as to avoid misleading the reader. It should be known that some velocities were rounded to the nearest whole velocity—i.e., 1,405 fps appears as 1,400 fps, in deference to the computer program used to compute the downrange pellet velocities and energy. Neither the shooter nor the game will know the difference. It should be noted that downrange pellet velocities and energy are the *average* of the load based on a perfectly round pellet at the exact velocity. Even with the most carefully loaded ammunition, shotshells seldom produce the exact velocities advertised—the same occurs with rifle ammunition—so the data represented are based on ideal ammunition under ideal conditions.

Slugs presented a unique challenge since each company uses different range delineations for its own ammunition. Attempting to tailor their data to a uniform set of ranges proved to be less than genuine. While a shotshell lends itself to being interpreted through a computer program that yields average values, as its tables show, slugs travel in precise trajectories and therefore do not lend themselves to being put into general tables. The slug tables represent the data supplied by the manufacturers regarding slug performance. However, when data were not available or forthcoming from a manufacturer, it was possible to determine ballistic coefficients with a computer program. By linking these derived ballistic coefficients with slug diameter and weight, it was possible to generate downrange velocity, energy, and trajectory tables for ammunition for which data were not available from the maker.

As you peruse these tables, be they on fine shot, buckshot, or slug, use them to influence your shooting. Look at downrange pellet energy—that's what does the job. Too little energy results in crippling, and crippling is not good sportsmanship. Conversely, using a too-powerful load will result in excessive recoil and, within a few shots, diminished marksmanship and, ultimately, flinching. Flinching is a condition in which part of the brain says, "Shoot," while another part says, "Don't shoot; it hurts." Competitive shooters develop flinching, and it's obvious when they do. When a hunter flinches, it's not as obvious, except that he or she misses. So, look over the tables and determine what load best fits your situation. Helping the reader find a load that's just right for the conditions and application could be the strongest benefit of this book, and that's my hope.

SHOTGUN GAUGES:
A HISTORICAL PERSPECTIVE

Historically, shotgun gauges were determined not by specific measurement but by the number of equal-sized balls made from one pound of lead that would pass through the bore. The simplest way to visualize this measurement is to view the 16-gauge's bore as being of a size through which sixteen one-ounce lead balls would pass. The bore diameters of the other gauges were similarly determined, and it was essentially up to individual gunmakers to make their shotguns adhere to this rule. In the era of muzzleloading shotguns, bore standardization was not critical. Certainly, wads had to be cut to tightly seal the bore, and many muzzleloaders came with individual cutters so their owners could form wads of the proper diameter. However, with the advent of the breechloading shotgun, standardization of bore diameters became a necessity. Once shooters could purchase cartridges from many sources, it was absolutely necessary that some standard be set, and bore diameters became established as fractions of an inch.

Although American gunmakers were firmly established, the formalization of shotgun gauges originated with the British gun industry. In that nation, and for that matter throughout Europe, all firearms must be submitted to "proof" through the officially designated proof house. In this country, proofing of shotguns is left to the individual manufacturers. We'll look at proofing more closely when we discuss pressures. The government proof houses in London and Birmingham, England, do not deal solely with how much pressure a shotgun can withstand. In fact, proof houses are tasked with examining every aspect governing the performance of firearms, including the diameter of the bore. Under the 1925 Rules of Proof, shotgun barrels were stamped with what Major Sir Charles Burrard, in his text *The Modern Shotgun,* called "vulgar fractions." Using this method, a shotgun whose barrel measured .729 inch was proofed as a 12-bore. If it was larger than .729, but less than .740 inch, it was proofed as a $\frac{12}{1}$; if larger than .740, an 11-bore. On the narrow side, a bore that measured .719 was marked as a $\frac{13}{1}$ and a .710 was a 13-bore. These measurements are determined by measuring the bore exactly nine inches from the breech. The British proof houses insert a .729-inch plug into the bore, and if it fits snugly nine inches from the breech, the gun is determined to be a 12-gauge. A .740-inch plug is used for $\frac{12}{1}$, etc.

Today we accept the 10-, 12-, 16-, 20- and 28-gauges as normal. The .410 is actually a bore diameter, not a gauge. If it were, it would be about a 67-gauge. However, it wasn't always so. In England punt guns of 2-gauge and larger are still in use. Shoulder guns include the 4-, 6- and 8-gauge, and, on the smaller end of the spectrum, 24-, 32-, 36-gauges and 9mm. Certainly there are others, but these were the main variants. In Europe, some of these shells are still loaded for commercial sale.

The following are the nominal bore diameters, in inches, of the most common gauges. It should be noted that variations are allowed, as cited above in the proofing of bores. However, under today's tightly controlled manufacturing processes, tolerances are very close and variances deviate very slightly from these nominal dimensions.

10	.775
12	.729
16	.662
20	.615
24	.579
28	.550
32	.526
36	.506

Often one of these odd gauges will be encountered at a gun show or estate sale. They can be fun to shoot,

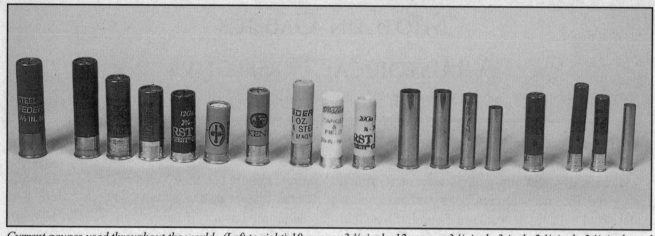

Current gauges used throughout the world. (Left to right) 10-gauge: 3 ½-inch; 12-gauge: 3 ½-inch, 3-inch, 2 ¾-inch, 2 ½-inch, and 2-inch; 16-gauge: 2 ¾-inch; 20-gauge: 3-inch, 2 ¾-inch, 2 ½-inch; 24-gauge; 32-gauge; 36-gauge: 2 ½-inch and 2-inch; 28-gauge; 2 ¾-inch; .410-bore: 3-inch and 2 ½-inch; 9.1mm Flobert. With the exception of the 24-, 32-, 36-gauges, and 9.1mm Flobert, these cartridges are found and used throughout the world. However, the most commonly found cartridges are the 12-, 16-, and 20-gauge. Although the 16-gauge has lost ground in the United States, it r emains popular in Europe. The 3 ½-inch 10- and 12-gauge loads (and to some extent the 3-inch 12-gauge load) are indigenous to the United States and are often difficult to find abroad.

and Ballistic Products, Inc. offers handloading components for these gauges. Old Western Scrounger sells brass and paper hulls and sometimes loaded ammunition for these little-known gauges.

Although gauges are a rather straightforward matter, the waters can become murky when chamber length enters the equation, and that topic is worth its own chapter.

THE SPORTING ARMS AND AMMUNITION MANUFACTURERS' INSTITUTE (SAAMI)

In each nation that manufactures sporting arms and ammunition, there exists some form of governing body for that industry. In England and Europe the responsibility for safe arms and ammunition rests with the proof houses that are established by law. In the United States, no such laws exist. To ensure uniformity of manufacture and the safety of the shooting public, in 1926 the individual arms makers and importers established the Sporting Arms and Ammunition Manufacturers' Institute, best known as SAAMI. Under this body's auspices, uniform chamber and bore diameters, and equally uniform standards for acceptably safe pressures of ammunition to be used in these arms, were established. In addition, proof ammunition and proof pressures are dictated by SAAMI to ensure that all domestically produced firearms are safe under normal use with proper ammunition. SAAMI's standards are applied to domestically manufactured arms and recognize arms and ammunition manufactured to the proof standards of other nations and imported for sale in this country.

SAAMI's presence is not as prominent as the proof houses in Britain, where anyone selling a firearm must ensure that it is "in proof" prior to sale and submit it for proof if it is not. Nonetheless, SAAMI's standards are applied to the entire American arms and ammunition industry to ensure that newly manufactured firearms are safe to use, and that commercial ammunition purchased by the shooting public meets standards not only for safety but also for performance.

Cartridge and Chamber Dimensions

The Sporting Arms and Ammunition Manufacturers' Institute, in accord with similar bodies in other nations, has established standard dimensions for cartridges, chambers, and bores. In so doing, it has ensured that a box of shotshells bought at the corner gun shop, Wal-Mart, Purdey in London, or an outpost in Canada, Alaska, or Addis Ababa will perform in the chamber for which they were intended. Chambers differ in length, and that topic will be covered elsewhere. Here we'll provide the standard chamber and cartridge dimensions.

An accurate bore micrometer like this one from 100-Straight and precision chamber gauges like these from Galazan are necessary for the proper evaluation of shotgun barrels. The cylindrical Galazan choke gauge uses average choke dimensions and can be used to roughly check chokes. However, since the amount of choke is based on the cylindrical bore of a particular shotgun barrel, it is necessary to measure the bore and choke with a bore micrometer, leaving this type of gauge for rough evaluation.

CARTRIDGE & CHAMBER
10 GAUGE 3 1/2"

CARTRIDGE
UNLESS OTHERWISE NOTED
LENGTH TOL -.250(6.35)

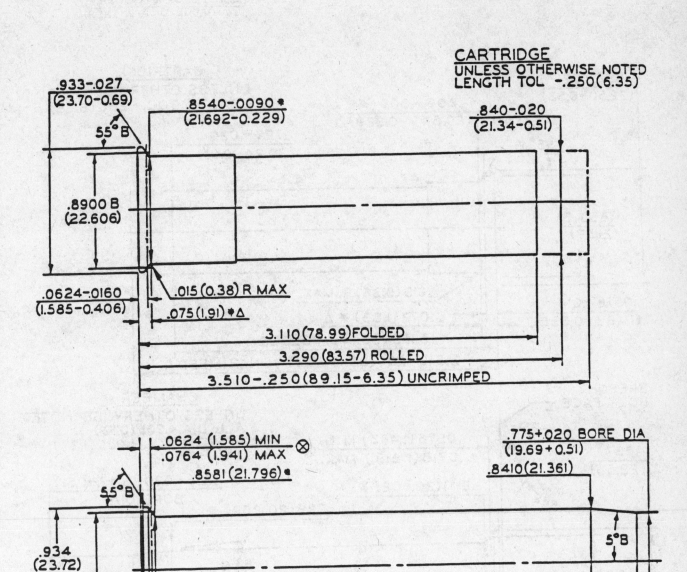

.933-.027
(23.70-0.69)

55°B

.8540-.0090 *
(21.692-0.229)

.840-.020
(21.34-0.51)

.8900 B
(22.606)

.0624-.0160
(1.585-0.406)

.015 (0.38) R MAX

.075 (1.91) *Δ

3.110 (78.99) FOLDED

3.290 (83.57) ROLLED

3.510-.250 (89.15-6.35) UNCRIMPED

.0624 (1.585) MIN ⊗
.0764 (1.941) MAX ⊗
.8581 (21.796) *

.775+.020 BORE DIA
(19.69+0.51)

.8410 (21.361)

55°B

5°B

.934
(23.72)

.8900 B ⊗
(22.606)

.0736 (1.869) *Δ

.020+.005 (0.51+0.13) R

3.500 (88.90)

3.8772 (98.481) Δ

BREECH
BOLT FACE

« 5

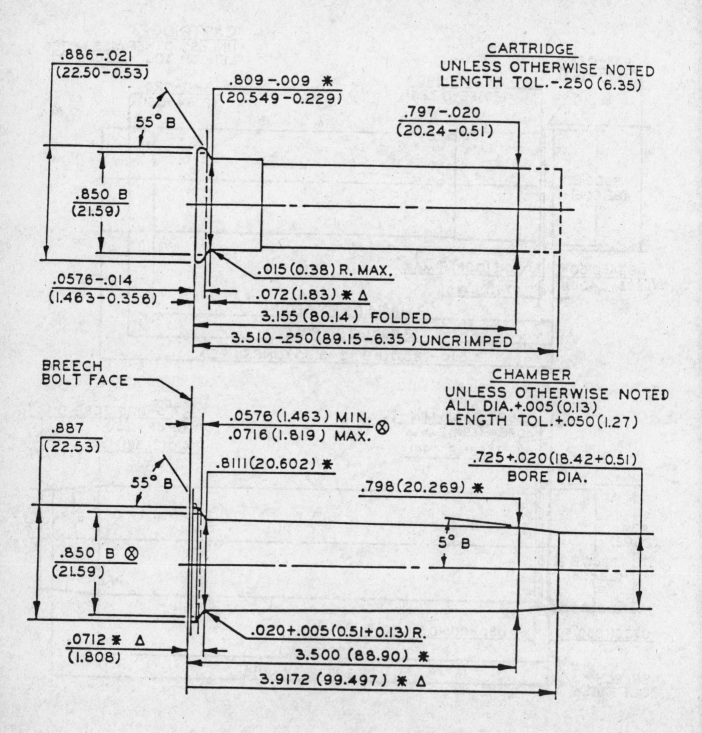

CARTRIDGE & CHAMBER
12 GAUGE 3 1/2 INCH

CARTRIDGE
UNLESS OTHERWISE NOTED
LENGTH TOL. -.250 (6.35)

.886 -.021
(22.50 - 0.53)

.809 -.009 ✳
(20.549 - 0.229)

.797 -.020
(20.24 - 0.51)

55° B

.850 B
(21.59)

.0576 -.014
(1.463 - 0.356)

.015 (0.38) R. MAX.

.072 (1.83) ✳ Δ

3.155 (80.14) FOLDED

3.510 -.250 (89.15 - 6.35) UNCRIMPED

BREECH
BOLT FACE

CHAMBER
UNLESS OTHERWISE NOTED
ALL DIA. +.005 (0.13)
LENGTH TOL. +.050 (1.27)

.887
(22.53)

.0576 (1.463) MIN. ⊗
.0716 (1.819) MAX.

.8111 (20.602) ✳

.725 +.020 (18.42 +0.51)
BORE DIA.

55° B

.798 (20.269) ✳

5° B

.850 B ⊗
(21.59)

.020 +.005 (0.51 +0.13) R.

.0712 ✳ Δ
(1.808)

3.500 (88.90) ✳

3.9172 (99.497) ✳ Δ

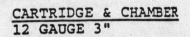

CARTRIDGE & CHAMBER
12 GAUGE 3"

CARTRIDGE
UNLESS OTHERWISE NOTED
LENGTH TOL −.250 (6.35)

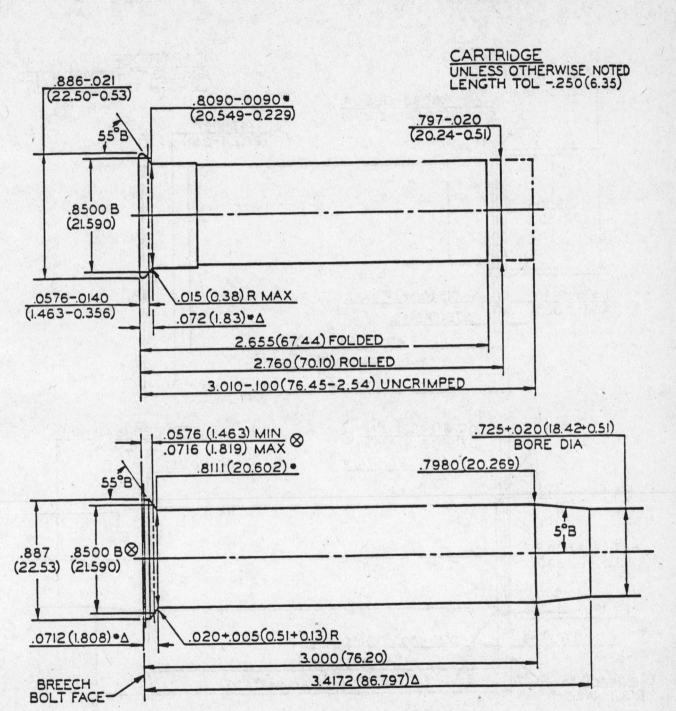

.886−.021
(22.50−0.53)

55°B

.8090−.0090 ⊛
(20.549−0.229)

.797−.020
(20.24−0.51)

.8500 B
(21.590)

.0576−.0140
(1.463−0.356)

.015 (0.38) R MAX

.072 (1.83) ⊛△

2.655 (67.44) FOLDED

2.760 (70.10) ROLLED

3.010−.100 (76.45−2.54) UNCRIMPED

.0576 (1.463) MIN ⊗
.0716 (1.819) MAX ⊗

.8111 (20.602) ⊛

.725+.020 (18.42+0.51)
BORE DIA

.7980 (20.269)

55°B

5°B

.887
(22.53)

.8500 B ⊗
(21.590)

.0712 (1.808) ⊛△

.020+.005 (0.51+0.13) R

3.000 (76.20)

3.4172 (86.797) △

BREECH
BOLT FACE

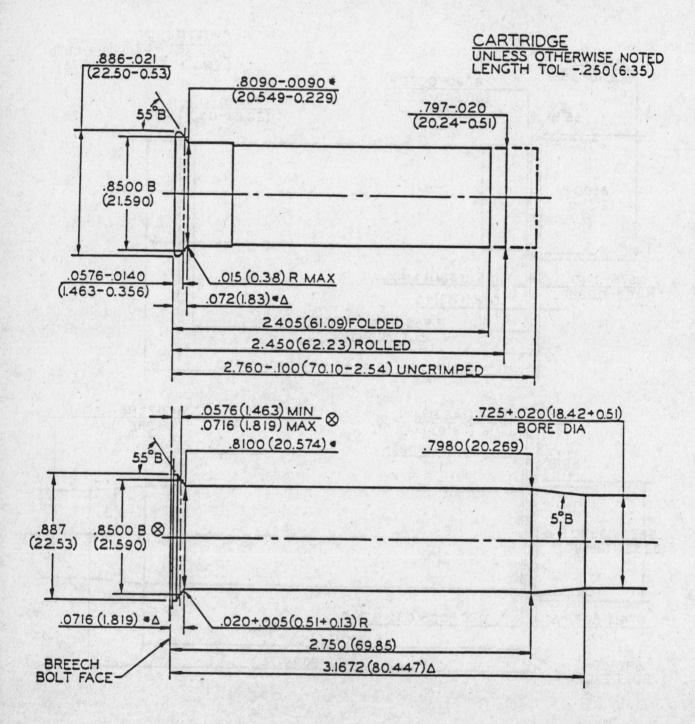

CARTRIDGE & CHAMBER
12 GAUGE 2 3/4"

CARTRIDGE
UNLESS OTHERWISE NOTED
LENGTH TOL -.250(6.35)

.886-.021
(22.50-0.53)

55°B

.8090-.0090 *
(20.549-0.229)

.797-.020
(20.24-0.51)

.8500 B
(21.590)

.0576-.0140
(1.463-0.356)

.015 (0.38) R MAX

.072(1.83) *Δ

2.405(61.09)FOLDED

2.450(62.23)ROLLED

2.760-.100(70.10-2.54) UNCRIMPED

.0576(1.463) MIN
.0716 (1.819) MAX ⊗

.725+.020(18.42+0.51)
BORE DIA

.8100 (20.574) *

.7980(20.269)

55°B

5°B

.887
(22.53)

.8500 B ⊗
(21.590)

.0716 (1.819) *Δ

.020+.005(0.51+0.13)R

2.750 (69.85)

3.1672(80.447)Δ

BREECH
BOLT FACE

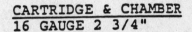

CARTRIDGE & CHAMBER
16 GAUGE 2 3/4"

CARTRIDGE
UNLESS OTHERWISE NOTED
LENGTH TOL -.250 (6.35)

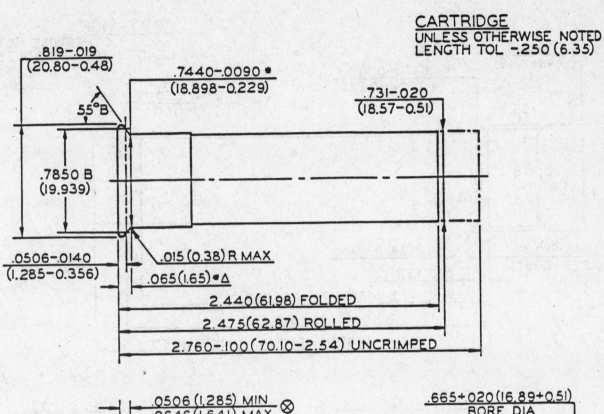

.819-.019
(20.80-0.48)

.7440-.0090 *
(18.898-0.229)

.731-.020
(18.57-0.51)

55°B

.7850 B
(19.939)

.0506-.0140
(1.285-0.356)

.015 (0.38) R MAX

.065 (1.65) * △

2.440 (61.98) FOLDED

2.475 (62.87) ROLLED

2.760-.100 (70.10-2.54) UNCRIMPED

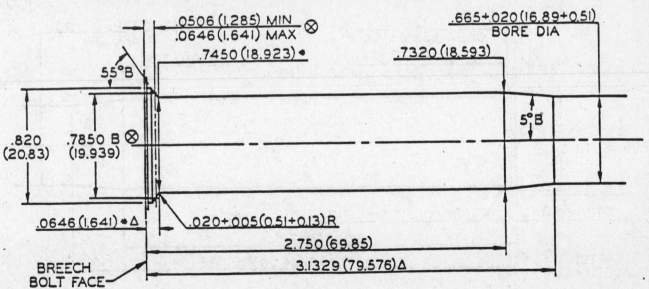

.0506 (1.285) MIN ⊗
.0646 (1.641) MAX ⊗

.7450 (18.923) *

.7320 (18.593)

.665+.020 (16.89+0.51)
BORE DIA

55°B

5°B

.820
(20.83)

.7850 B ⊗
(19.939)

.0646 (1.641) * △

.020+.005 (0.51+0.13) R

2.750 (69.85)

3.1329 (79.576) △

BREECH
BOLT FACE

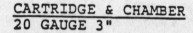

CARTRIDGE & CHAMBER
20 GAUGE 3"

CARTRIDGE
UNLESS OTHERWISE NOTED
LENGTH TOL -.250 (6.35)

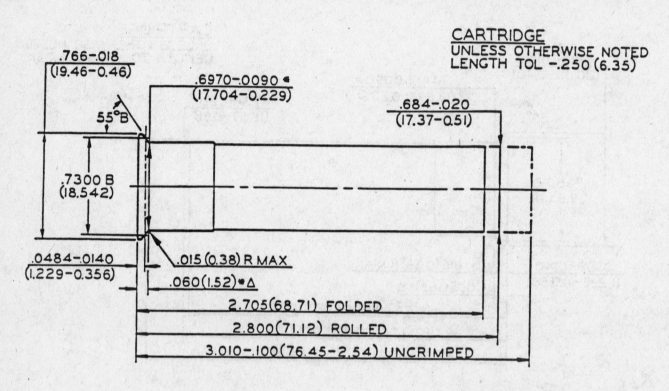

.766-.018
(19.46-0.46)

.6970-.0090 ◄
(17.704-0.229)

55°B

.684-.020
(17.37-0.51)

.7300 B
(18.542)

.0484-.0140
(1.229-0.356)

.015 (0.38) R MAX

.060 (1.52) ✱△

2.705 (68.71) FOLDED

2.800 (71.12) ROLLED

3.010-.100 (76.45-2.54) UNCRIMPED

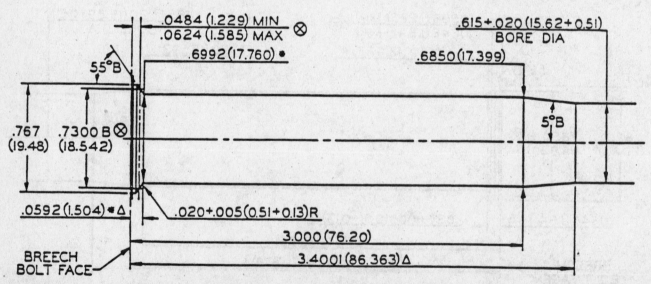

.0484 (1.229) MIN ⊗
.0624 (1.585) MAX ⊗
.6992 (17.760) ✱

.615+.020 (15.62+0.51)
BORE DIA

.6850 (17.399)

55°B

.767
(19.48)

.7300 B ⊗
(18.542)

5°B

.0592 (1.504) ✱△

.020+.005 (0.51+0.13) R

3.000 (76.20)

3.4001 (86.363) △

BREECH
BOLT FACE

CARTRIDGE & CHAMBER
20 GAUGE 2 3/4"

CARTRIDGE
UNLESS OTHERWISE NOTED
LENGTH TOL -.250(6.35)

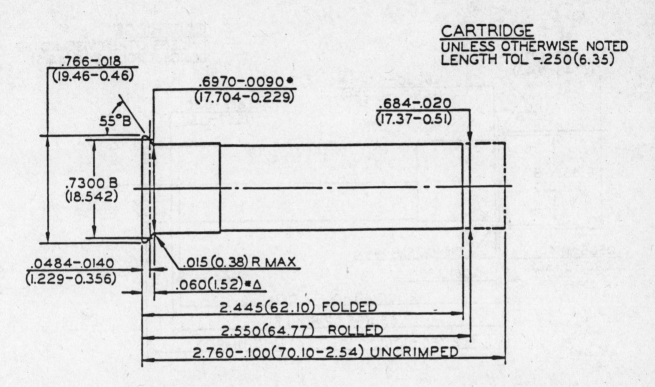

.766-.018
(19.46-0.46)

.6970-.0090*
(17.704-0.229)

.684-.020
(17.37-0.51)

55°B

.7300 B
(18.542)

.0484-.0140
(1.229-0.356)

.015(0.38) R MAX

.060(1.52)*△

2.445(62.10) FOLDED

2.550(64.77) ROLLED

2.760-.100(70.10-2.54) UNCRIMPED

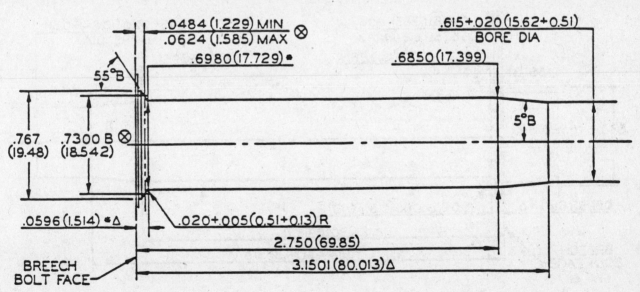

.0484(1.229) MIN ⊗
.0624(1.585) MAX ⊗
.6980(17.729)*

.615+.020(15.62+0.51)
BORE DIA

.6850(17.399)

55°B

5°B

.767   .7300 B ⊗
(19.48)   (18.542)

.0596(1.514)*△

.020+.005(0.51+0.13)R

2.750(69.85)

3.1501(80.013)△

BREECH
BOLT FACE

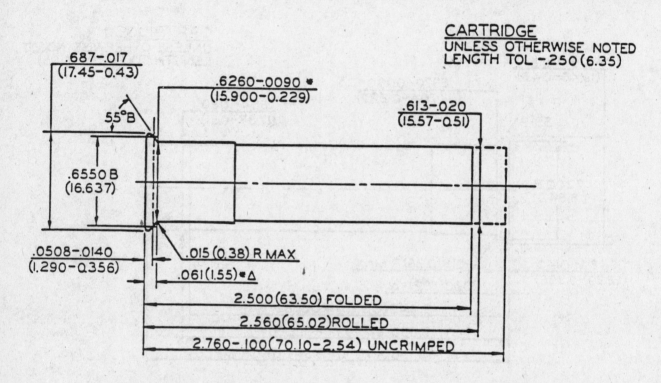

CARTRIDGE & CHAMBER
28 GAUGE 2 3/4"

CARTRIDGE
UNLESS OTHERWISE NOTED
LENGTH TOL -.250 (6.35)

.687-.017
(17.45-0.43)

.6260-.0090 *
(15.900-0.229)

.613-.020
(15.57-0.51)

55°B

.6550 B
(16.637)

.0508-.0140
(1.290-0.356)

.015 (0.38) R MAX

.061(1.55) *Δ

2.500 (63.50) FOLDED

2.560 (65.02) ROLLED

2.760-.100 (70.10-2.54) UNCRIMPED

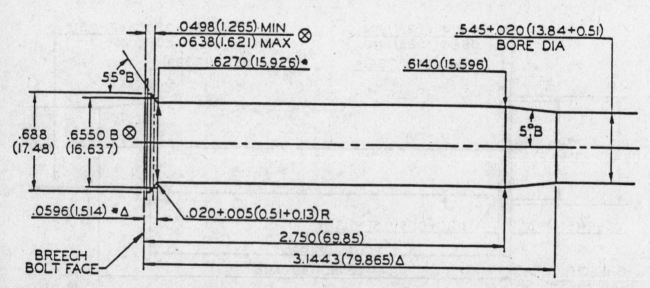

.0498 (1.265) MIN ⊗
.0638 (1.621) MAX ⊗

.545+.020 (13.84+0.51)
BORE DIA

.6270 (15.926) *

.6140 (15.596)

55°B

.688   .6550 B ⊗
(17.48)   (16.637)

5°B

.0596 (1.514) *Δ

.020+.005 (0.51+0.13) R

2.750 (69.85)

3.1443 (79.865) Δ

BREECH
BOLT FACE

CARTRIDGE & CHAMBER
410 BORE 3"

CARTRIDGE
UNLESS OTHERWISE NOTED
LENGTH TOL -.250 (6.35)

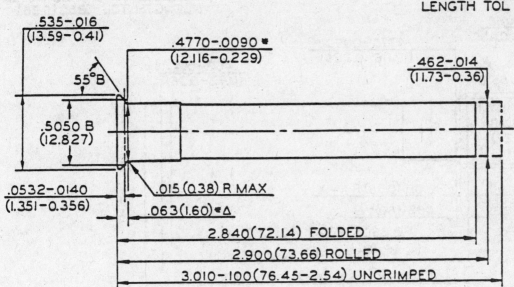

.535-.016
(13.59-0.41)

.4770-.0090 ✱
(12.116-0.229)

55°B

.462-.014
(11.73-0.36)

.5050 B
(12.827)

.0532-.0140
(1.351-0.356)

.015 (0.38) R MAX

.063 (1.60) ✱△

2.840 (72.14) FOLDED

2.900 (73.66) ROLLED

3.010-.100 (76.45-2.54) UNCRIMPED

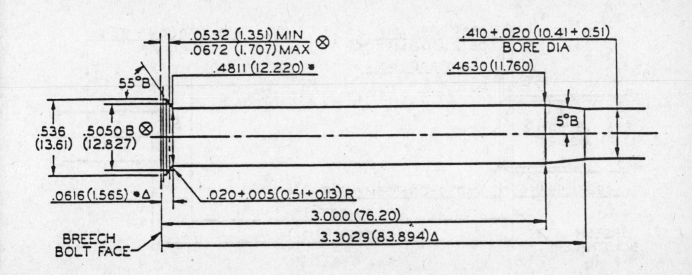

.0532 (1.351) MIN ⊗
.0672 (1.707) MAX ⊗
.4811 (12.220) ✱

.410+.020 (10.41+0.51)
BORE DIA

.4630 (11.760)

55°B

.536
(13.61)

.5050 B ⊗
(12.827)

5°B

.0616 (1.565) ✱△

.020+.005 (0.51+0.13) R

3.000 (76.20)

3.3029 (83.894) △

BREECH
BOLT FACE

CARTRIDGE & CHAMBER
410 BORE 2 1/2"

CARTRIDGE
UNLESS OTHERWISE NOTED
LENGTH TOL −.250 (6.35)

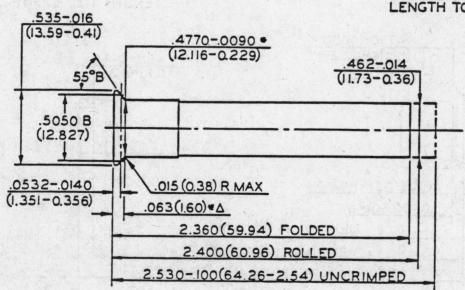

.535−.016
(13.59−0.41)

55°B

.4770−.0090 *
(12.116−0.229)

.462−.014
(11.73−0.36)

.5050 B
(12.827)

.0532−.0140
(1.351−0.356)

.015 (0.38) R MAX

.063 (1.60) * △

2.360 (59.94) FOLDED

2.400 (60.96) ROLLED

2.530−.100 (64.26−2.54) UNCRIMPED

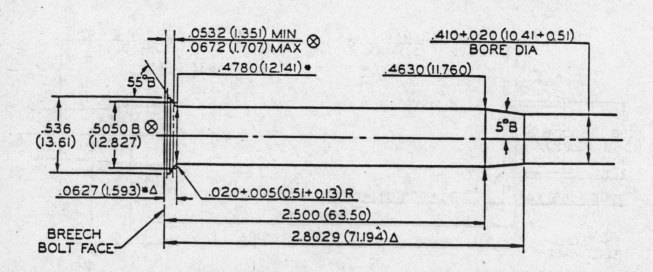

.0532 (1.351) MIN ⊗
.0672 (1.707) MAX ⊗

.410+.020 (10.41+0.51)
BORE DIA

.4780 (12.141) *

.4630 (11.760)

55°B

.536
(13.61)

.5050 B ⊗
(12.827)

5°B

.0627 (1.593) * △

.020+.005 (0.51+0.13) R

2.500 (63.50)

2.8029 (71.194) △

BREECH
BOLT FACE

Shotgun Bores

It is impossible to discuss shotshells without a discourse on the barrel through which they are fired. Regardless of the style of action, barrels are essentially the same. At the breech end they have the chamber into which the unfired cartridge is inserted and the forcing cone that serves as the transition area between the chamber and the bore. At the muzzle is the choke, which regulates the shot charge, and it, too, has a forcing cone that transitions the shot from the cylinder bore to the choke constriction.

Numerous gauges and devices are used to measure bores. Simple gauges are made that can be carried by potential gun buyers to check chamber depth; however, these gauges are not infallible should the gun have a tightly or rapidly tapering chamber and choke. Choke gauges provide nominal dimensions but cannot accurately determine choke. However, they allow us to quickly check to see whether a chamber is as marked and whether the choke has been drastically altered from the designation stamped on the barrel. Most reliable are bore micrometers that employ either a dial or a digital readout. Many include a carefully marked stem that can be used to check chamber depth, both chamber and choke forcing-cone length, and true bore diameter, which is measured precisely nine inches from the breech-end of the chamber. Although micrometers are expensive, averaging from just less than $100 for a single gauge to over $500 for a set that will measure 12-gauge through the .410-bore, there is no substitute for the shotgun enthusiast or professional.

Chamber diameters are regulated by SAAMI in the United States and by the various proof houses throughout the remainder of the world. Although each entity has its own unique regulations, all agree on the basic dimensions of chambers and bores of the various gauges and the .410 bore. Certainly, you may encounter chambers that are larger than specified. These are virtually all traceable to severe pitting or corrosion that has been polished out by a gunsmith.

In practice, with few exceptions, chambers begin with a shallow rebate cut to accommodate the rim of the shell. At the end of the rim rebate, the chamber proper begins and then gradually tapers throughout its length to the beginning of the forcing cone. With the exception of the few all-plastic shotshells that have come and gone, all cartridges have a prominent head made of brass or steel of varying length. Because there is no need to support these metal heads and since they are of nonstandard lengths, no accommodation is made for them in the chamber. One can quickly refer to SAAMI-standard chamber drawings to determine what the taper is and use a proper bore micrometer to measure individual chambers.

A number of gauges exist that quickly determine chamber depth. There are, however, some exceptions. Perhaps the most notable are the three hundred or so side-by-sides made by Ansley H. Fox (A. H. Fox) called the HE-Grade Super Fox. Begun in the 1920s, these shotguns were bored to shoot extremely tight patterns. Initially, Fox guaranteed them to shoot 80-percent patterns. However, there was a gap between what Fox guaranteed and what the shooting public perceived. Fox bored the Super Fox barrels to shoot these 80-percent patterns with Western Super-X ammunition, which employed the then-new progressive-burning powder and copper-plated Lubaloy shot. When John Q. Public shot low-quality dropped shot through his new Super Fox, less than the guaranteed 80-percent patterns resulted. Subsequently, barrels were stamped "not guaranteed" in a neat little oval on the barrel flats. Many observers have construed this to mean that the barrels were second-rate, but the stamp refers solely to the advertising gaffe.

However, one aspect of these shotguns was the tightly tapered chambers Fox used. The company found that with the paper cartridges of the 1920s, a more tightly tapered chamber added to overall downrange performance. I suspect that what this tighter chamber did was to help prevent gas leakage, which was a serious detriment to good pattern performance. Inserting a normal chamber gauge into a Super Fox chamber results in a reading of 2½-inch chamber. According to research by Michael McIntosh, about half of the Super Foxes were made with 2¾-inch chambers and the remainder with 3-inch, the discrepancies resulting from the rapid taper. Though the various agencies set the standards, the above serves to illustrate that variation is permitted and often occurs.

Perhaps the most important aspect of chambers to the shooting public is length. As a contributing editor to several outdoor and shooting publications, I receive a constant stream of inquiries regarding shotguns that don't seem to work with newly purchased shotshells. In virtually every case, the individual is attempting to shoot shells longer than those for which the shotgun was constructed. All involve repeaters that will not eject fired cases because until the late 1920s, chambers for the 10-, 12-, 16-, and 20-gauge were shorter than what are now considered standard.

Repeaters are not immune to having short chambers. For the record, since, say, 1930, chamber lengths in the United States have standardized at 2¾ inches for the 12-, 16-, 20-, and 28-gauges. The 10-gauge became 3½ inches, and the .410 bore uses 2½-inch shells for skeet and 3-inch shells for field use. But it wasn't always so. For many years the 10-gauge was chambered for 2⅞-inch shells, the 16-gauge for 2⁹⁄₁₆-inch shells, early 20-gauge shotguns for 2½-inch shells, and some 28-gauge guns for a 2½-inch shell. Thousands of early Winchester Model 12 16-gauge shotguns were chambered for the 2⁹⁄₁₆-inch shell, and when Winchester changed to the longer chamber, guns were stamped 2¾ on the barrel sleeve.

Today, domestically manufactured shotguns are all of standard chamber length, with the 12-gauge offered in 2¾, 3, and 3½ inches. Twenty-gauge shotguns pretty much come chambered for the 3-inch shell, although many are available with standard 2¾-inch chambers. However, shotguns coming from the British Isles have a better than fifty-fifty chance of being chambered for 2½-inch shells, and a very few take the cute little 2-inch shell. In fact, older British-made shotguns of all gauges have a good chance of being chambered for shells shorter than today's standard.

Americans have become obsessed with magnum cartridges, while the British, who can still hunt waterfowl with large 4-, 6-, and 8-bore shotguns, prefer lighter models made to be shot with equally light loads. Because British- and European-made shotguns must have the barrels stamped with the chamber length and be submitted to re-proof should the chambers be lengthened and then so marked, it's an easy matter to check out chamber lengths by looking at the stamps on the barrel flats. However, I highly recommend that any older shotgun be carefully inspected by a competent gunsmith before being shot. I want to emphasize, moreover, that the gunsmith must carefully measure and verify chamber length during the inspection. Older British guns will have the chamber length stamped in inches. However, shotguns made in continental Europe will use metric lengths. Since 1989, when the European Common Market came into being, both chambers and shotshells have been marked in metric lengths. For quick reference, 3-inch shells are designated as 76mm, 2¾-inch shells measure 70mm, 2½-inch shells are marked 65mm and the little 2-inch shells are 50mm. Obviously, few of us will encounter a 2-inch-chambered shotgun, but if you ever do, you won't forget it. You might think that these shotguns would be little, spindly, ladies' guns, but, in fact, they balance beautifully, pattern well, and easily handle the light 24-gram (⅞-ounce) shot charge.

At the mouth of the chamber is the forcing cone, where the shot charge is funneled into the barrel. Muzzleloading shotguns had no forcing cone, but with the advent of breechloading shotguns, whose cartridge was fatter than the cylinder bore, it was necessary to provide a transitional section of the

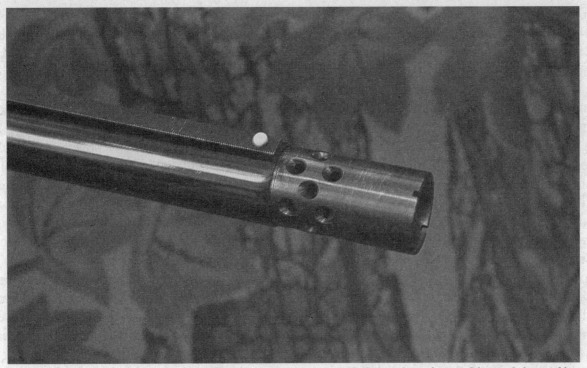

Screw-in chokes have revolutionized shotgunning. This experimental choke tube is designed for steel shot and has its maximum constriction beyond the muzzle. The ports bleed off the propellant gases, preventing their disrupting the shot column.

Porting is the placing of a series of holes, most often formed by electric-spark erosion that prevents internal burrs frequently left by common drilling, near the muzzle of a shotgun barrel that provides recoil attenuation and often better patterns due to the lessened gas pressure at the muzzle.

bore to compensate for the larger cartridge. Initially, only over-powder cards and felt spacer wads were available, and because these wads were, by necessity, of the internal diameter of the paper hull and cylinder bore, the potential was high for the hot propellant gases to leak past them and fuse pellets in the lead-shot charge. It wasn't until 1945 when Winchester-Western patented the first cup-shaped over-powder wad that gas leaking was eliminated. Because it was necessary to make the transition from the larger chamber to the bore quickly, the standard length of the forcing cones was set at five degrees or just a shade over ⅜ of an inch. Although they helped stop gas leakage, these short forcing cones—which are still used by many manufacturers because they are SAAMI standard and therefore provide an additional defense against liability lawsuits—battered the lead shot and produced numerous out-of-round pellets that quickly left the patterns and became what are called flyers. The notable exception—I'm sure there were others—was the HE-Grade Super Fox, made with ¾-inch-long forcing cones that complemented the tightly tapered chambers. This is not long by current standards, but because these cones weren't as sharply angled as the standard ⅜-inch cones, they eased the shot charge into the bore.

Today, some shotguns are manufactured with long forcing cones, and a cottage industry has grown up around barrel modifications. Depending on the gunsmith, current long forcing cones go from 1½ inches all the way to 5 inches. Each has its adherents, but in the main, forcing cones tend to fall between 1½ and 3 inches. Tests show that cones lengthened beyond 3 inches don't seem to provide any additional benefit. Outfits like Briley Manufacturing in Houston, Texas, prefer to cut their forcing cones at a 1½-degree angle to the bore, which in a standard shotgun bore works out to about a 3-inch-long cone. Other aspects, chiefly in shotshell construction, govern downrange performance, and shotshells and bore configuration are interrelated, but little has helped improve patterning more than the lengthening of forcing cones.

The bore itself is little more than a cylindrical tube. However, before we dismiss it totally, there are some things we should discuss. For years barrel length has been the topic of numerous gun shop and duck-blind conversations. In the days of black powder, long barrels were necessary to allow sufficient space for the powder to burn completely and hence develop maximum pressure and maximum velocity for the load. The same is true for black powder's direct descendant, bulk powder—an early smokeless powder that could be loaded by dram weight or volume with black-powder dippers. When smokeless powder came along, it was found that for the most part the powder charge reached its maximum pressure within the first 16 to 18 inches of the barrel, and thus longer barrels were not necessary to ensure maximum velocity for a given load. While ballistics are important, the fact remains that longer barrels make for better gun handling. In the 1960s and early '70s, American shooters went through a spasm of embracing short barrels for upland hunting and skeet. To this day, some hold on. Of course, when a 26-inch barrel is used on a repeater that has a 6- or 8-inch-long receiver, handling is very much like handling a 30-inch-barrel double. The trouble was that when 26-inch barrels were built on doubles, shooters suddenly had a very "whippy," hard-to-control shotgun. An old saying about these short-barreled guns was, "It's easy to start them swinging, but even easier to stop them." Longer barrels impart more inertia and consequently are harder to stop or slow. There's a lot of air around a clay target or a gamebird, and short barrels are just plain hard to swing smoothly.

The interior of a shotgun barrel appears highly polished. However, polishing methods vary from long strokes that polish lengthwise to rotary hones that leave microscopic concentric rings. Handmade, bespoke British, Spanish, Italian, and the American-made Galazan shotguns that carry astronomical price tags have their bores polished this way: The barrels are mounted in a fixture; then a lap carried on a sliding trolley is inserted, and a workman moves the trolley back and forth, polishing the bore with long strokes. Most guns that we mere mortals buy are mass-produced and their bores polished with a rotary lap that is powered by the industrial equivalent of a power drill, and the polishing is essentially done at a right angle to the bore.

Once polished, some bores are chrome-plated. This provides two benefits; the first is that the bore is virtually impervious to rust and corrosion. The second is that chrome-plating provides a slicker surface than plain polished steel, though the difference in velocity is negligible. Sometimes chrome-plated bores show up in odd places. I have a handmade AyA 53E that has chrome-plated bores, so plated bores are not part and parcel of inexpensive shotguns.

Bore diameter was discussed earlier; however, some interesting observations can be made here. In general, American- and British-made 12-gauge shotguns will normally have bore diameters very close to the established .729. Although the Super Fox was a harbinger with its .740-inch bore, today's shotguns such as the Winchester Super X 2 and the Browning 3½ Gold also have .740-inch bores, which pattern better with large shot and steel shot. Shotguns made in Belgium, Germany, and Italy tend to have bores that are on the tight side. I have a new Beretta Urika 391 whose bore measures .7195, which under the old British proof laws would be very close to a $^{13}/_1$ bore. Neither has much effect on velocity, but tests at the patterning board show that enlarged bores shoot consistently better patterns, especially with large shot.

Once the shot charge has traversed the bore and approaches the muzzle, it encounters the forcing cone of the choke. This section of the bore gradually tapers to the actual choke constriction. Before screw-in chokes became common, better shotguns were carefully choked, using long forcing cones leading to the constriction, followed by a parallel section at the muzzle. More expensive to cut, the parallel-style choke is found on better guns such as the Winchester Model 12 and others. A simpler yet equally effective style of choke also involved the forcing cone but without the parallel. This choke simply tapered to the muzzle, where the constriction was applied. For years mass-produced shotguns used this style of choke, formed by boring the barrels all the same with a very tight constriction at the muzzle. Then a reamer was inserted, and material was cut away until the proper amount of choke was produced. Normally no measuring was done; rather, a reamer marked for full, modified, and improved cylinder was run into the muzzle to whichever mark produced the amount of choke stamped on the barrel.

The last style of inexpensive choke was the swaged choke. When the barrel was made, an extra thickness of metal was left at the muzzle. The barrel was then drawn through a die that made the exterior uniform and squeezed the extra metal into the choke constriction.

Over the years, adjustable chokes came into use, and their popularity ebbed and flowed. Some were factory-installed on new shotguns, while the bulk were mounted by the individual manufacturers and gunsmiths. There were two types: The Cutts Compensator that had a steel cage onto which were screwed interchangeable choke tubes, and the collet-style, typified by the Poly-Choke, which offered "nine degrees of choke." In truth, neither performed completely to expectations. Perhaps the Cutts Compensator, extrapolated from the muzzle device designed by Marine Colonel Richard M. Cutts to control muzzle climb of the Thompson submachine gun, worked the best, but it lacked the convenience of the collet-style choke device. Made by Lyman, the Cutts Compensator did help attenuate recoil and offered choke tubes ranging from spreader for skeet through extra-full. The Poly-Choke, and copies made by Herter's, Weaver, and so on, used a collet that compressed six steel fingers into a tighter constriction when tightened. Both devices offered pretty good open patterns but did not provide the tight full and extra-full patterns they promised.

One of the least attractive aspects of these early chokes was their tendency to shoot anywhere but on target. Because the chokes raised the front bead, guns almost always shot low. Lyman and Poly-Choke assured hunters that their guns would not shoot low, since the companies "straightened" the barrel as part of the installation. This straightening involved simply bending the barrel up. Herter's recommended the simultaneous installation of a ventilated rib to prevent shooting low. Though some independent gunsmiths installed these devices in a workmanlike manner, many were installed by incompetent individuals who should have stuck to sharpening lawnmowers. These guns shot off to the right or left, up or down—anywhere but on target. In the end, variable-choke devices lost out to screw-in chokes. Some skeet shooters cling to compensator-style muzzle devices, and Poly-Chokes continue to be made, but screw-in chokes provide patterns that deliver the percentages they should without altering the appearance of the gun with a big metal blob at the muzzle. Screw-in choke tubes are centered on the bore and provide excellent performance.

It should always be borne in mind that choke constriction is related to the cylinder bore. The old test of measuring full choke with a dime tells you only that you have a shotgun and ten cents. The standard full-choke dimension applied to a shotgun with a cylinder bore of .740 will fool a fixed gauge anytime, because these gauges and dimes are predicated on a cylinder bore of .729. Those whose business it is to install screw-in chokes always base the chokes supplied with a particular job on the gun's cylinder bore, not on a wall chart.

The shotgun barrel is an arcane device: No two are the same. Even those from the same manufacturer can produce different downrange results. However, as this is being written, shotgunners have at their disposal the very best barrels that incorporate the results of years of improvements in forcing cones and choking. We still have to hit the target, and when we don't, we cannot in good conscience blame the barrel or ammunition.

Table 4.1 Nominal (SAAMI) Choke Dimensions

Gauge/Bore	Choke diameter in inches	Choke	Constriction in inches
10	0.775	full	0.036
		improved modified	0.027
		modified	0.018
		improved cylinder	0.009
12	0.729	full	0.036
		improved modified	0.027
		modified	0.021
		improved cylinder	0.011
16	0.662	full	0.030
		improved modified	0.022
		modified	0.015
		improved cylinder	0.008
20	0.615	full	0.025
		improved modified	0.017
		modified	0.011
		improved cylinder	0.007
28	0.550	full	0.023
		improved modified	0.015
		modified	0.010
		improved cylinder	0.006
.410	0.410	full	0.020
		modified	0.010
		improved cylinder	0.005

PATTERNING

There are two separate and distinct uses for the patterning board. The first is to test and determine gun fit. The second is to test ammunition performance.

When we consistently miss with a shotgun, there are two reasons: faulty shooting technique and improper gun fit. The two are interrelated, and it's difficult to check fit without first establishing a consistent gun mount. However, this book is about ammunition, and there are several other texts that completely cover shooting technique and gun mount (e.g., Michael Barnes' *Gunfitting: The Shotgun*). At the patterning board, though, we can discover whether a gunstock is improperly made for an individual and, if so, learn how to correct it.

By carefully measuring exactly 16 yards from the shooter to the patterning board and then smoothly mounting the gun and firing a series of shots at a mark, we can determine faults. Once several shots have been fired—I normally recommend using the tightest choke available—and a trend is established, the pattern sheets are evaluated. The centers of the patterns are determined, and then the distance from the patterns' centers to the center of the aim points is measured. For every inch the patterns deviate from the aiming mark, the stock must be adjusted by one-sixteenth of an inch. One shotgun I really like consistently shot one inch low and two inches left. I'm having a new stock made for it that is a quarter-inch higher and has an eighth-inch of cast-off. This should get me dead-on side-to-side, and about 60 percent of my pattern will be above the sight plane so that I never have to block out a target below the barrel, save for straight overhead shots. Once I get my new stock, I'll go back and run the same test again, just to be sure. By having the comb made just a

bit high, I can always take a little off, but I don't think I'll need to.

The other, and far more common, use of the patterning board is to evaluate ammunition. The only way to really determine how well a particular load performs in a particular shotgun barrel is to pattern it. The established range is exactly 40 yards from the muzzle. When the most common choke was full, 40 yards was (and still is) considered the range at which a properly bored full-choke barrel would put 70 percent or more of its shot charge into a 30-inch circle. Other ranges accommodate 70 percent of the shot charge of other chokes, but for all eternity, 40 yards is *the* distance for patterning. To be 100 percent accurate, the distance should be *exactly* 40 yards from the *muzzle* to the face of the patterning board. A few inches one way or the other is critical; distances should be as accurate as possible. I use a Bushnell or Leica rangefinder to verify the distance, even though my gun club's patterning range has distance markers that are quite close.

A means of securing a 40-inch-square sheet of paper to a backer is essential. For informal patterning, a large piece of cardboard from an appliance carton works well. For more intense patterning, something permanent with the space to hang two or more sheets is important.

Targets can be made from white butcher's paper, but buying a roll is fairly expensive, so I recommend using Hunter John Shotgun Pattern Targets (St. Louis, Missouri). They come preprinted in the choice of a turkey head, duck, or clay targets with the center marked by a 3³/₄-inch red circle. In addition, several 30-inch rings are printed on the target so that the hits can be counted without having to own a 30-inch template. When I'm in a hurry, I use the preprinted rings, but I own a 30-inch Plexiglas template with a

The author shooting patterns. The 40-yard target is secured to a solid and safe backstop, and the gun is supported so as to deliver an accurate shot to the target. Also used are pads to soften recoil and plenty of ammunition.

Two patterns showing good, even shot distribution.

2$1^3/_8$-inch center circle. To fully evaluate a pattern, both circles are drawn to encompass the maximum number of pellet hits. Then hits in the center and the outer ring are counted separately.

When it comes time to evaluate the patterns, there are three approaches. First is the overall percentage of the total pellets that fall within the 30-inch circle. Then there is the core pattern represented by the smaller, inner circle. And finally there is the distribution of pellets in the outer ring. The total-count pattern will provide a basis for evaluating how close that particular choke/load combination comes to the pattern standards. The 2$1^3/_8$-inch core pattern will show how dense the shell/choke combination is and is particularly valuable when working with turkey loads, in which a tight concentration of the whole shot charge is important. Perhaps more valuable than the two others to the wingshooter, however, is the pellet distribution in the outer ring. If the distribution is patchy, with numerous holes through which a gamebird or clay can escape, look further. The ideal shotgun pattern is one that evenly fills the 30-inch circle with no apparent holes. Does it exist? I doubt it. I've shot thousands of patterns and don't ever remember a perfect one; some have come close, but I can't recall one that was perfectly symmetrical and perfectly distributed. So we do the best we can.

When you get a series of patterns that provide even distribution, look at the core to check that it, too, is evenly spread across the sheet. These core pellets become fringe pellets as the pattern travels downrange.

The 40-yard range standard is a bit deceiving. Yes, it is the standard, but hunters and sporting-clay enthusiasts need also to shoot patterns at distances appropriate to the game and targets they prefer. In short, a southern quail hunter ought to check out his No. 7½ or 8 load and his improved-cylinder barrel at 20, 25, and 30 yards. The pheasant hunter ought to shoot his favorite load of 4s, 5s, or 6s at 30, 35, and 40 yards, etc. In each instance, valuable information can thus be harvested.

The eternal question is how many patterns to shoot. The ballisticians at Winchester-Western once said that shooting 100 patterns would give an "indication" of how a particular barrel/choke/shell combination worked. I once did a story that entailed shooting and counting fifty patterns, and it about wore me out. In practical terms, three patterns will give you fair information, five will do you better, and ten patterns, while not definitive, will give you a pretty good idea of how your shotgun performs with a particular load. Wide variation is not necessarily a cause for alarm—some loads in some barrels and chokes will vary by over a hundred pellets. If you experience this, it's a clear indicator that you need to shoot more patterns until a trend emerges. *However*, if the patterns continue to be erratic, particularly if it's a handload, it's time to research another load. Erratic performance normally indicates a shell problem, although a change in choke tube, particularly if it's to a more- open, less-constricted tube, can often make a difference. With today's shotshell technology, older shotguns with extremely tight choke constrictions often do not perform especially well. I have a Fox Sterlingworth marked full (choke) on both barrels that initially had .045-inch constriction. I shot it and at 40 yards got patchy, 50-percent patterns. Following a trip to Briley Manufacturing, where the chokes were opened to about .035 inch, the patterns tightened to an acceptable 70 to 75 percent with Kent's No. 5 Tungsten Matrix waterfowl loads.

SHOT STRING

One negative aspect of patterning is that it can lull us into thinking of shotshell performance as simply a flat circle of shot on paper. However, the shot pattern, although represented as a two-dimensional entity having only height and width, is actually a fluid cloud of shot. Best thought of as a sausage-shaped cluster of shot, the pattern is three-dimensional. We seldom see today's ammunition manufacturers touting "short shot strings," but in the days before plastic shot-protecting cups and wrappers, shot string was a *big* issue. Even today, when we have the advantage of all this technology, shot stringing is still an issue.

When lead shot is handled, loaded, and especially when it's subjected to the forces of being thrust violently forward when the shell is fired, it deforms. The harder the shot in terms of antimony and, to a lesser extent, plating, the less it deforms. This deformation essentially flattens the pellets. As lead shot travels the length of the bore, it is further damaged by friction against the bore and finally as it is compressed by the choke. These deformed pellets are less aerodynamically stable than their round companions and therefore either rapidly slip to the side or, because of the drag of the air, lag far behind the round pellets. As the deformed pellets continue to drop behind, the string of shot lengthens. In terms of hitting a moving target, shot string is a clear advantage. If we were dealing only with a flat pancake of shot, we'd have to be dead on each time we shot. But because the shot is stringing out four to ten feet, having a little too much lead is not disastrous—the bird may well fly into the shot string. However, as Bob Brister so incisively points out in his landmark book, *Shotgunning—the Art and Science*, anytime you take shot from one part of the pattern, another suffers. There are only so many pellets in the load, and the farther they string out, the fewer there are in our theoretical 30-inch circle. What we see on the pattern board is a cumulative measure of the pattern, but if we string the shot over ten feet, suddenly there are far fewer pellets available to strike the target. Think about it.

So while stringing allows for errors in lead (nothing compensates for shooting behind), its downside is loss of lethality. When we really smoke a clay target or "dishrag" a duck, our lead was just right and the pattern, in both cross-section and length, caught the target squarely on with the maximum number of pellets. By the way, steel shot is so hard that it does not deform and tends to string very little. Regardless, when evaluating patterns, keep in mind that what is on the sheet is only a representation of two dimensions of the shot pattern, and that there is also length. A thin, patchy pattern on paper is a sure indicator of a bad performer in the field, because when the element of length is added, insufficient pellets will be available throughout the pattern's length to be lethal. That load/choke combination should be immediately abandoned.

Patterning is the key to understanding how your shotgun performs with its own unique choke or chokes and the load you prefer to use for a given application. Patterning is time-consuming, sometimes boring, and tedious, but in the end, if you keep notes and are honest with the results, it can lead you to the best loads you can use in your own equipment. For the handloader, patterning is invaluable because it will quickly lead to loads that really perform in a given gun.

Table 5.1 Nominal 40-Yard Pattern Percentages

British	European	U.S.	Percentage
Cylinder	Cylinder	Cylinder	40 percent
¼	++++	Improved cylinder	50 percent
½	+++	Modified	60 percent
¾	++	Improved modified	65 percent
Full	+	Full	70 percent

SHOTSHELL COMPONENTS

A shotshell consists of many parts, but essentially it is a hull that holds all of the various components in a convenient package. The convenience of this package allows us to carry a bunch of shells around, load them into both chamber and magazine, and, after they are fired, keep them for reloading and reuse. Into the hull is inserted a primer that is the source of ignition of the propellant or powder. Once ignited, modern progressive-burning powders release an ever-expanding quantity of gas that forces the wad and the shot forward against the crimp. When sufficient pressure has built, the crimp is forced open, and the shot charge is thrust through the barrel toward the target. In every instance, these components must be carefully matched so that they interact both safely and efficiently.

CASES

Historically, shotshell cases were all brass. The first expendable hulls were made of paper to which a brass head was crimped to hold the side walls of the case to the base wad and to provide a firm surface for the extractor to grip. In about 1962, Remington introduced the first case that had plastic sides, a wound-fiber base wad, and a brass head.

Winchester followed suit in 1964 and in 1965 introduced the first one-piece, compression-formed hull. Today nearly all hulls are either two-piece or one-piece compression-formed plastic. A few manufacturers—Federal, Kent-Gamebore, and Eley—still load shells with paper hulls. Numerous clay-target competitors, especially trapshooters, feel they get better gas sealing from the more pliable paper hull; consequently, Federal still produces the paper-hulled Champion. In recent years, shooters in

Great Britain and Europe have come under pressure from various "green" factions and landowners regarding discarded plastic hulls and wads left on farmlands. In answer to this criticism, and to promote hunters and shooters as the true friends of the environment that they are, Kent-Gamebore, Bismuth, Eley, and others are loading cartridges with paper hulls and card and felt wads. Kent-Gamebore's general manager, Stephen Dales, has developed a fiber shot cup that serves the same ballistic purpose as a plastic shot cup (see *Wads*) but also biodegrades, leaving no trace.

Plastic hulls come in two basic designs, a two-piece hull that has straight-sided walls and a separate basewad, and an injection-molded or compression-formed one-piece hull that is integral with the basewad. Made by the Riefenhauser process, two-piece cases have a metal head that binds together the exterior tube and the internal basewad. Federal, Winchester, and Remington primarily use two-piece Riefenhauser-style hulls in their field loads. Compression-formed hulls combine the case walls and basewad all in one. In addition, compression-formed cases normally have tapered walls. At one time, ACTIV was a brand of ammunition that used all-plastic hulls with a reinforcing steel web molded into the head. But these hulls did not have the traditional external metal (brass) head and never caught the eye of American sportsmen. The truth is that compression-formed hulls would function equally well without a metal head; but nevertheless, sportsmen's acceptance is not promising.

One of the great myths of shotshell lore has to do with high- and low-brass shell heads. For some reason, there is a perception that if a shotshell has a high-brass metal head, it is powerful; if it has a low-brass head, it's a mild load. As a contributing editor for *American Rifleman* and *American Hunter* magazines, I answer numerous letters about old shotguns, many with Damascus or twist-steel barrels. In some cases the owners have taken them to their local gunsmiths—apparently part of the group the late Jack O'Connor identified as "lawnmower sharpeners"—who told them to go ahead and shoot their Damascus-barrel heirloom with "low-brass shells." Advice is free, but that's downright *bad* advice. Some low-brass loads push the top end of the pressure curve and are as inappropriate for these old guns as a modern proof load.

Part of the myth of high and low brass is attributable to a misunderstanding of the more technical description of the internal capacity of hulls. When the change was made from black powder to bulk or semi-smokeless powder and ultimately to smokeless powder, different hulls were made to accommodate the different powders or propellants. Black powder is bulky; it takes up a lot of space in the case, and hence needed a hull with a *low basewad* or low-base case. When smokeless powder came along, its first generation available to handloaders was called bulk powder. Loaded bulk for bulk the same as black powder, it, too, needed lots of room in the case, and again, low-base cases were needed to accommodate its volume. However, real smokeless powder, especially John Olin's new progressive-burning propellant, needed far less space in the case; consequently, cases were made that had high basewads and thus less internal space.

One problem with these early shotshells was that when higher-pressure smokeless powder was fired, often the gases, whose force is exerted in all directions, would cut around the edges of the base wad, dramatically swelling the case head and making extraction difficult. I have an old-time hand extractor that has on one end a three-pronged claw that can be slipped over the head of a stuck shell and, with the help of a finger inserted into the loop, will pull the swollen hull from the breech. If the head pulls off, there's a hook on the end opposite the claw that can be inserted through the primer hole and used to pull out the remainder of the obstinate case. In 1936, Winchester-Western addressed the problem of high-pressure gas leakage by developing an overlay base wad that sealed the gases within the hull and prevented their migration between the base wad and the metal head. Somehow that helped generate a myth equating the internal case capacity—i.e., high or low basewads—with high and low exterior metal heads. For all eternity, the promise of a metal head on the outside of *any* shotshell is simply to add stiffness—especially important with paper cases—to the head of the shell, and primarily to provide a firm surface for the extractor to grip, ensuring positive extraction and ejection.

PRIMERS

The primer is inserted into the head of whatever case we have. Historically, primers took on different forms and sizes. As late as the 1960s, they were still made in two sizes, No. 157 Remington and No. 209 Winchester. The 209 Winchester was used universally, while the 157 was confined to Remington shotshells. Finally Remington gave in and adopted the 209-size primer. Though these two had different diameters, primers differ in far more ways. The primer is the source of ignition of the propellent charge, and while they are all the same size, they differ greatly in their individual ignition characteristics. Below is the result of a series of tests performed for this book by Hodgdon Powder Company's chief ballistician, Ron Reiber.

PRIMER COMPARISON TESTS

The following charts were created using Winchester (compression-formed) AA cases and Winchester AA wads. Cases were crimped excessively deeply to create the highest pressure possible for a given load. Powder charges were the same throughout. As the tests reveal, not only do primer changes make drastic differences, but changing shot quantities also changes the way primers perform. Therefore, let me repeat the always-present warning to reloaders: *Use only those components listed, and do not interchange components.*

As Table 6.1 shows, there are wide pressure swings when primers are interchanged. Issues here include not only safety but also performance. Hot

Table 6.1

Primer	1⅛-oz. shot test Velocity(fps)	Pressure(psi)	Primer	⅞-oz. shot test Velocity	Pressure (psi)
Win. AATP	1,176	11,200	Win. 209	1,214	10,300
Fed. 209H	1,172	11,100	CCI 209M	1,217	10,200
Win. 209	1,173	10,900	Fed. 209	1,195	9,100
Fiocchi 616	1,171	10,800	Fiocchi 616	1,196	9,000
CCI 2069M	1,171	10,400	Win. AATP	1,191	8,400
Rem. 209P	1,156	8,500	Rem. 209P	1,187	8,200
CCI 209	1,162	8,400	CCI 209	1,180	7,700

Win. = Winchester; Fed. = Federal; Rem. = Remington

weather can drive pressures even higher, and cold weather makes powders harder to ignite.

The earliest shotguns fired black powder, which was a combination of approximately 15 percent charcoal, 10 percent sulfur, and 75 percent potassium nitrate, commonly known as saltpeter. The proportions were not exact, and variations in percentages probably didn't affect performance. Black powder, once blended, was ground to various-size granules; the finest was for priming, and coarseness increased for rifles, shotguns, and on up to artillery. Black powder had several disadvantages: It readily absorbed moisture to the point that it would cake and have to be recrushed into usable form, and if transported for any distance, black powder would separate into its original components. Add to this the thick clouds of smoke it generated and the gummy, moisture- and corrosion-attracting residue left in the barrel and on the user's hands, face, and clothing, and black powder was less than great. Black powder is also a low-grade explosive, and instead of burning, it in fact exploded, giving a pressure spike.

Smokeless powder attempted to address black powder's faults, and did so easily, though it generated much higher pressures. While smokeless powder does create smoke, even in the heaviest humidity, its smoke is nowhere near that of black powder. Smokeless powder also absorbs moisture, but does so in moderation, and when it becomes moist, it does not clump and cake. Even when shaken and jostled, smokeless retains its integrity and does not separate. Smokeless powder will, however, go bad. Fresh smokeless powder has a sweet smell; old, bad smokeless powder has a sharp, acrid, acidic smell, and should be discarded.

In the transition period, smokeless powder was initially called semi-smokeless or bulk powder. Black powder was loaded by dram weight. A dram is equal to 60 grains, but black powder, unlike modern smokeless powder, was not commonly loaded by grains. Usually it was measured with a dipper marked in drams. Only commercial loading operations used measures similar to those in use today. Initially, semi-smokeless or bulk powder was manufactured to be loaded volume for volume or bulk for bulk, to provide the same ballistic result as a similar volume of black powder. In the early 1900s, Union Metallic Cartridge Company made what it called the "Standard 3-dram Bulk Powder Measure." It listed a 3-dram volume as 1.1250 cubic inches. From 1894 through 1942, Winchester-Western manufactured shotshells loaded with bulk powder, and the following were some of the brands of bulk powder used:

Alarm Smokeless
American Wood Smokeless
Dead Shot Smokeless
Diamond Grain Smokeless
DuPont Smokeless
DuPont No. 2 Smokeless
DuPont Gray Smokeless
E. C. Smokeless
E. C. No. 1 Smokeless
E. C. No. 2 Smokeless
Empire Smokeless
Hazard Blue Ribbon Smokeless
Mullerite Smokeless
Oriental Smokeless
Schultze Smokeless
New Schultze Smokeless
Sea Shooting (S. S.) Smokeless
Wolf Smokeless

As a boy, I wanted to reload shotshells, and I read in one of the sporting magazines of the day about making a set of handloading tools for use with bulk powder. Herter's offered a similar set, but I was never able to convince my parents that it was safe and economical. Still, it sounded like fun. At any rate, the whole deal was predicated on loading bulk powder dram for dram, and that's how smokeless powder came into being.

In 1922, the Western Super-X shell hit the market. The Olin family, who owned Western and later Winchester, sought a better propellant, one that could achieve higher velocities than bulk powders. The result was progressive-burning smokeless powder that, rather than quickly reaching its peak pressure as black powder and bulk powder did, would build its peak pressure slowly. This new powder, instead of burning quickly and producing a limited volume of propellant gases, would continue to produce expanding gas, thus pushing the shot charge faster and faster. Olin's development led the way for today's variety of powders that fulfill a broad swath of ballistic needs. For example, clay-target shooters shoot light loads and expect a certain level of performance. Included in their requirements are uniform velocity and clean burning. Though clean burning isn't a major factor in the operation of a single-barrel trap gun or double gun, it matters when the shooter uses one of the popular gas-operated semi-automatics that are prone to malfunction when used with a "dirty" powder.

On the other end of the spectrum are heavy magnum loads that require a very slow-burning powder whose peak pressure is very slow to rise, giving time for the extra-heavy shot charge to get into motion. These slow-burning powders are very dirty. They leave lots of unburned residue in the barrel, although that's not a great problem. The average waterfowl or turkey hunter shoots many fewer shots than a down-the-line trap, skeet, or sporting-clays aficionado, and stoppages are rare, provided the hunter cleans his shotgun at reasonable intervals.

Between these two extremes are lots of powders. And their placement on a burn-rate chart doesn't fully explain their uses. As with every other component of a shotshell, their burn rates

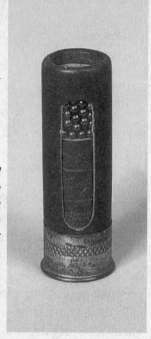

This salesman's cutaway shell from the 1920s shows all the components of a shotshell. The brass-headed hull contains (from bottom to top) the primer (hidden), propellant or powder, an over-powder card wad and two felt spacer wads, the shot, which in this case is No. 4 chilled shot, and the over-shot wad that is roll-crimped atop the shell.

can change when combined with different shot charges, primers, and so on. However, Table 6.2, graciously supplied by Hodgdon, gives some idea of the relative burning rates of several powders. These burn rates are only approximate and do not indicate exact placement. However, they do give a good idea of where individual powders familiar to handloaders and shotgunners lie in relation to each other and their applications. Even a cursory knowledge of the burn rates of various powders can wave a flag when a powder doesn't seem appropriate for a load for a given application. For example, I'd ignore someone who says he heard of a great turkey load that combined two ounces of shot with 70 grains of Hodgdon Clays. Such are the formulae for disaster.

Handloaders need to be extremely attentive not only to what powder is being loaded but also to what weight. Those who purchase their ammo should be aware that certain powders used in certain loads often leave unburned powder in the barrel, but that alone does not indicate an inferior load.

WADS

Simply put, the purpose of shotshell wads is to separate the extremely hot propellant or powder gases from the shot charge. In 1929, personnel at

Table 6.2
Shotshell Powder Relative Burn Rates

(Powders shown from fastest to slowest)

Hodgdon	Alliant	IMR	Winchester	Accurate
Clays	Bullseye			Nitro 100
Titewad	Red Dot			
		"Hi-Skor" 700X		
International Titegroup	Green Dot American Select		WAAP WST WSL	Solo 1000 Royal Scot D
		PB		
Universal	Unique Herco	Hi-Skor 800X		Solo 1250
			WSF	
		SR7625 SR4756		
HS-6			540	
	Blue Dot			
HS-7			571	
Longshot	2400			
H110				4100
Lil' Gun			296	

the U.S. Army's Frankfort Arsenal conducted a test using a .30-06 Browning Mechanical (Automatic) Rifle. They determined that a .30-06 cartridge generated 598.6 calories of gas overall and 2,864 calories overall when fired. One calorie raises the temperature of one gram of water one degree Celsius. Using a simple conversion from Celsius to Fahrenheit of doubling the Celsius temperature and adding 28 means that the gas generated by a single .30-06 round is around 1,206 degrees F. The overall heat is 5,756 degrees F. I'm no mathematician, but even if my calculations are off, propellent gases are more than hot enough to melt lead, which has a melting point of 327.4 degrees C. (682.8 F.) and boils at 1,770 C. (3,568 F.). If exposed unprotected to hot powder gases, many of a shotshell's lead pellets would melt. Of course, there are more obvious reasons for using wads. Since a shot charge is porous, if it were fired without a wad, the gases would simply flow through the pellets—thus the need to separate the powder and shot charges.

Early wads were just that, a wad of whatever material the gunner had—literally! I won't go into the gory details. As breechloaders came onto the scene, more formal wads were used—an over-shot card and felt spacers. The card wads, which are still sold for specialized loading, were very dense, stiff cardboard cut to tightly fit into the brass shell or, later, paper hull. Above these were one or more wads cut from varying thicknesses of felt of various resilience. While these felt wads provided some cushioning for the shot, their main purpose was to fill the case sufficiently to ensure a good crimp.

In 1945, the first real breakthrough came when Winchester-Western began loading ammunition with a cup-shaped over-powder wad. Loading this inverse cup wad is complicated, yet nearly sixty years after its introduction, it is still being used, although it is being phased out in some loads in favor of the simpler-to-make-and-load one-piece plastic wad. The cup wad is made of a special grade and thickness of treated kraft paper, and officials at Winchester state it is still the best wad for many of the company's premium high-performance loads. The use of this wad began the evolution of over-powder wads that truly sealed the hot powder gases behind the shot column.

The production of the many various materials for World War II quickly increased the use of

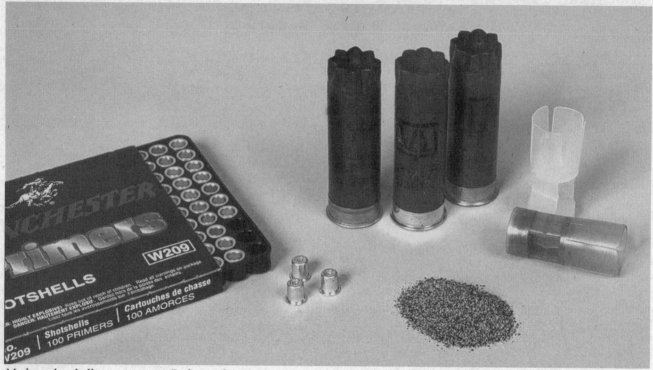

Modern shotshell components. (Left to right) non-corrosive primers, plastic hulls, propellant or powder, and plastic wads.

plastics for a multitude of applications. One of those was as a highly efficient gas-sealing over-powder wad. It was first made as a single gas seal, but with the increased use of plastic shot wrappers, the plastic seal soon became part of a single wad that incorporated both a gas seal and a shot-protecting cup in one easy-to-handle unit.

Just as with primers and powders, the changing of wads can influence ballistics. To ensure safe pressures and uniform downrange ballistics, ammunition companies carefully control each step of manufacture. However, handloaders easily fall victim to changing wads. Hodgdon powders ran a series of tests in its laboratory similar to the primer substitution test, and the results show a significant spread of pressures and velocity. Hodgdon's

sophisticated pressure guns use piezo-electric transducers that read out in pounds per square inch. These readouts are highly accurate, and in the loads tested all the components are weighed to ensure that the data are unquestionable.

The test in Table 6.3 was performed using a 12-gauge Winchester AA hull (the old compression-formed hull), a Federal 209A primer, 16.0 grains of Hodgdon Clays powder, and 1⅛ ounces of lead shot. Only the wad was changed. It is interesting to note that when the Federal 12 S2 was substituted, the pressure actually rose as the velocity dropped.

Looking at the chart, one could ask, "So what?" The problem might not seem to be grave with *this* load; however, when loading steel shot and heavy

Table 6.3

Wad	Velocity (fps)	Pressure (psi)
Winchester WAA 12	1,145	10,800
Hornady Versalite	1,114	10,800
Remington Figure 8	1,113	9,300
Windjammer	1,112	8,500
Federal 12 S2	1,105	9,500
Pattern Control Red	1,050	8,100

field and turkey loads, pressures can be very high and any tinkering with the load data or component substitution could be dangerous.

One component that is not generally used but rather reserved for special high-performance lead and nontoxic shot loads is buffer. Buffer is finely ground polyethylene or other soft plastic that is sifted in among the shot load. It supports the pellets and makes them less prone to deforming during firing. Although it looks benign, buffer cannot be indiscriminately added to a load. Because it adds weight to the shot load and also affects the fluid dynamics of the shot charge, buffering must be added only to those loads developed especially for its use.

We'll deal with shot separately, so all that remains to cover here is how the shell is closed. The crimp, as it's called, serves two purposes. The most obvious is to seal the end of the shell and prevent the shot from coming out. However, it also serves the very important function of keeping the powder compressed until it is properly ignited. It is vitally important that the combustion chamber formed by the base wad, shell sides, and over-powder wad or gas seal remains tight for a split second while the primer fully ignites the powder. Handloaders who have inadvertently omitted the powder charge in one of their reloads have observed that the primer is sufficiently strong by itself to push the wad partially up the bore and eject the shot load through the muzzle. Although it appears that the primer itself will thrust the wad and shot forward

and open the crimp, if the crimp is sufficiently firm, the powder will be properly ignited. Old, worn-out hulls that have been reloaded to exhaustion often exhibit flame at the muzzle, through the ejection port, and even around the edges of a break-action shotgun. This flame is due to the crimp opening too fast and the powder charge not being properly ignited within the combustion chamber. So the crimp serves a far more important purpose than just keeping the shot within the shell.

Early brass shells used a thin card wad over the shot that was held in place with water glass, a thin solution of sodium silicate or potassium silicate—essentially a glue. Because water glass fractures easily, it did not significantly raise pressures.

When paper hulls were adopted, black powder was the propellant. Because the powder was bulky and required lots of room in the shell, the only crimp that would allow a feasible combination of black powder, wads, and the shot charge was the rolled crimp. Still using an over-shot wad, this crimp rolled the hull back on itself and down onto the edges of the over-shot card. Using only a quarter-inch of hull, it was the best way to accommodate the large volume of powder and other components. When smokeless powder came along, it took up far less room in the hull, hence the development of hulls with high-base wads. Too, more of the open end of the hull was available for the crimp. For years some evidence and lots of hearsay attributed missing to the pattern-

The historic progression of wads. (Left to right) card and spacers, Winchester's over-shot cup wad that was first introduced in 1945 and spacers, Winchester's Mark-V shot wrapper, and, finally, today's plastic wads that combine an over-powder gas-sealing cup, a collapsible cushioning section, and protective shot cup.

Two styles of crimp currently in use. On the left is the more familiar folded or pie-crimp. On the right is the older rolled crimp that requires an over-shot card to retain the shot in the shell. Thought to disrupt patterns, rolled crimping fell from use in the late 1940s. However, because a rolled crimp uses less hull, they are still used for some waterfowl loads, for 2- and 2½-inch 12-gauge loads and slugs, where a folded crimp is not practical.

disturbing effect of the over-shot wad. All manner of doughnut patterns were ascribed to the use of over-shot wads and rolled crimps. When the folded or pie-style crimp came along, overall performance was enhanced.

Folded crimps come in two types, six- and eight-segment. Six-segment crimps are commonly found on field or hunting loads and small-gauge shells, while the eight-segment crimp is common to 12- and 20-gauge target loads. The reason is that eight-segment crimps provide a tighter closing of the shell with small shot. In the 28-gauge and .410-bore, there isn't sufficient room to bring together all the material, so those shells by necessity use a six-segment crimp.

When first developed, the folded crimp had several different appearances. Some were flat across the top and used a varnish to ensure stability, while others retained part of the rolled crimp and pushed the folds down into the shell. In either case the folded segments took over the function of the over-shot wad and held the shot in the shell, yet did not contribute the extra wad to the shot string when the shell was fired.

The modern folded crimp is functional and, like the other components, sensitive to adjustment. In fact, changing the depth of the crimp can change pressures far more than one might expect. As with the other components, Ron Reiber, Hodgdon's chief ballistician, ran tests for this book that emphasize the synergy of the crimp in the overall load. As Hodgdon's data points out, individual ammunition manufacturers use differing crimp depths with different loads; however, Hodgdon recommends an average depth of .055 inch as a good average. The tests gradually increased crimp depth by .020-inch intervals, and the results are revealing (Table 6.4).

The loads were assembled using the following components: Winchester 12-gauge AA (compression-formed) hull, Winchester 209 primer, 20.0 grains of Hodgdon Clays powder, ⅞-ounce lead shot.

From these data it is easy to understand how an improper crimp affects performance and, most importantly, pressure. Note that pressure on the last crimp depth of 13,100 psi is *above* the service pressure of the 2¾-inch 12-gauge.

All of the components of any shotshell interrelate, and each is dependent upon the others to provide safe pressures and appropriate downrange performance. Today's shotshells are excellent, and even the cheapest on sale at the various marts and discount-priced at gun shops perform well for their intended purpose.

Table 6.4

Crimp depth	Velocity (fps)	Pressure (psi)
0.030	1,308	9,300
0.050	1,329	10,500
0.070	1,351	11,900
0.090	1,363	13,100

SHOT

Shooting moving targets with shot is the shotgun's primary purpose. We'll look at slugs and buckshot in another section, but fine shot, the subject here, is the traditional shotgun projectile. Today we have lead shot and several variants of nontoxic shot. Lead shot was the only kind until the 1970s, when steel shot was developed to prevent lead poisoning of waterfowl. We'll look at them all, but we'll start with lead shot.

Historically, shot wasn't very sophisticated. Whatever was at hand was dropped down the barrel and fired at the hunter's quarry. As the shotgun developed, so did shot. By the last half of the nineteenth century, the techniques of dropping shot had been perfected or at least developed to the point where the individual pellets were of more-or-less uniform size, and began to appear in various grades. Shot was and still is made by hoisting lead ingots up a 100-foot or higher tower, melting them in a furnace, adding whatever alloy is necessary for that batch, and then pouring the molten lead alloy through a sieve perforated with precisely sized holes appropriate to the size of shot being made. The pellets then fall the 100 feet into a pool of water. "Chilled" shot became so named because cool air was blown across the dropping pellets; "dropped" shot was the term used when the chilling effect was not employed. (At one time shot towers were prevalent across the nation. There is still a shot tower near the bustling Inner Harbor in downtown Baltimore, Maryland, and it is viewed as a historically significant landmark. Winchester and Remington maintain traditional shot towers. Owners of other, independent shot towers supply shot to some manufacturers and the reloading market.) Federal Cartridge Company, Bismuth Cartridge, and many foreign companies use the Bleimeister process, in which lead or bismuth

alloys are melted, dropped through a sieve, and then fall about three feet into hot water. Easily housed in a warehouse, the Bleimeister process has consolidated shot-making into a more manageable environment.

The basic and historic material used for shot was and remains lead. Early shotshell advertisements of the late nineteenth century offered dropped and chilled shot. Later, extra-hard pellets came along as magnum shot and under other names. The basic difference is in the alloy or, more specifically, the amount of alloy. Two metals are alloyed with pure lead: Antimony hardens the lead, and in large shot, arsenic serves as a surfactant, which causes the pellets to form as perfectly round spheres. Historically, it has been widely written that the higher the antimony content, the better the shot. Dropped shot is simply pure lead with perhaps half a percent antimony; chilled shot has 1 to 3 percent antimony; and magnum or extra-hard shot has 4 to 6 percent antimony. Pattern performance rises dramatically when as little as 1 percent antimony is added to pure lead. Little extra is gained by adding more antimony, and in fact, only the very top target loads and some high-performance hunting loads have more than 3 percent.

Arsenic was used in early shot as a hardener, but because of its extreme toxicity, it was dropped in favor of the more benign antimony. However, in making very hard shot with lots of antimony, a trace of arsenic is added as a surfactant. Arsenic is also used for that reason in making buckshot and for lead air-rifle shot used at carnivals.

Much of dropped shot was pure lead. However, most that was commercially produced in the twentieth century had about half a percent of antimony alloyed with the lead. John Olin, one of the sons of the founder of Western Cartridge (now the Winchester division of Olin) always said that Winchester-Western used a half-percent of antimony in its softest shot. The reason was ease of manufacture. Pure lead did not easily form perfectly round pellets, but with a little antimony added, it did. Hoisting large numbers of poorly formed pellets back up the 100-foot shot tower to fall again as out-of-round pellets was hardly expedient, so a little antimony made sense.

It was argued long and loud by hunters that dropped or soft shot was more lethal than harder shot. They said that because the soft pellets flattened when they struck game, more impact was delivered and hence more lethality. I suspect that their ability to down more game with soft shot had a lot to do with it. In an era of full-choke shotguns, soft shot deformed far more than harder shot and gave those early hunters wider patterns. The same argument was heard when steel shot became law. Hunters who were used to knocking down ducks with wide patterns consisting largely of deformed pellets suddenly began missing birds or just nicking them with their tighter steel-shot patterns, and steel shot got off to a bad start. Nothing was felt to be better for bobwhite quail in the South than soft or dropped shot. Because of its propensity to become deformed, soft shot is ideal for short-range targets, and what better choice for close-range shots at Mr. Bob?

While upland hunters were content with very soft shot and the wide-open patterns it threw, waterfowl hunters wanted the opposite—shot that would pattern tightly out to forty and fifty yards. Certainly, soft, dropped shot didn't fill the bill, but hard shot with more antimony would help. Then John Olin decided that plating would also help. Actually Olin didn't invent plated shot, but he certainly put it to the forefront. In his monumental two-volume treatise *The Modern Shotgun,* Major Sir Gerald Burrard says, "I have explained the impossibility of preventing pellet deformation by giving the pellets a thin coating of copper, in itself a soft metal, and will not refer to it again." So there . . . take that! Burrard missed the fact that though copper plating will not prevent lead pellets from being deformed during firing, it did protect them from fusing when the hot propellant gases blasted and squirted around the card and felt spacer wads.

At this point I should explain that shot deforms during several phases of being fired. It all happens in a split second, but it happens. As the powder burns, it begins pushing the shot charge up the barrel. At the moment of initial acceleration, the pellets at the rear of the load begin to move, but those at the front are still stationary. In a process called setback, the rearmost pellets are crushed together and, if they are soft, flatten against each other. Then, as the shot exits the hull, it meets the sharp taper of the chamber forcing cone, and the pellets on the outside are battered against the hard barrel steel. As the pellets pass through the bore, they are further abraded by friction against the barrel walls. Finally, they are squeezed by the choke forcing cone and the choke constriction, becoming further deformed. When polyethylene shot wrappers and plastic wads came along, they greatly reduced pellet deformation, but setback is still a problem despite the cushioning sections of collapsible plastic wads. One item did help: buffering. By the addition of finely ground polyethylene—originally ground-up mold flashing and imperfect wads—pellets are held more firmly within the shot cup and tend not to deform, or to deform less, from setback.

All of these advancements, including plastic wads and buffering, have come along during the past fifty or sixty years. Previously, the powder and the extremely hot gases it produces were separated only by a hard card wad and as many felt wads as were necessary to properly fill the case to ensure a good crimp. When John Olin developed his progressive-burning powder and the resulting Super-X loads, he included copper-plated shot, which he named Lubaloy. This copper-plated shot not only was less prone to fuse if hot propellent gases leaked forward of the wad column, it also made the pellets a little more slippery and hence they tended to abrade less against the barrel walls. I know gas does leak because in 1975 I was chosen to shoot on the U.S. skeet team at the pre-Olympic games in Montreal. There we had the opportunity to shoot some practice with European shells, among which were East German shells loaded with felt wads made of horsehair, and boy, did they burn and smell! We could see the smoldering wads lying on the ground. So Lubaloy shot was used primarily to stop fusing, but it also supplied a small amount of lubricity to the shot so that it slipped more easily through the bore.

Today, copper-plated shot is still available, but in truth, nickel-plated shot works even better. Nickel is harder and more slippery than lead or copper, and it's used in high-performance loads for upland hunting and pigeon loads. Thousands of dollars, pesos, francs, pesetas, lira, etc., can ride on a single pigeon at a big shoot, and competitors rely almost exclusively on nickel-plated shot to ensure that the most shot stays in the pattern and reaches the rapidly fleeing pigeons.

Before we leave plating, it should be mentioned that steel shot is often plated, especially in the premium loads. Steel pellets are very prone to rusting, and coating them with copper, zinc, or another metal or alloy that does not rust greatly diminishes or eliminates the threat of their rusting into a solid lump.

For the most part, you get what you're paying for so far as shot is concerned. Promotional loads that sell for less than $5 a box in the various marts and gun shops are loaded with soft shot, and that's not all bad. Because it deforms, soft shot tends to open patterns and provides a little more margin for error. More expensive field loads tend to be loaded with harder shot, and premium field loads use hard shot, often plated. Very hard, plated shot is used in high-performance turkey loads to enhance their performance.

Nontoxic Shot

It used to be easy to describe nontoxic shot. One word would do: steel. Actually, steel shot is soft iron formed by snipping off prescribed lengths of steel wire that is annealed and then rolled into spheres, just like ball bearings are made. Until 1992, steel shot was it. And its evolution was painful, to say the least. Then along came bismuth/tin shot, then tungsten/polymer, and the latest versions are blends of tungsten and iron or tungsten, iron, and nickel.

Lakes of ink have been used to describe the evolution of nontoxic shot; here's the short version. Initially planned for use in areas identified as "hotspots" by the U.S. Fish and Wildlife Service (USFWS), nontoxic shot was not a big item for ammunition makers. Its market was guaranteed to be small, since it would be required in a mere handful of locations. Then lawsuits arose, and suddenly the hotspot philosophy went out the window. Although there were some detours and states' rights and other philosophies were debated, finally the USFWS mandated the use of nontoxic shot for the taking of all waterfowl regardless of where. Years later, Canada, too, came on line.

I shot some of the very first steel loads at Blackwater National Wildlife Refuge's Fishing Bay public hunting area in Virginia. Their use was voluntary, and as I recall, the shot size was No. 1. In a place set up strictly as a pass-shooting area, I shot at a couple of rapidly climbing Canadas, and the new steel pellets seemed to have no effect other than to increase the birds' rate of climb.

Essentially, steel is about 65 percent as dense as lead. The laws of physics, which are absolute, dictate that a lighter projectile will slow faster than a heavier one and, more importantly, carry less kinetic energy. It's kinetic energy that kills, and the less energy a pellet carries, the less lethal it is. When steel shot came along, it was quickly determined that the lag in kinetic energy could be made up, at least partially, by using a larger pellet. The rule of thumb is one size larger than lead—that is, if your favorite duck load was No. 4 lead, then No. 2 steel would perform about the same. Goose hunters needed large pellets, and many settled on very large T-size shot as the ultimate pellet for big Canada geese. Because these large pellets don't flow very well through smaller bores, the 10-gauge made a miraculous rebound from near oblivion.

Through the years since the steel-shot requirement became law, the ammunition companies have rallied and, through their extensive ballistic research and development laboratories, have elevated steel-pellet shotshells to a new level. Designing a new shotshell or family thereof is a delicate balancing act. Since steel shot is considerably lighter than lead, ratcheting up the velocity while maintaining safe pressures was the challenge. New powders were developed based on John Olin's historic progressive-burning powders, which burn slowly and continue to burn and increase pressure as the shot charge moves up the barrel. However, Boyle's Law in physics states that as the volume is doubled, the pressure is halved; so powder that continues to burn and develop pressure is managed by the ever-expanding space in the barrel as the shot and wad move toward the muzzle. The trick is to manage the burning rate of the powder to maintain the elevated pressure for a longer time. As I said, it's a delicate balancing act. To their credit, the ammunition makers constantly researched and developed increasingly more lethal shotshells. As we see in the data section, the latest high-performance steel loads leave the muzzle at velocities only imagined in the 1970s, when steel shot came into being.

The problems associated with steel shot didn't stop with its inferior ballistic properties as measured against lead shot. A shotgun barrel is made of mild steel that is relatively soft. Add to this the fact that virtually every shotgun made for waterfowl hunting was choked full, and the problems grew. Unlike lead shot, which in its hardest, plated manifestation is many times softer than barrel steel, steel shot's hardness approaches that of barrel steel.

Then there's the problem of flow. Because of its softness and lubricity, lead shot flows through a barrel much like water through a hose. When lead shot met the constriction of the choke, it elongated and slipped through the tight orifice. Steel shot is a horse of a different color. It resists flowing, preferring to stick together and move as a hard clump. When this lump of hard steel met the choke constriction, something had to go, and as ballisticians described it, it peened the choke area much like a hammer peens steel in the process of riveting or shaping metal. The result was that within five to ten shots, the barrel showed a slight ring at the muzzle over the point of choke constriction. Normally .008 to .010 inches, this ring bulge was cosmetic, for all intents and purposes. Although it opened the choke to light full, it caused no real problem, so long as it was on a single-barrel shotgun. When it appeared on a double gun, whose barrels are closely jointed at the muzzle, the result was to force the barrels apart, damaging the gun and necessitating a very expensive repair to rejoin the barrels. Added to this was the possibility of scoring the barrel if one of the steel pellets came in direct contact with it. This problem was solved by the universal adoption of extremely thick shot cups that, instead of protecting the shot from the barrel as with lead shot, protected the barrel from the hard steel shot.

Performance was further improved by the addition of copper, zinc, or other pellet coatings. This added lubricity, prevented rusting, and helped steel shot flow better. Still, steel shot rendered obsolete some of the finest shotguns ever made. No longer did hunters wish to subject their Belgian-made Browning Auto-5s, Winchester Model 12s, A. H. Foxes, L. C. Smiths, Parkers, etc., to the ravages of steel shot. Like the Red phobia of the 1950s, many saw this move to steel shot as a cabal of the government and arms manufacturers to rearm the shooting public; others painted it as an anti-hunting movement. None of this was really true. The facts were that lead was poisoning some ducks, and a group of environmental zealots led by the National Wildlife Federation, which was once a conservation group but is increasingly an extremist preservationist organization, brought suit based on alleged lead poisoning of bald eagles brought on by eagles eating dead ducks.

In retrospect, one can say that steel shot was but a blip in the road that ultimately had some very positive results, not the least of which is the near universal application of screw-in chokes to new shotguns. In fact, the adoption of steel shot brought about a complete rethinking of shotguns and led to the rebirth of the 10-gauge and such improvements in shotgun technology as factory-lengthened forcing cones and over- or back-bored barrels that pattern better regardless of the kind of shot used. Too, steel shot has led manufacturers to seek and find answers to barrel-separation and other problems. The period of 1893 through 1930 could truly be called the Golden Age of shotgun development—the time of the Winchester 1893 and improved 1897, Browning Auto-5, Winchester Model 12, Remington's bottom-ejecting Model 10, the HE-grade Super Fox, Winchester 21, progressive-burning powder, and the Super-X. And one could easily call the period from 1971 through 2000 the Second Golden Age. It was during this period that shotguns leaped into the twenty-first century, driven by computer-based technology. We initially heaped derision and invective on steel shot, but in retrospect, we really have to thank this hard interloper for many improvements. Still, all those wonderful old shotguns lie fallow.

Those who explore and invent see things like the requirement of steel shot as an opportunity, while the rest of us see them as dark doom. For example, Canadian carpenter and dreamer John Brown had an idea. If a benign metal that was heavier and yet softer than steel could be made into pellets, he reasoned, perhaps this could be a viable alternative to steel shot and, because it was softer than steel, could be usable in older shotguns. Brown began investigating bismuth, which lies below lead in weight but well above iron, the prime ingredient of steel shot. Following several years of experimenting and rejection by the major ammunition companies, publishing magnate Robert Petersen stepped in and gave Brown's research an infusion of cash that was needed for toxicity testing and production. Finally the Bismuth Cartridge Company was officially founded, and formal application was made to USFWS for approval of bismuth shot as an alternative nontoxic shot.

On the face of it, bismuth seemed to need little testing—after all, it's the main ingredient in Pepto Bismol, a commonly used over-the-counter stomach and gastric distress remedy. Bismuth Cartridge and Petersen persevered through a long and tortuous series of toxicity tests on live ducks that finally ended when bismuth shot was approved as a nontoxic shot.

During that period, I was associate editor of *American Hunter* magazine and worked on very early bismuth research, including lab, patterning, and penetration tests, culminating in a four-day duck hunt in Mexico, where there were no nontoxic-shot requirements. We determined that bismuth shot was brittle and tended to lack uniformity because the pellets are formed by the Bleimeister process, which uses a very short drop

into hot water. These factors were viewed with trepidation, and one colleague voiced the opinion that bismuth shot might not even work. The results of the lab tests were OK, but nothing to inspire rapture. In the field, though, the results were striking. It's been almost ten years, but I believe we lost only two or three crippled ducks in three days of hunting. Although I was short my gun, since Continental Airlines chose to send all of my gear and guns to Mexico City and they didn't arrive until the last day, we three shooters didn't miss many and tended to center the birds in the pattern. Ducks were shot at all ranges, and bismuth proved its worth to us and ultimately to the magazine's readers. Finally there was a nontoxic alternative to steel shot that was also usable in older shotguns.

Just as bismuth came along, British ballisticians at the Royal Ordnance establishment were working on a shotgun pellet that could be made even heavier than lead. Intended to shoot the rotor blades from helicopters, these pellets used micro-fine tungsten blended into a polymer similar to nylon. For a short time, Eley, one of England's leading ammunition manufacturers, experimented with loading these pellets, called Molyshot. The problem with this early tungsten/polymer pellet was that the tungsten was not uniformly distributed throughout the pellet. The polymer was too thin to keep the tungsten suspended while the pellet hardened. The result was a pellet that spun erratically, much like a ball that is weighted on one side. Molyshot was available for only a very brief time, but the idea remained alive.

Researchers at Kent Cartridge in Hull, England, continued to experiment with tungsten/polymer pellets. In 1996, a group of Canadian investors, seeing the distinct possibility of nontoxic shot becoming law in Canada, became interested in the tungsten/polymer pellet. If successful, it could be manufactured to replicate the density of lead and yet, because of the elasticity of the polymer, could be used in any shotgun without barrel damage. When the Canadian group bought Kent Cartridge, it decided to go full-speed ahead with tungsten/polymer shot and employed the services of a

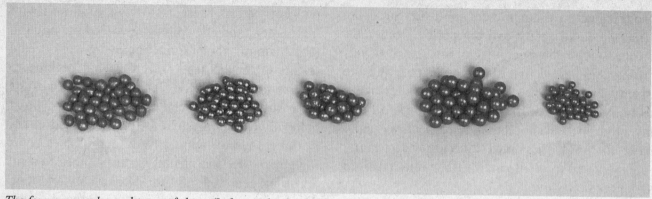

The four commonly used types of shot. (Left to right) lead, steel, bismuth, tungsten-polymer, and tungsten-nickel-iron. While lead shot remains the mainstay of upland and target loads, steel, bismuth, and the tungsten blends are required and approved for waterfowl hunting.

research chemist at Pennsylvania State University who specialized in polymers. He recommended a very thick polymer—Kent officials call it a "goo"—that would uniformly suspend the micro-fine tungsten particles while the polymer hardened, producing ballistically viable pellets. These pellets possess two important properties: They are ballistically identical to lead, and because they are somewhat elastic, they are safe to shoot in any shotgun that is safe with modern smokeless-powder ammunition.

I've shot many, many ducks and geese using Kent tungsten/polymer pellets in a variety of shotguns. These shotguns ranged from a 1920-vintage HE-grade Super Fox and a 1926 Parker to the new Winchester Super X 2 and Beretta AL391 Urika, and if I was on target, I filled my limit.

In the search for heavier steel shot, Federal Cartridge Company introduced its tungsten/iron blend that mixes micro-fine tungsten and iron in specific proportions that are then sintered into pellets. Sintering involves compressing materials at high pressure and high heat. Canadian Industries Limited (CIL), at the request of the Canadian Wildlife Service, experimented with sintered steel pellets when nontoxic shot became an issue in the late 1960s and early '70s. However, CIL never developed the pellet, and the project was largely forgotten until it was resurrected by Federal in the 1990s. These pellets are intended to be shot only in shotguns specifically designed to shoot steel shot. In use, these heavier pellets have proven to be excellent in the field, ensuring clean kills at acceptable shotgun ranges.

The newest pellet, Hevi-Shot, combines iron, nickel, and tungsten into pellets that are even heavier and denser than lead, and very hard. Hevi-Shot contends that because this pellet is heavier, smaller shot can be used, thus providing denser patterns with velocities equal to much larger shot. Again, this shot is for use only in steel-shot-compatible shotguns, and in brief field tests it did provide good lethality.

Since the birth of the shotgun centuries ago, the composition of shot has been the subject of debate, experimentation, and evolution. Today, there are developments yet to be made in the realm of nontoxic pellets. There is a real need for a ballistically viable pellet that can be shot in any shotgun and will deliver the downrange results of the common-denominator lead pellet, yet be as affordable as lead. The tungsten derivatives are expensive, and even steel is not as reasonable as lead because of the extra cost of making steel pellets. As we head into the twenty-first century, nontoxic shot will continue to be a factor that will increasingly affect all aspects of shotgunning, and the need for an inexpensive and yet effective pellet will remain the challenge.

PRESSURE AND VELOCITY

We frequently talk of pressure: safe pressures, service pressure, proof pressure—all of which greatly affect shotshell performance and safety. When powders burn, they combine with oxygen to create an ever-expanding volume of gas that continues to be generated until all of the powder is consumed or the ejecta—wad and shot—exit the muzzle. Pressures must be engineered so that the volume of gas, which generates the pressure, is balanced with the ever-expanding chamber created as the wad and shot column move down the barrel. Essentially, powders are grouped by their burning rates. Those that burn quickly are intended for light loads of moderate velocity. Slow-burning powders are intended to propel heavy shot charges at higher velocities. That is an oversimplification, of course, but the important factor is that powders are matched to their task so that the resulting pressures remain below the service pressure.

Anytime pressures exceed those that firearms are designed to safely contain, a very dangerous situation is at hand. One of the worst horror stories I've ever heard was related by a warden who had to investigate a Christmas-morning tragedy. A husband had asked his wife for a Lee Loader for Christmas. His particular model was manufactured essentially like turn-of-the-century reloading equipment. This all-manual unit was a very inexpensive way to reload hunting ammunition, but it was in no way to blame for the disastrous outcome. The wife shopped for the loader and also bought components so her husband could try it out right away. Unwittingly, she disregarded the advice of the shop owner and, thinking powders to be all the same, put back the milder shotgun powder in favor of a can of pistol powder. In the rush of Christmas shoppers, the gun shop clerk didn't notice that she had selected a canister of pistol powder. As she later stated, "I had no idea they were different—one was cheaper than the other."

Christmas morning came, and her excited husband quickly assembled a couple of shells, stepped onto their front porch, loaded one into his single-barrel break-action 10-bore shotgun, and fired it. When he did, the top of the standing breech came off to the rear, along with the majority of the man's head above his eyebrows. It's a ghastly story, but it reminds us that any casual approach to loading ammunition can be a one-way ticket to disaster. And it vividly demonstrates why pressure is such an important facet of ammunition research, development, and safe loading.

With this in mind, the ammunition companies are very careful when they load ammunition for us, their consumers. Certainly, some loads generate close to the maximum allowable pressures, but those and every other commercially produced load are frequently tested and evaluated as loading takes place. Random lots of ammunition are continually taken from the loading machines and checked with highly sensitive pressure guns. During the research and development phase of any load, it is further tested at extreme temperatures, both hot and cold, all to ensure safety.

In consort with other national proof and standards associations, the Sporting Arms and Ammunition Manufacturers' Institute (SAAMI) publishes a set of service pressures that all arms makers must use in designing and building shotguns, to ensure the safety of the individual arms to the shooting public. All arms are proof-tested as one of the final steps of manufacture. In England and Europe, where government proof houses proof-test all arms, whether made in that country or imported, barrels are frequently proof-

This pressure gun, owned by Hodgdon Powders and used in their laboratory in Shawnee Mission, Kansas, can accurately measure the pressure generated by a particular cartridge. Similar guns are used by all ammunition and component manufacturers to test loaded ammunition to ensure that it meets all requirements of safe pressure and velocity. This particular pressure gun is fired with compressed air so that each strike of the primer is uniform.

tested prior to being built into complete shotguns then proof-tested again when the gun is completed and nearly ready for delivery. Foreign proof marks often show both provisional proof of barrels and definitive proof for the entire firearm. In America, the responsibility for proofing arms lies with the individual manufacturers. In lockstep with the arms makers, the ammunition companies load their products to the same set of data, ensuring that the shooting public is in no way endangered when firearms and ammo come together. Table 8.1 illustrates the SAAMI service pressures used to ensure that the pressures of manufactured ammunition remain within the safe limits of each particular gauge.

These pressures are at the very top of the allowable measure for any round, and manufacturers and those who provide handloading

data endeavor to keep pressures well below the precipice. However, there are loads that approach these pressures, and all handloaders are advised to use extreme care when assembling ammunition that approaches these thresholds.

Proof pressure is about one-third to one-half more than service pressures. Shotguns are normally tested with one or two proof rounds, then carefully examined for any signs of stress or damage. Any arm showing any negative effects from the testing is rejected—very few are, although some old shotguns submitted for re-proof or nitro-proof of Damascus barrels can fail proof-testing. In England, any shotgun sold must be in proof, and if any work has been done on any part of the barrel, except perhaps very minor polishing of the bore, the gun must be re-proofed by either the London or the Birmingham proof house prior to any type of sale.

SAAMI standards for definitive proof loads are quoted in Table 8.2. It should be pointed out that ammunition companies very carefully control the sale and distribution of proof loads. Furthermore, proof loads are very specially marked so that they cannot be confused with loads of normal pressures.

The preamble to the section on proof loads in the SAAMI standards manual states:

SAAMI Definitive Proof Loads are shells commercially loaded by SAAMI member companies to develop pressures substantially

Table 8.1

Gauge/bore	Chamber length in inches	Maximum service pressure in psi
10	3½	11,000
12	3½	14,000
12	3	11,500
12	2¾	11,500
16	2¾	11,500
20	3	12,000
20	2¾	12,000
28	2¾	12,500
.410	3	13,500
.410	2½	12,500

Table 8.2

Gauge/bore	Chamber length (in.)	Shot weight (oz.)	Minimum average (psi)	Maximum average (psi)
10	2⁷/₈	1⁵/₈ oz.	18,000	19,500
10	3¹/₂	2 oz.	18,000	19,500
12	2³/₄ and 3	1¹/₂ oz.	19,000	20,500
12	3¹/₂	1⁹/₁₆ oz.	22,800	24,500
16	2³/₄	1¹/₄ oz.	19,000	20,200
20	2³/₄ and 3	1¹/₈ oz.	19,500	21,000
28	2³/₄	1 oz.	20,500	22,000
.410	2¹/₂	¹/₂ oz.	20,500	22,000
.410	3	¹¹/₁₆ oz.	22,000	23,500

exceeding those developed by normal service loads. The pressure levels are designed to assure firearms safety when using ammunition loaded to service pressures in accord with accepted American practices.

Proof loads are designed to stress firearms components which contain the cartridge in order to assure safety in the recommended use of [the] firearm during its service life. Definitive proof loads are loaded with the heaviest shot charge commercially available for the particular gauge and shell length. The slowest [burning rate] powder that will meet the pressure values is used in order to maintain effective pressure-distance relationships.

SAAMI further states, "Shotshell Definitive Proof Loads should be used for one purpose only: The proof testing of shotguns." All proof cartridges are labeled: *DANGER—High Pressure.* Some are also stamped: *For use by Gun Makers for testing strength of Guns or Danger Proof Load* or *Danger High Pressure Proof Load.* In Table 8.2 are the minimum and maximum average pressures used in proof loads.

Obviously, these proof pressures are far in excess of the nominal service pressures and in no way imply that shells loaded in excess of service pressures are safe. *They are not.*

While ammunition manufacturers do not publish pressures, they are increasingly publishing velocity data. However, it should be kept in mind that the heavier the load, the slower-burning the powder used. Because pressure, hence velocity, is affected by temperature, ammunition is routinely tested at about 65 degrees F. When the temperature

dips below 32 degrees, powder, especially slow-burning powders used in steel shot and other waterfowl loads, becomes harder to ignite and burns slower than it does at 65 degrees and higher. The fluctuation is minor, and even the most experienced shots cannot detect the slight drop in velocity. However, often more unburned powder is left in the barrel and blown back into the action. In the case of gas-operated semiautomatic shotguns, the accumulation of unburned powder can necessitate more frequent cleaning.

In the section containing the ballistic tables, manufacturer-stated velocities are listed whenever possible. When it comes down to it, velocity is one of the two most important aspects of shotshell performance, the other being pattern efficiency (including shot string). It is difficult to divorce pattern efficiency from velocity—if there aren't enough pellets striking the target, be it clay, furred, or feathered, it matters little how fast the pellets are going. But the reverse is also true, at least to an extent—if the pellets aren't going fast enough to penetrate, there is little likelihood they will prove lethal. However, velocity can be overrated. In rifle shooting, velocity governs long-range accuracy and also lethality; in the world of shotguns, everything save rifle slugs is short-range, and though pellets certainly are affected by gravity, pellet drop is seldom a consideration to shotgunners. Pellets simply run out of energy before drop becomes a factor. Bullets intended for long-range rifle shooting are aerodynamically designed to cut through the resistance of air, but round pellets are inefficient from the start, and therefore loss of velocity occurs before trajectory factors come into play.

In shotgunning, there is a downside to high-velocity loss of pattern efficiency. When lead shot

Velocity is measured by means of a chronograph such as this one manufactured by PACT. The shot charge, or, in the case of a rifle, the projectile, flies through the openings created by the arched plastic diffusers. Beneath each diffuser is a highly sensitive photoelectric cell. When the shot cluster crosses the first photocell, it turns the chronograph on, and when the light is interrupted by the shot charge crossing the second cell, the circuit is turned off. The computer then calculates the velocity at which the charge crossed the two cells and displays the result on the screen in feet per second or meters per second, depending on how the computer is programmed.

is driven at very high velocity, so many of the pellets are crushed against each other and deformed that pattern density suffers. Although modern, progressive-burning powders can propel shot at blistering velocities—as witness the new 1,900-fps slug loads—the resulting damage to the shot, even when buffered, makes such velocities impractical. However, in steel shot, which is immensely harder than the hardest 6-percent-antimony, nickel-plated lead shot, high velocity is not only possible but necessary. Steel shot is only about 65 percent as heavy as lead, and to compete in the lethality arena, it must be launched at higher velocity to have any chance to perform at long ranges.

In examining the tables that accompany each load, it is easy to see how quickly velocities drop off as ranges lengthen.

One aspect of velocity is the apparent need to increase or decrease lead or forward allowance according to velocity. However, anyone who advocates lead adjustment based on velocity is playing in micro-measurements. In short, lead differences are minuscule. Certainly, you can work out leads mathematically, but such minor differences should never be the basis of a shooting style. I shoot lots of different loads every year, and I cannot honestly state that I can tell the difference in required lead from one to another. It would seem that a high-velocity load should really make a difference, but I can't tell if it does, and I doubt you can, either. The best advice is to establish a good, sound approach to shotgun shooting and allow velocity to provide lethality. Whether a target is hit by a truck or by five No. 7½ pellets, it's the transmitted energy established by velocity that provides lethality.

Each component of a shotshell interrelates with each other component, and when they interact efficiently as a whole, the result is proper velocity over the intended range of the load. Shotshells have become highly specialized, and though you can shoot pheasants with a trap load, doves with a duck load, and so on, each shotshell essentially fills a niche for which its ballistic designers have intended it. Velocity is one of the most important facets of the equation, and in designing loads, it is one of the primary considerations. The tables make it easy to compare velocities and their effect on the loads' downrange pellet performance.

RECOIL

For every action there is an equal reaction. Sir Isaac Newton's law, while not precisely stated here, essentially says that if we fire a shotgun, we have to expect some recoil. Numerous variables govern how unpleasant it is. First is the shotshell. With a light payload at a low velocity, recoil can be almost nothing. Conversely, a heavy, maximum payload fired at high velocity will cause maximum recoil. Then there's the gun. The heavier it is, the slower it will be pushed backward by recoil. But recoil can be made endurable by the combination of gun weight and the unique ability of semiautomatic shotguns to spread out the sensation of recoil. Other methods to attenuate recoil include barrel porting and add-on recoil reducers such as pads, shock-absorbing stocks, and weights.

Recoil in its simplest form is indeed explained by Newton, and you can calculate free recoil by using a formula discussed by Gen. Julian S. Hatcher, former officer-in-charge of the Experimental Department of the Springfield Armory, in his book, *Hatcher's Notebook*. Free recoil is the recoil energy or recoil velocity developed by the gun alone without any outside factors—in short, kick. The formula Hatcher and everyone else uses is:

$$(E+1.75P)Mv \div W \div 7,000$$

In this equation E equals the weight of the ejecta (powder, wad, and shot) in grains. The powder weight is multiplied by 1.75 to compensate for the fact that the expanding powder gases are moving faster than the shot when they exit the muzzle, and Mv is muzzle velocity. The figure derived by multiplying all of these factors is then divided by W, the weight of the gun, and the final answer is attained by dividing the above by 7,000, the number of grains in a pound, yielding recoil velocity in foot-pounds. I ran several popular loads in a couple of average-weight shotguns through E. D. Lowry's ballistics program, which does all the math for me, and the findings are in Table 9.1.

The mathematics reveal recoil energy, a measure of what we feel. However, recoil velocity tells us how fast that gun is coming back against our shoulder—and up into our cheek, given a poorly designed stock that has too much drop or too little pitch.

In the reference section of this book, I've used only two gun weights, eight and ten pounds. The ten-pound shotgun was used solely with 10-gauge loads, since that's an appropriate weight for those guns. An eight-pound shotgun was used for all the other loads. Although plenty of lighter and heavier guns are used with the various gauges,

Table 9.1

Gauge	Length	Velocity (fps)	Shot charge/type	Gun weight (lbs)	Recoil (ft.-lbs)	Energy Velocity (fps)
12	2¾	1,200	1⅛ lead	7	23.3	14.6
12	2¾	1,260	1⅛ lead	8	20.4	12.8
12	2¾	1,260	1¼ lead	7	32.7	17.3
12	2¾	1,260	1¼ lead	8	28.8	15.2
12	3½	1,150	2¼ lead	7½	77.8	25.8
12	3½	1,450	1⅜ steel	7½	53.8	21.5
20	2¾	1,220	1 lead	6	22.4	15.5
20	3	1,330	1 steel	6	28.2	17.4

there needed to be a standard for comparison of all loads. In general, Americans like semiautos and pumps, and many of these weigh in the eight-pound range. Recoil energy and velocity are included for the sake of comparison, and therefore a standard was selected and universally applied.

When we shoot at game, we often don't remember the recoil, regardless of how heavy—our attention is directed at the target. However, when we shoot at the pattern board or in a long competitive tournament, we do notice recoil. Too, one bad experience with a particular shotgun will cause us, consciously or not, to be afraid to shoot that gun. An ill-fitting stock, especially in a situation where a youngster or slightly built female is started with a shotgun designed for a large male, can also cause a heightened sense of recoil. Everyone has his or her own threshold of tolerance to recoil. Some become toughened to it, others become more sensitized. From years of shooting at clays, game, and the patterning board, I find that unpleasantness starts at thirty foot-pounds of recoil and goes up rapidly from there. One of my least favorite tasks is shooting patterns with one of the current crop of 7- or 7½-pound pumps, using 3½-inch 12-gauge magnum loads. Check out the 12-gauge 3½-inch recoil figures. People have broken collarbones shooting such magnum loads through light turkey guns while propped against a tree. Pads and porting can do only so much. I'll freely admit that I used to lust after the latest magnum load, feeling that more was better—it's the American way. We've always looked for the giant economy size, the long-range load, the magnum super thumper. The fact is, though, that if you shoot well, light or moderate loads fill the bill pretty well, all at a great decrease in recoil.

Recoil pads are the most familiar way we have of softening recoil. Walter Scott of Birmingham, England, patented the first "India-rubber" pad in 1871. Perhaps the most famous of the early pads was made by Hugh Silver, who patented his design in 1874. Known by their all-red appearance, Silver's pads were used on shotguns well into the twentieth century. My old Super Fox has a red Silver-style pad, and when Greg Wolf restocks it, he's going to put the same style pad on, this one probably made by Galazan in New Britain,

Connecticut. So the idea of something soft and squishy on the butt to ease recoil isn't really new, but as time marches on, so does progress.

In the past couple of decades or so, big strides have been made in recoil pads that are either permanently attached to a stock or simply slip over the existing butt. If you need a longer stock, one of the slip-on models is a good bet. If the stock is OK as is or needs to be shorter, the services of a good gunsmith should be enlisted to cut the stock and attach and trim the pad to look as if it grew onto the stock. Traditional recoil pads like the venerable Pachmayr are made of rubber, and though they provided some cushioning, it wasn't until the advent of Sorbothane, which is used as the padding in ejection seats and similar products, that recoil pads really got cooking. These new pads require some special handling when it comes to trimming them to size, but when in place, they provide superior recoil attenuation. Pachmayr, 100-Straight, Kick-Eez, and others make these high-performance pads. At this writing, Beretta has just released a new gel-filled pad for its current over/under and semiauto shotguns that works very well.

One of the oldest ways to reduce felt recoil is to make the gun heavier. Adding lead shot embedded in glue or lead golf-club tape to the inside of the buttstock and fore-end can help. Many tout the recoil reducers that you can purchase and insert into the magazines of pumps and semiautos, or others like the venerable Edwards that can be inserted into the buttstock of about any shotgun. They all add weight, and that is the primary reason they reduce the recoil.

Barrel porting is relatively new. It redirects the propellant gases up and partially to the rear, greatly reducing the upward recoil of the gun. The difference between ported and unported barrels is fairly dramatic. Although porting's attenuation of the *rearward* movement of the gun is minimal, its ability to stop the barrel from rising is immediately apparent. Keeping the muzzle down makes follow-up shots much easier to control and target acquisition much easier.

Recoil is an important factor to consider when selecting ammunition. Remember, when you approach the ammo counter or check loads in the ballistics section of this book, those shells that offer enlarged payloads or higher velocity come

Recoil can be tamed by pads such as these, pads permanently mounted to the buttstock, barrel porting, or adding weight to the gun.

at a price: increased recoil. For the hunter who may shoot only a few rounds a day, it's not a big factor, but for the beginner, or those who will shoot many shots, lighter loads carrying less shot or somewhat slower velocities are a better choice. A well-made, appropriately choked shotgun whose stock fits the shooter, and adequate but relatively light loads, may well bring better results than a super magnum that carries a fear factor. The first requirement is to hit the target, and poor shooting spawned by excessive recoil is a prime enemy of good marksmanship.

HANDLOADING

In previous sections, especially the one about components, I've covered much that is germane to the handloading of shotshells. Reloading, or handloading, offers the shotgunner economy and the ability to tailor loads to individual circumstances. For example, a die-hard duck hunter I once met puts together special loads that he uses in only one, unique place, a pond that is barely twenty yards across. Because all of his shots are within that range, he puts together one-ounce loads of steel No. 5s that he shoots through a cylinder barrel. Other waterfowlers whose shots at geese are at the fringe of steel-shot range put up ultra-high-velocity loads equal to that situation. Shooters who pursue clay birds with passion use handloading to ease the bite on their wallet.

As a basic definition, shotshell reloading is the replacing of the components—primer, powder, wad, and shot—consumed when the shot is fired. Although the concept is simple, these components must be replaced with care, and in accord with established data from a reputable source, to assure ballistically excellent loads.

Shotgunners deal with much lower pressures than their rifle-shooting buddies do, but there are still hazards if data are not carefully followed. I witnessed the destruction of a Remington 11-48 .410 at the hands of a basement ballistician who, rather than following established data, decided to make his own "special" load. It was special, all right! Too, improperly assembled loads, even if they do not prove hazardous, are often so inefficient that loading and using them is a waste of time and money. The first step toward safe, sane, quality reloads is a good data manual. The *Hodgdon Shotshell Data Manual* contains everything a novice handloader needs to know, and everything an experienced handloader *ought* to know. Before investing in equipment, get the book, read it, then proceed.

Beyond a manual, any handloader needs only two pieces of equipment, a loader and a powder scale. Loader prices run from less than $50 for a Lee to close to $1,000 for the Spolar Gold; the popular MEC and Hornady tools run between $150 and $300; the new RCBS Grand American goes for about $650. The differences in price have something to do with materials and construction, but more to do with convenience. The less expensive loaders produce one shell at a time, while the more expensive ones drop a loaded shell into the bucket with each pull of the lever. Beginners should start with a basic single-station loader. Once they know the ropes, and if the demand for ammunition dictates, they can move up to one of the faster progressive loaders.

The steps of reloading begin with resizing, during which the metal head—they often look like brass, but most are mostly plated steel—is squeezed back to factory dimensions. Next, the spent primer is punched out and replaced with a fresh one. The powder is then charged, the wad inserted, the shot dropped, and the mouth of the shell is first partially closed and then finally crimped.

Resizing is accomplished by either forcing the shell into a die or by the action of MEC's fingered collet that squeezes the metal back to standard dimensions. If shells are fired repeatedly in the same gun, they may not need resizing, especially if it's a double. However, nearly all loaders incorporate resizing so smoothly into the process that omitting the step is not worth considering. Contrary to reloading rifle cartridges, there is no wear and tear on the brass; I don't remember ever cracking a shotshell's head by resizing.

The question often arises: How many times can a hull be reloaded? Hodgdon's chief ballistician, Ron Reiber, says, "I load 'em until the crimps split." Hodgdon did some tests over the fifteen-reload life of a particular hull. By shot Number 7 pinholes appeared around the crimp fold, and by the time it had been reloaded ten times, the crimp folds began splitting. Following the fifteenth reloading, the hull split. Surprisingly, over the course of the test, velocity remained consistent at 1,150 fps, dropping only four feet. Pressures dropped consistently from 11,100 psi to a low of 10,600 psi on the thirteenth firing, but in view of the consistent velocity, that's insignificant. Contrary to commonly held beliefs, so long as loading procedure and crimp depth remain consistent, hulls seem to cause little variation. However, if you plan to hunt or compete at clays with your reloads, and especially if you shoot a pump or semiautomatic, I'd use once- or twice-fired hulls to prevent a bulged crimp from hanging up and not chambering. This way, you wouldn't miss the day's only chance at game or lose a competition.

Punching out the old primer normally occurs at the same stage at which the new primer is inserted. At one time there were different-sized primers, but save for some European shells that are unlikely candidates for reloading, all are now of the same dimension. However, as pointed out in the section on components, *no two brands or types of primers are the same*. Primers should never be substituted. Yes, some are similar, and yes, almost identical data exist for loads using different primers, but primers are nonetheless different and not interchangeable. Switching primers can raise pressure or at the very least unbalance an otherwise good load. How? The crimp must remain tight for the fraction of a second needed to efficiently and uniformly light the powder. A heavier-than-specified primer can prematurely blow open the crimp, robbing the shell of the compression necessary to properly build pressure. This discussion could go on for pages. Simply put, don't substitute primers. Ditto for powders and wads.

Next in line is charging the powder. Shotshell loaders measure powder with bushings of differing capacity. All loaders come with literature that includes a chart listing the various bushings and the amounts of different powders they drop. These charts are only a guide. Once a load and the appropriate powder are selected and the bushing inserted in the loader, the powder drop *must* be verified with a good powder scale. It is generally accepted that a variation of no more than three-tenths (.3) of a grain will produce good, reliable loads, but it is possible to narrow that to as little as one-tenth (.1). Much depends upon how

the loader is cycled. Operators who gently lower and raise the loader's handle and gently cycle the bar that holds the powder bushing will drop consistently lighter powder charges than those who are rougher and consequently cause heavier charges to drop. Regardless, the powder drop needs to be checked with a good scale.

I normally load the powder hopper, cycle the handle three or four times, resize, de-prime, and re-prime a hull, and drop the powder. Then I remove the charged hull from the loader and deposit the powder onto the pan of my zeroed PAST electronic scale. Tapping the side of the hull away from the primer with a wooden dowel ensures that all the powder gets into the pan. Then I weigh the charge. If it's not within .2 or .3 grains of the data, check it again. If it's still off the mark, you'll have to change the bushing to a larger or smaller one based on the scale's reading. You need to do this each time you change powder brands or even use a different lot of the same powder; it ensures safety and provides the best load for your time and money.

Once the powder is charged, the wad is inserted. Time was when we loaded over-powder card and felt spacers and a specific pressure had to be applied to the wad column. That's no longer necessary. All that's needed is to firmly seat the wad atop the powder. Some hunting loads will compress the wad, but most will not. Though wads are not interchangeable, some made by various manufacturers are intended to interchange with specific brand-name wads. These come with data, which should be compared with the data for the brand-name wad to be sure that they match. Hunting loads normally do not permit wad interchanges, and steel-shot loads are so specific that wad changes aren't possible.

Once the wad is inserted, the shot is charged. Shot charging is the easiest part of the reloading process but still requires a one-time check of the shot drop with a scale just to be sure that the loader is dropping the proper amount. Very rarely a bushing will be mis-stamped, so it's best to verify the drop the first time you use it. Loading a lighter- or heavier-than-specified shot charge can be as serious as substituting other components.

The next station is the crimp starter, which partially folds the crimp in so that the final crimp stage can neatly fold it back to its factory-new appearance. The importance of obtaining a good crimp of proper depth cannot be overemphasized, but too much of a good thing can also be bad. According to research by Hodgdon's ballistic lab, good crimps ought to be right at .050 inch deep, just short of one-sixteenth of an inch. Increasing the crimp depth of a test load by as little as .020 to a depth of .070 raised a common target load into the high-pressure range at 11,900 psi, and a crimp of .090 raised the pressure into the dangerous zone at 13,100 psi. Both are beyond the service pressure (see the chapter on pressure and velocity). Most loaders come adjusted from the factory to crimp at the correct depth, and adjustment from there should be carefully done.

Traditionally, the crimp station was it, but more recently, manufacturers have added a final station that applies a cone to the crimp. At one time, the crimps of many handloaded shotshells were fatter than the metal base and had to be "assisted" into the chamber. This final coning by modern loaders ensures positive chambering, provided you use good hulls that allow a firm crimp.

There you have it, a stage-by-stage, blow-by-blow of how shotshells are reloaded. Each loading machine does it a little differently, but they all perform the same tasks. The speed at which they perform them is the big difference. I've known handloaders who could really turn out the reloads with a single-stage MEC, Jr., but when volume becomes a must, it's time to look at the progressive-style loaders. These machines are designed to produce lots of ammunition in a short amount of time. They perform the same operations as single-stage loaders—they just do them all at the same time. Once the platen or shell plate is full and the powder and shot are turned on, these loaders perform all of the steps each time the machine cycles. Many of these progressive loaders can be attached to a hydraulic operating system that cycles the machine each time a foot pedal is pressed. An even faster way to produce ammo with a

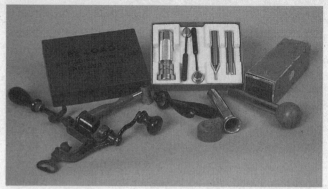

Handloading is simply replacing the components consumed when the shell is fired. Although we now use sophisticated loading presses, these early loading tools that include a roll-crimping device and the 1950s Lee loader essentially accomplish the goal.

progressive loader is to have two operators, one cycling the handle and inserting the hull or wad, the other inserting whatever component the handle puller doesn't insert and keeping the hoppers full of powder and shot. And, boy, can a progressive gobble up the components!

Loaders that have approached nirvana in terms of rapidly producing lots of quality ammo are the Spolar Gold, which incorporates a vibrator to keep the primer track full and also settles the powder in the bushing for very accurate drops, the Dillon SL900, and the RCBS Grand American. None is cheap, but they can really put out the shells. The Dillon has the added advantage of a mechanical hopper that drops a hull onto the platen each time the machine cycles, leaving the operator to insert only the wad and pull the handle.

Any way you slice it, reloading your own ammo can save upward of 50 percent of the cost of store-bought shells. Selecting components carefully, choosing a good, balanced load, and assembling it with care can put shells in your shotgun that can rival the best, and that's the idea.

(The above originally appeared in the July 2000 issue of *American Rifleman*.)

SELECTING THE CORRECT LOAD

The loads shown in the data section cover the widest range of uses. Many, such as nontoxic loads, fill niche purposes, while others can be used on virtually any game. Prior to the implementation of nontoxic shot for hunting waterfowl, the shotshell ammunition catalog was considerably simpler and of less breadth. It broke down into heavy and light waterfowl and field loads, target loads, buckshot, and rifled slugs. A heavy load like Winchester-Western's Super-X or Remington's Express could easily be found in a waterfowler's shell box or a pheasant hunter's coat. A trap load was as likely to be found in a quail hunter's coat as a competitor's vest at the Grand American. The only slotted ammunition was buckshot and rifled slugs intended for big game. However, many misguided goose hunters shot buckshot at out-of-range geese, hoping for a lucky pellet to break a wing. If they had ever shot buckshot on paper, that poke-and-hope tradition would have died. As it was, most game departments, or at least those with any sense, made the use of buckshot for waterfowl illegal. Today, there is virtually no crossover between waterfowlers' nontoxic shotshells and lead loads. Field loads still have crossover users, as do target loads.

Perhaps the biggest mystery load is the "promotional" load. These are the shotshells sold primarily at the various marts, gun clubs, and gun shops for very low prices. Identified as "dove and quail," "pheasant," or other generic names implying their best potential use, these loads carry an ounce of relatively soft shot in 12-gauge and 7/8 ounce in 20-gauge. They do, however, possess good velocity and give good value for the money, though they are put up in a hull that is not intended to be reloaded. These loads use quality wads and are ballistically balanced. The cost savings are in the one-way hull and softer shot. The advantages these shells provide the hunter include good velocity, which helps keep him ahead of his target, and the wider pattern provided by the softer shot. The major ammunition companies are now loading similar shells with steel shot.

The specifics of nontoxic shot are covered elsewhere, but its use needs to be viewed as an ever-expanding horizon. The flip side of that coin is lead: As its use in our everyday life is further restricted, so, too, will be its use as shot.

Certainly, steel shot is adequate for short-range applications, but how will it work for the various clay-target games? Skeet is shot at short range, and distance is not a factor, except that it is probably not possible to successfully load steel shot in the diminutive .410 and difficult at best for the 28-gauge. But handicap trap, live-pigeon shooting, and other long-range games could be impacted by the increasing use of steel. Steel is the least expensive shot to produce; tungsten/polymer and bismuth pellets are more expensive because of the cost of tungsten, and the blends of steel, iron, nickel, and other metals still hover at the expensive level. My hope is that we can continue to use lead shot for the majority of the clay-target games and allowable hunting. By the time nontoxic shot is required for everything (and that could be generations away though it is likely to be sooner), perhaps the cost of producing nontoxic shot will drop or a cheap alternative will be found. Although shooting might not be the direct target, the drive to eliminate lead in automobile batteries and other common applications will indeed impact its use for shot. It is good that ammunition manufacturers have taken the lead in searching for viable alternatives. Who knows—as the twenty-first century progresses, we may be using ray guns à la *Star Wars*!

Turning to more positive thoughts, here is a breakdown of what loads work best for what game

(Table 11.1) Don't forget, though, that whenever a light load is specified, target loads are equally acceptable and often provide better performance in terms of pattern and consistency. Too, in some places traditional loads are preferred by the locals, and often the use of these loads is well grounded in fact; sometimes, however, a local preference has no basis in ballistics and is best forgotten.

The below are based on manufacturers' recommendations and experience. In any situation, a more open choke is probably the best choice since it provides a little more room for error. Only in the case of turkeys should extremely tight full chokes be used; they are highly recommended because of their ability to put the maximum number of pellets into the tennis-ball-sized head.

Table 11.1

Game	Shot	Recommended shot size	Choke	Gauge
Large geese	steel	T, BBB, BB	Modified	10, 12
Large geese	bismuth	BB, 2	Mod., Full	10, 12
Large geese	tung./polymer	1	Mod., I. Mod., Full	12
Small geese	steel	BB, 1	Mod.	10, 12
Small geese	bismuth	2, 4	Mod., I. Mod., Full	12
Small geese	tung./polymer	1, 2	Mod., I. Mod., Full	12
Ducks	steel	1, 2, 3	Imp. Cyl., Mod., I. Mod	10, 12, 20
Ducks	bismuth	2, 4, 5, 6	Imp. Cyl., Mod.	10, 12, 20
Ducks	tung./polymer	2, 3, 4, 5, 6	Imp. Cyl., Mod.	12, 16, 20
Turkeys	lead	4, 5, 6	Full, Extra full	10, 12, 16, 20
Pheasants	steel	4	Imp. Cyl.	12, 20
Pheasants	lead	4, 5, 6, 7½	I.C., Mod., Full	12, 16, 20
Pheasants	bismuth	2, 4, 6	Imp. Cyl., Mod., Full	12, 16, 20
Pheasants	tung./polymer	4, 5, 6	Imp. Cyl., Mod., Full	12, 16
Grouse/Partridge	lead	6, 7½	Imp. Cyl., Mod.	12, 16, 20, 28
Woodcock	steel	4, 6, 7	Imp. Cyl.,	12, 16, 20
Woodcock	bismuth	6, 7½	Skeet, I.C., Mod.	12, 16, 20, 28
Woodcock	tung./polymer	6	Skeet, I.C., Mod.	12, 16, 20
Woodcock	lead	6, 7½, 8	Skeet, I.C., Mod.	12, 16, 20, 28
Snipe/Rail	steel	6, 7	Skeet, I.C.	12, 16
Snipe/Rail	bismuth	7½, 8	Skeet, I.C.	12, 16, 20, 28
Snipe/Rail	tung./polymer	6	Skeet, I.C.	12, 16, 20
Quail	lead	7½, 8	Skeet, I.C.	12, 16, 20, 28
Quail	bismuth	7½	Skeet, I.C.	12, 16, 20, 28
Quail	tung./polymer	6	Skeet, I.C.	12, 16, 20
Dove	lead	7½, 8	I.C., Mod., I. Mod.	12, 16, 20, 28
Dove	steel	6, 7	Skeet, I.C., Mod.	12, 20
Dove	bismuth	7½	I.C., Mod., I. Mod.	12, 16, 20, 28
Dove	tung./polymer	6	I.C., Mod., I. Mod.	12, 16, 20
Rabbit	lead	4, 5, 6	I.C., Mod.	12, 16, 20, 28, .410
Squirrel	lead	4, 5, 6	Mod., I. Mod., Full	12, 16, 20, 28. .410

Chokes abbreviations:
I.C. = Improved Cylinder; Mod. = modified; I. Mod. = improved modified.

LOADS FOR BIG GAME

The original shotgun was, in fact, a smoothbore rifle that shot a single round ball. Many Civil War weapons shot round balls, yet troops often loaded their smoothbores with "buck and ball," which combined a single ball with a charge of buckshot. While these firearms were intended as rifles, the fact that they lacked rifling made them de facto shotguns. At Gettysburg, buck and ball were used by infantry against cavalry. As things became more sophisticated, rifles and shotguns went their separate ways, and better firearms and projectiles evolved.

SLUGS

Around the turn of the twentieth century, the British introduced the Paradox gun, a shotgun whose bore is mostly smooth but has rifling in the last few inches (normally the last two). In theory, this gun is capable of firing either shot or a slug; the ball or bullet engages sufficient rifling to provide the spin necessary for accurate shooting. Intended to replace multibarrel guns such as drillings, Paradox guns seem to have been effective as big-game rifles, while providing the user with the handling qualities of a shotgun. Although the popularity of these guns waned following World War I, firms such as Holland & Holland continued to catalog and manufacture them until the 1950s.

Paradox guns seemed to work well for those who could afford them, but most shotgunners needed more. These enthusiasts who had the opportunity to take the occasional crack at a buck and yet used their shotguns primarily for upland and waterfowl hunting needed a solid projectile that would provide accuracy without the need for a rifled barrel. The Foster-style slug, which came along in the 1920s, has several aspects that, at least

in theory, make it a viable projectile for taking big game. Intended for and limited to white-tailed deer, European boar, black bear, and other animals classified as "light big game" taken at ranges of less than a hundred yards, the Foster-style slug is cast of soft lead with a hollow base. These factors allow it to expand under the pressures of the propellant gases, sealing the bore and centering it in the bore. Cast into the sides of the slug are slanted grooves that may cause it to spin when it hits the air. Spinning stabilizes solid projectiles in flight and provides accuracy.

Foster-style slugs perform reasonably well when fired through tight cylinder bores. One of the most accurate smoothbore barrels I ever tested with slugs was a Browning Auto-5 slug barrel that, true to Browning's and European standards, was bored on the tight side. Ithaca Model 37 slug guns have become hunters' favorites because their barrels, too, are bored on the tight side. In any case, for the very best performance, barrels for shooting Foster-style slugs should be choked cylinder and bored slightly tighter than standard: The tighter the fit, within safe limits, the better the accuracy.

Though the Foster-style slug set the standard for years, shooters who constantly sought better performance looked to the military for answers. Although rifling became a very important aspect of artillery, in more recent years sabot (pronounced *sá bow*) rounds fired through smoothbore artillery and tank guns have proven ultra-accurate. Applying that technology to shotgun slugs has brought about yet another revolution in scattergun technology. Sabot is a French word for shoe, and this shoe is used to encase the projectile and center it in the bore. Made of tough plastic, the sabot, contrary to those used in smoothbore artillery, works best in rifled

Today big-game slugs take advantage of a protective sabot to deliver superior accuracy. The Winchester Supreme uses a Nosler Partition slug derived from Nosler's highly successful rifle bullet. So too does Federal Cartridge use a proven Barnes bullet design in their sabot round. Lightfield uses a sabot, yet secures the wad to the base of the projectile, which acts as a stabilizer when the slug reenters subsonic flight. Also shown is the original Foster-style rifled slug that is designed for smooth-bored barrels; sabot rounds are exclusively intended for partially or fully rifled barrels.

shotgun barrels. The technology is not new. Early attempts to rifle shotgun barrels included screw-in choke tubes that were rifled à la the Paradox gun, but it soon became apparent that fully rifled barrels were the answer to real sabot-slug accuracy. Foster-style slugs, however, do not gain any accuracy when fired through a rifled barrel, which seldom handles them as well as a tightly bored cylinder-choke barrel does.

As with any rifle, one brand of slugs will shoot better through a given shotgun barrel than others, and it's necessary that some accuracy testing take place to evaluate the possibilities and determine the best combination of barrel and slug. It might be added that several of the ammunition companies have recently joined forces with major rifle-bullet makers to produce sabot slugs that fly at previously uncharted velocities and provide improved aerodynamic performance and terminal upset or expansion that ensures positive kills.

BUCKSHOT

Buckshot remains a part of the hunting tradition in selected areas of the nation, mainly the Southeast. In these states, deer are driven by both humans and dogs, and buckshot is used both to provide the traditional shotgun's role of hitting a moving target with a pattern of pellets and for safety, since buckshot is a relatively short-range projectile. I say relatively because, though a centerfire rifle is lethal for hundreds of yards, buckshot is lethal out to and beyond 300 yards, and will pierce skin beyond 350 yards, so the idea that it's safe in deer-drive situations is a myth. Any firearm is dangerous, and careless use cannot be condoned.

Buckshot's failing is that its *effective* range is far less than its lethal range. The problem is that although buckshot's weight and retained energy make it capable of delivering killing energy at long range, not enough of the twelve or fifteen pellets in a 12-gauge shell strike the target at longer ranges to provide the cumulative energy necessary to bring down a whitetail. The vital zone on a whitetail is only about six or eight inches in diameter, and it's slightly less on a black bear. To concentrate four or five 00-buckshot pellets into that zone requires that the range be very short. Buckshot should be fired only through a full-choke barrel, and testing shows that the effective range—the range at which sufficient pellets strike the six-or eight-inch target to ensure a clean kill—is only thirty or thirty-five yards at the most. Too often hunters take shots with buckshot that have no chance of cleanly killing a deer or other game. Only short-range shots taken at the ideal broadside exposure, where pellets can penetrate the heart/lung area, are considered lethal with buckshot.

One egregious use of buckshot was perpetrated by those who hunted so-called firing-line geese. Areas were established along state and federal refuge boundaries where hunters could pass-shoot geese as they gained altitude while flying out to feed. Hunters in these and similar areas fired buckshot at high-altitude geese in the hope that one or two pellets would break a wing and down a bird, which might or might not be retrievable. Unethical by any definition, the practice is now outlawed, rendered dead and buried by the short effective range of steel shot. On the other hand, many are the African professional hunters, pursuing a wounded lion or leopard in thick cover,

whose lives have been saved by a shotgun charged with 00 or the British-equivalent SSG buckshot. At very short range on thin-skinned dangerous game, few weapons are as effective as a shotgun loaded with buckshot. Only when its limits are stretched does it become ineffective.

Seeking big game with a shotgun is a way of life for hunters in areas of high-density human populations and on many military reservations. Because of their relative short range, compared with centerfire rifles, slugs are ideally suited to these areas. Sabot slugs, especially the newest high-velocity rounds that have a muzzle velocity of 1,900 fps in fully rifled barrels, provide both the accuracy and near-centerfire-rifle performance needed to cleanly take big game.

DOWNRANGE BALLISTICS

Here's the heart of this book: What happens to all those pellets once they leave a shotgun's barrel? Some questions we need to ask ourselves: How are they affected by choke, how far out can they effectively bring game to bag, and how far can they do damage? We need to be eternally attentive to safety. Though gun clubs usually have plenty of safe space, casual clay shooting and hunting dictate care when firing. For example, dove shoots often take place near farm buildings, and pheasant hunts involve drives with standers or blockers and drivers who eventually converge, as do beaters and shooters in driven-game shooting. Knowing that pellets can wreak havoc at extended ranges seems to me to be valuable information. The fact that pellets will break skin implies that they will also blind an unfortunate who is struck in his or her eye. I've been shot in the face from across a dove field, and it hurts. Fortunately, I was wearing shooting glasses, and my eyes were protected, but though the fine shot didn't break my skin, it sure stung, and I don't recommend it.

Shotgun pellets are ballistically poor projectiles. A sharp-pointed boattail bullet slices through the atmosphere and is far more aerodynamically viable than the roundest, smoothest pellet. Because round pellets present so much surface area to the air, they produce drag and slow much faster than a bullet. Too, shotguns must swing and be near-living things in the hands—to be sure there are plenty that swing (or are swung) like a railroad tie—and therefore, unlike rifles, must have thin barrels that cannot withstand pressures that would produce ultra-high velocities. We've gotten to the point today where we can launch pellets at 1,500 fps (still well below rifle velocities), but pellets still slow far quicker than more aerodynamically viable projectiles. It

should also be kept in mind that these new high-velocity loads are specifically for steel shot. Steel is very hard and doesn't deform when fired, as does lead, and therefore can be fired at higher velocities. The upward end of lead-shot-loaded shells is about 1,400 fps—Federal Cartridge in 2001 released a new pheasant load that fires 1$\frac{3}{8}$ ounces of hard, copper-plated shot at 1,400 fps—but for the most part, the highest velocities are reserved for steel shot.

When shotshells are fired, lead shot undergoes severe stresses that, if sufficient, can deform the hardest alloyed and plated shot. As the primer ignites the powder, the bottom pellets begin moving, squeezing against the pellets that are near the crimp. Called setback, these bottommost pellets become flattened or dented on several sides. In the late 1960s, it was discovered that adding buffer to the shot—first common baking flour, which when exposed to moisture congealed into a hard slug, and then granulated polyethylene—cut down deformation due to setback. Before the advent of plastic gas seals, there was also the possibility that gas would leak around the card and felt wads and fuse the pellets near the bottom and on the sides of the shot charge. Without protection, shot also deformed as it skidded along the shotgun's bore. Winchester was the first to protect lead shot from the bore with its polyethylene Mark-V shot wrapper. Plastic shot cups followed and, when combined with buffer, greatly reduced bore scrubbing and kept even more pellets round. Long chamber forcing cones help ease the shot into the bore and eliminate another shot deformation point.

Given all the bore and shotshell improvements of the past fifty years, the higher velocities are now possible without robbing the pattern of shot through deformation. To be sure, some lead shot still deforms through the forces of firing and during its travel through the bore and choke, but far fewer pellets are damaged. Still, there is a limit to practical velocities. An old wives' tale held that high velocity blew patterns open. Not true. What high velocity did was to deform more pellets, resulting in poor patterns. However, with all of the improvements made in shotshell and shotgun barrel technology, high velocity with good patterns is now possible. It is neither cheap nor easy, but certainly possible.

As shot travels from the muzzle to the target and beyond, the forces of gravity pull it toward the earth and the resistance or drag of the atmosphere drastically slows it. As mentioned earlier, although gravity affects long-range rifle shooting, shotshell pellets slow so quickly and their range is so limited that there is little need to consider gravity's pull. Yes, the pellets drop and ultimately fall to earth, but their energy is expended so quickly that drop due to gravity is of little consequence in terms of effectively taking game. Table 13.1 shows the drop of a once-popular duck load. These statistics are for No. 4 lead duck load, having a velocity of 1,260 fps. As this table clearly shows, drop is negligible since the pattern is continually expanding, and even at seventy yards there is still room for error. Considering that most shotguns are built to shoot slightly high, placing about sixty percent of their pattern above the center of the pattern at forty yards, the whole problem is moot.

Steel shot, because it is only about 65 percent as heavy as lead, runs out of energy much faster than lead. Similarly, rifled and sabot slugs have very large frontal areas that cause them to slow rapidly in the atmosphere. As we'll see in the slug section, trajectories are quite high. Still, pellets do travel long distances—at an optimum angle they can travel beyond 300 yards. It is interesting to

watch the resident deer herd at our gun club. When our night skeet league shoots, deer frequently graze anywhere from 50 to 300 yards from the fields. Under normal wind and atmospheric conditions, skeet targets are normally shot at above the horizon, and the fine shot falls much like rain at 150 to 200 yards. Dropping No. 9 pellets are calculated as traveling at 71 fps, and the deer react as they would to rain, looking up but seldom moving, rarely running as if spooked. No. 9 shot fired at 1,200 fps will break skin out to 113 yards, but at longer ranges, when it's dropping from the height of its trajectory, it's more like rain.

Regardless of how far shot carries, the vital statistic for this book's purposes is the point at which it strikes the target. Many years ago Winchester ran tests using mallard ducks suspended in a harness that was run along a wire. The process permitted accurate tests on live ducks at carefully measured distances, precisely calculated leads that ensured the ducks were centered in the pattern, and selected test ammunition. Winchester's ballisticians determined that at sixty yards—about the edge of practical shotgun range—hits within the vitals by five No. 4 lead pellets were necessary to cleanly kill a mallard. At the same range, Winchester's people determined that even if twice that number (ten) of No. 7½ pellets struck the mallard, only enough energy was imparted to wound the bird, which would probably die later, but *not* to bring it to bag.

Running several pellets through E. D. Lowry's shotshell ballistics program, which is used to derive the tables found elsewhere in this book, reveals the data in Table 13.2

If lead shot were still the only pellets in use, it would be easy to continue to select the same ammunition year in and year out, but nontoxic shot has considerably changed the playing field. Using the familiar No. 4 lead pellet as a yardstick, it's easy to see that no nontoxic pellet of the same size delivers the same energy at sixty yards. There is an exception, the new Hevi-Shot, which is concocted of tungsten, nickel, and iron and is heavier than lead. Still, it is obvious that nontoxic shot must be selected with care if we're to be sporting and avoid needlessly wounding game.

Table 13.1

Range in yards	Drop in inches
30	1.2
40	2.4
50	4.2
60	6.6
70	9.9

Table 13.2

Pellet size	Type	Velocity (fps)	Pellet energy (ft-lb) at 60 yards
No. 4	lead	1,265	2.58
No. 4	steel	1,400	1.22
No. 4	Federal tungsten/polymer	1,330	2.35
No. 2	steel	1,400	2.33
No. 4	bismuth	1,280	1.92
No. 2	bismuth	1,280	3.53
No. 5	Kent tungsten/polymer	1,330	1.71
No. 3	Kent tungsten/polymer	1,330	3.29

At this point, I'll bluntly state that most duck hunters don't shoot well enough to be firing at ducks from sixty yards. Sorry. On the other hand, the art of waterfowl hunting (with the exception of jump-shooting) calls for bringing the birds within thirty yards or less with good decoy spreads and calling. Upland hunters using good dogs have the same obligation.

In the study of ballistics, temperature, barometric pressure, wind, and other factors must be considered. However, because shotguns are short-range-application firearms, atmospheric conditions have little or at least a diminished effect on downrange ballistics.

Standard atmospheric conditions used in calculating ballistic charts, etc., are: a temperature of 59 degrees F. or 15 degrees C., a barometric pressure of 29.54 inches or 75 centimeters of mercury at sea level, no wind, and a relative humidity of 50 percent. Changes from these conditions will have the following effects on ballistic performance:

Temperature: Higher temperature results in less dense air and therefore less drag on pellets and thus a slightly higher velocity, causing the pellets to disperse a bit faster. This can affect patterning, but only in a very minor way.

Wind: Winds moving directly at or away from the shooter (head wind or tail wind) have almost no effect on velocity, ballistics, or patterning. Similarly, crosswinds have negligible effect on either velocity or patterning, though strong winds can laterally move the pattern or shot cluster.

In Table 13.3 are some statistics regarding drift, using the same duck load as above. These statistics are for No. 4 lead duck load, having a velocity of 1,260 fps in a 10-mile-per-hour crosswind:

Though these figures show considerable drift at long ranges, at practical ranges where we can reasonably expect to hit something—fifty yards and less—the amount of drift isn't excessive. In very high winds, some little compensation might be in order, but in terms of actual adjustment of the sight picture, it's a minuscule correction.

Humidity: High humidity and rain have virtually no effect on downrange ballistics. Though you'd think driving rain might slow pellets, the fact is that it doesn't.

In the ballistic-table section of this book, you will be able to compare various loads and the performance of their pellets at various ranges from the muzzle. These calculations are based on perfectly round pellets. It is impossible to compensate or skew the figures to include deformed pellets since each load is unique at the moment of firing. It is folly to assume that 100 percent of the pellets will travel downrange and strike the target. In fact, depending on the load, wad, quality of shot, plating or absence of plating, and all the other factors discussed in this book, those pellets that actually strike the target may be many or few. Therefore, the calculations should be viewed as applying to only one perfect pellet from the load of potentially hundreds of pellets that fly downrange. However, this is a rather gloomy way to look at the data. What is available here

Table 13.3

Range in yards	Drift in inches
30	3.5
40	6.2
50	9.8
60	14.2
70	19.5
80	25.9

Bagging one of these wily, tough birds requires heavy loads and very tight chokes. This Rio Grande gobbler was shot in Texas using Winchester's high-velocity turkey load shooting No. 5 shot.

to the shooter, hunter, or ballistic explorer is the *potential* of each load. The data will reveal how much energy our pellet delivers to the target, and at what range that load delivers insufficient pellet energy to be a viable choice in the field.

Shotshell ballistics is a continually evolving science. As new pellet materials evolve and as propellants and other components continue to change and complement these new pellet materials, we'll certainly see a further evolution in downrange ballistics. I fervently hope this book will serve as a guide for casual comparison of loads and more intense exploration of the mystery of shotshell ballistics.

Shotshell Manufacturers

Aguila Ammunition
c/o Centurion Ordnance, Inc.
11614 Rainbow Ridge
Helotes, TX 78023
210-695-4602
cordance@aol.com
www.aguilaammo.com

Armscor
Arms Corporation of the Philippines
Parang, Marikina, Metro Manila, 1800
Philippines
www.armscor.com.ph

ARMUSA
La Calzada de Zubiete, 6
48192 Gordexola (Bizkaia) Spain
94-679-9702
227 Bridge Crest Blvd.
Houston, TX 77082
281-381-7773
carmusa@carmusa.com

Baschieri & Pellagri
B&P America
12321 Brittany Circle
Dallas, TX 75230
972-726-9073
info@baschieri-pellagri.com
www.baschieri-pellagri.com

Bismuth Cartridge Company
11650 Riverside Drive
N. Hollywood, CA 91602
800-759-3333
bismuth@bismuth-notox.com
www.bismuth-notox.com

Brenneke of America
P.O. Box 1481
Clinton, IA 52733-1481
800-753-9733
www.brennekeusa.com

Clever s.r.l.
Via A. Da Legnago, 9
Ponte Florio di Montorio
37033 Verona, Italy
011-39-45-8840770
www.clevervr.com

Dionisi Cartridge s.r.l.
Via Bonifica, 34
63040 Maltignano (AP) Italy
J.F. International LLC
P.O. Box 5703
Vernon Hills, IL 60061
847-821-7731
dap@dionisi.com
www.dionisi.com

Eley Hawk
c/o Zanders Sporting Goods
7525 State Route 154
Baldwin, IL 62217
618-785-2235
sales@eley.co.uk
www.eley.co.uk

Estate Cartridge, Inc.
P.O. Box 3702
Conroe, TX 77305
409-856-7277
www.estatecartridge.com

Federal Cartridge Company
900 Ehlen Drive
Anoka, MN 55303-7503
612-323-2300
800-322-2342
www.federalcartridge.com

Fiocchi of America, Inc.
6930 Fremont Road
Ozark, MO 65721
417-725-4118
www.fiocchiusa.com

Hevi-Shot (See Remington)
Environ-Metal, Inc.
P.O. Box 834
Sweet Home, OR 97386
541-367-3522
www.hevishot.com

Kent Cartridge America/Canada
Kent-Gamebore
P.O. Box 849
Kearneysville, WV 25430
888-311-KENT (5368)
www.kentgamebore.com

Lightfield Ammunition Corp.
Slug Group, Inc.
101 Dogtown Road
Bloomsburg, PA 17815
570-784-6557

Precision Made Cartridges
PMC
P.O. Box 62508
Boulder City, NV 89006
702-294-0025
pmcecc@aol.com
www.pmcammo.com

Polywad Shotgun Shells
P.O. Box 7916
Macon, GA 31209
800-998-0669
www.polywad.com

RIO Cartridges
ITC International, Inc.
3619 Cantrell Industrial Parkway
Acworth, GA 30101
770-966-0600
itclint@aol.com

RST, Ltd.
P.O. Box 127
7 Weston Way
Center Conway, NH 03813-0127
603-447-6770

Remington Arms Company
P.O. Box 700
870 Remington Dr.
Madison, NC 27025-0700
800-243-9700
www.remington.com

Sellier & Bellot, USA
P.O. Box 7307
Shawnee Mission, KS 66207-0307
800-690-2422
grasso@sb-usa.com
www.sb-usa.com

Winchester Ammunition Division, Olin Industries
427 N. Shamrock
East Alton, IL 62024
618-258-2000
www.winchester.com

Other Useful Addresses:

Hunter John Patterning Targets
P.O. Box 771457
St. Louis, MO 63177-2457
314-531-7250

Briley Manufacturing
1230 Lumpkin
Houston, TX 77430
800-331-5718

Reloading Supplies:

Ballistic Products, Inc.
20015 75th Ave. North
Corcoran, MN 55340
888-273-5623

Precision Reloading
P.O. Box 122
Stafford Springs, CT 06076-0122
860-684-5680

Old Western Scrounger
12924 Highway A-12
Montague, CA 96064
800-UPS-AMMO
www.ows-ammunition.com

To the Reader

This book contains a wealth of information on many different gauges, shot sizes, and shot materials as well as hull lengths, weights of shot charge, and velocities. We have arranged the tables in this book as follows.

1- **QUARY**—All shells for shooting birds or small mammals are listed first; slugs and buckshot are listed at the back of the book.

2- **GAUGE**—A 10-gauge shell is listed before a 12-gauge shell, which in turn is listed before a 16-gauge shell, etc.

3- **SHOT MATERIAL**—Within the gauges, the order of the shot material is as follows: lead, steel, tungsten-iron, bismuth, tungsten-polymer, and finally tin.

4- **HULL LENGTH**—Within the shot-material categories, the shortest hull length is listed first and the longest hull length last.

5- **SHOT SIZE**—Within the hull length categories, the largest shot size (FF) is listed first and the smallest shot size (9) is listed last. Slugs are listed from lightest to heaviest projectile, and buckshot is listed from smallest to biggest pellet size.

6- **WEIGHT OF SHOT CHARGE**—Within the shot size categories, the weight of the shot load is listed with the lightest first and the heaviest last.

7- **VELOCITY**—Within the weight of the shot load categories, the slowest muzzle velocity is listed first and the highest muzzle velocity is listed last.

The table of contents on page vi is detailed and will help the reader find the information that is wanted quickly.

NO. BB LEAD PELLETS—2 OUNCES—140 PELLETS
Mfg: Eley Hawk **Manufacturer's code:** Magnum
Recoil energy in 10-lb. shotgun: 60.5 ft./lbs. **Recoil velocity in 10-lb. shotgun:** 19.7 ft./sec.

Distance in yards:	Muzzle	20	30	40	50	60	70
Velocity in fps:	1,335	1,041	938	852	779	716	661
Average pellet energy in ft-lbs:	33.94	20.64	16.74	13.81	11.55	9.76	8.31
Time of flight in seconds:	0	.0513	.0817	.1153	.1521	.1923	.2360

Type of load: Field
Three-foot velocity: 1,275 ft./sec.
Hull: 3½-inch plastic
Wad: Plastic
Shot: Lead
Buffered: No
Test barrel length: 32 inch
Pellets will pierce skin up to 236 yards.

NO. 3 LEAD PELLETS—2 OUNCES—280 PELLETS
Mfg: Eley Hawk **Manufacturer's code:** Magnum
Recoil energy in 10-lb. shotgun: 60.5 ft./lbs. **Recoil velocity in 10-lb. shotgun:** 19.7 ft./sec.

Distance in yards:	Muzzle	20	30	40	50	60	70
Velocity in fps:	1,357	991	873	777	698	631	572
Average pellet energy in ft-lbs:	16.49	8.81	6.82	5.41	4.36	3.56	2.93
Time of flight in seconds:	0	.0523	.0847	.1211	.1619	.2072	.2571

Type of load: Field
Three-foot velocity: 1,275 ft./sec.
Hull: 3½-inch plastic
Wad: Plastic
Shot: Copper-plated, hard lead
Buffered: Yes
Test barrel length: 32 inch
Pellets will pierce skin up to 184 yards.

NO. 4 LEAD PELLETS—2 OUNCES—270 PELLETS
Mfg: Federal Cartridge Co. **Manufacturer's code:** PT101
Recoil energy in 10-lb. shotgun: 63.7 ft./lbs. **Recoil velocity in 10-lb. shotgun:** 20.2 ft./sec.

Distance in yards:	Muzzle	20	30	40	50	60	70
Velocity in fps:	1390	989	863	762	680	611	551
Average pellet energy in ft-lbs:	13.86	7.01	5.34	4.17	3.32	2.67	2.18
Time of flight in seconds:	0	.0519	.0844	.1215	.1632	.2098	.2615

Type of load: Turkey
Three-foot velocity: 1,300 ft./sec.
Hull: 3½-inch plastic
Wad: Plastic
Shot: Copper-plated, hard lead
Buffered: Yes
Test barrel length: 32 inch
Pellets will pierce skin up to 172 yards.

NO. 4 LEAD PELLETS—2 OUNCES—270 PELLETS
Mfg: Olin/Winchester **Manufacturer's code:** STH10
Recoil energy in 10-lb. shotgun: 63.7 ft./lbs. **Recoil velocity in 10-lb. shotgun:** 20.2 ft./sec.

Distance in yards:	Muzzle	20	30	40	50	60	70
Velocity in fps:	1390	989	863	762	680	611	551
Average pellet energy in ft-lbs:	13.86	7.01	5.34	4.17	3.32	2.67	2.18
Time of flight in seconds:	0	.0519	.0844	.1215	.1632	.2098	.2615

Type of load: Turkey
Three-foot velocity: 1,300 ft./sec.
Hull: 3½-inch plastic
Wad: Plastic
Shot: Copper-plated, hard lead
Buffered: Yes
Test barrel length: 32 inch
Pellets will pierce skin up to 172 yards.

NO. 4 LEAD PELLETS—2¼ OUNCES—304 PELLETS
Mfg: Federal Cartridge Co. **Manufacturer's code:** PT109
Recoil energy in 10-lb. shotgun: 66.7 ft./lbs. **Recoil velocity in 10-lb. shotgun:** 20.7 ft./sec.

Distance in yards:	Muzzle	20	30	40	50	60	70
Velocity in fps:	1,281	931	817	725	649	584	528
Average pellet energy in ft-lbs:	11.77	6.21	4.79	3.77	3.02	2.45	2.00
Time of flight in seconds:	0	.0556	.0901	.01291	.1729	.2216	.2757

Type of load: Turkey
Three-foot velocity: 1,210 ft./sec.
Hull: 3½-inch plastic
Wad: Plastic
Shot: Copper-plated, hard lead
Buffered: No
Test barrel length: 32 inch
Pellets will pierce skin up to 168 yards.

NO. 4 LEAD PELLETS—2¼ OUNCES—304 PELLETS
Mfg: Remington Arms Co. **Manufacturer's code:** P10HM
Recoil energy in 10-lb. shotgun: 66.7 ft./lbs. **Recoil velocity in 10-lb. shotgun:** 20.7 ft./sec.

Distance in yards:	Muzzle	20	30	40	50	60	70
Velocity in fps:	1,281	931	817	725	649	584	528
Average pellet energy in ft-lbs:	11.77	6.21	4.79	3.77	3.02	2.45	2.00
Time of flight in seconds:	0	.0556	.0901	.01291	.1729	.2216	.2757

Type of load: Turkey
Three-foot velocity: 1,210 ft./sec.
Hull: 3½-inch plastic
Wad: Plastic
Shot: Hard lead
Buffered: Yes
Test barrel length: 32 inch
Pellets will pierce skin up to 168 yards.

NO. 4 LEAD PELLETS—2¼ OUNCES—304 PELLETS
Mfg: Remington Arms Co. **Manufacturer's code:** P10HM
Recoil energy in 10-lb. shotgun: 66.7 ft./lbs. **Recoil velocity in 10-lb. shotgun:** 20.7 ft./sec.

Distance in yards:	Muzzle	20	30	40	50	60	70
Velocity in fps:	1,281	931	817	725	649	584	528
Average pellet energy in ft-lbs:	11.77	6.21	4.79	3.77	3.02	2.45	2.00
Time of flight in seconds:	0	.0556	.0901	.01291	.1729	.2216	.2757

Type of load: Turkey
Three-foot velocity: 1,210 ft./sec.
Hull: 3½-inch plastic
Wad: Plastic
Shot: Copper-plated, hard lead
Buffered: Yes
Test barrel length: 32 inch
Pellets will pierce skin up to 168 yards.

NO. 5 LEAD PELLETS—2 OUNCES—340 PELLETS

Mfg: Federal Cartridge Co. **Manufacturer's code:** PT101
Recoil energy in 10-lb. shotgun: 63.7 ft./lbs. **Recoil velocity in 10-lb. shotgun:** 20.2 ft./sec.

Distance in yards:	Muzzle	20	30	40	50	60	70
Velocity in fps:	1,396	969	838	735	651	581	521
Average pellet energy in ft-lbs:	11.00	5.29	3.96	3.05	2.39	1.90	1.53
Time of flight in seconds:	0	.0524	.0858	.1241	.1675	.2163	.2708

Type of load: Turkey
Three-foot velocity: 1,300 ft./sec.
Hull: 3½-inch plastic
Wad: Plastic
Shot: Copper-plated, hard lead
Buffered: Yes
Test barrel length: 32 inch
Pellets will pierce skin up to 159 yards.

NO. 5 LEAD PELLETS—2 OUNCES—340 PELLETS

Mfg: Olin/Winchester **Manufacturer's code:** STH10
Recoil energy in 10-lb. shotgun: 63.7 ft./lbs. **Recoil velocity in 10-lb. shotgun:** 20.2 ft./sec.

Distance in yards:	Muzzle	20	30	40	50	60	70
Velocity in fps:	1,396	969	838	735	651	581	521
Average pellet energy in ft-lbs:	11.00	5.29	3.96	3.05	2.39	1.90	1.53
Time of flight in seconds:	0	.0524	.0858	.1241	.1675	.2163	.2708

Type of load: Turkey
Three-foot velocity: 1,300 ft./sec.
Hull: 3½-inch plastic
Wad: Plastic
Shot: Copper-plated, hard lead
Buffered: Yes
Test barrel length: 32 inch
Pellets will pierce skin up to 159 yards.

NO. 6 LEAD PELLETS—2 OUNCES—450 PELLETS

Mfg: Federal Cartridge Co. **Manufacturer's code:** PT101
Recoil energy in 10-lb. shotgun: 63.7 ft./lbs. **Recoil velocity in 10-lb. shotgun:** 20.2 ft./sec.

Distance in yards:	Muzzle	20	30	40	50	60	70
Velocity in fps:	1,403	945	810	705	620	548	487
Average pellet energy in ft-lbs:	8.55	3.88	2.85	2.16	1.67	1.31	1.03
Time of flight in seconds:	0	.0531	.0875	.1272	.1727	.2242	.2723

Type of load: Turkey
Three-foot velocity: 1,300 ft./sec.
Hull: 3½-inch plastic
Wad: Plastic
Shot: Copper-plated, hard lead
Buffered: Yes
Test barrel length: 32 inch
Pellets will pierce skin up to 146 yards.

NO. 6 LEAD PELLETS—2 OUNCES—450 PELLETS

Mfg: Olin/Winchester **Manufacturer's code:** STH10
Recoil energy in 10-lb. shotgun: 63.7 ft./lbs. **Recoil velocity in 10-lb. shotgun:** 20.2 ft./sec.

Distance in yards:	Muzzle	20	30	40	50	60	70
Velocity in fps:	1,403	945	810	705	620	548	487
Average pellet energy in ft-lbs:	8.55	3.88	2.85	2.16	1.67	1.31	1.03
Time of flight in seconds:	0	.0531	.0875	.1272	.1727	.2242	.2723

Type of load: Turkey
Three-foot velocity: 1,300 ft./sec.
Hull: 3½-inch plastic
Wad: Plastic
Shot: Copper-plated, hard lead
Buffered: Yes
Test barrel length: 32 inch
Pellets will pierce skin up to 146 yards.

NO. 6 LEAD PELLETS—2¼ OUNCES—506 PELLETS

Mfg: Federal Cartridge Co. **Manufacturer's code:** PT109
Recoil energy in 10-lb. shotgun: 66.7 ft./lbs. **Recoil velocity in 10-lb. shotgun:** 20.7 ft./sec.

Distance in yards:	Muzzle	20	30	40	50	60	70
Velocity in fps:	1,292	892	769	672	593	525	467
Average pellet energy in ft-lbs:	7.26	3.46	2.57	1.96	1.53	1.20	.095
Time of flight in seconds:	0	.0568	.0931	.01349	.1825	.2363	.2969

Type of load: Turkey
Three-foot velocity: 1,210 ft./sec.
Hull: 3½-inch plastic
Wad: Plastic
Shot: Copper-plated, hard lead
Buffered: No
Test barrel length: 32 inch
Pellets will pierce skin up to 157 yards.

NO. 6 LEAD PELLETS—2¼ OUNCES—506 PELLETS

Mfg: Remington Arms Co. **Manufacturer's code:** P10HM
Recoil energy in 10-lb. shotgun: 66.7 ft./lbs. **Recoil velocity in 10-lb. shotgun:** 20.7 ft./sec.

Distance in yards:	Muzzle	20	30	40	50	60	70
Velocity in fps:	1,292	892	769	672	593	525	467
Average pellet energy in ft-lbs:	7.26	3.46	2.57	1.96	1.53	1.20	.095
Time of flight in seconds:	0	.0568	.0931	.01349	.1825	.2363	.2969

Type of load: Turkey
Three-foot velocity: 1,210 ft./sec.
Hull: 3½-inch plastic
Wad: Plastic
Shot: Copper-plated, hard lead
Buffered: Yes
Test barrel length: 32 inch
Pellets will pierce skin up to 157 yards.

NO. F STEEL PELLETS—65 PELLETS
Mfg: Federal Cartridge Co. **Manufacturer's code:** W104
Recoil energy in 10-lb. shotgun: 46.5 ft./lbs. **Recoil velocity in 10-lb. shotgun:** 17.3 ft./sec.

Distance in yards:	Muzzle	20	30	40	50	60	70
Velocity in fps:	1,402	1,046	927	831	751	683	624
Average pellet energy in ft-lbs:	48.41	26.92	21.15	17.00	13.89	11.48	9.58
Time of flight in seconds:	0	.0500	.0806	.1148	.1528	.1947	.2407

Type of load: Nontoxic
Three-foot velocity: 1,350 ft./sec.
Hull: 3½-inch plastic
Wad: Plastic
Shot: Steel
Buffered: No
Test barrel length: 32 inch
Pellets will pierce skin up to 207 yards.

NO. TT STEEL PELLETS—1¾ OUNCES—79 PELLETS
Mfg: Remington Arms Co. **Manufacturer's code:** NS10M
Recoil energy in 10-lb. shotgun: 38.7 ft./lbs. **Recoil velocity in 10-lb. shotgun:** 15.8 ft./sec.

Distance in yards:	Muzzle	20	30	40	50	60	70
Velocity in fps:	1,311	981	871	781	705	641	584
Average pellet energy in ft-lbs:	36.80	20.62	16.24	13.05	10.65	8.79	7.31
Time of flight in seconds:	0	.0534	.0860	.1224	.1628	.2075	.2566

Type of load: Nontoxic
Three-foot velocity: 1,260 ft./sec.
Hull: 3½-inch plastic
Wad: Plastic
Shot: Zinc-galvanized steel
Buffered: No
Test barrel length: 32 inch
Pellets will pierce skin up to 194 yards.

NO. T STEEL PELLETS—1⅝ OUNCES—84 PELLETS
Mfg: Federal Cartridge Co. **Manufacturer's code:** W104
Recoil energy in 10-lb. shotgun: 46.5 ft./lbs. **Recoil velocity in 10-lb. shotgun:** 17.3 ft./sec.

Distance in yards:	Muzzle	20	30	40	50	60	70
Velocity in fps:	1,411	1,024	900	800	718	649	589
Average pellet energy in ft-lbs:	36.81	19.41	14.97	11.85	9.54	7.78	6.41
Time of flight in seconds:	0	.0505	.0818	.1172	.1568	.2008	.2494

Type of load: Nontoxic
Three-foot velocity: 1,350 ft./sec.
Hull: 3½-inch plastic
Wad: Plastic
Shot: Steel
Buffered: No
Test barrel length: 32 inch
Pellets will pierce skin up to 188 yards.

NO. T STEEL PELLETS—1⅝ OUNCES—84 PELLETS
Mfg: Olin/Winchester **Manufacturer's code:** XSC10
Recoil energy in 10-lb. shotgun: 46.5 ft./lbs. **Recoil velocity in 10-lb. shotgun:** 17.3 ft./sec.

Distance in yards:	Muzzle	20	30	40	50	60	70
Velocity in fps:	1,411	1,024	900	800	718	649	589
Average pellet energy in ft-lbs:	36.81	19.41	14.97	11.85	9.54	7.78	6.41
Time of flight in seconds:	0	.0505	.0818	.1172	.1568	.2008	.2494

Type of load: Nontoxic
Three-foot velocity: 1,350 ft./sec.
Hull: 3½-inch plastic
Wad: Plastic
Shot: Steel
Buffered: No
Test barrel length: 32 inch
Pellets will pierce skin up to 188 yards.

NO. T STEEL PELLETS—1¾ OUNCES—101 PELLETS
Mfg: Remington Arms Co. **Manufacturer's code:** NS10M
Recoil energy in 10-lb. shotgun: 38.7 ft./lbs. **Recoil velocity in 10-lb. shotgun:** 15.8 ft./sec.

Distance in yards:	Muzzle	20	30	40	50	60	70
Velocity in fps:	1,304	965	853	762	686	621	565
Average pellet energy in ft-lbs:	31.46	17.24	13.46	10.74	8.71	7.14	5.90
Time of flight in seconds:	0	.0541	.0872	.1244	.1660	.2119	.2626

Type of load: Nontoxic
Three-foot velocity: 1,260 ft./sec.
Hull: 3½-inch plastic
Wad: Plastic
Shot: Zinc-galvanized steel
Buffered: No
Test barrel length: 32 inch
Pellets will pierce skin up to 184 yards.

NO. BBB STEEL PELLETS
Mfg: Federal Cartridge Co. **Manufacturer's code:** PW102
Recoil energy in 10-lb. shotgun: 38.5 ft./lbs. **Recoil velocity in 10-lb. shotgun:** 15.7 ft./sec.

Distance in yards:	Muzzle	20	30	40	50	60	70
Velocity in fps:	1496	1055	918	810	722	649	586
Average pellet energy in ft-lbs:	35.47	17.66	13.36	10.41	8.28	6.68	5.45
Time of flight in seconds:	0	.0484	.0789	.1138	.1531	.1969	.2456

Type of load: Nontoxic
Three-foot velocity: 1,425 ft./sec.
Hull: 3½-inch plastic
Wad: Plastic
Shot: Steel
Buffered: No
Test barrel length: 32 inch
Pellets will pierce skin up to 182 yards.

NO. BBB STEEL PELLETS—1⅜ OUNCES—85 PELLETS
Mfg: Olin/Winchester **Manufacturer's code:** SSH10
Recoil energy in 10-lb. shotgun: 40.4 ft./lbs. **Recoil velocity in 10-lb. shotgun:** 16.1 ft./sec.

Distance in yards:	Muzzle	20	30	40	50	60	70
Velocity in fps:	1,522	1,070	929	819	730	655	591
Average pellet energy in ft-lbs:	36.75	18.15	13.68	10.64	8.44	6.80	5.55
Time of flight in seconds:	0	.0476	.0778	.1122	.1511	.1945	.2428

Type of load: Nontoxic
Three-foot velocity: 1,450 ft./sec.
Hull: 3½-inch plastic
Wad: Plastic
Shot: Steel
Buffered: No
Test barrel length: 32 inch
Pellets will pierce skin up to 183 yards.

NO. BBB STEEL PELLETS—1⅝ OUNCES—101 PELLETS
Mfg: Federal Cartridge Co. **Manufacturer's code:** W104
Recoil energy in 10-lb. shotgun: 46.5 ft./lbs. **Recoil velocity in 10-lb. shotgun:** 17.3 ft./sec.

Distance in yards:	Muzzle	20	30	40	50	60	70
Velocity in fps:	1,415	1,012	884	783	700	630	570
Average pellet energy in ft-lbs:	31.75	16.24	12.40	9.73	7.77	6.29	5.14
Time of flight in seconds:	0	.0508	.0826	.1187	.1592	.2044	.2546

Type of load: Nontoxic
Three-foot velocity: 1,350 ft./sec.
Hull: 3½-inch plastic
Wad: Plastic
Shot: Steel
Buffered: No
Test barrel length: 32 inch
Pellets will pierce skin up to 179 yards.

NO. BBB STEEL PELLETS—1⅝ OUNCES—101 PELLETS
Mfg: Olin/Winchester **Manufacturer's code:** XSC10
Recoil energy in 10-lb. shotgun: 46.5 ft./lbs. **Recoil velocity in 10-lb. shotgun:** 17.3 ft./sec.

Distance in yards:	Muzzle	20	30	40	50	60	70
Velocity in fps:	1,415	1,012	884	783	700	630	570
Average pellet energy in ft-lbs:	31.75	16.24	12.40	9.73	7.77	6.29	5.14
Time of flight in seconds:	0	.0508	.0826	.1187	.1592	.2044	.2546

Type of load: Nontoxic
Three-foot velocity: 1,350 ft./sec.
Hull: 3½-inch plastic
Wad: Plastic
Shot: Steel
Buffered: No
Test barrel length: 32 inch
Pellets will pierce skin up to 179 yards.

NO. BBB STEEL PELLETS—1¾ OUNCES—109 PELLETS
Mfg: Remington Arms Co. **Manufacturer's code:** NS10M
Recoil energy in 10-lb. shotgun: 38.7 ft./lbs. **Recoil velocity in 10-lb. shotgun:** 15.8 ft./sec.

Distance in yards:	Muzzle	20	30	40	50	60	70
Velocity in fps:	1308	954	839	746	669	604	547
Average pellet energy in ft-lbs:	27.13	14.44	11.17	8.84	7.10	6.40	4.47
Time of flight in seconds:	0	.0544	.0879	.1259	.1684	.2156	.2679

Type of load: Nontoxic
Three-foot velocity: 1,260 ft./sec.
Hull: 3½-inch plastic
Wad: Plastic
Shot: Zinc-galvanized steel
Buffered: No
Test barrel length: 32 inch
Pellets will pierce skin up to 175 yards.

NO. BB STEEL PELLETS—1¾ OUNCES—126 PELLETS
Mfg: Remington Arms Co. **Manufacturer's code:** NS10M
Recoil energy in 10-lb. shotgun: 38.7 ft./lbs. **Recoil velocity in 10-lb. shotgun:** 15.8 ft./sec.

Distance in yards:	Muzzle	20	30	40	50	60	70
Velocity in fps:	1,312	942	824	730	651	585	527
Average pellet energy in ft-lbs:	23.21	11.97	9.16	7.18	5.72	4.61	3.75
Time of flight in seconds:	0	.0547	.0888	.1275	.1711	.2198	.2738

Type of load: Nontoxic
Three-foot velocity: 1,260 ft./sec.
Hull: 3½-inch plastic
Wad: Plastic
Shot: Zinc-galvanized steel
Buffered: No
Test barrel length: 32 inch
Pellets will pierce skin up to 166 yards.

NO. BB STEEL PELLETS—1⅜ OUNCES—99 PELLETS
Mfg: Olin/Winchester **Manufacturer's code:** SSH10
Recoil energy in 10-lb. shotgun: 40.4 ft./lbs. **Recoil velocity in 10-lb. shotgun:** 16.1 ft./sec.

Distance in yards:	Muzzle	20	30	40	50	60	70
Velocity in fps:	1,527	1,055	911	799	709	634	570
Average pellet energy in ft-lbs:	31.45	15.00	11.18	8.61	6.78	5.42	4.38
Time of flight in seconds:	0	.0480	.0786	.1139	.1538	.1986	.2485

Type of load: Nontoxic
Three-foot velocity: 1,450 ft./sec.
Hull: 3½-inch plastic
Wad: Plastic
Shot: Steel
Buffered: No
Test barrel length: 32 inch
Pellets will pierce skin up to 173 yards.

NO. BB STEEL PELLETS
Mfg: Federal Cartridge Co. **Manufacturer's code:** PW102
Recoil energy in 10-lb. shotgun: 38.5 ft./lbs. **Recoil velocity in 10-lb. shotgun:** 15.7 ft./sec.

Distance in yards:	Muzzle	20	30	40	50	60	70
Velocity in fps:	1500	1041	900	791	702	628	565
Average pellet energy in ft-lbs:	30.35	14.60	10.92	8.43	6.64	5.32	4.30
Time of flight in seconds:	0	.0487	.0798	.1154	.1557	.2010	.2514

Type of load: Nontoxic
Three-foot velocity: 1,425 ft./sec.
Hull: 3½-inch plastic
Wad: Plastic
Shot: Steel
Buffered: No
Test barrel length: 32 inch
Pellets will pierce skin up to 173 yards.

NO. BB STEEL PELLETS—117 PELLETS
Mfg: Federal Cartridge Co. **Manufacturer's code:** W104
Recoil energy in 10-lb. shotgun: 46.5 ft./lbs. **Recoil velocity in 10-lb. shotgun:** 17.3 ft./sec.

Distance in yards:	Muzzle	20	30	40	50	60	70
Velocity in fps:	1,420	998	868	765	681	610	549
Average pellet energy in ft-lbs:	27.17	13.44	10.15	7.89	6.25	5.01	4.07
Time of flight in seconds:	0	.0511	.0834	.1203	.1619	.2085	.2604

Type of load: Nontoxic
Three-foot velocity: 1,350 ft./sec.
Hull: 3½-inch plastic
Wad: Plastic
Shot: Steel
Buffered: No
Test barrel length: 32 inch
Pellets will pierce skin up to 170 yards.

NO. BB STEEL PELLETS—1¾ OUNCES—126 PELLETS
Mfg: Olin/Winchester **Manufacturer's code:** XSM10
Recoil energy in 10-lb. shotgun: 38.7 ft./lbs. **Recoil velocity in 10-lb. shotgun:** 15.8 ft./sec.

Distance in yards:	Muzzle	20	30	40	50	60	70
Velocity in fps:	1,312	942	824	730	651	585	527
Average pellet energy in ft-lbs:	23.21	11.97	9.16	7.18	5.72	4.61	3.75
Time of flight in seconds:	0	.0547	.0888	.1275	.1711	.2198	.2738

Type of load: Nontoxic
Three-foot velocity: 1,260 ft./sec.
Hull: 3½-inch plastic
Wad: Plastic
Shot: Steel
Buffered: No
Test barrel length: 32 inch
Pellets will pierce skin up to 166 yards.

NO. 1 STEEL PELLETS—1⅝ OUNCES—167 PELLETS
Mfg: Federal Cartridge Co. **Manufacturer's code:** W104
Recoil energy in 10-lb. shotgun: 46.5 ft./lbs. **Recoil velocity in 10-lb. shotgun:** 17.3 ft./sec.

Distance in yards:	Muzzle	20	30	40	50	60	70
Velocity in fps:	1,429	967	830	724	637	565	504
Average pellet energy in ft-lbs:	19.34	8.86	6.52	4.96	3.85	3.03	2.40
Time of flight in seconds:	0	.0520	.0855	1243	.1685	.2186	.2848

Type of load: Nontoxic
Three-foot velocity: 1,350 ft./sec.
Hull: 3½-inch plastic
Wad: Plastic
Shot: Steel
Buffered: No
Test barrel length: 32 inch
Pellets will pierce skin up to 166 yards.

NO. 1 STEEL PELLETS—1¾ OUNCES—180 PELLETS
Mfg: Remington Arms Co. **Manufacturer's code:** NS10M
Recoil energy in 10-lb. shotgun: 38.7 ft./lbs. **Recoil velocity in 10-lb. shotgun:** 15.8 ft./sec.

Distance in yards:	Muzzle	20	30	40	50	60	70
Velocity in fps:	1,321	914	790	691	611	543	484
Average pellet energy in ft-lbs:	16.51	7.91	5.90	4.52	3.53	2.79	2.22
Time of flight in seconds:	0	.0555	.0909	.1316	.1778	.2300	.2886

Type of load: Nontoxic
Three-foot velocity: 1,260 ft./sec.
Hull: 3½-inch plastic
Wad: Plastic
Shot: Zinc-galvanized steel
Buffered: Yes
Test barrel length: 32 inch
Pellets will pierce skin up to 148 yards.

NO. 1 STEEL PELLETS—1¾ OUNCES—180 PELLETS
Mfg: Olin/Winchester **Manufacturer's code:** XSM10
Recoil energy in 10-lb. shotgun: 38.7 ft./lbs. **Recoil velocity in 10-lb. shotgun:** 15.8 ft./sec.

Distance in yards:	Muzzle	20	30	40	50	60	70
Velocity in fps:	1,321	914	790	691	611	543	484
Average pellet energy in ft-lbs:	16.51	7.91	5.90	4.52	3.53	2.79	2.22
Time of flight in seconds:	0	.0555	.0909	.1316	.1778	.2300	.2886

Type of load: Nontoxic
Three-foot velocity: 1,260 ft./sec.
Hull: 3½-inch plastic
Wad: Plastic
Shot: Steel
Buffered: No
Test barrel length: 32 inch
Pellets will pierce skin up to 148 yards.

NO. 2 STEEL PELLETS—1⅜ OUNCES—172 PELLETS
Mfg: Federal Cartridge Co. **Manufacturer's code:** PW102/W102
Recoil energy in 10-lb. shotgun: 38.5 ft./lbs. **Recoil velocity in 10-lb. shotgun:** 15.7 ft./sec.

Distance in yards:	Muzzle	20	30	40	50	60	70
Velocity in fps:	1516	987	837	723	631	556	492
Average pellet energy in ft-lbs:	17.93	7.60	5.46	4.07	3.11	2.41	1.89
Time of flight in seconds:	0	.0501	.0832	.1218	.1663	.2170	.2744

Type of load: Nontoxic
Three-foot velocity: 1,425 ft./sec.
Hull: 3½-inch plastic
Wad: Plastic
Shot: Steel
Buffered: No
Test barrel length: 32 inch
Pellets will pierce skin up to 144 yards.

NO. 2 STEEL PELLETS—1⅝ OUNCES—203 PELLETS
Mfg: Federal Cartridge Co. **Manufacturer's code:** W104
Recoil energy in 10-lb. shotgun: 46.5 ft./lbs. **Recoil velocity in 10-lb. shotgun:** 17.3 ft./sec.

Distance in yards:	Muzzle	20	30	40	50	60	70
Velocity in fps:	1,434	949	808	700	613	541	479
Average pellet energy in ft-lbs:	16.04	7.02	2.10	3.3	2.93	2.28	1.79
Time of flight in seconds:	0	.0525	.0868	.1268	.1726	.2248	.2838

Type of load: Nontoxic
Three-foot velocity: 1,350 ft./sec.
Hull: 3½-inch plastic
Wad: Plastic
Shot: Steel
Buffered: No
Test barrel length: 32 inch
Pellets will pierce skin up to 142 yards.

NO. 2 STEEL PELLETS—1⅜ OUNCES—172 PELLETS
Mfg: Olin/Winchester **Manufacturer's code:** SSH10
Recoil energy in 10-lb. shotgun: 40.4 ft./lbs. **Recoil velocity in 10-lb. shotgun:** 16.1 ft./sec.

Distance in yards:	Muzzle	20	30	40	50	60	70
Velocity in fps:	1,543	1,000	846	730	637	561	496
Average pellet energy in ft-lbs:	18.58	7.80	5.59	4.16	3.17	2.46	1.92
Time of flight in seconds:	0	.0493	.0820	.1203	.1643	.2146	.2715

Type of load: Nontoxic
Three-foot velocity: 1,450 ft./sec.
Hull: 3½-inch plastic
Wad: Plastic
Shot: Steel
Buffered: No
Test barrel length: 32 inch
Pellets will pierce skin up to 145 yards.

NO. 2 STEEL PELLETS—1¾ OUNCES—219 PELLETS

Mfg: Remington Arms Co. **Manufacturer's code:** NS10M
Recoil energy in 10-lb. shotgun: 38.7 ft./lbs. **Recoil velocity in 10-lb. shotgun:** 15.8 ft./sec.

Distance in yards:	Muzzle	20	30	40	50	60	70
Velocity in fps:	1,325	977	770	669	588	519	460
Average pellet energy in ft-lbs:	13.70	6.29	4.62	3.50	2.70	2.10	1.65
Time of flight in seconds:	0	.0560	.0922	.1341	.1819	.2363	.2977

Type of load: Nontoxic
Three-foot velocity: 1,260 ft./sec.
Hull: 3½-inch plastic
Wad: Plastic
Shot: Zinc-galvanized steel
Buffered: Yes
Test barrel length: 32 inch
Pellets will pierce skin up to 139 yards.

NO. 2 STEEL PELLETS—1¾ OUNCES—219 PELLETS

Mfg: Olin/Winchester **Manufacturer's code:** XSM10
Recoil energy in 10-lb. shotgun: 38.7 ft./lbs. **Recoil velocity in 10-lb. shotgun:** 15.8 ft./sec.

Distance in yards:	Muzzle	20	30	40	50	60	70
Velocity in fps:	1,325	977	770	669	588	519	460
Average pellet energy in ft-lbs:	13.70	6.29	4.62	3.50	2.70	2.10	1.65
Time of flight in seconds:	0	.0560	.0922	.1341	.1819	.2363	.2977

Type of load: Nontoxic
Three-foot velocity: 1,260 ft./sec.
Hull: 3½-inch plastic
Wad: Plastic
Shot: Zinc-galvanized steel
Buffered: No
Test barrel length: 32 inch
Pellets will pierce skin up to 139 yards.

NO. 3 STEEL PELLETS—1¾ OUNCES—277 PELLETS

Mfg: Olin/Winchester **Manufacturer's code:** XSM10
Recoil energy in 10-lb. shotgun: 38.7 ft./lbs. **Recoil velocity in 10-lb. shotgun:** 15.8 ft./sec.

Distance in yards:	Muzzle	20	30	40	50	60	70
Velocity in fps:	1,330	879	748	646	563	494	433
Average pellet energy in ft-lbs:	11.22	4.91	3.55	2.65	2.01	1.55	1.19
Time of flight in seconds:	0	.0566	.0937	.1370	.1868	.2437	.3086

Type of load: Nontoxic
Three-foot velocity: 1,260 ft./sec.
Hull: 3½-inch plastic
Wad: Plastic
Shot: Zinc-galvanized steel
Buffered: No
Test barrel length: 32 inch
Pellets will pierce skin up to 130 yards.

These geese were bagged on the shores of James Bay using No. 2 and BB bismuth shot. Alternative nontoxic shot such as bismuth and tungsten/polymer offers hunters the option of using their classic shotguns with these softer, more leadlike pellets or steel shot with shotguns designed for it.

NO. BBB TUNGSTEN-IRON PELLETS—1⅜ OUNCES—63 PELLETS

Mfg: Federal Cartridge Co. **Manufacturer's code:** PWT105
Recoil energy in 10-lb. shotgun: 40.4 ft./lbs. **Recoil velocity in 10-lb. shotgun:** 16.1 ft./sec.

Distance in yards:	Muzzle	20	30	40	50	60	70
Velocity in fps:	1,496	1,138	1,041	914	831	761	699
Average pellet energy in ft-lbs:	46.86	27.12	21.54	17.51	14.47	12.11	10.23
Time of flight in seconds:	0	.0463	.0743	.1055	.1399	.1777	.2188

Type of load: Nontoxic
Three-foot velocity: 1,450 ft./sec.
Hull: 3½-inch plastic
Wad: Plastic
Shot: Tungsten-iron
Buffered: Yes
Test barrel length: 32 inch
Pellets will pierce skin up to 263 yards.

NO. BBB TUNGSTEN-IRON PELLETS—1⅝ OUNCES—75 PELLETS

Mfg: Federal Cartridge Co. **Manufacturer's code:** PWT106
Recoil energy in 10-lb. shotgun: 42.0 ft./lbs. **Recoil velocity in 10-lb. shotgun:** 16.4 ft./sec.

Distance in yards:	Muzzle	20	30	40	50	60	70
Velocity in fps:	1,339	1,040	936	849	776	713	657
Average pellet energy in ft-lbs:	37.53	22.67	17.34	15.10	13.61	10.63	9.04
Time of flight in seconds:	0	.0512	.0817	.1154	.1523	.1927	.2366

Type of load: Nontoxic
Three-foot velocity: 1,300 ft./sec.
Hull: 3½-inch plastic
Wad: Plastic
Shot: Tungsten-iron
Buffered: Yes
Test barrel length: 32 inch
Pellets will pierce skin up to 255 yards.

NO. BB TUNGSTEN-IRON PELLETS—1⅜ OUNCES—75 PELLETS

Mfg: Federal Cartridge Co. **Manufacturer's code:** PWT105
Recoil energy in 10-lb. shotgun: 40.4 ft./lbs. **Recoil velocity in 10-lb. shotgun:** 16.1 ft./sec.

Distance in yards:	Muzzle	20	30	40	50	60	70
Velocity in fps:	1,500	1,125	998	896	812	740	678
Average pellet energy in ft-lbs:	40.04	22.54	17.73	14.30	11.73	9.76	8.19
Time of flight in seconds:	0	.0466	.0749	.1067	.1419	.1806	.2230

Type of load: Nontoxic
Three-foot velocity: 1,450 ft./sec.
Hull: 3½-inch plastic
Wad: Plastic
Shot: Tungsten-iron
Buffered: Yes
Test barrel length: 32 inch
Pellets will pierce skin up to 249 yards.

NO. BB TUNGSTEN-IRON PELLETS—1⅝ OUNCES—88 PELLETS

Mfg: Federal Cartridge Co. **Manufacturer's code:** PWT106
Recoil energy in 10-lb. shotgun: 42.0 ft./lbs. **Recoil velocity in 10-lb. shotgun:** 16.4 ft./sec.

Distance in yards:	Muzzle	20	30	40	50	60	70
Velocity in fps:	1,342	1,030	922	833	759	694	638
Average pellet energy in ft-lbs:	32.06	18.87	15.13	12.36	10.24	8.58	7.24
Time of flight in seconds:	0	.0516	.0823	.1166	.1543	.1957	.2408

Type of load: Nontoxic
Three-foot velocity: 1,300 ft./sec.
Hull: 3½-inch plastic
Wad: Plastic
Shot: Tungsten-iron
Buffered: Yes
Test barrel length: 32 inch
Pellets will pierce skin up to 242 yards.

NO. 2 TUNGSTEN-IRON PELLETS—1⅜ OUNCES—129 PELLETS

Mfg: Federal Cartridge Co. **Manufacturer's code:** PWT105
Recoil energy in 10-lb. shotgun: 40.4 ft./lbs. **Recoil velocity in 10-lb. shotgun:** 16.1 ft./sec.

Distance in yards:	Muzzle	20	30	40	50	60	70
Velocity in fps:	1,511	1,077	939	831	743	670	785
Average pellet energy in ft-lbs:	23.53	11.96	9.09	7.12	5.69	4.62	3.79
Time of flight in seconds:	0	.0476	.0775	.1115	.1497	.1922	.2394

Type of load: Nontoxic
Three-foot velocity: 1,450 ft./sec.
Hull: 3½-inch plastic
Wad: Plastic
Shot: Tungsten-iron
Buffered: Yes
Test barrel length: 32 inch
Pellets will pierce skin up to 208 yards.

NO. 2 TUNGSTEN-IRON PELLETS—1⅝ OUNCES—153 PELLETS

Mfg: Federal Cartridge Co. **Manufacturer's code:** PWT106
Recoil energy in 10-lb. shotgun: 42.0 ft./lbs. **Recoil velocity in 10-lb. shotgun:** 16.4 ft./sec.

Distance in yards:	Muzzle	20	30	40	50	60	70
Velocity in fps:	1,352	989	871	776	697	630	572
Average pellet energy in ft-lbs:	18.83	10.08	7.82	6.21	5.01	4.09	3.37
Time of flight in seconds:	0	.0525	.0849	.1214	.1622	.2075	.2575

Type of load: Nontoxic
Three-foot velocity: 1,300 ft./sec.
Hull: 3½-inch plastic
Wad: Plastic
Shot: Tungsten-iron
Buffered: Yes
Test barrel length: 32 inch
Pellets will pierce skin up to 202 yards.

NO. 4 TUNGSTEN-IRON PELLETS—1⅜ OUNCES—199 PELLETS

Mfg: Federal Cartridge Co. **Manufacturer's code:** PWT105
Recoil energy in 10-lb. shotgun: 40.4 ft./lbs. **Recoil velocity in 10-lb. shotgun:** 16.1 ft./sec.

Distance in yards:	Muzzle	20	30	40	50	60	70
Velocity in fps:	1,520	1,035	890	778	688	613	549
Average pellet energy in ft-lbs:	15.49	7.18	5.31	4.06	3.17	2.52	2.02
Time of flight in seconds:	0	.0486	.0799	.1161	.1571	.2034	.2552

Type of load: Nontoxic
Three-foot velocity: 1,450 ft./sec.
Hull: 3½-inch plastic
Wad: Plastic
Shot: Tungsten-iron
Buffered: Yes
Test barrel length: 32 inch
Pellets will pierce skin up to 181 yards.

NO. 4 TUNGSTEN-IRON PELLETS—1⅝ OUNCES—235 PELLETS

Mfg: Federal Cartridge Co. **Manufacturer's code:** PWT106
Recoil energy in 10-lb. shotgun: 42.0 ft./lbs. **Recoil velocity in 10-lb. shotgun:** 16.4 ft./sec.

Distance in yards:	Muzzle	20	30	40	50	60	70
Velocity in fps:	1,359	954	828	728	647	578	519
Average pellet energy in ft-lbs:	12.39	6.10	4.60	3.56	2.80	2.24	1.80
Time of flight in seconds:	0	.0535	.0873	.1260	.1698	.2189	.2738

Type of load: Nontoxic
Three-foot velocity: 1,300 ft./sec.
Hull: 3½-inch plastic
Wad: Plastic
Shot: Tungsten-iron
Buffered: Yes
Test barrel length: 32 inch
Pellets will pierce skin up to 176 yards.

NO. 2 TUNGSTEN-IRON PELLETS ON THE BOTTOM TOPPED
WITH A LAYER OF BB STEEL SHOT—1½ OUNCES

Mfg: Federal Cartridge Company **Manufacturer's code:** PWT100
Recoil energy in 10-lb. shotgun: 41.6 ft./lbs. **Recoil velocity in 10-lb. shotgun:** 16.4 ft./sec.

NO. 2 TUNGSTEN-IRON PELLETS

Distance in yards:	Muzzle	20	30	40	50	60	70
Velocity in fps:	1,417	1,025	899	799	717	647	586
Average pellet energy in ft-lbs:	20.70	10.83	8.33	6.58	5.29	4.31	3.54
Time of flight in seconds:	0	.0504	.0817	.1171	.1568	.2009	.2497

NO. BB STEEL PELLETS

Distance in yards:	Muzzle	20	30	40	50	60	70
Velocity in fps:	1,446	1,012	879	774	688	616	554
Average pellet energy in ft-lbs:	28.21	13.82	10.41	8.07	6.38	5.12	4.14
Time of flight in seconds:	0	.0503	.0822	.1186	.1598	.2059	.2573

Type of load: Nontoxic
Three-foot velocity: 1,375 ft./sec.
Hull: 3½-inch plastic
Wad: Plastic
Shot: Steel
Buffered: No
Test barrel length: 32 inch

Pellets will pierce skin up to 187 yards.

Pellets will pierce skin up to 171 yards.

Screw-in chokes have been called the greatest development since the invention of the breechloading shotgun. Although many choke tubes are flush with the muzzle, these have some or all of the constriction beyond the muzzle. The tube on the right is designed to shoot steel and has all of the constriction beyond the muzzle, eliminating any possible strain on the barrel.

NO. 2 BISMUTH PELLETS—1¼ OUNCES—126 PELLETS
Mfg: Bismuth Cartridge Co.   **Manufacturer's code:** BGL-107
Recoil energy in 10-lb. shotgun: 21.0 ft./lbs.   **Recoil velocity in 10-lb. shotgun:** 11.6 ft./sec.

Distance in yards:	Muzzle	20	30	40	50	60	70
Velocity in fps:	1,409	1,001	873	771	688	618	558
Average pellet energy in ft-lbs:	19.09	9.63	7.32	5.72	4.55	3.67	2.99
Time of flight in seconds:	0	.0512	.0834	.1200	.1612	.2073	.2584

Type of load: Field
Three-foot velocity: 1,320 ft./sec.
Hull: 2⅞-inch plastic
Wad: Plastic
Shot: Bismuth
Buffered: No
Test barrel length: 32 inch
Pellets will pierce skin up to 174 yards.

NO. 5 BISMUTH PELLETS—1¼ OUNCES—246 PELLETS
Mfg: Bismuth Cartridge Co.   **Manufacturer's code:** BGL-107
Recoil energy in 10-lb. shotgun: 21.0 ft./lbs.   **Recoil velocity in 10-lb. shotgun:** 11.6 ft./sec.

Distance in yards:	Muzzle	20	30	40	50	60	70
Velocity in fps:	1,428	942	801	693	606	534	472
Average pellet energy in ft-lbs:	10.05	4.36	3.16	2.37	1.81	1.40	1.10
Time of flight in seconds:	0	.0528	.0874	.1278	.1741	.2269	.2867

Type of load: Field
Three-foot velocity: 1,320 ft./sec.
Hull: 2⅞-inch plastic
Wad: Plastic
Shot: Bismuth
Buffered: No
Test barrel length: 32 inch
Pellets will pierce skin up to 140 yards.

Mfg: Olin/Winchester   **Manufacturer's code:** XBP10
Recoil energy in 10-lb. shotgun: 0 ft./lbs.   **Recoil velocity in 10-lb. shotgun:** 0 ft./sec.

Type of load: Blank
Three-foot velocity: 0 ft./sec.
Hull: 2⅞-inch plastic
Wad: Plastic
Drams of black powder: 8

Hunting waterfowl in severe weather calls for good shooting and good ammunition. Extreme cold causes propellants to be more difficult to ignite and slower to burn, resulting in slightly lower velocities and often more unburned powder left in the bore.

NO. BB BISMUTH PELLETS—1⅝ OUNCES—95 PELLETS
Mfg: Bismuth Cartridge Co. **Manufacturer's code:** MBHV-10
Recoil energy in 10-lb. shotgun: 41.6 ft./lbs. **Recoil velocity in 10-lb. shotgun:** 16.4 ft./sec.

Distance in yards:	Muzzle	20	30	40	50	60	70
Velocity in fps:	1,445	1,073	949	850	768	698	637
Average pellet energy in ft-lbs:	34.71	19.13	14.97	12.01	9.80	8.09	6.75
Time of flight in seconds:	0	.0497	.0784	.1119	.1490	.1901	.2351

Type of load: Field
Three-foot velocity: 1,375 ft./sec.
Hull: 3½-inch plastic
Wad: Plastic
Shot: Bismuth
Buffered: Yes
Test barrel length: 32 inch
Pellets will pierce skin up to 210 yards.

NO. BB BISMUTH PELLETS—1⅞ OUNCES—51 PELLETS
Mfg: Bismuth Cartridge Co. **Manufacturer's code:** MBGL-10
Recoil energy in 10-lb. shotgun: 41.7 ft./lbs. **Recoil velocity in 10-lb. shotgun:** 16.4 ft./sec.

Distance in yards:	Muzzle	20	30	40	50	60	70
Velocity in fps:	1,285	979	874	788	715	653	598
Average pellet energy in ft-lbs:	27.42	15.93	12.71	10.32	8.50	7.08	5.94
Time of flight in seconds:	0	.0540	.0865	.1226	.1626	.2065	.2546

Type of load: Field
Three-foot velocity: 1,225 ft./sec.
Hull: 3½-inch plastic
Wad: Plastic
Shot: Bismuth
Buffered: Yes
Test barrel length: 32 inch
Pellets will pierce skin up to 203 yards.

NO. 2 BISMUTH PELLETS—1⅝ OUNCES—164 PELLETS
Mfg: Bismuth Cartridge Co. **Manufacturer's code:** MBHV-10
Recoil energy in 10-lb. shotgun: 41.7 ft./lbs. **Recoil velocity in 10-lb. shotgun:** 16.4 ft./sec.

Distance in yards:	Muzzle	20	30	40	50	60	70
Velocity in fps:	1,464	1,030	895	789	703	630	568
Average pellet energy in ft-lbs:	20.60	10.19	7.70	5.99	4.75	3.82	3.11
Time of flight in seconds:	0	.0496	.0809	.1166	.1570	.2021	.2522

Type of load: Field
Three-foot velocity: 1,375 ft./sec.
Hull: 3½-inch plastic
Wad: Plastic
Shot: Bismuth
Buffered: Yes
Test barrel length: 32 inch
Pellets will pierce skin up to 176 yards.

NO. 2 BISMUTH PELLETS—1⅞ OUNCES—88 PELLETS
Mfg: Bismuth Cartridge Co. **Manufacturer's code:** MBGL-10
Recoil energy in 10-lb. shotgun: 41.7 ft./lbs. **Recoil velocity in 10-lb. shotgun:** 16.4 ft./sec.

Distance in yards:	Muzzle	20	30	40	50	60	70
Velocity in fps:	1,300	943	828	735	657	592	535
Average pellet energy in ft-lbs:	16.26	8.55	6.59	5.19	4.15	3.36	2.75
Time of flight in seconds:	0	.0549	.0889	.1274	.1706	.2188	.2722

Type of load: Field
Three-foot velocity: 1,225 ft./sec.
Hull: 3½-inch plastic
Wad: One-piece plastic
Shot: Bismuth
Buffered: Yes
Test barrel length: 32 inch
Pellets will pierce skin up to 170 yards.

NO. 4 BISMUTH PELLETS—1⅝ OUNCES—252 PELLETS
Mfg: Bismuth Cartridge Co. **Manufacturer's code:** MBHV-10
Recoil energy in 10-lb. shotgun: 41.6 ft./lbs. **Recoil velocity in 10-lb. shotgun:** 16.4 ft./sec.

Distance in yards:	Muzzle	20	30	40	50	60	70
Velocity in fps:	1,477	991	848	738	649	576	513
Average pellet energy in ft-lbs:	13.65	6.14	4.50	3.41	2.64	2.07	1.65
Time of flight in seconds:	0	.0505	.0833	.1213	.1647	.2138	.2691

Type of load: Field
Three-foot velocity: 1,375 ft./sec.
Hull: 3½-inch plastic
Wad: Plastic
Shot: Bismuth
Buffered: Yes
Test barrel length: 32 inch
Pellets will pierce skin up to 153 yards.

NO. 4 BISMUTH PELLETS—1⅞ OUNCES—135 PELLETS
Mfg: Bismuth Cartridge Co. **Manufacturer's code:** MBGL-10
Recoil energy in 10-lb. shotgun: 41.7 ft./lbs. **Recoil velocity in 10-lb. shotgun:** 16.4 ft./sec.

Distance in yards:	Muzzle	20	30	40	50	60	70
Velocity in fps:	1,312	910	787	689	609	541	483
Average pellet energy in ft-lbs:	10.77	5.19	3.87	2.97	2.32	1.83	1.46
Time of flight in seconds:	0	.0558	.0913	.1322	.1785	.2309	.2896

Type of load: Field
Three-foot velocity: 1,225 ft./sec.
Hull: 3½-inch plastic
Wad: One-piece plastic
Shot: Bismuth
Buffered: Yes
Test barrel length: 32 inch
Pellets will pierce skin up to 148 yards.

NO. 6 LEAD PELLETS—7/8 OUNCE—236 PELLETS
Mfg: Eley Hawk **Manufacturer's code:** Two Inch
Recoil energy in 8-lb. shotgun: 12.9 ft./lbs. **Recoil velocity in 8-lb. shotgun:** 10.2 ft./sec.

Distance in yards:	Muzzle	20	30	40	50	60	70
Velocity in fps:	1,314	903	778	679	598	530	471
Average pellet energy in ft-lbs:	7.51	3.54	2.63	2.00	1.55	1.22	.97
Time of flight in seconds:	0	.0560	.0919	.1333	.1804	.2337	.2938

Type of load: Field
Three-foot velocity: 1,220 ft./sec.
Hull: 2-inch plastic
Wad: Fiber
Shot: Lead
Buffered: No
Test barrel length: 30 inch
Pellets will pierce skin up to 143 yards.

NO. 6 LEAD PELLETS—7/8 OUNCE—236 PELLETS
Mfg: Kent-Gamebore **Manufacturer's code:** G1220SG24
Recoil energy in 8-lb. shotgun: 12.9 ft./lbs. **Recoil velocity in 8-lb. shotgun:** 10.2 ft./sec.

Distance in yards:	Muzzle	20	30	40	50	60	70
Velocity in fps:	1,314	903	778	679	598	530	471
Average pellet energy in ft-lbs:	7.51	3.54	2.63	2.00	1.55	1.22	.97
Time of flight in seconds:	0	.0560	.0919	.1333	.1804	.2337	.2938

Type of load: Field
Three-foot velocity: 1,220 ft./sec.
Hull: 2-inch plastic
Wad: Fiber
Shot: Lead
Buffered: No
Test barrel length: 30 inch
Pellets will pierce skin up to 143 yards.

NO. 6 LEAD PELLETS—15/16 OUNCE—211 PELLETS
Mfg: RST, Ltd. **Manufacturer's code:** N/A
Recoil energy in 8-lb. shotgun: 18.2 ft./lbs. **Recoil velocity in 8-lb. shotgun:** 12.1 ft./sec.

Distance in yards:	Muzzle	20	30	40	50	60	70
Velocity in fps:	1,237	865	748	655	578	513	456
Average pellet energy in ft-lbs:	6.65	3.25	2.43	1.86	1.45	1.14	.90
Time of flight in seconds:	0	.0589	.0963	.1392	.1880	.2431	.3051

Type of load: Target
Three-foot velocity: 1,150 ft./sec.
Hull: 2-inch plastic
Wad: Plastic
Shot: Lead
Buffered: No
Test barrel length: 30 inch
Pellets will pierce skin up to 140 yards.

NO. 7½ LEAD PELLETS—7/8 OUNCE—306 PELLETS
Mfg: Kent-Gamebore **Manufacturer's code:** G1220SG24
Recoil energy in 8-lb. shotgun: 12.9 ft./lbs. **Recoil velocity in 8-lb. shotgun:** 10.9 ft./sec.

Distance in yards:	Muzzle	20	30	40	50	60	70
Velocity in fps:	1,324	864	731	629	546	476	416
Average pellet energy in ft-lbs:	4.91	2.09	1.50	1.11	.83	.63	.48
Time of flight in seconds:	0	.0573	.0952	.1395	.1908	.2497	.3172

Type of load: Field
Three-foot velocity: 1,220 ft./sec.
Hull: 2-inch plastic
Wad: Fiber
Shot: Lead
Buffered: No
Test barrel length: 30 inch
Pellets will pierce skin up to 124 yards.

NO. 7½ LEAD PELLETS—15/16 OUNCE—328 PELLETS
Mfg: RST, Ltd. **Manufacturer's code:** N/A
Recoil energy in 8-lb. shotgun: 18.2 ft./lbs. **Recoil velocity in 8-lb. shotgun:** 12.1 ft./sec.

Distance in yards:	Muzzle	20	30	40	50	60	70
Velocity in fps:	1,246	829	705	607	528	461	402
Average pellet energy in ft-lbs:	4.35	1.92	1.39	1.03	.78	.59	.45
Time of flight in seconds:	0	.0602	.0996	.1455	.1985	.2594	.3290

Type of load: Target
Three-foot velocity: 1,150 ft./sec.
Hull: 2-inch plastic
Wad: Plastic
Shot: Lead
Buffered: No
Test barrel length: 30 inch
Pellets will pierce skin up to 122 yards.

NO. 8 LEAD PELLETS—15/16 OUNCE—385 PELLETS
Mfg: RST, Ltd. **Manufacturer's code:** N/A
Recoil energy in 8-lb. shotgun: 18.2 ft./lbs. **Recoil velocity in 8-lb. shotgun:** 12.1 ft./sec.

Distance in yards:	Muzzle	20	30	40	50	60	70
Velocity in fps:	1,249	815	688	589	509	441	382
Average pellet energy in ft-lbs:	3.71	1.58	1.13	.83	.62	.46	.35
Time of flight in seconds:	0	.0608	.1010	.1482	.2030	.2663	.3394

Type of load: Target
Three-foot velocity: 1,150 ft./sec.
Hull: 2-inch plastic
Wad: Plastic
Shot: Lead
Buffered: No
Test barrel length: 30 inch
Pellets will pierce skin up to 115 yards.

NO. 6 LEAD PELLETS—1 OUNCE—225 PELLETS
Mfg: RST, Ltd.   **Manufacturer's code:** N/A
Recoil energy in 8-lb. shotgun: 15.2 ft./lbs.   **Recoil velocity in 8-lb. shotgun:** 11.1 ft./sec.

Distance in yards:	Muzzle	20	30	40	50	60	70
Velocity in fps:	1,265	878	759	664	585	519	462
Average pellet energy in ft-lbs:	6.95	3.35	2.50	1.91	1.9	1.17	.93
Time of flight in seconds:	0	.0578	.0947	.1370	.1852	.2396	.3009

Type of load: Target
Three-foot velocity: 1,175 ft./sec.
Hull: 2½-inch plastic
Wad: Plastic
Shot: Lead
Buffered: No
Test barrel length: 30 inch
Pellets will pierce skin up to 141 yards.

NO. 6 LEAD PELLETS—1 OUNCE—270 PELLETS
Mfg: Eley Hawk **Manufacturer's code:** Impax
Recoil energy in 8-lb. shotgun: 16.8 ft./lbs.   **Recoil velocity in 8-lb. shotgun:** 11.6 ft./sec.

Distance in yards:	Muzzle	20	30	40	50	60	70
Velocity in fps:	1,314	903	778	679	598	530	471
Average pellet energy in ft-lbs:	7.51	3.54	2.63	2.00	1.55	1.22	.97
Time of flight in seconds:	0	.0560	.0919	.1333	.1804	.2337	.2938

Type of load: Field
Three-foot velocity: 1,220 ft./sec.
Hull: 2½-inch plastic
Wad: Fiber
Shot: Lead
Buffered: No
Test barrel length: 30 inch
Pellets will pierce skin up to 143 yards.

NO. 6 LEAD PELLETS—1 OUNCE—270 PELLETS
Mfg: Eley Hawk **Manufacturer's code:** Impax
Recoil energy in 8-lb. shotgun: 16.8 ft./lbs.   **Recoil velocity in 8-lb. shotgun:** 11.6 ft./sec.

Distance in yards:	Muzzle	20	30	40	50	60	70
Velocity in fps:	1,314	903	778	679	598	530	471
Average pellet energy in ft-lbs:	7.51	3.54	2.63	2.00	1.55	1.22	.97
Time of flight in seconds:	0	.0560	.0919	.1333	.1804	.2337	.2938

Type of load: Field
Three-foot velocity: 1,220 ft./sec.
Hull: 2½-inch paper
Wad: Fiber
Shot: Lead
Buffered: No
Test barrel length: 30 inch
Pellets will pierce skin up to 143 yards.

NO. 6 LEAD PELLETS—1 OUNCE—270 PELLETS
Mfg: Eley Hawk **Manufacturer's code:** VIP Game
Recoil energy in 8-lb. shotgun: 19.9 ft./lbs.   **Recoil velocity in 8-lb. shotgun:** 12.6 ft./sec.

Distance in yards:	Muzzle	20	30	40	50	60	70
Velocity in fps:	1,403	945	810	705	620	548	487
Average pellet energy in ft-lbs:	8.55	3.88	2.85	2.16	1.67	1.31	1.03
Time of flight in seconds:	0	.0531	.0875	.1272	.1727	.2242	.2723

Type of load: Field
Three-foot velocity: 1,300 ft./sec.
Hull: 2½-inch plastic
Wad: Fiber or Photo-degradable plastic
Shot: Lead
Buffered: No
Test barrel length: 30 inch
Pellets will pierce skin up to 146 yards.

NO. 6 LEAD PELLETS—1¹/₁₆ OUNCES—287 PELLETS
Mfg: Eley Hawk **Manufacturer's code:** Grand Prix
Recoil energy in 8-lb. shotgun: 17.9 ft./lbs.   **Recoil velocity in 8-lb. shotgun:** 12.0 ft./sec.

Distance in yards:	Muzzle	20	30	40	50	60	70
Velocity in fps:	1,348	919	790	689	606	537	477
Average pellet energy in ft-lbs:	7.89	3.67	2.71	2.06	1.60	1.25	.99
Time of flight in seconds:	0	.0549	.0902	.1309	.1774	.2300	.2893

Type of load: Field
Three-foot velocity: 1,250 ft./sec.
Hull: 2½-inch plastic
Wad: Fiber
Shot: Lead
Buffered: No
Test barrel length: 30 inch
Pellets will pierce skin up to 144 yards.

NO. 6 LEAD PELLETS—1¹/₁₆ OUNCES—287 PELLETS
Mfg: Eley Hawk **Manufacturer's code:** Grand Prix
Recoil energy in 8-lb. shotgun: 17.9 ft./lbs.   **Recoil velocity in 8-lb. shotgun:** 12.0 ft./sec.

Distance in yards:	Muzzle	20	30	40	50	60	70
Velocity in fps:	1,348	919	790	689	606	537	477
Average pellet energy in ft-lbs:	7.89	3.67	2.71	2.06	1.60	1.25	.99
Time of flight in seconds:	0	.0549	.0902	.1309	.1774	.2300	.2893

Type of load: Field
Three-foot velocity: 1,250 ft./sec.
Hull: 2½-inch paper
Wad: Fiber
Shot: Lead
Buffered: No
Test barrel length: 30 inch
Pellets will pierce skin up to 144 yards.

NO. 6 LEAD PELLETS—1¹/₁₆ OUNCES—239 PELLETS
Mfg: Baschieri & Pellagri **Manufacturer's code:**
Recoil energy in 8-lb. shotgun: 19.1 ft./lbs.   **Recoil velocity in 8-lb. shotgun:** 12.4 ft./sec.

Distance in yards:	Muzzle	20	30	40	50	60	70
Velocity in fps:	1375	932	800	697	613	543	482
Average pellet energy in ft-lbs:	8.22	3.77	2.78	2.11	1.63	1.28	1.01
Time of flight in seconds:	0	.0540	.0888	.1290	.1750	.2271	.2858

Type of load: High Pheasant
Three-foot velocity: 1,275 ft./sec.
Hull: 2½-inch plastic
Wad: Plastic
Shot: Lead
Buffered: No
Test barrel length: 30 inch
Pellets will pierce skin up to 145 yards.

NO. 6 LEAD PELLETS—1¹/₁₆ OUNCES—287 PELLETS
Mfg: Eley Hawk **Manufacturer's code:** Classic Game
Recoil energy in 8-lb. shotgun: 23.9 ft./lbs. **Recoil velocity in 8-lb. shotgun:** 13.9 ft./sec.

Distance in yards:	Muzzle	20	30	40	50	60	70
Velocity in fps:	1,375	932	800	697	613	543	482
Average pellet energy in ft-lbs:	8.22	3.77	2.78	2.11	1.63	1.28	1.01
Time of flight in seconds:	0	.0540	.0888	.1290	.1750	.2271	.2858

Type of load: Field
Three-foot velocity: 1,275 ft./sec.
Hull: 2½-inch plastic
Wad: Fiber
Shot: Copper-plated lead
Buffered: No
Test barrel length: 30 inch
Pellets will pierce skin up to 145 yards.

NO. 6 LEAD PELLETS—1¹/₁₆ OUNCES—287 PELLETS
Mfg: Eley Hawk **Manufacturer's code:** VIP Game
Recoil energy in 8-lb. shotgun: 23.5 ft./lbs. **Recoil velocity in 8-lb. shotgun:** 13.4 ft./sec.

Distance in yards:	Muzzle	20	30	40	50	60	70
Velocity in fps:	1,403	945	810	705	620	548	487
Average pellet energy in ft-lbs:	8.55	3.88	2.85	2.16	1.67	1.31	1.03
Time of flight in seconds:	0	.0531	.0875	.1272	.1727	.2242	.2723

Type of load: Field
Three-foot velocity: 1,300 ft./sec.
Hull: 2½-inch plastic
Wad: Fiber or Photo-degradable plastic
Shot: Lead
Buffered: No
Test barrel length: 30 inch
Pellets will pierce skin up to 146 yards.

NO. 6 LEAD PELLETS—1⅛ OUNCES—304 PELLETS
Mfg: Eley Hawk **Manufacturer's code:** Super Game
Recoil energy in 8-lb. shotgun: 25.5 ft./lbs. **Recoil velocity in 8-lb. shotgun:** 14.2 ft./sec.

Distance in yards:	Muzzle	20	30	40	50	60	70
Velocity in fps:	1,403	945	810	705	620	548	487
Average pellet energy in ft-lbs:	8.55	3.88	2.85	2.16	1.67	1.31	1.03
Time of flight in seconds:	0	.0531	.0875	.1272	.1727	.2242	.2723

Type of load: Field
Three-foot velocity: 1,300 ft./sec.
Hull: 2½-inch plastic
Wad: Plastic
Shot: Lead
Buffered: No
Test barrel length: 30 inch
Pellets will pierce skin up to 146 yards.

NO. 7 LEAD PELLETS—1 OUNCE—340 PELLETS
Mfg: Eley Hawk **Manufacturer's code:** VIP Game
Recoil energy in 8-lb. shotgun: 19.9 ft./lbs. **Recoil velocity in 8-lb. shotgun:** 12.6 ft./sec.

Distance in yards:	Muzzle	20	30	40	50	60	70
Velocity in fps:	1,410	918	778	670	584	512	450
Average pellet energy in ft-lbs:	6.49	2.75	1.98	1.47	1.11	.86	.66
Time of flight in seconds:	0	.0539	.0895	.1311	.1791	.2340	.2966

Type of load: Field
Three-foot velocity: 1,300 ft./sec.
Hull: 2½-inch plastic
Wad: Fiber or Photo-degradable plastic
Shot: Lead
Buffered: No
Test barrel length: 30 inch
Pellets will pierce skin up to 133 yards.

NO. 7 LEAD PELLETS—1¹/₁₆ OUNCES—318 PELLETS
Mfg: Baschieri & Pellagri **Manufacturer's code:**
Recoil energy in 8-lb. shotgun: 19.1 ft./lbs. **Recoil velocity in 8-lb. shotgun:** 12.4 ft./sec.

Distance in yards:	Muzzle	20	30	40	50	60	70
Velocity in fps:	1,382	906	769	663	578	507	446
Average pellet energy in ft-lbs:	6.23	2.68	1.93	1.44	1.09	.84	.65
Time of flight in seconds:	0	.0548	.0908	.1329	.1815	.2370	.3349

Type of load: High Pheasant
Three-foot velocity: 1,275 ft./sec.
Hull: 2½-inch plastic
Wad: Plastic
Shot: Lead
Buffered: No
Test barrel length: 30 inch
Pellets will pierce skin up to 132 yards.

NO. 7 LEAD PELLETS—1¹/₁₆ OUNCES—361 PELLETS
Mfg: Eley Hawk **Manufacturer's code:** VIP Game
Recoil energy in 8-lb. shotgun: 23.5 ft./lbs. **Recoil velocity in 8-lb. shotgun:** 13.4 ft./sec.

Distance in yards:	Muzzle	20	30	40	50	60	70
Velocity in fps:	1,410	918	778	670	584	512	450
Average pellet energy in ft-lbs:	6.49	2.75	1.98	1.47	1.11	.86	.66
Time of flight in seconds:	0	.0539	.0895	.1311	.1791	.2340	.2966

Type of load: Field
Three-foot velocity: 1,300 ft./sec.
Hull: 2½-inch plastic
Wad: Fiber or Photo-degradable plastic
Shot: Lead
Buffered: No
Test barrel length: 30 inch
Pellets will pierce skin up to 133 yards.

NO. 7½ LEAD PELLETS—1 OUNCE—350 PELLETS
Mfg: RST, Ltd. **Manufacturer's code:** N/A
Recoil energy in 8-lb. shotgun: 14.4 ft./lbs. **Recoil velocity in 8-lb. shotgun:** 9.6 ft./sec.

Distance in yards:	Muzzle	20	30	40	50	60	70
Velocity in fps:	1,135	776	664	575	501	437	382
Average pellet energy in ft-lbs:	3.61	1.69	1.23	.92	.70	.53	.41
Time of flight in seconds:	0	.0650	.1068	.1555	.2114	.2756	.3490

Type of load: Target
Three-foot velocity: 1,050 ft./sec.
Hull: 2½-inch plastic
Wad: Plastic
Shot: Lead
Buffered: No
Test barrel length: 30 inch
Pellets will pierce skin up to 118 yards.

NO. 7½ LEAD PELLETS—1 OUNCE—350 PELLETS

Mfg: RST, Ltd.   **Manufacturer's code:** N/A
Recoil energy in 8-lb. shotgun: 15.2 ft./lbs.   **Recoil velocity in 8-lb. shotgun:** 11.1 ft./sec.

Distance in yards:	Muzzle	20	30	40	50	60	70
Velocity in fps:	1,274	841	714	615	535	466	407
Average pellet energy in ft-lbs:	4.54	1.98	1.43	1.06	.80	.61	.46
Time of flight in seconds:	0	.0592	.0980	.1433	.1957	.2558	.3246

Type of load: Target
Three-foot velocity: 1,175 ft./sec.
Hull: 2½-inch plastic
Wad: Plastic
Shot: Lead
Buffered: No
Test barrel length: 30 inch
Pellets will pierce skin up to 122 yards.

NO. 7½ LEAD PELLETS—1 OUNCE—350 PELLETS

Mfg: Eley Hawk   **Manufacturer's code:** Impax
Recoil energy in 8-lb. shotgun: 16.8 ft./lbs.   **Recoil velocity in 8-lb. shotgun:** 11.6 ft./sec.

Distance in yards:	Muzzle	20	30	40	50	60	70
Velocity in fps:	1,324	864	731	629	546	476	416
Average pellet energy in ft-lbs:	4.91	2.09	1.50	1.11	.83	.63	.48
Time of flight in seconds:	0	.0573	.0952	.1395	.1908	.2497	.3172

Type of load: Field
Three-foot velocity: 1,220 ft./sec.
Hull: 2½-inch plastic
Wad: Fiber
Shot: Lead
Buffered: No
Test barrel length: 30 inch
Pellets will pierce skin up to 124 yards.

NO. 7½ LEAD PELLETS—1 OUNCE—350 PELLETS

Mfg: Eley Hawk   **Manufacturer's code:** Impax
Recoil energy in 8-lb. shotgun: 16.8 ft./lbs.   **Recoil velocity in 8-lb. shotgun:** 11.6 ft./sec.

Distance in yards:	Muzzle	20	30	40	50	60	70
Velocity in fps:	1,324	864	731	629	546	476	416
Average pellet energy in ft-lbs:	4.91	2.09	1.50	1.11	.83	.63	.48
Time of flight in seconds:	0	.0573	.0952	.1395	.1908	.2497	.3172

Type of load: Field
Three-foot velocity: 1,220 ft./sec.
Hull: 2½-inch plastic
Wad: Fiber
Shot: Lead
Buffered: No
Test barrel length: 30 inch
Pellets will pierce skin up to 124 yards.

NO. 7½ LEAD PELLETS—1¹/₁₆ OUNCES—372 PELLETS

Mfg: Baschieri & Pellagri   **Manufacturer's code:** N/A
Recoil energy in 8-lb. shotgun: 12.8 ft./lbs.   **Recoil velocity in 8-lb. shotgun:** 10.2 ft./sec.

Distance in yards:	Muzzle	20	30	40	50	60	70
Velocity in fps:	1,191	803	685	592	515	449	392
Average pellet energy in ft-lbs:	3.97	1.81	1.31	.98	.74	.57	.43
Time of flight in seconds:	0	.0625	.1030	.1502	.2047	.2671	.3385

Type of load: High Pheasant Target
Three-foot velocity: 1,100 ft./sec.
Hull: 2½-inch plastic
Wad: Plastic
Shot: Hard lead
Buffered: No
Test barrel length: 30 inch
Pellets will pierce skin up to 132 yards.

NO. 7½ LEAD PELLETS—1¹/₁₆ OUNCES—372 PELLETS

Mfg: Eley Hawk   **Manufacturer's code:** Grand Prix
Recoil energy in 8-lb. shotgun: 17.9 ft./lbs.   **Recoil velocity in 8-lb. shotgun:** 12.0 ft./sec.

Distance in yards:	Muzzle	20	30	40	50	60	70
Velocity in fps:	1,357	878	742	637	553	482	421
Average pellet energy in ft-lbs:	5.16	2.16	1.54	1.14	.86	.65	.50
Time of flight in seconds:	0	.0562	.0935	.1372	.1878	.2459	.3126

Type of load: Field
Three-foot velocity: 1,250 ft./sec.
Hull: 2½-inch plastic
Wad: Fiber
Shot: Lead
Buffered: No
Test barrel length: 30 inch
Pellets will pierce skin up to 125 yards.

NO. 8 LEAD PELLETS—1 OUNCE—410 PELLETS

Mfg: RST, Ltd.   **Manufacturer's code:** N/A
Recoil energy in 8-lb. shotgun: 14.4 ft./lbs.   **Recoil velocity in 8-lb. shotgun:** 9.6 ft./sec.

Distance in yards:	Muzzle	20	30	40	50	60	70
Velocity in fps:	1,138	764	649	558	483	418	363
Average pellet energy in ft-lbs:	3.08	1.39	1.00	.74	.55	.42	.31
Time of flight in seconds:	0	.0655	.1082	.1582	.2160	.2828	.3599

Type of load: Target
Three-foot velocity: 1,050 ft./sec.
Hull: 2½-inch plastic
Wad: Plastic
Shot: Lead
Buffered: No
Test barrel length: 30 inch
Pellets will pierce skin up to 112 yards.

NO. 8 LEAD PELLETS—1 OUNCE—410 PELLETS

Mfg: RST, Ltd.   **Manufacturer's code:** N/A
Recoil energy in 8-lb. shotgun: 15.2 ft./lbs.   **Recoil velocity in 8-lb. shotgun:** 11.1 ft./sec.

Distance in yards:	Muzzle	20	30	40	50	60	70
Velocity in fps:	1,277	827	697	597	515	446	387
Average pellet energy in ft-lbs:	3.88	1.63	1.16	.85	.63	.47	.36
Time of flight in seconds:	0	.0597	.0993	.1459	.2001	.2627	.3349

Type of load: Target
Three-foot velocity: 1,175 ft./sec.
Hull: 2½-inch plastic
Wad: Plastic
Shot: Lead
Buffered: No
Test barrel length: 30 inch
Pellets will pierce skin up to 116 yards.

NO. 8 LEAD PELLETS—1¹/₁₆ OUNCES—435 PELLETS

Mfg: Baschieri & Pellagri **Manufacturer's code:** N/A
Recoil energy in 8-lb. shotgun: 12.8 ft./lbs. **Recoil velocity in 8-lb. shotgun:** 10.2 ft./sec.

Distance in yards:	Muzzle	20	30	40	50	60	70
Velocity in fps:	1,193	790	669	574	496	430	373
Average pellet energy in ft-lbs:	3.39	1.48	1.06	.78	.59	.44	.33
Time of flight in seconds:	0	.0630	.1044	.1529	.2092	.2741	.3491

Type of load: High Pheasant Target
Three-foot velocity: 1,100 ft./sec.
Hull: 2½-inch plastic
Wad: Plastic
Shot: Hard lead
Buffered: No
Test barrel length: 30 inch
Pellets will pierce skin up to 125 yards.

Winchester's Mike Jordan with his morning's limit of ducks taken shooting bismuth shot during the period of Winchester's and Bismuth Cartridge Company's joint venture of loading and distributing this ammunition. Hunting ducks in flooded timber and Mississippi River backwater sloughs does not require extra-heavy magnum loads; lighter 2³/₄-inch loads of No. 2 steel or No. 4 bismuth or Kent's Impact tungsten/polymer ammo are just right.

NO. BB LEAD PELLETS—1¼ OUNCES—62 PELLETS
Mfg: Eley Hawk **Manufacturer's code:** Alphamax
Recoil energy in 8-lb. shotgun: 31.1 ft./lbs. **Recoil velocity in 8-lb. shotgun:** 15.8 ft./sec.

Distance in yards:	Muzzle	20	30	40	50	60	70
Velocity in fps:	1,362	1,058	951	863	789	724	668
Average pellet energy in ft-lbs:	35.30	21.30	17.22	14.18	11.84	9.99	8.50
Time of flight in seconds:	0	.0504	.0803	.1135	.1499	.1896	.2327

Type of load: Field
Three-foot velocity: 1,300 ft./sec.
Hull: 2¾-inch plastic
Wad: Plastic
Shot: Lead
Buffered: No
Test barrel length: 30 inch
Pellets will pierce skin up to 237 yards.

NO. BB LEAD PELLETS—1¼ OUNCES—62 PELLETS
Mfg: Remington Arms Co. **Manufacturer's code:** SP12
Recoil energy in 8-lb. shotgun: 33.0 ft./lbs. **Recoil velocity in 8-lb. shotgun:** 16.3 ft./sec.

Distance in yards:	Muzzle	20	30	40	50	60	70
Velocity in fps:	1,394	1,078	967	877	800	734	677
Average pellet energy in ft-lbs:	36.98	22.11	17.81	14.63	12.91	10.27	8.72
Time of flight in seconds:	0	.0493	.0788	.1114	.1472	.1864	.2289

Type of load: Field
Three-foot velocity: 1,330 ft./sec.
Hull: 2¾-inch plastic
Wad: Plastic
Shot: Lead
Buffered: No
Test barrel length: 30 inch
Pellets will pierce skin up to 239 yards.

NO. BB LEAD PELLETS—1½ OUNCES—75 PELLETS
Mfg: Federal Cartridge Co. **Manufacturer's code:** F130
Recoil energy in 8-lb. shotgun: 40.4 ft./lbs. **Recoil velocity in 8-lb. shotgun:** 18.0 ft./sec.

Distance in yards:	Muzzle	20	30	40	50	60	70
Velocity in fps:	1,309	1,025	924	840	769	707	653
Average pellet energy in ft-lbs:	32.60	19.99	16.26	13.45	11.27	9.53	8.12
Time of flight in seconds:	0	.0522	.0831	.1171	.1545	.1952	.2393

Type of load: Field
Three-foot velocity: 1,250 ft./sec.
Hull: 2¾-inch plastic
Wad: Plastic
Shot: Lead
Buffered: No
Test barrel length: 30 inch
Pellets will pierce skin up to 234 yards.

NO. BB LEAD PELLETS—1½ OUNCES—75 PELLETS
Mfg: Eley Hawk **Manufacturer's code:** Magnum 70
Recoil energy in 8-lb. shotgun: 42.5 ft./lbs. **Recoil velocity in 8-lb. shotgun:** 18.5 ft./sec.

Distance in yards:	Muzzle	20	30	40	50	60	70
Velocity in fps:	1,335	1,041	938	852	779	716	661
Average pellet energy in ft-lbs:	33.94	20.64	16.74	13.81	11.55	9.76	8.31
Time of flight in seconds:	0	.0513	.0817	.1153	.1521	.1923	.2360

Type of load: Field
Three-foot velocity: 1,275 ft./sec.
Hull: 2¾-inch plastic
Wad: Plastic
Shot: Lead
Buffered: No
Test barrel length: 30 inch
Pellets will pierce skin up to 236 yards.

NO. BB LEAD PELLETS—1½ OUNCES—75 PELLETS
Mfg: Federal Cartridge Co. **Manufacturer's code:** P156
Recoil energy in 8-lb. shotgun: 44.8 ft./lbs. **Recoil velocity in 8-lb. shotgun:** 19.0 ft./sec.

Distance in yards:	Muzzle	20	30	40	50	60	70
Velocity in fps:	1,362	1,058	951	863	789	724	668
Average pellet energy in ft-lbs:	35.30	21.30	17.22	14.18	11.84	9.99	8.50
Time of flight in seconds:	0	.0504	.0803	.1135	.1499	.1896	.2327

Type of load: Field
Three-foot velocity: 1,300 ft./sec.
Hull: 2¾-inch plastic
Wad: Plastic
Shot: Lead
Buffered: No
Test barrel length: 30 inch
Pellets will pierce skin up to 237 yards.

NO. 2 LEAD PELLETS—1 OUNCE—82 PELLETS
Mfg: Aguila **Manufacturer's code:** N/A
Recoil energy in 8-lb. shotgun: 20.4 ft./lbs. **Recoil velocity in 8-lb. shotgun:** 12.8 ft./sec.

Distance in yards:	Muzzle	20	30	40	50	60	70
Velocity in fps:	1,270	960	855	768	695	632	577
Average pellet energy in ft-lbs:	17.78	10.16	8.05	6.50	5.32	4.40	3.67
Time of flight in seconds:	0	.0549	.0880	.01261	.1662	.2115	.2612

Type of load: Field
Three-foot velocity: 1,200 ft./sec.
Hull: 2¾-inch plastic
Wad: Two-piece, ribbed plastic
Shot: Lead
Buffered: No
Test barrel length: 30 inch
Pellets will pierce skin up to 213 yards.

NO. 2 LEAD PELLETS—1⅛ OUNCES—99 PELLETS
Mfg: Aguila **Manufacturer's code:** N/A
Recoil energy in 8-lb. shotgun: 20.4 ft./lbs. **Recoil velocity in 8-lb. shotgun:** 12.8 ft./sec.

Distance in yards:	Muzzle	20	30	40	50	60	70
Velocity in fps:	1,270	960	855	768	695	632	577
Average pellet energy in ft-lbs:	17.78	10.16	8.05	6.50	5.32	4.40	3.67
Time of flight in seconds:	0	.0549	.0880	.01261	.1662	.2115	.2612

Type of load: Field
Three-foot velocity: 1,200 ft./sec.
Hull: 2¾-inch plastic
Wad: Plastic
Shot: Lead
Buffered: No
Test barrel length: 30 inch
Pellets will pierce skin up to 213 yards.

NO. 2 LEAD PELLETS—1⅛ OUNCES—99 PELLETS
Mfg: Clever **Manufacturer's code:** T2 Light Game
Recoil energy in 8-lb. shotgun: 27.9 ft./lbs. **Recoil velocity in 8-lb. shotgun:** 15.0 ft./sec.

Distance in yards:	Muzzle	20	30	40	50	60	70
Velocity in fps:	1,432	1,053	928	829	746	676	616
Average pellet energy in ft-lbs:	22.61	12.21	9.49	7.57	6.14	5.04	4.18
Time of flight in seconds:	0	.0494	.0798	.1140	.1522	.1945	.2410

Type of load: Field
Three-foot velocity: 1,350 ft./sec.
Hull: 2¾-inch plastic
Wad: Plastic
Shot: Lead
Buffered: No
Test barrel length: 30 inch
Pellets will pierce skin up to 200 yards.

NO. 2 LEAD PELLETS—1³/₁₆ OUNCES—105 PELLETS
Mfg: Clever **Manufacturer's code:** T2 Caccia
Recoil energy in 8-lb. shotgun: 25.2 ft./lbs. **Recoil velocity in 8-lb. shotgun:** 14.2 ft./sec.

Distance in yards:	Muzzle	20	30	40	50	60	70
Velocity in fps:	1,378	1,022	904	809	730	662	604
Average pellet energy in ft-lbs:	20.93	11.50	9.00	7.21	5.87	4.83	4.01
Time of flight in seconds:	0	.0511	.0824	.1175	.1566	.1988	.2473

Type of load: Field
Three-foot velocity: 1,300 ft./sec.
Hull: 2¾-inch plastic
Wad: Plastic
Shot: Lead
Buffered: No
Test barrel length: 30 inch
Pellets will pierce skin up to 198 yards.

NO. 2 LEAD PELLETS—1¼ OUNCES—110 PELLETS
Mfg: ARMUSA **Manufacturer's code:** N/A
Recoil energy in 8-lb. shotgun: 31.1 ft./lbs. **Recoil velocity in 8-lb. shotgun:** 15.8 ft./sec.

Distance in yards:	Muzzle	20	30	40	50	60	70
Velocity in fps:	1,378	1,022	904	809	730	662	604
Average pellet energy in ft-lbs:	20.93	11.50	9.00	7.21	5.87	4.83	4.01
Time of flight in seconds:	0	.0511	.0824	.1175	.1566	.1988	.2473

Type of load: Field
Three-foot velocity: 1,300 ft./sec.
Hull: 2¾-inch plastic
Wad: Plastic
Shot: Lead
Buffered: No
Test barrel length: 30 inch
Pellets will pierce skin up to 198 yards.

NO. 2 LEAD PELLETS—1¼ OUNCES—110 PELLETS
Mfg: Clever **Manufacturer's code:** T4 High Velocity
Recoil energy in 8-lb. shotgun: 31.1 ft./lbs. **Recoil velocity in 8-lb. shotgun:** 15.8 ft./sec.

Distance in yards:	Muzzle	20	30	40	50	60	70
Velocity in fps:	1,378	1,022	904	809	730	662	604
Average pellet energy in ft-lbs:	20.93	11.50	9.00	7.21	5.87	4.83	4.01
Time of flight in seconds:	0	.0511	.0824	.1175	.1566	.1988	.2473

Type of load: Field
Three-foot velocity: 1,300 ft./sec.
Hull: 2¾-inch plastic
Wad: Plastic
Shot: Lead
Buffered: No
Test barrel length: 30 inch
Pellets will pierce skin up to 198 yards.

NO. 2 LEAD PELLETS—1¼ OUNCES—110 PELLETS
Mfg: Aguila **Manufacturer's code:** N/A
Recoil energy in 8-lb. shotgun: 33.0 ft./lbs. **Recoil velocity in 8-lb. shotgun:** 16.3 ft./sec.

Distance in yards:	Muzzle	20	30	40	50	60	70
Velocity in fps:	1,411	1,040	919	821	740	671	611
Average pellet energy in ft-lbs:	21.93	11.92	9.30	7.42	6.03	7.96	4.12
Time of flight in seconds:	0	.0501	.0808	.1154	.1539	.1966	.2434

Type of load: Field
Three-foot velocity: 1,330 ft./sec.
Hull: 2¾-inch plastic
Wad: Plastic
Shot: Lead
Buffered: No
Test barrel length: 30 inch
Pellets will pierce skin up to 219 yards.

NO. 2 LEAD PELLETS—1¼ OUNCES—110 PELLETS
Mfg: Baschieri & Pellagri **Manufacturer's code:** MB Long Range
Recoil energy in 8-lb. shotgun: 33.0 ft./lbs. **Recoil velocity in 8-lb. shotgun:** 16.3 ft./sec.

Distance in yards:	Muzzle	20	30	40	50	60	70
Velocity in fps:	1,411	1,040	919	821	740	671	611
Average pellet energy in ft-lbs:	21.93	11.92	9.30	7.42	6.03	7.96	4.12
Time of flight in seconds:	0	.0501	.0808	.1154	.1539	.1966	.2434

Type of load: Field
Three-foot velocity: 1,330 ft./sec.
Hull: 2¾-inch plastic
Wad: Plastic
Shot: Lead
Buffered: No
Test barrel length: 30 inch
Pellets will pierce skin up to 219 yards.

NO. 2 LEAD PELLETS—1¼ OUNCES—110 PELLETS
Mfg: Federal Cartridge Co. **Manufacturer's code:** H126
Recoil energy in 8-lb. shotgun: 33.0 ft./lbs. **Recoil velocity in 8-lb. shotgun:** 16.3 ft./sec.

Distance in yards:	Muzzle	20	30	40	50	60	70
Velocity in fps:	1,411	1,040	919	821	740	671	611
Average pellet energy in ft-lbs:	21.93	11.92	9.30	7.42	6.03	7.96	4.12
Time of flight in seconds:	0	.0501	.0808	.1154	.1539	.1966	.2434

Type of load: Field
Three-foot velocity: 1,330 ft./sec.
Hull: 2¾-inch plastic
Wad: Plastic
Shot: Lead
Buffered: No
Test barrel length: 30 inch
Pellets will pierce skin up to 219 yards.

NO. 2 LEAD PELLETS—1¼ OUNCES—110 PELLETS
Mfg: Remington Arms Co. **Manufacturer's code:** SP12
Recoil energy in 8-lb. shotgun: 33.0 ft./lbs. **Recoil velocity in 8-lb. shotgun:** 16.3 ft./sec.

Distance in yards:	Muzzle	20	30	40	50	60	70
Velocity in fps:	1,411	1,040	919	821	740	671	611
Average pellet energy in ft-lbs:	21.93	11.92	9.30	7.42	6.03	7.96	4.12
Time of flight in seconds:	0	.0501	.0808	.1154	.1539	.1966	.2434

Type of load: Field
Three-foot velocity: 1,330 ft./sec.
Hull: 2¾-inch plastic
Wad: Plastic
Shot: Lead
Buffered: No
Test barrel length: 30 inch
Pellets will pierce skin up to 219 yards.

NO. 2 LEAD PELLETS—1⅜ OUNCES—121 PELLETS
Mfg: Clever **Manufacturer's code:** T4 Caccia
Recoil energy in 8-lb. shotgun: 35.7 ft./lbs. **Recoil velocity in 8-lb. shotgun:** 16.9 ft./sec.

Distance in yards:	Muzzle	20	30	40	50	60	70
Velocity in fps:	1,351	1,006	892	799	721	655	597
Average pellet energy in ft-lbs:	20.12	11.16	8.76	7.03	5.73	4.72	3.93
Time of flight in seconds:	0	.0520	.0837	.1193	.1589	.2026	.2506

Type of load: Field
Three-foot velocity: 1,275 ft./sec.
Hull: 2¾-inch plastic
Wad: Plastic
Shot: Lead
Buffered: No
Test barrel length: 30 inch
Pellets will pierce skin up to 197 yards.

NO. 2 LEAD PELLETS—1½ OUNCES—130 PELLETS
Mfg: Federal Cartridge Co. **Manufacturer's code:** F130
Recoil energy in 8-lb. shotgun: 40.4 ft./lbs. **Recoil velocity in 8-lb. shotgun:** 18.0 ft./sec.

Distance in yards:	Muzzle	20	30	40	50	60	70
Velocity in fps:	1,324	991	879	789	713	647	591
Average pellet energy in ft-lbs:	19.32	10.82	8.52	6.85	5.59	4.62	3.84
Time of flight in seconds:	0	.0529	.0851	.1212	.1612	.2054	.2540

Type of load: Field
Three-foot velocity: 1,250 ft./sec.
Hull: 2¾-inch plastic
Wad: Plastic
Shot: Lead
Buffered: No
Test barrel length: 30 inch
Pellets will pierce skin up to 196 yards.

NO. 2 LEAD PELLETS—1½ OUNCES—130 PELLETS
Mfg: Remington Arms Co. **Manufacturer's code:** NM12S
Recoil energy in 8-lb. shotgun: 40.4 ft./lbs. **Recoil velocity in 8-lb. shotgun:** 18.0 ft./sec.

Distance in yards:	Muzzle	20	30	40	50	60	70
Velocity in fps:	1,324	991	879	789	713	647	591
Average pellet energy in ft-lbs:	19.32	10.82	8.52	6.85	5.59	4.62	3.84
Time of flight in seconds:	0	.0529	.0851	.1212	.1612	.2054	.2540

Type of load: Field
Three-foot velocity: 1,250 ft./sec.
Hull: 2¾-inch plastic
Wad: Plastic
Shot: Lead
Buffered: No
Test barrel length: 30 inch
Pellets will pierce skin up to 196 yards.

NO. 2 LEAD PELLETS—1½ OUNCES—130 PELLETS
Mfg: Clever **Manufacturer's code:** Magnum 42
Recoil energy in 8-lb. shotgun: 42.5 ft./lbs. **Recoil velocity in 8-lb. shotgun:** 18.5 ft./sec.

Distance in yards:	Muzzle	20	30	40	50	60	70
Velocity in fps:	1,351	1,006	892	799	721	655	597
Average pellet energy in ft-lbs:	20.12	11.16	8.76	7.03	5.73	4.72	3.93
Time of flight in seconds:	0	.0520	.0837	.1193	.1589	.2026	.2506

Type of load: Field
Three-foot velocity: 1,275 ft./sec.
Hull: 2¾-inch plastic
Wad: Plastic
Shot: Lead
Buffered: No
Test barrel length: 30 inch
Pellets will pierce skin up to 197 yards.

NO. 2 LEAD PELLETS—1½ OUNCES—130 PELLETS
Mfg: Federal Cartridge Co. **Manufacturer's code:** P156
Recoil energy in 8-lb. shotgun: 44.8 ft./lbs. **Recoil velocity in 8-lb. shotgun:** 19.0 ft./sec.

Distance in yards:	Muzzle	20	30	40	50	60	70
Velocity in fps:	1,378	1,022	904	809	730	662	604
Average pellet energy in ft-lbs:	20.93	11.50	9.00	7.21	5.87	4.83	4.01
Time of flight in seconds:	0	.0511	.0824	.1175	.1566	.1988	.2473

Type of load: Field
Three-foot velocity: 1,300 ft./sec.
Hull: 2¾-inch plastic
Wad: Plastic
Shot: Lead
Buffered: No
Test barrel length: 30 inch
Pellets will pierce skin up to 198 yards.

NO. 2 LEAD PELLETS—1¾ OUNCES—154 PELLETS
Mfg: Clever **Manufacturer's code:** Magnum 76
Recoil energy in 8-lb. shotgun: 54.9 ft./lbs. **Recoil velocity in 8-lb. shotgun:** 21.0 ft./sec.

Distance in yards:	Muzzle	20	30	40	50	60	70
Velocity in fps:	1,324	991	879	789	713	647	591
Average pellet energy in ft-lbs:	19.32	10.82	8.52	6.85	5.59	4.62	3.84
Time of flight in seconds:	0	.0529	.0851	.1212	.1612	.2054	.2540

Type of load: Field
Three-foot velocity: 1,250 ft./sec.
Hull: 2¾-inch plastic
Wad: Plastic
Shot: Lead
Buffered: No
Test barrel length: 30 inch
Pellets will pierce skin up to 196 yards.

NO. 3 LEAD PELLETS—1¼ OUNCES—136 PELLETS
Mfg: Eley Hawk **Manufacturer's code:** Alphamax
Recoil energy in 8-lb. shotgun: 31.1 ft./lbs. **Recoil velocity in 8-lb. shotgun:** 15.8 ft./sec.

Distance in yards:	Muzzle	20	30	40	50	60	70
Velocity in fps:	1,384	1,006	884	787	706	638	578
Average pellet energy in ft-lbs:	17.16	9.07	7.01	5.55	4.47	3.64	3.00
Time of flight in seconds:	0	.0514	.0833	.1193	.1596	.2044	.2538

Type of load: Field
Three-foot velocity: 1,300 ft./sec.
Hull: 2¾-inch plastic
Wad: Plastic
Shot: Lead
Buffered: No
Test barrel length: 30 inch
Pellets will pierce skin up to 185 yards.

NO. 3 LEAD PELLETS—1¼ OUNCES—136 PELLETS
Mfg: Baschieri & Pellagri **Manufacturer's code:** MB/F2 Long Range
Recoil energy in 8-lb. shotgun: 33.0 ft./lbs. **Recoil velocity in 8-lb. shotgun:** 16.3 ft./sec.

Distance in yards:	Muzzle	20	30	40	50	60	70
Velocity in fps:	1,417	1,024	898	798	716	646	586
Average pellet energy in ft-lbs:	17.98	9.40	7.23	5.71	4.59	3.73	3.07
Time of flight in seconds:	0	.0504	.0817	.1172	.1570	.2011	.2499

Type of load: Field
Three-foot velocity: 1,330 ft./sec.
Hull: 2¾-inch plastic
Wad: Plastic
Shot: Lead
Buffered: No
Test barrel length: 30 inch
Pellets will pierce skin up to 205 yards.

NO. 3 LEAD PELLETS—1⅜ OUNCES—150 PELLETS
Mfg: Baschieri & Pellagri **Manufacturer's code:** MB Winter
Recoil energy in 8-lb. shotgun: 35.7 ft./lbs. **Recoil velocity in 8-lb. shotgun:** 16.9 ft./sec.

Distance in yards:	Muzzle	20	30	40	50	60	70
Velocity in fps:	1,357	991	873	777	698	631	572
Average pellet energy in ft-lbs:	16.49	8.81	6.82	5.41	4.36	3.56	2.93
Time of flight in seconds:	0	.0523	.0847	.1211	.1619	.2072	.2571

Type of load: Field
Three-foot velocity: 1,275 ft./sec.
Hull: 2¾-inch plastic
Wad: Plastic
Shot: Hard lead
Buffered: No
Test barrel length: 30 inch
Pellets will pierce skin up to 202 yards.

NO. 3 LEAD PELLETS—1½ OUNCES—164 PELLETS
Mfg: Eley Hawk **Manufacturer's code:** Magnum 70
Recoil energy in 8-lb. shotgun: 42.5 ft./lbs. **Recoil velocity in 8-lb. shotgun:** 18.5 ft./sec.

Distance in yards:	Muzzle	20	30	40	50	60	70
Velocity in fps:	1,357	991	873	777	698	631	572
Average pellet energy in ft-lbs:	16.49	8.81	6.82	5.41	4.36	3.56	2.93
Time of flight in seconds:	0	.0523	.0847	.1211	.1619	.2072	.2571

Type of load: Field
Three-foot velocity: 1,275 ft./sec.
Hull: 2¾-inch plastic
Wad: Plastic
Shot: Lead
Buffered: No
Test barrel length: 30 inch
Pellets will pierce skin up to 184 yards.

NO. 4 LEAD PELLETS—1 OUNCE—136 PELLETS
Mfg: Aguila **Manufacturer's code:** N/A
Recoil energy in 8-lb. shotgun: 20.4 ft./lbs. **Recoil velocity in 8-lb. shotgun:** 12.8 ft./sec.

Distance in yards:	Muzzle	20	30	40	50	60	70
Velocity in fps:	1,281	931	817	725	649	584	528
Average pellet energy in ft-lbs:	11.77	6.21	4.79	3.77	3.02	2.45	2.00
Time of flight in seconds:	0	.0556	.0901	.01291	.1729	.2216	.2757

Type of load: Field
Three-foot velocity: 1,200 ft./sec.
Hull: 2¾-inch plastic
Wad: Two-piece, ribbed plastic
Shot: Lead
Buffered: No
Test barrel length: 30 inch
Pellets will pierce skin up to 168 yards.

NO. 4 LEAD PELLETS—1 OUNCE—136 PELLETS
Mfg: Estate Cartridge **Manufacturer's code:** DQ12
Recoil energy in 8-lb. shotgun: 19.9 ft./lbs. **Recoil velocity in 8-lb. shotgun:** 12.6 ft./sec.

Distance in yards:	Muzzle	20	30	40	50	60	70
Velocity in fps:	1,390	989	863	762	680	611	551
Average pellet energy in ft-lbs:	13.86	7.01	5.34	4.17	3.32	2.67	2.18
Time of flight in seconds:	0	.0519	.0844	.1215	.1632	.2098	.2615

Type of load: Field
Three-foot velocity: 1,300 ft./sec.5
Hull: 2¾-inch plastic
Wad: Plastic
Shot: Hard lead
Buffered: No
Test barrel length: 30 inch
Pellets will pierce skin up to 172 yards.

NO. 4 LEAD PELLETS—1⅛ OUNCES—153 PELLETS
Mfg: Armscor **Manufacturer's code:** N/A
Recoil energy in 8-lb. shotgun: 18.0 ft./lbs. **Recoil velocity in 8-lb. shotgun:** 12.0 ft./sec.

Distance in yards:	Muzzle	20	30	40	50	60	70
Velocity in fps:	1,221	898	791	704	631	569	514
Average pellet energy in ft-lbs:	10.69	5.79	4.49	3.56	2.86	2.32	1.90
Time of flight in seconds:	0	.0579	.0936	.1338	.1789	.2290	.2845

Type of load: Field
Three-foot velocity: 1,145 ft./sec.
Hull: 2¾-inch plastic
Wad: Plastic
Shot: Lead
Buffered: No
Test barrel length: 30 inch
Pellets will pierce skin up to 165 yards.

NO. 4 LEAD PELLETS—1⅛ OUNCES—153 PELLETS
Mfg: Aguila **Manufacturer's code:** N/A
Recoil energy in 8-lb. shotgun: 20.4 ft./lbs. **Recoil velocity in 8-lb. shotgun:** 12.8 ft./sec.

Distance in yards:	Muzzle	20	30	40	50	60	70
Velocity in fps:	1,281	931	817	725	649	584	528
Average pellet energy in ft-lbs:	11.77	6.21	4.79	3.77	3.02	2.45	2.00
Time of flight in seconds:	0	.0556	.0901	.01291	.1729	.2216	.2757

Type of load: Field
Three-foot velocity: 1,200 ft./sec.
Hull: 2¾-inch plastic
Wad: Plastic
Shot: Lead
Buffered: No
Test barrel length: 30 inch
Pellets will pierce skin up to 168 yards.

NO. 4 LEAD PELLETS—1⅛ OUNCES—153 PELLETS
Mfg: Estate Cartridge **Manufacturer's code:** HG12
Recoil energy in 8-lb. shotgun: 22.7 ft./lbs. **Recoil velocity in 8-lb. shotgun:** 13.5 ft./sec.

Distance in yards:	Muzzle	20	30	40	50	60	70
Velocity in fps:	1,336	960	840	744	665	598	540
Average pellet energy in ft-lbs:	12.79	6.61	5.06	3.97	3.17	2.56	2.09
Time of flight in seconds:	0	.0537	.0872	.1252	.1679	.2155	.2684

Type of load: Field
Three-foot velocity: 1,250 ft./sec.
Hull: 2¾-inch plastic
Wad: Plastic
Shot: Hard lead
Buffered: No
Test barrel length: 30 inch
Pellets will pierce skin up to 170 yards.

NO. 4 LEAD PELLETS—1⅛ OUNCES—153 PELLETS
Mfg: Federal Cartridge Co. **Manufacturer's code:** H123
Recoil energy in 8-lb. shotgun: 22.7 ft./lbs. **Recoil velocity in 8-lb. shotgun:** 13.5 ft./sec.

Distance in yards:	Muzzle	20	30	40	50	60	70
Velocity in fps:	1,336	960	840	744	665	598	540
Average pellet energy in ft-lbs:	12.79	6.61	5.06	3.97	3.17	2.56	2.09
Time of flight in seconds:	0	.0537	.0872	.1252	.1679	.2155	.2684

Type of load: Field
Three-foot velocity: 1,250 ft./sec.
Hull: 2¾-inch plastic
Wad: Plastic
Shot: Lead
Buffered: No
Test barrel length: 30 inch
Pellets will pierce skin up to 170 yards.

NO. 4 LEAD PELLETS—1⅛ OUNCES—153 PELLETS
Mfg: Winchester **Manufacturer's code:** XU12H
Recoil energy in 8-lb. shotgun: 22.7 ft./lbs. **Recoil velocity in 8-lb. shotgun:** 13.5 ft./sec.

Distance in yards:	Muzzle	20	30	40	50	60	70
Velocity in fps:	1,336	960	840	744	665	598	540
Average pellet energy in ft-lbs:	12.79	6.61	5.06	3.97	3.17	2.56	2.09
Time of flight in seconds:	0	.0537	.0872	.1252	.1679	.2155	.2684

Type of load: Field
Three-foot velocity: 1,250 ft./sec.
Hull: 2¾-inch plastic
Wad: Plastic
Shot: Lead
Buffered: No
Test barrel length: 30 inch
Pellets will pierce skin up to 170 yards.

NO. 4 LEAD PELLETS—1⅛ OUNCES—153 PELLETS
Mfg: Baschieri & Pellagri **Manufacturer's code:** F2 Long Range
Recoil energy in 8-lb. shotgun: 26.8 ft./lbs. **Recoil velocity in 8-lb. shotgun:** 14.7 ft./sec.

Distance in yards:	Muzzle	20	30	40	50	60	70
Velocity in fps:	1,445	1018	885	780	695	623	562
Average pellet energy in ft-lbs:	14.97	7.43	5.61	4.37	3.46	2.79	2.26
Time of flight in seconds:	0	.0502	.0819	.1180	.1588	.2044	.2551

Type of load: Field
Three-foot velocity: 1,350 ft./sec.
Hull: 2¾-inch plastic
Wad: Plastic
Shot: Lead
Buffered: No
Test barrel length: 30 inch
Pellets will pierce skin up to 174 yards.

NO. 4 LEAD PELLETS—1⅛ OUNCES—153 PELLETS
Mfg: Clever **Manufacturer's code:** T2 Light Game
Recoil energy in 8-lb. shotgun: 27.9 ft./lbs. **Recoil velocity in 8-lb. shotgun:** 15.0 ft./sec.

Distance in yards:	Muzzle	20	30	40	50	60	70
Velocity in fps:	1,445	1,018	885	780	695	623	562
Average pellet energy in ft-lbs:	14.97	7.43	5.61	4.37	3.46	2.79	2.26
Time of flight in seconds:	0	.0502	.0819	.1180	.1588	.2044	.2551

Type of load: Field
Three-foot velocity: 1,350 ft./sec.
Hull: 2¾-inch plastic
Wad: Plastic
Shot: Lead
Buffered: No
Test barrel length: 30 inch
Pellets will pierce skin up to 174 yards.

NO. 4 LEAD PELLETS—1⅛ OUNCES—153 PELLETS
Mfg: Federal Cartridge Co. **Manufacturer's code:** P128
Recoil energy in 8-lb. shotgun: 30.7 ft./lbs. **Recoil velocity in 8-lb. shotgun:** 15.7 ft./sec.

Distance in yards:	Muzzle	20	30	40	50	60	70
Velocity in fps:	1,500	1,134	907	798	710	636	573
Average pellet energy in ft-lbs:	16.13	7.86	5.90	4.57	3.61	2.90	2.35
Time of flight in seconds:	0	.0486	.0794	.1147	.1547	.1994	.2491

Type of load: Field
Three-foot velocity: 1,400 ft./sec.
Hull: 2¾-inch plastic
Wad: Plastic
Shot: Lead
Buffered: No
Test barrel length: 30 inch
Pellets will pierce skin up to 176 yards.

NO. 4 LEAD PELLETS—1³/₁₆ OUNCES—162 PELLETS
Mfg: Clever **Manufacturer's code:** T2 Caccia
Recoil energy in 8-lb. shotgun: 25.2 ft./lbs. **Recoil velocity in 8-lb. shotgun:** 14.2 ft./sec.

Distance in yards:	Muzzle	20	30	40	50	60	70
Velocity in fps:	1,390	989	863	762	680	611	551
Average pellet energy in ft-lbs:	13.86	7.01	5.34	4.17	3.32	2.67	2.18
Time of flight in seconds:	0	.0519	.0844	.1215	.1632	.2098	.2615

Type of load: Field
Three-foot velocity: 1,300 ft./sec.
Hull: 2¾-inch plastic
Wad: Plastic
Shot: Lead
Buffered: No
Test barrel length: 30 inch
Pellets will pierce skin up to 172 yards.

NO. 4 LEAD PELLETS—1¼ OUNCES—170 PELLETS
Mfg: Estate Cartridge **Manufacturer's code:** XHG12
Recoil energy in 8-lb. shotgun: 26.3 ft./lbs. **Recoil velocity in 8-lb. shotgun:** 14.5 ft./sec.

Distance in yards:	Muzzle	20	30	40	50	60	70
Velocity in fps:	1,303	943	826	733	655	590	532
Average pellet energy in ft-lbs:	12.17	6.37	4.90	3.85	3.08	2.49	2.03
Time of flight in seconds:	0	.0548	.0889	.1275	.1708	.2191	.2727

Type of load: Field
Three-foot velocity: 1,220 ft./sec.
Hull: 2¾-inch plastic
Wad: Plastic
Shot: Hard lead
Buffered: No
Test barrel length: 30 inch
Pellets will pierce skin up to 169 yards.

NO. 4 LEAD PELLETS—1¼ OUNCES—170 PELLETS
Mfg: Federal Cartridge Co. **Manufacturer's code:** H127
Recoil energy in 8-lb. shotgun: 29.5 ft./lbs. **Recoil velocity in 8-lb. shotgun:** 15.4 ft./sec.

Distance in yards:	Muzzle	20	30	40	50	60	70
Velocity in fps:	1,363	1,049	851	753	672	604	545
Average pellet energy in ft-lbs:	13.32	6.81	5.20	4.07	3.24	2.62	2.13
Time of flight in seconds:	0	.0528	.0858	.1233	.1655	.2126	.2649

Type of load: Field
Three-foot velocity: 1,275 ft./sec.
Hull: 2¾-inch plastic
Wad: Plastic
Shot: Lead
Buffered: No
Test barrel length: 30 inch
Pellets will pierce skin up to 171 yards.

NO. 4 LEAD PELLETS—1¼ OUNCES—170 PELLETS
Mfg: ARMUSA **Manufacturer's code:** N/A
Recoil energy in 8-lb. shotgun: 31.1 ft./lbs. **Recoil velocity in 8-lb. shotgun:** 15.8 ft./sec.

Distance in yards:	Muzzle	20	30	40	50	60	70
Velocity in fps:	1,390	989	863	762	680	611	551
Average pellet energy in ft-lbs:	13.86	7.01	5.34	4.17	3.32	2.67	2.18
Time of flight in seconds:	0	.0519	.0844	.1215	.1632	.2098	.2615

Type of load: Field
Three-foot velocity: 1,300 ft./sec.
Hull: 2¾-inch plastic
Wad: Plastic
Shot: Lead
Buffered: No
Test barrel length: 30 inch
Pellets will pierce skin up to 172 yards.

NO. 4 LEAD PELLETS—1¼ OUNCES—170 PELLETS
Mfg: Baschieri & Pellagri **Manufacturer's code:** MB Extra
Recoil energy in 8-lb. shotgun: 31.1 ft./lbs. **Recoil velocity in 8-lb. shotgun:** 15.8 ft./sec.

Distance in yards:	Muzzle	20	30	40	50	60	70
Velocity in fps:	1,390	989	863	762	680	611	551
Average pellet energy in ft-lbs:	13.86	7.01	5.34	4.17	3.32	2.67	2.18
Time of flight in seconds:	0	.0519	.0844	.1215	.1632	.2098	.2615

Type of load: Field
Three-foot velocity: 1,300 ft./sec.
Hull: 2¾-inch plastic
Wad: Plastic
Shot: Lead
Buffered: No
Test barrel length: 30 inch
Pellets will pierce skin up to 172 yards.

NO. 4 LEAD PELLETS—1¼ OUNCES—170 PELLETS
Mfg: Clever **Manufacturer's code:** T4 High Velocity
Recoil energy in 8-lb. shotgun: 31.1 ft./lbs. **Recoil velocity in 8-lb. shotgun:** 15.8 ft./sec.

Distance in yards:	Muzzle	20	30	40	50	60	70
Velocity in fps:	1,390	989	863	762	680	611	551
Average pellet energy in ft-lbs:	13.86	7.01	5.34	4.17	3.32	2.67	2.18
Time of flight in seconds:	0	.0519	.0844	.1215	.1632	.2098	.2615

Type of load: Field
Three-foot velocity: 1,300 ft./sec.
Hull: 2¾-inch plastic
Wad: Plastic
Shot: Lead
Buffered: No
Test barrel length: 30 inch
Pellets will pierce skin up to 172 yards.

NO. 4 LEAD PELLETS—1¼ OUNCES—170 PELLETS
Mfg: Eley Hawk **Manufacturer's code:** Alphamax
Recoil energy in 8-lb. shotgun: 31.1 ft./lbs. **Recoil velocity in 8-lb. shotgun:** 15.8 ft./sec.

Distance in yards:	Muzzle	20	30	40	50	60	70
Velocity in fps:	1,390	989	863	762	680	611	551
Average pellet energy in ft-lbs:	13.86	7.01	5.34	4.17	3.32	2.67	2.18
Time of flight in seconds:	0	.0519	.0844	.1215	.1632	.2098	.2615

Type of load: Field
Three-foot velocity: 1,300 ft./sec.
Hull: 2¾-inch plastic
Wad: Plastic
Shot: Lead
Buffered: No
Test barrel length: 30 inch
Pellets will pierce skin up to 172 yards.

NO. 4 LEAD PELLETS—1¼ OUNCES—170 PELLETS
Mfg: Aguila **Manufacturer's code:** N/A
Recoil energy in 8-lb. shotgun: 33.0 ft./lbs. **Recoil velocity in 8-lb. shotgun:** 16.3 ft./sec.

Distance in yards:	Muzzle	20	30	40	50	60	70
Velocity in fps:	1,423	1006	876	773	689	618	558
Average pellet energy in ft-lbs:	14.52	7.26	5.50	4.29	3.41	2.74	2.23
Time of flight in seconds:	0	.0508	.0829	.1194	.1605	.2065	.2576

Type of load: Field
Three-foot velocity: 1,330 ft./sec.
Hull: 2¾-inch plastic
Wad: Plastic
Shot: Lead
Buffered: No
Test barrel length: 30 inch
Pellets will pierce skin up to 173 yards.

NO. 4 LEAD PELLETS—1¼ OUNCES—170 PELLETS
Mfg: Baschieri & Pellagri **Manufacturer's code:** MB/F2 Long Range
Recoil energy in 8-lb. shotgun: 33.0 ft./lbs. **Recoil velocity in 8-lb. shotgun:** 16.3 ft./sec.

Distance in yards:	Muzzle	20	30	40	50	60	70
Velocity in fps:	1,423	1006	876	773	689	618	558
Average pellet energy in ft-lbs:	14.52	7.26	5.50	4.29	3.41	2.74	2.23
Time of flight in seconds:	0	.0508	.0829	.1194	.1605	.2065	.2576

Type of load: Field
Three-foot velocity: 1,330 ft./sec.
Hull: 2¾-inch plastic
Wad: Plastic
Shot: Lead
Buffered: No
Test barrel length: 30 inch
Pellets will pierce skin up to 173 yards.

NO. 4 LEAD PELLETS—1¼ OUNCES—170 PELLETS
Mfg: Dionisi **Manufacturer's code:** D 12 SLR
Recoil energy in 8-lb. shotgun: 33.0 ft./lbs. **Recoil velocity in 8-lb. shotgun:** 16.3 ft./sec.

Distance in yards:	Muzzle	20	30	40	50	60	70
Velocity in fps:	1,423	1006	876	773	689	618	558
Average pellet energy in ft-lbs:	14.52	7.26	5.50	4.29	3.41	2.74	2.23
Time of flight in seconds:	0	.0508	.0829	.1194	.1605	.2065	.2576

Type of load: Field
Three-foot velocity: 1,330 ft./sec.
Hull: 2¾-inch plastic
Wad: Plastic
Shot: Lead
Buffered: No
Test barrel length: 30 inch
Pellets will pierce skin up to 173 yards.

NO. 4 LEAD PELLETS—1¼ OUNCES—170 PELLETS
Mfg: Federal Cartridge Co. **Manufacturer's code:** P154/H126
Recoil energy in 8-lb. shotgun: 33.0 ft./lbs. **Recoil velocity in 8-lb. shotgun:** 16.3 ft./sec.

Distance in yards:	Muzzle	20	30	40	50	60	70
Velocity in fps:	1,423	1006	876	773	689	618	558
Average pellet energy in ft-lbs:	14.52	7.26	5.50	4.29	3.41	2.74	2.23
Time of flight in seconds:	0	.0508	.0829	.1194	.1605	.2065	.2576

Type of load: Field
Three-foot velocity: 1,330 ft./sec.
Hull: 2¾-inch plastic
Wad: Plastic
Shot: Lead
Buffered: No
Test barrel length: 30 inch
Pellets will pierce skin up to 173 yards.

NO. 4 LEAD PELLETS—1¼ OUNCES—170 PELLETS
Mfg: Fiocchi **Manufacturer's code:** 12HV
Recoil energy in 8-lb. shotgun: 33.0 ft./lbs. **Recoil velocity in 8-lb. shotgun:** 16.3 ft./sec.

Distance in yards:	Muzzle	20	30	40	50	60	70
Velocity in fps:	1,423	1006	876	773	689	618	558
Average pellet energy in ft-lbs:	14.52	7.26	5.50	4.29	3.41	2.74	2.23
Time of flight in seconds:	0	.0508	.0829	.1194	.1605	.2065	.2576

Type of load: Field
Three-foot velocity: 1,330 ft./sec.
Hull: 2¾-inch plastic
Wad: Plastic
Shot: Lead
Buffered: No
Test barrel length: 30 inch
Pellets will pierce skin up to 173 yards.

NO. 4 LEAD PELLETS—1¼ OUNCES—170 PELLETS
Mfg: Fiocchi **Manufacturer's code:** 12HVN
Recoil energy in 8-lb. shotgun: 33.0 ft./lbs. **Recoil velocity in 8-lb. shotgun:** 17.9 ft./sec.

Distance in yards:	Muzzle	20	30	40	50	60	70
Velocity in fps:	1,423	1006	876	773	689	618	558
Average pellet energy in ft-lbs:	14.52	7.26	5.50	4.29	3.41	2.74	2.23
Time of flight in seconds:	0	.0508	.0829	.1194	.1605	.2065	.2576

Type of load: Field
Three-foot velocity: 1,330 ft./sec.
Hull: 2¾-inch plastic
Wad: Plastic
Shot: Nickel-plated lead
Buffered: No
Test barrel length: 30 inch
Pellets will pierce skin up to 173 yards.

NO. 4 LEAD PELLETS—1¼ OUNCES—170 PELLETS
Mfg: Kent Cartridge America/Canada **Manufacturer's code:** K122UG36
Recoil energy in 8-lb. shotgun: 31.1 ft./lbs. **Recoil velocity in 8-lb. shotgun:** 15.8 ft./sec.

Distance in yards:	Muzzle	20	30	40	50	60	70
Velocity in fps:	1,423	1006	876	773	689	618	558
Average pellet energy in ft-lbs:	14.52	7.26	5.50	4.29	3.41	2.74	2.23
Time of flight in seconds:	0	.0508	.0829	.1194	.1605	.2065	.2576

Type of load: Field
Three-foot velocity: 1,330 ft./sec.
Hull: 2¾-inch plastic
Wad: Plastic
Shot: Lead
Buffered: No
Test barrel length: 30 inch
Pellets will pierce skin up to 173 yards.

NO. 4 LEAD PELLETS—1¼ OUNCES—170 PELLETS
Mfg: PMC (Eldorado Cartridge Corp.) **Manufacturer's code:** HF12
Recoil energy in 8-lb. shotgun: 31.1 ft./lbs. **Recoil velocity in 8-lb. shotgun:** 15.8 ft./sec.

Distance in yards:	Muzzle	20	30	40	50	60	70
Velocity in fps:	1,423	1006	876	773	689	618	558
Average pellet energy in ft-lbs:	14.52	7.26	5.50	4.29	3.41	2.74	2.23
Time of flight in seconds:	0	.0508	.0829	.1194	.1605	.2065	.2576

Type of load: Field
Three-foot velocity: 1,330 ft./sec.
Hull: 2¾-inch plastic
Wad: Plastic
Shot: Lead
Buffered: No
Test barrel length: 30 inch
Pellets will pierce skin up to 173 yards.

NO. 4 LEAD PELLETS—1¼ OUNCES—170 PELLETS
Mfg: Remington Arms Co. **Manufacturer's code:** SP12/HGL12
Recoil energy in 8-lb. shotgun: 33.0 ft./lbs. **Recoil velocity in 8-lb. shotgun:** 16.3 ft./sec.

Distance in yards:	Muzzle	20	30	40	50	60	70
Velocity in fps:	1,423	1006	876	773	689	618	558
Average pellet energy in ft-lbs:	14.52	7.26	5.50	4.29	3.41	2.74	2.23
Time of flight in seconds:	0	.0508	.0829	.1194	.1605	.2065	.2576

Type of load: Field
Three-foot velocity: 1,330 ft./sec.
Hull: 2¾-inch plastic
Wad: Plastic
Shot: Lead
Buffered: No
Test barrel length: 30 inch
Pellets will pierce skin up to 173 yards.

NO. 4 LEAD PELLETS—1¼ OUNCES—170 PELLETS
Mfg: Winchester **Manufacturer's code:** X12
Recoil energy in 8-lb. shotgun: 33.0 ft./lbs. **Recoil velocity in 8-lb. shotgun:** 16.3 ft./sec.

Distance in yards:	Muzzle	20	30	40	50	60	70
Velocity in fps:	1,423	1006	876	773	689	618	558
Average pellet energy in ft-lbs:	14.52	7.26	5.50	4.29	3.41	2.74	2.23
Time of flight in seconds:	0	.0508	.0829	.1194	.1605	.2065	.2576

Type of load: Field
Three-foot velocity: 1,330 ft./sec.
Hull: 2¾-inch plastic
Wad: Plastic
Shot: Lead
Buffered: No
Test barrel length: 30 inch
Pellets will pierce skin up to 173 yards.

NO. 4 LEAD PELLETS—1¼ OUNCES—170 PELLETS
Mfg: Remington Arms Co. **Manufacturer's code:** SPHV12
Recoil energy in 8-lb. shotgun: 37.9 ft./lbs. **Recoil velocity in 8-lb. shotgun:** 17.5 ft./sec.

Distance in yards:	Muzzle	20	30	40	50	60	70
Velocity in fps:	1,500	1,134	907	798	710	636	573
Average pellet energy in ft-lbs:	16.13	7.86	5.90	4.57	3.61	2.90	2.35
Time of flight in seconds:	0	.0486	.0794	.1147	.1547	.1994	.2491

Type of load: Field
Three-foot velocity: 1,400 ft./sec.
Hull: 2¾-inch plastic
Wad: Plastic
Shot: Lead
Buffered: No
Test barrel length: 30 inch
Pellets will pierce skin up to 176 yards.

NO. 4 LEAD PELLETS—1¼ OUNCES—170 PELLETS
Mfg: Winchester **Manufacturer's code:** SFH12
Recoil energy in 8-lb. shotgun: 37.9 ft./lbs. **Recoil velocity in 8-lb. shotgun:** 17.5 ft./sec.

Distance in yards:	Muzzle	20	30	40	50	60	70
Velocity in fps:	1,500	1,134	907	798	710	636	573
Average pellet energy in ft-lbs:	16.13	7.86	5.90	4.57	3.61	2.90	2.35
Time of flight in seconds:	0	.0486	.0794	.1147	.1547	.1994	.2491

Type of load: Field
Three-foot velocity: 1,400 ft./sec.
Hull: 2¾-inch plastic
Wad: Plastic
Shot: Copper-plated lead
Buffered: Yes
Test barrel length: 30 inch
Pellets will pierce skin up to 176 yards.

NO. 4 LEAD PELLETS—1⅜ OUNCES—187 PELLETS
Mfg: Fiocchi **Manufacturer's code:** 12HGP/12TT
Recoil energy in 8-lb. shotgun: 33.9 ft./lbs. **Recoil velocity in 8-lb. shotgun:** 16.5 ft./sec.

Distance in yards:	Muzzle	20	30	40	50	60	70
Velocity in fps:	1,336	960	840	744	665	598	540
Average pellet energy in ft-lbs:	12.79	6.61	5.06	3.97	3.17	2.56	2.09
Time of flight in seconds:	0	.0537	.0872	.1252	.1679	.2155	.2684

Type of load: Field & Turkey
Three-foot velocity: 1,250 ft./sec.
Hull: 2¾-inch plastic
Wad: Plastic
Shot: Nickel-plated lead
Buffered: No
Test barrel length: 30 inch
Pellets will pierce skin up to 170 yards.

NO. 4 LEAD PELLETS—1⅜ OUNCES—187 PELLETS
Mfg: Baschieri & Pellagri **Manufacturer's code:** MB Winter
Recoil energy in 8-lb. shotgun: 35.7 ft./lbs. **Recoil velocity in 8-lb. shotgun:** 16.9 ft./sec.

Distance in yards:	Muzzle	20	30	40	50	60	70
Velocity in fps:	1,363	1,049	851	753	672	604	545
Average pellet energy in ft-lbs:	13.32	6.81	5.20	4.07	3.24	2.62	2.13
Time of flight in seconds:	0	.0528	.0858	.1233	.1655	.2126	.2649

Type of load: Field
Three-foot velocity: 1,275 ft./sec.
Hull: 2¾-inch plastic
Wad: Plastic
Shot: Hard lead
Buffered: No
Test barrel length: 30 inch
Pellets will pierce skin up to 171 yards.

NO. 4 LEAD PELLETS—1⅜ OUNCES—187 PELLETS
Mfg: Clever Manufacturer's code: T4 Caccia
Recoil energy in 8-lb. shotgun: 35.7 ft./lbs. Recoil velocity in 8-lb. shotgun: 16.9 ft./sec.

Distance in yards:	Muzzle	20	30	40	50	60	70
Velocity in fps:	1,363	1,049	851	753	672	604	545
Average pellet energy in ft-lbs:	13.32	6.81	5.20	4.07	3.24	2.62	2.13
Time of flight in seconds:	0	.0528	.0858	.1233	.1655	.2126	.2649

Type of load: Field
Three-foot velocity: 1,275 ft./sec.
Hull: 2¾-inch plastic
Wad: Plastic
Shot: Lead
Buffered: No
Test barrel length: 30 inch
Pellets will pierce skin up to 171 yards.

NO. 4 LEAD PELLETS—1⅜ OUNCES—187 PELLETS
Mfg: Federal Cartridge Co. Manufacturer's code: P138
Recoil energy in 8-lb. shotgun: 45.9 ft./lbs. Recoil velocity in 8-lb. shotgun: 19.2 ft./sec.

Distance in yards:	Muzzle	20	30	40	50	60	70
Velocity in fps:	1,500	1,134	907	798	710	636	573
Average pellet energy in ft-lbs:	16.13	7.86	5.90	4.57	3.61	2.90	2.35
Time of flight in seconds:	0	.0486	.0794	.1147	.1547	.1994	.2491

Type of load: Field
Three-foot velocity: 1,400 ft./sec.
Hull: 2¾-inch plastic
Wad: Plastic
Shot: Lead
Buffered: No
Test barrel length: 30 inch
Pellets will pierce skin up to 176 yards.

NO. 4 LEAD PELLETS—1½ OUNCES—204 PELLETS
Mfg: Dionisi Manufacturer's code: D 12G
Recoil energy in 8-lb. shotgun: 40.4 ft./lbs. Recoil velocity in 8-lb. shotgun: 18.0 ft./sec.

Distance in yards:	Muzzle	20	30	40	50	60	70
Velocity in fps:	1,336	960	840	744	665	598	540
Average pellet energy in ft-lbs:	12.79	6.61	5.06	3.97	3.17	2.56	2.09
Time of flight in seconds:	0	.0537	.0872	.1252	.1679	.2155	.2684

Type of load: Field
Three-foot velocity: 1,250 ft./sec.
Hull: 2¾-inch plastic
Wad: Plastic
Shot: Lead
Buffered: No
Test barrel length: 30 inch
Pellets will pierce skin up to 170 yards.

NO. 4 LEAD PELLETS—1½ OUNCES—204 PELLETS
Mfg: Federal Cartridge Co. Manufacturer's code: F130
Recoil energy in 8-lb. shotgun: 40.4 ft./lbs. Recoil velocity in 8-lb. shotgun: 18.0 ft./sec.

Distance in yards:	Muzzle	20	30	40	50	60	70
Velocity in fps:	1,336	960	840	744	665	598	540
Average pellet energy in ft-lbs:	12.79	6.61	5.06	3.97	3.17	2.56	2.09
Time of flight in seconds:	0	.0537	.0872	.1252	.1679	.2155	.2684

Type of load: Field
Three-foot velocity: 1,250 ft./sec.
Hull: 2¾-inch plastic
Wad: Plastic
Shot: Lead
Buffered: No
Test barrel length: 30 inch
Pellets will pierce skin up to 170 yards.

NO. 4 LEAD PELLETS—1½ OUNCES—204 PELLETS
Mfg: Remington Arms Co. Manufacturer's code: P12SM/NM12S
Recoil energy in 8-lb. shotgun: 40.4 ft./lbs. Recoil velocity in 8-lb. shotgun: 18.0 ft./sec.

Distance in yards:	Muzzle	20	30	40	50	60	70
Velocity in fps:	1,336	960	840	744	665	598	540
Average pellet energy in ft-lbs:	12.79	6.61	5.06	3.97	3.17	2.56	2.09
Time of flight in seconds:	0	.0537	.0872	.1252	.1679	.2155	.2684

Type of load: Turkey & Field
Three-foot velocity: 1,250 ft./sec.
Hull: 2¾-inch plastic
Wad: Plastic
Shot: Copper-plated lead/lead
Buffered: Yes
Test barrel length: 30 inch
Pellets will pierce skin up to 170 yards.

NO. 4 LEAD PELLETS—1½ OUNCES—204 PELLETS
Mfg: Winchester Manufacturer's code: X12XC
Recoil energy in 8-lb. shotgun: 40.4 ft./lbs. Recoil velocity in 8-lb. shotgun: 18.0 ft./sec.

Distance in yards:	Muzzle	20	30	40	50	60	70
Velocity in fps:	1,336	960	840	744	665	598	540
Average pellet energy in ft-lbs:	12.79	6.61	5.06	3.97	3.17	2.56	2.09
Time of flight in seconds:	0	.0537	.0872	.1252	.1679	.2155	.2684

Type of load: Field
Three-foot velocity: 1,250 ft./sec.
Hull: 2¾-inch plastic
Wad: Plastic
Shot: Copper-plated lead
Buffered: Yes
Test barrel length: 30 inch
Pellets will pierce skin up to 170 yards.

NO. 4 LEAD PELLETS—1½ OUNCES—204 PELLETS
Mfg: Clever Manufacturer's code: Magnum 42
Recoil energy in 8-lb. shotgun: 42.5 ft./lbs. Recoil velocity in 8-lb. shotgun: 18.5 ft./sec.

Distance in yards:	Muzzle	20	30	40	50	60	70
Velocity in fps:	1,363	1,049	851	753	672	604	545
Average pellet energy in ft-lbs:	13.32	6.81	5.20	4.07	3.24	2.62	2.13
Time of flight in seconds:	0	.0528	.0858	.1233	.1655	.2126	.2649

Type of load: Field
Three-foot velocity: 1,275 ft./sec.
Hull: 2¾-inch plastic
Wad: Plastic
Shot: Lead
Buffered: No
Test barrel length: 30 inch
Pellets will pierce skin up to 171 yards.

NO. 4 LEAD PELLETS—1½ OUNCES—204 PELLETS

Mfg: Federal Cartridge Co. **Manufacturer's code:** P156
Recoil energy in 8-lb. shotgun: 44.8 ft./lbs. **Recoil velocity in 8-lb. shotgun:** 19.0 ft./sec.

Distance in yards:	Muzzle	20	30	40	50	60	70
Velocity in fps:	1,390	989	863	762	680	611	551
Average pellet energy in ft-lbs:	13.86	7.01	5.34	4.17	3.32	2.67	2.18
Time of flight in seconds:	0	.0519	.0844	.1215	.1632	.2098	.2615

Type of load: Field
Three-foot velocity: 1,300 ft./sec.
Hull: 2¾-inch plastic
Wad: Plastic
Shot: Lead
Buffered: No
Test barrel length: 30 inch
Pellets will pierce skin up to 172 yards.

NO. 4 LEAD PELLETS—1½ OUNCES—204 PELLETS

Mfg: Estate Cartridge **Manufacturer's code:** HV12SMAG
Recoil energy in 8-lb. shotgun: 47.6 ft./lbs. **Recoil velocity in 8-lb. shotgun:** 19.6 ft./sec.

Distance in yards:	Muzzle	20	30	40	50	60	70
Velocity in fps:	1,423	1006	876	773	689	618	558
Average pellet energy in ft-lbs:	14.52	7.26	5.50	4.29	3.41	2.74	2.23
Time of flight in seconds:	0	.0508	.0829	.1194	.1605	.2065	.2576

Type of load: Field
Three-foot velocity: 1,330 ft./sec.
Hull: 2¾-inch plastic
Wad: Plastic
Shot: Hard lead
Buffered: Yes
Test barrel length: 30 inch
Pellets will pierce skin up to 173 yards.

NO. 4 LEAD PELLETS—1⅝ OUNCES—221 PELLETS

Mfg: Federal Cartridge Co. **Manufacturer's code:** PT155
Recoil energy in 8-lb. shotgun: 47.4 ft./lbs. **Recoil velocity in 8-lb. shotgun:** 19.5 ft./sec.

Distance in yards:	Muzzle	20	30	40	50	60	70
Velocity in fps:	1,336	960	840	744	665	598	540
Average pellet energy in ft-lbs:	12.79	6.61	5.06	3.97	3.17	2.56	2.09
Time of flight in seconds:	0	.0537	.0872	.1252	.1679	.2155	.2684

Type of load: Turkey
Three-foot velocity: 1,250 ft./sec.
Hull: 2¾-inch plastic
Wad: Plastic
Shot: Copper-plated lead
Buffered: Yes
Test barrel length: 30 inch
Pellets will pierce skin up to 170 yards.

NO. 4 LEAD PELLETS—1⅝ OUNCES—221 PELLETS

Mfg: Winchester **Manufacturer's code:** X12HXCT
Recoil energy in 8-lb. shotgun: 47.4 ft./lbs. **Recoil velocity in 8-lb. shotgun:** 19.5 ft./sec.

Distance in yards:	Muzzle	20	30	40	50	60	70
Velocity in fps:	1,336	960	840	744	665	598	540
Average pellet energy in ft-lbs:	12.79	6.61	5.06	3.97	3.17	2.56	2.09
Time of flight in seconds:	0	.0537	.0872	.1252	.1679	.2155	.2684

Type of load: Turkey
Three-foot velocity: 1,250 ft./sec.
Hull: 2¾-inch plastic
Wad: Plastic
Shot: Copper-plated lead
Buffered: Yes
Test barrel length: 30 inch
Pellets will pierce skin up to 170 yards.

These snow geese are among the group of geese that includes brant, Richardson's, blue, whitefronted, and Ross's geese, classified as "small geese," that can be taken with smaller pellets and lighter loads than big Canada geese require. When they decoy as close as these, good shooting is more important than the load selected.

NO. 4 LEAD PELLETS—1⅝ OUNCES—221 PELLETS
Mfg: Kent Cartridge America/Canada **Manufacturer's code:** K122TK46
Recoil energy in 8-lb. shotgun: 49.4 ft./lbs. **Recoil velocity in 8-lb. shotgun:** 20.0 ft./sec.

Distance in yards:	Muzzle	20	30	40	50	60	70
Velocity in fps:	1,363	1,049	851	753	672	604	545
Average pellet energy in ft-lbs:	13.32	6.81	5.20	4.07	3.24	2.62	2.13
Time of flight in seconds:	0	.0528	.0858	.1233	.1655	.2126	.2649

Type of load: Turkey
Three-foot velocity: 1,275 ft./sec.
Hull: 2¾-inch plastic
Wad: Plastic
Shot: Lead
Buffered: No
Test barrel length: 30 inch
Pellets will pierce skin up to 171 yards.

NO. 4 LEAD PELLETS LAYERED OVER NO. 6 LEAD PELLETS—1½ OUNCES
Mfg: Remington Arms Co. **Manufacturer's code:** MP12S
Recoil energy in 8-lb. shotgun: 40.4 ft./lbs. **Recoil velocity in 8-lb. shotgun:** 18.0 ft./sec.

Distance in yards:	Muzzle	20	30	40	50	60	70
Velocity in fps:	1,336	960	840	744	665	598	540
Average pellet energy in ft-lbs:	12.79	6.61	5.06	3.97	3.17	2.56	2.09
Time of flight in seconds:	0	.0537	.0872	.1252	.1679	.2155	.2684

Type of load: Duplex Field
Three-foot velocity: 1,250 ft./sec.
Hull: 2¾-inch plastic
Wad: Plastic
Shot: Copper-plated lead
Buffered: Yes
Test barrel length: 30 inch
Pellets will pierce skin up to 170 yards.

NO. 6 LEAD PELLETS

Distance in yards:	Muzzle	20	30	40	50	60	70
Velocity in fps:	1,348	919	790	689	606	537	477
Average pellet energy in ft-lbs:	7.8	3.67	2.71	2.06	1.60	1.25	.99
Time of flight in seconds:	0	.0549	.0902	.1309	.1774	.2300	.2893

Pellets will pierce skin up to 170 yards.

NO. 5 LEAD PELLETS—1⅛ OUNCES—194 PELLETS
Mfg: Armscor **Manufacturer's code:** N/A
Recoil energy in 8-lb. shotgun: 18.0 ft./lbs. **Recoil velocity in 8-lb. shotgun:** 12.0 ft./sec.

Distance in yards:	Muzzle	20	30	40	50	60	70
Velocity in fps:	1,226	882	770	680	605	542	486
Average pellet energy in ft-lbs:	8.48	4.38	3.35	2.61	2.07	1.66	1.33
Time of flight in seconds:	0	.0585	.0949	.1364	.1832	.2357	.2941

Type of load: Field
Three-foot velocity: 1,145 ft./sec.
Hull: 2¾-inch plastic
Wad: Plastic
Shot: Lead
Buffered: No
Test barrel length: 30 inch
Pellets will pierce skin up to 153 yards.

NO. 5 LEAD PELLETS—1⅛ OUNCES—194 PELLETS
Mfg: Kent Cartridge America/Canada **Manufacturer's code:** K122UG32
Recoil energy in 8-lb. shotgun: 22.7 ft./lbs. **Recoil velocity in 8-lb. shotgun:** 13.5 ft./sec.

Distance in yards:	Muzzle	20	30	40	50	60	70
Velocity in fps:	1,341	941	817	718	637	569	510
Average pellet energy in ft-lbs:	10.15	4.99	3.76	2.91	2.29	1.83	1.47
Time of flight in seconds:	0	.0542	.0885	.1278	.1722	.2221	.2778

Type of load: Field
Three-foot velocity: 1,250 ft./sec.
Hull: 2¾-inch plastic
Wad: Plastic
Shot: Lead
Buffered: No
Test barrel length: 30 inch
Pellets will pierce skin up to 157 yards.

NO. 5 LEAD PELLETS—1⅛ OUNCES—194 PELLETS
Mfg: Baschieri & Pellagri **Manufacturer's code:** F2 Long Range
Recoil energy in 8-lb. shotgun: 26.8 ft./lbs. **Recoil velocity in 8-lb. shotgun:** 14.7 ft./sec.

Distance in yards:	Muzzle	20	30	40	50	60	70
Velocity in fps:	1,451	1,082	859	752	665	593	531
Average pellet energy in ft-lbs:	11.88	5.60	4.16	3.19	2.50	1.98	1.59
Time of flight in seconds:	0	.0507	.0832	.1206	.1631	.2109	.2644

Type of load: Field
Three-foot velocity: 1,350 ft./sec.
Hull: 2¾-inch plastic
Wad: Plastic
Shot: Lead
Buffered: No
Test barrel length: 30 inch
Pellets will pierce skin up to 161 yards.

NO. 5 LEAD PELLETS—1⅛ OUNCES—194 PELLETS
Mfg: Clever **Manufacturer's code:** T2 Light Game
Recoil energy in 8-lb. shotgun: 27.9 ft./lbs. **Recoil velocity in 8-lb. shotgun:** 15.0 ft./sec.

Distance in yards:	Muzzle	20	30	40	50	60	70
Velocity in fps:	1,451	1,082	859	752	665	593	531
Average pellet energy in ft-lbs:	11.88	5.60	4.16	3.19	2.50	1.98	1.59
Time of flight in seconds:	0	.0507	.0832	.1206	.1631	.2109	.2644

Type of load: Field
Three-foot velocity: 1,350 ft./sec.
Hull: 2¾-inch plastic
Wad: Plastic
Shot: Lead
Buffered: No
Test barrel length: 30 inch
Pellets will pierce skin up to 161 yards.

NO. 5 LEAD PELLETS—1³/₁₆ OUNCES—205 PELLETS
Mfg: Clever **Manufacturer's code:** T2 Felt Wad
Recoil energy in 8-lb. shotgun: 23.9 ft./lbs. **Recoil velocity in 8-lb. shotgun:** 13.9 ft./sec.

Distance in yards:	Muzzle	20	30	40	50	60	70
Velocity in fps:	1,369	955	827	727	644	575	515
Average pellet energy in ft-lbs:	10.57	5.14	3.86	2.98	2.34	1.87	1.50
Time of flight in seconds:	0	.0533	.0871	.1259	.1698	.2191	.2743

Type of load: Field
Three-foot velocity: 1,275 ft./sec.
Hull: 2¾-inch plastic
Wad: Felt/fiber
Shot: Lead
Buffered: No
Test barrel length: 30 inch
Pellets will pierce skin up to 158 yards.

NO. 5 LEAD PELLETS—1³/₁₆ OUNCES—205 PELLETS
Mfg: Clever **Manufacturer's code:** T2 Caccia
Recoil energy in 8-lb. shotgun: 25.2 ft./lbs. **Recoil velocity in 8-lb. shotgun:** 14.2 ft./sec.

Distance in yards:	Muzzle	20	30	40	50	60	70
Velocity in fps:	1,396	969	838	735	651	581	521
Average pellet energy in ft-lbs:	11.00	5.29	3.96	3.05	2.39	1.90	1.53
Time of flight in seconds:	0	.0524	.0858	.1241	.1675	.2163	.2708

Type of load: Field
Three-foot velocity: 1,300 ft./sec.
Hull: 2¾-inch plastic
Wad: Plastic
Shot: Lead
Buffered: No
Test barrel length: 30 inch
Pellets will pierce skin up to 159 yards.

NO. 5 LEAD PELLETS—1¼ OUNCES—215 PELLETS
Mfg: Federal Cartridge Co. **Manufacturer's code:** H120
Recoil energy in 8-lb. shotgun: 26.3 ft./lbs. **Recoil velocity in 8-lb. shotgun:** 14.5 ft./sec.

Distance in yards:	Muzzle	20	30	40	50	60	70
Velocity in fps:	1,309	924	804	707	628	561	503
Average pellet energy in ft-lbs:	9.66	4.82	3.64	2.82	2.23	1.78	1.43
Time of flight in seconds:	0	.0554	.0903	.1301	.1752	.2257	.2822

Type of load: Field
Three-foot velocity: 1,220 ft./sec.
Hull: 2¾-inch plastic
Wad: Plastic
Shot: Lead
Buffered: No
Test barrel length: 30 inch
Pellets will pierce skin up to 156 yards.

NO. 5 LEAD PELLETS—1¼ OUNCES—215 PELLETS
Mfg: Baschieri & Pellagri **Manufacturer's code:** MB Extra
Recoil energy in 8-lb. shotgun: 31.1 ft./lbs. **Recoil velocity in 8-lb. shotgun:** 15.8 ft./sec.

Distance in yards:	Muzzle	20	30	40	50	60	70
Velocity in fps:	1,396	969	838	735	651	581	521
Average pellet energy in ft-lbs:	11.00	5.29	3.96	3.05	2.39	1.90	1.53
Time of flight in seconds:	0	.0524	.0858	.1241	.1675	.2163	.2708

Type of load: Field
Three-foot velocity: 1,300 ft./sec.
Hull: 2¾-inch plastic
Wad: Plastic
Shot: Lead
Buffered: No
Test barrel length: 30 inch
Pellets will pierce skin up to 159 yards.

NO. 5 LEAD PELLETS—1¼ OUNCES—215 PELLETS
Mfg: Clever **Manufacturer's code:** T4 High Velocity
Recoil energy in 8-lb. shotgun: 31.1 ft./lbs. **Recoil velocity in 8-lb. shotgun:** 15.8 ft./sec.

Distance in yards:	Muzzle	20	30	40	50	60	70
Velocity in fps:	1,396	969	838	735	651	581	521
Average pellet energy in ft-lbs:	11.00	5.29	3.96	3.05	2.39	1.90	1.53
Time of flight in seconds:	0	.0524	.0858	.1241	.1675	.2163	.2708

Type of load: Field
Three-foot velocity: 1,300 ft./sec.
Hull: 2¾-inch plastic
Wad: Plastic
Shot: Lead
Buffered: No
Test barrel length: 30 inch
Pellets will pierce skin up to 159 yards.

NO. 5 LEAD PELLETS—1¼ OUNCES—215 PELLETS
Mfg: Eley Hawk **Manufacturer's code:** Alphamax
Recoil energy in 8-lb. shotgun: 31.1 ft./lbs. **Recoil velocity in 8-lb. shotgun:** 15.8 ft./sec.

Distance in yards:	Muzzle	20	30	40	50	60	70
Velocity in fps:	1,396	969	838	735	651	581	521
Average pellet energy in ft-lbs:	11.00	5.29	3.96	3.05	2.39	1.90	1.53
Time of flight in seconds:	0	.0524	.0858	.1241	.1675	.2163	.2708

Type of load: Field
Three-foot velocity: 1,300 ft./sec.
Hull: 2¾-inch plastic
Wad: Plastic
Shot: Lead
Buffered: No
Test barrel length: 30 inch
Pellets will pierce skin up to 159 yards.

NO. 5 LEAD PELLETS—1¼ OUNCES—215 PELLETS
Mfg: Baschieri & Pellagri **Manufacturer's code:** MB/F2 Long Range
Recoil energy in 8-lb. shotgun: 33.0 ft./lbs. **Recoil velocity in 8-lb. shotgun:** 16.3 ft./sec.

Distance in yards:	Muzzle	20	30	40	50	60	70
Velocity in fps:	1,429	985	851	745	660	588	527
Average pellet energy in ft-lbs:	11.53	5.47	4.08	3.13	2.46	1.95	1.57
Time of flight in seconds:	0	.0514	.0842	.1220	.1648	.2130	.2669

Type of load: Field
Three-foot velocity: 1,330 ft./sec.
Hull: 2¾-inch plastic
Wad: Plastic
Shot: Lead
Buffered: No
Test barrel length: 30 inch
Pellets will pierce skin up to 160 yards.

NO. 5 LEAD PELLETS—1¼ OUNCES—215 PELLETS
Mfg: Dionisi **Manufacturer's code:** D 12 SLR
Recoil energy in 8-lb. shotgun: 33.0 ft./lbs. **Recoil velocity in 8-lb. shotgun:** 16.3 ft./sec.

Distance in yards:	Muzzle	20	30	40	50	60	70
Velocity in fps:	1,429	985	851	745	660	588	527
Average pellet energy in ft-lbs:	11.53	5.47	4.08	3.13	2.46	1.95	1.57
Time of flight in seconds:	0	.0514	.0842	.1220	.1648	.2130	.2669

Type of load: Field
Three-foot velocity: 1,330 ft./sec.
Hull: 2¾-inch plastic
Wad: Plastic
Shot: Lead
Buffered: No
Test barrel length: 30 inch
Pellets will pierce skin up to 160 yards.

NO. 5 LEAD PELLETS—1¼ OUNCES—215 PELLETS
Mfg: Federal Cartridge Co. **Manufacturer's code:** H126
Recoil energy in 8-lb. shotgun: 33.0 ft./lbs. **Recoil velocity in 8-lb. shotgun:** 16.3 ft./sec.

Distance in yards:	Muzzle	20	30	40	50	60	70
Velocity in fps:	1,429	985	851	745	660	588	527
Average pellet energy in ft-lbs:	11.53	5.47	4.08	3.13	2.46	1.95	1.57
Time of flight in seconds:	0	.0514	.0842	.1220	.1648	.2130	.2669

Type of load: Field
Three-foot velocity: 1,330 ft./sec.
Hull: 2¾-inch plastic
Wad: Plastic
Shot: Lead
Buffered: No
Test barrel length: 30 inch
Pellets will pierce skin up to 160 yards.

NO. 5 LEAD PELLETS—1¼ OUNCES—215 PELLETS
Mfg: Fiocchi **Manufacturer's code:** 12HV
Recoil energy in 8-lb. shotgun: 40.0 ft./lbs. **Recoil velocity in 8-lb. shotgun:** 17.9 ft./sec.

Distance in yards:	Muzzle	20	30	40	50	60	70
Velocity in fps:	1,429	985	851	745	660	588	527
Average pellet energy in ft-lbs:	11.53	5.47	4.08	3.13	2.46	1.95	1.57
Time of flight in seconds:	0	.0514	.0842	.1220	.1648	.2130	.2669

Type of load: Field
Three-foot velocity: 1,330 ft./sec.
Hull: 2¾-inch plastic
Wad: Plastic
Shot: Lead
Buffered: No
Test barrel length: 30 inch
Pellets will pierce skin up to 160 yards.

NO. 5 LEAD PELLETS—1¼ OUNCES—215 PELLETS
Mfg: Fiocchi **Manufacturer's code:** 12HVN
Recoil energy in 8-lb. shotgun: 40.0 ft./lbs. **Recoil velocity in 8-lb. shotgun:** 17.9 ft./sec.

Distance in yards:	Muzzle	20	30	40	50	60	70
Velocity in fps:	1,429	985	851	745	660	588	527
Average pellet energy in ft-lbs:	11.53	5.47	4.08	3.13	2.46	1.95	1.57
Time of flight in seconds:	0	.0514	.0842	.1220	.1648	.2130	.2669

Type of load: Field
Three-foot velocity: 1,330 ft./sec.
Hull: 2¾-inch plastic
Wad: Plastic
Shot: Nickel-plated lead
Buffered: No
Test barrel length: 30 inch
Pellets will pierce skin up to 160 yards.

NO. 5 LEAD PELLETS—1¼ OUNCES—215 PELLETS
Mfg: Kent Cartridge America/Canada **Manufacturer's code:** K122UG36
Recoil energy in 8-lb. shotgun: 31.1 ft./lbs. **Recoil velocity in 8-lb. shotgun:** 15.8 ft./sec.

Distance in yards:	Muzzle	20	30	40	50	60	70
Velocity in fps:	1,429	985	851	745	660	588	527
Average pellet energy in ft-lbs:	11.53	5.47	4.08	3.13	2.46	1.95	1.57
Time of flight in seconds:	0	.0514	.0842	.1220	.1648	.2130	.2669

Type of load: Field
Three-foot velocity: 1,330 ft./sec.
Hull: 2¾-inch plastic
Wad: Plastic
Shot: Lead
Buffered: No
Test barrel length: 30 inch
Pellets will pierce skin up to 160 yards.

NO. 5 LEAD PELLETS—1¼ OUNCES—215 PELLETS
Mfg: PMC (Eldorado Cartridge Corp.) **Manufacturer's code:** HF12
Recoil energy in 8-lb. shotgun: 31.1 ft./lbs. **Recoil velocity in 8-lb. shotgun:** 15.8 ft./sec.

Distance in yards:	Muzzle	20	30	40	50	60	70
Velocity in fps:	1,429	985	851	745	660	588	527
Average pellet energy in ft-lbs:	11.53	5.47	4.08	3.13	2.46	1.95	1.57
Time of flight in seconds:	0	.0514	.0842	.1220	.1648	.2130	.2669

Type of load: Field
Three-foot velocity: 1,330 ft./sec.
Hull: 2¾-inch plastic
Wad: Plastic
Shot: Lead
Buffered: No
Test barrel length: 30 inch
Pellets will pierce skin up to 160 yards.

NO. 5 LEAD PELLETS—1¼ OUNCES—215 PELLETS
Mfg: Remington Arms Co. **Manufacturer's code:** SP12
Recoil energy in 8-lb. shotgun: 33.0 ft./lbs. **Recoil velocity in 8-lb. shotgun:** 16.3 ft./sec.

Distance in yards:	Muzzle	20	30	40	50	60	70
Velocity in fps:	1,429	985	851	745	660	588	527
Average pellet energy in ft-lbs:	11.53	5.47	4.08	3.13	2.46	1.95	1.57
Time of flight in seconds:	0	.0514	.0842	.1220	.1648	.2130	.2669

Type of load: Field
Three-foot velocity: 1,330 ft./sec.
Hull: 2¾-inch plastic
Wad: Plastic
Shot: Lead
Buffered: No
Test barrel length: 30 inch
Pellets will pierce skin up to 160 yards.

NO. 5 LEAD PELLETS—1¼ OUNCES—215 PELLETS
Mfg: RIO **Manufacturer's code:** Extra Game
Recoil energy in 8-lb. shotgun: 33.0 ft./lbs. **Recoil velocity in 8-lb. shotgun:** 16.3 ft./sec.

Distance in yards:	Muzzle	20	30	40	50	60	70
Velocity in fps:	1,429	985	851	745	660	588	527
Average pellet energy in ft-lbs:	11.53	5.47	4.08	3.13	2.46	1.95	1.57
Time of flight in seconds:	0	.0514	.0842	.1220	.1648	.2130	.2669

Type of load: Field
Three-foot velocity: 1,330 ft./sec.
Hull: 2¾-inch plastic
Wad: Plastic
Shot: Hard lead
Buffered: No
Test barrel length: 30 inch
Pellets will pierce skin up to 160 yards.

NO. 5 LEAD PELLETS—1¼ OUNCES—215 PELLETS
Mfg: Winchester **Manufacturer's code:** X12
Recoil energy in 8-lb. shotgun: 33.0 ft./lbs. **Recoil velocity in 8-lb. shotgun:** 16.3 ft./sec.

Distance in yards:	Muzzle	20	30	40	50	60	70
Velocity in fps:	1,429	985	851	745	660	588	527
Average pellet energy in ft-lbs:	11.53	5.47	4.08	3.13	2.46	1.95	1.57
Time of flight in seconds:	0	.0514	.0842	.1220	.1648	.2130	.2669

Type of load: Field
Three-foot velocity: 1,330 ft./sec.
Hull: 2¾-inch plastic
Wad: Plastic
Shot: Lead
Buffered: No
Test barrel length: 30 inch
Pellets will pierce skin up to 160 yards.

NO. 5 LEAD PELLETS—1⅜ OUNCES—237 PELLETS
Mfg: Fiocchi **Manufacturer's code:** 12HGP/12TT
Recoil energy in 8-lb. shotgun: 33.9 ft./lbs. **Recoil velocity in 8-lb. shotgun:** 16.5 ft./sec.

Distance in yards:	Muzzle	20	30	40	50	60	70
Velocity in fps:	1,341	941	817	718	637	569	510
Average pellet energy in ft-lbs:	10.15	4.99	3.76	2.91	2.29	1.83	1.47
Time of flight in seconds:	0	.0542	.0885	.1278	.1722	.2221	.2778

Type of load: Field & Turkey
Three-foot velocity: 1,250 ft./sec.
Hull: 2¾-inch plastic
Wad: Plastic
Shot: Nickel-plated lead
Buffered: No
Test barrel length: 30 inch
Pellets will pierce skin up to 157 yards.

NO. 5 LEAD PELLETS—1⅜ OUNCES—237 PELLETS
Mfg: Baschieri & Pellagri **Manufacturer's code:** MB Winter
Recoil energy in 8-lb. shotgun: 35.7 ft./lbs. **Recoil velocity in 8-lb. shotgun:** 16.9 ft./sec.

Distance in yards:	Muzzle	20	30	40	50	60	70
Velocity in fps:	1,369	955	827	727	644	575	515
Average pellet energy in ft-lbs:	10.57	5.14	3.86	2.98	2.34	1.87	1.50
Time of flight in seconds:	0	.0533	.0871	.1259	.1698	.2191	.2743

Type of load: Field
Three-foot velocity: 1,275 ft./sec.
Hull: 2¾-inch plastic
Wad: Plastic
Shot: Hard lead
Buffered: No
Test barrel length: 30 inch
Pellets will pierce skin up to 158 yards.

NO. 5 LEAD PELLETS—1⅜ OUNCES—237 PELLETS
Mfg: Clever **Manufacturer's code:** T4 Caccia
Recoil energy in 8-lb. shotgun: 35.7 ft./lbs. **Recoil velocity in 8-lb. shotgun:** 16.9 ft./sec.

Distance in yards:	Muzzle	20	30	40	50	60	70
Velocity in fps:	1,369	955	827	727	644	575	515
Average pellet energy in ft-lbs:	10.57	5.14	3.86	2.98	2.34	1.87	1.50
Time of flight in seconds:	0	.0533	.0871	.1259	.1698	.2191	.2743

Type of load: Field
Three-foot velocity: 1,275 ft./sec.
Hull: 2¾-inch plastic
Wad: Plastic
Shot: Lead
Buffered: No
Test barrel length: 30 inch
Pellets will pierce skin up to 158 yards.

NO. 5 LEAD PELLETS—1⅜ OUNCES—237 PELLETS
Mfg: Federal Cartridge Co. **Manufacturer's code:** P138
Recoil energy in 8-lb. shotgun: 45.9 ft./lbs. **Recoil velocity in 8-lb. shotgun:** 19.2 ft./sec.

Distance in yards:	Muzzle	20	30	40	50	60	70
Velocity in fps:	1,507	1,024	880	769	679	605	541
Average pellet energy in ft-lbs:	12.80	5.91	4.37	3.33	2.60	2.06	1.65
Time of flight in seconds:	0	.0491	.0808	.1173	.1589	.2058	.2583

Type of load: Field
Three-foot velocity: 1,400 ft./sec.
Hull: 2¾-inch plastic
Wad: Plastic
Shot: Lead
Buffered: No
Test barrel length: 30 inch
Pellets will pierce skin up to 163 yards.

NO. 5 LEAD PELLETS—1½ OUNCES—258 PELLETS
Mfg: Dionisi **Manufacturer's code:** D 12G
Recoil energy in 8-lb. shotgun: 40.4 ft./lbs. **Recoil velocity in 8-lb. shotgun:** 18.0 ft./sec.

Distance in yards:	Muzzle	20	30	40	50	60	70
Velocity in fps:	1,341	941	817	718	637	569	510
Average pellet energy in ft-lbs:	10.15	4.99	3.76	2.91	2.29	1.83	1.47
Time of flight in seconds:	0	.0542	.0885	.1278	.1722	.2221	.2778

Type of load: Field
Three-foot velocity: 1,250 ft./sec.
Hull: 2¾-inch plastic
Wad: Plastic
Shot: Lead
Buffered: No
Test barrel length: 30 inch
Pellets will pierce skin up to 157 yards.

NO. 5 LEAD PELLETS—1½ OUNCES—258 PELLETS
Mfg: Federal Cartridge Co. **Manufacturer's code:** F130
Recoil energy in 8-lb. shotgun: 40.4 ft./lbs. **Recoil velocity in 8-lb. shotgun:** 18.0 ft./sec.

Distance in yards:	Muzzle	20	30	40	50	60	70
Velocity in fps:	1,341	941	817	718	637	569	510
Average pellet energy in ft-lbs:	10.15	4.99	3.76	2.91	2.29	1.83	1.47
Time of flight in seconds:	0	.0542	.0885	.1278	.1722	.2221	.2778

Type of load: Field
Three-foot velocity: 1,250 ft./sec.
Hull: 2¾-inch plastic
Wad: Plastic
Shot: Lead
Buffered: No
Test barrel length: 30 inch
Pellets will pierce skin up to 157 yards.

NO. 5 LEAD PELLETS—1½ OUNCES—258 PELLETS
Mfg: Remington Arms Co. **Manufacturer's code:** P12SM
Recoil energy in 8-lb. shotgun: 40.4 ft./lbs. **Recoil velocity in 8-lb. shotgun:** 18.0 ft./sec.

Distance in yards:	Muzzle	20	30	40	50	60	70
Velocity in fps:	1,341	941	817	718	637	569	510
Average pellet energy in ft-lbs:	10.15	4.99	3.76	2.91	2.29	1.83	1.47
Time of flight in seconds:	0	.0542	.0885	.1278	.1722	.2221	.2778

Type of load: Turkey
Three-foot velocity: 1,250 ft./sec.
Hull: 2¾-inch plastic
Wad: Plastic
Shot: Copper-plated lead
Buffered: Yes
Test barrel length: 30 inch
Pellets will pierce skin up to 157 yards.

NO. 5 LEAD PELLETS—1½ OUNCES—258 PELLETS
Mfg: Winchester **Manufacturer's code:** X12XC
Recoil energy in 8-lb. shotgun: 40.4 ft./lbs. **Recoil velocity in 8-lb. shotgun:** 18.0 ft./sec.

Distance in yards:	Muzzle	20	30	40	50	60	70
Velocity in fps:	1,341	941	817	718	637	569	510
Average pellet energy in ft-lbs:	10.15	4.99	3.76	2.91	2.29	1.83	1.47
Time of flight in seconds:	0	.0542	.0885	.1278	.1722	.2221	.2778

Type of load: Field
Three-foot velocity: 1,250 ft./sec.
Hull: 2¾-inch plastic
Wad: Plastic
Shot: Copper-plated lead
Buffered: Yes
Test barrel length: 30 inch
Pellets will pierce skin up to 157 yards.

NO. 5 LEAD PELLETS—1½ OUNCES—258 PELLETS
Mfg: Eley Hawk **Manufacturer's code:** Magnum 70
Recoil energy in 8-lb. shotgun: 42.5 ft./lbs. **Recoil velocity in 8-lb. shotgun:** 18.5 ft./sec.

Distance in yards:	Muzzle	20	30	40	50	60	70
Velocity in fps:	1,369	955	827	727	644	575	515
Average pellet energy in ft-lbs:	10.57	5.14	3.86	2.98	2.34	1.87	1.50
Time of flight in seconds:	0	.0533	.0871	.1259	.1698	.2191	.2743

Type of load: Field
Three-foot velocity: 1,275 ft./sec.
Hull: 2¾-inch plastic
Wad: Plastic
Shot: Lead
Buffered: No
Test barrel length: 30 inch
Pellets will pierce skin up to 158 yards.

NO. 5 LEAD PELLETS—1⅝ OUNCES—280 PELLETS
Mfg: Federal Cartridge Co. **Manufacturer's code:** PT155
Recoil energy in 8-lb. shotgun: 47.4 ft./lbs. **Recoil velocity in 8-lb. shotgun:** 19.5 ft./sec.

Distance in yards:	Muzzle	20	30	40	50	60	70
Velocity in fps:	1,341	941	817	718	637	569	510
Average pellet energy in ft-lbs:	10.15	4.99	3.76	2.91	2.29	1.83	1.47
Time of flight in seconds:	0	.0542	.0885	.1278	.1722	.2221	.2778

Type of load: Turkey
Three-foot velocity: 1,250 ft./sec.
Hull: 2¾-inch plastic
Wad: Plastic
Shot: Copper-plated lead
Buffered: Yes
Test barrel length: 30 inch
Pellets will pierce skin up to 157 yards.

NO. 5 LEAD PELLETS—1⅝ OUNCES—280 PELLETS
Mfg: Winchester **Manufacturer's code:** X12HXCT
Recoil energy in 8-lb. shotgun: 47.4 ft./lbs. **Recoil velocity in 8-lb. shotgun:** 19.5 ft./sec.

Distance in yards:	Muzzle	20	30	40	50	60	70
Velocity in fps:	1,341	941	817	718	637	569	510
Average pellet energy in ft-lbs:	10.15	4.99	3.76	2.91	2.29	1.83	1.47
Time of flight in seconds:	0	.0542	.0885	.1278	.1722	.2221	.2778

Type of load: Turkey
Three-foot velocity: 1,250 ft./sec.
Hull: 2¾-inch plastic
Wad: Plastic
Shot: Copper-plated lead
Buffered: Yes
Test barrel length: 30 inch
Pellets will pierce skin up to 157 yards.

NO. 5 LEAD PELLETS—1⅝ OUNCES—280 PELLETS
Mfg: Kent Cartridge America/Canada **Manufacturer's code:** K122TK46
Recoil energy in 8-lb. shotgun: 49.4 ft./lbs. **Recoil velocity in 8-lb. shotgun:** 20.0 ft./sec.

Distance in yards:	Muzzle	20	30	40	50	60	70
Velocity in fps:	1,369	955	827	727	644	575	515
Average pellet energy in ft-lbs:	10.57	5.14	3.86	2.98	2.34	1.87	1.50
Time of flight in seconds:	0	.0533	.0871	.1259	.1698	.2191	.2743

Type of load: Turkey
Three-foot velocity: 1,275 ft./sec.
Hull: 2¾-inch plastic
Wad: Plastic
Shot: Lead
Buffered: No
Test barrel length: 30 inch
Pellets will pierce skin up to 158 yards.

NO. 6 LEAD PELLETS—1 OUNCE—223 PELLETS
Mfg: Kent Cartridge America/Canada **Manufacturer's code:** K122UG28
Recoil energy in 8-lb. shotgun: 16.1 ft./lbs. **Recoil velocity in 8-lb. shotgun:** 11.4 ft./sec.

Distance in yards:	Muzzle	20	30	40	50	60	70
Velocity in fps:	1,292	892	769	672	593	525	467
Average pellet energy in ft-lbs:	7.26	3.46	2.57	1.96	1.53	1.20	.095
Time of flight in seconds:	0	.0568	.0931	.01349	.1825	.2363	.2969

Type of load: Field
Three-foot velocity: 1,200 ft./sec.
Hull: 2¾-inch plastic
Wad: Plastic
Shot: Lead
Buffered: No
Test barrel length: 30 inch
Pellets will pierce skin up to 157 yards.

NO. 6 LEAD PELLETS—1 OUNCE—223 PELLETS
Mfg: Aguila **Manufacturer's code:** N/A
Recoil energy in 8-lb. shotgun: 20.4 ft./lbs. **Recoil velocity in 8-lb. shotgun:** 12.8 ft./sec.

Distance in yards:	Muzzle	20	30	40	50	60	70
Velocity in fps:	1,292	892	769	672	593	525	467
Average pellet energy in ft-lbs:	7.26	3.46	2.57	1.96	1.53	1.20	.095
Time of flight in seconds:	0	.0568	.0931	.01349	.1825	.2363	.2969

Type of load: Field
Three-foot velocity: 1,200 ft./sec.
Hull: 2¾-inch plastic
Wad: Two-piece, ribbed plastic
Shot: Lead
Buffered: No
Test barrel length: 30 inch
Pellets will pierce skin up to 157 yards.

NO. 6 LEAD PELLETS—1 OUNCE—223 PELLETS
Mfg: Estate Cartridge **Manufacturer's code:** DQ12
Recoil energy in 8-lb. shotgun: 19.9 ft./lbs. **Recoil velocity in 8-lb. shotgun:** 12.6 ft./sec.

Distance in yards:	Muzzle	20	30	40	50	60	70
Velocity in fps:	1,403	945	810	705	620	548	487
Average pellet energy in ft-lbs:	8.55	3.88	2.85	2.16	1.67	1.31	1.03
Time of flight in seconds:	0	.0531	.0875	.1272	.1727	.2242	.2723

Type of load: Field
Three-foot velocity: 1,300 ft./sec.5
Hull: 2¾-inch plastic
Wad: Plastic
Shot: Hard lead
Buffered: No
Test barrel length: 30 inch
Pellets will pierce skin up to 146 yards.

NO. 6 LEAD PELLETS—1 OUNCE—223 PELLETS
Mfg: Federal Cartridge Co. **Manufacturer's code:** H121
Recoil energy in 8-lb. shotgun: 19.9 ft./lbs. **Recoil velocity in 8-lb. shotgun:** 12.6 ft./sec.

Distance in yards:	Muzzle	20	30	40	50	60	70
Velocity in fps:	1,403	945	810	705	620	548	487
Average pellet energy in ft-lbs:	8.55	3.88	2.85	2.16	1.67	1.31	1.03
Time of flight in seconds:	0	.0531	.0875	.1272	.1727	.2242	.2723

Type of load: Field
Three-foot velocity: 1,300 ft./sec.
Hull: 2¾-inch plastic
Wad: Plastic
Shot: Lead
Buffered: No
Test barrel length: 30 inch
Pellets will pierce skin up to 146 yards.

NO. 6 LEAD PELLETS—1 OUNCE—223 PELLETS
Mfg: Fiocchi **Manufacturer's code:** 12GT1
Recoil energy in 8-lb. shotgun: 19.9 ft./lbs. **Recoil velocity in 8-lb. shotgun:** 12.6 ft./sec.

Distance in yards:	Muzzle	20	30	40	50	60	70
Velocity in fps:	1,403	945	810	705	620	548	487
Average pellet energy in ft-lbs:	8.55	3.88	2.85	2.16	1.67	1.31	1.03
Time of flight in seconds:	0	.0531	.0875	.1272	.1727	.2242	.2723

Type of load: Game & Target
Three-foot velocity: 1,300 ft./sec.
Hull: 2¾-inch plastic
Wad: Plastic
Shot: Lead
Buffered: No
Test barrel length: 30 inch
Pellets will pierce skin up to 146 yards.

NO. 6 LEAD PELLETS—1 OUNCE—223 PELLETS
Mfg: PMC (Eldorado Cartridge Corp.) **Manufacturer's code:** PL12
Recoil energy in 8-lb. shotgun: 19.9 ft./lbs. **Recoil velocity in 8-lb. shotgun:** 12.6 ft./sec.

Distance in yards:	Muzzle	20	30	40	50	60	70
Velocity in fps:	1,403	945	810	705	620	548	487
Average pellet energy in ft-lbs:	8.55	3.88	2.85	2.16	1.67	1.31	1.03
Time of flight in seconds:	0	.0531	.0875	.1272	.1727	.2242	.2723

Type of load: Quail & Dove
Three-foot velocity: 1,300 ft./sec.
Hull: 2¾-inch plastic
Wad: Plastic
Shot: Lead
Buffered: No
Test barrel length: 30 inch
Pellets will pierce skin up to 146 yards.

NO. 6 LEAD PELLETS—1 OUNCE—223 PELLETS
Mfg: Remington Arms Co. **Manufacturer's code:** GL12
Recoil energy in 8-lb. shotgun: 19.9 ft./lbs. **Recoil velocity in 8-lb. shotgun:** 12.6 ft./sec.

Distance in yards:	Muzzle	20	30	40	50	60	70
Velocity in fps:	1,403	945	810	705	620	548	487
Average pellet energy in ft-lbs:	8.55	3.88	2.85	2.16	1.67	1.31	1.03
Time of flight in seconds:	0	.0531	.0875	.1272	.1727	.2242	.2723

Type of load: Field
Three-foot velocity: 1,300 ft./sec.
Hull: 2¾-inch plastic
Wad: Plastic
Shot: Lead
Buffered: No
Test barrel length: 30 inch
Pellets will pierce skin up to 146 yards.

12 Gauge—Lead 2¾ inch

NO. 6 LEAD PELLETS—1 OUNCE—223 PELLETS
Mfg: Winchester **Manufacturer's code:** XU12
Recoil energy in 8-lb. shotgun: 19.9 ft./lbs. **Recoil velocity in 8-lb. shotgun:** 12.6 ft./sec.

Distance in yards:	Muzzle	20	30	40	50	60	70
Velocity in fps:	1,403	945	810	705	620	548	487
Average pellet energy in ft-lbs:	8.55	3.88	2.85	2.16	1.67	1.31	1.03
Time of flight in seconds:	0	.0531	.0875	.1272	.1727	.2242	.2723

Type of load: Field
Three-foot velocity: 1,300 ft./sec.
Hull: 2¾-inch plastic
Wad: Plastic
Shot: Lead
Buffered: No
Test barrel length: 30 inch
Pellets will pierce skin up to 146 yards.

NO. 6 LEAD PELLETS—1 OUNCE—223 PELLETS
Mfg: RIO **Manufacturer's code:** Basic Game
Recoil energy in 8-lb. shotgun: 16.2 ft./lbs. **Recoil velocity in 8-lb. shotgun:** 11.4 ft./sec.

Distance in yards:	Muzzle	20	30	40	50	60	70
Velocity in fps:	1,436	961	822	714	627	555	493
Average pellet energy in ft-lbs:	8.96	4.01	2.94	2.22	1.71	1.34	1.06
Time of flight in seconds:	0	.0520	.0859	.1251	.1700	.2209	.2782

Type of load: Field
Three-foot velocity: 1,330 ft./sec.
Hull: 2¾-inch plastic
Wad: Plastic
Shot: Hard lead
Buffered: No
Test barrel length: 30 inch
Pellets will pierce skin up to 147 yards.

NO. 6 LEAD PELLETS—1 OUNCE—237 PELLETS
Mfg: RIO **Manufacturer's code:** Extra Game
Recoil energy in 8-lb. shotgun: 16.2 ft./lbs. **Recoil velocity in 8-lb. shotgun:** 11.4 ft./sec.

Distance in yards:	Muzzle	20	30	40	50	60	70
Velocity in fps:	1,436	961	822	714	627	555	493
Average pellet energy in ft-lbs:	8.96	4.01	2.94	2.22	1.71	1.34	1.06
Time of flight in seconds:	0	.0520	.0859	.1251	.1700	.2209	.2782

Type of load: Field
Three-foot velocity: 1,330 ft./sec.
Hull: 2¾-inch plastic
Wad: Plastic
Shot: Hard lead
Buffered: No
Test barrel length: 30 inch
Pellets will pierce skin up to 147 yards.

NO. 6 LEAD PELLETS—1⅛ OUNCES—251 PELLETS
Mfg: Armscor **Manufacturer's code:** N/A
Recoil energy in 8-lb. shotgun: 18.0 ft./lbs. **Recoil velocity in 8-lb. shotgun:** 12.0 ft./sec.

Distance in yards:	Muzzle	20	30	40	50	60	70
Velocity in fps:	1,232	862	746	653	577	512	455
Average pellet energy in ft-lbs:	6.59	3.23	2.11	1.85	1.45	1.14	.90
Time of flight in seconds:	0	.0591	.0966	.1396	.1886	.2438	.3060

Type of load: Field
Three-foot velocity: 1,145 ft./sec.
Hull: 2¾-inch plastic
Wad: Plastic
Shot: Lead
Buffered: No
Test barrel length: 30 inch
Pellets will pierce skin up to 140 yards.

NO. 6 LEAD PELLETS—1⅛ OUNCES—251 PELLETS
Mfg: Aguila **Manufacturer's code:** N/A
Recoil energy in 8-lb. shotgun: 20.4 ft./lbs. **Recoil velocity in 8-lb. shotgun:** 12.8 ft./sec.

Distance in yards:	Muzzle	20	30	40	50	60	70
Velocity in fps:	1,292	892	769	672	593	525	467
Average pellet energy in ft-lbs:	7.26	3.46	2.57	1.96	1.53	1.20	.095
Time of flight in seconds:	0	.0568	.0931	.01349	.1825	.2363	.2969

Type of load: Field
Three-foot velocity: 1,200 ft./sec.
Hull: 2¾-inch plastic
Wad: Plastic
Shot: Lead
Buffered: No
Test barrel length: 30 inch
Pellets will pierce skin up to 157 yards.

NO. 6 LEAD PELLETS—1⅛ OUNCES—251 PELLETS
Mfg: Polywad **Manufacturer's code:** SRH126
Recoil energy in 8-lb. shotgun: 20.4 ft./lbs. **Recoil velocity in 8-lb. shotgun:** 12.8 ft./sec.

Distance in yards:	Muzzle	20	30	40	50	60	70
Velocity in fps:	1,292	892	769	672	593	525	467
Average pellet energy in ft-lbs:	7.26	3.46	2.57	1.96	1.53	1.20	.095
Time of flight in seconds:	0	.0568	.0931	.01349	.1825	.2363	.2969

Type of load: Field
Three-foot velocity: 1,200 ft./sec.
Hull: 2¾-inch plastic
Wad: Plastic
Shot: Lead
Buffered: No
Test barrel length: 30 inch
Pellets will pierce skin up to 157 yards.

NO. 6 LEAD PELLETS—1⅛ OUNCES—251 PELLETS
Mfg: Estate Cartridge **Manufacturer's code:** HG12
Recoil energy in 8-lb. shotgun: 22.7 ft./lbs. **Recoil velocity in 8-lb. shotgun:** 13.5 ft./sec.

Distance in yards:	Muzzle	20	30	40	50	60	70
Velocity in fps:	1,348	919	790	689	606	537	477
Average pellet energy in ft-lbs:	7.89	3.67	2.71	2.06	1.60	1.25	.99
Time of flight in seconds:	0	.0549	.0902	.1309	.1774	.2300	.2893

Type of load: Field
Three-foot velocity: 1,250 ft./sec.
Hull: 2¾-inch plastic
Wad: Plastic
Shot: Hard lead
Buffered: No
Test barrel length: 30 inch
Pellets will pierce skin up to 144 yards.

NO. 6 LEAD PELLETS—1⅛ OUNCES—251 PELLETS
Mfg: Federal Cartridge Co. **Manufacturer's code:** H123/HGL12
Recoil energy in 8-lb. shotgun: 22.7 ft./lbs. **Recoil velocity in 8-lb. shotgun:** 13.5 ft./sec.

Distance in yards:	Muzzle	20	30	40	50	60	70
Velocity in fps:	1,348	919	790	689	606	537	477
Average pellet energy in ft-lbs:	7.89	3.67	2.71	2.06	1.60	1.25	.99
Time of flight in seconds:	0	.0549	.0902	.1309	.1774	.2300	.2893

Type of load: Field
Three-foot velocity: 1,250 ft./sec.
Hull: 2¾-inch plastic
Wad: Plastic
Shot: Lead
Buffered: No
Test barrel length: 30 inch
Pellets will pierce skin up to 144 yards.

NO. 6 LEAD PELLETS—1⅛ OUNCES—251 PELLETS
Mfg: Fiocchi **Manufacturer's code:** 12FLD
Recoil energy in 8-lb. shotgun: 22.7 ft./lbs. **Recoil velocity in 8-lb. shotgun:** 13.5 ft./sec.

Distance in yards:	Muzzle	20	30	40	50	60	70
Velocity in fps:	1,348	919	790	689	606	537	477
Average pellet energy in ft-lbs:	7.89	3.67	2.71	2.06	1.60	1.25	.99
Time of flight in seconds:	0	.0549	.0902	.1309	.1774	.2300	.2893

Type of load: Field
Three-foot velocity: 1,250 ft./sec.
Hull: 2¾-inch plastic
Wad: Plastic
Shot: Lead
Buffered: No
Test barrel length: 30 inch
Pellets will pierce skin up to 144 yards.

NO. 6 LEAD PELLETS—1⅛ OUNCES—251 PELLETS
Mfg: Kent Cartridge America/Canada **Manufacturer's code:** K122UG32
Recoil energy in 8-lb. shotgun: 22.7 ft./lbs. **Recoil velocity in 8-lb. shotgun:** 13.5 ft./sec.

Distance in yards:	Muzzle	20	30	40	50	60	70
Velocity in fps:	1,348	919	790	689	606	537	477
Average pellet energy in ft-lbs:	7.89	3.67	2.71	2.06	1.60	1.25	.99
Time of flight in seconds:	0	.0549	.0902	.1309	.1774	.2300	.2893

Type of load: Field
Three-foot velocity: 1,250 ft./sec.
Hull: 2¾-inch plastic
Wad: Plastic
Shot: Lead
Buffered: No
Test barrel length: 30 inch
Pellets will pierce skin up to 144 yards.

NO. 6 LEAD PELLETS—1⅛ OUNCES—251 PELLETS
Mfg: Remington Arms Co. **Manufacturer's code:** RP12HD
Recoil energy in 8-lb. shotgun: 22.7 ft./lbs. **Recoil velocity in 8-lb. shotgun:** 13.5 ft./sec.

Distance in yards:	Muzzle	20	30	40	50	60	70
Velocity in fps:	1,348	919	790	689	606	537	477
Average pellet energy in ft-lbs:	7.89	3.67	2.71	2.06	1.60	1.25	.99
Time of flight in seconds:	0	.0549	.0902	.1309	.1774	.2300	.2893

Type of load: Field
Three-foot velocity: 1,250 ft./sec.
Hull: 2¾-inch plastic
Wad: Plastic
Shot: Lead
Buffered: No
Test barrel length: 30 inch
Pellets will pierce skin up to 144 yards.

NO. 6 LEAD PELLETS—1⅛ OUNCES—251 PELLETS
Mfg: Winchester **Manufacturer's code:** XU12H
Recoil energy in 8-lb. shotgun: 22.7 ft./lbs. **Recoil velocity in 8-lb. shotgun:** 13.5 ft./sec.

Distance in yards:	Muzzle	20	30	40	50	60	70
Velocity in fps:	1,348	919	790	689	606	537	477
Average pellet energy in ft-lbs:	7.89	3.67	2.71	2.06	1.60	1.25	.99
Time of flight in seconds:	0	.0549	.0902	.1309	.1774	.2300	.2893

Type of load: Target
Three-foot velocity: 1,250 ft./sec.
Hull: 2¾-inch plastic
Wad: Plastic
Shot: Lead
Buffered: No
Test barrel length: 30 inch
Pellets will pierce skin up to 144 yards.

NO. 6 LEAD PELLETS—1⅛ OUNCES—251 PELLETS
Mfg: RST, Ltd. **Manufacturer's code:** N/A
Recoil energy in 8-lb. shotgun: 25.2 ft./lbs. **Recoil velocity in 8-lb. shotgun:** 14.2 ft./sec.

Distance in yards:	Muzzle	20	30	40	50	60	70
Velocity in fps:	1,403	945	810	705	620	548	487
Average pellet energy in ft-lbs:	8.55	3.88	2.85	2.16	1.67	1.31	1.03
Time of flight in seconds:	0	.0531	.0875	.1272	.1727	.2242	.2723

Type of load: Target
Three-foot velocity: 1,300 ft./sec.
Hull: 2¾-inch plastic
Wad: Plastic
Shot: Lead
Buffered: No
Test barrel length: 30 inch
Pellets will pierce skin up to 146 yards.

NO. 6 LEAD PELLETS—1⅛ OUNCES—251 PELLETS
Mfg: ARMUSA **Manufacturer's code:** PLA-32
Recoil energy in 8-lb. shotgun: 26.8 ft./lbs. **Recoil velocity in 8-lb. shotgun:** 14.7 ft./sec.

Distance in yards:	Muzzle	20	30	40	50	60	70
Velocity in fps:	1,436	961	822	714	627	555	493
Average pellet energy in ft-lbs:	8.96	4.01	2.94	2.22	1.71	1.34	1.06
Time of flight in seconds:	0	.0520	.0859	.1251	.1700	.2209	.2782

Type of load: Sporting Clay
Three-foot velocity: 1,330 ft./sec.
Hull: 2¾-inch plastic
Wad: Plastic
Shot: Lead
Buffered: No
Test barrel length: 30 inch
Pellets will pierce skin up to 147 yards.

NO. 6 LEAD PELLETS—1⅛ OUNCES—251 PELLETS
Mfg: RIO **Manufacturer's code:** Super Game
Recoil energy in 8-lb. shotgun: 21.2 ft./lbs. **Recoil velocity in 8-lb. shotgun:** 13.0 ft./sec.

Distance in yards:	Muzzle	20	30	40	50	60	70
Velocity in fps:	1,436	961	822	714	627	555	493
Average pellet energy in ft-lbs:	8.96	4.01	2.94	2.22	1.71	1.34	1.06
Time of flight in seconds:	0	.0520	.0859	.1251	.1700	.2209	.2782

Type of load: Field
Three-foot velocity: 1,330 ft./sec.
Hull: 2¾-inch plastic
Wad: Plastic
Shot: Hard lead
Buffered: No
Test barrel length: 30 inch
Pellets will pierce skin up to 147 yards.

NO. 6 LEAD PELLETS—1⅛ OUNCES—251 PELLETS
Mfg: Baschieri & Pellagri **Manufacturer's code:** F2 Long Range
Recoil energy in 8-lb. shotgun: 26.8 ft./lbs. **Recoil velocity in 8-lb. shotgun:** 14.7 ft./sec.

Distance in yards:	Muzzle	20	30	40	50	60	70
Velocity in fps:	1,458	972	830	721	633	559	497
Average pellet energy in ft-lbs:	9.24	4.10	2.99	2.26	1.74	1.36	1.07
Time of flight in seconds:	0	.0514	.0849	.1237	.1682	.2187	.2757

Type of load: Field
Three-foot velocity: 1,350 ft./sec.
Hull: 2¾-inch plastic
Wad: Plastic
Shot: Lead
Buffered: No
Test barrel length: 30 inch
Pellets will pierce skin up to 148 yards.

NO. 6 LEAD PELLETS—1⅛ OUNCES—251 PELLETS
Mfg: Clever **Manufacturer's code:** T2 Light Game
Recoil energy in 8-lb. shotgun: 27.9 ft./lbs. **Recoil velocity in 8-lb. shotgun:** 15.0 ft./sec.

Distance in yards:	Muzzle	20	30	40	50	60	70
Velocity in fps:	1,458	972	830	721	633	559	497
Average pellet energy in ft-lbs:	9.24	4.10	2.99	2.26	1.74	1.36	1.07
Time of flight in seconds:	0	.0514	.0849	.1237	.1682	.2187	.2757

Type of load: Field
Three-foot velocity: 1,350 ft./sec.
Hull: 2¾-inch plastic
Wad: Plastic
Shot: Lead
Buffered: No
Test barrel length: 30 inch
Pellets will pierce skin up to 148 yards.

NO. 6 LEAD PELLETS—1⅛ OUNCES—251 PELLETS
Mfg: Federal Cartridge Co. **Manufacturer's code:** P128
Recoil energy in 8-lb. shotgun: 30.7 ft./lbs. **Recoil velocity in 8-lb. shotgun:** 15.7 ft./sec.

Distance in yards:	Muzzle	20	30	40	50	60	70
Velocity in fps:	1,514	998	850	736	645	570	506
Average pellet energy in ft-lbs:	9.96	4.33	3.14	2.35	1.81	1.41	1.11
Time of flight in seconds:	0	.0498	.0824	.1204	.1640	.2136	.2694

Type of load: Field
Three-foot velocity: 1,400 ft./sec.
Hull: 2¾-inch plastic
Wad: Plastic
Shot: Lead
Buffered: No
Test barrel length: 30 inch
Pellets will pierce skin up to 149 yards.

NO. 6 LEAD PELLETS—1³/₁₆ OUNCES—265 PELLETS
Mfg: Clever **Manufacturer's code:** T2 Felt Wad
Recoil energy in 8-lb. shotgun: 23.9 ft./lbs. **Recoil velocity in 8-lb. shotgun:** 13.9 ft./sec.

Distance in yards:	Muzzle	20	30	40	50	60	70
Velocity in fps:	1,375	932	800	697	613	543	482
Average pellet energy in ft-lbs:	8.22	3.77	2.78	2.11	1.63	1.28	1.01
Time of flight in seconds:	0	.0540	.0888	.1290	.1750	.2271	.2858

Type of load: Field
Three-foot velocity: 1,275 ft./sec.
Hull: 2¾-inch plastic
Wad: Felt/fiber
Shot: Lead
Buffered: No
Test barrel length: 30 inch
Pellets will pierce skin up to 145 yards.

NO. 6 LEAD PELLETS—1³/₁₆ OUNCES—265 PELLETS
Mfg: Clever **Manufacturer's code:** T2 Caccia
Recoil energy in 8-lb. shotgun: 25.2 ft./lbs. **Recoil velocity in 8-lb. shotgun:** 14.2 ft./sec.

Distance in yards:	Muzzle	20	30	40	50	60	70
Velocity in fps:	1,403	945	810	705	620	548	487
Average pellet energy in ft-lbs:	8.55	3.88	2.85	2.16	1.67	1.31	1.03
Time of flight in seconds:	0	.0531	.0875	.1272	.1727	.2242	.2723

Type of load: Field
Three-foot velocity: 1,300 ft./sec.
Hull: 2¾-inch plastic
Wad: Plastic
Shot: Lead
Buffered: No
Test barrel length: 30 inch
Pellets will pierce skin up to 146 yards.

NO. 6 LEAD PELLETS—1³/₁₆ OUNCES—265 PELLETS
Mfg: RIO **Manufacturer's code:** Extra Game
Recoil energy in 8-lb. shotgun: 16.2 ft./lbs. **Recoil velocity in 8-lb. shotgun:** 11.4 ft./sec.

Distance in yards:	Muzzle	20	30	40	50	60	70
Velocity in fps:	1,436	961	822	714	627	555	493
Average pellet energy in ft-lbs:	8.96	4.01	2.94	2.22	1.71	1.34	1.06
Time of flight in seconds:	0	.0520	.0859	.1251	.1700	.2209	.2782

Type of load: Field
Three-foot velocity: 1,330 ft./sec.
Hull: 2¾-inch plastic
Wad: Plastic
Shot: Hard lead
Buffered: No
Test barrel length: 30 inch
Pellets will pierce skin up to 147 yards.

NO. 6 LEAD PELLETS—1¼ OUNCES—279 PELLETS
Mfg: Estate Cartridge **Manufacturer's code:** XHG12
Recoil energy in 8-lb. shotgun: 26.3 ft./lbs. **Recoil velocity in 8-lb. shotgun:** 14.5 ft./sec.

Distance in yards:	Muzzle	20	30	40	50	60	70
Velocity in fps:	1,314	903	778	679	598	530	471
Average pellet energy in ft-lbs:	7.51	3.54	2.63	2.00	1.55	1.22	.97
Time of flight in seconds:	0	.0560	.0919	.1333	.1804	.2337	.2938

Type of load: Field
Three-foot velocity: 1,220 ft./sec.
Hull: 2¾-inch plastic
Wad: Plastic
Shot: Hard lead
Buffered: No
Test barrel length: 30 inch
Pellets will pierce skin up to 143 yards.

NO. 6 LEAD PELLETS—1¼ OUNCES—279 PELLETS
Mfg: Federal Cartridge Co. **Manufacturer's code:** H125/H120
Recoil energy in 8-lb. shotgun: 26.3 ft./lbs. **Recoil velocity in 8-lb. shotgun:** 14.5 ft./sec.

Distance in yards:	Muzzle	20	30	40	50	60	70
Velocity in fps:	1,314	903	778	679	598	530	471
Average pellet energy in ft-lbs:	7.51	3.54	2.63	2.00	1.55	1.22	.97
Time of flight in seconds:	0	.0560	.0919	.1333	.1804	.2337	.2938

Type of load: Field
Three-foot velocity: 1,220 ft./sec.
Hull: 2¾-inch plastic
Wad: Plastic
Shot: Lead
Buffered: No
Test barrel length: 30 inch
Pellets will pierce skin up to 143 yards.

NO. 6 LEAD PELLETS—1¼ OUNCES—279 PELLETS
Mfg: Fiocchi **Manufacturer's code:** 12HF
Recoil energy in 8-lb. shotgun: 26.3 ft./lbs. **Recoil velocity in 8-lb. shotgun:** 14.5 ft./sec.

Distance in yards:	Muzzle	20	30	40	50	60	70
Velocity in fps:	1,314	903	778	679	598	530	471
Average pellet energy in ft-lbs:	7.51	3.54	2.63	2.00	1.55	1.22	.97
Time of flight in seconds:	0	.0560	.0919	.1333	.1804	.2337	.2938

Type of load: Field
Three-foot velocity: 1,220 ft./sec.
Hull: 2¾-inch plastic
Wad: Plastic
Shot: Lead
Buffered: No
Test barrel length: 30 inch
Pellets will pierce skin up to 143 yards.

NO. 6 LEAD PELLETS—1¼ OUNCES—279 PELLETS
Mfg: Remington Arms Co. **Manufacturer's code:** RP12H
Recoil energy in 8-lb. shotgun: 26.3 ft./lbs. **Recoil velocity in 8-lb. shotgun:** 14.5 ft./sec.

Distance in yards:	Muzzle	20	30	40	50	60	70
Velocity in fps:	1,314	903	778	679	598	530	471
Average pellet energy in ft-lbs:	7.51	3.54	2.63	2.00	1.55	1.22	.97
Time of flight in seconds:	0	.0560	.0919	.1333	.1804	.2337	.2938

Type of load: Field
Three-foot velocity: 1,220 ft./sec.
Hull: 2¾-inch plastic
Wad: Plastic
Shot: Lead
Buffered: No
Test barrel length: 30 inch
Pellets will pierce skin up to 143 yards.

NO. 6 LEAD PELLETS—1¼ OUNCES—279 PELLETS
Mfg: Sellier & Bellot **Manufacturer's code:** SBA01210
Recoil energy in 8-lb. shotgun: 26.3 ft./lbs. **Recoil velocity in 8-lb. shotgun:** 14.5 ft./sec.

Distance in yards:	Muzzle	20	30	40	50	60	70
Velocity in fps:	1,314	903	778	679	598	530	471
Average pellet energy in ft-lbs:	7.51	3.54	2.63	2.00	1.55	1.22	.97
Time of flight in seconds:	0	.0560	.0919	.1333	.1804	.2337	.2938

Type of load: Field
Three-foot velocity: 1,220 ft./sec.
Hull: 2¾-inch plastic
Wad: Plastic
Shot: Lead
Buffered: No
Test barrel length: 30 inch
Pellets will pierce skin up to 143 yards.

NO. 6 LEAD PELLETS—1¼ OUNCES—279 PELLETS
Mfg: Winchester **Manufacturer's code:** XU12SP/AA12SP
Recoil energy in 8-lb. shotgun: 26.3 ft./lbs. **Recoil velocity in 8-lb. shotgun:** 14.5 ft./sec.

Distance in yards:	Muzzle	20	30	40	50	60	70
Velocity in fps:	1,314	903	778	679	598	530	471
Average pellet energy in ft-lbs:	7.51	3.54	2.63	2.00	1.55	1.22	.97
Time of flight in seconds:	0	.0560	.0919	.1333	.1804	.2337	.2938

Type of load: Field & Target
Three-foot velocity: 1,220 ft./sec.
Hull: 2¾-inch plastic
Wad: Plastic
Shot: Lead
Buffered: No
Test barrel length: 30 inch
Pellets will pierce skin up to 143 yards.

NO. 6 LEAD PELLETS—1¼ OUNCES—279 PELLETS
Mfg: Rottweil **Manufacturer's code:** Super Game
Recoil energy in 8-lb. shotgun: 26.3 ft./lbs. **Recoil velocity in 8-lb. shotgun:** 14.5 ft./sec.

Distance in yards:	Muzzle	20	30	40	50	60	70
Velocity in fps:	1,331	911	784	684	602	534	474
Average pellet energy in ft-lbs:	7.70	3.60	2.67	2.03	1.58	1.24	.98
Time of flight in seconds:	0	.0555	.0911	.1321	.1789	.2319	.2915

Type of load: Field
Three-foot velocity: 1,235 ft./sec.
Hull: 2¾-inch plastic
Wad: Plastic
Shot: Lead
Buffered: No
Test barrel length: 30 inch
Pellets will pierce skin up to 144 yards.

NO. 6 LEAD PELLETS—1¼ OUNCES—279 PELLETS

Mfg: Federal Cartridge Co. **Manufacturer's code:** H127
Recoil energy in 8-lb. shotgun: 29.5 ft./lbs. **Recoil velocity in 8-lb. shotgun:** 15.4 ft./sec.

Distance in yards:	Muzzle	20	30	40	50	60	70
Velocity in fps:	1,375	932	800	697	613	543	482
Average pellet energy in ft-lbs:	8.22	3.77	2.78	2.11	1.63	1.28	1.01
Time of flight in seconds:	0	.0540	.0888	.1290	.1750	.2271	.2858

Type of load: Field
Three-foot velocity: 1,275 ft./sec.
Hull: 2¾-inch plastic
Wad: Plastic
Shot: Lead
Buffered: No
Test barrel length: 30 inch
Pellets will pierce skin up to 145 yards.

NO. 6 LEAD PELLETS—1¼ OUNCES—279 PELLETS

Mfg: ARMUSA **Manufacturer's code:** N/A
Recoil energy in 8-lb. shotgun: 31.1 ft./lbs. **Recoil velocity in 8-lb. shotgun:** 15.8 ft./sec.

Distance in yards:	Muzzle	20	30	40	50	60	70
Velocity in fps:	1,403	945	810	705	620	548	487
Average pellet energy in ft-lbs:	8.55	3.88	2.85	2.16	1.67	1.31	1.03
Time of flight in seconds:	0	.0531	.0875	.1272	.1727	.2242	.2723

Type of load: Field
Three-foot velocity: 1,300 ft./sec.
Hull: 2¾-inch plastic
Wad: Plastic
Shot: Lead
Buffered: No
Test barrel length: 30 inch
Pellets will pierce skin up to 146 yards.

NO. 6 LEAD PELLETS—1¼ OUNCES—279 PELLETS

Mfg: Baschieri & Pellagri **Manufacturer's code:** MB Extra
Recoil energy in 8-lb. shotgun: 31.1 ft./lbs. **Recoil velocity in 8-lb. shotgun:** 15.8 ft./sec.

Distance in yards:	Muzzle	20	30	40	50	60	70
Velocity in fps:	1,403	945	810	705	620	548	487
Average pellet energy in ft-lbs:	8.55	3.88	2.85	2.16	1.67	1.31	1.03
Time of flight in seconds:	0	.0531	.0875	.1272	.1727	.2242	.2723

Type of load: Field
Three-foot velocity: 1,300 ft./sec.
Hull: 2¾-inch plastic
Wad: Plastic
Shot: Lead
Buffered: No
Test barrel length: 30 inch
Pellets will pierce skin up to 146 yards.

NO. 6 LEAD PELLETS—1¼ OUNCES—279 PELLETS

Mfg: Clever **Manufacturer's code:** T4 High Velocity
Recoil energy in 8-lb. shotgun: 31.1 ft./lbs. **Recoil velocity in 8-lb. shotgun:** 15.8 ft./sec.

Distance in yards:	Muzzle	20	30	40	50	60	70
Velocity in fps:	1,403	945	810	705	620	548	487
Average pellet energy in ft-lbs:	8.55	3.88	2.85	2.16	1.67	1.31	1.03
Time of flight in seconds:	0	.0531	.0875	.1272	.1727	.2242	.2723

Type of load: Field
Three-foot velocity: 1,300 ft./sec.
Hull: 2¾-inch plastic
Wad: Plastic
Shot: Lead
Buffered: No
Test barrel length: 30 inch
Pellets will pierce skin up to 146 yards.

NO. 6 LEAD PELLETS—1¼ OUNCES—279 PELLETS

Mfg: Eley Hawk **Manufacturer's code:** Alphamax
Recoil energy in 8-lb. shotgun: 31.1 ft./lbs. **Recoil velocity in 8-lb. shotgun:** 15.8 ft./sec.

Distance in yards:	Muzzle	20	30	40	50	60	70
Velocity in fps:	1,403	945	810	705	620	548	487
Average pellet energy in ft-lbs:	8.55	3.88	2.85	2.16	1.67	1.31	1.03
Time of flight in seconds:	0	.0531	.0875	.1272	.1727	.2242	.2723

Type of load: Field
Three-foot velocity: 1,300 ft./sec.
Hull: 2¾-inch plastic
Wad: Plastic
Shot: Lead
Buffered: No
Test barrel length: 30 inch
Pellets will pierce skin up to 146 yards.

NO. 6 LEAD PELLETS—1¼ OUNCES—279 PELLETS

Mfg: Aguila **Manufacturer's code:** N/A
Recoil energy in 8-lb. shotgun: 33.0 ft./lbs. **Recoil velocity in 8-lb. shotgun:** 16.3 ft./sec.

Distance in yards:	Muzzle	20	30	40	50	60	70
Velocity in fps:	1,436	961	822	714	627	555	493
Average pellet energy in ft-lbs:	8.96	4.01	2.94	2.22	1.71	1.34	1.06
Time of flight in seconds:	0	.0520	.0859	.1251	.1700	.2209	.2782

Type of load: Field
Three-foot velocity: 1,330 ft./sec.
Hull: 2¾-inch plastic
Wad: Plastic
Shot: Lead
Buffered: No
Test barrel length: 30 inch
Pellets will pierce skin up to 147 yards.

NO. 6 LEAD PELLETS—1¼ OUNCES—279 PELLETS

Mfg: Baschieri & Pellagri **Manufacturer's code:** MB/F2 Long Range
Recoil energy in 8-lb. shotgun: 33.0 ft./lbs. **Recoil velocity in 8-lb. shotgun:** 16.3 ft./sec.

Distance in yards:	Muzzle	20	30	40	50	60	70
Velocity in fps:	1,436	961	822	714	627	555	493
Average pellet energy in ft-lbs:	8.96	4.01	2.94	2.22	1.71	1.34	1.06
Time of flight in seconds:	0	.0520	.0859	.1251	.1700	.2209	.2782

Type of load: Field
Three-foot velocity: 1,330 ft./sec.
Hull: 2¾-inch plastic
Wad: Plastic
Shot: Lead
Buffered: No
Test barrel length: 30 inch
Pellets will pierce skin up to 147 yards.

NO. 6 LEAD PELLETS—1¼ OUNCES—279 PELLETS
Mfg: Dionisi Manufacturer's code: D 12 SLR
Recoil energy in 8-lb. shotgun: 33.0 ft./lbs. **Recoil velocity in 8-lb. shotgun:** 16.3 ft./sec.

Distance in yards:	Muzzle	20	30	40	50	60	70
Velocity in fps:	1,436	961	822	714	627	555	493
Average pellet energy in ft-lbs:	8.96	4.01	2.94	2.22	1.71	1.34	1.06
Time of flight in seconds:	0	.0520	.0859	.1251	.1700	.2209	.2782

Type of load: Field
Three-foot velocity: 1,330 ft./sec.
Hull: 2¾-inch plastic
Wad: Plastic
Shot: Lead
Buffered: No
Test barrel length: 30 inch
Pellets will pierce skin up to 147 yards.

NO. 6 LEAD PELLETS—1¼ OUNCES—279 PELLETS
Mfg: Estate Cartridge Manufacturer's code: HV12
Recoil energy in 8-lb. shotgun: 33.0 ft./lbs. **Recoil velocity in 8-lb. shotgun:** 16.3 ft./sec.

Distance in yards:	Muzzle	20	30	40	50	60	70
Velocity in fps:	1,436	961	822	714	627	555	493
Average pellet energy in ft-lbs:	8.96	4.01	2.94	2.22	1.71	1.34	1.06
Time of flight in seconds:	0	.0520	.0859	.1251	.1700	.2209	.2782

Type of load: Field
Three-foot velocity: 1,330 ft./sec.
Hull: 2¾-inch plastic
Wad: Plastic
Shot: Hard lead
Buffered: No
Test barrel length: 30 inch
Pellets will pierce skin up to 147 yards.

NO. 6 LEAD PELLETS—1¼ OUNCES—279 PELLETS
Mfg: Federal Cartridge Co. Manufacturer's code: P154/H126
Recoil energy in 8-lb. shotgun: 33.0 ft./lbs. **Recoil velocity in 8-lb. shotgun:** 16.3 ft./sec.

Distance in yards:	Muzzle	20	30	40	50	60	70
Velocity in fps:	1,436	961	822	714	627	555	493
Average pellet energy in ft-lbs:	8.96	4.01	2.94	2.22	1.71	1.34	1.06
Time of flight in seconds:	0	.0520	.0859	.1251	.1700	.2209	.2782

Type of load: Field
Three-foot velocity: 1,330 ft./sec.
Hull: 2¾-inch plastic
Wad: Plastic
Shot: Lead
Buffered: No
Test barrel length: 30 inch
Pellets will pierce skin up to 147 yards.

NO. 6 LEAD PELLETS—1¼ OUNCES—279 PELLETS
Mfg: Fiocchi Manufacturer's code: 12HV
Recoil energy in 8-lb. shotgun: 40.0 ft./lbs. **Recoil velocity in 8-lb. shotgun:** 17.9 ft./sec.

Distance in yards:	Muzzle	20	30	40	50	60	70
Velocity in fps:	1,436	961	822	714	627	555	493
Average pellet energy in ft-lbs:	8.96	4.01	2.94	2.22	1.71	1.34	1.06
Time of flight in seconds:	0	.0520	.0859	.1251	.1700	.2209	.2782

Type of load: Field
Three-foot velocity: 1,330 ft./sec.
Hull: 2¾-inch plastic
Wad: Plastic
Shot: Lead
Buffered: No
Test barrel length: 30 inch
Pellets will pierce skin up to 147 yards.

Hunting pheasants in large, harvested grain fields often calls for hefty 1¼- or 1⅜-ounce loads of No. 4 or 6 lead shot. When hunting a mixed bag that includes quail and partridge, No. 6 shot is probably the best compromise. If pen-reared birds are the only quarry, then No. 7½ shot will be the best choice.

NO. 6 LEAD PELLETS—1¼ OUNCES—279 PELLETS
Mfg: Fiocchi **Manufacturer's code:** 12HVN
Recoil energy in 8-lb. shotgun: 40.0 ft./lbs. **Recoil velocity in 8-lb. shotgun:** 17.9 ft./sec.

Distance in yards:	Muzzle	20	30	40	50	60	70
Velocity in fps:	1,436	961	822	714	627	555	493
Average pellet energy in ft-lbs:	8.96	4.01	2.94	2.22	1.71	1.34	1.06
Time of flight in seconds:	0	.0520	.0859	.1251	.1700	.2209	.2782

Type of load: Field
Three-foot velocity: 1,330 ft./sec.
Hull: 2¾-inch plastic
Wad: Plastic
Shot: Nickel-plated lead
Buffered: No
Test barrel length: 30 inch
Pellets will pierce skin up to 147 yards.

NO. 6 LEAD PELLETS—1¼ OUNCES—279 PELLETS
Mfg: Kent Cartridge America/Canada **Manufacturer's code:** K122UG36
Recoil energy in 8-lb. shotgun: 31.1 ft./lbs. **Recoil velocity in 8-lb. shotgun:** 15.8 ft./sec.

Distance in yards:	Muzzle	20	30	40	50	60	70
Velocity in fps:	1,436	961	822	714	627	555	493
Average pellet energy in ft-lbs:	8.96	4.01	2.94	2.22	1.71	1.34	1.06
Time of flight in seconds:	0	.0520	.0859	.1251	.1700	.2209	.2782

Type of load: Field
Three-foot velocity: 1,330 ft./sec.
Hull: 2¾-inch plastic
Wad: Plastic
Shot: Lead
Buffered: No
Test barrel length: 30 inch
Pellets will pierce skin up to 147 yards.

NO. 6 LEAD PELLETS—1¼ OUNCES—279 PELLETS
Mfg: PMC (Eldorado Cartridge Corp.) **Manufacturer's code:** HF12
Recoil energy in 8-lb. shotgun: 31.1 ft./lbs. **Recoil velocity in 8-lb. shotgun:** 15.8 ft./sec.

Distance in yards:	Muzzle	20	30	40	50	60	70
Velocity in fps:	1,436	961	822	714	627	555	493
Average pellet energy in ft-lbs:	8.96	4.01	2.94	2.22	1.71	1.34	1.06
Time of flight in seconds:	0	.0520	.0859	.1251	.1700	.2209	.2782

Type of load: Field
Three-foot velocity: 1,330 ft./sec.
Hull: 2¾-inch plastic
Wad: Plastic
Shot: Lead
Buffered: No
Test barrel length: 30 inch
Pellets will pierce skin up to 147 yards.

NO. 6 LEAD PELLETS—1¼ OUNCES—279 PELLETS
Mfg: Remington Arms Co. **Manufacturer's code:** SP12/HGL12
Recoil energy in 8-lb. shotgun: 33.0 ft./lbs. **Recoil velocity in 8-lb. shotgun:** 16.3 ft./sec.

Distance in yards:	Muzzle	20	30	40	50	60	70
Velocity in fps:	1,436	961	822	714	627	555	493
Average pellet energy in ft-lbs:	8.96	4.01	2.94	2.22	1.71	1.34	1.06
Time of flight in seconds:	0	.0520	.0859	.1251	.1700	.2209	.2782

Type of load: Field
Three-foot velocity: 1,330 ft./sec.
Hull: 2¾-inch plastic
Wad: Plastic
Shot: Lead
Buffered: No
Test barrel length: 30 inch
Pellets will pierce skin up to 147 yards.

NO. 6 LEAD PELLETS—1¼ OUNCES—279 PELLETS
Mfg: RIO **Manufacturer's code:** Extra Game
Recoil energy in 8-lb. shotgun: 33.0 ft./lbs. **Recoil velocity in 8-lb. shotgun:** 16.3 ft./sec.

Distance in yards:	Muzzle	20	30	40	50	60	70
Velocity in fps:	1,436	961	822	714	627	555	493
Average pellet energy in ft-lbs:	8.96	4.01	2.94	2.22	1.71	1.34	1.06
Time of flight in seconds:	0	.0520	.0859	.1251	.1700	.2209	.2782

Type of load: Field
Three-foot velocity: 1,330 ft./sec.
Hull: 2¾-inch plastic
Wad: Plastic
Shot: Hard lead
Buffered: No
Test barrel length: 30 inch
Pellets will pierce skin up to 147 yards.

NO. 6 LEAD PELLETS—1¼ OUNCES—279 PELLETS
Mfg: Winchester **Manufacturer's code:** X12
Recoil energy in 8-lb. shotgun: 33.0 ft./lbs. **Recoil velocity in 8-lb. shotgun:** 16.3 ft./sec.

Distance in yards:	Muzzle	20	30	40	50	60	70
Velocity in fps:	1,436	961	822	714	627	555	493
Average pellet energy in ft-lbs:	8.96	4.01	2.94	2.22	1.71	1.34	1.06
Time of flight in seconds:	0	.0520	.0859	.1251	.1700	.2209	.2782

Type of load: Field
Three-foot velocity: 1,330 ft./sec.
Hull: 2¾-inch plastic
Wad: Plastic
Shot: Lead
Buffered: No
Test barrel length: 30 inch
Pellets will pierce skin up to 147 yards.

NO. 6 LEAD PELLETS—1¼ OUNCES—279 PELLETS
Mfg: Remington Arms Co. **Manufacturer's code:** SPHV12
Recoil energy in 8-lb. shotgun: 37.9 ft./lbs. **Recoil velocity in 8-lb. shotgun:** 17.5 ft./sec.

Distance in yards:	Muzzle	20	30	40	50	60	70
Velocity in fps:	1,514	998	850	736	645	570	506
Average pellet energy in ft-lbs:	9.96	4.33	3.14	2.35	1.81	1.41	1.11
Time of flight in seconds:	0	.0498	.0824	.1204	.1640	.2136	.2694

Type of load: Field
Three-foot velocity: 1,400 ft./sec.
Hull: 2¾-inch plastic
Wad: Plastic
Shot: Lead
Buffered: No
Test barrel length: 30 inch
Pellets will pierce skin up to 149 yards.

NO. 6 LEAD PELLETS—1¼ OUNCES—279 PELLETS
Mfg: Winchester **Manufacturer's code:** SFH12
Recoil energy in 8-lb. shotgun: 37.9 ft./lbs. **Recoil velocity in 8-lb. shotgun:** 17.5 ft./sec.

Distance in yards:	Muzzle	20	30	40	50	60	70
Velocity in fps:	1,514	998	850	736	645	570	506
Average pellet energy in ft-lbs:	9.96	4.33	3.14	2.35	1.81	1.41	1.11
Time of flight in seconds:	0	.0498	.0824	.1204	.1640	.2136	.2694

Type of load: Field
Three-foot velocity: 1,400 ft./sec.
Hull: 2¾-inch plastic
Wad: Plastic
Shot: Copper-plated lead
Buffered: Yes
Test barrel length: 30 inch
Pellets will pierce skin up to 149 yards.

NO. 6 LEAD PELLETS—1⅜ OUNCES—307 PELLETS
Mfg: Fiocchi **Manufacturer's code:** 12HGP/12TT
Recoil energy in 8-lb. shotgun: 33.9 ft./lbs. **Recoil velocity in 8-lb. shotgun:** 16.5 ft./sec.

Distance in yards:	Muzzle	20	30	40	50	60	70
Velocity in fps:	1,348	919	790	689	606	537	477
Average pellet energy in ft-lbs:	7.89	3.67	2.71	2.06	1.60	1.25	.99
Time of flight in seconds:	0	.0549	.0902	.1309	.1774	.2300	.2893

Type of load: Field & Turkey
Three-foot velocity: 1,250 ft./sec.
Hull: 2¾-inch plastic
Wad: Plastic
Shot: Nickel-plated lead
Buffered: No
Test barrel length: 30 inch
Pellets will pierce skin up to 144 yards.

NO. 6 LEAD PELLETS—1⅜ OUNCES—307 PELLETS
Mfg: Baschieri & Pellagri **Manufacturer's code:** MB Winter
Recoil energy in 8-lb. shotgun: 35.7 ft./lbs. **Recoil velocity in 8-lb. shotgun:** 16.9 ft./sec.

Distance in yards:	Muzzle	20	30	40	50	60	70
Velocity in fps:	1,375	932	800	697	613	543	482
Average pellet energy in ft-lbs:	8.22	3.77	2.78	2.11	1.63	1.28	1.01
Time of flight in seconds:	0	.0540	.0888	.1290	.1750	.2271	.2858

Type of load: Field
Three-foot velocity: 1,275 ft./sec.
Hull: 2¾-inch plastic
Wad: Plastic
Shot: Hard lead
Buffered: No
Test barrel length: 30 inch
Pellets will pierce skin up to 145 yards.

NO. 6 LEAD PELLETS—1⅜ OUNCES—307 PELLETS
Mfg: Clever **Manufacturer's code:** T4 Caccia
Recoil energy in 8-lb. shotgun: 35.7 ft./lbs. **Recoil velocity in 8-lb. shotgun:** 16.9 ft./sec.

Distance in yards:	Muzzle	20	30	40	50	60	70
Velocity in fps:	1,375	932	800	697	613	543	482
Average pellet energy in ft-lbs:	8.22	3.77	2.78	2.11	1.63	1.28	1.01
Time of flight in seconds:	0	.0540	.0888	.1290	.1750	.2271	.2858

Type of load: Field
Three-foot velocity: 1,275 ft./sec.
Hull: 2¾-inch plastic
Wad: Plastic
Shot: Lead
Buffered: No
Test barrel length: 30 inch
Pellets will pierce skin up to 145 yards.

NO. 6 LEAD PELLETS—1⅜ OUNCES—307 PELLETS
Mfg: Federal Cartridge Co. **Manufacturer's code:** P138
Recoil energy in 8-lb. shotgun: 45.9 ft./lbs. **Recoil velocity in 8-lb. shotgun:** 19.2 ft./sec.

Distance in yards:	Muzzle	20	30	40	50	60	70
Velocity in fps:	1,514	998	850	736	645	570	506
Average pellet energy in ft-lbs:	9.96	4.33	3.14	2.35	1.81	1.41	1.11
Time of flight in seconds:	0	.0498	.0824	.1204	.1640	.2136	.2694

Type of load: Field
Three-foot velocity: 1,400 ft./sec.
Hull: 2¾-inch plastic
Wad: Plastic
Shot: Lead
Buffered: No
Test barrel length: 30 inch
Pellets will pierce skin up to 149 yards.

NO. 6 LEAD PELLETS—1½ OUNCES—335 PELLETS
Mfg: Dionisi **Manufacturer's code:** D 12G
Recoil energy in 8-lb. shotgun: 40.4 ft./lbs. **Recoil velocity in 8-lb. shotgun:** 18.0 ft./sec.

Distance in yards:	Muzzle	20	30	40	50	60	70
Velocity in fps:	1,348	919	790	689	606	537	477
Average pellet energy in ft-lbs:	7.89	3.67	2.71	2.06	1.60	1.25	.99
Time of flight in seconds:	0	.0549	.0902	.1309	.1774	.2300	.2893

Type of load: Field
Three-foot velocity: 1,250 ft./sec.
Hull: 2¾-inch plastic
Wad: Plastic
Shot: Lead
Buffered: No
Test barrel length: 30 inch
Pellets will pierce skin up to 144 yards.

NO. 6 LEAD PELLETS—1½ OUNCES—335 PELLETS
Mfg: Federal Cartridge Co. **Manufacturer's code:** F130
Recoil energy in 8-lb. shotgun: 40.4 ft./lbs. **Recoil velocity in 8-lb. shotgun:** 18.0 ft./sec.

Distance in yards:	Muzzle	20	30	40	50	60	70
Velocity in fps:	1,348	919	790	689	606	537	477
Average pellet energy in ft-lbs:	7.89	3.67	2.71	2.06	1.60	1.25	.99
Time of flight in seconds:	0	.0549	.0902	.1309	.1774	.2300	.2893

Type of load: Field
Three-foot velocity: 1,250 ft./sec.
Hull: 2¾-inch plastic
Wad: Plastic
Shot: Lead
Buffered: No
Test barrel length: 30 inch
Pellets will pierce skin up to 144 yards.

NO. 6 LEAD PELLETS—1½ OUNCES—335 PELLETS
Mfg: Remington Arms Co. **Manufacturer's code:** P12SM/NM12S
Recoil energy in 8-lb. shotgun: 40.4 ft./lbs. **Recoil velocity in 8-lb. shotgun:** 18.0 ft./sec.

Distance in yards:	Muzzle	20	30	40	50	60	70
Velocity in fps:	1,348	919	790	689	606	537	477
Average pellet energy in ft-lbs:	7.89	3.67	2.71	2.06	1.60	1.25	.99
Time of flight in seconds:	0	.0549	.0902	.1309	.1774	.2300	.2893

Type of load: Turkey & Field
Three-foot velocity: 1,250 ft./sec.
Hull: 2¾-inch plastic
Wad: Plastic
Shot: Copper-plated lead/lead
Buffered: Yes
Test barrel length: 30 inch
Pellets will pierce skin up to 144 yards.

NO. 6 LEAD PELLETS—1½ OUNCES—335 PELLETS
Mfg: Clever **Manufacturer's code:** Magnum 42
Recoil energy in 8-lb. shotgun: 42.5 ft./lbs. **Recoil velocity in 8-lb. shotgun:** 18.5 ft./sec.

Distance in yards:	Muzzle	20	30	40	50	60	70
Velocity in fps:	1,375	932	800	697	613	543	482
Average pellet energy in ft-lbs:	8.22	3.77	2.78	2.11	1.63	1.28	1.01
Time of flight in seconds:	0	.0540	.0888	.1290	.1750	.2271	.2858

Type of load: Field
Three-foot velocity: 1,275 ft./sec.
Hull: 2¾-inch plastic
Wad: Plastic
Shot: Lead
Buffered: No
Test barrel length: 30 inch
Pellets will pierce skin up to 145 yards.

NO. 6 LEAD PELLETS—1½ OUNCES—335 PELLETS
Mfg: Federal Cartridge Co. **Manufacturer's code:** P156
Recoil energy in 8-lb. shotgun: 44.8 ft./lbs. **Recoil velocity in 8-lb. shotgun:** 19.0 ft./sec.

Distance in yards:	Muzzle	20	30	40	50	60	70
Velocity in fps:	1,403	945	810	705	620	548	487
Average pellet energy in ft-lbs:	8.55	3.88	2.85	2.16	1.67	1.31	1.03
Time of flight in seconds:	0	.0531	.0875	.1272	.1727	.2242	.2723

Type of load: Field
Three-foot velocity: 1,300 ft./sec.
Hull: 2¾-inch plastic
Wad: Plastic
Shot: Lead
Buffered: No
Test barrel length: 30 inch
Pellets will pierce skin up to 146 yards.

NO. 6 LEAD PELLETS—1½ OUNCES—335 PELLETS
Mfg: Estate Cartridge **Manufacturer's code:** HV12SMAG
Recoil energy in 8-lb. shotgun: 47.6 ft./lbs. **Recoil velocity in 8-lb. shotgun:** 19.6 ft./sec.

Distance in yards:	Muzzle	20	30	40	50	60	70
Velocity in fps:	1,436	961	822	714	627	555	493
Average pellet energy in ft-lbs:	8.96	4.01	2.94	2.22	1.71	1.34	1.06
Time of flight in seconds:	0	.0520	.0859	.1251	.1700	.2209	.2782

Type of load: Field
Three-foot velocity: 1,330 ft./sec.
Hull: 2¾-inch plastic
Wad: Plastic
Shot: Hard lead
Buffered: Yes
Test barrel length: 30 inch
Pellets will pierce skin up to 147 yards.

NO. 6 LEAD PELLETS—1⅝ OUNCES—362 PELLETS
Mfg: Federal Cartridge Co. **Manufacturer's code:** PT155
Recoil energy in 8-lb. shotgun: 47.4 ft./lbs. **Recoil velocity in 8-lb. shotgun:** 19.5 ft./sec.

Distance in yards:	Muzzle	20	30	40	50	60	70
Velocity in fps:	1,348	919	790	689	606	537	477
Average pellet energy in ft-lbs:	7.89	3.67	2.71	2.06	1.60	1.25	.99
Time of flight in seconds:	0	.0549	.0902	.1309	.1774	.2300	.2893

Type of load: Turkey
Three-foot velocity: 1,250 ft./sec.
Hull: 2¾-inch plastic
Wad: Plastic
Shot: Copper-plated lead
Buffered: Yes
Test barrel length: 30 inch
Pellets will pierce skin up to 144 yards.

NO. 6 LEAD PELLETS—1⅝ OUNCES—362 PELLETS
Mfg: Winchester **Manufacturer's code:** X12HXCT
Recoil energy in 8-lb. shotgun: 47.4 ft./lbs. **Recoil velocity in 8-lb. shotgun:** 19.5 ft./sec.

Distance in yards:	Muzzle	20	30	40	50	60	70
Velocity in fps:	1,348	919	790	689	606	537	477
Average pellet energy in ft-lbs:	7.89	3.67	2.71	2.06	1.60	1.25	.99
Time of flight in seconds:	0	.0549	.0902	.1309	.1774	.2300	.2893

Type of load: Turkey
Three-foot velocity: 1,250 ft./sec.
Hull: 2¾-inch plastic
Wad: Plastic
Shot: Copper-plated lead
Buffered: Yes
Test barrel length: 30 inch
Pellets will pierce skin up to 144 yards.

NO. 6 LEAD PELLETS—1⅝ OUNCES—362 PELLETS
Mfg: Kent Cartridge America/Canada **Manufacturer's code:** K122TK46
Recoil energy in 8-lb. shotgun: 49.4 ft./lbs. **Recoil velocity in 8-lb. shotgun:** 20.0 ft./sec.

Distance in yards:	Muzzle	20	30	40	50	60	70
Velocity in fps:	1,375	932	800	697	613	543	482
Average pellet energy in ft-lbs:	8.22	3.77	2.78	2.11	1.63	1.28	1.01
Time of flight in seconds:	0	.0540	.0888	.1290	.1750	.2271	.2858

Type of load: Turkey
Three-foot velocity: 1,275 ft./sec.
Hull: 2¾-inch plastic
Wad: Plastic
Shot: Lead
Buffered: No
Test barrel length: 30 inch
Pellets will pierce skin up to 145 yards.

NO. 7 LEAD PELLETS—⅞ OUNCE—262 PELLETS
Mfg: Eley Hawk **Manufacturer's code:** VIP
Recoil energy in 8-lb. shotgun: 16.2 ft./lbs. **Recoil velocity in 8-lb. shotgun:** 11.4 ft./sec.

Distance in yards:	Muzzle	20	30	40	50	60	70
Velocity in fps:	1,443	933	789	679	591	518	455
Average pellet energy in ft-lbs:	6.80	2.84	2.03	1.51	1.14	.88	.68
Time of flight in seconds:	0	.0529	.0879	.1290	.1764	.2306	.2925

Type of load: Target
Three-foot velocity: 1,330 ft./sec.
Hull: 2¾-inch plastic
Wad: Plastic
Shot: Hard lead
Buffered: No
Test barrel length: 30 inch
Pellets will pierce skin up to 134 yards.

NO. 7 LEAD PELLETS—1 OUNCE—299 PELLETS
Mfg: Eley Hawk **Manufacturer's code:** VIP
Recoil energy in 8-lb. shotgun: 16.2 ft./lbs. **Recoil velocity in 8-lb. shotgun:** 11.4 ft./sec.

Distance in yards:	Muzzle	20	30	40	50	60	70
Velocity in fps:	1,443	933	789	679	591	518	455
Average pellet energy in ft-lbs:	6.80	2.84	2.03	1.51	1.14	.88	.68
Time of flight in seconds:	0	.0529	.0879	.1290	.1764	.2306	.2925

Type of load: Target
Three-foot velocity: 1,330 ft./sec.
Hull: 2¾-inch plastic
Wad: Plastic
Shot: Hard lead
Buffered: No
Test barrel length: 30 inch
Pellets will pierce skin up to 134 yards.

NO. 7 LEAD PELLETS—1 OUNCE—299 PELLETS
Mfg: RIO **Manufacturer's code:** Basic Game
Recoil energy in 8-lb. shotgun: 16.2 ft./lbs. **Recoil velocity in 8-lb. shotgun:** 11.4 ft./sec.

Distance in yards:	Muzzle	20	30	40	50	60	70
Velocity in fps:	1,443	933	789	679	591	518	455
Average pellet energy in ft-lbs:	6.80	2.84	2.03	1.51	1.14	.88	.68
Time of flight in seconds:	0	.0529	.0879	.1290	.1764	.2306	.2925

Type of load: Field
Three-foot velocity: 1,330 ft./sec.
Hull: 2¾-inch plastic
Wad: Plastic
Shot: Hard lead
Buffered: No
Test barrel length: 30 inch
Pellets will pierce skin up to 134 yards.

NO. 7 LEAD PELLETS—1⅛ OUNCES—336 PELLETS
Mfg: ARMUSA **Manufacturer's code:** PLA-32
Recoil energy in 8-lb. shotgun: 26.8 ft./lbs. **Recoil velocity in 8-lb. shotgun:** 14.7 ft./sec.

Distance in yards:	Muzzle	20	30	40	50	60	70
Velocity in fps:	1,443	933	789	679	591	518	455
Average pellet energy in ft-lbs:	6.80	2.84	2.03	1.51	1.14	.88	.68
Time of flight in seconds:	0	.0529	.0879	.1290	.1764	.2306	.2925

Type of load: Sporting Clay
Three-foot velocity: 1,330 ft./sec.
Hull: 2¾-inch plastic
Wad: Plastic
Shot: Lead
Buffered: No
Test barrel length: 30 inch
Pellets will pierce skin up to 134 yards.

NO. 7 LEAD PELLETS—1⅛ OUNCES—336 PELLETS
Mfg: Baschieri & Pellagri **Manufacturer's code:** F2/MB Disperante
Recoil energy in 8-lb. shotgun: 21.2 ft./lbs. **Recoil velocity in 8-lb. shotgun:** 13.0 ft./sec.

Distance in yards:	Muzzle	20	30	40	50	60	70
Velocity in fps:	1,443	933	789	679	591	518	455
Average pellet energy in ft-lbs:	6.80	2.84	2.03	1.51	1.14	.88	.68
Time of flight in seconds:	0	.0529	.0879	.1290	.1764	.2306	.2925

Type of load: Sporting Clay
Three-foot velocity: 1,330 ft./sec.
Hull: 2¾-inch plastic
Wad: Plastic
Shot: Hard lead
Buffered: No
Test barrel length: 30 inch
Pellets will pierce skin up to 134 yards.

NO. 7 LEAD PELLETS—1⅛ OUNCES—336 PELLETS
Mfg: RIO **Manufacturer's code:** Super Game
Recoil energy in 8-lb. shotgun: 21.2 ft./lbs. **Recoil velocity in 8-lb. shotgun:** 13.0 ft./sec.

Distance in yards:	Muzzle	20	30	40	50	60	70
Velocity in fps:	1,443	933	789	679	591	518	455
Average pellet energy in ft-lbs:	6.80	2.84	2.03	1.51	1.14	.88	.68
Time of flight in seconds:	0	.0529	.0879	.1290	.1764	.2306	.2925

Type of load: Field
Three-foot velocity: 1,330 ft./sec.
Hull: 2¾-inch plastic
Wad: Plastic
Shot: Hard lead
Buffered: No
Test barrel length: 30 inch
Pellets will pierce skin up to 134 yards.

NO. 7 LEAD PELLETS—1⅛ OUNCES—336 PELLETS
Mfg: Baschieri & Pellagri **Manufacturer's code:** F2 Long Range
Recoil energy in 8-lb. shotgun: 26.8 ft./lbs. **Recoil velocity in 8-lb. shotgun:** 14.7 ft./sec.

Distance in yards:	Muzzle	20	30	40	50	60	70
Velocity in fps:	1,466	943	797	685	596	522	459
Average pellet energy in ft-lbs:	7.01	2.90	2.07	1.53	1.16	.89	.69
Time of flight in seconds:	0	.0522	.0869	.1276	.1746	.2285	.2898

Type of load: Field
Three-foot velocity: 1,350 ft./sec.
Hull: 2¾-inch plastic
Wad: Plastic
Shot: Lead
Buffered: No
Test barrel length: 30 inch
Pellets will pierce skin up to 134 yards.

NO. 7 LEAD PELLETS—1⅛ OUNCES—336 PELLETS
Mfg: Clever **Manufacturer's code:** T2 Light Game
Recoil energy in 8-lb. shotgun: 27.9 ft./lbs. **Recoil velocity in 8-lb. shotgun:** 15.0 ft./sec.

Distance in yards:	Muzzle	20	30	40	50	60	70
Velocity in fps:	1,466	943	797	685	596	522	459
Average pellet energy in ft-lbs:	7.01	2.90	2.07	1.53	1.16	.89	.69
Time of flight in seconds:	0	.0522	.0869	.1276	.1746	.2285	.2898

Type of load: Field
Three-foot velocity: 1,350 ft./sec.
Hull: 2¾-inch plastic
Wad: Plastic
Shot: Lead
Buffered: No
Test barrel length: 30 inch
Pellets will pierce skin up to 134 yards.

NO. 7 LEAD PELLETS—1³⁄₁₆ OUNCES—355 PELLETS
Mfg: Clever **Manufacturer's code:** T2 Felt Wad
Recoil energy in 8-lb. shotgun: 23.9 ft./lbs. **Recoil velocity in 8-lb. shotgun:** 13.9 ft./sec.

Distance in yards:	Muzzle	20	30	40	50	60	70
Velocity in fps:	1,382	906	769	663	578	507	446
Average pellet energy in ft-lbs:	6.23	2.68	1.93	1.44	1.09	.84	.65
Time of flight in seconds:	0	.0548	.0908	.1329	.1815	.2370	.3349

Type of load: Field
Three-foot velocity: 1,275 ft./sec.
Hull: 2¾-inch plastic
Wad: Felt/fiber
Shot: Lead
Buffered: No
Test barrel length: 30 inch
Pellets will pierce skin up to 132 yards.

NO. 7 LEAD PELLETS—1³⁄₁₆ OUNCES—355 PELLETS
Mfg: Clever **Manufacturer's code:** T2 Caccia
Recoil energy in 8-lb. shotgun: 25.2 ft./lbs. **Recoil velocity in 8-lb. shotgun:** 14.2 ft./sec.

Distance in yards:	Muzzle	20	30	40	50	60	70
Velocity in fps:	1,410	918	778	670	584	512	450
Average pellet energy in ft-lbs:	6.49	2.75	1.98	1.47	1.11	.86	.66
Time of flight in seconds:	0	.0539	.0895	.1311	.1791	.2340	.2966

Type of load: Field
Three-foot velocity: 1,300 ft./sec.
Hull: 2¾-inch plastic
Wad: Plastic
Shot: Lead
Buffered: No
Test barrel length: 30 inch
Pellets will pierce skin up to 133 yards.

NO. 7 LEAD PELLETS—1³⁄₁₆ OUNCES—355 PELLETS
Mfg: Clever **Manufacturer's code:** T2 34 Disperante
Recoil energy in 8-lb. shotgun: 25.2 ft./lbs. **Recoil velocity in 8-lb. shotgun:** 14.2 ft./sec.

Distance in yards:	Muzzle	20	30	40	50	60	70
Velocity in fps:	1,410	918	778	670	584	512	450
Average pellet energy in ft-lbs:	6.49	2.75	1.98	1.47	1.11	.86	.66
Time of flight in seconds:	0	.0539	.0895	.1311	.1791	.2340	.2966

Type of load: Field
Three-foot velocity: 1,300 ft./sec.
Hull: 2¾-inch plastic
Wad: Plastic spreader
Shot: Lead
Buffered: No
Test barrel length: 30 inch
Pellets will pierce skin up to 133 yards.

NO. 7 LEAD PELLETS—1³⁄₁₆ OUNCES—355 PELLETS
Mfg: RIO **Manufacturer's code:** Extra Game
Recoil energy in 8-lb. shotgun: 16.2 ft./lbs. **Recoil velocity in 8-lb. shotgun:** 11.4 ft./sec.

Distance in yards:	Muzzle	20	30	40	50	60	70
Velocity in fps:	1,443	933	789	679	591	518	455
Average pellet energy in ft-lbs:	6.80	2.84	2.03	1.51	1.14	.88	.68
Time of flight in seconds:	0	.0529	.0879	.1290	.1764	.2306	.2925

Type of load: Field
Three-foot velocity: 1,330 ft./sec.
Hull: 2¾-inch plastic
Wad: Plastic
Shot: Hard lead
Buffered: No
Test barrel length: 30 inch
Pellets will pierce skin up to 134 yards.

NO. 7 LEAD PELLETS—1¼ OUNCES—374 PELLETS
Mfg: ARMUSA **Manufacturer's code:** Live Pigeon
Recoil energy in 8-lb. shotgun: 31.1 ft./lbs. **Recoil velocity in 8-lb. shotgun:** 15.8 ft./sec.

Distance in yards:	Muzzle	20	30	40	50	60	70
Velocity in fps:	1,410	918	778	670	584	512	450
Average pellet energy in ft-lbs:	6.49	2.75	1.98	1.47	1.11	.86	.66
Time of flight in seconds:	0	.0539	.0895	.1311	.1791	.2340	.2966

Type of load: Target
Three-foot velocity: 1,300 ft./sec.
Hull: 2¾-inch plastic
Wad: Plastic
Shot: Nickel-plated lead
Buffered: No
Test barrel length: 30 inch
Pellets will pierce skin up to 133 yards.

NO. 7 LEAD PELLETS—1¼ OUNCES—374 PELLETS
Mfg: Baschieri & Pellagri **Manufacturer's code:** MB Extra
Recoil energy in 8-lb. shotgun: 31.1 ft./lbs. **Recoil velocity in 8-lb. shotgun:** 15.8 ft./sec.

Distance in yards:	Muzzle	20	30	40	50	60	70
Velocity in fps:	1,410	918	778	670	584	512	450
Average pellet energy in ft-lbs:	6.49	2.75	1.98	1.47	1.11	.86	.66
Time of flight in seconds:	0	.0539	.0895	.1311	.1791	.2340	.2966

Type of load: Field
Three-foot velocity: 1,300 ft./sec.
Hull: 2¾-inch plastic
Wad: Plastic
Shot: Lead
Buffered: No
Test barrel length: 30 inch
Pellets will pierce skin up to 133 yards.

NO. 7 LEAD PELLETS—1¼ OUNCES—374 PELLETS
Mfg: Clever **Manufacturer's code:** T4 High Velocity
Recoil energy in 8-lb. shotgun: 31.1 ft./lbs. **Recoil velocity in 8-lb. shotgun:** 15.8 ft./sec.

Distance in yards:	Muzzle	20	30	40	50	60	70
Velocity in fps:	1,410	918	778	670	584	512	450
Average pellet energy in ft-lbs:	6.49	2.75	1.98	1.47	1.11	.86	.66
Time of flight in seconds:	0	.0539	.0895	.1311	.1791	.2340	.2966

Type of load: Field
Three-foot velocity: 1,300 ft./sec.
Hull: 2¾-inch plastic
Wad: Plastic
Shot: Lead
Buffered: No
Test barrel length: 30 inch
Pellets will pierce skin up to 133 yards.

NO. 7 LEAD PELLETS—1¼ OUNCES—374 PELLETS
Mfg: Eley Hawk **Manufacturer's code:** Alphamax
Recoil energy in 8-lb. shotgun: 31.1 ft./lbs. **Recoil velocity in 8-lb. shotgun:** 15.8 ft./sec.

Distance in yards:	Muzzle	20	30	40	50	60	70
Velocity in fps:	1,410	918	778	670	584	512	450
Average pellet energy in ft-lbs:	6.49	2.75	1.98	1.47	1.11	.86	.66
Time of flight in seconds:	0	.0539	.0895	.1311	.1791	.2340	.2966

Type of load: Field
Three-foot velocity: 1,300 ft./sec.
Hull: 2¾-inch plastic
Wad: Plastic
Shot: Lead
Buffered: No
Test barrel length: 30 inch
Pellets will pierce skin up to 133 yards.

NO. 7 LEAD PELLETS—1¼ OUNCES—374 PELLETS
Mfg: Baschieri & Pellagri **Manufacturer's code:** F2 Long Range
Recoil energy in 8-lb. shotgun: 33.0 ft./lbs. **Recoil velocity in 8-lb. shotgun:** 16.3 ft./sec.

Distance in yards:	Muzzle	20	30	40	50	60	70
Velocity in fps:	1,443	933	789	679	591	518	455
Average pellet energy in ft-lbs:	6.80	2.84	2.03	1.51	1.14	.88	.68
Time of flight in seconds:	0	.0529	.0879	.1290	.1764	.2306	.2925

Type of load: Field
Three-foot velocity: 1,330 ft./sec.
Hull: 2¾-inch plastic
Wad: Plastic
Shot: Nickel-plated lead
Buffered: No
Test barrel length: 30 inch
Pellets will pierce skin up to 134 yards.

NO. 7 LEAD PELLETS—1¼ OUNCES—374 PELLETS
Mfg: Baschieri & Pellagri **Manufacturer's code:** Star Rossa High Velocity
Recoil energy in 8-lb. shotgun: 36.1 ft./lbs. **Recoil velocity in 8-lb. shotgun:** 17.0 ft./sec.

Distance in yards:	Muzzle	20	30	40	50	60	70
Velocity in fps:	1,443	933	789	679	591	518	455
Average pellet energy in ft-lbs:	6.80	2.84	2.03	1.51	1.14	.88	.68
Time of flight in seconds:	0	.0529	.0879	.1290	.1764	.2306	.2925

Type of load: Target
Three-foot velocity: 1,330 ft./sec.
Hull: 2¾-inch plastic
Wad: Plastic
Shot: Hard lead
Buffered: No
Test barrel length: 30 inch
Pellets will pierce skin up to 134 yards.

NO. 7 LEAD PELLETS—1¼ OUNCES—374 PELLETS
Mfg: RIO **Manufacturer's code:** Extra Game
Recoil energy in 8-lb. shotgun: 33.0 ft./lbs. **Recoil velocity in 8-lb. shotgun:** 16.3 ft./sec.

Distance in yards:	Muzzle	20	30	40	50	60	70
Velocity in fps:	1,443	933	789	679	591	518	455
Average pellet energy in ft-lbs:	6.80	2.84	2.03	1.51	1.14	.88	.68
Time of flight in seconds:	0	.0529	.0879	.1290	.1764	.2306	.2925

Type of load: Field
Three-foot velocity: 1,330 ft./sec.
Hull: 2¾-inch plastic
Wad: Plastic
Shot: Hard lead
Buffered: No
Test barrel length: 30 inch
Pellets will pierce skin up to 134 yards.

NO. 7 LEAD PELLETS—1⅜ OUNCES—411 PELLETS
Mfg: Clever **Manufacturer's code:** T4 Caccia
Recoil energy in 8-lb. shotgun: 35.7 ft./lbs. **Recoil velocity in 8-lb. shotgun:** 16.9 ft./sec.

Distance in yards:	Muzzle	20	30	40	50	60	70
Velocity in fps:	1,382	906	769	663	578	507	446
Average pellet energy in ft-lbs:	6.23	2.68	1.93	1.44	1.09	.84	.65
Time of flight in seconds:	0	.0548	.0908	.1329	.1815	.2370	.3349

Type of load: Field
Three-foot velocity: 1,275 ft./sec.
Hull: 2¾-inch plastic
Wad: Plastic
Shot: Lead
Buffered: No
Test barrel length: 30 inch
Pellets will pierce skin up to 132 yards.

NO. 7½ LEAD PELLETS—⅞ OUNCES—302 PELLETS
Mfg: Fiocchi **Manufacturer's code:** 1278OZ
Recoil energy in 8-lb. shotgun: 12.3 ft./lbs. **Recoil velocity in 8-lb. shotgun:** 10.0 ft./sec.

Distance in yards:	Muzzle	20	30	40	50	60	70
Velocity in fps:	1,302	854	724	623	541	472	412
Average pellet energy in ft-lbs:	4.74	2.04	1.47	1.09	.82	.62	.47
Time of flight in seconds:	0	.0581	.0964	.1412	.1930	.2524	.3204

Type of load: Target & Trainer
Three-foot velocity: 1,200 ft./sec.
Hull: 2¾-inch plastic
Wad: Plastic
Shot: Hard lead
Buffered: No
Test barrel length: 30 inch
Pellets will pierce skin up to 136 yards.

NO. 7½ LEAD PELLETS—⅞ OUNCE—302 PELLETS
Mfg: Estate Cartridge **Manufacturer's code:** ML12
Recoil energy in 8-lb. shotgun: 13.7 ft./lbs. **Recoil velocity in 8-lb. shotgun:** 10.5 ft./sec.

Distance in yards:	Muzzle	20	30	40	50	60	70
Velocity in fps:	1,357	878	742	637	553	482	421
Average pellet energy in ft-lbs:	5.16	2.16	1.54	1.14	.86	.65	.50
Time of flight in seconds:	0	.0562	.0935	.1372	.1878	.2459	.3126

Type of load: Target
Three-foot velocity: 1,250 ft./sec.
Hull: 2¾-inch plastic
Wad: Plastic
Shot: Hard lead
Buffered: No
Test barrel length: 30 inch
Pellets will pierce skin up to 125 yards.

NO. 7½ LEAD PELLETS—⅞ OUNCE—302 PELLETS
Mfg: Eley Hawk **Manufacturer's code:** Olympic 2000
Recoil energy in 8-lb. shotgun: 15.2 ft./lbs. **Recoil velocity in 8-lb. shotgun:** 11.1 ft./sec.

Distance in yards:	Muzzle	20	30	40	50	60	70
Velocity in fps:	1,413	903	761	652	565	492	430
Average pellet energy in ft-lbs:	5.59	2.28	1.62	1.19	.89	.68	.52
Time of flight in seconds:	0	.0544	.0907	.1334	.1829	.2399	.3052

Type of load: Target
Three-foot velocity: 1,300 ft./sec.
Hull: 2¾-inch plastic
Wad: Plastic
Shot: Lead
Buffered: No
Test barrel length: 30 inch
Pellets will pierce skin up to 126 yards.

NO. 7½ LEAD PELLETS—⅞ OUNCE—302 PELLETS
Mfg: Eley Hawk **Manufacturer's code:** VIP
Recoil energy in 8-lb. shotgun: 16.2 ft./lbs. **Recoil velocity in 8-lb. shotgun:** 11.4 ft./sec.

Distance in yards:	Muzzle	20	30	40	50	60	70
Velocity in fps:	1,447	917	771	660	571	498	435
Average pellet energy in ft-lbs:	5.86	2.36	1.66	1.22	.91	.69	.53
Time of flight in seconds:	0	.0534	.0891	.1313	.1802	.2365	.3010

Type of load: Target
Three-foot velocity: 1,330 ft./sec.
Hull: 2¾-inch plastic
Wad: Plastic
Shot: Hard lead
Buffered: No
Test barrel length: 30 inch
Pellets will pierce skin up to 127 yards.

NO. 7½ LEAD PELLETS—⅞ OUNCE—302 PELLETS
Mfg: Federal Cartridge Co. **Manufacturer's code:** N110
Recoil energy in 8-lb. shotgun: 16.2 ft./lbs. **Recoil velocity in 8-lb. shotgun:** 11.4 ft./sec.

Distance in yards:	Muzzle	20	30	40	50	60	70
Velocity in fps:	1,447	917	771	660	571	498	435
Average pellet energy in ft-lbs:	5.86	2.36	1.66	1.22	.91	.69	.53
Time of flight in seconds:	0	.0534	.0891	.1313	.1802	.2365	.3010

Type of load: Target
Three-foot velocity: 1,330 ft./sec.
Hull: 2¾-inch plastic
Wad: Plastic
Shot: Copper-plated lead
Buffered: No
Test barrel length: 30 inch
Pellets will pierce skin up to 127 yards.

NO. 7½ LEAD PELLETS—⅞ OUNCE—302 PELLETS
Mfg: Federal Cartridge Co. **Manufacturer's code:** N119
Recoil energy in 8-lb. shotgun: 16.2 ft./lbs. **Recoil velocity in 8-lb. shotgun:** 11.4 ft./sec.

Distance in yards:	Muzzle	20	30	40	50	60	70
Velocity in fps:	1,447	917	771	660	571	498	435
Average pellet energy in ft-lbs:	5.86	2.36	1.66	1.22	.91	.69	.53
Time of flight in seconds:	0	.0534	.0891	.1313	.1802	.2365	.3010

Type of load: Target
Three-foot velocity: 1,330 ft./sec.
Hull: 2¾-inch paper
Wad: Plastic
Shot: Copper-plated lead
Buffered: No
Test barrel length: 30 inch
Pellets will pierce skin up to 127 yards.

NO. 7½ LEAD PELLETS—⅞ OUNCE—302 PELLETS
Mfg: Remington Arms Co. **Manufacturer's code:** STS12IT
Recoil energy in 8-lb. shotgun: 16.2 ft./lbs. **Recoil velocity in 8-lb. shotgun:** 11.4 ft./sec.

Distance in yards:	Muzzle	20	30	40	50	60	70
Velocity in fps:	1,447	917	771	660	571	498	435
Average pellet energy in ft-lbs:	5.86	2.36	1.66	1.22	.91	.69	.53
Time of flight in seconds:	0	.0534	.0891	.1313	.1802	.2365	.3010

Type of load: Target
Three-foot velocity: 1,330 ft./sec.
Hull: 2¾-inch plastic
Wad: Plastic
Shot: Hard lead
Buffered: No
Test barrel length: 30 inch
Pellets will pierce skin up to 127 yards.

NO. 7½ LEAD PELLETS—⅞ OUNCE—302 PELLETS
Mfg: Sellier & Bellot **Manufacturer's code:** SBA01241
Recoil energy in 8-lb. shotgun: 16.2 ft./lbs. **Recoil velocity in 8-lb. shotgun:** 11.4 ft./sec.

Distance in yards:	Muzzle	20	30	40	50	60	70
Velocity in fps:	1,447	917	771	660	571	498	435
Average pellet energy in ft-lbs:	5.86	2.36	1.66	1.22	.91	.69	.53
Time of flight in seconds:	0	.0534	.0891	.1313	.1802	.2365	.3010

Type of load: Target
Three-foot velocity: 1,330 ft./sec.
Hull: 2¾-inch plastic
Wad: Plastic
Shot: Lead
Buffered: No
Test barrel length: 30 inch
Pellets will pierce skin up to 127 yards.

NO. 7½ LEAD PELLETS—⅞ OUNCE—302 PELLETS
Mfg: Winchester **Manufacturer's code:** AANL12
Recoil energy in 8-lb. shotgun: 16.2 ft./lbs. **Recoil velocity in 8-lb. shotgun:** 11.4 ft./sec.

Distance in yards:	Muzzle	20	30	40	50	60	70
Velocity in fps:	1,447	917	771	660	571	498	435
Average pellet energy in ft-lbs:	5.86	2.36	1.66	1.22	.91	.69	.53
Time of flight in seconds:	0	.0534	.0891	.1313	.1802	.2365	.3010

Type of load: Target
Three-foot velocity: 1,330 ft./sec.
Hull: 2¾-inch plastic
Wad: Plastic
Shot: Hard lead
Buffered: No
Test barrel length: 30 inch
Pellets will pierce skin up to 127 yards.

NO. 7½ LEAD PELLETS—⅞ OUNCE—302 PELLETS
Mfg: Baschieri & Pellagri **Manufacturer's code:** N/A
Recoil energy in 8-lb. shotgun: 22.0 ft./lbs. **Recoil velocity in 8-lb. shotgun:** 13.3 ft./sec.

Distance in yards:	Muzzle	20	30	40	50	60	70
Velocity in fps:	1,469	927	778	666	576	502	438
Average pellet energy in ft-lbs:	6.04	2.41	1.70	1.24	.93	.70	.54
Time of flight in seconds:	0	.0527	.0881	.1299	.1784	.2343	.2983

Type of load: Comp-2000 24 gr.
Three-foot velocity: 1,350 ft./sec.
Hull: 2¾-inch plastic
Wad: Plastic
Shot: Hard lead
Buffered: No
Test barrel length: 30 inch
Pellets will pierce skin up to 128 yards.

NO. 7½ LEAD PELLETS—⅞ OUNCE—302 PELLETS
Mfg: Fiocchi **Manufacturer's code:** 12IN24
Recoil energy in 8-lb. shotgun: 16.9 ft./lbs. **Recoil velocity in 8-lb. shotgun:** 11.6 ft./sec.

Distance in yards:	Muzzle	20	30	40	50	60	70
Velocity in fps:	1,469	927	778	666	576	502	438
Average pellet energy in ft-lbs:	6.04	2.41	1.70	1.24	.93	.70	.54
Time of flight in seconds:	0	.0527	.0881	.1299	.1784	.2343	.2983

Type of load: Target
Three-foot velocity: 1,350 ft./sec.
Hull: 2¾-inch plastic
Wad: Plastic
Shot: Hard lead
Buffered: No
Test barrel length: 30 inch
Pellets will pierce skin up to 128 yards.

NO.7½ LEAD PELLETS—⅞ OUNCE—302 PELLETS
Mfg: Kent Cartridge America/Canada **Manufacturer's code:** K122ITR24
Recoil energy in 8-lb. shotgun: 16.9 ft./lbs. **Recoil velocity in 8-lb. shotgun:** 11.6 ft./sec.

Distance in yards:	Muzzle	20	30	40	50	60	70
Velocity in fps:	1,469	927	778	666	576	502	438
Average pellet energy in ft-lbs:	6.04	2.41	1.70	1.24	.93	.70	.54
Time of flight in seconds:	0	.0527	.0881	.1299	.1784	.2343	.2983

Type of load: Target
Three-foot velocity: 1,350 ft./sec.
Hull: 2¾-inch plastic
Wad: Plastic
Shot: Lead
Buffered: No
Test barrel length: 30 inch
Pellets will pierce skin up to 128 yards.

NO. 7½ LEAD PELLETS—⅞ OUNCE—302 PELLETS
Mfg: Estate Cartridge **Manufacturer's code:** INT24
Recoil energy in 8-lb. shotgun: 17.7 ft./lbs. **Recoil velocity in 8-lb. shotgun:** 11.9 ft./sec.

Distance in yards:	Muzzle	20	30	40	50	60	70
Velocity in fps:	1,497	939	787	673	582	506	442
Average pellet energy in ft-lbs:	6.27	2.47	1.73	1.27	.95	.72	.55
Time of flight in seconds:	0	.0519	.0869	.1282	.1762	.2316	.2950

Type of load: Target
Three-foot velocity: 1,375 ft./sec.
Hull: 2¾-inch plastic
Wad: Plastic
Shot: Hard lead
Buffered: No
Test barrel length: 30 inch
Pellets will pierce skin up to 129 yards.

NO. 7½ LEAD PELLETS—⅞ OUNCE—302 PELLETS
Mfg: RIO **Manufacturer's code:** Trap 24
Recoil energy in 8-lb. shotgun: 17.7 ft./lbs. **Recoil velocity in 8-lb. shotgun:** 11.9 ft./sec.

Distance in yards:	Muzzle	20	30	40	50	60	70
Velocity in fps:	1,497	939	787	673	582	506	442
Average pellet energy in ft-lbs:	6.27	2.47	1.73	1.27	.95	.72	.55
Time of flight in seconds:	0	.0519	.0869	.1282	.1762	.2316	.2950

Type of load: Field
Three-foot velocity: 1,375 ft./sec.
Hull: 2¾-inch plastic
Wad: Plastic
Shot: Hard lead
Buffered: No
Test barrel length: 30 inch
Pellets will pierce skin up to 129 yards.

NO. 7½ LEAD PELLETS—⅞ OUNCE—302 PELLETS
Mfg: RST, Ltd. **Manufacturer's code:** N/A
Recoil energy in 8-lb. shotgun: 18.6 ft./lbs. **Recoil velocity in 8-lb. shotgun:** 12.2 ft./sec.

Distance in yards:	Muzzle	20	30	40	50	60	70
Velocity in fps:	1,525	951	796	679	587	511	446
Average pellet energy in ft-lbs:	6.51	2.53	1.77	1.29	.96	.73	.56
Time of flight in seconds:	0	.0511	.0857	.1265	.1741	.2290	.2918

Type of load: Target
Three-foot velocity: 1,400 ft./sec.
Hull: 2¾-inch plastic
Wad: Plastic
Shot: Lead
Buffered: No
Test barrel length: 30 inch
Pellets will pierce skin up to 129 yards.

NO. 7½ LEAD PELLETS—1 OUNCE—350 PELLETS
Mfg: Eley Hawk **Manufacturer's code:** Subsonic
Recoil energy in 8-lb. shotgun: 9.8 ft./lbs. **Recoil velocity in 8-lb. shotgun:** 8.9 ft./sec.

Distance in yards:	Muzzle	20	30	40	50	60	70
Velocity in fps:	1,021	846	618	537	468	409	357
Average pellet energy in ft-lbs:	2.92	1.44	1.07	.81	.61	.47	.36
Time of flight in seconds:	0	.0710	.1161	.1683	.2282	.2967	.3753

Type of load: Target
Three-foot velocity: 1,000 ft./sec.
Hull: 2¾-inch plastic
Wad: Plastic
Shot: Lead
Buffered: No
Test barrel length: 30 inch
Pellets will pierce skin up to 113 yards.

NO. 7½ LEAD PELLETS—1 OUNCE—350 PELLETS
Mfg: RST, Ltd. **Manufacturer's code:** N/A
Recoil energy in 8-lb. shotgun: 11.4 ft./lbs. **Recoil velocity in 8-lb. shotgun:** 9.6 ft./sec.

Distance in yards:	Muzzle	20	30	40	50	60	70
Velocity in fps:	1,135	776	664	575	501	437	382
Average pellet energy in ft-lbs:	3.61	1.69	1.23	.92	.70	.53	.41
Time of flight in seconds:	0	.0650	.1068	.1555	.2114	.2756	.3490

Type of load: Target
Three-foot velocity: 1,050 ft./sec.
Hull: 2¾-inch plastic
Wad: Plastic
Shot: Lead
Buffered: No
Test barrel length: 30 inch
Pellets will pierce skin up to 118 yards.

NO. 7½ LEAD PELLETS—1 OUNCE—350 PELLETS
Mfg: Baschieri & Pellagri **Manufacturer's code:** N/A
Recoil energy in 8-lb. shotgun: 13.9 ft./lbs. **Recoil velocity in 8-lb. shotgun:** 10.6 ft./sec.

Distance in yards:	Muzzle	20	30	40	50	60	70
Velocity in fps:	1,229	821	699	603	524	458	400
Average pellet energy in ft-lbs:	4.23	1089	1.37	1.02	.077	.59	.45
Time of flight in seconds:	0	.0609	.1006	.1469	.2003	.2616	.3318

Type of load: F2 Target
Three-foot velocity: 1,135 ft./sec.
Hull: 2¾-inch plastic
Wad: Plastic
Shot: Hard lead
Buffered: No
Test barrel length: 30 inch
Pellets will pierce skin up to 121 yards.

NO. 7½ LEAD PELLETS—1 OUNCE—350 PELLETS
Mfg: Federal Cartridge Co. **Manufacturer's code:** T175
Recoil energy in 8-lb. shotgun: 14.2 ft./lbs. **Recoil velocity in 8-lb. shotgun:** 10.7 ft./sec.

Distance in yards:	Muzzle	20	30	40	50	60	70
Velocity in fps:	1,241	826	703	606	527	460	401
Average pellet energy in ft-lbs:	4.31	1.91	1.38	1.03	.78	.59	.45
Time of flight in seconds:	0	.0604	.0999	.1460	.1991	.2601	.3300

Type of load: Target
Three-foot velocity: 1,145 ft./sec.
Hull: 2¾-inch paper
Wad: Plastic
Shot: Hard lead
Buffered: No
Test barrel length: 30 inch
Pellets will pierce skin up to 121 yards.

NO. 7½ LEAD PELLETS—1 OUNCE—350 PELLETS
Mfg: Fiocchi **Manufacturer's code:** 12TL
Recoil energy in 8-lb. shotgun: 18.2 ft./lbs. **Recoil velocity in 8-lb. shotgun:** 12.1 ft./sec.

Distance in yards:	Muzzle	20	30	40	50	60	70
Velocity in fps:	1,246	829	705	607	528	461	402
Average pellet energy in ft-lbs:	4.35	1.92	1.39	1.03	.78	.59	.45
Time of flight in seconds:	0	.0602	.0996	.1455	.1985	.2594	.3290

Type of load: Target
Three-foot velocity: 1,150 ft./sec.
Hull: 2¾-inch plastic
Wad: Plastic
Shot: Hard lead
Buffered: No
Test barrel length: 30 inch
Pellets will pierce skin up to 122 yards.

NO. 7½ LEAD PELLETS—1 OUNCE—350 PELLETS
Mfg: Dionisi **Manufacturer's code:** D 12 TLX
Recoil energy in 8-lb. shotgun: 15.2 ft./lbs. **Recoil velocity in 8-lb. shotgun:** 11.1 ft./sec.

Distance in yards:	Muzzle	20	30	40	50	60	70
Velocity in fps:	1,274	841	714	615	535	466	407
Average pellet energy in ft-lbs:	4.54	1.98	1.43	1.06	.80	.61	.46
Time of flight in seconds:	0	.0592	.0980	.1433	.1957	.2558	.3246

Type of load: Target
Three-foot velocity: 1,175 ft./sec.
Hull: 2¾-inch plastic
Wad: Plastic
Shot: Lead
Buffered: No
Test barrel length: 30 inch
Pellets will pierce skin up to 122 yards.

NO. 7½ LEAD PELLETS—1 OUNCE—350 PELLETS
Mfg: Estate Cartridge **Manufacturer's code:** CT12L1/SS12L1
Recoil energy in 8-lb. shotgun: 15.2 ft./lbs. **Recoil velocity in 8-lb. shotgun:** 11.1 ft./sec.

Distance in yards:	Muzzle	20	30	40	50	60	70
Velocity in fps:	1,274	841	714	615	535	466	407
Average pellet energy in ft-lbs:	4.54	1.98	1.43	1.06	.80	.61	.46
Time of flight in seconds:	0	.0592	.0980	.1433	.1957	.2558	.3246

Type of load: Target
Three-foot velocity: 1,175 ft./sec.
Hull: 2¾-inch plastic
Wad: Plastic
Shot: Hard lead
Buffered: No
Test barrel length: 30 inch
Pellets will pierce skin up to 122 yards.

NO. 7½ LEAD PELLETS—1 OUNCE—350 PELLETS
Mfg: Federal Cartridge Co. **Manufacturer's code:** T113
Recoil energy in 8-lb. shotgun: 15.2 ft./lbs. **Recoil velocity in 8-lb. shotgun:** 11.1 ft./sec.

Distance in yards:	Muzzle	20	30	40	50	60	70
Velocity in fps:	1,274	841	714	615	535	466	407
Average pellet energy in ft-lbs:	4.54	1.98	1.43	1.06	.80	.61	.46
Time of flight in seconds:	0	.0592	.0980	.1433	.1957	.2558	.3246

Type of load: Target
Three-foot velocity: 1,175 ft./sec.
Hull: 2¾-inch plastic
Wad: Plastic
Shot: Hard lead
Buffered: No
Test barrel length: 30 inch
Pellets will pierce skin up to 122 yards.

NO. 7½ LEAD PELLETS—1 OUNCE—350 PELLETS
Mfg: PMC (Eldorado Cartridge Corp.) **Manufacturer's code:** CB127.5
Recoil energy in 8-lb. shotgun: 15.2 ft./lbs. **Recoil velocity in 8-lb. shotgun:** 11.1 ft./sec.

Distance in yards:	Muzzle	20	30	40	50	60	70
Velocity in fps:	1,274	841	714	615	535	466	407
Average pellet energy in ft-lbs:	4.54	1.98	1.43	1.06	.80	.61	.46
Time of flight in seconds:	0	.0592	.0980	.1433	.1957	.2558	.3246

Type of load: Cowboy
Three-foot velocity: 1,175 ft./sec.
Hull: 2¾-inch plastic
Wad: Plastic
Shot: Lead
Buffered: No
Test barrel length: 30 inch
Pellets will pierce skin up to 122 yards.

NO. 7½ LEAD PELLETS—1 OUNCE—350 PELLETS
Mfg: Polywad **Manufacturer's code:** SRL127
Recoil energy in 8-lb. shotgun: 15.2 ft./lbs. **Recoil velocity in 8-lb. shotgun:** 11.1 ft./sec.

Distance in yards:	Muzzle	20	30	40	50	60	70
Velocity in fps:	1,274	841	714	615	535	466	407
Average pellet energy in ft-lbs:	4.54	1.98	1.43	1.06	.80	.61	.46
Time of flight in seconds:	0	.0592	.0980	.1433	.1957	.2558	.3246

Type of load: Field
Three-foot velocity: 1,175 ft./sec.
Hull: 2¾-inch plastic
Wad: Plastic
Shot: Lead
Buffered: No
Test barrel length: 30 inch
Pellets will pierce skin up to 122 yards.

NO. 7½ LEAD PELLETS—1 OUNCE—350 PELLETS
Mfg: Remington Arms Co. **Manufacturer's code:** STS121
Recoil energy in 8-lb. shotgun: 15.2 ft./lbs. **Recoil velocity in 8-lb. shotgun:** 11.1 ft./sec.

Distance in yards:	Muzzle	20	30	40	50	60	70
Velocity in fps:	1,274	841	714	615	535	466	407
Average pellet energy in ft-lbs:	4.54	1.98	1.43	1.06	.80	.61	.46
Time of flight in seconds:	0	.0592	.0980	.1433	.1957	.2558	.3246

Type of load: Target
Three-foot velocity: 1,175 ft./sec.
Hull: 2¾-inch plastic
Wad: Plastic
Shot: Hard lead
Buffered: No
Test barrel length: 30 inch
Pellets will pierce skin up to 122 yards.

NO. 7½ LEAD PELLETS—1 OUNCE—350 PELLETS
Mfg: RST, Ltd. **Manufacturer's code:** N/A
Recoil energy in 8-lb. shotgun: 15.2 ft./lbs. **Recoil velocity in 8-lb. shotgun:** 11.1 ft./sec.

Distance in yards:	Muzzle	20	30	40	50	60	70
Velocity in fps:	1,274	841	714	615	535	466	407
Average pellet energy in ft-lbs:	4.54	1.98	1.43	1.06	.80	.61	.46
Time of flight in seconds:	0	.0592	.0980	.1433	.1957	.2558	.3246

Type of load: Target
Three-foot velocity: 1,175 ft./sec.
Hull: 2¾-inch plastic
Wad: Plastic
Shot: Lead
Buffered: No
Test barrel length: 30 inch
Pellets will pierce skin up to 122 yards.

NO. 7½ LEAD PELLETS—1 OUNCE—350 PELLETS
Mfg: Winchester **Manufacturer's code:** AAL12
Recoil energy in 8-lb. shotgun: 15.2 ft./lbs. **Recoil velocity in 8-lb. shotgun:** 11.1 ft./sec.

Distance in yards:	Muzzle	20	30	40	50	60	70
Velocity in fps:	1,274	841	714	615	535	466	407
Average pellet energy in ft-lbs:	4.54	1.98	1.43	1.06	.80	.61	.46
Time of flight in seconds:	0	.0592	.0980	.1433	.1957	.2558	.3246

Type of load: Target
Three-foot velocity: 1,175 ft./sec.
Hull: 2¾-inch plastic
Wad: Plastic
Shot: Hard lead
Buffered: No
Test barrel length: 30 inch
Pellets will pierce skin up to 122 yards.

NO. 7½ LEAD PELLETS—1 OUNCE—350 PELLETS
Mfg: Fiocchi **Manufacturer's code:** 12TH
Recoil energy in 8-lb. shotgun: 16.1 ft./lbs. **Recoil velocity in 8-lb. shotgun:** 11.4 ft./sec.

Distance in yards:	Muzzle	20	30	40	50	60	70
Velocity in fps:	1,302	854	724	623	541	472	412
Average pellet energy in ft-lbs:	4.74	2.04	1.47	1.09	.82	.62	.47
Time of flight in seconds:	0	.0581	.0964	.1412	.1930	.2524	.3204

Type of load: Target
Three-foot velocity: 1,200 ft./sec.
Hull: 2¾-inch plastic
Wad: Plastic
Shot: Hard lead
Buffered: No
Test barrel length: 30 inch
Pellets will pierce skin up to 136 yards.

NO. 7½ LEAD PELLETS—1 OUNCE—350 PELLETS
Mfg: Kent Cartridge America/Canada **Manufacturer's code:** K122UG28
Recoil energy in 8-lb. shotgun: 16.1 ft./lbs. **Recoil velocity in 8-lb. shotgun:** 11.4 ft./sec.

Distance in yards:	Muzzle	20	30	40	50	60	70
Velocity in fps:	1,302	854	724	623	541	472	412
Average pellet energy in ft-lbs:	4.74	2.04	1.47	1.09	.82	.62	.47
Time of flight in seconds:	0	.0581	.0964	.1412	.1930	.2524	.3204

Type of load: Field
Three-foot velocity: 1,200 ft./sec.
Hull: 2¾-inch plastic
Wad: Plastic
Shot: Lead
Buffered: No
Test barrel length: 30 inch
Pellets will pierce skin up to 136 yards.

NO. 7½ LEAD PELLETS—1 OUNCE—350 PELLETS
Mfg: Kent Cartridge America/Canada **Manufacturer's code:** K122LSC28
Recoil energy in 8-lb. shotgun: 16.1 ft./lbs. **Recoil velocity in 8-lb. shotgun:** 11.4 ft./sec.

Distance in yards:	Muzzle	20	30	40	50	60	70
Velocity in fps:	1,302	854	724	623	541	472	412
Average pellet energy in ft-lbs:	4.74	2.04	1.47	1.09	.82	.62	.47
Time of flight in seconds:	0	.0581	.0964	.1412	.1930	.2524	.3204

Type of load: Target
Three-foot velocity: 1,200 ft./sec.
Hull: 2¾-inch plastic
Wad: Plastic
Shot: Lead
Buffered: No
Test barrel length: 30 inch
Pellets will pierce skin up to 136 yards.

NO. 7½ LEAD PELLETS—1 OUNCE—350 PELLETS
Mfg: Aguila **Manufacturer's code:** N/A
Recoil energy in 8-lb. shotgun: 20.4 ft./lbs. **Recoil velocity in 8-lb. shotgun:** 12.8 ft./sec.

Distance in yards:	Muzzle	20	30	40	50	60	70
Velocity in fps:	1,302	854	724	623	541	472	412
Average pellet energy in ft-lbs:	4.74	2.04	1.47	1.09	.82	.62	.47
Time of flight in seconds:	0	.0581	.0964	.1412	.1930	.2524	.3204

Type of load: Field
Three-foot velocity: 1,200 ft./sec.
Hull: 2¾-inch plastic
Wad: Plastic
Shot: Lead
Buffered: No
Test barrel length: 30 inch
Pellets will pierce skin up to 136 yards.

NO. 7½ LEAD PELLETS—1 OUNCE—350 PELLETS
Mfg: Baschieri & Pellagri **Manufacturer's code:** N/A
Recoil energy in 8-lb. shotgun: 17.4 ft./lbs. **Recoil velocity in 8-lb. shotgun:** 11.8 ft./sec.

Distance in yards:	Muzzle	20	30	40	50	60	70
Velocity in fps:	1,341	871	737	633	549	479	418
Average pellet energy in ft-lbs:	5.03	2.12	1.52	1.12	.84	.64	.49
Time of flight in seconds:	0	.0568	.0943	.1383	.1893	.2478	.3149

Type of load: Comp-2000 32 gr.
Three-foot velocity: 1,235 ft./sec.
Hull: 2¾-inch plastic
Wad: Plastic
Shot: Hard lead
Buffered: No
Test barrel length: 30 inch
Pellets will pierce skin up to 124 yards.

NO. 7½ LEAD PELLETS—1 OUNCE—350 PELLETS
Mfg: Dionisi **Manufacturer's code:** D 12 GT
Recoil energy in 8-lb. shotgun: 16.8 ft./lbs. **Recoil velocity in 8-lb. shotgun:** 11.6 ft./sec.

Distance in yards:	Muzzle	20	30	40	50	60	70
Velocity in fps:	1,341	871	737	633	549	479	418
Average pellet energy in ft-lbs:	5.03	2.12	1.52	1.12	.84	.64	.49
Time of flight in seconds:	0	.0568	.0943	.1383	.1893	.2478	.3149

Type of load: Game & Target
Three-foot velocity: 1,235 ft./sec.
Hull: 2¾-inch plastic
Wad: Plastic
Shot: Lead
Buffered: No
Test barrel length: 30 inch
Pellets will pierce skin up to 124 yards.

NO. 7½ LEAD PELLETS—1 OUNCE—350 PELLETS
Mfg: Estate Cartridge **Manufacturer's code:** CT12H1/SS12H1
Recoil energy in 8-lb. shotgun: 17.4 ft./lbs. **Recoil velocity in 8-lb. shotgun:** 11.8 ft./sec.

Distance in yards:	Muzzle	20	30	40	50	60	70
Velocity in fps:	1,341	871	737	633	549	479	418
Average pellet energy in ft-lbs:	5.03	2.12	1.52	1.12	.84	.64	.49
Time of flight in seconds:	0	.0568	.0943	.1383	.1893	.2478	.3149

Type of load: Target
Three-foot velocity: 1,235 ft./sec.
Hull: 2¾-inch plastic
Wad: Plastic
Shot: Hard lead
Buffered: No
Test barrel length: 30 inch
Pellets will pierce skin up to 124 yards.

NO. 7½ LEAD PELLETS—1 OUNCE—350 PELLETS
Mfg: Fiocchi **Manufacturer's code:** 12MS3
Recoil energy in 8-lb. shotgun: 17.9 ft./lbs. **Recoil velocity in 8-lb. shotgun:** 12.0 ft./sec.

Distance in yards:	Muzzle	20	30	40	50	60	70
Velocity in fps:	1,357	878	742	637	553	482	421
Average pellet energy in ft-lbs:	5.16	2.16	1.54	1.14	.86	.65	.50
Time of flight in seconds:	0	.0562	.0935	.1372	.1878	.2459	.3126

Type of load: Field
Three-foot velocity: 1,250 ft./sec.
Hull: 2¾-inch plastic
Wad: Plastic
Shot: Lead
Buffered: No
Test barrel length: 30 inch
Pellets will pierce skin up to 125 yards.

NO. 7½ LEAD PELLETS—1 OUNCE—350 PELLETS
Mfg: Fiocchi **Manufacturer's code:** 12TX
Recoil energy in 8-lb. shotgun: 17.9 ft./lbs. **Recoil velocity in 8-lb. shotgun:** 12.0 ft./sec.

Distance in yards:	Muzzle	20	30	40	50	60	70
Velocity in fps:	1,357	878	742	637	553	482	421
Average pellet energy in ft-lbs:	5.16	2.16	1.54	1.14	.86	.65	.50
Time of flight in seconds:	0	.0562	.0935	.1372	.1878	.2459	.3126

Type of load: Target
Three-foot velocity: 1,250 ft./sec.
Hull: 2¾-inch plastic
Wad: Plastic
Shot: Hard lead
Buffered: No
Test barrel length: 30 inch
Pellets will pierce skin up to 125 yards.

NO. 7½ LEAD PELLETS—1 OUNCE—350 PELLETS
Mfg: Eley Hawk **Manufacturer's code:** Black Trap
Recoil energy in 8-lb. shotgun: 18.9 ft./lbs. **Recoil velocity in 8-lb. shotgun:** 12.3 ft./sec.

Distance in yards:	Muzzle	20	30	40	50	60	70
Velocity in fps:	1,385	891	752	645	559	487	425
Average pellet energy in ft-lbs:	5.37	2.22	1.58	1.16	.87	.66	.51
Time of flight in seconds:	0	.0553	.0921	.1652	.1853	.2429	.3088

Type of load: Target
Three-foot velocity: 1,275 ft./sec.
Hull: 2¾-inch plastic
Wad: Plastic
Shot: Lead
Buffered: No
Test barrel length: 30 inch
Pellets will pierce skin up to 126 yards.

NO. 7½ LEAD PELLETS—1 OUNCE—350 PELLETS
Mfg: Dionisi **Manufacturer's code:** D 12 DQ
Recoil energy in 8-lb. shotgun: 19.9 ft./lbs. **Recoil velocity in 8-lb. shotgun:** 12.6 ft./sec.

Distance in yards:	Muzzle	20	30	40	50	60	70
Velocity in fps:	1,413	903	761	652	565	492	430
Average pellet energy in ft-lbs:	5.59	2.28	1.62	1.19	.89	.68	.52
Time of flight in seconds:	0	.0544	.0907	.1334	.1829	.2399	.3052

Type of load: Dove & Quail
Three-foot velocity: 1,300 ft./sec.
Hull: 2¾-inch plastic
Wad: Plastic
Shot: Lead
Buffered: No
Test barrel length: 30 inch
Pellets will pierce skin up to 126 yards.

NO. 7½ LEAD PELLETS—1 OUNCE—350 PELLETS
Mfg: Eley Hawk **Manufacturer's code:** Olympic 2000
Recoil energy in 8-lb. shotgun: 19.9 ft./lbs. **Recoil velocity in 8-lb. shotgun:** 12.6 ft./sec.

Distance in yards:	Muzzle	20	30	40	50	60	70
Velocity in fps:	1,413	903	761	652	565	492	430
Average pellet energy in ft-lbs:	5.59	2.28	1.62	1.19	.89	.68	.52
Time of flight in seconds:	0	.0544	.0907	.1334	.1829	.2399	.3052

Type of load: Target
Three-foot velocity: 1,300 ft./sec.
Hull: 2¾-inch plastic
Wad: Plastic
Shot: Lead
Buffered: No
Test barrel length: 30 inch
Pellets will pierce skin up to 126 yards.

NO. 7½ LEAD PELLETS—1 OUNCE—350 PELLETS
Mfg: Eley Hawk **Manufacturer's code:** VIP Sporting Fibre
Recoil energy in 8-lb. shotgun: 19.9 ft./lbs. **Recoil velocity in 8-lb. shotgun:** 12.6 ft./sec.

Distance in yards:	Muzzle	20	30	40	50	60	70
Velocity in fps:	1,413	903	761	652	565	492	430
Average pellet energy in ft-lbs:	5.59	2.28	1.62	1.19	.89	.68	.52
Time of flight in seconds:	0	.0544	.0907	.1334	.1829	.2399	.3052

Type of load: Target
Three-foot velocity: 1,300 ft./sec.
Hull: 2¾-inch plastic
Wad: Fiber
Shot: Lead
Buffered: No
Test barrel length: 30 inch
Pellets will pierce skin up to 126 yards.

NO. 7½ LEAD PELLETS—1 OUNCE—350 PELLETS
Mfg: Estate Cartridge **Manufacturer's code:** DQ12
Recoil energy in 8-lb. shotgun: 19.9 ft./lbs. **Recoil velocity in 8-lb. shotgun:** 12.6 ft./sec.

Distance in yards:	Muzzle	20	30	40	50	60	70
Velocity in fps:	1,413	903	761	652	565	492	430
Average pellet energy in ft-lbs:	5.59	2.28	1.62	1.19	.89	.68	.52
Time of flight in seconds:	0	.0544	.0907	.1334	.1829	.2399	.3052

Type of load: Field
Three-foot velocity: 1,300 ft./sec.5
Hull: 2¾-inch plastic
Wad: Plastic
Shot: Hard lead
Buffered: No
Test barrel length: 30 inch
Pellets will pierce skin up to 126 yards.

NO. 7½ LEAD PELLETS—1 OUNCE—350 PELLETS
Mfg: Federal Cartridge Co. **Manufacturer's code:** H121
Recoil energy in 8-lb. shotgun: 19.9 ft./lbs. **Recoil velocity in 8-lb. shotgun:** 12.6 ft./sec.

Distance in yards:	Muzzle	20	30	40	50	60	70
Velocity in fps:	1,413	903	761	652	565	492	430
Average pellet energy in ft-lbs:	5.59	2.28	1.62	1.19	.89	.68	.52
Time of flight in seconds:	0	.0544	.0907	.1334	.1829	.2399	.3052

Type of load: Field
Three-foot velocity: 1,300 ft./sec.
Hull: 2¾-inch plastic
Wad: Plastic
Shot: Lead
Buffered: No
Test barrel length: 30 inch
Pellets will pierce skin up to 126 yards.

NO. 7½ LEAD PELLETS—1 OUNCE—350 PELLETS

Mfg: Federal Cartridge Co. **Manufacturer's code:** FD12
Recoil energy in 8-lb. shotgun: 19.9 ft./lbs. **Recoil velocity in 8-lb. shotgun:** 12.6 ft./sec.

Distance in yards:	Muzzle	20	30	40	50	60	70
Velocity in fps:	1,413	903	761	652	565	492	430
Average pellet energy in ft-lbs:	5.59	2.28	1.62	1.19	.89	.68	.52
Time of flight in seconds:	0	.0544	.0907	.1334	.1829	.2399	.3052

Type of load: Field
Three-foot velocity: 1,300 ft./sec.
Hull: 2¾-inch plastic
Wad: Plastic
Shot: Hard lead
Buffered: No
Test barrel length: 30 inch
Pellets will pierce skin up to 126 yards.

NO. 7½ LEAD PELLETS—1 OUNCE—350 PELLETS

Mfg: Fiocchi **Manufacturer's code:** 12GT1
Recoil energy in 8-lb. shotgun: 19.9 ft./lbs. **Recoil velocity in 8-lb. shotgun:** 12.6 ft./sec.

Distance in yards:	Muzzle	20	30	40	50	60	70
Velocity in fps:	1,413	903	761	652	565	492	430
Average pellet energy in ft-lbs:	5.59	2.28	1.62	1.19	.89	.68	.52
Time of flight in seconds:	0	.0544	.0907	.1334	.1829	.2399	.3052

Type of load: Game & Target
Three-foot velocity: 1,300 ft./sec.
Hull: 2¾-inch plastic
Wad: Plastic
Shot: Lead
Buffered: No
Test barrel length: 30 inch
Pellets will pierce skin up to 126 yards.

NO. 7½ LEAD PELLETS—1 OUNCE—350 PELLETS

Mfg: Fiocchi **Manufacturer's code:** 12CPTR
Recoil energy in 8-lb. shotgun: 19.9 ft./lbs. **Recoil velocity in 8-lb. shotgun:** 12.6 ft./sec.

Distance in yards:	Muzzle	20	30	40	50	60	70
Velocity in fps:	1,413	903	761	652	565	492	430
Average pellet energy in ft-lbs:	5.59	2.28	1.62	1.19	.89	.68	.52
Time of flight in seconds:	0	.0544	.0907	.1334	.1829	.2399	.3052

Type of load: Target/spreader
Three-foot velocity: 1,300 ft./sec.
Hull: 2¾-inch plastic
Wad: Plastic
Shot: Hard lead
Buffered: No
Test barrel length: 30 inch
Pellets will pierce skin up to 126 yards.

NO. 7½ LEAD PELLETS—1 OUNCE—350 PELLETS

Mfg: Fiocchi **Manufacturer's code:** 12CRSR
Recoil energy in 8-lb. shotgun: 19.9 ft./lbs. **Recoil velocity in 8-lb. shotgun:** 12.6 ft./sec.

Distance in yards:	Muzzle	20	30	40	50	60	70
Velocity in fps:	1,413	903	761	652	565	492	430
Average pellet energy in ft-lbs:	5.59	2.28	1.62	1.19	.89	.68	.52
Time of flight in seconds:	0	.0544	.0907	.1334	.1829	.2399	.3052

Type of load: Target
Three-foot velocity: 1,300 ft./sec.
Hull: 2¾-inch plastic
Wad: Plastic
Shot: Hard lead
Buffered: No
Test barrel length: 30 inch
Pellets will pierce skin up to 126 yards.

NO. 7½ LEAD PELLETS—1 OUNCE—350 PELLETS

Mfg: Kent Cartridge America/Canada **Manufacturer's code:** K122HV28
Recoil energy in 8-lb. shotgun: 19.9 ft./lbs. **Recoil velocity in 8-lb. shotgun:** 12.6 ft./sec.

Distance in yards:	Muzzle	20	30	40	50	60	70
Velocity in fps:	1,413	903	761	652	565	492	430
Average pellet energy in ft-lbs:	5.59	2.28	1.62	1.19	.89	.68	.52
Time of flight in seconds:	0	.0544	.0907	.1334	.1829	.2399	.3052

Type of load: Target
Three-foot velocity: 1,300 ft./sec.
Hull: 2¾-inch plastic
Wad: Plastic
Shot: Lead
Buffered: No
Test barrel length: 30 inch
Pellets will pierce skin up to 126 yards.

NO. 7½ LEAD PELLETS—1 OUNCE—350 PELLETS

Mfg: PMC (Eldorado Cartridge Corp.) **Manufacturer's code:** PL12
Recoil energy in 8-lb. shotgun: 19.9 ft./lbs. **Recoil velocity in 8-lb. shotgun:** 12.6 ft./sec.

Distance in yards:	Muzzle	20	30	40	50	60	70
Velocity in fps:	1,413	903	761	652	565	492	430
Average pellet energy in ft-lbs:	5.59	2.28	1.62	1.19	.89	.68	.52
Time of flight in seconds:	0	.0544	.0907	.1334	.1829	.2399	.3052

Type of load: Quail & Dove
Three-foot velocity: 1,300 ft./sec.
Hull: 2¾-inch plastic
Wad: Plastic
Shot: Lead
Buffered: No
Test barrel length: 30 inch
Pellets will pierce skin up to 126 yards.

NO. 7½ LEAD PELLETS—1 OUNCE—350 PELLETS

Mfg: Remington Arms Co. **Manufacturer's code:** GL12
Recoil energy in 8-lb. shotgun: 19.9 ft./lbs. **Recoil velocity in 8-lb. shotgun:** 12.6 ft./sec.

Distance in yards:	Muzzle	20	30	40	50	60	70
Velocity in fps:	1,413	903	761	652	565	492	430
Average pellet energy in ft-lbs:	5.59	2.28	1.62	1.19	.89	.68	.52
Time of flight in seconds:	0	.0544	.0907	.1334	.1829	.2399	.3052

Type of load: Field
Three-foot velocity: 1,300 ft./sec.
Hull: 2¾-inch plastic
Wad: Plastic
Shot: Lead
Buffered: No
Test barrel length: 30 inch
Pellets will pierce skin up to 126 yards.

NO. 7½ LEAD PELLETS—1 OUNCE—350 PELLETS
Mfg: Remington Arms Co. **Manufacturer's code:** STS12NH1
Recoil energy in 8-lb. shotgun: 19.9 ft./lbs. **Recoil velocity in 8-lb. shotgun:** 12.6 ft./sec.

Distance in yards:	Muzzle	20	30	40	50	60	70
Velocity in fps:	1,413	903	761	652	565	492	430
Average pellet energy in ft-lbs:	5.59	2.28	1.62	1.19	.89	.68	.52
Time of flight in seconds:	0	.0544	.0907	.1334	.1829	.2399	.3052

Type of load: Target
Three-foot velocity: 1,300 ft./sec.
Hull: 2¾-inch plastic
Wad: Plastic
Shot: Hard lead
Buffered: No
Test barrel length: 30 inch
Pellets will pierce skin up to 126 yards.

NO. 7½ LEAD PELLETS—1 OUNCE—350 PELLETS
Mfg: Rottweil **Manufacturer's code:** Game
Recoil energy in 8-lb. shotgun: 25.2 ft./lbs. **Recoil velocity in 8-lb. shotgun:** 14.2 ft./sec.

Distance in yards:	Muzzle	20	30	40	50	60	70
Velocity in fps:	1,413	903	761	652	565	492	430
Average pellet energy in ft-lbs:	5.59	2.28	1.62	1.19	.89	.68	.52
Time of flight in seconds:	0	.0544	.0907	.1334	.1829	.2399	.3052

Type of load: Field
Three-foot velocity: 1,300 ft./sec.
Hull: 2¾-inch plastic
Wad: Plastic
Shot: Lead
Buffered: No
Test barrel length: 30 inch
Pellets will pierce skin up to 126 yards.

NO. 7½ LEAD PELLETS—1 OUNCE—350 PELLETS
Mfg: RST, Ltd. **Manufacturer's code:** N/A
Recoil energy in 8-lb. shotgun: 19.9 ft./lbs. **Recoil velocity in 8-lb. shotgun:** 12.6 ft./sec.

Distance in yards:	Muzzle	20	30	40	50	60	70
Velocity in fps:	1,413	903	761	652	565	492	430
Average pellet energy in ft-lbs:	5.59	2.28	1.62	1.19	.89	.68	.52
Time of flight in seconds:	0	.0544	.0907	.1334	.1829	.2399	.3052

Type of load: Target
Three-foot velocity: 1,300 ft./sec.
Hull: 2¾-inch plastic
Wad: Plastic
Shot: Lead
Buffered: No
Test barrel length: 30 inch
Pellets will pierce skin up to 126 yards.

NO. 7½ LEAD PELLETS—1 OUNCE—350 PELLETS
Mfg: Sellier & Bellot **Manufacturer's code:** SBA01244
Recoil energy in 8-lb. shotgun: 19.9 ft./lbs. **Recoil velocity in 8-lb. shotgun:** 12.6 ft./sec.

Distance in yards:	Muzzle	20	30	40	50	60	70
Velocity in fps:	1,413	903	761	652	565	492	430
Average pellet energy in ft-lbs:	5.59	2.28	1.62	1.19	.89	.68	.52
Time of flight in seconds:	0	.0544	.0907	.1334	.1829	.2399	.3052

Type of load: Target
Three-foot velocity: 1,300 ft./sec.
Hull: 2¾-inch plastic
Wad: Plastic
Shot: Lead
Buffered: No
Test barrel length: 30 inch
Pellets will pierce skin up to 126 yards.

NO. 7½ LEAD PELLETS—1 OUNCE—350 PELLETS
Mfg: Winchester **Manufacturer's code:** XU12
Recoil energy in 8-lb. shotgun: 19.9 ft./lbs. **Recoil velocity in 8-lb. shotgun:** 12.6 ft./sec.

Distance in yards:	Muzzle	20	30	40	50	60	70
Velocity in fps:	1,413	903	761	652	565	492	430
Average pellet energy in ft-lbs:	5.59	2.28	1.62	1.19	.89	.68	.52
Time of flight in seconds:	0	.0544	.0907	.1334	.1829	.2399	.3052

Type of load: Field
Three-foot velocity: 1,300 ft./sec.
Hull: 2¾-inch plastic
Wad: Plastic
Shot: Lead
Buffered: No
Test barrel length: 30 inch
Pellets will pierce skin up to 126 yards.

NO. 7½ LEAD PELLETS—1 OUNCE—350 PELLETS
Mfg: Winchester **Manufacturer's code:** AAHLA12
Recoil energy in 8-lb. shotgun: 19.9 ft./lbs. **Recoil velocity in 8-lb. shotgun:** 12.6 ft./sec.

Distance in yards:	Muzzle	20	30	40	50	60	70
Velocity in fps:	1,413	903	761	652	565	492	430
Average pellet energy in ft-lbs:	5.59	2.28	1.62	1.19	.89	.68	.52
Time of flight in seconds:	0	.0544	.0907	.1334	.1829	.2399	.3052

Type of load: Target
Three-foot velocity: 1,300 ft./sec.
Hull: 2¾-inch plastic
Wad: Plastic
Shot: Hard lead
Buffered: No
Test barrel length: 30 inch
Pellets will pierce skin up to 126 yards.

NO. 7½ LEAD PELLETS—1 OUNCE—350 PELLETS
Mfg: Baschieri & Pellagri **Manufacturer's code:** N/A
Recoil energy in 8-lb. shotgun: 21.2 ft./lbs. **Recoil velocity in 8-lb. shotgun:** 13.0 ft./sec.

Distance in yards:	Muzzle	20	30	40	50	60	70
Velocity in fps:	1,447	917	771	660	571	498	435
Average pellet energy in ft-lbs:	5.86	2.36	1.66	1.22	.91	.69	.53
Time of flight in seconds:	0	.0534	.0891	.1313	.1802	.2365	.3010

Type of load: F2 Sporting Clay
Three-foot velocity: 1,330 ft./sec.
Hull: 2¾-inch plastic
Wad: Plastic
Shot: Hard lead
Buffered: No
Test barrel length: 30 inch
Pellets will pierce skin up to 127 yards.

NO. 7½ LEAD PELLETS—1 OUNCE—350 PELLETS
Mfg: Eley Hawk **Manufacturer's code:** VIP
Recoil energy in 8-lb. shotgun: 16.2 ft./lbs. **Recoil velocity in 8-lb. shotgun:** 11.4 ft./sec.

Distance in yards:	Muzzle	20	30	40	50	60	70
Velocity in fps:	1,447	917	771	660	571	498	435
Average pellet energy in ft-lbs:	5.86	2.36	1.66	1.22	.91	.69	.53
Time of flight in seconds:	0	.0534	.0891	.1313	.1802	.2365	.3010

Type of load: Target
Three-foot velocity: 1,330 ft./sec.
Hull: 2¾-inch plastic
Wad: Plastic
Shot: Hard lead
Buffered: No
Test barrel length: 30 inch
Pellets will pierce skin up to 127 yards

NO. 7½ LEAD PELLETS—1 OUNCE—350 PELLETS
Mfg: Estate Cartridge **Manufacturer's code:** CT12XH1/SS12XH1
Recoil energy in 8-lb. shotgun: 21.2 ft./lbs. **Recoil velocity in 8-lb. shotgun:** 13.0 ft./sec.

Distance in yards:	Muzzle	20	30	40	50	60	70
Velocity in fps:	1,447	917	771	660	571	498	435
Average pellet energy in ft-lbs:	5.86	2.36	1.66	1.22	.91	.69	.53
Time of flight in seconds:	0	.0534	.0891	.1313	.1802	.2365	.3010

Type of load: Target
Three-foot velocity: 1,330 ft./sec.
Hull: 2¾-inch plastic
Wad: Plastic
Shot: Hard lead
Buffered: No
Test barrel length: 30 inch
Pellets will pierce skin up to 127 yards

NO. 7½ LEAD PELLETS—1 OUNCE—350 PELLETS
Mfg: Estate Cartridge **Manufacturer's code:** INT28
Recoil energy in 8-lb. shotgun: 21.2 ft./lbs. **Recoil velocity in 8-lb. shotgun:** 13.0 ft./sec.

Distance in yards:	Muzzle	20	30	40	50	60	70
Velocity in fps:	1,447	917	771	660	571	498	435
Average pellet energy in ft-lbs:	5.86	2.36	1.66	1.22	.91	.69	.53
Time of flight in seconds:	0	.0534	.0891	.1313	.1802	.2365	.3010

Type of load: Target
Three-foot velocity: 1,330 ft./sec.
Hull: 2¾-inch plastic
Wad: Plastic
Shot: Hard lead
Buffered: No
Test barrel length: 30 inch
Pellets will pierce skin up to 127 yards.

NO. 7½ LEAD PELLETS—1 OUNCE—350 PELLETS
Mfg: RST, Ltd. **Manufacturer's code:** N/A
Recoil energy in 8-lb. shotgun: 16.2 ft./lbs. **Recoil velocity in 8-lb. shotgun:** 11.4 ft./sec.

Distance in yards:	Muzzle	20	30	40	50	60	70
Velocity in fps:	1,447	917	771	660	571	498	435
Average pellet energy in ft-lbs:	5.86	2.36	1.66	1.22	.91	.69	.53
Time of flight in seconds:	0	.0534	.0891	.1313	.1802	.2365	.3010

Type of load: Target
Three-foot velocity: 1,330 ft./sec.
Hull: 2¾-inch plastic
Wad: Plastic
Shot: Lead
Buffered: No
Test barrel length: 30 inch
Pellets will pierce skin up to 127 yards.

NO. 7½ LEAD PELLETS—1 OUNCE—350 PELLETS
Mfg: Winchester **Manufacturer's code:** AASCL12
Recoil energy in 8-lb. shotgun: 12.0 ft./lbs. **Recoil velocity in 8-lb. shotgun:** 13.3 ft./sec.

Distance in yards:	Muzzle	20	30	40	50	60	70
Velocity in fps:	1,469	927	778	666	576	502	438
Average pellet energy in ft-lbs:	6.04	2.41	1.70	1.24	.93	.70	.54
Time of flight in seconds:	0	.0527	.0881	.1299	.1784	.2343	.2983

Type of load: Target
Three-foot velocity: 1,350 ft./sec.
Hull: 2¾-inch plastic
Wad: Plastic
Shot: Hard lead
Buffered: No
Test barrel length: 30 inch
Pellets will pierce skin up to 128 yards.

NO. 7½ LEAD PELLETS—1 OUNCE—350 PELLETS
Mfg: RIO **Manufacturer's code:** Trap 24
Recoil energy in 8-lb. shotgun: 17.7 ft./lbs. **Recoil velocity in 8-lb. shotgun:** 11.9 ft./sec.

Distance in yards:	Muzzle	20	30	40	50	60	70
Velocity in fps:	1,497	939	787	673	582	506	442
Average pellet energy in ft-lbs:	6.27	2.47	1.73	1.27	.95	.72	.55
Time of flight in seconds:	0	.0519	.0869	.1282	.1762	.2316	.2950

Type of load: Field
Three-foot velocity: 1,375 ft./sec.
Hull: 2¾-inch plastic
Wad: Plastic
Shot: Hard lead
Buffered: No
Test barrel length: 30 inch
Pellets will pierce skin up to 129 yards.

NO. 7½ LEAD PELLETS—1 OUNCE—350 PELLETS
Mfg: Baschieri & Pellagri **Manufacturer's code:** N/A
Recoil energy in 8-lb. shotgun: 24.3 ft./lbs. **Recoil velocity in 8-lb. shotgun:** 14.0 ft./sec.

Distance in yards:	Muzzle	20	30	40	50	60	70
Velocity in fps:	1,525	951	796	679	587	511	446
Average pellet energy in ft-lbs:	6.51	2.53	1.77	1.29	.96	.73	.56
Time of flight in seconds:	0	.0511	.0857	.1265	.1741	.2290	.2918

Type of load: F2 Ultra Velocity
Three-foot velocity: 1,400 ft./sec.
Hull: 2¾-inch plastic
Wad: Plastic
Shot: Hard lead
Buffered: No
Test barrel length: 30 inch
Pellets will pierce skin up to 129 yards.

NO. 7½ LEAD PELLETS—1¹⁄₁₆ OUNCES—372 PELLETS

Mfg: Kent Cartridge America/Canada **Manufacturer's code:** K122TR30
Recoil energy in 8-lb. shotgun: 17.4 ft./lbs. **Recoil velocity in 8-lb. shotgun:** 11.8 ft./sec.

Distance in yards:	Muzzle	20	30	40	50	60	70
Velocity in fps:	1,341	871	737	633	549	479	418
Average pellet energy in ft-lbs:	5.03	2.12	1.52	1.12	.84	.64	.49
Time of flight in seconds:	0	.0568	.0943	.1383	.1893	.2478	.3149

Type of load: Target
Three-foot velocity: 1,235 ft./sec.
Hull: 2¾-inch plastic
Wad: Plastic
Shot: Lead
Buffered: No
Test barrel length: 30 inch
Pellets will pierce skin up to 124 yards.

NO. 7½ LEAD PELLETS—1⅛ OUNCES—394 PELLETS

Mfg: Dionisi **Manufacturer's code:** D 12 TL
Recoil energy in 8-lb. shotgun: 12.7 ft./lbs. **Recoil velocity in 8-lb. shotgun:** 10.1 ft./sec.

Distance in yards:	Muzzle	20	30	40	50	60	70
Velocity in fps:	1,021	846	618	537	468	409	357
Average pellet energy in ft-lbs:	2.92	1.44	1.07	.81	.61	.47	.36
Time of flight in seconds:	0	.0710	.1161	.1683	.2282	.2967	.3753

Type of load: Target Low Noise
Three-foot velocity: 1,000 ft./sec.
Hull: 2¾-inch plastic
Wad: Plastic
Shot: Lead
Buffered: No
Test barrel length: 30 inch
Pellets will pierce skin up to 113 yards.

NO. 7½ LEAD PELLETS—1⅛ OUNCES—394 PELLETS

Mfg: RST, Ltd. **Manufacturer's code:** N/A
Recoil energy in 8-lb. shotgun: 12.7 ft./lbs. **Recoil velocity in 8-lb. shotgun:** 10.1 ft./sec.

Distance in yards:	Muzzle	20	30	40	50	60	70
Velocity in fps:	1,021	846	618	537	468	409	357
Average pellet energy in ft-lbs:	2.92	1.44	1.07	.81	.61	.47	.36
Time of flight in seconds:	0	.0710	.1161	.1683	.2282	.2967	.3753

Type of load: Target
Three-foot velocity: 1,000 ft./sec.
Hull: 2¾-inch plastic
Wad: Plastic
Shot: Lead
Buffered: No
Test barrel length: 30 inch
Pellets will pierce skin up to 113 yards.

NO. 7½ LEAD PELLETS—1⅛ OUNCES—394 PELLETS

Mfg: Federal Cartridge Co. **Manufacturer's code:** T114
Recoil energy in 8-lb. shotgun: 16.2 ft./lbs. **Recoil velocity in 8-lb. shotgun:** 11.4 ft./sec.

Distance in yards:	Muzzle	20	30	40	50	60	70
Velocity in fps:	1,191	803	685	592	515	449	392
Average pellet energy in ft-lbs:	3.97	1.81	1.31	.98	.74	.57	.43
Time of flight in seconds:	0	.0625	.1030	.1502	.2047	.2671	.3385

Type of load: Target
Three-foot velocity: 1,100 ft./sec.
Hull: 2¾-inch plastic
Wad: Plastic
Shot: Hard lead
Buffered: No
Test barrel length: 30 inch
Pellets will pierce skin up to 132 yards.

NO. 7½ LEAD PELLETS—1⅛ OUNCES—394 PELLETS

Mfg: Federal Cartridge Co. **Manufacturer's code:** T172
Recoil energy in 8-lb. shotgun: 16.2 ft./lbs. **Recoil velocity in 8-lb. shotgun:** 11.4 ft./sec.

Distance in yards:	Muzzle	20	30	40	50	60	70
Velocity in fps:	1,191	803	685	592	515	449	392
Average pellet energy in ft-lbs:	3.97	1.81	1.31	.98	.74	.57	.43
Time of flight in seconds:	0	.0625	.1030	.1502	.2047	.2671	.3385

Type of load: Target
Three-foot velocity: 1,100 ft./sec.
Hull: 2¾-inch plastic
Wad: Plastic
Shot: Hard lead
Buffered: No
Test barrel length: 30 inch
Pellets will pierce skin up to 132 yards.

NO. 7½ LEAD PELLETS—1⅛ OUNCES—394 PELLETS

Mfg: Remington Arms Co. **Manufacturer's code:** STS12LR
Recoil energy in 8-lb. shotgun: 16.2 ft./lbs. **Recoil velocity in 8-lb. shotgun:** 11.4 ft./sec.

Distance in yards:	Muzzle	20	30	40	50	60	70
Velocity in fps:	1,191	803	685	592	515	449	392
Average pellet energy in ft-lbs:	3.97	1.81	1.31	.98	.74	.57	.43
Time of flight in seconds:	0	.0625	.1030	.1502	.2047	.2671	.3385

Type of load: Target
Three-foot velocity: 1,100 ft./sec.
Hull: 2¾-inch plastic
Wad: Plastic
Shot: Hard lead
Buffered: No
Test barrel length: 30 inch
Pellets will pierce skin up to 132 yards.

NO. 7½ LEAD PELLETS—1⅛ OUNCES—394 PELLETS

Mfg: Estate Cartridge **Manufacturer's code:** CT12XL
Recoil energy in 8-lb. shotgun: 17.2 ft./lbs. **Recoil velocity in 8-lb. shotgun:** 11.8 ft./sec.

Distance in yards:	Muzzle	20	30	40	50	60	70
Velocity in fps:	1,218	816	695	600	522	455	398
Average pellet energy in ft-lbs:	4.15	1.86	1.35	1.01	.76	.58	.44
Time of flight in seconds:	0	.0613	.1013	.1478	.2015	.2631	.3337

Type of load: Target
Three-foot velocity: 1,125 ft./sec.
Hull: 2¾-inch plastic
Wad: Plastic
Shot: Hard lead
Buffered: No
Test barrel length: 30 inch
Pellets will pierce skin up to 121 yards.

NO. 7½ LEAD PELLETS—1⅛ OUNCES—394 PELLETS
Mfg: Fiocchi **Manufacturer's code:** 12TRAPL
Recoil energy in 8-lb. shotgun: 17.6 ft./lbs. **Recoil velocity in 8-lb. shotgun:** 11.9 ft./sec.

Distance in yards:	Muzzle	20	30	40	50	60	70
Velocity in fps:	1,229	821	699	603	524	458	400
Average pellet energy in ft-lbs:	4.23	1089	1.37	1.02	.077	.59	.45
Time of flight in seconds:	0	.0609	.1006	.1469	.2003	.2616	.3318

Type of load: Target
Three-foot velocity: 1,135 ft./sec.
Hull: 2¾-inch plastic
Wad: Plastic
Shot: Hard lead
Buffered: No
Test barrel length: 30 inch
Pellets will pierce skin up to 121 yards.

NO. 7½ LEAD PELLETS—1⅛ OUNCES—394 PELLETS
Mfg: Armscor **Manufacturer's code:** N/A
Recoil energy in 8-lb. shotgun: 18.0 ft./lbs. **Recoil velocity in 8-lb. shotgun:** 12.0 ft./sec.

Distance in yards:	Muzzle	20	30	40	50	60	70
Velocity in fps:	1,241	826	703	606	527	460	401
Average pellet energy in ft-lbs:	4.31	1.91	1.38	1.03	.78	.59	.45
Time of flight in seconds:	0	.0604	.0999	.1460	.1991	.2601	.3300

Type of load: Field
Three-foot velocity: 1,145 ft./sec.
Hull: 2¾-inch plastic
Wad: Plastic
Shot: Lead
Buffered: No
Test barrel length: 30 inch
Pellets will pierce skin up to 121 yards.

NO. 7½ LEAD PELLETS—1⅛ OUNCES—394 PELLETS
Mfg: Dionisi **Manufacturer's code:** D 12 TD
Recoil energy in 8-lb. shotgun: 18.0 ft./lbs. **Recoil velocity in 8-lb. shotgun:** 12.0 ft./sec.

Distance in yards:	Muzzle	20	30	40	50	60	70
Velocity in fps:	1,241	826	703	606	527	460	401
Average pellet energy in ft-lbs:	4.31	1.91	1.38	1.03	.78	.59	.45
Time of flight in seconds:	0	.0604	.0999	.1460	.1991	.2601	.3300

Type of load: Target
Three-foot velocity: 1,145 ft./sec.
Hull: 2¾-inch plastic
Wad: Plastic
Shot: Lead
Buffered: No
Test barrel length: 30 inch
Pellets will pierce skin up to 121 yards.

NO. 7½ LEAD PELLETS—1⅛ OUNCES—394 PELLETS
Mfg: Estate Cartridge **Manufacturer's code:** CT12L/SS12L
Recoil energy in 8-lb. shotgun: 18.0 ft./lbs. **Recoil velocity in 8-lb. shotgun:** 12.0 ft./sec.

Distance in yards:	Muzzle	20	30	40	50	60	70
Velocity in fps:	1,241	826	703	606	527	460	401
Average pellet energy in ft-lbs:	4.31	1.91	1.38	1.03	.78	.59	.45
Time of flight in seconds:	0	.0604	.0999	.1460	.1991	.2601	.3300

Type of load: Target
Three-foot velocity: 1,145 ft./sec.
Hull: 2¾-inch plastic
Wad: Plastic
Shot: Hard lead
Buffered: No
Test barrel length: 30 inch
Pellets will pierce skin up to 121 yards.

NO. 7½ LEAD PELLETS—1⅛ OUNCES—394 PELLETS
Mfg: Federal Cartridge Co. **Manufacturer's code:** T115
Recoil energy in 8-lb. shotgun: 18.0 ft./lbs. **Recoil velocity in 8-lb. shotgun:** 12.0 ft./sec.

Distance in yards:	Muzzle	20	30	40	50	60	70
Velocity in fps:	1,241	826	703	606	527	460	401
Average pellet energy in ft-lbs:	4.31	1.91	1.38	1.03	.78	.59	.45
Time of flight in seconds:	0	.0604	.0999	.1460	.1991	.2601	.3300

Type of load: Target
Three-foot velocity: 1,145 ft./sec.
Hull: 2¾-inch plastic
Wad: Plastic
Shot: Hard lead
Buffered: No
Test barrel length: 30 inch
Pellets will pierce skin up to 121 yards.

NO. 7½ LEAD PELLETS—1⅛ OUNCES—394 PELLETS
Mfg: Federal Cartridge Co. **Manufacturer's code:** T117
Recoil energy in 8-lb. shotgun: 18.0 ft./lbs. **Recoil velocity in 8-lb. shotgun:** 12.0 ft./sec.

Distance in yards:	Muzzle	20	30	40	50	60	70
Velocity in fps:	1,241	826	703	606	527	460	401
Average pellet energy in ft-lbs:	4.31	1.91	1.38	1.03	.78	.59	.45
Time of flight in seconds:	0	.0604	.0999	.1460	.1991	.2601	.3300

Type of load: Target
Three-foot velocity: 1,145 ft./sec.
Hull: 2¾-inch paper
Wad: Plastic
Shot: Hard lead
Buffered: No
Test barrel length: 30 inch
Pellets will pierce skin up to 121 yards.

NO. 7½ LEAD PELLETS—1⅛ OUNCES—394 PELLETS
Mfg: Remington Arms Co. **Manufacturer's code:** STS12L
Recoil energy in 8-lb. shotgun: 18.0 ft./lbs. **Recoil velocity in 8-lb. shotgun:** 12.0 ft./sec.

Distance in yards:	Muzzle	20	30	40	50	60	70
Velocity in fps:	1,241	826	703	606	527	460	401
Average pellet energy in ft-lbs:	4.31	1.91	1.38	1.03	.78	.59	.45
Time of flight in seconds:	0	.0604	.0999	.1460	.1991	.2601	.3300

Type of load: Target
Three-foot velocity: 1,145 ft./sec.
Hull: 2¾-inch plastic
Wad: Plastic
Shot: Hard lead
Buffered: No
Test barrel length: 30 inch
Pellets will pierce skin up to 121 yards.

NO. 7½ LEAD PELLETS—1⅛ OUNCES—394 PELLETS
Mfg: RST, Ltd. **Manufacturer's code:** N/A
Recoil energy in 8-lb. shotgun: 18.0 ft./lbs. **Recoil velocity in 8-lb. shotgun:** 12.0 ft./sec.

Distance in yards:	Muzzle	20	30	40	50	60	70
Velocity in fps:	1,241	826	703	606	527	460	401
Average pellet energy in ft-lbs:	4.31	1.91	1.38	1.03	.78	.59	.45
Time of flight in seconds:	0	.0604	.0999	.1460	.1991	.2601	.3300

Type of load: Target
Three-foot velocity: 1,145 ft./sec.
Hull: 2¾-inch plastic
Wad: Plastic
Shot: Lead
Buffered: No
Test barrel length: 30 inch
Pellets will pierce skin up to 121 yards.

NO. 7½ LEAD PELLETS—1⅛ OUNCES—394 PELLETS
Mfg: Sellier & Bellot **Manufacturer's code:** SBA1272
Recoil energy in 8-lb. shotgun: 18.0 ft./lbs. **Recoil velocity in 8-lb. shotgun:** 12.0 ft./sec.

Distance in yards:	Muzzle	20	30	40	50	60	70
Velocity in fps:	1,241	826	703	606	527	460	401
Average pellet energy in ft-lbs:	4.31	1.91	1.38	1.03	.78	.59	.45
Time of flight in seconds:	0	.0604	.0999	.1460	.1991	.2601	.3300

Type of load: Target
Three-foot velocity: 1,145 ft./sec.
Hull: 2¾-inch paper
Wad: Plastic
Shot: Lead
Buffered: No
Test barrel length: 30 inch
Pellets will pierce skin up to 121 yards.

NO. 7½ LEAD PELLETS—1⅛ OUNCES—394 PELLETS
Mfg: Winchester **Manufacturer's code:** AA12/WEST12
Recoil energy in 8-lb. shotgun: 18.0 ft./lbs. **Recoil velocity in 8-lb. shotgun:** 12.0 ft./sec.

Distance in yards:	Muzzle	20	30	40	50	60	70
Velocity in fps:	1,241	826	703	606	527	460	401
Average pellet energy in ft-lbs:	4.31	1.91	1.38	1.03	.78	.59	.45
Time of flight in seconds:	0	.0604	.0999	.1460	.1991	.2601	.3300

Type of load: Field & Target
Three-foot velocity: 1,145 ft./sec.
Hull: 2¾-inch plastic
Wad: Plastic
Shot: Lead
Buffered: No
Test barrel length: 30 inch
Pellets will pierce skin up to 121 yards.

NO. 7½ LEAD PELLETS—1⅛ OUNCES—394 PELLETS
Mfg: Fiocchi **Manufacturer's code:** 12VIPL
Recoil energy in 8-lb. shotgun: 18.2 ft./lbs. **Recoil velocity in 8-lb. shotgun:** 12.1 ft./sec.

Distance in yards:	Muzzle	20	30	40	50	60	70
Velocity in fps:	1,246	829	705	607	528	461	402
Average pellet energy in ft-lbs:	4.35	1.92	1.39	1.03	.78	.59	.45
Time of flight in seconds:	0	.0602	.0996	.1455	.1985	.2594	.3290

Type of load: Target
Three-foot velocity: 1,150 ft./sec.
Hull: 2¾-inch plastic
Wad: Plastic
Shot: Hard lead
Buffered: No
Test barrel length: 30 inch
Pellets will pierce skin up to 122 yards.

NO. 7½ LEAD PELLETS—1⅛ OUNCES—394 PELLETS
Mfg: Kent Cartridge America/Canada **Manufacturer's code:** K122LTR32
Recoil energy in 8-lb. shotgun: 18.2 ft./lbs. **Recoil velocity in 8-lb. shotgun:** 12.1 ft./sec.

Distance in yards:	Muzzle	20	30	40	50	60	70
Velocity in fps:	1,246	829	705	607	528	461	402
Average pellet energy in ft-lbs:	4.35	1.92	1.39	1.03	.78	.59	.45
Time of flight in seconds:	0	.0602	.0996	.1455	.1985	.2594	.3290

Type of load: Target
Three-foot velocity: 1,150 ft./sec.
Hull: 2¾-inch plastic
Wad: Plastic
Shot: Lead
Buffered: No
Test barrel length: 30 inch
Pellets will pierce skin up to 122 yards.

NO. 7½ LEAD PELLETS—1⅛ OUNCES—394 PELLETS
Mfg: Rottweil **Manufacturer's code:** Sport
Recoil energy in 8-lb. shotgun: 18.2 ft./lbs. **Recoil velocity in 8-lb. shotgun:** 12.1 ft./sec.

Distance in yards:	Muzzle	20	30	40	50	60	70
Velocity in fps:	1,246	829	705	607	528	461	402
Average pellet energy in ft-lbs:	4.35	1.92	1.39	1.03	.78	.59	.45
Time of flight in seconds:	0	.0602	.0996	.1455	.1985	.2594	.3290

Type of load: Target
Three-foot velocity: 1,150 ft./sec.
Hull: 2¾-inch plastic
Wad: Plastic
Shot: Lead
Buffered: No
Test barrel length: 30 inch
Pellets will pierce skin up to 122 yards.

NO. 7½ LEAD PELLETS—1⅛ OUNCES—394 PELLETS
Mfg: Fiocchi **Manufacturer's code:** 12LITE
Recoil energy in 8-lb. shotgun: 19.9 ft./lbs. **Recoil velocity in 8-lb. shotgun:** 12.6 ft./sec.

Distance in yards:	Muzzle	20	30	40	50	60	70
Velocity in fps:	1,263	836	710	612	532	464	405
Average pellet energy in ft-lbs:	4.46	1.96	1.41	1.05	.79	.60	.46
Time of flight in seconds:	0	.0596	.0986	.1442	.1968	.2572	.3264

Type of load: Target
Three-foot velocity: 1,165 ft./sec.
Hull: 2¾-inch plastic
Wad: Plastic
Shot: Hard lead
Buffered: No
Test barrel length: 30 inch
Pellets will pierce skin up to 122 yards.

NO. 7½ LEAD PELLETS—1⅛ OUNCES—394 PELLETS
Mfg: Fiocchi **Manufacturer's code:** 12TRAPH
Recoil energy in 8-lb. shotgun: 19.3 ft./lbs. **Recoil velocity in 8-lb. shotgun:** 12.5 ft./sec.

Distance in yards:	Muzzle	20	30	40	50	60	70
Velocity in fps:	1,274	841	714	615	535	466	407
Average pellet energy in ft-lbs:	4.54	1.98	1.43	1.06	.80	.61	.46
Time of flight in seconds:	0	.0592	.0980	.1433	.1957	.2558	.3246

Type of load: Target
Three-foot velocity: 1,175 ft./sec.
Hull: 2¾-inch plastic
Wad: Plastic
Shot: Hard lead
Buffered: No
Test barrel length: 30 inch
Pellets will pierce skin up to 122 yards.

NO. 7½ LEAD PELLETS—1⅛ OUNCES—394 PELLETS
Mfg: PMC (Eldorado Cartridge Corp.) **Manufacturer's code:** LCT12
Recoil energy in 8-lb. shotgun: 19.3 ft./lbs. **Recoil velocity in 8-lb. shotgun:** 12.5 ft./sec.

Distance in yards:	Muzzle	20	30	40	50	60	70
Velocity in fps:	1,274	841	714	615	535	466	407
Average pellet energy in ft-lbs:	4.54	1.98	1.43	1.06	.80	.61	.46
Time of flight in seconds:	0	.0592	.0980	.1433	.1957	.2558	.3246

Type of load: Target
Three-foot velocity: 1,175 ft./sec.
Hull: 2¾-inch plastic
Wad: Plastic
Shot: Lead
Buffered: No
Test barrel length: 30 inch
Pellets will pierce skin up to 122 yards.

NO. 7½ LEAD PELLETS—1⅛ OUNCES—394 PELLETS
Mfg: Aguila **Manufacturer's code:** N/A
Recoil energy in 8-lb. shotgun: 20.4 ft./lbs. **Recoil velocity in 8-lb. shotgun:** 12.8 ft./sec.

Distance in yards:	Muzzle	20	30	40	50	60	70
Velocity in fps:	1,302	854	724	623	541	472	412
Average pellet energy in ft-lbs:	4.74	2.04	1.47	1.09	.82	.62	.47
Time of flight in seconds:	0	.0581	.0964	.1412	.1930	.2524	.3204

Type of load: Field
Three-foot velocity: 1,200 ft./sec.
Hull: 2¾-inch plastic
Wad: Plastic
Shot: Lead
Buffered: No
Test barrel length: 30 inch
Pellets will pierce skin up to 124 yards.

NO. 7½ LEAD PELLETS—1⅛ OUNCES—394 PELLETS
Mfg: Dionisi **Manufacturer's code:** D 12 GTX
Recoil energy in 8-lb. shotgun: 20.4 ft./lbs. **Recoil velocity in 8-lb. shotgun:** 12.8 ft./sec.

Distance in yards:	Muzzle	20	30	40	50	60	70
Velocity in fps:	1,302	854	724	623	541	472	412
Average pellet energy in ft-lbs:	4.74	2.04	1.47	1.09	.82	.62	.47
Time of flight in seconds:	0	.0581	.0964	.1412	.1930	.2524	.3204

Type of load: Game & Target
Three-foot velocity: 1,200 ft./sec.
Hull: 2¾-inch plastic
Wad: Plastic
Shot: Lead
Buffered: No
Test barrel length: 30 inch
Pellets will pierce skin up to 124 yards.

NO. 7½ LEAD PELLETS—1⅛ OUNCES—394 PELLETS
Mfg: Dionisi **Manufacturer's code:** D 12 TDX
Recoil energy in 8-lb. shotgun: 20.4 ft./lbs. **Recoil velocity in 8-lb. shotgun:** 12.8 ft./sec.

Distance in yards:	Muzzle	20	30	40	50	60	70
Velocity in fps:	1,302	854	724	623	541	472	412
Average pellet energy in ft-lbs:	4.74	2.04	1.47	1.09	.82	.62	.47
Time of flight in seconds:	0	.0581	.0964	.1412	.1930	.2524	.3204

Type of load: Target & Pigeon
Three-foot velocity: 1,200 ft./sec.
Hull: 2¾-inch plastic
Wad: Plastic
Shot: Lead
Buffered: No
Test barrel length: 30 inch
Pellets will pierce skin up to 124 yards.

NO. 7½ LEAD PELLETS—1⅛ OUNCES—394 PELLETS
Mfg: Estate Cartridge **Manufacturer's code:** CT12H/SS12H
Recoil energy in 8-lb. shotgun: 20.4 ft./lbs. **Recoil velocity in 8-lb. shotgun:** 12.8 ft./sec.

Distance in yards:	Muzzle	20	30	40	50	60	70
Velocity in fps:	1,302	854	724	623	541	472	412
Average pellet energy in ft-lbs:	4.74	2.04	1.47	1.09	.82	.62	.47
Time of flight in seconds:	0	.0581	.0964	.1412	.1930	.2524	.3204

Type of load: Target
Three-foot velocity: 1,200 ft./sec.
Hull: 2¾-inch plastic
Wad: Plastic
Shot: Hard lead
Buffered: No
Test barrel length: 30 inch
Pellets will pierce skin up to 124 yards.

NO. 7½ LEAD PELLETS—1⅛ OUNCES—394 PELLETS
Mfg: Estate Cartridge **Manufacturer's code:** CT12HS
Recoil energy in 8-lb. shotgun: 20.4 ft./lbs. **Recoil velocity in 8-lb. shotgun:** 12.8 ft./sec.

Distance in yards:	Muzzle	20	30	40	50	60	70
Velocity in fps:	1,302	854	724	623	541	472	412
Average pellet energy in ft-lbs:	4.74	2.04	1.47	1.09	.82	.62	.47
Time of flight in seconds:	0	.0581	.0964	.1412	.1930	.2524	.3204

Type of load: Target
Three-foot velocity: 1,200 ft./sec.
Hull: 2¾-inch plastic
Wad: Plastic
Shot: Hard lead
Buffered: No
Test barrel length: 30 inch
Pellets will pierce skin up to 124 yards.

NO. 7½ LEAD PELLETS—1⅛ OUNCES—394 PELLETS
Mfg: Federal Cartridge Co. **Manufacturer's code:** T116
Recoil energy in 8-lb. shotgun: 20.4 ft./lbs. **Recoil velocity in 8-lb. shotgun:** 12.8 ft./sec.

Distance in yards:	Muzzle	20	30	40	50	60	70
Velocity in fps:	1,302	854	724	623	541	472	412
Average pellet energy in ft-lbs:	4.74	2.04	1.47	1.09	.82	.62	.47
Time of flight in seconds:	0	.0581	.0964	.1412	.1930	.2524	.3204

Type of load: Target
Three-foot velocity: 1,200 ft./sec.
Hull: 2¾-inch plastic
Wad: Plastic
Shot: Hard lead
Buffered: No
Test barrel length: 30 inch
Pellets will pierce skin up to 123 yards.

NO. 7½ LEAD PELLETS—1⅛ OUNCES—394 PELLETS
Mfg: Federal Cartridge Co. **Manufacturer's code:** T118
Recoil energy in 8-lb. shotgun: 20.4 ft./lbs. **Recoil velocity in 8-lb. shotgun:** 12.8 ft./sec.

Distance in yards:	Muzzle	20	30	40	50	60	70
Velocity in fps:	1,302	854	724	623	541	472	412
Average pellet energy in ft-lbs:	4.74	2.04	1.47	1.09	.82	.62	.47
Time of flight in seconds:	0	.0581	.0964	.1412	.1930	.2524	.3204

Type of load: Target
Three-foot velocity: 1,200 ft./sec.
Hull: 2¾-inch paper
Wad: Plastic
Shot: Hard lead
Buffered: No
Test barrel length: 30 inch
Pellets will pierce skin up to 123 yards.

NO. 7½ LEAD PELLETS—1⅛ OUNCES—394 PELLETS
Mfg: Fiocchi **Manufacturer's code:** 12GT118
Recoil energy in 8-lb. shotgun: 20.4 ft./lbs. **Recoil velocity in 8-lb. shotgun:** 12.8 ft./sec.

Distance in yards:	Muzzle	20	30	40	50	60	70
Velocity in fps:	1,302	854	724	623	541	472	412
Average pellet energy in ft-lbs:	4.74	2.04	1.47	1.09	.82	.62	.47
Time of flight in seconds:	0	.0581	.0964	.1412	.1930	.2524	.3204

Type of load: Game & Target
Three-foot velocity: 1,200 ft./sec.
Hull: 2¾-inch plastic
Wad: Plastic
Shot: Lead
Buffered: No
Test barrel length: 30 inch
Pellets will pierce skin up to 123 yards.

NO. 7½ LEAD PELLETS—1⅛ OUNCES—394 PELLETS
Mfg: Fiocchi **Manufacturer's code:** 12SSCH
Recoil energy in 8-lb. shotgun: 20.4 ft./lbs. **Recoil velocity in 8-lb. shotgun:** 12.8 ft./sec.

Distance in yards:	Muzzle	20	30	40	50	60	70
Velocity in fps:	1,302	854	724	623	541	472	412
Average pellet energy in ft-lbs:	4.74	2.04	1.47	1.09	.82	.62	.47
Time of flight in seconds:	0	.0581	.0964	.1412	.1930	.2524	.3204

Type of load: Target & Spreader
Three-foot velocity: 1,200 ft./sec.
Hull: 2¾-inch plastic
Wad: Plastic
Shot: Hard lead
Buffered: No
Test barrel length: 30 inch
Pellets will pierce skin up to 123 yards.

NO. 7½ LEAD PELLETS—1⅛ OUNCES—394 PELLETS
Mfg: Fiocchi **Manufacturer's code:** 12VIPH
Recoil energy in 8-lb. shotgun: 20.4 ft./lbs. **Recoil velocity in 8-lb. shotgun:** 12.8 ft./sec.

Distance in yards:	Muzzle	20	30	40	50	60	70
Velocity in fps:	1,302	854	724	623	541	472	412
Average pellet energy in ft-lbs:	4.74	2.04	1.47	1.09	.82	.62	.47
Time of flight in seconds:	0	.0581	.0964	.1412	.1930	.2524	.3204

Type of load: Target
Three-foot velocity: 1,200 ft./sec.
Hull: 2¾-inch plastic
Wad: Plastic
Shot: Hard lead
Buffered: No
Test barrel length: 30 inch
Pellets will pierce skin up to 123 yards.

NO. 7½ LEAD PELLETS—1⅛ OUNCES—394 PELLETS
Mfg: Kent Cartridge America/Canada **Manufacturer's code:** K122RTR32
Recoil energy in 8-lb. shotgun: 20.4 ft./lbs. **Recoil velocity in 8-lb. shotgun:** 12.8 ft./sec.

Distance in yards:	Muzzle	20	30	40	50	60	70
Velocity in fps:	1,302	854	724	623	541	472	412
Average pellet energy in ft-lbs:	4.74	2.04	1.47	1.09	.82	.62	.47
Time of flight in seconds:	0	.0581	.0964	.1412	.1930	.2524	.3204

Type of load: Target
Three-foot velocity: 1,200 ft./sec.
Hull: 2¾-inch plastic
Wad: Plastic
Shot: Lead
Buffered: No
Test barrel length: 30 inch
Pellets will pierce skin up to 123 yards.

NO. 7½ LEAD PELLETS—1⅛ OUNCES—394 PELLETS
Mfg: Polywad **Manufacturer's code:** SRH127
Recoil energy in 8-lb. shotgun: 20.4 ft./lbs. **Recoil velocity in 8-lb. shotgun:** 12.8 ft./sec.

Distance in yards:	Muzzle	20	30	40	50	60	70
Velocity in fps:	1,302	854	724	623	541	472	412
Average pellet energy in ft-lbs:	4.74	2.04	1.47	1.09	.82	.62	.47
Time of flight in seconds:	0	.0581	.0964	.1412	.1930	.2524	.3204

Type of load: Field
Three-foot velocity: 1,200 ft./sec.
Hull: 2¾-inch plastic
Wad: Plastic
Shot: Lead
Buffered: No
Test barrel length: 30 inch
Pellets will pierce skin up to 123 yards.

NO. 7½ LEAD PELLETS—1⅛ OUNCES—394 PELLETS
Mfg: Remington Arms Co. **Manufacturer's code:** STS12LH
Recoil energy in 8-lb. shotgun: 20.4 ft./lbs. **Recoil velocity in 8-lb. shotgun:** 12.8 ft./sec.

Distance in yards:	Muzzle	20	30	40	50	60	70
Velocity in fps:	1,302	854	724	623	541	472	412
Average pellet energy in ft-lbs:	4.74	2.04	1.47	1.09	.82	.62	.47
Time of flight in seconds:	0	.0581	.0964	.1412	.1930	.2524	.3204

Type of load: Target
Three-foot velocity: 1,200 ft./sec.
Hull: 2¾-inch plastic
Wad: Plastic
Shot: Hard lead
Buffered: No
Test barrel length: 30 inch
Pellets will pierce skin up to 123 yards.

NO. 7½ LEAD PELLETS—1⅛ OUNCES—394 PELLETS
Mfg: RST, Ltd. **Manufacturer's code:** N/A
Recoil energy in 8-lb. shotgun: 20.4 ft./lbs. **Recoil velocity in 8-lb. shotgun:** 12.8 ft./sec.

Distance in yards:	Muzzle	20	30	40	50	60	70
Velocity in fps:	1,302	854	724	623	541	472	412
Average pellet energy in ft-lbs:	4.74	2.04	1.47	1.09	.82	.62	.47
Time of flight in seconds:	0	.0581	.0964	.1412	.1930	.2524	.3204

Type of load: Target
Three-foot velocity: 1,200 ft./sec.
Hull: 2¾-inch plastic
Wad: Plastic
Shot: Lead
Buffered: No
Test barrel length: 30 inch
Pellets will pierce skin up to 123 yards.

NO. 7½ LEAD PELLETS—1⅛ OUNCES—394 PELLETS
Mfg: Sellier & Bellot **Manufacturer's code:** SBA1264
Recoil energy in 8-lb. shotgun: 20.4 ft./lbs. **Recoil velocity in 8-lb. shotgun:** 12.8 ft./sec.

Distance in yards:	Muzzle	20	30	40	50	60	70
Velocity in fps:	1,302	854	724	623	541	472	412
Average pellet energy in ft-lbs:	4.74	2.04	1.47	1.09	.82	.62	.47
Time of flight in seconds:	0	.0581	.0964	.1412	.1930	.2524	.3204

Type of load: Target
Three-foot velocity: 1,200 ft./sec.
Hull: 2¾-inch paper
Wad: Plastic
Shot: Lead
Buffered: No
Test barrel length: 30 inch
Pellets will pierce skin up to 123 yards.

NO. 7½ LEAD PELLETS—1⅛ OUNCES—394 PELLETS
Mfg: Winchester **Manufacturer's code:** AAM12
Recoil energy in 8-lb. shotgun: 20.4 ft./lbs. **Recoil velocity in 8-lb. shotgun:** 12.8 ft./sec.

Distance in yards:	Muzzle	20	30	40	50	60	70
Velocity in fps:	1,302	854	724	623	541	472	412
Average pellet energy in ft-lbs:	4.74	2.04	1.47	1.09	.82	.62	.47
Time of flight in seconds:	0	.0581	.0964	.1412	.1930	.2524	.3204

Type of load: Target
Three-foot velocity: 1,200 ft./sec.
Hull: 2¾-inch plastic
Wad: Plastic
Shot: Hard lead
Buffered: No
Test barrel length: 30 inch
Pellets will pierce skin up to 123 yards.

NO. 7½ LEAD PELLETS—1⅛ OUNCES—394 PELLETS
Mfg: Kent Cartridge America/Canada **Manufacturer's code:** K122HTR32
Recoil energy in 8-lb. shotgun: 21.3 ft./lbs. **Recoil velocity in 8-lb. shotgun:** 13.1 ft./sec.

Distance in yards:	Muzzle	20	30	40	50	60	70
Velocity in fps:	1,324	864	731	629	546	476	416
Average pellet energy in ft-lbs:	4.91	2.09	1.50	1.11	.83	.63	.48
Time of flight in seconds:	0	.0573	.0952	.1395	.1908	.2497	.3172

Type of load: Target
Three-foot velocity: 1,220 ft./sec.
Hull: 2¾-inch plastic
Wad: Plastic
Shot: Lead
Buffered: No
Test barrel length: 30 inch
Pellets will pierce skin up to 124 yards.

NO. 7½ LEAD PELLETS—1⅛ OUNCES—394 PELLETS
Mfg: Aguila **Manufacturer's code:** N/A
Recoil energy in 8-lb. shotgun: 22.0 ft./lbs. **Recoil velocity in 8-lb. shotgun:** 13.3 ft./sec.

Distance in yards:	Muzzle	20	30	40	50	60	70
Velocity in fps:	1,341	871	737	633	549	479	418
Average pellet energy in ft-lbs:	5.03	2.12	1.52	1.12	.84	.64	.49
Time of flight in seconds:	0	.0568	.0943	.1383	.1893	.2478	.3149

Type of load: Sporting Clays
Three-foot velocity: 1,235 ft./sec.
Hull: 2¾-inch plastic
Wad: Plastic
Shot: Nickel-plated lead
Buffered: No
Test barrel length: 30 inch
Pellets will pierce skin up to 124 yards.

NO. 7½ LEAD PELLETS—1⅛ OUNCES—394 PELLETS
Mfg: Baschieri & Pellagri **Manufacturer's code:** N/A
Recoil energy in 8-lb. shotgun: 22.0 ft./lbs. **Recoil velocity in 8-lb. shotgun:** 13.3 ft./sec.

Distance in yards:	Muzzle	20	30	40	50	60	70
Velocity in fps:	1,341	871	737	633	549	479	418
Average pellet energy in ft-lbs:	5.03	2.12	1.52	1.12	.84	.64	.49
Time of flight in seconds:	0	.0568	.0943	.1383	.1893	.2478	.3149

Type of load: Comp-2000 32 gr.
Three-foot velocity: 1,235 ft./sec.
Hull: 2¾-inch plastic
Wad: Plastic
Shot: Hard lead
Buffered: No
Test barrel length: 30 inch
Pellets will pierce skin up to 124 yards.

NO. 7½ LEAD PELLETS—1⅛ OUNCES—394 PELLETS

Mfg: Federal Cartridge Co. **Manufacturer's code:** T178
Recoil energy in 8-lb. shotgun: 22.0 ft./lbs. **Recoil velocity in 8-lb. shotgun:** 13.3 ft./sec.

Distance in yards:	Muzzle	20	30	40	50	60	70
Velocity in fps:	1,341	871	737	633	549	479	418
Average pellet energy in ft-lbs:	5.03	2.12	1.52	1.12	.84	.64	.49
Time of flight in seconds:	0	.0568	.0943	.1383	.1893	.2478	.3149

Type of load: Target
Three-foot velocity: 1,235 ft./sec.
Hull: 2¾-inch plastic
Wad: Plastic
Shot: Hard lead
Buffered: No
Test barrel length: 30 inch
Pellets will pierce skin up to 124 yards.

NO. 7½ LEAD PELLETS—1⅛ OUNCES—394 PELLETS

Mfg: Federal Cartridge Co. **Manufacturer's code:** T171
Recoil energy in 8-lb. shotgun: 22.0 ft./lbs. **Recoil velocity in 8-lb. shotgun:** 13.3 ft./sec.

Distance in yards:	Muzzle	20	30	40	50	60	70
Velocity in fps:	1,341	871	737	633	549	479	418
Average pellet energy in ft-lbs:	5.03	2.12	1.52	1.12	.84	.64	.49
Time of flight in seconds:	0	.0568	.0943	.1383	.1893	.2478	.3149

Type of load: Target
Three-foot velocity: 1,235 ft./sec.
Hull: 2¾-inch paper
Wad: Plastic
Shot: Hard lead
Buffered: No
Test barrel length: 30 inch
Pellets will pierce skin up to 124 yards.

NO. 7½ LEAD PELLETS—1⅛ OUNCES—394 PELLETS

Mfg: PMC (Eldorado Cartridge Corp.) **Mfg's code:** HD12/CT12/GCT
Recoil energy in 8-lb. shotgun: 22.0 ft./lbs. **Recoil velocity in 8-lb. shotgun:** 13.3 ft./sec.

Distance in yards:	Muzzle	20	30	40	50	60	70
Velocity in fps:	1,341	871	737	633	549	479	418
Average pellet energy in ft-lbs:	5.03	2.12	1.52	1.12	.84	.64	.49
Time of flight in seconds:	0	.0568	.0943	.1383	.1893	.2478	.3149

Type of load: Heavy Dove & Target
Three-foot velocity: 1,235 ft./sec.
Hull: 2¾-inch plastic
Wad: Plastic
Shot: Lead
Buffered: No
Test barrel length: 30 inch
Pellets will pierce skin up to 124 yards.

NO. 7½ LEAD PELLETS—1⅛ OUNCES—394 PELLETS

Mfg: Estate Cartridge **Manufacturer's code:** CT12XH/SS12XH
Recoil energy in 8-lb. shotgun: 22.7 ft./lbs. **Recoil velocity in 8-lb. shotgun:** 13.5 ft./sec.

Distance in yards:	Muzzle	20	30	40	50	60	70
Velocity in fps:	1,357	878	742	637	553	482	421
Average pellet energy in ft-lbs:	5.16	2.16	1.54	1.14	.86	.65	.50
Time of flight in seconds:	0	.0562	.0935	.1372	.1878	.2459	.3126

Type of load: Target
Three-foot velocity: 1,250 ft./sec.
Hull: 2¾-inch plastic
Wad: Plastic
Shot: Hard lead
Buffered: No
Test barrel length: 30 inch
Pellets will pierce skin up to 125 yards.

NO. 7½ LEAD PELLETS—1⅛ OUNCES—394 PELLETS

Mfg: Estate Cartridge **Manufacturer's code:** HG12
Recoil energy in 8-lb. shotgun: 22.7 ft./lbs. **Recoil velocity in 8-lb. shotgun:** 13.5 ft./sec.

Distance in yards:	Muzzle	20	30	40	50	60	70
Velocity in fps:	1,357	878	742	637	553	482	421
Average pellet energy in ft-lbs:	5.16	2.16	1.54	1.14	.86	.65	.50
Time of flight in seconds:	0	.0562	.0935	.1372	.1878	.2459	.3126

Type of load: Field
Three-foot velocity: 1,250 ft./sec.
Hull: 2¾-inch plastic
Wad: Plastic
Shot: Hard lead
Buffered: No
Test barrel length: 30 inch
Pellets will pierce skin up to 125 yards.

NO. 7½ LEAD PELLETS—1⅛ OUNCES—394 PELLETS

Mfg: Federal Cartridge Co. **Manufacturer's code:** H123/HGL12
Recoil energy in 8-lb. shotgun: 22.7 ft./lbs. **Recoil velocity in 8-lb. shotgun:** 13.5 ft./sec.

Distance in yards:	Muzzle	20	30	40	50	60	70
Velocity in fps:	1,357	878	742	637	553	482	421
Average pellet energy in ft-lbs:	5.16	2.16	1.54	1.14	.86	.65	.50
Time of flight in seconds:	0	.0562	.0935	.1372	.1878	.2459	.3126

Type of load: Field
Three-foot velocity: 1,250 ft./sec.
Hull: 2¾-inch plastic
Wad: Plastic
Shot: Lead
Buffered: No
Test barrel length: 30 inch
Pellets will pierce skin up to 125 yards.

NO. 7½ LEAD PELLETS—1⅛ OUNCES—394 PELLETS

Mfg: Fiocchi **Manufacturer's code:** 12FLD
Recoil energy in 8-lb. shotgun: 22.7 ft./lbs. **Recoil velocity in 8-lb. shotgun:** 13.5 ft./sec.

Distance in yards:	Muzzle	20	30	40	50	60	70
Velocity in fps:	1,357	878	742	637	553	482	421
Average pellet energy in ft-lbs:	5.16	2.16	1.54	1.14	.86	.65	.50
Time of flight in seconds:	0	.0562	.0935	.1372	.1878	.2459	.3126

Type of load: Field
Three-foot velocity: 1,250 ft./sec.
Hull: 2¾-inch plastic
Wad: Plastic
Shot: Lead
Buffered: No
Test barrel length: 30 inch
Pellets will pierce skin up to 125 yards.

NO. 7½ LEAD PELLETS—1⅛ OUNCES—394 PELLETS
Mfg: Fiocchi **Manufacturer's code:** 12WRNO
Recoil energy in 8-lb. shotgun: 22.7 ft./lbs. **Recoil velocity in 8-lb. shotgun:** 13.5 ft./sec.

Distance in yards:	Muzzle	20	30	40	50	60	70
Velocity in fps:	1,357	878	742	637	553	482	421
Average pellet energy in ft-lbs:	5.16	2.16	1.54	1.14	.86	.65	.50
Time of flight in seconds:	0	.0562	.0935	.1372	.1878	.2459	.3126

Type of load: Target
Three-foot velocity: 1,250 ft./sec.
Hull: 2¾-inch plastic
Wad: Plastic
Shot: Hard lead
Buffered: No
Test barrel length: 30 inch
Pellets will pierce skin up to 125 yards.

NO. 7½ LEAD PELLETS—1⅛ OUNCES—394 PELLETS
Mfg: Kent Cartridge America/Canada **Manufacturer's code:** K122UG32
Recoil energy in 8-lb. shotgun: 22.7 ft./lbs. **Recoil velocity in 8-lb. shotgun:** 13.5 ft./sec.

Distance in yards:	Muzzle	20	30	40	50	60	70
Velocity in fps:	1,357	878	742	637	553	482	421
Average pellet energy in ft-lbs:	5.16	2.16	1.54	1.14	.86	.65	.50
Time of flight in seconds:	0	.0562	.0935	.1372	.1878	.2459	.3126

Type of load: Field
Three-foot velocity: 1,250 ft./sec.
Hull: 2¾-inch plastic
Wad: Plastic
Shot: Lead
Buffered: No
Test barrel length: 30 inch
Pellets will pierce skin up to 125 yards.

NO. 7½ LEAD PELLETS—1⅛ OUNCES—394 PELLETS
Mfg: Kent Cartridge America/Canada **Manufacturer's code:** K122RSC32
Recoil energy in 8-lb. shotgun: 22.7 ft./lbs. **Recoil velocity in 8-lb. shotgun:** 13.5 ft./sec.

Distance in yards:	Muzzle	20	30	40	50	60	70
Velocity in fps:	1,357	878	742	637	553	482	421
Average pellet energy in ft-lbs:	5.16	2.16	1.54	1.14	.86	.65	.50
Time of flight in seconds:	0	.0562	.0935	.1372	.1878	.2459	.3126

Type of load: Target
Three-foot velocity: 1,250 ft./sec.
Hull: 2¾-inch plastic
Wad: Plastic
Shot: Lead
Buffered: No
Test barrel length: 30 inch
Pellets will pierce skin up to 125 yards.

NO. 7½ LEAD PELLETS—1⅛ OUNCES—394 PELLETS
Mfg: Remington Arms Co. **Manufacturer's code:** RP12HD
Recoil energy in 8-lb. shotgun: 22.7 ft./lbs. **Recoil velocity in 8-lb. shotgun:** 13.5 ft./sec.

Distance in yards:	Muzzle	20	30	40	50	60	70
Velocity in fps:	1,357	878	742	637	553	482	421
Average pellet energy in ft-lbs:	5.16	2.16	1.54	1.14	.86	.65	.50
Time of flight in seconds:	0	.0562	.0935	.1372	.1878	.2459	.3126

Type of load: Field
Three-foot velocity: 1,250 ft./sec.
Hull: 2¾-inch plastic
Wad: Plastic
Shot: Lead
Buffered: No
Test barrel length: 30 inch
Pellets will pierce skin up to 125 yards.

NO. 7½ LEAD PELLETS—1⅛ OUNCES—394 PELLETS
Mfg: Rottweil **Manufacturer's code:** Super Sport
Recoil energy in 8-lb. shotgun: 22.7 ft./lbs. **Recoil velocity in 8-lb. shotgun:** 13.5 ft./sec.

Distance in yards:	Muzzle	20	30	40	50	60	70
Velocity in fps:	1,357	878	742	637	553	482	421
Average pellet energy in ft-lbs:	5.16	2.16	1.54	1.14	.86	.65	.50
Time of flight in seconds:	0	.0562	.0935	.1372	.1878	.2459	.3126

Type of load: Target
Three-foot velocity: 1,250 ft./sec.
Hull: 2¾-inch plastic
Wad: Plastic
Shot: Lead
Buffered: No
Test barrel length: 30 inch
Pellets will pierce skin up to 125 yards.

NO. 7½ LEAD PELLETS—1⅛ OUNCES—394 PELLETS
Mfg: RST, Ltd. **Manufacturer's code:** N/A
Recoil energy in 8-lb. shotgun: 22.7 ft./lbs. **Recoil velocity in 8-lb. shotgun:** 13.5 ft./sec.

Distance in yards:	Muzzle	20	30	40	50	60	70
Velocity in fps:	1,357	878	742	637	553	482	421
Average pellet energy in ft-lbs:	5.16	2.16	1.54	1.14	.86	.65	.50
Time of flight in seconds:	0	.0562	.0935	.1372	.1878	.2459	.3126

Type of load: Target
Three-foot velocity: 1,250 ft./sec.
Hull: 2¾-inch plastic
Wad: Plastic
Shot: Lead
Buffered: No
Test barrel length: 30 inch
Pellets will pierce skin up to 125 yards.

NO. 7½ LEAD PELLETS—1⅛ OUNCES—394 PELLETS
Mfg: Winchester **Manufacturer's code:** XU12H
Recoil energy in 8-lb. shotgun: 22.7 ft./lbs. **Recoil velocity in 8-lb. shotgun:** 13.5 ft./sec.

Distance in yards:	Muzzle	20	30	40	50	60	70
Velocity in fps:	1,357	878	742	637	553	482	421
Average pellet energy in ft-lbs:	5.16	2.16	1.54	1.14	.86	.65	.50
Time of flight in seconds:	0	.0562	.0935	.1372	.1878	.2459	.3126

Type of load: Field
Three-foot velocity: 1,250 ft./sec.
Hull: 2¾-inch plastic
Wad: Plastic
Shot: Lead
Buffered: No
Test barrel length: 30 inch
Pellets will pierce skin up to 125 yards.

NO. 7½ LEAD PELLETS—1⅛ OUNCES—394 PELLETS
Mfg: Winchester **Manufacturer's code:** AAHA12
Recoil energy in 8-lb. shotgun: 22.7 ft./lbs. **Recoil velocity in 8-lb. shotgun:** 13.7 ft./sec.

Distance in yards:	Muzzle	20	30	40	50	60	70
Velocity in fps:	1,357	878	742	637	553	482	421
Average pellet energy in ft-lbs:	5.16	2.16	1.54	1.14	.86	.65	.50
Time of flight in seconds:	0	.0562	.0935	.1372	.1878	.2459	.3126

Type of load: Target
Three-foot velocity: 1,250 ft./sec.
Hull: 2¾-inch plastic
Wad: Plastic
Shot: Hard lead
Buffered: No
Test barrel length: 30 inch
Pellets will pierce skin up to 125 yards.

NO. 7½ LEAD PELLETS—1⅛ OUNCES—394 PELLETS
Mfg: Sellier & Bellot **Manufacturer's code:** SBA01247
Recoil energy in 8-lb. shotgun: 23.9 ft./lbs. **Recoil velocity in 8-lb. shotgun:** 13.9 ft./sec.

Distance in yards:	Muzzle	20	30	40	50	60	70
Velocity in fps:	1,385	891	752	645	559	487	425
Average pellet energy in ft-lbs:	5.37	2.22	1.58	1.16	.87	.66	.51
Time of flight in seconds:	0	.0553	.0921	.1652	.1853	.2429	.3088

Type of load: Target
Three-foot velocity: 1,275 ft./sec.
Hull: 2¾-inch plastic
Wad: Plastic
Shot: Lead
Buffered: No
Test barrel length: 30 inch
Pellets will pierce skin up to 126 yards.

NO. 7½ LEAD PELLETS—1⅛ OUNCES—394 PELLETS
Mfg: RST, Ltd. **Manufacturer's code:** N/A
Recoil energy in 8-lb. shotgun: 25.2 ft./lbs. **Recoil velocity in 8-lb. shotgun:** 14.2 ft./sec.

Distance in yards:	Muzzle	20	30	40	50	60	70
Velocity in fps:	1,413	903	761	652	565	492	430
Average pellet energy in ft-lbs:	5.59	2.28	1.62	1.19	.89	.68	.52
Time of flight in seconds:	0	.0544	.0907	.1334	.1829	.2399	.3052

Type of load: Target
Three-foot velocity: 1,300 ft./sec.
Hull: 2¾-inch plastic
Wad: Plastic
Shot: Lead
Buffered: No
Test barrel length: 30 inch
Pellets will pierce skin up to 126 yards.

NO. 7½ LEAD PELLETS—1⅛ OUNCES—394 PELLETS
Mfg: Winchester **Manufacturer's code:** AASC12
Recoil energy in 8-lb. shotgun: 25.2 ft./lbs. **Recoil velocity in 8-lb. shotgun:** 14.2 ft./sec.

Distance in yards:	Muzzle	20	30	40	50	60	70
Velocity in fps:	1,413	903	761	652	565	492	430
Average pellet energy in ft-lbs:	5.59	2.28	1.62	1.19	.89	.68	.52
Time of flight in seconds:	0	.0544	.0907	.1334	.1829	.2399	.3052

Type of load: Target
Three-foot velocity: 1,300 ft./sec.
Hull: 2¾-inch plastic
Wad: Plastic
Shot: Lead
Buffered: No
Test barrel length: 30 inch
Pellets will pierce skin up to 126 yards.

NO. 7½ LEAD PELLETS—1⅛ OUNCES—394 PELLETS
Mfg: ARMUSA **Manufacturer's code:** PLA-32
Recoil energy in 8-lb. shotgun: 26.8 ft./lbs. **Recoil velocity in 8-lb. shotgun:** 14.7 ft./sec.

Distance in yards:	Muzzle	20	30	40	50	60	70
Velocity in fps:	1,447	917	771	660	571	498	435
Average pellet energy in ft-lbs:	5.86	2.36	1.66	1.22	.91	.69	.53
Time of flight in seconds:	0	.0534	.0891	.1313	.1802	.2365	.3010

Type of load: Sporting Clay
Three-foot velocity: 1,330 ft./sec.
Hull: 2¾-inch plastic
Wad: Plastic
Shot: Lead
Buffered: No
Test barrel length: 30 inch
Pellets will pierce skin up to 127 yards.

NO. 7½ LEAD PELLETS—1⅛ OUNCES—394 PELLETS
Mfg: Baschieri & Pellagri **Manufacturer's code:** F2
Recoil energy in 8-lb. shotgun: 21.2 ft./lbs. **Recoil velocity in 8-lb. shotgun:** 13.0 ft./sec.

Distance in yards:	Muzzle	20	30	40	50	60	70
Velocity in fps:	1,447	917	771	660	571	498	435
Average pellet energy in ft-lbs:	5.86	2.36	1.66	1.22	.91	.69	.53
Time of flight in seconds:	0	.0534	.0891	.1313	.1802	.2365	.3010

Type of load: Sporting Clay
Three-foot velocity: 1,330 ft./sec.
Hull: 2¾-inch plastic
Wad: Plastic
Shot: Hard lead
Buffered: No
Test barrel length: 30 inch
Pellets will pierce skin up to 127 yards.

NO. 7½ LEAD PELLETS—1⅛ OUNCES—394 PELLETS
Mfg: Eley Hawk **Manufacturer's code:** VIP
Recoil energy in 8-lb. shotgun: 26.8 ft./lbs. **Recoil velocity in 8-lb. shotgun:** 14.7 ft./sec.

Distance in yards:	Muzzle	20	30	40	50	60	70
Velocity in fps:	1,447	917	771	660	571	498	435
Average pellet energy in ft-lbs:	5.86	2.36	1.66	1.22	.91	.69	.53
Time of flight in seconds:	0	.0534	.0891	.1313	.1802	.2365	.3010

Type of load: Target
Three-foot velocity: 1,330 ft./sec.
Hull: 2¾-inch plastic
Wad: Plastic
Shot: Hard lead
Buffered: No
Test barrel length: 30 inch
Pellets will pierce skin up to 127 yards.

NO. 7½ LEAD PELLETS—1⅛ OUNCES—388 PELLETS

Mfg: Kent Cartridge America/Canada **Manufacturer's code:** K122SSC32
Recoil energy in 8-lb. shotgun: 21.2 ft./lbs. **Recoil velocity in 8-lb. shotgun:** 13.0 ft./sec.

Distance in yards:	Muzzle	20	30	40	50	60	70
Velocity in fps:	1,447	917	771	660	571	498	435
Average pellet energy in ft-lbs:	5.86	2.36	1.66	1.22	.91	.69	.53
Time of flight in seconds:	0	.0534	.0891	.1313	.1802	.2365	.3010

Type of load: Target
Three-foot velocity: 1,330 ft./sec.
Hull: 2¾-inch plastic
Wad: Plastic
Shot: Lead
Buffered: No
Test barrel length: 30 inch
Pellets will pierce skin up to 127 yards.

NO. 7½ LEAD PELLETS—1⅛ OUNCES—394 PELLETS

Mfg: Federal Cartridge Co. **Manufacturer's code:** P128
Recoil energy in 8-lb. shotgun: 30.7 ft./lbs. **Recoil velocity in 8-lb. shotgun:** 15.7 ft./sec.

Distance in yards:	Muzzle	20	30	40	50	60	70
Velocity in fps:	1,525	951	796	679	587	511	446
Average pellet energy in ft-lbs:	6.51	2.53	1.77	1.29	.96	.73	.56
Time of flight in seconds:	0	.0511	.0857	.1265	.1741	.2290	.2918

Type of load: Field
Three-foot velocity: 1,400 ft./sec.
Hull: 2¾-inch plastic
Wad: Plastic
Shot: Lead
Buffered: No
Test barrel length: 30 inch
Pellets will pierce skin up to 129 yards.

NO. 7½ LEAD PELLETS—1¼ OUNCES—437 PELLETS

Mfg: Estate Cartridge **Manufacturer's code:** XHG12
Recoil energy in 8-lb. shotgun: 26.3 ft./lbs. **Recoil velocity in 8-lb. shotgun:** 14.5 ft./sec.

Distance in yards:	Muzzle	20	30	40	50	60	70
Velocity in fps:	1,324	864	731	629	546	476	416
Average pellet energy in ft-lbs:	4.91	2.09	1.50	1.11	.83	.63	.48
Time of flight in seconds:	0	.0573	.0952	.1395	.1908	.2497	.3172

Type of load: Field
Three-foot velocity: 1,220 ft./sec.
Hull: 2¾-inch plastic
Wad: Plastic
Shot: Hard lead
Buffered: No
Test barrel length: 30 inch
Pellets will pierce skin up to 124 yards.

NO. 7½ LEAD PELLETS—1¼ OUNCES—437 PELLETS

Mfg: Federal Cartridge Co. **Manufacturer's code:** P153/H125/H120
Recoil energy in 8-lb. shotgun: 26.3 ft./lbs. **Recoil velocity in 8-lb. shotgun:** 14.5 ft./sec.

Distance in yards:	Muzzle	20	30	40	50	60	70
Velocity in fps:	1,324	864	731	629	546	476	416
Average pellet energy in ft-lbs:	4.91	2.09	1.50	1.11	.83	.63	.48
Time of flight in seconds:	0	.0573	.0952	.1395	.1908	.2497	.3172

Type of load: Field
Three-foot velocity: 1,220 ft./sec.
Hull: 2¾-inch plastic
Wad: Plastic
Shot: Lead
Buffered: No
Test barrel length: 30 inch
Pellets will pierce skin up to 124 yards.

NO. 7½ LEAD PELLETS—1¼ OUNCES—437 PELLETS

Mfg: Fiocchi **Manufacturer's code:** 12HF
Recoil energy in 8-lb. shotgun: 26.3 ft./lbs. **Recoil velocity in 8-lb. shotgun:** 14.5 ft./sec.

Distance in yards:	Muzzle	20	30	40	50	60	70
Velocity in fps:	1,324	864	731	629	546	476	416
Average pellet energy in ft-lbs:	4.91	2.09	1.50	1.11	.83	.63	.48
Time of flight in seconds:	0	.0573	.0952	.1395	.1908	.2497	.3172

Type of load: Field
Three-foot velocity: 1,220 ft./sec.
Hull: 2¾-inch plastic
Wad: Plastic
Shot: Lead
Buffered: No
Test barrel length: 30 inch
Pellets will pierce skin up to 124 yards.

NO. 7½ LEAD PELLETS—1¼ OUNCES—437 PELLETS

Mfg: Fiocchi **Manufacturer's code:** 12HFN
Recoil energy in 8-lb. shotgun: 26.3 ft./lbs. **Recoil velocity in 8-lb. shotgun:** 14.5 ft./sec.

Distance in yards:	Muzzle	20	30	40	50	60	70
Velocity in fps:	1,324	864	731	629	546	476	416
Average pellet energy in ft-lbs:	4.91	2.09	1.50	1.11	.83	.63	.48
Time of flight in seconds:	0	.0573	.0952	.1395	.1908	.2497	.3172

Type of load: Field
Three-foot velocity: 1,220 ft./sec.
Hull: 2¾-inch plastic
Wad: Plastic
Shot: Nickel-plated lead
Buffered: No
Test barrel length: 30 inch
Pellets will pierce skin up to 124 yards.

NO. 7½ LEAD PELLETS—1¼ OUNCES—437 PELLETS

Mfg: Kent Cartridge America/Canada **Manufacturer's code:** K122PL36
Recoil energy in 8-lb. shotgun: 26.3 ft./lbs. **Recoil velocity in 8-lb. shotgun:** 14.5 ft./sec.

Distance in yards:	Muzzle	20	30	40	50	60	70
Velocity in fps:	1,324	864	731	629	546	476	416
Average pellet energy in ft-lbs:	4.91	2.09	1.50	1.11	.83	.63	.48
Time of flight in seconds:	0	.0573	.0952	.1395	.1908	.2497	.3172

Type of load: Target
Three-foot velocity: 1,220 ft./sec.
Hull: 2¾-inch plastic
Wad: Plastic
Shot: Lead
Buffered: No
Test barrel length: 30 inch
Pellets will pierce skin up to 124 yards.

NO. 7½ LEAD PELLETS—1¼ OUNCES—437 PELLETS

Mfg: Remington Arms Co. **Manufacturer's code:** RP12H
Recoil energy in 8-lb. shotgun: 26.3 ft./lbs. **Recoil velocity in 8-lb. shotgun:** 14.5 ft./sec.

Distance in yards:	Muzzle	20	30	40	50	60	70
Velocity in fps:	1,324	864	731	629	546	476	416
Average pellet energy in ft-lbs:	4.91	2.09	1.50	1.11	.83	.63	.48
Time of flight in seconds:	0	.0573	.0952	.1395	.1908	.2497	.3172

Type of load: Field
Three-foot velocity: 1,220 ft./sec.
Hull: 2¾-inch plastic
Wad: Plastic
Shot: Lead
Buffered: No
Test barrel length: 30 inch
Pellets will pierce skin up to 124 yards.

NO. 7½ LEAD PELLETS—1¼ OUNCES—437 PELLETS

Mfg: Remington Arms Co. **Manufacturer's code:** STS12P
Recoil energy in 8-lb. shotgun: 26.3 ft./lbs. **Recoil velocity in 8-lb. shotgun:** 14.5 ft./sec.

Distance in yards:	Muzzle	20	30	40	50	60	70
Velocity in fps:	1,324	864	731	629	546	476	416
Average pellet energy in ft-lbs:	4.91	2.09	1.50	1.11	.83	.63	.48
Time of flight in seconds:	0	.0573	.0952	.1395	.1908	.2497	.3172

Type of load: Target
Three-foot velocity: 1,220 ft./sec.
Hull: 2¾-inch plastic
Wad: Plastic
Shot: Hard lead
Buffered: No
Test barrel length: 30 inch
Pellets will pierce skin up to 124 yards.

NO. 7½ LEAD PELLETS—1¼ OUNCES—437 PELLETS

Mfg: Sellier & Bellot **Manufacturer's code:** SBA01207
Recoil energy in 8-lb. shotgun: 26.3 ft./lbs. **Recoil velocity in 8-lb. shotgun:** 14.5 ft./sec.

Distance in yards:	Muzzle	20	30	40	50	60	70
Velocity in fps:	1,324	864	731	629	546	476	416
Average pellet energy in ft-lbs:	4.91	2.09	1.50	1.11	.83	.63	.48
Time of flight in seconds:	0	.0573	.0952	.1395	.1908	.2497	.3172

Type of load: Field
Three-foot velocity: 1,220 ft./sec.
Hull: 2¾-inch plastic
Wad: Plastic
Shot: Lead
Buffered: No
Test barrel length: 30 inch
Pellets will pierce skin up to 124 yards.

NO. 7½ LEAD PELLETS—1¼ OUNCES—437 PELLETS

Mfg: Winchester **Manufacturer's code:** XU12SP/AA12SP
Recoil energy in 8-lb. shotgun: 26.3 ft./lbs. **Recoil velocity in 8-lb. shotgun:** 14.5 ft./sec.

Distance in yards:	Muzzle	20	30	40	50	60	70
Velocity in fps:	1,324	864	731	629	546	476	416
Average pellet energy in ft-lbs:	4.91	2.09	1.50	1.11	.83	.63	.48
Time of flight in seconds:	0	.0573	.0952	.1395	.1908	.2497	.3172

Type of load: Field & Target
Three-foot velocity: 1,220 ft./sec.
Hull: 2¾-inch plastic
Wad: Plastic
Shot: Lead
Buffered: No
Test barrel length: 30 inch
Pellets will pierce skin up to 124 yards.

NO. 7½ LEAD PELLETS—1¼ OUNCES—437 PELLETS

Mfg: Rottweil **Manufacturer's code:** Super Game
Recoil energy in 8-lb. shotgun: 26.3 ft./lbs. **Recoil velocity in 8-lb. shotgun:** 14.5 ft./sec.

Distance in yards:	Muzzle	20	30	40	50	60	70
Velocity in fps:	1,341	871	737	633	549	479	418
Average pellet energy in ft-lbs:	5.03	2.12	1.52	1.12	.84	.64	.49
Time of flight in seconds:	0	.0568	.0943	.1383	.1893	.2478	.3149

Type of load: Field
Three-foot velocity: 1,235 ft./sec.
Hull: 2¾-inch plastic
Wad: Plastic
Shot: Lead
Buffered: No
Test barrel length: 30 inch
Pellets will pierce skin up to 124 yards.

NO. 7½ LEAD PELLETS—1¼ OUNCES—437 PELLETS

Mfg: Baschieri & Pellagri **Manufacturer's code:** F2 Flash
Recoil energy in 8-lb. shotgun: 29.5 ft./lbs. **Recoil velocity in 8-lb. shotgun:** 15.4 ft./sec.

Distance in yards:	Muzzle	20	30	40	50	60	70
Velocity in fps:	1,385	891	752	645	559	487	425
Average pellet energy in ft-lbs:	5.37	2.22	1.58	1.16	.87	.66	.51
Time of flight in seconds:	0	.0553	.0921	.1652	.1853	.2429	.3088

Type of load: Target
Three-foot velocity: 1,275 ft./sec.
Hull: 2¾-inch plastic
Wad: Plastic
Shot: Hard lead
Buffered: No
Test barrel length: 30 inch
Pellets will pierce skin up to 126 yards.

NO. 7½ LEAD PELLETS—1¼ OUNCES—437 PELLETS

Mfg: Federal Cartridge Co. **Manufacturer's code:** H127
Recoil energy in 8-lb. shotgun: 29.5 ft./lbs. **Recoil velocity in 8-lb. shotgun:** 15.4 ft./sec.

Distance in yards:	Muzzle	20	30	40	50	60	70
Velocity in fps:	1,385	891	752	645	559	487	425
Average pellet energy in ft-lbs:	5.37	2.22	1.58	1.16	.87	.66	.51
Time of flight in seconds:	0	.0553	.0921	.1652	.1853	.2429	.3088

Type of load: Field
Three-foot velocity: 1,275 ft./sec.
Hull: 2¾-inch plastic
Wad: Plastic
Shot: Lead
Buffered: No
Test barrel length: 30 inch
Pellets will pierce skin up to 126 yards.

NO. 7½ LEAD PELLETS—1¼ OUNCES—437 PELLETS

Mfg: ARMUSA **Manufacturer's code:** Live Pigeon
Recoil energy in 8-lb. shotgun: 31.1 ft./lbs. **Recoil velocity in 8-lb. shotgun:** 15.8 ft./sec.

Distance in yards:	Muzzle	20	30	40	50	60	70
Velocity in fps:	1,413	903	761	652	565	492	430
Average pellet energy in ft-lbs:	5.59	2.28	1.62	1.19	.89	.68	.52
Time of flight in seconds:	0	.0544	.0907	.1334	.1829	.2399	.3052

Type of load: Target
Three-foot velocity: 1,300 ft./sec.
Hull: 2¾-inch plastic
Wad: Plastic
Shot: Nickel-plated lead
Buffered: No
Test barrel length: 30 inch
Pellets will pierce skin up to 126 yards.

NO. 7½ LEAD PELLETS—1¼ OUNCES—437 PELLETS

Mfg: ARMUSA **Manufacturer's code:** N/A
Recoil energy in 8-lb. shotgun: 31.1 ft./lbs. **Recoil velocity in 8-lb. shotgun:** 15.8 ft./sec.

Distance in yards:	Muzzle	20	30	40	50	60	70
Velocity in fps:	1,413	903	761	652	565	492	430
Average pellet energy in ft-lbs:	5.59	2.28	1.62	1.19	.89	.68	.52
Time of flight in seconds:	0	.0544	.0907	.1334	.1829	.2399	.3052

Type of load: Field
Three-foot velocity: 1,300 ft./sec.
Hull: 2¾-inch plastic
Wad: Plastic
Shot: Lead
Buffered: No
Test barrel length: 30 inch
Pellets will pierce skin up to 126 yards.

NO. 7½ LEAD PELLETS—1¼ OUNCES—437 PELLETS

Mfg: Aguila **Manufacturer's code:** N/A
Recoil energy in 8-lb. shotgun: 33.0 ft./lbs. **Recoil velocity in 8-lb. shotgun:** 16.3 ft./sec.

Distance in yards:	Muzzle	20	30	40	50	60	70
Velocity in fps:	1,447	917	771	660	571	498	435
Average pellet energy in ft-lbs:	5.86	2.36	1.66	1.22	.91	.69	.53
Time of flight in seconds:	0	.0534	.0891	.1313	.1802	.2365	.3010

Type of load: Field & Target
Three-foot velocity: 1,330 ft./sec.
Hull: 2¾-inch plastic
Wad: Plastic
Shot: Lead
Buffered: No
Test barrel length: 30 inch
Pellets will pierce skin up to 127 yards.

NO. 7½ LEAD PELLETS—1¼ OUNCES—437 PELLETS

Mfg: Dionisi **Manufacturer's code:** D 12 SLR
Recoil energy in 8-lb. shotgun: 33.0 ft./lbs. **Recoil velocity in 8-lb. shotgun:** 16.3 ft./sec.

Distance in yards:	Muzzle	20	30	40	50	60	70
Velocity in fps:	1,447	917	771	660	571	498	435
Average pellet energy in ft-lbs:	5.86	2.36	1.66	1.22	.91	.69	.53
Time of flight in seconds:	0	.0534	.0891	.1313	.1802	.2365	.3010

Type of load: Field
Three-foot velocity: 1,330 ft./sec.
Hull: 2¾-inch plastic
Wad: Plastic
Shot: Lead
Buffered: No
Test barrel length: 30 inch
Pellets will pierce skin up to 127 yards.

NO. 7½ LEAD PELLETS—1¼ OUNCES—437 PELLETS

Mfg: Estate Cartridge **Manufacturer's code:** HV12
Recoil energy in 8-lb. shotgun: 33.0 ft./lbs. **Recoil velocity in 8-lb. shotgun:** 16.3 ft./sec.

Distance in yards:	Muzzle	20	30	40	50	60	70
Velocity in fps:	1,447	917	771	660	571	498	435
Average pellet energy in ft-lbs:	5.86	2.36	1.66	1.22	.91	.69	.53
Time of flight in seconds:	0	.0534	.0891	.1313	.1802	.2365	.3010

Type of load: Field
Three-foot velocity: 1,330 ft./sec.
Hull: 2¾-inch plastic
Wad: Plastic
Shot: Hard lead
Buffered: No
Test barrel length: 30 inch
Pellets will pierce skin up to 127 yards.

NO. 7½ LEAD PELLETS—1¼ OUNCES—437 PELLETS

Mfg: Federal Cartridge Co. **Manufacturer's code:** P154/H126
Recoil energy in 8-lb. shotgun: 33.0 ft./lbs. **Recoil velocity in 8-lb. shotgun:** 16.3 ft./sec.

Distance in yards:	Muzzle	20	30	40	50	60	70
Velocity in fps:	1,447	917	771	660	571	498	435
Average pellet energy in ft-lbs:	5.86	2.36	1.66	1.22	.91	.69	.53
Time of flight in seconds:	0	.0534	.0891	.1313	.1802	.2365	.3010

Type of load: Field
Three-foot velocity: 1,330 ft./sec.
Hull: 2¾-inch plastic
Wad: Plastic
Shot: Lead
Buffered: No
Test barrel length: 30 inch
Pellets will pierce skin up to 127 yards.

NO. 7½ LEAD PELLETS—1¼ OUNCES—437 PELLETS

Mfg: Fiocchi **Manufacturer's code:** 12HV
Recoil energy in 8-lb. shotgun: 40.0 ft./lbs. **Recoil velocity in 8-lb. shotgun:** 17.9 ft./sec.

Distance in yards:	Muzzle	20	30	40	50	60	70
Velocity in fps:	1,447	917	771	660	571	498	435
Average pellet energy in ft-lbs:	5.86	2.36	1.66	1.22	.91	.69	.53
Time of flight in seconds:	0	.0534	.0891	.1313	.1802	.2365	.3010

Type of load: Field
Three-foot velocity: 1,330 ft./sec.
Hull: 2¾-inch plastic
Wad: Plastic
Shot: Lead
Buffered: No
Test barrel length: 30 inch
Pellets will pierce skin up to 127 yards.

NO. 7½ LEAD PELLETS—1¼ OUNCES—437 PELLETS
Mfg: Fiocchi **Manufacturer's code:** 12HVN
Recoil energy in 8-lb. shotgun: 40.0 ft./lbs. **Recoil velocity in 8-lb. shotgun:** 17.9 ft./sec.

Distance in yards:	Muzzle	20	30	40	50	60	70
Velocity in fps:	1,447	917	771	660	571	498	435
Average pellet energy in ft-lbs:	5.86	2.36	1.66	1.22	.91	.69	.53
Time of flight in seconds:	0	.0534	.0891	.1313	.1802	.2365	.3010

Type of load: Field
Three-foot velocity: 1,330 ft./sec.
Hull: 2¾-inch plastic
Wad: Plastic
Shot: Nickel-plated lead
Buffered: No
Test barrel length: 30 inch
Pellets will pierce skin up to 127 yards.

NO. 7½ LEAD PELLETS—1¼ OUNCES—437 PELLETS
Mfg: Kent Cartridge America/Canada **Manufacturer's code:** K122UG36
Recoil energy in 8-lb. shotgun: 33.0 ft./lbs. **Recoil velocity in 8-lb. shotgun:** 16.3 ft./sec.

Distance in yards:	Muzzle	20	30	40	50	60	70
Velocity in fps:	1,447	917	771	660	571	498	435
Average pellet energy in ft-lbs:	5.86	2.36	1.66	1.22	.91	.69	.53
Time of flight in seconds:	0	.0534	.0891	.1313	.1802	.2365	.3010

Type of load: Field
Three-foot velocity: 1,330 ft./sec.
Hull: 2¾-inch plastic
Wad: Plastic
Shot: Lead
Buffered: No
Test barrel length: 30 inch
Pellets will pierce skin up to 127 yards.

NO. 7½ LEAD PELLETS—1¼ OUNCES—437 PELLETS
Mfg: PMC (Eldorado Cartridge Corp.) **Manufacturer's code:** HF12
Recoil energy in 8-lb. shotgun: 31.1 ft./lbs. **Recoil velocity in 8-lb. shotgun:** 15.8 ft./sec.

Distance in yards:	Muzzle	20	30	40	50	60	70
Velocity in fps:	1,447	917	771	660	571	498	435
Average pellet energy in ft-lbs:	5.86	2.36	1.66	1.22	.91	.69	.53
Time of flight in seconds:	0	.0534	.0891	.1313	.1802	.2365	.3010

Type of load: Field
Three-foot velocity: 1,330 ft./sec.
Hull: 2¾-inch plastic
Wad: Plastic
Shot: Lead
Buffered: No
Test barrel length: 30 inch
Pellets will pierce skin up to 127 yards.

NO. 7½ LEAD PELLETS—1¼ OUNCES—437 PELLETS
Mfg: Remington Arms Co. **Manufacturer's code:** SP12/HGL12
Recoil energy in 8-lb. shotgun: 33.0 ft./lbs. **Recoil velocity in 8-lb. shotgun:** 16.3 ft./sec.

Distance in yards:	Muzzle	20	30	40	50	60	70
Velocity in fps:	1,447	917	771	660	571	498	435
Average pellet energy in ft-lbs:	5.86	2.36	1.66	1.22	.91	.69	.53
Time of flight in seconds:	0	.0534	.0891	.1313	.1802	.2365	.3010

Type of load: Field
Three-foot velocity: 1,330 ft./sec.
Hull: 2¾-inch plastic
Wad: Plastic
Shot: Lead
Buffered: No
Test barrel length: 30 inch
Pellets will pierce skin up to 127 yards.

NO. 7½ LEAD PELLETS—1¼ OUNCES—437 PELLETS
Mfg: Winchester **Manufacturer's code:** X12
Recoil energy in 8-lb. shotgun: 33.0 ft./lbs. **Recoil velocity in 8-lb. shotgun:** 16.3 ft./sec.

Distance in yards:	Muzzle	20	30	40	50	60	70
Velocity in fps:	1,447	917	771	660	571	498	435
Average pellet energy in ft-lbs:	5.86	2.36	1.66	1.22	.91	.69	.53
Time of flight in seconds:	0	.0534	.0891	.1313	.1802	.2365	.3010

Type of load: Field
Three-foot velocity: 1,330 ft./sec.
Hull: 2¾-inch plastic
Wad: Plastic
Shot: Lead
Buffered: No
Test barrel length: 30 inch
Pellets will pierce skin up to 127 yards.

NO. 7½ LEAD PELLETS—1¼ OUNCES—437 PELLETS
Mfg: Baschieri & Pellagri **Manufacturer's code:** Star Rossa High Velocity
Recoil energy in 8-lb. shotgun: 36.1 ft./lbs. **Recoil velocity in 8-lb. shotgun:** 17.0 ft./sec.

Distance in yards:	Muzzle	20	30	40	50	60	70
Velocity in fps:	1,497	939	787	673	582	506	442
Average pellet energy in ft-lbs:	6.72	2.47	1.73	1.27	.96	.72	.55
Time of flight in seconds:	0	.0519	.0869	.1282	.1762	.2316	.2950

Type of load: Target
Three-foot velocity: 1,375 ft./sec.
Hull: 2¾-inch plastic
Wad: Plastic
Shot: Hard lead
Buffered: No
Test barrel length: 30 inch
Pellets will pierce skin up to 141 yards.

NO. 7½ LEAD PELLETS—1¼ OUNCES—437 PELLETS
Mfg: Remington Arms Co. **Manufacturer's code:** SPHV12
Recoil energy in 8-lb. shotgun: 37.9 ft./lbs. **Recoil velocity in 8-lb. shotgun:** 17.5 ft./sec.

Distance in yards:	Muzzle	20	30	40	50	60	70
Velocity in fps:	1,525	951	796	679	587	511	446
Average pellet energy in ft-lbs:	6.51	2.53	1.77	1.29	.96	.73	.56
Time of flight in seconds:	0	.0511	.0857	.1265	.1741	.2290	.2918

Type of load: Field
Three-foot velocity: 1,400 ft./sec.
Hull: 2¾-inch plastic
Wad: Plastic
Shot: Lead
Buffered: No
Test barrel length: 30 inch
Pellets will pierce skin up to 129 yards.

NO. 7½ LEAD PELLETS—1¼ OUNCES—437 PELLETS
Mfg: Winchester **Manufacturer's code:** SFH12
Recoil energy in 8-lb. shotgun: 37.9 ft./lbs. **Recoil velocity in 8-lb. shotgun:** 17.5 ft./sec.

Distance in yards:	Muzzle	20	30	40	50	60	70
Velocity in fps:	1,525	951	796	679	587	511	446
Average pellet energy in ft-lbs:	6.51	2.53	1.77	1.29	.96	.73	.56
Time of flight in seconds:	0	.0511	.0857	.1265	.1741	.2290	.2918

Type of load: Field
Three-foot velocity: 1,400 ft./sec.
Hull: 2¾-inch plastic
Wad: Plastic
Shot: Copper-plated lead
Buffered: Yes
Test barrel length: 30 inch
Pellets will pierce skin up to 129 yards.

NO. 8 LEAD PELLETS—⅞ OUNCE—359 PELLETS
Mfg: Federal Cartridge Co. **Manufacturer's code:** T176
Recoil energy in 8-lb. shotgun: 12.3 ft./lbs. **Recoil velocity in 8-lb. shotgun:** 10.0 ft./sec.

Distance in yards:	Muzzle	20	30	40	50	60	70
Velocity in fps:	1,305	839	706	604	521	452	391
Average pellet energy in ft-lbs:	4.05	1.67	1.19	.87	.65	.49	.36
Time of flight in seconds:	0	.0587	.0978	.1438	.1973	.2593	.3307

Type of load: Target
Three-foot velocity: 1,200 ft./sec.
Hull: 2¾-inch plastic
Wad: Plastic
Shot: Hard lead
Buffered: No
Test barrel length: 30 inch
Pellets will pierce skin up to 129 yards.

NO. 8 LEAD PELLETS—⅞ OUNCES—359 PELLETS
Mfg: Fiocchi **Manufacturer's code:** 1278OZ
Recoil energy in 8-lb. shotgun: 12.3 ft./lbs. **Recoil velocity in 8-lb. shotgun:** 10.0 ft./sec.

Distance in yards:	Muzzle	20	30	40	50	60	70
Velocity in fps:	1,305	839	706	604	521	452	391
Average pellet energy in ft-lbs:	4.05	1.67	1.19	.87	.65	.49	.36
Time of flight in seconds:	0	.0587	.0978	.1438	.1973	.2593	.3307

Type of load: Target & Trainer
Three-foot velocity: 1,200 ft./sec.
Hull: 2¾-inch plastic
Wad: Plastic
Shot: Hard lead
Buffered: No
Test barrel length: 30 inch
Pellets will pierce skin up to 129 yards.

NO. 8 LEAD PELLETS—⅞ OUNCE—359 PELLETS
Mfg: Estate Cartridge **Manufacturer's code:** ML12
Recoil energy in 8-lb. shotgun: 13.7 ft./lbs. **Recoil velocity in 8-lb. shotgun:** 10.5 ft./sec.

Distance in yards:	Muzzle	20	30	40	50	60	70
Velocity in fps:	1,361	863	724	618	533	461	400
Average pellet energy in ft-lbs:	4.41	1.77	1.25	.91	.68	.51	.38
Time of flight in seconds:	0	.0568	.0948	.1398	.1921	.2527	.3225

Type of load: Target
Three-foot velocity: 1,250 ft./sec.
Hull: 2¾-inch plastic
Wad: Plastic
Shot: Hard lead
Buffered: No
Test barrel length: 30 inch
Pellets will pierce skin up to 118 yards.

NO. 8 LEAD PELLETS—⅞ OUNCE—359 PELLETS
Mfg: Eley Hawk **Manufacturer's code:** Olympic 2000
Recoil energy in 8-lb. shotgun: 15.2 ft./lbs. **Recoil velocity in 8-lb. shotgun:** 11.1 ft./sec.

Distance in yards:	Muzzle	20	30	40	50	60	70
Velocity in fps:	1,417	886	742	632	544	471	408
Average pellet energy in ft-lbs:	4.78	1.87	1.31	.95	.70	.53	.40
Time of flight in seconds:	0	.0549	.0921	.1360	.1873	.2466	.3150

Type of load: Target
Three-foot velocity: 1,300 ft./sec.
Hull: 2¾-inch plastic
Wad: Plastic
Shot: Lead
Buffered: No
Test barrel length: 30 inch
Pellets will pierce skin up to 132 yards.

NO. 8 LEAD PELLETS—⅞ OUNCE—359 PELLETS
Mfg: Dionisi **Manufacturer's code:** D 12 INT
Recoil energy in 8-lb. shotgun: 16.2 ft./lbs. **Recoil velocity in 8-lb. shotgun:** 11.4 ft./sec.

Distance in yards:	Muzzle	20	30	40	50	60	70
Velocity in fps:	1,451	900	752	640	551	477	413
Average pellet energy in ft-lbs:	5.01	1.93	1.35	.97	.72	.54	.41
Time of flight in seconds:	0	.0539	.0905	.1338	.1845	.2431	.3108

Type of load: Target International
Three-foot velocity: 1,330 ft./sec.
Hull: 2¾-inch plastic
Wad: Plastic
Shot: Lead
Buffered: No
Test barrel length: 30 inch
Pellets will pierce skin up to 134 yards.

NO. 8 LEAD PELLETS—⅞ OUNCE—359 PELLETS
Mfg: Eley Hawk **Manufacturer's code:** VIP
Recoil energy in 8-lb. shotgun: 16.2 ft./lbs. **Recoil velocity in 8-lb. shotgun:** 11.4 ft./sec.

Distance in yards:	Muzzle	20	30	40	50	60	70
Velocity in fps:	1,451	900	752	640	551	477	413
Average pellet energy in ft-lbs:	5.01	1.93	1.35	.97	.72	.54	.41
Time of flight in seconds:	0	.0539	.0905	.1338	.1845	.2431	.3108

Type of load: Target
Three-foot velocity: 1,330 ft./sec.
Hull: 2¾-inch plastic
Wad: Plastic
Shot: Hard lead
Buffered: No
Test barrel length: 30 inch
Pellets will pierce skin up to 134 yards.

NO. 8 LEAD PELLETS—⅞ OUNCE—359 PELLETS
Mfg: Sellier & Bellot **Manufacturer's code:** SBA01242
Recoil energy in 8-lb. shotgun: 16.2 ft./lbs. **Recoil velocity in 8-lb. shotgun:** 11.4 ft./sec.

Distance in yards:	Muzzle	20	30	40	50	60	70
Velocity in fps:	1,451	900	752	640	551	477	413
Average pellet energy in ft-lbs:	5.01	1.93	1.35	.97	.72	.54	.41
Time of flight in seconds:	0	.0539	.0905	.1338	.1845	.2431	.3108

Type of load: Target
Three-foot velocity: 1,330 ft./sec.
Hull: 2¾-inch plastic
Wad: Plastic
Shot: Lead
Buffered: No
Test barrel length: 30 inch
Pellets will pierce skin up to 134 yards.

NO. 8 LEAD PELLETS—⅞ OUNCE—359 PELLETS
Mfg: Baschieri & Pellagri **Manufacturer's code:** N/A
Recoil energy in 8-lb. shotgun: 22.0 ft./lbs. **Recoil velocity in 8-lb. shotgun:** 13.3 ft./sec.

Distance in yards:	Muzzle	20	30	40	50	60	70
Velocity in fps:	1,473	910	759	645	555	480	416
Average pellet energy in ft-lbs:	5.16	1.97	1.37	.99	.73	.55	.41
Time of flight in seconds:	0	.0532	.0895	.1324	.1827	.2409	.3080

Type of load: Comp-2000 24 gr.
Three-foot velocity: 1,350 ft./sec.
Hull: 2¾-inch plastic
Wad: Plastic
Shot: Hard lead
Buffered: No
Test barrel length: 30 inch
Pellets will pierce skin up to 134 yards.

NO. 8 LEAD PELLETS—⅞ OUNCE—359 PELLETS
Mfg: Fiocchi **Manufacturer's code:** 12IN24
Recoil energy in 8-lb. shotgun: 16.9 ft./lbs. **Recoil velocity in 8-lb. shotgun:** 11.6 ft./sec.

Distance in yards:	Muzzle	20	30	40	50	60	70
Velocity in fps:	1,473	910	759	645	555	480	416
Average pellet energy in ft-lbs:	5.16	1.97	1.37	.99	.73	.55	.41
Time of flight in seconds:	0	.0532	.0895	.1324	.1827	.2409	.3080

Type of load: Target
Three-foot velocity: 1,350 ft./sec.
Hull: 2¾-inch plastic
Wad: Plastic
Shot: Hard lead
Buffered: No
Test barrel length: 30 inch
Pellets will pierce skin up to 135 yards.

NO. 8 LEAD PELLETS—⅞ OUNCE—359 PELLETS
Mfg: Kent Cartridge America/Canada **Manufacturer's code:** K122ITR24
Recoil energy in 8-lb. shotgun: 16.9 ft./lbs. **Recoil velocity in 8-lb. shotgun:** 11.6 ft./sec.

Distance in yards:	Muzzle	20	30	40	50	60	70
Velocity in fps:	1,473	910	759	645	555	480	416
Average pellet energy in ft-lbs:	5.16	1.97	1.37	.99	.73	.55	.41
Time of flight in seconds:	0	.0532	.0895	.1324	.1827	.2409	.3080

Type of load: Target
Three-foot velocity: 1,350 ft./sec.
Hull: 2¾-inch plastic
Wad: Plastic
Shot: Lead
Buffered: No
Test barrel length: 30 inch
Pellets will pierce skin up to 135 yards.

NO. 8 LEAD PELLETS—⅞ OUNCE—359 PELLETS
Mfg: Estate Cartridge **Manufacturer's code:** INT24
Recoil energy in 8-lb. shotgun: 17.7 ft./lbs. **Recoil velocity in 8-lb. shotgun:** 11.9 ft./sec.

Distance in yards:	Muzzle	20	30	40	50	60	70
Velocity in fps:	1,501	921	767	652	560	485	420
Average pellet energy in ft-lbs:	5.36	2.02	1.40	1.01	.75	.65	.42
Time of flight in seconds:	0	.0524	.0882	.1308	.1805	.2381	.3047

Type of load: Target
Three-foot velocity: 1,375 ft./sec.
Hull: 2¾-inch plastic
Wad: Plastic
Shot: Hard lead
Buffered: No
Test barrel length: 30 inch
Pellets will pierce skin up to 138 yards.

NO. 8 LEAD PELLETS—⅞ OUNCE—357 PELLETS
Mfg: RIO **Manufacturer's code:** Trap 24
Recoil energy in 8-lb. shotgun: 17.7 ft./lbs. **Recoil velocity in 8-lb. shotgun:** 11.9 ft./sec.

Distance in yards:	Muzzle	20	30	40	50	60	70
Velocity in fps:	1,501	921	767	652	560	485	420
Average pellet energy in ft-lbs:	5.36	2.02	1.40	1.01	.75	.65	.42
Time of flight in seconds:	0	.0524	.0882	.1308	.1805	.2381	.3047

Type of load: Field
Three-foot velocity: 1,375 ft./sec.
Hull: 2¾-inch plastic
Wad: Plastic
Shot: Hard lead
Buffered: No
Test barrel length: 30 inch
Pellets will pierce skin up to 138 yards.

NO. 8 LEAD PELLETS—⅞ OUNCE—357 PELLETS
Mfg: RST, Ltd. **Manufacturer's code:** N/A
Recoil energy in 8-lb. shotgun: 18.6 ft./lbs. **Recoil velocity in 8-lb. shotgun:** 12.2 ft./sec.

Distance in yards:	Muzzle	20	30	40	50	60	70
Velocity in fps:	1,525	951	796	679	587	511	446
Average pellet energy in ft-lbs:	6.51	2.53	1.77	1.29	.96	.73	.56
Time of flight in seconds:	0	.0511	.0857	.1265	.1741	.2290	.2918

Type of load: Target
Three-foot velocity: 1,400 ft./sec.
Hull: 2¾-inch plastic
Wad: Plastic
Shot: Lead
Buffered: No
Test barrel length: 30 inch
Pellets will pierce skin up to 140 yards.

NO. 8 LEAD PELLETS—1 OUNCE—410 PELLETS
Mfg: Eley Hawk **Manufacturer's code:** Subsonic
Recoil energy in 8-lb. shotgun: 9.8 ft./lbs. **Recoil velocity in 8-lb. shotgun:** 8.9 ft./sec.

Distance in yards:	Muzzle	20	30	40	50	60	70
Velocity in fps:	1,022	706	603	521	451	391	339
Average pellet energy in ft-lbs:	2.48	1.19	.87	.65	.48	.36	.27
Time of flight in seconds:	0	.0717	.1177	.1713	.2332	.2047	.3871

Type of load: Target
Three-foot velocity: 1,000 ft./sec.
Hull: 2¾-inch plastic
Wad: Plastic
Shot: Lead
Buffered: No
Test barrel length: 30 inch
Pellets will pierce skin up to 107 yards.

NO. 8 LEAD PELLETS—1 OUNCE—410 PELLETS
Mfg: Winchester **Manufacturer's code:** AA12FL
Recoil energy in 8-lb. shotgun: 9.8 ft./lbs. **Recoil velocity in 8-lb. shotgun:** 8.9 ft./sec.

Distance in yards:	Muzzle	20	30	40	50	60	70
Velocity in fps:	1,022	706	603	521	451	391	339
Average pellet energy in ft-lbs:	2.48	1.19	.87	.65	.48	.36	.27
Time of flight in seconds:	0	.0717	.1177	.1713	.2332	.2047	.3871

Type of load: Target
Three-foot velocity: 1,000 ft./sec.
Hull: 2¾-inch plastic
Wad: Plastic
Shot: Hard lead
Buffered: No
Test barrel length: 30 inch
Pellets will pierce skin up to 107 yards.

NO. 8 LEAD PELLETS—1 OUNCE—410 PELLETS
Mfg: RST, Ltd. **Manufacturer's code:** N/A
Recoil energy in 8-lb. shotgun: 11.4 ft./lbs. **Recoil velocity in 8-lb. shotgun:** 9.6 ft./sec.

Distance in yards:	Muzzle	20	30	40	50	60	70
Velocity in fps:	1,138	764	649	558	483	418	363
Average pellet energy in ft-lbs:	3.08	1.39	1.00	.74	.55	.42	.31
Time of flight in seconds:	0	.0655	.1082	.1582	.2160	.2828	.3599

Type of load: Target
Three-foot velocity: 1,050 ft./sec.
Hull: 2¾-inch plastic
Wad: Plastic
Shot: Lead
Buffered: No
Test barrel length: 30 inch
Pellets will pierce skin up to 112 yards.

NO. 8 LEAD PELLETS—1 OUNCE—410 PELLETS
Mfg: Baschieri & Pellagri **Manufacturer's code:** N/A
Recoil energy in 8-lb. shotgun: 13.9 ft./lbs. **Recoil velocity in 8-lb. shotgun:** 10.6 ft./sec.

Distance in yards:	Muzzle	20	30	40	50	60	70
Velocity in fps:	1,232	807	682	585	505	438	380
Average pellet energy in ft-lbs:	3.61	1.55	1.11	.81	.61	.46	.34
Time of flight in seconds:	0	.0614	.1020	.1495	.2048	.2686	.3422

Type of load: F2 Target
Three-foot velocity: 1,135 ft./sec.
Hull: 2¾-inch plastic
Wad: Plastic
Shot: Hard lead
Buffered: No
Test barrel length: 30 inch
Pellets will pierce skin up to 112 yards.

NO. 8 LEAD PELLETS—1 OUNCE—410 PELLETS
Mfg: Federal Cartridge Co. **Manufacturer's code:** T175
Recoil energy in 8-lb. shotgun: 14.2 ft./lbs. **Recoil velocity in 8-lb. shotgun:** 10.7 ft./sec.

Distance in yards:	Muzzle	20	30	40	50	60	70
Velocity in fps:	1,244	812	686	588	508	440	381
Average pellet energy in ft-lbs:	3.68	1.57	1.12	.82	.61	.46	.35
Time of flight in seconds:	0	.0616	.1013	.1486	.2036	.2671	.3403

Type of load: Target
Three-foot velocity: 1,145 ft./sec.
Hull: 2¾-inch paper
Wad: Plastic
Shot: Hard lead
Buffered: No
Test barrel length: 30 inch
Pellets will pierce skin up to 115 yards.

NO. 8 LEAD PELLETS—1 OUNCE—410 PELLETS
Mfg: Fiocchi **Manufacturer's code:** 12TL
Recoil energy in 8-lb. shotgun: 18.2 ft./lbs. **Recoil velocity in 8-lb. shotgun:** 12.1 ft./sec.

Distance in yards:	Muzzle	20	30	40	50	60	70
Velocity in fps:	1,249	815	688	589	509	441	382
Average pellet energy in ft-lbs:	3.71	1.58	1.13	.83	.62	.46	.35
Time of flight in seconds:	0	.0608	.1010	.1482	.2030	.2663	.3394

Type of load: Target
Three-foot velocity: 1,150 ft./sec.
Hull: 2¾-inch plastic
Wad: Plastic
Shot: Hard lead
Buffered: No
Test barrel length: 30 inch
Pellets will pierce skin up to 115 yards.

NO. 8 LEAD PELLETS—1 OUNCE—410 PELLETS
Mfg: Dionisi **Manufacturer's code:** D 12 TLX
Recoil energy in 8-lb. shotgun: 15.2 ft./lbs. **Recoil velocity in 8-lb. shotgun:** 11.1 ft./sec.

Distance in yards:	Muzzle	20	30	40	50	60	70
Velocity in fps:	1,277	827	697	597	515	446	387
Average pellet energy in ft-lbs:	3.88	1.63	1.16	.85	.63	.47	.36
Time of flight in seconds:	0	.0597	.0993	.1459	.2001	.2627	.3349

Type of load: Target
Three-foot velocity: 1,175 ft./sec.
Hull: 2¾-inch plastic
Wad: Plastic
Shot: Lead
Buffered: No
Test barrel length: 30 inch
Pellets will pierce skin up to 116 yards.

NO. 8 LEAD PELLETS—1 OUNCE—410 PELLETS

Mfg: Estate Cartridge **Manufacturer's code:** CT12L1/SS12L1
Recoil energy in 8-lb. shotgun: 15.2 ft./lbs. **Recoil velocity in 8-lb. shotgun:** 11.1 ft./sec.

Distance in yards:	Muzzle	20	30	40	50	60	70
Velocity in fps:	1,277	827	697	597	515	446	387
Average pellet energy in ft-lbs:	3.88	1.63	1.16	.85	.63	.47	.36
Time of flight in seconds:	0	.0597	.0993	.1459	.2001	.2627	.3349

Type of load: Target
Three-foot velocity: 1,175 ft./sec.
Hull: 2¾-inch plastic
Wad: Plastic
Shot: Hard lead
Buffered: No
Test barrel length: 30 inch
Pellets will pierce skin up to 116 yards.

NO. 8 LEAD PELLETS—1 OUNCE—410 PELLETS

Mfg: Federal Cartridge Co. **Manufacturer's code:** T113
Recoil energy in 8-lb. shotgun: 15.2 ft./lbs. **Recoil velocity in 8-lb. shotgun:** 11.1 ft./sec.

Distance in yards:	Muzzle	20	30	40	50	60	70
Velocity in fps:	1,277	827	697	597	515	446	387
Average pellet energy in ft-lbs:	3.88	1.63	1.16	.85	.63	.47	.36
Time of flight in seconds:	0	.0597	.0993	.1459	.2001	.2627	.3349

Type of load: Target
Three-foot velocity: 1,175 ft./sec.
Hull: 2¾-inch plastic
Wad: Plastic
Shot: Hard lead
Buffered: No
Test barrel length: 30 inch
Pellets will pierce skin up to 116 yards.

NO. 8 LEAD PELLETS—1 OUNCE—410 PELLETS

Mfg: Polywad **Manufacturer's code:** SRL128
Recoil energy in 8-lb. shotgun: 15.2 ft./lbs. **Recoil velocity in 8-lb. shotgun:** 11.1 ft./sec.

Distance in yards:	Muzzle	20	30	40	50	60	70
Velocity in fps:	1,277	827	697	597	515	446	387
Average pellet energy in ft-lbs:	3.88	1.63	1.16	.85	.63	.47	.36
Time of flight in seconds:	0	.0597	.0993	.1459	.2001	.2627	.3349

Type of load: Field
Three-foot velocity: 1,175 ft./sec.
Hull: 2¾-inch plastic
Wad: Plastic
Shot: Lead
Buffered: No
Test barrel length: 30 inch
Pellets will pierce skin up to 116 yards.

NO. 8 LEAD PELLETS—1 OUNCE—410 PELLETS

Mfg: Remington Arms Co. **Manufacturer's code:** STS121
Recoil energy in 8-lb. shotgun: 15.2 ft./lbs. **Recoil velocity in 8-lb. shotgun:** 11.1 ft./sec.

Distance in yards:	Muzzle	20	30	40	50	60	70
Velocity in fps:	1,277	827	697	597	515	446	387
Average pellet energy in ft-lbs:	3.88	1.63	1.16	.85	.63	.47	.36
Time of flight in seconds:	0	.0597	.0993	.1459	.2001	.2627	.3349

Type of load: Target
Three-foot velocity: 1,175 ft./sec.
Hull: 2¾-inch plastic
Wad: Plastic
Shot: Hard lead
Buffered: No
Test barrel length: 30 inch
Pellets will pierce skin up to 116 yards.

NO. 8 LEAD PELLETS—1 OUNCE—410 PELLETS

Mfg: RST, Ltd. **Manufacturer's code:** N/A
Recoil energy in 8-lb. shotgun: 15.2 ft./lbs. **Recoil velocity in 8-lb. shotgun:** 11.1 ft./sec.

Distance in yards:	Muzzle	20	30	40	50	60	70
Velocity in fps:	1,277	827	697	597	515	446	387
Average pellet energy in ft-lbs:	3.88	1.63	1.16	.85	.63	.47	.36
Time of flight in seconds:	0	.0597	.0993	.1459	.2001	.2627	.3349

Type of load: Target
Three-foot velocity: 1,175 ft./sec.
Hull: 2¾-inch plastic
Wad: Plastic
Shot: Lead
Buffered: No
Test barrel length: 30 inch
Pellets will pierce skin up to 116 yards.

NO. 8 LEAD PELLETS—1 OUNCE—410 PELLETS

Mfg: Winchester **Manufacturer's code:** AAL12
Recoil energy in 8-lb. shotgun: 15.2 ft./lbs. **Recoil velocity in 8-lb. shotgun:** 11.1 ft./sec.

Distance in yards:	Muzzle	20	30	40	50	60	70
Velocity in fps:	1,277	827	697	597	515	446	387
Average pellet energy in ft-lbs:	3.88	1.63	1.16	.85	.63	.47	.36
Time of flight in seconds:	0	.0597	.0993	.1459	.2001	.2627	.3349

Type of load: Target
Three-foot velocity: 1,175 ft./sec.
Hull: 2¾-inch plastic
Wad: Plastic
Shot: Hard lead
Buffered: No
Test barrel length: 30 inch
Pellets will pierce skin up to 116 yards.

NO. 8 LEAD PELLETS—1 OUNCE—410 PELLETS

Mfg: Fiocchi **Manufacturer's code:** 12TH
Recoil energy in 8-lb. shotgun: 16.1 ft./lbs. **Recoil velocity in 8-lb. shotgun:** 11.4 ft./sec.

Distance in yards:	Muzzle	20	30	40	50	60	70
Velocity in fps:	1,305	839	706	604	521	452	391
Average pellet energy in ft-lbs:	4.05	1.67	1.19	.87	.65	.49	.36
Time of flight in seconds:	0	.0587	.0978	.1438	.1973	.2593	.3307

Type of load: Target
Three-foot velocity: 1,200 ft./sec.
Hull: 2¾-inch plastic
Wad: Plastic
Shot: Hard lead
Buffered: No
Test barrel length: 30 inch
Pellets will pierce skin up to 129 yards.

NO. 8 LEAD PELLETS—1 OUNCE—410 PELLETS
Mfg: Kent Cartridge América/Canada **Manufacturer's code:** K122UG28
Recoil energy in 8-lb. shotgun: 16.1 ft./lbs. **Recoil velocity in 8-lb. shotgun:** 11.4 ft./sec.

Distance in yards:	Muzzle	20	30	40	50	60	70
Velocity in fps:	1,305	839	706	604	521	452	391
Average pellet energy in ft-lbs:	4.05	1.67	1.19	.87	.65	.49	.36
Time of flight in seconds:	0	.0587	.0978	.1438	.1973	.2593	.3307

Type of load: Field
Three-foot velocity: 1,200 ft./sec.
Hull: 2¾-inch plastic
Wad: Plastic
Shot: Lead
Buffered: No
Test barrel length: 30 inch
Pellets will pierce skin up to 129 yards.

NO. 8 LEAD PELLETS—1 OUNCE—410 PELLETS
Mfg: Kent Cartridge América/Canada **Manufacturer's code:** K122LSC28
Recoil energy in 8-lb. shotgun: 16.1 ft./lbs. **Recoil velocity in 8-lb. shotgun:** 11.4 ft./sec.

Distance in yards:	Muzzle	20	30	40	50	60	70
Velocity in fps:	1,305	839	706	604	521	452	391
Average pellet energy in ft-lbs:	4.05	1.67	1.19	.87	.65	.49	.36
Time of flight in seconds:	0	.0587	.0978	.1438	.1973	.2593	.3307

Type of load: Target
Three-foot velocity: 1,200 ft./sec.
Hull: 2¾-inch plastic
Wad: Plastic
Shot: Lead
Buffered: No
Test barrel length: 30 inch
Pellets will pierce skin up to 129 yards.

NO. 8 LEAD PELLETS—1 OUNCE—410 PELLETS
Mfg: Aguila **Manufacturer's code:** N/A
Recoil energy in 8-lb. shotgun: 20.4 ft./lbs. **Recoil velocity in 8-lb. shotgun:** 12.8 ft./sec.

Distance in yards:	Muzzle	20	30	40	50	60	70
Velocity in fps:	1,305	839	706	604	521	452	391
Average pellet energy in ft-lbs:	4.05	1.67	1.19	.87	.65	.49	.36
Time of flight in seconds:	0	.0587	.0978	.1438	.1973	.2593	.3307

Type of load: Field
Three-foot velocity: 1,200 ft./sec.
Hull: 2¾-inch plastic
Wad: Plastic
Shot: Lead
Buffered: No
Test barrel length: 30 inch
Pellets will pierce skin up to 129 yards.

NO. 8 LEAD PELLETS—1 OUNCE—410 PELLETS
Mfg: Baschieri & Pellagri **Manufacturer's code:** N/A
Recoil energy in 8-lb. shotgun: 17.4 ft./lbs. **Recoil velocity in 8-lb. shotgun:** 11.8 ft./sec.

Distance in yards:	Muzzle	20	30	40	50	60	70
Velocity in fps:	1,344	856	719	614	529	459	397
Average pellet energy in ft-lbs:	4.30	1.74	1.23	.90	.67	.50	.38
Time of flight in seconds:	0	.0573	.0957	.1409	.1936	.2546	.3249

Type of load: Comp-2000 28 gr.
Three-foot velocity: 1,235 ft./sec.
Hull: 2¾-inch plastic
Wad: Plastic
Shot: Hard lead
Buffered: No
Test barrel length: 30 inch
Pellets will pierce skin up to 118 yards.

NO. 8 LEAD PELLETS—1 OUNCE—410 PELLETS
Mfg: Dionisi **Manufacturer's code:** D 12 GT
Recoil energy in 8-lb. shotgun: 16.8 ft./lbs. **Recoil velocity in 8-lb. shotgun:** 11.6 ft./sec.

Distance in yards:	Muzzle	20	30	40	50	60	70
Velocity in fps:	1,344	856	719	614	529	459	397
Average pellet energy in ft-lbs:	4.30	1.74	1.23	.90	.67	.50	.38
Time of flight in seconds:	0	.0573	.0957	.1409	.1936	.2546	.3249

Type of load: Game & Target
Three-foot velocity: 1,235 ft./sec.
Hull: 2¾-inch plastic
Wad: Plastic
Shot: Lead
Buffered: No
Test barrel length: 30 inch
Pellets will pierce skin up to 118 yards.

NO. 8 LEAD PELLETS—1 OUNCE—410 PELLETS
Mfg: Estate Cartridge **Manufacturer's code:** CT12H1/SS12H1
Recoil energy in 8-lb. shotgun: 17.4 ft./lbs. **Recoil velocity in 8-lb. shotgun:** 11.8 ft./sec.

Distance in yards:	Muzzle	20	30	40	50	60	70
Velocity in fps:	1,344	856	719	614	529	459	397
Average pellet energy in ft-lbs:	4.30	1.74	1.23	.90	.67	.50	.38
Time of flight in seconds:	0	.0573	.0957	.1409	.1936	.2546	.3249

Type of load: Target
Three-foot velocity: 1,235 ft./sec.
Hull: 2¾-inch plastic
Wad: Plastic
Shot: Hard lead
Buffered: No
Test barrel length: 30 inch
Pellets will pierce skin up to 118 yards.

NO. 8 LEAD PELLETS—1 OUNCE—410 PELLETS
Mfg: Fiocchi **Manufacturer's code:** 12MS3
Recoil energy in 8-lb. shotgun: 17.9 ft./lbs. **Recoil velocity in 8-lb. shotgun:** 12.0 ft./sec.

Distance in yards:	Muzzle	20	30	40	50	60	70
Velocity in fps:	1,361	863	724	618	533	461	400
Average pellet energy in ft-lbs:	4.41	1.77	1.25	.91	.68	.51	.38
Time of flight in seconds:	0	.0568	.0948	.1398	.1921	.2527	.3225

Type of load: Field
Three-foot velocity: 1,250 ft./sec.
Hull: 2¾-inch plastic
Wad: Plastic
Shot: Lead
Buffered: No
Test barrel length: 30 inch
Pellets will pierce skin up to 118 yards.

NO. 8 LEAD PELLETS—1 OUNCE—410 PELLETS
Mfg: Fiocchi **Manufacturer's code:** 12TX
Recoil energy in 8-lb. shotgun: 17.9 ft./lbs. **Recoil velocity in 8-lb. shotgun:** 12.0 ft./sec.

Distance in yards:	Muzzle	20	30	40	50	60	70
Velocity in fps:	1,361	863	724	618	533	461	400
Average pellet energy in ft-lbs:	4.41	1.77	1.25	.91	.68	.51	.38
Time of flight in seconds:	0	.0568	.0948	.1398	.1921	.2527	.3225

Type of load: Target
Three-foot velocity: 1,250 ft./sec.
Hull: 2¾-inch plastic
Wad: Plastic
Shot: Hard lead
Buffered: No
Test barrel length: 30 inch
Pellets will pierce skin up to 118 yards.

NO. 8 LEAD PELLETS—1 OUNCE—410 PELLETS
Mfg: Eley Hawk **Manufacturer's code:** Black Trap
Recoil energy in 8-lb. shotgun: 18.9 ft./lbs. **Recoil velocity in 8-lb. shotgun:** 12.3 ft./sec.

Distance in yards:	Muzzle	20	30	40	50	60	70
Velocity in fps:	1,389	875	733	625	538	466	404
Average pellet energy in ft-lbs:	4.59	1.82	1.28	.93	.63	.52	.39
Time of flight in seconds:	0	.0558	.0934	.1378	.1897	.2496	.3187

Type of load: Target
Three-foot velocity: 1,275 ft./sec.
Hull: 2¾-inch plastic
Wad: Plastic
Shot: Lead
Buffered: No
Test barrel length: 30 inch
Pellets will pierce skin up to 131 yards.

NO. 8 LEAD PELLETS—1 OUNCE—410 PELLETS
Mfg: Dionisi **Manufacturer's code:** D 12 DQ
Recoil energy in 8-lb. shotgun: 19.9 ft./lbs. **Recoil velocity in 8-lb. shotgun:** 12.6 ft./sec.

Distance in yards:	Muzzle	20	30	40	50	60	70
Velocity in fps:	1,417	886	742	632	544	471	408
Average pellet energy in ft-lbs:	4.78	1.87	1.31	.95	.70	.53	.40
Time of flight in seconds:	0	.0549	.0921	.1360	.1873	.2466	.3150

Type of load: Dove & Quail
Three-foot velocity: 1,300 ft./sec.
Hull: 2¾-inch plastic
Wad: Plastic
Shot: Lead
Buffered: No
Test barrel length: 30 inch
Pellets will pierce skin up to 132 yards.

NO. 8 LEAD PELLETS—1 OUNCE—410 PELLETS
Mfg: Eley Hawk **Manufacturer's code:** Olympic 2000
Recoil energy in 8-lb. shotgun: 19.9 ft./lbs. **Recoil velocity in 8-lb. shotgun:** 12.6 ft./sec.

Distance in yards:	Muzzle	20	30	40	50	60	70
Velocity in fps:	1,417	886	742	632	544	471	408
Average pellet energy in ft-lbs:	4.78	1.87	1.31	.95	.70	.53	.40
Time of flight in seconds:	0	.0549	.0921	.1360	.1873	.2466	.3150

Type of load: Target
Three-foot velocity: 1,300 ft./sec.
Hull: 2¾-inch plastic
Wad: Plastic
Shot: Lead
Buffered: No
Test barrel length: 30 inch
Pellets will pierce skin up to 132 yards.

NO. 8 LEAD PELLETS—1 OUNCE—410 PELLETS
Mfg: Eley Hawk **Manufacturer's code:** VIP Fibre
Recoil energy in 8-lb. shotgun: 19.9 ft./lbs. **Recoil velocity in 8-lb. shotgun:** 12.6 ft./sec.

Distance in yards:	Muzzle	20	30	40	50	60	70
Velocity in fps:	1,417	886	742	632	544	471	408
Average pellet energy in ft-lbs:	4.78	1.87	1.31	.95	.70	.53	.40
Time of flight in seconds:	0	.0549	.0921	.1360	.1873	.2466	.3150

Type of load: Target
Three-foot velocity: 1,300 ft./sec.
Hull: 2¾-inch plastic
Wad: Fiber
Shot: Lead
Buffered: No
Test barrel length: 30 inch
Pellets will pierce skin up to 132 yards.

NO. 8 LEAD PELLETS—1 OUNCE—410 PELLETS
Mfg: Estate Cartridge **Manufacturer's code:** CT12XH1
Recoil energy in 8-lb. shotgun: 16.1 ft./lbs. **Recoil velocity in 8-lb. shotgun:** 11.4 ft./sec.

Distance in yards:	Muzzle	20	30	40	50	60	70
Velocity in fps:	1,451	900	752	640	551	477	413
Average pellet energy in ft-lbs:	5.01	1.93	1.35	.97	.72	.54	.41
Time of flight in seconds:	0	.0539	.0905	.1338	.1845	.2431	.3108

Type of load: Target
Three-foot velocity: 1,300 ft./sec.
Hull: 2¾-inch plastic
Wad: Plastic
Shot: Hard lead
Buffered: No
Test barrel length: 30 inch
Pellets will pierce skin up to 121 yards.

NO. 8 LEAD PELLETS—1 OUNCE—410 PELLETS
Mfg: Estate Cartridge **Manufacturer's code:** DQ12
Recoil energy in 8-lb. shotgun: 19.9 ft./lbs. **Recoil velocity in 8-lb. shotgun:** 12.6 ft./sec.

Distance in yards:	Muzzle	20	30	40	50	60	70
Velocity in fps:	1,417	886	742	632	544	471	408
Average pellet energy in ft-lbs:	4.78	1.87	1.31	.95	.70	.53	.40
Time of flight in seconds:	0	.0549	.0921	.1360	.1873	.2466	.3150

Type of load: Field
Three-foot velocity: 1,300 ft./sec.5
Hull: 2¾-inch plastic
Wad: Plastic
Shot: Hard lead
Buffered: No
Test barrel length: 30 inch
Pellets will pierce skin up to 132 yards.

NO. 8 LEAD PELLETS—1 OUNCE—410 PELLETS
Mfg: Federal Cartridge Co. **Manufacturer's code:** H121
Recoil energy in 8-lb. shotgun: 19.9 ft./lbs. **Recoil velocity in 8-lb. shotgun:** 12.6 ft./sec.

Distance in yards:	Muzzle	20	30	40	50	60	70
Velocity in fps:	1,417	886	742	632	544	471	408
Average pellet energy in ft-lbs:	4.78	1.87	1.31	.95	.70	.53	.40
Time of flight in seconds:	0	.0549	.0921	.1360	.1873	.2466	.3150

Type of load: Field
Three-foot velocity: 1,300 ft./sec.
Hull: 2¾-inch plastic
Wad: Plastic
Shot: Lead
Buffered: No
Test barrel length: 30 inch
Pellets will pierce skin up to 132 yards.

NO. 8 LEAD PELLETS—1 OUNCE—410 PELLETS
Mfg: Federal Cartridge Co. **Manufacturer's code:** FD12
Recoil energy in 8-lb. shotgun: 19.9 ft./lbs. **Recoil velocity in 8-lb. shotgun:** 12.6 ft./sec.

Distance in yards:	Muzzle	20	30	40	50	60	70
Velocity in fps:	1,417	886	742	632	544	471	408
Average pellet energy in ft-lbs:	4.78	1.87	1.31	.95	.70	.53	.40
Time of flight in seconds:	0	.0549	.0921	.1360	.1873	.2466	.3150

Type of load: Field
Three-foot velocity: 1,300 ft./sec.
Hull: 2¾-inch plastic
Wad: Plastic
Shot: Hard lead
Buffered: No
Test barrel length: 30 inch
Pellets will pierce skin up to 132 yards.

NO. 8 LEAD PELLETS—1 OUNCE—410 PELLETS
Mfg: Fiocchi **Manufacturer's code:** 12GT1
Recoil energy in 8-lb. shotgun: 19.9 ft./lbs. **Recoil velocity in 8-lb. shotgun:** 12.6 ft./sec.

Distance in yards:	Muzzle	20	30	40	50	60	70
Velocity in fps:	1,417	886	742	632	544	471	408
Average pellet energy in ft-lbs:	4.78	1.87	1.31	.95	.70	.53	.40
Time of flight in seconds:	0	.0549	.0921	.1360	.1873	.2466	.3150

Type of load: Game & Target
Three-foot velocity: 1,300 ft./sec.
Hull: 2¾-inch plastic
Wad: Plastic
Shot: Lead
Buffered: No
Test barrel length: 30 inch
Pellets will pierce skin up to 132 yards.

NO. 8 LEAD PELLETS—1 OUNCE—410 PELLETS
Mfg: Fiocchi **Manufacturer's code:** 12CPTR
Recoil energy in 8-lb. shotgun: 19.9 ft./lbs. **Recoil velocity in 8-lb. shotgun:** 12.6 ft./sec.

Distance in yards:	Muzzle	20	30	40	50	60	70
Velocity in fps:	1,417	886	742	632	544	471	408
Average pellet energy in ft-lbs:	4.78	1.87	1.31	.95	.70	.53	.40
Time of flight in seconds:	0	.0549	.0921	.1360	.1873	.2466	.3150

Type of load: Target & Spreader
Three-foot velocity: 1,300 ft./sec.
Hull: 2¾-inch plastic
Wad: Plastic
Shot: Hard lead
Buffered: No
Test barrel length: 30 inch
Pellets will pierce skin up to 132 yards.

NO. 8 LEAD PELLETS—1 OUNCE—410 PELLETS
Mfg: Fiocchi **Manufacturer's code:** 12CRSR
Recoil energy in 8-lb. shotgun: 19.9 ft./lbs. **Recoil velocity in 8-lb. shotgun:** 12.6 ft./sec.

Distance in yards:	Muzzle	20	30	40	50	60	70
Velocity in fps:	1,417	886	742	632	544	471	408
Average pellet energy in ft-lbs:	4.78	1.87	1.31	.95	.70	.53	.40
Time of flight in seconds:	0	.0549	.0921	.1360	.1873	.2466	.3150

Type of load: Target
Three-foot velocity: 1,300 ft./sec.
Hull: 2¾-inch plastic
Wad: Plastic
Shot: Hard lead
Buffered: No
Test barrel length: 30 inch
Pellets will pierce skin up to 132 yards.

NO. 8 LEAD PELLETS—1 OUNCE—410 PELLETS
Mfg: Kent Cartridge America/Canada **Manufacturer's code:** K122HV28
Recoil energy in 8-lb. shotgun: 19.9 ft./lbs. **Recoil velocity in 8-lb. shotgun:** 12.6 ft./sec.

Distance in yards:	Muzzle	20	30	40	50	60	70
Velocity in fps:	1,417	886	742	632	544	471	408
Average pellet energy in ft-lbs:	4.78	1.87	1.31	.95	.70	.53	.40
Time of flight in seconds:	0	.0549	.0921	.1360	.1873	.2466	.3150

Type of load: Target
Three-foot velocity: 1,300 ft./sec.
Hull: 2¾-inch plastic
Wad: Plastic
Shot: Lead
Buffered: No
Test barrel length: 30 inch
Pellets will pierce skin up to 132 yards.

NO. 8 LEAD PELLETS—1 OUNCE—410 PELLETS
Mfg: PMC (Eldorado Cartridge Corp.) **Manufacturer's code:** PL12
Recoil energy in 8-lb. shotgun: 19.9 ft./lbs. **Recoil velocity in 8-lb. shotgun:** 12.6 ft./sec.

Distance in yards:	Muzzle	20	30	40	50	60	70
Velocity in fps:	1,417	886	742	632	544	471	408
Average pellet energy in ft-lbs:	4.78	1.87	1.31	.95	.70	.53	.40
Time of flight in seconds:	0	.0549	.0921	.1360	.1873	.2466	.3150

Type of load: Quail & Dove
Three-foot velocity: 1,300 ft./sec.
Hull: 2¾-inch plastic
Wad: Plastic
Shot: Lead
Buffered: No
Test barrel length: 30 inch
Pellets will pierce skin up to 132 yards.

NO. 8 LEAD PELLETS—1 OUNCE—410 PELLETS

Mfg: Remington Arms Co. **Manufacturer's code:** GL12
Recoil energy in 8-lb. shotgun: 19.9 ft./lbs. **Recoil velocity in 8-lb. shotgun:** 12.6 ft./sec.

Distance in yards:	Muzzle	20	30	40	50	60	70
Velocity in fps:	1,417	886	742	632	544	471	408
Average pellet energy in ft-lbs:	4.78	1.87	1.31	.95	.70	.53	.40
Time of flight in seconds:	0	.0549	.0921	.1360	.1873	.2466	.3150

Type of load: Field
Three-foot velocity: 1,300 ft./sec.
Hull: 2¾-inch plastic
Wad: Plastic
Shot: Lead
Buffered: No
Test barrel length: 30 inch
Pellets will pierce skin up to 132 yards.

NO. 8 LEAD PELLETS—1 OUNCE—410 PELLETS

Mfg: Remington Arms Co. **Manufacturer's code:** R12SL
Recoil energy in 8-lb. shotgun: 19.9 ft./lbs. **Recoil velocity in 8-lb. shotgun:** 12.6 ft./sec.

Distance in yards:	Muzzle	20	30	40	50	60	70
Velocity in fps:	1,417	886	742	632	544	471	408
Average pellet energy in ft-lbs:	4.78	1.87	1.31	.95	.70	.53	.40
Time of flight in seconds:	0	.0549	.0921	.1360	.1873	.2466	.3150

Type of load: Field
Three-foot velocity: 1,300 ft./sec.
Hull: 2¾-inch plastic
Wad: Plastic
Shot: Lead
Buffered: No
Test barrel length: 30 inch
Pellets will pierce skin up to 132 yards.

NO. 8 LEAD PELLETS—1 OUNCE—410 PELLETS

Mfg: Remington Arms Co. **Manufacturer's code:** STS12NH1
Recoil energy in 8-lb. shotgun: 19.9 ft./lbs. **Recoil velocity in 8-lb. shotgun:** 12.6 ft./sec.

Distance in yards:	Muzzle	20	30	40	50	60	70
Velocity in fps:	1,417	886	742	632	544	471	408
Average pellet energy in ft-lbs:	4.78	1.87	1.31	.95	.70	.53	.40
Time of flight in seconds:	0	.0549	.0921	.1360	.1873	.2466	.3150

Type of load: Target
Three-foot velocity: 1,300 ft./sec.
Hull: 2¾-inch plastic
Wad: Plastic
Shot: Hard lead
Buffered: No
Test barrel length: 30 inch
Pellets will pierce skin up to 132 yards.

NO. 8 LEAD PELLETS—1 OUNCE—410 PELLETS

Mfg: Rottweil **Manufacturer's code:** Game
Recoil energy in 8-lb. shotgun: 25.2 ft./lbs. **Recoil velocity in 8-lb. shotgun:** 14.2 ft./sec.

Distance in yards:	Muzzle	20	30	40	50	60	70
Velocity in fps:	1,417	886	742	632	544	471	408
Average pellet energy in ft-lbs:	4.78	1.87	1.31	.95	.70	.53	.40
Time of flight in seconds:	0	.0549	.0921	.1360	.1873	.2466	.3150

Type of load: Field
Three-foot velocity: 1,300 ft./sec.
Hull: 2¾-inch plastic
Wad: Plastic
Shot: Lead
Buffered: No
Test barrel length: 30 inch
Pellets will pierce skin up to 132 yards.

NO. 8 LEAD PELLETS—1 OUNCE—410 PELLETS

Mfg: RST, Ltd. **Manufacturer's code:** N/A
Recoil energy in 8-lb. shotgun: 19.9 ft./lbs. **Recoil velocity in 8-lb. shotgun:** 12.6 ft./sec.

Distance in yards:	Muzzle	20	30	40	50	60	70
Velocity in fps:	1,417	886	742	632	544	471	408
Average pellet energy in ft-lbs:	4.78	1.87	1.31	.95	.70	.53	.40
Time of flight in seconds:	0	.0549	.0921	.1360	.1873	.2466	.3150

Type of load: Target
Three-foot velocity: 1,300 ft./sec.
Hull: 2¾-inch plastic
Wad: Plastic
Shot: Lead
Buffered: No
Test barrel length: 30 inch
Pellets will pierce skin up to 132 yards.

NO. 8 LEAD PELLETS—1 OUNCE—410 PELLETS

Mfg: Sellier & Bellot **Manufacturer's code:** SBA01245
Recoil energy in 8-lb. shotgun: 19.9 ft./lbs. **Recoil velocity in 8-lb. shotgun:** 12.6 ft./sec.

Distance in yards:	Muzzle	20	30	40	50	60	70
Velocity in fps:	1,417	886	742	632	544	471	408
Average pellet energy in ft-lbs:	4.78	1.87	1.31	.95	.70	.53	.40
Time of flight in seconds:	0	.0549	.0921	.1360	.1873	.2466	.3150

Type of load: Target
Three-foot velocity: 1,300 ft./sec.
Hull: 2¾-inch plastic
Wad: Plastic
Shot: Lead
Buffered: No
Test barrel length: 30 inch
Pellets will pierce skin up to 132 yards.

NO. 8 LEAD PELLETS—1 OUNCE—410 PELLETS

Mfg: Winchester **Manufacturer's code:** XU12
Recoil energy in 8-lb. shotgun: 19.9 ft./lbs. **Recoil velocity in 8-lb. shotgun:** 12.6 ft./sec.

Distance in yards:	Muzzle	20	30	40	50	60	70
Velocity in fps:	1,417	886	742	632	544	471	408
Average pellet energy in ft-lbs:	4.78	1.87	1.31	.95	.70	.53	.40
Time of flight in seconds:	0	.0549	.0921	.1360	.1873	.2466	.3150

Type of load: Field
Three-foot velocity: 1,300 ft./sec.
Hull: 2¾-inch plastic
Wad: Plastic
Shot: Lead
Buffered: No
Test barrel length: 30 inch
Pellets will pierce skin up to 132 yards.

NO. 8 LEAD PELLETS—1 OUNCE—410 PELLETS
Mfg: Winchester **Manufacturer's code:** AAHLA12
Recoil energy in 8-lb. shotgun: 19.9 ft./lbs. **Recoil velocity in 8-lb. shotgun:** 12.6 ft./sec.

Distance in yards:	Muzzle	20	30	40	50	60	70
Velocity in fps:	1,417	886	742	632	544	471	408
Average pellet energy in ft-lbs:	4.78	1.87	1.31	.95	.70	.53	.40
Time of flight in seconds:	0	.0549	.0921	.1360	.1873	.2466	.3150

Type of load: Target
Three-foot velocity: 1,300 ft./sec.
Hull: 2¾-inch plastic
Wad: Plastic
Shot: Hard lead
Buffered: No
Test barrel length: 30 inch
Pellets will pierce skin up to 132 yards.

NO. 8 LEAD PELLETS—1 OUNCE—410 PELLETS
Mfg: Baschieri & Pellagri **Manufacturer's code:** N/A
Recoil energy in 8-lb. shotgun: 21.2 ft./lbs. **Recoil velocity in 8-lb. shotgun:** 13.0 ft./sec.

Distance in yards:	Muzzle	20	30	40	50	60	70
Velocity in fps:	1,451	900	752	640	551	477	413
Average pellet energy in ft-lbs:	5.01	1.93	1.35	.97	.72	.54	.41
Time of flight in seconds:	0	.0539	.0905	.1338	.1845	.2431	.3108

Type of load: F2 Sporting Clay
Three-foot velocity: 1,330 ft./sec.
Hull: 2¾-inch plastic
Wad: Plastic
Shot: Hard lead
Buffered: No
Test barrel length: 30 inch
Pellets will pierce skin up to 133 yards.

NO. 8 LEAD PELLETS—1 OUNCE—410 PELLETS
Mfg: Eley Hawk **Manufacturer's code:** VIP
Recoil energy in 8-lb. shotgun: 16.2 ft./lbs. **Recoil velocity in 8-lb. shotgun:** 11.4 ft./sec.

Distance in yards:	Muzzle	20	30	40	50	60	70
Velocity in fps:	1,451	900	752	640	551	477	413
Average pellet energy in ft-lbs:	5.01	1.93	1.35	.97	.72	.54	.41
Time of flight in seconds:	0	.0539	.0905	.1338	.1845	.2431	.3108

Type of load: Target
Three-foot velocity: 1,330 ft./sec.
Hull: 2¾-inch plastic
Wad: Plastic
Shot: Hard lead
Buffered: No
Test barrel length: 30 inch
Pellets will pierce skin up to 133 yards.

NO. 8 LEAD PELLETS—1 OUNCE—410 PELLETS
Mfg: Estate Cartridge **Manufacturer's code:** CT12XH1/SS12XH1
Recoil energy in 8-lb. shotgun: 21.2 ft./lbs. **Recoil velocity in 8-lb. shotgun:** 13.0 ft./sec.

Distance in yards:	Muzzle	20	30	40	50	60	70
Velocity in fps:	1,451	900	752	640	551	477	413
Average pellet energy in ft-lbs:	5.01	1.93	1.35	.97	.72	.54	.41
Time of flight in seconds:	0	.0539	.0905	.1338	.1845	.2431	.3108

Type of load: Target
Three-foot velocity: 1,330 ft./sec.
Hull: 2¾-inch plastic
Wad: Plastic
Shot: Hard lead
Buffered: No
Test barrel length: 30 inch
Pellets will pierce skin up to 133 yards.

NO. 8 LEAD PELLETS—1 OUNCE—410 PELLETS
Mfg: Estate Cartridge **Manufacturer's code:** INT28
Recoil energy in 8-lb. shotgun: 21.2 ft./lbs. **Recoil velocity in 8-lb. shotgun:** 13.0 ft./sec.

Distance in yards:	Muzzle	20	30	40	50	60	70
Velocity in fps:	1,451	900	752	640	551	477	413
Average pellet energy in ft-lbs:	5.01	1.93	1.35	.97	.72	.54	.41
Time of flight in seconds:	0	.0539	.0905	.1338	.1845	.2431	.3108

Type of load: Target
Three-foot velocity: 1,330 ft./sec.
Hull: 2¾-inch plastic
Wad: Plastic
Shot: Hard lead
Buffered: No
Test barrel length: 30 inch
Pellets will pierce skin up to 133 yards.

NO. 8 LEAD PELLETS—1 OUNCE—410 PELLETS
Mfg: RIO **Manufacturer's code:** Basic Game
Recoil energy in 8-lb. shotgun: 16.2 ft./lbs. **Recoil velocity in 8-lb. shotgun:** 11.4 ft./sec.

Distance in yards:	Muzzle	20	30	40	50	60	70
Velocity in fps:	1,451	900	752	640	551	477	413
Average pellet energy in ft-lbs:	5.01	1.93	1.35	.97	.72	.54	.41
Time of flight in seconds:	0	.0539	.0905	.1338	.1845	.2431	.3108

Type of load: Field
Three-foot velocity: 1,330 ft./sec.
Hull: 2¾-inch plastic
Wad: Plastic
Shot: Hard lead
Buffered: No
Test barrel length: 30 inch
Pellets will pierce skin up to 133 yards.

NO. 8 LEAD PELLETS—1 OUNCE—410 PELLETS
Mfg: RST, Ltd. **Manufacturer's code:** N/A
Recoil energy in 8-lb. shotgun: 16.2 ft./lbs. **Recoil velocity in 8-lb. shotgun:** 11.4 ft./sec.

Distance in yards:	Muzzle	20	30	40	50	60	70
Velocity in fps:	1,451	900	752	640	551	477	413
Average pellet energy in ft-lbs:	5.01	1.93	1.35	.97	.72	.54	.41
Time of flight in seconds:	0	.0539	.0905	.1338	.1845	.2431	.3108

Type of load: Target
Three-foot velocity: 1,330 ft./sec.
Hull: 2¾-inch plastic
Wad: Plastic
Shot: Lead
Buffered: No
Test barrel length: 30 inch
Pellets will pierce skin up to 133 yards.

NO. 8 LEAD PELLETS—1 OUNCE—410 PELLETS
Mfg: Winchester **Manufacturer's code:** AASCL12
Recoil energy in 8-lb. shotgun: 12.0 ft./lbs. **Recoil velocity in 8-lb. shotgun:** 13.3 ft./sec.

Distance in yards:	Muzzle	20	30	40	50	60	70
Velocity in fps:	1,473	910	759	645	555	480	416
Average pellet energy in ft-lbs:	5.16	1.97	1.37	.99	.73	.55	.41
Time of flight in seconds:	0	.0532	.0895	.1324	.1827	.2409	.3080

Type of load: Target
Three-foot velocity: 1,350 ft./sec.
Hull: 2¾-inch plastic
Wad: Plastic
Shot: Hard lead
Buffered: No
Test barrel length: 30 inch
Pellets will pierce skin up to 134 yards.

NO. 8 LEAD PELLETS—1¹⁄₁₆ OUNCES—436 PELLETS
Mfg: Kent Cartridge America/Canada **Manufacturer's code:** K122TR30
Recoil energy in 8-lb. shotgun: 17.4 ft./lbs. **Recoil velocity in 8-lb. shotgun:** 11.8 ft./sec.

Distance in yards:	Muzzle	20	30	40	50	60	70
Velocity in fps:	1,344	856	719	614	529	459	397
Average pellet energy in ft-lbs:	4.30	1.74	1.23	.90	.67	.50	.38
Time of flight in seconds:	0	.0573	.0957	.1409	.1936	.2546	.3249

Type of load: Target
Three-foot velocity: 1,230 ft./sec.
Hull: 2¾-inch plastic
Wad: Plastic
Shot: Lead
Buffered: No
Test barrel length: 30 inch
Pellets will pierce skin up to 118 yards.

NO. 8 LEAD PELLETS—1¹⁄₁₆ OUNCES—436 PELLETS
Mfg: Kent Cartridge America/Canada **Manufacturer's code:** K202SK24
Recoil energy in 8-lb. shotgun: 17.4 ft./lbs. **Recoil velocity in 8-lb. shotgun:** 11.8 ft./sec.

Distance in yards:	Muzzle	20	30	40	50	60	70
Velocity in fps:	1,344	856	719	614	529	459	397
Average pellet energy in ft-lbs:	4.30	1.74	1.23	.90	.67	.50	.38
Time of flight in seconds:	0	.0573	.0957	.1409	.1936	.2546	.3249

Type of load: Target
Three-foot velocity: 1,235 ft./sec.
Hull: 2¾-inch plastic
Wad: Plastic
Shot: Lead
Buffered: No
Test barrel length: 30 inch
Pellets will pierce skin up to 118 yards.

NO. 8 LEAD PELLETS—1¹⁄₈ OUNCES—461 PELLETS
Mfg: Dionisi **Manufacturer's code:** D 12 TL
Recoil energy in 8-lb. shotgun: 12.7 ft./lbs. **Recoil velocity in 8-lb. shotgun:** 10.1 ft./sec.

Distance in yards:	Muzzle	20	30	40	50	60	70
Velocity in fps:	1,022	706	603	521	451	391	339
Average pellet energy in ft-lbs:	2.48	1.19	.87	.65	.48	.36	.27
Time of flight in seconds:	0	.0717	.1177	.1713	.2332	.2047	.3871

Type of load: Target Low Noise
Three-foot velocity: 1,000 ft./sec.
Hull: 2¾-inch plastic
Wad: Plastic
Shot: Lead
Buffered: No
Test barrel length: 30 inch
Pellets will pierce skin up to 107 yards.

NO. 8 LEAD PELLETS—1¹⁄₈ OUNCES—461 PELLETS
Mfg: RST, Ltd. **Manufacturer's code:** N/A
Recoil energy in 8-lb. shotgun: 12.7 ft./lbs. **Recoil velocity in 8-lb. shotgun:** 10.1 ft./sec.

Distance in yards:	Muzzle	20	30	40	50	60	70
Velocity in fps:	1,022	706	603	521	451	391	339
Average pellet energy in ft-lbs:	2.48	1.19	.87	.65	.48	.36	.27
Time of flight in seconds:	0	.0717	.1177	.1713	.2332	.2047	.3871

Type of load: Target
Three-foot velocity: 1,000 ft./sec.
Hull: 2¾-inch plastic
Wad: Plastic
Shot: Lead
Buffered: No
Test barrel length: 30 inch
Pellets will pierce skin up to 107 yards.

NO. 8 LEAD PELLETS—1¹⁄₈ OUNCES—461 PELLETS
Mfg: Federal Cartridge Co. **Manufacturer's code:** T114
Recoil energy in 8-lb. shotgun: 16.2 ft./lbs. **Recoil velocity in 8-lb. shotgun:** 11.4 ft./sec.

Distance in yards:	Muzzle	20	30	40	50	60	70
Velocity in fps:	1,193	790	669	574	496	430	373
Average pellet energy in ft-lbs:	3.39	1.48	1.06	.78	.59	.44	.33
Time of flight in seconds:	0	.0630	.1044	.1529	.2092	.2741	.3491

Type of load: Target
Three-foot velocity: 1,100 ft./sec.
Hull: 2¾-inch plastic
Wad: Plastic
Shot: Hard lead
Buffered: No
Test barrel length: 30 inch
Pellets will pierce skin up to 125 yards.

NO. 8 LEAD PELLETS—1¹⁄₈ OUNCES—461 PELLETS
Mfg: Federal Cartridge Co. **Manufacturer's code:** T172
Recoil energy in 8-lb. shotgun: 16.2 ft./lbs. **Recoil velocity in 8-lb. shotgun:** 11.4 ft./sec.

Distance in yards:	Muzzle	20	30	40	50	60	70
Velocity in fps:	1,193	790	669	574	496	430	373
Average pellet energy in ft-lbs:	3.39	1.48	1.06	.78	.59	.44	.33
Time of flight in seconds:	0	.0630	.1044	.1529	.2092	.2741	.3491

Type of load: Target
Three-foot velocity: 1,100 ft./sec.
Hull: 2¾-inch plastic
Wad: Plastic
Shot: Hard lead
Buffered: No
Test barrel length: 30 inch
Pellets will pierce skin up to 125 yards.

NO. 8 LEAD PELLETS—1⅛ OUNCES—461 PELLETS
Mfg: Remington Arms Co. **Manufacturer's code:** STS12LR
Recoil energy in 8-lb. shotgun: 16.2 ft./lbs. **Recoil velocity in 8-lb. shotgun:** 11.4 ft./sec.

Distance in yards:	Muzzle	20	30	40	50	60	70
Velocity in fps:	1,193	790	669	574	496	430	373
Average pellet energy in ft-lbs:	3.39	1.48	1.06	.78	.59	.44	.33
Time of flight in seconds:	0	.0630	.1044	.1529	.2092	.2741	.3491

Type of load: Target
Three-foot velocity: 1,100 ft./sec.
Hull: 2¾-inch plastic
Wad: Plastic
Shot: Hard lead
Buffered: No
Test barrel length: 30 inch
Pellets will pierce skin up to 114 yards.

NO. 8 LEAD PELLETS—1⅛ OUNCES—461 PELLETS
Mfg: Estate Cartridge **Manufacturer's code:** CT12XL
Recoil energy in 8-lb. shotgun: 17.2 ft./lbs. **Recoil velocity in 8-lb. shotgun:** 11.8 ft./sec.

Distance in yards:	Muzzle	20	30	40	50	60	70
Velocity in fps:	1,221	802	678	582	503	436	378
Average pellet energy in ft-lbs:	3.55	1.53	1.10	.81	.60	.45	.34
Time of flight in seconds:	0	.0619	.1026	.1505	.2060	.2701	.3441

Type of load: Target
Three-foot velocity: 1,125 ft./sec.
Hull: 2¾-inch plastic
Wad: Plastic
Shot: Hard lead
Buffered: No
Test barrel length: 30 inch
Pellets will pierce skin up to 114 yards.

NO. 8 LEAD PELLETS—1⅛ OUNCES—461 PELLETS
Mfg: Fiocchi **Manufacturer's code:** 12TRAPL
Recoil energy in 8-lb. shotgun: 17.6 ft./lbs. **Recoil velocity in 8-lb. shotgun:** 11.9 ft./sec.

Distance in yards:	Muzzle	20	30	40	50	60	70
Velocity in fps:	1,232	807	682	585	505	438	380
Average pellet energy in ft-lbs:	3.61	1.55	1.11	.81	.61	.46	.34
Time of flight in seconds:	0	.0614	.1020	.1495	.2048	.2686	.3422

Type of load: Target
Three-foot velocity: 1,135 ft./sec.
Hull: 2¾-inch plastic
Wad: Plastic
Shot: Hard lead
Buffered: No
Test barrel length: 30 inch
Pellets will pierce skin up to 115 yards.

NO. 8 LEAD PELLETS—1⅛ OUNCES—461 PELLETS
Mfg: Armscor **Manufacturer's code:** N/A
Recoil energy in 8-lb. shotgun: 18.0 ft./lbs. **Recoil velocity in 8-lb. shotgun:** 12.0 ft./sec.

Distance in yards:	Muzzle	20	30	40	50	60	70
Velocity in fps:	1,244	812	686	588	508	440	381
Average pellet energy in ft-lbs:	3.68	1.57	1.12	.82	.61	.46	.35
Time of flight in seconds:	0	.0616	.1013	.1486	.2036	.2671	.3403

Type of load: Field
Three-foot velocity: 1,145 ft./sec.
Hull: 2¾-inch plastic
Wad: Plastic
Shot: Lead
Buffered: No
Test barrel length: 30 inch
Pellets will pierce skin up to 115 yards.

NO. 8 LEAD PELLETS—1⅛ OUNCES—461 PELLETS
Mfg: Dionisi **Manufacturer's code:** D 12 TD
Recoil energy in 8-lb. shotgun: 18.0 ft./lbs. **Recoil velocity in 8-lb. shotgun:** 12.0 ft./sec.

Distance in yards:	Muzzle	20	30	40	50	60	70
Velocity in fps:	1,244	812	686	588	508	440	381
Average pellet energy in ft-lbs:	3.68	1.57	1.12	.82	.61	.46	.35
Time of flight in seconds:	0	.0616	.1013	.1486	.2036	.2671	.3403

Type of load: Target
Three-foot velocity: 1,145 ft./sec.
Hull: 2¾-inch plastic
Wad: Plastic
Shot: Lead
Buffered: No
Test barrel length: 30 inch
Pellets will pierce skin up to 115 yards.

NO. 8 LEAD PELLETS—1⅛ OUNCES—461 PELLETS
Mfg: Estate Cartridge **Manufacturer's code:** CT12L/SS12L
Recoil energy in 8-lb. shotgun: 18.0 ft./lbs. **Recoil velocity in 8-lb. shotgun:** 12.0 ft./sec.

Distance in yards:	Muzzle	20	30	40	50	60	70
Velocity in fps:	1,244	812	686	588	508	440	381
Average pellet energy in ft-lbs:	3.68	1.57	1.12	.82	.61	.46	.35
Time of flight in seconds:	0	.0616	.1013	.1486	.2036	.2671	.3403

Type of load: Target
Three-foot velocity: 1,145 ft./sec.
Hull: 2¾-inch plastic
Wad: Plastic
Shot: Hard lead
Buffered: No
Test barrel length: 30 inch
Pellets will pierce skin up to 115 yards.

NO. 8 LEAD PELLETS—1⅛ OUNCES—461 PELLETS
Mfg: Federal Cartridge Co. **Manufacturer's code:** T115
Recoil energy in 8-lb. shotgun: 18.0 ft./lbs. **Recoil velocity in 8-lb. shotgun:** 12.0 ft./sec.

Distance in yards:	Muzzle	20	30	40	50	60	70
Velocity in fps:	1,244	812	686	588	508	440	381
Average pellet energy in ft-lbs:	3.68	1.57	1.12	.82	.61	.46	.35
Time of flight in seconds:	0	.0616	.1013	.1486	.2036	.2671	.3403

Type of load: Target
Three-foot velocity: 1,145 ft./sec.
Hull: 2¾-inch plastic
Wad: Plastic
Shot: Hard lead
Buffered: No
Test barrel length: 30 inch
Pellets will pierce skin up to 115 yards.

NO. 8 LEAD PELLETS—1⅛ OUNCES—461 PELLETS
Mfg: Federal Cartridge Co. **Manufacturer's code:** T117
Recoil energy in 8-lb. shotgun: 18.0 ft./lbs. **Recoil velocity in 8-lb. shotgun:** 12.0 ft./sec.

Distance in yards:	Muzzle	20	30	40	50	60	70
Velocity in fps:	1,244	812	686	588	508	440	381
Average pellet energy in ft-lbs:	3.68	1.57	1.12	.82	.61	.46	.35
Time of flight in seconds:	0	.0616	.1013	.1486	.2036	.2671	.3403

Type of load: Target
Three-foot velocity: 1,145 ft./sec.
Hull: 2¾-inch paper
Wad: Plastic
Shot: Hard lead
Buffered: No
Test barrel length: 30 inch
Pellets will pierce skin up to 115 yards.

NO. 8 LEAD PELLETS—1⅛ OUNCES—461 PELLETS
Mfg: Remington Arms Co. **Manufacturer's code:** STS12L
Recoil energy in 8-lb. shotgun: 18.0 ft./lbs. **Recoil velocity in 8-lb. shotgun:** 12.0 ft./sec.

Distance in yards:	Muzzle	20	30	40	50	60	70
Velocity in fps:	1,244	812	686	588	508	440	381
Average pellet energy in ft-lbs:	3.68	1.57	1.12	.82	.61	.46	.35
Time of flight in seconds:	0	.0616	.1013	.1486	.2036	.2671	.3403

Type of load: Target
Three-foot velocity: 1,145 ft./sec.
Hull: 2¾-inch plastic
Wad: Plastic
Shot: Hard lead
Buffered: No
Test barrel length: 30 inch
Pellets will pierce skin up to 115 yards.

NO. 8 LEAD PELLETS—1⅛ OUNCES—461 PELLETS
Mfg: RST, Ltd. **Manufacturer's code:** N/A
Recoil energy in 8-lb. shotgun: 18.0 ft./lbs. **Recoil velocity in 8-lb. shotgun:** 12.0 ft./sec.

Distance in yards:	Muzzle	20	30	40	50	60	70
Velocity in fps:	1,244	812	686	588	508	440	381
Average pellet energy in ft-lbs:	3.68	1.57	1.12	.82	.61	.46	.35
Time of flight in seconds:	0	.0616	.1013	.1486	.2036	.2671	.3403

Type of load: Target
Three-foot velocity: 1,145 ft./sec.
Hull: 2¾-inch plastic
Wad: Plastic
Shot: Lead
Buffered: No
Test barrel length: 30 inch
Pellets will pierce skin up to 115 yards.

NO. 8 LEAD PELLETS—1⅛ OUNCES—461 PELLETS
Mfg: Sellier & Bellot **Manufacturer's code:** SBA1273
Recoil energy in 8-lb. shotgun: 18.0 ft./lbs. **Recoil velocity in 8-lb. shotgun:** 12.0 ft./sec.

Distance in yards:	Muzzle	20	30	40	50	60	70
Velocity in fps:	1,244	812	686	588	508	440	381
Average pellet energy in ft-lbs:	3.68	1.57	1.12	.82	.61	.46	.35
Time of flight in seconds:	0	.0616	.1013	.1486	.2036	.2671	.3403

Type of load: Target
Three-foot velocity: 1,145 ft./sec.
Hull: 2¾-inch paper
Wad: Plastic
Shot: Lead
Buffered: No
Test barrel length: 30 inch
Pellets will pierce skin up to 115 yards.

NO. 8 LEAD PELLETS—1⅛ OUNCES—461 PELLETS
Mfg: Winchester **Manufacturer's code:** AA12/WEST12
Recoil energy in 8-lb. shotgun: 18.0 ft./lbs. **Recoil velocity in 8-lb. shotgun:** 12.0 ft./sec.

Distance in yards:	Muzzle	20	30	40	50	60	70
Velocity in fps:	1,244	812	686	588	508	440	381
Average pellet energy in ft-lbs:	3.68	1.57	1.12	.82	.61	.46	.35
Time of flight in seconds:	0	.0616	.1013	.1486	.2036	.2671	.3403

Type of load: Field & Target
Three-foot velocity: 1,145 ft./sec.
Hull: 2¾-inch plastic
Wad: Plastic
Shot: Lead
Buffered: No
Test barrel length: 30 inch
Pellets will pierce skin up to 115 yards.

NO. 8 LEAD PELLETS—1⅛ OUNCES—461 PELLETS
Mfg: Fiocchi **Manufacturer's code:** 12VIPL
Recoil energy in 8-lb. shotgun: 18.2 ft./lbs. **Recoil velocity in 8-lb. shotgun:** 12.1 ft./sec.

Distance in yards:	Muzzle	20	30	40	50	60	70
Velocity in fps:	1,249	815	688	589	509	441	382
Average pellet energy in ft-lbs:	3.71	1.58	1.13	.83	.62	.46	.35
Time of flight in seconds:	0	.0608	.1010	.1482	.2030	.2663	.3394

Type of load: Target
Three-foot velocity: 1,150 ft./sec.
Hull: 2¾-inch plastic
Wad: Plastic
Shot: Hard lead
Buffered: No
Test barrel length: 30 inch
Pellets will pierce skin up to 115 yards.

NO. 8 LEAD PELLETS—1⅛ OUNCES—461 PELLETS
Mfg: Kent Cartridge America/Canada **Manufacturer's code:** K122LTR32
Recoil energy in 8-lb. shotgun: 18.2 ft./lbs. **Recoil velocity in 8-lb. shotgun:** 12.1 ft./sec.

Distance in yards:	Muzzle	20	30	40	50	60	70
Velocity in fps:	1,249	815	688	589	509	441	382
Average pellet energy in ft-lbs:	3.71	1.58	1.13	.83	.62	.46	.35
Time of flight in seconds:	0	.0608	.1010	.1482	.2030	.2663	.3394

Type of load: Target
Three-foot velocity: 1,150 ft./sec.
Hull: 2¾-inch plastic
Wad: Plastic
Shot: Lead
Buffered: No
Test barrel length: 30 inch
Pellets will pierce skin up to 115 yards.

NO. 8 LEAD PELLETS—1⅛ OUNCES—461 PELLETS
Mfg: Rottweil **Manufacturer's code:** Sport
Recoil energy in 8-lb. shotgun: 18.2 ft./lbs. **Recoil velocity in 8-lb. shotgun:** 12.1 ft./sec.

Distance in yards:	Muzzle	20	30	40	50	60	70
Velocity in fps:	1,249	815	688	589	509	441	382
Average pellet energy in ft-lbs:	3.71	1.58	1.13	.83	.62	.46	.35
Time of flight in seconds:	0	.0608	.1010	.1482	.2030	.2663	.3394

Type of load: Target
Three-foot velocity: 1,150 ft./sec.
Hull: 2¾-inch plastic
Wad: Plastic
Shot: Lead
Buffered: No
Test barrel length: 30 inch
Pellets will pierce skin up to 115 yards.

NO. 8 LEAD PELLETS—1⅛ OUNCES—461 PELLETS
Mfg: Fiocchi **Manufacturer's code:** 12LITE
Recoil energy in 8-lb. shotgun: 19.9 ft./lbs. **Recoil velocity in 8-lb. shotgun:** 12.6 ft./sec.

Distance in yards:	Muzzle	20	30	40	50	60	70
Velocity in fps:	1,266	822	693	594	513	444	385
Average pellet energy in ft-lbs:	3.81	1.61	1.14	.84	.63	.47	.35
Time of flight in seconds:	0	.0601	.1000	.1468	.2013	.2641	.3367

Type of load: Target
Three-foot velocity: 1,165 ft./sec.
Hull: 2¾-inch plastic
Wad: Plastic
Shot: Hard lead
Buffered: No
Test barrel length: 30 inch
Pellets will pierce skin up to 116 yards.

NO. 8 LEAD PELLETS—1⅛ OUNCES—461 PELLETS
Mfg: Fiocchi **Manufacturer's code:** 12TRAPH
Recoil energy in 8-lb. shotgun: 19.3 ft./lbs. **Recoil velocity in 8-lb. shotgun:** 12.5 ft./sec.

Distance in yards:	Muzzle	20	30	40	50	60	70
Velocity in fps:	1,277	827	697	597	515	446	387
Average pellet energy in ft-lbs:	3.88	1.63	1.16	.85	.63	.47	.36
Time of flight in seconds:	0	.0597	.0993	.1459	.2001	.2627	.3349

Type of load: Target
Three-foot velocity: 1,175 ft./sec.
Hull: 2¾-inch plastic
Wad: Plastic
Shot: Hard lead
Buffered: No
Test barrel length: 30 inch
Pellets will pierce skin up to 116 yards.

NO. 8 LEAD PELLETS—1⅛ OUNCES—461 PELLETS
Mfg: PMC (Eldorado Cartridge Corp.) **Manufacturer's code:** LCT12
Recoil energy in 8-lb. shotgun: 19.3 ft./lbs. **Recoil velocity in 8-lb. shotgun:** 12.5 ft./sec.

Distance in yards:	Muzzle	20	30	40	50	60	70
Velocity in fps:	1,277	827	697	597	515	446	387
Average pellet energy in ft-lbs:	3.88	1.63	1.16	.85	.63	.47	.36
Time of flight in seconds:	0	.0597	.0993	.1459	.2001	.2627	.3349

Type of load: Target
Three-foot velocity: 1,175 ft./sec.
Hull: 2¾-inch plastic
Wad: Plastic
Shot: Lead
Buffered: No
Test barrel length: 30 inch
Pellets will pierce skin up to 116 yards.

NO. 8 LEAD PELLETS—1⅛ OUNCES—461 PELLETS
Mfg: Aguila **Manufacturer's code:** N/A
Recoil energy in 8-lb. shotgun: 20.4 ft./lbs. **Recoil velocity in 8-lb. shotgun:** 12.8 ft./sec.

Distance in yards:	Muzzle	20	30	40	50	60	70
Velocity in fps:	1,305	839	706	604	521	452	391
Average pellet energy in ft-lbs:	4.05	1.67	1.19	.87	.65	.49	.36
Time of flight in seconds:	0	.0587	.0978	.1438	.1973	.2593	.3307

Type of load: Field
Three-foot velocity: 1,200 ft./sec.
Hull: 2¾-inch plastic
Wad: Plastic
Shot: Lead
Buffered: No
Test barrel length: 30 inch
Pellets will pierce skin up to 129 yards.

NO. 8 LEAD PELLETS—1⅛ OUNCES—461 PELLETS
Mfg: Dionisi **Manufacturer's code:** D 12 GTX
Recoil energy in 8-lb. shotgun: 20.4 ft./lbs. **Recoil velocity in 8-lb. shotgun:** 12.8 ft./sec.

Distance in yards:	Muzzle	20	30	40	50	60	70
Velocity in fps:	1,305	839	706	604	521	452	391
Average pellet energy in ft-lbs:	4.05	1.67	1.19	.87	.65	.49	.36
Time of flight in seconds:	0	.0587	.0978	.1438	.1973	.2593	.3307

Type of load: Game & Target
Three-foot velocity: 1,200 ft./sec.
Hull: 2¾-inch plastic
Wad: Plastic
Shot: Lead
Buffered: No
Test barrel length: 30 inch
Pellets will pierce skin up to 129 yards.

NO. 8 LEAD PELLETS—1⅛ OUNCES—461 PELLETS
Mfg: Dionisi **Manufacturer's code:** D 12 TDX
Recoil energy in 8-lb. shotgun: 20.4 ft./lbs. **Recoil velocity in 8-lb. shotgun:** 12.8 ft./sec.

Distance in yards:	Muzzle	20	30	40	50	60	70
Velocity in fps:	1,305	839	706	604	521	452	391
Average pellet energy in ft-lbs:	4.05	1.67	1.19	.87	.65	.49	.36
Time of flight in seconds:	0	.0587	.0978	.1438	.1973	.2593	.3307

Type of load: Target & Pigeon
Three-foot velocity: 1,200 ft./sec.
Hull: 2¾-inch plastic
Wad: Plastic
Shot: Lead
Buffered: No
Test barrel length: 30 inch
Pellets will pierce skin up to 129 yards.

NO. 8 LEAD PELLETS—1⅛ OUNCES—461 PELLETS
Mfg: Estate Cartridge **Manufacturer's code:** CT12H/SS12H
Recoil energy in 8-lb. shotgun: 20.4 ft./lbs. **Recoil velocity in 8-lb. shotgun:** 12.8 ft./sec.

Distance in yards:	Muzzle	20	30	40	50	60	70
Velocity in fps:	1,305	839	706	604	521	452	391
Average pellet energy in ft-lbs:	4.05	1.67	1.19	.87	.65	.49	.36
Time of flight in seconds:	0	.0587	.0978	.1438	.1973	.2593	.3307

Type of load: Target
Three-foot velocity: 1,200 ft./sec.
Hull: 2¾-inch plastic
Wad: Plastic
Shot: Hard lead
Buffered: No
Test barrel length: 30 inch
Pellets will pierce skin up to 129 yards.

NO. 8 LEAD PELLETS—1⅛ OUNCES—461 PELLETS
Mfg: Estate Cartridge **Manufacturer's code:** CT12HS
Recoil energy in 8-lb. shotgun: 20.4 ft./lbs. **Recoil velocity in 8-lb. shotgun:** 12.8 ft./sec.

Distance in yards:	Muzzle	20	30	40	50	60	70
Velocity in fps:	1,305	839	706	604	521	452	391
Average pellet energy in ft-lbs:	4.05	1.67	1.19	.87	.65	.49	.36
Time of flight in seconds:	0	.0587	.0978	.1438	.1973	.2593	.3307

Type of load: Target
Three-foot velocity: 1,200 ft./sec.
Hull: 2¾-inch plastic
Wad: Plastic
Shot: Hard lead
Buffered: No
Test barrel length: 30 inch
Pellets will pierce skin up to 129 yards.

NO. 8 LEAD PELLETS—1⅛ OUNCES—461 PELLETS
Mfg: Federal Cartridge Co. **Manufacturer's code:** T116
Recoil energy in 8-lb. shotgun: 20.4 ft./lbs. **Recoil velocity in 8-lb. shotgun:** 12.8 ft./sec.

Distance in yards:	Muzzle	20	30	40	50	60	70
Velocity in fps:	1,305	839	706	604	521	452	391
Average pellet energy in ft-lbs:	4.05	1.67	1.19	.87	.65	.49	.36
Time of flight in seconds:	0	.0587	.0978	.1438	.1973	.2593	.3307

Type of load: Target
Three-foot velocity: 1,200 ft./sec.
Hull: 2¾-inch plastic
Wad: Plastic
Shot: Hard lead
Buffered: No
Test barrel length: 30 inch
Pellets will pierce skin up to 129 yards.

NO. 8 LEAD PELLETS—1⅛ OUNCES—461 PELLETS
Mfg: Federal Cartridge Co. **Manufacturer's code:** T118
Recoil energy in 8-lb. shotgun: 20.4 ft./lbs. **Recoil velocity in 8-lb. shotgun:** 12.8 ft./sec.

Distance in yards:	Muzzle	20	30	40	50	60	70
Velocity in fps:	1,305	839	706	604	521	452	391
Average pellet energy in ft-lbs:	4.05	1.67	1.19	.87	.65	.49	.36
Time of flight in seconds:	0	.0587	.0978	.1438	.1973	.2593	.3307

Type of load: Target
Three-foot velocity: 1,200 ft./sec.
Hull: 2¾-inch paper
Wad: Plastic
Shot: Hard lead
Buffered: No
Test barrel length: 30 inch
Pellets will pierce skin up to 129 yards.

NO. 8 LEAD PELLETS—1⅛ OUNCES—461 PELLETS
Mfg: Federal Cartridge Co. **Manufacturer's code:** T177
Recoil energy in 8-lb. shotgun: 20.4 ft./lbs. **Recoil velocity in 8-lb. shotgun:** 12.8 ft./sec.

Distance in yards:	Muzzle	20	30	40	50	60	70
Velocity in fps:	1,305	839	706	604	521	452	391
Average pellet energy in ft-lbs:	4.05	1.67	1.19	.87	.65	.49	.36
Time of flight in seconds:	0	.0587	.0978	.1438	.1973	.2593	.3307

Type of load: Target & Spreader
Three-foot velocity: 1,200 ft./sec.
Hull: 2¾-inch plastic
Wad: Plastic
Shot: Hard lead
Buffered: No
Test barrel length: 30 inch
Pellets will pierce skin up to 129 yards.

NO. 8 LEAD PELLETS—1⅛ OUNCES—461 PELLETS
Mfg: Fiocchi **Manufacturer's code:** 12GT118
Recoil energy in 8-lb. shotgun: 20.4 ft./lbs. **Recoil velocity in 8-lb. shotgun:** 12.8 ft./sec.

Distance in yards:	Muzzle	20	30	40	50	60	70
Velocity in fps:	1,305	839	706	604	521	452	391
Average pellet energy in ft-lbs:	4.05	1.67	1.19	.87	.65	.49	.36
Time of flight in seconds:	0	.0587	.0978	.1438	.1973	.2593	.3307

Type of load: Game & Target
Three-foot velocity: 1,200 ft./sec.
Hull: 2¾-inch plastic
Wad: Plastic
Shot: Lead
Buffered: No
Test barrel length: 30 inch
Pellets will pierce skin up to 129 yards.

NO. 8 LEAD PELLETS—1⅛ OUNCES—461 PELLETS
Mfg: Fiocchi **Manufacturer's code:** 12SSCH
Recoil energy in 8-lb. shotgun: 20.4 ft./lbs. **Recoil velocity in 8-lb. shotgun:** 12.8 ft./sec.

Distance in yards:	Muzzle	20	30	40	50	60	70
Velocity in fps:	1,305	839	706	604	521	452	391
Average pellet energy in ft-lbs:	4.05	1.67	1.19	.87	.65	.49	.36
Time of flight in seconds:	0	.0587	.0978	.1438	.1973	.2593	.3307

Type of load: Target & Spreader
Three-foot velocity: 1,200 ft./sec.
Hull: 2¾-inch plastic
Wad: Plastic
Shot: Hard lead
Buffered: No
Test barrel length: 30 inch
Pellets will pierce skin up to 129 yards.

NO. 8 LEAD PELLETS—1⅛ OUNCES—461 PELLETS
Mfg: Fiocchi **Manufacturer's code:** 12VIPH
Recoil energy in 8-lb. shotgun: 20.4 ft./lbs. **Recoil velocity in 8-lb. shotgun:** 12.8 ft./sec.

Distance in yards:	Muzzle	20	30	40	50	60	70
Velocity in fps:	1,305	839	706	604	521	452	391
Average pellet energy in ft-lbs:	4.05	1.67	1.19	.87	.65	.49	.36
Time of flight in seconds:	0	.0587	.0978	.1438	.1973	.2593	.3307

Type of load: Target
Three-foot velocity: 1,200 ft./sec.
Hull: 2¾-inch plastic
Wad: Plastic
Shot: Hard lead
Buffered: No
Test barrel length: 30 inch
Pellets will pierce skin up to 129 yards.

NO. 8 LEAD PELLETS—1⅛ OUNCES—461 PELLETS
Mfg: Kent Cartridge America/Canada **Manufacturer's code:** K122RTR32
Recoil energy in 8-lb. shotgun: 20.4 ft./lbs. **Recoil velocity in 8-lb. shotgun:** 12.8 ft./sec.

Distance in yards:	Muzzle	20	30	40	50	60	70
Velocity in fps:	1,305	839	706	604	521	452	391
Average pellet energy in ft-lbs:	4.05	1.67	1.19	.87	.65	.49	.36
Time of flight in seconds:	0	.0587	.0978	.1438	.1973	.2593	.3307

Type of load: Target
Three-foot velocity: 1,200 ft./sec.
Hull: 2¾-inch plastic
Wad: Plastic
Shot: Lead
Buffered: No
Test barrel length: 30 inch
Pellets will pierce skin up to 129 yards.

NO. 8 LEAD PELLETS—1⅛ OUNCES—461 PELLETS
Mfg: Kent Cartridge America/Canada **Manufacturer's code:** K122SK32
Recoil energy in 8-lb. shotgun: 20.4 ft./lbs. **Recoil velocity in 8-lb. shotgun:** 12.8 ft./sec.

Distance in yards:	Muzzle	20	30	40	50	60	70
Velocity in fps:	1,305	839	706	604	521	452	391
Average pellet energy in ft-lbs:	4.05	1.67	1.19	.87	.65	.49	.36
Time of flight in seconds:	0	.0587	.0978	.1438	.1973	.2593	.3307

Type of load: Target
Three-foot velocity: 1,200 ft./sec.
Hull: 2¾-inch plastic
Wad: Plastic
Shot: Lead
Buffered: No
Test barrel length: 30 inch
Pellets will pierce skin up to 129 yards.

NO. 8 LEAD PELLETS—1⅛ OUNCES—461 PELLETS
Mfg: Polywad **Manufacturer's code:** SRH128
Recoil energy in 8-lb. shotgun: 20.4 ft./lbs. **Recoil velocity in 8-lb. shotgun:** 12.8 ft./sec.

Distance in yards:	Muzzle	20	30	40	50	60	70
Velocity in fps:	1,305	839	706	604	521	452	391
Average pellet energy in ft-lbs:	4.05	1.67	1.19	.87	.65	.49	.36
Time of flight in seconds:	0	.0587	.0978	.1438	.1973	.2593	.3307

Type of load: Field
Three-foot velocity: 1,200 ft./sec.
Hull: 2¾-inch plastic
Wad: Plastic
Shot: Lead
Buffered: No
Test barrel length: 30 inch
Pellets will pierce skin up to 129 yards.

NO. 8 LEAD PELLETS—1⅛ OUNCES—461 PELLETS
Mfg: Remington Arms Co. **Manufacturer's code:** STS12LH
Recoil energy in 8-lb. shotgun: 20.4 ft./lbs. **Recoil velocity in 8-lb. shotgun:** 12.8 ft./sec.

Distance in yards:	Muzzle	20	30	40	50	60	70
Velocity in fps:	1,305	839	706	604	521	452	391
Average pellet energy in ft-lbs:	4.05	1.67	1.19	.87	.65	.49	.36
Time of flight in seconds:	0	.0587	.0978	.1438	.1973	.2593	.3307

Type of load: Target
Three-foot velocity: 1,200 ft./sec.
Hull: 2¾-inch plastic
Wad: Plastic
Shot: Hard lead
Buffered: No
Test barrel length: 30 inch
Pellets will pierce skin up to 129 yards.

NO. 8 LEAD PELLETS—1⅛ OUNCES—461 PELLETS
Mfg: RST, Ltd. **Manufacturer's code:** N/A
Recoil energy in 8-lb. shotgun: 20.4 ft./lbs. **Recoil velocity in 8-lb. shotgun:** 12.8 ft./sec.

Distance in yards:	Muzzle	20	30	40	50	60	70
Velocity in fps:	1,305	839	706	604	521	452	391
Average pellet energy in ft-lbs:	4.05	1.67	1.19	.87	.65	.49	.36
Time of flight in seconds:	0	.0587	.0978	.1438	.1973	.2593	.3307

Type of load: Target
Three-foot velocity: 1,200 ft./sec.
Hull: 2¾-inch plastic
Wad: Plastic
Shot: Lead
Buffered: No
Test barrel length: 30 inch
Pellets will pierce skin up to 129 yards.

NO. 8 LEAD PELLETS—1⅛ OUNCES—461 PELLETS
Mfg: Sellier & Bellot **Manufacturer's code:** SBA1265
Recoil energy in 8-lb. shotgun: 20.4 ft./lbs. **Recoil velocity in 8-lb. shotgun:** 12.8 ft./sec.

Distance in yards:	Muzzle	20	30	40	50	60	70
Velocity in fps:	1,305	839	706	604	521	452	391
Average pellet energy in ft-lbs:	4.05	1.67	1.19	.87	.65	.49	.36
Time of flight in seconds:	0	.0587	.0978	.1438	.1973	.2593	.3307

Type of load: Target
Three-foot velocity: 1,200 ft./sec.
Hull: 2¾-inch paper
Wad: Plastic
Shot: Lead
Buffered: No
Test barrel length: 30 inch
Pellets will pierce skin up to 129 yards.

NO. 8 LEAD PELLETS—1⅛ OUNCES—461 PELLETS
Mfg: Winchester **Manufacturer's code:** AAM12
Recoil energy in 8-lb. shotgun: 20.4 ft./lbs. **Recoil velocity in 8-lb. shotgun:** 12.8 ft./sec.

Distance in yards:	Muzzle	20	30	40	50	60	70
Velocity in fps:	1,305	839	706	604	521	452	391
Average pellet energy in ft-lbs:	4.05	1.67	1.19	.87	.65	.49	.36
Time of flight in seconds:	0	.0587	.0978	.1438	.1973	.2593	.3307

Type of load: Target
Three-foot velocity: 1,200 ft./sec.
Hull: 2¾-inch plastic
Wad: Plastic
Shot: Hard lead
Buffered: No
Test barrel length: 30 inch
Pellets will pierce skin up to 129 yards.

NO. 8 LEAD PELLETS—1⅛ OUNCES—461 PELLETS
Mfg: Kent Cartridge America/Canada **Manufacturer's code:** K122HTR32
Recoil energy in 8-lb. shotgun: 21.3 ft./lbs. **Recoil velocity in 8-lb. shotgun:** 13.1 ft./sec.

Distance in yards:	Muzzle	20	30	40	50	60	70
Velocity in fps:	1,327	934	713	610	526	456	395
Average pellet energy in ft-lbs:	4.19	1.71	1.21	.88	.66	.49	.37
Time of flight in seconds:	0	.0579	.0966	.1422	.1952	.2566	.3273

Type of load: Target
Three-foot velocity: 1,220 ft./sec.
Hull: 2¾-inch plastic
Wad: Plastic
Shot: Lead
Buffered: No
Test barrel length: 30 inch
Pellets will pierce skin up to 130 yards.

NO. 8 LEAD PELLETS—1⅛ OUNCES—461 PELLETS
Mfg: Aguila **Manufacturer's code:** N/A
Recoil energy in 8-lb. shotgun: 22.0 ft./lbs. **Recoil velocity in 8-lb. shotgun:** 13.3 ft./sec.

Distance in yards:	Muzzle	20	30	40	50	60	70
Velocity in fps:	1,344	856	719	614	529	459	397
Average pellet energy in ft-lbs:	4.30	1.74	1.23	.90	.67	.50	.38
Time of flight in seconds:	0	.0573	.0957	.1409	.1936	.2546	.3249

Type of load: Sporting Clay
Three-foot velocity: 1,235 ft./sec.
Hull: 2¾-inch plastic
Wad: Plastic
Shot: Nickel-plated lead
Buffered: No
Test barrel length: 30 inch
Pellets will pierce skin up to 130 yards.

NO. 8 LEAD PELLETS—1⅛ OUNCES—461 PELLETS
Mfg: Baschieri & Pellagri **Manufacturer's code:** N/A
Recoil energy in 8-lb. shotgun: 22.0 ft./lbs. **Recoil velocity in 8-lb. shotgun:** 13.3 ft./sec.

Distance in yards:	Muzzle	20	30	40	50	60	70
Velocity in fps:	1,344	856	719	614	529	459	397
Average pellet energy in ft-lbs:	4.30	1.74	1.23	.90	.67	.50	.38
Time of flight in seconds:	0	.0573	.0957	.1409	.1936	.2546	.3249

Type of load: Comp-2000 32 gr.
Three-foot velocity: 1,235 ft./sec.
Hull: 2¾-inch plastic
Wad: Plastic
Shot: Hard lead
Buffered: No
Test barrel length: 30 inch
Pellets will pierce skin up to 130 yards.

NO. 8 LEAD PELLETS—1⅛ OUNCES—461 PELLETS
Mfg: Federal Cartridge Co. **Manufacturer's code:** T178
Recoil energy in 8-lb. shotgun: 22.0 ft./lbs. **Recoil velocity in 8-lb. shotgun:** 13.3 ft./sec.

Distance in yards:	Muzzle	20	30	40	50	60	70
Velocity in fps:	1,344	856	719	614	529	459	397
Average pellet energy in ft-lbs:	4.30	1.74	1.23	.90	.67	.50	.38
Time of flight in seconds:	0	.0573	.0957	.1409	.1936	.2546	.3249

Type of load: Target
Three-foot velocity: 1,235 ft./sec.
Hull: 2¾-inch plastic
Wad: Plastic
Shot: Hard lead
Buffered: No
Test barrel length: 30 inch
Pellets will pierce skin up to 130 yards.

NO. 8 LEAD PELLETS—1⅛ OUNCES—461 PELLETS
Mfg: Federal Cartridge Co. **Manufacturer's code:** T171
Recoil energy in 8-lb. shotgun: 22.0 ft./lbs. **Recoil velocity in 8-lb. shotgun:** 13.3 ft./sec.

Distance in yards:	Muzzle	20	30	40	50	60	70
Velocity in fps:	1,344	856	719	614	529	459	397
Average pellet energy in ft-lbs:	4.30	1.74	1.23	.90	.67	.50	.38
Time of flight in seconds:	0	.0573	.0957	.1409	.1936	.2546	.3249

Type of load: Target
Three-foot velocity: 1,235 ft./sec.
Hull: 2¾-inch paper
Wad: Plastic
Shot: Hard lead
Buffered: No
Test barrel length: 30 inch
Pellets will pierce skin up to 130 yards.

NO. 8 LEAD PELLETS—1⅛ OUNCES—461 PELLETS
Mfg: Estate Cartridge **Manufacturer's code:** CT12XH/SS12XH
Recoil energy in 8-lb. shotgun: 22.7 ft./lbs. **Recoil velocity in 8-lb. shotgun:** 13.5 ft./sec.

Distance in yards:	Muzzle	20	30	40	50	60	70
Velocity in fps:	1,361	863	724	618	533	461	400
Average pellet energy in ft-lbs:	4.41	1.77	1.25	.91	.68	.51	.38
Time of flight in seconds:	0	.0568	.0948	.1398	.1921	.2527	.3225

Type of load: Target
Three-foot velocity: 1,250 ft./sec.
Hull: 2¾-inch plastic
Wad: Plastic
Shot: Hard lead
Buffered: No
Test barrel length: 30 inch
Pellets will pierce skin up to 131 yards.

NO. 8 LEAD PELLETS—1⅛ OUNCES—461 PELLETS
Mfg: Estate Cartridge **Manufacturer's code:** HG12
Recoil energy in 8-lb. shotgun: 22.7 ft./lbs. **Recoil velocity in 8-lb. shotgun:** 13.5 ft./sec.

Distance in yards:	Muzzle	20	30	40	50	60	70
Velocity in fps:	1,361	863	724	618	533	461	400
Average pellet energy in ft-lbs:	4.41	1.77	1.25	.91	.68	.51	.38
Time of flight in seconds:	0	.0568	.0948	.1398	.1921	.2527	.3225

Type of load: Field
Three-foot velocity: 1,250 ft./sec.
Hull: 2¾-inch plastic
Wad: Plastic
Shot: Hard lead
Buffered: No
Test barrel length: 30 inch
Pellets will pierce skin up to 131 yards.

NO. 8 LEAD PELLETS—1⅛ OUNCES—461 PELLETS
Mfg: PMC (Eldorado Cartridge Corp.) **Manufacturer's code:** HD12/CT12/GCT
Recoil energy in 8-lb. shotgun: 22.0 ft./lbs. **Recoil velocity in 8-lb. shotgun:** 13.3 ft./sec.

Distance in yards:	Muzzle	20	30	40	50	60	70
Velocity in fps:	1,344	856	719	614	529	459	397
Average pellet energy in ft-lbs:	4.30	1.74	1.23	.90	.67	.50	.38
Time of flight in seconds:	0	.0573	.0957	.1409	.1936	.2546	.3249

Type of load: Heavy Dove & Target
Three-foot velocity: 1,235 ft./sec.
Hull: 2¾-inch plastic
Wad: Plastic
Shot: Lead
Buffered: No
Test barrel length: 30 inch
Pellets will pierce skin up to 130 yards.

NO. 8 LEAD PELLETS—1⅛ OUNCES—461 PELLETS
Mfg: Federal Cartridge Co. **Manufacturer's code:** H123/HGL12
Recoil energy in 8-lb. shotgun: 22.7 ft./lbs. **Recoil velocity in 8-lb. shotgun:** 13.5 ft./sec.

Distance in yards:	Muzzle	20	30	40	50	60	70
Velocity in fps:	1,361	863	724	618	533	461	400
Average pellet energy in ft-lbs:	4.41	1.77	1.25	.91	.68	.51	.38
Time of flight in seconds:	0	.0568	.0948	.1398	.1921	.2527	.3225

Type of load: Field
Three-foot velocity: 1,250 ft./sec.
Hull: 2¾-inch plastic
Wad: Plastic
Shot: Lead
Buffered: No
Test barrel length: 30 inch
Pellets will pierce skin up to 131 yards.

NO. 8 LEAD PELLETS—1⅛ OUNCES—461 PELLETS
Mfg: Fiocchi **Manufacturer's code:** 12FLD
Recoil energy in 8-lb. shotgun: 22.7 ft./lbs. **Recoil velocity in 8-lb. shotgun:** 13.5 ft./sec.

Distance in yards:	Muzzle	20	30	40	50	60	70
Velocity in fps:	1,361	863	724	618	533	461	400
Average pellet energy in ft-lbs:	4.41	1.77	1.25	.91	.68	.51	.38
Time of flight in seconds:	0	.0568	.0948	.1398	.1921	.2527	.3225

Type of load: Field
Three-foot velocity: 1,250 ft./sec.
Hull: 2¾-inch plastic
Wad: Plastic
Shot: Lead
Buffered: No
Test barrel length: 30 inch
Pellets will pierce skin up to 131 yards.

NO. 8 LEAD PELLETS—1⅛ OUNCES—461 PELLETS
Mfg: Fiocchi **Manufacturer's code:** 12SSCX
Recoil energy in 8-lb. shotgun: 22.7 ft./lbs. **Recoil velocity in 8-lb. shotgun:** 13.5 ft./sec.

Distance in yards:	Muzzle	20	30	40	50	60	70
Velocity in fps:	1,361	863	724	618	533	461	400
Average pellet energy in ft-lbs:	4.41	1.77	1.25	.91	.68	.51	.38
Time of flight in seconds:	0	.0568	.0948	.1398	.1921	.2527	.3225

Type of load: Target & Spreader
Three-foot velocity: 1,250 ft./sec.
Hull: 2¾-inch plastic
Wad: Plastic
Shot: Hard lead
Buffered: No
Test barrel length: 30 inch
Pellets will pierce skin up to 131 yards.

NO. 8 LEAD PELLETS—1⅛ OUNCES—461 PELLETS
Mfg: Fiocchi **Manufacturer's code:** 12WRNO
Recoil energy in 8-lb. shotgun: 22.7 ft./lbs. **Recoil velocity in 8-lb. shotgun:** 13.5 ft./sec.

Distance in yards:	Muzzle	20	30	40	50	60	70
Velocity in fps:	1,361	863	724	618	533	461	400
Average pellet energy in ft-lbs:	4.41	1.77	1.25	.91	.68	.51	.38
Time of flight in seconds:	0	.0568	.0948	.1398	.1921	.2527	.3225

Type of load: Target
Three-foot velocity: 1,250 ft./sec.
Hull: 2¾-inch plastic
Wad: Plastic
Shot: Hard lead
Buffered: No
Test barrel length: 30 inch
Pellets will pierce skin up to 131 yards.

NO. 8 LEAD PELLETS—1⅛ OUNCES—461 PELLETS
Mfg: Kent Cartridge America/Canada **Manufacturer's code:** K122SL32
Recoil energy in 8-lb. shotgun: 22.7 ft./lbs. **Recoil velocity in 8-lb. shotgun:** 13.5 ft./sec.

Distance in yards:	Muzzle	20	30	40	50	60	70
Velocity in fps:	1,361	863	724	618	533	461	400
Average pellet energy in ft-lbs:	4.41	1.77	1.25	.91	.68	.51	.38
Time of flight in seconds:	0	.0568	.0948	.1398	.1921	.2527	.3225

Type of load: Target
Three-foot velocity: 1,250 ft./sec.
Hull: 2¾-inch plastic
Wad: Plastic
Shot: Lead
Buffered: No
Test barrel length: 30 inch
Pellets will pierce skin up to 131 yards.

NO. 8 LEAD PELLETS—1⅛ OUNCES—461 PELLETS
Mfg: Kent Cartridge America/Canada **Manufacturer's code:** K122RSC32
Recoil energy in 8-lb. shotgun: 22.7 ft./lbs. **Recoil velocity in 8-lb. shotgun:** 13.5 ft./sec.

Distance in yards:	Muzzle	20	30	40	50	60	70
Velocity in fps:	1,361	863	724	618	533	461	400
Average pellet energy in ft-lbs:	4.41	1.77	1.25	.91	.68	.51	.38
Time of flight in seconds:	0	.0568	.0948	.1398	.1921	.2527	.3225

Type of load: Target
Three-foot velocity: 1,250 ft./sec.
Hull: 2¾-inch plastic
Wad: Plastic
Shot: Lead
Buffered: No
Test barrel length: 30 inch
Pellets will pierce skin up to 131 yards.

NO. 8 LEAD PELLETS—1⅛ OUNCES—461 PELLETS
Mfg: Remington Arms Co. **Manufacturer's code:** RP12HD
Recoil energy in 8-lb. shotgun: 22.7 ft./lbs. **Recoil velocity in 8-lb. shotgun:** 13.5 ft./sec.

Distance in yards:	Muzzle	20	30	40	50	60	70
Velocity in fps:	1,361	863	724	618	533	461	400
Average pellet energy in ft-lbs:	4.41	1.77	1.25	.91	.68	.51	.38
Time of flight in seconds:	0	.0568	.0948	.1398	.1921	.2527	.3225

Type of load: Field
Three-foot velocity: 1,250 ft./sec.
Hull: 2¾-inch plastic
Wad: Plastic
Shot: Lead
Buffered: No
Test barrel length: 30 inch
Pellets will pierce skin up to 131 yards.

NO. 8 LEAD PELLETS—1⅛ OUNCES—461 PELLETS
Mfg: Rottweil **Manufacturer's code:** Super Sport
Recoil energy in 8-lb. shotgun: 22.7 ft./lbs. **Recoil velocity in 8-lb. shotgun:** 13.5 ft./sec.

Distance in yards:	Muzzle	20	30	40	50	60	70
Velocity in fps:	1,361	863	724	618	533	461	400
Average pellet energy in ft-lbs:	4.41	1.77	1.25	.91	.68	.51	.38
Time of flight in seconds:	0	.0568	.0948	.1398	.1921	.2527	.3225

Type of load: Target
Three-foot velocity: 1,250 ft./sec.
Hull: 2¾-inch plastic
Wad: Plastic
Shot: Lead
Buffered: No
Test barrel length: 30 inch
Pellets will pierce skin up to 131 yards.

NO. 8 LEAD PELLETS—1⅛ OUNCES—461 PELLETS
Mfg: RST, Ltd. **Manufacturer's code:** N/A
Recoil energy in 8-lb. shotgun: 22.7 ft./lbs. **Recoil velocity in 8-lb. shotgun:** 13.5 ft./sec.

Distance in yards:	Muzzle	20	30	40	50	60	70
Velocity in fps:	1,361	863	724	618	533	461	400
Average pellet energy in ft-lbs:	4.41	1.77	1.25	.91	.68	.51	.38
Time of flight in seconds:	0	.0568	.0948	.1398	.1921	.2527	.3225

Type of load: Target
Three-foot velocity: 1,250 ft./sec.
Hull: 2¾-inch plastic
Wad: Plastic
Shot: Lead
Buffered: No
Test barrel length: 30 inch
Pellets will pierce skin up to 131 yards.

NO. 8 LEAD PELLETS—1⅛ OUNCES—461 PELLETS
Mfg: Winchester **Manufacturer's code:** XU12H
Recoil energy in 8-lb. shotgun: 22.7 ft./lbs. **Recoil velocity in 8-lb. shotgun:** 13.5 ft./sec.

Distance in yards:	Muzzle	20	30	40	50	60	70
Velocity in fps:	1,361	863	724	618	533	461	400
Average pellet energy in ft-lbs:	4.41	1.77	1.25	.91	.68	.51	.38
Time of flight in seconds:	0	.0568	.0948	.1398	.1921	.2527	.3225

Type of load: Field
Three-foot velocity: 1,250 ft./sec.
Hull: 2¾-inch plastic
Wad: Plastic
Shot: Lead
Buffered: No
Test barrel length: 30 inch
Pellets will pierce skin up to 131 yards.

NO. 8 LEAD PELLETS—1⅛ OUNCES—461 PELLETS
Mfg: Winchester **Manufacturer's code:** AAHA12
Recoil energy in 8-lb. shotgun: 22.7 ft./lbs. **Recoil velocity in 8-lb. shotgun:** 13.7 ft./sec.

Distance in yards:	Muzzle	20	30	40	50	60	70
Velocity in fps:	1,361	863	724	618	533	461	400
Average pellet energy in ft-lbs:	4.41	1.77	1.25	.91	.68	.51	.38
Time of flight in seconds:	0	.0568	.0948	.1398	.1921	.2527	.3225

Type of load: Target
Three-foot velocity: 1,250 ft./sec.
Hull: 2¾-inch plastic
Wad: Plastic
Shot: Hard lead
Buffered: No
Test barrel length: 30 inch
Pellets will pierce skin up to 131 yards.

NO. 8 LEAD PELLETS—1⅛ OUNCES—461 PELLETS
Mfg: Sellier & Bellot **Manufacturer's code:** SBA01247
Recoil energy in 8-lb. shotgun: 23.9 ft./lbs. **Recoil velocity in 8-lb. shotgun:** 13.9 ft./sec.

Distance in yards:	Muzzle	20	30	40	50	60	70
Velocity in fps:	1,389	875	733	625	538	466	404
Average pellet energy in ft-lbs:	4.59	1.82	1.28	.93	.69	.52	.39
Time of flight in seconds:	0	.0558	.0934	.1378	.1897	.2496	.3181

Type of load: Target
Three-foot velocity: 1,275 ft./sec.
Hull: 2¾-inch plastic
Wad: Plastic
Shot: Lead
Buffered: No
Test barrel length: 30 inch
Pellets will pierce skin up to 131 yards.

NO. 8 LEAD PELLETS—1⅛ OUNCES—461 PELLETS

Mfg: RST, Ltd. **Manufacturer's code:** N/A
Recoil energy in 8-lb. shotgun: 25.2 ft./lbs. **Recoil velocity in 8-lb. shotgun:** 14.2 ft./sec.

Distance in yards:	Muzzle	20	30	40	50	60	70
Velocity in fps:	1,417	886	742	632	544	471	408
Average pellet energy in ft-lbs:	4.78	1.87	1.31	.95	.70	.53	.40
Time of flight in seconds:	0	.0549	.0921	.1360	.1873	.2466	.3150

Type of load: Target
Three-foot velocity: 1,300 ft./sec.
Hull: 2¾-inch plastic
Wad: Plastic
Shot: Lead
Buffered: No
Test barrel length: 30 inch
Pellets will pierce skin up to 132 yards.

NO. 8 LEAD PELLETS—1⅛ OUNCES—461 PELLETS

Mfg: Winchester **Manufacturer's code:** AASC12
Recoil energy in 8-lb. shotgun: 25.2 ft./lbs. **Recoil velocity in 8-lb. shotgun:** 14.2 ft./sec.

Distance in yards:	Muzzle	20	30	40	50	60	70
Velocity in fps:	1,417	886	742	632	544	471	408
Average pellet energy in ft-lbs:	4.78	1.87	1.31	.95	.70	.53	.40
Time of flight in seconds:	0	.0549	.0921	.1360	.1873	.2466	.3150

Type of load: Target
Three-foot velocity: 1,300 ft./sec.
Hull: 2¾-inch plastic
Wad: Plastic
Shot: Lead
Buffered: No
Test barrel length: 30 inch
Pellets will pierce skin up to 132 yards.

NO. 8 LEAD PELLETS—1⅛ OUNCES—461 PELLETS

Mfg: ARMUSA **Manufacturer's code:** PLA-32
Recoil energy in 8-lb. shotgun: 26.8 ft./lbs. **Recoil velocity in 8-lb. shotgun:** 14.7 ft./sec.

Distance in yards:	Muzzle	20	30	40	50	60	70
Velocity in fps:	1,451	900	752	640	551	477	413
Average pellet energy in ft-lbs:	5.01	1.93	1.35	.97	.72	.54	.41
Time of flight in seconds:	0	.0539	.0905	.1338	.1845	.2431	.3108

Type of load: Sporting clay
Three-foot velocity: 1,330 ft./sec.
Hull: 2¾-inch plastic
Wad: Plastic
Shot: Lead
Buffered: No
Test barrel length: 30 inch
Pellets will pierce skin up to 133 yards.

NO. 8 LEAD PELLETS—1⅛ OUNCES—461 PELLETS

Mfg: Baschieri & Pellagri **Manufacturer's code:** F2/MB Disperante
Recoil energy in 8-lb. shotgun: 21.2 ft./lbs. **Recoil velocity in 8-lb. shotgun:** 13.0 ft./sec.

Distance in yards:	Muzzle	20	30	40	50	60	70
Velocity in fps:	1,451	900	752	640	551	477	413
Average pellet energy in ft-lbs:	5.01	1.93	1.35	.97	.72	.54	.41
Time of flight in seconds:	0	.0539	.0905	.1338	.1845	.2431	.3108

Type of load: Sporting Clay
Three-foot velocity: 1,330 ft./sec.
Hull: 2¾-inch plastic
Wad: Plastic
Shot: Hard lead
Buffered: No
Test barrel length: 30 inch
Pellets will pierce skin up to 133 yards.

NO. 8 LEAD PELLETS—1⅛ OUNCES—461 PELLETS

Mfg: Eley Hawk **Manufacturer's code:** VIP
Recoil energy in 8-lb. shotgun: 26.8 ft./lbs. **Recoil velocity in 8-lb. shotgun:** 14.7 ft./sec.

Distance in yards:	Muzzle	20	30	40	50	60	70
Velocity in fps:	1,451	900	752	640	551	477	413
Average pellet energy in ft-lbs:	5.01	1.93	1.35	.97	.72	.54	.41
Time of flight in seconds:	0	.0539	.0905	.1338	.1845	.2431	.3108

Type of load: Target
Three-foot velocity: 1,330 ft./sec.
Hull: 2¾-inch plastic
Wad: Plastic
Shot: Hard lead
Buffered: No
Test barrel length: 30 inch
Pellets will pierce skin up to 133 yards.

NO. 8 LEAD PELLETS—1⅛ OUNCES—461 PELLETS

Mfg: Kent Cartridge America/Canada **Manufacturer's code:** K122SSC32
Recoil energy in 8-lb. shotgun: 21.2 ft./lbs. **Recoil velocity in 8-lb. shotgun:** 13.0 ft./sec.

Distance in yards:	Muzzle	20	30	40	50	60	70
Velocity in fps:	1,451	900	752	640	551	477	413
Average pellet energy in ft-lbs:	5.01	1.93	1.35	.97	.72	.54	.41
Time of flight in seconds:	0	.0539	.0905	.1338	.1845	.2431	.3108

Type of load: Field
Three-foot velocity: 1,330 ft./sec.
Hull: 2¾-inch plastic
Wad: Plastic
Shot: Lead
Buffered: No
Test barrel length: 30 inch
Pellets will pierce skin up to 133 yards.

NO. 8 LEAD PELLETS—1⅛ OUNCES—461 PELLETS

Mfg: RIO **Manufacturer's code:** Super Game
Recoil energy in 8-lb. shotgun: 21.2 ft./lbs. **Recoil velocity in 8-lb. shotgun:** 13.0 ft./sec.

Distance in yards:	Muzzle	20	30	40	50	60	70
Velocity in fps:	1,451	900	752	640	551	477	413
Average pellet energy in ft-lbs:	5.01	1.93	1.35	.97	.72	.54	.41
Time of flight in seconds:	0	.0539	.0905	.1338	.1845	.2431	.3108

Type of load: Field
Three-foot velocity: 1,330 ft./sec.
Hull: 2¾-inch plastic
Wad: Plastic
Shot: Hard lead
Buffered: No
Test barrel length: 30 inch
Pellets will pierce skin up to 133 yards.

NO. 8 LEAD PELLETS—1⅛ OUNCES—461 PELLETS
Mfg: Clever Manufacturer's code: T2 Light Game
Recoil energy in 8-lb. shotgun: 27.9 ft./lbs. Recoil velocity in 8-lb. shotgun: 15.0 ft./sec.

Distance in yards:	Muzzle	20	30	40	50	60	70
Velocity in fps:	1,473	910	759	645	555	480	416
Average pellet energy in ft-lbs:	5.16	1.97	1.37	.99	.73	.55	.41
Time of flight in seconds:	0	.0532	.0895	.1324	.1827	.2409	.3080

Type of load: Field
Three-foot velocity: 1,350 ft./sec.
Hull: 2¾-inch plastic
Wad: Plastic
Shot: Lead
Buffered: No
Test barrel length: 30 inch
Pellets will pierce skin up to 135 yards.

NO. 8 LEAD PELLETS—1⅛ OUNCES—461 PELLETS
Mfg: Federal Cartridge Co. Manufacturer's code: P128
Recoil energy in 8-lb. shotgun: 30.7 ft./lbs. Recoil velocity in 8-lb. shotgun: 15.7 ft./sec.

Distance in yards:	Muzzle	20	30	40	50	60	70
Velocity in fps:	1,525	951	796	679	587	511	446
Average pellet energy in ft-lbs:	6.51	2.53	1.77	1.29	.96	.73	.56
Time of flight in seconds:	0	.0511	.0857	.1265	.1741	.2290	.2918

Type of load: Field
Three-foot velocity: 1,400 ft./sec.
Hull: 2¾-inch plastic
Wad: Plastic
Shot: Lead
Buffered: No
Test barrel length: 30 inch
Pellets will pierce skin up to 136 yards.

NO. 8 LEAD PELLETS—1³⁄₁₆ OUNCES—486 PELLETS
Mfg: Clever Manufacturer's code: T2 Caccia
Recoil energy in 8-lb. shotgun: 25.2 ft./lbs. Recoil velocity in 8-lb. shotgun: 14.2 ft./sec.

Distance in yards:	Muzzle	20	30	40	50	60	70
Velocity in fps:	1,417	886	742	632	544	471	408
Average pellet energy in ft-lbs:	4.78	1.87	1.31	.95	.70	.53	.40
Time of flight in seconds:	0	.0549	.0921	.1360	.1873	.2466	.3150

Type of load: Field
Three-foot velocity: 1,300 ft./sec.
Hull: 2¾-inch plastic
Wad: Plastic
Shot: Lead
Buffered: No
Test barrel length: 30 inch
Pellets will pierce skin up to 132 yards.

NO. 8 LEAD PELLETS—1³⁄₁₆ OUNCES—486 PELLETS
Mfg: RIO Manufacturer's code: Basic Game
Recoil energy in 8-lb. shotgun: 16.2 ft./lbs. Recoil velocity in 8-lb. shotgun: 11.4 ft./sec.

Distance in yards:	Muzzle	20	30	40	50	60	70
Velocity in fps:	1,451	900	752	640	551	477	413
Average pellet energy in ft-lbs:	5.01	1.93	1.35	.97	.72	.54	.41
Time of flight in seconds:	0	.0539	.0905	.1338	.1845	.2431	.3108

Type of load: Field
Three-foot velocity: 1,330 ft./sec.
Hull: 2¾-inch plastic
Wad: Plastic
Shot: Hard lead
Buffered: No
Test barrel length: 30 inch
Pellets will pierce skin up to 133 yards.

NO. 8 LEAD PELLETS—1¼ OUNCES—512 PELLETS
Mfg: Estate Cartridge Manufacturer's code: XHG12
Recoil energy in 8-lb. shotgun: 26.3 ft./lbs. Recoil velocity in 8-lb. shotgun: 14.5 ft./sec.

Distance in yards:	Muzzle	20	30	40	50	60	70
Velocity in fps:	1,327	934	713	610	526	456	395
Average pellet energy in ft-lbs:	4.19	1.71	1.21	.88	.66	.49	.37
Time of flight in seconds:	0	.0579	.0966	.1422	.1952	.2566	.3273

Type of load: Field
Three-foot velocity: 1,220 ft./sec.
Hull: 2¾-inch plastic
Wad: Plastic
Shot: Hard lead
Buffered: No
Test barrel length: 30 inch
Pellets will pierce skin up to 118 yards.

NO. 8 LEAD PELLETS—1¼ OUNCES—512 PELLETS
Mfg: Federal Cartridge Co. Manufacturer's code: P153/H125/H120
Recoil energy in 8-lb. shotgun: 26.3 ft./lbs. Recoil velocity in 8-lb. shotgun: 14.5 ft./sec.

Distance in yards:	Muzzle	20	30	40	50	60	70
Velocity in fps:	1,327	934	713	610	526	456	395
Average pellet energy in ft-lbs:	4.19	1.71	1.21	.88	.66	.49	.37
Time of flight in seconds:	0	.0579	.0966	.1422	.1952	.2566	.3273

Type of load: Field
Three-foot velocity: 1,220 ft./sec.
Hull: 2¾-inch plastic
Wad: Plastic
Shot: Lead
Buffered: No
Test barrel length: 30 inch
Pellets will pierce skin up to 118 yards.

NO. 8 LEAD PELLETS—1¼ OUNCES—512 PELLETS
Mfg: Fiocchi Manufacturer's code: 12HF
Recoil energy in 8-lb. shotgun: 26.3 ft./lbs. Recoil velocity in 8-lb. shotgun: 14.5 ft./sec.

Distance in yards:	Muzzle	20	30	40	50	60	70
Velocity in fps:	1,327	934	713	610	526	456	395
Average pellet energy in ft-lbs:	4.19	1.71	1.21	.88	.66	.49	.37
Time of flight in seconds:	0	.0579	.0966	.1422	.1952	.2566	.3273

Type of load: Field
Three-foot velocity: 1,220 ft./sec.
Hull: 2¾-inch plastic
Wad: Plastic
Shot: Lead
Buffered: No
Test barrel length: 30 inch
Pellets will pierce skin up to 118 yards.

NO. 8 LEAD PELLETS—1¼ OUNCES—512 PELLETS
Mfg: Fiocchi **Manufacturer's code:** 12HFN
Recoil energy in 8-lb. shotgun: 26.3 ft./lbs. **Recoil velocity in 8-lb. shotgun:** 14.5 ft./sec.

Distance in yards:	Muzzle	20	30	40	50	60	70
Velocity in fps:	1,327	934	713	610	526	456	395
Average pellet energy in ft-lbs:	4.19	1.71	1.21	.88	.66	.49	.37
Time of flight in seconds:	0	.0579	.0966	.1422	.1952	.2566	.3273

Type of load: Field
Three-foot velocity: 1,220 ft./sec.
Hull: 2¾-inch plastic
Wad: Plastic
Shot: Nickel-plated lead
Buffered: No
Test barrel length: 30 inch
Pellets will pierce skin up to 118 yards.

NO. 8 LEAD PELLETS—1¼ OUNCES—512 PELLETS
Mfg: Kent Cartridge America/Canada **Manufacturer's code:** K122PL36
Recoil energy in 8-lb. shotgun: 26.3 ft./lbs. **Recoil velocity in 8-lb. shotgun:** 14.5 ft./sec.

Distance in yards:	Muzzle	20	30	40	50	60	70
Velocity in fps:	1,327	934	713	610	526	456	395
Average pellet energy in ft-lbs:	4.19	1.71	1.21	.88	.66	.49	.37
Time of flight in seconds:	0	.0579	.0966	.1422	.1952	.2566	.3273

Type of load: Target
Three-foot velocity: 1,220 ft./sec.
Hull: 2¾-inch plastic
Wad: Plastic
Shot: Lead
Buffered: No
Test barrel length: 30 inch
Pellets will pierce skin up to 118 yards.

NO. 8 LEAD PELLETS—1¼ OUNCES—512 PELLETS
Mfg: Remington Arms Co. **Manufacturer's code:** RP12H
Recoil energy in 8-lb. shotgun: 26.3 ft./lbs. **Recoil velocity in 8-lb. shotgun:** 14.5 ft./sec.

Distance in yards:	Muzzle	20	30	40	50	60	70
Velocity in fps:	1,327	934	713	610	526	456	395
Average pellet energy in ft-lbs:	4.19	1.71	1.21	.88	.66	.49	.37
Time of flight in seconds:	0	.0579	.0966	.1422	.1952	.2566	.3273

Type of load: Field
Three-foot velocity: 1,220 ft./sec.
Hull: 2¾-inch plastic
Wad: Plastic
Shot: Lead
Buffered: No
Test barrel length: 30 inch
Pellets will pierce skin up to 118 yards.

NO. 8 LEAD PELLETS—1¼ OUNCES—512 PELLETS
Mfg: Remington Arms Co. **Manufacturer's code:** STS12P
Recoil energy in 8-lb. shotgun: 26.3 ft./lbs. **Recoil velocity in 8-lb. shotgun:** 14.5 ft./sec.

Distance in yards:	Muzzle	20	30	40	50	60	70
Velocity in fps:	1,327	934	713	610	526	456	395
Average pellet energy in ft-lbs:	4.19	1.71	1.21	.88	.66	.49	.37
Time of flight in seconds:	0	.0579	.0966	.1422	.1952	.2566	.3273

Type of load: Target
Three-foot velocity: 1,220 ft./sec.
Hull: 2¾-inch plastic
Wad: Plastic
Shot: Hard lead
Buffered: No
Test barrel length: 30 inch
Pellets will pierce skin up to 118 yards.

NO. 8 LEAD PELLETS—1¼ OUNCES—512 PELLETS
Mfg: Sellier & Bellot **Manufacturer's code:** SBA01208
Recoil energy in 8-lb. shotgun: 26.3 ft./lbs. **Recoil velocity in 8-lb. shotgun:** 14.5 ft./sec.

Distance in yards:	Muzzle	20	30	40	50	60	70
Velocity in fps:	1,327	934	713	610	526	456	395
Average pellet energy in ft-lbs:	4.19	1.71	1.21	.88	.66	.49	.37
Time of flight in seconds:	0	.0579	.0966	.1422	.1952	.2566	.3273

Type of load: Field
Three-foot velocity: 1,220 ft./sec.
Hull: 2¾-inch plastic
Wad: Plastic
Shot: Lead
Buffered: No
Test barrel length: 30 inch
Pellets will pierce skin up to 118 yards.

NO. 8 LEAD PELLETS—1¼ OUNCES—512 PELLETS
Mfg: Winchester **Manufacturer's code:** XU12SP/AA12SP
Recoil energy in 8-lb. shotgun: 26.3 ft./lbs. **Recoil velocity in 8-lb. shotgun:** 14.5 ft./sec.

Distance in yards:	Muzzle	20	30	40	50	60	70
Velocity in fps:	1,327	934	713	610	526	456	395
Average pellet energy in ft-lbs:	4.19	1.71	1.21	.88	.66	.49	.37
Time of flight in seconds:	0	.0579	.0966	.1422	.1952	.2566	.3273

Type of load: Field & Target
Three-foot velocity: 1,220 ft./sec.
Hull: 2¾-inch plastic
Wad: Plastic
Shot: Lead
Buffered: No
Test barrel length: 30 inch
Pellets will pierce skin up to 118 yards.

NO. 8 LEAD PELLETS—1¼ OUNCES—512 PELLETS
Mfg: Baschieri & Pellagri **Manufacturer's code:** F2 Flash
Recoil energy in 8-lb. shotgun: 29.5 ft./lbs. **Recoil velocity in 8-lb. shotgun:** 15.4 ft./sec.

Distance in yards:	Muzzle	20	30	40	50	60	70
Velocity in fps:	1,389	875	733	625	538	466	404
Average pellet energy in ft-lbs:	4.59	1.82	1.28	.93	.69	.52	.39
Time of flight in seconds:	0	.0558	.0934	.1378	.1897	.2496	.3181

Type of load: Target
Three-foot velocity: 1,275 ft./sec.
Hull: 2¾-inch plastic
Wad: Plastic
Shot: Polished lead
Buffered: No
Test barrel length: 30 inch
Pellets will pierce skin up to 131 yards.

NO. 8 LEAD PELLETS—1¼ OUNCES—512 PELLETS
Mfg: ARMUSA **Manufacturer's code:** Live Pigeon
Recoil energy in 8-lb. shotgun: 31.1 ft./lbs. **Recoil velocity in 8-lb. shotgun:** 15.8 ft./sec.

Distance in yards:	Muzzle	20	30	40	50	60	70
Velocity in fps:	1,417	886	742	632	544	471	408
Average pellet energy in ft-lbs:	4.78	1.87	1.31	.95	.70	.53	.40
Time of flight in seconds:	0	.0549	.0921	.1360	.1873	.2466	.3150

Type of load: Target
Three-foot velocity: 1,300 ft./sec.
Hull: 2¾-inch plastic
Wad: Plastic
Shot: Nickel-plated lead
Buffered: No
Test barrel length: 30 inch
Pellets will pierce skin up to 132 yards.

NO. 8 LEAD PELLETS—1¼ OUNCES—512 PELLETS
Mfg: Clever **Manufacturer's code:** T4 High Velocity
Recoil energy in 8-lb. shotgun: 31.1 ft./lbs. **Recoil velocity in 8-lb. shotgun:** 15.8 ft./sec.

Distance in yards:	Muzzle	20	30	40	50	60	70
Velocity in fps:	1,417	886	742	632	544	471	408
Average pellet energy in ft-lbs:	4.78	1.87	1.31	.95	.70	.53	.40
Time of flight in seconds:	0	.0549	.0921	.1360	.1873	.2466	.3150

Type of load: Field
Three-foot velocity: 1,300 ft./sec.
Hull: 2¾-inch plastic
Wad: Plastic
Shot: Lead
Buffered: No
Test barrel length: 30 inch
Pellets will pierce skin up to 132 yards.

NO. 8 LEAD PELLETS—1¼ OUNCES—512 PELLETS
Mfg: Aguila **Manufacturer's code:** N/A
Recoil energy in 8-lb. shotgun: 33.0 ft./lbs. **Recoil velocity in 8-lb. shotgun:** 16.3 ft./sec.

Distance in yards:	Muzzle	20	30	40	50	60	70
Velocity in fps:	1,451	900	752	640	551	477	413
Average pellet energy in ft-lbs:	5.01	1.93	1.35	.97	.72	.54	.41
Time of flight in seconds:	0	.0539	.0905	.1338	.1845	.2431	.3108

Type of load: Field & Target
Three-foot velocity: 1,330 ft./sec.
Hull: 2¾-inch plastic
Wad: Plastic
Shot: Lead
Buffered: No
Test barrel length: 30 inch
Pellets will pierce skin up to 133 yards.

NO. 8 LEAD PELLETS—1¼ OUNCES—512 PELLETS
Mfg: Baschieri & Pellagri **Manufacturer's code:** Star Rossa High Velocity
Recoil energy in 8-lb. shotgun: 36.1 ft./lbs. **Recoil velocity in 8-lb. shotgun:** 17.0 ft./sec.

Distance in yards:	Muzzle	20	30	40	50	60	70
Velocity in fps:	1,451	900	752	640	551	477	413
Average pellet energy in ft-lbs:	5.01	1.93	1.35	.97	.72	.54	.41
Time of flight in seconds:	0	.0539	.0905	.1338	.1845	.2431	.3108

Type of load: Target
Three-foot velocity: 1,330 ft./sec.
Hull: 2¾-inch plastic
Wad: Plastic
Shot: Hard lead
Buffered: No
Test barrel length: 30 inch
Pellets will pierce skin up to 133 yards.

NO. 8 LEAD PELLETS—1¼ OUNCES—512 PELLETS
Mfg: Estate Cartridge **Manufacturer's code:** HV12
Recoil energy in 8-lb. shotgun: 33.0 ft./lbs. **Recoil velocity in 8-lb. shotgun:** 16.3 ft./sec.

Distance in yards:	Muzzle	20	30	40	50	60	70
Velocity in fps:	1,451	900	752	640	551	477	413
Average pellet energy in ft-lbs:	5.01	1.93	1.35	.97	.72	.54	.41
Time of flight in seconds:	0	.0539	.0905	.1338	.1845	.2431	.3108

Type of load: Field
Three-foot velocity: 1,330 ft./sec.
Hull: 2¾-inch plastic
Wad: Plastic
Shot: Hard lead
Buffered: No
Test barrel length: 30 inch
Pellets will pierce skin up to 133 yards.

NO. 8 LEAD PELLETS—1¼ OUNCES—512 PELLETS
Mfg: Federal Cartridge Co. **Manufacturer's code:** P154/H126
Recoil energy in 8-lb. shotgun: 33.0 ft./lbs. **Recoil velocity in 8-lb. shotgun:** 16.3 ft./sec.

Distance in yards:	Muzzle	20	30	40	50	60	70
Velocity in fps:	1,451	900	752	640	551	477	413
Average pellet energy in ft-lbs:	5.01	1.93	1.35	.97	.72	.54	.41
Time of flight in seconds:	0	.0539	.0905	.1338	.1845	.2431	.3108

Type of load: Field
Three-foot velocity: 1,330 ft./sec.
Hull: 2¾-inch plastic
Wad: Plastic
Shot: Lead
Buffered: No
Test barrel length: 30 inch
Pellets will pierce skin up to 133 yards.

NO. 8 LEAD PELLETS—1¼ OUNCES—512 PELLETS
Mfg: Fiocchi **Manufacturer's code:** 12HV
Recoil energy in 8-lb. shotgun: 40.0 ft./lbs. **Recoil velocity in 8-lb. shotgun:** 17.9 ft./sec.

Distance in yards:	Muzzle	20	30	40	50	60	70
Velocity in fps:	1,451	900	752	640	551	477	413
Average pellet energy in ft-lbs:	5.01	1.93	1.35	.97	.72	.54	.41
Time of flight in seconds:	0	.0539	.0905	.1338	.1845	.2431	.3108

Type of load: Field
Three-foot velocity: 1,330 ft./sec.
Hull: 2¾-inch plastic
Wad: Plastic
Shot: Lead
Buffered: No
Test barrel length: 30 inch
Pellets will pierce skin up to 133 yards.

NO. 8 LEAD PELLETS—1¼ OUNCES—512 PELLETS
Mfg: Fiocchi **Manufacturer's code:** 12HVN
Recoil energy in 8-lb. shotgun: 40.0 ft./lbs. **Recoil velocity in 8-lb. shotgun:** 17.9 ft./sec.

Distance in yards:	Muzzle	20	30	40	50	60	70
Velocity in fps:	1,451	900	752	640	551	477	413
Average pellet energy in ft-lbs:	5.01	1.93	1.35	.97	.72	.54	.41
Time of flight in seconds:	0	.0539	.0905	.1338	.1845	.2431	.3108

Type of load: Field
Three-foot velocity: 1,330 ft./sec.
Hull: 2¾-inch plastic
Wad: Plastic
Shot: Nickel-plated lead
Buffered: No
Test barrel length: 30 inch
Pellets will pierce skin up to 133 yards.

NO. 8 LEAD PELLETS—1¼ OUNCES—512 PELLETS
Mfg: RIO **Manufacturer's code:** Extra Game
Recoil energy in 8-lb. shotgun: 33.0 ft./lbs. **Recoil velocity in 8-lb. shotgun:** 16.3 ft./sec.

Distance in yards:	Muzzle	20	30	40	50	60	70
Velocity in fps:	1,451	900	752	640	551	477	413
Average pellet energy in ft-lbs:	5.01	1.93	1.35	.97	.72	.54	.41
Time of flight in seconds:	0	.0539	.0905	.1338	.1845	.2431	.3108

Type of load: Field
Three-foot velocity: 1,330 ft./sec.
Hull: 2¾-inch plastic
Wad: Plastic
Shot: Hard lead
Buffered: No
Test barrel length: 30 inch
Pellets will pierce skin up to 133 yards.

NO. 8 LEAD PELLETS—1¼ OUNCES—512 PELLETS
Mfg: Winchester **Manufacturer's code:** X12
Recoil energy in 8-lb. shotgun: 33.0 ft./lbs. **Recoil velocity in 8-lb. shotgun:** 16.3 ft./sec.

Distance in yards:	Muzzle	20	30	40	50	60	70
Velocity in fps:	1,451	900	752	640	551	477	413
Average pellet energy in ft-lbs:	5.01	1.93	1.35	.97	.72	.54	.41
Time of flight in seconds:	0	.0539	.0905	.1338	.1845	.2431	.3108

Type of load: Field
Three-foot velocity: 1,330 ft./sec.
Hull: 2¾-inch plastic
Wad: Plastic
Shot: Lead
Buffered: No
Test barrel length: 30 inch
Pellets will pierce skin up to 133 yards.

NO. 8½ LEAD PELLETS—⅞ OUNCE—435 PELLETS
Mfg: Estate Cartridge **Manufacturer's code:** ML12
Recoil energy in 8-lb. shotgun: 13.7 ft./lbs. **Recoil velocity in 8-lb. shotgun:** 10.5 ft./sec.

Distance in yards:	Muzzle	20	30	40	50	60	70
Velocity in fps:	1,364	846	705	597	511	439	378
Average pellet energy in ft-lbs:	9.73	1.43	1.00	.71	.52	.39	.29
Time of flight in seconds:	0	.0574	.0964	.1427	.1971	.2604	.3341

Type of load: Target
Three-foot velocity: 1,250 ft./sec.
Hull: 2¾-inch plastic
Wad: Plastic
Shot: Hard lead
Buffered: No
Test barrel length: 30 inch
Pellets will pierce skin up to 112 yards.

NO. 8½ LEAD PELLETS—⅞ OUNCE—435 PELLETS
Mfg: Federal Cartridge Co. **Manufacturer's code:** N110
Recoil energy in 8-lb. shotgun: 16.2 ft./lbs. **Recoil velocity in 8-lb. shotgun:** 11.4 ft./sec.

Distance in yards:	Muzzle	20	30	40	50	60	70
Velocity in fps:	1,455	882	731	618	528	454	390
Average pellet energy in ft-lbs:	4.24	1.56	1.07	.77	.56	.41	.30
Time of flight in seconds:	0	.0545	.0920	.1368	.1894	.2507	.3221

Type of load: Target
Three-foot velocity: 1,330 ft./sec.
Hull: 2¾-inch plastic
Wad: Plastic
Shot: Copper-plated lead
Buffered: No
Test barrel length: 30 inch
Pellets will pierce skin up to 114 yards.

NO. 8½ LEAD PELLETS—⅞ OUNCE—435 PELLETS
Mfg: Federal Cartridge Co. **Manufacturer's code:** N119
Recoil energy in 8-lb. shotgun: 16.2 ft./lbs. **Recoil velocity in 8-lb. shotgun:** 11.4 ft./sec.

Distance in yards:	Muzzle	20	30	40	50	60	70
Velocity in fps:	1,455	882	731	618	528	454	390
Average pellet energy in ft-lbs:	4.24	1.56	1.07	.77	.56	.41	.30
Time of flight in seconds:	0	.0545	.0920	.1368	.1894	.2507	.3221

Type of load: Target
Three-foot velocity: 1,330 ft./sec.
Hull: 2¾-inch paper
Wad: Plastic
Shot: Copper-plated lead
Buffered: No
Test barrel length: 30 inch
Pellets will pierce skin up to 114 yards.

NO. 8½ LEAD PELLETS—⅞ OUNCE—435 PELLETS
Mfg: Remington Arms Co. **Manufacturer's code:** STS12IT
Recoil energy in 8-lb. shotgun: 16.2 ft./lbs. **Recoil velocity in 8-lb. shotgun:** 11.4 ft./sec.

Distance in yards:	Muzzle	20	30	40	50	60	70
Velocity in fps:	1,455	882	731	618	528	454	390
Average pellet energy in ft-lbs:	4.24	1.56	1.07	.77	.56	.41	.30
Time of flight in seconds:	0	.0545	.0920	.1368	.1894	.2507	.3221

Type of load: Target
Three-foot velocity: 1,330 ft./sec.
Hull: 2¾-inch plastic
Wad: Plastic
Shot: Hard lead
Buffered: No
Test barrel length: 30 inch
Pellets will pierce skin up to 114 yards.

NO. 8½ LEAD PELLETS—24 GRAMS (⅞ OUNCE)—435 PELLETS

Mfg: Fiocchi **Manufacturer's code:** 12IN24
Recoil energy in 8-lb. shotgun: 16.9 ft./lbs. **Recoil velocity in 8-lb. shotgun:** 11.6 ft./sec.

Distance in yards:	Muzzle	20	30	40	50	60	70
Velocity in fps:	1,477	891	738	623	532	457	393
Average pellet energy in ft-lbs:	4.37	1.59	1.09	.78	.66	.42	.31
Time of flight in seconds:	0	.0539	.0910	.1354	.1876	.2484	.3193

Type of load: Target
Three-foot velocity: 1,350 ft./sec.
Hull: 2¾-inch plastic
Wad: Plastic
Shot: Hard lead
Buffered: No
Test barrel length: 30 inch
Pellets will pierce skin up to 115 yards.

NO. 8½ LEAD PELLETS—⅞ OUNCE—435 PELLETS

Mfg: Estate Cartridge **Manufacturer's code:** INT24
Recoil energy in 8-lb. shotgun: 17.7 ft./lbs. **Recoil velocity in 8-lb. shotgun:** 11.9 ft./sec.

Distance in yards:	Muzzle	20	30	40	50	60	70
Velocity in fps:	1,505	902	746	629	537	461	397
Average pellet energy in ft-lbs:	4.54	1.63	1.11	.79	.58	.43	.32
Time of flight in seconds:	0	.0531	.0898	.1337	.1854	.2457	.3157

Type of load: Target
Three-foot velocity: 1,375 ft./sec.
Hull: 2¾-inch plastic
Wad: Plastic
Shot: Hard lead
Buffered: No
Test barrel length: 30 inch
Pellets will pierce skin up to 115 yards.

NO. 8½ LEAD PELLETS—1 OUNCE—497 PELLETS

Mfg: Federal Cartridge Co. **Manufacturer's code:** T175
Recoil energy in 8-lb. shotgun: 14.2 ft./lbs. **Recoil velocity in 8-lb. shotgun:** 10.7 ft./sec.

Distance in yards:	Muzzle	20	30	40	50	60	70
Velocity in fps:	1,247	797	668	568	488	419	360
Average pellet energy in ft-lbs:	3.12	1.27	.89	.65	.48	.35	.26
Time of flight in seconds:	0	.0616	.1029	.1516	.2087	.2751	.3525

Type of load: Target
Three-foot velocity: 1,145 ft./sec.
Hull: 2¾-inch paper
Wad: Plastic
Shot: Hard lead
Buffered: No
Test barrel length: 30 inch
Pellets will pierce skin up to 109 yards.

NO. 8½ LEAD PELLETS—1 OUNCE—497 PELLETS

Mfg: Fiocchi **Manufacturer's code:** 12TL
Recoil energy in 8-lb. shotgun: 18.2 ft./lbs. **Recoil velocity in 8-lb. shotgun:** 12.1 ft./sec.

Distance in yards:	Muzzle	20	30	40	50	60	70
Velocity in fps:	1,252	799	670	570	489	420	361
Average pellet energy in ft-lbs:	3.14	1.28	.90	.65	.48	.35	.26
Time of flight in seconds:	0	.0614	.1025	.1512	.2081	.2744	.3515

Type of load: Target
Three-foot velocity: 1,150 ft./sec.
Hull: 2¾-inch plastic
Wad: Plastic
Shot: Hard lead
Buffered: No
Test barrel length: 30 inch
Pellets will pierce skin up to 109 yards.

NO. 8½ LEAD PELLETS—1 OUNCE—497 PELLETS

Mfg: Estate Cartridge **Manufacturer's code:** CT12L1/SS12L1
Recoil energy in 8-lb. shotgun: 15.2 ft./lbs. **Recoil velocity in 8-lb. shotgun:** 11.1 ft./sec.

Distance in yards:	Muzzle	20	30	40	50	60	70
Velocity in fps:	1,280	811	679	577	495	425	365
Average pellet energy in ft-lbs:	3.29	1.32	.92	.67	.49	.36	.27
Time of flight in seconds:	0	.0604	.1009	.1489	.2052	.2707	.3469

Type of load: Target
Three-foot velocity: 1,175 ft./sec.
Hull: 2¾-inch plastic
Wad: Plastic
Shot: Hard lead
Buffered: No
Test barrel length: 30 inch
Pellets will pierce skin up to 110 yards.

NO. 8½ LEAD PELLETS—1 OUNCE—497 PELLETS

Mfg: Federal Cartridge Co. **Manufacturer's code:** T113
Recoil energy in 8-lb. shotgun: 15.2 ft./lbs. **Recoil velocity in 8-lb. shotgun:** 11.1 ft./sec.

Distance in yards:	Muzzle	20	30	40	50	60	70
Velocity in fps:	1,280	811	679	577	495	425	365
Average pellet energy in ft-lbs:	3.29	1.32	.92	.67	.49	.36	.27
Time of flight in seconds:	0	.0604	.1009	.1489	.2052	.2707	.3469

Type of load: Target
Three-foot velocity: 1,175 ft./sec.
Hull: 2¾-inch plastic
Wad: Plastic
Shot: Hard lead
Buffered: No
Test barrel length: 30 inch
Pellets will pierce skin up to 110 yards.

NO. 8½ LEAD PELLETS—1 OUNCE—497 PELLETS

Mfg: Polywad **Manufacturer's code:** SRL1285
Recoil energy in 8-lb. shotgun: 15.2 ft./lbs. **Recoil velocity in 8-lb. shotgun:** 11.1 ft./sec.

Distance in yards:	Muzzle	20	30	40	50	60	70
Velocity in fps:	1,280	811	679	577	495	425	365
Average pellet energy in ft-lbs:	3.29	1.32	.92	.67	.49	.36	.27
Time of flight in seconds:	0	.0604	.1009	.1489	.2052	.2707	.3469

Type of load: Field
Three-foot velocity: 1,175 ft./sec.
Hull: 2¾-inch plastic
Wad: Plastic
Shot: Lead
Buffered: No
Test barrel length: 30 inch
Pellets will pierce skin up to 110 yards.

NO. 8½ LEAD PELLETS—1 OUNCE—497 PELLETS

Mfg: Remington Arms Co. **Manufacturer's code:** STS121
Recoil energy in 8-lb. shotgun: 15.2 ft./lbs. **Recoil velocity in 8-lb. shotgun:** 11.1 ft./sec.

Distance in yards:	Muzzle	20	30	40	50	60	70
Velocity in fps:	1,280	811	679	577	495	425	365
Average pellet energy in ft-lbs:	3.29	1.32	.92	.67	.49	.36	.27
Time of flight in seconds:	0	.0604	.1009	.1489	.2052	.2707	.3469

Type of load: Target
Three-foot velocity: 1,175 ft./sec.
Hull: 2¾-inch plastic
Wad: Plastic
Shot: Hard lead
Buffered: No
Test barrel length: 30 inch
Pellets will pierce skin up to 110 yards.

NO. 8½ LEAD PELLETS—1 OUNCE—497 PELLETS

Mfg: Fiocchi **Manufacturer's code:** 12TH
Recoil energy in 8-lb. shotgun: 16.1 ft./lbs. **Recoil velocity in 8-lb. shotgun:** 11.4 ft./sec.

Distance in yards:	Muzzle	20	30	40	50	60	70
Velocity in fps:	1,308	823	687	584	500	430	369
Average pellet energy in ft-lbs:	1.36	1.13	.95	.68	.50	.37	.325
Time of flight in seconds:	0	.0593	.0993	.1468	.2024	.2671	.3423

Type of load: Target
Three-foot velocity: 1,200 ft./sec.
Hull: 2¾-inch plastic
Wad: Plastic
Shot: Hard lead
Buffered: No
Test barrel length: 30 inch
Pellets will pierce skin up to 111 yards.

NO. 8½ LEAD PELLETS—1 OUNCE—497 PELLETS

Mfg: Estate Cartridge **Manufacturer's code:** CT12H1
Recoil energy in 8-lb. shotgun: 17.4 ft./lbs. **Recoil velocity in 8-lb. shotgun:** 11.8 ft./sec.

Distance in yards:	Muzzle	20	30	40	50	60	70
Velocity in fps:	1,348	839	699	593	508	437	375
Average pellet energy in ft-lbs:	3.64	1.41	.98	.71	.52	.38	.28
Time of flight in seconds:							

Type of load: Target
Three-foot velocity: 1,235 ft./sec.
Hull: 2¾-inch plastic
Wad: Plastic
Shot: Hard lead
Buffered: No
Test barrel length: 30 inch
Pellets will pierce skin up to 112 yards.

These Kent Impact™ tungsten/polymer loads can be shot in any shotgun, including this $40,000 Holland & Holland sporting-clays/game gun.

NO. 8½ LEAD PELLETS—1 OUNCE—497 PELLETS
Mfg: Fiocchi **Manufacturer's code:** 12TX
Recoil energy in 8-lb. shotgun: 17.9 ft./lbs. **Recoil velocity in 8-lb. shotgun:** 12.0 ft./sec.

Distance in yards:	Muzzle	20	30	40	50	60	70
Velocity in fps:	1,364	846	705	597	511	439	378
Average pellet energy in ft-lbs:	9.73	1.43	1.00	.71	.52	.39	.29
Time of flight in seconds:	0	.0574	.0964	.1427	.1971	.2604	.3341

Type of load: Target
Three-foot velocity: 1,250 ft./sec.
Hull: 2¾-inch plastic
Wad: Plastic
Shot: Hard lead
Buffered: No
Test barrel length: 30 inch
Pellets will pierce skin up to 112 yards.

NO. 8½ LEAD PELLETS—1 OUNCE—497 PELLETS
Mfg: Fiocchi **Manufacturer's code:** 12CPTR
Recoil energy in 8-lb. shotgun: 19.9 ft./lbs. **Recoil velocity in 8-lb. shotgun:** 12.6 ft./sec.

Distance in yards:	Muzzle	20	30	40	50	60	70
Velocity in fps:	1,421	868	721	610	622	448	385
Average pellet energy in ft-lbs:	4.05	1.51	1.04	.75	.55	.40	.30
Time of flight in seconds:	0	.0556	.0936	.1389	.1922	.2543	.3265

Type of load: Target & Spreader
Three-foot velocity: 1,300 ft./sec.
Hull: 2¾-inch plastic
Wad: Plastic
Shot: Hard lead
Buffered: No
Test barrel length: 30 inch
Pellets will pierce skin up to 124 yards.

NO. 8½ LEAD PELLETS—1 OUNCE—497 PELLETS
Mfg: Fiocchi **Manufacturer's code:** 12CRSR
Recoil energy in 8-lb. shotgun: 19.9 ft./lbs. **Recoil velocity in 8-lb. shotgun:** 12.6 ft./sec.

Distance in yards:	Muzzle	20	30	40	50	60	70
Velocity in fps:	1,421	868	721	610	622	448	385
Average pellet energy in ft-lbs:	4.05	1.51	1.04	.75	.55	.40	.30
Time of flight in seconds:	0	.0556	.0936	.1389	.1922	.2543	.3265

Type of load: Target
Three-foot velocity: 1,300 ft./sec.
Hull: 2¾-inch plastic
Wad: Plastic
Shot: Hard lead
Buffered: No
Test barrel length: 30 inch
Pellets will pierce skin up to 124 yards.

NO. 8½ LEAD PELLETS—1 OUNCE—497 PELLETS
Mfg: Estate Cartridge **Manufacturer's code:** CT12XH1
Recoil energy in 8-lb. shotgun: 21.2 ft./lbs. **Recoil velocity in 8-lb. shotgun:** 13.0 ft./sec.

Distance in yards:	Muzzle	20	30	40	50	60	70
Velocity in fps:	1,455	882	731	618	528	454	390
Average pellet energy in ft-lbs:	4.24	1.56	1.07	.77	.56	.41	.30
Time of flight in seconds:	0	.0545	.0920	.1368	.1894	.2507	.3221

Type of load: Target
Three-foot velocity: 1,330 ft./sec.
Hull: 2¾-inch plastic
Wad: Plastic
Shot: Hard lead
Buffered: No
Test barrel length: 30 inch
Pellets will pierce skin up to 124 yards.

NO. 8½ LEAD PELLETS—1 OUNCE—497 PELLETS
Mfg: Estate Cartridge **Manufacturer's code:** INT28
Recoil energy in 8-lb. shotgun: 21.2 ft./lbs. **Recoil velocity in 8-lb. shotgun:** 13.0 ft./sec.

Distance in yards:	Muzzle	20	30	40	50	60	70
Velocity in fps:	1,455	882	731	618	528	454	390
Average pellet energy in ft-lbs:	4.24	1.56	1.07	.77	.56	.41	.30
Time of flight in seconds:	0	.0545	.0920	.1368	.1894	.2507	.3221

Type of load: Target
Three-foot velocity: 1,330 ft./sec.
Hull: 2¾-inch plastic
Wad: Plastic
Shot: Hard lead
Buffered: No
Test barrel length: 30 inch
Pellets will pierce skin up to 124 yards.

NO. 8½ LEAD PELLETS—1⅛ OUNCES—559 PELLETS
Mfg: Federal Cartridge Co. **Manufacturer's code:** T114
Recoil energy in 8-lb. shotgun: 16.2 ft./lbs. **Recoil velocity in 8-lb. shotgun:** 11.4 ft./sec.

Distance in yards:	Muzzle	20	30	40	50	60	70
Velocity in fps:	1,196	775	652	555	477	410	352
Average pellet energy in ft-lbs:	2.87	1.20	.85	.62	.46	.34	.25
Time of flight in seconds:	0	.0637	.1060	.1560	.2144	.2823	.3613

Type of load: Target
Three-foot velocity: 1,100 ft./sec.
Hull: 2¾-inch plastic
Wad: Plastic
Shot: Hard lead
Buffered: No
Test barrel length: 30 inch
Pellets will pierce skin up to 107 yards.

NO. 8½ LEAD PELLETS—1⅛ OUNCES—559 PELLETS
Mfg: Federal Cartridge Co. **Manufacturer's code:** T172
Recoil energy in 8-lb. shotgun: 16.2 ft./lbs. **Recoil velocity in 8-lb. shotgun:** 11.4 ft./sec.

Distance in yards:	Muzzle	20	30	40	50	60	70
Velocity in fps:	1,196	775	652	555	477	410	352
Average pellet energy in ft-lbs:	2.87	1.20	.85	.62	.46	.34	.25
Time of flight in seconds:	0	.0637	.1060	.1560	.2144	.2823	.3613

Type of load: Target
Three-foot velocity: 1,100 ft./sec.
Hull: 2¾-inch plastic
Wad: Plastic
Shot: Hard lead
Buffered: No
Test barrel length: 30 inch
Pellets will pierce skin up to 107 yards.

NO. 8½ LEAD PELLETS—1⅛ OUNCES—559 PELLETS

Mfg: Estate Cartridge **Manufacturer's code:** CT12XL
Recoil energy in 8-lb. shotgun: 17.2 ft./lbs. **Recoil velocity in 8-lb. shotgun:** 11.8 ft./sec.

Distance in yards:	Muzzle	20	30	40	50	60	70
Velocity in fps:	1,224	787	661	563	483	415	357
Average pellet energy in ft-lbs:	3.01	1.24	.88	.63	.47	.35	.25
Time of flight in seconds:	0	.0625	.1042	.1535	.2112	.2782	.3563

Type of load: Target
Three-foot velocity: 1,125 ft./sec.
Hull: 2¾-inch plastic
Wad: Plastic
Shot: Hard lead
Buffered: No
Test barrel length: 30 inch
Pellets will pierce skin up to 108 yards

NO. 8½ LEAD PELLETS—1⅛ OUNCES—559 PELLETS

Mfg: Estate Cartridge **Manufacturer's code:** CT12L
Recoil energy in 8-lb. shotgun: 18.0 ft./lbs. **Recoil velocity in 8-lb. shotgun:** 12.0 ft./sec.

Distance in yards:	Muzzle	20	30	40	50	60	70
Velocity in fps:	1,247	797	668	568	488	419	360
Average pellet energy in ft-lbs:	3.12	1.27	.89	.65	.48	.35	.26
Time of flight in seconds:	0	.0616	.1029	.1516	.2087	.2751	.3525

Type of load: Target
Three-foot velocity: 1,145 ft./sec.
Hull: 2¾-inch plastic
Wad: Plastic
Shot: Hard lead
Buffered: No
Test barrel length: 30 inch
Pellets will pierce skin up to 109 yards.

NO. 8½ LEAD PELLETS—1⅛ OUNCES—559 PELLETS

Mfg: Remington Arms Co. **Manufacturer's code:** STS12L
Recoil energy in 8-lb. shotgun: 18.0 ft./lbs. **Recoil velocity in 8-lb. shotgun:** 12.0 ft./sec.

Distance in yards:	Muzzle	20	30	40	50	60	70
Velocity in fps:	1,247	797	668	568	488	419	360
Average pellet energy in ft-lbs:	3.12	1.27	.89	.65	.48	.35	.26
Time of flight in seconds:	0	.0616	.1029	.1516	.2087	.2751	.3525

Type of load: Target
Three-foot velocity: 1,145 ft./sec.
Hull: 2¾-inch plastic
Wad: Plastic
Shot: Hard lead
Buffered: No
Test barrel length: 30 inch
Pellets will pierce skin up to 109 yards.

NO. 8½ LEAD PELLETS—1⅛ OUNCES—559 PELLETS

Mfg: Estate Cartridge **Manufacturer's code:** CT12H
Recoil energy in 8-lb. shotgun: 20.4 ft./lbs. **Recoil velocity in 8-lb. shotgun:** 12.8 ft./sec.

Distance in yards:	Muzzle	20	30	40	50	60	70
Velocity in fps:	1,308	823	687	584	500	430	369
Average pellet energy in ft-lbs:	1.36	1.13	.95	.68	.50	.37	.325
Time of flight in seconds:	0	.0593	.0993	.1468	.2024	.2671	.3423

Type of load: Target
Three-foot velocity: 1,200 ft./sec.
Hull: 2¾-inch plastic
Wad: Plastic
Shot: Hard lead
Buffered: No
Test barrel length: 30 inch
Pellets will pierce skin up to 111 yards.

NO. 8½ LEAD PELLETS—1⅛ OUNCES—559 PELLETS

Mfg: Estate Cartridge **Manufacturer's code:** CT12HS
Recoil energy in 8-lb. shotgun: 20.4 ft./lbs. **Recoil velocity in 8-lb. shotgun:** 12.8 ft./sec.

Distance in yards:	Muzzle	20	30	40	50	60	70
Velocity in fps:	1,308	823	687	584	500	430	369
Average pellet energy in ft-lbs:	1.36	1.13	.95	.68	.50	.37	.325
Time of flight in seconds:	0	.0593	.0993	.1468	.2024	.2671	.3423

Type of load: Target
Three-foot velocity: 1,200 ft./sec.
Hull: 2¾-inch plastic
Wad: Plastic
Shot: Hard lead
Buffered: No
Test barrel length: 30 inch
Pellets will pierce skin up to 111 yards.

NO. 8½ LEAD PELLETS—1⅛ OUNCES—559 PELLETS

Mfg: Federal Cartridge Co. **Manufacturer's code:** T177
Recoil energy in 8-lb. shotgun: 20.4 ft./lbs. **Recoil velocity in 8-lb. shotgun:** 12.8 ft./sec.

Distance in yards:	Muzzle	20	30	40	50	60	70
Velocity in fps:	1,308	823	687	584	500	430	369
Average pellet energy in ft-lbs:	1.36	1.13	.95	.68	.50	.37	.325
Time of flight in seconds:	0	.0593	.0993	.1468	.2024	.2671	.3423

Type of load: Target & Spreader
Three-foot velocity: 1,200 ft./sec.
Hull: 2¾-inch plastic
Wad: Plastic
Shot: Hard lead
Buffered: No
Test barrel length: 30 inch
Pellets will pierce skin up to 111 yards.

NO. 8½ LEAD PELLETS—1⅛ OUNCES—559 PELLETS

Mfg: Fiocchi **Manufacturer's code:** 12SSCH
Recoil energy in 8-lb. shotgun: 20.4 ft./lbs. **Recoil velocity in 8-lb. shotgun:** 12.8 ft./sec.

Distance in yards:	Muzzle	20	30	40	50	60	70
Velocity in fps:	1,308	823	687	584	500	430	369
Average pellet energy in ft-lbs:	1.36	1.13	.95	.68	.50	.37	.325
Time of flight in seconds:	0	.0593	.0993	.1468	.2024	.2671	.3423

Type of load: Target & Spreader
Three-foot velocity: 1,200 ft./sec.
Hull: 2¾-inch plastic
Wad: Plastic
Shot: Hard lead
Buffered: No
Test barrel length: 30 inch
Pellets will pierce skin up to 111 yards.

NO. 8½ LEAD PELLETS—1⅛ OUNCES—559 PELLETS
Mfg: Estate Cartridge **Manufacturer's code:** CT12XH/SS12XH
Recoil energy in 8-lb. shotgun: 22.7 ft./lbs. **Recoil velocity in 8-lb. shotgun:** 13.5 ft./sec.

Distance in yards:	Muzzle	20	30	40	50	60	70
Velocity in fps:	1,364	846	705	597	511	439	378
Average pellet energy in ft-lbs:	9.73	1.43	1.00	.71	.52	.39	.29
Time of flight in seconds:	0	.0574	.0964	.1427	.1971	.2604	.3341

Type of load: Target
Three-foot velocity: 1,250 ft./sec.
Hull: 2¾-inch plastic
Wad: Plastic
Shot: Hard lead
Buffered: No
Test barrel length: 30 inch
Pellets will pierce skin up to 112 yards.

NO. 8½ LEAD PELLETS—1⅛ OUNCES—559 PELLETS
Mfg: Fiocchi **Manufacturer's code:** 12SSCX
Recoil energy in 8-lb. shotgun: 22.7 ft./lbs. **Recoil velocity in 8-lb. shotgun:** 13.5 ft./sec.

Distance in yards:	Muzzle	20	30	40	50	60	70
Velocity in fps:	1,364	846	705	597	511	439	378
Average pellet energy in ft-lbs:	9.73	1.43	1.00	.71	.52	.39	.29
Time of flight in seconds:	0	.0574	.0964	.1427	.1971	.2604	.3341

Type of load: Target & Spreader
Three-foot velocity: 1,250 ft./sec.
Hull: 2¾-inch plastic
Wad: Plastic
Shot: Hard lead
Buffered: No
Test barrel length: 30 inch
Pellets will pierce skin up to 112 yards.

NO. 8½ LEAD PELLETS—1⅛ OUNCES—559 PELLETS
Mfg: Fiocchi **Manufacturer's code:** 12WRNO
Recoil energy in 8-lb. shotgun: 22.7 ft./lbs. **Recoil velocity in 8-lb. shotgun:** 13.5 ft./sec.

Distance in yards:	Muzzle	20	30	40	50	60	70
Velocity in fps:	1,364	846	705	597	511	439	378
Average pellet energy in ft-lbs:	9.73	1.43	1.00	.71	.52	.39	.29
Time of flight in seconds:	0	.0574	.0964	.1427	.1971	.2604	.3341

Type of load: Target
Three-foot velocity: 1,250 ft./sec.
Hull: 2¾-inch plastic
Wad: Plastic
Shot: Hard lead
Buffered: No
Test barrel length: 30 inch
Pellets will pierce skin up to 112 yards.

NO. 8½ LEAD PELLETS—1¼ OUNCES—621 PELLETS
Mfg: ARMUSA **Manufacturer's code:** Live Pigeon
Recoil energy in 8-lb. shotgun: 31.1 ft./lbs. **Recoil velocity in 8-lb. shotgun:** 15.8 ft./sec.

Distance in yards:	Muzzle	20	30	40	50	60	70
Velocity in fps:	1,421	868	721	610	622	448	385
Average pellet energy in ft-lbs:	4.05	1.51	1.04	.75	.55	.40	.30
Time of flight in seconds:	0	.0556	.0936	.1389	.1922	.2543	.3265

Type of load: Target
Three-foot velocity: 1,300 ft./sec.
Hull: 2¾-inch plastic
Wad: Plastic
Shot: Nickel-plated lead
Buffered: No
Test barrel length: 30 inch
Pellets will pierce skin up to 124 yards.

NO. 9 LEAD PELLETS—24 GRAMS (⅞ OUNCE)—512 PELLETS
Mfg: Kent Cartridge America/Canada **Manufacturer's code:** K202SK24
Recoil energy in 8-lb. shotgun: 13.3 ft./lbs. **Recoil velocity in 8-lb. shotgun:** 10.3 ft./sec.

Distance in yards:	Muzzle	20	30	40	50	60	70
Velocity in fps:	1,351	820	678	571	485	413	352
Average pellet energy in ft-lbs:	3.05	1.12	.77	.55	.39	.29	.21
Time of flight in seconds:	0	.0687	.0990	.1473	.2044	.2716	.3502

Type of load: Target
Three-foot velocity: 1,235 ft./sec.
Hull: 2¾-inch plastic
Wad: Plastic
Shot: Lead
Buffered: No
Test barrel length: 30 inch
Pellets will pierce skin up to 116 yards.

NO. 9 LEAD PELLETS—24 GRAMS (⅞ OUNCE)—512 PELLETS
Mfg: Kent Cartridge America/Canada **Manufacturer's code:** K122TR30
Recoil energy in 8-lb. shotgun: 13.3 ft./lbs. **Recoil velocity in 8-lb. shotgun:** 10.3 ft./sec.

Distance in yards:	Muzzle	20	30	40	50	60	70
Velocity in fps:	1,351	820	678	571	485	413	352
Average pellet energy in ft-lbs:	3.05	1.12	.77	.55	.39	.29	.21
Time of flight in seconds:	0	.0687	.0990	.1473	.2044	.2716	.3502

Type of load: Target
Three-foot velocity: 1,235 ft./sec.
Hull: 2¾-inch plastic
Wad: Plastic
Shot: Lead
Buffered: No
Test barrel length: 30 inch
Pellets will pierce skin up to 116 yards.

NO. 9 LEAD PELLETS—⅞ OUNCE—512 PELLETS
Mfg: Estate Cartridge **Manufacturer's code:** ML12
Recoil energy in 8-lb. shotgun: 13.7 ft./lbs. **Recoil velocity in 8-lb. shotgun:** 10.5 ft./sec.

Distance in yards:	Muzzle	20	30	40	50	60	70
Velocity in fps:	1,368	827	683	575	488	416	354
Average pellet energy in ft-lbs:	3.13	1.14	.78	.55	.40	.29	.21
Time of flight in seconds:	0	.0581	.0982	.1461	.2028	.2695	.3477

Type of load: Target
Three-foot velocity: 1,250 ft./sec.
Hull: 2¾-inch plastic
Wad: Plastic
Shot: Hard lead
Buffered: No
Test barrel length: 30 inch
Pellets will pierce skin up to 105 yards.

NO. 9 LEAD PELLETS—⅞ OUNCE—512 PELLETS
Mfg: Eley Hawk **Manufacturer's code:** Olympic 2000
Recoil energy in 8-lb. shotgun: 15.2 ft./lbs. **Recoil velocity in 8-lb. shotgun:** 11.1 ft./sec.

Distance in yards:	Muzzle	20	30	40	50	60	70
Velocity in fps:	1,426	849	699	587	498	424	361
Average pellet energy in ft-lbs:	3.39	1.20	.82	.58	.42	.30	.22
Time of flight in seconds:	0	.0563	.0954	.1423	.1978	.2632	.3399

Type of load: Target
Three-foot velocity: 1,300 ft./sec.
Hull: 2¾-inch plastic
Wad: Plastic
Shot: Lead
Buffered: No
Test barrel length: 30 inch
Pellets will pierce skin up to 117 yards.

NO. 9 LEAD PELLETS—⅞ OUNCE—512 PELLETS
Mfg: Dionisi **Manufacturer's code:** D 12 INT
Recoil energy in 8-lb. shotgun: 16.2 ft./lbs. **Recoil velocity in 8-lb. shotgun:** 11.4 ft./sec.

Distance in yards:	Muzzle	20	30	40	50	60	70
Velocity in fps:	1,459	862	709	594	504	429	365
Average pellet energy in ft-lbs:	3.56	1.24	.84	.59	.42	.31	.22
Time of flight in seconds:	0	.0553	.0938	.1401	.2260	.2596	.3354

Type of load: Target International
Three-foot velocity: 1,330 ft./sec.
Hull: 2¾-inch plastic
Wad: Plastic
Shot: Lead
Buffered: No
Test barrel length: 30 inch
Pellets will pierce skin up to 107 yards.

NO. 9 LEAD PELLETS—⅞ OUNCE—512 PELLETS
Mfg: Eley Hawk **Manufacturer's code:** VIP
Recoil energy in 8-lb. shotgun: 16.2 ft./lbs. **Recoil velocity in 8-lb. shotgun:** 11.4 ft./sec.

Distance in yards:	Muzzle	20	30	40	50	60	70
Velocity in fps:	1,459	862	709	594	504	429	365
Average pellet energy in ft-lbs:	3.56	1.24	.84	.59	.42	.31	.22
Time of flight in seconds:	0	.0553	.0938	.1401	.2260	.2596	.3354

Type of load: Target
Three-foot velocity: 1,330 ft./sec.
Hull: 2¾-inch plastic
Wad: Plastic
Shot: Hard lead
Buffered: No
Test barrel length: 30 inch
Pellets will pierce skin up to 107 yards.

NO. 9 LEAD PELLETS—⅞ OUNCE—512 PELLETS
Mfg: Sellier & Bellot **Manufacturer's code:** SBA01243
Recoil energy in 8-lb. shotgun: 16.2 ft./lbs. **Recoil velocity in 8-lb. shotgun:** 11.4 ft./sec.

Distance in yards:	Muzzle	20	30	40	50	60	70
Velocity in fps:	1,459	862	709	594	504	429	365
Average pellet energy in ft-lbs:	3.56	1.24	.84	.59	.42	.31	.22
Time of flight in seconds:	0	.0553	.0938	.1401	.2260	.2596	.3354

Type of load: Target
Three-foot velocity: 1,330 ft./sec.
Hull: 2¾-inch plastic
Wad: Plastic
Shot: Lead
Buffered: No
Test barrel length: 30 inch
Pellets will pierce skin up to 107 yards.

NO. 9 LEAD PELLETS—⅞ OUNCE—512 PELLETS
Mfg: Winchester **Manufacturer's code:** AANL12
Recoil energy in 8-lb. shotgun: 16.2 ft./lbs. **Recoil velocity in 8-lb. shotgun:** 11.4 ft./sec.

Distance in yards:	Muzzle	20	30	40	50	60	70
Velocity in fps:	1,459	862	709	594	504	429	365
Average pellet energy in ft-lbs:	3.56	1.24	.84	.59	.42	.31	.22
Time of flight in seconds:	0	.0553	.0938	.1401	.2260	.2596	.3354

Type of load: Target
Three-foot velocity: 1,330 ft./sec.
Hull: 2¾-inch plastic
Wad: Plastic
Shot: Hard lead
Buffered: No
Test barrel length: 30 inch
Pellets will pierce skin up to 107 yards.

NO. 9 LEAD PELLETS—⅞ OUNCE—512 PELLETS
Mfg: Baschieri & Pellagri **Manufacturer's code:** N/A
Recoil energy in 8-lb. shotgun: 22.0 ft./lbs. **Recoil velocity in 8-lb. shotgun:** 13.3 ft./sec.

Distance in yards:	Muzzle	20	30	40	50	60	70
Velocity in fps:	1,481	870	715	599	508	432	368
Average pellet energy in ft-lbs:	3.67	1.27	.85	.60	.43	.31	.23
Time of flight in seconds:	0	.0546	.0928	.1387	.1932	.2572	.3325

Type of load: Comp-2000 24 gr.
Three-foot velocity: 1,350 ft./sec.
Hull: 2¾-inch plastic
Wad: Plastic
Shot: Hard lead
Buffered: No
Test barrel length: 30 inch
Pellets will pierce skin up to 108 yards.

NO. 9 LEAD PELLETS—24 GRAMS (⅞ OUNCE)—512 PELLETS
Mfg: Fiocchi **Manufacturer's code:** 12IN24
Recoil energy in 8-lb. shotgun: 16.9 ft./lbs. **Recoil velocity in 8-lb. shotgun:** 11.6 ft./sec.

Distance in yards:	Muzzle	20	30	40	50	60	70
Velocity in fps:	1,481	870	715	599	508	432	368
Average pellet energy in ft-lbs:	3.67	1.27	.85	.60	.43	.31	.23
Time of flight in seconds:	0	.0546	.0928	.1387	.1932	.2572	.3325

Type of load: Target
Three-foot velocity: 1,350 ft./sec.
Hull: 2¾-inch plastic
Wad: Plastic
Shot: Hard lead
Buffered: No
Test barrel length: 30 inch
Pellets will pierce skin up to 108 yards.

NO. 9 LEAD PELLETS—24 GRAMS (⅞ OUNCE)—512 PELLETS

Mfg: Kent Cartridge America/Canada **Manufacturer's code:** K122ISK24
Recoil energy in 8-lb. shotgun: 16.9 ft./lbs. **Recoil velocity in 8-lb. shotgun:** 11.6 ft./sec.

Distance in yards:	Muzzle	20	30	40	50	60	70
Velocity in fps:	1,481	870	715	599	508	432	368
Average pellet energy in ft-lbs:	3.67	1.27	.85	.60	.43	.31	.23
Time of flight in seconds:	0	.0546	.0928	.1387	.1932	.2572	.3325

Type of load: Target
Three-foot velocity: 1,350 ft./sec.
Hull: 2¾-inch plastic
Wad: Plastic
Shot: Lead
Buffered: No
Test barrel length: 30 inch
Pellets will pierce skin up to 108 yards.

NO. 9 LEAD PELLETS—⅞ OUNCE—512 PELLETS

Mfg: Estate Cartridge **Manufacturer's code:** INT24
Recoil energy in 8-lb. shotgun: 17.7 ft./lbs. **Recoil velocity in 8-lb. shotgun:** 11.9 ft./sec.

Distance in yards:	Muzzle	20	30	40	50	60	70
Velocity in fps:	1,510	881	723	605	513	437	372
Average pellet energy in ft-lbs:	3.81	1.30	.87	.61	.44	.32	.23
Time of flight in seconds:	0	.0538	.0915	.1370	.1909	.2544	.3289

Type of load: Target
Three-foot velocity: 1,375 ft./sec.
Hull: 2¾-inch plastic
Wad: Plastic
Shot: Hard lead
Buffered: No
Test barrel length: 30 inch
Pellets will pierce skin up to 109 yards.

NO. 9 LEAD PELLETS—⅞ OUNCE—512 PELLETS

Mfg: RST, Ltd. **Manufacturer's code:** N/A
Recoil energy in 8-lb. shotgun: 18.6 ft./lbs. **Recoil velocity in 8-lb. shotgun:** 12.2 ft./sec.

Distance in yards:	Muzzle	20	30	40	50	60	70
Velocity in fps:	1,538	892	730	611	518	441	375
Average pellet energy in ft-lbs:	3.95	1.33	.89	.62	.45	.32	.24
Time of flight in seconds:	0	.0530	.0903	.1353	.1888	.2516	.3255

Type of load: Target
Three-foot velocity: 1,400 ft./sec.
Hull: 2¾-inch plastic
Wad: Plastic
Shot: Lead
Buffered: No
Test barrel length: 30 inch
Pellets will pierce skin up to 109 yards.

NO. 9 LEAD PELLETS—1 OUNCE—585 PELLETS

Mfg: Eley Hawk **Manufacturer's code:** Subsonic
Recoil energy in 8-lb. shotgun: 9.8 ft./lbs. **Recoil velocity in 8-lb. shotgun:** 8.9 ft./sec.

Distance in yards:	Muzzle	20	30	40	50	60	70
Velocity in fps:	1,023	679	571	485	413	352	299
Average pellet energy in ft-lbs:	1.75	.77	.55	.39	.29	.21	.15
Time of flight in seconds:	0	.0732	.1215	.1786	.2456	.3244	.4170

Type of load: Target
Three-foot velocity: 1,000 ft./sec.
Hull: 2¾-inch plastic
Wad: Plastic
Shot: Lead
Buffered: No
Test barrel length: 30 inch
Pellets will pierce skin up to 95 yards.

NO. 9 LEAD PELLETS—1 OUNCE—585 PELLETS

Mfg: Federal Cartridge Co. **Manufacturer's code:** T175
Recoil energy in 8-lb. shotgun: 14.2 ft./lbs. **Recoil velocity in 8-lb. shotgun:** 10.7 ft./sec.

Distance in yards:	Muzzle	20	30	40	50	60	70
Velocity in fps:	1,176	749	625	529	450	383	326
Average pellet energy in ft-lbs:	2.31	.94	.65	.47	.34	.25	.18
Time of flight in seconds:	0	.0654	.1094	.1617	.2233	.2955	.3805

Type of load: Target
Three-foot velocity: 1,145 ft./sec.
Hull: 2¾-inch paper
Wad: Plastic
Shot: Hard lead
Buffered: No
Test barrel length: 30 inch
Pellets will pierce skin up to 100 yards.

NO. 9 LEAD PELLETS—1 OUNCE—585 PELLETS

Mfg: Fiocchi **Manufacturer's code:** 12TL
Recoil energy in 8-lb. shotgun: 18.2 ft./lbs. **Recoil velocity in 8-lb. shotgun:** 12.1 ft./sec.

Distance in yards:	Muzzle	20	30	40	50	60	70
Velocity in fps:	1,256	782	650	549	467	397	338
Average pellet energy in ft-lbs:	2.64	1.02	.71	.50	.36	.26	.19
Time of flight in seconds:	0	.0621	.1043	.1546	.2140	.2837	.3656

Type of load: Target
Three-foot velocity: 1,150 ft./sec.
Hull: 2¾-inch plastic
Wad: Plastic
Shot: Hard lead
Buffered: No
Test barrel length: 30 inch
Pellets will pierce skin up to 103 yards.

NO. 9 LEAD PELLETS—1 OUNCE—585 PELLETS

Mfg: Estate Cartridge **Manufacturer's code:** CT12L1/SS12L1
Recoil energy in 8-lb. shotgun: 15.2 ft./lbs. **Recoil velocity in 8-lb. shotgun:** 11.1 ft./sec.

Distance in yards:	Muzzle	20	30	40	50	60	70
Velocity in fps:	1,284	794	659	556	472	402	342
Average pellet energy in ft-lbs:	2.75	1.05	.73	.52	.37	.27	.20
Time of flight in seconds:	0	.0611	.1027	.1524	.2110	.2799	.3608

Type of load: Target
Three-foot velocity: 1,175 ft./sec.
Hull: 2¾-inch plastic
Wad: Plastic
Shot: Hard lead
Buffered: No
Test barrel length: 30 inch
Pellets will pierce skin up to 103 yards.

NO. 9 LEAD PELLETS—1 OUNCE—585 PELLETS
Mfg: Federal Cartridge Co. **Manufacturer's code:** T113
Recoil energy in 8-lb. shotgun: 15.2 ft./lbs. **Recoil velocity in 8-lb. shotgun:** 11.1 ft./sec.

Distance in yards:	Muzzle	20	30	40	50	60	70
Velocity in fps:	1,284	794	659	556	472	402	342
Average pellet energy in ft-lbs:	2.75	1.05	.73	.52	.37	.27	.20
Time of flight in seconds:	0	.0611	.1027	.1524	.2110	.2799	.3608

Type of load: Target
Three-foot velocity: 1,175 ft./sec.
Hull: 2¾-inch plastic
Wad: Plastic
Shot: Hard lead
Buffered: No
Test barrel length: 30 inch
Pellets will pierce skin up to 103 yards

NO. 9 LEAD PELLETS—1 OUNCE—585 PELLETS
Mfg: Polywad **Manufacturer's code:** SRL129
Recoil energy in 8-lb. shotgun: 15.2 ft./lbs. **Recoil velocity in 8-lb. shotgun:** 11.1 ft./sec.

Distance in yards:	Muzzle	20	30	40	50	60	70
Velocity in fps:	1,284	794	659	556	472	402	342
Average pellet energy in ft-lbs:	2.75	1.05	.73	.52	.37	.27	.20
Time of flight in seconds:	0	.0611	.1027	.1524	.2110	.2799	.3608

Type of load: Field
Three-foot velocity: 1,175 ft./sec.
Hull: 2¾-inch plastic
Wad: Plastic
Shot: Lead
Buffered: No
Test barrel length: 30 inch
Pellets will pierce skin up to 103 yards

NO. 9 LEAD PELLETS—1 OUNCE—585 PELLETS
Mfg: Remington Arms Co. **Manufacturer's code:** STS121
Recoil energy in 8-lb. shotgun: 15.2 ft./lbs. **Recoil velocity in 8-lb. shotgun:** 11.1 ft./sec.

Distance in yards:	Muzzle	20	30	40	50	60	70
Velocity in fps:	1,284	794	659	556	472	402	342
Average pellet energy in ft-lbs:	2.75	1.05	.73	.52	.37	.27	.20
Time of flight in seconds:	0	.0611	.1027	.1524	.2110	.2799	.3608

Type of load: Target
Three-foot velocity: 1,175 ft./sec.
Hull: 2¾-inch plastic
Wad: Plastic
Shot: Hard lead
Buffered: No
Test barrel length: 30 inch
Pellets will pierce skin up to 103 yards.

NO. 9 LEAD PELLETS—1 OUNCE—585 PELLETS
Mfg: RST, Ltd. **Manufacturer's code:** N/A
Recoil energy in 8-lb. shotgun: 15.2 ft./lbs. **Recoil velocity in 8-lb. shotgun:** 11.1 ft./sec.

Distance in yards:	Muzzle	20	30	40	50	60	70
Velocity in fps:	1,284	794	659	556	472	402	342
Average pellet energy in ft-lbs:	2.75	1.05	.73	.52	.37	.27	.20
Time of flight in seconds:	0	.0611	.1027	.1524	.2110	.2799	.3608

Type of load: Target
Three-foot velocity: 1,175 ft./sec.
Hull: 2¾-inch plastic
Wad: Plastic
Shot: Lead
Buffered: No
Test barrel length: 30 inch
Pellets will pierce skin up to 103 yards.

NO. 9 LEAD PELLETS—1 OUNCE—585 PELLETS
Mfg: Winchester **Manufacturer's code:** AAL12
Recoil energy in 8-lb. shotgun: 15.2 ft./lbs. **Recoil velocity in 8-lb. shotgun:** 11.1 ft./sec.

Distance in yards:	Muzzle	20	30	40	50	60	70
Velocity in fps:	1,284	794	659	556	472	402	342
Average pellet energy in ft-lbs:	2.75	1.05	.73	.52	.37	.27	.20
Time of flight in seconds:	0	.0611	.1027	.1524	.2110	.2799	.3608

Type of load: Target
Three-foot velocity: 1,175 ft./sec.
Hull: 2¾-inch plastic
Wad: Plastic
Shot: Hard lead
Buffered: No
Test barrel length: 30 inch
Pellets will pierce skin up to 103 yards.

NO. 9 LEAD PELLETS—1 OUNCE—585 PELLETS
Mfg: Aguila **Manufacturer's code:** N/A
Recoil energy in 8-lb. shotgun: 20.4 ft./lbs. **Recoil velocity in 8-lb. shotgun:** 12.8 ft./sec.

Distance in yards:	Muzzle	20	30	40	50	60	70
Velocity in fps:	1,312	805	667	562	478	407	346
Average pellet energy in ft-lbs:	2.88	1.08	.74	.53	.38	.28	.20
Time of flight in seconds:	0	.0601	.1011	.1502	.2082	.2763	.3562

Type of load: Field
Three-foot velocity: 1,200 ft./sec.
Hull: 2¾-inch plastic
Wad: Plastic
Shot: Lead
Buffered: No
Test barrel length: 30 inch
Pellets will pierce skin up to 115 yards.

NO. 9 LEAD PELLETS—1 OUNCE—585 PELLETS
Mfg: Estate Cartridge **Manufacturer's code:** CT12H1/SS12H1
Recoil energy in 8-lb. shotgun: 17.4 ft./lbs. **Recoil velocity in 8-lb. shotgun:** 11.8 ft./sec.

Distance in yards:	Muzzle	20	30	40	50	60	70
Velocity in fps:	1,351	820	678	571	485	413	352
Average pellet energy in ft-lbs:	3.05	1.12	.77	.55	.39	.29	.21
Time of flight in seconds:	0	.0687	.0990	.1473	.2044	.2716	.3502

Type of load: Target
Three-foot velocity: 1,235 ft./sec.
Hull: 2¾-inch plastic
Wad: Plastic
Shot: Hard lead
Buffered: No
Test barrel length: 30 inch
Pellets will pierce skin up to 116 yards.

NO. 9 LEAD PELLETS—1 OUNCE—585 PELLETS
Mfg: Fiocchi **Manufacturer's code:** 12MS3
Recoil energy in 8-lb. shotgun: 17.9 ft./lbs. **Recoil velocity in 8-lb. shotgun:** 12.0 ft./sec.

Distance in yards:	Muzzle	20	30	40	50	60	70
Velocity in fps:	1,368	827	683	575	488	416	354
Average pellet energy in ft-lbs:	3.13	1.14	.78	.55	.40	.29	.21
Time of flight in seconds:	0	.0581	.0982	.1461	.2028	.2695	.3477

Type of load: Field
Three-foot velocity: 1,250 ft./sec.
Hull: 2¾-inch plastic
Wad: Plastic
Shot: Lead
Buffered: No
Test barrel length: 30 inch
Pellets will pierce skin up to 116 yards.

NO. 9 LEAD PELLETS—1 OUNCE—585 PELLETS
Mfg: Eley Hawk **Manufacturer's code:** Black Trap
Recoil energy in 8-lb. shotgun: 18.9 ft./lbs. **Recoil velocity in 8-lb. shotgun:** 12.3 ft./sec.

Distance in yards:	Muzzle	20	30	40	50	60	70
Velocity in fps:	1,396	838	691	581	493	420	358
Average pellet energy in ft-lbs:	3.26	1.17	.80	.56	.41	.29	.21
Time of flight in seconds:	0	.0572	.0967	.1442	.2003	.2663	.3438

Type of load: Target
Three-foot velocity: 1,275 ft./sec.
Hull: 2¾-inch plastic
Wad: Plastic
Shot: Lead
Buffered: No
Test barrel length: 30 inch
Pellets will pierce skin up to 117 yards.

NO. 9 LEAD PELLETS—1 OUNCE—585 PELLETS
Mfg: Eley Hawk **Manufacturer's code:** Olympic 2000
Recoil energy in 8-lb. shotgun: 19.9 ft./lbs. **Recoil velocity in 8-lb. shotgun:** 12.6 ft./sec.

Distance in yards:	Muzzle	20	30	40	50	60	70
Velocity in fps:	1,426	849	699	587	498	424	361
Average pellet energy in ft-lbs:	3.39	1.20	.82	.58	.42	.30	.22
Time of flight in seconds:	0	.0563	.0954	.1423	.1978	.2632	.3399

Type of load: Target
Three-foot velocity: 1,300 ft./sec.
Hull: 2¾-inch plastic
Wad: Plastic
Shot: Lead
Buffered: No
Test barrel length: 30 inch
Pellets will pierce skin up to 117 yards.

NO. 9 LEAD PELLETS—1 OUNCE—585 PELLETS
Mfg: Eley Hawk **Manufacturer's code:** VIP Sporting Fibre
Recoil energy in 8-lb. shotgun: 19.9 ft./lbs. **Recoil velocity in 8-lb. shotgun:** 12.6 ft./sec.

Distance in yards:	Muzzle	20	30	40	50	60	70
Velocity in fps:	1,426	849	699	587	498	424	361
Average pellet energy in ft-lbs:	3.39	1.20	.82	.58	.42	.30	.22
Time of flight in seconds:	0	.0563	.0954	.1423	.1978	.2632	.3399

Type of load: Target
Three-foot velocity: 1,300 ft./sec.
Hull: 2¾-inch plastic
Wad: Fiber
Shot: Lead
Buffered: No
Test barrel length: 30 inch
Pellets will pierce skin up to 117 yards.

NO. 9 LEAD PELLETS—1 OUNCE—585 PELLETS
Mfg: Estate Cartridge **Manufacturer's code:** DQ12
Recoil energy in 8-lb. shotgun: 19.9 ft./lbs. **Recoil velocity in 8-lb. shotgun:** 12.6 ft./sec.

Distance in yards:	Muzzle	20	30	40	50	60	70
Velocity in fps:	1,426	849	699	587	498	424	361
Average pellet energy in ft-lbs:	3.39	1.20	.82	.58	.42	.30	.22
Time of flight in seconds:	0	.0563	.0954	.1423	.1978	.2632	.3399

Type of load: Field
Three-foot velocity: 1,300 ft./sec.5
Hull: 2¾-inch plastic
Wad: Plastic
Shot: Hard lead
Buffered: No
Test barrel length: 30 inch
Pellets will pierce skin up to 117 yards.

NO. 9 LEAD PELLETS—1 OUNCE—585 PELLETS
Mfg: Fiocchi **Manufacturer's code:** 12GT1
Recoil energy in 8-lb. shotgun: 19.9 ft./lbs. **Recoil velocity in 8-lb. shotgun:** 12.6 ft./sec.

Distance in yards:	Muzzle	20	30	40	50	60	70
Velocity in fps:	1,426	849	699	587	498	424	361
Average pellet energy in ft-lbs:	3.39	1.20	.82	.58	.42	.30	.22
Time of flight in seconds:	0	.0563	.0954	.1423	.1978	.2632	.3399

Type of load: Game & Target
Three-foot velocity: 1,300 ft./sec.
Hull: 2¾-inch plastic
Wad: Plastic
Shot: Lead
Buffered: No
Test barrel length: 30 inch
Pellets will pierce skin up to 117 yards.

NO. 9 LEAD PELLETS—1 OUNCE—585 PELLETS
Mfg: Fiocchi **Manufacturer's code:** 12CPTR
Recoil energy in 8-lb. shotgun: 19.9 ft./lbs. **Recoil velocity in 8-lb. shotgun:** 12.6 ft./sec.

Distance in yards:	Muzzle	20	30	40	50	60	70
Velocity in fps:	1,426	849	699	587	498	424	361
Average pellet energy in ft-lbs:	3.39	1.20	.82	.58	.42	.30	.22
Time of flight in seconds:	0	.0563	.0954	.1423	.1978	.2632	.3399

Type of load: Target & Spreader
Three-foot velocity: 1,300 ft./sec.
Hull: 2¾-inch plastic
Wad: Plastic
Shot: Hard lead
Buffered: No
Test barrel length: 30 inch
Pellets will pierce skin up to 117 yards.

NO. 9 LEAD PELLETS—1 OUNCE—585 PELLETS
Mfg: Fiocchi **Manufacturer's code:** 12CRSR
Recoil energy in 8-lb. shotgun: 19.9 ft./lbs. **Recoil velocity in 8-lb. shotgun:** 12.6 ft./sec.

Distance in yards:	Muzzle	20	30	40	50	60	70
Velocity in fps:	1,426	849	699	587	498	424	361
Average pellet energy in ft-lbs:	3.39	1.20	.82	.58	.42	.30	.22
Time of flight in seconds:	0	.0563	.0954	.1423	.1978	.2632	.3399

Type of load: Target
Three-foot velocity: 1,300 ft./sec.
Hull: 2¾-inch plastic
Wad: Plastic
Shot: Hard lead
Buffered: No
Test barrel length: 30 inch
Pellets will pierce skin up to 117 yards.

NO. 9 LEAD PELLETS—1 OUNCE—585 PELLETS
Mfg: PMC (Eldorado Cartridge Corp.) **Manufacturer's code:** PL12
Recoil energy in 8-lb. shotgun: 19.9 ft./lbs. **Recoil velocity in 8-lb. shotgun:** 12.6 ft./sec.

Distance in yards:	Muzzle	20	30	40	50	60	70
Velocity in fps:	1,426	849	699	587	498	424	361
Average pellet energy in ft-lbs:	3.39	1.20	.82	.58	.42	.30	.22
Time of flight in seconds:	0	.0563	.0954	.1423	.1978	.2632	.3399

Type of load: Quail & Dove
Three-foot velocity: 1,300 ft./sec.
Hull: 2¾-inch plastic
Wad: Plastic
Shot: Lead
Buffered: No
Test barrel length: 30 inch
Pellets will pierce skin up to 117 yards.

NO. 9 LEAD PELLETS—1 OUNCE—585 PELLETS
Mfg: Rottweil **Manufacturer's code:** Game
Recoil energy in 8-lb. shotgun: 25.2 ft./lbs. **Recoil velocity in 8-lb. shotgun:** 14.2 ft./sec.

Distance in yards:	Muzzle	20	30	40	50	60	70
Velocity in fps:	1,426	849	699	587	498	424	361
Average pellet energy in ft-lbs:	3.39	1.20	.82	.58	.42	.30	.22
Time of flight in seconds:	0	.0563	.0954	.1423	.1978	.2632	.3399

Type of load: Field
Three-foot velocity: 1,300 ft./sec.
Hull: 2¾-inch plastic
Wad: Plastic
Shot: Lead
Buffered: No
Test barrel length: 30 inch
Pellets will pierce skin up to 117 yards.

NO. 9 LEAD PELLETS—1 OUNCE—585 PELLETS
Mfg: RST, Ltd. **Manufacturer's code:** N/A
Recoil energy in 8-lb. shotgun: 19.9 ft./lbs. **Recoil velocity in 8-lb. shotgun:** 12.6 ft./sec.

Distance in yards:	Muzzle	20	30	40	50	60	70
Velocity in fps:	1,426	849	699	587	498	424	361
Average pellet energy in ft-lbs:	3.39	1.20	.82	.58	.42	.30	.22
Time of flight in seconds:	0	.0563	.0954	.1423	.1978	.2632	.3399

Type of load: Target
Three-foot velocity: 1,300 ft./sec.
Hull: 2¾-inch plastic
Wad: Plastic
Shot: Lead
Buffered: No
Test barrel length: 30 inch
Pellets will pierce skin up to 117 yards.

NO. 9 LEAD PELLETS—1 OUNCE—585 PELLETS
Mfg: Sellier & Bellot **Manufacturer's code:** SBA01246
Recoil energy in 8-lb. shotgun: 19.9 ft./lbs. **Recoil velocity in 8-lb. shotgun:** 12.6 ft./sec.

Distance in yards:	Muzzle	20	30	40	50	60	70
Velocity in fps:	1,426	849	699	587	498	424	361
Average pellet energy in ft-lbs:	3.39	1.20	.82	.58	.42	.30	.22
Time of flight in seconds:	0	.0563	.0954	.1423	.1978	.2632	.3399

Type of load: Target
Three-foot velocity: 1,300 ft./sec.
Hull: 2¾-inch plastic
Wad: Plastic
Shot: Lead
Buffered: No
Test barrel length: 30 inch
Pellets will pierce skin up to 117 yards.

NO. 9 LEAD PELLETS—1 OUNCE—585 PELLETS
Mfg: Baschieri & Pellagri **Manufacturer's code:** N/A
Recoil energy in 8-lb. shotgun: 21.2 ft./lbs. **Recoil velocity in 8-lb. shotgun:** 13.0 ft./sec.

Distance in yards:	Muzzle	20	30	40	50	60	70
Velocity in fps:	1,459	862	709	594	504	429	365
Average pellet energy in ft-lbs:	3.56	1.24	.84	.59	.42	.31	.22
Time of flight in seconds:	0	.0553	.0938	.1401	.2260	.2596	.3354

Type of load: F2 Sporting Clay
Three-foot velocity: 1,330 ft./sec.
Hull: 2¾-inch plastic
Wad: Plastic
Shot: Hard lead
Buffered: No
Test barrel length: 30 inch
Pellets will pierce skin up to 118 yards.

NO. 9 LEAD PELLETS—1 OUNCE—585 PELLETS
Mfg: Eley Hawk **Manufacturer's code:** VIP
Recoil energy in 8-lb. shotgun: 16.2 ft./lbs. **Recoil velocity in 8-lb. shotgun:** 11.4 ft./sec.

Distance in yards:	Muzzle	20	30	40	50	60	70
Velocity in fps:	1,459	862	709	594	504	429	365
Average pellet energy in ft-lbs:	3.56	1.24	.84	.59	.42	.31	.22
Time of flight in seconds:	0	.0553	.0938	.1401	.2260	.2596	.3354

Type of load: Target
Three-foot velocity: 1,330 ft./sec.
Hull: 2¾-inch plastic
Wad: Plastic
Shot: Hard lead
Buffered: No
Test barrel length: 30 inch
Pellets will pierce skin up to 118 yards.

NO. 9 LEAD PELLETS—1 OUNCE—585 PELLETS
Mfg: Estate Cartridge Manufacturer's code: CT12XH1/SS12H1
Recoil energy in 8-lb. shotgun: 21.2 ft./lbs. **Recoil velocity in 8-lb. shotgun:** 13.0 ft./sec.

Distance in yards:	Muzzle	20	30	40	50	60	70
Velocity in fps:	1,459	862	709	594	504	429	365
Average pellet energy in ft-lbs:	3.56	1.24	.84	.59	.42	.31	.22
Time of flight in seconds:	0	.0553	.0938	.1401	.2260	.2596	.3354

Type of load: Target
Three-foot velocity: 1,330 ft./sec.
Hull: 2¾-inch plastic
Wad: Plastic
Shot: Hard lead
Buffered: No
Test barrel length: 30 inch
Pellets will pierce skin up to 118 yards.

NO. 9 LEAD PELLETS—1 OUNCE—585 PELLETS
Mfg: Estate Cartridge Manufacturer's code: INT28
Recoil energy in 8-lb. shotgun: 21.2 ft./lbs. **Recoil velocity in 8-lb. shotgun:** 13.0 ft./sec.

Distance in yards:	Muzzle	20	30	40	50	60	70
Velocity in fps:	1,459	862	709	594	504	429	365
Average pellet energy in ft-lbs:	3.56	1.24	.84	.59	.42	.31	.22
Time of flight in seconds:	0	.0553	.0938	.1401	.2260	.2596	.3354

Type of load: Target
Three-foot velocity: 1,330 ft./sec.
Hull: 2¾-inch plastic
Wad: Plastic
Shot: Hard lead
Buffered: No
Test barrel length: 30 inch
Pellets will pierce skin up to 118 yards.

NO. 9 LEAD PELLETS—1 OUNCE—585 PELLETS
Mfg: RIO Manufacturer's code: Basic Game
Recoil energy in 8-lb. shotgun: 16.2 ft./lbs. **Recoil velocity in 8-lb. shotgun:** 11.4 ft./sec.

Distance in yards:	Muzzle	20	30	40	50	60	70
Velocity in fps:	1,459	862	709	594	504	429	365
Average pellet energy in ft-lbs:	3.56	1.24	.84	.59	.42	.31	.22
Time of flight in seconds:	0	.0553	.0938	.1401	.2260	.2596	.3354

Type of load: Field
Three-foot velocity: 1,330 ft./sec.
Hull: 2¾-inch plastic
Wad: Plastic
Shot: Hard lead
Buffered: No
Test barrel length: 30 inch
Pellets will pierce skin up to 118 yards.

NO. 9 LEAD PELLETS—1⅛ OUNCES—658 PELLETS
Mfg: Dionisi Manufacturer's code: D 12 TL
Recoil energy in 8-lb. shotgun: 12.7 ft./lbs. **Recoil velocity in 8-lb. shotgun:** 10.1 ft./sec.

Distance in yards:	Muzzle	20	30	40	50	60	70
Velocity in fps:	1,023	679	571	485	413	352	299
Average pellet energy in ft-lbs:	1.75	.77	.55	.39	.29	.21	.15
Time of flight in seconds:	0	.0732	.1215	.1786	.2456	.3244	.4170

Type of load: Target Low Noise
Three-foot velocity: 1,000 ft./sec.
Hull: 2¾-inch plastic
Wad: Plastic
Shot: Lead
Buffered: No
Test barrel length: 30 inch
Pellets will pierce skin up to 95 yards.

NO. 9 LEAD PELLETS—1⅛ OUNCES—658 PELLETS
Mfg: Federal Cartridge Co. Manufacturer's code: T114
Recoil energy in 8-lb. shotgun: 16.2 ft./lbs. **Recoil velocity in 8-lb. shotgun:** 11.4 ft./sec.

Distance in yards:	Muzzle	20	30	40	50	60	70
Velocity in fps:	1,200	759	633	535	455	387	330
Average pellet energy in ft-lbs:	2.40	.96	.67	.48	.35	.25	.18
Time of flight in seconds:	0	.0644	.1078	.1595	.2203	.2918	.3758

Type of load: Target
Three-foot velocity: 1,100 ft./sec.
Hull: 2¾-inch plastic
Wad: Plastic
Shot: Hard lead
Buffered: No
Test barrel length: 30 inch
Pellets will pierce skin up to 107 yards.

NO. 9 LEAD PELLETS—1⅛ OUNCES—658 PELLETS
Mfg: Estate Cartridge Manufacturer's code: CT12XL
Recoil energy in 8-lb. shotgun: 17.2 ft./lbs. **Recoil velocity in 8-lb. shotgun:** 11.8 ft./sec.

Distance in yards:	Muzzle	20	30	40	50	60	70
Velocity in fps:	1,154	740	618	523	445	379	323
Average pellet energy in ft-lbs:	2.23	.91	.64	.46	.33	.24	.17
Time of flight in seconds:	0	.0664	.1109	.1637	.2259	.2990	.3848

Type of load: Target
Three-foot velocity: 1,125 ft./sec.
Hull: 2¾-inch plastic
Wad: Plastic
Shot: Hard lead
Buffered: No
Test barrel length: 30 inch
Pellets will pierce skin up to 100 yards.

NO. 9 LEAD PELLETS—1⅛ OUNCES—658 PELLETS
Mfg: Dionisi Manufacturer's code: D 12 TD
Recoil energy in 8-lb. shotgun: 18.0 ft./lbs. **Recoil velocity in 8-lb. shotgun:** 12.0 ft./sec.

Distance in yards:	Muzzle	20	30	40	50	60	70
Velocity in fps:	1,176	749	625	529	450	383	326
Average pellet energy in ft-lbs:	2.31	.94	.65	.47	.34	.25	.18
Time of flight in seconds:	0	.0654	.1094	.1617	.2233	.2955	.3805

Type of load: Target
Three-foot velocity: 1,145 ft./sec.
Hull: 2¾-inch plastic
Wad: Plastic
Shot: Lead
Buffered: No
Test barrel length: 30 inch
Pellets will pierce skin up to 100 yards.

NO. 9 LEAD PELLETS—1⅛ OUNCES—658 PELLETS

Mfg: Estate Cartridge **Manufacturer's code:** CT12L/SS12L
Recoil energy in 8-lb. shotgun: 18.0 ft./lbs. **Recoil velocity in 8-lb. shotgun:** 12.0 ft./sec.

Distance in yards:	Muzzle	20	30	40	50	60	70
Velocity in fps:	1,176	749	625	529	450	383	326
Average pellet energy in ft-lbs:	2.31	.94	.65	.47	.34	.25	.18
Time of flight in seconds:	0	.0654	.1094	.1617	.2233	.2955	.3805

Type of load: Target
Three-foot velocity: 1,145 ft./sec.
Hull: 2¾-inch plastic
Wad: Plastic
Shot: Hard lead
Buffered: No
Test barrel length: 30 inch
Pellets will pierce skin up to 100 yards.

NO. 9 LEAD PELLETS—1⅛ OUNCES—658 PELLETS

Mfg: Federal Cartridge Co. **Manufacturer's code:** T115
Recoil energy in 8-lb. shotgun: 18.0 ft./lbs. **Recoil velocity in 8-lb. shotgun:** 12.0 ft./sec.

Distance in yards:	Muzzle	20	30	40	50	60	70
Velocity in fps:	1,176	749	625	529	450	383	326
Average pellet energy in ft-lbs:	2.31	.94	.65	.47	.34	.25	.18
Time of flight in seconds:	0	.0654	.1094	.1617	.2233	.2955	.3805

Type of load: Target
Three-foot velocity: 1,145 ft./sec.
Hull: 2¾-inch plastic
Wad: Plastic
Shot: Hard lead
Buffered: No
Test barrel length: 30 inch
Pellets will pierce skin up to 100 yards.

NO. 9 LEAD PELLETS—1⅛ OUNCES—658 PELLETS

Mfg: Federal Cartridge Co. **Manufacturer's code:** T117
Recoil energy in 8-lb. shotgun: 18.0 ft./lbs. **Recoil velocity in 8-lb. shotgun:** 12.0 ft./sec.

Distance in yards:	Muzzle	20	30	40	50	60	70
Velocity in fps:	1,176	749	625	529	450	383	326
Average pellet energy in ft-lbs:	2.31	.94	.65	.47	.34	.25	.18
Time of flight in seconds:	0	.0654	.1094	.1617	.2233	.2955	.3805

Type of load: Target
Three-foot velocity: 1,145 ft./sec.
Hull: 2¾-inch paper
Wad: Plastic
Shot: Hard lead
Buffered: No
Test barrel length: 30 inch
Pellets will pierce skin up to 100 yards.

NO. 9 LEAD PELLETS—1⅛ OUNCES—658 PELLETS

Mfg: Remington Arms Co. **Manufacturer's code:** STS12L
Recoil energy in 8-lb. shotgun: 18.0 ft./lbs. **Recoil velocity in 8-lb. shotgun:** 12.0 ft./sec.

Distance in yards:	Muzzle	20	30	40	50	60	70
Velocity in fps:	1,176	749	625	529	450	383	326
Average pellet energy in ft-lbs:	2.31	.94	.65	.47	.34	.25	.18
Time of flight in seconds:	0	.0654	.1094	.1617	.2233	.2955	.3805

Type of load: Target
Three-foot velocity: 1,145 ft./sec.
Hull: 2¾-inch plastic
Wad: Plastic
Shot: Hard lead
Buffered: No
Test barrel length: 30 inch
Pellets will pierce skin up to 100 yards.

NO. 9 LEAD PELLETS—1⅛ OUNCES—658 PELLETS

Mfg: RST, Ltd. **Manufacturer's code:** N/A
Recoil energy in 8-lb. shotgun: 18.0 ft./lbs. **Recoil velocity in 8-lb. shotgun:** 12.0 ft./sec.

Distance in yards:	Muzzle	20	30	40	50	60	70
Velocity in fps:	1,176	749	625	529	450	383	326
Average pellet energy in ft-lbs:	2.31	.94	.65	.47	.34	.25	.18
Time of flight in seconds:	0	.0654	.1094	.1617	.2233	.2955	.3805

Type of load: Target
Three-foot velocity: 1,145 ft./sec.
Hull: 2¾-inch plastic
Wad: Plastic
Shot: Lead
Buffered: No
Test barrel length: 30 inch
Pellets will pierce skin up to 100 yards.

NO. 9 LEAD PELLETS—1⅛ OUNCES—658 PELLETS

Mfg: Winchester **Manufacturer's code:** AA12
Recoil energy in 8-lb. shotgun: 18.0 ft./lbs. **Recoil velocity in 8-lb. shotgun:** 12.0 ft./sec.

Distance in yards:	Muzzle	20	30	40	50	60	70
Velocity in fps:	1,176	749	625	529	450	383	326
Average pellet energy in ft-lbs:	2.31	.94	.65	.47	.34	.25	.18
Time of flight in seconds:	0	.0654	.1094	.1617	.2233	.2955	.3805

Type of load: Target
Three-foot velocity: 1,145 ft./sec.
Hull: 2¾-inch plastic
Wad: Plastic
Shot: Hard lead
Buffered: No
Test barrel length: 30 inch
Pellets will pierce skin up to 110 yards.

NO. 9 LEAD PELLETS—1⅛ OUNCES—658 PELLETS

Mfg: Fiocchi **Manufacturer's code:** 12VIPL
Recoil energy in 8-lb. shotgun: 18.2 ft./lbs. **Recoil velocity in 8-lb. shotgun:** 12.1 ft./sec.

Distance in yards:	Muzzle	20	30	40	50	60	70
Velocity in fps:	1,256	782	650	549	467	397	338
Average pellet energy in ft-lbs:	2.64	1.02	.71	.50	.36	.26	.19
Time of flight in seconds:	0	.0621	.1043	.1546	.2140	.2837	.3656

Type of load: Target
Three-foot velocity: 1,150 ft./sec.
Hull: 2¾-inch plastic
Wad: Plastic
Shot: Hard lead
Buffered: No
Test barrel length: 30 inch
Pellets will pierce skin up to 103 yards.

NO. 9 LEAD PELLETS—1⅛ OUNCES—658 PELLETS
Mfg: Kent Cartridge America/Canada **Manufacturer's code:** K122LSK32
Recoil energy in 8-lb. shotgun: 18.2 ft./lbs. **Recoil velocity in 8-lb. shotgun:** 12.1 ft./sec.

Distance in yards:	Muzzle	20	30	40	50	60	70
Velocity in fps:	1,256	782	650	549	467	397	338
Average pellet energy in ft-lbs:	2.64	1.02	.71	.50	.36	.26	.19
Time of flight in seconds:	0	.0621	.1043	.1546	.2140	.2837	.3656

Type of load: Target
Three-foot velocity: 1,150 ft./sec.
Hull: 2¾-inch plastic
Wad: Plastic
Shot: Lead
Buffered: No
Test barrel length: 30 inch
Pellets will pierce skin up to 103 yards.

NO. 9 LEAD PELLETS—1⅛ OUNCES—658 PELLETS
Mfg: Rottweil **Manufacturer's code:** Sport
Recoil energy in 8-lb. shotgun: 18.2 ft./lbs. **Recoil velocity in 8-lb. shotgun:** 12.1 ft./sec.

Distance in yards:	Muzzle	20	30	40	50	60	70
Velocity in fps:	1,256	782	650	549	467	397	338
Average pellet energy in ft-lbs:	2.64	1.02	.71	.50	.36	.26	.19
Time of flight in seconds:	0	.0621	.1043	.1546	.2140	.2837	.3656

Type of load: Target
Three-foot velocity: 1,150 ft./sec.
Hull: 2¾-inch plastic
Wad: Plastic
Shot: Lead
Buffered: No
Test barrel length: 30 inch
Pellets will pierce skin up to 103 yards.

NO. 9 LEAD PELLETS—1⅛ OUNCES—658 PELLETS
Mfg: Fiocchi **Manufacturer's code:** 12LITE
Recoil energy in 8-lb. shotgun: 19.9 ft./lbs. **Recoil velocity in 8-lb. shotgun:** 12.6 ft./sec.

Distance in yards:	Muzzle	20	30	40	50	60	70
Velocity in fps:	1,272	789	655	553	470	400	341
Average pellet energy in ft-lbs:	2.71	1.04	.72	.51	.37	.27	.19
Time of flight in seconds:	0	.0615	.1033	.1533	.2122	.2814	.3627

Type of load: Target
Three-foot velocity: 1,165 ft./sec.
Hull: 2¾-inch plastic
Wad: Plastic
Shot: Hard lead
Buffered: No
Test barrel length: 30 inch
Pellets will pierce skin up to 103 yards.

NO. 9 LEAD PELLETS—1⅛ OUNCES—658 PELLETS
Mfg: PMC (Eldorado Cartridge Corp.) **Manufacturer's code:** LCT12
Recoil energy in 8-lb. shotgun: 19.3 ft./lbs. **Recoil velocity in 8-lb. shotgun:** 12.5 ft./sec.

Distance in yards:	Muzzle	20	30	40	50	60	70
Velocity in fps:	1,284	794	659	556	472	402	342
Average pellet energy in ft-lbs:	2.75	1.05	.73	.52	.37	.27	.20
Time of flight in seconds:	0	.0611	.1027	.1524	.2110	.2799	.3608

Type of load: Target
Three-foot velocity: 1,175 ft./sec.
Hull: 2¾-inch plastic
Wad: Plastic
Shot: Lead
Buffered: No
Test barrel length: 30 inch
Pellets will pierce skin up to 103 yards.

NO. 9 LEAD PELLETS—1⅛ OUNCES—658 PELLETS
Mfg: Aguila **Manufacturer's code:** N/A
Recoil energy in 8-lb. shotgun: 20.4 ft./lbs. **Recoil velocity in 8-lb. shotgun:** 12.8 ft./sec.

Distance in yards:	Muzzle	20	30	40	50	60	70
Velocity in fps:	1,312	805	667	562	478	407	346
Average pellet energy in ft-lbs:	2.88	1.08	.74	.53	.38	.28	.20
Time of flight in seconds:	0	.0601	.1011	.1502	.2082	.2763	.3562

Type of load: Field
Three-foot velocity: 1,200 ft./sec.
Hull: 2¾-inch plastic
Wad: Plastic
Shot: Lead
Buffered: No
Test barrel length: 30 inch
Pellets will pierce skin up to 115 yards.

NO. 9 LEAD PELLETS—1⅛ OUNCES—658 PELLETS
Mfg: Estate Cartridge **Manufacturer's code:** CT12H/SS12H
Recoil energy in 8-lb. shotgun: 20.4 ft./lbs. **Recoil velocity in 8-lb. shotgun:** 12.8 ft./sec.

Distance in yards:	Muzzle	20	30	40	50	60	70
Velocity in fps:	1,312	805	667	562	478	407	346
Average pellet energy in ft-lbs:	2.88	1.08	.74	.53	.38	.28	.20
Time of flight in seconds:	0	.0601	.1011	.1502	.2082	.2763	.3562

Type of load: Target
Three-foot velocity: 1,200 ft./sec.
Hull: 2¾-inch plastic
Wad: Plastic
Shot: Hard lead
Buffered: No
Test barrel length: 30 inch
Pellets will pierce skin up to 115 yards.

NO. 9 LEAD PELLETS—1⅛ OUNCES—658 PELLETS
Mfg: Estate Cartridge **Manufacturer's code:** CT12HS
Recoil energy in 8-lb. shotgun: 20.4 ft./lbs. **Recoil velocity in 8-lb. shotgun:** 12.8 ft./sec.

Distance in yards:	Muzzle	20	30	40	50	60	70
Velocity in fps:	1,312	805	667	562	478	407	346
Average pellet energy in ft-lbs:	2.88	1.08	.74	.53	.38	.28	.20
Time of flight in seconds:	0	.0601	.1011	.1502	.2082	.2763	.3562

Type of load: Target
Three-foot velocity: 1,200 ft./sec.
Hull: 2¾-inch plastic
Wad: Plastic
Shot: Hard lead
Buffered: No
Test barrel length: 30 inch
Pellets will pierce skin up to 115 yards.

NO. 9 LEAD PELLETS—1⅛ OUNCES—658 PELLETS
Mfg: Federal Cartridge Co. **Manufacturer's code:** T116
Recoil energy in 8-lb. shotgun: 20.4 ft./lbs. **Recoil velocity in 8-lb. shotgun:** 12.8 ft./sec.

Distance in yards:	Muzzle	20	30	40	50	60	70
Velocity in fps:	1,312	805	667	562	478	407	346
Average pellet energy in ft-lbs:	2.88	1.08	.74	.53	.38	.28	.20
Time of flight in seconds:	0	.0601	.1011	.1502	.2082	.2763	.3562

Type of load: Target
Three-foot velocity: 1,200 ft./sec.
Hull: 2¾-inch plastic
Wad: Plastic
Shot: Hard lead
Buffered: No
Test barrel length: 30 inch
Pellets will pierce skin up to 115 yards.

NO. 9 LEAD PELLETS—1⅛ OUNCES—658 PELLETS
Mfg: Federal Cartridge Co. **Manufacturer's code:** T118
Recoil energy in 8-lb. shotgun: 20.4 ft./lbs. **Recoil velocity in 8-lb. shotgun:** 12.8 ft./sec.

Distance in yards:	Muzzle	20	30	40	50	60	70
Velocity in fps:	1,312	805	667	562	478	407	346
Average pellet energy in ft-lbs:	2.88	1.08	.74	.53	.38	.28	.20
Time of flight in seconds:	0	.0601	.1011	.1502	.2082	.2763	.3562

Type of load: Target
Three-foot velocity: 1,200 ft./sec.
Hull: 2¾-inch paper
Wad: Plastic
Shot: Hard lead
Buffered: No
Test barrel length: 30 inch
Pellets will pierce skin up to 115 yards.

NO. 9 LEAD PELLETS—1⅛ OUNCES—658 PELLETS
Mfg: Fiocchi **Manufacturer's code:** 12SSCH
Recoil energy in 8-lb. shotgun: 20.4 ft./lbs. **Recoil velocity in 8-lb. shotgun:** 12.8 ft./sec.

Distance in yards:	Muzzle	20	30	40	50	60	70
Velocity in fps:	1,312	805	667	562	478	407	346
Average pellet energy in ft-lbs:	2.88	1.08	.74	.53	.38	.28	.20
Time of flight in seconds:	0	.0601	.1011	.1502	.2082	.2763	.3562

Type of load: Target/spreader
Three-foot velocity: 1,200 ft./sec.
Hull: 2¾-inch plastic
Wad: Plastic
Shot: Hard lead
Buffered: No
Test barrel length: 30 inch
Pellets will pierce skin up to 115 yards.

NO. 9 LEAD PELLETS—1⅛ OUNCES—658 PELLETS
Mfg: Fiocchi **Manufacturer's code:** 12VIPH
Recoil energy in 8-lb. shotgun: 20.4 ft./lbs. **Recoil velocity in 8-lb. shotgun:** 12.8 ft./sec.

Distance in yards:	Muzzle	20	30	40	50	60	70
Velocity in fps:	1,312	805	667	562	478	407	346
Average pellet energy in ft-lbs:	2.88	1.08	.74	.53	.38	.28	.20
Time of flight in seconds:	0	.0601	.1011	.1502	.2082	.2763	.3562

Type of load: Target
Three-foot velocity: 1,200 ft./sec.
Hull: 2¾-inch plastic
Wad: Plastic
Shot: Hard lead
Buffered: No
Test barrel length: 30 inch
Pellets will pierce skin up to 115 yards.

NO. 9 LEAD PELLETS—1⅛ OUNCES—658 PELLETS
Mfg: Kent Cartridge America/Canada **Manufacturer's code:** K122SK32
Recoil energy in 8-lb. shotgun: 20.4 ft./lbs. **Recoil velocity in 8-lb. shotgun:** 12.8 ft./sec.

Distance in yards:	Muzzle	20	30	40	50	60	70
Velocity in fps:	1,312	805	667	562	478	407	346
Average pellet energy in ft-lbs:	2.88	1.08	.74	.53	.38	.28	.20
Time of flight in seconds:	0	.0601	.1011	.1502	.2082	.2763	.3562

Type of load: Target
Three-foot velocity: 1,200 ft./sec.
Hull: 2¾-inch plastic
Wad: Plastic
Shot: Lead
Buffered: No
Test barrel length: 30 inch
Pellets will pierce skin up to 115 yards.

NO. 9 LEAD PELLETS—1⅛ OUNCES—658 PELLETS
Mfg: Polywad **Manufacturer's code:** SRH129
Recoil energy in 8-lb. shotgun: 20.4 ft./lbs. **Recoil velocity in 8-lb. shotgun:** 12.8 ft./sec.

Distance in yards:	Muzzle	20	30	40	50	60	70
Velocity in fps:	1,312	805	667	562	478	407	346
Average pellet energy in ft-lbs:	2.88	1.08	.74	.53	.38	.28	.20
Time of flight in seconds:	0	.0601	.1011	.1502	.2082	.2763	.3562

Type of load: Field
Three-foot velocity: 1,200 ft./sec.
Hull: 2¾-inch plastic
Wad: Plastic
Shot: Lead
Buffered: No
Test barrel length: 30 inch
Pellets will pierce skin up to 115 yards.

NO. 9 LEAD PELLETS—1⅛ OUNCES—658 PELLETS
Mfg: Remington Arms Co. **Manufacturer's code:** STS12H
Recoil energy in 8-lb. shotgun: 20.4 ft./lbs. **Recoil velocity in 8-lb. shotgun:** 12.8 ft./sec.

Distance in yards:	Muzzle	20	30	40	50	60	70
Velocity in fps:	1,312	805	667	562	478	407	346
Average pellet energy in ft-lbs:	2.88	1.08	.74	.53	.38	.28	.20
Time of flight in seconds:	0	.0601	.1011	.1502	.2082	.2763	.3562

Type of load: Target
Three-foot velocity: 1,200 ft./sec.
Hull: 2¾-inch plastic
Wad: Plastic
Shot: Hard lead
Buffered: No
Test barrel length: 30 inch
Pellets will pierce skin up to 115 yards.

NO. 9 LEAD PELLETS—1⅛ OUNCES—658 PELLETS
Mfg: RST, Ltd. **Manufacturer's code:** N/A
Recoil energy in 8-lb. shotgun: 20.4 ft./lbs. **Recoil velocity in 8-lb. shotgun:** 12.8 ft./sec.

Distance in yards:	Muzzle	20	30	40	50	60	70
Velocity in fps:	1,312	805	667	562	478	407	346
Average pellet energy in ft-lbs:	2.88	1.08	.74	.53	.38	.28	.20
Time of flight in seconds:	0	.0601	.1011	.1502	.2082	.2763	.3562

Type of load: Target
Three-foot velocity: 1,200 ft./sec.
Hull: 2¾-inch plastic
Wad: Plastic
Shot: Lead
Buffered: No
Test barrel length: 30 inch
Pellets will pierce skin up to 115 yards.

NO. 9 LEAD PELLETS—1⅛ OUNCES—658 PELLETS
Mfg: Sellier & Bellot **Manufacturer's code:** SBA1266
Recoil energy in 8-lb. shotgun: 20.4 ft./lbs. **Recoil velocity in 8-lb. shotgun:** 12.8 ft./sec.

Distance in yards:	Muzzle	20	30	40	50	60	70
Velocity in fps:	1,312	805	667	562	478	407	346
Average pellet energy in ft-lbs:	2.88	1.08	.74	.53	.38	.28	.20
Time of flight in seconds:	0	.0601	.1011	.1502	.2082	.2763	.3562

Type of load: Target
Three-foot velocity: 1,200 ft./sec.
Hull: 2¾-inch paper
Wad: Plastic
Shot: Lead
Buffered: No
Test barrel length: 30 inch
Pellets will pierce skin up to 115 yards.

NO. 9 LEAD PELLETS—1⅛ OUNCES—658 PELLETS
Mfg: Aguila **Manufacturer's code:** N/A
Recoil energy in 8-lb. shotgun: 22.0 ft./lbs. **Recoil velocity in 8-lb. shotgun:** 13.3 ft./sec.

Distance in yards:	Muzzle	20	30	40	50	60	70
Velocity in fps:	1,351	820	678	571	485	413	352
Average pellet energy in ft-lbs:	3.05	1.12	.77	.55	.39	.29	.21
Time of flight in seconds:	0	.0687	.0990	.1473	.2044	.2716	.3502

Type of load: Sporting Clays
Three-foot velocity: 1,235 ft./sec.
Hull: 2¾-inch plastic
Wad: Plastic
Shot: Nickel-plated lead
Buffered: No
Test barrel length: 30 inch
Pellets will pierce skin up to 116 yards.

NO. 9 LEAD PELLETS—1⅛ OUNCES—658 PELLETS
Mfg: PMC (Eldorado Cartridge Corp.) **Manufacturer's code:** CT12/GCT
Recoil energy in 8-lb. shotgun: 22.0 ft./lbs. **Recoil velocity in 8-lb. shotgun:** 13.3 ft./sec.

Distance in yards:	Muzzle	20	30	40	50	60	70
Velocity in fps:	1,351	820	678	571	485	413	352
Average pellet energy in ft-lbs:	3.05	1.12	.77	.55	.39	.29	.21
Time of flight in seconds:	0	.0687	.0990	.1473	.2044	.2716	.3502

Type of load: Target
Three-foot velocity: 1,235 ft./sec.
Hull: 2¾-inch plastic
Wad: Plastic
Shot: Lead
Buffered: No
Test barrel length: 30 inch
Pellets will pierce skin up to 116 yards.

NO. 9 LEAD PELLETS—1⅛ OUNCES—658 PELLETS
Mfg: Estate Cartridge **Manufacturer's code:** CT12XH
Recoil energy in 8-lb. shotgun: 22.7 ft./lbs. **Recoil velocity in 8-lb. shotgun:** 13.5 ft./sec.

Distance in yards:	Muzzle	20	30	40	50	60	70
Velocity in fps:	1,368	827	683	575	488	416	354
Average pellet energy in ft-lbs:	3.13	1.14	.78	.55	.40	.29	.21
Time of flight in seconds:	0	.0581	.0982	.1461	.2028	.2695	.3477

Type of load: Target
Three-foot velocity: 1,250 ft./sec.
Hull: 2¾-inch plastic
Wad: Plastic
Shot: Hard lead
Buffered: No
Test barrel length: 30 inch
Pellets will pierce skin up to 118 yards.

NO. 9 LEAD PELLETS—1⅛ OUNCES—658 PELLETS
Mfg: Estate Cartridge **Manufacturer's code:** HG12
Recoil energy in 8-lb. shotgun: 22.7 ft./lbs. **Recoil velocity in 8-lb. shotgun:** 13.5 ft./sec.

Distance in yards:	Muzzle	20	30	40	50	60	70
Velocity in fps:	1,368	827	683	575	488	416	354
Average pellet energy in ft-lbs:	3.13	1.14	.78	.55	.40	.29	.21
Time of flight in seconds:	0	.0581	.0982	.1461	.2028	.2695	.3477

Type of load: Field
Three-foot velocity: 1,250 ft./sec.
Hull: 2¾-inch plastic
Wad: Plastic
Shot: Hard lead
Buffered: No
Test barrel length: 30 inch
Pellets will pierce skin up to 118 yards.

NO. 9 LEAD PELLETS—1⅛ OUNCES—658 PELLETS
Mfg: Fiocchi **Manufacturer's code:** 12FLD
Recoil energy in 8-lb. shotgun: 22.7 ft./lbs. **Recoil velocity in 8-lb. shotgun:** 13.5 ft./sec.

Distance in yards:	Muzzle	20	30	40	50	60	70
Velocity in fps:	1,368	827	683	575	488	416	354
Average pellet energy in ft-lbs:	3.13	1.14	.78	.55	.40	.29	.21
Time of flight in seconds:	0	.0581	.0982	.1461	.2028	.2695	.3477

Type of load: Field
Three-foot velocity: 1,250 ft./sec.
Hull: 2¾-inch plastic
Wad: Plastic
Shot: Lead
Buffered: No
Test barrel length: 30 inch
Pellets will pierce skin up to 118 yards.

NO. 9 LEAD PELLETS—1⅛ OUNCES—658 PELLETS
Mfg: Fiocchi **Manufacturer's code:** 12SSCX
Recoil energy in 8-lb. shotgun: 22.7 ft./lbs. **Recoil velocity in 8-lb. shotgun:** 13.5 ft./sec.

Distance in yards:	Muzzle	20	30	40	50	60	70
Velocity in fps:	1,368	827	683	575	488	416	354
Average pellet energy in ft-lbs:	3.13	1.14	.78	.55	.40	.29	.21
Time of flight in seconds:	0	.0581	.0982	.1461	.2028	.2695	.3477

Type of load: Target & Spreader
Three-foot velocity: 1,250 ft./sec.
Hull: 2¾-inch plastic
Wad: Plastic
Shot: Hard lead
Buffered: No
Test barrel length: 30 inch
Pellets will pierce skin up to 118 yards.

NO. 9 LEAD PELLETS—1⅛ OUNCES—658 PELLETS
Mfg: Fiocchi **Manufacturer's code:** 12WRNO
Recoil energy in 8-lb. shotgun: 22.7 ft./lbs. **Recoil velocity in 8-lb. shotgun:** 13.5 ft./sec.

Distance in yards:	Muzzle	20	30	40	50	60	70
Velocity in fps:	1,368	827	683	575	488	416	354
Average pellet energy in ft-lbs:	3.13	1.14	.78	.55	.40	.29	.21
Time of flight in seconds:	0	.0581	.0982	.1461	.2028	.2695	.3477

Type of load: Target
Three-foot velocity: 1,250 ft./sec.
Hull: 2¾-inch plastic
Wad: Plastic
Shot: Hard lead
Buffered: No
Test barrel length: 30 inch
Pellets will pierce skin up to 118 yards.

NO. 9 LEAD PELLETS—1⅛ OUNCES—658 PELLETS
Mfg: Rottweil **Manufacturer's code:** Super Sport
Recoil energy in 8-lb. shotgun: 22.7 ft./lbs. **Recoil velocity in 8-lb. shotgun:** 13.5 ft./sec.

Distance in yards:	Muzzle	20	30	40	50	60	70
Velocity in fps:	1,368	827	683	575	488	416	354
Average pellet energy in ft-lbs:	3.13	1.14	.78	.55	.40	.29	.21
Time of flight in seconds:	0	.0581	.0982	.1461	.2028	.2695	.3477

Type of load: Target
Three-foot velocity: 1,250 ft./sec.
Hull: 2¾-inch plastic
Wad: Plastic
Shot: Lead
Buffered: No
Test barrel length: 30 inch
Pellets will pierce skin up to 118 yards.

NO. 9 LEAD PELLETS—1⅛ OUNCES—658 PELLETS
Mfg: RST, Ltd. **Manufacturer's code:** N/A
Recoil energy in 8-lb. shotgun: 25.2 ft./lbs. **Recoil velocity in 8-lb. shotgun:** 14.2 ft./sec.

Distance in yards:	Muzzle	20	30	40	50	60	70
Velocity in fps:	1,426	849	699	587	498	424	361
Average pellet energy in ft-lbs:	3.39	1.20	.82	.58	.42	.30	.22
Time of flight in seconds:	0	.0563	.0954	.1423	.1978	.2632	.3399

Type of load: Target
Three-foot velocity: 1,300 ft./sec.
Hull: 2¾-inch plastic
Wad: Plastic
Shot: Lead
Buffered: No
Test barrel length: 30 inch
Pellets will pierce skin up to 119 yards.

NO. 9 LEAD PELLETS—1⅛ OUNCES—658 PELLETS
Mfg: Baschieri & Pellagri **Manufacturer's code:** F2/MB Disperante
Recoil energy in 8-lb. shotgun: 21.2 ft./lbs. **Recoil velocity in 8-lb. shotgun:** 13.0 ft./sec.

Distance in yards:	Muzzle	20	30	40	50	60	70
Velocity in fps:	1,459	862	709	594	504	429	365
Average pellet energy in ft-lbs:	3.56	1.24	.84	.59	.42	.31	.22
Time of flight in seconds:	0	.0553	.0938	.1401	.2260	.2596	.3354

Type of load: Sporting Clay
Three-foot velocity: 1,330 ft./sec.
Hull: 2¾-inch plastic
Wad: Plastic
Shot: Hard lead
Buffered: No
Test barrel length: 30 inch
Pellets will pierce skin up to 120 yards.

NO. 9 LEAD PELLETS—1⅛ OUNCES—658 PELLETS
Mfg: RIO **Manufacturer's code:** Extra Game
Recoil energy in 8-lb. shotgun: 21.2 ft./lbs. **Recoil velocity in 8-lb. shotgun:** 13.0 ft./sec.

Distance in yards:	Muzzle	20	30	40	50	60	70
Velocity in fps:	1,459	862	709	594	504	429	365
Average pellet energy in ft-lbs:	3.56	1.24	.84	.59	.42	.31	.22
Time of flight in seconds:	0	.0553	.0938	.1401	.2260	.2596	.3354

Type of load: Field
Three-foot velocity: 1,330 ft./sec.
Hull: 2¾-inch plastic
Wad: Plastic
Shot: Hard lead
Buffered: No
Test barrel length: 30 inch
Pellets will pierce skin up to 120 yards.

NO. 9 LEAD PELLETS—1⅛ OUNCES—658 PELLETS
Mfg: Clever **Manufacturer's code:** T2 Light Game
Recoil energy in 8-lb. shotgun: 27.9 ft./lbs. **Recoil velocity in 8-lb. shotgun:** 15.0 ft./sec.

Distance in yards:	Muzzle	20	30	40	50	60	70
Velocity in fps:	1,481	870	715	599	508	432	368
Average pellet energy in ft-lbs:	3.67	1.27	.85	.60	.43	.31	.23
Time of flight in seconds:	0	.0546	.0928	.1387	.1932	.2572	.3325

Type of load: Field
Three-foot velocity: 1,350 ft./sec.
Hull: 2¾-inch plastic
Wad: Plastic
Shot: Lead
Buffered: No
Test barrel length: 30 inch
Pellets will pierce skin up to 121 yards.

NO. 9 LEAD PELLETS—1³/₁₆ OUNCES—695 PELLETS
Mfg: Clever **Manufacturer's code:** T2 Caccia
Recoil energy in 8-lb. shotgun: 25.2 ft./lbs. **Recoil velocity in 8-lb. shotgun:** 14.2 ft./sec.

Distance in yards:	Muzzle	20	30	40	50	60	70
Velocity in fps:	1,426	849	699	587	498	424	361
Average pellet energy in ft-lbs:	3.39	1.20	.82	.58	.42	.30	.22
Time of flight in seconds:	0	.0563	.0954	.1423	.1978	.2632	.3399

Type of load: Field
Three-foot velocity: 1,300 ft./sec.
Hull: 2¾-inch plastic
Wad: Plastic
Shot: Lead
Buffered: No
Test barrel length: 30 inch
Pellets will pierce skin up to 119 yards.

NO. 9 LEAD PELLETS—1³/₁₆ OUNCES—695 PELLETS
Mfg: RIO **Manufacturer's code:** Extra Game
Recoil energy in 8-lb. shotgun: 21.2 ft./lbs. **Recoil velocity in 8-lb. shotgun:** 13.0 ft./sec.

Distance in yards:	Muzzle	20	30	40	50	60	70
Velocity in fps:	1,459	862	709	594	504	429	365
Average pellet energy in ft-lbs:	3.56	1.24	.84	.59	.42	.31	.22
Time of flight in seconds:	0	.0553	.0938	.1401	.2260	.2596	.3354

Type of load: Field
Three-foot velocity: 1,330 ft./sec.
Hull: 2¾-inch plastic
Wad: Plastic
Shot: Hard lead
Buffered: No
Test barrel length: 30 inch
Pellets will pierce skin up to 120 yards.

NO. 9 LEAD PELLETS—1¼ OUNCES—731 PELLETS
Mfg: Estate Cartridge **Manufacturer's code:** XHG12
Recoil energy in 8-lb. shotgun: 26.3 ft./lbs. **Recoil velocity in 8-lb. shotgun:** 14.5 ft./sec.

Distance in yards:	Muzzle	20	30	40	50	60	70
Velocity in fps:	1,334	814	674	567	482	410	349
Average pellet energy in ft-lbs:	2.98	1.11	.76	.54	.39	.28	.20
Time of flight in seconds:	0	.0593	.0999	.1486	.2060	.2735	.3528

Type of load: Field
Three-foot velocity: 1,220 ft./sec.
Hull: 2¾-inch plastic
Wad: Plastic
Shot: Hard lead
Buffered: No
Test barrel length: 30 inch
Pellets will pierce skin up to 105 yards.

NO. 9 LEAD PELLETS—1¼ OUNCES—731 PELLETS
Mfg: Federal Cartridge Co. **Manufacturer's code:** H125
Recoil energy in 8-lb. shotgun: 26.3 ft./lbs. **Recoil velocity in 8-lb. shotgun:** 14.5 ft./sec.

Distance in yards:	Muzzle	20	30	40	50	60	70
Velocity in fps:	1,334	814	674	567	482	410	349
Average pellet energy in ft-lbs:	2.98	1.11	.76	.54	.39	.28	.20
Time of flight in seconds:	0	.0593	.0999	.1486	.2060	.2735	.3528

Type of load: Field
Three-foot velocity: 1,220 ft./sec.
Hull: 2¾-inch plastic
Wad: Plastic
Shot: Lead
Buffered: No
Test barrel length: 30 inch
Pellets will pierce skin up to 105 yards.

NO. 9 LEAD PELLETS—1¼ OUNCES—731 PELLETS
Mfg: Fiocchi **Manufacturer's code:** 12HF
Recoil energy in 8-lb. shotgun: 26.3 ft./lbs. **Recoil velocity in 8-lb. shotgun:** 14.5 ft./sec.

Distance in yards:	Muzzle	20	30	40	50	60	70
Velocity in fps:	1,334	814	674	567	482	410	349
Average pellet energy in ft-lbs:	2.98	1.11	.76	.54	.39	.28	.20
Time of flight in seconds:	0	.0593	.0999	.1486	.2060	.2735	.3528

Type of load: Field
Three-foot velocity: 1,220 ft./sec.
Hull: 2¾-inch plastic
Wad: Plastic
Shot: Lead
Buffered: No
Test barrel length: 30 inch
Pellets will pierce skin up to 105 yards.

NO. 9 LEAD PELLETS—1¼ OUNCES—731 PELLETS
Mfg: Aguila **Manufacturer's code:** N/A
Recoil energy in 8-lb. shotgun: 33.0 ft./lbs. **Recoil velocity in 8-lb. shotgun:** 16.3 ft./sec.

Distance in yards:	Muzzle	20	30	40	50	60	70
Velocity in fps:	1,459	862	709	594	504	429	365
Average pellet energy in ft-lbs:	3.56	1.24	.84	.59	.42	.31	.22
Time of flight in seconds:	0	.0553	.0938	.1401	.2260	.2596	.3354

Type of load: Field/Target
Three-foot velocity: 1,330 ft./sec.
Hull: 2¾-inch plastic
Wad: Plastic
Shot: Lead
Buffered: No
Test barrel length: 30 inch
Pellets will pierce skin up to 120 yards.

NO. 9 LEAD PELLETS—1¼ OUNCES—731 PELLETS
Mfg: ARMUSA **Manufacturer's code:** Live Pigeon
Recoil energy in 8-lb. shotgun: 31.1 ft./lbs. **Recoil velocity in 8-lb. shotgun:** 15.8 ft./sec.

Distance in yards:	Muzzle	20	30	40	50	60	70
Velocity in fps:	1,426	849	699	587	498	424	361
Average pellet energy in ft-lbs:	3.39	1.20	.82	.58	.42	.30	.22
Time of flight in seconds:	0	.0563	.0954	.1423	.1978	.2632	.3399

Type of load: Target
Three-foot velocity: 1,330 ft./sec.
Hull: 2¾-inch plastic
Wad: Plastic
Shot: Nickel-plated lead
Buffered: No
Test barrel length: 30 inch
Pellets will pierce skin up to 120 yards.

NO. 9 LEAD PELLETS—1¼ OUNCES—731 PELLETS
Mfg: Estate Cartridge **Manufacturer's code:** HV12
Recoil energy in 8-lb. shotgun: 33.0 ft./lbs. **Recoil velocity in 8-lb. shotgun:** 16.3 ft./sec.

Distance in yards:	Muzzle	20	30	40	50	60	70
Velocity in fps:	1,459	862	709	594	504	429	365
Average pellet energy in ft-lbs:	3.56	1.24	.84	.59	.42	.31	.22
Time of flight in seconds:	0	.0553	.0938	.1401	.2260	.2596	.3354

Type of load: Field
Three-foot velocity: 1,330 ft./sec.
Hull: 2¾-inch plastic
Wad: Plastic
Shot: Hard lead
Buffered: No
Test barrel length: 30 inch
Pellets will pierce skin up to 120 yards.

NO. 9 LEAD PELLETS—1¼ OUNCES—731 PELLETS
Mfg: Federal Cartridge Co. **Manufacturer's code:** H126
Recoil energy in 8-lb. shotgun: 33.0 ft./lbs. **Recoil velocity in 8-lb. shotgun:** 16.3 ft./sec.

Distance in yards:	Muzzle	20	30	40	50	60	70
Velocity in fps:	1,459	862	709	594	504	429	365
Average pellet energy in ft-lbs:	3.56	1.24	.84	.59	.42	.31	.22
Time of flight in seconds:	0	.0553	.0938	.1401	.2260	.2596	.3354

Type of load: Field
Three-foot velocity: 1,330 ft./sec.
Hull: 2¾-inch plastic
Wad: Plastic
Shot: Lead
Buffered: No
Test barrel length: 30 inch
Pellets will pierce skin up to 120 yards.

NO. 9 LEAD PELLETS—1¼ OUNCES—731 PELLETS
Mfg: Fiocchi **Manufacturer's code:** 12HV
Recoil energy in 8-lb. shotgun: 40.0 ft./lbs. **Recoil velocity in 8-lb. shotgun:** 17.9 ft./sec.

Distance in yards:	Muzzle	20	30	40	50	60	70
Velocity in fps:	1,459	862	709	594	504	429	365
Average pellet energy in ft-lbs:	3.56	1.24	.84	.59	.42	.31	.22
Time of flight in seconds:	0	.0553	.0938	.1401	.2260	.2596	.3354

Type of load: Field
Three-foot velocity: 1,330 ft./sec.
Hull: 2¾-inch plastic
Wad: Plastic
Shot: Lead
Buffered: No
Test barrel length: 30 inch
Pellets will pierce skin up to 120 yards.

NO. 9 LEAD PELLETS—1¼ OUNCES—731 PELLETS
Mfg: Fiocchi **Manufacturer's code:** 12HVN
Recoil energy in 8-lb. shotgun: 40.0 ft./lbs. **Recoil velocity in 8-lb. shotgun:** 17.9 ft./sec.

Distance in yards:	Muzzle	20	30	40	50	60	70
Velocity in fps:	1,459	862	709	594	504	429	365
Average pellet energy in ft-lbs:	3.56	1.24	.84	.59	.42	.31	.22
Time of flight in seconds:	0	.0553	.0938	.1401	.2260	.2596	.3354

Type of load: Field
Three-foot velocity: 1,330 ft./sec.
Hull: 2¾-inch plastic
Wad: Plastic
Shot: Nickel-plated lead
Buffered: No
Test barrel length: 30 inch
Pellets will pierce skin up to 120 yards.

NO. 9 LEAD PELLETS—1¼ OUNCES—731 PELLETS
Mfg: Kent Cartridge America/Canada **Manufacturer's code:** K122UG36
Recoil energy in 8-lb. shotgun: 31.1 ft./lbs. **Recoil velocity in 8-lb. shotgun:** 15.8 ft./sec.

Distance in yards:	Muzzle	20	30	40	50	60	70
Velocity in fps:	1,459	862	709	594	504	429	365
Average pellet energy in ft-lbs:	3.56	1.24	.84	.59	.42	.31	.22
Time of flight in seconds:	0	.0553	.0938	.1401	.2260	.2596	.3354

Type of load: Field
Three-foot velocity: 1,330 ft./sec.
Hull: 2¾-inch plastic
Wad: Plastic
Shot: Lead
Buffered: No
Test barrel length: 30 inch
Pellets will pierce skin up to 120 yards.

NO. 9 LEAD PELLETS—1¼ OUNCES—731 PELLETS
Mfg: Remington Arms Co. **Manufacturer's code:** SP12
Recoil energy in 8-lb. shotgun: 33.0 ft./lbs. **Recoil velocity in 8-lb. shotgun:** 16.3 ft./sec.

Distance in yards:	Muzzle	20	30	40	50	60	70
Velocity in fps:	1,459	862	709	594	504	429	365
Average pellet energy in ft-lbs:	3.56	1.24	.84	.59	.42	.31	.22
Time of flight in seconds:	0	.0553	.0938	.1401	.2260	.2596	.3354

Type of load: Field
Three-foot velocity: 1,330 ft./sec.
Hull: 2¾-inch plastic
Wad: Plastic
Shot: Lead
Buffered: No
Test barrel length: 30 inch
Pellets will pierce skin up to 120 yards.

NO. 9 LEAD PELLETS—1¼ OUNCES—731 PELLETS
Mfg: RIO **Manufacturer's code:** Extra Game
Recoil energy in 8-lb. shotgun: 33.0 ft./lbs. **Recoil velocity in 8-lb. shotgun:** 16.3 ft./sec.

Distance in yards:	Muzzle	20	30	40	50	60	70
Velocity in fps:	1,459	862	709	594	504	429	365
Average pellet energy in ft-lbs:	3.56	1.24	.84	.59	.42	.31	.22
Time of flight in seconds:	0	.0553	.0938	.1401	.2260	.2596	.3354

Type of load: Field
Three-foot velocity: 1,330 ft./sec.
Hull: 2¾-inch plastic
Wad: Plastic
Shot: Hard lead
Buffered: No
Test barrel length: 30 inch
Pellets will pierce skin up to 120 yards.

NO. BB LEAD PELLETS—1⅝ OUNCES—81 PELLETS
Mfg: Eley Hawk **Manufacturer's code:** Magnum 75
Recoil energy in 8-lb. shotgun: 49.9 ft./lbs. **Recoil velocity in 8-lb. shotgun:** 20.0 ft./sec.

Distance in yards:	Muzzle	20	30	40	50	60	70
Velocity in fps:	1,335	1,041	938	852	779	716	661
Average pellet energy in ft-lbs:	33.94	20.64	16.74	13.81	11.55	9.76	8.31
Time of flight in seconds:	0	.0513	.0817	.1153	.1521	.1923	.2360

Type of load: Field
Three-foot velocity: 1,275 ft./sec.
Hull: 3-inch plastic
Wad: Plastic
Shot: Lead
Buffered: No
Test barrel length: 30 inch
Pellets will pierce skin up to 236 yards.

NO. BB LEAD PELLETS—1⅞ OUNCES—94 PELLETS
Mfg: Federal Cartridge Co. **Manufacturer's code:** P158/F131
Recoil energy in 8-lb. shotgun: 56.6 ft./lbs. **Recoil velocity in 8-lb. shotgun:** 22.3 ft./sec.

Distance in yards:	Muzzle	20	30	40	50	60	70
Velocity in fps:	1,255	991	897	817	749	690	638
Average pellet energy in ft-lbs:	30.00	18.72	15.31	12.72	10.69	9.06	7.74
Time of flight in seconds:	0	.0542	.0860	.1211	.1594	.2012	.2464

Type of load: Field
Three-foot velocity: 1,200 ft./sec.
Hull: 3-inch plastic
Wad: Plastic
Shot: Lead
Buffered: No
Test barrel length: 30 inch
Pellets will pierce skin up to 231 yards.

NO. BB LEAD PELLETS—2 OUNCES—100 PELLETS
Mfg: Federal Cartridge Co. **Manufacturer's code:** P159
Recoil energy in 8-lb. shotgun: 61.0 ft./lbs. **Recoil velocity in 8-lb. shotgun:** 22.1 ft./sec.

Distance in yards:	Muzzle	20	30	40	50	60	70
Velocity in fps:	1,229	975	883	806	739	681	630
Average pellet energy in ft-lbs:	28.74	18.09	14.84	12.36	10.40	8.83	7.55
Time of flight in seconds:	0	.0552	.0876	.1232	.1621	.2044	.2502

Type of load: Turkey
Three-foot velocity: 1,175 ft./sec.
Hull: 3-inch plastic
Wad: Plastic
Shot: Lead
Buffered: No
Test barrel length: 30 inch
Pellets will pierce skin up to 229 yards.

NO. 2 LEAD PELLETS—1⅝ OUNCES—141 PELLETS
Mfg: Federal Cartridge Co. **Manufacturer's code:** F129
Recoil energy in 8-lb. shotgun: 49.9 ft./lbs. **Recoil velocity in 8-lb. shotgun:** 20.0 ft./sec.

Distance in yards:	Muzzle	20	30	40	50	60	70
Velocity in fps:	1,351	1,006	892	799	721	655	597
Average pellet energy in ft-lbs:	20.12	11.16	8.76	7.03	5.73	4.72	3.93
Time of flight in seconds:	0	.0520	.0837	.1193	.1589	.2026	.2506

Type of load: Field
Three-foot velocity: 1,275 ft./sec.
Hull: 3-inch plastic
Wad: Plastic
Shot: Lead
Buffered: No
Test barrel length: 30 inch
Pellets will pierce skin up to 197 yards.

NO. 2 LEAD PELLETS—1⅞ OUNCES—163 PELLETS
Mfg: Federal Cartridge Co. **Manufacturer's code:** P158/F131
Recoil energy in 8-lb. shotgun: 56.6 ft./lbs. **Recoil velocity in 8-lb. shotgun:** 22.3 ft./sec.

Distance in yards:	Muzzle	20	30	40	50	60	70
Velocity in fps:	1,270	960	855	768	695	632	577
Average pellet energy in ft-lbs:	17.78	10.16	8.05	6.50	5.32	4.40	3.67
Time of flight in seconds:	0	.0549	.0880	.01261	.1662	.2115	.2612

Type of load: Field
Three-foot velocity: 1,200 ft./sec.
Hull: 3-inch plastic
Wad: Plastic
Shot: Lead
Buffered: No
Test barrel length: 30 inch
Pellets will pierce skin up to 213 yards.

NO. 2 LEAD PELLETS—1⅞ OUNCES—163 PELLETS
Mfg: Remington Arms Co. **Manufacturer's code:** NM12H
Recoil energy in 8-lb. shotgun: 56.6 ft./lbs. **Recoil velocity in 8-lb. shotgun:** 22.3 ft./sec.

Distance in yards:	Muzzle	20	30	40	50	60	70
Velocity in fps:	1,270	960	855	768	695	632	577
Average pellet energy in ft-lbs:	17.78	10.16	8.05	6.50	5.32	4.40	3.67
Time of flight in seconds:	0	.0549	.0880	.01261	.1662	.2115	.2612

Type of load: Field
Three-foot velocity: 1,200 ft./sec.
Hull: 3-inch plastic
Wad: Plastic
Shot: Lead
Buffered: No
Test barrel length: 30 inch
Pellets will pierce skin up to 213 yards.

NO. 2 LEAD PELLETS—2 OUNCES—174 PELLETS
Mfg: Federal Cartridge Co. **Manufacturer's code:** P159
Recoil energy in 8-lb. shotgun: 61.0 ft./lbs. **Recoil velocity in 8-lb. shotgun:** 22.1 ft./sec.

Distance in yards:	Muzzle	20	30	40	50	60	70
Velocity in fps:	1,243	945	842	757	686	624	571
Average pellet energy in ft-lbs:	17.03	9.83	7.81	6.32	5.18	4.30	3.59
Time of flight in seconds:	0	.0559	.0896	.1272	.1688	.2147	.2650

Type of load: Turkey
Three-foot velocity: 1,175 ft./sec.
Hull: 3-inch plastic
Wad: Plastic
Shot: Lead
Buffered: No
Test barrel length: 30 inch
Pellets will pierce skin up to 192 yards.

NO. 3 LEAD PELLETS—1⅝ OUNCES—177 PELLETS

Mfg: Eley Hawk **Manufacturer's code:** Magnum 75
Recoil energy in 8-lb. shotgun: 49.9 ft./lbs. **Recoil velocity in 8-lb. shotgun:** 20.0 ft./sec.

Distance in yards:	Muzzle	20	30	40	50	60	70
Velocity in fps:	1,357	991	873	777	698	631	572
Average pellet energy in ft-lbs:	16.49	8.81	6.82	5.41	4.36	3.56	2.93
Time of flight in seconds:	0	.0523	.0847	.1211	.1619	.2072	.2571

Type of load: Field
Three-foot velocity: 1,275 ft./sec.
Hull: 3-inch plastic
Wad: Plastic
Shot: Lead
Buffered: No
Test barrel length: 30 inch
Pellets will pierce skin up to 184 yards.

NO. 4 LEAD PELLETS—1⅝ OUNCES—221 PELLETS

Mfg: Dionisi **Manufacturer's code:** D 12 MG 3
Recoil energy in 8-lb. shotgun: 49.9 ft./lbs. **Recoil velocity in 8-lb. shotgun:** 20.0 ft./sec.

Distance in yards:	Muzzle	20	30	40	50	60	70
Velocity in fps:	1,363	1,049	851	753	672	604	545
Average pellet energy in ft-lbs:	13.32	6.81	5.20	4.07	3.24	2.62	2.13
Time of flight in seconds:	0	.0528	.0858	.1233	.1655	.2126	.2649

Type of load: Field
Three-foot velocity: 1,275 ft./sec.
Hull: 3-inch plastic
Wad: Plastic
Shot: Lead
Buffered: No
Test barrel length: 30 inch
Pellets will pierce skin up to 171 yards.

NO. 4 LEAD PELLETS—1⅝ OUNCES—219 PELLETS

Mfg: Federal Cartridge Co. **Manufacturer's code:** F129
Recoil energy in 8-lb. shotgun: 49.9 ft./lbs. **Recoil velocity in 8-lb. shotgun:** 20.0 ft./sec.

Distance in yards:	Muzzle	20	30	40	50	60	70
Velocity in fps:	1,363	1,049	851	753	672	604	545
Average pellet energy in ft-lbs:	13.32	6.81	5.20	4.07	3.24	2.62	2.13
Time of flight in seconds:	0	.0528	.0858	.1233	.1655	.2126	.2649

Type of load: Field
Three-foot velocity: 1,275 ft./sec.
Hull: 3-inch plastic
Wad: Plastic
Shot: Lead
Buffered: No
Test barrel length: 30 inch
Pellets will pierce skin up to 171 yards.

NO. 4 LEAD PELLETS—1⅝ OUNCES—219 PELLETS

Mfg: Remington Arms Co. **Manufacturer's code:** NM12
Recoil energy in 8-lb. shotgun: 49.9 ft./lbs. **Recoil velocity in 8-lb. shotgun:** 20.0 ft./sec.

Distance in yards:	Muzzle	20	30	40	50	60	70
Velocity in fps:	1,363	1,049	851	753	672	604	545
Average pellet energy in ft-lbs:	13.32	6.81	5.20	4.07	3.24	2.62	2.13
Time of flight in seconds:	0	.0528	.0858	.1233	.1655	.2126	.2649

Type of load: Field
Three-foot velocity: 1,275 ft./sec.
Hull: 3-inch plastic
Wad: Plastic
Shot: Lead
Buffered: No
Test barrel length: 30 inch
Pellets will pierce skin up to 171 yards.

NO. 4 LEAD PELLETS—1⅝ OUNCES—219 PELLETS

Mfg: Winchester **Manufacturer's code:** X12MXC
Recoil energy in 8-lb. shotgun: 49.9 ft./lbs. **Recoil velocity in 8-lb. shotgun:** 20.0 ft./sec.

Distance in yards:	Muzzle	20	30	40	50	60	70
Velocity in fps:	1,363	1,049	851	753	672	604	545
Average pellet energy in ft-lbs:	13.32	6.81	5.20	4.07	3.24	2.62	2.13
Time of flight in seconds:	0	.0528	.0858	.1233	.1655	.2126	.2649

Type of load: Field
Three-foot velocity: 1,275 ft./sec.
Hull: 3-inch plastic
Wad: Plastic
Shot: Copper-plated lead
Buffered: Yes
Test barrel length: 30 inch
Pellets will pierce skin up to 171 yards.

NO. 4 LEAD PELLETS—1¾ OUNCES—238 PELLETS

Mfg: Fiocchi **Manufacturer's code:** 123TT
Recoil energy in 8-lb. shotgun: 44.1 ft./lbs. **Recoil velocity in 8-lb. shotgun:** 18.8 ft./sec.

Distance in yards:	Muzzle	20	30	40	50	60	70
Velocity in fps:	1,227	901	794	706	633	570	515
Average pellet energy in ft-lbs:	10.79	5.83	4.52	3.58	2.87	2.33	1.90
Time of flight in seconds:	0	.0577	.0933	.1334	.1783	.2283	.2837

Type of load: Turkey
Three-foot velocity: 1,150 ft./sec.
Hull: 3-inch plastic
Wad: Plastic
Shot: Nickel-plated lead
Buffered: No
Test barrel length: 30 inch
Pellets will pierce skin up to 166 yards.

NO. 4 LEAD PELLETS—1¾ OUNCES—238 PELLETS

Mfg: Clever **Manufacturer's code:** Magnum 76
Recoil energy in 8-lb. shotgun: 54.9 ft./lbs. **Recoil velocity in 8-lb. shotgun:** 21.0 ft./sec.

Distance in yards:	Muzzle	20	30	40	50	60	70
Velocity in fps:	1,336	960	840	744	665	598	540
Average pellet energy in ft-lbs:	12.79	6.61	5.06	3.97	3.17	2.56	2.09
Time of flight in seconds:	0	.0537	.0872	.1252	.1679	.2155	.2684

Type of load: Field
Three-foot velocity: 1,250 ft./sec.
Hull: 3-inch plastic
Wad: Plastic
Shot: Lead
Buffered: No
Test barrel length: 30 inch
Pellets will pierce skin up to 170 yards.

NO. 4 LEAD PELLETS—1¾ OUNCES—238 PELLETS

Mfg: Federal Cartridge Co. **Manufacturer's code:** PT157
Recoil energy in 8-lb. shotgun: 61.0 ft./lbs. **Recoil velocity in 8-lb. shotgun:** 22.1 ft./sec.

Distance in yards:	Muzzle	20	30	40	50	60	70
Velocity in fps:	1,390	989	863	762	680	611	551
Average pellet energy in ft-lbs:	13.86	7.01	5.34	4.17	3.32	2.67	2.18
Time of flight in seconds:	0	.0519	.0844	.1215	.1632	.2098	.261

Type of load: Turkey
Three-foot velocity: 1,300 ft./sec.
Hull: 3-inch plastic
Wad: Plastic
Shot: Copper-plated lead
Buffered: Yes
Test barrel length: 30 inch
Pellets will pierce skin up to 172 yards.

NO. 4 LEAD PELLETS—1¾ OUNCES—238 PELLETS

Mfg: Remington Arms Co. **Manufacturer's code:** PHV12M
Recoil energy in 8-lb. shotgun: 61.0 ft./lbs. **Recoil velocity in 8-lb. shotgun:** 22.1 ft./sec.

Distance in yards:	Muzzle	20	30	40	50	60	70
Velocity in fps:	1,390	989	863	762	680	611	551
Average pellet energy in ft-lbs:	13.86	7.01	5.34	4.17	3.32	2.67	2.18
Time of flight in seconds:	0	.0519	.0844	.1215	.1632	.2098	.2615

Type of load: Turkey
Three-foot velocity: 1,300 ft./sec.
Hull: 3-inch plastic
Wad: Plastic
Shot: Copper-plated lead
Buffered: Yes
Test barrel length: 30 inch
Pellets will pierce skin up to 172 yards.

NO. 4 LEAD PELLETS—1¾ OUNCES—238 PELLETS

Mfg: Winchester **Manufacturer's code:** STH123
Recoil energy in 8-lb. shotgun: 61.0 ft./lbs. **Recoil velocity in 8-lb. shotgun:** 22.1 ft./sec.

Distance in yards:	Muzzle	20	30	40	50	60	70
Velocity in fps:	1,390	989	863	762	680	611	551
Average pellet energy in ft-lbs:	13.86	7.01	5.34	4.17	3.32	2.67	2.18
Time of flight in seconds:	0	.0519	.0844	.1215	.1632	.2098	.2615

Type of load: Turkey
Three-foot velocity: 1,300 ft./sec.
Hull: 3-inch plastic
Wad: Plastic
Shot: Copper-plated lead
Buffered: Yes
Test barrel length: 30 inch
Pellets will pierce skin up to 172 yards.

NO. 4 LEAD PELLETS—1⅞ OUNCES—253 PELLETS

Mfg: Federal Cartridge Co. **Manufacturer's code:** P158/F131
Recoil energy in 8-lb. shotgun: 56.6 ft./lbs. **Recoil velocity in 8-lb. shotgun:** 22.3 ft./sec.

Distance in yards:	Muzzle	20	30	40	50	60	70
Velocity in fps:	1,281	931	817	725	649	584	528
Average pellet energy in ft-lbs:	11.77	6.21	4.79	3.77	3.02	2.45	2.00
Time of flight in seconds:	0	.0556	.0901	.01291	.1729	.2216	.2757

Type of load: Field
Three-foot velocity: 1,200 ft./sec.
Hull: 3-inch plastic
Wad: Plastic
Shot: Lead
Buffered: No
Test barrel length: 30 inch
Pellets will pierce skin up to 168 yards.

NO. 4 LEAD PELLETS—1⅞ OUNCES—253 PELLETS

Mfg: Remington Arms Co. **Manufacturer's code:** NM12H
Recoil energy in 8-lb. shotgun: 56.6 ft./lbs. **Recoil velocity in 8-lb. shotgun:** 22.3 ft./sec.

Distance in yards:	Muzzle	20	30	40	50	60	70
Velocity in fps:	1,281	931	817	725	649	584	528
Average pellet energy in ft-lbs:	11.77	6.21	4.79	3.77	3.02	2.45	2.00
Time of flight in seconds:	0	.0556	.0901	.01291	.1729	.2216	.2757

Type of load: Field
Three-foot velocity: 1,200 ft./sec.
Hull: 3-inch plastic
Wad: Plastic
Shot: Lead
Buffered: No
Test barrel length: 30 inch
Pellets will pierce skin up to 168 yards.

NO. 4 LEAD PELLETS—1⅞ OUNCES—253 PELLETS

Mfg: Winchester **Manufacturer's code:** X123XC
Recoil energy in 8-lb. shotgun: 56.6 ft./lbs. **Recoil velocity in 8-lb. shotgun:** 22.3 ft./sec.

Distance in yards:	Muzzle	20	30	40	50	60	70
Velocity in fps:	1,281	931	817	725	649	584	528
Average pellet energy in ft-lbs:	11.77	6.21	4.79	3.77	3.02	2.45	2.00
Time of flight in seconds:	0	.0556	.0901	.01291	.1729	.2216	.2757

Type of load: Field
Three-foot velocity: 1,200 ft./sec.
Hull: 3-inch plastic
Wad: Plastic
Shot: Copper-plated lead
Buffered: Yes
Test barrel length: 30 inch
Pellets will pierce skin up to 168 yards.

NO. 4 LEAD PELLETS—1⅞ OUNCES—253 PELLETS

Mfg: Estate Cartridge **Manufacturer's code:** HV12HMAG
Recoil energy in 8-lb. shotgun: 59.1 ft./lbs. **Recoil velocity in 8-lb. shotgun:** 21.8 ft./sec.

Distance in yards:	Muzzle	20	30	40	50	60	70
Velocity in fps:	1,303	943	826	733	655	590	532
Average pellet energy in ft-lbs:	12.17	6.37	4.90	3.85	3.08	2.49	2.03
Time of flight in seconds:	0	.0548	.0889	.1275	.1708	.2191	.2727

Type of load: Field
Three-foot velocity: 1,220 ft./sec.
Hull: 3-inch plastic
Wad: Plastic
Shot: Hard lead
Buffered: Yes
Test barrel length: 30 inch
Pellets will pierce skin up to 169 yards.

NO. 4 LEAD PELLETS—2 OUNCES—270 PELLETS

Mfg: Winchester **Manufacturer's code:** X123MXCT
Recoil energy in 8-lb. shotgun: 54.4 ft./lbs. **Recoil velocity in 8-lb. shotgun:** 20.9 ft./sec.

Distance in yards:	Muzzle	20	30	40	50	60	70
Velocity in fps:	1,199	887	782	696	624	563	509
Average pellet energy in ft-lbs:	10.32	5.64	4.38	3.48	2.80	2.27	1.86
Time of flight in seconds:	0	.0588	.0949	.1356	.1812	.2318	.287

Type of load: Turkey
Three-foot velocity: 1,125 ft./sec.
Hull: 3-inch plastic
Wad: Plastic
Shot: Copper-plated lead
Buffered: Yes
Test barrel length: 30 inch
Pellets will pierce skin up to 164 yards.

NO. 4 LEAD PELLETS—2 OUNCES—270 PELLETS

Mfg: Federal Cartridge Co. **Manufacturer's code:** PT159/P159
Recoil energy in 8-lb. shotgun: 61.0 ft./lbs. **Recoil velocity in 8-lb. shotgun:** 22.1 ft./sec.

Distance in yards:	Muzzle	20	30	40	50	60	70
Velocity in fps:	1,254	916	806	716	641	577	522
Average pellet energy in ft-lbs:	11.27	6.02	4.65	3.68	2.95	2.39	1.95
Time of flight in seconds:	0	.0567	.0916	.1312	.1755	.2249	.2796

Type of load: Turkey
Three-foot velocity: 1,175 ft./sec.
Hull: 3-inch plastic
Wad: Plastic
Shot: Copper-plated lead
Buffered: Yes
Test barrel length: 30 inch
Pellets will pierce skin up to 167 yards.

NO. 4 LEAD PELLETS—2 OUNCES—270 PELLETS

Mfg: Kent Cartridge America/Canada **Manufacturer's code:** K123TK56
Recoil energy in 8-lb. shotgun: 61.0 ft./lbs. **Recoil velocity in 8-lb. shotgun:** 22.1 ft./sec.

Distance in yards:	Muzzle	20	30	40	50	60	70
Velocity in fps:	1,254	916	806	716	641	577	522
Average pellet energy in ft-lbs:	11.27	6.02	4.65	3.68	2.95	2.39	1.95
Time of flight in seconds:	0	.0567	.0916	.1312	.1755	.2249	.2796

Type of load: Turkey
Three-foot velocity: 1,175 ft./sec.
Hull: 3-inch plastic
Wad: Plastic
Shot: Lead
Buffered: No
Test barrel length: 30 inch
Pellets will pierce skin up to 167 yards.

NO. 4 LEAD PELLETS—2 OUNCES—270 PELLETS

Mfg: Remington Arms Co. **Manufacturer's code:** P12XHM
Recoil energy in 8-lb. shotgun: 61.0 ft./lbs. **Recoil velocity in 8-lb. shotgun:** 22.1 ft./sec.

Distance in yards:	Muzzle	20	30	40	50	60	70
Velocity in fps:	1,254	916	806	716	641	577	522
Average pellet energy in ft-lbs:	11.27	6.02	4.65	3.68	2.95	2.39	1.95
Time of flight in seconds:	0	.0567	.0916	.1312	.1755	.2249	.2796

Type of load: Turkey
Three-foot velocity: 1,175 ft./sec.
Hull: 3-inch plastic
Wad: Plastic
Shot: Copper-plated lead
Buffered: Yes
Test barrel length: 30 inch
Pellets will pierce skin up to 167 yards.

NO. 4 LEAD PELLETS—2 OUNCES—270 PELLETS

Mfg: PMC (Eldorado Cartridge Corp.) **Manufacturer's code:** TL124/6
Recoil energy in 8-lb. shotgun: 64.4 ft./lbs. **Recoil velocity in 8-lb. shotgun:** 22.8 ft./sec.

Distance in yards:	Muzzle	20	30	40	50	60	70
Velocity in fps:	1,281	931	817	725	649	584	528
Average pellet energy in ft-lbs:	11.77	6.21	4.79	3.77	3.02	2.45	2.00
Time of flight in seconds:	0	.0556	.0901	.01291	.1729	.2216	.2757

Type of load: Turkey
Three-foot velocity: 1,200 ft./sec.
Hull: 3-inch plastic
Wad: Plastic
Shot: Lead
Buffered: Yes
Test barrel length: 30 inch
Pellets will pierce skin up to 168 yards.

NO. 4 LEAD PELLETS LAYERED OVER
NO. 6 LEAD PELLETS—1⅞ OUNCES

Mfg: Remington Arms Co. **Manufacturer's code:** MP12H
Recoil energy in 8-lb. shotgun: 56.6 ft./lbs. **Recoil velocity in 8-lb. shotgun:** 22.3 ft./sec.

NO. 4 LEAD PELLETS

Distance in yards:	Muzzle	20	30	40	50	60	70
Velocity in fps:	1,281	931	817	725	649	584	528
Average pellet energy in ft-lbs:	11.77	6.21	4.79	3.77	3.02	2.45	2.00
Time of flight in seconds:	0	.0556	.0901	.01291	.1729	.2216	.2757

NO. 6 LEAD PELLETS

Distance in yards:	Muzzle	20	30	40	50	60	70
Velocity in fps:	1,292	892	769	672	593	525	467
Average pellet energy in ft-lbs:	7.26	3.46	2.57	1.96	1.53	1.20	.095
Time of flight in seconds:	0	.0568	.0931	.01349	.1825	.2363	.2969

Type of load: Duplex Field
Three-foot velocity: 1,200 ft./sec.
Hull: 3-inch plastic
Wad: Plastic
Shot: Copper-plated lead
Buffered: Yes
Test barrel length: 30 inch

Pellets will pierce skin up to 168 yards.

Pellets will pierce skin up to 157 yards.

NO. 5 LEAD PELLETS—1⅝ OUNCES—276 PELLETS
Mfg: Dionisi **Manufacturer's code:** D 12 MG 3
Recoil energy in 8-lb. shotgun: 49.9 ft./lbs. **Recoil velocity in 8-lb. shotgun:** 20.0 ft./sec.

Distance in yards:	Muzzle	20	30	40	50	60	70
Velocity in fps:	1,369	955	827	727	644	575	515
Average pellet energy in ft-lbs:	10.57	5.14	3.86	2.98	2.34	1.87	1.50
Time of flight in seconds:	0	.0533	.0871	.1259	.1698	.2191	.2743

Type of load: Field
Three-foot velocity: 1,275 ft./sec.
Hull: 3-inch plastic
Wad: Plastic
Shot: Lead
Buffered: No
Test barrel length: 30 inch
Pellets will pierce skin up to 158 yards.

NO. 5 LEAD PELLETS—1⅝ OUNCES—276 PELLETS
Mfg: Eley Hawk **Manufacturer's code:** Magnum 75
Recoil energy in 8-lb. shotgun: 49.9 ft./lbs. **Recoil velocity in 8-lb. shotgun:** 20.0 ft./sec.

Distance in yards:	Muzzle	20	30	40	50	60	70
Velocity in fps:	1,369	955	827	727	644	575	515
Average pellet energy in ft-lbs:	10.57	5.14	3.86	2.98	2.34	1.87	1.50
Time of flight in seconds:	0	.0533	.0871	.1259	.1698	.2191	.2743

Type of load: Field
Three-foot velocity: 1,275 ft./sec.
Hull: 3-inch plastic
Wad: Plastic
Shot: Lead
Buffered: No
Test barrel length: 30 inch
Pellets will pierce skin up to 158 yards.

NO. 5 LEAD PELLETS—1¾ OUNCES—301 PELLETS
Mfg: Fiocchi **Manufacturer's code:** 123TT
Recoil energy in 8-lb. shotgun: 44.1 ft./lbs. **Recoil velocity in 8-lb. shotgun:** 18.8 ft./sec.

Distance in yards:	Muzzle	20	30	40	50	60	70
Velocity in fps:	1,232	885	772	682	607	543	487
Average pellet energy in ft-lbs:	8.56	4.41	3.37	2.62	2.08	1.66	1.34
Time of flight in seconds:	0	.0583	.0946	.2.62	.1827	.2350	.2933

Type of load: Turkey
Three-foot velocity: 1,150 ft./sec.
Hull: 3-inch plastic
Wad: Plastic
Shot: Nickel-plated lead
Buffered: No
Test barrel length: 30 inch
Pellets will pierce skin up to 153 yards.

NO. 5 LEAD PELLETS—1¾ OUNCES—301 PELLETS
Mfg: Federal Cartridge Co. **Manufacturer's code:** PT157
Recoil energy in 8-lb. shotgun: 61.0 ft./lbs. **Recoil velocity in 8-lb. shotgun:** 22.1 ft./sec.

Distance in yards:	Muzzle	20	30	40	50	60	70
Velocity in fps:	1,396	969	838	735	651	581	521
Average pellet energy in ft-lbs:	11.00	5.29	3.96	3.05	2.39	1.90	1.53
Time of flight in seconds:	0	.0524	.0858	.1241	.1675	.2163	.2708

Type of load: Turkey
Three-foot velocity: 1,300 ft./sec.
Hull: 3-inch plastic
Wad: Plastic
Shot: Copper-plated lead
Buffered: Yes
Test barrel length: 30 inch
Pellets will pierce skin up to 159 yards.

NO. 5 LEAD PELLETS—1¾ OUNCES—301 PELLETS
Mfg: Remington Arms Co. **Manufacturer's code:** PHV12M
Recoil energy in 8-lb. shotgun: 61.0 ft./lbs. **Recoil velocity in 8-lb. shotgun:** 22.1 ft./sec.

Distance in yards:	Muzzle	20	30	40	50	60	70
Velocity in fps:	1,396	969	838	735	651	581	521
Average pellet energy in ft-lbs:	11.00	5.29	3.96	3.05	2.39	1.90	1.53
Time of flight in seconds:	0	.0524	.0858	.1241	.1675	.2163	.2708

Type of load: Turkey
Three-foot velocity: 1,300 ft./sec.
Hull: 3-inch plastic
Wad: Plastic
Shot: Copper-plated lead
Buffered: Yes
Test barrel length: 30 inch
Pellets will pierce skin up to 159 yards.

NO. 5 LEAD PELLETS—1¾ OUNCES—301 PELLETS
Mfg: Winchester **Manufacturer's code:** STH123
Recoil energy in 8-lb. shotgun: 61.0 ft./lbs. **Recoil velocity in 8-lb. shotgun:** 22.1 ft./sec.

Distance in yards:	Muzzle	20	30	40	50	60	70
Velocity in fps:	1,396	969	838	735	651	581	521
Average pellet energy in ft-lbs:	11.00	5.29	3.96	3.05	2.39	1.90	1.53
Time of flight in seconds:	0	.0524	.0858	.1241	.1675	.2163	.2708

Type of load: Turkey
Three-foot velocity: 1,300 ft./sec.
Hull: 3-inch plastic
Wad: Plastic
Shot: Copper-plated lead
Buffered: Yes
Test barrel length: 30 inch
Pellets will pierce skin up to 159 yards.

NO. 5 LEAD PELLETS—2 OUNCES—340 PELLETS
Mfg: Winchester **Manufacturer's code:** X123MXCT
Recoil energy in 8-lb. shotgun: 54.4 ft./lbs. **Recoil velocity in 8-lb. shotgun:** 20.9 ft./sec.

Distance in yards:	Muzzle	20	30	40	50	60	70
Velocity in fps:	1,205	870	760	673	599	536	481
Average pellet energy in ft-lbs:	8.81	4.27	3.27	2.55	2.02	1.62	1.31
Time of flight in seconds:	0	.0594	.0963	.1383	.1856	.2385	.2976

Type of load: Turkey
Three-foot velocity: 1,125 ft./sec.
Hull: 3-inch plastic
Wad: Plastic
Shot: Copper-plated lead
Buffered: Yes
Test barrel length: 30 inch
Pellets will pierce skin up to 152 yards.

NO. 5 LEAD PELLETS—2 OUNCES—340 PELLETS
Mfg: Federal Cartridge Co. **Manufacturer's code:** PT159
Recoil energy in 8-lb. shotgun: 61.0 ft./lbs. **Recoil velocity in 8-lb. shotgun:** 22.1 ft./sec.

Distance in yards:	Muzzle	20	30	40	50	60	70
Velocity in fps:	1,259	899	784	691	615	550	493
Average pellet energy in ft-lbs:	8.94	4.56	3.46	2.70	2.13	1.70	1.37
Time of flight in seconds:	0	.0572	.0930	.1338	.1799	.2315	.3204

Type of load: Turkey
Three-foot velocity: 1,175 ft./sec.
Hull: 3-inch plastic
Wad: Plastic
Shot: Copper-plated lead
Buffered: Yes
Test barrel length: 30 inch
Pellets will pierce skin up to 154 yards.

NO. 5 LEAD PELLETS—2 OUNCES—340 PELLETS
Mfg: Kent Cartridge America/Canada **Manufacturer's code:** K123TK56
Recoil energy in 8-lb. shotgun: 61.0 ft./lbs. **Recoil velocity in 8-lb. shotgun:** 22.1 ft./sec.

Distance in yards:	Muzzle	20	30	40	50	60	70
Velocity in fps:	1,259	899	784	691	615	550	493
Average pellet energy in ft-lbs:	8.94	4.56	3.46	2.70	2.13	1.70	1.37
Time of flight in seconds:	0	.0572	.0930	.1338	.1799	.2315	.3204

Type of load: Turkey
Three-foot velocity: 1,175 ft./sec.
Hull: 3-inch plastic
Wad: Plastic
Shot: Lead
Buffered: No
Test barrel length: 30 inch
Pellets will pierce skin up to 154 yards.

NO. 5 LEAD PELLETS—2 OUNCES—340 PELLETS
Mfg: Remington Arms Co. **Manufacturer's code:** P12XHM
Recoil energy in 8-lb. shotgun: 61.0 ft./lbs. **Recoil velocity in 8-lb. shotgun:** 22.1 ft./sec.

Distance in yards:	Muzzle	20	30	40	50	60	70
Velocity in fps:	1,259	899	784	691	615	550	493
Average pellet energy in ft-lbs:	8.94	4.56	3.46	2.70	2.13	1.70	1.37
Time of flight in seconds:	0	.0572	.0930	.1338	.1799	.2315	.3204

Type of load: Turkey
Three-foot velocity: 1,175 ft./sec.
Hull: 3-inch plastic
Wad: Plastic
Shot: Copper-plated lead
Buffered: Yes
Test barrel length: 30 inch
Pellets will pierce skin up to 154 yards.

NO. 6 LEAD PELLETS—1⅝ OUNCES—362 PELLETS
Mfg: Dionisi **Manufacturer's code:** D 12 MG 3
Recoil energy in 8-lb. shotgun: 49.9 ft./lbs. **Recoil velocity in 8-lb. shotgun:** 20.0 ft./sec.

Distance in yards:	Muzzle	20	30	40	50	60	70
Velocity in fps:	1,375	932	800	697	613	543	482
Average pellet energy in ft-lbs:	8.22	3.77	2.78	2.11	1.63	1.28	1.01
Time of flight in seconds:	0	.0540	.0888	.1290	.1750	.2271	.2858

Type of load: Field
Three-foot velocity: 1,275 ft./sec.
Hull: 3-inch plastic
Wad: Plastic
Shot: Lead
Buffered: No
Test barrel length: 30 inch
Pellets will pierce skin up to 145 yards.

NO. 6 LEAD PELLETS—1⅝ OUNCES—366 PELLETS
Mfg: Federal Cartridge Co. **Manufacturer's code:** F129
Recoil energy in 8-lb. shotgun: 49.9 ft./lbs. **Recoil velocity in 8-lb. shotgun:** 20.0 ft./sec.

Distance in yards:	Muzzle	20	30	40	50	60	70
Velocity in fps:	1,375	932	800	697	613	543	482
Average pellet energy in ft-lbs:	8.22	3.77	2.78	2.11	1.63	1.28	1.01
Time of flight in seconds:	0	.0540	.0888	.1290	.1750	.2271	.2858

Type of load: Field
Three-foot velocity: 1,275 ft./sec.
Hull: 3-inch plastic
Wad: Plastic
Shot: Lead
Buffered: No
Test barrel length: 30 inch
Pellets will pierce skin up to 145 yards.

NO. 6 LEAD PELLETS—1⅝ OUNCES—366 PELLETS
Mfg: Remington Arms Co. **Manufacturer's code:** NM12
Recoil energy in 8-lb. shotgun: 49.9 ft./lbs. **Recoil velocity in 8-lb. shotgun:** 20.0 ft./sec.

Distance in yards:	Muzzle	20	30	40	50	60	70
Velocity in fps:	1,375	932	800	697	613	543	482
Average pellet energy in ft-lbs:	8.22	3.77	2.78	2.11	1.63	1.28	1.01
Time of flight in seconds:	0	.0540	.0888	.1290	.1750	.2271	.2858

Type of load: Field
Three-foot velocity: 1,275 ft./sec.
Hull: 3-inch plastic
Wad: Plastic
Shot: Lead
Buffered: No
Test barrel length: 30 inch
Pellets will pierce skin up to 145 yards.

NO. 6 LEAD PELLETS—1⅝ OUNCES—366 PELLETS
Mfg: Winchester **Manufacturer's code:** X12MXC
Recoil energy in 8-lb. shotgun: 49.9 ft./lbs. **Recoil velocity in 8-lb. shotgun:** 20.0 ft./sec.

Distance in yards:	Muzzle	20	30	40	50	60	70
Velocity in fps:	1,375	932	800	697	613	543	482
Average pellet energy in ft-lbs:	8.22	3.77	2.78	2.11	1.63	1.28	1.01
Time of flight in seconds:	0	.0540	.0888	.1290	.1750	.2271	.2858

Type of load: Field
Three-foot velocity: 1,275 ft./sec.
Hull: 3-inch plastic
Wad: Plastic
Shot: Copper-plated lead
Buffered: Yes
Test barrel length: 30 inch
Pellets will pierce skin up to 145 yards.

NO. 6 LEAD PELLETS—1¾ OUNCES—390 PELLETS
Mfg: Clever **Manufacturer's code:** Magnum 76
Recoil energy in 8-lb. shotgun: 54.9 ft./lbs. **Recoil velocity in 8-lb. shotgun:** 21.0 ft./sec.

Distance in yards:	Muzzle	20	30	40	50	60	70
Velocity in fps:	1,348	919	790	689	606	537	477
Average pellet energy in ft-lbs:	7.89	3.67	2.71	2.06	1.60	1.25	.99
Time of flight in seconds:	0	.0549	.0902	.1309	.1774	.2300	.2893

Type of load: Field
Three-foot velocity: 1,250 ft./sec.
Hull: 3-inch plastic
Wad: Plastic
Shot: Lead
Buffered: No
Test barrel length: 30 inch
Pellets will pierce skin up to 144 yards.

NO. 6 LEAD PELLETS—1¾ OUNCES—390 PELLETS
Mfg: Fiocchi **Manufacturer's code:** 123TT
Recoil energy in 8-lb. shotgun: 44.1 ft./lbs. **Recoil velocity in 8-lb. shotgun:** 18.8 ft./sec.

Distance in yards:	Muzzle	20	30	40	50	60	70
Velocity in fps:	1,237	865	748	655	578	513	456
Average pellet energy in ft-lbs:	6.65	3.25	2.43	1.86	1.45	1.14	.90
Time of flight in seconds:	0	.0589	.0963	.1392	.1880	.2431	.3051

Type of load: Turkey
Three-foot velocity: 1,150 ft./sec.
Hull: 3-inch plastic
Wad: Plastic
Shot: Nickel-plated lead
Buffered: No
Test barrel length: 30 inch
Pellets will pierce skin up to 140 yards.

NO. 6 LEAD PELLETS—1¾ OUNCES—390 PELLETS
Mfg: Federal Cartridge Co. **Manufacturer's code:** PT157
Recoil energy in 8-lb. shotgun: 61.0 ft./lbs. **Recoil velocity in 8-lb. shotgun:** 22.1 ft./sec.

Distance in yards:	Muzzle	20	30	40	50	60	70
Velocity in fps:	1,403	945	810	705	620	548	487
Average pellet energy in ft-lbs:	8.55	3.88	2.85	2.16	1.67	1.31	1.03
Time of flight in seconds:	0	.0531	.0875	.1272	.1727	.2242	.2723

Type of load: Turkey
Three-foot velocity: 1,300 ft./sec.
Hull: 3-inch plastic
Wad: Plastic
Shot: Copper-plated lead
Buffered: Yes
Test barrel length: 30 inch
Pellets will pierce skin up to 146 yards.

NO. 6 LEAD PELLETS—1¾ OUNCES—390 PELLETS
Mfg: Remington Arms Co. **Manufacturer's code:** PHV12M
Recoil energy in 8-lb. shotgun: 61.0 ft./lbs. **Recoil velocity in 8-lb. shotgun:** 22.1 ft./sec.

Distance in yards:	Muzzle	20	30	40	50	60	70
Velocity in fps:	1,403	945	810	705	620	548	487
Average pellet energy in ft-lbs:	8.55	3.88	2.85	2.16	1.67	1.31	1.03
Time of flight in seconds:	0	.0531	.0875	.1272	.1727	.2242	.2723

Type of load: Turkey
Three-foot velocity: 1,300 ft./sec.
Hull: 3-inch plastic
Wad: Plastic
Shot: Copper-plated lead
Buffered: Yes
Test barrel length: 30 inch
Pellets will pierce skin up to 146 yards.

NO. 6 LEAD PELLETS—1¾ OUNCES—390 PELLETS
Mfg: Winchester **Manufacturer's code:** STH123
Recoil energy in 8-lb. shotgun: 61.0 ft./lbs. **Recoil velocity in 8-lb. shotgun:** 22.1 ft./sec.

Distance in yards:	Muzzle	20	30	40	50	60	70
Velocity in fps:	1,403	945	810	705	620	548	487
Average pellet energy in ft-lbs:	8.55	3.88	2.85	2.16	1.67	1.31	1.03
Time of flight in seconds:	0	.0531	.0875	.1272	.1727	.2242	.2723

Type of load: Turkey
Three-foot velocity: 1,300 ft./sec.
Hull: 3-inch plastic
Wad: Plastic
Shot: Copper-plated lead
Buffered: Yes
Test barrel length: 30 inch
Pellets will pierce skin up to 146 yards.

NO. 6 LEAD PELLETS—1⅞ OUNCES—422 PELLETS
Mfg: Federal Cartridge Co. **Manufacturer's code:** P158
Recoil energy in 8-lb. shotgun: 56.6 ft./lbs. **Recoil velocity in 8-lb. shotgun:** 22.3 ft./sec.

Distance in yards:	Muzzle	20	30	40	50	60	70
Velocity in fps:	1,292	892	769	672	593	525	467
Average pellet energy in ft-lbs:	7.26	3.46	2.57	1.96	1.53	1.20	.095
Time of flight in seconds:	0	.0568	.0931	.01349	.1825	.2363	.2969

Type of load: Field
Three-foot velocity: 1,200 ft./sec.
Hull: 3-inch plastic
Wad: Plastic
Shot: Lead
Buffered: No
Test barrel length: 30 inch
Pellets will pierce skin up to 157 yards.

NO. 6 LEAD PELLETS—1⅞ OUNCES—422 PELLETS
Mfg: Remington Arms Co. **Manufacturer's code:** NM12H
Recoil energy in 8-lb. shotgun: 56.6 ft./lbs. **Recoil velocity in 8-lb. shotgun:** 22.3 ft./sec.

Distance in yards:	Muzzle	20	30	40	50	60	70
Velocity in fps:	1,292	892	769	672	593	525	467
Average pellet energy in ft-lbs:	7.26	3.46	2.57	1.96	1.53	1.20	.095
Time of flight in seconds:	0	.0568	.0931	.01349	.1825	.2363	.2969

Type of load: Field
Three-foot velocity: 1,200 ft./sec.
Hull: 3-inch plastic
Wad: Plastic
Shot: Lead
Buffered: No
Test barrel length: 30 inch
Pellets will pierce skin up to 157 yards.

NO. 6 LEAD PELLETS—1⅞ OUNCES—422 PELLETS
Mfg: Winchester **Manufacturer's code:** X123XC
Recoil energy in 8-lb. shotgun: 56.6 ft./lbs. **Recoil velocity in 8-lb. shotgun:** 22.3 ft./sec.

Distance in yards:	Muzzle	20	30	40	50	60	70
Velocity in fps:	1,292	892	769	672	593	525	467
Average pellet energy in ft-lbs:	7.26	3.46	2.57	1.96	1.53	1.20	.095
Time of flight in seconds:	0	.0568	.0931	.01349	.1825	.2363	.2969

Type of load: Field
Three-foot velocity: 1,200 ft./sec.
Hull: 3-inch plastic
Wad: Plastic
Shot: Copper-plated lead
Buffered: Yes
Test barrel length: 30 inch
Pellets will pierce skin up to 157 yards.

NO. 6 LEAD PELLETS—1⅞ OUNCES—422 PELLETS
Mfg: Estate Cartridge **Manufacturer's code:** HV12HMAG
Recoil energy in 8-lb. shotgun: 59.1 ft./lbs. **Recoil velocity in 8-lb. shotgun:** 21.8 ft./sec.

Distance in yards:	Muzzle	20	30	40	50	60	70
Velocity in fps:	1,314	903	778	679	598	530	471
Average pellet energy in ft-lbs:	7.51	3.54	2.63	2.00	1.55	1.22	.97
Time of flight in seconds:	0	.0560	.0919	.1333	.1804	.2337	.2938

Type of load: Field
Three-foot velocity: 1,220 ft./sec.
Hull: 3-inch plastic
Wad: Plastic
Shot: Hard lead
Buffered: Yes
Test barrel length: 30 inch
Pellets will pierce skin up to 143 yards.

NO. 6 LEAD PELLETS—2 OUNCES—450 PELLETS
Mfg: Winchester **Manufacturer's code:** X123MXCT
Recoil energy in 8-lb. shotgun: 54.4 ft./lbs. **Recoil velocity in 8-lb. shotgun:** 20.9 ft./sec.

Distance in yards:	Muzzle	20	30	40	50	60	70
Velocity in fps:	1,210	851	737	646	571	507	451
Average pellet energy in ft-lbs:	6.36	3.15	2.36	1.81	1.42	1.12	.88
Time of flight in seconds:	0	.0600	.0980	.1415	.1909	.2467	.3096

Type of load: Turkey
Three-foot velocity: 1,125 ft./sec.
Hull: 3-inch plastic
Wad: Plastic
Shot: Copper-plated lead
Buffered: Yes
Test barrel length: 30 inch
Pellets will pierce skin up to 139 yards.

NO. 6 LEAD PELLETS—2 OUNCES—450 PELLETS
Mfg: Federal Cartridge Co. **Manufacturer's code:** PT159/P159
Recoil energy in 8-lb. shotgun: 61.0 ft./lbs. **Recoil velocity in 8-lb. shotgun:** 22.1 ft./sec.

Distance in yards:	Muzzle	20	30	40	50	60	70
Velocity in fps:	1,265	878	759	664	585	519	462
Average pellet energy in ft-lbs:	6.95	3.35	2.50	1.91	1.9	1.17	.93
Time of flight in seconds:	0	.0578	.0947	.1370	.1852	.2396	.3009

Type of load: Turkey
Three-foot velocity: 1,175 ft./sec.
Hull: 3-inch plastic
Wad: Plastic
Shot: Copper-plated lead
Buffered: Yes
Test barrel length: 30 inch
Pellets will pierce skin up to 141 yards.

NO. 6 LEAD PELLETS—2 OUNCES—450 PELLETS
Mfg: Kent Cartridge America/Canada **Manufacturer's code:** K123TK56
Recoil energy in 8-lb. shotgun: 61.0 ft./lbs. **Recoil velocity in 8-lb. shotgun:** 22.1 ft./sec.

Distance in yards:	Muzzle	20	30	40	50	60	70
Velocity in fps:	1,265	878	759	664	585	519	462
Average pellet energy in ft-lbs:	6.95	3.35	2.50	1.91	1.9	1.17	.93
Time of flight in seconds:	0	.0578	.0947	.1370	.1852	.2396	.3009

Type of load: Turkey
Three-foot velocity: 1,175 ft./sec.
Hull: 3-inch plastic
Wad: Plastic
Shot: Lead
Buffered: No
Test barrel length: 30 inch
Pellets will pierce skin up to 141 yards.

NO. 6 LEAD PELLETS—2 OUNCES—450 PELLETS
Mfg: Remington Arms Co. **Manufacturer's code:** P12XHM
Recoil energy in 8-lb. shotgun: 61.0 ft./lbs. **Recoil velocity in 8-lb. shotgun:** 22.1 ft./sec.

Distance in yards:	Muzzle	20	30	40	50	60	70
Velocity in fps:	1,265	878	759	664	585	519	462
Average pellet energy in ft-lbs:	6.95	3.35	2.50	1.91	1.9	1.17	.93
Time of flight in seconds:	0	.0578	.0947	.1370	.1852	.2396	.3009

Type of load: Turkey
Three-foot velocity: 1,175 ft./sec.
Hull: 3-inch plastic
Wad: Plastic
Shot: Copper-plated lead
Buffered: Yes
Test barrel length: 30 inch
Pellets will pierce skin up to 141 yards.

NO. 6 LEAD PELLETS—2 OUNCES—450 PELLETS
Mfg: PMC (Eldorado Cartridge Corp.) **Manufacturer's code:** TL124/6
Recoil energy in 8-lb. shotgun: 64.4 ft./lbs. **Recoil velocity in 8-lb. shotgun:** 22.8 ft./sec.

Distance in yards:	Muzzle	20	30	40	50	60	70
Velocity in fps:	1,292	892	769	672	593	525	467
Average pellet energy in ft-lbs:	7.26	3.46	2.57	1.96	1.53	1.20	.095
Time of flight in seconds:	0	.0568	.0931	.01349	.1825	.2363	.2969

Type of load: Turkey
Three-foot velocity: 1,200 ft./sec.
Hull: 3-inch plastic
Wad: Plastic
Shot: Lead
Buffered: Yes
Test barrel length: 30 inch
Pellets will pierce skin up to 157 yards.

NO. 7½ LEAD PELLETS—2 OUNCES—700 PELLETS

Mfg: Federal Cartridge Co. **Manufacturer's code:** PT159
Recoil energy in 8-lb. shotgun: 61.0 ft./lbs. **Recoil velocity in 8-lb. shotgun:** 22.1 ft./sec.

Distance in yards:	Muzzle	20	30	40	50	60	70
Velocity in fps:	1,274	841	714	615	535	466	407
Average pellet energy in ft-lbs:	4.54	1.98	1.43	1.06	.80	.61	.46
Time of flight in seconds:	0	.0592	.0980	.1433	.1957	.2558	.3246

Type of load: Turkey
Three-foot velocity: 1,175 ft./sec.
Hull: 3-inch plastic
Wad: Plastic
Shot: Copper-plated lead
Buffered: Yes
Test barrel length: 30 inch
Pellets will pierce skin up to 122 yards.

This little guy has his mouth full of this South Dakota pheasant, but he's proud of making a good retrieve. The value of a good dog when we head afield cannot be emphasized enough.

NO. 2 LEAD PELLETS—2⅜ OUNCES—206 PELLETS
Mfg: Clever **Manufacturer's code:** Magnum 89
Recoil energy in 8-lb. shotgun: 68.9 ft./lbs. **Recoil velocity in 8-lb. shotgun:** 23.5 ft./sec.

Distance in yards:	Muzzle	20	30	40	50	60	70
Velocity in fps:	1,190	913	816	736	667	308	556
Average pellet energy in ft-lbs:	15.59	9.18	7.34	5.97	4.91	4.08	3.41
Time of flight in seconds:	0	.0581	.0929	.1316	.1745	.2216	.2731

Type of load: Field
Three-foot velocity: 1,125 ft./sec.
Hull: 3½-inch plastic
Wad: Plastic
Shot: Lead
Buffered: No
Test barrel length: 30 inch
Pellets will pierce skin up to 208 yards.

NO. 4 LEAD PELLETS—2 OUNCES—270 PELLETS
Mfg: Federal Cartridge Co. **Manufacturer's code:** PT139
Recoil energy in 8-lb. shotgun: 75.6 ft./lbs. **Recoil velocity in 8-lb. shotgun:** 24.7 ft./sec.

Distance in yards:	Muzzle	20	30	40	50	60	70
Velocity in fps:	1,363	1,049	851	753	672	604	545
Average pellet energy in ft-lbs:	13.32	6.81	5.20	4.07	3.24	2.62	2.13
Time of flight in seconds:	0	.0528	.0858	.1233	.1655	.2126	.2649

Type of load: Turkey
Three-foot velocity: 1,275 ft./sec.
Hull: 3½-inch plastic
Wad: Plastic
Shot: Copper-plated lead
Buffered: Yes
Test barrel length: 30 inch
Pellets will pierce skin up to 171 yards.

NO. 4 LEAD PELLETS—2 OUNCES—270 PELLETS
Mfg: Remington Arms Co. **Manufacturer's code:** PHV1235M
Recoil energy in 8-lb. shotgun: 79.6 ft./lbs. **Recoil velocity in 8-lb. shotgun:** 25.3 ft./sec.

Distance in yards:	Muzzle	20	30	40	50	60	70
Velocity in fps:	1,390	989	863	762	680	611	551
Average pellet energy in ft-lbs:	13.86	7.01	5.34	4.17	3.32	2.67	2.18
Time of flight in seconds:	0	.0519	.0844	.1215	.1632	.2098	.2615

Type of load: Turkey
Three-foot velocity: 1,300 ft./sec.
Hull: 3½-inch plastic
Wad: Plastic
Shot: Copper-plated lead
Buffered: Yes
Test barrel length: 30 inch
Pellets will pierce skin up to 172 yards.

NO. 4 LEAD PELLETS—2 OUNCES—270 PELLETS
Mfg: Winchester **Manufacturer's code:** STH1235
Recoil energy in 8-lb. shotgun: 79.6 ft./lbs. **Recoil velocity in 8-lb. shotgun:** 25.3 ft./sec.

Distance in yards:	Muzzle	20	30	40	50	60	70
Velocity in fps:	1,390	989	863	762	680	611	551
Average pellet energy in ft-lbs:	13.86	7.01	5.34	4.17	3.32	2.67	2.18
Time of flight in seconds:	0	.0519	.0844	.1215	.1632	.2098	.2615

Type of load: Turkey
Three-foot velocity: 1,300 ft./sec.
Hull: 3½-inch plastic
Wad: Plastic
Shot: Copper-plated lead
Buffered: Yes
Test barrel length: 30 inch
Pellets will pierce skin up to 172 yards.

NO. 4 LEAD PELLETS—2¼ OUNCES—304 PELLETS
Mfg: Federal Cartridge Co. **Manufacturer's code:** PT135
Recoil energy in 8-lb. shotgun: 72.9 ft./lbs. **Recoil velocity in 8-lb. shotgun:** 24.2 ft./sec.

Distance in yards:	Muzzle	20	30	40	50	60	70
Velocity in fps:	1,227	901	794	706	633	570	515
Average pellet energy in ft-lbs:	10.79	5.83	4.52	3.58	2.87	2.33	1.90
Time of flight in seconds:	0	.0577	.0933	.1334	.1783	.2283	.2837

Type of load: Turkey
Three-foot velocity: 1,150 ft./sec.
Hull: 3½-inch plastic
Wad: Plastic
Shot: Copper-plated lead
Buffered: Yes
Test barrel length: 30 inch
Pellets will pierce skin up to 166 yards.

NO. 4 LEAD PELLETS—2¼ OUNCES—304 PELLETS
Mfg: Kent Cartridge America/Canada **Manufacturer's code:** K1235TK63
Recoil energy in 8-lb. shotgun: 72.9 ft./lbs. **Recoil velocity in 8-lb. shotgun:** 24.2 ft./sec.

Distance in yards:	Muzzle	20	30	40	50	60	70
Velocity in fps:	1,227	901	794	706	633	570	515
Average pellet energy in ft-lbs:	10.79	5.83	4.52	3.58	2.87	2.33	1.90
Time of flight in seconds:	0	.0577	.0933	.1334	.1783	.2283	.2837

Type of load: Turkey
Three-foot velocity: 1,150 ft./sec.
Hull: 3½-inch plastic
Wad: Plastic
Shot: Lead
Buffered: No
Test barrel length: 30 inch
Pellets will pierce skin up to 166 yards.

NO. 4 LEAD PELLETS—2¼ OUNCES—304 PELLETS
Mfg: Remington Arms Co. **Manufacturer's code:** P1235M
Recoil energy in 8-lb. shotgun: 72.9 ft./lbs. **Recoil velocity in 8-lb. shotgun:** 24.2 ft./sec.

Distance in yards:	Muzzle	20	30	40	50	60	70
Velocity in fps:	1,227	901	794	706	633	570	515
Average pellet energy in ft-lbs:	10.79	5.83	4.52	3.58	2.87	2.33	1.90
Time of flight in seconds:	0	.0577	.0933	.1334	.1783	.2283	.2837

Type of load: Turkey
Three-foot velocity: 1,150 ft./sec.
Hull: 3½-inch plastic
Wad: Plastic
Shot: Copper-plated lead
Buffered: Yes
Test barrel length: 30 inch
Pellets will pierce skin up to 166 yards.

NO. 4 LEAD PELLETS—2¼ OUNCES—304 PELLETS
Mfg: Winchester **Manufacturer's code:** XXT12L
Recoil energy in 8-lb. shotgun: 72.9 ft./lbs. **Recoil velocity in 8-lb. shotgun:** 24.2 ft./sec.

Distance in yards:	Muzzle	20	30	40	50	60	70
Velocity in fps:	1,227	901	794	706	633	570	515
Average pellet energy in ft-lbs:	10.79	5.83	4.52	3.58	2.87	2.33	1.90
Time of flight in seconds:	0	.0577	.0933	.1334	.1783	.2283	.2837

Type of load: Turkey
Three-foot velocity: 1,150 ft./sec.
Hull: 3½-inch plastic
Wad: Plastic
Shot: Copper-plated lead
Buffered: Yes
Test barrel length: 30 inch
Pellets will pierce skin up to 166 yards.

NO. 4 LEAD PELLETS—2⅜ OUNCES—321 PELLETS
Mfg: Clever **Manufacturer's code:** Magnum 89
Recoil energy in 8-lb. shotgun: 68.9 ft./lbs. **Recoil velocity in 8-lb. shotgun:** 23.5 ft./sec.

Distance in yards:	Muzzle	20	30	40	50	60	70
Velocity in fps:	1,199	887	782	696	624	563	509
Average pellet energy in ft-lbs:	10.32	5.64	4.38	3.48	2.80	2.27	1.86
Time of flight in seconds:	0	.0588	.0949	.1356	.1812	.2318	.2879

Type of load: Field
Three-foot velocity: 1,125 ft./sec.
Hull: 3½-inch plastic
Wad: Plastic
Shot: Lead
Buffered: No
Test barrel length: 30 inch
Pellets will pierce skin up to 164 yards.

NO. 5 LEAD PELLETS—2 OUNCES—340 PELLETS
Mfg: Federal Cartridge Co. **Manufacturer's code:** PT139
Recoil energy in 8-lb. shotgun: 75.6 ft./lbs. **Recoil velocity in 8-lb. shotgun:** 24.7 ft./sec.

Distance in yards:	Muzzle	20	30	40	50	60	70
Velocity in fps:	1,369	955	827	727	644	575	515
Average pellet energy in ft-lbs:	10.57	5.14	3.86	2.98	2.34	1.87	1.50
Time of flight in seconds:	0	.0533	.0871	.1259	.1698	.2191	.2743

Type of load: Turkey
Three-foot velocity: 1,275 ft./sec.
Hull: 3½-inch plastic
Wad: Plastic
Shot: Copper-plated lead
Buffered: Yes
Test barrel length: 30 inch
Pellets will pierce skin up to 158 yards.

NO. 5 LEAD PELLETS—2 OUNCES—340 PELLETS
Mfg: Winchester **Manufacturer's code:** STH1235
Recoil energy in 8-lb. shotgun: 79.6 ft./lbs. **Recoil velocity in 8-lb. shotgun:** 25.3 ft./sec.

Distance in yards:	Muzzle	20	30	40	50	60	70
Velocity in fps:	1,396	969	838	735	651	581	521
Average pellet energy in ft-lbs:	11.00	5.29	3.96	3.05	2.39	1.90	1.53
Time of flight in seconds:	0	.0524	.0858	.1241	.1675	.2163	.2708

Type of load: Turkey
Three-foot velocity: 1,300 ft./sec.
Hull: 3½-inch plastic
Wad: Plastic
Shot: Copper-plated lead
Buffered: Yes
Test barrel length: 30 inch
Pellets will pierce skin up to 159 yards.

NO. 5 LEAD PELLETS—2¼ OUNCES—382 PELLETS
Mfg: Federal Cartridge Co. **Manufacturer's code:** PT135
Recoil energy in 8-lb. shotgun: 72.9 ft./lbs. **Recoil velocity in 8-lb. shotgun:** 24.2 ft./sec.

Distance in yards:	Muzzle	20	30	40	50	60	70
Velocity in fps:	1,232	885	772	682	607	543	487
Average pellet energy in ft-lbs:	8.56	4.41	3.37	2.62	2.08	1.66	1.34
Time of flight in seconds:	0	.0583	.0946	.2.62	.1827	.2350	.2933

Type of load: Turkey
Three-foot velocity: 1,150 ft./sec.
Hull: 3½-inch plastic
Wad: Plastic
Shot: Copper-plated lead
Buffered: Yes
Test barrel length: 30 inch
Pellets will pierce skin up to 153 yards.

NO. 5 LEAD PELLETS—2¼ OUNCES—382 PELLETS
Mfg: Kent Cartridge America/Canada **Manufacturer's code:** K1235TK63
Recoil energy in 8-lb. shotgun: 72.9 ft./lbs. **Recoil velocity in 8-lb. shotgun:** 24.2 ft./sec.

Distance in yards:	Muzzle	20	30	40	50	60	70
Velocity in fps:	1,232	885	772	682	607	543	487
Average pellet energy in ft-lbs:	8.56	4.41	3.37	2.62	2.08	1.66	1.34
Time of flight in seconds:	0	.0583	.0946	.2.62	.1827	.2350	.2933

Type of load: Turkey
Three-foot velocity: 1,150 ft./sec.
Hull: 3½-inch plastic
Wad: Plastic
Shot: Lead
Buffered: No
Test barrel length: 30 inch
Pellets will pierce skin up to 153 yards.

NO. 5 LEAD PELLETS—2¼ OUNCES—382 PELLETS
Mfg: Winchester **Manufacturer's code:** XXT12L
Recoil energy in 8-lb. shotgun: 72.9 ft./lbs. **Recoil velocity in 8-lb. shotgun:** 24.2 ft./sec.

Distance in yards:	Muzzle	20	30	40	50	60	70
Velocity in fps:	1,232	885	772	682	607	543	487
Average pellet energy in ft-lbs:	8.56	4.41	3.37	2.62	2.08	1.66	1.34
Time of flight in seconds:	0	.0583	.0946	.2.62	.1827	.2350	.2933

Type of load: Turkey
Three-foot velocity: 1,150 ft./sec.
Hull: 3½-inch plastic
Wad: Plastic
Shot: Copper-plated lead
Buffered: Yes
Test barrel length: 30 inch
Pellets will pierce skin up to 153 yards.

NO. 6 LEAD PELLETS—2 OUNCES—450 PELLETS
Mfg: Federal Cartridge Co. **Manufacturer's code:** PT139
Recoil energy in 8-lb. shotgun: 75.6 ft./lbs. **Recoil velocity in 8-lb. shotgun:** 24.7 ft./sec.

Distance in yards:	Muzzle	20	30	40	50	60	70
Velocity in fps:	1,375	932	800	697	613	543	482
Average pellet energy in ft-lbs:	8.22	3.77	2.78	2.11	1.63	1.28	1.01
Time of flight in seconds:	0	.0540	.0888	.1290	.1750	.2271	.2858

Type of load: Turkey
Three-foot velocity: 1,275 ft./sec.
Hull: 3½-inch plastic
Wad: Plastic
Shot: Copper-plated lead
Buffered: Yes
Test barrel length: 30 inch
Pellets will pierce skin up to 145 yards.

NO. 6 LEAD PELLETS—2 OUNCES—450 PELLETS
Mfg: Remington Arms Co. **Manufacturer's code:** PHV1235M
Recoil energy in 8-lb. shotgun: 79.6 ft./lbs. **Recoil velocity in 8-lb. shotgun:** 25.3 ft./sec.

Distance in yards:	Muzzle	20	30	40	50	60	70
Velocity in fps:	1,403	945	810	705	620	548	487
Average pellet energy in ft-lbs:	8.55	3.88	2.85	2.16	1.67	1.31	1.03
Time of flight in seconds:	0	.0531	.0875	.1272	.1727	.2242	.2723

Type of load: Turkey
Three-foot velocity: 1,300 ft./sec.
Hull: 3½-inch plastic
Wad: Plastic
Shot: Copper-plated lead
Buffered: Yes
Test barrel length: 30 inch
Pellets will pierce skin up to 146 yards.

NO. 6 LEAD PELLETS—2 OUNCES—450 PELLETS
Mfg: Winchester **Manufacturer's code:** STH1235
Recoil energy in 8-lb. shotgun: 79.6 ft./lbs. **Recoil velocity in 8-lb. shotgun:** 25.3 ft./sec.

Distance in yards:	Muzzle	20	30	40	50	60	70
Velocity in fps:	1,403	945	810	705	620	548	487
Average pellet energy in ft-lbs:	8.55	3.88	2.85	2.16	1.67	1.31	1.03
Time of flight in seconds:	0	.0531	.0875	.1272	.1727	.2242	.2723

Type of load: Turkey
Three-foot velocity: 1,300 ft./sec.
Hull: 3½-inch plastic
Wad: Plastic
Shot: Copper-plated lead
Buffered: Yes
Test barrel length: 30 inch
Pellets will pierce skin up to 146 yards.

NO. 6 LEAD PELLETS—2¼ OUNCES—506 PELLETS
Mfg: Kent Cartridge America/Canada **Manufacturer's code:** K1235TK63
Recoil energy in 8-lb. shotgun: 72.9 ft./lbs. **Recoil velocity in 8-lb. shotgun:** 24.2 ft./sec.

Distance in yards:	Muzzle	20	30	40	50	60	70
Velocity in fps:	1,237	865	748	655	578	513	456
Average pellet energy in ft-lbs:	6.65	3.25	2.43	1.86	1.45	1.14	.90
Time of flight in seconds:	0	.0589	.0963	.1392	.1880	.2431	.3051

Type of load: Turkey
Three-foot velocity: 1,150 ft./sec.
Hull: 3½-inch plastic
Wad: Plastic
Shot: Lead
Buffered: No
Test barrel length: 30 inch
Pellets will pierce skin up to 140 yards.

NO. 6 LEAD PELLETS—2¼ OUNCES—506 PELLETS
Mfg: Federal Cartridge Co. **Manufacturer's code:** PT135
Recoil energy in 8-lb. shotgun: 72.9 ft./lbs. **Recoil velocity in 8-lb. shotgun:** 24.2 ft./sec.

Distance in yards:	Muzzle	20	30	40	50	60	70
Velocity in fps:	1,237	865	748	655	578	513	456
Average pellet energy in ft-lbs:	6.65	3.25	2.43	1.86	1.45	1.14	.90
Time of flight in seconds:	0	.0589	.0963	.1392	.1880	.2431	.3051

Type of load: Turkey
Three-foot velocity: 1,150 ft./sec.
Hull: 3½-inch plastic
Wad: Plastic
Shot: Copper-plated lead
Buffered: Yes
Test barrel length: 30 inch
Pellets will pierce skin up to 140 yards.

NO. 6 LEAD PELLETS—2¼ OUNCES—506 PELLETS
Mfg: Remington Arms Co. **Manufacturer's code:** P1235M
Recoil energy in 8-lb. shotgun: 72.9 ft./lbs. **Recoil velocity in 8-lb. shotgun:** 24.2 ft./sec.

Distance in yards:	Muzzle	20	30	40	50	60	70
Velocity in fps:	1,237	865	748	655	578	513	456
Average pellet energy in ft-lbs:	6.65	3.25	2.43	1.86	1.45	1.14	.90
Time of flight in seconds:	0	.0589	.0963	.1392	.1880	.2431	.3051

Type of load: Turkey
Three-foot velocity: 1,150 ft./sec.
Hull: 3½-inch plastic
Wad: Plastic
Shot: Copper-plated lead
Buffered: Yes
Test barrel length: 30 inch
Pellets will pierce skin up to 140 yards.

NO. 6 LEAD PELLETS—2¼ OUNCES—506 PELLETS
Mfg: Winchester **Manufacturer's code:** XXT12L
Recoil energy in 8-lb. shotgun: 72.9 ft./lbs. **Recoil velocity in 8-lb. shotgun:** 24.2 ft./sec.

Distance in yards:	Muzzle	20	30	40	50	60	70
Velocity in fps:	1,237	865	748	655	578	513	456
Average pellet energy in ft-lbs:	6.65	3.25	2.43	1.86	1.45	1.14	.90
Time of flight in seconds:	0	.0589	.0963	.1392	.1880	.2431	.3051

Type of load: Turkey
Three-foot velocity: 1,150 ft./sec.
Hull: 3½-inch plastic
Wad: Plastic
Shot: Copper-plated lead
Buffered: Yes
Test barrel length: 30 inch
Pellets will pierce skin up to 140 yards.

NO. 6 LEAD PELLETS—2⅜ OUNCES—534 PELLETS

Mfg: Clever **Manufacturer's code:** Magnum 89
Recoil energy in 8-lb. shotgun: 68.9 ft./lbs. **Recoil velocity in 8-lb. shotgun:** 23.5 ft./sec.

Distance in yards:	Muzzle	20	30	40	50	60	70
Velocity in fps:	1,210	851	737	646	571	507	451
Average pellet energy in ft-lbs:	6.36	3.15	2.36	1.81	1.42	1.12	.88
Time of flight in seconds:	0	.0600	.0980	.1415	.1909	.2467	.3096

Type of load: Field & Turkey
Three-foot velocity: 1,125 ft./sec.
Hull: 3½-inch plastic
Wad: Plastic
Shot: Lead
Buffered: No
Test barrel length: 30 inch
Pellets will pierce skin up to 139 yards.

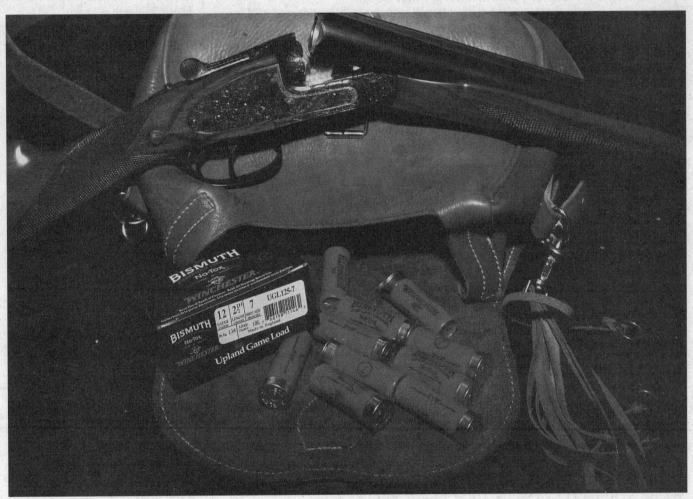

Although the AyA 53 is chambered for 2¾-inch shells, these 2½-inch bismuth loads are comfortable to shoot and pack plenty of wallop for doves, quail, and even pen-reared pheasants.

NO. T STEEL PELLETS—1¼ OUNCES—65 PELLETS

Mfg: Federal Cartridge Company **Manufacturer's code:** W148
Recoil energy in 8-lb. shotgun: 29.5 ft./lbs. **Recoil velocity in 8-lb. shotgun:** 15.4 ft./sec.

Distance in yards:	Muzzle	20	30	40	50	60	70
Velocity in fps:	1,331	980	865	772	694	628	751
Average pellet energy in ft-lbs:	32.76	17.77	13.84	11.02	8.92	7.30	6.03
Time of flight in seconds:	0	.0531	.0858	.1225	.1636	.2090	.2592

Type of load: Nontoxic
Three-foot velocity: 1,275 ft./sec.
Hull: 2¾-inch plastic
Wad: Plastic
Shot: Steel
Buffered: No
Test barrel length: 30 inch
Pellets will pierce skin up to 185 yards.

NO. T STEEL PELLETS—1¼ OUNCES—65 PELLETS

Mfg: Remington Arms Co. **Manufacturer's code:** NS12S
Recoil energy in 8-lb. shotgun: 29.5 ft./lbs. **Recoil velocity in 8-lb. shotgun:** 15.4 ft./sec.

Distance in yards:	Muzzle	20	30	40	50	60	70
Velocity in fps:	1,331	980	865	772	694	628	751
Average pellet energy in ft-lbs:	32.76	17.77	13.84	11.02	8.92	7.30	6.03
Time of flight in seconds:	0	.0531	.0858	.1225	.1636	.2090	.2592

Type of load: Nontoxic
Three-foot velocity: 1,275 ft./sec.
Hull: 2¾-inch plastic
Wad: Plastic
Shot: Zinc-galvanized steel
Buffered: No
Test barrel length: 30 inch
Pellets will pierce skin up to 185 yards.

NO. BBB STEEL PELLETS—1¼ OUNCES—77 PELLETS

Mfg: Federal Cartridge Company **Manufacturer's code:** W148
Recoil energy in 8-lb. shotgun: 29.5 ft./lbs. **Recoil velocity in 8-lb. shotgun:** 15.4 ft./sec.

Distance in yards:	Muzzle	20	30	40	50	60	70
Velocity in fps:	1,335	969	851	756	677	610	552
Average pellet energy in ft-lbs:	28.25	14.88	11.48	9.06	7.27	5.91	4.84
Time of flight in seconds:	0	.0534	0.865	.1240	.1660	.2127	.2644

Type of load: Nontoxic
Three-foot velocity: 1,275 ft./sec.
Hull: 2¾-inch plastic
Wad: Plastic
Shot: Steel
Buffered: No
Test barrel length: 30 inch
Pellets will pierce skin up to 176 yards.

NO. BBB STEEL PELLETS—1¼ OUNCES—77 PELLETS

Mfg: Remington Arms Co. **Manufacturer's code:** NS12S
Recoil energy in 8-lb. shotgun: 29.5 ft./lbs. **Recoil velocity in 8-lb. shotgun:** 15.4 ft./sec.

Distance in yards:	Muzzle	20	30	40	50	60	70
Velocity in fps:	1,335	969	851	756	677	610	552
Average pellet energy in ft-lbs:	28.25	14.88	11.48	9.06	7.27	5.91	4.84
Time of flight in seconds:	0	.0534	0.865	.1240	.1660	.2127	.2644

Type of load: Nontoxic
Three-foot velocity: 1,275 ft./sec.
Hull: 2¾-inch plastic
Wad: Plastic
Shot: Zinc-galvanized steel
Buffered: No
Test barrel length: 30 inch
Pellets will pierce skin up to 176 yards.

NO. BBB STEEL PELLETS—1¼ OUNCES—77 PELLETS

Mfg: Estate Cartridge **Manufacturer's code:** HVST12SM
Recoil energy in 8-lb. shotgun: 37.9 ft./lbs. **Recoil velocity in 8-lb. shotgun:** 17.5 ft./sec.

Distance in yards:	Muzzle	20	30	40	50	60	70
Velocity in fps:	1,469	1,041	907	8014	715	643	581
Average pellet energy in ft-lbs:	34.20	17.18	1.04	10.18	8.11	6.55	5.35
Time of flight in seconds:	0	.0492	.0801	.1154	.1551	.1993	.2485

Type of load: Nontoxic
Three-foot velocity: 1,400 ft./sec.
Hull: 2¾-inch plastic
Wad: Plastic
Shot: Steel
Buffered: No
Test barrel length: 30 inch
Pellets will pierce skin up to 181 yards.

NO. BB STEEL PELLETS—1¹⁄₁₆ OUNCES—77 PELLETS

Mfg: Kent Cartridge America/Canada **Manufacturer's code:** K122ST30
Recoil energy in 8-lb. shotgun: 40.5 ft./lbs. **Recoil velocity in 8-lb. shotgun:** 18.1 ft./sec.

Distance in yards:	Muzzle	20	30	40	50	60	70
Velocity in fps:	1,635	1,112	953	833	737	657	590
Average pellet energy in ft-lbs:	36.06	16.68	12.26	9.35	7.32	5.82	4.69
Time of flight in seconds:	0	.0451	.0743	.1080	.1464	.1896	.2378

Type of load: Field
Three-foot velocity: 1,550 ft./sec.
Hull: 2¾-inch plastic
Wad: Plastic
Shot: Steel
Buffered: No
Test barrel length: 30 inch
Pellets will pierce skin up to 177 yards.

NO. BB STEEL PELLETS—1⅛ OUNCES—81 PELLETS

Mfg: Dionisi **Manufacturer's code:** D 12 ST
Recoil energy in 8-lb. shotgun: 27.9 ft./lbs. **Recoil velocity in 8-lb. shotgun:** 15.0 ft./sec.

Distance in yards:	Muzzle	20	30	40	50	60	70
Velocity in fps:	1,420	998	868	765	681	610	549
Average pellet energy in ft-lbs:	27.17	13.44	10.15	7.89	6.25	5.01	4.07
Time of flight in seconds:	0	.0511	.0834	.1203	.1619	.2085	.2604

Type of load: Nontoxic
Three-foot velocity: 1,350 ft./sec.
Hull: 2¾-inch plastic
Wad: Plastic
Shot: Steel
Buffered: No
Test barrel length: 30 inch
Pellets will pierce skin up to 170 yards.

NO. BB STEEL PELLETS—1⅛ OUNCES—81 PELLETS
Mfg: Federal Cartridge Co. **Manufacturer's code:** PW147
Recoil energy in 8-lb. shotgun: 29.3 ft./lbs. **Recoil velocity in 8-lb. shotgun:** 15.3 ft./sec.

Distance in yards:	Muzzle	20	30	40	50	60	70
Velocity in fps:	1,446	1,012	879	774	688	616	554
Average pellet energy in ft-lbs:	28.21	13.82	10.41	8.07	6.38	5.12	4.14
Time of flight in seconds:	0	.0503	.0822	.1186	.1598	.2059	.2573

Type of load: Nontoxic
Three-foot velocity: 1,375 ft./sec.
Hull: 2¾-inch plastic
Wad: Plastic
Shot: Steel
Buffered: No
Test barrel length: 30 inch
Pellets will pierce skin up to 171 yards.

NO. BB STEEL PELLETS—1⅛ OUNCES—81 PELLETS
Mfg: Fiocchi **Manufacturer's code:** 12S118
Recoil energy in 8-lb. shotgun: 29.3 ft./lbs. **Recoil velocity in 8-lb. shotgun:** 15.3 ft./sec.

Distance in yards:	Muzzle	20	30	40	50	60	70
Velocity in fps:	1,446	1,012	879	774	688	616	554
Average pellet energy in ft-lbs:	28.21	13.82	10.41	8.07	6.38	5.12	4.14
Time of flight in seconds:	0	.0503	.0822	.1186	.1598	.2059	.2573

Type of load: Nontoxic
Three-foot velocity: 1,375 ft./sec.
Hull: 2¾-inch plastic
Wad: Plastic
Shot: Steel
Buffered: No
Test barrel length: 30 inch
Pellets will pierce skin up to 171 yards.

NO. BB STEEL PELLETS—1⅛ OUNCES—81 PELLETS
Mfg: PMC (Eldorado Cartridge Corp.) **Manufacturer's code:** SS12
Recoil energy in 8-lb. shotgun: 29.3 ft./lbs. **Recoil velocity in 8-lb. shotgun:** 15.3 ft./sec.

Distance in yards:	Muzzle	20	30	40	50	60	70
Velocity in fps:	1,446	1,012	879	774	688	616	554
Average pellet energy in ft-lbs:	28.21	13.82	10.41	8.07	6.38	5.12	4.14
Time of flight in seconds:	0	.0503	.0822	.1186	.1598	.2059	.2573

Type of load: Nontoxic
Three-foot velocity: 1,375 ft./sec.
Hull: 2¾-inch plastic
Wad: Plastic
Shot: Steel
Buffered: No
Test barrel length: 30 inch
Pellets will pierce skin up to 171 yards.

NO. BB STEEL PELLETS—1⅛ OUNCES—81 PELLETS
Mfg: Remington Arms Co. **Manufacturer's code:** SSP12
Recoil energy in 8-lb. shotgun: 29.3 ft./lbs. **Recoil velocity in 8-lb. shotgun:** 15.3 ft./sec.

Distance in yards:	Muzzle	20	30	40	50	60	70
Velocity in fps:	1,446	1,012	879	774	688	616	554
Average pellet energy in ft-lbs:	28.21	13.82	10.41	8.07	6.38	5.12	4.14
Time of flight in seconds:	0	.0503	.0822	.1186	.1598	.2059	.2573

Type of load: Nontoxic
Three-foot velocity: 1,375 ft./sec.
Hull: 2¾-inch plastic
Wad: Plastic
Shot: Zinc-galvanized steel
Buffered: No
Test barrel length: 30 inch
Pellets will pierce skin up to 171 yards.

NO. BB STEEL PELLETS—1⅛ OUNCES—81 PELLETS
Mfg: Estate Cartridge **Manufacturer's code:** HVST12
Recoil energy in 8-lb. shotgun: 30.7 ft./lbs. **Recoil velocity in 8-lb. shotgun:** 15.7 ft./sec.

Distance in yards:	Muzzle	20	30	40	50	60	70
Velocity in fps:	1,473	1,026	889	782	695	622	560
Average pellet energy in ft-lbs:	29.27	14.21	10.66	8.25	6.51	5.22	4.22
Time of flight in seconds:	0	.0495	.0810	.1170	.1577	.2034	.2543

Type of load: Nontoxic
Three-foot velocity: 1,400 ft./sec.
Hull: 2¾-inch plastic
Wad: Plastic
Shot: Steel
Buffered: No
Test barrel length: 30 inch
Pellets will pierce skin up to 172 yards.

NO. BB STEEL PELLETS—1⅛ OUNCES—81 PELLETS
Mfg: Kent Cartridge America/Canada **Manufacturer's code:** K122ST32
Recoil energy in 8-lb. shotgun: 30.7 ft./lbs. **Recoil velocity in 8-lb. shotgun:** 15.7 ft./sec.

Distance in yards:	Muzzle	20	30	40	50	60	70
Velocity in fps:	1,473	1,026	889	782	695	622	560
Average pellet energy in ft-lbs:	29.27	14.21	10.66	8.25	6.51	5.22	4.22
Time of flight in seconds:	0	.0495	.0810	.1170	.1577	.2034	.2543

Type of load: Field
Three-foot velocity: 1,400 ft./sec.
Hull: 2¾-inch plastic
Wad: Plastic
Shot: Steel
Buffered: No
Test barrel length: 30 inch
Pellets will pierce skin up to 172 yards.

NO. BB STEEL PELLETS—1⅛ OUNCES—81 PELLETS
Mfg: Federal Cartridge Company **Manufacturer's code:** W144
Recoil energy in 8-lb. shotgun: 32.2 ft./lbs. **Recoil velocity in 8-lb. shotgun:** 16.1 ft./sec.

Distance in yards:	Muzzle	20	30	40	50	60	70
Velocity in fps:	1,500	1,041	900	791	702	628	565
Average pellet energy in ft-lbs:	30.35	14.60	10.92	8.43	6.64	5.32	4.30
Time of flight in seconds:	0	.0487	.0798	.1154	.1557	.2010	.2514

Type of load: Nontoxic
Three-foot velocity: 1,425 ft./sec.
Hull: 2¾-inch plastic
Wad: Plastic
Shot: Steel
Buffered: No
Test barrel length: 30 inch
Pellets will pierce skin up to 173 yards.

NO. BB STEEL PELLETS—1¼ OUNCES—90 PELLETS
Mfg: Federal Cartridge Company **Manufacturer's code:** PWT148/W148
Recoil energy in 8-lb. shotgun: 29.5 ft./lbs. **Recoil velocity in 8-lb. shotgun:** 15.4 ft./sec.

Distance in yards:	Muzzle	20	30	40	50	60	70
Velocity in fps:	1,339	956	835	739	659	591	533
Average pellet energy in ft-lbs:	24.17	12.33	9.41	7.35	5.85	4.71	3.83
Time of flight in seconds:	0	.0538	.0874	.1256	.1687	.2168	.2703

Type of load: Nontoxic
Three-foot velocity: 1,275 ft./sec.
Hull: 2¾-inch plastic
Wad: Plastic
Shot: Steel
Buffered: No
Test barrel length: 30 inch
Pellets will pierce skin up to 167 yards.

NO. BB STEEL PELLETS—1¼ OUNCES—90 PELLETS
Mfg: Kent Cartridge America/Canada **Manufacturer's code:** K122ST36
Recoil energy in 8-lb. shotgun: 29.5 ft./lbs. **Recoil velocity in 8-lb. shotgun:** 15.4 ft./sec.

Distance in yards:	Muzzle	20	30	40	50	60	70
Velocity in fps:	1,339	956	835	739	659	591	533
Average pellet energy in ft-lbs:	24.17	12.33	9.41	7.35	5.85	4.71	3.83
Time of flight in seconds:	0	.0538	.0874	.1256	.1687	.2168	.2703

Type of load: Field
Three-foot velocity: 1,275 ft./sec.
Hull: 2¾-inch plastic
Wad: Plastic
Shot: Steel
Buffered: No
Test barrel length: 30 inch
Pellets will pierce skin up to 167 yards.

NO. BB STEEL PELLETS—1¼ OUNCES—90 PELLETS
Mfg: Remington Arms Co. **Manufacturer's code:** NS12S
Recoil energy in 8-lb. shotgun: 29.5 ft./lbs. **Recoil velocity in 8-lb. shotgun:** 15.4 ft./sec.

Distance in yards:	Muzzle	20	30	40	50	60	70
Velocity in fps:	1,339	956	835	739	659	591	533
Average pellet energy in ft-lbs:	24.17	12.33	9.41	7.35	5.85	4.71	3.83
Time of flight in seconds:	0	.0538	.0874	.1256	.1687	.2168	.2703

Type of load: Nontoxic
Three-foot velocity: 1,275 ft./sec.
Hull: 2¾-inch plastic
Wad: Plastic
Shot: Zinc-galvanized steel
Buffered: No
Test barrel length: 30 inch
Pellets will pierce skin up to 167 yards.

NO. BB STEEL PELLETS—1¼ OUNCES—90 PELLETS
Mfg: Winchester **Manufacturer's code:** XSM12
Recoil energy in 8-lb. shotgun: 29.5 ft./lbs. **Recoil velocity in 8-lb. shotgun:** 15.4 ft./sec.

Distance in yards:	Muzzle	20	30	40	50	60	70
Velocity in fps:	1,339	956	835	739	659	591	533
Average pellet energy in ft-lbs:	24.17	12.33	9.41	7.35	5.85	4.71	3.83
Time of flight in seconds:	0	.0538	.0874	.1256	.1687	.2168	.2703

Type of load: Nontoxic
Three-foot velocity: 1,275 ft./sec.
Hull: 2¾-inch plastic
Wad: Two-piece plastic
Shot: Steel
Buffered: No
Test barrel length: 30 inch
Pellets will pierce skin up to 167 yards.

NO. BB STEEL PELLETS—1¼ OUNCES—90 PELLETS
Mfg: Dionisi **Manufacturer's code:** D 12 STX
Recoil energy in 8-lb. shotgun: 33.0 ft./lbs. **Recoil velocity in 8-lb. shotgun:** 16.3 ft./sec.

Distance in yards:	Muzzle	20	30	40	50	60	70
Velocity in fps:	1,398	987	859	758	675	605	545
Average pellet energy in ft-lbs:	26.35	13.14	9.95	7.75	6.14	4.93	4.00
Time of flight in seconds:	0	.0518	.0844	.1217	.1637	.2107	.2630

Type of load: Nontoxic
Three-foot velocity: 1,330 ft./sec.
Hull: 2¾-inch plastic
Wad: Plastic
Shot: Steel
Buffered: No
Test barrel length: 30 inch
Pellets will pierce skin up to 169 yards.

NO. BB STEEL PELLETS—1¼ OUNCES—90 PELLETS
Mfg: Estate Cartridge **Manufacturer's code:** HVST12SM
Recoil energy in 8-lb. shotgun: 37.9 ft./lbs. **Recoil velocity in 8-lb. shotgun:** 17.5 ft./sec.

Distance in yards:	Muzzle	20	30	40	50	60	70
Velocity in fps:	1,473	1,026	889	782	695	622	560
Average pellet energy in ft-lbs:	29.27	14.21	10.66	8.25	6.51	5.22	4.22
Time of flight in seconds:	0	.0495	.0810	.1170	.1577	.2034	.2543

Type of load: Nontoxic
Three-foot velocity: 1,400 ft./sec.
Hull: 2¾-inch plastic
Wad: Plastic
Shot: Steel
Buffered: No
Test barrel length: 30 inch
Pellets will pierce skin up to 172 yards.

NO. 1 STEEL PELLETS—1¹/₁₆ OUNCES—109 PELLETS
Mfg: Kent Cartridge America/Canada **Manufacturer's code:** K122ST30
Recoil energy in 8-lb. shotgun: 40.5 ft./lbs. **Recoil velocity in 8-lb. shotgun:** 18.1 ft./sec.

Distance in yards:	Muzzle	20	30	40	50	60	70
Velocity in fps:	1,647	1,073	909	786	688	608	540
Average pellet energy in ft-lbs:	25.68	10.91	7.82	5.84	4.48	3.50	2.76
Time of flight in seconds:	0	.0459	.0764	.1120	.1529	.1993	.2417

Type of load: Field
Three-foot velocity: 1,550 ft./sec.
Hull: 2¾-inch plastic
Wad: Plastic
Shot: Steel
Buffered: No
Test barrel length: 30 inch
Pellets will pierce skin up to 157 yards.

NO. 1 STEEL PELLETS—1⅛ OUNCES—116 PELLETS
Mfg: Fiocchi **Manufacturer's code:** 12S118
Recoil energy in 8-lb. shotgun: 29.3 ft./lbs. **Recoil velocity in 8-lb. shotgun:** 15.3 ft./sec.

Distance in yards:	Muzzle	20	30	40	50	60	70
Velocity in fps:	1,456	980	840	731	644	571	509
Average pellet energy in ft-lbs:	20.08	9.10	6.68	5.07	3.93	3.09	2.45
Time of flight in seconds:	0	.0511	.0843	.1226	.1664	.2159	.2717

Type of load: Nontoxic
Three-foot velocity: 1,375 ft./sec.
Hull: 2¾-inch plastic
Wad: Plastic
Shot: Steel
Buffered: No
Test barrel length: 30 inch
Pellets will pierce skin up to 152 yards.

NO. 1 STEEL PELLETS—1⅛ OUNCES—116 PELLETS
Mfg: Remington Arms Co. **Manufacturer's code:** SSP12
Recoil energy in 8-lb. shotgun: 29.3 ft./lbs. **Recoil velocity in 8-lb. shotgun:** 15.3 ft./sec.

Distance in yards:	Muzzle	20	30	40	50	60	70
Velocity in fps:	1,456	980	840	731	644	571	509
Average pellet energy in ft-lbs:	20.08	9.10	6.68	5.07	3.93	3.09	2.45
Time of flight in seconds:	0	.0511	.0843	.1226	.1664	.2159	.2717

Type of load: Nontoxic
Three-foot velocity: 1,375 ft./sec.
Hull: 2¾-inch plastic
Wad: Plastic
Shot: Zinc-galvanized steel
Buffered: No
Test barrel length: 30 inch
Pellets will pierce skin up to 152 yards.

NO. 1 STEEL PELLETS—1⅛ OUNCES—116 PELLETS
Mfg: Estate Cartridge **Manufacturer's code:** HVST12
Recoil energy in 8-lb. shotgun: 30.7 ft./lbs. **Recoil velocity in 8-lb. shotgun:** 15.7 ft./sec.

Distance in yards:	Muzzle	20	30	40	50	60	70
Velocity in fps:	1,483	993	850	739	650	576	513
Average pellet energy in ft-lbs:	20.83	9.34	6.84	5.18	4.00	3.15	2.49
Time of flight in seconds:	0	.0503	.0831	.1210	.1643	.2134	.2686

Type of load: Nontoxic
Three-foot velocity: 1,400 ft./sec.
Hull: 2¾-inch plastic
Wad: Plastic
Shot: Steel
Buffered: No
Test barrel length: 30 inch
Pellets will pierce skin up to 153 yards.

NO. 1 STEEL PELLETS—1⅛ OUNCES—116 PELLETS
Mfg: Kent Cartridge America/Canada **Manufacturer's code:** K122ST32
Recoil energy in 8-lb. shotgun: 30.7 ft./lbs. **Recoil velocity in 8-lb. shotgun:** 15.7 ft./sec.

Distance in yards:	Muzzle	20	30	40	50	60	70
Velocity in fps:	1,483	993	850	739	650	576	513
Average pellet energy in ft-lbs:	20.83	9.34	6.84	5.18	4.00	3.15	2.49
Time of flight in seconds:	0	.0503	.0831	.1210	.1643	.2134	.2686

Type of load: Nontoxic
Three-foot velocity: 1,400 ft./sec.
Hull: 2¾-inch plastic
Wad: Plastic
Shot: Steel
Buffered: No
Test barrel length: 30 inch
Pellets will pierce skin up to 153 yards.

NO. 1 STEEL PELLETS—1¼ OUNCES—129 PELLETS
Mfg: Federal Cartridge Company **Manufacturer's code:** W148
Recoil energy in 8-lb. shotgun: 29.5 ft./lbs. **Recoil velocity in 8-lb. shotgun:** 15.4 ft./sec.

Distance in yards:	Muzzle	20	30	40	50	60	70
Velocity in fps:	1,348	927	800	699	617	548	489
Average pellet energy in ft-lbs:	17.20	8.15	6.06	4.63	3.61	2.85	2.26
Time of flight in seconds:	0	.0546	.0895	.1297	.1754	.2270	.2849

Type of load: Nontoxic
Three-foot velocity: 1,275 ft./sec.
Hull: 2¾-inch plastic
Wad: Plastic
Shot: Steel
Buffered: No
Test barrel length: 30 inch
Pellets will pierce skin up to 149 yards.

NO. 1 STEEL PELLETS—1¼ OUNCES—129 PELLETS
Mfg: Fiocchi **Manufacturer's code:** 12S114
Recoil energy in 8-lb. shotgun: 29.5 ft./lbs. **Recoil velocity in 8-lb. shotgun:** 15.4 ft./sec.

Distance in yards:	Muzzle	20	30	40	50	60	70
Velocity in fps:	1,348	927	800	699	617	548	489
Average pellet energy in ft-lbs:	17.20	8.15	6.06	4.63	3.61	2.85	2.26
Time of flight in seconds:	0	.0546	.0895	.1297	.1754	.2270	.2849

Type of load: Nontoxic
Three-foot velocity: 1,275 ft./sec.
Hull: 2¾-inch plastic
Wad: Plastic
Shot: Steel
Buffered: No
Test barrel length: 30 inch
Pellets will pierce skin up to 149 yards.

NO. 1 STEEL PELLETS—1¼ OUNCES—129 PELLETS
Mfg: Kent Cartridge America/Canada **Manufacturer's code:** K122ST36
Recoil energy in 8-lb. shotgun: 29.5 ft./lbs. **Recoil velocity in 8-lb. shotgun:** 15.4 ft./sec.

Distance in yards:	Muzzle	20	30	40	50	60	70
Velocity in fps:	1,348	927	800	699	617	548	489
Average pellet energy in ft-lbs:	17.20	8.15	6.06	4.63	3.61	2.85	2.26
Time of flight in seconds:	0	.0546	.0895	.1297	.1754	.2270	.2849

Type of load: Field
Three-foot velocity: 1,275 ft./sec.
Hull: 2¾-inch plastic
Wad: Plastic
Shot: Steel
Buffered: No
Test barrel length: 30 inch
Pellets will pierce skin up to 149 yards.

NO. 1 STEEL PELLETS—1¼ OUNCES—129 PELLETS
Mfg: Remington Arms Co. **Manufacturer's code:** NS12S
Recoil energy in 8-lb. shotgun: 29.5 ft./lbs. **Recoil velocity in 8-lb. shotgun:** 15.4 ft./sec.

Distance in yards:	Muzzle	20	30	40	50	60	70
Velocity in fps:	1,348	927	800	699	617	548	489
Average pellet energy in ft-lbs:	17.20	8.15	6.06	4.63	3.61	2.85	2.26
Time of flight in seconds:	0	.0546	.0895	.1297	.1754	.2270	.2849

Type of load: Nontoxic
Three-foot velocity: 1,275 ft./sec.
Hull: 2¾-inch plastic
Wad: Plastic
Shot: Zinc-galvanized steel
Buffered: No
Test barrel length: 30 inch
Pellets will pierce skin up to 149 yards.

NO. 1 STEEL PELLETS—1¼ OUNCES—129 PELLETS
Mfg: Winchester **Manufacturer's code:** XS12
Recoil energy in 8-lb. shotgun: 29.5 ft./lbs. **Recoil velocity in 8-lb. shotgun:** 15.4 ft./sec.

Distance in yards:	Muzzle	20	30	40	50	60	70
Velocity in fps:	1,348	927	800	699	617	548	489
Average pellet energy in ft-lbs:	17.20	8.15	6.06	4.63	3.61	2.85	2.26
Time of flight in seconds:	0	.0546	.0895	.1297	.1754	.2270	.2849

Type of load: Nontoxic
Three-foot velocity: 1,275 ft./sec.
Hull: 2¾-inch plastic
Wad: Two-piece plastic
Shot: Steel
Buffered: No
Test barrel length: 30 inch
Pellets will pierce skin up to 149 yards.

NO. 1 STEEL PELLETS—1¼ OUNCES—129 PELLETS
Mfg: Dionisi **Manufacturer's code:** D 12 STX
Recoil energy in 8-lb. shotgun: 33.0 ft./lbs. **Recoil velocity in 8-lb. shotgun:** 16.3 ft./sec.

Distance in yards:	Muzzle	20	30	40	50	60	70
Velocity in fps:	1,407	956	822	717	632	561	500
Average pellet energy in ft-lbs:	18.75	8.66	6.40	4.87	3.78	2.98	2.37
Time of flight in seconds:	0	.0526	.0865	.1257	.1703	.2207	.0774

Type of load: Nontoxic
Three-foot velocity: 1,330 ft./sec.
Hull: 2¾-inch plastic
Wad: Plastic
Shot: Steel
Buffered: No
Test barrel length: 30 inch
Pellets will pierce skin up to 151 yards.

NO. 1 STEEL PELLETS—1¼ OUNCES—129 PELLETS
Mfg: Estate Cartridge **Manufacturer's code:** HVST12SM
Recoil energy in 8-lb. shotgun: 37.9 ft./lbs. **Recoil velocity in 8-lb. shotgun:** 17.5 ft./sec.

Distance in yards:	Muzzle	20	30	40	50	60	70
Velocity in fps:	1,483	993	850	739	650	576	513
Average pellet energy in ft-lbs:	20.83	9.34	6.84	5.18	4.00	3.15	2.49
Time of flight in seconds:	0	.0503	.0831	.1210	.1643	.2134	.2686

Type of load: Nontoxic
Three-foot velocity: 1,400 ft./sec.
Hull: 2¾-inch plastic
Wad: Plastic
Shot: Steel
Buffered: No
Test barrel length: 30 inch
Pellets will pierce skin up to 153 yards.

NO. 2 STEEL PELLETS—1 OUNCE—125 PELLETS
Mfg: Federal Cartridge Co. **Manufacturer's code:** W146
Recoil energy in 8-lb. shotgun: 23.1 ft./lbs. **Recoil velocity in 8-lb. shotgun:** 13.6 ft./sec.

Distance in yards:	Muzzle	20	30	40	50	60	70
Velocity in fps:	1,461	961	818	708	619	546	483
Average pellet energy in ft-lbs:	16.66	7.21	5.22	3.91	2.99	2.32	1.82
Time of flight in seconds:	0	.0517	.0856	.1251	.1705	.2221	.2806

Type of load: Nontoxic
Three-foot velocity: 1,375 ft./sec.
Hull: 2¾-inch plastic
Wad: Plastic
Shot: Steel
Buffered: No
Test barrel length: 30 inch
Pellets will pierce skin up to 143 yards.

NO. 2 STEEL PELLETS—1 OUNCE—125 PELLETS
Mfg: Remington Arms Co. **Manufacturer's code:** SSP12L
Recoil energy in 8-lb. shotgun: 23.1 ft./lbs. **Recoil velocity in 8-lb. shotgun:** 13.6 ft./sec.

Distance in yards:	Muzzle	20	30	40	50	60	70
Velocity in fps:	1,461	961	818	708	619	546	483
Average pellet energy in ft-lbs:	16.66	7.21	5.22	3.91	2.99	2.32	1.82
Time of flight in seconds:	0	.0517	.0856	.1251	.1705	.2221	.2806

Type of load: Nontoxic
Three-foot velocity: 1,375 ft./sec.
Hull: 2¾-inch plastic
Wad: Plastic
Shot: Zinc-galvanized steel
Buffered: No
Test barrel length: 30 inch
Pellets will pierce skin up to 143 yards.

NO. 2 STEEL PELLETS—1¹⁄₁₆ OUNCES—133 PELLETS
Mfg: Kent Cartridge America/Canada **Manufacturer's code:** K122ST30
Recoil energy in 8-lb. shotgun: 40.5 ft./lbs. **Recoil velocity in 8-lb. shotgun:** 18.1 ft./sec.

Distance in yards:	Muzzle	20	30	40	50	60	70
Velocity in fps:	1,653	1,051	884	759	661	581	513
Average pellet energy in ft-lbs:	21.32	8.62	3.09	4.49	3.41	2.63	2.05
Time of flight in seconds:	0	.0465	.0777	.1145	.1569	.2054	.2604

Type of load: Nontoxic
Three-foot velocity: 1,550 ft./sec.
Hull: 2¾-inch plastic
Wad: Plastic
Shot: Steel
Buffered: No
Test barrel length: 30 inch
Pellets will pierce skin up to 148 yards.

NO. 2 STEEL PELLETS—1⅛ OUNCES—141 PELLETS
Mfg: Clever **Manufacturer's code:** Magnum load
Recoil energy in 8-lb. shotgun: 28.0 ft./lbs. **Recoil velocity in 8-lb. shotgun:** 15.0 ft./sec.

Distance in yards:	Muzzle	20	30	40	50	60	70
Velocity in fps:	1,325	977	770	669	588	519	460
Average pellet energy in ft-lbs:	13.70	6.29	4.62	3.50	2.70	2.10	1.65
Time of flight in seconds:	0	.0560	.0922	.1341	.1819	.2363	.2977

Type of load: Nontoxic
Three-foot velocity: 1,250 ft./sec.
Hull: 2¾-inch plastic
Wad: Plastic
Shot: Steel
Buffered: No
Test barrel length: 30 inch
Pellets will pierce skin up to 139 yards.

NO. 2 STEEL PELLETS—1⅛ OUNCES—141 PELLETS
Mfg: Winchester **Manufacturer's code:** WE12H
Recoil energy in 8-lb. shotgun: 25.2 ft./lbs. **Recoil velocity in 8-lb. shotgun:** 14.2 ft./sec.

Distance in yards:	Muzzle	20	30	40	50	60	70
Velocity in fps:	1,379	923	789	685	601	530	469
Average pellet energy in ft-lbs:	14.85	6.65	4.86	3.66	2.81	2.19	1.72
Time of flight in seconds:	0	.0542	.0894	.1303	.1771	.2303	.2905

Type of load: Nontoxic
Three-foot velocity: 1,300 ft./sec.
Hull: 2¾-inch plastic
Wad: Plastic
Shot: Steel
Buffered: No
Test barrel length: 30 inch
Pellets will pierce skin up to 140 yards.

NO. 2 STEEL PELLETS—1⅛ OUNCES—141 PELLETS
Mfg: Dionisi **Manufacturer's code:** D 12 ST
Recoil energy in 8-lb. shotgun: 27.9 ft./lbs. **Recoil velocity in 8-lb. shotgun:** 15.0 ft./sec.

Distance in yards:	Muzzle	20	30	40	50	60	70
Velocity in fps:	1,434	949	808	700	613	541	479
Average pellet energy in ft-lbs:	16.04	7.02	2.10	3.3	2.93	2.28	1.79
Time of flight in seconds:	0	.0525	.0868	.1268	.1726	.2248	.2838

Type of load: Nontoxic
Three-foot velocity: 1,350 ft./sec.
Hull: 2¾-inch plastic
Wad: Plastic
Shot: Steel
Buffered: No
Test barrel length: 30 inch
Pellets will pierce skin up to 142 yards.

NO. 2 STEEL PELLETS—1⅛ OUNCES—141 PELLETS
Mfg: Federal Cartridge Co. **Manufacturer's code:** PW147/W147
Recoil energy in 8-lb. shotgun: 29.3 ft./lbs. **Recoil velocity in 8-lb. shotgun:** 15.3 ft./sec.

Distance in yards:	Muzzle	20	30	40	50	60	70
Velocity in fps:	1,461	961	818	708	619	546	483
Average pellet energy in ft-lbs:	16.66	7.21	5.22	3.91	2.99	2.32	1.82
Time of flight in seconds:	0	.0517	.0856	.1251	.1705	.2221	.2806

Type of load: Nontoxic
Three-foot velocity: 1,375 ft./sec.
Hull: 2¾-inch plastic
Wad: Plastic
Shot: Steel
Buffered: No
Test barrel length: 30 inch
Pellets will pierce skin up to 143 yards.

NO. 2 STEEL PELLETS—1⅛ OUNCES—141 PELLETS
Mfg: Fiocchi **Manufacturer's code:** 12S118
Recoil energy in 8-lb. shotgun: 29.3 ft./lbs. **Recoil velocity in 8-lb. shotgun:** 15.3 ft./sec.

Distance in yards:	Muzzle	20	30	40	50	60	70
Velocity in fps:	1,461	961	818	708	619	546	483
Average pellet energy in ft-lbs:	16.66	7.21	5.22	3.91	2.99	2.32	1.82
Time of flight in seconds:	0	.0517	.0856	.1251	.1705	.2221	.2806

Type of load: Nontoxic
Three-foot velocity: 1,375 ft./sec.
Hull: 2¾-inch plastic
Wad: Plastic
Shot: Steel
Buffered: No
Test barrel length: 30 inch
Pellets will pierce skin up to 143 yards.

NO. 2 STEEL PELLETS—1⅛ OUNCES—141 PELLETS
Mfg: PMC (Eldorado Cartridge Corp.) **Manufacturer's code:** SS12
Recoil energy in 8-lb. shotgun: 29.3 ft./lbs. **Recoil velocity in 8-lb. shotgun:** 15.3 ft./sec.

Distance in yards:	Muzzle	20	30	40	50	60	70
Velocity in fps:	1,461	961	818	708	619	546	483
Average pellet energy in ft-lbs:	16.66	7.21	5.22	3.91	2.99	2.32	1.82
Time of flight in seconds:	0	.0517	.0856	.1251	.1705	.2221	.2806

Type of load: Nontoxic
Three-foot velocity: 1,375 ft./sec.
Hull: 2¾-inch plastic
Wad: Plastic
Shot: Steel
Buffered: No
Test barrel length: 30 inch
Pellets will pierce skin up to 143 yards.

NO. 2 STEEL PELLETS—1⅛ OUNCES—141 PELLETS
Mfg: Winchester **Manufacturer's code:** XS12
Recoil energy in 8-lb. shotgun: 29.3 ft./lbs. **Recoil velocity in 8-lb. shotgun:** 15.3 ft./sec.

Distance in yards:	Muzzle	20	30	40	50	60	70
Velocity in fps:	1,461	961	818	708	619	546	483
Average pellet energy in ft-lbs:	16.66	7.21	5.22	3.91	2.99	2.32	1.82
Time of flight in seconds:	0	.0517	.0856	.1251	.1705	.2221	.2806

Type of load: Nontoxic
Three-foot velocity: 1,375 ft./sec.
Hull: 2¾-inch plastic
Wad: Two-piece plastic
Shot: Steel
Buffered: No
Test barrel length: 30 inch
Pellets will pierce skin up to 143 yards.

NO. 2 STEEL PELLETS—1⅛ OUNCES—141 PELLETS
Mfg: Estate Cartridge **Manufacturer's code:** HVST12
Recoil energy in 8-lb. shotgun: 30.7 ft./lbs. **Recoil velocity in 8-lb. shotgun:** 15.7 ft./sec.

Distance in yards:	Muzzle	20	30	40	50	60	70
Velocity in fps:	1,488	974	827	715	625	551	487
Average pellet energy in ft-lbs:	17.29	7.40	5.34	3.99	3.05	2.37	1.85
Time of flight in seconds:	0	.0509	.0844	.1234	.1684	.2195	.2775

Type of load: Nontoxic
Three-foot velocity: 1,400 ft./sec.
Hull: 2¾-inch plastic
Wad: Plastic
Shot: Steel
Buffered: No
Test barrel length: 30 inch
Pellets will pierce skin up to 144 yards.

NO. 2 STEEL PELLETS—1⅛ OUNCES—141 PELLETS
Mfg: Kent Cartridge America/Canada **Manufacturer's code:** K122ST32
Recoil energy in 8-lb. shotgun: 30.7 ft./lbs. **Recoil velocity in 8-lb. shotgun:** 15.7 ft./sec.

Distance in yards:	Muzzle	20	30	40	50	60	70
Velocity in fps:	1,488	974	827	715	625	551	487
Average pellet energy in ft-lbs:	17.29	7.40	5.34	3.99	3.05	2.37	1.85
Time of flight in seconds:	0	.0509	.0844	.1234	.1684	.2195	.2775

Type of load: Field
Three-foot velocity: 1,400 ft./sec.
Hull: 2¾-inch plastic
Wad: Plastic
Shot: Steel
Buffered: No
Test barrel length: 30 inch
Pellets will pierce skin up to 144 yards.

NO. 2 STEEL PELLETS—1⅛ OUNCES—141 PELLETS
Mfg: Federal Cartridge Company **Manufacturer's code:** W144
Recoil energy in 8-lb. shotgun: 32.2 ft./lbs. **Recoil velocity in 8-lb. shotgun:** 16.1 ft./sec.

Distance in yards:	Muzzle	20	30	40	50	60	70
Velocity in fps:	1,516	987	837	723	631	556	492
Average pellet energy in ft-lbs:	17.93	7.60	5.46	4.07	3.11	2.41	1.89
Time of flight in seconds:	0	.0501	.0832	.1218	.1663	.2170	.2744

Type of load: Nontoxic
Three-foot velocity: 1,425 ft./sec.
Hull: 2¾-inch plastic
Wad: Plastic
Shot: Steel
Buffered: No
Test barrel length: 30 inch
Pellets will pierce skin up to 144 yards.

NO. 2 STEEL PELLETS—1¼ OUNCES—156 PELLETS
Mfg: Federal Cartridge Company **Manufacturer's code:** PWT148/W148
Recoil energy in 8-lb. shotgun: 29.5 ft./lbs. **Recoil velocity in 8-lb. shotgun:** 15.4 ft./sec.

Distance in yards:	Muzzle	20	30	40	50	60	70
Velocity in fps:	1,352	911	780	677	594	525	465
Average pellet energy in ft-lbs:	14.27	6.47	4.74	3.58	2.76	2.15	1.68
Time of flight in seconds:	0	.0551	.0908	.1321	.1795	.2333	.2941

Type of load: Nontoxic
Three-foot velocity: 1,275 ft./sec.
Hull: 2¾-inch plastic
Wad: Plastic
Shot: Steel
Buffered: No
Test barrel length: 30 inch
Pellets will pierce skin up to 140 yards.

NO. 2 STEEL PELLETS—1¼ OUNCES—156 PELLETS
Mfg: Fiocchi **Manufacturer's code:** 12S114
Recoil energy in 8-lb. shotgun: 29.5 ft./lbs. **Recoil velocity in 8-lb. shotgun:** 15.4 ft./sec.

Distance in yards:	Muzzle	20	30	40	50	60	70
Velocity in fps:	1,352	911	780	677	594	525	465
Average pellet energy in ft-lbs:	14.27	6.47	4.74	3.58	2.76	2.15	1.68
Time of flight in seconds:	0	.0551	.0908	.1321	.1795	.2333	.2941

Type of load: Nontoxic
Three-foot velocity: 1,275 ft./sec.
Hull: 2¾-inch plastic
Wad: Plastic
Shot: Steel
Buffered: No
Test barrel length: 30 inch
Pellets will pierce skin up to 140 yards.

NO. 2 STEEL PELLETS—1¼ OUNCES—156 PELLETS
Mfg: Kent Cartridge America/Canada **Manufacturer's code:** K122ST36
Recoil energy in 8-lb. shotgun: 29.5 ft./lbs. **Recoil velocity in 8-lb. shotgun:** 15.4 ft./sec.

Distance in yards:	Muzzle	20	30	40	50	60	70
Velocity in fps:	1,352	911	780	677	594	525	465
Average pellet energy in ft-lbs:	14.27	6.47	4.74	3.58	2.76	2.15	1.68
Time of flight in seconds:	0	.0551	.0908	.1321	.1795	.2333	.2941

Type of load: Nontoxic
Three-foot velocity: 1,275 ft./sec.
Hull: 2¾-inch plastic
Wad: Plastic
Shot: Steel
Buffered: No
Test barrel length: 30 inch
Pellets will pierce skin up to 140 yards.

NO. 2 STEEL PELLETS—1¼ OUNCES—156 PELLETS
Mfg: Remington Arms Co. **Manufacturer's code:** NS12S
Recoil energy in 8-lb. shotgun: 29.5 ft./lbs. **Recoil velocity in 8-lb. shotgun:** 15.4 ft./sec.

Distance in yards:	Muzzle	20	30	40	50	60	70
Velocity in fps:	1,352	911	780	677	594	525	465
Average pellet energy in ft-lbs:	14.27	6.47	4.74	3.58	2.76	2.15	1.68
Time of flight in seconds:	0	.0551	.0908	.1321	.1795	.2333	.2941

Type of load: Nontoxic
Three-foot velocity: 1,275 ft./sec.
Hull: 2¾-inch plastic
Wad: Plastic
Shot: Zinc-galvanized steel
Buffered: No
Test barrel length: 30 inch
Pellets will pierce skin up to 140 yards.

NO. 2 STEEL PELLETS—1¼ OUNCES—156 PELLETS
Mfg: Winchester **Manufacturer's code:** XSM12
Recoil energy in 8-lb. shotgun: 29.5 ft./lbs. **Recoil velocity in 8-lb. shotgun:** 15.4 ft./sec.

Distance in yards:	Muzzle	20	30	40	50	60	70
Velocity in fps:	1,352	911	780	677	594	525	465
Average pellet energy in ft-lbs:	14.27	6.47	4.74	3.58	2.76	2.15	1.68
Time of flight in seconds:	0	.0551	.0908	.1321	.1795	.2333	.2941

Type of load: Nontoxic
Three-foot velocity: 1,275 ft./sec.
Hull: 2¾-inch plastic
Wad: Plastic
Shot: Steel
Buffered: No
Test barrel length: 30 inch
Pellets will pierce skin up to 140 yards.

NO. 2 STEEL PELLETS—1¼ OUNCES—156 PELLETS
Mfg: Dionisi **Manufacturer's code:** D 12 STX
Recoil energy in 8-lb. shotgun: 33.0 ft./lbs. **Recoil velocity in 8-lb. shotgun:** 16.3 ft./sec.

Distance in yards:	Muzzle	20	30	40	50	60	70
Velocity in fps:	1,412	939	801	694	608	536	475
Average pellet energy in ft-lbs:	15.56	6.87	5.00	3.76	2.89	2.25	1.76
Time of flight in seconds:	0	.0532	.0878	.1282	.1744	.2270	.2864

Type of load: Nontoxic
Three-foot velocity: 1,330 ft./sec.
Hull: 2¾-inch plastic
Wad: Plastic
Shot: Steel
Buffered: No
Test barrel length: 30 inch
Pellets will pierce skin up to 141 yards.

NO. 2 STEEL PELLETS—1¼ OUNCES—156 PELLETS
Mfg: Estate Cartridge **Manufacturer's code:** HVST12SM
Recoil energy in 8-lb. shotgun: 37.9 ft./lbs. **Recoil velocity in 8-lb. shotgun:** 17.5 ft./sec.

Distance in yards:	Muzzle	20	30	40	50	60	70
Velocity in fps:	1,488	974	827	715	625	551	487
Average pellet energy in ft-lbs:	17.29	7.40	5.34	3.99	3.05	2.37	1.85
Time of flight in seconds:	0	.0509	.0844	.1234	.1684	.2195	.2775

Type of load: Nontoxic
Three-foot velocity: 1,400 ft./sec.
Hull: 2¾-inch plastic
Wad: Plastic
Shot: Steel
Buffered: No
Test barrel length: 30 inch
Pellets will pierce skin up to 144 yards.

NO. 3 STEEL PELLETS—1 OUNCE—158 PELLETS
Mfg: Remington Arms Co. **Manufacturer's code:** SSP12L
Recoil energy in 8-lb. shotgun: 23.1 ft./lbs. **Recoil velocity in 8-lb. shotgun:** 13.6 ft./sec.

Distance in yards:	Muzzle	20	30	40	50	60	70
Velocity in fps:	1,466	941	794	682	593	519	455
Average pellet energy in ft-lbs:	13.64	5.61	4.00	2.95	2.23	1.71	1.32
Time of flight in seconds:	0	.0523	.0871	.1279	.1752	.2294	.2911

Type of load: Nontoxic
Three-foot velocity: 1,375 ft./sec.
Hull: 2¾-inch plastic
Wad: Plastic
Shot: Zinc-galvanized steel
Buffered: No
Test barrel length: 30 inch
Pellets will pierce skin up to 133 yards.

NO. 3 STEEL PELLETS—1 OUNCE—158 PELLETS
Mfg: Federal Cartridge Company **Manufacturer's code:** W 141
Recoil energy in 8-lb. shotgun: 29.3 ft./lbs. **Recoil velocity in 8-lb. shotgun:** 15.3 ft./sec.

Distance in yards:	Muzzle	20	30	40	50	60	70
Velocity in fps:	1,604	1002	838	717	621	542	476
Average pellet energy in ft-lbs:	16.32	6.36	4.46	3.26	2.44	1.87	1.44
Time of flight in seconds:	0	.0484	.0813	.1201	.1651	.2169	.2760

Type of load: Nontoxic
Three-foot velocity: 1,500 ft./sec.
Hull: 2¾-inch plastic
Wad: Plastic
Shot: Steel
Buffered: No
Test barrel length: 30 inch
Pellets will pierce skin up to 137 yards.

NO. 3 STEEL PELLETS—1¹⁄₁₆ OUNCES—168 PELLETS
Mfg: Kent Cartridge America/Canada **Manufacturer's code:** K122ST30
Recoil energy in 8-lb. shotgun: 40.5 ft./lbs. **Recoil velocity in 8-lb. shotgun:** 18.1 ft./sec.

Distance in yards:	Muzzle	20	30	40	50	60	70
Velocity in fps:	1,659	1,026	856	730	632	551	484
Average pellet energy in ft-lbs:	17.47	6.68	4.65	3.38	2.53	1.93	1.48
Time of flight in seconds:	0	.0473	.0794	.1174	.1617	.2126	.2707

Type of load: Field
Three-foot velocity: 1,550 ft./sec.
Hull: 2¾-inch plastic
Wad: Plastic
Shot: Steel
Buffered: No
Test barrel length: 30 inch
Pellets will pierce skin up to 138 yards.

NO. 3 STEEL PELLETS—1⅛ OUNCES—178 PELLETS
Mfg: Winchester **Manufacturer's code:** WE12H
Recoil energy in 8-lb. shotgun: 25.2 ft./lbs. **Recoil velocity in 8-lb. shotgun:** 14.2 ft./sec.

Distance in yards:	Muzzle	20	30	40	50	60	70
Velocity in fps:	1,384	904	767	661	575	504	442
Average pellet energy in ft-lbs:	12.16	5.18	3.73	2.77	2.10	1.61	1.24
Time of flight in seconds:	0	.0548	.0909	.1332	.1819	.2377	.3013

Type of load: Nontoxic
Three-foot velocity: 1,300 ft./sec.
Hull: 2¾-inch plastic
Wad: Plastic
Shot: Steel
Buffered: No
Test barrel length: 30 inch
Pellets will pierce skin up to 131 yards.

NO. 3 STEEL PELLETS—1⅛ OUNCES—178 PELLETS
Mfg: Dionisi **Manufacturer's code:** D 12 ST
Recoil energy in 8-lb. shotgun: 27.9 ft./lbs. **Recoil velocity in 8-lb. shotgun:** 15.0 ft./sec.

Distance in yards:	Muzzle	20	30	40	50	60	70
Velocity in fps:	1,439	928	785	675	587	514	451
Average pellet energy in ft-lbs:	13.14	5.47	3.91	2.89	2.19	1.68	1.29
Time of flight in seconds:	0	.0531	.0883	.1296	.1774	.2321	.2944

Type of load: Nontoxic
Three-foot velocity: 1,350 ft./sec.
Hull: 2¾-inch plastic
Wad: Plastic
Shot: Steel
Buffered: No
Test barrel length: 30 inch
Pellets will pierce skin up to 133 yards.

NO. 3 STEEL PELLETS—1⅛ OUNCES—178 PELLETS
Mfg: Federal Cartridge Co. **Manufacturer's code:** W147
Recoil energy in 8-lb. shotgun: 29.3 ft./lbs. **Recoil velocity in 8-lb. shotgun:** 15.3 ft./sec.

Distance in yards:	Muzzle	20	30	40	50	60	70
Velocity in fps:	1,466	941	794	682	593	519	455
Average pellet energy in ft-lbs:	13.64	5.61	4.00	2.95	2.23	1.71	1.32
Time of flight in seconds:	0	.0523	.0871	.1279	.1752	.2294	.2911

Type of load: Nontoxic
Three-foot velocity: 1,375 ft./sec.
Hull: 2¾-inch plastic
Wad: Plastic
Shot: Steel
Buffered: No
Test barrel length: 30 inch
Pellets will pierce skin up to 133 yards.

NO. 3 STEEL PELLETS—1⅛ OUNCES—178 PELLETS
Mfg: Fiocchi **Manufacturer's code:** 12S118
Recoil energy in 8-lb. shotgun: 29.3 ft./lbs. **Recoil velocity in 8-lb. shotgun:** 15.3 ft./sec.

Distance in yards:	Muzzle	20	30	40	50	60	70
Velocity in fps:	1,466	941	794	682	593	519	455
Average pellet energy in ft-lbs:	13.64	5.61	4.00	2.95	2.23	1.71	1.32
Time of flight in seconds:	0	.0523	.0871	.1279	.1752	.2294	.2911

Type of load: Nontoxic
Three-foot velocity: 1,375 ft./sec.
Hull: 2¾-inch plastic
Wad: Plastic
Shot: Steel
Buffered: No
Test barrel length: 30 inch
Pellets will pierce skin up to 133 yards.

NO. 3 STEEL PELLETS—1⅛ OUNCES—178 PELLETS
Mfg: PMC (Eldorado Cartridge Corp.) **Manufacturer's code:** SS12
Recoil energy in 8-lb. shotgun: 29.3 ft./lbs. **Recoil velocity in 8-lb. shotgun:** 15.3 ft./sec.

Distance in yards:	Muzzle	20	30	40	50	60	70
Velocity in fps:	1,466	941	794	682	593	519	455
Average pellet energy in ft-lbs:	13.64	5.61	4.00	2.95	2.23	1.71	1.32
Time of flight in seconds:	0	.0523	.0871	.1279	.1752	.2294	.2911

Type of load: Nontoxic
Three-foot velocity: 1,375 ft./sec.
Hull: 2¾-inch plastic
Wad: Plastic
Shot: Steel
Buffered: No
Test barrel length: 30 inch
Pellets will pierce skin up to 133 yards.

NO. 3 STEEL PELLETS—1⅛ OUNCES—178 PELLETS
Mfg: Estate Cartridge **Manufacturer's code:** HVST12
Recoil energy in 8-lb. shotgun: 30.7 ft./lbs. **Recoil velocity in 8-lb. shotgun:** 15.7 ft./sec.

Distance in yards:	Muzzle	20	30	40	50	60	70
Velocity in fps:	1,494	953	803	689	598	524	460
Average pellet energy in ft-lbs:	14.16	5.76	4.09	3.01	2.27	1.74	1.34
Time of flight in seconds:	0	.0515	.0859	.1263	.1731	.2267	.2879

Type of load: Nontoxic
Three-foot velocity: 1,400 ft./sec.
Hull: 2¾-inch plastic
Wad: Plastic
Shot: Steel
Buffered: No
Test barrel length: 30 inch
Pellets will pierce skin up to 134 yards.

NO. 3 STEEL PELLETS—1⅛ OUNCES—178 PELLETS
Mfg: Kent Cartridge America/Canada **Manufacturer's code:** K122ST32
Recoil energy in 8-lb. shotgun: 30.7 ft./lbs. **Recoil velocity in 8-lb. shotgun:** 15.7 ft./sec.

Distance in yards:	Muzzle	20	30	40	50	60	70
Velocity in fps:	1,494	953	803	689	598	524	460
Average pellet energy in ft-lbs:	14.16	5.76	4.09	3.01	2.27	1.74	1.34
Time of flight in seconds:	0	.0515	.0859	.1263	.1731	.2267	.2879

Type of load: Nontoxic
Three-foot velocity: 1,400 ft./sec.
Hull: 2¾-inch plastic
Wad: Plastic
Shot: Steel
Buffered: No
Test barrel length: 30 inch
Pellets will pierce skin up to 134 yards.

NO. 3 STEEL PELLETS—1¼ OUNCES—197 PELLETS
Mfg: Federal Cartridge Company **Manufacturer's code:** W148
Recoil energy in 8-lb. shotgun: 29.5 ft./lbs. **Recoil velocity in 8-lb. shotgun:** 15.4 ft./sec.

Distance in yards:	Muzzle	20	30	40	50	60	70
Velocity in fps:	1,357	892	757	653	569	499	438
Average pellet energy in ft-lbs:	11.68	5.04	3.64	2.71	2.06	1.58	1.22
Time of flight in seconds:	0	.0557	.0923	.1350	.1843	.2407	.3049

Type of load: Nontoxic
Three-foot velocity: 1,275 ft./sec.
Hull: 2¾-inch plastic
Wad: Plastic
Shot: Steel
Buffered: No
Test barrel length: 30 inch
Pellets will pierce skin up to 130 yards.

NO. 3 STEEL PELLETS—1¼ OUNCES—197 PELLETS
Mfg: Fiocchi **Manufacturer's code:** 12S114
Recoil energy in 8-lb. shotgun: 29.5 ft./lbs. **Recoil velocity in 8-lb. shotgun:** 15.4 ft./sec.

Distance in yards:	Muzzle	20	30	40	50	60	70
Velocity in fps:	1,357	892	757	653	569	499	438
Average pellet energy in ft-lbs:	11.68	5.04	3.64	2.71	2.06	1.58	1.22
Time of flight in seconds:	0	.0557	.0923	.1350	.1843	.2407	.3049

Type of load: Nontoxic
Three-foot velocity: 1,275 ft./sec.
Hull: 2¾-inch plastic
Wad: Plastic
Shot: Steel
Buffered: No
Test barrel length: 30 inch
Pellets will pierce skin up to 130 yards.

NO. 3 STEEL PELLETS—1¼ OUNCES—197 PELLETS
Mfg: Kent Cartridge America/Canada **Manufacturer's code:** K122ST36
Recoil energy in 8-lb. shotgun: 29.5 ft./lbs. **Recoil velocity in 8-lb. shotgun:** 15.4 ft./sec.

Distance in yards:	Muzzle	20	30	40	50	60	70
Velocity in fps:	1,357	892	757	653	569	499	438
Average pellet energy in ft-lbs:	11.68	5.04	3.64	2.71	2.06	1.58	1.22
Time of flight in seconds:	0	.0557	.0923	.1350	.1843	.2407	.3049

Type of load: Nontoxic
Three-foot velocity: 1,275 ft./sec.
Hull: 2¾-inch plastic
Wad: Plastic
Shot: Steel
Buffered: No
Test barrel length: 30 inch
Pellets will pierce skin up to 130 yards.

NO. 3 STEEL PELLETS—1¼ OUNCES—197 PELLETS
Mfg: Remington Arms Co. **Manufacturer's code:** NS12S
Recoil energy in 8-lb. shotgun: 29.5 ft./lbs. **Recoil velocity in 8-lb. shotgun:** 15.4 ft./sec.

Distance in yards:	Muzzle	20	30	40	50	60	70
Velocity in fps:	1,357	892	757	653	569	499	438
Average pellet energy in ft-lbs:	11.68	5.04	3.64	2.71	2.06	1.58	1.22
Time of flight in seconds:	0	.0557	.0923	.1350	.1843	.2407	.3049

Type of load: Nontoxic
Three-foot velocity: 1,275 ft./sec.
Hull: 2¾-inch plastic
Wad: Plastic
Shot: Zinc-galvanized steel
Buffered: No
Test barrel length: 30 inch
Pellets will pierce skin up to 130 yards.

NO. 3 STEEL PELLETS—1¼ OUNCES—197 PELLETS
Mfg: Winchester **Manufacturer's code:** XSM12
Recoil energy in 8-lb. shotgun: 29.5 ft./lbs. **Recoil velocity in 8-lb. shotgun:** 15.4 ft./sec.

Distance in yards:	Muzzle	20	30	40	50	60	70
Velocity in fps:	1,357	892	757	653	569	499	438
Average pellet energy in ft-lbs:	11.68	5.04	3.64	2.71	2.06	1.58	1.22
Time of flight in seconds:	0	.0557	.0923	.1350	.1843	.2407	.3049

Type of load: Nontoxic
Three-foot velocity: 1,275 ft./sec.
Hull: 2¾-inch plastic
Wad: Two-piece plastic
Shot: Steel
Buffered: No
Test barrel length: 30 inch
Pellets will pierce skin up to 130 yards.

NO. 3 STEEL PELLETS—1¼ OUNCES—197 PELLETS
Mfg: Dionisi **Manufacturer's code:** D 12 STX
Recoil energy in 8-lb. shotgun: 33.0 ft./lbs. **Recoil velocity in 8-lb. shotgun:** 16.3 ft./sec.

Distance in yards:	Muzzle	20	30	40	50	60	70
Velocity in fps:	1,417	919	778	669	582	510	448
Average pellet energy in ft-lbs:	12.74	5.35	3.84	2.84	2.15	1.65	1.27
Time of flight in seconds:	0	.0538	.0894	.1310	.1792	.2343	.2971

Type of load: Nontoxic
Three-foot velocity: 1,330 ft./sec.
Hull: 2¾-inch plastic
Wad: Plastic
Shot: Steel
Buffered: No
Test barrel length: 30 inch
Pellets will pierce skin up to 132 yards.

NO. 3 STEEL PELLETS—1¼ OUNCES—197 PELLETS
Mfg: Estate Cartridge **Manufacturer's code:** HVST12SM
Recoil energy in 8-lb. shotgun: 37.9 ft./lbs. **Recoil velocity in 8-lb. shotgun:** 17.5 ft./sec.

Distance in yards:	Muzzle	20	30	40	50	60	70
Velocity in fps:	1,494	953	803	689	598	524	460
Average pellet energy in ft-lbs:	14.16	5.76	4.09	3.01	2.27	1.74	1.34
Time of flight in seconds:	0	.0515	.0859	.1263	.1731	.2267	.2879

Type of load: Nontoxic
Three-foot velocity: 1,400 ft./sec.
Hull: 2¾-inch plastic
Wad: Plastic
Shot: Steel
Buffered: No
Test barrel length: 30 inch
Pellets will pierce skin up to 134 yards.

NO. 4 STEEL PELLETS—1 OUNCE—192 PELLETS
Mfg: Estate Cartridge **Manufacturer's code:** STL12H1
Recoil energy in 8-lb. shotgun: 16.8 ft./lbs. **Recoil velocity in 8-lb. shotgun:** 11.6 ft./sec.

Distance in yards:	Muzzle	20	30	40	50	60	70
Velocity in fps:	1,302	844	713	611	529	460	400
Average pellet energy in ft-lbs:	8.61	3.62	2.58	1.90	1.42	1.07	.81
Time of flight in seconds:	0	.0585	.0973	.1428	.1956	.2565	.3265

Type of load: Nontoxic
Three-foot velocity: 1,220 ft./sec.
Hull: 2¾-inch plastic
Wad: Plastic
Shot: Steel
Buffered: No
Test barrel length: 30 inch
Pellets will pierce skin up to 120 yards.

NO. 4 STEEL PELLETS—1 OUNCE—192 PELLETS
Mfg: Federal Cartridge Co. Manufacturer's code: W146
Recoil energy in 8-lb. shotgun: 23.1 ft./lbs. Recoil velocity in 8-lb. shotgun: 13.6 ft./sec.

Distance in yards:	Muzzle	20	30	40	50	60	70
Velocity in fps:	1,472	917	767	654	465	489	425
Average pellet energy in ft-lbs:	11.01	4.27	2.99	2.17	1.61	1.22	.92
Time of flight in seconds:	0	.0530	.0889	.1313	.1808	.2380	.3038

Type of load: Nontoxic
Three-foot velocity: 1,375 ft./sec.
Hull: 2¾-inch plastic
Wad: Plastic
Shot: Steel
Buffered: No
Test barrel length: 30 inch
Pellets will pierce skin up to 124 yards.

NO. 4 STEEL PELLETS—1 OUNCE—192 PELLETS
Mfg: Remington Arms Co. Manufacturer's code: SSP12L
Recoil energy in 8-lb. shotgun: 23.1 ft./lbs. Recoil velocity in 8-lb. shotgun: 13.6 ft./sec.

Distance in yards:	Muzzle	20	30	40	50	60	70
Velocity in fps:	1,472	917	767	654	465	489	425
Average pellet energy in ft-lbs:	11.01	4.27	2.99	2.17	1.61	1.22	.92
Time of flight in seconds:	0	.0530	.0889	.1313	.1808	.2380	.3038

Type of load: Nontoxic
Three-foot velocity: 1,375 ft./sec.
Hull: 2¾-inch plastic
Wad: Plastic
Shot: Zinc-galvanized steel
Buffered: No
Test barrel length: 30 inch
Pellets will pierce skin up to 124 yards.

NO. 4 STEEL PELLETS—1 OUNCE—192 PELLETS
Mfg: Fiocchi Manufacturer's code: 12S1OZ
Recoil energy in 8-lb. shotgun: 24.3 ft./lbs. Recoil velocity in 8-lb. shotgun: 14.0 ft./sec.

Distance in yards:	Muzzle	20	30	40	50	60	70
Velocity in fps:	1,500	929	776	660	569	494	429
Average pellet energy in ft-lbs:	11.42	4.38	3.06	2.22	1.65	1.24	.94
Time of flight in seconds:	0	.0522	.0876	.1297	.1787	.2353	.3005

Type of load: Nontoxic
Three-foot velocity: 1,400 ft./sec.
Hull: 2¾-inch plastic
Wad: Plastic
Shot: Steel
Buffered: No
Test barrel length: 30 inch
Pellets will pierce skin up to 125 yards.

NO. 4 STEEL PELLETS—1 OUNCE—192 PELLETS
Mfg: Federal Cartridge Company Manufacturer's code: W 141
Recoil energy in 8-lb. shotgun: 29.3 ft./lbs. Recoil velocity in 8-lb. shotgun: 15.3 ft./sec.

Distance in yards:	Muzzle	20	30	40	50	60	70
Velocity in fps:	1,610	975	809	686	590	511	444
Average pellet energy in ft-lbs:	13.17	4.83	3.33	2.39	1.77	1.33	1.00
Time of flight in seconds:	0	.0492	.0831	.1234	.1706	.2253	.2883

Type of load: Nontoxic
Three-foot velocity: 1,500 ft./sec.
Hull: 2¾-inch plastic
Wad: Plastic
Shot: Steel
Buffered: No
Test barrel length: 30 inch
Pellets will pierce skin up to 127 yards.

NO. 4 STEEL PELLETS—1¹/₁₆ OUNCES—204 PELLETS
Mfg: Kent Cartridge America/Canada Manufacturer's code: K122ST30
Recoil energy in 8-lb. shotgun: 40.5 ft./lbs. Recoil velocity in 8-lb. shotgun: 18.1 ft./sec.

Distance in yards:	Muzzle	20	30	40	50	60	70
Velocity in fps:	1,666	999	826	699	600	520	452
Average pellet energy in ft-lbs:	14.10	5.07	3.46	2.48	1.83	1.37	1.04
Time of flight in seconds:	0	.0482	.0813	.1209	.1673	.2211	.2831

Type of load: Nontoxic
Three-foot velocity: 1,550 ft./sec.
Hull: 2¾-inch plastic
Wad: Plastic
Shot: Steel
Buffered: No
Test barrel length: 30 inch
Pellets will pierce skin up to 128 yards.

NO. 4 STEEL PELLETS—1⅛ OUNCES—216 PELLETS
Mfg: Clever Manufacturer's code: Steel load
Recoil energy in 8-lb. shotgun: 22.7 ft./lbs. Recoil velocity in 8-lb. shotgun: 13.5 ft./sec.

Distance in yards:	Muzzle	20	30	40	50	60	70
Velocity in fps:	1,335	859	724	620	536	466	405
Average pellet energy in ft-lbs:	9.05	3.75	2.66	1.95	1.46	1.10	.83
Time of flight in seconds:	0	.0574	.0955	.1404	.1925	.2526	.3217

Type of load: Nontoxic
Three-foot velocity: 1,250 ft./sec.
Hull: 2¾-inch plastic
Wad: Plastic
Shot: Steel
Buffered: No
Test barrel length: 30 inch
Pellets will pierce skin up to 120 yards.

NO. 4 STEEL PELLETS—1⅛ OUNCES—216 PELLETS
Mfg: Winchester Manufacturer's code: WE12H
Recoil energy in 8-lb. shotgun: 25.2 ft./lbs. Recoil velocity in 8-lb. shotgun: 14.2 ft./sec.

Distance in yards:	Muzzle	20	30	40	50	60	70
Velocity in fps:	1,389	882	741	634	547	475	413
Average pellet energy in ft-lbs:	9.81	3.95	2.79	2.04	1.52	1.32	.87
Time of flight in seconds:	0	.0555	.0927	.1366	.1876	.2465	.3142

Type of load: Nontoxic
Three-foot velocity: 1,300 ft./sec.
Hull: 2¾-inch plastic
Wad: Plastic
Shot: Steel
Buffered: No
Test barrel length: 30 inch
Pellets will pierce skin up to 122 yards.

NO. 4 STEEL PELLETS—1⅛ OUNCES—216 PELLETS

Mfg: Dionisi **Manufacturer's code:** D 12 ST
Recoil energy in 8-lb. shotgun: 27.9 ft./lbs. **Recoil velocity in 8-lb. shotgun:** 15.0 ft./sec.

Distance in yards:	Muzzle	20	30	40	50	60	70
Velocity in fps:	1,445	906	759	647	558	485	422
Average pellet energy in ft-lbs:	10.60	4.17	2.92	2.13	1.58	1.19	.90
Time of flight in seconds:	0	.0538	.0901	.1130	.1830	.2407	.3071

Type of load: Nontoxic
Three-foot velocity: 1,350 ft./sec.
Hull: 2¾-inch plastic
Wad: Plastic
Shot: Steel
Buffered: No
Test barrel length: 30 inch
Pellets will pierce skin up to 123 yards.

NO. 4 STEEL PELLETS—1⅛ OUNCES—216 PELLETS

Mfg: Federal Cartridge Co. **Manufacturer's code:** W147
Recoil energy in 8-lb. shotgun: 29.3 ft./lbs. **Recoil velocity in 8-lb. shotgun:** 15.3 ft./sec.

Distance in yards:	Muzzle	20	30	40	50	60	70
Velocity in fps:	1,472	917	767	654	465	489	425
Average pellet energy in ft-lbs:	11.01	4.27	2.99	2.17	1.61	1.22	.92
Time of flight in seconds:	0	.0530	.0889	.1313	.1808	.2380	.3038

Type of load: Nontoxic
Three-foot velocity: 1,375 ft./sec.
Hull: 2¾-inch plastic
Wad: Plastic
Shot: Steel
Buffered: No
Test barrel length: 30 inch
Pellets will pierce skin up to 124 yards.

The over/under has become widely used both in the field and for clays. Here the author draws a bead on a decoying Uruguayan spot-winged pigeon with a friend's Holland & Holland sporting/game gun.

NO. 4 STEEL PELLETS—1⅛ OUNCES—216 PELLETS
Mfg: Fiocchi **Manufacturer's code:** 12S118
Recoil energy in 8-lb. shotgun: 29.3 ft./lbs. **Recoil velocity in 8-lb. shotgun:** 15.3 ft./sec.

Distance in yards:	Muzzle	20	30	40	50	60	70
Velocity in fps:	1,472	917	767	654	465	489	425
Average pellet energy in ft-lbs:	11.01	4.27	2.99	2.17	1.61	1.22	.92
Time of flight in seconds:	0	.0530	.0889	.1313	.1808	.2380	.3038

Type of load: Nontoxic
Three-foot velocity: 1,375 ft./sec.
Hull: 2¾-inch plastic
Wad: Plastic
Shot: Steel
Buffered: No
Test barrel length: 30 inch
Pellets will pierce skin up to 124 yards.

NO. 4 STEEL PELLETS—1⅛ OUNCES—216 PELLETS
Mfg: PMC (Eldorado Cartridge Corp.) **Manufacturer's code:** SS12
Recoil energy in 8-lb. shotgun: 29.3 ft./lbs. **Recoil velocity in 8-lb. shotgun:** 15.3 ft./sec.

Distance in yards:	Muzzle	20	30	40	50	60	70
Velocity in fps:	1,472	917	767	654	465	489	425
Average pellet energy in ft-lbs:	11.01	4.27	2.99	2.17	1.61	1.22	.92
Time of flight in seconds:	0	.0530	.0889	.1313	.1808	.2380	.3038

Type of load: Nontoxic
Three-foot velocity: 1,375 ft./sec.
Hull: 2¾-inch plastic
Wad: Plastic
Shot: Steel
Buffered: No
Test barrel length: 30 inch
Pellets will pierce skin up to 124 yards.

NO. 4 STEEL PELLETS—1⅛ OUNCES—216 PELLETS
Mfg: Winchester **Manufacturer's code:** XS12
Recoil energy in 8-lb. shotgun: 29.3 ft./lbs. **Recoil velocity in 8-lb. shotgun:** 15.3 ft./sec.

Distance in yards:	Muzzle	20	30	40	50	60	70
Velocity in fps:	1,472	917	767	654	465	489	425
Average pellet energy in ft-lbs:	11.01	4.27	2.99	2.17	1.61	1.22	.92
Time of flight in seconds:	0	.0530	.0889	.1313	.1808	.2380	.3038

Type of load: Nontoxic
Three-foot velocity: 1,375 ft./sec.
Hull: 2¾-inch plastic
Wad: Two-piece plastic
Shot: Steel
Buffered: No
Test barrel length: 30 inch
Pellets will pierce skin up to 124 yards.

NO. 4 STEEL PELLETS—1⅛ OUNCES—216 PELLETS
Mfg: Estate Cartridge **Manufacturer's code:** HVST12
Recoil energy in 8-lb. shotgun: 30.7 ft./lbs. **Recoil velocity in 8-lb. shotgun:** 15.7 ft./sec.

Distance in yards:	Muzzle	20	30	40	50	60	70
Velocity in fps:	1,500	929	776	660	569	494	429
Average pellet energy in ft-lbs:	11.42	4.38	3.06	2.22	1.65	1.24	.94
Time of flight in seconds:	0	.0522	.0876	.1297	.1787	.2353	.3005

Type of load: Nontoxic
Three-foot velocity: 1,400 ft./sec.
Hull: 2¾-inch plastic
Wad: Plastic
Shot: Steel
Buffered: No
Test barrel length: 30 inch
Pellets will pierce skin up to 125 yards.

NO. 4 STEEL PELLETS—1⅛ OUNCES—216 PELLETS
Mfg: Kent Cartridge America/Canada **Manufacturer's code:** K122ST32
Recoil energy in 8-lb. shotgun: 30.7 ft./lbs. **Recoil velocity in 8-lb. shotgun:** 15.7 ft./sec.

Distance in yards:	Muzzle	20	30	40	50	60	70
Velocity in fps:	1,500	929	776	660	569	494	429
Average pellet energy in ft-lbs:	11.42	4.38	3.06	2.22	1.65	1.24	.94
Time of flight in seconds:	0	.0522	.0876	.1297	.1787	.2353	.3005

Type of load: Nontoxic
Three-foot velocity: 1,400 ft./sec.
Hull: 2¾-inch plastic
Wad: Plastic
Shot: Steel
Buffered: No
Test barrel length: 30 inch
Pellets will pierce skin up to 125 yards.

NO. 4 STEEL PELLETS—1⅛ OUNCES—216 PELLETS
Mfg: Federal Cartridge Company **Manufacturer's code:** W144
Recoil energy in 8-lb. shotgun: 32.2 ft./lbs. **Recoil velocity in 8-lb. shotgun:** 16.1 ft./sec.

Distance in yards:	Muzzle	20	30	40	50	60	70
Velocity in fps:	1,527	940	784	667	574	498	433
Average pellet energy in ft-lbs:	11.85	4.49	3.12	2.26	1.68	1.26	.95
Time of flight in seconds:	0	.0514	.0865	.1280	.1766	.2327	.2973

Type of load: Nontoxic
Three-foot velocity: 1,425 ft./sec.
Hull: 2¾-inch plastic
Wad: Plastic
Shot: Steel
Buffered: No
Test barrel length: 30 inch
Pellets will pierce skin up to 125 yards.

NO. 4 STEEL PELLETS—1¼ OUNCES—240 PELLETS
Mfg: Federal Cartridge Company **Manufacturer's code:** W148
Recoil energy in 8-lb. shotgun: 29.5 ft./lbs. **Recoil velocity in 8-lb. shotgun:** 15.4 ft./sec.

Distance in yards:	Muzzle	20	30	40	50	60	70
Velocity in fps:	1,362	871	733	627	542	471	409
Average pellet energy in ft-lbs:	9.42	3.85	2.73	2.00	1.49	1.13	.85
Time of flight in seconds:	0	.0564	.0941	.1385	.1900	.2495	.3178

Type of load: Nontoxic
Three-foot velocity: 1,275 ft./sec.
Hull: 2¾-inch plastic
Wad: Plastic
Shot: Steel
Buffered: No
Test barrel length: 30 inch
Pellets will pierce skin up to 121 yards.

NO. 4 STEEL PELLETS—1¼ OUNCES—240 PELLETS
Mfg: Fiocchi Manufacturer's code: 12S114
Recoil energy in 8-lb. shotgun: 29.5 ft./lbs. Recoil velocity in 8-lb. shotgun: 15.4 ft./sec.

Distance in yards:	Muzzle	20	30	40	50	60	70
Velocity in fps:	1,362	871	733	627	542	471	409
Average pellet energy in ft-lbs:	9.42	3.85	2.73	2.00	1.49	1.13	.85
Time of flight in seconds:	0	.0564	.0941	.1385	.1900	.2495	.3178

Type of load: Nontoxic
Three-foot velocity: 1,275 ft./sec.
Hull: 2¾-inch plastic
Wad: Plastic
Shot: Steel
Buffered: No
Test barrel length: 30 inch
Pellets will pierce skin up to 121 yards.

NO. 4 STEEL PELLETS—1¼ OUNCES—240 PELLETS
Mfg: Kent Cartridge America/Canada Manufacturer's code: K122ST36
Recoil energy in 8-lb. shotgun: 29.5 ft./lbs. Recoil velocity in 8-lb. shotgun: 15.4 ft./sec.

Distance in yards:	Muzzle	20	30	40	50	60	70
Velocity in fps:	1,362	871	733	627	542	471	409
Average pellet energy in ft-lbs:	9.42	3.85	2.73	2.00	1.49	1.13	.85
Time of flight in seconds:	0	.0564	.0941	.1385	.1900	.2495	.3178

Type of load: Nontoxic
Three-foot velocity: 1,275 ft./sec.
Hull: 2¾-inch plastic
Wad: Plastic
Shot: Steel
Buffered: No
Test barrel length: 30 inch
Pellets will pierce skin up to 121 yards.

NO. 4 STEEL PELLETS—1¼ OUNCES—240 PELLETS
Mfg: Remington Arms Co. Manufacturer's code: NS12S
Recoil energy in 8-lb. shotgun: 29.5 ft./lbs. Recoil velocity in 8-lb. shotgun: 15.4 ft./sec.

Distance in yards:	Muzzle	20	30	40	50	60	70
Velocity in fps:	1,362	871	733	627	542	471	409
Average pellet energy in ft-lbs:	9.42	3.85	2.73	2.00	1.49	1.13	.85
Time of flight in seconds:	0	.0564	.0941	.1385	.1900	.2495	.3178

Type of load: Nontoxic
Three-foot velocity: 1,275 ft./sec.
Hull: 2¾-inch plastic
Wad: Plastic
Shot: Zinc-galvanized steel
Buffered: No
Test barrel length: 30 inch
Pellets will pierce skin up to 121 yards.

NO. 4 STEEL PELLETS—1¼ OUNCES—240 PELLETS
Mfg: Winchester Manufacturer's code: XSM12
Recoil energy in 8-lb. shotgun: 29.5 ft./lbs. Recoil velocity in 8-lb. shotgun: 15.4 ft./sec.

Distance in yards:	Muzzle	20	30	40	50	60	70
Velocity in fps:	1,362	871	733	627	542	471	409
Average pellet energy in ft-lbs:	9.42	3.85	2.73	2.00	1.49	1.13	.85
Time of flight in seconds:	0	.0564	.0941	.1385	.1900	.2495	.3178

Type of load: Nontoxic
Three-foot velocity: 1,275 ft./sec.
Hull: 2¾-inch plastic
Wad: Two-piece plastic
Shot: Steel
Buffered: No
Test barrel length: 30 inch
Pellets will pierce skin up to 121 yards.

NO. 4 STEEL PELLETS—1¼ OUNCES—240 PELLETS
Mfg: Dionisi Manufacturer's code: D 12 STX
Recoil energy in 8-lb. shotgun: 33.0 ft./lbs. Recoil velocity in 8-lb. shotgun: 16.3 ft./sec.

Distance in yards:	Muzzle	20	30	40	50	60	70
Velocity in fps:	1,422	896	752	642	554	481	418
Average pellet energy in ft-lbs:	10.28	4.08	2.87	2.09	1.56	1.18	.89
Time of flight in seconds:	0	.0545	.0912	.1344	.1848	.2403	.3099

Type of load: Nontoxic
Three-foot velocity: 1,330 ft./sec.
Hull: 2¾-inch plastic
Wad: Plastic
Shot: Steel
Buffered: No
Test barrel length: 30 inch
Pellets will pierce skin up to 123 yards.

NO. 4 STEEL PELLETS—1¼ OUNCES—240 PELLETS
Mfg: Estate Cartridge Manufacturer's code: HVST12SM
Recoil energy in 8-lb. shotgun: 37.9 ft./lbs. Recoil velocity in 8-lb. shotgun: 17.5 ft./sec.

Distance in yards:	Muzzle	20	30	40	50	60	70
Velocity in fps:	1,500	929	776	660	569	494	429
Average pellet energy in ft-lbs:	11.42	4.38	3.06	2.22	1.65	1.24	.94
Time of flight in seconds:	0	.0522	.0876	.1297	.1787	.2353	.3005

Type of load: Nontoxic
Three-foot velocity: 1,400 ft./sec.
Hull: 2¾-inch plastic
Wad: Plastic
Shot: Steel
Buffered: No
Test barrel length: 30 inch
Pellets will pierce skin up to 125 yards.

NO. 6 STEEL PELLETS—1 OUNCE—315 PELLETS
Mfg: Estate Cartridge Manufacturer's code: STL12H1
Recoil energy in 8-lb. shotgun: 16.8 ft./lbs. Recoil velocity in 8-lb. shotgun: 11.6 ft./sec.

Distance in yards:	Muzzle	20	30	40	50	60	70
Velocity in fps:	1,312	796	658	552	467	396	336
Average pellet energy in ft-lbs:	5.30	1.95	1.33	.94	.67	.48	.35
Time of flight in seconds:	0	.0604	.1020	.1519	.2110	.2808	.3631

Type of load: Nontoxic
Three-foot velocity: 1,220 ft./sec.
Hull: 2¾-inch plastic
Wad: Plastic
Shot: Steel
Buffered: No
Test barrel length: 30 inch
Pellets will pierce skin up to 101 yards.

NO. 6 STEEL PELLETS—1 OUNCE—315 PELLETS

Mfg: Winchester **Manufacturer's code:** WE12
Recoil energy in 8-lb. shotgun: 19.9 ft./lbs. **Recoil velocity in 8-lb. shotgun:** 12.6 ft./sec.

Distance in yards:	Muzzle	20	30	40	50	60	70
Velocity in fps:	1,401	830	683	572	483	410	347
Average pellet energy in ft-lbs:	6.04	2.12	1.43	1.01	.72	.52	.37
Time of flight in seconds:	0	.0574	.0974	.1456	.2027	.2703	.3497

Type of load: Nontoxic
Three-foot velocity: 1,300 ft./sec.
Hull: 2¾-inch plastic
Wad: Plastic
Shot: Steel
Buffered: No
Test barrel length: 30 inch
Pellets will pierce skin up to 103 yards.

NO. 6 STEEL PELLETS—1 OUNCE—315 PELLETS

Mfg: Federal Cartridge Co. **Manufacturer's code:** W146
Recoil energy in 8-lb. shotgun: 23.1 ft./lbs. **Recoil velocity in 8-lb. shotgun:** 13.6 ft./sec.

Distance in yards:	Muzzle	20	30	40	50	60	70
Velocity in fps:	1,484	862	705	589	498	422	358
Average pellet energy in ft-lbs:	6.78	2.28	1.53	1.07	.76	.55	.39
Time of flight in seconds:	0	.0549	.0935	.1402	.1957	.2613	.3386

Type of load: Nontoxic
Three-foot velocity: 1,375 ft./sec.
Hull: 2¾-inch plastic
Wad: Plastic
Shot: Steel
Buffered: No
Test barrel length: 30 inch
Pellets will pierce skin up to 105 yards.

NO. 6 STEEL PELLETS—1 OUNCE—315 PELLETS

Mfg: Fiocchi **Manufacturer's code:** 12S1OZ
Recoil energy in 8-lb. shotgun: 24.3 ft./lbs. **Recoil velocity in 8-lb. shotgun:** 14.0 ft./sec.

Distance in yards:	Muzzle	20	30	40	50	60	70
Velocity in fps:	1,512	872	713	595	502	426	361
Average pellet energy in ft-lbs:	7.04	2.34	1.56	1.09	.78	.56	.40
Time of flight in seconds:	0	.0541	.0923	.1385	.1935	.2584	.3351

Type of load: Nontoxic
Three-foot velocity: 1,400 ft./sec.
Hull: 2¾-inch plastic
Wad: Plastic
Shot: Steel
Buffered: No
Test barrel length: 30 inch
Pellets will pierce skin up to 106 yards.

NO. 6 STEEL PELLETS—1 OUNCE—315 PELLETS

Mfg: Federal Cartridge Company **Manufacturer's code:** W 141
Recoil energy in 8-lb. shotgun: 29.3 ft./lbs. **Recoil velocity in 8-lb. shotgun:** 15.3 ft./sec.

Distance in yards:	Muzzle	20	30	40	50	60	70
Velocity in fps:	1,624	913	742	617	520	441	374
Average pellet energy in ft-lbs:	8.12	2.57	1.69	1.17	.83	.60	.43
Time of flight in seconds:	0	.0510	.0877	.1321	.1852	.2479	.3219

Type of load: Nontoxic
Three-foot velocity: 1,500 ft./sec.
Hull: 2¾-inch plastic
Wad: Plastic
Shot: Steel
Buffered: No
Test barrel length: 30 inch
Pellets will pierce skin up to 108 yards.

NO. 6 STEEL PELLETS—1⅛ OUNCES—354 PELLETS

Mfg: Winchester **Manufacturer's code:** WE12H
Recoil energy in 8-lb. shotgun: 25.2 ft./lbs. **Recoil velocity in 8-lb. shotgun:** 14.2 ft./sec.

Distance in yards:	Muzzle	20	30	40	50	60	70
Velocity in fps:	1,401	830	683	572	483	410	347
Average pellet energy in ft-lbs:	6.04	2.12	1.43	1.01	.72	.52	.37
Time of flight in seconds:	0	.0574	.0974	.1456	.2027	.2703	.3497

Type of load: Nontoxic
Three-foot velocity: 1,300 ft./sec.
Hull: 2¾-inch plastic
Wad: Plastic
Shot: Steel
Buffered: No
Test barrel length: 30 inch
Pellets will pierce skin up to 103 yards.

NO. 6 STEEL PELLETS—1⅛ OUNCES—354 PELLETS

Mfg: Federal Cartridge Co. **Manufacturer's code:** SSP12
Recoil energy in 8-lb. shotgun: 29.3 ft./lbs. **Recoil velocity in 8-lb. shotgun:** 15.3 ft./sec.

Distance in yards:	Muzzle	20	30	40	50	60	70
Velocity in fps:	1,484	862	705	589	498	422	358
Average pellet energy in ft-lbs:	6.78	2.28	1.53	1.07	.76	.55	.39
Time of flight in seconds:	0	.0549	.0935	.1402	.1957	.2613	.3386

Type of load: Nontoxic
Three-foot velocity: 1,375 ft./sec.
Hull: 2¾-inch plastic
Wad: Plastic
Shot: Zinc-galvanized steel
Buffered: No
Test barrel length: 30 inch
Pellets will pierce skin up to 105 yards.

NO. 6 STEEL PELLETS—1⅛ OUNCES—354 PELLETS

Mfg: Fiocchi **Manufacturer's code:** 12S118
Recoil energy in 8-lb. shotgun: 29.3 ft./lbs. **Recoil velocity in 8-lb. shotgun:** 15.3 ft./sec.

Distance in yards:	Muzzle	20	30	40	50	60	70
Velocity in fps:	1,484	862	705	589	498	422	358
Average pellet energy in ft-lbs:	6.78	2.28	1.53	1.07	.76	.55	.39
Time of flight in seconds:	0	.0549	.0935	.1402	.1957	.2613	.3386

Type of load: Nontoxic
Three-foot velocity: 1,375 ft./sec.
Hull: 2¾-inch plastic
Wad: Plastic
Shot: Steel
Buffered: No
Test barrel length: 30 inch
Pellets will pierce skin up to 105 yards.

NO. 6 STEEL PELLETS—1⅛ OUNCES—354 PELLETS
Mfg: Remington Arms Co. **Manufacturer's code:** SSP12
Recoil energy in 8-lb. shotgun: 29.3 ft./lbs. **Recoil velocity in 8-lb. shotgun:** 15.3 ft./sec.

Distance in yards:	Muzzle	20	30	40	50	60	70
Velocity in fps:	1,484	862	705	589	498	422	358
Average pellet energy in ft-lbs:	6.78	2.28	1.53	1.07	.76	.55	.39
Time of flight in seconds:	0	.0549	.0935	.1402	.1957	.2613	.3386

Type of load: Nontoxic
Three-foot velocity: 1,375 ft./sec.
Hull: 2¾-inch plastic
Wad: Plastic
Shot: Zinc-galvanized steel
Buffered: No
Test barrel length: 30 inch
Pellets will pierce skin up to 105 yards.

NO. 6 STEEL PELLETS—1⅛ OUNCES—354 PELLETS
Mfg: Winchester **Manufacturer's code:** XS12
Recoil energy in 8-lb. shotgun: 29.3 ft./lbs. **Recoil velocity in 8-lb. shotgun:** 15.3 ft./sec.

Distance in yards:	Muzzle	20	30	40	50	60	70
Velocity in fps:	1,484	862	705	589	498	422	358
Average pellet energy in ft-lbs:	6.78	2.28	1.53	1.07	.76	.55	.39
Time of flight in seconds:	0	.0549	.0935	.1402	.1957	.2613	.3386

Type of load: Nontoxic
Three-foot velocity: 1,375 ft./sec.
Hull: 2¾-inch plastic
Wad: Two-piece plastic
Shot: Steel
Buffered: No
Test barrel length: 30 inch
Pellets will pierce skin up to 105 yards.

NO. 6 STEEL PELLETS—1⅛ OUNCES—354 PELLETS
Mfg: Estate Cartridge **Manufacturer's code:** HVST12
Recoil energy in 8-lb. shotgun: 30.7 ft./lbs. **Recoil velocity in 8-lb. shotgun:** 15.7 ft./sec.

Distance in yards:	Muzzle	20	30	40	50	60	70
Velocity in fps:	1,512	872	713	595	502	426	361
Average pellet energy in ft-lbs:	7.04	2.34	1.56	1.09	.78	.56	.40
Time of flight in seconds:	0	.0541	.0923	.1385	.1935	.2584	.3351

Type of load: Nontoxic
Three-foot velocity: 1,400 ft./sec.
Hull: 2¾-inch plastic
Wad: Plastic
Shot: Steel
Buffered: No
Test barrel length: 30 inch
Pellets will pierce skin up to 106 yards.

NO. 6 STEEL PELLETS—1⅛ OUNCES—354 PELLETS
Mfg: Kent Cartridge America/Canada **Manufacturer's code:** K122ST32
Recoil energy in 8-lb. shotgun: 30.7 ft./lbs. **Recoil velocity in 8-lb. shotgun:** 15.7 ft./sec.

Distance in yards:	Muzzle	20	30	40	50	60	70
Velocity in fps:	1,512	872	713	595	502	426	361
Average pellet energy in ft-lbs:	7.04	2.34	1.56	1.09	.78	.56	.40
Time of flight in seconds:	0	.0541	.0923	.1385	.1935	.2584	.3351

Type of load: Nontoxic
Three-foot velocity: 1,400 ft./sec.
Hull: 2¾-inch plastic
Wad: Plastic
Shot: Steel
Buffered: No
Test barrel length: 30 inch
Pellets will pierce skin up to 106 yards.

NO. 6 STEEL PELLETS—1⅛ OUNCES—354 PELLETS
Mfg: Federal Cartridge Company **Manufacturer's code:** W144
Recoil energy in 8-lb. shotgun: 32.2 ft./lbs. **Recoil velocity in 8-lb. shotgun:** 16.1 ft./sec.

Distance in yards:	Muzzle	20	30	40	50	60	70
Velocity in fps:	1,540	882	720	600	507	429	364
Average pellet energy in ft-lbs:	7.30	2.40	1.59	1.11	.79	.57	.41
Time of flight in seconds:	0	.0533	.0911	.1369	.1913	.2557	.3317

Type of load: Nontoxic
Three-foot velocity: 1,425 ft./sec.
Hull: 2¾-inch plastic
Wad: Plastic
Shot: Steel
Buffered: No
Test barrel length: 30 inch
Pellets will pierce skin up to 106 yards.

NO. 6 STEEL PELLETS—1¼ OUNCES—394 PELLETS
Mfg: Kent Cartridge America/Canada **Manufacturer's code:** K122ST36
Recoil energy in 8-lb. shotgun: 29.5 ft./lbs. **Recoil velocity in 8-lb. shotgun:** 15.4 ft./sec.

Distance in yards:	Muzzle	20	30	40	50	60	70
Velocity in fps:	1373	820	675	566	479	406	344
Average pellet energy in ft-lbs:	5.80	2.07	1.40	.98	.70	.51	.36
Time of flight in seconds:	0	.0584	.0988	.1475	.2052	.2733	.3537

Type of load: Nontoxic
Three-foot velocity: 1,275 ft./sec.
Hull: 2¾-inch plastic
Wad: Plastic
Shot: Steel
Buffered: No
Test barrel length: 30 inch
Pellets will pierce skin up to 103 yards.

NO. 6 STEEL PELLETS—1¼ OUNCES—394 PELLETS
Mfg: Estate Cartridge **Manufacturer's code:** HVST12SM
Recoil energy in 8-lb. shotgun: 37.9 ft./lbs. **Recoil velocity in 8-lb. shotgun:** 17.5 ft./sec.

Distance in yards:	Muzzle	20	30	40	50	60	70
Velocity in fps:	1,512	872	713	595	502	426	361
Average pellet energy in ft-lbs:	7.04	2.34	1.56	1.09	.78	.56	.40
Time of flight in seconds:	0	.0541	.0923	.1385	.1935	.2584	.3351

Type of load: Nontoxic
Three-foot velocity: 1,400 ft./sec.
Hull: 2¾-inch plastic
Wad: Plastic
Shot: Steel
Buffered: No
Test barrel length: 30 inch
Pellets will pierce skin up to 106 yards.

NO. 6½ STEEL PELLETS—1⅛ OUNCES—408 PELLETS
Mfg: Remington Arms Co. **Manufacturer's code:** STS12HS
Recoil energy in 8-lb. shotgun: 20.4 ft./lbs. **Recoil velocity in 8-lb. shotgun:** 12.8 ft./sec.

Distance in yards:	Muzzle	20	30	40	50	60	70
Velocity in fps:	1,292	774	635	531	446	375	315
Average pellet energy in ft-lbs:	4.47	1.60	1.08	.75	.53	.38	.27
Time of flight in seconds:	0	.0619	.1048	.1566	.2183	.2917	.3790

Type of load: Nontoxic Target
Three-foot velocity: 1,200 ft./sec.
Hull: 2¾-inch plastic
Wad: Plastic
Shot: Steel
Buffered: No
Test barrel length: 30 inch
Pellets will pierce skin up to 96 yards.

NO. 7 STEEL PELLETS—⅞ OUNCES—369 PELLETS
Mfg: Fiocchi **Manufacturer's code:** 12S78
Recoil energy in 8-lb. shotgun: 20.4 ft./lbs. **Recoil velocity in 8-lb. shotgun:** 12.8 ft./sec.

Distance in yards:	Muzzle	20	30	40	50	60	70
Velocity in fps:	1,575	857	689	567	472	393	328
Average pellet energy in ft-lbs:	5.74	1.70	1.10	.74	.51	.36	.25
Time of flight in seconds:	0	.0538	.0930	.1412	.1993	.2690	.3526

Type of load: Nontoxic Target
Three-foot velocity: 1,450 ft./sec.
Hull: 2¾-inch plastic
Wad: Plastic
Shot: Steel
Buffered: No
Test barrel length: 30 inch
Pellets will pierce skin up to 97 yards.

NO. 7 STEEL PELLETS—1 OUNCE—422 PELLETS
Mfg: Estate Cartridge **Manufacturer's code:** STL12H1
Recoil energy in 8-lb. shotgun: 16.8 ft./lbs. **Recoil velocity in 8-lb. shotgun:** 11.6 ft./sec.

Distance in yards:	Muzzle	20	30	40	50	60	70
Velocity in fps:	1,317	767	625	518	431	360	300
Average pellet energy in ft-lbs:	4.01	1.36	.90	.62	.43	.30	.21
Time of flight in seconds:	0	.0617	.1052	.1581	.2217	.2980	.3895

Type of load: Nontoxic Target
Three-foot velocity: 1,220 ft./sec.
Hull: 2¾-inch plastic
Wad: Plastic
Shot: Steel
Buffered: No
Test barrel length: 30 inch
Pellets will pierce skin up to 92 yards.

NO. 7 STEEL PELLETS—1 OUNCE—422 PELLETS
Mfg: Winchester **Manufacturer's code:** AAST12
Recoil energy in 8-lb. shotgun: 16.8 ft./lbs. **Recoil velocity in 8-lb. shotgun:** 11.6 ft./sec.

Distance in yards:	Muzzle	20	30	40	50	60	70
Velocity in fps:	1,317	767	625	518	431	360	300
Average pellet energy in ft-lbs:	4.01	1.36	.90	.62	.43	.30	.21
Time of flight in seconds:	0	.0617	.1052	.1581	.2217	.2980	.3895

Type of load: Nontoxic Target
Three-foot velocity: 1,235 ft./sec.
Hull: 2¾-inch plastic
Wad: Plastic
Shot: Steel
Buffered: No
Test barrel length: 30 inch
Pellets will pierce skin up to 92 yards.

NO. 7 STEEL PELLETS—1 OUNCE—422 PELLETS
Mfg: Federal Cartridge Co. **Manufacturer's code:** W146
Recoil energy in 8-lb. shotgun: 19.9 ft./lbs. **Recoil velocity in 8-lb. shotgun:** 12.6 ft./sec.

Distance in yards:	Muzzle	20	30	40	50	60	70
Velocity in fps:	1,344	777	632	523	436	363	303
Average pellet energy in ft-lbs:	4.17	1.39	.92	.63	.44	.31	.21
Time of flight in seconds:	0	.0608	.1038	.1561	.2191	.2946	.3851

Type of load: Nontoxic Target
Three-foot velocity: 1,300 ft./sec.
Hull: 2¾-inch plastic
Wad: Plastic
Shot: Steel
Buffered: No
Test barrel length: 30 inch
Pellets will pierce skin up to 93 yards.

NO. 7 STEEL PELLETS—1 OUNCE—422 PELLETS
Mfg: Winchester **Manufacturer's code:** WE12
Recoil energy in 8-lb. shotgun: 19.9 ft./lbs. **Recoil velocity in 8-lb. shotgun:** 12.6 ft./sec.

Distance in yards:	Muzzle	20	30	40	50	60	70
Velocity in fps:	1,344	777	632	523	436	363	303
Average pellet energy in ft-lbs:	4.17	1.39	.92	.63	.44	.31	.21
Time of flight in seconds:	0	.0608	.1038	.1561	.2191	.2946	.3851

Type of load: Nontoxic Target
Three-foot velocity: 1,300 ft./sec.
Hull: 2¾-inch plastic
Wad: Plastic
Shot: Steel
Buffered: No
Test barrel length: 30 inch
Pellets will pierce skin up to 93 yards.

NO. 7 STEEL PELLETS—1 OUNCE—422 PELLETS
Mfg: Remington Arms Co. **Manufacturer's code:** GSTL12
Recoil energy in 8-lb. shotgun: 21.2 ft./lbs. **Recoil velocity in 8-lb. shotgun:** 13.0 ft./sec.

Distance in yards:	Muzzle	20	30	40	50	60	70
Velocity in fps:	1,440	811	656	542	451	376	314
Average pellet energy in ft-lbs:	4.80	1.52	1.00	.68	.47	.33	.23
Time of flight in seconds:	0	.0577	.0990	.1494	.2102	.2830	.3704

Type of load: Nontoxic Target
Three-foot velocity: 1,330 ft./sec.
Hull: 2¾-inch plastic
Wad: Plastic
Shot: Steel
Buffered: No
Test barrel length: 30 inch
Pellets will pierce skin up to 95 yards.

NO. 7 STEEL PELLETS—1 OUNCE—422 PELLETS
Mfg: Fiocchi **Manufacturer's code:** 12S1OZ
Recoil energy in 8-lb. shotgun: 24.3 ft./lbs. **Recoil velocity in 8-lb. shotgun:** 14.0 ft./sec.

Distance in yards:	Muzzle	20	30	40	50	60	70
Velocity in fps:	1,519	838	675	557	463	386	322
Average pellet energy in ft-lbs:	5.34	1.62	1.05	.72	.50	.35	.24
Time of flight in seconds:	0	.0554	.0954	.1445	.2036	.2746	.3597

Type of load: Nontoxic Target
Three-foot velocity: 1,400 ft./sec.
Hull: 2¾-inch plastic
Wad: Plastic
Shot: Steel
Buffered: No
Test barrel length: 30 inch
Pellets will pierce skin up to 96 yards.

NO. 7 STEEL PELLETS—1 OUNCE—422 PELLETS
Mfg: Federal Cartridge Company **Manufacturer's code:** W 141
Recoil energy in 8-lb. shotgun: 29.3 ft./lbs. **Recoil velocity in 8-lb. shotgun:** 15.3 ft./sec.

Distance in yards:	Muzzle	20	30	40	50	60	70
Velocity in fps:	1,632	876	702	577	480	400	333
Average pellet energy in ft-lbs:	6.16	1.78	1.14	.77	.53	.37	.26
Time of flight in seconds:	0	.0523	.0907	.1380	.1952	.2637	.3459

Type of load: Nontoxic Target
Three-foot velocity: 1,500 ft./sec.
Hull: 2¾-inch plastic
Wad: Plastic
Shot: Steel
Buffered: No
Test barrel length: 30 inch
Pellets will pierce skin up to 98 yards.

NO. 7 STEEL PELLETS—1⅛ OUNCES—475 PELLETS
Mfg: Remington Arms Co. **Manufacturer's code:** STS12LS
Recoil energy in 8-lb. shotgun: 18.0 ft./lbs. **Recoil velocity in 8-lb. shotgun:** 12.0 ft./sec.

Distance in yards:	Muzzle	20	30	40	50	60	70
Velocity in fps:	1,234	736	602	500	417	347	290
Average pellet energy in ft-lbs:	3.52	1.25	.84	.58	.40	.28	.19
Time of flight in seconds:	0	.0649	.1101	.1649	.2308	.3097	.4043

Type of load: Nontoxic Target
Three-foot velocity: 1,145 ft./sec.
Hull: 2¾-inch plastic
Wad: Plastic
Shot: Steel
Buffered: No
Test barrel length: 30 inch
Pellets will pierce skin up to 90 yards.

NO. 7 STEEL PELLETS—1⅛ OUNCES—475 PELLETS
Mfg: Remington Arms Co. **Manufacturer's code:** STS12HS
Recoil energy in 8-lb. shotgun: 20.4 ft./lbs. **Recoil velocity in 8-lb. shotgun:** 12.8 ft./sec.

Distance in yards:	Muzzle	20	30	40	50	60	70
Velocity in fps:	1,295	759	619	513	428	356	297
Average pellet energy in ft-lbs:	3.88	1.33	.88	.61	.42	.29	.20
Time of flight in seconds:	0	.0625	.1065	.1599	.2240	.3009	.3932

Type of load: Nontoxic Target
Three-foot velocity: 1,200 ft./sec.
Hull: 2¾-inch plastic
Wad: Plastic
Shot: Steel
Buffered: No
Test barrel length: 30 inch
Pellets will pierce skin up to 92 yards.

Skeet is a short-range clay-target game that lends itself to very light loads. Because targets are taken at 25 yards and less, subsonic shells and loads with less than standard shot charges are as effective as heavier loads.

NO. F STEEL PELLETS—1¼ OUNCES—50 PELLETS
Mfg: Sellier & Bellot **Manufacturer's code:** SBA12001
Recoil energy in 8-lb. shotgun: 36.1 ft./lbs. **Recoil velocity in 8-lb. shotgun:** 17.0 ft./sec.

Distance in yards:	Muzzle	20	30	40	50	60	70
Velocity in fps:	1,429	1,061	939	841	760	690	630
Average pellet energy in ft-lbs:	50.26	27.72	21.71	17.41	14.20	11.73	9.78
Time of flight in seconds:	0	.0492	.0793	.1131	.1507	.1922	.2377

Type of load: Nontoxic
Three-foot velocity: 1,375 ft./sec.
Hull: 3-inch plastic
Wad: Plastic
Shot: Steel
Buffered: No
Test barrel length: 30 inch
Pellets will pierce skin up to 208 yards.

NO. F STEEL PELLETS—1⅜ OUNCES—55 PELLETS
Mfg: Federal Cartridge Company **Manufacturer's code:** W149
Recoil energy in 8-lb. shotgun: 35.7 ft./lbs. **Recoil velocity in 8-lb. shotgun:** 16.9 ft./sec.

Distance in yards:	Muzzle	20	30	40	50	60	70
Velocity in fps:	1,323	1,000	890	801	725	661	604
Average pellet energy in ft-lbs:	43.09	24.60	19.50	15.78	12.95	10.75	9.00
Time of flight in seconds:	0	.0527	.0845	.1018	.1595	.2029	.2504

Type of load: Nontoxic
Three-foot velocity: 1,275 ft./sec.
Hull: 3-inch plastic
Wad: Plastic
Shot: Steel
Buffered: No
Test barrel length: 30 inch
Pellets will pierce skin up to 203 yards.

NO. TT STEEL PELLETS—1⅜ OUNCES—62 PELLETS
Mfg: Remington Arms Co. **Manufacturer's code:** NS12HM
Recoil energy in 8-lb. shotgun: 35.7 ft./lbs. **Recoil velocity in 8-lb. shotgun:** 16.9 ft./sec.

Distance in yards:	Muzzle	20	30	40	50	60	70
Velocity in fps:	1,327	990	878	787	710	645	588
Average pellet energy in ft-lbs:	37.69	21.00	16.51	13.25	10.80	8.91	7.41
Time of flight in seconds:	0	.0529	.0851	.1213	.1614	.2058	.2545

Type of load: Nontoxic
Three-foot velocity: 1,275 ft./sec.
Hull: 3-inch plastic
Wad: Plastic
Shot: Zinc-galvanized steel
Buffered: No
Test barrel length: 30 inch
Pellets will pierce skin up to 194 yards.

NO. T STEEL PELLETS—1⅛ OUNCES—58 PELLETS
Mfg: Federal Cartridge Company **Manufacturer's code:** PWT143/W143
Recoil energy in 8-lb. shotgun: 37.0 ft./lbs. **Recoil velocity in 8-lb. shotgun:** 17.3 ft./sec.

Distance in yards:	Muzzle	20	30	40	50	60	70
Velocity in fps:	1,571	1,114	969	856	764	688	623
Average pellet energy in ft-lbs:	45.66	22.94	17.35	13.54	10.80	8.75	7.17
Time of flight in seconds:	0	.0459	.0748	.1078	.1450	.1864	.2323

Type of load: Nontoxic
Three-foot velocity: 1,500 ft./sec.
Hull: 3-inch plastic
Wad: Plastic
Shot: Steel
Buffered: No
Test barrel length: 30 inch
Pellets will pierce skin up to 194 yards.

NO. T STEEL PELLETS—1¼ OUNCES—65 PELLETS
Mfg: Fiocchi **Manufacturer's code:** 123S
Recoil energy in 8-lb. shotgun: 33.0 ft./lbs. **Recoil velocity in 8-lb. shotgun:** 16.3 ft./sec.

Distance in yards:	Muzzle	20	30	40	50	60	70
Velocity in fps:	1,389	1,013	890	793	712	643	584
Average pellet energy in ft-lbs:	35.70	18.96	14.67	11.63	9.37	7.65	6.31
Time of flight in seconds:	0	.0512	.0828	.1186	.1586	.2029	.2519

Type of load: Nontoxic
Three-foot velocity: 1,330 ft./sec.
Hull: 3-inch plastic
Wad: Plastic
Shot: Steel
Buffered: No
Test barrel length: 30 inch
Pellets will pierce skin up to 188 yards.

NO. T STEEL PELLETS—1¼ OUNCES—65 PELLETS
Mfg: Federal Cartridge Company **Manufacturer's code:** W140
Recoil energy in 8-lb. shotgun: 36.1 ft./lbs. **Recoil velocity in 8-lb. shotgun:** 17.0 ft./sec.

Distance in yards:	Muzzle	20	30	40	50	60	70
Velocity in fps:	1,437	1,039	911	810	726	655	595
Average pellet energy in ft-lbs:	38.21	19.97	15.36	12.13	9.75	7.94	6.54
Time of flight in seconds:	0	.0497	.0806	.1156	.1547	.1982	.2463

Type of load: Nontoxic
Three-foot velocity: 1,375 ft./sec.
Hull: 3-inch plastic
Wad: Plastic
Shot: Steel
Buffered: No
Test barrel length: 30 inch
Pellets will pierce skin up to 189 yards.

NO. T STEEL PELLETS—1¼ OUNCES—65 PELLETS
Mfg: Remington Arms Co. **Manufacturer's code:** NS12H
Recoil energy in 8-lb. shotgun: 36.1 ft./lbs. **Recoil velocity in 8-lb. shotgun:** 17.0 ft./sec.

Distance in yards:	Muzzle	20	30	40	50	60	70
Velocity in fps:	1,437	1,039	911	810	726	655	595
Average pellet energy in ft-lbs:	38.21	19.97	15.36	12.13	9.75	7.94	6.54
Time of flight in seconds:	0	.0497	.0806	.1156	.1547	.1982	.2463

Type of load: Nontoxic
Three-foot velocity: 1,375 ft./sec.
Hull: 3-inch plastic
Wad: Plastic
Shot: Zinc-galvanized steel
Buffered: No
Test barrel length: 30 inch
Pellets will pierce skin up to 189 yards.

NO. T STEEL PELLETS—1¼ OUNCES—65 PELLETS
Mfg: Sellier & Bellot **Manufacturer's code:** SBA12001
Recoil energy in 8-lb. shotgun: 36.1 ft./lbs. **Recoil velocity in 8-lb. shotgun:** 17.0 ft./sec.

Distance in yards:	Muzzle	20	30	40	50	60	70
Velocity in fps:	1,437	1,039	911	810	726	655	595
Average pellet energy in ft-lbs:	38.21	19.97	15.36	12.13	9.75	7.94	6.54
Time of flight in seconds:	0	.0497	.0806	.1156	.1547	.1982	.2463

Type of load: Nontoxic
Three-foot velocity: 1,375 ft./sec.
Hull: 3-inch plastic
Wad: Plastic
Shot: Steel
Buffered: No
Test barrel length: 30 inch
Pellets will pierce skin up to 189 yards.

NO. T STEEL PELLETS—1¼ OUNCES—65 PELLETS
Mfg: Winchester **Manufacturer's code:** XSV123
Recoil energy in 8-lb. shotgun: 36.1 ft./lbs. **Recoil velocity in 8-lb. shotgun:** 17.0 ft./sec.

Distance in yards:	Muzzle	20	30	40	50	60	70
Velocity in fps:	1,437	1,039	911	810	726	655	595
Average pellet energy in ft-lbs:	38.21	19.97	15.36	12.13	9.75	7.94	6.54
Time of flight in seconds:	0	.0497	.0806	.1156	.1547	.1982	.2463

Type of load: Nontoxic
Three-foot velocity: 1,375 ft./sec.
Hull: 3-inch plastic
Wad: Two-piece plastic
Shot: Copper-plated steel
Buffered: No
Test barrel length: 30 inch
Pellets will pierce skin up to 189 yards.

The toughest clay target game may be sporting clays. Targets vary in size, and many trick targets can be used. Although trap and skeet provide their own challenges, sporting clays offer the hunter the best tune-up for the game season.

NO. T STEEL PELLETS—1⅜ OUNCES—71 PELLETS
Mfg: Federal Cartridge Company **Manufacturer's code:** W149
Recoil energy in 8-lb. shotgun: 35.7 ft./lbs. **Recoil velocity in 8-lb. shotgun:** 16.9 ft./sec.

Distance in yards:	Muzzle	20	30	40	50	60	70
Velocity in fps:	1,331	980	865	772	694	628	751
Average pellet energy in ft-lbs:	32.76	17.77	13.84	11.02	8.92	7.30	6.03
Time of flight in seconds:	0	.0531	.0858	.1225	.1636	.2090	.2592

Type of load: Nontoxic
Three-foot velocity: 1,275 ft./sec.
Hull: 3-inch plastic
Wad: Plastic
Shot: Steel
Buffered: No
Test barrel length: 30 inch
Pellets will pierce skin up to 185 yards.

NO. T STEEL PELLETS—1⅜ OUNCES—71 PELLETS
Mfg: Remington Arms Co. **Manufacturer's code:** NS12HM
Recoil energy in 8-lb. shotgun: 35.7 ft./lbs. **Recoil velocity in 8-lb. shotgun:** 16.9 ft./sec.

Distance in yards:	Muzzle	20	30	40	50	60	70
Velocity in fps:	1,331	980	865	772	694	628	751
Average pellet energy in ft-lbs:	32.76	17.77	13.84	11.02	8.92	7.30	6.03
Time of flight in seconds:	0	.0531	.0858	.1225	.1636	.2090	.2592

Type of load: Nontoxic
Three-foot velocity: 1,275 ft./sec.
Hull: 3-inch plastic
Wad: Plastic
Shot: Zinc-galvanized steel
Buffered: No
Test barrel length: 30 inch
Pellets will pierce skin up to 185 yards.

NO. BBB STEEL PELLETS—1⅛ OUNCES—70 PELLETS
Mfg: Fiocchi **Manufacturer's code:** 123ST
Recoil energy in 8-lb. shotgun: 35.4 ft./lbs. **Recoil velocity in 8-lb. shotgun:** 16.9 ft./sec.

Distance in yards:	Muzzle	20	30	40	50	60	70
Velocity in fps:	1,549	1,084	940	828	737	661	597
Average pellet energy in ft-lbs:	38.06	18.65	14.01	10.87	9.61	6.93	5.65
Time of flight in seconds:	0	.0469	.0767	.1107	.1492	.1922	.2400

Type of load: Nontoxic
Three-foot velocity: 1,475 ft./sec.
Hull: 3-inch plastic
Wad: Plastic
Shot: Steel
Buffered: No
Test barrel length: 30 inch
Pellets will pierce skin up to 184 yards.

NO. BBB STEEL PELLETS—1⅛ OUNCES—70 PELLETS
Mfg: Federal Cartridge Company **Manufacturer's code:** PWT143/W143
Recoil energy in 8-lb. shotgun: 37.0 ft./lbs. **Recoil velocity in 8-lb. shotgun:** 17.3 ft./sec.

Distance in yards:	Muzzle	20	30	40	50	60	70
Velocity in fps:	1,576	1,099	951	837	744	667	602
Average pellet energy in ft-lbs:	39.39	19.16	14.34	11.10	8.78	7.06	5.75
Time of flight in seconds:	0	.0462	.0756	.1093	.1473	.1900	.2373

Type of load: Nontoxic
Three-foot velocity: 1,500 ft./sec.
Hull: 3-inch plastic
Wad: Plastic
Shot: Steel
Buffered: No
Test barrel length: 30 inch
Pellets will pierce skin up to 185 yards.

NO. BBB STEEL PELLETS—1¼ OUNCES—77 PELLETS
Mfg: Fiocchi **Manufacturer's code:** 123S
Recoil energy in 8-lb. shotgun: 33.0 ft./lbs. **Recoil velocity in 8-lb. shotgun:** 16.3 ft./sec.

Distance in yards:	Muzzle	20	30	40	50	60	70
Velocity in fps:	1,394	1,000	875	776	694	625	656
Average pellet energy in ft-lbs:	30.80	15.87	12.15	9.55	7.64	6.19	5.06
Time of flight in seconds:	0	.0515	.0836	.1200	.1610	.2066	.2571

Type of load: Nontoxic
Three-foot velocity: 1,330 ft./sec.
Hull: 3-inch plastic
Wad: Plastic
Shot: Steel
Buffered: No
Test barrel length: 30 inch
Pellets will pierce skin up to 178 yards.

NO. BBB STEEL PELLETS—1¼ OUNCES—77 PELLETS
Mfg: Federal Cartridge Company **Manufacturer's code:** W140
Recoil energy in 8-lb. shotgun: 36.1 ft./lbs. **Recoil velocity in 8-lb. shotgun:** 17.0 ft./sec.

Distance in yards:	Muzzle	20	30	40	50	60	70
Velocity in fps:	1,442	1026	896	792	708	636	575
Average pellet energy in ft-lbs:	32.97	16.71	12.72	9.95	7.94	6.42	5.25
Time of flight in seconds:	0	.0500	..0813	.1170	.1571	.2019	.2515

Type of load: Nontoxic
Three-foot velocity: 1,375 ft./sec.
Hull: 3-inch plastic
Wad: Plastic
Shot: Steel
Buffered: No
Test barrel length: 30 inch
Pellets will pierce skin up to 180 yards.

NO. BBB STEEL PELLETS—1¼ OUNCES—77 PELLETS
Mfg: Remington Arms Co. **Manufacturer's code:** NS12H
Recoil energy in 8-lb. shotgun: 36.1 ft./lbs. **Recoil velocity in 8-lb. shotgun:** 17.0 ft./sec.

Distance in yards:	Muzzle	20	30	40	50	60	70
Velocity in fps:	1,442	1026	896	792	708	636	575
Average pellet energy in ft-lbs:	32.97	16.71	12.72	9.95	7.94	6.42	5.25
Time of flight in seconds:	0	.0500	..0813	.1170	.1571	.2019	.2515

Type of load: Nontoxic
Three-foot velocity: 1,375 ft./sec.
Hull: 3-inch plastic
Wad: Plastic
Shot: Zinc-galvanized steel
Buffered: No
Test barrel length: 30 inch
Pellets will pierce skin up to 180 yards.

NO. BBB STEEL PELLETS—1¼ OUNCES—77 PELLETS
Mfg: Sellier & Bellot **Manufacturer's code:** SBA12001
Recoil energy in 8-lb. shotgun: 36.1 ft./lbs. **Recoil velocity in 8-lb. shotgun:** 17.0 ft./sec.

Distance in yards:	Muzzle	20	30	40	50	60	70
Velocity in fps:	1,442	1026	896	792	708	636	575
Average pellet energy in ft-lbs:	32.97	16.71	12.72	9.95	7.94	6.42	5.25
Time of flight in seconds:	0	.0500	..0813	.1170	.1571	.2019	.2515

Type of load: Nontoxic
Three-foot velocity: 1,375 ft./sec.
Hull: 3-inch plastic
Wad: Plastic
Shot: Steel
Buffered: No
Test barrel length: 30 inch
Pellets will pierce skin up to 180 yards.

NO. BBB STEEL PELLETS—1¼ OUNCES—77 PELLETS
Mfg: Winchester **Manufacturer's code:** XSC123
Recoil energy in 8-lb. shotgun: 36.1 ft./lbs. **Recoil velocity in 8-lb. shotgun:** 17.0 ft./sec.

Distance in yards:	Muzzle	20	30	40	50	60	70
Velocity in fps:	1,442	1026	896	792	708	636	575
Average pellet energy in ft-lbs:	32.97	16.71	12.72	9.95	7.94	6.42	5.25
Time of flight in seconds:	0	.0500	..0813	.1170	.1571	.2019	.2515

Type of load: Nontoxic
Three-foot velocity: 1,375 ft./sec.
Hull: 3-inch plastic
Wad: Two-piece plastic
Shot: Copper-plated steel
Buffered: No
Test barrel length: 30 inch
Pellets will pierce skin up to 180 yards.

NO. BBB STEEL PELLETS—1¼ OUNCES—77 PELLETS
Mfg: Estate Cartridge **Manufacturer's code:** HVST12M
Recoil energy in 8-lb. shotgun: 39.8 ft./lbs. **Recoil velocity in 8-lb. shotgun:** 17.9 ft./sec.

Distance in yards:	Muzzle	20	30	40	50	60	70
Velocity in fps:	1,496	1,055	918	810	722	649	586
Average pellet energy in ft-lbs:	35.47	17.66	13.36	10.41	8.28	6.68	5.45
Time of flight in seconds:	0	.0484	.0789	.1138	.1531	.1969	.2456

Type of load: Nontoxic Field
Three-foot velocity: 1,425 ft./sec.
Hull: 3-inch plastic
Wad: Plastic
Shot: Steel
Buffered: No
Test barrel length: 30 inch
Pellets will pierce skin up to 182 yards.

NO. BBB STEEL PELLETS—1¼ OUNCES—77 PELLETS
Mfg: PMC (Eldorado Cartridge Corp.) **Manufacturer's code:** SS12M
Recoil energy in 8-lb. shotgun: 39.8 ft./lbs. **Recoil velocity in 8-lb. shotgun:** 17.9 ft./sec.

Distance in yards:	Muzzle	20	30	40	50	60	70
Velocity in fps:	1,496	1,055	918	810	722	649	586
Average pellet energy in ft-lbs:	35.47	17.66	13.36	10.41	8.28	6.68	5.45
Time of flight in seconds:	0	.0484	.0789	.1138	.1531	.1969	.2456

Type of load: Nontoxic
Three-foot velocity: 1,425 ft./sec.
Hull: 3-inch plastic
Wad: Plastic
Shot: Steel
Buffered: No
Test barrel length: 30 inch
Pellets will pierce skin up to 182 yards.

NO. BBB STEEL PELLETS—1⅜ OUNCES—85 PELLETS
Mfg: Federal Cartridge Company **Manufacturer's code:** W149
Recoil energy in 8-lb. shotgun: 35.7 ft./lbs. **Recoil velocity in 8-lb. shotgun:** 16.9 ft./sec.

Distance in yards:	Muzzle	20	30	40	50	60	70
Velocity in fps:	1,335	969	851	756	677	610	552
Average pellet energy in ft-lbs:	28.25	14.88	11.48	9.06	7.27	5.91	4.84
Time of flight in seconds:	0	.0534	0.865	.1240	.1660	.2127	.2644

Type of load: Nontoxic
Three-foot velocity: 1,275 ft./sec.
Hull: 3-inch plastic
Wad: Plastic
Shot: Steel
Buffered: No
Test barrel length: 30 inch
Pellets will pierce skin up to 176 yards.

NO. BBB STEEL PELLETS—1⅜ OUNCES—85 PELLETS
Mfg: Remington Arms Co. **Manufacturer's code:** NS12HM
Recoil energy in 8-lb. shotgun: 35.7 ft./lbs. **Recoil velocity in 8-lb. shotgun:** 16.9 ft./sec.

Distance in yards:	Muzzle	20	30	40	50	60	70
Velocity in fps:	1,335	969	851	756	677	610	552
Average pellet energy in ft-lbs:	28.25	14.88	11.48	9.06	7.27	5.91	4.84
Time of flight in seconds:	0	.0534	0.865	.1240	.1660	.2127	.2644

Type of load: Nontoxic
Three-foot velocity: 1,275 ft./sec.
Hull: 3-inch plastic
Wad: Plastic
Shot: Zinc-galvanized steel
Buffered: No
Test barrel length: 30 inch
Pellets will pierce skin up to 176 yards.

NO. BBB STEEL PELLETS—1⅜ OUNCES—85 PELLETS
Mfg: Estate Cartridge **Manufacturer's code:** HVST12MM
Recoil energy in 8-lb. shotgun: 54.6 ft./lbs. **Recoil velocity in 8-lb. shotgun:** 21.0 ft./sec.

Distance in yards:	Muzzle	20	30	40	50	60	70
Velocity in fps:	1,442	1,026	896	792	708	636	575
Average pellet energy in ft-lbs:	32.97	16.71	12.72	9.95	7.94	6.42	5.25
Time of flight in seconds:	0	.0500	..0813	.1170	.1571	.2019	.2515

Type of load: Nontoxic
Three-foot velocity: 1,400 ft./sec.
Hull: 3-inch plastic
Wad: Plastic
Shot: Steel
Buffered: No
Test barrel length: 30 inch
Pellets will pierce skin up to 180 yards.

NO. BB STEEL PELLETS—1⅛ OUNCES—81 PELLETS
Mfg: Fiocchi **Manufacturer's code:** 123ST
Recoil energy in 8-lb. shotgun: 35.4 ft./lbs. **Recoil velocity in 8-lb. shotgun:** 16.9 ft./sec.

Distance in yards:	Muzzle	20	30	40	50	60	70
Velocity in fps:	1,554	1,069	921	808	716	640	575
Average pellet energy in ft-lbs:	32.57	15.40	11.45	8.80	6.91	5.52	4.46
Time of flight in seconds:	0	.0472	.0775	.1124	.1519	.1962	.2458

Type of load: Nontoxic
Three-foot velocity: 1,475 ft./sec.
Hull: 3-inch plastic
Wad: Plastic
Shot: Steel
Buffered: No
Test barrel length: 30 inch
Pellets will pierce skin up to 174 yards.

NO. BB STEEL PELLETS—1⅛ OUNCES—81 PELLETS
Mfg: Federal Cartridge Company **Manufacturer's code:** PWT143/W143
Recoil energy in 8-lb. shotgun: 37.0 ft./lbs. **Recoil velocity in 8-lb. shotgun:** 17.3 ft./sec.

Distance in yards:	Muzzle	20	30	40	50	60	70
Velocity in fps:	1,581	1,083	932	816	723	646	580
Average pellet energy in ft-lbs:	33.72	15.82	11.71	8.98	7.05	5.62	4.53
Time of flight in seconds:	0	.0465	.0764	.1109	.1500	.1940	.2430

Type of load: Nontoxic
Three-foot velocity: 1,500 ft./sec.
Hull: 3-inch plastic
Wad: Plastic
Shot: Steel
Buffered: No
Test barrel length: 30 inch
Pellets will pierce skin up to 175 yards.

NO. BB STEEL PELLETS—1⅛ OUNCES—81 PELLETS
Mfg: Kent Cartridge America/Canada **Manufacturer's code:** K123ST32
Recoil energy in 8-lb. shotgun: 37.0 ft./lbs. **Recoil velocity in 8-lb. shotgun:** 17.3 ft./sec.

Distance in yards:	Muzzle	20	30	40	50	60	70
Velocity in fps:	1,581	1,083	932	816	723	646	580
Average pellet energy in ft-lbs:	33.72	15.82	11.71	8.98	7.05	5.62	4.53
Time of flight in seconds:	0	.0465	.0764	.1109	.1500	.1940	.2430

Type of load: Nontoxic
Three-foot velocity: 1,500 ft./sec.
Hull: 3-inch plastic
Wad: Plastic
Shot: Steel
Buffered: No
Test barrel length: 30 inch
Pellets will pierce skin up to 175 yards.

NO. BB STEEL PELLETS—1⅛ OUNCES—81 PELLETS
Mfg: Remington Arms Co. **Manufacturer's code:** NS12HV
Recoil energy in 8-lb. shotgun: 37.0 ft./lbs. **Recoil velocity in 8-lb. shotgun:** 17.3 ft./sec.

Distance in yards:	Muzzle	20	30	40	50	60	70
Velocity in fps:	1,581	1,083	932	816	723	646	580
Average pellet energy in ft-lbs:	33.72	15.82	11.71	8.98	7.05	5.62	4.53
Time of flight in seconds:	0	.0465	.0764	.1109	.1500	.1940	.2430

Type of load: Nontoxic
Three-foot velocity: 1,500 ft./sec.
Hull: 3-inch plastic
Wad: Plastic
Shot: Zinc-galvanized steel
Buffered: No
Test barrel length: 30 inch
Pellets will pierce skin up to 175 yards.

NO. BB STEEL PELLETS—1⅛ OUNCES—81 PELLETS
Mfg: Dionisi **Manufacturer's code:** D 12 ST3
Recoil energy in 8-lb. shotgun: 40.5 ft./lbs. **Recoil velocity in 8-lb. shotgun:** 18.1 ft./sec.

Distance in yards:	Muzzle	20	30	40	50	60	70
Velocity in fps:	1,635	1,112	953	833	737	657	590
Average pellet energy in ft-lbs:	36.06	16.68	12.26	9.35	7.32	5.82	4.69
Time of flight in seconds:	0	.0451	.0743	.1080	.1464	.1896	.2378

Type of load: Nontoxic
Three-foot velocity: 1,550 ft./sec.
Hull: 3-inch plastic
Wad: Plastic
Shot: Steel
Buffered: No
Test barrel length: 30 inch
Pellets will pierce skin up to 177 yards.

NO. BB STEEL PELLETS—1¼ OUNCES—90 PELLETS
Mfg: Fiocchi **Manufacturer's code:** 123S
Recoil energy in 8-lb. shotgun: 33.0 ft./lbs. **Recoil velocity in 8-lb. shotgun:** 16.3 ft./sec.

Distance in yards:	Muzzle	20	30	40	50	60	70
Velocity in fps:	1,398	987	859	758	675	605	545
Average pellet energy in ft-lbs:	26.35	13.14	9.95	7.75	6.14	4.93	4.00
Time of flight in seconds:	0	.0518	.0844	.1217	.1637	.2107	.2630

Type of load: Nontoxic
Three-foot velocity: 1,330 ft./sec.
Hull: 3-inch plastic
Wad: Plastic
Shot: Steel
Buffered: No
Test barrel length: 30 inch
Pellets will pierce skin up to 169 yards.

NO. BB STEEL PELLETS—1¼ OUNCES—90 PELLETS
Mfg: Federal Cartridge Company **Manufacturer's code:** W140
Recoil energy in 8-lb. shotgun: 36.1 ft./lbs. **Recoil velocity in 8-lb. shotgun:** 17.0 ft./sec.

Distance in yards:	Muzzle	20	30	40	50	60	70
Velocity in fps:	1,446	1,012	879	774	688	616	554
Average pellet energy in ft-lbs:	28.21	13.82	10.41	8.07	6.38	5.12	4.14
Time of flight in seconds:	0	.0503	.0822	.1186	.1598	.2059	.2573

Type of load: Nontoxic
Three-foot velocity: 1,375 ft./sec.
Hull: 3-inch plastic
Wad: Plastic
Shot: Steel
Buffered: No
Test barrel length: 30 inch
Pellets will pierce skin up to 171 yards.

NO. BB STEEL PELLETS—1¼ OUNCES—90 PELLETS
Mfg: Remington Arms Co. **Manufacturer's code:** NS12H
Recoil energy in 8-lb. shotgun: 36.1 ft./lbs. **Recoil velocity in 8-lb. shotgun:** 17.0 ft./sec.

Distance in yards:	Muzzle	20	30	40	50	60	70
Velocity in fps:	1,446	1,012	879	774	688	616	554
Average pellet energy in ft-lbs:	28.21	13.82	10.41	8.07	6.38	5.12	4.14
Time of flight in seconds:	0	.0503	.0822	.1186	.1598	.2059	.2573

Type of load: Nontoxic
Three-foot velocity: 1,375 ft./sec.
Hull: 3-inch plastic
Wad: Plastic
Shot: Zinc-galvanized steel
Buffered: No
Test barrel length: 30 inch
Pellets will pierce skin up to 171 yards.

NO. BB STEEL PELLETS—1¼ OUNCES—90 PELLETS
Mfg: Winchester **Manufacturer's code:** XSV123
Recoil energy in 8-lb. shotgun: 36.1 ft./lbs. **Recoil velocity in 8-lb. shotgun:** 17.0 ft./sec.

Distance in yards:	Muzzle	20	30	40	50	60	70
Velocity in fps:	1,446	1,012	879	774	688	616	554
Average pellet energy in ft-lbs:	28.21	13.82	10.41	8.07	6.38	5.12	4.14
Time of flight in seconds:	0	.0503	.0822	.1186	.1598	.2059	.2573

Type of load: Nontoxic
Three-foot velocity: 1,375 ft./sec.
Hull: 3-inch plastic
Wad: Two-piece plastic
Shot: Steel
Buffered: No
Test barrel length: 30 inch
Pellets will pierce skin up to 171 yards.

NO. BB STEEL PELLETS—1¼ OUNCES—90 PELLETS
Mfg: Dionisi **Manufacturer's code:** D 12 ST3X
Recoil energy in 8-lb. shotgun: 37.9 ft./lbs. **Recoil velocity in 8-lb. shotgun:** 17.5 ft./sec.

Distance in yards:	Muzzle	20	30	40	50	60	70
Velocity in fps:	1,473	1,026	889	782	695	622	560
Average pellet energy in ft-lbs:	29.27	14.21	10.66	8.25	6.51	5.22	4.22
Time of flight in seconds:	0	.0495	.0810	.1170	.1577	.2034	.2543

Type of load: Nontoxic
Three-foot velocity: 1,400 ft./sec.
Hull: 3-inch plastic
Wad: Plastic
Shot: Steel
Buffered: No
Test barrel length: 30 inch
Pellets will pierce skin up to 172 yards.

NO. BB STEEL PELLETS—1¼ OUNCES—90 PELLETS
Mfg: Kent Cartridge America/Canada **Manufacturer's code:** K123ST36
Recoil energy in 8-lb. shotgun: 37.9 ft./lbs. **Recoil velocity in 8-lb. shotgun:** 17.5 ft./sec.

Distance in yards:	Muzzle	20	30	40	50	60	70
Velocity in fps:	1,473	1,026	889	782	695	622	560
Average pellet energy in ft-lbs:	29.27	14.21	10.66	8.25	6.51	5.22	4.22
Time of flight in seconds:	0	.0495	.0810	.1170	.1577	.2034	.2543

Type of load: Nontoxic
Three-foot velocity: 1,400 ft./sec.
Hull: 3-inch plastic
Wad: Plastic
Shot: Steel
Buffered: No
Test barrel length: 30 inch
Pellets will pierce skin up to 172 yards.

NO. BB STEEL PELLETS—1¼ OUNCES—90 PELLETS
Mfg: Estate Cartridge **Manufacturer's code:** HVST12M
Recoil energy in 8-lb. shotgun: 39.8 ft./lbs. **Recoil velocity in 8-lb. shotgun:** 17.9 ft./sec.

Distance in yards:	Muzzle	20	30	40	50	60	70
Velocity in fps:	1,500	1,041	900	791	702	628	565
Average pellet energy in ft-lbs:	30.35	14.60	10.92	8.43	6.64	5.32	4.30
Time of flight in seconds:	0	.0487	.0798	.1154	.1557	.2010	.2514

Type of load: Nontoxic
Three-foot velocity: 1,425 ft./sec.
Hull: 3-inch plastic
Wad: Plastic
Shot: Steel
Buffered: No
Test barrel length: 30 inch
Pellets will pierce skin up to 173 yards.

NO. BB STEEL PELLETS—1¼ OUNCES—90 PELLETS
Mfg: PMC (Eldorado Cartridge Corp.) **Manufacturer's code:** SS12M
Recoil energy in 8-lb. shotgun: 39.8 ft./lbs. **Recoil velocity in 8-lb. shotgun:** 17.9 ft./sec.

Distance in yards:	Muzzle	20	30	40	50	60	70
Velocity in fps:	1,500	1,041	900	791	702	628	565
Average pellet energy in ft-lbs:	30.35	14.60	10.92	8.43	6.64	5.32	4.30
Time of flight in seconds:	0	.0487	.0798	.1154	.1557	.2010	.2514

Type of load: Nontoxic
Three-foot velocity: 1,425 ft./sec.
Hull: 3-inch plastic
Wad: Plastic
Shot: Steel
Buffered: No
Test barrel length: 30 inch
Pellets will pierce skin up to 173 yards.

NO. BB STEEL PELLETS—1¼ OUNCES—90 PELLETS
Mfg: Winchester **Manufacturer's code:** SSH123
Recoil energy in 8-lb. shotgun: 41.7 ft./lbs. **Recoil velocity in 8-lb. shotgun:** 18.3 ft./sec.

Distance in yards:	Muzzle	20	30	40	50	60	70
Velocity in fps:	1,527	1,055	911	799	709	634	570
Average pellet energy in ft-lbs:	31.45	15.00	11.18	8.61	6.78	5.42	4.38
Time of flight in seconds:	0	.0480	.0786	.1139	.1538	.1986	.2485

Type of load: Nontoxic
Three-foot velocity: 1,450 ft./sec.
Hull: 3-inch plastic
Wad: Two-piece plastic
Shot: Steel
Buffered: No
Test barrel length: 30 inch
Pellets will pierce skin up to 173 yards.

NO. BB STEEL PELLETS—1⅜ OUNCES—99 PELLETS
Mfg: Federal Cartridge Company **Manufacturer's code:** W149
Recoil energy in 8-lb. shotgun: 35.7 ft./lbs. **Recoil velocity in 8-lb. shotgun:** 16.9 ft./sec.

Distance in yards:	Muzzle	20	30	40	50	60	70
Velocity in fps:	1,339	956	835	739	659	591	533
Average pellet energy in ft-lbs:	24.17	12.33	9.41	7.35	5.85	4.71	3.83
Time of flight in seconds:	0	.0538	.0874	.1256	.1687	.2168	.2703

Type of load: Nontoxic
Three-foot velocity: 1,275 ft./sec.
Hull: 3-inch plastic
Wad: Plastic
Shot: Steel
Buffered: No
Test barrel length: 30 inch
Pellets will pierce skin up to 167 yards.

NO. BB STEEL PELLETS—1⅜ OUNCES—99 PELLETS
Mfg: Remington Arms Co. **Manufacturer's code:** NS12HM
Recoil energy in 8-lb. shotgun: 35.7 ft./lbs. **Recoil velocity in 8-lb. shotgun:** 16.9 ft./sec.

Distance in yards:	Muzzle	20	30	40	50	60	70
Velocity in fps:	1,339	956	835	739	659	591	533
Average pellet energy in ft-lbs:	24.17	12.33	9.41	7.35	5.85	4.71	3.83
Time of flight in seconds:	0	.0538	.0874	.1256	.1687	.2168	.2703

Type of load: Nontoxic
Three-foot velocity: 1,275 ft./sec.
Hull: 3-inch plastic
Wad: Plastic
Shot: Zinc-galvanized steel
Buffered: No
Test barrel length: 30 inch
Pellets will pierce skin up to 167 yards.

NO. BB STEEL PELLETS—1⅜ OUNCES—99 PELLETS
Mfg: Winchester **Manufacturer's code:** XSM123
Recoil energy in 8-lb. shotgun: 35.7 ft./lbs. **Recoil velocity in 8-lb. shotgun:** 16.9 ft./sec.

Distance in yards:	Muzzle	20	30	40	50	60	70
Velocity in fps:	1,339	956	835	739	659	591	533
Average pellet energy in ft-lbs:	24.17	12.33	9.41	7.35	5.85	4.71	3.83
Time of flight in seconds:	0	.0538	.0874	.1256	.1687	.2168	.2703

Type of load: Nontoxic
Three-foot velocity: 1,275 ft./sec.
Hull: 3-inch plastic
Wad: Two-piece plastic
Shot: Steel
Buffered: No
Test barrel length: 30 inch
Pellets will pierce skin up to 167 yards.

NO. BB STEEL PELLETS—1⅜ OUNCES—99 PELLETS
Mfg: Kent Cartridge America/Canada **Manufacturer's code:** K123ST40
Recoil energy in 8-lb. shotgun: 37.6 ft./lbs. **Recoil velocity in 8-lb. shotgun:** 17.4 ft./sec.

Distance in yards:	Muzzle	20	30	40	50	60	70
Velocity in fps:	1,366	970	846	747	666	597	538
Average pellet energy in ft-lbs:	25.15	12.70	9.65	7.53	5.98	4.81	3.91
Time of flight in seconds:	0	.0529	.0860	.1238	.1664	.2140	.2669

Type of load: Nontoxic
Three-foot velocity: 1,300 ft./sec.
Hull: 3-inch plastic
Wad: Plastic
Shot: Steel
Buffered: No
Test barrel length: 30 inch
Pellets will pierce skin up to 168 yards.

NO. BB STEEL PELLETS—1⅜ OUNCES—99 PELLETS
Mfg: Estate Cartridge **Manufacturer's code:** HVST12MM
Recoil energy in 8-lb. shotgun: 54.6 ft./lbs. **Recoil velocity in 8-lb. shotgun:** 21.0 ft./sec.

Distance in yards:	Muzzle	20	30	40	50	60	70
Velocity in fps:	1,446	1,012	879	774	688	616	554
Average pellet energy in ft-lbs:	28.21	13.82	10.41	8.07	6.38	5.12	4.14
Time of flight in seconds:	0	.0503	.0822	.1186	.1598	.2059	.2573

Type of load: Nontoxic
Three-foot velocity: 1,400 ft./sec.
Hull: 3-inch plastic
Wad: Plastic
Shot: Steel
Buffered: No
Test barrel length: 30 inch
Pellets will pierce skin up to 171 yards.

NO. 1 STEEL PELLETS—1⅛ OUNCES—116 PELLETS
Mfg: Fiocchi **Manufacturer's code:** 123ST
Recoil energy in 8-lb. shotgun: 35.4 ft./lbs. **Recoil velocity in 8-lb. shotgun:** 16.9 ft./sec.

Distance in yards:	Muzzle	20	30	40	50	60	70
Velocity in fps:	1,565	1,033	879	763	669	558	527
Average pellet energy in ft-lbs:	23.19	10.11	7.32	5.51	4.24	3.32	2.63
Time of flight in seconds:	0	.0480	.0796	.1163	.1584	.2061	.2598

Type of load: Nontoxic
Three-foot velocity: 1,475 ft./sec.
Hull: 3-inch plastic
Wad: Plastic
Shot: Steel
Buffered: No
Test barrel length: 30 inch
Pellets will pierce skin up to 155 yards.

NO. 1 STEEL PELLETS—1⅛ OUNCES—116 PELLETS
Mfg: Kent Cartridge America/Canada **Manufacturer's code:** K123ST32
Recoil energy in 8-lb. shotgun: 37.0 ft./lbs. **Recoil velocity in 8-lb. shotgun:** 17.3 ft./sec.

Distance in yards:	Muzzle	20	30	40	50	60	70
Velocity in fps:	1,592	1,046	889	770	675	597	531
Average pellet energy in ft-lbs:	24.01	10.37	7.49	5.62	4.32	3.38	2.67
Time of flight in seconds:	0	.0473	.0785	.1148	.1565	.2038	.2570

Type of load: Nontoxic
Three-foot velocity: 1,500 ft./sec.
Hull: 3-inch plastic
Wad: Plastic
Shot: Steel
Buffered: No
Test barrel length: 30 inch
Pellets will pierce skin up to 156 yards.

NO. 1 STEEL PELLETS—1⅛ OUNCES—116 PELLETS
Mfg: Dionisi **Manufacturer's code:** D 12 ST3
Recoil energy in 8-lb. shotgun: 40.5 ft./lbs. **Recoil velocity in 8-lb. shotgun:** 18.1 ft./sec.

Distance in yards:	Muzzle	20	30	40	50	60	70
Velocity in fps:	1,647	1,073	909	786	688	608	540
Average pellet energy in ft-lbs:	25.68	10.91	7.82	5.84	4.48	3.50	2.76
Time of flight in seconds:	0	.0459	.0764	.1120	.1529	.1993	.2417

Type of load: Nontoxic
Three-foot velocity: 1,550 ft./sec.
Hull: 3-inch plastic
Wad: Plastic
Shot: Steel
Buffered: No
Test barrel length: 30 inch
Pellets will pierce skin up to 157 yards.

NO. 1 STEEL PELLETS—1¼ OUNCES—129 PELLETS
Mfg: Winchester **Manufacturer's code:** WE123
Recoil energy in 8-lb. shotgun: 25.2 ft./lbs. **Recoil velocity in 8-lb. shotgun:** 14.2 ft./sec.

Distance in yards:	Muzzle	20	30	40	50	60	70
Velocity in fps:	1,375	941	810	708	624	554	494
Average pellet energy in ft-lbs:	17.90	8.38	6.21	4.74	3.69	2.91	2.31
Time of flight in seconds:	0	.0537	.0881	.1278	.1930	.2241	.2814

Type of load: Nontoxic
Three-foot velocity: 1,300 ft./sec.
Hull: 3-inch plastic
Wad: Plastic
Shot: Steel
Buffered: No
Test barrel length: 30 inch
Pellets will pierce skin up to 150 yards.

NO. 1 STEEL PELLETS—1¼ OUNCES—129 PELLETS
Mfg: Fiocchi **Manufacturer's code:** 123S
Recoil energy in 8-lb. shotgun: 33.0 ft./lbs. **Recoil velocity in 8-lb. shotgun:** 16.3 ft./sec.

Distance in yards:	Muzzle	20	30	40	50	60	70
Velocity in fps:	1,407	956	822	717	632	561	500
Average pellet energy in ft-lbs:	18.75	8.66	6.40	4.87	3.78	2.98	2.37
Time of flight in seconds:	0	.0526	.0865	.1257	.1703	.2207	.0774

Type of load: Nontoxic
Three-foot velocity: 1,330 ft./sec.
Hull: 3-inch plastic
Wad: Plastic
Shot: Steel
Buffered: No
Test barrel length: 30 inch
Pellets will pierce skin up to 151 yards.

NO. 1 STEEL PELLETS—1¼ OUNCES—129 PELLETS
Mfg: Federal Cartridge Company **Manufacturer's code:** W140
Recoil energy in 8-lb. shotgun: 36.1 ft./lbs. **Recoil velocity in 8-lb. shotgun:** 17.0 ft./sec.

Distance in yards:	Muzzle	20	30	40	50	60	70
Velocity in fps:	1,456	980	840	731	644	571	509
Average pellet energy in ft-lbs:	20.08	9.10	6.68	5.07	3.93	3.09	2.45
Time of flight in seconds:	0	.0511	.0843	.1226	.1664	.2159	.2717

Type of load: Nontoxic
Three-foot velocity: 1,375 ft./sec.
Hull: 3-inch plastic
Wad: Plastic
Shot: Steel
Buffered: No
Test barrel length: 30 inch
Pellets will pierce skin up to 152 yards.

NO. 1 STEEL PELLETS—1¼ OUNCES—129 PELLETS
Mfg: Remington Arms Co. **Manufacturer's code:** NS12H
Recoil energy in 8-lb. shotgun: 36.1 ft./lbs. **Recoil velocity in 8-lb. shotgun:** 17.0 ft./sec.

Distance in yards:	Muzzle	20	30	40	50	60	70
Velocity in fps:	1,456	980	840	731	644	571	509
Average pellet energy in ft-lbs:	20.08	9.10	6.68	5.07	3.93	3.09	2.45
Time of flight in seconds:	0	.0511	.0843	.1226	.1664	.2159	.2717

Type of load: Nontoxic
Three-foot velocity: 1,375 ft./sec.
Hull: 3-inch plastic
Wad: Plastic
Shot: Zinc-galvanized steel
Buffered: No
Test barrel length: 30 inch
Pellets will pierce skin up to 152 yards.

NO. 1 STEEL PELLETS—1¼ OUNCES—129 PELLETS
Mfg: Winchester **Manufacturer's code:** XSC123
Recoil energy in 8-lb. shotgun: 36.1 ft./lbs. **Recoil velocity in 8-lb. shotgun:** 17.0 ft./sec.

Distance in yards:	Muzzle	20	30	40	50	60	70
Velocity in fps:	1,456	980	840	731	644	571	509
Average pellet energy in ft-lbs:	20.08	9.10	6.68	5.07	3.93	3.09	2.45
Time of flight in seconds:	0	.0511	.0843	.1226	.1664	.2159	.2717

Type of load: Nontoxic
Three-foot velocity: 1,375 ft./sec.
Hull: 3-inch plastic
Wad: Two-piece plastic
Shot: Steel
Buffered: No
Test barrel length: 30 inch
Pellets will pierce skin up to 152 yards.

NO. 1 STEEL PELLETS—1¼ OUNCES—129 PELLETS
Mfg: Dionisi **Manufacturer's code:** D 12 ST3X
Recoil energy in 8-lb. shotgun: 37.9 ft./lbs. **Recoil velocity in 8-lb. shotgun:** 17.5 ft./sec.

Distance in yards:	Muzzle	20	30	40	50	60	70
Velocity in fps:	1,483	993	850	739	650	576	513
Average pellet energy in ft-lbs:	20.83	9.34	6.84	5.18	4.00	3.15	2.49
Time of flight in seconds:	0	.0503	.0831	.1210	.1643	.2134	.2686

Type of load: Nontoxic
Three-foot velocity: 1,400 ft./sec.
Hull: 3-inch plastic
Wad: Plastic
Shot: Steel
Buffered: No
Test barrel length: 30 inch
Pellets will pierce skin up to 153 yards.

NO. 1 STEEL PELLETS—1¼ OUNCES—129 PELLETS
Mfg: Kent Cartridge America/Canada **Manufacturer's code:** K123ST36
Recoil energy in 8-lb. shotgun: 37.9 ft./lbs. **Recoil velocity in 8-lb. shotgun:** 17.5 ft./sec.

Distance in yards:	Muzzle	20	30	40	50	60	70
Velocity in fps:	1,483	993	850	739	650	576	513
Average pellet energy in ft-lbs:	20.83	9.34	6.84	5.18	4.00	3.15	2.49
Time of flight in seconds:	0	.0503	.0831	.1210	.1643	.2134	.2686

Type of load: Nontoxic
Three-foot velocity: 1,400 ft./sec.
Hull: 3-inch plastic
Wad: Plastic
Shot: Steel
Buffered: No
Test barrel length: 30 inch
Pellets will pierce skin up to 153 yards.

NO. 1 STEEL PELLETS—1¼ OUNCES—129 PELLETS
Mfg: Estate Cartridge **Manufacturer's code:** HVST12M
Recoil energy in 8-lb. shotgun: 39.8 ft./lbs. **Recoil velocity in 8-lb. shotgun:** 17.9 ft./sec.

Distance in yards:	Muzzle	20	30	40	50	60	70
Velocity in fps:	1,510	1,007	860	747	657	582	518
Average pellet energy in ft-lbs:	21.60	9.59	7.00	5.29	4.08	3.20	2.54
Time of flight in seconds:	0	.0496	.0819	.1194	.1623	.2109	.2656

Type of load: Nontoxic
Three-foot velocity: 1,425 ft./sec.
Hull: 3-inch plastic
Wad: Plastic
Shot: Steel
Buffered: No
Test barrel length: 30 inch
Pellets will pierce skin up to 154 yards.

NO. 1 STEEL PELLETS—1⅜ OUNCES—142 PELLETS
Mfg: Federal Cartridge Company **Manufacturer's code:** W149
Recoil energy in 8-lb. shotgun: 35.7 ft./lbs. **Recoil velocity in 8-lb. shotgun:** 16.9 ft./sec.

Distance in yards:	Muzzle	20	30	40	50	60	70
Velocity in fps:	1,348	927	800	699	617	548	489
Average pellet energy in ft-lbs:	17.20	8.15	6.06	4.63	3.61	2.85	2.26
Time of flight in seconds:	0	.0546	.0895	.1297	.1754	.2270	.2849

Type of load: Nontoxic
Three-foot velocity: 1,275 ft./sec.
Hull: 3-inch plastic
Wad: Plastic
Shot: Steel
Buffered: No
Test barrel length: 30 inch
Pellets will pierce skin up to 149 yards.

NO. 1 STEEL PELLETS—1⅜ OUNCES—142 PELLETS
Mfg: Remington Arms Co. **Manufacturer's code:** NS12HM
Recoil energy in 8-lb. shotgun: 35.7 ft./lbs. **Recoil velocity in 8-lb. shotgun:** 16.9 ft./sec.

Distance in yards:	Muzzle	20	30	40	50	60	70
Velocity in fps:	1,348	927	800	699	617	548	489
Average pellet energy in ft-lbs:	17.20	8.15	6.06	4.63	3.61	2.85	2.26
Time of flight in seconds:	0	.0546	.0895	.1297	.1754	.2270	.2849

Type of load: Nontoxic
Three-foot velocity: 1,275 ft./sec.
Hull: 3-inch plastic
Wad: Plastic
Shot: Zinc-galvanized steel
Buffered: No
Test barrel length: 30 inch
Pellets will pierce skin up to 149 yards.

NO. 1 STEEL PELLETS—1⅜ OUNCES—142 PELLETS
Mfg: Winchester **Manufacturer's code:** XSM123
Recoil energy in 8-lb. shotgun: 35.7 ft./lbs. **Recoil velocity in 8-lb. shotgun:** 16.9 ft./sec.

Distance in yards:	Muzzle	20	30	40	50	60	70
Velocity in fps:	1,348	927	800	699	617	548	489
Average pellet energy in ft-lbs:	17.20	8.15	6.06	4.63	3.61	2.85	2.26
Time of flight in seconds:	0	.0546	.0895	.1297	.1754	.2270	.2849

Type of load: Nontoxic
Three-foot velocity: 1,275 ft./sec.
Hull: 3-inch plastic
Wad: Two-piece plastic
Shot: Steel
Buffered: No
Test barrel length: 30 inch
Pellets will pierce skin up to 149 yards.

NO. 1 STEEL PELLETS—1⅜ OUNCES—142 PELLETS
Mfg: Kent Cartridge America/Canada **Manufacturer's code:** K123ST40
Recoil energy in 8-lb. shotgun: 37.6 ft./lbs. **Recoil velocity in 8-lb. shotgun:** 17.4 ft./sec.

Distance in yards:	Muzzle	20	30	40	50	60	70
Velocity in fps:	1,375	941	810	708	624	554	494
Average pellet energy in ft-lbs:	17.90	8.38	6.21	4.74	3.69	2.91	2.31
Time of flight in seconds:	0	.0537	.0881	.1278	.1930	.2241	.2814

Type of load: Nontoxic
Three-foot velocity: 1,300 ft./sec.
Hull: 3-inch plastic
Wad: Plastic
Shot: Steel
Buffered: No
Test barrel length: 30 inch
Pellets will pierce skin up to 150 yards.

NO. 1 STEEL PELLETS—1⅜ OUNCES—142 PELLETS
Mfg: Estate Cartridge **Manufacturer's code:** HVST12MM
Recoil energy in 8-lb. shotgun: 54.6 ft./lbs. **Recoil velocity in 8-lb. shotgun:** 21.0 ft./sec.

Distance in yards:	Muzzle	20	30	40	50	60	70
Velocity in fps:	1,456	980	840	731	644	571	509
Average pellet energy in ft-lbs:	20.08	9.10	6.68	5.07	3.93	3.09	2.45
Time of flight in seconds:	0	.0511	.0843	.1226	.1664	.2159	.2717

Type of load: Nontoxic
Three-foot velocity: 1,375 ft./sec.
Hull: 3-inch plastic
Wad: Plastic
Shot: Steel
Buffered: No
Test barrel length: 30 inch
Pellets will pierce skin up to 152 yards.

NO. 2 STEEL PELLETS—1⅛ OUNCES—141 PELLETS
Mfg: Fiocchi **Manufacturer's code:** 123ST
Recoil energy in 8-lb. shotgun: 35.4 ft./lbs. **Recoil velocity in 8-lb. shotgun:** 16.9 ft./sec.

Distance in yards:	Muzzle	20	30	40	50	60	70
Velocity in fps:	1,571	1,012	856	737	643	566	500
Average pellet energy in ft-lbs:	19.25	8.00	5.71	4.24	3.23	2.50	1.95
Time of flight in seconds:	0	.0486	.0809	.1188	.1624	.2122	.2686

Type of load: Nontoxic
Three-foot velocity: 1,475 ft./sec.
Hull: 3-inch plastic
Wad: Plastic
Shot: Steel
Buffered: No
Test barrel length: 30 inch
Pellets will pierce skin up to 146 yards.

NO. 2 STEEL PELLETS—1⅛ OUNCES—141 PELLETS
Mfg: Federal Cartridge Company **Manufacturer's code:** PWT143/W143
Recoil energy in 8-lb. shotgun: 37.0 ft./lbs. **Recoil velocity in 8-lb. shotgun:** 17.3 ft./sec.

Distance in yards:	Muzzle	20	30	40	50	60	70
Velocity in fps:	1,598	1,025	865	745	649	608	505
Average pellet energy in ft-lbs:	19.92	8.20	5.84	4.33	3.29	2.54	1.99
Time of flight in seconds:	0	.0478	.0798	.1173	.1605	.2098	.2658

Type of load: Nontoxic
Three-foot velocity: 1,500 ft./sec.
Hull: 3-inch plastic
Wad: Plastic
Shot: Steel
Buffered: No
Test barrel length: 30 inch
Pellets will pierce skin up to 146 yards.

NO. 2 STEEL PELLETS—1⅛ OUNCES—141 PELLETS
Mfg: Kent Cartridge America/Canada **Manufacturer's code:** K123ST32
Recoil energy in 8-lb. shotgun: 37.0 ft./lbs. **Recoil velocity in 8-lb. shotgun:** 17.3 ft./sec.

Distance in yards:	Muzzle	20	30	40	50	60	70
Velocity in fps:	1,598	1,025	865	745	649	608	505
Average pellet energy in ft-lbs:	19.92	8.20	5.84	4.33	3.29	2.54	1.99
Time of flight in seconds:	0	.0478	.0798	.1173	.1605	.2098	.2658

Type of load: Nontoxic
Three-foot velocity: 1,500 ft./sec.
Hull: 3-inch plastic
Wad: Plastic
Shot: Steel
Buffered: No
Test barrel length: 30 inch
Pellets will pierce skin up to 146 yards.

NO. 2 STEEL PELLETS—1⅛ OUNCES—141 PELLETS
Mfg: Remington Arms Co. **Manufacturer's code:** NS12HV
Recoil energy in 8-lb. shotgun: 37.0 ft./lbs. **Recoil velocity in 8-lb. shotgun:** 17.3 ft./sec.

Distance in yards:	Muzzle	20	30	40	50	60	70
Velocity in fps:	1,598	1,025	865	745	649	608	505
Average pellet energy in ft-lbs:	19.92	8.20	5.84	4.33	3.29	2.54	1.99
Time of flight in seconds:	0	.0478	.0798	.1173	.1605	.2098	.2658

Type of load: Nontoxic
Three-foot velocity: 1,500 ft./sec.
Hull: 3-inch plastic
Wad: Plastic
Shot: Zinc-galvanized steel
Buffered: No
Test barrel length: 30 inch
Pellets will pierce skin up to 146 yards.

NO. 2 STEEL PELLETS—1⅛ OUNCES—141 PELLETS
Mfg: Dionisi **Manufacturer's code:** D 12 ST3
Recoil energy in 8-lb. shotgun: 40.5 ft./lbs. **Recoil velocity in 8-lb. shotgun:** 18.1 ft./sec.

Distance in yards:	Muzzle	20	30	40	50	60	70
Velocity in fps:	1,653	1,051	884	759	661	581	513
Average pellet energy in ft-lbs:	21.32	8.62	3.09	4.49	3.41	2.63	2.05
Time of flight in seconds:	0	.0465	.0777	.1145	.1569	.2054	.2604

Type of load: Nontoxic
Three-foot velocity: 1,550 ft./sec.
Hull: 3-inch plastic
Wad: Plastic
Shot: Steel
Buffered: No
Test barrel length: 30 inch
Pellets will pierce skin up to 148 yards.

NO. 2 STEEL PELLETS—1¼ OUNCES—156 PELLETS
Mfg: Clever **Manufacturer's code:** Magnum load
Recoil energy in 8-lb. shotgun: 28.0 ft./lbs. **Recoil velocity in 8-lb. shotgun:** 15.0 ft./sec.

Distance in yards:	Muzzle	20	30	40	50	60	70
Velocity in fps:	1,325	977	770	669	588	519	460
Average pellet energy in ft-lbs:	13.70	6.29	4.62	3.50	2.70	2.10	1.65
Time of flight in seconds:	0	.0560	.0922	.1341	.1819	.2363	.2977

Type of load: Nontoxic
Three-foot velocity: 1,250 ft./sec.
Hull: 3-inch plastic
Wad: Plastic
Shot: Steel
Buffered: No
Test barrel length: 30 inch
Pellets will pierce skin up to 139 yards.

NO. 2 STEEL PELLETS—1¼ OUNCES—156 PELLETS
Mfg: Winchester **Manufacturer's code:** WE123
Recoil energy in 8-lb. shotgun: 25.2 ft./lbs. **Recoil velocity in 8-lb. shotgun:** 14.2 ft./sec.

Distance in yards:	Muzzle	20	30	40	50	60	70
Velocity in fps:	1,379	923	789	685	601	530	469
Average pellet energy in ft-lbs:	14.85	6.65	4.86	3.66	2.81	2.19	1.72
Time of flight in seconds:	0	.0542	.0894	.1303	.1771	.2303	.2905

Type of load: Nontoxic
Three-foot velocity: 1,300 ft./sec.
Hull: 3-inch plastic
Wad: Plastic
Shot: Steel
Buffered: No
Test barrel length: 30 inch
Pellets will pierce skin up to 140 yards.

NO. 2 STEEL PELLETS—1¼ OUNCES—156 PELLETS
Mfg: Fiocchi **Manufacturer's code:** 123S
Recoil energy in 8-lb. shotgun: 33.0 ft./lbs. **Recoil velocity in 8-lb. shotgun:** 16.3 ft./sec.

Distance in yards:	Muzzle	20	30	40	50	60	70
Velocity in fps:	1,412	939	801	694	608	536	475
Average pellet energy in ft-lbs:	15.56	6.87	5.00	3.76	2.89	2.25	1.76
Time of flight in seconds:	0	.0532	.0878	.1282	.1744	.2270	.2864

Type of load: Nontoxic
Three-foot velocity: 1,330 ft./sec.
Hull: 3-inch plastic
Wad: Plastic
Shot: Steel
Buffered: No
Test barrel length: 30 inch
Pellets will pierce skin up to 145 yards.

NO. 2 STEEL PELLETS—1¼ OUNCES—156 PELLETS
Mfg: Federal Cartridge Company **Manufacturer's code:** W140
Recoil energy in 8-lb. shotgun: 36.1 ft./lbs. **Recoil velocity in 8-lb. shotgun:** 17.0 ft./sec.

Distance in yards:	Muzzle	20	30	40	50	60	70
Velocity in fps:	1,461	961	818	708	619	546	483
Average pellet energy in ft-lbs:	16.66	7.21	5.22	3.91	2.99	2.32	1.82
Time of flight in seconds:	0	.0517	.0856	.1251	.1705	.2221	.2806

Type of load: Nontoxic
Three-foot velocity: 1,375 ft./sec.
Hull: 3-inch plastic
Wad: Plastic
Shot: Steel
Buffered: No
Test barrel length: 30 inch
Pellets will pierce skin up to 143 yards.

NO. 2 STEEL PELLETS—1¼ OUNCES—156 PELLETS
Mfg: Remington Arms Co. **Manufacturer's code:** NS12H
Recoil energy in 8-lb. shotgun: 36.1 ft./lbs. **Recoil velocity in 8-lb. shotgun:** 17.0 ft./sec.

Distance in yards:	Muzzle	20	30	40	50	60	70
Velocity in fps:	1,461	961	818	708	619	546	483
Average pellet energy in ft-lbs:	16.66	7.21	5.22	3.91	2.99	2.32	1.82
Time of flight in seconds:	0	.0517	.0856	.1251	.1705	.2221	.2806

Type of load: Nontoxic
Three-foot velocity: 1,375 ft./sec.
Hull: 3-inch plastic
Wad: Plastic
Shot: Zinc-galvanized steel
Buffered: No
Test barrel length: 30 inch
Pellets will pierce skin up to 143 yards.

NO. 2 STEEL PELLETS—1¼ OUNCES—156 PELLETS
Mfg: Sellier & Bellot **Manufacturer's code:** SBA12001
Recoil energy in 8-lb. shotgun: 36.1 ft./lbs. **Recoil velocity in 8-lb. shotgun:** 17.0 ft./sec.

Distance in yards:	Muzzle	20	30	40	50	60	70
Velocity in fps:	1,461	961	818	708	619	546	483
Average pellet energy in ft-lbs:	16.66	7.21	5.22	3.91	2.99	2.32	1.82
Time of flight in seconds:	0	.0517	.0856	.1251	.1705	.2221	.2806

Type of load: Nontoxic
Three-foot velocity: 1,375 ft./sec.
Hull: 3-inch plastic
Wad: Plastic
Shot: Steel
Buffered: No
Test barrel length: 30 inch
Pellets will pierce skin up to 143 yards.

NO. 2 STEEL PELLETS—1¼ OUNCES—156 PELLETS
Mfg: Winchester **Manufacturer's code:** XSC123
Recoil energy in 8-lb. shotgun: 36.1 ft./lbs. **Recoil velocity in 8-lb. shotgun:** 17.0 ft./sec.

Distance in yards:	Muzzle	20	30	40	50	60	70
Velocity in fps:	1,461	961	818	708	619	546	483
Average pellet energy in ft-lbs:	16.66	7.21	5.22	3.91	2.99	2.32	1.82
Time of flight in seconds:	0	.0517	.0856	.1251	.1705	.2221	.2806

Type of load: Nontoxic
Three-foot velocity: 1,375 ft./sec.
Hull: 3-inch plastic
Wad: Two-piece plastic
Shot: Steel
Buffered: No
Test barrel length: 30 inch
Pellets will pierce skin up to 143 yards.

NO. 2 STEEL PELLETS—1¼ OUNCES—156 PELLETS
Mfg: Dionisi **Manufacturer's code:** D 12 ST3X
Recoil energy in 8-lb. shotgun: 37.9 ft./lbs. **Recoil velocity in 8-lb. shotgun:** 17.5 ft./sec.

Distance in yards:	Muzzle	20	30	40	50	60	70
Velocity in fps:	1,488	974	827	715	625	551	487
Average pellet energy in ft-lbs:	17.29	7.40	5.34	3.99	3.05	2.37	1.85
Time of flight in seconds:	0	.0509	.0844	.1234	.1684	.2195	.2775

Type of load: Nontoxic
Three-foot velocity: 1,400 ft./sec.
Hull: 3-inch plastic
Wad: Plastic
Shot: Steel
Buffered: No
Test barrel length: 30 inch
Pellets will pierce skin up to 144 yards.

NO. 2 STEEL PELLETS—1¼ OUNCES—156 PELLETS
Mfg: Kent Cartridge America/Canada **Manufacturer's code:** K123ST36
Recoil energy in 8-lb. shotgun: 37.9 ft./lbs. **Recoil velocity in 8-lb. shotgun:** 17.5 ft./sec.

Distance in yards:	Muzzle	20	30	40	50	60	70
Velocity in fps:	1,488	974	827	715	625	551	487
Average pellet energy in ft-lbs:	17.29	7.40	5.34	3.99	3.05	2.37	1.85
Time of flight in seconds:	0	.0509	.0844	.1234	.1684	.2195	.2775

Type of load: Nontoxic
Three-foot velocity: 1,400 ft./sec.
Hull: 3-inch plastic
Wad: Plastic
Shot: Steel
Buffered: No
Test barrel length: 30 inch
Pellets will pierce skin up to 144 yards.

NO. 2 STEEL PELLETS—1¼ OUNCES—156 PELLETS
Mfg: Estate Cartridge **Manufacturer's code:** HVST12M
Recoil energy in 8-lb. shotgun: 39.8 ft./lbs. **Recoil velocity in 8-lb. shotgun:** 17.9 ft./sec.

Distance in yards:	Muzzle	20	30	40	50	60	70
Velocity in fps:	1,516	987	837	723	631	556	492
Average pellet energy in ft-lbs:	17.93	7.60	5.46	4.07	3.11	2.41	1.89
Time of flight in seconds:	0	.0501	.0832	.1218	.1663	.2170	.2744

Type of load: Nontoxic
Three-foot velocity: 1,425 ft./sec.
Hull: 3-inch plastic
Wad: Plastic
Shot: Steel
Buffered: No
Test barrel length: 30 inch
Pellets will pierce skin up to 144 yards.

NO. 2 STEEL PELLETS—1¼ OUNCES—156 PELLETS
Mfg: PMC (Eldorado Cartridge Corp.) **Manufacturer's code:** SS12M
Recoil energy in 8-lb. shotgun: 39.8 ft./lbs. **Recoil velocity in 8-lb. shotgun:** 17.9 ft./sec.

Distance in yards:	Muzzle	20	30	40	50	60	70
Velocity in fps:	1,516	987	837	723	631	556	492
Average pellet energy in ft-lbs:	17.93	7.60	5.46	4.07	3.11	2.41	1.89
Time of flight in seconds:	0	.0501	.0832	.1218	.1663	.2170	.2744

Type of load: Nontoxic
Three-foot velocity: 1,425 ft./sec.
Hull: 3-inch plastic
Wad: Plastic
Shot: Steel
Buffered: No
Test barrel length: 30 inch
Pellets will pierce skin up to 144 yards.

NO. 2 STEEL PELLETS—1¼ OUNCES—156 PELLETS
Mfg: Winchester **Manufacturer's code:** SSH123
Recoil energy in 8-lb. shotgun: 41.7 ft./lbs. **Recoil velocity in 8-lb. shotgun:** 18.3 ft./sec.

Distance in yards:	Muzzle	20	30	40	50	60	70
Velocity in fps:	1,543	1,000	846	730	637	561	496
Average pellet energy in ft-lbs:	18.58	7.80	5.59	4.16	3.17	2.46	1.92
Time of flight in seconds:	0	.0493	.0820	.1203	.1643	.2146	.2715

Type of load: Nontoxic
Three-foot velocity: 1,450 ft./sec.
Hull: 3-inch plastic
Wad: Two-piece plastic
Shot: Steel
Buffered: No
Test barrel length: 30 inch
Pellets will pierce skin up to 145 yards.

NO. 2 STEEL PELLETS—1⅜ OUNCES—172 PELLETS
Mfg: Federal Cartridge Company **Manufacturer's code:** W149
Recoil energy in 8-lb. shotgun: 35.7 ft./lbs. **Recoil velocity in 8-lb. shotgun:** 16.9 ft./sec.

Distance in yards:	Muzzle	20	30	40	50	60	70
Velocity in fps:	1,352	911	780	677	594	525	465
Average pellet energy in ft-lbs:	14.27	6.47	4.74	3.58	2.76	2.15	1.68
Time of flight in seconds:	0	.0551	.0908	.1321	.1795	.2333	.2941

Type of load: Nontoxic
Three-foot velocity: 1,275 ft./sec.
Hull: 3-inch plastic
Wad: Plastic
Shot: Steel
Buffered: No
Test barrel length: 30 inch
Pellets will pierce skin up to 140 yards.

NO. 2 STEEL PELLETS—1⅜ OUNCES—172 PELLETS
Mfg: Remington Arms Co. **Manufacturer's code:** NS12HM
Recoil energy in 8-lb. shotgun: 35.7 ft./lbs. **Recoil velocity in 8-lb. shotgun:** 16.9 ft./sec.

Distance in yards:	Muzzle	20	30	40	50	60	70
Velocity in fps:	1,352	911	780	677	594	525	465
Average pellet energy in ft-lbs:	14.27	6.47	4.74	3.58	2.76	2.15	1.68
Time of flight in seconds:	0	.0551	.0908	.1321	.1795	.2333	.2941

Type of load: Nontoxic
Three-foot velocity: 1,275 ft./sec.
Hull: 3-inch plastic
Wad: Plastic
Shot: Zinc-galvanized steel
Buffered: No
Test barrel length: 30 inch
Pellets will pierce skin up to 140 yards.

NO. 2 STEEL PELLETS—1⅜ OUNCES—172 PELLETS
Mfg: Winchester **Manufacturer's code:** XSM123
Recoil energy in 8-lb. shotgun: 35.7 ft./lbs. **Recoil velocity in 8-lb. shotgun:** 16.9 ft./sec.

Distance in yards:	Muzzle	20	30	40	50	60	70
Velocity in fps:	1,352	911	780	677	594	525	465
Average pellet energy in ft-lbs:	14.27	6.47	4.74	3.58	2.76	2.15	1.68
Time of flight in seconds:	0	.0551	.0908	.1321	.1795	.2333	.2941

Type of load: Nontoxic
Three-foot velocity: 1,275 ft./sec.
Hull: 3-inch plastic
Wad: Two-piece plastic
Shot: Steel
Buffered: No
Test barrel length: 30 inch
Pellets will pierce skin up to 140 yards.

NO. 2 STEEL PELLETS—1⅜ OUNCES—172 PELLETS
Mfg: Fiocchi **Manufacturer's code:** 123SH
Recoil energy in 8-lb. shotgun: 37.6 ft./lbs. **Recoil velocity in 8-lb. shotgun:** 17.4 ft./sec.

Distance in yards:	Muzzle	20	30	40	50	60	70
Velocity in fps:	1,379	923	789	685	601	530	469
Average pellet energy in ft-lbs:	14.85	6.65	4.86	3.66	2.81	2.19	1.72
Time of flight in seconds:	0	.0542	.0894	.1303	.1771	.2303	.2905

Type of load: Nontoxic
Three-foot velocity: 1,300 ft./sec.
Hull: 3-inch plastic
Wad: Plastic
Shot: Steel
Buffered: No
Test barrel length: 30 inch
Pellets will pierce skin up to 140 yards.

NO. 2 STEEL PELLETS—1³/₈ OUNCES—172 PELLETS
Mfg: Kent Cartridge America/Canada **Manufacturer's code:** K123ST40
Recoil energy in 8-lb. shotgun: 37.6 ft./lbs. **Recoil velocity in 8-lb. shotgun:** 17.4 ft./sec.

Distance in yards:	Muzzle	20	30	40	50	60	70
Velocity in fps:	1,379	923	789	685	601	530	469
Average pellet energy in ft-lbs:	14.85	6.65	4.86	3.66	2.81	2.19	1.72
Time of flight in seconds:	0	.0542	.0894	.1303	.1771	.2303	.2905

Type of load: Nontoxic
Three-foot velocity: 1,300 ft./sec.
Hull: 3-inch plastic
Wad: Plastic
Shot: Steel
Buffered: No
Test barrel length: 30 inch
Pellets will pierce skin up to 140 yards.

NO. 2 STEEL PELLETS—1³/₈ OUNCES—172 PELLETS
Mfg: Estate Cartridge **Manufacturer's code:** HVST12MM
Recoil energy in 8-lb. shotgun: 54.6 ft./lbs. **Recoil velocity in 8-lb. shotgun:** 21.0 ft./sec.

Distance in yards:	Muzzle	20	30	40	50	60	70
Velocity in fps:	1,461	961	818	708	619	546	483
Average pellet energy in ft-lbs:	16.66	7.21	5.22	3.91	2.99	2.32	1.82
Time of flight in seconds:	0	.0517	.0856	.1251	.1705	.2221	.2806

Type of load: Nontoxic
Three-foot velocity: 1,375 ft./sec.
Hull: 3-inch plastic
Wad: Plastic
Shot: Steel
Buffered: No
Test barrel length: 30 inch
Pellets will pierce skin up to 143 yards.

NO. 3 STEEL PELLETS—1¹/₈ OUNCES—178 PELLETS
Mfg: Fiocchi **Manufacturer's code:** 123ST
Recoil energy in 8-lb. shotgun: 35.4 ft./lbs. **Recoil velocity in 8-lb. shotgun:** 16.9 ft./sec.

Distance in yards:	Muzzle	20	30	40	50	60	70
Velocity in fps:	1,576	1,093	829	710	615	538	472
Average pellet energy in ft-lbs:	15.77	6.21	4.36	3.20	2.40	1.83	1.41
Time of flight in seconds:	0	.0492	.0824	.1216	.1671	.2193	.2789

Type of load: Nontoxic
Three-foot velocity: 1,475 ft./sec.
Hull: 3-inch plastic
Wad: Plastic
Shot: Steel
Buffered: No
Test barrel length: 30 inch
Pellets will pierce skin up to 136 yards.

NO. 3 STEEL PELLETS—1¹/₈ OUNCES—178 PELLETS
Mfg: Federal Cartridge Company **Manufacturer's code:** PWT143
Recoil energy in 8-lb. shotgun: 37.0 ft./lbs. **Recoil velocity in 8-lb. shotgun:** 17.3 ft./sec.

Distance in yards:	Muzzle	20	30	40	50	60	70
Velocity in fps:	1,604	1002	838	717	621	542	476
Average pellet energy in ft-lbs:	16.32	6.36	4.46	3.26	2.44	1.87	1.44
Time of flight in seconds:	0	.0484	.0813	.1201	.1651	.2169	.2760

Type of load: Nontoxic
Three-foot velocity: 1,500 ft./sec.
Hull: 3-inch plastic
Wad: Plastic
Shot: Steel
Buffered: No
Test barrel length: 30 inch
Pellets will pierce skin up to 137 yards.

NO. 3 STEEL PELLETS—1¹/₈ OUNCES—178 PELLETS
Mfg: Kent Cartridge America/Canada **Manufacturer's code:** K123ST32
Recoil energy in 8-lb. shotgun: 37.0 ft./lbs. **Recoil velocity in 8-lb. shotgun:** 17.3 ft./sec.

Distance in yards:	Muzzle	20	30	40	50	60	70
Velocity in fps:	1,604	1002	838	717	621	542	476
Average pellet energy in ft-lbs:	16.32	6.36	4.46	3.26	2.44	1.87	1.44
Time of flight in seconds:	0	.0484	.0813	.1201	.1651	.2169	.2760

Type of load: Nontoxic
Three-foot velocity: 1,500 ft./sec.
Hull: 3-inch plastic
Wad: Plastic
Shot: Steel
Buffered: No
Test barrel length: 30 inch
Pellets will pierce skin up to 137 yards.

NO. 3 STEEL PELLETS—1¹/₈ OUNCES—178 PELLETS
Mfg: Dionisi **Manufacturer's code:** D 12 ST3
Recoil energy in 8-lb. shotgun: 40.5 ft./lbs. **Recoil velocity in 8-lb. shotgun:** 18.1 ft./sec.

Distance in yards:	Muzzle	20	30	40	50	60	70
Velocity in fps:	1,659	1,026	856	730	632	551	484
Average pellet energy in ft-lbs:	17.47	6.68	4.65	3.38	2.53	1.93	1.48
Time of flight in seconds:	0	.0473	.0794	.1174	.1617	.2126	.2707

Type of load: Nontoxic
Three-foot velocity: 1,550 ft./sec.
Hull: 3-inch plastic
Wad: Plastic
Shot: Steel
Buffered: No
Test barrel length: 30 inch
Pellets will pierce skin up to 138 yards.

NO. 3 STEEL PELLETS—1¹/₄ OUNCES—197 PELLETS
Mfg: Winchester **Manufacturer's code:** WE123
Recoil energy in 8-lb. shotgun: 25.2 ft./lbs. **Recoil velocity in 8-lb. shotgun:** 14.2 ft./sec.

Distance in yards:	Muzzle	20	30	40	50	60	70
Velocity in fps:	1,384	904	767	661	575	504	442
Average pellet energy in ft-lbs:	12.16	5.18	3.73	2.77	2.10	1.61	1.24
Time of flight in seconds:	0	.0548	.0909	.1332	.1819	.2377	.3013

Type of load: Nontoxic
Three-foot velocity: 1,300 ft./sec.
Hull: 3-inch plastic
Wad: Plastic
Shot: Steel
Buffered: No
Test barrel length: 30 inch
Pellets will pierce skin up to 131 yards.

NO. 3 STEEL PELLETS—1¼ OUNCES—197 PELLETS
Mfg: Fiocchi **Manufacturer's code:** 123S
Recoil energy in 8-lb. shotgun: 33.0 ft./lbs. **Recoil velocity in 8-lb. shotgun:** 16.3 ft./sec.

Distance in yards:	Muzzle	20	30	40	50	60	70
Velocity in fps:	1,417	919	778	669	582	510	448
Average pellet energy in ft-lbs:	12.74	5.35	3.84	2.84	2.15	1.65	1.27
Time of flight in seconds:	0	.0538	.0894	.1310	.1792	.2343	.2971

Type of load: Nontoxic
Three-foot velocity: 1,330 ft./sec.
Hull: 3-inch plastic
Wad: Plastic
Shot: Steel
Buffered: No
Test barrel length: 30 inch
Pellets will pierce skin up to 132 yards.

NO. 3 STEEL PELLETS—1¼ OUNCES—197 PELLETS
Mfg: Federal Cartridge Company **Manufacturer's code:** W140
Recoil energy in 8-lb. shotgun: 36.1 ft./lbs. **Recoil velocity in 8-lb. shotgun:** 17.0 ft./sec.

Distance in yards:	Muzzle	20	30	40	50	60	70
Velocity in fps:	1,466	941	794	682	593	519	455
Average pellet energy in ft-lbs:	13.64	5.61	4.00	2.95	2.23	1.71	1.32
Time of flight in seconds:	0	.0523	.0871	.1279	.1752	.2294	.2911

Type of load: Nontoxic
Three-foot velocity: 1,375 ft./sec.
Hull: 3-inch plastic
Wad: Plastic
Shot: Steel
Buffered: No
Test barrel length: 30 inch
Pellets will pierce skin up to 133 yards.

NO. 3 STEEL PELLETS—1¼ OUNCES—197 PELLETS
Mfg: Remington Arms Co. **Manufacturer's code:** NS12H
Recoil energy in 8-lb. shotgun: 36.1 ft./lbs. **Recoil velocity in 8-lb. shotgun:** 17.0 ft./sec.

Distance in yards:	Muzzle	20	30	40	50	60	70
Velocity in fps:	1,466	941	794	682	593	519	455
Average pellet energy in ft-lbs:	13.64	5.61	4.00	2.95	2.23	1.71	1.32
Time of flight in seconds:	0	.0523	.0871	.1279	.1752	.2294	.2911

Type of load: Nontoxic
Three-foot velocity: 1,375 ft./sec.
Hull: 3-inch plastic
Wad: Plastic
Shot: Zinc-galvanized steel
Buffered: No
Test barrel length: 30 inch
Pellets will pierce skin up to 133 yards.

NO. 3 STEEL PELLETS—1¼ OUNCES—197 PELLETS
Mfg: Sellier & Bellot **Manufacturer's code:** SBA12001
Recoil energy in 8-lb. shotgun: 36.1 ft./lbs. **Recoil velocity in 8-lb. shotgun:** 17.0 ft./sec.

Distance in yards:	Muzzle	20	30	40	50	60	70
Velocity in fps:	1,466	941	794	682	593	519	455
Average pellet energy in ft-lbs:	13.64	5.61	4.00	2.95	2.23	1.71	1.32
Time of flight in seconds:	0	.0523	.0871	.1279	.1752	.2294	.2911

Type of load: Nontoxic
Three-foot velocity: 1,375 ft./sec.
Hull: 3-inch plastic
Wad: Plastic
Shot: Steel
Buffered: No
Test barrel length: 30 inch
Pellets will pierce skin up to 133 yards.

NO. 3 STEEL PELLETS—1¼ OUNCES—197 PELLETS
Mfg: Winchester **Manufacturer's code:** XSV123
Recoil energy in 8-lb. shotgun: 36.1 ft./lbs. **Recoil velocity in 8-lb. shotgun:** 17.0 ft./sec.

Distance in yards:	Muzzle	20	30	40	50	60	70
Velocity in fps:	1,466	941	794	682	593	519	455
Average pellet energy in ft-lbs:	13.64	5.61	4.00	2.95	2.23	1.71	1.32
Time of flight in seconds:	0	.0523	.0871	.1279	.1752	.2294	.2911

Type of load: Nontoxic
Three-foot velocity: 1,375 ft./sec.
Hull: 3-inch plastic
Wad: Two-piece plastic
Shot: Steel
Buffered: No
Test barrel length: 30 inch
Pellets will pierce skin up to 133 yards.

NO. 3 STEEL PELLETS—1¼ OUNCES—197 PELLETS
Mfg: Dionisi **Manufacturer's code:** D 12 ST3X
Recoil energy in 8-lb. shotgun: 37.9 ft./lbs. **Recoil velocity in 8-lb. shotgun:** 17.5 ft./sec.

Distance in yards:	Muzzle	20	30	40	50	60	70
Velocity in fps:	1,494	953	803	689	598	524	460
Average pellet energy in ft-lbs:	14.16	5.76	4.09	3.01	2.27	1.74	1.34
Time of flight in seconds:	0	.0515	.0859	.1263	.1731	.2267	.2879

Type of load: Nontoxic
Three-foot velocity: 1,400 ft./sec.
Hull: 3-inch plastic
Wad: Plastic
Shot: Steel
Buffered: No
Test barrel length: 30 inch
Pellets will pierce skin up to 134 yards.

NO. 3 STEEL PELLETS—1¼ OUNCES—197 PELLETS
Mfg: Kent Cartridge America/Canada **Manufacturer's code:** K123ST36
Recoil energy in 8-lb. shotgun: 37.9 ft./lbs. **Recoil velocity in 8-lb. shotgun:** 17.5 ft./sec.

Distance in yards:	Muzzle	20	30	40	50	60	70
Velocity in fps:	1,494	953	803	689	598	524	460
Average pellet energy in ft-lbs:	14.16	5.76	4.09	3.01	2.27	1.74	1.34
Time of flight in seconds:	0	.0515	.0859	.1263	.1731	.2267	.2879

Type of load: Nontoxic
Three-foot velocity: 1,400 ft./sec.
Hull: 3-inch plastic
Wad: Plastic
Shot: Steel
Buffered: No
Test barrel length: 30 inch
Pellets will pierce skin up to 134 yards.

NO. 3 STEEL PELLETS—1¼ OUNCES—197 PELLETS
Mfg: Estate Cartridge **Manufacturer's code:** HVST12M
Recoil energy in 8-lb. shotgun: 39.8 ft./lbs. **Recoil velocity in 8-lb. shotgun:** 17.9 ft./sec.

Distance in yards:	Muzzle	20	30	40	50	60	70
Velocity in fps:	1,521	965	812	696	604	528	464
Average pellet energy in ft-lbs:	14.68	5.91	4.18	3.07	2.31	1.77	1.36
Time of flight in seconds:	0	.0507	.0847	.1247	.1710	.2242	.2848

Type of load: Nontoxic
Three-foot velocity: 1,425 ft./sec.
Hull: 3-inch plastic
Wad: Plastic
Shot: Steel
Buffered: No
Test barrel length: 30 inch
Pellets will pierce skin up to 135 yards.

NO. 3 STEEL PELLETS—1¼ OUNCES—197 PELLETS
Mfg: PMC (Eldorado Cartridge Corp.) **Manufacturer's code:** SS12M
Recoil energy in 8-lb. shotgun: 39.8 ft./lbs. **Recoil velocity in 8-lb. shotgun:** 17.9 ft./sec.

Distance in yards:	Muzzle	20	30	40	50	60	70
Velocity in fps:	1,521	965	812	696	604	528	464
Average pellet energy in ft-lbs:	14.68	5.91	4.18	3.07	2.31	1.77	1.36
Time of flight in seconds:	0	.0507	.0847	.1247	.1710	.2242	.2848

Type of load: Nontoxic
Three-foot velocity: 1,425 ft./sec.
Hull: 3-inch plastic
Wad: Plastic
Shot: Steel
Buffered: No
Test barrel length: 30 inch
Pellets will pierce skin up to 135 yards.

NO. 3 STEEL PELLETS—1¼ OUNCES—197 PELLETS
Mfg: Winchester **Manufacturer's code:** SSH123
Recoil energy in 8-lb. shotgun: 41.7 ft./lbs. **Recoil velocity in 8-lb. shotgun:** 18.3 ft./sec.

Distance in yards:	Muzzle	20	30	40	50	60	70
Velocity in fps:	1,549	977	821	703	610	533	468
Average pellet energy in ft-lbs:	15.22	6.06	4.27	3.13	2.36	1.80	1.39
Time of flight in seconds:	0	.0499	.0835	.1231	.1690	.2217	.2818

Type of load: Nontoxic
Three-foot velocity: 1,450 ft./sec.
Hull: 3-inch plastic
Wad: Two-piece plastic
Shot: Steel
Buffered: No
Test barrel length: 30 inch
Pellets will pierce skin up to 135 yards.

NO. 3 STEEL PELLETS—1⅜ OUNCES—217 PELLETS
Mfg: Federal Cartridge Company **Manufacturer's code:** W149
Recoil energy in 8-lb. shotgun: 35.7 ft./lbs. **Recoil velocity in 8-lb. shotgun:** 16.9 ft./sec.

Distance in yards:	Muzzle	20	30	40	50	60	70
Velocity in fps:	1,357	892	757	653	569	499	438
Average pellet energy in ft-lbs:	11.68	5.04	3.64	2.71	2.06	1.58	1.22
Time of flight in seconds:	0	.0557	.0923	.1350	.1843	.2407	.3049

Type of load: Nontoxic
Three-foot velocity: 1,275 ft./sec.
Hull: 3-inch plastic
Wad: Plastic
Shot: Steel
Buffered: No
Test barrel length: 30 inch
Pellets will pierce skin up to 130 yards.

NO. 3 STEEL PELLETS—1⅜ OUNCES—217 PELLETS
Mfg: Remington Arms Co. **Manufacturer's code:** NS12HM
Recoil energy in 8-lb. shotgun: 35.7 ft./lbs. **Recoil velocity in 8-lb. shotgun:** 16.9 ft./sec.

Distance in yards:	Muzzle	20	30	40	50	60	70
Velocity in fps:	1,357	892	757	653	569	499	438
Average pellet energy in ft-lbs:	11.68	5.04	3.64	2.71	2.06	1.58	1.22
Time of flight in seconds:	0	.0557	.0923	.1350	.1843	.2407	.3049

Type of load: Nontoxic
Three-foot velocity: 1,275 ft./sec.
Hull: 3-inch plastic
Wad: Plastic
Shot: Zinc-galvanized steel
Buffered: No
Test barrel length: 30 inch
Pellets will pierce skin up to 130 yards.

NO. 3 STEEL PELLETS—1⅜ OUNCES—217 PELLETS
Mfg: Winchester **Manufacturer's code:** XSM123
Recoil energy in 8-lb. shotgun: 35.7 ft./lbs. **Recoil velocity in 8-lb. shotgun:** 16.9 ft./sec.

Distance in yards:	Muzzle	20	30	40	50	60	70
Velocity in fps:	1,357	892	757	653	569	499	438
Average pellet energy in ft-lbs:	11.68	5.04	3.64	2.71	2.06	1.58	1.22
Time of flight in seconds:	0	.0557	.0923	.1350	.1843	.2407	.3049

Type of load: Nontoxic
Three-foot velocity: 1,275 ft./sec.
Hull: 3-inch plastic
Wad: Two-piece plastic
Shot: Steel
Buffered: No
Test barrel length: 30 inch
Pellets will pierce skin up to 130 yards.

NO. 3 STEEL PELLETS—1⅜ OUNCES—217 PELLETS
Mfg: Fiocchi **Manufacturer's code:** 123SH
Recoil energy in 8-lb. shotgun: 37.6 ft./lbs. **Recoil velocity in 8-lb. shotgun:** 17.4 ft./sec.

Distance in yards:	Muzzle	20	30	40	50	60	70
Velocity in fps:	1,384	904	767	661	575	504	442
Average pellet energy in ft-lbs:	12.16	5.18	3.73	2.77	2.10	1.61	1.24
Time of flight in seconds:	0	.0548	.0909	.1332	.1819	.2377	.3013

Type of load: Nontoxic
Three-foot velocity: 1,300 ft./sec.
Hull: 3-inch plastic
Wad: Plastic
Shot: Steel
Buffered: No
Test barrel length: 30 inch
Pellets will pierce skin up to 131 yards.

NO. 3 STEEL PELLETS—1⅜ OUNCES—217 PELLETS
Mfg: Kent Cartridge America/Canada **Manufacturer's code:** K123ST40
Recoil energy in 8-lb. shotgun: 37.6 ft./lbs. **Recoil velocity in 8-lb. shotgun:** 17.4 ft./sec.

Distance in yards:	Muzzle	20	30	40	50	60	70
Velocity in fps:	1,384	904	767	661	575	504	442
Average pellet energy in ft-lbs:	12.16	5.18	3.73	2.77	2.10	1.61	1.24
Time of flight in seconds:	0	.0548	.0909	.1332	.1819	.2377	.3013

Type of load: Nontoxic
Three-foot velocity: 1,300 ft./sec.
Hull: 3-inch plastic
Wad: Plastic
Shot: Steel
Buffered: No
Test barrel length: 30 inch
Pellets will pierce skin up to 131 yards.

NO. 3 STEEL PELLETS—1⅜ OUNCES—217 PELLETS
Mfg: Estate Cartridge **Manufacturer's code:** HVST12MM
Recoil energy in 8-lb. shotgun: 54.6 ft./lbs. **Recoil velocity in 8-lb. shotgun:** 21.0 ft./sec.

Distance in yards:	Muzzle	20	30	40	50	60	70
Velocity in fps:	1,466	941	794	682	593	519	455
Average pellet energy in ft-lbs:	13.64	5.61	4.00	2.95	2.23	1.71	1.32
Time of flight in seconds:	0	.0523	.0871	.1279	.1752	.2294	.2911

Type of load: Nontoxic
Three-foot velocity: 1,375 ft./sec.
Hull: 3-inch plastic
Wad: Plastic
Shot: Steel
Buffered: No
Test barrel length: 30 inch
Pellets will pierce skin up to 133 yards.

NO. 4 STEEL PELLETS—1⅛ OUNCES—216 PELLETS
Mfg: Fiocchi **Manufacturer's code:** 123ST
Recoil energy in 8-lb. shotgun: 35.4 ft./lbs. **Recoil velocity in 8-lb. shotgun:** 16.9 ft./sec.

Distance in yards:	Muzzle	20	30	40	50	60	70
Velocity in fps:	1,583	1,204	801	680	585	507	441
Average pellet energy in ft-lbs:	12.72	4.72	3.26	2.35	1.74	1.31	.99
Time of flight in seconds:	0	.0499	.0842	.1249	.1726	.2277	.2912

Type of load: Nontoxic
Three-foot velocity: 1,475 ft./sec.
Hull: 3-inch plastic
Wad: Plastic
Shot: Steel
Buffered: No
Test barrel length: 30 inch
Pellets will pierce skin up to 127 yards.

NO. 4 STEEL PELLETS—1⅛ OUNCES—216 PELLETS
Mfg: Federal Cartridge Company **Manufacturer's code:** PWT143/W143
Recoil energy in 8-lb. shotgun: 37.0 ft./lbs. **Recoil velocity in 8-lb. shotgun:** 17.3 ft./sec.

Distance in yards:	Muzzle	20	30	40	50	60	70
Velocity in fps:	1,610	975	809	686	590	511	444
Average pellet energy in ft-lbs:	13.17	4.83	3.33	2.39	1.77	1.33	1.00
Time of flight in seconds:	0	.0492	.0831	.1234	.1706	.2253	.2883

Type of load: Nontoxic
Three-foot velocity: 1,500 ft./sec.
Hull: 3-inch plastic
Wad: Plastic
Shot: Steel
Buffered: No
Test barrel length: 30 inch
Pellets will pierce skin up to 127 yards.

NO. 4 STEEL PELLETS—1⅛ OUNCES—216 PELLETS
Mfg: Kent Cartridge America/Canada **Manufacturer's code:** K123ST32
Recoil energy in 8-lb. shotgun: 37.0 ft./lbs. **Recoil velocity in 8-lb. shotgun:** 17.3 ft./sec.

Distance in yards:	Muzzle	20	30	40	50	60	70
Velocity in fps:	1,610	975	809	686	590	511	444
Average pellet energy in ft-lbs:	13.17	4.83	3.33	2.39	1.77	1.33	1.00
Time of flight in seconds:	0	.0492	.0831	.1234	.1706	.2253	.2883

Type of load: Nontoxic
Three-foot velocity: 1,500 ft./sec.
Hull: 3-inch plastic
Wad: Plastic
Shot: Steel
Buffered: No
Test barrel length: 30 inch
Pellets will pierce skin up to 127 yards.

NO. 4 STEEL PELLETS—1⅛ OUNCES—216 PELLETS
Mfg: Remington Arms Co. **Manufacturer's code:** NS12HV
Recoil energy in 8-lb. shotgun: 37.0 ft./lbs. **Recoil velocity in 8-lb. shotgun:** 17.3 ft./sec.

Distance in yards:	Muzzle	20	30	40	50	60	70
Velocity in fps:	1,610	975	809	686	590	511	444
Average pellet energy in ft-lbs:	13.17	4.83	3.33	2.39	1.77	1.33	1.00
Time of flight in seconds:	0	.0492	.0831	.1234	.1706	.2253	.2883

Type of load: Nontoxic
Three-foot velocity: 1,500 ft./sec.
Hull: 3-inch plastic
Wad: Plastic
Shot: Zinc-galvanized steel
Buffered: No
Test barrel length: 30 inch
Pellets will pierce skin up to 127 yards.

NO. 4 STEEL PELLETS—1⅛ OUNCES—216 PELLETS
Mfg: Dionisi **Manufacturer's code:** D 12 ST3
Recoil energy in 8-lb. shotgun: 40.5 ft./lbs. **Recoil velocity in 8-lb. shotgun:** 18.1 ft./sec.

Distance in yards:	Muzzle	20	30	40	50	60	70
Velocity in fps:	1,666	999	826	699	600	520	452
Average pellet energy in ft-lbs:	14.10	5.07	3.46	2.48	1.83	1.37	1.04
Time of flight in seconds:	0	.0482	.0813	.1209	.1673	.2211	.2831

Type of load: Nontoxic
Three-foot velocity: 1,550 ft./sec.
Hull: 3-inch plastic
Wad: Plastic
Shot: Steel
Buffered: No
Test barrel length: 30 inch
Pellets will pierce skin up to 128 yards.

NO. 4 STEEL PELLETS—1¼ OUNCES—240 PELLETS
Mfg: Clever **Manufacturer's code:** Magnum load
Recoil energy in 8-lb. shotgun: 28.0 ft./lbs. **Recoil velocity in 8-lb. shotgun:** 15.0 ft./sec.

Distance in yards:	Muzzle	20	30	40	50	60	70
Velocity in fps:	1,335	859	724	620	536	466	405
Average pellet energy in ft-lbs:	9.05	3.75	2.66	1.95	1.46	1.10	.83
Time of flight in seconds:	0	.0574	.0955	.1404	.1925	.2526	.3217

Type of load: Nontoxic Field
Three-foot velocity: 1,250 ft./sec.
Hull: 3-inch plastic
Wad: Plastic
Shot: Steel
Buffered: No
Test barrel length: 30 inch
Pellets will pierce skin up to 120 yards.

NO. 4 STEEL PELLETS—1¼ OUNCES—240 PELLETS
Mfg: Winchester **Manufacturer's code:** WE123
Recoil energy in 8-lb. shotgun: 25.2 ft./lbs. **Recoil velocity in 8-lb. shotgun:** 14.2 ft./sec.

Distance in yards:	Muzzle	20	30	40	50	60	70
Velocity in fps:	1,389	882	741	634	547	475	413
Average pellet energy in ft-lbs:	9.81	3.95	2.79	2.04	1.52	1.32	.87
Time of flight in seconds:	0	.0555	.0927	.1366	.1876	.2465	.3142

Type of load: Nontoxic
Three-foot velocity: 1,300 ft./sec.
Hull: 3-inch plastic
Wad: Plastic
Shot: Steel
Buffered: No
Test barrel length: 30 inch
Pellets will pierce skin up to 122 yards.

NO. 4 STEEL PELLETS—1¼ OUNCES—240 PELLETS
Mfg: Fiocchi **Manufacturer's code:** 123S
Recoil energy in 8-lb. shotgun: 33.0 ft./lbs. **Recoil velocity in 8-lb. shotgun:** 16.3 ft./sec.

Distance in yards:	Muzzle	20	30	40	50	60	70
Velocity in fps:	1,422	896	752	642	554	481	418
Average pellet energy in ft-lbs:	10.28	4.08	2.87	2.09	1.56	1.18	.89
Time of flight in seconds:	0	.0545	.0912	.1344	.1848	.2403	.3099

Type of load: Nontoxic
Three-foot velocity: 1,330 ft./sec.
Hull: 3-inch plastic
Wad: Plastic
Shot: Steel
Buffered: No
Test barrel length: 30 inch
Pellets will pierce skin up to 123 yards.

NO. 4 STEEL PELLETS—1¼ OUNCES—240 PELLETS
Mfg: Federal Cartridge Company **Manufacturer's code:** W140
Recoil energy in 8-lb. shotgun: 36.1 ft./lbs. **Recoil velocity in 8-lb. shotgun:** 17.0 ft./sec.

Distance in yards:	Muzzle	20	30	40	50	60	70
Velocity in fps:	1,472	917	767	654	465	489	425
Average pellet energy in ft-lbs:	11.01	4.27	2.99	2.17	1.61	1.22	.92
Time of flight in seconds:	0	.0530	.0889	.1313	.1808	.2380	.3038

Type of load: Nontoxic
Three-foot velocity: 1,375 ft./sec.
Hull: 3-inch plastic
Wad: Plastic
Shot: Steel
Buffered: No
Test barrel length: 30 inch
Pellets will pierce skin up to 124 yards.

NO. 4 STEEL PELLETS—1¼ OUNCES—240 PELLETS
Mfg: Remington Arms Co. **Manufacturer's code:** NS12H
Recoil energy in 8-lb. shotgun: 36.1 ft./lbs. **Recoil velocity in 8-lb. shotgun:** 17.0 ft./sec.

Distance in yards:	Muzzle	20	30	40	50	60	70
Velocity in fps:	1,472	917	767	654	465	489	425
Average pellet energy in ft-lbs:	11.01	4.27	2.99	2.17	1.61	1.22	.92
Time of flight in seconds:	0	.0530	.0889	.1313	.1808	.2380	.3038

Type of load: Nontoxic
Three-foot velocity: 1,375 ft./sec.
Hull: 3-inch plastic
Wad: Plastic
Shot: Zinc-galvanized steel
Buffered: No
Test barrel length: 30 inch
Pellets will pierce skin up to 124 yards.

NO. 4 STEEL PELLETS—1¼ OUNCES—240 PELLETS
Mfg: Sellier & Bellot **Manufacturer's code:** SBA12001
Recoil energy in 8-lb. shotgun: 36.1 ft./lbs. **Recoil velocity in 8-lb. shotgun:** 17.0 ft./sec.

Distance in yards:	Muzzle	20	30	40	50	60	70
Velocity in fps:	1,472	917	767	654	465	489	425
Average pellet energy in ft-lbs:	11.01	4.27	2.99	2.17	1.61	1.22	.92
Time of flight in seconds:	0	.0530	.0889	.1313	.1808	.2380	.3038

Type of load: Nontoxic
Three-foot velocity: 1,375 ft./sec.
Hull: 3-inch plastic
Wad: Plastic
Shot: Steel
Buffered: No
Test barrel length: 30 inch
Pellets will pierce skin up to 124 yards.

NO. 4 STEEL PELLETS—1¼ OUNCES—240 PELLETS
Mfg: Winchester **Manufacturer's code:** XSV123
Recoil energy in 8-lb. shotgun: 36.1 ft./lbs. **Recoil velocity in 8-lb. shotgun:** 17.0 ft./sec.

Distance in yards:	Muzzle	20	30	40	50	60	70
Velocity in fps:	1,472	917	767	654	465	489	425
Average pellet energy in ft-lbs:	11.01	4.27	2.99	2.17	1.61	1.22	.92
Time of flight in seconds:	0	.0530	.0889	.1313	.1808	.2380	.3038

Type of load: Nontoxic
Three-foot velocity: 1,375 ft./sec.
Hull: 3-inch plastic
Wad: Two-piece plastic
Shot: Steel
Buffered: No
Test barrel length: 30 inch
Pellets will pierce skin up to 124 yards.

NO. 4 STEEL PELLETS—1¼ OUNCES—240 PELLETS
Mfg: Dionisi **Manufacturer's code:** D 12 ST3X
Recoil energy in 8-lb. shotgun: 37.9 ft./lbs. **Recoil velocity in 8-lb. shotgun:** 17.5 ft./sec.

Distance in yards:	Muzzle	20	30	40	50	60	70
Velocity in fps:	1,500	929	776	660	569	494	429
Average pellet energy in ft-lbs:	11.42	4.38	3.06	2.22	1.65	1.24	.94
Time of flight in seconds:	0	.0522	.0876	.1297	.1787	.2353	.3005

Type of load: Nontoxic
Three-foot velocity: 1,400 ft./sec.
Hull: 3-inch plastic
Wad: Plastic
Shot: Steel
Buffered: No
Test barrel length: 30 inch
Pellets will pierce skin up to 125 yards.

NO. 4 STEEL PELLETS—1¼ OUNCES—240 PELLETS
Mfg: Kent Cartridge America/Canada **Manufacturer's code:** K123ST36
Recoil energy in 8-lb. shotgun: 37.9 ft./lbs. **Recoil velocity in 8-lb. shotgun:** 17.5 ft./sec.

Distance in yards:	Muzzle	20	30	40	50	60	70
Velocity in fps:	1,500	929	776	660	569	494	429
Average pellet energy in ft-lbs:	11.42	4.38	3.06	2.22	1.65	1.24	.94
Time of flight in seconds:	0	.0522	.0876	.1297	.1787	.2353	.3005

Type of load: Nontoxic
Three-foot velocity: 1,400 ft./sec.
Hull: 3-inch plastic
Wad: Plastic
Shot: Steel
Buffered: No
Test barrel length: 30 inch
Pellets will pierce skin up to 125 yards.

NO. 4 STEEL PELLETS—1¼ OUNCES—240 PELLETS
Mfg: Estate Cartridge **Manufacturer's code:** HVST12M
Recoil energy in 8-lb. shotgun: 39.8 ft./lbs. **Recoil velocity in 8-lb. shotgun:** 17.9 ft./sec.

Distance in yards:	Muzzle	20	30	40	50	60	70
Velocity in fps:	1,527	940	784	667	574	498	433
Average pellet energy in ft-lbs:	11.85	4.49	3.12	2.26	1.68	1.26	.95
Time of flight in seconds:	0	.0514	.0865	.1280	.1766	.2327	.2973

Type of load: Nontoxic
Three-foot velocity: 1,425 ft./sec.
Hull: 3-inch plastic
Wad: Plastic
Shot: Steel
Buffered: No
Test barrel length: 30 inch
Pellets will pierce skin up to 125 yards.

NO. 4 STEEL PELLETS—1¼ OUNCES—240 PELLETS
Mfg: PMC (Eldorado Cartridge Corp.) **Manufacturer's code:** SS12M
Recoil energy in 8-lb. shotgun: 39.8 ft./lbs. **Recoil velocity in 8-lb. shotgun:** 17.9 ft./sec.

Distance in yards:	Muzzle	20	30	40	50	60	70
Velocity in fps:	1,527	940	784	667	574	498	433
Average pellet energy in ft-lbs:	11.85	4.49	3.12	2.26	1.68	1.26	.95
Time of flight in seconds:	0	.0514	.0865	.1280	.1766	.2327	.2973

Type of load: Nontoxic
Three-foot velocity: 1,425 ft./sec.
Hull: 3-inch plastic
Wad: Plastic
Shot: Steel
Buffered: No
Test barrel length: 30 inch
Pellets will pierce skin up to 125 yards.

NO. 4 STEEL PELLETS—1¼ OUNCES—240 PELLETS
Mfg: Winchester **Manufacturer's code:** SSH123
Recoil energy in 8-lb. shotgun: 41.7 ft./lbs. **Recoil velocity in 8-lb. shotgun:** 18.3 ft./sec.

Distance in yards:	Muzzle	20	30	40	50	60	70
Velocity in fps:	1,555	952	793	673	580	503	437
Average pellet energy in ft-lbs:	12.28	4.60	3.19	2.30	1.71	1.28	.97
Time of flight in seconds:	0	.0506	.0853	.1265	.1745	.2302	.2942

Type of load: Nontoxic
Three-foot velocity: 1,450 ft./sec.
Hull: 3-inch plastic
Wad: Two-piece plastic
Shot: Steel
Buffered: No
Test barrel length: 30 inch
Pellets will pierce skin up to 126 yards.

NO. 4 STEEL PELLETS—1⅜ OUNCES—264 PELLETS
Mfg: Federal Cartridge Company **Manufacturer's code:** W149
Recoil energy in 8-lb. shotgun: 35.7 ft./lbs. **Recoil velocity in 8-lb. shotgun:** 16.9 ft./sec.

Distance in yards:	Muzzle	20	30	40	50	60	70
Velocity in fps:	1,362	871	733	627	542	471	409
Average pellet energy in ft-lbs:	9.42	3.85	2.73	2.00	1.49	1.13	.85
Time of flight in seconds:	0	.0564	.0941	.1385	.1900	.2495	.3178

Type of load: Nontoxic
Three-foot velocity: 1,275 ft./sec.
Hull: 3-inch plastic
Wad: Plastic
Shot: Steel
Buffered: No
Test barrel length: 30 inch
Pellets will pierce skin up to 121 yards.

NO. 4 STEEL PELLETS—1⅜ OUNCES—264 PELLETS
Mfg: Remington Arms Co. **Manufacturer's code:** NS12HM
Recoil energy in 8-lb. shotgun: 35.7 ft./lbs. **Recoil velocity in 8-lb. shotgun:** 16.9 ft./sec.

Distance in yards:	Muzzle	20	30	40	50	60	70
Velocity in fps:	1,362	871	733	627	542	471	409
Average pellet energy in ft-lbs:	9.42	3.85	2.73	2.00	1.49	1.13	.85
Time of flight in seconds:	0	.0564	.0941	.1385	.1900	.2495	.3178

Type of load: Nontoxic
Three-foot velocity: 1,275 ft./sec.
Hull: 3-inch plastic
Wad: Plastic
Shot: Zinc-galvanized steel
Buffered: No
Test barrel length: 30 inch
Pellets will pierce skin up to 121 yards.

NO. 4 STEEL PELLETS—1³⁄₈ OUNCES—264 PELLETS

Mfg: Winchester **Manufacturer's code:** XSM123
Recoil energy in 8-lb. shotgun: 35.7 ft./lbs. **Recoil velocity in 8-lb. shotgun:** 16.9 ft./sec.

Distance in yards:	Muzzle	20	30	40	50	60	70
Velocity in fps:	1,362	871	733	627	542	471	409
Average pellet energy in ft-lbs:	9.42	3.85	2.73	2.00	1.49	1.13	.85
Time of flight in seconds:	0	.0564	.0941	.1385	.1900	.2495	.3178

Type of load: Nontoxic
Three-foot velocity: 1,275 ft./sec.
Hull: 3-inch plastic
Wad: Two-piece plastic
Shot: Steel
Buffered: No
Test barrel length: 30 inch
Pellets will pierce skin up to 121 yards.

NO. 4 STEEL PELLETS—1³⁄₈ OUNCES—264 PELLETS

Mfg: Fiocchi **Manufacturer's code:** 123SH
Recoil energy in 8-lb. shotgun: 37.6 ft./lbs. **Recoil velocity in 8-lb. shotgun:** 17.4 ft./sec.

Distance in yards:	Muzzle	20	30	40	50	60	70
Velocity in fps:	1,389	882	741	634	547	475	413
Average pellet energy in ft-lbs:	9.81	3.95	2.79	2.04	1.52	1.32	.87
Time of flight in seconds:	0	.0555	.0927	.1366	.1876	.2465	.3142

Type of load: Nontoxic
Three-foot velocity: 1,300 ft./sec.
Hull: 3-inch plastic
Wad: Plastic
Shot: Steel
Buffered: No
Test barrel length: 30 inch
Pellets will pierce skin up to 122 yards.

NO. 4 STEEL PELLETS—1³⁄₈ OUNCES—264 PELLETS

Mfg: Kent Cartridge America/Canada **Manufacturer's code:** K123ST40
Recoil energy in 8-lb. shotgun: 37.6 ft./lbs. **Recoil velocity in 8-lb. shotgun:** 17.4 ft./sec.

Distance in yards:	Muzzle	20	30	40	50	60	70
Velocity in fps:	1,389	882	741	634	547	475	413
Average pellet energy in ft-lbs:	9.81	3.95	2.79	2.04	1.52	1.32	.87
Time of flight in seconds:	0	.0555	.0927	.1366	.1876	.2465	.3142

Type of load: Nontoxic
Three-foot velocity: 1,300 ft./sec.
Hull: 3-inch plastic
Wad: Plastic
Shot: Steel
Buffered: No
Test barrel length: 30 inch
Pellets will pierce skin up to 122 yards.

NO. 4 STEEL PELLETS—1³⁄₈ OUNCES—264 PELLETS

Mfg: Estate Cartridge **Manufacturer's code:** HVST12MM
Recoil energy in 8-lb. shotgun: 54.6 ft./lbs. **Recoil velocity in 8-lb. shotgun:** 21.0 ft./sec.

Distance in yards:	Muzzle	20	30	40	50	60	70
Velocity in fps:	1,472	917	767	654	465	489	425
Average pellet energy in ft-lbs:	11.01	4.27	2.99	2.17	1.61	1.22	.92
Time of flight in seconds:	0	.0530	.0889	.1313	.1808	.2380	.3038

Type of load: Nontoxic
Three-foot velocity: 1,375 ft./sec.
Hull: 3-inch plastic
Wad: Plastic
Shot: Steel
Buffered: No
Test barrel length: 30 inch
Pellets will pierce skin up to 124 yards.

NO. 6 STEEL PELLETS—1¹⁄₈ OUNCES—354 PELLETS

Mfg: Federal Cartridge Company **Manufacturer's code:** PWT143/W143
Recoil energy in 8-lb. shotgun: 37.0 ft./lbs. **Recoil velocity in 8-lb. shotgun:** 17.3 ft./sec.

Distance in yards:	Muzzle	20	30	40	50	60	70
Velocity in fps:	1,624	913	742	617	520	441	374
Average pellet energy in ft-lbs:	8.12	2.57	1.69	1.17	.83	.60	.43
Time of flight in seconds:	0	.0510	.0877	.1321	.1852	.2479	.3219

Type of load: Nontoxic
Three-foot velocity: 1,500 ft./sec.
Hull: 3-inch plastic
Wad: Plastic
Shot: Steel
Buffered: No
Test barrel length: 30 inch
Pellets will pierce skin up to 108 yards.

NO. 6 STEEL PELLETS—1¹⁄₈ OUNCES—354 PELLETS

Mfg: Kent Cartridge America/Canada **Manufacturer's code:** K123ST32
Recoil energy in 8-lb. shotgun: 37.0 ft./lbs. **Recoil velocity in 8-lb. shotgun:** 17.3 ft./sec.

Distance in yards:	Muzzle	20	30	40	50	60	70
Velocity in fps:	1,624	913	742	617	520	441	374
Average pellet energy in ft-lbs:	8.12	2.57	1.69	1.17	.83	.60	.43
Time of flight in seconds:	0	.0510	.0877	.1321	.1852	.2479	.3219

Type of load: Nontoxic
Three-foot velocity: 1,500 ft./sec.
Hull: 3-inch plastic
Wad: Plastic
Shot: Steel
Buffered: No
Test barrel length: 30 inch
Pellets will pierce skin up to 108 yards.

NO. 6 STEEL PELLETS—1¹⁄₄ OUNCES—394 PELLETS

Mfg: Clever **Manufacturer's code:** Magnum load
Recoil energy in 8-lb. shotgun: 28.0 ft./lbs. **Recoil velocity in 8-lb. shotgun:** 15.0 ft./sec.

Distance in yards:	Muzzle	20	30	40	50	60	70
Velocity in fps:	1,345	809	667	560	474	401	340
Average pellet energy in ft-lbs:	5.57	2.01	1.37	.96	.69	.50	.36
Time of flight in seconds:	0	.0593	.1003	.1495	.2078	.2767	.3579

Type of load: Nontoxic
Three-foot velocity: 1,250 ft./sec.
Hull: 3-inch plastic
Wad: Plastic
Shot: Steel
Buffered: No
Test barrel length: 30 inch
Pellets will pierce skin up to 102 yards.

NO. 6 STEEL PELLETS—1¼ OUNCES—394 PELLETS

Mfg: Estate Cartridge **Manufacturer's code:** HVST12M
Recoil energy in 8-lb. shotgun: 39.8 ft./lbs. **Recoil velocity in 8-lb. shotgun:** 17.9 ft./sec.

Distance in yards:	Muzzle	20	30	40	50	60	70
Velocity in fps:	1,540	882	720	600	507	429	364
Average pellet energy in ft-lbs:	7.30	2.40	1.59	1.11	.79	.57	.41
Time of flight in seconds:	0	.0533	.0911	.1369	.1913	.2557	.3317

Type of load: Nontoxic
Three-foot velocity: 1,425 ft./sec.
Hull: 3-inch plastic
Wad: Plastic
Shot: Steel
Buffered: No
Test barrel length: 30 inch
Pellets will pierce skin up to 106 yards.

NO. 6 STEEL PELLETS—1⅜ OUNCES—433 PELLETS

Mfg: Estate Cartridge **Manufacturer's code:** HVST12MM
Recoil energy in 8-lb. shotgun: 54.6 ft./lbs. **Recoil velocity in 8-lb. shotgun:** 21.0 ft./sec.

Distance in yards:	Muzzle	20	30	40	50	60	70
Velocity in fps:	1,484	862	705	589	498	422	358
Average pellet energy in ft-lbs:	6.78	2.28	1.53	1.07	.76	.55	.39
Time of flight in seconds:	0	.0549	.0935	.1402	.1957	.2613	.3386

Type of load: Nontoxic
Three-foot velocity: 1,375 ft./sec.
Hull: 3-inch plastic
Wad: Plastic
Shot: Steel
Buffered: No
Test barrel length: 30 inch
Pellets will pierce skin up to 105 yards.

Kent Cartridge's CEO, Bob Cove, pauses in the setting sun following a duck hunt using Kent's Impact™ Tungsten/Matrix ammunition. As soft as lead, Impact can be shot in any shotgun safe to shoot with modern smokeless powder.

NO. F STEEL PELLETS—1⁹/₁₆ OUNCES—62 PELLETS

Mfg: Federal Cartridge Company **Manufacturer's code:** W135
Recoil energy in 8-lb. shotgun: 48.6 ft./lbs. **Recoil velocity in 8-lb. shotgun:** 19.8 ft./sec.

Distance in yards:	Muzzle	20	30	40	50	60	70
Velocity in fps:	1,349	1,015	902	811	734	668	611
Average pellet energy in ft-lbs:	44.83	25.36	20.05	16.18	13.26	10.99	9.19
Time of flight in seconds:	0	.0518	.0832	.1183	.1572	.2001	.2470

Type of load: Nontoxic
Three-foot velocity: 1,300 ft./sec.
Hull: 3½-inch plastic
Wad: Plastic
Shot: Steel
Buffered: No
Test barrel length: 30 inch
Pellets will pierce skin up to 205 yards.

NO. T STEEL PELLETS—1³/₈ OUNCES—71 PELLETS

Mfg: Federal Cartridge Company **Manufacturer's code:** PWT133/W133
Recoil energy in 8-lb. shotgun: 50.5 ft./lbs. **Recoil velocity in 8-lb. shotgun:** 20.1 ft./sec.

Distance in yards:	Muzzle	20	30	40	50	60	70
Velocity in fps:	1,518	1,084	946	837	749	675	612
Average pellet energy in ft-lbs:	42.60	21.72	16.54	12.97	10.38	8.43	6.92
Time of flight in seconds:	0	.0473	.0770	.1108	.1487	.1901	.2377

Type of load: Nontoxic
Three-foot velocity: 1,450 ft./sec.
Hull: 3½-inch plastic
Wad: Plastic
Shot: Steel
Buffered: No
Test barrel length: 30 inch
Pellets will pierce skin up to 192 yards.

NO. T STEEL PELLETS—1³/₈ OUNCES—71 PELLETS

Mfg: PMC (Eldorado Cartridge Corp.) **Manufacturer's code:** SSG12
Recoil energy in 8-lb. shotgun: 50.5 ft./lbs. **Recoil velocity in 8-lb. shotgun:** 20.1 ft./sec.

Distance in yards:	Muzzle	20	30	40	50	60	70
Velocity in fps:	1,518	1,084	946	837	749	675	612
Average pellet energy in ft-lbs:	42.60	21.72	16.54	12.97	10.38	8.43	6.92
Time of flight in seconds:	0	.0473	.0770	.1108	.1487	.1901	.2377

Type of load: Nontoxic
Three-foot velocity: 1,450 ft./sec.
Hull: 3½-inch plastic
Wad: Plastic
Shot: Steel
Buffered: No
Test barrel length: 30 inch
Pellets will pierce skin up to 192 yards.

NO. T STEEL PELLETS—1³/₈ OUNCES—71 PELLETS

Mfg: Fiocchi **Manufacturer's code:** 1235ST
Recoil energy in 8-lb. shotgun: 55.3 ft./lbs. **Recoil velocity in 8-lb. shotgun:** 21.1 ft./sec.

Distance in yards:	Muzzle	20	30	40	50	60	70
Velocity in fps:	1,571	1,114	969	856	764	688	623
Average pellet energy in ft-lbs:	45.66	22.94	17.35	13.54	10.80	8.75	7.17
Time of flight in seconds:	0	.0459	.0748	.1078	.1450	.1864	.2323

Type of load: Nontoxic
Three-foot velocity: 1,500 ft./sec.
Hull: 3½-inch plastic
Wad: Plastic
Shot: Steel
Buffered: No
Test barrel length: 30 inch
Pellets will pierce skin up to 194 yards.

NO. T STEEL PELLETS—1⁹/₁₆ OUNCES—81 PELLETS

Mfg: Federal Cartridge Company **Manufacturer's code:** W135
Recoil energy in 8-lb. shotgun: 48.6 ft./lbs. **Recoil velocity in 8-lb. shotgun:** 19.8 ft./sec.

Distance in yards:	Muzzle	20	30	40	50	60	70
Velocity in fps:	1,357	995	877	781	702	635	577
Average pellet energy in ft-lbs:	34.08	18.31	14.21	11.30	9.12	7.46	6.16
Time of flight in seconds:	0	.0522	.0844	.1207	.1612	.2062	.2558

Type of load: Nontoxic
Three-foot velocity: 1,300 ft./sec.
Hull: 3½-inch plastic
Wad: Plastic
Shot: Steel
Buffered: No
Test barrel length: 30 inch
Pellets will pierce skin up to 186 yards.

NO. T STEEL PELLETS—1⁹/₁₆ OUNCES—81 PELLETS

Mfg: Remington Arms Co. **Manufacturer's code:** NS1235
Recoil energy in 8-lb. shotgun: 48.6 ft./lbs. **Recoil velocity in 8-lb. shotgun:** 19.8 ft./sec.

Distance in yards:	Muzzle	20	30	40	50	60	70
Velocity in fps:	1,357	995	877	781	702	635	577
Average pellet energy in ft-lbs:	34.08	18.31	14.21	11.30	9.12	7.46	6.16
Time of flight in seconds:	0	.0522	.0844	.1207	.1612	.2062	.2558

Type of load: Nontoxic
Three-foot velocity: 1,300 ft./sec.
Hull: 3½-inch plastic
Wad: Plastic
Shot: Zinc-galvanized steel
Buffered: No
Test barrel length: 30 inch
Pellets will pierce skin up to 186 yards.

NO. T STEEL PELLETS—1⁹/₁₆ OUNCES—81 PELLETS

Mfg: Winchester **Manufacturer's code:** XSC12L
Recoil energy in 8-lb. shotgun: 48.6 ft./lbs. **Recoil velocity in 8-lb. shotgun:** 19.8 ft./sec.

Distance in yards:	Muzzle	20	30	40	50	60	70
Velocity in fps:	1,357	995	877	781	702	635	577
Average pellet energy in ft-lbs:	34.08	18.31	14.21	11.30	9.12	7.46	6.16
Time of flight in seconds:	0	.0522	.0844	.1207	.1612	.2062	.2558

Type of load: Nontoxic
Three-foot velocity: 1,300 ft./sec.
Hull: 3½-inch plastic
Wad: Two-piece plastic
Shot: Copper-plated steel
Buffered: No
Test barrel length: 30 inch
Pellets will pierce skin up to 186 yards.

NO. T STEEL PELLETS—1⁹/₁₆ OUNCES—81 PELLETS
Mfg: Fiocchi **Manufacturer's code:** 1235SH
Recoil energy in 8-lb. shotgun: 68.3 ft./lbs. **Recoil velocity in 8-lb. shotgun:** 23.4 ft./sec.

Distance in yards:	Muzzle	20	30	40	50	60	70
Velocity in fps:	1,544	1,099	957	847	757	681	617
Average pellet energy in ft-lbs:	44.11	22.32	16.94	13.26	10.59	8.59	7.04
Time of flight in seconds:	0	.0466	.0759	.1093	.1468	.1886	.2349

Type of load: Nontoxic
Three-foot velocity: 1,475 ft./sec.
Hull: 3½-inch plastic
Wad: Plastic
Shot: Steel
Buffered: No
Test barrel length: 30 inch
Pellets will pierce skin up to 193 yards.

NO. BBB STEEL PELLETS—1³/₈ OUNCES—85 PELLETS
Mfg: Federal Cartridge Company **Manufacturer's code:** PWT133/W133
Recoil energy in 8-lb. shotgun: 50.5 ft./lbs. **Recoil velocity in 8-lb. shotgun:** 20.1 ft./sec.

Distance in yards:	Muzzle	20	30	40	50	60	70
Velocity in fps:	1,522	1,070	929	819	730	655	591
Average pellet energy in ft-lbs:	36.75	18.15	13.68	10.64	8.44	6.80	5.55
Time of flight in seconds:	0	.0476	.0778	.1122	.1511	.1945	.2428

Type of load: Nontoxic
Three-foot velocity: 1,450 ft./sec.
Hull: 3½-inch plastic
Wad: Plastic
Shot: Steel
Buffered: No
Test barrel length: 30 inch
Pellets will pierce skin up to 183 yards.

NO. BBB STEEL PELLETS—1³/₈ OUNCES—85 PELLETS
Mfg: Winchester **Manufacturer's code:** SSH1235
Recoil energy in 8-lb. shotgun: 50.5 ft./lbs. **Recoil velocity in 8-lb. shotgun:** 20.1 ft./sec.

Distance in yards:	Muzzle	20	30	40	50	60	70
Velocity in fps:	1,522	1,070	929	819	730	655	591
Average pellet energy in ft-lbs:	36.75	18.15	13.68	10.64	8.44	6.80	5.55
Time of flight in seconds:	0	.0476	.0778	.1122	.1511	.1945	.2428

Type of load: Nontoxic
Three-foot velocity: 1,450 ft./sec.
Hull: 3½-inch plastic
Wad: Two-piece plastic
Shot: Steel
Buffered: No
Test barrel length: 30 inch
Pellets will pierce skin up to 183 yards.

NO. BBB STEEL PELLETS—1³/₈ OUNCES—85 PELLETS
Mfg: Fiocchi **Manufacturer's code:** 1235ST
Recoil energy in 8-lb. shotgun: 55.3 ft./lbs. **Recoil velocity in 8-lb. shotgun:** 21.1 ft./sec.

Distance in yards:	Muzzle	20	30	40	50	60	70
Velocity in fps:	1,576	1,099	951	837	744	667	602
Average pellet energy in ft-lbs:	39.39	19.16	14.34	11.10	8.78	7.06	5.75
Time of flight in seconds:	0	.0462	.0756	.1093	.1473	.1900	.2373

Type of load: Nontoxic
Three-foot velocity: 1,500 ft./sec.
Hull: 3½-inch plastic
Wad: Plastic
Shot: Steel
Buffered: No
Test barrel length: 30 inch
Pellets will pierce skin up to 185 yards.

NO. BBB STEEL PELLETS—1½ OUNCES—93 PELLETS
Mfg: Estate Cartridge **Manufacturer's code:** HVST1235M
Recoil energy in 8-lb. shotgun: 54.6 ft./lbs. **Recoil velocity in 8-lb. shotgun:** 21.0 ft./sec.

Distance in yards:	Muzzle	20	30	40	50	60	70
Velocity in fps:	1,469	1,041	907	8014	715	643	581
Average pellet energy in ft-lbs:	34.20	17.18	1.04	10.18	8.11	6.55	5.35
Time of flight in seconds:	0	.0492	.0801	.1154	.1551	.1993	.2485

Type of load: Nontoxic
Three-foot velocity: 1,400 ft./sec.
Hull: 3½-inch plastic
Wad: Plastic
Shot: Steel
Buffered: No
Test barrel length: 30 inch
Pellets will pierce skin up to 181 yards.

NO. BBB STEEL PELLETS—1⁹/₁₆ OUNCES—97 PELLETS
Mfg: Federal Cartridge Company **Manufacturer's code:** W135
Recoil energy in 8-lb. shotgun: 48.6 ft./lbs. **Recoil velocity in 8-lb. shotgun:** 19.8 ft./sec.

Distance in yards:	Muzzle	20	30	40	50	60	70
Velocity in fps:	1,362	983	862	765	685	671	558
Average pellet energy in ft-lbs:	29.40	15.33	11.78	9.28	7.44	6.03	4.94
Time of flight in seconds:	0	.0525	.0852	.1222	.1636	.2098	.2610

Type of load: Nontoxic
Three-foot velocity: 1,300 ft./sec.
Hull: 3½-inch plastic
Wad: Plastic
Shot: Steel
Buffered: No
Test barrel length: 30 inch
Pellets will pierce skin up to 177 yards.

NO. BBB STEEL PELLETS—1⁹/₁₆ OUNCES—97 PELLETS
Mfg: Kent Cartridge America/Canada **Manufacturer's code:** K1235ST44
Recoil energy in 8-lb. shotgun: 48.6 ft./lbs. **Recoil velocity in 8-lb. shotgun:** 19.8 ft./sec.

Distance in yards:	Muzzle	20	30	40	50	60	70
Velocity in fps:	1,362	983	862	765	685	671	558
Average pellet energy in ft-lbs:	29.40	15.33	11.78	9.28	7.44	6.03	4.94
Time of flight in seconds:	0	.0525	.0852	.1222	.1636	.2098	.2610

Type of load: Nontoxic
Three-foot velocity: 1,300 ft./sec.
Hull: 3½-inch plastic
Wad: Plastic
Shot: Steel
Buffered: No
Test barrel length: 30 inch
Pellets will pierce skin up to 177 yards.

NO. BBB STEEL PELLETS—1⁹/₁₆ OUNCES—97 PELLETS

Mfg: Remington Arms Co. **Manufacturer's code:** NS1235
Recoil energy in 8-lb. shotgun: 48.6 ft./lbs. **Recoil velocity in 8-lb. shotgun:** 19.8 ft./sec.

Distance in yards:	Muzzle	20	30	40	50	60	70
Velocity in fps:	1,362	983	862	765	685	671	558
Average pellet energy in ft-lbs:	29.40	15.33	11.78	9.28	7.44	6.03	4.94
Time of flight in seconds:	0	.0525	.0852	.1222	.1636	.2098	.2610

Type of load: Nontoxic
Three-foot velocity: 1,300 ft./sec.
Hull: 3½-inch plastic
Wad: Plastic
Shot: Zinc-galvanized steel
Buffered: No
Test barrel length: 30 inch
Pellets will pierce skin up to 177 yards.

NO. BBB STEEL PELLETS—1⁹/₁₆ OUNCES—97 PELLETS

Mfg: Winchester **Manufacturer's code:** XSC12L
Recoil energy in 8-lb. shotgun: 48.6 ft./lbs. **Recoil velocity in 8-lb. shotgun:** 19.8 ft./sec.

Distance in yards:	Muzzle	20	30	40	50	60	70
Velocity in fps:	1,362	983	862	765	685	671	558
Average pellet energy in ft-lbs:	29.40	15.33	11.78	9.28	7.44	6.03	4.94
Time of flight in seconds:	0	.0525	.0852	.1222	.1636	.2098	.2610

Type of load: Nontoxic
Three-foot velocity: 1,300 ft./sec.
Hull: 3½-inch plastic
Wad: Two-piece plastic
Shot: Copper-plated steel
Buffered: No
Test barrel length: 30 inch
Pellets will pierce skin up to 177 yards.

NO. BBB STEEL PELLETS—1⁹/₁₆ OUNCES—97 PELLETS

Mfg: Fiocchi **Manufacturer's code:** 1235SH
Recoil energy in 8-lb. shotgun: 68.3 ft./lbs. **Recoil velocity in 8-lb. shotgun:** 23.4 ft./sec.

Distance in yards:	Muzzle	20	30	40	50	60	70
Velocity in fps:	1,549	1,084	940	828	737	661	597
Average pellet energy in ft-lbs:	38.06	18.65	14.01	10.87	9.61	6.93	5.65
Time of flight in seconds:	0	.0469	.0767	.1107	.1492	.1922	.2400

Type of load: Nontoxic
Three-foot velocity: 1,475 ft./sec.
Hull: 3½-inch plastic
Wad: Plastic
Shot: Steel
Buffered: No
Test barrel length: 30 inch
Pellets will pierce skin up to 184 yards.

NO. BB STEEL PELLETS—1³/₈ OUNCES—99 PELLETS

Mfg: Federal Cartridge Company **Manufacturer's code:** PWT133/W133
Recoil energy in 8-lb. shotgun: 50.5 ft./lbs. **Recoil velocity in 8-lb. shotgun:** 20.1 ft./sec.

Distance in yards:	Muzzle	20	30	40	50	60	70
Velocity in fps:	1,527	1,055	911	799	709	634	570
Average pellet energy in ft-lbs:	31.45	15.00	11.18	8.61	6.78	5.42	4.38
Time of flight in seconds:	0	.0480	.0786	.1139	.1538	.1986	.2485

Type of load: Nontoxic
Three-foot velocity: 1,450 ft./sec.
Hull: 3½-inch plastic
Wad: Plastic
Shot: Steel
Buffered: No
Test barrel length: 30 inch
Pellets will pierce skin up to 173 yards.

NO. BB STEEL PELLETS—1³/₈ OUNCES—99 PELLETS

Mfg: PMC (Eldorado Cartridge Corp.) **Manufacturer's code:** SSG12
Recoil energy in 8-lb. shotgun: 50.5 ft./lbs. **Recoil velocity in 8-lb. shotgun:** 20.1 ft./sec.

Distance in yards:	Muzzle	20	30	40	50	60	70
Velocity in fps:	1,527	1,055	911	799	709	634	570
Average pellet energy in ft-lbs:	31.45	15.00	11.18	8.61	6.78	5.42	4.38
Time of flight in seconds:	0	.0480	.0786	.1139	.1538	.1986	.2485

Type of load: Nontoxic
Three-foot velocity: 1,450 ft./sec.
Hull: 3½-inch plastic
Wad: Plastic
Shot: Steel
Buffered: No
Test barrel length: 30 inch
Pellets will pierce skin up to 173 yards.

NO. BB STEEL PELLETS—1³/₈ OUNCES—99 PELLETS

Mfg: Remington Arms Co. **Manufacturer's code:** NS1235HV
Recoil energy in 8-lb. shotgun: 50.5 ft./lbs. **Recoil velocity in 8-lb. shotgun:** 20.1 ft./sec.

Distance in yards:	Muzzle	20	30	40	50	60	70
Velocity in fps:	1,527	1,055	911	799	709	634	570
Average pellet energy in ft-lbs:	31.45	15.00	11.18	8.61	6.78	5.42	4.38
Time of flight in seconds:	0	.0480	.0786	.1139	.1538	.1986	.2485

Type of load: Nontoxic
Three-foot velocity: 1,450 ft./sec.
Hull: 3½-inch plastic
Wad: Plastic
Shot: Steel
Buffered: No
Test barrel length: 30 inch
Pellets will pierce skin up to 173 yards.

NO. BB STEEL PELLETS—1³/₈ OUNCES—99 PELLETS

Mfg: Winchester **Manufacturer's code:** SSH1235
Recoil energy in 8-lb. shotgun: 50.5 ft./lbs. **Recoil velocity in 8-lb. shotgun:** 20.1 ft./sec.

Distance in yards:	Muzzle	20	30	40	50	60	70
Velocity in fps:	1,527	1,055	911	799	709	634	570
Average pellet energy in ft-lbs:	31.45	15.00	11.18	8.61	6.78	5.42	4.38
Time of flight in seconds:	0	.0480	.0786	.1139	.1538	.1986	.2485

Type of load: Nontoxic
Three-foot velocity: 1,450 ft./sec.
Hull: 3½-inch plastic
Wad: Two-piece plastic
Shot: Steel
Buffered: No
Test barrel length: 30 inch
Pellets will pierce skin up to 173 yards.

NO. BB STEEL PELLETS—1⅜ OUNCES—99 PELLETS
Mfg: Fiocchi Manufacturer's code: 1235ST
Recoil energy in 8-lb. shotgun: 55.3 ft./lbs. Recoil velocity in 8-lb. shotgun: 21.1 ft./sec.

Distance in yards:	Muzzle	20	30	40	50	60	70
Velocity in fps:	1,581	1,083	932	816	723	646	580
Average pellet energy in ft-lbs:	33.72	15.82	11.71	8.98	7.05	5.62	4.53
Time of flight in seconds:	0	.0465	.0764	.1109	.1500	.1940	.2430

Type of load: Nontoxic
Three-foot velocity: 1,500 ft./sec.
Hull: 3½-inch plastic
Wad: Plastic
Shot: Steel
Buffered: No
Test barrel length: 30 inch
Pellets will pierce skin up to 175 yards.

NO. BB STEEL PELLETS—1½ OUNCES—108 PELLETS
Mfg: Estate Cartridge Manufacturer's code: HVST1235M
Recoil energy in 8-lb. shotgun: 54.6 ft./lbs. Recoil velocity in 8-lb. shotgun: 21.0 ft./sec.

		30	40	50	60	70
		889	782	695	622	560
		.66	8.25	6.51	5.22	4.22
		810	.1170	.1577	.2034	.2543

Type of load: Nontoxic
Three-foot velocity: 1,400 ft./sec.
Hull: 3½-inch plastic
Wad: Plastic
Shot: Steel
Buffered: No
Test barrel length: 30 inch
Pellets will pierce skin up to 172 yards.

...12 PELLETS
...'s code: W135
...velocity in 8-lb. shotgun: 19.8 ft./sec.

		30	40	50	60	70
		846	747	666	597	538
		.65	7.53	5.98	4.81	3.91
		860	.1238	.1664	.2140	.2669

Type of load: Nontoxic
Three-foot velocity: 1,300 ft./sec.
Hull: 3½-inch plastic
Wad: Plastic
Shot: Steel
Buffered: No
Test barrel length: 30 inch
Pellets will pierce skin up to 168 yards.

...12 PELLETS
...s code: K1235ST44
...velocity in 8-lb. shotgun: 19.8 ft./sec.

		30	40	50	60	70
		846	747	666	597	538
		.65	7.53	5.98	4.81	3.91
		860	.1238	.1664	.2140	.2669

Type of load: Nontoxic
Three-foot velocity: 1,300 ft./sec.
Hull: 3½-inch plastic
Wad: Plastic
Shot: Steel
Buffered: No
Test barrel length: 30 inch
Pellets will pierce skin up to 168 yards.

...12 PELLETS
...: NS1235
...velocity in 8-lb. shotgun: 19.8 ft./sec.

		30	40	50	60	70
		846	747	666	597	538
		.65	7.53	5.98	4.81	3.91
		860	.1238	.1664	.2140	.2669

Type of load: Nontoxic
Three-foot velocity: 1,300 ft./sec.
Hull: 3½-inch plastic
Wad: Plastic
Shot: Zinc-galvanized steel
Buffered: No
Test barrel length: 30 inch
Pellets will pierce skin up to 168 yards.

...12 PELLETS
...velocity in 8-lb. shotgun: 19.8 ft./sec.

		30	40	50	60	70
		846	747	666	597	538
		.65	7.53	5.98	4.81	3.91
		860	.1238	.1664	.2140	.2669

Type of load: Nontoxic
Three-foot velocity: 1,300 ft./sec.
Hull: 3½-inch plastic
Wad: Two-piece plastic
Shot: Steel
Buffered: No
Test barrel length: 30 inch
Pellets will pierce skin up to 168 yards.

NO. BB STEEL PELLETS—1⁹⁄₁₆ OUNCES—112 PELLETS
Mfg: Fiocchi Manufacturer's code: 1235SH
Recoil energy in 8-lb. shotgun: 68.3 ft./lbs. Recoil velocity in 8-lb. shotgun: 23.4 ft./sec.

Distance in yards:	Muzzle	20	30	40	50	60	70
Velocity in fps:	1,554	1,069	921	808	716	640	575
Average pellet energy in ft-lbs:	32.57	15.40	11.45	8.80	6.91	5.52	4.46
Time of flight in seconds:	0	.0472	.0775	.1124	.1519	.1962	.2458

Type of load: Nontoxic
Three-foot velocity: 1,475 ft./sec.
Hull: 3½-inch plastic
Wad: Plastic
Shot: Steel
Buffered: No
Test barrel length: 30 inch
Pellets will pierce skin up to 174 yards.

NO. 1 STEEL PELLETS—1³⁄₈ OUNCES—142 PELLETS
Mfg: Winchester **Manufacturer's code:** WE12L
Recoil energy in 8-lb. shotgun: 41.6 ft./lbs. **Recoil velocity in 8-lb. shotgun:** 18.3 ft./sec.

Distance in yards:	Muzzle	20	30	40	50	60	70
Velocity in fps:	1,429	967	830	724	637	565	504
Average pellet energy in ft-lbs:	19.34	8.86	6.52	4.96	3.85	3.03	2.40
Time of flight in seconds:	0	.0520	.0855	.1243	.1685	.2186	.2748

Type of load: Nontoxic
Three-foot velocity: 1,350 ft./sec.
Hull: 3½-inch plastic
Wad: Plastic
Shot: Steel
Buffered: No
Test barrel length: 30 inch
Pellets will pierce skin up to 151 yards.

NO. 1 STEEL PELLETS—1³⁄₈ OUNCES—142 PELLETS
Mfg: Fiocchi **Manufacturer's code:** 1235ST
Recoil energy in 8-lb. shotgun: 55.3 ft./lbs. **Recoil velocity in 8-lb. shotgun:** 21.1 ft./sec.

Distance in yards:	Muzzle	20	30	40	50	60	70
Velocity in fps:	1,592	1,046	889	770	675	597	531
Average pellet energy in ft-lbs:	24.01	10.37	7.49	5.62	4.32	3.38	2.67
Time of flight in seconds:	0	.0473	.0785	.1148	.1565	.2038	.2570

Type of load: Nontoxic
Three-foot velocity: 1,500 ft./sec.
Hull: 3½-inch plastic
Wad: Plastic
Shot: Steel
Buffered: No
Test barrel length: 30 inch
Pellets will pierce skin up to 156 yards.

NO. 1 STEEL PELLETS—1½ OUNCES—154 PELLETS
Mfg: Estate Cartridge **Manufacturer's code:** HVST1235M
Recoil energy in 8-lb. shotgun: 54.6 ft./lbs. **Recoil velocity in 8-lb. shotgun:** 21.0 ft./sec.

Distance in yards:	Muzzle	20	30	40	50	60	70
Velocity in fps:	1,483	993	850	739	650	576	513
Average pellet energy in ft-lbs:	20.83	9.34	6.84	5.18	4.00	3.15	2.49
Time of flight in seconds:	0	.0503	.0831	.1210	.1643	.2134	.2686

Type of load: Nontoxic
Three-foot velocity: 1,400 ft./sec.
Hull: 3½-inch plastic
Wad: Plastic
Shot: Steel
Buffered: No
Test barrel length: 30 inch
Pellets will pierce skin up to 153 yards.

NO. 1 STEEL PELLETS—1⁹⁄₁₆ OUNCES—161 PELLETS
Mfg: Federal Cartridge Company **Manufacturer's code:** W135
Recoil energy in 8-lb. shotgun: 48.6 ft./lbs. **Recoil velocity in 8-lb. shotgun:** 19.8 ft./sec.

Distance in yards:	Muzzle	20	30	40	50	60	70
Velocity in fps:	1,375	941	810	708	624	554	494
Average pellet energy in ft-lbs:	17.90	8.38	6.21	4.74	3.69	2.91	2.31
Time of flight in seconds:	0	.0537	.0881	.1278	.1930	.2241	.2814

Type of load: Nontoxic
Three-foot velocity: 1,300 ft./sec.
Hull: 3½-inch plastic
Wad: Plastic
Shot: Steel
Buffered: No
Test barrel length: 30 inch
Pellets will pierce skin up to 150 yards.

NO. 1 STEEL PELLETS—1⁹⁄₁₆ OUNCES—161 PELLETS
Mfg: Kent Cartridge America/Canada **Manufacturer's code:** K1235ST44
Recoil energy in 8-lb. shotgun: 48.6 ft./lbs. **Recoil velocity in 8-lb. shotgun:** 19.8 ft./sec.

Distance in yards:	Muzzle	20	30	40	50	60	70
Velocity in fps:	1,375	941	810	708	624	554	494
Average pellet energy in ft-lbs:	17.90	8.38	6.21	4.74	3.69	2.91	2.31
Time of flight in seconds:	0	.0537	.0881	.1278	.1930	.2241	.2814

Type of load: Nontoxic
Three-foot velocity: 1,300 ft./sec.
Hull: 3½-inch plastic
Wad: Plastic
Shot: Steel
Buffered: No
Test barrel length: 30 inch
Pellets will pierce skin up to 150 yards.

NO. 1 STEEL PELLETS—1⁹⁄₁₆ OUNCES—161 PELLETS
Mfg: Remington Arms Co. **Manufacturer's code:** NS1235
Recoil energy in 8-lb. shotgun: 48.6 ft./lbs. **Recoil velocity in 8-lb. shotgun:** 19.8 ft./sec.

Distance in yards:	Muzzle	20	30	40	50	60	70
Velocity in fps:	1,375	941	810	708	624	554	494
Average pellet energy in ft-lbs:	17.90	8.38	6.21	4.74	3.69	2.91	2.31
Time of flight in seconds:	0	.0537	.0881	.1278	.1930	.2241	.2814

Type of load: Nontoxic
Three-foot velocity: 1,300 ft./sec.
Hull: 3½-inch plastic
Wad: Plastic
Shot: Zinc-galvanized steel
Buffered: No
Test barrel length: 30 inch
Pellets will pierce skin up to 150 yards.

NO. 1 STEEL PELLETS—1⁹⁄₁₆ OUNCES—161 PELLETS
Mfg: Winchester **Manufacturer's code:** XSM12L
Recoil energy in 8-lb. shotgun: 48.6 ft./lbs. **Recoil velocity in 8-lb. shotgun:** 19.8 ft./sec.

Distance in yards:	Muzzle	20	30	40	50	60	70
Velocity in fps:	1,375	941	810	708	624	554	494
Average pellet energy in ft-lbs:	17.90	8.38	6.21	4.74	3.69	2.91	2.31
Time of flight in seconds:	0	.0537	.0881	.1278	.1930	.2241	.2814

Type of load: Nontoxic
Three-foot velocity: 1,300 ft./sec.
Hull: 3½-inch plastic
Wad: Two-piece plastic
Shot: Steel
Buffered: No
Test barrel length: 30 inch
Pellets will pierce skin up to 150 yards.

NO. 1 STEEL PELLETS—1⁹/₁₆ OUNCES—161 PELLETS
Mfg: Fiocchi **Manufacturer's code:** 1235SH
Recoil energy in 8-lb. shotgun: 68.3 ft./lbs. **Recoil velocity in 8-lb. shotgun:** 23.4 ft./sec.

Distance in yards:	Muzzle	20	30	40	50	60	70
Velocity in fps:	1,565	1,033	879	763	669	558	527
Average pellet energy in ft-lbs:	23.19	10.11	7.32	5.51	4.24	3.32	2.63
Time of flight in seconds:	0	.0480	.0796	.1163	.1584	.2061	.2598

Type of load: Nontoxic
Three-foot velocity: 1,475 ft./sec.
Hull: 3½-inch plastic
Wad: Plastic
Shot: Steel
Buffered: No
Test barrel length: 30 inch
Pellets will pierce skin up to 155 yards.

NO. 2 STEEL PELLETS—1³/₈ OUNCES—172 PELLETS
Mfg: Winchester **Manufacturer's code:** WE12L
Recoil energy in 8-lb. shotgun: 41.6 ft./lbs. **Recoil velocity in 8-lb. shotgun:** 18.3 ft./sec.

Distance in yards:	Muzzle	20	30	40	50	60	70
Velocity in fps:	1,434	949	808	700	613	541	479
Average pellet energy in ft-lbs:	16.04	7.02	5.10	3.83	2.93	2.28	1.79
Time of flight in seconds:	0	.0525	.0868	.1268	.1726	.2248	.2838

Type of load: Nontoxic
Three-foot velocity: 1,350 ft./sec.
Hull: 3½-inch plastic
Wad: Plastic
Shot: Steel
Buffered: No
Test barrel length: 30 inch
Pellets will pierce skin up to 142 yards.

NO. 2 STEEL PELLETS—1³/₈ OUNCES—172 PELLETS
Mfg: Federal Cartridge Company **Manufacturer's code:** PWT133/W133
Recoil energy in 8-lb. shotgun: 50.5 ft./lbs. **Recoil velocity in 8-lb. shotgun:** 20.1 ft./sec.

Distance in yards:	Muzzle	20	30	40	50	60	70
Velocity in fps:	1,543	1,000	846	730	637	561	496
Average pellet energy in ft-lbs:	18.58	7.80	5.59	4.16	3.17	2.46	1.92
Time of flight in seconds:	0	.0493	.0820	.1203	.1643	.2146	.2715

Type of load: Nontoxic
Three-foot velocity: 1,450 ft./sec.
Hull: 3½-inch plastic
Wad: Plastic
Shot: Steel
Buffered: No
Test barrel length: 30 inch
Pellets will pierce skin up to 145 yards.

NO. 2 STEEL PELLETS—1³/₈ OUNCES—172 PELLETS
Mfg: PMC (Eldorado Cartridge Corp.) **Manufacturer's code:** SSG12
Recoil energy in 8-lb. shotgun: 50.5 ft./lbs. **Recoil velocity in 8-lb. shotgun:** 20.1 ft./sec.

Distance in yards:	Muzzle	20	30	40	50	60	70
Velocity in fps:	1,543	1,000	846	730	637	561	496
Average pellet energy in ft-lbs:	18.58	7.80	5.59	4.16	3.17	2.46	1.92
Time of flight in seconds:	0	.0493	.0820	.1203	.1643	.2146	.2715

Type of load: Nontoxic
Three-foot velocity: 1,450 ft./sec.
Hull: 3½-inch plastic
Wad: Plastic
Shot: Steel
Buffered: No
Test barrel length: 30 inch
Pellets will pierce skin up to 145 yards.

NO. 2 STEEL PELLETS—1³/₈ OUNCES—172 PELLETS
Mfg: Winchester **Manufacturer's code:** SSH1235
Recoil energy in 8-lb. shotgun: 50.5 ft./lbs. **Recoil velocity in 8-lb. shotgun:** 20.1 ft./sec.

Distance in yards:	Muzzle	20	30	40	50	60	70
Velocity in fps:	1,543	1,000	846	730	637	561	496
Average pellet energy in ft-lbs:	18.58	7.80	5.59	4.16	3.17	2.46	1.92
Time of flight in seconds:	0	.0493	.0820	.1203	.1643	.2146	.2715

Type of load: Nontoxic
Three-foot velocity: 1,450 ft./sec.
Hull: 3½-inch plastic
Wad: Two-piece plastic
Shot: Steel
Buffered: No
Test barrel length: 30 inch
Pellets will pierce skin up to 145 yards.

NO. 2 STEEL PELLETS—1³/₈ OUNCES—172 PELLETS
Mfg: Fiocchi **Manufacturer's code:** 1235ST
Recoil energy in 8-lb. shotgun: 55.3 ft./lbs. **Recoil velocity in 8-lb. shotgun:** 21.1 ft./sec.

Distance in yards:	Muzzle	20	30	40	50	60	70
Velocity in fps:	1,598	1,025	865	745	649	608	505
Average pellet energy in ft-lbs:	19.92	8.20	5.84	4.33	3.29	2.54	1.99
Time of flight in seconds:	0	.0478	.0798	.1173	.1605	.2098	.2658

Type of load: Nontoxic
Three-foot velocity: 1,500 ft./sec.
Hull: 3½-inch plastic
Wad: Plastic
Shot: Steel
Buffered: No
Test barrel length: 30 inch
Pellets will pierce skin up to 146 yards.

NO. 2 STEEL PELLETS—1½ OUNCES—187 PELLETS
Mfg: Estate Cartridge **Manufacturer's code:** HVST1235M
Recoil energy in 8-lb. shotgun: 54.6 ft./lbs. **Recoil velocity in 8-lb. shotgun:** 21.0 ft./sec.

Distance in yards:	Muzzle	20	30	40	50	60	70
Velocity in fps:	1,488	974	827	715	625	551	487
Average pellet energy in ft-lbs:	17.29	7.40	5.34	3.99	3.05	2.37	1.85
Time of flight in seconds:	0	.0509	.0844	.1234	.1684	.2195	.2775

Type of load: Nontoxic & Field
Three-foot velocity: 1,400 ft./sec.
Hull: 3½-inch plastic
Wad: Plastic
Shot: Steel
Buffered: No
Test barrel length: 30 inch
Pellets will pierce skin up to 144 yards.

NO. 2 STEEL PELLETS—1⁹⁄₁₆ OUNCES—195 PELLETS

Mfg: Federal Cartridge Company   **Manufacturer's code:** W135
Recoil energy in 8-lb. shotgun: 48.6 ft./lbs.   **Recoil velocity in 8-lb. shotgun:** 19.8 ft./sec.

Distance in yards:	Muzzle	20	30	40	50	60	70
Velocity in fps:	1,379	923	789	685	601	530	469
Average pellet energy in ft-lbs:	14.85	6.65	4.86	3.66	2.81	2.19	1.72
Time of flight in seconds:	0	.0542	.0894	.1303	.1771	.2303	.2905

Type of load: Nontoxic
Three-foot velocity: 1,300 ft./sec.
Hull: 3½-inch plastic
Wad: Plastic
Shot: Steel
Buffered: No
Test barrel length: 30 inch
Pellets will pierce skin up to 140 yards.

NO. 2 STEEL PELLETS—1⁹⁄₁₆ OUNCES—195 PELLETS

Mfg: Kent Cartridge America/Canada   **Manufacturer's code:** K1235ST44
Recoil energy in 8-lb. shotgun: 48.6 ft./lbs.   **Recoil velocity in 8-lb. shotgun:** 19.8 ft./sec.

Distance in yards:	Muzzle	20	30	40	50	60	70
Velocity in fps:	1,379	923	789	685	601	530	469
Average pellet energy in ft-lbs:	14.85	6.65	4.86	3.66	2.81	2.19	1.72
Time of flight in seconds:	0	.0542	.0894	.1303	.1771	.2303	.2905

Type of load: Nontoxic
Three-foot velocity: 1,300 ft./sec.
Hull: 3½-inch plastic
Wad: Plastic
Shot: Steel
Buffered: No
Test barrel length: 30 inch
Pellets will pierce skin up to 140 yards.

NO. 2 STEEL PELLETS—1⁹⁄₁₆ OUNCES—195 PELLETS

Mfg: Remington Arms Co.   **Manufacturer's code:** NS1235
Recoil energy in 8-lb. shotgun: 48.6 ft./lbs.   **Recoil velocity in 8-lb. shotgun:** 19.8 ft./sec.

Distance in yards:	Muzzle	20	30	40	50	60	70
Velocity in fps:	1,379	923	789	685	601	530	469
Average pellet energy in ft-lbs:	14.85	6.65	4.86	3.66	2.81	2.19	1.72
Time of flight in seconds:	0	.0542	.0894	.1303	.1771	.2303	.2905

Type of load: Nontoxic
Three-foot velocity: 1,300 ft./sec.
Hull: 3½-inch plastic
Wad: Plastic
Shot: Zinc-galvanized steel
Buffered: No
Test barrel length: 30 inch
Pellets will pierce skin up to 140 yards.

The author with a limit of Colorado mallards bagged with a modified Damascus-barreled hammer gun. Employing steel chamber sleeves installed by Briley Manufacturing, this old 10-bore was made into a 12-gauge and provided a great morning's hunting. There is a renewed interest in shooting old shotguns such as this J. P. Clabrough, and outfits like Briley are able to modify many of them so they can be enjoyed in their second hundred years.

NO. 2 STEEL PELLETS—1⁹/₁₆ OUNCES—195 PELLETS
Mfg: Winchester **Manufacturer's code:** XSM12L
Recoil energy in 8-lb. shotgun: 48.6 ft./lbs. **Recoil velocity in 8-lb. shotgun:** 19.8 ft./sec.

Distance in yards:	Muzzle	20	30	40	50	60	70
Velocity in fps:	1,379	923	789	685	601	530	469
Average pellet energy in ft-lbs:	14.85	6.65	4.86	3.66	2.81	2.19	1.72
Time of flight in seconds:	0	.0542	.0894	.1303	.1771	.2303	.2905

Type of load: Nontoxic
Three-foot velocity: 1,300 ft./sec.
Hull: 3½-inch plastic
Wad: Two-piece plastic
Shot: Steel
Buffered: No
Test barrel length: 30 inch
Pellets will pierce skin up to 140 yards.

NO. 3 STEEL PELLETS—1½ OUNCES—237 PELLETS
Mfg: Estate Cartridge **Manufacturer's code:** HVST1235M
Recoil energy in 8-lb. shotgun: 54.6 ft./lbs. **Recoil velocity in 8-lb. shotgun:** 21.0 ft./sec.

Distance in yards:	Muzzle	20	30	40	50	60	70
Velocity in fps:	1,494	953	803	689	598	524	460
Average pellet energy in ft-lbs:	14.16	5.76	4.09	3.01	2.27	1.74	1.34
Time of flight in seconds:	0	.0515	.0859	.1263	.1731	.2267	.2879

Type of load: Nontoxic
Three-foot velocity: 1,400 ft./sec.
Hull: 3½-inch plastic
Wad: Plastic
Shot: Steel
Buffered: No
Test barrel length: 30 inch
Pellets will pierce skin up to 134 yards.

NO. 3 STEEL PELLETS—1⁹/₁₆ OUNCES—247 PELLETS
Mfg: Kent Cartridge America/Canada **Manufacturer's code:** K1235ST44
Recoil energy in 8-lb. shotgun: 48.6 ft./lbs. **Recoil velocity in 8-lb. shotgun:** 19.8 ft./sec.

Distance in yards:	Muzzle	20	30	40	50	60	70
Velocity in fps:	1,384	904	767	661	575	504	442
Average pellet energy in ft-lbs:	12.16	5.18	3.73	2.77	2.10	1.61	1.24
Time of flight in seconds:	0	.0548	.0909	.1332	.1819	.2377	.3013

Type of load: Nontoxic
Three-foot velocity: 1,300 ft./sec.
Hull: 3½-inch plastic
Wad: Plastic
Shot: Steel
Buffered: No
Test barrel length: 30 inch
Pellets will pierce skin up to 131 yards.

NO. 3 STEEL PELLETS—1⁹/₁₆ OUNCES—247 PELLETS
Mfg: Winchester **Manufacturer's code:** XSM12L
Recoil energy in 8-lb. shotgun: 48.6 ft./lbs. **Recoil velocity in 8-lb. shotgun:** 19.8 ft./sec.

Distance in yards:	Muzzle	20	30	40	50	60	70
Velocity in fps:	1,384	904	767	661	575	504	442
Average pellet energy in ft-lbs:	12.16	5.18	3.73	2.77	2.10	1.61	1.24
Time of flight in seconds:	0	.0548	.0909	.1332	.1819	.2377	.3013

Type of load: Nontoxic
Three-foot velocity: 1,300 ft./sec.
Hull: 3½-inch plastic
Wad: Two-piece plastic
Shot: Steel
Buffered: No
Test barrel length: 30 inch
Pellets will pierce skin up to 131 yards.

NO. 4 STEEL PELLETS—1⅜ OUNCES—264 PELLETS
Mfg: Federal Cartridge Company **Manufacturer's code:** PWT133/W133
Recoil energy in 8-lb. shotgun: 50.5 ft./lbs. **Recoil velocity in 8-lb. shotgun:** 20.1 ft./sec.

Distance in yards:	Muzzle	20	30	40	50	60	70
Velocity in fps:	1,555	952	793	673	580	503	437
Average pellet energy in ft-lbs:	12.28	4.60	3.19	2.30	1.71	1.28	.97
Time of flight in seconds:	0	.0506	.0853	.1265	.1745	.2302	.2942

Type of load: Nontoxic
Three-foot velocity: 1,450 ft./sec.
Hull: 3½-inch plastic
Wad: Plastic
Shot: Steel
Buffered: No
Test barrel length: 30 inch
Pellets will pierce skin up to 126 yards.

NO. 4 STEEL PELLETS—1½ OUNCES—288 PELLETS
Mfg: Estate Cartridge **Manufacturer's code:** HVST1235M
Recoil energy in 8-lb. shotgun: 54.6 ft./lbs. **Recoil velocity in 8-lb. shotgun:** 21.0 ft./sec.

Distance in yards:	Muzzle	20	30	40	50	60	70
Velocity in fps:	1,500	929	776	660	569	494	429
Average pellet energy in ft-lbs:	11.42	4.38	3.06	2.22	1.65	1.24	.94
Time of flight in seconds:	0	.0522	.0876	.1297	.1787	.2353	.3005

Type of load: Nontoxic
Three-foot velocity: 1,400 ft./sec.
Hull: 3½-inch plastic
Wad: Plastic
Shot: Steel
Buffered: No
Test barrel length: 30 inch
Pellets will pierce skin up to 125 yards.

NO. BBB TUNGSTEN-IRON PELLETS—1⅜ OUNCES—63 PELLETS
Mfg: Federal Cartridge Company **Manufacturer's code:** PWT 136
Recoil energy in 8-lb. shotgun: 45.9 ft./lbs. **Recoil velocity in 8-lb. shotgun:** 19.2 ft./sec.

Distance in yards:	Muzzle	20	30	40	50	60	70
Velocity in fps:	1,444	1,105	988	893	813	745	685
Average pellet energy in ft-lbs:	43.63	25.58	20.45	16.69	13.84	11.62	9.83
Time of flight in seconds:	0	.0479	.0766	.1086	.1438	.1824	.2244

Type of load: Nontoxic
Three-foot velocity: 1,400 ft./sec.
Hull: 3½-inch plastic
Wad: Plastic
Shot: Tungsten-iron
Buffered: Yes
Test barrel length: 30 inch
Pellets will pierce skin up to 238 yards.

NO. BB TUNGSTEN-IRON PELLETS—1⅜ OUNCES—74 PELLETS
Mfg: Federal Cartridge Company **Manufacturer's code:** PWT 136
Recoil energy in 8-lb. shotgun: 45.9 ft./lbs. **Recoil velocity in 8-lb. shotgun:** 19.2 ft./sec.

Distance in yards:	Muzzle	20	30	40	50	60	70
Velocity in fps:	1,447	1,093	973	875	794	725	665
Average pellet energy in ft-lbs:	37.28	21.27	16.84	13.64	11.23	9.36	7.87
Time of flight in seconds:	0	.0481	.0773	.1398	.1458	.1854	.2286

Type of load: Nontoxic
Three-foot velocity: 1,400 ft./sec.
Hull: 3½-inch plastic
Wad: Plastic
Shot: Tungsten-iron
Buffered: Yes
Test barrel length: 30 inch
Pellets will pierce skin up to 226 yards.

NO. 2 TUNGSTEN-IRON PELLETS—1⅜ OUNCES—129 PELLETS
Mfg: Federal Cartridge Company **Manufacturer's code:** PWT 136
Recoil energy in 8-lb. shotgun: 45.9 ft./lbs. **Recoil velocity in 8-lb. shotgun:** 19.2 ft./sec.

Distance in yards:	Muzzle	20	30	40	50	60	70
Velocity in fps:	1,458	1,348	917	813	728	657	595
Average pellet energy in ft-lbs:	21.90	11.31	8.66	6.81	5.46	4.44	3.65
Time of flight in seconds:	0	.0491	.0798	.1146	.1536	.1971	.2451

Type of load: Nontoxic
Three-foot velocity: 1,400 ft./sec.
Hull: 3½-inch plastic
Wad: Plastic
Shot: Tungsten-iron
Buffered: Yes
Test barrel length: 30 inch
Pellets will pierce skin up to 188 yards.

NO. 4 TUNGSTEN-IRON PELLETS—1⅜ OUNCES—199 PELLETS
Mfg: Federal Cartridge Company **Manufacturer's code:** PWT 136
Recoil energy in 8-lb. shotgun: 45.9 ft./lbs. **Recoil velocity in 8-lb. shotgun:** 19.2 ft./sec.

Distance in yards:	Muzzle	20	30	40	50	60	70
Velocity in fps:	1,466	1,008	869	762	674	601	539
Average pellet energy in ft-lbs:	14.42	6.81	5.07	3.89	3.05	2.42	1.95
Time of flight in seconds:	0	.0501	.0823	.1192	.1611	.2083	.2610

Type of load: Nontoxic
Three-foot velocity: 1,400 ft./sec.
Hull: 3½-inch plastic
Wad: Plastic
Shot: Tungsten-iron
Buffered: Yes
Test barrel length: 30 inch
Pellets will pierce skin up to 164 yards.

NO. 2 TUNGSTEN-IRON PELLETS ON THE BOTTOM TOPPED
WITH A LAYER OF BB STEEL SHOT—1⅜ OUNCES
Mfg: Federal Cartridge Company **Manufacturer's code:** PWT132
Recoil energy in 8-lb. shotgun: 43.7 ft./lbs. **Recoil velocity in 8-lb. shotgun:** 18.7 ft./sec.

NO. 2 TUNGSTEN-IRON PELLETS

Distance in yards:	Muzzle	20	30	40	50	60	70
Velocity in fps:	1,417	1,025	899	799	717	647	586
Average pellet energy in ft-lbs:	20.70	10.83	8.33	6.58	5.29	4.31	3.54
Time of flight in seconds:	0	.0504	.0817	.1171	.1568	.2009	.2497

Type of load: Nontoxic
Three-foot velocity: 1,375 ft./sec.
Hull: 3½-inch plastic
Wad: Plastic
Shot: Steel/Tungsten-iron
Buffered: No
Test barrel length: 30 inch

Pellets will pierce skin up to 187 yards.

NO. BB STEEL PELLETS

Distance in yards:	Muzzle	20	30	40	50	60	70
Velocity in fps:	1,446	1,012	879	774	688	616	554
Average pellet energy in ft-lbs:	28.21	13.82	10.41	8.07	6.38	5.12	4.14
Time of flight in seconds:	0	.0503	.0822	.1186	.1598	.2059	.2573

Pellets will pierce skin up to 171 yards.

NO. 4 BISMUTH PELLETS—1 OUNCE—170 PELLETS

Mfg: Bismuth Cartridge Co. **Manufacturer's code:** Sporting Game
Recoil energy in 8-lb. shotgun: 19.9 ft./lbs. **Recoil velocity in 8-lb. shotgun:** 12.6 ft./sec.

Distance in yards:	Muzzle	20	30	40	50	60	70
Velocity in fps:	1,394	951	818	714	629	559	498
Average pellet energy in ft-lbs:	12.17	5.66	4.19	3.19	2.48	1.95	1.55
Time of flight in seconds:	0	.0530	.0871	.1265	.1713	.2219	.2788

Type of load: Nontoxic
Three-foot velocity: 1,300 ft./sec.
Hull: 2½-inch plastic
Wad: Plastic
Shot: Bismuth
Buffered: No
Test barrel length: 30 inch
Pellets will pierce skin up to 150 yards.

NO. 4 BISMUTH PELLETS—1⅛ OUNCES—191 PELLETS

Mfg: Eley Hawk **Manufacturer's code:** Grand Prix High Velocity
Recoil energy in 8-lb. shotgun: 23.9 ft./lbs. **Recoil velocity in 8-lb. shotgun:** 13.9 ft./sec.

Distance in yards:	Muzzle	20	30	40	50	60	70
Velocity in fps:	1,367	937	807	706	623	553	493
Average pellet energy in ft-lbs:	11.69	5.50	4.08	3.12	2.43	1.91	1.52
Time of flight in seconds:	0	.0539	.0885	.1283	.1736	.2248	.2823

Type of load: Nontoxic
Three-foot velocity: 1,275 ft./sec.
Hull: 2½-inch plastic
Wad: Fiber or plastic
Shot: Bismuth
Buffered: No
Test barrel length: 30 inch
Pellets will pierce skin up to 150 yards.

NO. 5 BISMUTH PELLETS—1⅛ OUNCES—248 PELLETS

Mfg: Eley Hawk **Manufacturer's code:** Grand Prix High Velocity
Recoil energy in 8-lb. shotgun: 23.9 ft./lbs. **Recoil velocity in 8-lb. shotgun:** 13.9 ft./sec.

Distance in yards:	Muzzle	20	30	40	50	60	70
Velocity in fps:	1,373	916	782	678	594	523	463
Average pellet energy in ft-lbs:	9.28	4.13	3.01	2.26	1.74	1.35	1.05
Time of flight in seconds:	0	.0546	.0901	.1314	.1787	.2326	.2936

Type of load: Nontoxic
Three-foot velocity: 1,275 ft./sec.
Hull: 2½-inch plastic
Wad: Fiber or plastic
Shot: Bismuth
Buffered: No
Test barrel length: 30 inch
Pellets will pierce skin up to 138 yards.

NO. 6 BISMUTH PELLETS—1 OUNCE—270 PELLETS

Mfg: Bismuth Cartridge Co. **Manufacturer's code:** Sporting Game
Recoil energy in 8-lb. shotgun: 19.9 ft./lbs. **Recoil velocity in 8-lb. shotgun:** 12.6 ft./sec.

Distance in yards:	Muzzle	20	30	40	50	60	70
Velocity in fps:	1,408	904	763	654	568	495	433
Average pellet energy in ft-lbs:	7.51	3.10	2.21	1.62	1.22	.93	.71
Time of flight in seconds:	0	.0544	.0907	.1332	.1826	.2392	.3040

Type of load: Nontoxic
Three-foot velocity: 1,300 ft./sec.
Hull: 2½-inch plastic
Wad: Plastic
Shot: Bismuth
Buffered: No
Test barrel length: 30 inch
Pellets will pierce skin up to 128 yards.

NO. 6 BISMUTH PELLETS—1⅛ OUNCES—304 PELLETS

Mfg: Eley Hawk **Manufacturer's code:** Grand Prix High Velocity
Recoil energy in 8-lb. shotgun: 23.9 ft./lbs. **Recoil velocity in 8-lb. shotgun:** 13.9 ft./sec.

Distance in yards:	Muzzle	20	30	40	50	60	70
Velocity in fps:	1,380	892	753	647	562	490	429
Average pellet energy in ft-lbs:	7.22	3.01	2.15	1.59	1.20	.91	.70
Time of flight in seconds:	0	.0553	.0920	.1351	.1849	.2421	.3076

Type of load: Nontoxic
Three-foot velocity: 1,275 ft./sec.
Hull: 2½-inch plastic
Wad: Fiber or plastic
Shot: Bismuth
Buffered: No
Test barrel length: 30 inch
Pellets will pierce skin up to 127 yards.

BB BISMUTH PELLETS—1¼ OUNCES—75 PELLETS
Mfg: Eley Hawk **Manufacturer's code:** Alphamax Bismuth
Recoil energy in 8-lb. shotgun: 31.1 ft./lbs. **Recoil velocity in 8-lb. shotgun:** 15.8 ft./sec.

Distance in yards:	Muzzle	20	30	40	50	60	70
Velocity in fps:	1,397	1,045	927	832	752	685	626
Average pellet energy in ft-lbs:	32.43	18.14	14.28	11.50	9.41	7.79	6.51
Time of flight in seconds:	0	.0502	.0807	.1149	.1528	.1947	.2405

Type of load: Nontoxic
Three-foot velocity: 1,330 ft./sec.
Hull: 2¾-inch plastic
Wad: Plastic
Shot: Bismuth
Buffered: No
Test barrel length: 30 inch
Pellets will pierce skin up to 229 yards.

BB BISMUTH PELLETS—1⅜ OUNCES—83 PELLETS
Mfg: Bismuth Cartridge Co. **Manufacturer's code:** Magnum Buffered Game
Recoil energy in 8-lb. shotgun: 35.7 ft./lbs. **Recoil velocity in 8-lb. shotgun:** 16.9 ft./sec.

Distance in yards:	Muzzle	20	30	40	50	60	70
Velocity in fps:	1,338	1,010	900	809	733	668	611
Average pellet energy in ft-lbs:	29.75	16.97	13.45	10.88	8.93	7.42	6.21
Time of flight in seconds:	0	.0521	.0836	.1188	.1578	.2007	.2476

Type of load: Nontoxic
Three-foot velocity: 1,275 ft./sec.
Hull: 2¾-inch plastic
Wad: Plastic
Shot: Bismuth
Buffered: Yes
Test barrel length: 30 inch
Pellets will pierce skin up to 206 yards.

NO. 2 BISMUTH PELLETS—1⅜ OUNCES—165 PELLETS
Mfg: Bismuth Cartridge Co. **Manufacturer's code:** Magnum Buffered Game
Recoil energy in 8-lb. shotgun: 35.7 ft./lbs. **Recoil velocity in 8-lb. shotgun:** 16.9 ft./sec.

Distance in yards:	Muzzle	20	30	40	50	60	70
Velocity in fps:	1,355	972	850	753	673	605	546
Average pellet energy in ft-lbs:	17.65	9.09	6.95	5.45	4.35	3.52	2.87
Time of flight in seconds:	0	.0530	.0860	.1236	.1658	.2128	.2651

Type of load: Nontoxic
Three-foot velocity: 1,275 ft./sec.
Hull: 2¾-inch plastic
Wad: Plastic
Shot: Bismuth
Buffered: Yes
Test barrel length: 30 inch
Pellets will pierce skin up to 172 yards.

NO. 3 BISMUTH PELLETS—1¼ OUNCES—155 PELLETS
Mfg: Eley Hawk **Manufacturer's code:** Alphamax Bismuth
Recoil energy in 8-lb. shotgun: 31.1 ft./lbs. **Recoil velocity in 8-lb. shotgun:** 15.8 ft./sec.

Distance in yards:	Muzzle	20	30	40	50	60	70
Velocity in fps:	1,421	986	854	750	665	594	533
Average pellet energy in ft-lbs:	15.78	7.61	5.70	4.39	3.45	2.75	2.22
Time of flight in seconds:	0	.0515	.0842	.1218	.1644	.2122	.2656

Type of load: Nontoxic
Three-foot velocity: 1,330 ft./sec.
Hull: 2¾-inch plastic
Wad: Plastic
Shot: Bismuth
Buffered: No
Test barrel length: 30 inch
Pellets will pierce skin up to 170 yards.

NO. 4 BISMUTH PELLETS—1¼ OUNCES—194 PELLETS
Mfg: Bismuth Cartridge Co. **Manufacturer's code:** Sporting Game
Recoil energy in 8-lb. shotgun: 26.3 ft./lbs. **Recoil velocity in 8-lb. shotgun:** 14.5 ft./sec.

Distance in yards:	Muzzle	20	30	40	50	60	70
Velocity in fps:	1,312	910	787	689	609	541	483
Average pellet energy in ft-lbs:	10.77	5.19	3.87	2.97	2.32	1.83	1.46
Time of flight in seconds:	0	.0558	.0913	.1322	.1785	.2309	.2896

Type of load: Nontoxic
Three-foot velocity: 1,225 ft./sec.
Hull: 2¾-inch plastic
Wad: Plastic
Shot: Bismuth
Buffered: No
Test barrel length: 30 inch
Pellets will pierce skin up to 148 yards.

NO. 4 BISMUTH PELLETS—1¼ OUNCES—194 PELLETS
Mfg: Bismuth Cartridge Co. **Manufacturer's code:** Eco
Recoil energy in 8-lb. shotgun: 31.1 ft./lbs. **Recoil velocity in 8-lb. shotgun:** 15.8 ft./sec.

Distance in yards:	Muzzle	20	30	40	50	60	70
Velocity in fps:	1,394	951	818	714	629	559	498
Average pellet energy in ft-lbs:	12.17	5.66	4.19	3.19	2.48	1.95	1.55
Time of flight in seconds:	0	.0530	.0871	.1265	.1713	.2219	.2788

Type of load: Nontoxic
Three-foot velocity: 1,300 ft./sec.
Hull: 2¾-inch lacquered paper
Wad: Fiber
Shot: Bismuth
Buffered: No
Test barrel length: 30 inch
Pellets will pierce skin up to 150 yards.

NO. 4 BISMUTH PELLETS—1¼ OUNCES—194 PELLETS
Mfg: Eley Hawk **Manufacturer's code:** Alphamax Bismuth
Recoil energy in 8-lb. shotgun: 31.1 ft./lbs. **Recoil velocity in 8-lb. shotgun:** 15.8 ft./sec.

Distance in yards:	Muzzle	20	30	40	50	60	70
Velocity in fps:	1,427	967	830	124	637	566	504
Average pellet energy in ft-lbs:	12.75	5.85	4.31	3.28	2.54	2.00	1.59
Time of flight in seconds:	0	.0520	.0856	.1244	.1686	.2186	.2748

Type of load: Nontoxic
Three-foot velocity: 1,330 ft./sec.
Hull: 2¾-inch plastic
Wad: Plastic
Shot: Bismuth
Buffered: No
Test barrel length: 30 inch
Pellets will pierce skin up to 158 yards.

NO. 4 BISMUTH PELLETS—1⅜ OUNCES—234 PELLETS
Mfg: Bismuth Cartridge Co. **Manufacturer's code:** Magnum Buffered Game
Recoil energy in 8-lb. shotgun: 35.7 ft./lbs. **Recoil velocity in 8-lb. shotgun:** 16.9 ft./sec.

Distance in yards:	Muzzle	20	30	40	50	60	70
Velocity in fps:	1,367	937	807	706	623	553	493
Average pellet energy in ft-lbs:	11.69	5.50	4.08	3.12.	2.43	1.91	1.52
Time of flight in seconds:	0	.0539	.0885	.1283	.1736	.2248	.2823

Type of load: Nontoxic
Three-foot velocity: 1,275 ft./sec.
Hull: 2¾-inch plastic
Wad: Plastic
Shot: Bismuth
Buffered: Yes
Test barrel length: 30 inch
Pellets will pierce skin up to 150 yards.

NO. 5 BISMUTH PELLETS—1 OUNCE—220 PELLETS
Mfg: Eley Hawk **Manufacturer's code:** Impax
Recoil energy in 8-lb. shotgun: 17.9 ft./lbs. **Recoil velocity in 8-lb. shotgun:** 12.0 ft./sec.

Distance in yards:	Muzzle	20	30	40	50	60	70
Velocity in fps:	1,345	984	772	670	587	518	458
Average pellet energy in ft-lbs:	8.91	4.02	2.94	2.21	1.70	1.32	1.03
Time of flight in seconds:	0	.0555	.0915	.1333	.1811	.2356	.2972

Type of load: Nontoxic
Three-foot velocity: 1,250 ft./sec.
Hull: 2¾-inch plastic
Wad: Fiber
Shot: Bismuth
Buffered: No
Test barrel length: 30 inch
Pellets will pierce skin up to 137 yards.

NO. 5 BISMUTH PELLETS—1¼ OUNCES—246 PELLETS
Mfg: Eley Hawk **Manufacturer's code:** Alphamax Bismuth
Recoil energy in 8-lb. shotgun: 31.1 ft./lbs. **Recoil velocity in 8-lb. shotgun:** 15.8 ft./sec.

Distance in yards:	Muzzle	20	30	40	50	60	70
Velocity in fps:	1,434	944	803	695	608	535	473
Average pellet energy in ft-lbs:	10.12	4.39	3.18	2.38	1.82	1.41	1.10
Time of flight in seconds:	0	.0526	.0872	.1274	.1736	.2263	.2860

Type of load: Nontoxic
Three-foot velocity: 1,330 ft./sec.
Hull: 2¾-inch plastic
Wad: Plastic
Shot: Bismuth
Buffered: No
Test barrel length: 30 inch
Pellets will pierce skin up to 146 yards.

NO. 5 BISMUTH PELLETS—1⅜ OUNCES—303 PELLETS
Mfg: Bismuth Cartridge Co. **Manufacturer's code:** Magnum Buffered Game
Recoil energy in 8-lb. shotgun: 35.7 ft./lbs. **Recoil velocity in 8-lb. shotgun:** 16.9 ft./sec.

Distance in yards:	Muzzle	20	30	40	50	60	70
Velocity in fps:	1,373	916	782	678	594	523	463
Average pellet energy in ft-lbs:	9.28	4.13	3.01	2.26	1.74	1.35	1.05
Time of flight in seconds:	0	.0546	.0901	.1314	.1787	.2326	.2936

Type of load: Nontoxic
Three-foot velocity: 1,275 ft./sec.
Hull: 2¾-inch plastic
Wad: Plastic
Shot: Bismuth
Buffered: Yes
Test barrel length: 30 inch
Pellets will pierce skin up to 138 yards.

NO. 6 BISMUTH PELLETS—1 OUNCE—270 PELLETS
Mfg: Eley Hawk **Manufacturer's code:** Impax
Recoil energy in 8-lb. shotgun: 17.9 ft./lbs. **Recoil velocity in 8-lb. shotgun:** 12.0 ft./sec.

Distance in yards:	Muzzle	20	30	40	50	60	70
Velocity in fps:	1,352	879	744	640	556	485	424
Average pellet energy in ft-lbs:	6.93	2.93	2.10	1.55	1.17	.89	.68
Time of flight in seconds:	0	.0563	.0934	.1370	.1874	.2452	.3114

Type of load: Nontoxic
Three-foot velocity: 1,250 ft./sec.
Hull: 2¾-inch plastic
Wad: Fiber
Shot: Bismuth
Buffered: No
Test barrel length: 30 inch
Pellets will pierce skin up to 127 yards.

NO. 6 BISMUTH PELLETS—1 OUNCE—270 PELLETS
Mfg: Bismuth Cartridge Co. **Manufacturer's code:** Sporting Game
Recoil energy in 8-lb. shotgun: 19.9 ft./lbs. **Recoil velocity in 8-lb. shotgun:** 12.6 ft./sec.

Distance in yards:	Muzzle	20	30	40	50	60	70
Velocity in fps:	1,408	904	763	654	568	495	433
Average pellet energy in ft-lbs:	7.51	3.10	2.21	1.62	1.22	.93	.71
Time of flight in seconds:	0	.0544	.0907	.1332	.1826	.2392	.3040

Type of load: Nontoxic
Three-foot velocity: 1,300 ft./sec.
Hull: 2¾-inch plastic
Wad: Plastic
Shot: Bismuth
Buffered: No
Test barrel length: 30 inch
Pellets will pierce skin up to 128 yards.

NO. 6 BISMUTH PELLETS—1¼ OUNCES—320 PELLETS
Mfg: Bismuth Cartridge Co. **Manufacturer's code:** Sporting Game
Recoil energy in 8-lb. shotgun: 26.3 ft./lbs. **Recoil velocity in 8-lb. shotgun:** 14.5 ft./sec.

Distance in yards:	Muzzle	20	30	40	50	60	70
Velocity in fps:	1,324	867	735	682	550	480	420
Average pellet energy in ft-lbs:	6.65	2.85	2.05	1.52	1.15	.87	.67
Time of flight in seconds:	0	.0572	.0949	.1390	.1899	.2484	.3153

Type of load: Nontoxic
Three-foot velocity: 1,225 ft./sec.
Hull: 2¾-inch plastic
Wad: Fiber
Shot: Bismuth
Buffered: No
Test barrel length: 30 inch
Pellets will pierce skin up to 125 yards.

NO. 6 BISMUTH PELLETS—1¼ OUNCES—338 PELLETS

Mfg: Bismuth Cartridge Co. **Manufacturer's code:** Eco
Recoil energy in 8-lb. shotgun: 31.1 ft./lbs. **Recoil velocity in 8-lb. shotgun:** 15.8 ft./sec.

Distance in yards:	Muzzle	20	30	40	50	60	70
Velocity in fps:	1,408	904	763	654	568	495	433
Average pellet energy in ft-lbs:	7.51	3.10	2.21	1.62	1.22	.93	.71
Time of flight in seconds:	0	.0544	.0907	.1332	.1826	.2392	.3040

Type of load: Nontoxic
Three-foot velocity: 1,300 ft./sec.
Hull: 2¾-inch lacquered paper
Wad: Fiber
Shot: Bismuth
Buffered: No
Test barrel length: 30 inch
Pellets will pierce skin up to 128 yards.

NO. 6 BISMUTH PELLETS—1¼ OUNCES—320 PELLETS

Mfg: Eley Hawk **Manufacturer's code:** Alphamax Bismuth
Recoil energy in 8-lb. shotgun: 31.1 ft./lbs. **Recoil velocity in 8-lb. shotgun:** 15.8 ft./sec.

Distance in yards:	Muzzle	20	30	40	50	60	70
Velocity in fps:	1,441	918	773	663	574	501	438
Average pellet energy in ft-lbs:	7.87	3.20	2.27	1.97	1.25	.95	.73
Time of flight in seconds:	0	.0534	.0891	.1311	.1798	.2357	.2998

Type of load: Nontoxic
Three-foot velocity: 1,330 ft./sec.
Hull: 2¾-inch plastic
Wad: Plastic
Shot: Bismuth
Buffered: No
Test barrel length: 30 inch
Pellets will pierce skin up to 134 yards.

NO. 6 BISMUTH PELLETS—1⅜ OUNCES—371 PELLETS

Mfg: Bismuth Cartridge Co. **Manufacturer's code:** Magnum Buffered Game
Recoil energy in 8-lb. shotgun: 35.7 ft./lbs. **Recoil velocity in 8-lb. shotgun:** 16.9 ft./sec.

Distance in yards:	Muzzle	20	30	40	50	60	70
Velocity in fps:	1,380	892	753	647	562	490	429
Average pellet energy in ft-lbs:	7.22	3.01	2.15	1.59	1.20	.91	.70
Time of flight in seconds:	0	.0553	.0920	.1351	.1849	.2421	.3076

Type of load: Nontoxic
Three-foot velocity: 1,275 ft./sec.
Hull: 2¾-inch plastic
Wad: Plastic
Shot: Bismuth
Buffered: Yes
Test barrel length: 30 inch
Pellets will pierce skin up to 127 yards.

NO. 7½ BISMUTH PELLETS—1 OUNCE—340 PELLETS

Mfg: Bismuth Cartridge Co. **Manufacturer's code:** Sporting Game
Recoil energy in 8-lb. shotgun: 19.9 ft./lbs. **Recoil velocity in 8-lb. shotgun:** 12.6 ft./sec.

Distance in yards:	Muzzle	20	30	40	50	60	70
Velocity in fps:	1,418	859	711	600	512	438	375
Average pellet energy in ft-lbs:	4.90	1.80	1.24	.88	.64	.47	.34
Time of flight in seconds:	0	.0560	.0945	.1405	.1948	.2582	.3323

Type of load: Nontoxic
Three-foot velocity: 1,300 ft./sec.
Hull: 2¾-inch plastic
Wad: Plastic
Shot: Bismuth
Buffered: No
Test barrel length: 30 inch
Pellets will pierce skin up to 110 yards.

NO. 7½ BISMUTH PELLETS—1¼ OUNCES—497 PELLETS

Mfg: Bismuth Cartridge Co. **Manufacturer's code:** Sporting Game
Recoil energy in 8-lb. shotgun: 26.3 ft./lbs. **Recoil velocity in 8-lb. shotgun:** 14.5 ft./sec.

Distance in yards:	Muzzle	20	30	40	50	60	70
Velocity in fps:	1,334	825	686	581	496	424	363
Average pellet energy in ft-lbs:	4.35	1.66	1.15	.82	.60	.44	.32
Time of flight in seconds:	0	.0588	.0987	.1464	.2023	.2678	.3443

Type of load: Nontoxic
Three-foot velocity: 1,225 ft./sec.
Hull: 2¾-inch plastic
Wad: Fiber
Shot: Bismuth
Buffered: No
Test barrel length: 30 inch
Pellets will pierce skin up to 108 yards.

NO. 7½ BISMUTH PELLETS—1¼ OUNCES—425 PELLETS

Mfg: Bismuth Cartridge Co. **Manufacturer's code:** Eco
Recoil energy in 8-lb. shotgun: 31.1 ft./lbs. **Recoil velocity in 8-lb. shotgun:** 15.8 ft./sec.

Distance in yards:	Muzzle	20	30	40	50	60	70
Velocity in fps:	1,418	859	711	600	512	438	375
Average pellet energy in ft-lbs:	4.90	1.80	1.24	.88	.64	.47	.34
Time of flight in seconds:	0	.0560	.0945	.1405	.1948	.2582	.3323

Type of load: Nontoxic
Three-foot velocity: 1,300 ft./sec.
Hull: 2¾-inch lacquered paper
Wad: Fiber
Shot: Bismuth
Buffered: No
Test barrel length: 30 inch
Pellets will pierce skin up to 110 yards.

NO. BB BISMUTH PELLETS—1⅜ OUNCES—83 PELLETS
Mfg: Bismuth Cartridge Co. **Manufacturer's code:** Magnum
Recoil energy in 8-lb. shotgun: 43.7 ft./lbs. **Recoil velocity in 8-lb. shotgun:** 18.7 ft./sec.

Distance in yards:	Muzzle	20	30	40	50	60	70
Velocity in fps:	1,445	1,073	949	850	768	698	637
Average pellet energy in ft-lbs:	34.71	19.13	14.97	12.01	9.80	8.09	6.75
Time of flight in seconds:	0	.0487	.0784	.1119	.1490	.1901	.2351

Type of load: Nontoxic
Three-foot velocity: 1,250 ft./sec.
Hull: 3-inch plastic
Wad: Plastic
Shot: Bismuth
Buffered: Yes
Test barrel length: 30 inch
Pellets will pierce skin up to 210 yards.

NO. BB BISMUTH PELLETS—1⅝ OUNCES—95 PELLETS
Mfg: Bismuth Cartridge Co. **Manufacturer's code:** Magnum Buffered Game
Recoil energy in 8-lb. shotgun: 47.4 ft./lbs. **Recoil velocity in 8-lb. shotgun:** 19.5 ft./sec.

Distance in yards:	Muzzle	20	30	40	50	60	70
Velocity in fps:	1,311	995	887	799	724	660	605
Average pellet energy in ft-lbs:	28.57	16.45	13.08	1.060	8.72	7.25	6.07
Time of flight in seconds:	0	.0530	.0850	.1207	.1602	.2036	.2511

Type of load: Nontoxic
Three-foot velocity: 1,250 ft./sec.
Hull: 3-inch plastic
Wad: Plastic
Shot: Bismuth
Buffered: Yes
Test barrel length: 30 inch
Pellets will pierce skin up to 204 yards.

NO. BB BISMUTH PELLETS—1⅝ OUNCES—95 PELLETS
Mfg: Eley Hawk **Manufacturer's code:** Magnum 75
Recoil energy in 8-lb. shotgun: 52.6 ft./lbs. **Recoil velocity in 8-lb. shotgun:** 20.6 ft./sec.

Distance in yards:	Muzzle	20	30	40	50	60	70
Velocity in fps:	1,365	1,026	912	820	742	676	618
Average pellet energy in ft-lbs:	30.95	22.83	13.82	11.16	9.15	7.59	6.35
Time of flight in seconds:	0	.0512	.0823	.1170	.1555	.1979	.2443

Type of load: Nontoxic
Three-foot velocity: 1,300 ft./sec.
Hull: 3-inch plastic
Wad: Plastic
Shot: Bismuth
Buffered: No
Test barrel length: 30 inch
Pellets will pierce skin up to 215 yards.

NO. 2 BISMUTH PELLETS—1⅜ OUNCES—138 PELLETS
Mfg: Bismuth Cartridge Co. **Manufacturer's code:** Magnum Buffered Game
Recoil energy in 8-lb. shotgun: 43.7 ft./lbs. **Recoil velocity in 8-lb. shotgun:** 18.7 ft./sec.

Distance in yards:	Muzzle	20	30	40	50	60	70
Velocity in fps:	1,464	1,030	895	789	703	630	568
Average pellet energy in ft-lbs:	20.60	10.19	7.70	5.99	4.75	3.82	3.11
Time of flight in seconds:	0	.0496	.0809	.1166	.1570	.2021	.2522

Type of load: Nontoxic
Three-foot velocity: 1,375 ft./sec.
Hull: 3-inch plastic
Wad: Plastic
Shot: Bismuth
Buffered: Yes
Test barrel length: 30 inch
Pellets will pierce skin up to 176 yards.

NO. 2 BISMUTH PELLETS—1⅝ OUNCES—164 PELLETS
Mfg: Bismuth Cartridge Co. **Manufacturer's code:** Magnum Buffered Game
Recoil energy in 8-lb. shotgun: 47.4 ft./lbs. **Recoil velocity in 8-lb. shotgun:** 19.5 ft./sec.

Distance in yards:	Muzzle	20	30	40	50	60	70
Velocity in fps:	1,328	958	839	744	665	598	540
Average pellet energy in ft-lbs:	16.95	8082	6.77	5.32	4.25	3.44	2.81
Time of flight in seconds:	0	.0539	.0874	.1255	.1682	.2158	.2686

Type of load: Nontoxic
Three-foot velocity: 1,250 ft./sec.
Hull: 3-inch plastic
Wad: Plastic
Shot: Bismuth
Buffered: Yes
Test barrel length: 30 inch
Pellets will pierce skin up to 171 yards.

NO. 3 BISMUTH PELLETS—1⅝ OUNCES—201 PELLETS
Mfg: Eley Hawk **Manufacturer's code:** Magnum 75
Recoil energy in 8-lb. shotgun: 52.6 ft./lbs. **Recoil velocity in 8-lb. shotgun:** 20.6 ft./sec.

Distance in yards:	Muzzle	20	30	40	50	60	70
Velocity in fps:	1,388	970	841	739	656	586	526
Average pellet energy in ft-lbs:	15.06	7.35	5.53	4.27	3.37	2.69	2.16
Time of flight in seconds:	0	.0525	.0858	.1239	.1671	.2155	.2695

Type of load: Nontoxic
Three-foot velocity: 1,300 ft./sec.
Hull: 3-inch plastic
Wad: Plastic
Shot: Bismuth
Buffered: No
Test barrel length: 30 inch
Pellets will pierce skin up to 169 yards.

NO. 4 BISMUTH PELLETS—1⅜ OUNCES—234 PELLETS
Mfg: Bismuth Cartridge Co. **Manufacturer's code:** Game
Recoil energy in 8-lb. shotgun: 43.7 ft./lbs. **Recoil velocity in 8-lb. shotgun:** 18.7 ft./sec.

Distance in yards:	Muzzle	20	30	40	50	60	70
Velocity in fps:	1,477	991	848	738	649	576	513
Average pellet energy in ft-lbs:	13.65	6.14	4.50	3.41	2.64	2.07	1.65
Time of flight in seconds:	0	.0505	.0833	.1213	.1647	.2138	.2691

Type of load: Nontoxic
Three-foot velocity: 1,250 ft./sec.
Hull: 3-inch plastic
Wad: Plastic
Shot: Bismuth
Buffered: Yes
Test barrel length: 30 inch
Pellets will pierce skin up to 153 yards.

NO. 4 BISMUTH PELLETS—1⅝ OUNCES—252 PELLETS
Mfg: Bismuth Cartridge Co. **Manufacturer's code:** Magnum Buffered Game
Recoil energy in 8-lb. shotgun: 47.4 ft./lbs. **Recoil velocity in 8-lb. shotgun:** 19.5 ft./sec.

Distance in yards:	Muzzle	20	30	40	50	60	70
Velocity in fps:	1,339	924	797	697	616	547	488
Average pellet energy in ft-lbs:	11.23	5.34	3.98	3.04	2.37	1.87	1.49
Time of flight in seconds:	0	.0549	.0899	.1302	.1760	.2278	.2859

Type of load: Nontoxic
Three-foot velocity: 1,250 ft./sec.
Hull: 3-inch plastic
Wad: Plastic
Shot: Bismuth
Buffered: Yes
Test barrel length: 30 inch
Pellets will pierce skin up to 149 yards.

NO. 4 BISMUTH PELLETS—1⅝ OUNCES—252 PELLETS
Mfg: Eley Hawk **Manufacturer's code:** Magnum 75
Recoil energy in 8-lb. shotgun: 52.6 ft./lbs. **Recoil velocity in 8-lb. shotgun:** 20.6 ft./sec.

Distance in yards:	Muzzle	20	30	40	50	60	70
Velocity in fps:	1,394	951	818	714	629	559	498
Average pellet energy in ft-lbs:	12.17	5.66	4.19	3.19	2.48	1.95	1.55
Time of flight in seconds:	0	.0530	.0871	.1265	.1713	.2219	.2788

Type of load: Nontoxic
Three-foot velocity: 1,300 ft./sec.
Hull: 3-inch plastic
Wad: Plastic
Shot: Bismuth
Buffered: No
Test barrel length: 30 inch
Pellets will pierce skin up to 157 yards.

NO. 5 BISMUTH PELLETS—1⅜ OUNCES—303 PELLETS
Mfg: Bismuth Cartridge Co. **Manufacturer's code:** Magnum Buffered Game
Recoil energy in 8-lb. shotgun: 43.7 ft./lbs. **Recoil velocity in 8-lb. shotgun:** 18.7 ft./sec.

Distance in yards:	Muzzle	20	30	40	50	60	70
Velocity in fps:	1,484	967	820	708	619	544	481
Average pellet energy in ft-lbs:	10.84	4.60	3.31	2.47	1.88	1.46	1.14
Time of flight in seconds:	0	.0511	.0849	.1243	.1697	.2215	.2802

Type of load: Nontoxic
Three-foot velocity: 1,250 ft./sec.
Hull: 3-inch plastic
Wad: Plastic
Shot: Bismuth
Buffered: Yes
Test barrel length: 30 inch
Pellets will pierce skin up to 141 yards.

NO. 5 BISMUTH PELLETS—1⅝ OUNCES—320 PELLETS
Mfg: Bismuth Cartridge Co. **Manufacturer's code:** Magnum Buffered Game
Recoil energy in 8-lb. shotgun: 47.4 ft./lbs. **Recoil velocity in 8-lb. shotgun:** 19.5 ft./sec.

Distance in yards:	Muzzle	20	30	40	50	60	70
Velocity in fps:	1,345	903	772	670	587	518	458
Average pellet energy in ft-lbs:	8.91	4.02	2.94	2.21	1.70	1.32	1.03
Time of flight in seconds:	0	.0555	.0915	.1333	.1811	.2356	.2972

Type of load: Nontoxic
Three-foot velocity: 1,250 ft./sec.
Hull: 3-inch plastic
Wad: Plastic
Shot: Bismuth
Buffered: Yes
Test barrel length: 30 inch
Pellets will pierce skin up to 137 yards.

NO. 5 BISMUTH PELLETS—1⅝ OUNCES—320 PELLETS
Mfg: Eley Hawk **Manufacturer's code:** Magnum 75 Bismuth
Recoil energy in 8-lb. shotgun: 52.6 ft./lbs. **Recoil velocity in 8-lb. shotgun:** 20.6 ft./sec.

Distance in yards:	Muzzle	20	30	40	50	60	70
Velocity in fps:	1,401	929	792	686	600	529	467
Average pellet energy in ft-lbs:	9.66	4.25	3.09	2.31	1.77	1.38	1.07
Time of flight in seconds:	0	.0537	.0887	.1295	.1764	.2297	.2901

Type of load: Nontoxic
Three-foot velocity: 1,300 ft./sec.
Hull: 3-inch plastic
Wad: Plastic
Shot: Bismuth
Buffered: No
Test barrel length: 30 inch
Pellets will pierce skin up to 133 yards.

NO. 6 BISMUTH PELLETS—1⅝ OUNCES—439 PELLETS
Mfg: Bismuth Cartridge Co. **Manufacturer's code:** Magnum Buffered Game
Recoil energy in 8-lb. shotgun: 47.4 ft./lbs. **Recoil velocity in 8-lb. shotgun:** 19.5 ft./sec.

Distance in yards:	Muzzle	20	30	40	50	60	70
Velocity in fps:	1,352	879	744	640	556	485	424
Average pellet energy in ft-lbs:	6.93	2.93	2.10	1.55	1.17	.89	.68
Time of flight in seconds:	0	.0563	.0934	.1613	.1874	.2452	.3114

Type of load: Nontoxic
Three-foot velocity: 1,250 ft./sec.
Hull: 3-inch plastic
Wad: Plastic
Shot: Bismuth
Buffered: Yes
Test barrel length: 30 inch
Pellets will pierce skin up to 126 yards.

NO. BB BISMUTH PELLETS—1⅝ OUNCES—95 PELLETS
Mfg: Bismuth Cartridge Co. **Manufacturer's code:** MBHV-1235
Recoil energy in 8-lb. shotgun: 41.6 ft./lbs. **Recoil velocity in 8-lb. shotgun:** 16.4 ft./sec.

Distance in yards:	Muzzle	20	30	40	50	60	70
Velocity in fps:	1,445	1,073	949	850	768	698	637
Average pellet energy in ft-lbs:	34.71	19.13	14.97	12.01	9.80	8.09	6.75
Time of flight in seconds:	0	.0497	.0784	.1119	.1490	.1901	.2351

Type of load: Nontoxic
Three-foot velocity: 1,375 ft./sec.
Hull: 3½-inch plastic
Wad: One-piece plastic
Shot: Bismuth
Buffered: Yes
Test barrel length: 30 inch
Pellets will pierce skin up to 210 yards.

NO. BB BISMUTH PELLETS—1⅞ OUNCES—109 PELLETS
Mfg: Bismuth Cartridge Co. **Manufacturer's code:** MBGL-1235
Recoil energy in 8-lb. shotgun: 41.7 ft./lbs. **Recoil velocity in 8-lb. shotgun:** 16.4 ft./sec.

Distance in yards:	Muzzle	20	30	40	50	60	70
Velocity in fps:	1,285	979	874	788	715	653	598
Average pellet energy in ft-lbs:	27.42	15.93	12.71	10.32	8.50	7.08	5.94
Time of flight in seconds:	0	.0540	.0865	.1226	.1626	.2065	.2546

Type of load: Nontoxic
Three-foot velocity: 1,225 ft./sec.
Hull: 3½-inch plastic
Wad: One-piece plastic
Shot: Bismuth
Buffered: Yes
Test barrel length: 30 inch
Pellets will pierce skin up to 203 yards.

NO. 2 BISMUTH PELLETS—1⅝ OUNCES—164 PELLETS
Mfg: Bismuth Cartridge Co. **Manufacturer's code:** MBHV-1235
Recoil energy in 8-lb. shotgun: 41.3 ft./lbs. **Recoil velocity in 8-lb. shotgun:** 16.4 ft./sec.

Distance in yards:	Muzzle	20	30	40	50	60	70
Velocity in fps:	1,464	1,030	895	789	703	630	568
Average pellet energy in ft-lbs:	20.60	10.19	7.70	5.99	4.75	3.82	3.11
Time of flight in seconds:	0	.0496	.0809	.1166	.1570	.2021	.2522

Type of load: Nontoxic
Three-foot velocity: 1,375 ft./sec.
Hull: 3½-inch plastic
Wad: One-piece plastic
Shot: Bismuth
Buffered: Yes
Test barrel length: 30 inch
Pellets will pierce skin up to 176 yards.

NO. 2 BISMUTH PELLETS—1⅞ OUNCES—189 PELLETS
Mfg: Bismuth Cartridge Co. **Manufacturer's code:** MBGL-1235
Recoil energy in 8-lb. shotgun: 41.7 ft./lbs. **Recoil velocity in 8-lb. shotgun:** 16.4 ft./sec.

Distance in yards:	Muzzle	20	30	40	50	60	70
Velocity in fps:	1,300	943	828	735	657	592	535
Average pellet energy in ft-lbs:	16.26	8.55	6.59	5.19	4.15	3.36	2.75
Time of flight in seconds:	0	.0549	.0889	.1274	.1706	.2188	.2722

Type of load: Nontoxic
Three-foot velocity: 1,225 ft./sec.
Hull: 3½-inch plastic
Wad: One-piece plastic
Shot: Bismuth
Buffered: Yes
Test barrel length: 30 inch
Pellets will pierce skin up to 170 yards.

NO. 4 BISMUTH PELLETS—1⅝ OUNCES—252 PELLETS
Mfg: Bismuth Cartridge Co. **Manufacturer's code:** MBHV-1235
Recoil energy in 8-lb. shotgun: 41.3 ft./lbs. **Recoil velocity in 8-lb. shotgun:** 16.4 ft./sec.

Distance in yards:	Muzzle	20	30	40	50	60	70
Velocity in fps:	1,477	991	848	738	649	576	513
Average pellet energy in ft-lbs:	13.65	6.14	4.50	3.41	2.64	2.07	1.65
Time of flight in seconds:	0	.0505	.0833	.1213	.1647	.2138	.2691

Type of load: Nontoxic
Three-foot velocity: 1,375 ft./sec.
Hull: 3½-inch plastic
Wad: One-piece plastic
Shot: Bismuth
Buffered: Yes
Test barrel length: 30 inch
Pellets will pierce skin up to 153 yards.

NO. 4 BISMUTH PELLETS—1⅞ OUNCES—291 PELLETS
Mfg: Bismuth Cartridge Co. **Manufacturer's code:** MBGL-1235
Recoil energy in 8-lb. shotgun: 41.7 ft./lbs. **Recoil velocity in 8-lb. shotgun:** 16.4 ft./sec.

Distance in yards:	Muzzle	20	30	40	50	60	70
Velocity in fps:	1,312	910	787	689	609	541	483
Average pellet energy in ft-lbs:	10.77	5.19	3.87	2.97	2.32	1.83	1.46
Time of flight in seconds:	0	.0558	.0913	.1322	.1785	.2309	.2896

Type of load: Nontoxic
Three-foot velocity: 1,225 ft./sec.
Hull: 3½-inch plastic
Wad: One-piece plastic
Shot: Bismuth
Buffered: Yes
Test barrel length: 30 inch
Pellets will pierce skin up to 148 yards.

NO. 5 BISMUTH PELLETS—1⅝ OUNCES—320 PELLETS
Mfg: Bismuth Cartridge Co. **Manufacturer's code:** MBHV-1235
Recoil energy in 8-lb. shotgun: 41.6 ft./lbs. **Recoil velocity in 8-lb. shotgun:** 16.4 ft./sec.

Distance in yards:	Muzzle	20	30	40	50	60	70
Velocity in fps:	1,484	967	820	708	619	544	481
Average pellet energy in ft-lbs:	10.84	4.60	3.31	2.47	1.88	1.46	1.14
Time of flight in seconds:	0	.0511	.0849	.1243	.1697	.2215	.2802

Type of load: Nontoxic
Three-foot velocity: 1,375 ft./sec.
Hull: 3½-inch plastic
Wad: One-piece plastic
Shot: Bismuth
Buffered: Yes
Test barrel length: 30 inch
Pellets will pierce skin up to 141 yards.

NO. 5 TUNGSTEN-POLYMER PELLETS—1¹/₁₆ OUNCES—152 PELLETS

Mfg: Gamebore **Manufacturer's code:** G1225NTF30
Recoil energy in 8-lb. shotgun: 15.6 ft./lbs. **Recoil velocity in 8-lb. shotgun:** 11.2 ft./sec.

Distance in yards:	Muzzle	20	30	40	50	60	70
Velocity in fps:	1,270	889	770	676	598	532	474
Average pellet energy in ft-lbs:	8.60	4.22	3.16	2.43	1.90	1.51	1.20
Time of flight in seconds:	0	.0573	.0936	.1353	.1825	.2358	.2955

Type of load: Nontoxic & Field
Three-foot velocity: 1,185 ft./sec.
Hull: 2½-inch paper
Wad: Biodegradable fiber shot cup
Shot: Tungsten-polymer
Buffered: No
Test barrel length: 30 inch
Pellets will pierce skin up to 146 yards.

NO. 6 TUNGSTEN-POLYMER PELLETS—1¹/₁₆ OUNCES—251 PELLETS

Mfg: Gamebore **Manufacturer's code:** G1225NTF30
Recoil energy in 8-lb. shotgun: 15.6 ft./lbs. **Recoil velocity in 8-lb. shotgun:** 11.2 ft./sec.

Distance in yards:	Muzzle	20	30	40	50	60	70
Velocity in fps:	1,276	868	745	647	568	501	442
Average pellet energy in ft-lbs:	6.68	3.10	2.28	1.72	1.32	1.03	.80
Time of flight in seconds:	0	.0580	.0954	.1387	.1882	.2445	.3083

Type of load: Nontoxic & Field
Three-foot velocity: 1,185 ft./sec.
Hull: 2½-inch paper
Wad: Biodegradable fiber shot cup
Shot: Tungsten-polymer
Buffered: No
Test barrel length: 30 inch
Pellets will pierce skin up to 134 yards.

Steel-shot wads before and after being fired. These heavy wads protect the bore from the very hard steel pellets they contain, and the imprint of the pellets can be seen on the petals of the fired wad.

NO. 1 TUNGSTEN-POLYMER PELLETS—1⅜ OUNCES—105 PELLETS

Mfg: Kent Cartridge America/Canada **Manufacturer's code:** K122NT40
Recoil energy in 8-lb. shotgun: 43.7 ft./lbs. **Recoil velocity in 8-lb. shotgun:** 18.7 ft./sec.

Distance in yards:	Muzzle	20	30	40	50	60	70
Velocity in fps:	1,453	1,067	940	839	756	685	624
Average pellet energy in ft-lbs:	26.70	14.39	11.17	8.90	7.22	5.93	4.92
Time of flight in seconds:	0	.0487	.0787	.1125	.1502	.1919	.2378

Type of load: Nontoxic
Three-foot velocity: 1,375 ft./sec.
Hull: 2¾-inch plastic
Wad: Plastic
Shot: Tungsten-polymer
Buffered: No
Test barrel length: 30 inch
Pellets will pierce skin up to 203 yards.

NO. 3 TUNGSTEN-POLYMER PELLETS—1¼ OUNCES—155 PELLETS

Mfg: Kent Cartridge America/Canada **Manufacturer's code:** K122NT36
Recoil energy in 8-lb. shotgun: 43.7 ft./lbs. **Recoil velocity in 8-lb. shotgun:** 18.7 ft./sec.

Distance in yards:	Muzzle	20	30	40	50	60	70
Velocity in fps:	1,493	1,049	911	803	715	641	579
Average pellet energy in ft-lbs:	18.87	9.31	7.02	5.46	4.33	3.48	2.83
Time of flight in seconds:	0	.0486	.0794	.1145	.1542	.1985	.2478

Type of load: Nontoxic
Three-foot velocity: 1,400 ft./sec.
Hull: 2¾-inch plastic
Wad: Plastic
Shot: Tungsten-polymer
Buffered: No
Test barrel length: 30 inch
Pellets will pierce skin up to 179 yards.

NO. 3 TUNGSTEN-POLYMER PELLETS—1⅜ OUNCES—170 PELLETS

Mfg: Kent Cartridge America/Canada **Manufacturer's code:** K122NT40
Recoil energy in 8-lb. shotgun: 43.7 ft./lbs. **Recoil velocity in 8-lb. shotgun:** 18.7 ft./sec.

Distance in yards:	Muzzle	20	30	40	50	60	70
Velocity in fps:	1,466	1,034	900	794	708	635	573
Average pellet energy in ft-lbs:	18.19	9.05	6.85	5.34	4.24	3.42	2.78
Time of flight in seconds:	0	.0494	.0806	.1161	.1562	.2010	.2507

Type of load: Nontoxic
Three-foot velocity: 1,375 ft./sec.
Hull: 2¾-inch plastic
Wad: Plastic
Shot: Tungsten-polymer
Buffered: No
Test barrel length: 30 inch
Pellets will pierce skin up to 178 yards.

NO. 5 TUNGSTEN-POLYMER PELLETS—1⅛ OUNCES—205 PELLETS

Mfg: Kent Cartridge America/Canada **Manufacturer's code:** K122UGNT32
Recoil energy in 8-lb. shotgun: 22.7 ft./lbs. **Recoil velocity in 8-lb. shotgun:** 13.5 ft./sec.

Distance in yards:	Muzzle	20	30	40	50	60	70
Velocity in fps:	1,341	925	798	698	616	547	488
Average pellet energy in ft-lbs:	9.59	4.56	3.39	2.60	2.02	1.60	1.27
Time of flight in seconds:	0	.0548	.0898	.1301	.1759	.2276	.2856

Type of load: Nontoxic
Three-foot velocity: 1,250 ft./sec.
Hull: 2¾-inch plastic
Wad: Plastic
Shot: Tungsten-polymer
Buffered: No
Test barrel length: 30 inch
Pellets will pierce skin up to 149 yards.

NO. 5 TUNGSTEN-POLYMER PELLETS—1¼ OUNCES—197 PELLETS

Mfg: Kent Cartridge America/Canada **Manufacturer's code:** K122UGNT36
Recoil energy in 8-lb. shotgun: 33.0 ft./lbs. **Recoil velocity in 8-lb. shotgun:** 16.3 ft./sec.

Distance in yards:	Muzzle	20	30	40	50	60	70
Velocity in fps:	1,429	968	831	724	638	566	504
Average pellet energy in ft-lbs:	10.89	4.99	3.68	2.80	2.17	1.71	1.36
Time of flight in seconds:	0	.0519	.0855	.1242	.1684	.2184	.2746

Type of load: Nontoxic
Three-foot velocity: 1,330 ft./sec.
Hull: 2¾-inch plastic
Wad: Plastic
Shot: Tungsten-polymer
Buffered: No
Test barrel length: 30 inch
Pellets will pierce skin up to 151 yards.

NO. 5 TUNGSTEN-POLYMER PELLETS—1¼ OUNCES—197 PELLETS

Mfg: Kent Cartridge America/Canada **Manufacturer's code:** K122NT36
Recoil energy in 8-lb. shotgun: 37.9 ft./lbs. **Recoil velocity in 8-lb. shotgun:** 17.5 ft./sec.

Distance in yards:	Muzzle	20	30	40	50	60	70
Velocity in fps:	1,507	1,005	859	746	656	581	518
Average pellet energy in ft-lbs:	12.10	5.38	3.93	2.97	2.29	1.80	1.43
Time of flight in seconds:	0	.0496	.0820	.1196	.1625	.2111	.2659

Type of load: Nontoxic
Three-foot velocity: 1,400 ft./sec.
Hull: 2¾-inch plastic
Wad: Plastic
Shot: Tungsten-polymer
Buffered: No
Test barrel length: 30 inch
Pellets will pierce skin up to 154 yards.

NO. 5 TUNGSTEN-POLYMER PELLETS—1⅜ OUNCES—217 PELLETS

Mfg: Kent Cartridge America/Canada **Manufacturer's code:** K122NT40
Recoil energy in 8-lb. shotgun: 37.9 ft./lbs. **Recoil velocity in 8-lb. shotgun:** 17.5 ft./sec.

Distance in yards:	Muzzle	20	30	40	50	60	70
Velocity in fps:	1,479	992	849	738	650	576	513
Average pellet energy in ft-lbs:	11.66	5.24	3.84	2.91	2.25	1.77	1.40
Time of flight in seconds:	0	.0504	.0832	.1212	.1646	.2137	.2689

Type of load: Nontoxic
Three-foot velocity: 1,375 ft./sec.
Hull: 2¾-inch plastic
Wad: Plastic
Shot: Tungsten-polymer
Buffered: No
Test barrel length: 30 inch
Pellets will pierce skin up to 153 yards.

NO. 6 TUNGSTEN-POLYMER PELLETS—1 OUNCE—236 PELLETS

Mfg: Kent Cartridge America/Canada **Manufacturer's code:** K122UGNT28
Recoil energy in 8-lb. shotgun: 16.1 ft./lbs. **Recoil velocity in 8-lb. shotgun:** 11.4 ft./sec.

Distance in yards:	Muzzle	20	30	40	50	60	70
Velocity in fps:	1,292	876	751	652	572	504	445
Average pellet energy in ft-lbs:	6.86	3.15	2.31	2.01	1.34	1.04	.81
Time of flight in seconds:	0	.0574	.0945	.1374	.1866	.2425	.3059

Type of load: Nontoxic
Three-foot velocity: 1,200 ft./sec.
Hull: 2¾-inch plastic
Wad: Plastic
Shot: Tungsten-polymer
Buffered: No
Test barrel length: 30 inch
Pellets will pierce skin up to 135 yards.

NO. 6 TUNGSTEN-POLYMER PELLETS—1⅛ OUNCES—266 PELLETS

Mfg: Kent Cartridge America/Canada **Manufacturer's code:** K122UGNT32
Recoil energy in 8-lb. shotgun: 22.7 ft./lbs. **Recoil velocity in 8-lb. shotgun:** 13.5 ft./sec.

Distance in yards:	Muzzle	20	30	40	50	60	70
Velocity in fps:	1,348	902	771	668	585	515	455
Average pellet energy in ft-lbs:	7.46	3.34	2.11	1.83	1.41	1.09	.85
Time of flight in seconds:	0	.0555	.0916	.1335	.1815	.2362	.2982

Type of load: Nontoxic
Three-foot velocity: 1,250 ft./sec.
Hull: 2¾-inch plastic
Wad: Plastic
Shot: Tungsten-polymer
Buffered: No
Test barrel length: 30 inch
Pellets will pierce skin up to 136 yards.

NO. 6 TUNGSTEN-POLYMER PELLETS—1¼ OUNCES—281 PELLETS

Mfg: Kent Cartridge America/Canada **Manufacturer's code:** K122UGNT36
Recoil energy in 8-lb. shotgun: 33.0 ft./lbs. **Recoil velocity in 8-lb. shotgun:** 16.3 ft./sec.

Distance in yards:	Muzzle	20	30	40	50	60	70
Velocity in fps:	1,436	943	801	693	605	532	470
Average pellet energy in ft-lbs:	8.47	3.65	2.64	1.97	1.50	1.16	.91
Time of flight in seconds:	0	.0526	.0873	.1276	.1740	.2269	.2869

Type of load: Nontoxic
Three-foot velocity: 1,330 ft./sec.
Hull: 2¾-inch plastic
Wad: Plastic
Shot: Tungsten-polymer
Buffered: No
Test barrel length: 30 inch
Pellets will pierce skin up to 139 yards.

This is one of the in-line loading machines in the Kent Cartridge America plant in Kearneysville, West Virginia. Made in Italy, all loading steps are done with great precision, ensuring the consumer the very best possible ammo.

NO. 1 TUNGSTEN-POLYMER PELLETS—1½ OUNCES—114 PELLETS

Mfg: Kent Cartridge America/Canada **Manufacturer's code:** K123NT42
Recoil energy in 8-lb. shotgun: 49.5 ft./lbs. **Recoil velocity in 8-lb. shotgun:** 20.0 ft./sec.

Distance in yards:	Muzzle	20	30	40	50	60	70
Velocity in fps:	1,427	1,052	928	829	748	678	618
Average pellet energy in ft-lbs:	25.72	13.97	10.89	8.69	7.06	5.81	4.83
Time of flight in seconds:	0	.0495	.0799	.1142	.1523	.1945	.2408

Type of load: Nontoxic
Three-foot velocity: 1,350 ft./sec.
Hull: 3-inch plastic
Wad: Plastic
Shot: Tungsten-polymer
Buffered: No
Test barrel length: 30 inch
Pellets will pierce skin up to 202 yards.

NO. 1 TUNGSTEN-POLYMER PELLETS—1⅝ OUNCES—124 PELLETS

Mfg: Kent Cartridge America/Canada **Manufacturer's code:** K123NT46
Recoil energy in 8-lb. shotgun: 55.9 ft./lbs. **Recoil velocity in 8-lb. shotgun:** 21.2 ft./sec.

Distance in yards:	Muzzle	20	30	40	50	60	70
Velocity in fps:	1,405	1,039	919	822	741	672	613
Average pellet energy in ft-lbs:	24.95	13.65	10.66	8.53	6.94	5.71	4.75
Time of flight in seconds:	0	.0502	.0809	.1155	.1540	.1965	.2433

Type of load: Nontoxic
Three-foot velocity: 1,330 ft./sec.
Hull: 3-inch plastic
Wad: Plastic
Shot: Tungsten-polymer
Buffered: No
Test barrel length: 30 inch
Pellets will pierce skin up to 201 yards.

NO. 3 TUNGSTEN-POLYMER PELLETS—1½ OUNCES—186 PELLETS

Mfg: Kent Cartridge America/Canada **Manufacturer's code:** K123NT42
Recoil energy in 8-lb. shotgun: 49.5 ft./lbs. **Recoil velocity in 8-lb. shotgun:** 20.0 ft./sec.

Distance in yards:	Muzzle	20	30	40	50	60	70
Velocity in fps:	1,439	1,020	888	785	700	629	568
Average pellet energy in ft-lbs:	17.52	8.80	6.68	5.22	4.15	3.35	2.73
Time of flight in seconds:	0	.0502	.0818	.1178	.1583	.2036	.2538

Type of load: Nontoxic
Three-foot velocity: 1,350 ft./sec.
Hull: 3-inch plastic
Wad: Plastic
Shot: Tungsten-polymer
Buffered: No
Test barrel length: 30 inch
Pellets will pierce skin up to 177 yards.

NO. 3 TUNGSTEN-POLYMER PELLETS—1⅝ OUNCES—201 PELLETS

Mfg: Kent Cartridge America/Canada **Manufacturer's code:** K123NT46
Recoil energy in 8-lb. shotgun: 55.9 ft./lbs. **Recoil velocity in 8-lb. shotgun:** 21.2 ft./sec.

Distance in yards:	Muzzle	20	30	40	50	60	70
Velocity in fps:	1,417	1,008	879	778	694	624	563
Average pellet energy in ft-lbs:	16.99	8.60	6.55	5.12	4.08	3.29	2.69
Time of flight in seconds:	0	.0509	.0828	.1191	.1066	.2056	.2563

Type of load: Nontoxic
Three-foot velocity: 1,330 ft./sec.
Hull: 3-inch plastic
Wad: Plastic
Shot: Tungsten-polymer
Buffered: No
Test barrel length: 30 inch
Pellets will pierce skin up to 176 yards.

NO. 5 TUNGSTEN-POLYMER PELLETS—1½ OUNCES—236 PELLETS

Mfg: Kent Cartridge America/Canada **Manufacturer's code:** K123NT42
Recoil energy in 8-lb. shotgun: 49.5 ft./lbs. **Recoil velocity in 8-lb. shotgun:** 20.0 ft./sec.

Distance in yards:	Muzzle	20	30	40	50	60	70
Velocity in fps:	1,451	978	839	730	643	570	508
Average pellet energy in ft-lbs:	11.23	5.10	3.75	2.84	2.20	1.73	1.38
Time of flight in seconds:	0	.0513	.0845	.1229	.1667	.2163	.2721

Type of load: Nontoxic
Three-foot velocity: 1,350 ft./sec.
Hull: 3-inch plastic
Wad: Plastic
Shot: Tungsten-polymer
Buffered: No
Test barrel length: 30 inch
Pellets will pierce skin up to 152 yards.

NO. 5 TUNGSTEN-POLYMER PELLETS—1⅝ OUNCES—256 PELLETS

Mfg: Kent Cartridge America/Canada **Manufacturer's code:** K123NT46
Recoil energy in 8-lb. shotgun: 55.9 ft./lbs. **Recoil velocity in 8-lb. shotgun:** 21.2 ft./sec.

Distance in yards:	Muzzle	20	30	40	50	60	70
Velocity in fps:	1,429	968	831	724	638	566	504
Average pellet energy in ft-lbs:	10.89	4.99	3.68	2.80	2.17	1.71	1.36
Time of flight in seconds:	0	.0519	.0855	.1242	.1684	.2184	.2746

Type of load: Nontoxic & Turkey
Three-foot velocity: 1,330 ft./sec.
Hull: 3-inch plastic
Wad: Plastic
Shot: Tungsten-polymer
Buffered: No
Test barrel length: 30 inch
Pellets will pierce skin up to 151 yards.

NO. 1 TUNGSTEN-POLYMER PELLETS—2 OUNCES—152 PELLETS

Mfg: Kent Cartridge America/Canada **Manufacturer's code:** K1235NT56
Recoil energy in 8-lb. shotgun: 73.3 ft./lbs. **Recoil velocity in 8-lb. shotgun:** 24.3 ft./sec.

Distance in yards:	Muzzle	20	30	40	50	60	70
Velocity in fps:	1,330	996	884	793	717	652	595
Average pellet energy in ft-lbs:	22.34	12.54	9.88	7.95	6.50	5.37	4.47
Time of flight in seconds:	0	.0527	.0847	.1205	.1604	.2043	.2525

Type of load: Nontoxic
Three-foot velocity: 1,260 ft./sec.
Hull: 3½-inch plastic
Wad: Two-piece plastic
Shot: Tungsten-polymer
Buffered: No
Test barrel length: 30 inch
Pellets will pierce skin up to 198 yards.

NO. 3 TUNGSTEN-POLYMER PELLETS—2 OUNCES—248 PELLETS

Mfg: Kent Cartridge America/Canada **Manufacturer's code:** K1235NT56
Recoil energy in 8-lb. shotgun: 73.3 ft./lbs. **Recoil velocity in 8-lb. shotgun:** 24.3 ft./sec.

Distance in yards:	Muzzle	20	30	40	50	60	70
Velocity in fps:	1,341	967	848	752	673	605	547
Average pellet energy in ft-lbs:	15.22	7.92	6.09	4.79	3.83	3.10	2.54
Time of flight in seconds:	0	.0534	.0866	.1242	.1664	.2135	.2656

Type of load: Nontoxic
Three-foot velocity: 1,260 ft./sec.
Hull: 3½-inch plastic
Wad: Two-piece plastic
Shot: Tungsten-polymer
Buffered: No
Test barrel length: 30 inch
Pellets will pierce skin up to 173 yards.

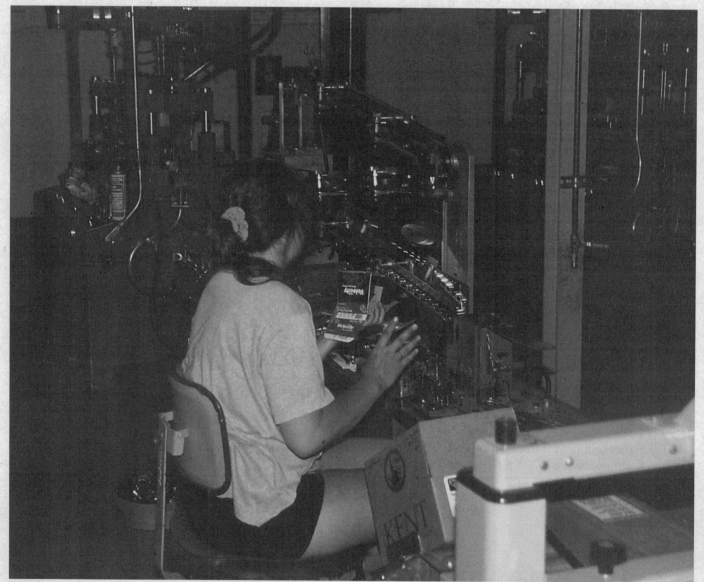

Although highly automated, each round loaded in Kent Cartridge America's Kearneysville, West Virginia, plant is inspected by a skilled worker before being boxed.

NO. 2 TUNGSTEN, IRON, NICKEL—1½ OUNCES—117 PELLETS

Mfg: Remington/Hevi-Shot **Manufacturer's code:** PRHSN12HM
Recoil energy in 8-lb. shotgun: 40.0 ft./lbs. **Recoil velocity in 8-lb. shotgun:** 17.9 ft./sec.

Distance in yards:	Muzzle	20	30	40	50	60	70
Velocity in fps:	1,370	1,025	910	817	739	672	614
Average pellet energy in ft-lbs:	21.35	11.96	9.42	7.59	6.20	5.13	4.29
Time of flight in seconds:	0	.0511	.0822	.1171	.1557	.1983	.2451

Type of load: Nontoxic
Three-foot velocity: 1,330 ft./sec.
Hull: 3-inch plastic
Wad: Plastic
Shot: Iron, tungsten, nickel
Buffered: No
Test barrel length: 30 inch
Pellets will pierce skin up to 204 yards.

NO. 4 TUNGSTEN, IRON, NICKEL—1¼ OUNCES—182 PELLETS

Mfg: Remington/Hevi-Shot **Manufacturer's code:** PRHSN12SM
Recoil energy in 8-lb. shotgun: 40.0 ft./lbs. **Recoil velocity in 8-lb. shotgun:** 17.9 ft./sec.

Distance in yards:	Muzzle	20	30	40	50	60	70
Velocity in fps:	1,375	990	867	769	688	619	560
Average pellet energy in ft-lbs:	14.01	7.26	5.57	4.38	3.50	2.84	2.32
Time of flight in seconds:	0	.0521	.0845	.1213	.1626	.2086	.2596

Type of load: Nontoxic
Three-foot velocity: 1,330 ft./sec.
Hull: 2¾- or 3-inch plastic
Wad: Plastic
Shot: Iron, tungsten, nickel
Buffered: No
Test barrel length: 30 inch
Pellets will pierce skin up to 177 yards.

NO. 6 TUNGSTEN, IRON, NICKEL—1¼ OUNCES—288 PELLETS

Mfg: Remington/Hevi-Shot **Manufacturer's code:** PRHSN12SM
Recoil energy in 8-lb. shotgun: 40.0 ft./lbs. **Recoil velocity in 8-lb. shotgun:** 17.9 ft./sec.

Distance in yards:	Muzzle	20	30	40	50	60	70
Velocity in fps:	1,382	945	813	710	627	557	496
Average pellet energy in ft-lbs:	8.56	4.00	2.97	2.26	1.76	1.39	1.10
Time of flight in seconds:	0	.0534	.0877	.1273	.1723	.2231	.2803

Type of load: Nontoxic
Three-foot velocity: 1,330 ft./sec.
Hull: 2¾- or 3-inch plastic
Wad: Plastic
Shot: Iron, tungsten, nickel
Buffered: No
Test barrel length: 30 inch
Pellets will pierce skin up to 150 yards.

NO. 7½ TUNGSTEN, IRON, NICKEL—1¼ OUNCES—440 PELLETS

Mfg: Remington/Hevi-Shot **Manufacturer's code:** PRHSN12SM
Recoil energy in 8-lb. shotgun: 40.0 ft./lbs. **Recoil velocity in 8-lb. shotgun:** 17.9 ft./sec.

Distance in yards:	Muzzle	20	30	40	50	60	70
Velocity in fps:	1,387	902	764	657	572	500	439
Average pellet energy in ft-lbs:	5.56	2.35	1.68	1.25	.94	.72	.56
Time of flight in seconds:	0	.0549	.0911	.1336	.1826	.2387	.3028

Type of load: Nontoxic
Three-foot velocity: 1,330 ft./sec.
Hull: 2¾- or 3-inch plastic
Wad: Plastic
Shot: Iron, tungsten, nickel
Buffered: No
Test barrel length: 30 inch
Pellets will pierce skin up to 130 yards.

Hunting ducks and geese on an open marsh calls for skill in decoy placement and calling in order to lure the birds close enough for killing shots. In areas like this, the temptation is to take shots that are too far, needlessly crippling birds that cannot be retrieved. Regardless of the "magnum" load used, shotshells are short range affairs and most effective inside 40 yards.

NO. BB LEAD PELLETS—¹³⁄₁₆ OUNCE—41 PELLETS
Mfg: Eley Hawk **Manufacturer's code:** Grand Prix
Recoil energy in 8-lb. shotgun: 13.7 ft./lbs. **Recoil velocity in 8-lb. shotgun:** 10.5 ft./sec.

Distance in yards:	Muzzle	20	30	40	50	60	70
Velocity in fps:	1,309	1,025	924	840	769	707	653
Average pellet energy in ft-lbs:	32.60	19.99	16.26	13.45	11.27	9.53	8.12
Time of flight in seconds:	0	.0522	.0831	.1171	.1545	.1952	.2393

Type of load: Field
Three-foot velocity: 1,250 ft./sec.
Hull: 2½-inch plastic
Wad: Fiber
Shot: Lead
Buffered: No
Test barrel length: 26 inch
Pellets will pierce skin up to 234 yards.

NO. 4 LEAD PELLETS—1 OUNCE—135 PELLETS
Mfg: ARMUSA **Manufacturer's code:** PLA-1
Recoil energy in 8-lb. shotgun: 19.9 ft./lbs. **Recoil velocity in 8-lb. shotgun:** 12.6 ft./sec.

Distance in yards:	Muzzle	20	30	40	50	60	70
Velocity in fps:	1,390	989	863	762	680	611	551
Average pellet energy in ft-lbs:	13.86	7.01	5.34	4.17	3.32	2.67	2.18
Time of flight in seconds:	0	.0519	.0844	.1215	.1632	.2098	.2615

Type of load: Field
Three-foot velocity: 1,300 ft./sec.
Hull: 2½-inch plastic
Wad: Plastic
Shot: Lead
Buffered: No
Test barrel length: 28 inch
Pellets will pierce skin up to 172 yards.

NO. 4 LEAD PELLETS—1¹⁄₃₂ OUNCES—138 PELLETS
Mfg: Baschieri & Pellagri **Manufacturer's code:** N/A
Recoil energy in 8-lb. shotgun: 21.2 ft./lbs. **Recoil velocity in 8-lb. shotgun:** 13.0 ft./sec.

Distance in yards:	Muzzle	20	30	40	50	60	70
Velocity in fps:	1,423	1006	876	773	689	618	558
Average pellet energy in ft-lbs:	14.52	7.26	5.50	4.29	3.41	2.74	2.23
Time of flight in seconds:	0	.0508	.0829	.1194	.1605	.2065	.2576

Type of load: Field
Three-foot velocity: 1,330 ft./sec.
Hull: 2½-inch plastic
Wad: Plastic
Shot: Lead
Buffered: No
Test barrel length: 28 inch
Pellets will pierce skin up to 173 yards.

NO. 5 LEAD PELLETS—1¹⁄₃₂ OUNCES—175 PELLETS
Mfg: Baschieri & Pellagri **Manufacturer's code:** N/A
Recoil energy in 8-lb. shotgun: 21.2 ft./lbs. **Recoil velocity in 8-lb. shotgun:** 13.0 ft./sec.

Distance in yards:	Muzzle	20	30	40	50	60	70
Velocity in fps:	1429	985	851	745	660	588	527
Average pellet energy in ft-lbs:	11.53	5.47	4.08	3.13	2.46	1.95	1.57
Time of flight in seconds:	0	.0514	.0842	.1220	.1648	.2130	.2669

Type of load: Field
Three-foot velocity: 1,330 ft./sec.
Hull: 2½-inch plastic
Wad: Plastic
Shot: Lead
Buffered: No
Test barrel length: 28 inch
Pellets will pierce skin up to 160 yards.

NO. 6 LEAD PELLETS—¹³⁄₁₆ OUNCE—183 PELLETS
Mfg: Eley Hawk **Manufacturer's code:** Grand Prix
Recoil energy in 8-lb. shotgun: 13.7 ft./lbs. **Recoil velocity in 8-lb. shotgun:** 10.5 ft./sec.

Distance in yards:	Muzzle	20	30	40	50	60	70
Velocity in fps:	1,348	919	790	689	606	537	477
Average pellet energy in ft-lbs:	7.89	3.67	2.71	2.06	1.60	1.25	.99
Time of flight in seconds:	0	.0549	.0902	.1309	.1774	.2300	.2893

Type of load: Field
Three-foot velocity: 1,250 ft./sec.
Hull: 2½-inch plastic
Wad: Fiber
Shot: Lead
Buffered: No
Test barrel length: 28 inch
Pellets will pierce skin up to 144 yards.

NO. 6 LEAD PELLETS—⁷⁄₈ OUNCE—197 PELLETS
Mfg: RST, Ltd. **Manufacturer's code:** N/A
Recoil energy in 8-lb. shotgun: 10.9 ft./lbs. **Recoil velocity in 8-lb. shotgun:** 9.4 ft./sec.

Distance in yards:	Muzzle	20	30	40	50	60	70
Velocity in fps:	1,232	862	746	653	577	512	455
Average pellet energy in ft-lbs:	6.59	3.23	2.11	1.85	1.45	1.14	.90
Time of flight in seconds:	0	.0591	.0966	.1396	.1886	.2438	.3060

Type of load: Target
Three-foot velocity: 1,145 ft./sec.
Hull: 2½-inch plastic
Wad: Plastic
Shot: Lead
Buffered: No
Test barrel length: 26 inch
Pellets will pierce skin up to 140 yards.

NO. 6 LEAD PELLETS—1 OUNCE—225 PELLETS
Mfg: RST, Ltd. **Manufacturer's code:** N/A
Recoil energy in 8-lb. shotgun: 13.6 ft./lbs. **Recoil velocity in 8-lb. shotgun:** 10.5 ft./sec.

Distance in yards:	Muzzle	20	30	40	50	60	70
Velocity in fps:	1,210	851	737	646	571	507	451
Average pellet energy in ft-lbs:	6.36	3.15	2.36	1.81	1.42	1.12	.88
Time of flight in seconds:	0	.0600	.0980	.1415	.1909	.2467	.3096

Type of load: Target
Three-foot velocity: 1,125 ft./sec.
Hull: 2½-inch plastic
Wad: Plastic
Shot: Lead
Buffered: No
Test barrel length: 26 inch
Pellets will pierce skin up to 139 yards.

NO. 6 LEAD PELLETS—1 OUNCE—225 PELLETS
Mfg: Eley Hawk **Manufacturer's code:** VIP Game
Recoil energy in 8-lb. shotgun: 18.9 ft./lbs. **Recoil velocity in 8-lb. shotgun:** 12.3 ft./sec.

Distance in yards:	Muzzle	20	30	40	50	60	70
Velocity in fps:	1,375	932	800	697	613	543	482
Average pellet energy in ft-lbs:	8.22	3.77	2.78	2.11	1.63	1.28	1.01
Time of flight in seconds:	0	.0540	.0888	.1290	.1750	.2271	.2858

Type of load: Field
Three-foot velocity: 1,275 ft./sec.
Hull: 2½-inch plastic
Wad: Fiber
Shot: Lead
Buffered: No
Test barrel length: 28 inch
Pellets will pierce skin up to 145 yards.

NO. 6 LEAD PELLETS—1 OUNCE—225 PELLETS
Mfg: ARMUSA **Manufacturer's code:** PLA-1
Recoil energy in 8-lb. shotgun: 19.9 ft./lbs. **Recoil velocity in 8-lb. shotgun:** 12.6 ft./sec.

Distance in yards:	Muzzle	20	30	40	50	60	70
Velocity in fps:	1,403	945	810	705	620	548	487
Average pellet energy in ft-lbs:	8.55	3.88	2.85	2.16	1.67	1.31	1.03
Time of flight in seconds:	0	.0531	.0875	.1272	.1727	.2242	.2723

Type of load: Field
Three-foot velocity: 1,300 ft./sec.
Hull: 2½-inch plastic
Wad: Plastic
Shot: Lead
Buffered: No
Test barrel length: 28 inch
Pellets will pierce skin up to 146 yards.

NO. 6 LEAD PELLETS—1 OUNCE—225 PELLETS
Mfg: Fiocchi **Manufacturer's code:** 16PL1
Recoil energy in 8-lb. shotgun: 21.2 ft./lbs. **Recoil velocity in 8-lb. shotgun:** 13.0 ft./sec.

Distance in yards:	Muzzle	20	30	40	50	60	70
Velocity in fps:	1,436	961	822	714	627	555	493
Average pellet energy in ft-lbs:	8.96	4.01	2.94	2.22	1.71	1.34	1.06
Time of flight in seconds:	0	.0520	.0859	.1251	.1700	.2209	.2782

Type of load: Game/Target
Three-foot velocity: 1,330 ft./sec.
Hull: 2½-inch plastic
Wad: Plastic
Shot: Lead
Buffered: No
Test barrel length: 26 inch
Pellets will pierce skin up to 147 yards.

NO. 6 LEAD PELLETS—1¹/₃₂ OUNCES—232 PELLETS
Mfg: Baschieri & Pellagri **Manufacturer's code:** N/A
Recoil energy in 8-lb. shotgun: 21.2 ft./lbs. **Recoil velocity in 8-lb. shotgun:** 13.0 ft./sec.

Distance in yards:	Muzzle	20	30	40	50	60	70
Velocity in fps:	1,436	961	822	714	627	555	493
Average pellet energy in ft-lbs:	8.96	4.01	2.94	2.22	1.71	1.34	1.06
Time of flight in seconds:	0	.0520	.0859	.1251	.1700	.2209	.2782

Type of load: Field
Three-foot velocity: 1,330 ft./sec.
Hull: 2½-inch plastic
Wad: Plastic
Shot: Lead
Buffered: No
Test barrel length: 28 inch
Pellets will pierce skin up to 147 yards.

NO. 7 LEAD PELLETS—1¹/₃₂ OUNCES—308 PELLETS
Mfg: Baschieri & Pellagri **Manufacturer's code:** N/A
Recoil energy in 8-lb. shotgun: 21.2 ft./lbs. **Recoil velocity in 8-lb. shotgun:** 13.0 ft./sec.

Distance in yards:	Muzzle	20	30	40	50	60	70
Velocity in fps:	1,443	933	789	679	591	518	455
Average pellet energy in ft-lbs:	6.80	2.84	2.03	1.51	1.14	.88	.68
Time of flight in seconds:	0	.0529	.0879	.1290	.1764	.2306	.2925

Type of load: Field
Three-foot velocity: 1,150 ft./sec.
Hull: 2½-inch plastic
Wad: Plastic
Shot: Lead
Buffered: No
Test barrel length: 28 inch
Pellets will pierce skin up to 147 yards.

NO. 7½ LEAD PELLETS—¹³/₁₆ OUNCE—285 PELLETS
Mfg: Eley Hawk **Manufacturer's code:** Grand Prix
Recoil energy in 8-lb. shotgun: 13.7 ft./lbs. **Recoil velocity in 8-lb. shotgun:** 10.5 ft./sec.

Distance in yards:	Muzzle	20	30	40	50	60	70
Velocity in fps:	1,357	878	742	637	553	482	421
Average pellet energy in ft-lbs:	5.16	2.16	1.54	1.14	.86	.65	.50
Time of flight in seconds:	0	.0562	.0935	.1372	.1878	.2459	.3126

Type of load: Field
Three-foot velocity: 1,250 ft./sec.
Hull: 2½-inch plastic
Wad: Fiber
Shot: Lead
Buffered: No
Test barrel length: 28 inch
Pellets will pierce skin up to 125 yards.

NO. 7½ LEAD PELLETS—1 OUNCE—350 PELLETS
Mfg: RST, Ltd. **Manufacturer's code:** N/A
Recoil energy in 8-lb. shotgun: 13.6 ft./lbs. **Recoil velocity in 8-lb. shotgun:** 10.5 ft./sec.

Distance in yards:	Muzzle	20	30	40	50	60	70
Velocity in fps:	1,218	816	695	600	522	455	398
Average pellet energy in ft-lbs:	4.15	1.86	1.35	1.01	.76	.58	.44
Time of flight in seconds:	0	.0613	.1013	.1478	.2015	.2631	.3337

Type of load: Target
Three-foot velocity: 1,125 ft./sec.
Hull: 2½-inch plastic
Wad: Plastic
Shot: Lead
Buffered: No
Test barrel length: 26 inch
Pellets will pierce skin up to 121 yards.

NO. 7½ LEAD PELLETS—1 OUNCE—350 PELLETS
Mfg: ARMUSA **Manufacturer's code:** PLA-1
Recoil energy in 8-lb. shotgun: 19.9 ft./lbs. **Recoil velocity in 8-lb. shotgun:** 12.6 ft./sec.

Distance in yards:	Muzzle	20	30	40	50	60	70
Velocity in fps:	1,413	903	761	652	565	492	430
Average pellet energy in ft-lbs:	5.59	2.28	1.62	1.19	.89	.68	.52
Time of flight in seconds:	0	.0544	.0907	.1334	.1829	.2399	.3052

Type of load: Field
Three-foot velocity: 1,300 ft./sec.
Hull: 2½-inch plastic
Wad: Plastic
Shot: Lead
Buffered: No
Test barrel length: 28 inch
Pellets will pierce skin up to 126 yards.

NO. 8 LEAD PELLETS—⅞ OUNCE—359 PELLETS
Mfg: RST, Ltd. **Manufacturer's code:** N/A
Recoil energy in 8-lb. shotgun: 10.9 ft./lbs. **Recoil velocity in 8-lb. shotgun:** 9.4 ft./sec.

Distance in yards:	Muzzle	20	30	40	50	60	70
Velocity in fps:	1,244	812	686	588	508	440	381
Average pellet energy in ft-lbs:	3.68	1.57	1.12	.82	.61	.46	.35
Time of flight in seconds:	0	.0616	.1013	.1486	.2036	.2671	.3403

Type of load: Target
Three-foot velocity: 1,145 ft./sec.
Hull: 2½-inch plastic
Wad: Plastic
Shot: Lead
Buffered: No
Test barrel length: 26 inch
Pellets will pierce skin up to 115 yards.

NO. 8 LEAD PELLETS—1 OUNCE—410 PELLETS
Mfg: RST, Ltd. **Manufacturer's code:** N/A
Recoil energy in 8-lb. shotgun: 13.6 ft./lbs. **Recoil velocity in 8-lb. shotgun:** 10.5 ft./sec.

Distance in yards:	Muzzle	20	30	40	50	60	70
Velocity in fps:	1,221	802	678	582	503	436	378
Average pellet energy in ft-lbs:	3.55	1.53	1.10	.81	.60	.45	.34
Time of flight in seconds:	0	.0619	.1026	.1505	.2060	.2701	.3441

Type of load: Target
Three-foot velocity: 1,125 ft./sec.
Hull: 2½-inch plastic
Wad: Plastic
Shot: Lead
Buffered: No
Test barrel length: 26 inch
Pellets will pierce skin up to 114 yards.

NO. 8 LEAD PELLETS—1 OUNCE—410 PELLETS
Mfg: Baschieri & Pellagri **Manufacturer's code:** N/A
Recoil energy in 8-lb. shotgun: 14.4 ft./lbs. **Recoil velocity in 8-lb. shotgun:** 10.8 ft./sec.

Distance in yards:	Muzzle	20	30	40	50	60	70
Velocity in fps:	1,249	815	688	589	509	441	382
Average pellet energy in ft-lbs:	3.71	1.58	1.13	.83	.62	.46	.35
Time of flight in seconds:	0	.0608	.1010	.1482	.2030	.2663	.3394

Type of load: Field
Three-foot velocity: 1,150 ft./sec.
Hull: 2½-inch plastic
Wad: Plastic
Shot: Lead
Buffered: No
Test barrel length: 28 inch
Pellets will pierce skin up to 115 yards.

NO. 8 LEAD PELLETS—1 OUNCE—410 PELLETS
Mfg: Fiocchi **Manufacturer's code:** 16PL1
Recoil energy in 8-lb. shotgun: 21.2 ft./lbs. **Recoil velocity in 8-lb. shotgun:** 13.0 ft./sec.

Distance in yards:	Muzzle	20	30	40	50	60	70
Velocity in fps:	1,451	900	752	640	551	477	413
Average pellet energy in ft-lbs:	5.01	1.93	1.35	.97	.72	.54	.41
Time of flight in seconds:	0	.0539	.0905	.1338	.1845	.2431	.3108

Type of load: Game & Target
Three-foot velocity: 1,330 ft./sec.
Hull: 2½-inch plastic
Wad: Plastic
Shot: Lead
Buffered: No
Test barrel length: 26 inch
Pellets will pierce skin up to 121 yards.

NO. 8 LEAD PELLETS—1 1/32 OUNCES—423 PELLETS
Mfg: Baschieri & Pellagri **Manufacturer's code:** N/A
Recoil energy in 8-lb. shotgun: 21.2 ft./lbs. **Recoil velocity in 8-lb. shotgun:** 13.0 ft./sec.

Distance in yards:	Muzzle	20	30	40	50	60	70
Velocity in fps:	1,451	900	752	640	551	477	413
Average pellet energy in ft-lbs:	5.01	1.93	1.35	.97	.72	.54	.41
Time of flight in seconds:	0	.0539	.0905	.1338	.1845	.2431	.3108

Type of load: Field
Three-foot velocity: 1,330 ft./sec.
Hull: 2½-inch plastic
Wad: Plastic
Shot: Lead
Buffered: No
Test barrel length: 28 inch
Pellets will pierce skin up to 121 yards.

NO. 9 LEAD PELLETS—1 1/32 OUNCES—603 PELLETS
Mfg: Baschieri & Pellagri **Manufacturer's code:** N/A
Recoil energy in 8-lb. shotgun: 21.2 ft./lbs. **Recoil velocity in 8-lb. shotgun:** 13.0 ft./sec.

Distance in yards:	Muzzle	20	30	40	50	60	70
Velocity in fps:	1,459	862	709	594	504	429	365
Average pellet energy in ft-lbs:	3.56	1.24	.84	.59	.42	.31	.22
Time of flight in seconds:	0	.0553	.0938	.1401	.2260	.2596	.3354

Type of load: Field
Three-foot velocity: 1,330 ft./sec.
Hull: 2½-inch plastic
Wad: Plastic
Shot: Lead
Buffered: No
Test barrel length: 28 inch
Pellets will pierce skin up to 107 yards.

NO. 2 LEAD PELLETS—1 OUNCE—87 PELLETS
Mfg: Aguila **Manufacturer's code:** N/A
Recoil energy in 8-lb. shotgun: 16.1 ft./lbs. **Recoil velocity in 8-lb. shotgun:** 11.4 ft./sec.

Distance in yards:	Muzzle	20	30	40	50	60	70
Velocity in fps:	1,270	960	855	768	695	632	577
Average pellet energy in ft-lbs:	17.78	10.16	8.05	6.50	5.32	4.40	3.67
Time of flight in seconds:	0	.0549	.0880	.01261	.1662	.2115	.2612

Type of load: Field
Three-foot velocity: 1,200 ft./sec.
Hull: 2¾-inch plastic
Wad: Plastic
Shot: Lead
Buffered: No
Test barrel length: 28 inch
Pellets will pierce skin up to 213 yards.

NO. 2 LEAD PELLETS—1¹/₁₆ OUNCES—92 PELLETS
Mfg: Clever **Manufacturer's code:** T1 Light Game
Recoil energy in 8-lb. shotgun: 21.2 ft./lbs. **Recoil velocity in 8-lb. shotgun:** 13.0 ft./sec.

Distance in yards:	Muzzle	20	30	40	50	60	70
Velocity in fps:	1,411	1,040	919	821	740	671	611
Average pellet energy in ft-lbs:	21.93	11.92	9.30	7.42	6.03	7.96	4.12
Time of flight in seconds:	0	.0501	.0808	.1154	.1539	.1966	.2434

Type of load: Field
Three-foot velocity: 1,330 ft./sec.
Hull: 2¾-inch plastic
Wad: Plastic
Shot: Lead
Buffered: No
Test barrel length: 28 inch
Pellets will pierce skin up to 219 yards.

NO. 2 LEAD PELLETS—1⅛ OUNCES—98 PELLETS
Mfg: Aguila **Manufacturer's code:** N/A
Recoil energy in 8-lb. shotgun: 22.7 ft./lbs. **Recoil velocity in 8-lb. shotgun:** 13.5 ft./sec.

Distance in yards:	Muzzle	20	30	40	50	60	70
Velocity in fps:	1,324	991	879	789	713	647	591
Average pellet energy in ft-lbs:	19.32	10.82	8.52	6.85	5.59	4.62	3.84
Time of flight in seconds:	0	.0529	.0851	.1212	.1612	.2054	.2540

Type of load: Field
Three-foot velocity: 1,250 ft./sec.
Hull: 2¾-inch plastic
Wad: Plastic
Shot: Lead
Buffered: No
Test barrel length: 28 inch
Pellets will pierce skin up to 196 yards.

NO. 4 LEAD PELLETS—1 OUNCE—135 PELLETS
Mfg: Aguila **Manufacturer's code:** N/A
Recoil energy in 8-lb. shotgun: 16.1 ft./lbs. **Recoil velocity in 8-lb. shotgun:** 11.4 ft./sec.

Distance in yards:	Muzzle	20	30	40	50	60	70
Velocity in fps:	1,281	931	817	725	649	584	528
Average pellet energy in ft-lbs:	11.77	6.21	4.79	3.77	3.02	2.45	2.00
Time of flight in seconds:	0	.0556	.0901	.01291	.1729	.2216	.2757

Type of load: Field
Three-foot velocity: 1,200 ft./sec.
Hull: 2¾-inch plastic
Wad: Plastic
Shot: Lead
Buffered: No
Test barrel length: 28 inch
Pellets will pierce skin up to 168 yards.

NO. 4 LEAD PELLETS—1¹/₁₆ OUNCES—143 PELLETS
Mfg: Clever **Manufacturer's code:** T1 Light Game
Recoil energy in 8-lb. shotgun: 21.2 ft./lbs. **Recoil velocity in 8-lb. shotgun:** 13.0 ft./sec.

Distance in yards:	Muzzle	20	30	40	50	60	70
Velocity in fps:	1,423	1006	876	773	689	618	558
Average pellet energy in ft-lbs:	14.52	7.26	5.50	4.29	3.41	2.74	2.23
Time of flight in seconds:	0	.0508	.0829	.1194	.1605	.2065	.2576

Type of load: Field
Three-foot velocity: 1,330 ft./sec.
Hull: 2¾-inch plastic
Wad: Plastic
Shot: Lead
Buffered: No
Test barrel length: 28 inch
Pellets will pierce skin up to 173 yards.

NO. 4 LEAD PELLETS—1⅛ OUNCES—152 PELLETS
Mfg: Aguila **Manufacturer's code:** N/A
Recoil energy in 8-lb. shotgun: 22.7 ft./lbs. **Recoil velocity in 8-lb. shotgun:** 13.5 ft./sec.

Distance in yards:	Muzzle	20	30	40	50	60	70
Velocity in fps:	1336	960	840	744	665	598	540
Average pellet energy in ft-lbs:	12.79	6.61	5.06	3.97	3.17	2.56	2.09
Time of flight in seconds:	0	.0537	.0872	.1252	.1679	.2155	.2684

Type of load: Field
Three-foot velocity: 1,250 ft./sec.
Hull: 2¾-inch plastic
Wad: Plastic
Shot: Lead
Buffered: No
Test barrel length: 28 inch
Pellets will pierce skin up to 170 yards.

NO. 4 LEAD PELLETS—1⅛ OUNCES—152 PELLETS
Mfg: Dionisi **Manufacturer's code:** D 16 SLR
Recoil energy in 8-lb. shotgun: 25.2 ft./lbs. **Recoil velocity in 8-lb. shotgun:** 14.2 ft./sec.

Distance in yards:	Muzzle	20	30	40	50	60	70
Velocity in fps:	1,390	989	863	762	680	611	551
Average pellet energy in ft-lbs:	13.86	7.01	5.34	4.17	3.32	2.67	2.18
Time of flight in seconds:	0	.0519	.0844	.1215	.1632	.2098	.2615

Type of load: Field
Three-foot velocity: 1,300 ft./sec.
Hull: 2¾-inch plastic
Wad: Plastic
Shot: Lead
Buffered: No
Test barrel length: 28 inch
Pellets will pierce skin up to 172 yards.

NO. 4 LEAD PELLETS—1⅛ OUNCES—152 PELLETS
Mfg: Federal Cartridge Co. **Manufacturer's code:** H463
Recoil energy in 8-lb. shotgun: 25.2 ft./lbs. **Recoil velocity in 8-lb. shotgun:** 14.2 ft./sec.

Distance in yards:	Muzzle	20	30	40	50	60	70
Velocity in fps:	1,390	989	863	762	680	611	551
Average pellet energy in ft-lbs:	13.86	7.01	5.34	4.17	3.32	2.67	2.18
Time of flight in seconds:	0	.0519	.0844	.1215	.1632	.2098	.2615

Type of load: Field
Three-foot velocity: 1,300 ft./sec.
Hull: 2¾-inch plastic
Wad: Plastic
Shot: Lead
Buffered: No
Test barrel length: 28 inch
Pellets will pierce skin up to 172 yards.

NO. 4 LEAD PELLETS—1⅛ OUNCES—152 PELLETS
Mfg: Fiocchi **Manufacturer's code:** 16HV
Recoil energy in 8-lb. shotgun: 25.2 ft./lbs. **Recoil velocity in 8-lb. shotgun:** 14.2 ft./sec.

Distance in yards:	Muzzle	20	30	40	50	60	70
Velocity in fps:	1,390	989	863	762	680	611	551
Average pellet energy in ft-lbs:	13.86	7.01	5.34	4.17	3.32	2.67	2.18
Time of flight in seconds:	0	.0519	.0844	.1215	.1632	.2098	.2615

Type of load: Field
Three-foot velocity: 1,300 ft./sec.
Hull: 2¾-inch plastic
Wad: Plastic
Shot: Lead
Buffered: No
Test barrel length: 28 inch
Pellets will pierce skin up to 172 yards.

NO. 4 LEAD PELLETS—1⅛ OUNCES—152 PELLETS
Mfg: PMC (Eldorado Cartridge Corp.) **Manufacturer's code:** HF16
Recoil energy in 8-lb. shotgun: 25.2 ft./lbs. **Recoil velocity in 8-lb. shotgun:** 14.2 ft./sec.

Distance in yards:	Muzzle	20	30	40	50	60	70
Velocity in fps:	1,390	989	863	762	680	611	551
Average pellet energy in ft-lbs:	13.86	7.01	5.34	4.17	3.32	2.67	2.18
Time of flight in seconds:	0	.0519	.0844	.1215	.1632	.2098	.2615

Type of load: Field
Three-foot velocity: 1,300 ft./sec.
Hull: 2¾-inch plastic
Wad: Plastic
Shot: Lead
Buffered: No
Test barrel length: 28 inch
Pellets will pierce skin up to 172 yards.

NO. 4 LEAD PELLETS—1⅛ OUNCES—152 PELLETS
Mfg: Remington Arms Co. **Manufacturer's code:** SP16
Recoil energy in 8-lb. shotgun: 25.2 ft./lbs. **Recoil velocity in 8-lb. shotgun:** 14.2 ft./sec.

Distance in yards:	Muzzle	20	30	40	50	60	70
Velocity in fps:	1,390	989	863	762	680	611	551
Average pellet energy in ft-lbs:	13.86	7.01	5.34	4.17	3.32	2.67	2.18
Time of flight in seconds:	0	.0519	.0844	.1215	.1632	.2098	.2615

Type of load: Field
Three-foot velocity: 1,300 ft./sec.
Hull: 2¾-inch plastic
Wad: Plastic
Shot: Lead
Buffered: No
Test barrel length: 28 inch
Pellets will pierce skin up to 172 yards.

NO. 4 LEAD PELLETS—1⅛ OUNCES—152 PELLETS
Mfg: Winchester **Manufacturer's code:** X16
Recoil energy in 8-lb. shotgun: 25.2 ft./lbs. **Recoil velocity in 8-lb. shotgun:** 14.2 ft./sec.

Distance in yards:	Muzzle	20	30	40	50	60	70
Velocity in fps:	1,390	989	863	762	680	611	551
Average pellet energy in ft-lbs:	13.86	7.01	5.34	4.17	3.32	2.67	2.18
Time of flight in seconds:	0	.0519	.0844	.1215	.1632	.2098	.2615

Type of load: Field
Three-foot velocity: 1,300 ft./sec.
Hull: 2¾-inch plastic
Wad: Plastic
Shot: Lead
Buffered: No
Test barrel length: 28 inch
Pellets will pierce skin up to 172 yards.

NO. 4 LEAD PELLETS—1¼ OUNCES—169 PELLETS
Mfg: Federal Cartridge Co. **Manufacturer's code:** P165
Recoil energy in 8-lb. shotgun: 29.5 ft./lbs. **Recoil velocity in 8-lb. shotgun:** 15.4 ft./sec.

Distance in yards:	Muzzle	20	30	40	50	60	70
Velocity in fps:	1,363	1,049	851	753	672	604	545
Average pellet energy in ft-lbs:	13.32	6.81	5.20	4.07	3.24	2.62	2.13
Time of flight in seconds:	0	.0528	.0858	.1233	.1655	.2126	.2649

Type of load: Field
Three-foot velocity: 1,275 ft./sec.
Hull: 2¾-inch plastic
Wad: Plastic
Shot: Lead
Buffered: No
Test barrel length: 28 inch
Pellets will pierce skin up to 171 yards.

NO. 5 LEAD PELLETS—1¹⁄₁₆ OUNCES—181 PELLETS
Mfg: Clever **Manufacturer's code:** T1 Light Game
Recoil energy in 8-lb. shotgun: 21.2 ft./lbs. **Recoil velocity in 8-lb. shotgun:** 13.0 ft./sec.

Distance in yards:	Muzzle	20	30	40	50	60	70
Velocity in fps:	1,429	985	851	745	660	588	527
Average pellet energy in ft-lbs:	11.53	5.47	4.08	3.13	2.46	1.95	1.57
Time of flight in seconds:	0	.0514	.0842	.1220	.1648	.2130	.2669

Type of load: Field
Three-foot velocity: 1,330 ft./sec.
Hull: 2¾-inch plastic
Wad: Plastic
Shot: Lead
Buffered: No
Test barrel length: 28 inch
Pellets will pierce skin up to 160 yards.

NO. 5 LEAD PELLETS—1⅛ OUNCES—191 PELLETS
Mfg: Dionisi Manufacturer's code: D 16 SLR
Recoil energy in 8-lb. shotgun: 25.2 ft./lbs. Recoil velocity in 8-lb. shotgun: 14.2 ft./sec.

Distance in yards:	Muzzle	20	30	40	50	60	70
Velocity in fps:	1,396	969	838	735	651	581	521
Average pellet energy in ft-lbs:	11.00	5.29	3.96	3.05	2.39	1.90	1.53
Time of flight in seconds:	0	.0524	.0858	.1241	.1675	.2163	.2708

Type of load: Field
Three-foot velocity: 1,300 ft./sec.
Hull: 2¾-inch plastic
Wad: Plastic
Shot: Lead
Buffered: No
Test barrel length: 28 inch
Pellets will pierce skin up to 159 yards.

NO. 6 LEAD PELLETS—1 OUNCE—225 PELLETS
Mfg: Federal Cartridge Co. Manufacturer's code: H166
Recoil energy in 8-lb. shotgun: 14.9 ft./lbs. Recoil velocity in 8-lb. shotgun: 10.9 ft./sec.

Distance in yards:	Muzzle	20	30	40	50	60	70
Velocity in fps:	1,254	873	755	660	583	517	460
Average pellet energy in ft-lbs:	6.83	3.31	2.47	1.89	1.47	1.16	.92
Time of flight in seconds:	0	.0583	.0953	.1379	.1863	.2410	.3026

Type of load: Field
Three-foot velocity: 1,165 ft./sec.
Hull: 2¾-inch plastic
Wad: Plastic
Shot: Lead
Buffered: No
Test barrel length: 28 inch
Pellets will pierce skin up to 141 yards.

NO. 6 LEAD PELLETS—1 OUNCE—225 PELLETS
Mfg: Fiocchi Manufacturer's code: 16GT
Recoil energy in 8-lb. shotgun: 14.9 ft./lbs. Recoil velocity in 8-lb. shotgun: 10.9 ft./sec.

Distance in yards:	Muzzle	20	30	40	50	60	70
Velocity in fps:	1,254	873	755	660	583	517	460
Average pellet energy in ft-lbs:	6.83	3.31	2.47	1.89	1.47	1.16	.92
Time of flight in seconds:	0	.0583	.0953	.1379	.1863	.2410	.3026

Type of load: Game & Target
Three-foot velocity: 1,156 ft./sec.
Hull: 2¾-inch plastic
Wad: Plastic
Shot: Lead
Buffered: No
Test barrel length: 26 inch
Pellets will pierce skin up to 141 yards.

NO. 6 LEAD PELLETS—1 OUNCE—225 PELLETS
Mfg: Winchester Manufacturer's code: XU16
Recoil energy in 8-lb. shotgun: 14.9 ft./lbs. Recoil velocity in 8-lb. shotgun: 10.9 ft./sec.

Distance in yards:	Muzzle	20	30	40	50	60	70
Velocity in fps:	1,254	873	755	660	583	517	460
Average pellet energy in ft-lbs:	6.83	3.31	2.47	1.89	1.47	1.16	.92
Time of flight in seconds:	0	.0583	.0953	.1379	.1863	.2410	.3026

Type of load: Field
Three-foot velocity: 1,165 ft./sec.
Hull: 2¾-inch plastic
Wad: Plastic
Shot: Lead
Buffered: No
Test barrel length: 28 inch
Pellets will pierce skin up to 141 yards.

NO. 6 LEAD PELLETS—1 OUNCE—225 PELLETS
Mfg: Aguila Manufacturer's code: N/A
Recoil energy in 8-lb. shotgun: 16.1 ft./lbs. Recoil velocity in 8-lb. shotgun: 11.4 ft./sec.

Distance in yards:	Muzzle	20	30	40	50	60	70
Velocity in fps:	1,292	892	769	672	593	525	467
Average pellet energy in ft-lbs:	7.26	3.46	2.57	1.96	1.53	1.20	.095
Time of flight in seconds:	0	.0568	.0931	.01349	.1825	.2363	.2969

Type of load: Field
Three-foot velocity: 1,200 ft./sec.
Hull: 2¾-inch plastic
Wad: Plastic
Shot: Lead
Buffered: No
Test barrel length: 28 inch
Pellets will pierce skin up to 157 yards.

NO. 6 LEAD PELLETS—1 OUNCE—225 PELLETS
Mfg: Kent Cartridge America/Canada Manufacturer's code: K162UG28
Recoil energy in 8-lb. shotgun: 16.1 ft./lbs. Recoil velocity in 8-lb. shotgun: 11.4 ft./sec.

Distance in yards:	Muzzle	20	30	40	50	60	70
Velocity in fps:	1,292	892	769	672	593	525	467
Average pellet energy in ft-lbs:	7.26	3.46	2.57	1.96	1.53	1.20	.095
Time of flight in seconds:	0	.0568	.0931	.01349	.1825	.2363	.2969

Type of load: Field
Three-foot velocity: 1,200 ft./sec.
Hull: 2¾-inch plastic
Wad: Plastic
Shot: Lead
Buffered: No
Test barrel length: 28 inch
Pellets will pierce skin up to 157 yards.

NO. 6 LEAD PELLETS—1 OUNCE—225 PELLETS
Mfg: Remington Arms Co. Manufacturer's code: GL16
Recoil energy in 8-lb. shotgun: 16.1 ft./lbs. Recoil velocity in 8-lb. shotgun: 11.4 ft./sec.

Distance in yards:	Muzzle	20	30	40	50	60	70
Velocity in fps:	1,292	892	769	672	593	525	467
Average pellet energy in ft-lbs:	7.26	3.46	2.57	1.96	1.53	1.20	.095
Time of flight in seconds:	0	.0568	.0931	.01349	.1825	.2363	.2969

Type of load: Field
Three-foot velocity: 1,200 ft./sec.
Hull: 2¾-inch plastic
Wad: Plastic
Shot: Lead
Buffered: No
Test barrel length: 28 inch
Pellets will pierce skin up to 157 yards.

NO. 6 LEAD PELLETS—1¹/₁₆ OUNCES—239 PELLETS
Mfg: Sellier & Bellot **Manufacturer's code:** SBA01602
Recoil energy in 8-lb. shotgun: 22.7 ft./lbs. **Recoil velocity in 8-lb. shotgun:** 13.5 ft./sec.

Distance in yards:	Muzzle	20	30	40	50	60	70
Velocity in fps:	1,348	919	790	689	606	537	477
Average pellet energy in ft-lbs:	7.89	3.67	2.71	2.06	1.60	1.25	.99
Time of flight in seconds:	0	.0549	.0902	.1309	.1774	.2300	.2893

Type of load: Field
Three-foot velocity: 1,250 ft./sec.
Hull: 2¾-inch plastic
Wad: Plastic
Shot: Lead
Buffered: No
Test barrel length: 28 inch
Pellets will pierce skin up to 144 yards.

NO. 6 LEAD PELLETS—1¹/₁₆ OUNCES—239 PELLETS
Mfg: Clever **Manufacturer's code:** T1 Light Game
Recoil energy in 8-lb. shotgun: 21.2 ft./lbs. **Recoil velocity in 8-lb. shotgun:** 13.0 ft./sec.

Distance in yards:	Muzzle	20	30	40	50	60	70
Velocity in fps:	1,436	961	822	714	627	555	493
Average pellet energy in ft-lbs:	8.96	4.01	2.94	2.22	1.71	1.34	1.06
Time of flight in seconds:	0	.0520	.0859	.1251	.1700	.2209	.2782

Type of load: Field
Three-foot velocity: 1,330 ft./sec.
Hull: 2¾-inch plastic
Wad: Plastic
Shot: Lead
Buffered: No
Test barrel length: 28 inch
Pellets will pierce skin up to 147 yards.

NO. 6 LEAD PELLETS—1¹/₈ OUNCES—253 PELLETS
Mfg: Federal Cartridge Co. **Manufacturer's code:** H162
Recoil energy in 8-lb. shotgun: 19.3 ft./lbs. **Recoil velocity in 8-lb. shotgun:** 12.5 ft./sec.

Distance in yards:	Muzzle	20	30	40	50	60	70
Velocity in fps:	1,265	878	759	664	585	519	462
Average pellet energy in ft-lbs:	6.95	3.35	2.50	1.91	1.9	1.17	.93
Time of flight in seconds:	0	.0578	.0947	.1370	.1852	.2396	.3009

Type of load: Field
Three-foot velocity: 1,175 ft./sec.
Hull: 2¾-inch plastic
Wad: Plastic
Shot: Lead
Buffered: No
Test barrel length: 28 inch
Pellets will pierce skin up to 141 yards.

NO. 6 LEAD PELLETS—1¹/₈ OUNCES—253 PELLETS
Mfg: Fiocchi **Manufacturer's code:** 16FLD
Recoil energy in 8-lb. shotgun: 19.3 ft./lbs. **Recoil velocity in 8-lb. shotgun:** 12.5 ft./sec.

Distance in yards:	Muzzle	20	30	40	50	60	70
Velocity in fps:	1,265	878	759	664	585	519	462
Average pellet energy in ft-lbs:	6.95	3.35	2.50	1.91	1.9	1.17	.93
Time of flight in seconds:	0	.0578	.0947	.1370	.1852	.2396	.3009

Type of load: Field
Three-foot velocity: 1,175 ft./sec.
Hull: 2¾-inch plastic
Wad: Plastic
Shot: Lead
Buffered: No
Test barrel length: 28 inch
Pellets will pierce skin up to 141 yards.

NO. 6 LEAD PELLETS—1¹/₈ OUNCES—253 PELLETS
Mfg: Aguila **Manufacturer's code:** N/A
Recoil energy in 8-lb. shotgun: 22.7 ft./lbs. **Recoil velocity in 8-lb. shotgun:** 13.5 ft./sec.

Distance in yards:	Muzzle	20	30	40	50	60	70
Velocity in fps:	1348	919	790	689	606	537	477
Average pellet energy in ft-lbs:	7.89	3.67	2.71	2.06	1.60	1.25	.99
Time of flight in seconds:	0	.0549	.0902	.1309	.1774	.2300	.2893

Type of load: Field
Three-foot velocity: 1,250 ft./sec.
Hull: 2¾-inch plastic
Wad: Plastic
Shot: Lead
Buffered: No
Test barrel length: 28 inch
Pellets will pierce skin up to 144 yards.

NO. 6 LEAD PELLETS—1¹/₈ OUNCES—253 PELLETS
Mfg: Federal Cartridge Co. **Manufacturer's code:** H164
Recoil energy in 8-lb. shotgun: 22.7 ft./lbs. **Recoil velocity in 8-lb. shotgun:** 13.5 ft./sec.

Distance in yards:	Muzzle	20	30	40	50	60	70
Velocity in fps:	1,348	919	790	689	606	537	477
Average pellet energy in ft-lbs:	7.89	3.67	2.71	2.06	1.60	1.25	.99
Time of flight in seconds:	0	.0549	.0902	.1309	.1774	.2300	.2893

Type of load: Field
Three-foot velocity: 1,250 ft./sec.
Hull: 2¾-inch plastic
Wad: Plastic
Shot: Lead
Buffered: No
Test barrel length: 28 inch
Pellets will pierce skin up to 144 yards.

NO. 6 LEAD PELLETS—1¹/₈ OUNCES—253 PELLETS
Mfg: Dionisi **Manufacturer's code:** D 16 SLR
Recoil energy in 8-lb. shotgun: 25.2 ft./lbs. **Recoil velocity in 8-lb. shotgun:** 14.2 ft./sec.

Distance in yards:	Muzzle	20	30	40	50	60	70
Velocity in fps:	1,403	945	810	705	620	548	487
Average pellet energy in ft-lbs:	8.55	3.88	2.85	2.16	1.67	1.31	1.03
Time of flight in seconds:	0	.0531	.0875	.1272	.1727	.2242	.2723

Type of load: Field
Three-foot velocity: 1,300 ft./sec.
Hull: 2¾-inch plastic
Wad: Plastic
Shot: Lead
Buffered: No
Test barrel length: 28 inch
Pellets will pierce skin up to 146 yards.

NO. 6 LEAD PELLETS—1⅛ OUNCES—253 PELLETS
Mfg: Federal Cartridge Co. **Manufacturer's code:** H463
Recoil energy in 8-lb. shotgun: 25.2 ft./lbs. **Recoil velocity in 8-lb. shotgun:** 14.2 ft./sec.

Distance in yards:	Muzzle	20	30	40	50	60	70
Velocity in fps:	1,403	945	810	705	620	548	487
Average pellet energy in ft-lbs:	8.55	3.88	2.85	2.16	1.67	1.31	1.03
Time of flight in seconds:	0	.0531	.0875	.1272	.1727	.2242	.2723

Type of load: Field
Three-foot velocity: 1,300 ft./sec.
Hull: 2¾-inch plastic
Wad: Plastic
Shot: Lead
Buffered: No
Test barrel length: 28 inch
Pellets will pierce skin up to 146 yards.

NO. 6 LEAD PELLETS—1⅛ OUNCES—253 PELLETS
Mfg: Fiocchi **Manufacturer's code:** 16HV
Recoil energy in 8-lb. shotgun: 25.2 ft./lbs. **Recoil velocity in 8-lb. shotgun:** 14.2 ft./sec.

Distance in yards:	Muzzle	20	30	40	50	60	70
Velocity in fps:	1,403	945	810	705	620	548	487
Average pellet energy in ft-lbs:	8.55	3.88	2.85	2.16	1.67	1.31	1.03
Time of flight in seconds:	0	.0531	.0875	.1272	.1727	.2242	.2723

Type of load: Field
Three-foot velocity: 1,300 ft./sec.
Hull: 2¾-inch plastic
Wad: Plastic
Shot: Lead
Buffered: No
Test barrel length: 28 inch
Pellets will pierce skin up to 146 yards.

NO. 6 LEAD PELLETS—1⅛ OUNCES—253 PELLETS
Mfg: PMC (Eldorado Cartridge Corp.) **Manufacturer's code:** HF16
Recoil energy in 8-lb. shotgun: 25.2 ft./lbs. **Recoil velocity in 8-lb. shotgun:** 14.2 ft./sec.

Distance in yards:	Muzzle	20	30	40	50	60	70
Velocity in fps:	1,403	945	810	705	620	548	487
Average pellet energy in ft-lbs:	8.55	3.88	2.85	2.16	1.67	1.31	1.03
Time of flight in seconds:	0	.0531	.0875	.1272	.1727	.2242	.2723

Type of load: Field
Three-foot velocity: 1,300 ft./sec.
Hull: 2¾-inch plastic
Wad: Plastic
Shot: Lead
Buffered: No
Test barrel length: 28 inch
Pellets will pierce skin up to 146 yards.

NO. 6 LEAD PELLETS—1⅛ OUNCES—253 PELLETS
Mfg: Remington Arms Co. **Manufacturer's code:** SP16/HGL16
Recoil energy in 8-lb. shotgun: 25.2 ft./lbs. **Recoil velocity in 8-lb. shotgun:** 14.2 ft./sec.

Distance in yards:	Muzzle	20	30	40	50	60	70
Velocity in fps:	1,403	945	810	705	620	548	487
Average pellet energy in ft-lbs:	8.55	3.88	2.85	2.16	1.67	1.31	1.03
Time of flight in seconds:	0	.0531	.0875	.1272	.1727	.2242	.2723

Type of load: Field
Three-foot velocity: 1,300 ft./sec.
Hull: 2¾-inch plastic
Wad: Plastic
Shot: Lead
Buffered: No
Test barrel length: 28 inch
Pellets will pierce skin up to 146 yards.

NO. 6 LEAD PELLETS—1⅛ OUNCES—253 PELLETS
Mfg: Winchester **Manufacturer's code:** X16
Recoil energy in 8-lb. shotgun: 25.2 ft./lbs. **Recoil velocity in 8-lb. shotgun:** 14.2 ft./sec.

Distance in yards:	Muzzle	20	30	40	50	60	70
Velocity in fps:	1,403	945	810	705	620	548	487
Average pellet energy in ft-lbs:	8.55	3.88	2.85	2.16	1.67	1.31	1.03
Time of flight in seconds:	0	.0531	.0875	.1272	.1727	.2242	.2723

Type of load: Field
Three-foot velocity: 1,300 ft./sec.
Hull: 2¾-inch plastic
Wad: Plastic
Shot: Lead
Buffered: No
Test barrel length: 28 inch
Pellets will pierce skin up to 146 yards.

NO. 6 LEAD PELLETS—1¼ OUNCES—281 PELLETS
Mfg: Federal Cartridge Co. **Manufacturer's code:** P165
Recoil energy in 8-lb. shotgun: 29.5 ft./lbs. **Recoil velocity in 8-lb. shotgun:** 15.4 ft./sec.

Distance in yards:	Muzzle	20	30	40	50	60	70
Velocity in fps:	1,375	932	800	697	613	543	482
Average pellet energy in ft-lbs:	8.22	3.77	2.78	2.11	1.63	1.28	1.01
Time of flight in seconds:	0	.0540	.0888	.1290	.1750	.2271	.2858

Type of load: Field
Three-foot velocity: 1,275 ft./sec.
Hull: 2¾-inch plastic
Wad: Plastic
Shot: Lead
Buffered: No
Test barrel length: 28 inch
Pellets will pierce skin up to 145 yards.

NO. 7 LEAD PELLETS—1¹⁄₁₆ OUNCES—318 PELLETS
Mfg: Clever **Manufacturer's code:** T1 Light Game
Recoil energy in 8-lb. shotgun: 21.2 ft./lbs. **Recoil velocity in 8-lb. shotgun:** 13.0 ft./sec.

Distance in yards:	Muzzle	20	30	40	50	60	70
Velocity in fps:	1,443	933	789	679	591	518	455
Average pellet energy in ft-lbs:	6.80	2.84	2.03	1.51	1.14	.88	.68
Time of flight in seconds:	0	.0529	.0879	.1290	.1764	.2306	.2925

Type of load: Field
Three-foot velocity: 1,330 ft./sec.
Hull: 2¾-inch plastic
Wad: Plastic
Shot: Lead
Buffered: No
Test barrel length: 28 inch
Pellets will pierce skin up to 134 yards.

NO. 7½ LEAD PELLETS—1 OUNCE—350 PELLETS
Mfg: Federal Cartridge Co. **Manufacturer's code:** H166
Recoil energy in 8-lb. shotgun: 14.9 ft./lbs. **Recoil velocity in 8-lb. shotgun:** 10.9 ft./sec.

Distance in yards:	Muzzle	20	30	40	50	60	70
Velocity in fps:	1,263	836	710	612	532	464	405
Average pellet energy in ft-lbs:	4.46	1.96	1.41	1.05	.79	.60	.46
Time of flight in seconds:	0	.0596	.0986	.1442	.1968	.2572	.3264

Type of load: Field
Three-foot velocity: 1,165 ft./sec.
Hull: 2¾-inch plastic
Wad: Plastic
Shot: Lead
Buffered: No
Test barrel length: 28 inch
Pellets will pierce skin up to 122 yards.

NO. 7½ LEAD PELLETS—1 OUNCE—350 PELLETS
Mfg: Fiocchi **Manufacturer's code:** 16GT
Recoil energy in 8-lb. shotgun: 14.9 ft./lbs. **Recoil velocity in 8-lb. shotgun:** 10.9 ft./sec.

Distance in yards:	Muzzle	20	30	40	50	60	70
Velocity in fps:	1,263	836	710	612	532	464	405
Average pellet energy in ft-lbs:	4.46	1.96	1.41	1.05	.79	.60	.46
Time of flight in seconds:	0	.0596	.0986	.1442	.1968	.2572	.3264

Type of load: Game & Target
Three-foot velocity: 1,156 ft./sec.
Hull: 2¾-inch plastic
Wad: Plastic
Shot: Lead
Buffered: No
Test barrel length: 26 inch
Pellets will pierce skin up to 122 yards.

NO. 7½ LEAD PELLETS—1 OUNCE—350 PELLETS
Mfg: Aguila **Manufacturer's code:** N/A
Recoil energy in 8-lb. shotgun: 16.1 ft./lbs. **Recoil velocity in 8-lb. shotgun:** 11.4 ft./sec.

Distance in yards:	Muzzle	20	30	40	50	60	70
Velocity in fps:	1,302	854	724	623	541	472	412
Average pellet energy in ft-lbs:	4.74	2.04	1.47	1.09	.82	.62	.47
Time of flight in seconds:	0	.0581	.0964	.1412	.1930	.2524	.3204

Type of load: Field
Three-foot velocity: 1,200 ft./sec.
Hull: 2¾-inch plastic
Wad: Plastic
Shot: Lead
Buffered: No
Test barrel length: 28 inch
Pellets will pierce skin up to 136 yards.

NO. 7½ LEAD PELLETS—1 OUNCE—350 PELLETS
Mfg: Dionisi **Manufacturer's code:** D 16 DQ
Recoil energy in 8-lb. shotgun: 16.1 ft./lbs. **Recoil velocity in 8-lb. shotgun:** 11.4 ft./sec.

Distance in yards:	Muzzle	20	30	40	50	60	70
Velocity in fps:	1,302	854	724	623	541	472	412
Average pellet energy in ft-lbs:	4.74	2.04	1.47	1.09	.82	.62	.47
Time of flight in seconds:	0	.0581	.0964	.1412	.1930	.2524	.3204

Type of load: Dove & Quail
Three-foot velocity: 1,200 ft./sec.
Hull: 2¾-inch plastic
Wad: Plastic
Shot: Lead
Buffered: No
Test barrel length: 28 inch
Pellets will pierce skin up to 136 yards.

NO. 7½ LEAD PELLETS—1 OUNCE—350 PELLETS
Mfg: Kent Cartridge America/Canada **Manufacturer's code:** K162UG28
Recoil energy in 8-lb. shotgun: 16.1 ft./lbs. **Recoil velocity in 8-lb. shotgun:** 11.4 ft./sec.

Distance in yards:	Muzzle	20	30	40	50	60	70
Velocity in fps:	1,302	854	724	623	541	472	412
Average pellet energy in ft-lbs:	4.74	2.04	1.47	1.09	.82	.62	.47
Time of flight in seconds:	0	.0581	.0964	.1412	.1930	.2524	.3204

Type of load: Field
Three-foot velocity: 1,200 ft./sec.
Hull: 2¾-inch plastic
Wad: Plastic
Shot: Lead
Buffered: No
Test barrel length: 28 inch
Pellets will pierce skin up to 136 yards.

NO. 7½ LEAD PELLETS—1 OUNCE—350 PELLETS
Mfg: Remington Arms Co. **Manufacturer's code:** GL16
Recoil energy in 8-lb. shotgun: 16.1 ft./lbs. **Recoil velocity in 8-lb. shotgun:** 11.4 ft./sec.

Distance in yards:	Muzzle	20	30	40	50	60	70
Velocity in fps:	1,302	854	724	623	541	472	412
Average pellet energy in ft-lbs:	4.74	2.04	1.47	1.09	.82	.62	.47
Time of flight in seconds:	0	.0581	.0964	.1412	.1930	.2524	.3204

Type of load: Field
Three-foot velocity: 1,200 ft./sec.
Hull: 2¾-inch plastic
Wad: Plastic
Shot: Lead
Buffered: No
Test barrel length: 28 inch
Pellets will pierce skin up to 136 yards.

NO. 7½ LEAD PELLETS—1¹⁄₁₆ OUNCES—372 PELLETS
Mfg: Sellier & Bellot **Manufacturer's code:** SBA01603
Recoil energy in 8-lb. shotgun: 22.7 ft./lbs. **Recoil velocity in 8-lb. shotgun:** 13.5 ft./sec.

Distance in yards:	Muzzle	20	30	40	50	60	70
Velocity in fps:	1357	878	742	637	553	482	421
Average pellet energy in ft-lbs:	5.16	2.16	1.54	1.14	.86	.65	.50
Time of flight in seconds:	0	.0562	.0935	.1372	.1878	.2459	.3126

Type of load: Field
Three-foot velocity: 1,250 ft./sec.
Hull: 2¾-inch plastic
Wad: Plastic
Shot: Lead
Buffered: No
Test barrel length: 28 inch
Pellets will pierce skin up to 125 yards.

NO. 7½ LEAD PELLETS—1⅛ OUNCES—394 PELLETS
Mfg: Federal Cartridge Co. **Manufacturer's code:** H162
Recoil energy in 8-lb. shotgun: 19.3 ft./lbs. **Recoil velocity in 8-lb. shotgun:** 12.5 ft./sec.

Distance in yards:	Muzzle	20	30	40	50	60	70
Velocity in fps:	1,274	841	714	615	535	466	407
Average pellet energy in ft-lbs:	4.54	1.98	1.43	1.06	.80	.61	.46
Time of flight in seconds:	0	.0592	.0980	.1433	.1957	.2558	.3246

Type of load: Field
Three-foot velocity: 1,175 ft./sec.
Hull: 2¾-inch plastic
Wad: Plastic
Shot: Lead
Buffered: No
Test barrel length: 28 inch
Pellets will pierce skin up to 122 yards.

NO. 7½ LEAD PELLETS—1⅛ OUNCES—394 PELLETS
Mfg: Fiocchi **Manufacturer's code:** 16FLD
Recoil energy in 8-lb. shotgun: 19.3 ft./lbs. **Recoil velocity in 8-lb. shotgun:** 12.5 ft./sec.

Distance in yards:	Muzzle	20	30	40	50	60	70
Velocity in fps:	1,274	841	714	615	535	466	407
Average pellet energy in ft-lbs:	4.54	1.98	1.43	1.06	.80	.61	.46
Time of flight in seconds:	0	.0592	.0980	.1433	.1957	.2558	.3246

Type of load: Field
Three-foot velocity: 1,175 ft./sec.
Hull: 2¾-inch plastic
Wad: Plastic
Shot: Lead
Buffered: No
Test barrel length: 28 inch
Pellets will pierce skin up to 122 yards.

NO. 7½ LEAD PELLETS—1⅛ OUNCES—394 PELLETS
Mfg: Aguila **Manufacturer's code:** N/A
Recoil energy in 8-lb. shotgun: 22.7 ft./lbs. **Recoil velocity in 8-lb. shotgun:** 13.5 ft./sec.

Distance in yards:	Muzzle	20	30	40	50	60	70
Velocity in fps:	1357	878	742	637	553	482	421
Average pellet energy in ft-lbs:	5.16	2.16	1.54	1.14	.86	.65	.50
Time of flight in seconds:	0	.0562	.0935	.1372	.1878	.2459	.3126

Type of load: Field
Three-foot velocity: 1,250 ft./sec.
Hull: 2¾-inch plastic
Wad: Plastic
Shot: Lead
Buffered: No
Test barrel length: 28 inch
Pellets will pierce skin up to 125 yards.

NO. 7½ LEAD PELLETS—1⅛ OUNCES—394 PELLETS
Mfg: Dionisi **Manufacturer's code:** D 16 SLR
Recoil energy in 8-lb. shotgun: 25.2 ft./lbs. **Recoil velocity in 8-lb. shotgun:** 14.2 ft./sec.

Distance in yards:	Muzzle	20	30	40	50	60	70
Velocity in fps:	1,413	903	761	652	565	492	430
Average pellet energy in ft-lbs:	5.59	2.28	1.62	1.19	.89	.68	.52
Time of flight in seconds:	0	.0544	.0907	.1334	.1829	.2399	.3052

Type of load: Field
Three-foot velocity: 1,300 ft./sec.
Hull: 2¾-inch plastic
Wad: Plastic
Shot: Lead
Buffered: No
Test barrel length: 26 inch
Pellets will pierce skin up to 126 yards.

NO. 7½ LEAD PELLETS—1⅛ OUNCES—394 PELLETS
Mfg: Federal Cartridge Co. **Manufacturer's code:** H463
Recoil energy in 8-lb. shotgun: 25.2 ft./lbs. **Recoil velocity in 8-lb. shotgun:** 14.2 ft./sec.

Distance in yards:	Muzzle	20	30	40	50	60	70
Velocity in fps:	1,413	903	761	652	565	492	430
Average pellet energy in ft-lbs:	5.59	2.28	1.62	1.19	.89	.68	.52
Time of flight in seconds:	0	.0544	.0907	.1334	.1829	.2399	.3052

Type of load: Field
Three-foot velocity: 1,300 ft./sec.
Hull: 2¾-inch plastic
Wad: Plastic
Shot: Lead
Buffered: No
Test barrel length: 28 inch
Pellets will pierce skin up to 126 yards.

NO. 7½ LEAD PELLETS—1⅛ OUNCES—394 PELLETS
Mfg: Fiocchi **Manufacturer's code:** 16HV
Recoil energy in 8-lb. shotgun: 25.2 ft./lbs. **Recoil velocity in 8-lb. shotgun:** 14.2 ft./sec.

Distance in yards:	Muzzle	20	30	40	50	60	70
Velocity in fps:	1,413	903	761	652	565	492	430
Average pellet energy in ft-lbs:	5.59	2.28	1.62	1.19	.89	.68	.52
Time of flight in seconds:	0	.0544	.0907	.1334	.1829	.2399	.3052

Type of load: Field
Three-foot velocity: 1,300 ft./sec.
Hull: 2¾-inch plastic
Wad: Plastic
Shot: Lead
Buffered: No
Test barrel length: 28 inch
Pellets will pierce skin up to 126 yards.

NO. 7½ LEAD PELLETS—1⅛ OUNCES—394 PELLETS
Mfg: PMC (Eldorado Cartridge Corp.) **Manufacturer's code:** HF16
Recoil energy in 8-lb. shotgun: 25.2 ft./lbs. **Recoil velocity in 8-lb. shotgun:** 14.2 ft./sec.

Distance in yards:	Muzzle	20	30	40	50	60	70
Velocity in fps:	1,413	903	761	652	565	492	430
Average pellet energy in ft-lbs:	5.59	2.28	1.62	1.19	.89	.68	.52
Time of flight in seconds:	0	.0544	.0907	.1334	.1829	.2399	.3052

Type of load: Field
Three-foot velocity: 1,300 ft./sec.
Hull: 2¾-inch plastic
Wad: Plastic
Shot: Lead
Buffered: No
Test barrel length: 28 inch
Pellets will pierce skin up to 126 yards.

NO. 7½ LEAD PELLETS—1⅛ OUNCES—394 PELLETS
Mfg: Remington Arms Co. **Manufacturer's code:** SP16
Recoil energy in 8-lb. shotgun: 25.2 ft./lbs. **Recoil velocity in 8-lb. shotgun:** 14.2 ft./sec.

Distance in yards:	Muzzle	20	30	40	50	60	70
Velocity in fps:	1,413	903	761	652	565	492	430
Average pellet energy in ft-lbs:	5.59	2.28	1.62	1.19	.89	.68	.52
Time of flight in seconds:	0	.0544	.0907	.1334	.1829	.2399	.3052

Type of load: Field
Three-foot velocity: 1,300 ft./sec.
Hull: 2¾-inch plastic
Wad: Plastic
Shot: Lead
Buffered: No
Test barrel length: 28 inch
Pellets will pierce skin up to 126 yards.

NO. 7½ LEAD PELLETS—1⅛ OUNCES—394 PELLETS
Mfg: Winchester **Manufacturer's code:** X16
Recoil energy in 8-lb. shotgun: 25.2 ft./lbs. **Recoil velocity in 8-lb. shotgun:** 14.2 ft./sec.

Distance in yards:	Muzzle	20	30	40	50	60	70
Velocity in fps:	1,413	903	761	652	565	492	430
Average pellet energy in ft-lbs:	5.59	2.28	1.62	1.19	.89	.68	.52
Time of flight in seconds:	0	.0544	.0907	.1334	.1829	.2399	.3052

Type of load: Field
Three-foot velocity: 1,300 ft./sec.
Hull: 2¾-inch plastic
Wad: Plastic
Shot: Lead
Buffered: No
Test barrel length: 28 inch
Pellets will pierce skin up to 126 yards.

NO. 8 LEAD PELLETS—1 OUNCE—410 PELLETS
Mfg: Federal Cartridge Co. **Manufacturer's code:** H166
Recoil energy in 8-lb. shotgun: 14.9 ft./lbs. **Recoil velocity in 8-lb. shotgun:** 10.9 ft./sec.

Distance in yards:	Muzzle	20	30	40	50	60	70
Velocity in fps:	1,266	822	693	594	513	444	385
Average pellet energy in ft-lbs:	3.81	1.61	1.14	.84	.63	.47	.35
Time of flight in seconds:	0	.0601	.1000	.1468	.2013	.2641	.3367

Type of load: Field
Three-foot velocity: 1,165 ft./sec.
Hull: 2¾-inch plastic
Wad: Plastic
Shot: Lead
Buffered: No
Test barrel length: 28 inch
Pellets will pierce skin up to 116 yards.

NO. 8 LEAD PELLETS—1 OUNCE—410 PELLETS
Mfg: Fiocchi **Manufacturer's code:** 16GT
Recoil energy in 8-lb. shotgun: 14.9 ft./lbs. **Recoil velocity in 8-lb. shotgun:** 10.9 ft./sec.

Distance in yards:	Muzzle	20	30	40	50	60	70
Velocity in fps:	1,266	822	693	594	513	444	385
Average pellet energy in ft-lbs:	3.81	1.61	1.14	.84	.63	.47	.35
Time of flight in seconds:	0	.0601	.1000	.1468	.2013	.2641	.3367

Type of load: Game & Target
Three-foot velocity: 1,156 ft./sec.
Hull: 2¾-inch plastic
Wad: Plastic
Shot: Lead
Buffered: No
Test barrel length: 28 inch
Pellets will pierce skin up to 116 yards.

NO. 8 LEAD PELLETS—1 OUNCE—410 PELLETS
Mfg: Winchester **Manufacturer's code:** XU16
Recoil energy in 8-lb. shotgun: 14.9 ft./lbs. **Recoil velocity in 8-lb. shotgun:** 10.9 ft./sec.

Distance in yards:	Muzzle	20	30	40	50	60	70
Velocity in fps:	1,266	822	693	594	513	444	385
Average pellet energy in ft-lbs:	3.81	1.61	1.14	.84	.63	.47	.35
Time of flight in seconds:	0	.0601	.1000	.1468	.2013	.2641	.3367

Type of load: Field
Three-foot velocity: 1,165 ft./sec.
Hull: 2¾-inch plastic
Wad: Plastic
Shot: Lead
Buffered: No
Test barrel length: 28 inch
Pellets will pierce skin up to 116 yards.

NO. 8 LEAD PELLETS—1 OUNCE—410 PELLETS
Mfg: Aguila **Manufacturer's code:** N/A
Recoil energy in 8-lb. shotgun: 16.1 ft./lbs. **Recoil velocity in 8-lb. shotgun:** 11.4 ft./sec.

Distance in yards:	Muzzle	20	30	40	50	60	70
Velocity in fps:	1,305	839	706	604	521	452	391
Average pellet energy in ft-lbs:	4.05	1.67	1.19	.87	.65	.49	.36
Time of flight in seconds:	0	.0587	.0978	.1438	.1973	.2593	.3307

Type of load: Field
Three-foot velocity: 1,200 ft./sec.
Hull: 2¾-inch plastic
Wad: Plastic
Shot: Lead
Buffered: No
Test barrel length: 28 inch
Pellets will pierce skin up to 129 yards.

NO. 8 LEAD PELLETS—1 OUNCE—410 PELLETS
Mfg: Dionisi **Manufacturer's code:** D 16 DQ
Recoil energy in 8-lb. shotgun: 16.1 ft./lbs. **Recoil velocity in 8-lb. shotgun:** 11.4 ft./sec.

Distance in yards:	Muzzle	20	30	40	50	60	70
Velocity in fps:	1,305	839	706	604	521	452	391
Average pellet energy in ft-lbs:	4.05	1.67	1.19	.87	.65	.49	.36
Time of flight in seconds:	0	.0587	.0978	.1438	.1973	.2593	.3307

Type of load: Dove & Quail
Three-foot velocity: 1,200 ft./sec.
Hull: 2¾-inch plastic
Wad: Plastic
Shot: Lead
Buffered: No
Test barrel length: 26 inch
Pellets will pierce skin up to 129 yards.

NO. 8 LEAD PELLETS—1 OUNCE—410 PELLETS
Mfg: Kent Cartridge America/Canada **Manufacturer's code:** K162UG28
Recoil energy in 8-lb. shotgun: 16.1 ft./lbs. **Recoil velocity in 8-lb. shotgun:** 11.4 ft./sec.

Distance in yards:	Muzzle	20	30	40	50	60	70
Velocity in fps:	1,305	839	706	604	521	452	391
Average pellet energy in ft-lbs:	4.05	1.67	1.19	.87	.65	.49	.36
Time of flight in seconds:	0	.0587	.0978	.1438	.1973	.2593	.3307

Type of load: Field
Three-foot velocity: 1,200 ft./sec.
Hull: 2¾-inch plastic
Wad: Plastic
Shot: Lead
Buffered: No
Test barrel length: 28 inch
Pellets will pierce skin up to 129 yards.

NO. 8 LEAD PELLETS—1 OUNCE—410 PELLETS
Mfg: Remington Arms Co. **Manufacturer's code:** GL16
Recoil energy in 8-lb. shotgun: 16.1 ft./lbs. **Recoil velocity in 8-lb. shotgun:** 11.4 ft./sec.

Distance in yards:	Muzzle	20	30	40	50	60	70
Velocity in fps:	1,305	839	706	604	521	452	391
Average pellet energy in ft-lbs:	4.05	1.67	1.19	.87	.65	.49	.36
Time of flight in seconds:	0	.0587	.0978	.1438	.1973	.2593	.3307

Type of load: Field
Three-foot velocity: 1,200 ft./sec.
Hull: 2¾-inch plastic
Wad: Plastic
Shot: Lead
Buffered: No
Test barrel length: 28 inch
Pellets will pierce skin up to 129 yards.

NO. 8 LEAD PELLETS—1¹/₁₆ OUNCES—435 PELLETS
Mfg: Sellier & Bellot **Manufacturer's code:** SBA01604
Recoil energy in 8-lb. shotgun: 22.7 ft./lbs. **Recoil velocity in 8-lb. shotgun:** 13.5 ft./sec.

Distance in yards:	Muzzle	20	30	40	50	60	70
Velocity in fps:	1,361	863	724	618	533	461	400
Average pellet energy in ft-lbs:	4.41	1.77	1.25	.91	.68	.51	.38
Time of flight in seconds:	0	.0568	.0948	.1398	.1921	.2527	.3225

Type of load: Field
Three-foot velocity: 1,250 ft./sec.
Hull: 2¾-inch plastic
Wad: Plastic
Shot: Lead
Buffered: No
Test barrel length: 28 inch
Pellets will pierce skin up to 118 yards.

NO. 8 LEAD PELLETS—1¹/₁₆ OUNCES—435 PELLETS
Mfg: Clever **Manufacturer's code:** T1 Light Game
Recoil energy in 8-lb. shotgun: 21.2 ft./lbs. **Recoil velocity in 8-lb. shotgun:** 13.0 ft./sec.

Distance in yards:	Muzzle	20	30	40	50	60	70
Velocity in fps:	1,451	900	752	640	551	477	413
Average pellet energy in ft-lbs:	5.01	1.93	1.35	.97	.72	.54	.41
Time of flight in seconds:	0	.0539	.0905	.1338	.1845	.2431	.3108

Type of load: Field
Three-foot velocity: 1,330 ft./sec.
Hull: 2¾-inch plastic
Wad: Plastic
Shot: Lead
Buffered: No
Test barrel length: 26 inch
Pellets will pierce skin up to 121 yards.

NO. 8 LEAD PELLETS—1¹/₈ OUNCES—461 PELLETS
Mfg: Federal Cartridge Co. **Manufacturer's code:** H162
Recoil energy in 8-lb. shotgun: 19.3 ft./lbs. **Recoil velocity in 8-lb. shotgun:** 12.5 ft./sec.

Distance in yards:	Muzzle	20	30	40	50	60	70
Velocity in fps:	1,277	827	697	597	515	446	387
Average pellet energy in ft-lbs:	3.88	1.63	1.16	.85	.63	.47	.36
Time of flight in seconds:	0	.0597	.0993	.1459	.2001	.2627	.3349

Type of load: Field
Three-foot velocity: 1,175 ft./sec.
Hull: 2¾-inch plastic
Wad: Plastic
Shot: Lead
Buffered: No
Test barrel length: 28 inch
Pellets will pierce skin up to 116 yards.

NO. 8 LEAD PELLETS—1¹/₈ OUNCES—461 PELLETS
Mfg: Fiocchi **Manufacturer's code:** 16FLD
Recoil energy in 8-lb. shotgun: 19.3 ft./lbs. **Recoil velocity in 8-lb. shotgun:** 12.5 ft./sec.

Distance in yards:	Muzzle	20	30	40	50	60	70
Velocity in fps:	1,277	827	697	597	515	446	387
Average pellet energy in ft-lbs:	3.88	1.63	1.16	.85	.63	.47	.36
Time of flight in seconds:	0	.0597	.0993	.1459	.2001	.2627	.3349

Type of load: Field
Three-foot velocity: 1,175 ft./sec.
Hull: 2¾-inch plastic
Wad: Plastic
Shot: Lead
Buffered: No
Test barrel length: 28 inch
Pellets will pierce skin up to 116 yards.

NO. 8 LEAD PELLETS—1¹/₈ OUNCES—461 PELLETS
Mfg: Fiocchi **Manufacturer's code:** 16HV
Recoil energy in 8-lb. shotgun: 25.2 ft./lbs. **Recoil velocity in 8-lb. shotgun:** 14.2 ft./sec.

Distance in yards:	Muzzle	20	30	40	50	60	70
Velocity in fps:	1,417	886	742	632	544	471	408
Average pellet energy in ft-lbs:	4.78	1.87	1.31	.95	.70	.53	.40
Time of flight in seconds:	0	.0549	.0921	.1360	.1873	.2466	.3150

Type of load: Field
Three-foot velocity: 1,300 ft./sec.
Hull: 2¾-inch plastic
Wad: Plastic
Shot: Lead
Buffered: No
Test barrel length: 28 inch
Pellets will pierce skin up to 132 yards.

NO. 9 LEAD PELLETS—1 OUNCE—585 PELLETS

Mfg: Fiocchi **Manufacturer's code:** 16GT
Recoil energy in 8-lb. shotgun: 14.9 ft./lbs. **Recoil velocity in 8-lb. shotgun:** 10.9 ft./sec.

Distance in yards:	Muzzle	20	30	40	50	60	70
Velocity in fps:	1,272	789	655	553	470	400	341
Average pellet energy in ft-lbs:	2.71	1.04	.72	.51	.37	.27	.19
Time of flight in seconds:	0	.0615	.1033	.1533	.2122	.2814	.3627

Type of load: Game & Target
Three-foot velocity: 1,156 ft./sec.
Hull: 2¾-inch plastic
Wad: Plastic
Shot: Lead
Buffered: No
Test barrel length: 26 inch
Pellets will pierce skin up to 103 yards.

NO. 9 LEAD PELLETS—1 1/16 OUNCES—622 PELLETS

Mfg: Clever **Manufacturer's code:** T1 Light Game
Recoil energy in 8-lb. shotgun: 21.2 ft./lbs. **Recoil velocity in 8-lb. shotgun:** 13.0 ft./sec.

Distance in yards:	Muzzle	20	30	40	50	60	70
Velocity in fps:	1,481	870	715	599	508	432	368
Average pellet energy in ft-lbs:	3.67	1.27	.85	.60	.43	.31	.23
Time of flight in seconds:	0	.0546	.0928	.1387	.1932	.2572	.3325

Type of load: Field
Three-foot velocity: 1,350 ft./sec.
Hull: 2¾-inch plastic
Wad: Plastic
Shot: Lead
Buffered: No
Test barrel length: 26 inch
Pellets will pierce skin up to 108 yards.

By using small-gauge tubes made by Briley Manufacturing and others, clay-target shooters can use one gun for every gauge from 12 through .410-bore by inserting the tubes of the appropriate gauge. Hunters can also use these tubes to enable them to use a small gauge for a given game or use an old shotgun such as this one for hunting and clays.

NO. 2 STEEL PELLETS—¹⁵/₁₆ OUNCE—117 PELLETS

Mfg: Federal Cartridge Co. **Manufacturer's code:** W168
Recoil energy in 8-lb. shotgun: 17.5 ft./lbs. **Recoil velocity in 8-lb. shotgun:** 11.9 ft./sec.

Distance in yards:	Muzzle	20	30	40	50	60	70
Velocity in fps:	1,379	923	789	685	601	530	469
Average pellet energy in ft-lbs:	14.85	6.65	4.86	3.66	2.81	2.19	1.72
Time of flight in seconds:	0	.0542	.0894	.1303	.1771	.2303	.2905

Type of load: Nontoxic
Three-foot velocity: 1,300 ft./sec.
Hull: 2¾-inch plastic
Wad: Plastic
Shot: Steel
Buffered: No
Test barrel length: 28 inch
Pellets will pierce skin up to 140 yards.

NO. 2 STEEL PELLETS—¹⁵/₁₆ OUNCE—117 PELLETS

Mfg: Remington Arms Co. **Manufacturer's code:** SSP16
Recoil energy in 8-lb. shotgun: 17.5 ft./lbs. **Recoil velocity in 8-lb. shotgun:** 11.9 ft./sec.

Distance in yards:	Muzzle	20	30	40	50	60	70
Velocity in fps:	1,379	923	789	685	601	530	469
Average pellet energy in ft-lbs:	14.85	6.65	4.86	3.66	2.81	2.19	1.72
Time of flight in seconds:	0	.0542	.0894	.1303	.1771	.2303	.2905

Type of load: Nontoxic
Three-foot velocity: 1,300 ft./sec.
Hull: 2¾-inch plastic
Wad: Plastic
Shot: Zinc-galvanized steel
Buffered: No
Test barrel length: 28 inch
Pellets will pierce skin up to 140 yards.

NO. 4 STEEL PELLETS—¹⁵/₁₆ OUNCE—180 PELLETS

Mfg: Federal Cartridge Co. **Manufacturer's code:** W168
Recoil energy in 8-lb. shotgun: 17.5 ft./lbs. **Recoil velocity in 8-lb. shotgun:** 11.9 ft./sec.

Distance in yards:	Muzzle	20	30	40	50	60	70
Velocity in fps:	1,389	882	741	634	547	475	413
Average pellet energy in ft-lbs:	9.81	3.95	2.79	2.04	1.52	1.32	.87
Time of flight in seconds:	0	.0555	.0927	.1366	.1876	.2465	.3142

Type of load: Nontoxic
Three-foot velocity: 1,300 ft./sec.
Hull: 2¾-inch plastic
Wad: Plastic
Shot: Steel
Buffered: No
Test barrel length: 28 inch
Pellets will pierce skin up to 122 yards.

NO. 4 STEEL PELLETS—¹⁵/₁₆ OUNCE—180 PELLETS

Mfg: Remington Arms Co. **Manufacturer's code:** SSP16
Recoil energy in 8-lb. shotgun: 17.5 ft./lbs. **Recoil velocity in 8-lb. shotgun:** 11.9 ft./sec.

Distance in yards:	Muzzle	20	30	40	50	60	70
Velocity in fps:	1,389	882	741	634	547	475	413
Average pellet energy in ft-lbs:	9.81	3.95	2.79	2.04	1.52	1.32	.87
Time of flight in seconds:	0	.0555	.0927	.1366	.1876	.2465	.3142

Type of load: Nontoxic
Three-foot velocity: 1,300 ft./sec.
Hull: 2¾-inch plastic
Wad: Plastic
Shot: Zinc-galvanized steel
Buffered: No
Test barrel length: 28 inch
Pellets will pierce skin up to 122 yards.

One of the reasons for smokeless powder was to avoid the heavy cloud of smoke and heavy barrel fouling following firing. This sporting-clay shooter is using black powder, and the smoke cloud is evident.

NO. 4 BISMUTH PELLETS—¹⁵/₁₆ OUNCE—159 PELLETS

Mfg: Eley Hawk **Manufacturer's code:** Grand Prix Bismuth
Recoil energy in 8-lb. shotgun: 18.9 ft./lbs. **Recoil velocity in 8-lb. shotgun:** 12.3 ft./sec.

Distance in yards:	Muzzle	20	30	40	50	60	70
Velocity in fps:	1,367	937	807	706	623	553	493
Average pellet energy in ft-lbs:	11.69	5.50	4.08	3.12	2.43	1.91	1.52
Time of flight in seconds:	0	.0539	.0885	.1283	.1736	.2248	.2823

Type of load: Nontoxic
Three-foot velocity: 1,275 ft./sec.
Hull: 2½-inch plastic
Wad: Fiber
Shot: Bismuth
Buffered: No
Test barrel length: 28 inch
Pellets will pierce skin up to 150 yards.

NO. 5 BISMUTH PELLETS—¹⁵/₁₆ OUNCE—206 PELLETS

Mfg: Eley Hawk **Manufacturer's code:** Grand Prix Bismuth
Recoil energy in 8-lb. shotgun: 18.9 ft./lbs. **Recoil velocity in 8-lb. shotgun:** 12.3 ft./sec.

Distance in yards:	Muzzle	20	30	40	50	60	70
Velocity in fps:	1,373	916	782	678	594	523	463
Average pellet energy in ft-lbs:	9.28	4.13	3.01	2.26	1.74	1.35	1.05
Time of flight in seconds:	0	.0546	.0901	.1314	.1787	.2326	.2936

Type of load: Nontoxic
Three-foot velocity: 1,275 ft./sec.
Hull: 2½-inch plastic
Wad: Fiber
Shot: Bismuth
Buffered: No
Test barrel length: 28 inch
Pellets will pierce skin up to 138 yards.

NO. 6 BISMUTH PELLETS—¹⁵/₁₆ OUNCE—253 PELLETS

Mfg: Eley Hawk **Manufacturer's code:** Grand Prix Bismuth
Recoil energy in 8-lb. shotgun: 18.9 ft./lbs. **Recoil velocity in 8-lb. shotgun:** 12.3 ft./sec.

Distance in yards:	Muzzle	20	30	40	50	60	70
Velocity in fps:	1,380	892	753	647	562	490	429
Average pellet energy in ft-lbs:	7.22	3.01	2.15	1.59	1.20	.91	.70
Time of flight in seconds:	0	.0553	.0920	.1351	.1849	.2421	.3076

Type of load: Nontoxic
Three-foot velocity: 1,275 ft./sec.
Hull: 2½-inch plastic
Wad: Fiber
Shot: Bismuth
Buffered: No
Test barrel length: 28 inch
Pellets will pierce skin up to 127 yards.

NO. 4 BISMUTH PELLETS—1⅛ OUNCES—191 PELLETS

Mfg: Bismuth Cartridge Co. **Manufacturer's code:** Sporting Game
Recoil energy in 8-lb. shotgun: 20.4 ft./lbs. **Recoil velocity in 8-lb. shotgun:** 12.8 ft./sec.

Distance in yards:	Muzzle	20	30	40	50	60	70
Velocity in fps:	1,284	897	776	680	602	535	477
Average pellet energy in ft-lbs:	10.33	5.03	3.77	2.90	2.27	1.79	1.43
Time of flight in seconds:	0	.0568	.0928	.1342	.1711	.2340	.2934

Type of load: Nontoxic
Three-foot velocity: 1,220 ft./sec.
Hull: 2¾-inch plastic
Wad: Plastic
Shot: Bismuth
Buffered: No
Test barrel length: 28 inch
Pellets will pierce skin up to 147 yards.

NO. 6 BISMUTH PELLETS—1⅛ OUNCES—304 PELLETS

Mfg: Bismuth Cartridge Co. **Manufacturer's code:** Sporting Game
Recoil energy in 8-lb. shotgun: 20.4 ft./lbs. **Recoil velocity in 8-lb. shotgun:** 12.8 ft./sec.

Distance in yards:	Muzzle	20	30	40	50	60	70
Velocity in fps:	1,296	855	726	625	543	475	415
Average pellet energy in ft-lbs:	6.37	2.77	2.00	1.48	1.12	.85	.65
Time of flight in seconds:	0	.0582	.0964	.1410	.1926	.2517	.3193

Type of load: Nontoxic
Three-foot velocity: 1,200 ft./sec.
Hull: 2¾-inch plastic
Wad: Plastic
Shot: Bismuth
Buffered: No
Test barrel length: 28 inch
Pellets will pierce skin up to 124 yards.

NO. 5 TUNGSTEN-POLYMER PELLETS—1 1/16 OUNCES—168 PELLETS

Mfg: Kent Cartridge America/Canada **Manufacturer's code:** K162UGNT36
Recoil energy in 8-lb. shotgun: 28.6 ft./lbs. **Recoil velocity in 8-lb. shotgun:** 15.2 ft./sec.

Distance in yards:	Muzzle	20	30	40	50	60	70
Velocity in fps:	1,413	960	824	719	634	562	501
Average pellet energy in ft-lbs:	10.64	4.91	3.62	2.76	2.14	1.69	1.34
Time of flight in seconds:	0	.0524	.0863	.1253	.1698	.2201	.2766

Type of load: Nontoxic
Three-foot velocity: 1,315 ft./sec.
Hull: 2¾-inch plastic
Wad: Plastic
Shot: Tungsten-polymer
Buffered: No
Test barrel length: 28 inch
Pellets will pierce skin up to 151 yards.

NO. 5 TUNGSTEN-POLYMER PELLETS—1 1/4 OUNCES—197 PELLETS

Mfg: Kent Cartridge America/Canada **Manufacturer's code:** K162UGNT36
Recoil energy in 8-lb. shotgun: 28.6 ft./lbs. **Recoil velocity in 8-lb. shotgun:** 15.2 ft./sec.

Distance in yards:	Muzzle	20	30	40	50	60	70
Velocity in fps:	1,358	933	804	703	620	551	491
Average pellet energy in ft-lbs:	9.83	4.64	3.45	2.63	2.05	1.62	1.29
Time of flight in seconds:	0	.0542	.0889	.1289	.1744	.2258	.2835

Type of load: Nontoxic
Three-foot velocity: 1,265 ft./sec.
Hull: 2¾-inch plastic
Wad: Plastic
Shot: Tungsten-polymer
Buffered: No
Test barrel length: 28 inch
Pellets will pierce skin up to 149 yards.

NO. 6 TUNGSTEN-POLYMER PELLETS—1 OUNCE—225 PELLETS

Mfg: Kent Cartridge America/Canada **Manufacturer's code:** K162UGNT28
Recoil energy in 8-lb. shotgun: 28.6 ft./lbs. **Recoil velocity in 8-lb. shotgun:** 15.2 ft./sec.

Distance in yards:	Muzzle	20	30	40	50	60	70
Velocity in fps:	1,348	902	771	668	585	515	455
Average pellet energy in ft-lbs:	7.46	3.34	2.44	1.83	1.41	1.09	.85
Time of flight in seconds:	0	.0555	.0916	.1335	.2080	.2362	.2982

Type of load: Nontoxic
Three-foot velocity: 1,250 ft./sec.
Hull: 2¾-inch plastic
Wad: Plastic
Shot: Tungsten-polymer
Buffered: No
Test barrel length: 28 inch
Pellets will pierce skin up to 136 yards.

NO. 6 TUNGSTEN-POLYMER PELLETS—1 1/4 OUNCES—281 PELLETS

Mfg: Kent Cartridge America/Canada **Manufacturer's code:** K162UGNT36
Recoil energy in 8-lb. shotgun: 28.6 ft./lbs. **Recoil velocity in 8-lb. shotgun:** 15.2 ft./sec.

Distance in yards:	Muzzle	20	30	40	50	60	70
Velocity in fps:	1,364	910	776	673	589	519	458
Average pellet energy in ft-lbs:	7.64	3.40	2.48	1.86	1.42	1.10	.86
Time of flight in seconds:	0	.0549	.0907	.1323	.1800	.2344	.2960

Type of load: Nontoxic
Three-foot velocity: 1,265 ft./sec.
Hull: 2¾-inch plastic
Wad: Plastic
Shot: Tungsten-polymer
Buffered: No
Test barrel length: 28 inch
Pellets will pierce skin up to 137 yards.

Hunting geese requires patience and the experience to allow the geese to get well within range before shooting. Although they look farther than they are, these Canada geese are only about 35 yards away and well within shotgun range.

NO. 5 LEAD PELLETS—⅞ OUNCE—149 PELLETS
Mfg: Eley Hawk **Manufacturer's code:** Grand Prix
Recoil energy in 8-lb. shotgun: 13.7 ft./lbs. **Recoil velocity in 8-lb. shotgun:** 10.5 ft./sec.

Distance in yards:	Muzzle	20	30	40	50	60	70
Velocity in fps:	1,341	941	817	718	637	569	510
Average pellet energy in ft-lbs:	10.15	4.99	3.76	2.91	2.29	1.83	1.47
Time of flight in seconds:	0	.0542	.0885	.1278	.1722	.2221	.2778

Type of load: Field
Three-foot velocity: 1,250 ft./sec.
Hull: 2½-inch plastic
Wad: Fiber
Shot: Lead
Buffered: No
Test barrel length: 26 inch
Pellets will pierce skin up to 157 yards.

NO. 5 LEAD PELLETS—¹⁵⁄₁₆ OUNCE—159 PELLETS
Mfg: Baschieri & Pellagri **Manufacturer's code:** High Pheasant
Recoil energy in 8-lb. shotgun: 21.1 ft./lbs. **Recoil velocity in 8-lb. shotgun:** 13.0 ft./sec.

Distance in yards:	Muzzle	20	30	40	50	60	70
Velocity in fps:	1,429	985	851	745	660	588	527
Average pellet energy in ft-lbs:	11.53	5.47	4.08	3.13	2.46	1.95	1.57
Time of flight in seconds:	0	.0514	.0842	.1220	.1648	.2130	.2669

Type of load: Field
Three-foot velocity: 1,320 ft./sec.
Hull: 2½-inch plastic
Wad: Plastic
Shot: Lead
Buffered: No
Test barrel length: 26 inch
Pellets will pierce skin up to 160 yards.

NO. 5 LEAD PELLETS—1 OUNCE—170 PELLETS
Mfg: Eley Hawk **Manufacturer's code:** VIP Game
Recoil energy in 8-lb. shotgun: 18.9 ft./lbs. **Recoil velocity in 8-lb. shotgun:** 12.3 ft./sec.

Distance in yards:	Muzzle	20	30	40	50	60	70
Velocity in fps:	1,369	955	827	727	644	575	515
Average pellet energy in ft-lbs:	10.57	5.14	3.86	2.98	2.34	1.87	1.50
Time of flight in seconds:	0	.0533	.0871	.1259	.1698	.2191	.2743

Type of load: Field
Three-foot velocity: 1,275 ft./sec.
Hull: 2½-inch plastic
Wad: Photo-degradable plastic
Shot: Lead
Buffered: No
Test barrel length: 26 inch
Pellets will pierce skin up to 158 yards.

NO. 5 LEAD PELLETS—1 OUNCE—170 PELLETS
Mfg: Eley Hawk **Manufacturer's code:** VIP Game
Recoil energy in 8-lb. shotgun: 18.9 ft./lbs. **Recoil velocity in 8-lb. shotgun:** 12.3 ft./sec.

Distance in yards:	Muzzle	20	30	40	50	60	70
Velocity in fps:	1,369	955	827	727	644	575	515
Average pellet energy in ft-lbs:	10.57	5.14	3.86	2.98	2.34	1.87	1.50
Time of flight in seconds:	0	.0533	.0871	.1259	.1698	.2191	.2743

Type of load: Field
Three-foot velocity: 1,275 ft./sec.
Hull: 2½-inch plastic
Wad: Fiber
Shot: Lead
Buffered: No
Test barrel length: 26 inch
Pellets will pierce skin up to 158 yards.

NO. 6 LEAD PELLETS—¹³⁄₁₆ OUNCE—182 PELLETS
Mfg: Eley Hawk **Manufacturer's code:** Classic Game
Recoil energy in 8-lb. shotgun: 13.7 ft./lbs. **Recoil velocity in 8-lb. shotgun:** 10.5 ft./sec.

Distance in yards:	Muzzle	20	30	40	50	60	70
Velocity in fps:	1,348	919	790	689	606	537	477
Average pellet energy in ft-lbs:	7.89	3.67	2.71	2.06	1.60	1.25	.99
Time of flight in seconds:	0	.0549	.0902	.1309	.1774	.2300	.2893

Type of load: Field
Three-foot velocity: 1,250 ft./sec.
Hull: 2½-inch plastic
Wad: Fiber
Shot: Copper-plated lead
Buffered: No
Test barrel length: 26 inch
Pellets will pierce skin up to 144 yards.

NO. 6 LEAD PELLETS—⅞ OUNCE—197 PELLETS
Mfg: RST, Ltd. **Manufacturer's code:** N/A
Recoil energy in 8-lb. shotgun: 12.3 ft./lbs. **Recoil velocity in 8-lb. shotgun:** 10.0 ft./sec.

Distance in yards:	Muzzle	20	30	40	50	60	70
Velocity in fps:	1,292	892	769	672	593	525	467
Average pellet energy in ft-lbs:	7.26	3.46	2.57	1.96	1.53	1.20	.095
Time of flight in seconds:	0	.0568	.0931	.01349	.1825	.2363	.2969

Type of load: Target
Three-foot velocity: 1,200 ft./sec.
Hull: 2½-inch plastic
Wad: Plastic
Shot: Lead
Buffered: No
Test barrel length: 26 inch
Pellets will pierce skin up to 157 yards.

NO. 6 LEAD PELLETS—⅞ OUNCE—197 PELLETS
Mfg: Eley Hawk **Manufacturer's code:** Grand Prix
Recoil energy in 8-lb. shotgun: 13.7 ft./lbs. **Recoil velocity in 8-lb. shotgun:** 10.5 ft./sec.

Distance in yards:	Muzzle	20	30	40	50	60	70
Velocity in fps:	1,348	919	790	689	606	537	477
Average pellet energy in ft-lbs:	7.89	3.67	2.71	2.06	1.60	1.25	.99
Time of flight in seconds:	0	.0549	.0902	.1309	.1774	.2300	.2893

Type of load: Field
Three-foot velocity: 1,250 ft./sec.
Hull: 2½-inch plastic
Wad: Fiber
Shot: Lead
Buffered: No
Test barrel length: 26 inch
Pellets will pierce skin up to 144 yards.

NO. 6 LEAD PELLETS—⅞ OUNCE—197 PELLETS
Mfg: Fiocchi **Manufacturer's code:** 20PL1
Recoil energy in 8-lb. shotgun: 15.2 ft./lbs. **Recoil velocity in 8-lb. shotgun:** 11.1 ft./sec.

Distance in yards:	Muzzle	20	30	40	50	60	70
Velocity in fps:	1,403	945	810	705	620	548	487
Average pellet energy in ft-lbs:	8.55	3.88	2.85	2.16	1.67	1.31	1.03
Time of flight in seconds:	0	.0531	.0875	.1272	.1727	.2242	.2723

Type of load: Game & Target
Three-foot velocity: 1,300 ft./sec.
Hull: 2½-inch plastic
Wad: Plastic
Shot: Lead
Buffered: No
Test barrel length: 26 inch
Pellets will pierce skin up to 146 yards.

NO. 6 LEAD PELLETS—¹⁵/₁₆ OUNCE—210 PELLETS
Mfg: Baschieri & Pellagri **Manufacturer's code:** High Pheasant
Recoil energy in 8-lb. shotgun: 21.1 ft./lbs. **Recoil velocity in 8-lb. shotgun:** 13.0 ft./sec.

Distance in yards:	Muzzle	20	30	40	50	60	70
Velocity in fps:	1,436	961	822	714	627	555	493
Average pellet energy in ft-lbs:	8.96	4.01	2.94	2.22	1.71	1.34	1.06
Time of flight in seconds:	0	.0520	.0859	.1251	.1700	.2209	.2782

Type of load: Field
Three-foot velocity: 1,320 ft./sec.
Hull: 2½-inch plastic
Wad: Plastic
Shot: Lead
Buffered: No
Test barrel length: 26 inch
Pellets will pierce skin up to 147 yards.

NO. 6 LEAD PELLETS—1 OUNCE—225 PELLETS
Mfg: Eley Hawk **Manufacturer's code:** VIP Game
Recoil energy in 8-lb. shotgun: 18.9 ft./lbs. **Recoil velocity in 8-lb. shotgun:** 12.3 ft./sec.

Distance in yards:	Muzzle	20	30	40	50	60	70
Velocity in fps:	1,375	932	800	697	613	543	482
Average pellet energy in ft-lbs:	8.22	3.77	2.78	2.11	1.63	1.28	1.01
Time of flight in seconds:	0	.0540	.0888	.1290	.1750	.2271	.2858

Type of load: Field
Three-foot velocity: 1,275 ft./sec.
Hull: 2½-inch plastic
Wad: Photo-degradable plastic
Shot: Lead
Buffered: No
Test barrel length: 26 inch
Pellets will pierce skin up to 145 yards.

NO. 6 LEAD PELLETS—1 OUNCE—225 PELLETS
Mfg: Eley Hawk **Manufacturer's code:** VIP Game
Recoil energy in 8-lb. shotgun: 18.9 ft./lbs. **Recoil velocity in 8-lb. shotgun:** 12.3 ft./sec.

Distance in yards:	Muzzle	20	30	40	50	60	70
Velocity in fps:	1,375	932	800	697	613	543	482
Average pellet energy in ft-lbs:	8.22	3.77	2.78	2.11	1.63	1.28	1.01
Time of flight in seconds:	0	.0540	.0888	.1290	.1750	.2271	.2858

Type of load: Field
Three-foot velocity: 1,275 ft./sec.
Hull: 2½-inch plastic
Wad: Fiber
Shot: Lead
Buffered: No
Test barrel length: 26 inch
Pellets will pierce skin up to 145 yards.

NO. 7 LEAD PELLETS—⅞ OUNCE—262 PELLETS
Mfg: Eley Hawk **Manufacturer's code:** Grand Prix
Recoil energy in 8-lb. shotgun: 13.7 ft./lbs. **Recoil velocity in 8-lb. shotgun:** 10.5 ft./sec.

Distance in yards:	Muzzle	20	30	40	50	60	70
Velocity in fps:	1,357	878	742	637	553	482	421
Average pellet energy in ft-lbs:	5.16	2.16	1.54	1.14	.86	.65	.50
Time of flight in seconds:	0	.0562	.0935	.1372	.1878	.2459	.3126

Type of load: Field
Three-foot velocity: 1,250 ft./sec.
Hull: 2½-inch plastic
Wad: Fiber
Shot: Lead
Buffered: No
Test barrel length: 26 inch
Pellets will pierce skin up to 125 yards.

NO. 7 LEAD PELLETS—¹⁵/₁₆ OUNCE—280 PELLETS
Mfg: Baschieri & Pellagri **Manufacturer's code:** High Pheasant
Recoil energy in 8-lb. shotgun: 21.1 ft./lbs. **Recoil velocity in 8-lb. shotgun:** 13.0 ft./sec.

Distance in yards:	Muzzle	20	30	40	50	60	70
Velocity in fps:	1,443	933	789	679	591	518	455
Average pellet energy in ft-lbs:	6.80	2.84	2.03	1.51	1.14	.88	.68
Time of flight in seconds:	0	.0529	.0879	.1290	.1764	.2306	.2925

Type of load: Field
Three-foot velocity: 1,320 ft./sec.
Hull: 2½-inch plastic
Wad: Plastic
Shot: Lead
Buffered: No
Test barrel length: 26 inch
Pellets will pierce skin up to 134 yards.

NO. 7½ LEAD PELLETS—⅞ OUNCE—306 PELLETS
Mfg: RST, Ltd. **Manufacturer's code:** N/A
Recoil energy in 8-lb. shotgun: 12.3 ft./lbs. **Recoil velocity in 8-lb. shotgun:** 10.0 ft./sec.

Distance in yards:	Muzzle	20	30	40	50	60	70
Velocity in fps:	1,302	854	724	623	541	472	412
Average pellet energy in ft-lbs:	4.74	2.04	1.47	1.09	.82	.62	.47
Time of flight in seconds:	0	.0581	.0964	.1412	.1930	.2524	.3204

Type of load: Target
Three-foot velocity: 1,200 ft./sec.
Hull: 2½-inch plastic
Wad: Plastic
Shot: Lead
Buffered: No
Test barrel length: 26 inch
Pellets will pierce skin up to 136 yards.

NO. 8 LEAD PELLETS—⁷⁄₈ OUNCE—359 PELLETS

Mfg: RST, Ltd. **Manufacturer's code:** N/A
Recoil energy in 8-lb. shotgun: 12.3 ft./lbs. **Recoil velocity in 8-lb. shotgun:** 10.0 ft./sec.

Distance in yards:	Muzzle	20	30	40	50	60	70
Velocity in fps:	1,305	839	706	604	521	452	391
Average pellet energy in ft-lbs:	4.05	1.67	1.19	.87	.65	.49	.36
Time of flight in seconds:	0	.0587	.0978	.1438	.1973	.2593	.3307

Type of load: Target
Three-foot velocity: 1,200 ft./sec.
Hull: 2½-inch plastic
Wad: Plastic
Shot: Lead
Buffered: No
Test barrel length: 26 inch
Pellets will pierce skin up to 129 yards.

NO. 8 LEAD PELLETS—⁷⁄₈ OUNCE—359 PELLETS

Mfg: Fiocchi **Manufacturer's code:** 20PL1
Recoil energy in 8-lb. shotgun: 15.2 ft./lbs. **Recoil velocity in 8-lb. shotgun:** 11.1 ft./sec.

Distance in yards:	Muzzle	20	30	40	50	60	70
Velocity in fps:	1,417	886	742	632	544	471	408
Average pellet energy in ft-lbs:	4.78	1.87	1.31	.95	.70	.53	.40
Time of flight in seconds:	0	.0549	.0921	.1360	.1873	.2466	.3150

Type of load: Game & Target
Three-foot velocity: 1,300 ft./sec.
Hull: 2½-inch plastic
Wad: Plastic
Shot: Lead
Buffered: No
Test barrel length: 26 inch
Pellets will pierce skin up to 132 yards.

NO. 9 LEAD PELLETS—⁷⁄₈ OUNCE—512 PELLETS

Mfg: RST, Ltd. **Manufacturer's code:** N/A
Recoil energy in 8-lb. shotgun: 12.3 ft./lbs. **Recoil velocity in 8-lb. shotgun:** 10.0 ft./sec.

Distance in yards:	Muzzle	20	30	40	50	60	70
Velocity in fps:	1,312	805	667	562	478	407	346
Average pellet energy in ft-lbs:	2.88	1.08	.74	.53	.38	.28	.20
Time of flight in seconds:	0	.0601	.1011	.1502	.2082	.2763	.3562

Type of load: Target
Three-foot velocity: 1,200 ft./sec.
Hull: 2½-inch plastic
Wad: Plastic
Shot: Lead
Buffered: No
Test barrel length: 26 inch
Pellets will pierce skin up to 115 yards.

Hunting ducks over flooded grain fields often calls for shots at the edge of practical shotgun range, which is about 40 yards. Although some claim long-range kills, most have no idea of the actual range, which, when accurately measured, normally falls within 40 yards.

NO. BB LEAD PELLETS—⅞ OUNCE—44 PELLETS
Mfg: Armscor **Manufacturer's code:** N/A
Recoil energy in 8-lb. shotgun: 12.6 ft./lbs. **Recoil velocity in 8-lb. shotgun:** 10.1 ft./sec.

Distance in yards:	Muzzle	20	30	40	50	60	70
Velocity in fps:	1,255	991	897	817	749	690	638
Average pellet energy in ft-lbs:	30.00	18.72	15.31	12.72	10.69	9.06	7.74
Time of flight in seconds:	0	.0542	.0860	.1211	.1594	.2012	.2464

Type of load: Field
Three-foot velocity: 1,210 ft./sec.
Hull: 2¾-inch plastic
Wad: Plastic
Shot: Lead
Buffered: No
Test barrel length: 26 inch
Pellets will pierce skin up to 231 yards.

NO. 2 LEAD PELLETS—1 OUNCE—87 PELLETS
Mfg: Aguila **Manufacturer's code:** N/A
Recoil energy in 8-lb. shotgun: 11.8 ft./lbs. **Recoil velocity in 8-lb. shotgun:** 11.8 ft./sec.

Distance in yards:	Muzzle	20	30	40	50	60	70
Velocity in fps:	1,308	982	872	783	707	643	587
Average pellet energy in ft-lbs:	18.85	10.62	9.38	6.75	5.51	4.55	3.79
Time of flight in seconds:	0	.0535	.0860	.1223	.1627	.2072	.2561

Type of load: Field
Three-foot velocity: 1,235 ft./sec.
Hull: 2¾-inch plastic
Wad: Plastic
Shot: Lead
Buffered: No
Test barrel length: 26 inch
Pellets will pierce skin up to 195 yards.

NO. 2 LEAD PELLETS—1 OUNCE—87 PELLETS
Mfg: ARMUSA **Manufacturer's code:** PLA-1
Recoil energy in 8-lb. shotgun: 18.9 ft./lbs. **Recoil velocity in 8-lb. shotgun:** 12.3 ft./sec.

Distance in yards:	Muzzle	20	30	40	50	60	70
Velocity in fps:	1,351	1,006	892	799	721	655	597
Average pellet energy in ft-lbs:	20.12	11.16	8.76	7.03	5.73	4.72	3.93
Time of flight in seconds:	0	.0520	.0837	.1193	.1589	.2026	.2506

Type of load: Field
Three-foot velocity: 1,275 ft./sec.
Hull: 2¾-inch plastic
Wad: Plastic
Shot: Lead
Buffered: No
Test barrel length: 26 inch
Pellets will pierce skin up to 197 yards.

NO. 2 LEAD PELLETS—1 OUNCE—87 PELLETS
Mfg: Clever **Manufacturer's code:** T1 Light Game
Recoil energy in 8-lb. shotgun: 19.9 ft./lbs. **Recoil velocity in 8-lb. shotgun:** 12.6 ft./sec.

Distance in yards:	Muzzle	20	30	40	50	60	70
Velocity in fps:	1,378	1,022	904	809	730	662	604
Average pellet energy in ft-lbs:	20.93	11.50	9.00	7.21	5.87	4.83	4.01
Time of flight in seconds:	0	.0511	.0824	.1175	.1566	.1988	.2473

Type of load: Field
Three-foot velocity: 1,300 ft./sec.
Hull: 2¾-inch plastic
Wad: Plastic
Shot: Lead
Buffered: No
Test barrel length: 26 inch
Pellets will pierce skin up to 198 yards.

NO. 4 LEAD PELLETS—⅞ OUNCE—118 PELLETS
Mfg: Aguila **Manufacturer's code:** N/A
Recoil energy in 8-lb. shotgun: 11.0 ft./lbs. **Recoil velocity in 8-lb. shotgun:** 9.4 ft./sec.

Distance in yards:	Muzzle	20	30	40	50	60	70
Velocity in fps:	1,227	901	794	706	633	570	515
Average pellet energy in ft-lbs:	10.79	5.83	4.52	3.58	2.87	2.33	1.90
Time of flight in seconds:	0	.0577	.0933	.1334	.1783	.2283	.2837

Type of load: Field
Three-foot velocity: 1,150 ft./sec.
Hull: 2¾-inch plastic
Wad: Plastic
Shot: Lead
Buffered: No
Test barrel length: 26 inch
Pellets will pierce skin up to 166 yards.

NO. 4 LEAD PELLETS—⅞ OUNCE—118 PELLETS
Mfg: Estate Cartridge **Manufacturer's code:** DQ20
Recoil energy in 8-lb. shotgun: 12.3 ft./lbs. **Recoil velocity in 8-lb. shotgun:** 10.0 ft./sec.

Distance in yards:	Muzzle	20	30	40	50	60	70
Velocity in fps:	1,281	931	817	725	649	584	528
Average pellet energy in ft-lbs:	11.77	6.21	4.79	3.77	3.02	2.45	2.00
Time of flight in seconds:	0	.0556	.0901	.01291	.1729	.2216	.2757

Type of load: Field
Three-foot velocity: 1,200 ft./sec.
Hull: 2¾-inch plastic
Wad: Plastic
Shot: Hard lead
Buffered: No
Test barrel length: 26 inch
Pellets will pierce skin up to 168 yards.

NO. 4 LEAD PELLETS—1 OUNCE—135 PELLETS
Mfg: Estate Cartridge **Manufacturer's code:** HG20
Recoil energy in 8-lb. shotgun: 18.9 ft./lbs. **Recoil velocity in 8-lb. shotgun:** 12.3 ft./sec.

Distance in yards:	Muzzle	20	30	40	50	60	70
Velocity in fps:	1,254	916	806	716	641	577	522
Average pellet energy in ft-lbs:	11.27	6.02	4.65	3.68	2.95	2.39	1.95
Time of flight in seconds:	0	.0567	.0916	.1312	.1755	.2249	.2796

Type of load: Field
Three-foot velocity: 1,175 ft./sec.5
Hull: 2¾-inch plastic
Wad: Plastic
Shot: Hard lead
Buffered: No
Test barrel length: 26 inch
Pellets will pierce skin up to 167 yards.

NO. 4 LEAD PELLETS—1 OUNCE—135 PELLETS
Mfg: Dionisi **Manufacturer's code:** D 20 SLR
Recoil energy in 8-lb. shotgun: 16.8 ft./lbs. **Recoil velocity in 8-lb. shotgun:** 11.6 ft./sec.

Distance in yards:	Muzzle	20	30	40	50	60	70
Velocity in fps:	1,303	943	826	733	655	590	532
Average pellet energy in ft-lbs:	12.17	6.37	4.90	3.85	3.08	2.49	2.03
Time of flight in seconds:	0	.0548	.0889	.1275	.1708	.2191	.2727

Type of load: Field
Three-foot velocity: 1,220 ft./sec.
Hull: 2¾-inch plastic
Wad: Plastic
Shot: Lead
Buffered: No
Test barrel length: 26 inch
Pellets will pierce skin up to 169 yards.

NO. 4 LEAD PELLETS—1 OUNCE—135 PELLETS
Mfg: Estate Cartridge **Manufacturer's code:** HV20
Recoil energy in 8-lb. shotgun: 16.8 ft./lbs. **Recoil velocity in 8-lb. shotgun:** 11.6 ft./sec.

Distance in yards:	Muzzle	20	30	40	50	60	70
Velocity in fps:	1,303	943	826	733	655	590	532
Average pellet energy in ft-lbs:	12.17	6.37	4.90	3.85	3.08	2.49	2.03
Time of flight in seconds:	0	.0548	.0889	.1275	.1708	.2191	.2727

Type of load: Field
Three-foot velocity: 1,220 ft./sec.
Hull: 2¾-inch plastic
Wad: Plastic
Shot: Hard lead
Buffered: No
Test barrel length: 26 inch
Pellets will pierce skin up to 169 yards.

NO. 4 LEAD PELLETS—1 OUNCE—135 PELLETS
Mfg: Federal Cartridge Co. **Manufacturer's code:** H204
Recoil energy in 8-lb. shotgun: 16.8 ft./lbs. **Recoil velocity in 8-lb. shotgun:** 11.6 ft./sec.

Distance in yards:	Muzzle	20	30	40	50	60	70
Velocity in fps:	1,303	943	826	733	655	590	532
Average pellet energy in ft-lbs:	12.17	6.37	4.90	3.85	3.08	2.49	2.03
Time of flight in seconds:	0	.0548	.0889	.1275	.1708	.2191	.2727

Type of load: Field
Three-foot velocity: 1,220 ft./sec.
Hull: 2¾-inch plastic
Wad: Plastic
Shot: Lead
Buffered: No
Test barrel length: 26 inch
Pellets will pierce skin up to 169 yards.

NO. 4 LEAD PELLETS—1 OUNCE—135 PELLETS
Mfg: Fiocchi **Manufacturer's code:** 20HV
Recoil energy in 8-lb. shotgun: 16.8 ft./lbs. **Recoil velocity in 8-lb. shotgun:** 11.6 ft./sec.

Distance in yards:	Muzzle	20	30	40	50	60	70
Velocity in fps:	1,303	943	826	733	655	590	532
Average pellet energy in ft-lbs:	12.17	6.37	4.90	3.85	3.08	2.49	2.03
Time of flight in seconds:	0	.0548	.0889	.1275	.1708	.2191	.2727

Type of load: Field
Three-foot velocity: 1,220 ft./sec.
Hull: 2¾-inch plastic
Wad: Plastic
Shot: Lead
Buffered: No
Test barrel length: 26 inch
Pellets will pierce skin up to 169 yards.

NO. 4 LEAD PELLETS—1 OUNCE—135 PELLETS
Mfg: Remington Arms Co. **Manufacturer's code:** SP20/HGL20
Recoil energy in 8-lb. shotgun: 16.8 ft./lbs. **Recoil velocity in 8-lb. shotgun:** 11.6 ft./sec.

Distance in yards:	Muzzle	20	30	40	50	60	70
Velocity in fps:	1,303	943	826	733	655	590	532
Average pellet energy in ft-lbs:	12.17	6.37	4.90	3.85	3.08	2.49	2.03
Time of flight in seconds:	0	.0548	.0889	.1275	.1708	.2191	.2727

Type of load: Field
Three-foot velocity: 1,220 ft./sec.
Hull: 2¾-inch plastic
Wad: Plastic
Shot: Lead
Buffered: No
Test barrel length: 26 inch
Pellets will pierce skin up to 169 yards.

NO. 4 LEAD PELLETS—1 OUNCE—136 PELLETS
Mfg: Aguila **Manufacturer's code:** N/A
Recoil energy in 8-lb. shotgun: 11.8 ft./lbs. **Recoil velocity in 8-lb. shotgun:** 11.8 ft./sec.

Distance in yards:	Muzzle	20	30	40	50	60	70
Velocity in fps:	1,319	951	833	739	660	594	536
Average pellet energy in ft-lbs:	12.48	6.49	4.98	3.91	3.13	2.53	2.06
Time of flight in seconds:	0	.0543	.0880	.1263	.1693	.2173	.2705

Type of load: Field
Three-foot velocity: 1,235 ft./sec.
Hull: 2¾-inch plastic
Wad: Plastic
Shot: Lead
Buffered: No
Test barrel length: 26 inch
Pellets will pierce skin up to 169 yards.

NO. 4 LEAD PELLETS—1 OUNCE—135 PELLETS
Mfg: ARMUSA **Manufacturer's code:** PLA-1
Recoil energy in 8-lb. shotgun: 18.9 ft./lbs. **Recoil velocity in 8-lb. shotgun:** 12.3 ft./sec.

Distance in yards:	Muzzle	20	30	40	50	60	70
Velocity in fps:	1,363	1,049	851	753	672	604	545
Average pellet energy in ft-lbs:	13.32	6.81	5.20	4.07	3.24	2.62	2.13
Time of flight in seconds:	0	.0528	.0858	.1233	.1655	.2126	.2649

Type of load: Field
Three-foot velocity: 1,275 ft./sec.
Hull: 2¾-inch plastic
Wad: Plastic
Shot: Lead
Buffered: No
Test barrel length: 26 inch
Pellets will pierce skin up to 171 yards.

NO. 4 LEAD PELLETS—1 OUNCE—135 PELLETS

Mfg: Clever **Manufacturer's code:** T1 Light Game
Recoil energy in 8-lb. shotgun: 19.9 ft./lbs. **Recoil velocity in 8-lb. shotgun:** 12.6 ft./sec.

Distance in yards:	Muzzle	20	30	40	50	60	70
Velocity in fps:	1,390	989	863	762	680	611	551
Average pellet energy in ft-lbs:	13.86	7.01	5.34	4.17	3.32	2.67	2.18
Time of flight in seconds:	0	.0519	.0844	.1215	.1632	.2098	.2615

Type of load: Field
Three-foot velocity: 1,300 ft./sec.
Hull: 2¾-inch plastic
Wad: Plastic
Shot: Lead
Buffered: No
Test barrel length: 26 inch
Pellets will pierce skin up to 172 yards.

NO. 4 LEAD PELLETS—1 OUNCE—135 PELLETS

Mfg: Remington Arms Co. **Manufacturer's code:** SPHV20
Recoil energy in 8-lb. shotgun: 19.9 ft./lbs. **Recoil velocity in 8-lb. shotgun:** 12.6 ft./sec.

Distance in yards:	Muzzle	20	30	40	50	60	70
Velocity in fps:	1,390	989	863	762	680	611	551
Average pellet energy in ft-lbs:	13.86	7.01	5.34	4.17	3.32	2.67	2.18
Time of flight in seconds:	0	.0519	.0844	.1215	.1632	.2098	.2615

Type of load: Field
Three-foot velocity: 1,300 ft./sec.
Hull: 2¾-inch plastic
Wad: Plastic
Shot: Lead
Buffered: No
Test barrel length: 26 inch
Pellets will pierce skin up to 172 yards.

NO. 4 LEAD PELLETS—1 OUNCE—135 PELLETS

Mfg: Winchester **Manufacturer's code:** SFH20
Recoil energy in 8-lb. shotgun: 19.9 ft./lbs. **Recoil velocity in 8-lb. shotgun:** 12.6 ft./sec.

Distance in yards:	Muzzle	20	30	40	50	60	70
Velocity in fps:	1,390	989	863	762	680	611	551
Average pellet energy in ft-lbs:	13.86	7.01	5.34	4.17	3.32	2.67	2.18
Time of flight in seconds:	0	.0519	.0844	.1215	.1632	.2098	.2615

Type of load: Field
Three-foot velocity: 1,300 ft./sec.
Hull: 2¾-inch plastic
Wad: Plastic
Shot: Copper-plated lead
Buffered: Yes
Test barrel length: 26 inch
Pellets will pierce skin up to 172 yards.

NO. 4 LEAD PELLETS—1⅛ OUNCES—152 PELLETS

Mfg: Federal Cartridge Co. **Manufacturer's code:** P256/F205/H203
Recoil energy in 8-lb. shotgun: 23.8 ft./lbs. **Recoil velocity in 8-lb. shotgun:** 13.8 ft./sec.

Distance in yards:	Muzzle	20	30	40	50	60	70
Velocity in fps:	1,254	916	806	716	641	577	522
Average pellet energy in ft-lbs:	11.27	6.02	4.65	3.68	2.95	2.39	1.95
Time of flight in seconds:	0	.0567	.0916	.1312	.1755	.2249	.2796

Type of load: Field
Three-foot velocity: 1,175 ft./sec.
Hull: 2¾-inch plastic
Wad: Plastic
Shot: Copper-plated lead/lead
Buffered: Yes
Test barrel length: 26 inch
Pellets will pierce skin up to 167 yards.

NO. 4 LEAD PELLETS—1⅛ OUNCES—152 PELLETS

Mfg: Remington Arms Co. **Manufacturer's code:** NM20S
Recoil energy in 8-lb. shotgun: 23.8 ft./lbs. **Recoil velocity in 8-lb. shotgun:** 13.8 ft./sec.

Distance in yards:	Muzzle	20	30	40	50	60	70
Velocity in fps:	1,254	916	806	716	641	577	522
Average pellet energy in ft-lbs:	11.27	6.02	4.65	3.68	2.95	2.39	1.95
Time of flight in seconds:	0	.0567	.0916	.1312	.1755	.2249	.2796

Type of load: Field
Three-foot velocity: 1,175 ft./sec.
Hull: 2¾-inch plastic
Wad: Plastic
Shot: Lead
Buffered: Yes
Test barrel length: 26 inch
Pellets will pierce skin up to 167 yards.

NO. 4 LEAD PELLETS—1⅛ OUNCES—152 PELLETS

Mfg: Estate Cartridge **Manufacturer's code:** HV20SMAG
Recoil energy in 8-lb. shotgun: 31.1 ft./lbs. **Recoil velocity in 8-lb. shotgun:** 15.8 ft./sec.

Distance in yards:	Muzzle	20	30	40	50	60	70
Velocity in fps:	1,336	960	840	744	665	598	540
Average pellet energy in ft-lbs:	12.79	6.61	5.06	3.97	3.17	2.56	2.09
Time of flight in seconds:	0	.0537	.0872	.1252	.1679	.2155	.2684

Type of load: Field
Three-foot velocity: 1,250 ft./sec.
Hull: 2¾-inch plastic
Wad: Plastic
Shot: Hard lead
Buffered: Yes
Test barrel length: 26 inch
Pellets will pierce skin up to 170 yards.

NO. 5 LEAD PELLETS—1 OUNCE—170 PELLETS

Mfg: Dionisi **Manufacturer's code:** D 20 SLR
Recoil energy in 8-lb. shotgun: 16.8 ft./lbs. **Recoil velocity in 8-lb. shotgun:** 11.6 ft./sec.

Distance in yards:	Muzzle	20	30	40	50	60	70
Velocity in fps:	1,309	924	804	707	628	561	503
Average pellet energy in ft-lbs:	9.66	4.82	3.64	2.82	2.23	1.78	1.43
Time of flight in seconds:	0	.0554	.0903	.1301	.1752	.2257	.2822

Type of load: Field
Three-foot velocity: 1,220 ft./sec.
Hull: 2¾-inch plastic
Wad: Plastic
Shot: Lead
Buffered: No
Test barrel length: 26 inch
Pellets will pierce skin up to 156 yards.

NO. 5 LEAD PELLETS—1 OUNCE—170 PELLETS
Mfg: Federal Cartridge Co. **Manufacturer's code:** H204
Recoil energy in 8-lb. shotgun: 16.8 ft./lbs. **Recoil velocity in 8-lb. shotgun:** 11.6 ft./sec.

Distance in yards:	Muzzle	20	30	40	50	60	70
Velocity in fps:	1,309	924	804	707	628	561	503
Average pellet energy in ft-lbs:	9.66	4.82	3.64	2.82	2.23	1.78	1.43
Time of flight in seconds:	0	.0554	.0903	.1301	.1752	.2257	.2822

Type of load: Field
Three-foot velocity: 1,220 ft./sec.
Hull: 2¾-inch plastic
Wad: Plastic
Shot: Lead
Buffered: No
Test barrel length: 26 inch
Pellets will pierce skin up to 156 yards.

NO. 5 LEAD PELLETS—1 OUNCE—170 PELLETS
Mfg: Fiocchi **Manufacturer's code:** 20HV
Recoil energy in 8-lb. shotgun: 16.8 ft./lbs. **Recoil velocity in 8-lb. shotgun:** 11.6 ft./sec.

Distance in yards:	Muzzle	20	30	40	50	60	70
Velocity in fps:	1,309	924	804	707	628	561	503
Average pellet energy in ft-lbs:	9.66	4.82	3.64	2.82	2.23	1.78	1.43
Time of flight in seconds:	0	.0554	.0903	.1301	.1752	.2257	.2822

Type of load: Field
Three-foot velocity: 1,220 ft./sec.
Hull: 2¾-inch plastic
Wad: Plastic
Shot: Lead
Buffered: No
Test barrel length: 26 inch
Pellets will pierce skin up to 156 yards.

NO. 5 LEAD PELLETS—1 OUNCE—170 PELLETS
Mfg: Remington Arms Co. **Manufacturer's code:** SP20
Recoil energy in 8-lb. shotgun: 16.8 ft./lbs. **Recoil velocity in 8-lb. shotgun:** 11.6 ft./sec.

Distance in yards:	Muzzle	20	30	40	50	60	70
Velocity in fps:	1,309	924	804	707	628	561	503
Average pellet energy in ft-lbs:	9.66	4.82	3.64	2.82	2.23	1.78	1.43
Time of flight in seconds:	0	.0554	.0903	.1301	.1752	.2257	.2822

Type of load: Field
Three-foot velocity: 1,220 ft./sec.
Hull: 2¾-inch plastic
Wad: Plastic
Shot: Lead
Buffered: No
Test barrel length: 26 inch
Pellets will pierce skin up to 156 yards.

NO. 5 LEAD PELLETS—1 OUNCE—170 PELLETS
Mfg: Winchester **Manufacturer's code:** X20
Recoil energy in 8-lb. shotgun: 16.8 ft./lbs. **Recoil velocity in 8-lb. shotgun:** 11.6 ft./sec.

Distance in yards:	Muzzle	20	30	40	50	60	70
Velocity in fps:	1,309	924	804	707	628	561	503
Average pellet energy in ft-lbs:	9.66	4.82	3.64	2.82	2.23	1.78	1.43
Time of flight in seconds:	0	.0554	.0903	.1301	.1752	.2257	.2822

Type of load: Field
Three-foot velocity: 1,220 ft./sec.
Hull: 2¾-inch plastic
Wad: Plastic
Shot: Lead
Buffered: No
Test barrel length: 26 inch
Pellets will pierce skin up to 156 yards.

NO. 5 LEAD PELLETS—1 OUNCE—170 PELLETS
Mfg: Clever **Manufacturer's code:** T1 Light Game
Recoil energy in 8-lb. shotgun: 19.9 ft./lbs. **Recoil velocity in 8-lb. shotgun:** 12.6 ft./sec.

Distance in yards:	Muzzle	20	30	40	50	60	70
Velocity in fps:	1,396	969	838	735	651	581	521
Average pellet energy in ft-lbs:	11.00	5.29	3.96	3.05	2.39	1.90	1.53
Time of flight in seconds:	0	.0524	.0858	.1241	.1675	.2163	.2708

Type of load: Field
Three-foot velocity: 1,300 ft./sec.
Hull: 2¾-inch plastic
Wad: Plastic
Shot: Lead
Buffered: No
Test barrel length: 26 inch
Pellets will pierce skin up to 159 yards.

NO. 5 LEAD PELLETS—1¹⁄₁₆ OUNCES—181 PELLETS
Mfg: Eley Hawk **Manufacturer's code:** VIP Game
Recoil energy in 8-lb. shotgun: 18.9 ft./lbs. **Recoil velocity in 8-lb. shotgun:** 12.3 ft./sec.

Distance in yards:	Muzzle	20	30	40	50	60	70
Velocity in fps:	1,309	924	804	707	628	561	503
Average pellet energy in ft-lbs:	9.66	4.82	3.64	2.82	2.23	1.78	1.43
Time of flight in seconds:	0	.0554	.0903	.1301	.1752	.2257	.2822

Type of load: Field
Three-foot velocity: 1,225 ft./sec.
Hull: 2¾-inch plastic
Wad: Plastic
Shot: Lead
Buffered: No
Test barrel length: 26 inch
Pellets will pierce skin up to 156 yards.

NO. 6 LEAD PELLETS—⁷⁄₈ OUNCE—197 PELLETS
Mfg: Aguila **Manufacturer's code:** N/A
Recoil energy in 8-lb. shotgun: 11.0 ft./lbs. **Recoil velocity in 8-lb. shotgun:** 9.4 ft./sec.

Distance in yards:	Muzzle	20	30	40	50	60	70
Velocity in fps:	1,237	865	748	655	578	513	456
Average pellet energy in ft-lbs:	6.65	3.25	2.43	1.86	1.45	1.14	.90
Time of flight in seconds:	0	.0589	.0963	.1392	.1880	.2431	.3051

Type of load: Field
Three-foot velocity: 1,150 ft./sec.
Hull: 2¾-inch plastic
Wad: Plastic
Shot: Lead
Buffered: No
Test barrel length: 26 inch
Pellets will pierce skin up to 140 yards.

NO. 6 LEAD PELLETS—⅞ OUNCE—197 PELLETS
Mfg: Estate Cartridge **Manufacturer's code:** DQ20
Recoil energy in 8-lb. shotgun: 12.3 ft./lbs. **Recoil velocity in 8-lb. shotgun:** 10.0 ft./sec.

Distance in yards:	Muzzle	20	30	40	50	60	70
Velocity in fps:	1,292	892	769	672	593	525	467
Average pellet energy in ft-lbs:	7.26	3.46	2.57	1.96	1.53	1.20	.095
Time of flight in seconds:	0	.0568	.0931	.01349	.1825	.2363	.2969

Type of load: Field
Three-foot velocity: 1,200 ft./sec.
Hull: 2¾-inch plastic
Wad: Plastic
Shot: Hard lead
Buffered: No
Test barrel length: 26 inch
Pellets will pierce skin up to 157 yards.

NO. 6 LEAD PELLETS—⅞ OUNCE—197 PELLETS
Mfg: Federal Cartridge Co. **Manufacturer's code:** H200
Recoil energy in 8-lb. shotgun: 12.3 ft./lbs. **Recoil velocity in 8-lb. shotgun:** 10.0 ft./sec.

Distance in yards:	Muzzle	20	30	40	50	60	70
Velocity in fps:	1,292	892	769	672	593	525	467
Average pellet energy in ft-lbs:	7.26	3.46	2.57	1.96	1.53	1.20	.095
Time of flight in seconds:	0	.0568	.0931	.01349	.1825	.2363	.2969

Type of load: Field
Three-foot velocity: 1,200 ft./sec.
Hull: 2¾-inch plastic
Wad: Plastic
Shot: Lead
Buffered: No
Test barrel length: 26 inch
Pellets will pierce skin up to 157 yards.

NO. 6 LEAD PELLETS—⅞ OUNCE—197 PELLETS
Mfg: Fiocchi **Manufacturer's code:** 20GT
Recoil energy in 8-lb. shotgun: 12.3 ft./lbs. **Recoil velocity in 8-lb. shotgun:** 10.0 ft./sec.

Distance in yards:	Muzzle	20	30	40	50	60	70
Velocity in fps:	1,292	892	769	672	593	525	467
Average pellet energy in ft-lbs:	7.26	3.46	2.57	1.96	1.53	1.20	.095
Time of flight in seconds:	0	.0568	.0931	.01349	.1825	.2363	.2969

Type of load: Game & Target
Three-foot velocity: 1,200 ft./sec.
Hull: 2¾-inch plastic
Wad: Plastic
Shot: Lead
Buffered: No
Test barrel length: 26 inch
Pellets will pierce skin up to 157 yards.

NO. 6 LEAD PELLETS—⅞ OUNCE—197 PELLETS
Mfg: Rottweil **Manufacturer's code:** Game
Recoil energy in 8-lb. shotgun: 12.3 ft./lbs. **Recoil velocity in 8-lb. shotgun:** 10.0 ft./sec.

Distance in yards:	Muzzle	20	30	40	50	60	70
Velocity in fps:	1,292	892	769	672	593	525	467
Average pellet energy in ft-lbs:	7.26	3.46	2.57	1.96	1.53	1.20	.095
Time of flight in seconds:	0	.0568	.0931	.01349	.1825	.2363	.2969

Type of load: Field
Three-foot velocity: 1,200 ft./sec.
Hull: 2¾-inch plastic
Wad: Plastic
Shot: Lead
Buffered: No
Test barrel length: 26 inch
Pellets will pierce skin up to 157 yards.

NO. 6 LEAD PELLETS—⅞ OUNCE—197 PELLETS
Mfg: Winchester **Manufacturer's code:** XU20
Recoil energy in 8-lb. shotgun: 12.3 ft./lbs. **Recoil velocity in 8-lb. shotgun:** 10.0 ft./sec.

Distance in yards:	Muzzle	20	30	40	50	60	70
Velocity in fps:	1,292	892	769	672	593	525	467
Average pellet energy in ft-lbs:	7.26	3.46	2.57	1.96	1.53	1.20	.095
Time of flight in seconds:	0	.0568	.0931	.01349	.1825	.2363	.2969

Type of load: Field
Three-foot velocity: 1,200 ft./sec.
Hull: 2¾-inch plastic
Wad: Plastic
Shot: Lead
Buffered: No
Test barrel length: 26 inch
Pellets will pierce skin up to 157 yards.

NO. 6 LEAD PELLETS—⅞ OUNCE—197 PELLETS
Mfg: PMC (Eldorado Cartridge Corp.) **Manufacturer's code:** PL20
Recoil energy in 8-lb. shotgun: 12.6 ft./lbs. **Recoil velocity in 8-lb. shotgun:** 10.1 ft./sec.

Distance in yards:	Muzzle	20	30	40	50	60	70
Velocity in fps:	1,314	903	778	679	598	530	471
Average pellet energy in ft-lbs:	7.51	3.54	2.63	2.00	1.55	1.22	.97
Time of flight in seconds:	0	.0560	.0919	.1333	.1804	.2337	.2938

Type of load: Quail & Dove
Three-foot velocity: 1,220 ft./sec.
Hull: 2¾-inch plastic
Wad: Plastic
Shot: Lead
Buffered: No
Test barrel length: 26 inch
Pellets will pierce skin up to 143 yards.

NO. 6 LEAD PELLETS—⅞ OUNCE—197 PELLETS
Mfg: Remington Arms Co. **Manufacturer's code:** GL20
Recoil energy in 8-lb. shotgun: 12.6 ft./lbs. **Recoil velocity in 8-lb. shotgun:** 10.1 ft./sec.

Distance in yards:	Muzzle	20	30	40	50	60	70
Velocity in fps:	1,314	903	778	679	598	530	471
Average pellet energy in ft-lbs:	7.51	3.54	2.63	2.00	1.55	1.22	.97
Time of flight in seconds:	0	.0560	.0919	.1333	.1804	.2337	.2938

Type of load: Field
Three-foot velocity: 1,220 ft./sec.
Hull: 2¾-inch plastic
Wad: Plastic
Shot: Lead
Buffered: No
Test barrel length: 26 inch
Pellets will pierce skin up to 143 yards.

NO. 6 LEAD PELLETS—⅞ OUNCE—197 PELLETS
Mfg: RST, Ltd. **Manufacturer's code:** N/A
Recoil energy in 8-lb. shotgun: 12.6 ft./lbs. **Recoil velocity in 8-lb. shotgun:** 10.1 ft./sec.

Distance in yards:	Muzzle	20	30	40	50	60	70
Velocity in fps:	1,314	903	778	679	598	530	471
Average pellet energy in ft-lbs:	7.51	3.54	2.63	2.00	1.55	1.22	.97
Time of flight in seconds:	0	.0560	.0919	.1333	.1804	.2337	.2938

Type of load: Target
Three-foot velocity: 1,220 ft./sec.
Hull: 2¾-inch plastic
Wad: Plastic
Shot: Lead
Buffered: No
Test barrel length: 26 inch
Pellets will pierce skin up to 143 yards.

NO. 6 LEAD PELLETS—1 OUNCE—225 PELLETS
Mfg: Federal CartridgeCo. **Manufacturer's code:** H202/HGL20
Recoil energy in 8-lb. shotgun: 14.9 ft./lbs. **Recoil velocity in 8-lb. shotgun:** 10.9 ft./sec.

Distance in yards:	Muzzle	20	30	40	50	60	70
Velocity in fps:	1,254	873	755	660	583	517	460
Average pellet energy in ft-lbs:	6.83	3.31	2.47	1.89	1.47	1.16	.92
Time of flight in seconds:	0	.0583	.0953	.1379	.1863	.2410	.3026

Type of load: Field
Three-foot velocity: 1,165 ft./sec.
Hull: 2¾-inch plastic
Wad: Plastic
Shot: Lead
Buffered: No
Test barrel length: 26 inch
Pellets will pierce skin up to 141 yards.

NO. 6 LEAD PELLETS—1 OUNCE—225 PELLETS
Mfg: Fiocchi **Manufacturer's code:** 20FLD
Recoil energy in 8-lb. shotgun: 14.9 ft./lbs. **Recoil velocity in 8-lb. shotgun:** 10.9 ft./sec.

Distance in yards:	Muzzle	20	30	40	50	60	70
Velocity in fps:	1,254	873	755	660	583	517	460
Average pellet energy in ft-lbs:	6.83	3.31	2.47	1.89	1.47	1.16	.92
Time of flight in seconds:	0	.0583	.0953	.1379	.1863	.2410	.3026

Type of load: Field
Three-foot velocity: 1,165 ft./sec.
Hull: 2¾-inch plastic
Wad: Plastic
Shot: Lead
Buffered: No
Test barrel length: 26 inch
Pellets will pierce skin up to 141 yards.

NO. 6 LEAD PELLETS—1 OUNCE—225 PELLETS
Mfg: Remington Arms Co. **Manufacturer's code:** RP20HD
Recoil energy in 8-lb. shotgun: 14.9 ft./lbs. **Recoil velocity in 8-lb. shotgun:** 10.9 ft./sec.

Distance in yards:	Muzzle	20	30	40	50	60	70
Velocity in fps:	1,254	873	755	660	583	517	460
Average pellet energy in ft-lbs:	6.83	3.31	2.47	1.89	1.47	1.16	.92
Time of flight in seconds:	0	.0583	.0953	.1379	.1863	.2410	.3026

Type of load: Field
Three-foot velocity: 1,165 ft./sec.
Hull: 2¾-inch plastic
Wad: Plastic
Shot: Lead
Buffered: No
Test barrel length: 26 inch
Pellets will pierce skin up to 141 yards.

NO. 6 LEAD PELLETS—1 OUNCE—225 PELLETS
Mfg: Winchester **Manufacturer's code:** XU20H
Recoil energy in 8-lb. shotgun: 14.9 ft./lbs. **Recoil velocity in 8-lb. shotgun:** 10.9 ft./sec.

Distance in yards:	Muzzle	20	30	40	50	60	70
Velocity in fps:	1,254	873	755	660	583	517	460
Average pellet energy in ft-lbs:	6.83	3.31	2.47	1.89	1.47	1.16	.92
Time of flight in seconds:	0	.0583	.0953	.1379	.1863	.2410	.3026

Type of load: Field
Three-foot velocity: 1,165 ft./sec.
Hull: 2¾-inch plastic
Wad: Plastic
Shot: Lead
Buffered: No
Test barrel length: 26 inch
Pellets will pierce skin up to 141 yards.

NO. 6 LEAD PELLETS—1 OUNCE—225 PELLETS
Mfg: Estate Cartridge **Manufacturer's code:** HG20
Recoil energy in 8-lb. shotgun: 18.9 ft./lbs. **Recoil velocity in 8-lb. shotgun:** 12.3 ft./sec.

Distance in yards:	Muzzle	20	30	40	50	60	70
Velocity in fps:	1,265	878	759	664	585	519	462
Average pellet energy in ft-lbs:	6.95	3.35	2.50	1.91	1.9	1.17	.93
Time of flight in seconds:	0	.0578	.0947	.1370	.1852	.2396	.3009

Type of load: Field
Three-foot velocity: 1,175 ft./sec.5
Hull: 2¾-inch plastic
Wad: Plastic
Shot: Hard lead
Buffered: No
Test barrel length: 26 inch
Pellets will pierce skin up to 141 yards.

NO. 6 LEAD PELLETS—1 OUNCE—225 PELLETS
Mfg: PMC (Eldorado Cartridge Corp.) **Manufacturer's code:** HF20
Recoil energy in 8-lb. shotgun: 16.1 ft./lbs. **Recoil velocity in 8-lb. shotgun:** 11.4 ft./sec.

Distance in yards:	Muzzle	20	30	40	50	60	70
Velocity in fps:	1,292	892	769	672	593	525	467
Average pellet energy in ft-lbs:	7.26	3.46	2.57	1.96	1.53	1.20	.095
Time of flight in seconds:	0	.0568	.0931	.01349	.1825	.2363	.2969

Type of load: Field
Three-foot velocity: 1,200 ft./sec.
Hull: 2¾-inch plastic
Wad: Plastic
Shot: Lead
Buffered: No
Test barrel length: 26 inch
Pellets will pierce skin up to 157 yards.

NO. 6 LEAD PELLETS—1 OUNCE—225 PELLETS
Mfg: Dionisi **Manufacturer's code:** D 20 SLR
Recoil energy in 8-lb. shotgun: 16.8 ft./lbs. **Recoil velocity in 8-lb. shotgun:** 11.6 ft./sec.

Distance in yards:	Muzzle	20	30	40	50	60	70
Velocity in fps:	1,314	903	778	679	598	530	471
Average pellet energy in ft-lbs:	7.51	3.54	2.63	2.00	1.55	1.22	.97
Time of flight in seconds:	0	.0560	.0919	.1333	.1804	.2337	.2938

Type of load: Field
Three-foot velocity: 1,220 ft./sec.
Hull: 2¾-inch plastic
Wad: Plastic
Shot: Lead
Buffered: No
Test barrel length: 26 inch
Pellets will pierce skin up to 143 yards.

NO. 6 LEAD PELLETS—1 OUNCE—225 PELLETS
Mfg: Estate Cartridge **Manufacturer's code:** HV20
Recoil energy in 8-lb. shotgun: 16.8 ft./lbs. **Recoil velocity in 8-lb. shotgun:** 11.6 ft./sec.

Distance in yards:	Muzzle	20	30	40	50	60	70
Velocity in fps:	1,314	903	778	679	598	530	471
Average pellet energy in ft-lbs:	7.51	3.54	2.63	2.00	1.55	1.22	.97
Time of flight in seconds:	0	.0560	.0919	.1333	.1804	.2337	.2938

Type of load: Field
Three-foot velocity: 1,220 ft./sec.
Hull: 2¾-inch plastic
Wad: Plastic
Shot: Hard lead
Buffered: No
Test barrel length: 26 inch
Pellets will pierce skin up to 143 yards.

NO. 6 LEAD PELLETS—1 OUNCE—225 PELLETS
Mfg: Federal Cartridge Co. **Manufacturer's code:** P254/H204
Recoil energy in 8-lb. shotgun: 16.8 ft./lbs. **Recoil velocity in 8-lb. shotgun:** 11.6 ft./sec.

Distance in yards:	Muzzle	20	30	40	50	60	70
Velocity in fps:	1,314	903	778	679	598	530	471
Average pellet energy in ft-lbs:	7.51	3.54	2.63	2.00	1.55	1.22	.97
Time of flight in seconds:	0	.0560	.0919	.1333	.1804	.2337	.2938

Type of load: Field
Three-foot velocity: 1,220 ft./sec.
Hull: 2¾-inch plastic
Wad: Plastic
Shot: Lead
Buffered: No
Test barrel length: 26 inch
Pellets will pierce skin up to 143 yards.

NO. 6 LEAD PELLETS—1 OUNCE—225 PELLETS
Mfg: Fiocchi **Manufacturer's code:** 20HV
Recoil energy in 8-lb. shotgun: 16.8 ft./lbs. **Recoil velocity in 8-lb. shotgun:** 11.6 ft./sec.

Distance in yards:	Muzzle	20	30	40	50	60	70
Velocity in fps:	1,314	903	778	679	598	530	471
Average pellet energy in ft-lbs:	7.51	3.54	2.63	2.00	1.55	1.22	.97
Time of flight in seconds:	0	.0560	.0919	.1333	.1804	.2337	.2938

Type of load: Field
Three-foot velocity: 1,220 ft./sec.
Hull: 2¾-inch plastic
Wad: Plastic
Shot: Lead
Buffered: No
Test barrel length: 26 inch
Pellets will pierce skin up to 143 yards.

NO. 6 LEAD PELLETS—1 OUNCE—225 PELLETS
Mfg: Remington Arms Co. **Manufacturer's code:** SP20/HGL20
Recoil energy in 8-lb. shotgun: 16.8 ft./lbs. **Recoil velocity in 8-lb. shotgun:** 11.6 ft./sec.

Distance in yards:	Muzzle	20	30	40	50	60	70
Velocity in fps:	1,314	903	778	679	598	530	471
Average pellet energy in ft-lbs:	7.51	3.54	2.63	2.00	1.55	1.22	.97
Time of flight in seconds:	0	.0560	.0919	.1333	.1804	.2337	.2938

Type of load: Field
Three-foot velocity: 1,220 ft./sec.
Hull: 2¾-inch plastic
Wad: Plastic
Shot: Lead
Buffered: No
Test barrel length: 26 inch
Pellets will pierce skin up to 143 yards.

NO. 6 LEAD PELLETS—1 OUNCE—225 PELLETS
Mfg: Sellier & Bellot **Manufacturer's code:** SBA02002
Recoil energy in 8-lb. shotgun: 16.8 ft./lbs. **Recoil velocity in 8-lb. shotgun:** 11.6 ft./sec.

Distance in yards:	Muzzle	20	30	40	50	60	70
Velocity in fps:	1,314	903	778	679	598	530	471
Average pellet energy in ft-lbs:	7.51	3.54	2.63	2.00	1.55	1.22	.97
Time of flight in seconds:	0	.0560	.0919	.1333	.1804	.2337	.2938

Type of load: Field
Three-foot velocity: 1,220 ft./sec.
Hull: 2¾-inch plastic
Wad: Plastic
Shot: Lead
Buffered: No
Test barrel length: 26 inch
Pellets will pierce skin up to 143 yards.

NO. 6 LEAD PELLETS—1 OUNCE—225 PELLETS
Mfg: Winchester **Manufacturer's code:** X20
Recoil energy in 8-lb. shotgun: 16.8 ft./lbs. **Recoil velocity in 8-lb. shotgun:** 11.6 ft./sec.

Distance in yards:	Muzzle	20	30	40	50	60	70
Velocity in fps:	1,314	903	778	679	598	530	471
Average pellet energy in ft-lbs:	7.51	3.54	2.63	2.00	1.55	1.22	.97
Time of flight in seconds:	0	.0560	.0919	.1333	.1804	.2337	.2938

Type of load: Field
Three-foot velocity: 1,220 ft./sec.
Hull: 2¾-inch plastic
Wad: Plastic
Shot: Lead
Buffered: No
Test barrel length: 26 inch
Pellets will pierce skin up to 143 yards.

NO. 6 LEAD PELLETS—1 OUNCE—225 PELLETS
Mfg: Aguila **Manufacturer's code:** N/A
Recoil energy in 8-lb. shotgun: 11.8 ft./lbs. **Recoil velocity in 8-lb. shotgun:** 11.8 ft./sec.

Distance in yards:	Muzzle	20	30	40	50	60	70
Velocity in fps:	1,331	911	784	684	602	534	474
Average pellet energy in ft-lbs:	7.70	3.60	2.67	2.03	1.58	1.24	.98
Time of flight in seconds:	0	.0555	.0911	.1321	.1789	.2319	.2915

Type of load: Field
Three-foot velocity: 1,235 ft./sec.
Hull: 2¾-inch plastic
Wad: Plastic
Shot: Lead
Buffered: No
Test barrel length: 26 inch
Pellets will pierce skin up to 144 yards.

NO. 6 LEAD PELLETS—1 OUNCE—225 PELLETS
Mfg: Federal Cartridge Co. **Manufacturer's code:** P204
Recoil energy in 8-lb. shotgun: 17.4 ft./lbs. **Recoil velocity in 8-lb. shotgun:** 11.8 ft./sec.

Distance in yards:	Muzzle	20	30	40	50	60	70
Velocity in fps:	1,331	911	784	684	602	534	474
Average pellet energy in ft-lbs:	7.70	3.60	2.67	2.03	1.58	1.24	.98
Time of flight in seconds:	0	.0555	.0911	.1321	.1789	.2319	.2915

Type of load: Field
Three-foot velocity: 1,235 ft./sec.
Hull: 2¾-inch plastic
Wad: Plastic
Shot: Lead
Buffered: No
Test barrel length: 26 inch
Pellets will pierce skin up to 144 yards.

NO. 6 LEAD PELLETS—1 OUNCE—225 PELLETS
Mfg: Kent Cartridge America/Canada **Manufacturer's code:** K202UG28
Recoil energy in 8-lb. shotgun: 17.4 ft./lbs. **Recoil velocity in 8-lb. shotgun:** 11.8 ft./sec.

Distance in yards:	Muzzle	20	30	40	50	60	70
Velocity in fps:	1,331	911	784	684	602	534	474
Average pellet energy in ft-lbs:	7.70	3.60	2.67	2.03	1.58	1.24	.98
Time of flight in seconds:	0	.0555	.0911	.1321	.1789	.2319	.2915

Type of load: Field
Three-foot velocity: 1,235 ft./sec.
Hull: 2¾-inch plastic
Wad: Plastic
Shot: Lead
Buffered: No
Test barrel length: 26 inch
Pellets will pierce skin up to 144 yards.

NO. 6 LEAD PELLETS—1 OUNCE—225 PELLETS
Mfg: ARMUSA **Manufacturer's code:** PLA-1
Recoil energy in 8-lb. shotgun: 18.9 ft./lbs. **Recoil velocity in 8-lb. shotgun:** 12.3 ft./sec.

Distance in yards:	Muzzle	20	30	40	50	60	70
Velocity in fps:	1,375	932	800	697	613	543	482
Average pellet energy in ft-lbs:	8.22	3.77	2.78	2.11	1.63	1.28	1.01
Time of flight in seconds:	0	.0540	.0888	.1290	.1750	.2271	.2858

Type of load: Field
Three-foot velocity: 1,275 ft./sec.
Hull: 2¾-inch plastic
Wad: Plastic
Shot: Lead
Buffered: No
Test barrel length: 26 inch
Pellets will pierce skin up to 145 yards.

NO. 6 LEAD PELLETS—1 OUNCE—225 PELLETS
Mfg: Eley Hawk **Manufacturer's code:** Competition 28
Recoil energy in 8-lb. shotgun: 18.9 ft./lbs. **Recoil velocity in 8-lb. shotgun:** 12.3 ft./sec.

Distance in yards:	Muzzle	20	30	40	50	60	70
Velocity in fps:	1,375	932	800	697	613	543	482
Average pellet energy in ft-lbs:	8.22	3.77	2.78	2.11	1.63	1.28	1.01
Time of flight in seconds:	0	.0540	.0888	.1290	.1750	.2271	.2858

Type of load: Target
Three-foot velocity: 1,275 ft./sec.
Hull: 2¾-inch plastic
Wad: Plastic or fiber
Shot: Lead
Buffered: No
Test barrel length: 26 inch
Pellets will pierce skin up to 160 yards.

NO. 6 LEAD PELLETS—1 OUNCE—225 PELLETS
Mfg: Clever **Manufacturer's code:** T1 Light Game
Recoil energy in 8-lb. shotgun: 19.9 ft./lbs. **Recoil velocity in 8-lb. shotgun:** 12.6 ft./sec.

Distance in yards:	Muzzle	20	30	40	50	60	70
Velocity in fps:	1,403	945	810	705	620	548	487
Average pellet energy in ft-lbs:	8.55	3.88	2.85	2.16	1.67	1.31	1.03
Time of flight in seconds:	0	.0531	.0875	.1272	.1727	.2242	.2723

Type of load: Field
Three-foot velocity: 1,300 ft./sec.
Hull: 2¾-inch plastic
Wad: Plastic
Shot: Lead
Buffered: No
Test barrel length: 26 inch
Pellets will pierce skin up to 146 yards.

NO. 6 LEAD PELLETS—1 OUNCE—225 PELLETS
Mfg: Remington Arms Co. **Manufacturer's code:** SPHV20
Recoil energy in 8-lb. shotgun: 19.9 ft./lbs. **Recoil velocity in 8-lb. shotgun:** 12.6 ft./sec.

Distance in yards:	Muzzle	20	30	40	50	60	70
Velocity in fps:	1,403	945	810	705	620	548	487
Average pellet energy in ft-lbs:	8.55	3.88	2.85	2.16	1.67	1.31	1.03
Time of flight in seconds:	0	.0531	.0875	.1272	.1727	.2242	.2723

Type of load: Field
Three-foot velocity: 1,300 ft./sec.
Hull: 2¾-inch plastic
Wad: Plastic
Shot: Lead
Buffered: No
Test barrel length: 26 inch
Pellets will pierce skin up to 146 yards.

NO. 6 LEAD PELLETS—1 OUNCE—225 PELLETS
Mfg: Winchester **Manufacturer's code:** SFH20
Recoil energy in 8-lb. shotgun: 19.9 ft./lbs. **Recoil velocity in 8-lb. shotgun:** 12.6 ft./sec.

Distance in yards:	Muzzle	20	30	40	50	60	70
Velocity in fps:	1,403	945	810	705	620	548	487
Average pellet energy in ft-lbs:	8.55	3.88	2.85	2.16	1.67	1.31	1.03
Time of flight in seconds:	0	.0531	.0875	.1272	.1727	.2242	.2723

Type of load: Field
Three-foot velocity: 1,300 ft./sec.
Hull: 2¾-inch plastic
Wad: Plastic
Shot: Copper-plated lead
Buffered: Yes
Test barrel length: 26 inch
Pellets will pierce skin up to 146 yards.

NO. 6 LEAD PELLETS—1¹/₁₆ OUNCES—239 PELLETS
Mfg: Eley Hawk **Manufacturer's code:** VIP Game
Recoil energy in 8-lb. shotgun: 18.9 ft./lbs. **Recoil velocity in 8-lb. shotgun:** 12.3 ft./sec.

Distance in yards:	Muzzle	20	30	40	50	60	70
Velocity in fps:	1,314	903	778	679	598	530	471
Average pellet energy in ft-lbs:	7.51	3.54	2.63	2.00	1.55	1.22	.97
Time of flight in seconds:	0	.0560	.0919	.1333	.1804	.2337	.2938

Type of load: Field
Three-foot velocity: 1,225 ft./sec.
Hull: 2¾-inch plastic
Wad: Plastic
Shot: Lead
Buffered: No
Test barrel length: 26 inch
Pellets will pierce skin up to 143 yards.

NO. 6 LEAD PELLETS—1¹/₈ OUNCES—253 PELLETS
Mfg: Federal Cartridge Co. **Manufacturer's code:** P256/F205/H203
Recoil energy in 8-lb. shotgun: 23.8 ft./lbs. **Recoil velocity in 8-lb. shotgun:** 13.8 ft./sec.

Distance in yards:	Muzzle	20	30	40	50	60	70
Velocity in fps:	1,265	878	759	664	585	519	462
Average pellet energy in ft-lbs:	6.95	3.35	2.50	1.91	1.9	1.17	.93
Time of flight in seconds:	0	.0578	.0947	.1370	.1852	.2396	.3009

Type of load: Field
Three-foot velocity: 1,175 ft./sec.
Hull: 2¾-inch plastic
Wad: Plastic
Shot: Copper-plated lead/lead
Buffered: Yes
Test barrel length: 26 inch
Pellets will pierce skin up to 141 yards.

NO. 6 LEAD PELLETS—1¹/₈ OUNCES—253 PELLETS
Mfg: Remington Arms Co. **Manufacturer's code:** NM20S
Recoil energy in 8-lb. shotgun: 23.8 ft./lbs. **Recoil velocity in 8-lb. shotgun:** 13.8 ft./sec.

Distance in yards:	Muzzle	20	30	40	50	60	70
Velocity in fps:	1,265	878	759	664	585	519	462
Average pellet energy in ft-lbs:	6.95	3.35	2.50	1.91	1.9	1.17	.93
Time of flight in seconds:	0	.0578	.0947	.1370	.1852	.2396	.3009

Type of load: Field
Three-foot velocity: 1,175 ft./sec.
Hull: 2¾-inch plastic
Wad: Plastic
Shot: Lead
Buffered: Yes
Test barrel length: 26 inch
Pellets will pierce skin up to 141 yards.

NO. 6 LEAD PELLETS—1¹/₈ OUNCES—253 PELLETS
Mfg: Winchester **Manufacturer's code:** X20XC
Recoil energy in 8-lb. shotgun: 23.8 ft./lbs. **Recoil velocity in 8-lb. shotgun:** 13.8 ft./sec.

Distance in yards:	Muzzle	20	30	40	50	60	70
Velocity in fps:	1,265	878	759	664	585	519	462
Average pellet energy in ft-lbs:	6.95	3.35	2.50	1.91	1.9	1.17	.93
Time of flight in seconds:	0	.0578	.0947	.1370	.1852	.2396	.3009

Type of load: Field
Three-foot velocity: 1,175 ft./sec.
Hull: 2¾-inch plastic
Wad: Plastic
Shot: Copper-plated lead
Buffered: Yes
Test barrel length: 26 inch
Pellets will pierce skin up to 141 yards.

NO. 6 LEAD PELLETS—1¹/₈ OUNCES—253 PELLETS
Mfg: Estate Cartridge **Manufacturer's code:** HV20SMAG
Recoil energy in 8-lb. shotgun: 31.1 ft./lbs. **Recoil velocity in 8-lb. shotgun:** 15.8 ft./sec.

Distance in yards:	Muzzle	20	30	40	50	60	70
Velocity in fps:	1,348	919	790	689	606	537	477
Average pellet energy in ft-lbs:	7.89	3.67	2.71	2.06	1.60	1.25	.99
Time of flight in seconds:	0	.0549	.0902	.1309	.1774	.2300	.2893

Type of load: Field
Three-foot velocity: 1,250 ft./sec.
Hull: 2¾-inch plastic
Wad: Plastic
Shot: Hard lead
Buffered: Yes
Test barrel length: 26 inch
Pellets will pierce skin up to 144 yards.

NO. 7 LEAD PELLETS—⁷/₈ OUNCE—262 PELLETS
Mfg: Eley Hawk **Manufacturer's code:** Competition 24
Recoil energy in 8-lb. shotgun: 14.5 ft./lbs. **Recoil velocity in 8-lb. shotgun:** 10.8 ft./sec.

Distance in yards:	Muzzle	20	30	40	50	60	70
Velocity in fps:	1,382	906	769	663	578	507	446
Average pellet energy in ft-lbs:	6.23	2.68	1.93	1.44	1.09	.84	.65
Time of flight in seconds:	0	.0548	.0908	.1329	.1815	.2370	.3001

Type of load: Target
Three-foot velocity: 1,275 ft./sec.
Hull: 2¾-inch plastic
Wad: Plastic or fiber
Shot: Lead
Buffered: No
Test barrel length: 26 inch
Pellets will pierce skin up to 145 yards.

NO. 7 LEAD PELLETS—1 OUNCE—299 PELLETS
Mfg: Clever **Manufacturer's code:** T1 Light Game
Recoil energy in 8-lb. shotgun: 19.9 ft./lbs. **Recoil velocity in 8-lb. shotgun:** 12.6 ft./sec.

Distance in yards:	Muzzle	20	30	40	50	60	70
Velocity in fps:	1,410	918	778	670	584	512	450
Average pellet energy in ft-lbs:	6.49	2.75	1.98	1.47	1.11	.86	.66
Time of flight in seconds:	0	.0539	.0895	.1311	.1791	.2340	.2966

Type of load: Field
Three-foot velocity: 1,300 ft./sec.
Hull: 2¾-inch plastic
Wad: Plastic
Shot: Lead
Buffered: No
Test barrel length: 26 inch
Pellets will pierce skin up to 133 yards.

NO. 7½ LEAD PELLETS—¾ OUNCE—262 PELLETS
Mfg: Estate Cartridge **Manufacturer's code:** ML20
Recoil energy in 8-lb. shotgun: 9.5 ft./lbs. **Recoil velocity in 8-lb. shotgun:** 8.7 ft./sec.

Distance in yards:	Muzzle	20	30	40	50	60	70
Velocity in fps:	1,324	864	731	629	546	476	416
Average pellet energy in ft-lbs:	4.91	2.09	1.50	1.11	.83	.63	.48
Time of flight in seconds:	0	.0573	.0952	.1395	.1908	.2497	.3172

Type of load: Target
Three-foot velocity: 1,220 ft./sec.
Hull: 2¾-inch plastic
Wad: Plastic
Shot: Hard lead
Buffered: No
Test barrel length: 26 inch
Pellets will pierce skin up to 124 yards.

NO. 7½ LEAD PELLETS—⅞ OUNCE—306 PELLETS
Mfg: Aguila **Manufacturer's code:** N/A
Recoil energy in 8-lb. shotgun: 11.0 ft./lbs. **Recoil velocity in 8-lb. shotgun:** 9.4 ft./sec.

Distance in yards:	Muzzle	20	30	40	50	60	70
Velocity in fps:	1,246	829	705	607	528	461	402
Average pellet energy in ft-lbs:	4.35	1.92	1.39	1.03	.78	.59	.45
Time of flight in seconds:	0	.0602	.0996	.1455	.1985	.2594	.3290

Type of load: Field
Three-foot velocity: 1,150 ft./sec.
Hull: 2¾-inch plastic
Wad: Plastic
Shot: Lead
Buffered: No
Test barrel length: 26 inch
Pellets will pierce skin up to 122 yards.

NO. 7½ LEAD PELLETS—⅞ OUNCE—306 PELLETS
Mfg: RST, Ltd. **Manufacturer's code:** N/A
Recoil energy in 8-lb. shotgun: 11.0 ft./lbs. **Recoil velocity in 8-lb. shotgun:** 9.4 ft./sec.

Distance in yards:	Muzzle	20	30	40	50	60	70
Velocity in fps:	1,246	829	705	607	528	461	402
Average pellet energy in ft-lbs:	4.35	1.92	1.39	1.03	.78	.59	.45
Time of flight in seconds:	0	.0602	.0996	.1455	.1985	.2594	.3290

Type of load: Target
Three-foot velocity: 1,150 ft./sec.
Hull: 2¾-inch plastic
Wad: Plastic
Shot: Lead
Buffered: No
Test barrel length: 26 inch
Pellets will pierce skin up to 122 yards.

NO. 7½ LEAD PELLETS—⅞ OUNCE—306 PELLETS
Mfg: Estate Cartridge **Manufacturer's code:** DQ20
Recoil energy in 8-lb. shotgun: 12.3 ft./lbs. **Recoil velocity in 8-lb. shotgun:** 10.0 ft./sec.

Distance in yards:	Muzzle	20	30	40	50	60	70
Velocity in fps:	1,302	854	724	623	541	472	412
Average pellet energy in ft-lbs:	4.74	2.04	1.47	1.09	.82	.62	.47
Time of flight in seconds:	0	.0581	.0964	.1412	.1930	.2524	.3204

Type of load: Field
Three-foot velocity: 1,200 ft./sec.
Hull: 2¾-inch plastic
Wad: Plastic
Shot: Hard lead
Buffered: No
Test barrel length: 26 inch
Pellets will pierce skin up to 136 yards.

NO. 7½ LEAD PELLETS—⅞ OUNCE—306 PELLETS
Mfg: Estate Cartridge **Manufacturer's code:** CT20/SS20
Recoil energy in 8-lb. shotgun: 12.3 ft./lbs. **Recoil velocity in 8-lb. shotgun:** 10.0 ft./sec.

Distance in yards:	Muzzle	20	30	40	50	60	70
Velocity in fps:	1,302	854	724	623	541	472	412
Average pellet energy in ft-lbs:	4.74	2.04	1.47	1.09	.82	.62	.47
Time of flight in seconds:	0	.0581	.0964	.1412	.1930	.2524	.3204

Type of load: Target
Three-foot velocity: 1,200 ft./sec.
Hull: 2¾-inch plastic
Wad: Plastic
Shot: Hard lead
Buffered: No
Test barrel length: 26 inch
Pellets will pierce skin up to 136 yards.

NO. 7½ LEAD PELLETS—⅞ OUNCE—306 PELLETS
Mfg: Federal Cartridge Co. **Manufacturer's code:** H200/FD20
Recoil energy in 8-lb. shotgun: 12.3 ft./lbs. **Recoil velocity in 8-lb. shotgun:** 10.0 ft./sec.

Distance in yards:	Muzzle	20	30	40	50	60	70
Velocity in fps:	1,302	854	724	623	541	472	412
Average pellet energy in ft-lbs:	4.74	2.04	1.47	1.09	.82	.62	.47
Time of flight in seconds:	0	.0581	.0964	.1412	.1930	.2524	.3204

Type of load: Field
Three-foot velocity: 1,200 ft./sec.
Hull: 2¾-inch plastic
Wad: Plastic
Shot: Lead
Buffered: No
Test barrel length: 26 inch
Pellets will pierce skin up to 136 yards.

NO. 7½ LEAD PELLETS—⅞ OUNCE—306 PELLETS
Mfg: Fiocchi **Manufacturer's code:** 20GT
Recoil energy in 8-lb. shotgun: 12.3 ft./lbs. **Recoil velocity in 8-lb. shotgun:** 10.0 ft./sec.

Distance in yards:	Muzzle	20	30	40	50	60	70
Velocity in fps:	1,302	854	724	623	541	472	412
Average pellet energy in ft-lbs:	4.74	2.04	1.47	1.09	.82	.62	.47
Time of flight in seconds:	0	.0581	.0964	.1412	.1930	.2524	.3204

Type of load: Game & Target
Three-foot velocity: 1,200 ft./sec.
Hull: 2¾-inch plastic
Wad: Plastic
Shot: Lead
Buffered: No
Test barrel length: 26 inch
Pellets will pierce skin up to 136 yards.

NO. 7½ LEAD PELLETS—⅞ OUNCE—306 PELLETS
Mfg: Fiocchi **Manufacturer's code:** 20VIP
Recoil energy in 8-lb. shotgun: 12.3 ft./lbs. **Recoil velocity in 8-lb. shotgun:** 10.0 ft./sec.

Distance in yards:	Muzzle	20	30	40	50	60	70
Velocity in fps:	1,302	854	724	623	541	472	412
Average pellet energy in ft-lbs:	4.74	2.04	1.47	1.09	.82	.62	.47
Time of flight in seconds:	0	.0581	.0964	.1412	.1930	.2524	.3204

Type of load: Target
Three-foot velocity: 1,200 ft./sec.
Hull: 2¾-inch plastic
Wad: Plastic
Shot: Hard lead
Buffered: No
Test barrel length: 26 inch
Pellets will pierce skin up to 136 yards.

NO. 7½ LEAD PELLETS—⅞ OUNCE—302 PELLETS
Mfg: Rottweil **Manufacturer's code:** Game
Recoil energy in 8-lb. shotgun: 12.3 ft./lbs. **Recoil velocity in 8-lb. shotgun:** 10.0 ft./sec.

Distance in yards:	Muzzle	20	30	40	50	60	70
Velocity in fps:	1,302	854	724	623	541	472	412
Average pellet energy in ft-lbs:	4.74	2.04	1.47	1.09	.82	.62	.47
Time of flight in seconds:	0	.0581	.0964	.1412	.1930	.2524	.3204

Type of load: Field
Three-foot velocity: 1,200 ft./sec.
Hull: 2¾-inch plastic
Wad: Plastic
Shot: Lead
Buffered: No
Test barrel length: 26 inch
Pellets will pierce skin up to 136 yards.

NO. 7½ LEAD PELLETS—⅞ OUNCE—306 PELLETS
Mfg: Winchester **Manufacturer's code:** XU20
Recoil energy in 8-lb. shotgun: 12.3 ft./lbs. **Recoil velocity in 8-lb. shotgun:** 10.0 ft./sec.

Distance in yards:	Muzzle	20	30	40	50	60	70
Velocity in fps:	1,302	854	724	623	541	472	412
Average pellet energy in ft-lbs:	4.74	2.04	1.47	1.09	.82	.62	.47
Time of flight in seconds:	0	.0581	.0964	.1412	.1930	.2524	.3204

Type of load: Field
Three-foot velocity: 1,200 ft./sec.
Hull: 2¾-inch plastic
Wad: Plastic
Shot: Lead
Buffered: No
Test barrel length: 26 inch
Pellets will pierce skin up to 136 yards.

NO. 7½ LEAD PELLETS—⅞ OUNCE—306 PELLETS
Mfg: Winchester **Manufacturer's code:** WEST20
Recoil energy in 8-lb. shotgun: 12.3 ft./lbs. **Recoil velocity in 8-lb. shotgun:** 10.0 ft./sec.

Distance in yards:	Muzzle	20	30	40	50	60	70
Velocity in fps:	1,302	854	724	623	541	472	412
Average pellet energy in ft-lbs:	4.74	2.04	1.47	1.09	.82	.62	.47
Time of flight in seconds:	0	.0581	.0964	.1412	.1930	.2524	.3204

Type of load: Field & Target
Three-foot velocity: 1,200 ft./sec.
Hull: 2¾-inch plastic
Wad: Plastic
Shot: Lead
Buffered: No
Test barrel length: 26 inch
Pellets will pierce skin up to 136 yards.

NO. 7½ LEAD PELLETS—⅞ OUNCE—306 PELLETS
Mfg: PMC (Eldorado Cartridge Corp.) **Manufacturer's code:** PL20/CT20
Recoil energy in 8-lb. shotgun: 12.6 ft./lbs. **Recoil velocity in 8-lb. shotgun:** 10.1 ft./sec.

Distance in yards:	Muzzle	20	30	40	50	60	70
Velocity in fps:	1,324	864	731	629	546	476	416
Average pellet energy in ft-lbs:	4.91	2.09	1.50	1.11	.83	.63	.48
Time of flight in seconds:	0	.0573	.0952	.1395	.1908	.2497	.3172

Type of load: Quail & Dove & Target
Three-foot velocity: 1,220 ft./sec.
Hull: 2¾-inch plastic
Wad: Plastic
Shot: Lead
Buffered: No
Test barrel length: 26 inch
Pellets will pierce skin up to 124 yards.

NO. 7½ LEAD PELLETS—⅞ OUNCE—306 PELLETS
Mfg: Remington Arms Co. **Manufacturer's code:** GL20
Recoil energy in 8-lb. shotgun: 12.6 ft./lbs. **Recoil velocity in 8-lb. shotgun:** 10.1 ft./sec.

Distance in yards:	Muzzle	20	30	40	50	60	70
Velocity in fps:	1,324	864	731	629	546	476	416
Average pellet energy in ft-lbs:	4.91	2.09	1.50	1.11	.83	.63	.48
Time of flight in seconds:	0	.0573	.0952	.1395	.1908	.2497	.3172

Type of load: Field
Three-foot velocity: 1,220 ft./sec.
Hull: 2¾-inch plastic
Wad: Plastic
Shot: Lead
Buffered: No
Test barrel length: 26 inch
Pellets will pierce skin up to 124 yards.

NO. 7½ LEAD PELLETS—⅞ OUNCE—306 PELLETS
Mfg: RST, Ltd. **Manufacturer's code:** N/A
Recoil energy in 8-lb. shotgun: 12.6 ft./lbs. **Recoil velocity in 8-lb. shotgun:** 10.1 ft./sec.

Distance in yards:	Muzzle	20	30	40	50	60	70
Velocity in fps:	1,324	864	731	629	546	476	416
Average pellet energy in ft-lbs:	4.91	2.09	1.50	1.11	.83	.63	.48
Time of flight in seconds:	0	.0573	.0952	.1395	.1908	.2497	.3172

Type of load: Target
Three-foot velocity: 1,220 ft./sec.
Hull: 2¾-inch plastic
Wad: Plastic
Shot: Lead
Buffered: No
Test barrel length: 26 inch
Pellets will pierce skin up to 124 yards.

NO. 7½ LEAD PELLETS—⅞ OUNCE—306 PELLETS
Mfg: Sellier & Bellot **Manufacturer's code:** SBA02020
Recoil energy in 8-lb. shotgun: 12.6 ft./lbs. **Recoil velocity in 8-lb. shotgun:** 10.1 ft./sec.

Distance in yards:	Muzzle	20	30	40	50	60	70
Velocity in fps:	1,324	864	731	629	546	476	416
Average pellet energy in ft-lbs:	4.91	2.09	1.50	1.11	.83	.63	.48
Time of flight in seconds:	0	.0573	.0952	.1395	.1908	.2497	.3172

Type of load: Target
Three-foot velocity: 1,220 ft./sec.
Hull: 2¾-inch plastic
Wad: Plastic
Shot: Lead
Buffered: No
Test barrel length: 26 inch
Pellets will pierce skin up to 124 yards.

NO. 7½ LEAD PELLETS—⅞ OUNCE—306 PELLETS
Mfg: Dionisi **Manufacturer's code:** D 20 DQ
Recoil energy in 8-lb. shotgun: 17.4 ft./lbs. **Recoil velocity in 8-lb. shotgun:** 11.8 ft./sec.

Distance in yards:	Muzzle	20	30	40	50	60	70
Velocity in fps:	1,341	871	737	633	549	479	418
Average pellet energy in ft-lbs:	5.03	2.12	1.52	1.12	.84	.64	.49
Time of flight in seconds:	0	.0568	.0943	.1383	.1893	.2478	.3149

Type of load: Dove & Quail
Three-foot velocity: 1,235 ft./sec.
Hull: 2¾-inch plastic
Wad: Plastic
Shot: Lead
Buffered: No
Test barrel length: 26 inch
Pellets will pierce skin up to 124 yards.

NO. 7½ LEAD PELLETS—⅞ OUNCE—306 PELLETS
Mfg: Kent Cartridge America/Canada **Manufacturer's code:** K202LSC24
Recoil energy in 8-lb. shotgun: 13.7 ft./lbs. **Recoil velocity in 8-lb. shotgun:** 10.5 ft./sec.

Distance in yards:	Muzzle	20	30	40	50	60	70
Velocity in fps:	1,357	878	742	637	553	482	421
Average pellet energy in ft-lbs:	5.16	2.16	1.54	1.14	.86	.65	.50
Time of flight in seconds:	0	.0562	.0935	.1372	.1878	.2459	.3126

Type of load: Target
Three-foot velocity: 1,250 ft./sec.
Hull: 2¾-inch plastic
Wad: Plastic
Shot: Lead
Buffered: No
Test barrel length: 26 inch
Pellets will pierce skin up to 125 yards.

NO. 7½ LEAD PELLETS—⅞ OUNCE—306 PELLETS
Mfg: Baschieri & Pellagri **Manufacturer's code:** F2
Recoil energy in 8-lb. shotgun: 16.2 ft./lbs. **Recoil velocity in 8-lb. shotgun:** 11.4 ft./sec.

Distance in yards:	Muzzle	20	30	40	50	60	70
Velocity in fps:	1,447	917	771	660	571	498	435
Average pellet energy in ft-lbs:	5.86	2.36	1.66	1.22	.91	.69	.53
Time of flight in seconds:	0	.0534	.0891	.1313	.1802	.2365	.3010

Type of load: Target
Three-foot velocity: 1,330 ft./sec.
Hull: 2¾-inch plastic
Wad: Plastic
Shot: Hard lead
Buffered: No
Test barrel length: 26 inch
Pellets will pierce skin up to 127 yards.

NO. 7½ LEAD PELLETS—1 OUNCE—350 PELLETS
Mfg: Federal Cartridge Co. **Manufacturer's code:** H202/HGL20
Recoil energy in 8-lb. shotgun: 14.9 ft./lbs. **Recoil velocity in 8-lb. shotgun:** 10.9 ft./sec.

Distance in yards:	Muzzle	20	30	40	50	60	70
Velocity in fps:	1,263	836	710	612	532	464	405
Average pellet energy in ft-lbs:	4.46	1.96	1.41	1.05	.79	.60	.46
Time of flight in seconds:	0	.0596	.0986	.1442	.1968	.2572	.3264

Type of load: Field
Three-foot velocity: 1,165 ft./sec.
Hull: 2¾-inch plastic
Wad: Plastic
Shot: Lead
Buffered: No
Test barrel length: 26 inch
Pellets will pierce skin up to 122 yards.

NO. 7½ LEAD PELLETS—1 OUNCE—350 PELLETS
Mfg: Fiocchi **Manufacturer's code:** 20FLD
Recoil energy in 8-lb. shotgun: 14.9 ft./lbs. **Recoil velocity in 8-lb. shotgun:** 10.9 ft./sec.

Distance in yards:	Muzzle	20	30	40	50	60	70
Velocity in fps:	1,263	836	710	612	532	464	405
Average pellet energy in ft-lbs:	4.46	1.96	1.41	1.05	.79	.60	.46
Time of flight in seconds:	0	.0596	.0986	.1442	.1968	.2572	.3264

Type of load: Field
Three-foot velocity: 1,165 ft./sec.
Hull: 2¾-inch plastic
Wad: Plastic
Shot: Lead
Buffered: No
Test barrel length: 26 inch
Pellets will pierce skin up to 122 yards.

NO. 7½ LEAD PELLETS—1 OUNCE—350 PELLETS
Mfg: Remington Arms Co. **Manufacturer's code:** RP20HD
Recoil energy in 8-lb. shotgun: 14.9 ft./lbs. **Recoil velocity in 8-lb. shotgun:** 10.9 ft./sec.

Distance in yards:	Muzzle	20	30	40	50	60	70
Velocity in fps:	1,263	836	710	612	532	464	405
Average pellet energy in ft-lbs:	4.46	1.96	1.41	1.05	.79	.60	.46
Time of flight in seconds:	0	.0596	.0986	.1442	.1968	.2572	.3264

Type of load: Field
Three-foot velocity: 1,165 ft./sec.
Hull: 2¾-inch plastic
Wad: Plastic
Shot: Lead
Buffered: No
Test barrel length: 26 inch
Pellets will pierce skin up to 122 yards.

NO. 7½ LEAD PELLETS—1 OUNCE—350 PELLETS
Mfg: Winchester **Manufacturer's code:** XU20H
Recoil energy in 8-lb. shotgun: 14.9 ft./lbs. **Recoil velocity in 8-lb. shotgun:** 10.9 ft./sec.

Distance in yards:	Muzzle	20	30	40	50	60	70
Velocity in fps:	1,263	836	710	612	532	464	405
Average pellet energy in ft-lbs:	4.46	1.96	1.41	1.05	.79	.60	.46
Time of flight in seconds:	0	.0596	.0986	.1442	.1968	.2572	.3264

Type of load: Field
Three-foot velocity: 1,165 ft./sec.
Hull: 2¾-inch plastic
Wad: Plastic
Shot: Lead
Buffered: No
Test barrel length: 26 inch
Pellets will pierce skin up to 122 yards.

NO. 7½ LEAD PELLETS—1 OUNCE—350 PELLETS
Mfg: Winchester **Manufacturer's code:** AAH20
Recoil energy in 8-lb. shotgun: 14.9 ft./lbs. **Recoil velocity in 8-lb. shotgun:** 10.9 ft./sec.

Distance in yards:	Muzzle	20	30	40	50	60	70
Velocity in fps:	1,263	836	710	612	532	464	405
Average pellet energy in ft-lbs:	4.46	1.96	1.41	1.05	.79	.60	.46
Time of flight in seconds:	0	.0596	.0986	.1442	.1968	.2572	.3264

Type of load: Target
Three-foot velocity: 1,165 ft./sec.
Hull: 2¾-inch plastic
Wad: Plastic
Shot: Hard lead
Buffered: No
Test barrel length: 26 inch
Pellets will pierce skin up to 122 yards.

NO. 7½ LEAD PELLETS—1 OUNCE—350 PELLETS
Mfg: Estate Cartridge **Manufacturer's code:** HG20
Recoil energy in 8-lb. shotgun: 18.9 ft./lbs. **Recoil velocity in 8-lb. shotgun:** 12.3 ft./sec.

Distance in yards:	Muzzle	20	30	40	50	60	70
Velocity in fps:	1,274	841	714	615	535	466	407
Average pellet energy in ft-lbs:	4.54	1.98	1.43	1.06	.80	.61	.46
Time of flight in seconds:	0	.0592	.0980	.1433	.1957	.2558	.3246

Type of load: Field
Three-foot velocity: 1,175 ft./sec.5
Hull: 2¾-inch plastic
Wad: Plastic
Shot: Hard lead
Buffered: No
Test barrel length: 26 inch
Pellets will pierce skin up to 122 yards.

NO. 7½ LEAD PELLETS—1 OUNCE—350 PELLETS
Mfg: Federal Cartridge Co. **Manufacturer's code:** P256/F205/H203
Recoil energy in 8-lb. shotgun: 15.2 ft./lbs. **Recoil velocity in 8-lb. shotgun:** 11.1 ft./sec.

Distance in yards:	Muzzle	20	30	40	50	60	70
Velocity in fps:	1,274	841	714	615	535	466	407
Average pellet energy in ft-lbs:	4.54	1.98	1.43	1.06	.80	.61	.46
Time of flight in seconds:	0	.0592	.0980	.1433	.1957	.2558	.3246

Type of load: Field
Three-foot velocity: 1,175 ft./sec.
Hull: 2¾-inch plastic
Wad: Plastic
Shot: Copper-plated lead/lead
Buffered: Yes
Test barrel length: 26 inch
Pellets will pierce skin up to 122 yards.

NO. 7½ LEAD PELLETS—1 OUNCE—350 PELLETS
Mfg: PMC (Eldorado Cartridge Corp.) **Manufacturer's code:** HF20
Recoil energy in 8-lb. shotgun: 16.1 ft./lbs. **Recoil velocity in 8-lb. shotgun:** 11.4 ft./sec.

Distance in yards:	Muzzle	20	30	40	50	60	70
Velocity in fps:	1,302	854	724	623	541	472	412
Average pellet energy in ft-lbs:	4.74	2.04	1.47	1.09	.82	.62	.47
Time of flight in seconds:	0	.0581	.0964	.1412	.1930	.2524	.3204

Type of load: Field
Three-foot velocity: 1,200 ft./sec.
Hull: 2¾-inch plastic
Wad: Plastic
Shot: Lead
Buffered: No
Test barrel length: 26 inch
Pellets will pierce skin up to 136 yards.

NO. 7½ LEAD PELLETS—1 OUNCE—350 PELLETS
Mfg: Dionisi **Manufacturer's code:** D 20 SLR
Recoil energy in 8-lb. shotgun: 16.8 ft./lbs. **Recoil velocity in 8-lb. shotgun:** 11.6 ft./sec.

Distance in yards:	Muzzle	20	30	40	50	60	70
Velocity in fps:	1,324	864	731	629	546	476	416
Average pellet energy in ft-lbs:	4.91	2.09	1.50	1.11	.83	.63	.48
Time of flight in seconds:	0	.0573	.0952	.1395	.1908	.2497	.3172

Type of load: Field
Three-foot velocity: 1,220 ft./sec.
Hull: 2¾-inch plastic
Wad: Plastic
Shot: Lead
Buffered: No
Test barrel length: 26 inch
Pellets will pierce skin up to 124 yards.

NO. 7½ LEAD PELLETS—1 OUNCE—350 PELLETS
Mfg: Estate Cartridge **Manufacturer's code:** HV20
Recoil energy in 8-lb. shotgun: 16.8 ft./lbs. **Recoil velocity in 8-lb. shotgun:** 11.6 ft./sec.

Distance in yards:	Muzzle	20	30	40	50	60	70
Velocity in fps:	1,324	864	731	629	546	476	416
Average pellet energy in ft-lbs:	4.91	2.09	1.50	1.11	.83	.63	.48
Time of flight in seconds:	0	.0573	.0952	.1395	.1908	.2497	.3172

Type of load: Target
Three-foot velocity: 1,220 ft./sec.
Hull: 2¾-inch plastic
Wad: Plastic
Shot: Hard lead
Buffered: No
Test barrel length: 26 inch
Pellets will pierce skin up to 124 yards.

NO. 7½ LEAD PELLETS—1 OUNCE—350 PELLETS
Mfg: Federal Cartridge Co. **Manufacturer's code:** H204
Recoil energy in 8-lb. shotgun: 16.8 ft./lbs. **Recoil velocity in 8-lb. shotgun:** 11.6 ft./sec.

Distance in yards:	Muzzle	20	30	40	50	60	70
Velocity in fps:	1,324	864	731	629	546	476	416
Average pellet energy in ft-lbs:	4.91	2.09	1.50	1.11	.83	.63	.48
Time of flight in seconds:	0	.0573	.0952	.1395	.1908	.2497	.3172

Type of load: Field
Three-foot velocity: 1,220 ft./sec.
Hull: 2¾-inch plastic
Wad: Plastic
Shot: Lead
Buffered: No
Test barrel length: 26 inch
Pellets will pierce skin up to 124 yards.

NO. 7½ LEAD PELLETS—1 OUNCE—350 PELLETS
Mfg: Fiocchi **Manufacturer's code:** 20HV
Recoil energy in 8-lb. shotgun: 16.8 ft./lbs. **Recoil velocity in 8-lb. shotgun:** 11.6 ft./sec.

Distance in yards:	Muzzle	20	30	40	50	60	70
Velocity in fps:	1,324	864	731	629	546	476	416
Average pellet energy in ft-lbs:	4.91	2.09	1.50	1.11	.83	.63	.48
Time of flight in seconds:	0	.0573	.0952	.1395	.1908	.2497	.3172

Type of load: Field
Three-foot velocity: 1,220 ft./sec.
Hull: 2¾-inch plastic
Wad: Plastic
Shot: Lead
Buffered: No
Test barrel length: 26 inch
Pellets will pierce skin up to 124 yards.

NO. 7½ LEAD PELLETS—1 OUNCE—350 PELLETS
Mfg: Remington Arms Co. **Manufacturer's code:** SP20/HGL20
Recoil energy in 8-lb. shotgun: 16.8 ft./lbs. **Recoil velocity in 8-lb. shotgun:** 11.6 ft./sec.

Distance in yards:	Muzzle	20	30	40	50	60	70
Velocity in fps:	1,324	864	731	629	546	476	416
Average pellet energy in ft-lbs:	4.91	2.09	1.50	1.11	.83	.63	.48
Time of flight in seconds:	0	.0573	.0952	.1395	.1908	.2497	.3172

Type of load: Field
Three-foot velocity: 1,220 ft./sec.
Hull: 2¾-inch plastic
Wad: Plastic
Shot: Lead
Buffered: No
Test barrel length: 26 inch
Pellets will pierce skin up to 124 yards.

NO. 7½ LEAD PELLETS—1 OUNCE—350 PELLETS
Mfg: Sellier & Bellot **Manufacturer's code:** SBA02004
Recoil energy in 8-lb. shotgun: 16.8 ft./lbs. **Recoil velocity in 8-lb. shotgun:** 11.6 ft./sec.

Distance in yards:	Muzzle	20	30	40	50	60	70
Velocity in fps:	1,324	864	731	629	546	476	416
Average pellet energy in ft-lbs:	4.91	2.09	1.50	1.11	.83	.63	.48
Time of flight in seconds:	0	.0573	.0952	.1395	.1908	.2497	.3172

Type of load: Field
Three-foot velocity: 1,220 ft./sec.
Hull: 2¾-inch plastic
Wad: Plastic
Shot: Lead
Buffered: No
Test barrel length: 26 inch
Pellets will pierce skin up to 124 yards.

NO. 7½ LEAD PELLETS—1 OUNCE—350 PELLETS
Mfg: Winchester **Manufacturer's code:** X20
Recoil energy in 8-lb. shotgun: 16.8 ft./lbs. **Recoil velocity in 8-lb. shotgun:** 11.6 ft./sec.

Distance in yards:	Muzzle	20	30	40	50	60	70
Velocity in fps:	1,324	864	731	629	546	476	416
Average pellet energy in ft-lbs:	4.91	2.09	1.50	1.11	.83	.63	.48
Time of flight in seconds:	0	.0573	.0952	.1395	.1908	.2497	.3172

Type of load: Field
Three-foot velocity: 1,220 ft./sec.
Hull: 2¾-inch plastic
Wad: Plastic
Shot: Lead
Buffered: No
Test barrel length: 26 inch
Pellets will pierce skin up to 124 yards.

NO. 7½ LEAD PELLETS—1 OUNCE—350 PELLETS
Mfg: Aguila **Manufacturer's code:** N/A
Recoil energy in 8-lb. shotgun: 11.8 ft./lbs. **Recoil velocity in 8-lb. shotgun:** 11.8 ft./sec.

Distance in yards:	Muzzle	20	30	40	50	60	70
Velocity in fps:	1,341	871	737	633	549	479	418
Average pellet energy in ft-lbs:	5.03	2.12	1.52	1.12	.84	.64	.49
Time of flight in seconds:	0	.0568	.0943	.1383	.1893	.2478	.3149

Type of load: Field
Three-foot velocity: 1,235 ft./sec.
Hull: 2¾-inch plastic
Wad: Plastic
Shot: Lead
Buffered: No
Test barrel length: 26 inch
Pellets will pierce skin up to 124 yards.

NO. 7½ LEAD PELLETS—1 OUNCE—350 PELLETS
Mfg: Federal Cartridge Co. **Manufacturer's code:** P204
Recoil energy in 8-lb. shotgun: 17.4 ft./lbs. **Recoil velocity in 8-lb. shotgun:** 11.8 ft./sec.

Distance in yards:	Muzzle	20	30	40	50	60	70
Velocity in fps:	1,341	871	737	633	549	479	418
Average pellet energy in ft-lbs:	5.03	2.12	1.52	1.12	.84	.64	.49
Time of flight in seconds:	0	.0568	.0943	.1383	.1893	.2478	.3149

Type of load: Field
Three-foot velocity: 1,235 ft./sec.
Hull: 2¾-inch plastic
Wad: Plastic
Shot: Lead
Buffered: No
Test barrel length: 26 inch
Pellets will pierce skin up to 124 yards.

NO. 7½ LEAD PELLETS—1 OUNCE—350 PELLETS
Mfg: Kent Cartridge America/Canada **Manufacturer's code:** K202UG28
Recoil energy in 8-lb. shotgun: 17.4 ft./lbs. **Recoil velocity in 8-lb. shotgun:** 11.8 ft./sec.

Distance in yards:	Muzzle	20	30	40	50	60	70
Velocity in fps:	1,341	871	737	633	549	479	418
Average pellet energy in ft-lbs:	5.03	2.12	1.52	1.12	.84	.64	.49
Time of flight in seconds:	0	.0568	.0943	.1383	.1893	.2478	.3149

Type of load: Field
Three-foot velocity: 1,235 ft./sec.
Hull: 2¾-inch plastic
Wad: Plastic
Shot: Lead
Buffered: No
Test barrel length: 26 inch
Pellets will pierce skin up to 124 yards.

NO. 7½ LEAD PELLETS—1 OUNCE—350 PELLETS
Mfg: ARMUSA **Manufacturer's code:** PLA-1
Recoil energy in 8-lb. shotgun: 18.9 ft./lbs. **Recoil velocity in 8-lb. shotgun:** 12.3 ft./sec.

Distance in yards:	Muzzle	20	30	40	50	60	70
Velocity in fps:	1,385	891	752	645	559	487	425
Average pellet energy in ft-lbs:	5.37	2.22	1.58	1.16	.87	.66	.51
Time of flight in seconds:	0	.0553	.0921	.1652	.1853	.2429	.3088

Type of load: Field
Three-foot velocity: 1,275 ft./sec.
Hull: 2¾-inch plastic
Wad: Plastic
Shot: Lead
Buffered: No
Test barrel length: 26 inch
Pellets will pierce skin up to 126 yards.

NO. 7½ LEAD PELLETS—1 OUNCE—350 PELLETS
Mfg: Eley Hawk **Manufacturer's code:** Competition 28
Recoil energy in 8-lb. shotgun: 18.9 ft./lbs. **Recoil velocity in 8-lb. shotgun:** 12.3 ft./sec.

Distance in yards:	Muzzle	20	30	40	50	60	70
Velocity in fps:	1,385	891	752	645	559	487	425
Average pellet energy in ft-lbs:	5.37	2.22	1.58	1.16	.87	.66	.51
Time of flight in seconds:	0	.0553	.0921	.1652	.1853	.2429	.3088

Type of load: Target
Three-foot velocity: 1,275 ft./sec.
Hull: 2¾-inch plastic
Wad: Plastic or fiber
Shot: Lead
Buffered: No
Test barrel length: 26 inch
Pellets will pierce skin up to 126 yards.

NO. 7½ LEAD PELLETS—1 OUNCE—350 PELLETS
Mfg: Baschieri & Pellagri **Manufacturer's code:** F2
Recoil energy in 8-lb. shotgun: 19.9 ft./lbs. **Recoil velocity in 8-lb. shotgun:** 12.6 ft./sec.

Distance in yards:	Muzzle	20	30	40	50	60	70
Velocity in fps:	1413	903	761	652	565	492	430
Average pellet energy in ft-lbs:	5.59	2.28	1.62	1.19	.89	.68	.52
Time of flight in seconds:	0	.0544	.0907	.1334	.1829	.2399	.3052

Type of load: Target
Three-foot velocity: 1,300 ft./sec.
Hull: 2¾-inch plastic
Wad: Plastic
Shot: Hard lead
Buffered: No
Test barrel length: 26 inch
Pellets will pierce skin up to 126 yards.

NO. 7½ LEAD PELLETS—1 OUNCE—350 PELLETS
Mfg: Remington Arms Co. **Manufacturer's code:** SPHV20
Recoil energy in 8-lb. shotgun: 19.9 ft./lbs. **Recoil velocity in 8-lb. shotgun:** 12.6 ft./sec.

Distance in yards:	Muzzle	20	30	40	50	60	70
Velocity in fps:	1413	903	761	652	565	492	430
Average pellet energy in ft-lbs:	5.59	2.28	1.62	1.19	.89	.68	.52
Time of flight in seconds:	0	.0544	.0907	.1334	.1829	.2399	.3052

Type of load: Field
Three-foot velocity: 1,300 ft./sec.
Hull: 2¾-inch plastic
Wad: Plastic
Shot: Lead
Buffered: No
Test barrel length: 26 inch
Pellets will pierce skin up to 126 yards.

NO. 7½ LEAD PELLETS—1 OUNCE—350 PELLETS
Mfg: Winchester **Manufacturer's code:** SFH20
Recoil energy in 8-lb. shotgun: 19.9 ft./lbs. **Recoil velocity in 8-lb. shotgun:** 12.6 ft./sec.

Distance in yards:	Muzzle	20	30	40	50	60	70
Velocity in fps:	1413	903	761	652	565	492	430
Average pellet energy in ft-lbs:	5.59	2.28	1.62	1.19	.89	.68	.52
Time of flight in seconds:	0	.0544	.0907	.1334	.1829	.2399	.3052

Type of load: Field
Three-foot velocity: 1,300 ft./sec.
Hull: 2¾-inch plastic
Wad: Plastic
Shot: Copper-plated lead
Buffered: Yes
Test barrel length: 26 inch
Pellets will pierce skin up to 126 yards.

NO. 7½ LEAD PELLETS—1⅛ OUNCES—394 PELLETS
Mfg: Winchester **Manufacturer's code:** X20XC
Recoil energy in 8-lb. shotgun: 23.8 ft./lbs. **Recoil velocity in 8-lb. shotgun:** 13.8 ft./sec.

Distance in yards:	Muzzle	20	30	40	50	60	70
Velocity in fps:	1,274	841	714	615	535	466	407
Average pellet energy in ft-lbs:	4.54	1.98	1.43	1.06	.80	.61	.46
Time of flight in seconds:	0	.0592	.0980	.1433	.1957	.2558	.3246

Type of load: Field
Three-foot velocity: 1,175 ft./sec.
Hull: 2¾-inch plastic
Wad: Plastic
Shot: Copper-plated lead
Buffered: Yes
Test barrel length: 26 inch
Pellets will pierce skin up to 122 yards.

NO. 8 LEAD PELLETS—¾ OUNCE—307 PELLETS
Mfg: Estate Cartridge **Manufacturer's code:** ML20
Recoil energy in 8-lb. shotgun: 9.5 ft./lbs. **Recoil velocity in 8-lb. shotgun:** 8.7 ft./sec.

Distance in yards:	Muzzle	20	30	40	50	60	70
Velocity in fps:	1,327	934	713	610	526	456	395
Average pellet energy in ft-lbs:	4.19	1.71	1.21	.88	.66	.49	.37
Time of flight in seconds:	0	.0579	.0966	.1422	.1952	.2566	.3273

Type of load: Target
Three-foot velocity: 1,220 ft./sec.
Hull: 2¾-inch plastic
Wad: Plastic
Shot: Hard lead
Buffered: No
Test barrel length: 26 inch
Pellets will pierce skin up to 118 yards.

NO. 8 LEAD PELLETS—⅞ OUNCE—359 PELLETS
Mfg: Aguila **Manufacturer's code:** N/A
Recoil energy in 8-lb. shotgun: 11.0 ft./lbs. **Recoil velocity in 8-lb. shotgun:** 9.4 ft./sec.

Distance in yards:	Muzzle	20	30	40	50	60	70
Velocity in fps:	1,249	815	688	589	509	441	382
Average pellet energy in ft-lbs:	3.71	1.58	1.13	.83	.62	.46	.35
Time of flight in seconds:	0	.0608	.1010	.1482	.2030	.2663	.3394

Type of load: Field
Three-foot velocity: 1,150 ft./sec.
Hull: 2¾-inch plastic
Wad: Plastic
Shot: Lead
Buffered: No
Test barrel length: 26 inch
Pellets will pierce skin up to 115 yards.

NO. 8 LEAD PELLETS—⅞ OUNCE—359 PELLETS
Mfg: RST, Ltd. **Manufacturer's code:** N/A
Recoil energy in 8-lb. shotgun: 11.0 ft./lbs. **Recoil velocity in 8-lb. shotgun:** 9.4 ft./sec.

Distance in yards:	Muzzle	20	30	40	50	60	70
Velocity in fps:	1,249	815	688	589	509	441	382
Average pellet energy in ft-lbs:	3.71	1.58	1.13	.83	.62	.46	.35
Time of flight in seconds:	0	.0608	.1010	.1482	.2030	.2663	.3394

Type of load: Target
Three-foot velocity: 1,150 ft./sec.
Hull: 2¾-inch plastic
Wad: Plastic
Shot: Lead
Buffered: No
Test barrel length: 26 inch
Pellets will pierce skin up to 115 yards.

NO. 8 LEAD PELLETS—⅞ OUNCE—359 PELLETS
Mfg: Federal Cartridge Co. **Manufacturer's code:** T206
Recoil energy in 8-lb. shotgun: 12.3 ft./lbs. **Recoil velocity in 8-lb. shotgun:** 10.0 ft./sec.

Distance in yards:	Muzzle	20	30	40	50	60	70
Velocity in fps:	1,305	839	706	604	521	452	391
Average pellet energy in ft-lbs:	4.05	1.67	1.19	.87	.65	.49	.36
Time of flight in seconds:	0	.0587	.0978	.1438	.1973	.2593	.3307

Type of load: Target
Three-foot velocity: 1,200 ft./sec.
Hull: 2¾-inch plastic
Wad: Plastic
Shot: Lead
Buffered: No
Test barrel length: 28 inch
Pellets will pierce skin up to 129 yards.

NO. 8 LEAD PELLETS—⅞ OUNCE—359 PELLETS
Mfg: Armscor **Manufacturer's code:** N/A
Recoil energy in 8-lb. shotgun: 12.6 ft./lbs. **Recoil velocity in 8-lb. shotgun:** 10.1 ft./sec.

Distance in yards:	Muzzle	20	30	40	50	60	70
Velocity in fps:	1,305	839	706	604	521	452	391
Average pellet energy in ft-lbs:	4.05	1.67	1.19	.87	.65	.49	.36
Time of flight in seconds:	0	.0587	.0978	.1438	.1973	.2593	.3307

Type of load: Field
Three-foot velocity: 1,200 ft./sec.
Hull: 2¾-inch plastic
Wad: Plastic
Shot: Lead
Buffered: No
Test barrel length: 26 inch
Pellets will pierce skin up to 129 yards.

NO. 8 LEAD PELLETS—⅞ OUNCE—359 PELLETS
Mfg: Estate Cartridge **Manufacturer's code:** DQ20
Recoil energy in 8-lb. shotgun: 12.3 ft./lbs. **Recoil velocity in 8-lb. shotgun:** 10.0 ft./sec.

Distance in yards:	Muzzle	20	30	40	50	60	70
Velocity in fps:	1,305	839	706	604	521	452	391
Average pellet energy in ft-lbs:	4.05	1.67	1.19	.87	.65	.49	.36
Time of flight in seconds:	0	.0587	.0978	.1438	.1973	.2593	.3307

Type of load: Field
Three-foot velocity: 1,200 ft./sec.
Hull: 2¾-inch plastic
Wad: Plastic
Shot: Hard lead
Buffered: No
Test barrel length: 26 inch
Pellets will pierce skin up to 129 yards.

NO. 8 LEAD PELLETS—⅞ OUNCE—359 PELLETS
Mfg: Estate Cartridge **Manufacturer's code:** CT20/SS20
Recoil energy in 8-lb. shotgun: 12.3 ft./lbs. **Recoil velocity in 8-lb. shotgun:** 10.0 ft./sec.

Distance in yards:	Muzzle	20	30	40	50	60	70
Velocity in fps:	1,305	839	706	604	521	452	391
Average pellet energy in ft-lbs:	4.05	1.67	1.19	.87	.65	.49	.36
Time of flight in seconds:	0	.0587	.0978	.1438	.1973	.2593	.3307

Type of load: Target
Three-foot velocity: 1,200 ft./sec.
Hull: 2¾-inch plastic
Wad: Plastic
Shot: Hard lead
Buffered: No
Test barrel length: 26 inch
Pellets will pierce skin up to 129 yards.

NO. 8 LEAD PELLETS—⅞ OUNCE—359 PELLETS
Mfg: Federal Cartridge Co. **Manufacturer's code:** H200/FD20
Recoil energy in 8-lb. shotgun: 12.3 ft./lbs. **Recoil velocity in 8-lb. shotgun:** 10.0 ft./sec.

Distance in yards:	Muzzle	20	30	40	50	60	70
Velocity in fps:	1,305	839	706	604	521	452	391
Average pellet energy in ft-lbs:	4.05	1.67	1.19	.87	.65	.49	.36
Time of flight in seconds:	0	.0587	.0978	.1438	.1973	.2593	.3307

Type of load: Field
Three-foot velocity: 1,200 ft./sec.
Hull: 2¾-inch plastic
Wad: Plastic
Shot: Lead
Buffered: No
Test barrel length: 26 inch
Pellets will pierce skin up to 129 yards.

NO. 8 LEAD PELLETS—⅞ OUNCE—359 PELLETS
Mfg: Fiocchi **Manufacturer's code:** 20GT
Recoil energy in 8-lb. shotgun: 12.3 ft./lbs. **Recoil velocity in 8-lb. shotgun:** 10.0 ft./sec.

Distance in yards:	Muzzle	20	30	40	50	60	70
Velocity in fps:	1,305	839	706	604	521	452	391
Average pellet energy in ft-lbs:	4.05	1.67	1.19	.87	.65	.49	.36
Time of flight in seconds:	0	.0587	.0978	.1438	.1973	.2593	.3307

Type of load: Game & Target
Three-foot velocity: 1,200 ft./sec.
Hull: 2¾-inch plastic
Wad: Plastic
Shot: Lead
Buffered: No
Test barrel length: 26 inch
Pellets will pierce skin up to 129 yards.

NO. 8 LEAD PELLETS—⅞ OUNCE—359 PELLETS
Mfg: Fiocchi **Manufacturer's code:** 20VIP
Recoil energy in 8-lb. shotgun: 12.3 ft./lbs. **Recoil velocity in 8-lb. shotgun:** 10.0 ft./sec.

Distance in yards:	Muzzle	20	30	40	50	60	70
Velocity in fps:	1,305	839	706	604	521	452	391
Average pellet energy in ft-lbs:	4.05	1.67	1.19	.87	.65	.49	.36
Time of flight in seconds:	0	.0587	.0978	.1438	.1973	.2593	.3307

Type of load: Target
Three-foot velocity: 1,200 ft./sec.
Hull: 2¾-inch plastic
Wad: Plastic
Shot: Hard lead
Buffered: No
Test barrel length: 26 inch
Pellets will pierce skin up to 129 yards.

NO. 8 LEAD PELLETS—⅞ OUNCE—359 PELLETS
Mfg: Remington Arms Co. **Manufacturer's code:** STS20SC
Recoil energy in 8-lb. shotgun: 12.3 ft./lbs. **Recoil velocity in 8-lb. shotgun:** 10.0 ft./sec.

Distance in yards:	Muzzle	20	30	40	50	60	70
Velocity in fps:	1,305	839	706	604	521	452	391
Average pellet energy in ft-lbs:	4.05	1.67	1.19	.87	.65	.49	.36
Time of flight in seconds:	0	.0587	.0978	.1438	.1973	.2593	.3307

Type of load: Target
Three-foot velocity: 1,200 ft./sec.
Hull: 2¾-inch plastic
Wad: Plastic
Shot: Hard lead
Buffered: No
Test barrel length: 26 inch
Pellets will pierce skin up to 129 yards.

NO. 8 LEAD PELLETS—⅞ OUNCE—359 PELLETS
Mfg: Rottweil **Manufacturer's code:** Game
Recoil energy in 8-lb. shotgun: 12.3 ft./lbs. **Recoil velocity in 8-lb. shotgun:** 10.0 ft./sec.

Distance in yards:	Muzzle	20	30	40	50	60	70
Velocity in fps:	1,305	839	706	604	521	452	391
Average pellet energy in ft-lbs:	4.05	1.67	1.19	.87	.65	.49	.36
Time of flight in seconds:	0	.0587	.0978	.1438	.1973	.2593	.3307

Type of load: Field
Three-foot velocity: 1,200 ft./sec.
Hull: 2¾-inch plastic
Wad: Plastic
Shot: Lead
Buffered: No
Test barrel length: 26 inch
Pellets will pierce skin up to 129 yards.

NO. 8 LEAD PELLETS—⅞ OUNCE—359 PELLETS
Mfg: Winchester **Manufacturer's code:** XU20
Recoil energy in 8-lb. shotgun: 12.3 ft./lbs. **Recoil velocity in 8-lb. shotgun:** 10.0 ft./sec.

Distance in yards:	Muzzle	20	30	40	50	60	70
Velocity in fps:	1,305	839	706	604	521	452	391
Average pellet energy in ft-lbs:	4.05	1.67	1.19	.87	.65	.49	.36
Time of flight in seconds:	0	.0587	.0978	.1438	.1973	.2593	.3307

Type of load: Field
Three-foot velocity: 1,200 ft./sec.
Hull: 2¾-inch plastic
Wad: Plastic
Shot: Lead
Buffered: No
Test barrel length: 26 inch
Pellets will pierce skin up to 129 yards.

NO. 8 LEAD PELLETS—⅞ OUNCE—359 PELLETS
Mfg: Winchester **Manufacturer's code:** AA20
Recoil energy in 8-lb. shotgun: 12.3 ft./lbs. **Recoil velocity in 8-lb. shotgun:** 10.0 ft./sec.

Distance in yards:	Muzzle	20	30	40	50	60	70
Velocity in fps:	1,305	839	706	604	521	452	391
Average pellet energy in ft-lbs:	4.05	1.67	1.19	.87	.65	.49	.36
Time of flight in seconds:	0	.0587	.0978	.1438	.1973	.2593	.3307

Type of load: Target
Three-foot velocity: 1,200 ft./sec.
Hull: 2¾-inch plastic
Wad: Plastic
Shot: Lead
Buffered: No
Test barrel length: 26 inch
Pellets will pierce skin up to 129 yards.

NO. 8 LEAD PELLETS—⅞ OUNCE—359 PELLETS
Mfg: Winchester **Manufacturer's code:** D 20 SLR
Recoil energy in 8-lb. shotgun: 12.3 ft./lbs. **Recoil velocity in 8-lb. shotgun:** 10.0 ft./sec.

Distance in yards:	Muzzle	20	30	40	50	60	70
Velocity in fps:	1,305	839	706	604	521	452	391
Average pellet energy in ft-lbs:	4.05	1.67	1.19	.87	.65	.49	.36
Time of flight in seconds:	0	.0587	.0978	.1438	.1973	.2593	.3307

Type of load: Field & Target
Three-foot velocity: 1,200 ft./sec.
Hull: 2¾-inch plastic
Wad: Plastic
Shot: Lead
Buffered: No
Test barrel length: 26 inch
Pellets will pierce skin up to 129 yards.

NO. 8 LEAD PELLETS—⅞ OUNCE—359 PELLETS
Mfg: PMC (Eldorado Cartridge Corp.) **Manufacturer's code:** PL20/CT20
Recoil energy in 8-lb. shotgun: 12.6 ft./lbs. **Recoil velocity in 8-lb. shotgun:** 10.1 ft./sec.

Distance in yards:	Muzzle	20	30	40	50	60	70
Velocity in fps:	1,327	934	713	610	526	456	395
Average pellet energy in ft-lbs:	4.19	1.71	1.21	.88	.66	.49	.37
Time of flight in seconds:	0	.0579	.0966	.1422	.1952	.2566	.3273

Type of load: Quail & Dove & Target
Three-foot velocity: 1,220 ft./sec.
Hull: 2¾-inch plastic
Wad: Plastic
Shot: Lead
Buffered: No
Test barrel length: 26 inch
Pellets will pierce skin up to 118 yards.

NO. 8 LEAD PELLETS—⅞ OUNCE—359 PELLETS
Mfg: Remington Arms Co. **Manufacturer's code:** GL20/R20SL
Recoil energy in 8-lb. shotgun: 12.6 ft./lbs. **Recoil velocity in 8-lb. shotgun:** 10.1 ft./sec.

Distance in yards:	Muzzle	20	30	40	50	60	70
Velocity in fps:	1,327	934	713	610	526	456	395
Average pellet energy in ft-lbs:	4.19	1.71	1.21	.88	.66	.49	.37
Time of flight in seconds:	0	.0579	.0966	.1422	.1952	.2566	.3273

Type of load: Field
Three-foot velocity: 1,220 ft./sec.
Hull: 2¾-inch plastic
Wad: Plastic
Shot: Lead
Buffered: No
Test barrel length: 26 inch
Pellets will pierce skin up to 118 yards.

NO. 8 LEAD PELLETS—⅞ OUNCE—359 PELLETS
Mfg: RST, Ltd. **Manufacturer's code:** N/A
Recoil energy in 8-lb. shotgun: 12.6 ft./lbs. **Recoil velocity in 8-lb. shotgun:** 10.1 ft./sec.

Distance in yards:	Muzzle	20	30	40	50	60	70
Velocity in fps:	1,327	934	713	610	526	456	395
Average pellet energy in ft-lbs:	4.19	1.71	1.21	.88	.66	.49	.37
Time of flight in seconds:	0	.0579	.0966	.1422	.1952	.2566	.3273

Type of load: Target
Three-foot velocity: 1,220 ft./sec.
Hull: 2¾-inch plastic
Wad: Plastic
Shot: Lead
Buffered: No
Test barrel length: 26 inch
Pellets will pierce skin up to 118 yards.

NO. 8 LEAD PELLETS—⅞ OUNCE—359 PELLETS
Mfg: Sellier & Bellot **Manufacturer's code:** SBA02021
Recoil energy in 8-lb. shotgun: 12.6 ft./lbs. **Recoil velocity in 8-lb. shotgun:** 10.1 ft./sec.

Distance in yards:	Muzzle	20	30	40	50	60	70
Velocity in fps:	1,327	934	713	610	526	456	395
Average pellet energy in ft-lbs:	4.19	1.71	1.21	.88	.66	.49	.37
Time of flight in seconds:	0	.0579	.0966	.1422	.1952	.2566	.3273

Type of load: Target
Three-foot velocity: 1,220 ft./sec.
Hull: 2¾-inch plastic
Wad: Plastic
Shot: Lead
Buffered: No
Test barrel length: 26 inch
Pellets will pierce skin up to 118 yards.

NO. 8 LEAD PELLETS—⅞ OUNCE—359 PELLETS
Mfg: Dionisi **Manufacturer's code:** D 20 DQ
Recoil energy in 8-lb. shotgun: 17.4 ft./lbs. **Recoil velocity in 8-lb. shotgun:** 11.8 ft./sec.

Distance in yards:	Muzzle	20	30	40	50	60	70
Velocity in fps:	1,344	856	719	614	529	459	397
Average pellet energy in ft-lbs:	4.30	1.74	1.23	.90	.67	.50	.38
Time of flight in seconds:	0	.0573	.0957	.1409	.1936	.2546	.3249

Type of load: Dove & Quail
Three-foot velocity: 1,235 ft./sec.
Hull: 2¾-inch plastic
Wad: Plastic
Shot: Lead
Buffered: No
Test barrel length: 26 inch
Pellets will pierce skin up to 118 yards.

NO. 8 LEAD PELLETS—⅞ OUNCE—359 PELLETS
Mfg: Kent Cartridge America/Canada **Manufacturer's code:** K202LSC24
Recoil energy in 8-lb. shotgun: 13.7 ft./lbs. **Recoil velocity in 8-lb. shotgun:** 10.5 ft./sec.

Distance in yards:	Muzzle	20	30	40	50	60	70
Velocity in fps:	1,361	863	724	618	533	461	400
Average pellet energy in ft-lbs:	4.41	1.77	1.25	.91	.68	.51	.38
Time of flight in seconds:	0	.0568	.0948	.1398	.1921	.2527	.3225

Type of load: Target
Three-foot velocity: 1,250 ft./sec.
Hull: 2¾-inch plastic
Wad: Plastic
Shot: Lead
Buffered: No
Test barrel length: 30 inch
Pellets will pierce skin up to 118 yards.

NO. 8 LEAD PELLETS—⅞ OUNCE—359 PELLETS
Mfg: Eley Hawk **Manufacturer's code:** Competition 24
Recoil energy in 8-lb. shotgun: 14.5 ft./lbs. **Recoil velocity in 8-lb. shotgun:** 10.8 ft./sec.

Distance in yards:	Muzzle	20	30	40	50	60	70
Velocity in fps:	1,389	875	733	625	538	466	404
Average pellet energy in ft-lbs:	4.59	1.82	1.28	.93	.63	.52	.39
Time of flight in seconds:	0	.0558	.0934	.1378	.1897	.2496	.3187

Type of load: Target
Three-foot velocity: 1,275 ft./sec.
Hull: 2¾-inch plastic
Wad: Plastic or fiber
Shot: Lead
Buffered: No
Test barrel length: 26 inch
Pellets will pierce skin up to 131 yards.

NO. 8 LEAD PELLETS—⅞ OUNCE—359 PELLETS
Mfg: Baschieri & Pellagri **Manufacturer's code:** F2
Recoil energy in 8-lb. shotgun: 16.2 ft./lbs. **Recoil velocity in 8-lb. shotgun:** 11.4 ft./sec.

Distance in yards:	Muzzle	20	30	40	50	60	70
Velocity in fps:	1,451	900	752	640	551	477	413
Average pellet energy in ft-lbs:	5.01	1.93	1.35	.97	.72	.54	.41
Time of flight in seconds:	0	.0539	.0905	.1338	.1845	.2431	.3108

Type of load: Target
Three-foot velocity: 1,330 ft./sec.
Hull: 2¾-inch plastic
Wad: Plastic
Shot: Hard lead
Buffered: No
Test barrel length: 26 inch
Pellets will pierce skin up to 121 yards.

NO. 8 LEAD PELLETS—1 OUNCE—410 PELLETS
Mfg: Federal Cartridge Co. **Manufacturer's code:** H202/HGL20
Recoil energy in 8-lb. shotgun: 14.9 ft./lbs. **Recoil velocity in 8-lb. shotgun:** 10.9 ft./sec.

Distance in yards:	Muzzle	20	30	40	50	60	70
Velocity in fps:	1,266	822	693	594	513	444	385
Average pellet energy in ft-lbs:	3.81	1.61	1.14	.84	.63	.47	.35
Time of flight in seconds:	0	.0601	.1000	.1468	.2013	.2641	.3367

Type of load: Field
Three-foot velocity: 1,165 ft./sec.
Hull: 2¾-inch plastic
Wad: Plastic
Shot: Lead
Buffered: No
Test barrel length: 26 inch
Pellets will pierce skin up to 116 yards.

NO. 8 LEAD PELLETS—1 OUNCE—410 PELLETS
Mfg: Fiocchi **Manufacturer's code:** 20FLD
Recoil energy in 8-lb. shotgun: 14.9 ft./lbs. **Recoil velocity in 8-lb. shotgun:** 10.9 ft./sec.

Distance in yards:	Muzzle	20	30	40	50	60	70
Velocity in fps:	1,266	822	693	594	513	444	385
Average pellet energy in ft-lbs:	3.81	1.61	1.14	.84	.63	.47	.35
Time of flight in seconds:	0	.0601	.1000	.1468	.2013	.2641	.3367

Type of load: Field
Three-foot velocity: 1,165 ft./sec.
Hull: 2¾-inch plastic
Wad: Plastic
Shot: Lead
Buffered: No
Test barrel length: 26 inch
Pellets will pierce skin up to 116 yards.

NO. 8 LEAD PELLETS—1 OUNCE—410 PELLETS
Mfg: Remington Arms Co. **Manufacturer's code:** RP20HD
Recoil energy in 8-lb. shotgun: 14.9 ft./lbs. **Recoil velocity in 8-lb. shotgun:** 10.9 ft./sec.

Distance in yards:	Muzzle	20	30	40	50	60	70
Velocity in fps:	1,266	822	693	594	513	444	385
Average pellet energy in ft-lbs:	3.81	1.61	1.14	.84	.63	.47	.35
Time of flight in seconds:	0	.0601	.1000	.1468	.2013	.2641	.3367

Type of load: Field
Three-foot velocity: 1,165 ft./sec.
Hull: 2¾-inch plastic
Wad: Plastic
Shot: Lead
Buffered: No
Test barrel length: 26 inch
Pellets will pierce skin up to 116 yards.

NO. 8 LEAD PELLETS—1 OUNCE—410 PELLETS
Mfg: Winchester **Manufacturer's code:** XU20H
Recoil energy in 8-lb. shotgun: 14.9 ft./lbs. **Recoil velocity in 8-lb. shotgun:** 10.9 ft./sec.

Distance in yards:	Muzzle	20	30	40	50	60	70
Velocity in fps:	1,266	822	693	594	513	444	385
Average pellet energy in ft-lbs:	3.81	1.61	1.14	.84	.63	.47	.35
Time of flight in seconds:	0	.0601	.1000	.1468	.2013	.2641	.3367

Type of load: Field
Three-foot velocity: 1,165 ft./sec.
Hull: 2¾-inch plastic
Wad: Plastic
Shot: Lead
Buffered: No
Test barrel length: 26 inch
Pellets will pierce skin up to 116 yards.

NO. 8 LEAD PELLETS—1 OUNCE—410 PELLETS
Mfg: Winchester **Manufacturer's code:** AAH20
Recoil energy in 8-lb. shotgun: 14.9 ft./lbs. **Recoil velocity in 8-lb. shotgun:** 10.9 ft./sec.

Distance in yards:	Muzzle	20	30	40	50	60	70
Velocity in fps:	1,266	822	693	594	513	444	385
Average pellet energy in ft-lbs:	3.81	1.61	1.14	.84	.63	.47	.35
Time of flight in seconds:	0	.0601	.1000	.1468	.2013	.2641	.3367

Type of load: Target
Three-foot velocity: 1,165 ft./sec.
Hull: 2¾-inch plastic
Wad: Plastic
Shot: Hard lead
Buffered: No
Test barrel length: 26 inch
Pellets will pierce skin up to 116 yards.

NO. 8 LEAD PELLETS—1 OUNCE—410 PELLETS
Mfg: Estate Cartridge **Manufacturer's code:** HG20
Recoil energy in 8-lb. shotgun: 18.9 ft./lbs. **Recoil velocity in 8-lb. shotgun:** 12.3 ft./sec.

Distance in yards:	Muzzle	20	30	40	50	60	70
Velocity in fps:	1,277	827	697	597	515	446	387
Average pellet energy in ft-lbs:	3.88	1.63	1.16	.85	.63	.47	.36
Time of flight in seconds:	0	.0597	.0993	.1459	.2001	.2627	.3349

Type of load: Field
Three-foot velocity: 1,175 ft./sec.5
Hull: 2¾-inch plastic
Wad: Plastic
Shot: Hard lead
Buffered: No
Test barrel length: 26 inch
Pellets will pierce skin up to 116 yards.

NO. 8 LEAD PELLETS—1 OUNCE—410 PELLETS
Mfg: PMC (Eldorado Cartridge Corp.) **Manufacturer's code:** HF20
Recoil energy in 8-lb. shotgun: 16.1 ft./lbs. **Recoil velocity in 8-lb. shotgun:** 11.4 ft./sec.

Distance in yards:	Muzzle	20	30	40	50	60	70
Velocity in fps:	1,305	839	706	604	521	452	391
Average pellet energy in ft-lbs:	4.05	1.67	1.19	.87	.65	.49	.36
Time of flight in seconds:	0	.0587	.0978	.1438	.1973	.2593	.3307

Type of load: Field
Three-foot velocity: 1,200 ft./sec.
Hull: 2¾-inch plastic
Wad: Plastic
Shot: Lead
Buffered: No
Test barrel length: 26 inch
Pellets will pierce skin up to 129 yards.

NO. 8 LEAD PELLETS—1 OUNCE—410 PELLETS
Mfg: Estate Cartridge **Manufacturer's code:** HV20
Recoil energy in 8-lb. shotgun: 16.8 ft./lbs. **Recoil velocity in 8-lb. shotgun:** 11.6 ft./sec.

Distance in yards:	Muzzle	20	30	40	50	60	70
Velocity in fps:	1,327	934	713	610	526	456	395
Average pellet energy in ft-lbs:	4.19	1.71	1.21	.88	.66	.49	.37
Time of flight in seconds:	0	.0579	.0966	.1422	.1952	.2566	.3273

Type of load: Field
Three-foot velocity: 1,220 ft./sec.
Hull: 2¾-inch plastic
Wad: Plastic
Shot: Hard lead
Buffered: No
Test barrel length: 26 inch
Pellets will pierce skin up to 118 yards.

NO. 8 LEAD PELLETS—1 OUNCE—410 PELLETS
Mfg: Federal Cartridge Co. **Manufacturer's code:** H204
Recoil energy in 8-lb. shotgun: 16.8 ft./lbs. **Recoil velocity in 8-lb. shotgun:** 11.6 ft./sec.

Distance in yards:	Muzzle	20	30	40	50	60	70
Velocity in fps:	1,327	934	713	610	526	456	395
Average pellet energy in ft-lbs:	4.19	1.71	1.21	.88	.66	.49	.37
Time of flight in seconds:	0	.0579	.0966	.1422	.1952	.2566	.3273

Type of load: Field
Three-foot velocity: 1,220 ft./sec.
Hull: 2¾-inch plastic
Wad: Plastic
Shot: Lead
Buffered: No
Test barrel length: 26 inch
Pellets will pierce skin up to 118 yards.

NO. 8 LEAD PELLETS—1 OUNCE—410 PELLETS
Mfg: Fiocchi **Manufacturer's code:** 20HV
Recoil energy in 8-lb. shotgun: 16.8 ft./lbs. **Recoil velocity in 8-lb. shotgun:** 11.6 ft./sec.

Distance in yards:	Muzzle	20	30	40	50	60	70
Velocity in fps:	1,327	934	713	610	526	456	395
Average pellet energy in ft-lbs:	4.19	1.71	1.21	.88	.66	.49	.37
Time of flight in seconds:	0	.0579	.0966	.1422	.1952	.2566	.3273

Type of load: Field
Three-foot velocity: 1,220 ft./sec.
Hull: 2¾-inch plastic
Wad: Plastic
Shot: Lead
Buffered: No
Test barrel length: 26 inch
Pellets will pierce skin up to 118 yards.

NO. 8 LEAD PELLETS—1 OUNCE—410 PELLETS
Mfg: Sellier & Bellot **Manufacturer's code:** SBA02003
Recoil energy in 8-lb. shotgun: 16.8 ft./lbs. **Recoil velocity in 8-lb. shotgun:** 11.6 ft./sec.

Distance in yards:	Muzzle	20	30	40	50	60	70
Velocity in fps:	1,327	934	713	610	526	456	395
Average pellet energy in ft-lbs:	4.19	1.71	1.21	.88	.66	.49	.37
Time of flight in seconds:	0	.0579	.0966	.1422	.1952	.2566	.3273

Type of load: Field
Three-foot velocity: 1,220 ft./sec.
Hull: 2¾-inch plastic
Wad: Plastic
Shot: Lead
Buffered: No
Test barrel length: 26 inch
Pellets will pierce skin up to 118 yards.

NO. 8 LEAD PELLETS—1 OUNCE—410 PELLETS
Mfg: Winchester **Manufacturer's code:** X20
Recoil energy in 8-lb. shotgun: 16.8 ft./lbs. **Recoil velocity in 8-lb. shotgun:** 11.6 ft./sec.

Distance in yards:	Muzzle	20	30	40	50	60	70
Velocity in fps:	1,327	934	713	610	526	456	395
Average pellet energy in ft-lbs:	4.19	1.71	1.21	.88	.66	.49	.37
Time of flight in seconds:	0	.0579	.0966	.1422	.1952	.2566	.3273

Type of load: Field
Three-foot velocity: 1,220 ft./sec.
Hull: 2¾-inch plastic
Wad: Plastic
Shot: Lead
Buffered: No
Test barrel length: 26 inch
Pellets will pierce skin up to 118 yards.

NO. 8 LEAD PELLETS—1 OUNCE—410 PELLETS
Mfg: Federal Cartridge Co. **Manufacturer's code:** P204
Recoil energy in 8-lb. shotgun: 17.4 ft./lbs. **Recoil velocity in 8-lb. shotgun:** 11.8 ft./sec.

Distance in yards:	Muzzle	20	30	40	50	60	70
Velocity in fps:	1,344	856	719	614	529	459	397
Average pellet energy in ft-lbs:	4.30	1.74	1.23	.90	.67	.50	.38
Time of flight in seconds:	0	.0573	.0957	.1409	.1936	.2546	.3249

Type of load: Field
Three-foot velocity: 1,235 ft./sec.
Hull: 2¾-inch plastic
Wad: Plastic
Shot: Lead
Buffered: No
Test barrel length: 26 inch
Pellets will pierce skin up to 118 yards.

NO. 8 LEAD PELLETS—1 OUNCE—410 PELLETS
Mfg: Kent Cartridge America/Canada **Manufacturer's code:** K202UG28
Recoil energy in 8-lb. shotgun: 17.4 ft./lbs. **Recoil velocity in 8-lb. shotgun:** 11.8 ft./sec.

Distance in yards:	Muzzle	20	30	40	50	60	70
Velocity in fps:	1,344	856	719	614	529	459	397
Average pellet energy in ft-lbs:	4.30	1.74	1.23	.90	.67	.50	.38
Time of flight in seconds:	0	.0573	.0957	.1409	.1936	.2546	.3249

Type of load: Field
Three-foot velocity: 1,235 ft./sec.
Hull: 2¾-inch plastic
Wad: Plastic
Shot: Lead
Buffered: No
Test barrel length: 26 inch
Pellets will pierce skin up to 118 yards.

NO. 8 LEAD PELLETS—1 OUNCE—410 PELLETS
Mfg: Eley Hawk **Manufacturer's code:** Competition 28
Recoil energy in 8-lb. shotgun: 18.9 ft./lbs. **Recoil velocity in 8-lb. shotgun:** 12.3 ft./sec.

Distance in yards:	Muzzle	20	30	40	50	60	70
Velocity in fps:	1,389	875	733	625	538	466	404
Average pellet energy in ft-lbs:	4.59	1.82	1.28	.93	.63	.52	.39
Time of flight in seconds:	0	.0558	.0934	.1378	.1897	.2496	.3187

Type of load: Target
Three-foot velocity: 1,275 ft./sec.
Hull: 2¾-inch plastic
Wad: Plastic or fiber
Shot: Lead
Buffered: No
Test barrel length: 26 inch
Pellets will pierce skin up to 131 yards.

NO. 8 LEAD PELLETS—1 OUNCE—410 PELLETS
Mfg: Baschieri & Pellagri **Manufacturer's code:** F2
Recoil energy in 8-lb. shotgun: 19.9 ft./lbs. **Recoil velocity in 8-lb. shotgun:** 12.6 ft./sec.

Distance in yards:	Muzzle	20	30	40	50	60	70
Velocity in fps:	1,417	886	742	632	544	471	408
Average pellet energy in ft-lbs:	4.78	1.87	1.31	.95	.70	.53	.40
Time of flight in seconds:	0	.0549	.0921	.1360	.1873	.2466	.3150

Type of load: Target
Three-foot velocity: 1,300 ft./sec.
Hull: 2¾-inch plastic
Wad: Plastic
Shot: Hard lead
Buffered: No
Test barrel length: 26 inch
Pellets will pierce skin up to 132 yards.

NO. 8 LEAD PELLETS—1 OUNCE—410 PELLETS
Mfg: Clever **Manufacturer's code:** T1 Light Game
Recoil energy in 8-lb. shotgun: 19.9 ft./lbs. **Recoil velocity in 8-lb. shotgun:** 12.6 ft./sec.

Distance in yards:	Muzzle	20	30	40	50	60	70
Velocity in fps:	1,417	886	742	632	544	471	408
Average pellet energy in ft-lbs:	4.78	1.87	1.31	.95	.70	.53	.40
Time of flight in seconds:	0	.0549	.0921	.1360	.1873	.2466	.3150

Type of load: Field
Three-foot velocity: 1,300 ft./sec.
Hull: 2¾-inch plastic
Wad: Plastic
Shot: Lead
Buffered: No
Test barrel length: 26 inch
Pellets will pierce skin up to 132 yards.

NO. 8½ LEAD PELLETS—¾ OUNCE—373 PELLETS
Mfg: Estate Cartridge **Manufacturer's code:** ML20
Recoil energy in 8-lb. shotgun: 9.5 ft./lbs. **Recoil velocity in 8-lb. shotgun:** 8.7 ft./sec.

Distance in yards:	Muzzle	20	30	40	50	60	70
Velocity in fps:	1,331	832	694	589	505	434	373
Average pellet energy in ft-lbs:	3.55	1.39	.97	.70	.51	.38	.28
Time of flight in seconds:	0	.0585	.0981	.1451	.2002	.2644	.3390

Type of load: Target
Three-foot velocity: 1,220 ft./sec.
Hull: 2¾-inch plastic
Wad: Plastic
Shot: Hard lead
Buffered: No
Test barrel length: 26 inch
Pellets will pierce skin up to 111 yards.

NO. 8½ LEAD PELLETS—⅞ OUNCE—435 PELLETS
Mfg: Estate Cartridge **Manufacturer's code:** CT20
Recoil energy in 8-lb. shotgun: 12.3 ft./lbs. **Recoil velocity in 8-lb. shotgun:** 10.0 ft./sec.

Distance in yards:	Muzzle	20	30	40	50	60	70
Velocity in fps:	1,308	823	687	584	500	430	369
Average pellet energy in ft-lbs:	1.36	1.13	.95	.68	.50	.37	.325
Time of flight in seconds:	0	.0593	.0993	.1468	.2024	.2671	.3423

Type of load: Target
Three-foot velocity: 1,200 ft./sec.
Hull: 2¾-inch plastic
Wad: Plastic
Shot: Hard lead
Buffered: No
Test barrel length: 26 inch
Pellets will pierce skin up to 111 yards.

NO. 8½ LEAD PELLETS—⅞ OUNCE—435 PELLETS
Mfg: Federal Cartridge Co. **Manufacturer's code:** T206
Recoil energy in 8-lb. shotgun: 12.3 ft./lbs. **Recoil velocity in 8-lb. shotgun:** 10.0 ft./sec.

Distance in yards:	Muzzle	20	30	40	50	60	70
Velocity in fps:	1,308	823	687	584	500	430	369
Average pellet energy in ft-lbs:	1.36	1.13	.95	.68	.50	.37	.325
Time of flight in seconds:	0	.0593	.0993	.1468	.2024	.2671	.3423

Type of load: Target
Three-foot velocity: 1,200 ft./sec.
Hull: 2¾-inch plastic
Wad: Plastic
Shot: Lead
Buffered: No
Test barrel length: 26 inch
Pellets will pierce skin up to 111 yards.

NO. 9 LEAD PELLETS—¾ OUNCE—439 PELLETS
Mfg: Estate Cartridge **Manufacturer's code:** ML20
Recoil energy in 8-lb. shotgun: 9.5 ft./lbs. **Recoil velocity in 8-lb. shotgun:** 8.7 ft./sec.

Distance in yards:	Muzzle	20	30	40	50	60	70
Velocity in fps:	1,334	814	674	567	482	410	349
Average pellet energy in ft-lbs:	2.98	1.11	.76	.54	.39	.28	.20
Time of flight in seconds:	0	.0593	.0999	.1486	.2060	.2735	.3528

Type of load: Target
Three-foot velocity: 1,220 ft./sec.
Hull: 2¾-inch plastic
Wad: Plastic
Shot: Hard lead
Buffered: No
Test barrel length: 26 inch
Pellets will pierce skin up to 105 yards.

NO. 9 LEAD PELLETS—⅞ OUNCE—512 PELLETS
Mfg: Estate Cartridge **Manufacturer's code:** DQ20
Recoil energy in 8-lb. shotgun: 12.3 ft./lbs. **Recoil velocity in 8-lb. shotgun:** 10.0 ft./sec.

Distance in yards:	Muzzle	20	30	40	50	60	70
Velocity in fps:	1,312	805	667	562	478	407	346
Average pellet energy in ft-lbs:	2.88	1.08	.74	.53	.38	.28	.20
Time of flight in seconds:	0	.0601	.1011	.1502	.2082	.2763	.3562

Type of load: Field
Three-foot velocity: 1,200 ft./sec.
Hull: 2¾-inch plastic
Wad: Plastic
Shot: Hard lead
Buffered: No
Test barrel length: 26 inch
Pellets will pierce skin up to 115 yards.

NO. 9 LEAD PELLETS—⅞ OUNCE—512 PELLETS
Mfg: Estate Cartridge **Manufacturer's code:** CT20/SS20
Recoil energy in 8-lb. shotgun: 12.3 ft./lbs. **Recoil velocity in 8-lb. shotgun:** 10.0 ft./sec.

Distance in yards:	Muzzle	20	30	40	50	60	70
Velocity in fps:	1,312	805	667	562	478	407	346
Average pellet energy in ft-lbs:	2.88	1.08	.74	.53	.38	.28	.20
Time of flight in seconds:	0	.0601	.1011	.1502	.2082	.2763	.3562

Type of load: Target
Three-foot velocity: 1,200 ft./sec.
Hull: 2¾-inch plastic
Wad: Plastic
Shot: Hard lead
Buffered: No
Test barrel length: 26 inch
Pellets will pierce skin up to 115 yards.

NO. 9 LEAD PELLETS—⅞ OUNCE—512 PELLETS
Mfg: Federal Cartridge Co. **Manufacturer's code:** T206
Recoil energy in 8-lb. shotgun: 12.3 ft./lbs. **Recoil velocity in 8-lb. shotgun:** 10.0 ft./sec.

Distance in yards:	Muzzle	20	30	40	50	60	70
Velocity in fps:	1,312	805	667	562	478	407	346
Average pellet energy in ft-lbs:	2.88	1.08	.74	.53	.38	.28	.20
Time of flight in seconds:	0	.0601	.1011	.1502	.2082	.2763	.3562

Type of load: Target
Three-foot velocity: 1,200 ft./sec.
Hull: 2¾-inch plastic
Wad: Plastic
Shot: Lead
Buffered: No
Test barrel length: 26 inch
Pellets will pierce skin up to 115 yards.

NO. 9 LEAD PELLETS—⅞ OUNCE—512 PELLETS
Mfg: Fiocchi **Manufacturer's code:** 20GT
Recoil energy in 8-lb. shotgun: 12.3 ft./lbs. **Recoil velocity in 8-lb. shotgun:** 10.0 ft./sec.

Distance in yards:	Muzzle	20	30	40	50	60	70
Velocity in fps:	1,312	805	667	562	478	407	346
Average pellet energy in ft-lbs:	2.88	1.08	.74	.53	.38	.28	.20
Time of flight in seconds:	0	.0601	.1011	.1502	.2082	.2763	.3562

Type of load: Game & Target
Three-foot velocity: 1,200 ft./sec.
Hull: 2¾-inch plastic
Wad: Plastic
Shot: Lead
Buffered: No
Test barrel length: 26 inch
Pellets will pierce skin up to 115 yards.

NO. 9 LEAD PELLETS—⅞ OUNCE—512 PELLETS
Mfg: Fiocchi **Manufacturer's code:** 20VIP
Recoil energy in 8-lb. shotgun: 12.3 ft./lbs. **Recoil velocity in 8-lb. shotgun:** 10.0 ft./sec.

Distance in yards:	Muzzle	20	30	40	50	60	70
Velocity in fps:	1,312	805	667	562	478	407	346
Average pellet energy in ft-lbs:	2.88	1.08	.74	.53	.38	.28	.20
Time of flight in seconds:	0	.0601	.1011	.1502	.2082	.2763	.3562

Type of load: Target
Three-foot velocity: 1,200 ft./sec.
Hull: 2¾-inch plastic
Wad: Plastic
Shot: Hard lead
Buffered: No
Test barrel length: 26 inch
Pellets will pierce skin up to 115 yards.

NO. 9 LEAD PELLETS—⅞ OUNCE—512 PELLETS
Mfg: Remington Arms Co. **Manufacturer's code:** STS20
Recoil energy in 8-lb. shotgun: 12.3 ft./lbs. **Recoil velocity in 8-lb. shotgun:** 10.0 ft./sec.

Distance in yards:	Muzzle	20	30	40	50	60	70
Velocity in fps:	1,312	805	667	562	478	407	346
Average pellet energy in ft-lbs:	2.88	1.08	.74	.53	.38	.28	.20
Time of flight in seconds:	0	.0601	.1011	.1502	.2082	.2763	.3562

Type of load: Target
Three-foot velocity: 1,200 ft./sec.
Hull: 2¾-inch plastic
Wad: Plastic
Shot: Hard lead
Buffered: No
Test barrel length: 26 inch
Pellets will pierce skin up to 115 yards.

NO. 9 LEAD PELLETS—⅞ OUNCE—512 PELLETS
Mfg: Winchester **Manufacturer's code:** AA20
Recoil energy in 8-lb. shotgun: 12.3 ft./lbs. **Recoil velocity in 8-lb. shotgun:** 10.0 ft./sec.

Distance in yards:	Muzzle	20	30	40	50	60	70
Velocity in fps:	1,312	805	667	562	478	407	346
Average pellet energy in ft-lbs:	2.88	1.08	.74	.53	.38	.28	.20
Time of flight in seconds:	0	.0601	.1011	.1502	.2082	.2763	.3562

Type of load: Target
Three-foot velocity: 1,200 ft./sec.
Hull: 2¾-inch plastic
Wad: Plastic
Shot: Hard lead
Buffered: No
Test barrel length: 26 inch
Pellets will pierce skin up to 115 yards.

NO. 9 LEAD PELLETS—⅞ OUNCE—512 PELLETS
Mfg: PMC (Eldorado Cartridge Corp.) **Manufacturer's code:** PL20/CT20
Recoil energy in 8-lb. shotgun: 12.6 ft./lbs. **Recoil velocity in 8-lb. shotgun:** 10.1 ft./sec.

Distance in yards:	Muzzle	20	30	40	50	60	70
Velocity in fps:	1,334	814	674	567	482	410	349
Average pellet energy in ft-lbs:	2.98	1.11	.76	.54	.39	.28	.20
Time of flight in seconds:	0	.0593	.0999	.1486	.2060	.2735	.3528

Type of load: Quail & Dove & Target
Three-foot velocity: 1,220 ft./sec.
Hull: 2¾-inch plastic
Wad: Plastic
Shot: Lead
Buffered: No
Test barrel length: 26 inch
Pellets will pierce skin up to 105 yards.

NO. 9 LEAD PELLETS—⅞ OUNCE—512 PELLETS
Mfg: RST, Ltd. **Manufacturer's code:** N/A
Recoil energy in 8-lb. shotgun: 12.6 ft./lbs. **Recoil velocity in 8-lb. shotgun:** 10.1 ft./sec.

Distance in yards:	Muzzle	20	30	40	50	60	70
Velocity in fps:	1,334	814	674	567	482	410	349
Average pellet energy in ft-lbs:	2.98	1.11	.76	.54	.39	.28	.20
Time of flight in seconds:	0	.0593	.0999	.1486	.2060	.2735	.3528

Type of load: Target
Three-foot velocity: 1,220 ft./sec.
Hull: 2¾-inch plastic
Wad: Plastic
Shot: Lead
Buffered: No
Test barrel length: 26 inch
Pellets will pierce skin up to 105 yards.

NO. 9 LEAD PELLETS—⅞ OUNCE—512 PELLETS
Mfg: Sellier & Bellot **Manufacturer's code:** SBA02025
Recoil energy in 8-lb. shotgun: 12.6 ft./lbs. **Recoil velocity in 8-lb. shotgun:** 10.1 ft./sec.

Distance in yards:	Muzzle	20	30	40	50	60	70
Velocity in fps:	1,334	814	674	567	482	410	349
Average pellet energy in ft-lbs:	2.98	1.11	.76	.54	.39	.28	.20
Time of flight in seconds:	0	.0593	.0999	.1486	.2060	.2735	.3528

Type of load: Target
Three-foot velocity: 1,220 ft./sec.
Hull: 2¾-inch plastic
Wad: Plastic
Shot: Lead
Buffered: No
Test barrel length: 26 inch
Pellets will pierce skin up to 105 yards.

NO. 9 LEAD PELLETS—1 OUNCE—585 PELLETS
Mfg: Fiocchi **Manufacturer's code:** 20FLD
Recoil energy in 8-lb. shotgun: 14.9 ft./lbs. **Recoil velocity in 8-lb. shotgun:** 10.9 ft./sec.

Distance in yards:	Muzzle	20	30	40	50	60	70
Velocity in fps:	1,272	789	655	553	470	400	341
Average pellet energy in ft-lbs:	2.71	1.04	.72	.51	.37	.27	.19
Time of flight in seconds:	0	.0615	.1033	.1533	.2122	.2814	.3627

Type of load: Field
Three-foot velocity: 1,165 ft./sec.
Hull: 2¾-inch plastic
Wad: Plastic
Shot: Lead
Buffered: No
Test barrel length: 26 inch
Pellets will pierce skin up to 103 yards.

NO. 9 LEAD PELLETS—1 OUNCE—585 PELLETS
Mfg: Estate Cartridge **Manufacturer's code:** HG20
Recoil energy in 8-lb. shotgun: 18.9 ft./lbs. **Recoil velocity in 8-lb. shotgun:** 12.3 ft./sec.

Distance in yards:	Muzzle	20	30	40	50	60	70
Velocity in fps:	1,284	794	659	556	472	402	342
Average pellet energy in ft-lbs:	2.75	1.05	.73	.52	.37	.27	.20
Time of flight in seconds:	0	.0611	.1027	.1524	.2110	.2799	.3608

Type of load: Field
Three-foot velocity: 1,175 ft./sec.5
Hull: 2¾-inch plastic
Wad: Plastic
Shot: Hard lead
Buffered: No
Test barrel length: 26 inch
Pellets will pierce skin up to 103 yards.

NO. 9 LEAD PELLETS—1 OUNCE—585 PELLETS
Mfg: Remington Arms Co. **Manufacturer's code:** STS20H
Recoil energy in 8-lb. shotgun: 16.1 ft./lbs. **Recoil velocity in 8-lb. shotgun:** 11.4 ft./sec.

Distance in yards:	Muzzle	20	30	40	50	60	70
Velocity in fps:	1,312	805	667	562	478	407	346
Average pellet energy in ft-lbs:	2.88	1.08	.74	.53	.38	.28	.20
Time of flight in seconds:	0	.0601	.1011	.1502	.2082	.2763	.3562

Type of load: Target
Three-foot velocity: 1,200 ft./sec.
Hull: 2¾-inch plastic
Wad: Plastic
Shot: Hard lead
Buffered: No
Test barrel length: 26 inch
Pellets will pierce skin up to 115 yards.

NO. 9 LEAD PELLETS—1 OUNCE—585 PELLETS
Mfg: Estate Cartridge **Manufacturer's code:** HV20
Recoil energy in 8-lb. shotgun: 16.8 ft./lbs. **Recoil velocity in 8-lb. shotgun:** 11.6 ft./sec.

Distance in yards:	Muzzle	20	30	40	50	60	70
Velocity in fps:	1,334	814	674	567	482	410	349
Average pellet energy in ft-lbs:	2.98	1.11	.76	.54	.39	.28	.20
Time of flight in seconds:	0	.0593	.0999	.1486	.2060	.2735	.3528

Type of load: Field
Three-foot velocity: 1,220 ft./sec.
Hull: 2¾-inch plastic
Wad: Plastic
Shot: Hard lead
Buffered: No
Test barrel length: 26 inch
Pellets will pierce skin up to 105 yards.

NO. 9 LEAD PELLETS—1 OUNCE—585 PELLETS
Mfg: Fiocchi **Manufacturer's code:** 20HV
Recoil energy in 8-lb. shotgun: 16.8 ft./lbs. **Recoil velocity in 8-lb. shotgun:** 11.6 ft./sec.

Distance in yards:	Muzzle	20	30	40	50	60	70
Velocity in fps:	1,334	814	674	567	482	410	349
Average pellet energy in ft-lbs:	2.98	1.11	.76	.54	.39	.28	.20
Time of flight in seconds:	0	.0593	.0999	.1486	.2060	.2735	.3528

Type of load: Field
Three-foot velocity: 1,220 ft./sec.
Hull: 2¾-inch plastic
Wad: Plastic
Shot: Lead
Buffered: No
Test barrel length: 26 inch
Pellets will pierce skin up to 105 yards.

NO. 9 LEAD PELLETS—1 OUNCE—585 PELLETS
Mfg: Remington Arms Co. **Manufacturer's code:** SP20
Recoil energy in 8-lb. shotgun: 16.8 ft./lbs. **Recoil velocity in 8-lb. shotgun:** 11.6 ft./sec.

Distance in yards:	Muzzle	20	30	40	50	60	70
Velocity in fps:	1,334	814	674	567	482	410	349
Average pellet energy in ft-lbs:	2.98	1.11	.76	.54	.39	.28	.20
Time of flight in seconds:	0	.0593	.0999	.1486	.2060	.2735	.3528

Type of load: Target
Three-foot velocity: 1,220 ft./sec.
Hull: 2¾-inch plastic
Wad: Plastic
Shot: Lead
Buffered: No
Test barrel length: 26 inch
Pellets will pierce skin up to 105 yards.

NO. 9 LEAD PELLETS—1 OUNCE—585 PELLETS
Mfg: Clever **Manufacturer's code:** T1 Light Game
Recoil energy in 8-lb. shotgun: 19.9 ft./lbs. **Recoil velocity in 8-lb. shotgun:** 12.6 ft./sec.

Distance in yards:	Muzzle	20	30	40	50	60	70
Velocity in fps:	1,426	849	699	587	498	424	361
Average pellet energy in ft-lbs:	3.39	1.20	.82	.58	.42	.30	.22
Time of flight in seconds:	0	.0563	.0954	.1423	.1978	.2632	.3399

Type of load: Field
Three-foot velocity: 1,300 ft./sec.
Hull: 2¾-inch plastic
Wad: Plastic
Shot: Lead
Buffered: No
Test barrel length: 26 inch
Pellets will pierce skin up to 117 yards.

NO. 2 LEAD PELLETS—1¼ OUNCES—109 PELLETS
Mfg: Federal Cartridge Co. **Manufacturer's code:** F207
Recoil energy in 8-lb. shotgun: 23.8 ft./lbs. **Recoil velocity in 8-lb. shotgun:** 13.8 ft./sec.

Distance in yards:	Muzzle	20	30	40	50	60	70
Velocity in fps:	1,243	945	842	757	686	624	571
Average pellet energy in ft-lbs:	17.03	9.83	7.81	6.32	5.18	4.30	3.59
Time of flight in seconds:	0	.0559	.0896	.1272	.1688	.2147	.2650

Type of load: Field
Three-foot velocity: 1,175 ft./sec.
Hull: 3-inch plastic
Wad: Plastic
Shot: Lead
Buffered: No
Test barrel length: 30 inch
Pellets will pierce skin up to 192 yards.

NO. 2 LEAD PELLETS—1¼ OUNCES—109 PELLETS
Mfg: Clever **Manufacturer's code:** Magnum 360
Recoil energy in 8-lb. shotgun: 27.1 ft./lbs. **Recoil velocity in 8-lb. shotgun:** 14.8 ft./sec.

Distance in yards:	Muzzle	20	30	40	50	60	70
Velocity in fps:	1,308	982	872	783	707	643	587
Average pellet energy in ft-lbs:	18.85	10.62	9.38	6.75	5.51	4.55	3.79
Time of flight in seconds:	0	.0535	.0860	.1223	.1627	.2072	.2561

Type of load: Field
Three-foot velocity: 1,235 ft./sec.
Hull: 3-inch plastic
Wad: Plastic
Shot: Lead
Buffered: No
Test barrel length: 30 inch
Pellets will pierce skin up to 195 yards.

NO. 4 LEAD PELLETS—1¼ OUNCES—169 PELLETS
Mfg: Federal Cartridge Co. **Manufacturer's code:** PT258/P258/F207
Recoil energy in 8-lb. shotgun: 23.8 ft./lbs. **Recoil velocity in 8-lb. shotgun:** 13.8 ft./sec.

Distance in yards:	Muzzle	20	30	40	50	60	70
Velocity in fps:	1,254	916	806	716	641	577	522
Average pellet energy in ft-lbs:	11.27	6.02	4.65	3.68	2.95	2.39	1.95
Time of flight in seconds:	0	.0567	.0916	.1312	.1755	.2249	.2796

Type of load: Turkey
Three-foot velocity: 1,175 ft./sec.
Hull: 3-inch plastic
Wad: Plastic
Shot: Copper-plated lead/lead
Buffered: Yes
Test barrel length: 30 inch
Pellets will pierce skin up to 167 yards.

NO. 4 LEAD PELLETS—1¼ OUNCES—169 PELLETS
Mfg: Remington Arms Co. **Manufacturer's code:** NM20H
Recoil energy in 8-lb. shotgun: 23.8 ft./lbs. **Recoil velocity in 8-lb. shotgun:** 13.8 ft./sec.

Distance in yards:	Muzzle	20	30	40	50	60	70
Velocity in fps:	1,254	916	806	716	641	577	522
Average pellet energy in ft-lbs:	11.27	6.02	4.65	3.68	2.95	2.39	1.95
Time of flight in seconds:	0	.0567	.0916	.1312	.1755	.2249	.2796

Type of load: Field
Three-foot velocity: 1,175 ft./sec.
Hull: 3-inch plastic
Wad: Plastic
Shot: Lead
Buffered: No
Test barrel length: 30 inch
Pellets will pierce skin up to 167 yards.

NO. 4 LEAD PELLETS—1¼ OUNCES—169 PELLETS
Mfg: Winchester **Manufacturer's code:** X203XC
Recoil energy in 8-lb. shotgun: 23.8 ft./lbs. **Recoil velocity in 8-lb. shotgun:** 13.8 ft./sec.

Distance in yards:	Muzzle	20	30	40	50	60	70
Velocity in fps:	1,254	916	806	716	641	577	522
Average pellet energy in ft-lbs:	11.27	6.02	4.65	3.68	2.95	2.39	1.95
Time of flight in seconds:	0	.0567	.0916	.1312	.1755	.2249	.2796

Type of load: Turkey & Field
Three-foot velocity: 1,175 ft./sec.
Hull: 3-inch plastic
Wad: Plastic
Shot: Copper-plated lead
Buffered: Yes
Test barrel length: 30 inch
Pellets will pierce skin up to 167 yards.

NO. 4 LEAD PELLETS—1¼ OUNCES—169 PELLETS
Mfg: Dionisi **Manufacturer's code:** D 20 MG3
Recoil energy in 8-lb. shotgun: 25.2 ft./lbs. **Recoil velocity in 8-lb. shotgun:** 14.2 ft./sec.

Distance in yards:	Muzzle	20	30	40	50	60	70
Velocity in fps:	1,281	931	817	725	649	584	528
Average pellet energy in ft-lbs:	11.77	6.21	4.79	3.77	3.02	2.45	2.00
Time of flight in seconds:	0	.0556	.0901	.01291	.1729	.2216	.2757

Type of load: Field
Three-foot velocity: 1,200 ft./sec.
Hull: 3-inch plastic
Wad: Plastic
Shot: Lead
Buffered: No
Test barrel length: 30 inch
Pellets will pierce skin up to 168 yards.

NO. 4 LEAD PELLETS—1¼ OUNCES—169 PELLETS
Mfg: Fiocchi **Manufacturer's code:** 203GP
Recoil energy in 8-lb. shotgun: 33.9 ft./lbs. **Recoil velocity in 8-lb. shotgun:** 16.5 ft./sec.

Distance in yards:	Muzzle	20	30	40	50	60	70
Velocity in fps:	1,281	931	817	725	649	584	528
Average pellet energy in ft-lbs:	11.77	6.21	4.79	3.77	3.02	2.45	2.00
Time of flight in seconds:	0	.0556	.0901	.01291	.1729	.2216	.2757

Type of load: Field
Three-foot velocity: 1,200 ft./sec.
Hull: 3-inch plastic
Wad: Plastic
Shot: Nickel-plated lead
Buffered: No
Test barrel length: 30 inch
Pellets will pierce skin up to 168 yards.

NO. 4 LEAD PELLETS—1¼ OUNCES—169 PELLETS
Mfg: Clever **Manufacturer's code:** Magnum 360
Recoil energy in 8-lb. shotgun: 27.1 ft./lbs. **Recoil velocity in 8-lb. shotgun:** 14.8 ft./sec.

Distance in yards:	Muzzle	20	30	40	50	60	70
Velocity in fps:	1,319	951	833	739	660	594	536
Average pellet energy in ft-lbs:	12.48	6.49	4.98	3.91	3.13	2.53	2.06
Time of flight in seconds:	0	.0543	.0880	.1263	.1693	.2173	.2705

Type of load: Field
Three-foot velocity: 1,235 ft./sec.
Hull: 3-inch plastic
Wad: Plastic
Shot: Lead
Buffered: No
Test barrel length: 30 inch
Pellets will pierce skin up to 169 yards.

NO. 4 LEAD PELLETS—1¼ OUNCES—169 PELLETS
Mfg: Estate Cartridge **Manufacturer's code:** HV20HMAG
Recoil energy in 8-lb. shotgun: 31.1 ft./lbs. **Recoil velocity in 8-lb. shotgun:** 15.8 ft./sec.

Distance in yards:	Muzzle	20	30	40	50	60	70
Velocity in fps:	1,390	989	863	762	680	611	551
Average pellet energy in ft-lbs:	13.86	7.01	5.34	4.17	3.32	2.67	2.18
Time of flight in seconds:	0	.0519	.0844	.1215	.1632	.2098	.2615

Type of load: Field
Three-foot velocity: 1,300 ft./sec.
Hull: 3-inch plastic
Wad: Plastic
Shot: Hard lead
Buffered: Yes
Test barrel length: 30 inch
Pellets will pierce skin up to 172 yards.

NO. 4 LEAD PELLETS—1¼ OUNCES—169 PELLETS
Mfg: Kent Cartridge America/Canada **Manufacturer's code:** K203TK36
Recoil energy in 8-lb. shotgun: 31.1 ft./lbs. **Recoil velocity in 8-lb. shotgun:** 15.8 ft./sec.

Distance in yards:	Muzzle	20	30	40	50	60	70
Velocity in fps:	1,390	989	863	762	680	611	551
Average pellet energy in ft-lbs:	13.86	7.01	5.34	4.17	3.32	2.67	2.18
Time of flight in seconds:	0	.0519	.0844	.1215	.1632	.2098	.2615

Type of load: Turkey
Three-foot velocity: 1,300 ft./sec.
Hull: 3-inch plastic
Wad: Plastic
Shot: Lead
Buffered: No
Test barrel length: 30 inch
Pellets will pierce skin up to 172 yards.

NO. 5 LEAD PELLETS—1¼ OUNCES—212 PELLETS
Mfg: Federal Cartridge Co. **Manufacturer's code:** PT258
Recoil energy in 8-lb. shotgun: 23.8 ft./lbs. **Recoil velocity in 8-lb. shotgun:** 13.8 ft./sec.

Distance in yards:	Muzzle	20	30	40	50	60	70
Velocity in fps:	1,259	899	784	691	615	550	493
Average pellet energy in ft-lbs:	8.94	4.56	3.46	2.70	2.13	1.70	1.37
Time of flight in seconds:	0	.0572	.0930	.1338	.1799	.2315	.3204

Type of load: Turkey
Three-foot velocity: 1,175 ft./sec.
Hull: 3-inch plastic
Wad: Plastic
Shot: Copper-plated lead
Buffered: Yes
Test barrel length: 30 inch
Pellets will pierce skin up to 154 yards.

NO. 5 LEAD PELLETS—1¼ OUNCES—212 PELLETS
Mfg: Dionisi **Manufacturer's code:** D 20 MG3
Recoil energy in 8-lb. shotgun: 25.2 ft./lbs. **Recoil velocity in 8-lb. shotgun:** 14.2 ft./sec.

Distance in yards:	Muzzle	20	30	40	50	60	70
Velocity in fps:	1,287	913	795	700	622	556	499
Average pellet energy in ft-lbs:	9.34	4.70	3.56	2.77	2.18	1.75	1.40
Time of flight in seconds:	0	.0562	.0915	.1317	.1772	.2282	.2852

Type of load: Field
Three-foot velocity: 1,200 ft./sec.
Hull: 3-inch plastic
Wad: Plastic
Shot: Lead
Buffered: No
Test barrel length: 30 inch
Pellets will pierce skin up to 155 yards.

NO. 5 LEAD PELLETS—1¼ OUNCES—212 PELLETS
Mfg: Fiocchi **Manufacturer's code:** 203GP
Recoil energy in 8-lb. shotgun: 33.9 ft./lbs. **Recoil velocity in 8-lb. shotgun:** 16.5 ft./sec.

Distance in yards:	Muzzle	20	30	40	50	60	70
Velocity in fps:	1,287	913	795	700	622	556	499
Average pellet energy in ft-lbs:	9.34	4.70	3.56	2.77	2.18	1.75	1.40
Time of flight in seconds:	0	.0562	.0915	.1317	.1772	.2282	.2852

Type of load: Field
Three-foot velocity: 1,200 ft./sec.
Hull: 3-inch plastic
Wad: Plastic
Shot: Nickel-plated lead
Buffered: No
Test barrel length: 30 inch
Pellets will pierce skin up to 155 yards.

NO. 5 LEAD PELLETS—1¼ OUNCES—212 PELLETS
Mfg: Kent Cartridge America/Canada **Manufacturer's code:** K203TK36
Recoil energy in 8-lb. shotgun: 31.1 ft./lbs. **Recoil velocity in 8-lb. shotgun:** 15.8 ft./sec.

Distance in yards:	Muzzle	20	30	40	50	60	70
Velocity in fps:	1,396	969	838	735	651	581	521
Average pellet energy in ft-lbs:	11.00	5.29	3.96	3.05	2.39	1.90	1.53
Time of flight in seconds:	0	.0524	.0858	.1241	.1675	.2163	.2708

Type of load: Turkey
Three-foot velocity: 1,300 ft./sec.
Hull: 3-inch plastic
Wad: Plastic
Shot: Lead
Buffered: No
Test barrel length: 30 inch
Pellets will pierce skin up to 159 yards.

NO. 6 LEAD PELLETS—1¼ OUNCES—281 PELLETS

Mfg: Federal Cartridge Co. **Manufacturer's code:** PT258/P258/F207
Recoil energy in 8-lb. shotgun: 23.8 ft./lbs. **Recoil velocity in 8-lb. shotgun:** 13.8 ft./sec.

Distance in yards:	Muzzle	20	30	40	50	60	70
Velocity in fps:	1,265	878	759	664	585	519	462
Average pellet energy in ft-lbs:	6.95	3.35	2.50	1.91	1.9	1.17	.93
Time of flight in seconds:	0	.0578	.0947	.1370	.1852	.2396	.3009

Type of load: Turkey
Three-foot velocity: 1,175 ft./sec.
Hull: 3-inch plastic
Wad: Plastic
Shot: Copper-plated lead/lead
Buffered: Yes
Test barrel length: 30 inch
Pellets will pierce skin up to 141 yards.

NO. 6 LEAD PELLETS—1¼ OUNCES—281 PELLETS

Mfg: Remington Arms Co. **Manufacturer's code:** P20XHM/NM20H
Recoil energy in 8-lb. shotgun: 23.8 ft./lbs. **Recoil velocity in 8-lb. shotgun:** 13.8 ft./sec.

Distance in yards:	Muzzle	20	30	40	50	60	70
Velocity in fps:	1,265	878	759	664	585	519	462
Average pellet energy in ft-lbs:	6.95	3.35	2.50	1.91	1.9	1.17	.93
Time of flight in seconds:	0	.0578	.0947	.1370	.1852	.2396	.3009

Type of load: Turkey & Field
Three-foot velocity: 1,175 ft./sec.
Hull: 3-inch plastic
Wad: Plastic
Shot: Copper-plated lead/lead
Buffered: Yes/no
Test barrel length: 30 inch
Pellets will pierce skin up to 141 yards.

NO. 6 LEAD PELLETS—1¼ OUNCES—281 PELLETS

Mfg: Winchester **Manufacturer's code:** X203XC
Recoil energy in 8-lb. shotgun: 23.8 ft./lbs. **Recoil velocity in 8-lb. shotgun:** 13.8 ft./sec.

Distance in yards:	Muzzle	20	30	40	50	60	70
Velocity in fps:	1,265	878	759	664	585	519	462
Average pellet energy in ft-lbs:	6.95	3.35	2.50	1.91	1.9	1.17	.93
Time of flight in seconds:	0	.0578	.0947	.1370	.1852	.2396	.3009

Type of load: Turkey & Field
Three-foot velocity: 1,175 ft./sec.
Hull: 3-inch plastic
Wad: Plastic
Shot: Copper-plated lead
Buffered: Yes
Test barrel length: 30 inch
Pellets will pierce skin up to 141 yards.

NO. 6 LEAD PELLETS—1¼ OUNCES—281 PELLETS

Mfg: Dionisi **Manufacturer's code:** D 20 MG3
Recoil energy in 8-lb. shotgun: 25.2 ft./lbs. **Recoil velocity in 8-lb. shotgun:** 14.2 ft./sec.

Distance in yards:	Muzzle	20	30	40	50	60	70
Velocity in fps:	1,292	892	769	672	593	525	467
Average pellet energy in ft-lbs:	7.26	3.46	2.57	1.96	1.53	1.20	.095
Time of flight in seconds:	0	.0568	.0931	.01349	.1825	.2363	.2969

Type of load: Field
Three-foot velocity: 1,200 ft./sec.
Hull: 3-inch plastic
Wad: Plastic
Shot: Lead
Buffered: No
Test barrel length: 30 inch
Pellets will pierce skin up to 157 yards.

NO. 6 LEAD PELLETS—1¼ OUNCES—281 PELLETS

Mfg: Fiocchi **Manufacturer's code:** 203GP
Recoil energy in 8-lb. shotgun: 33.9 ft./lbs. **Recoil velocity in 8-lb. shotgun:** 16.5 ft./sec.

Distance in yards:	Muzzle	20	30	40	50	60	70
Velocity in fps:	1,292	892	769	672	593	525	467
Average pellet energy in ft-lbs:	7.26	3.46	2.57	1.96	1.53	1.20	.095
Time of flight in seconds:	0	.0568	.0931	.01349	.1825	.2363	.2969

Type of load: Field
Three-foot velocity: 1,200 ft./sec.
Hull: 3-inch plastic
Wad: Plastic
Shot: Nickel-plated lead
Buffered: No
Test barrel length: 30 inch
Pellets will pierce skin up to 157 yards.

NO. 6 LEAD PELLETS—1¼ OUNCES—281 PELLETS

Mfg: Clever **Manufacturer's code:** Magnum 360
Recoil energy in 8-lb. shotgun: 27.1 ft./lbs. **Recoil velocity in 8-lb. shotgun:** 14.8 ft./sec.

Distance in yards:	Muzzle	20	30	40	50	60	70
Velocity in fps:	1,331	911	784	684	602	534	474
Average pellet energy in ft-lbs:	7.70	3.60	2.67	2.03	1.58	1.24	.9
Time of flight in seconds:	0	.0555	.0911	.1321	.1789	.2319	.2915

Type of load: Field
Three-foot velocity: 1,235 ft./sec.
Hull: 3-inch plastic
Wad: Plastic
Shot: Lead
Buffered: No
Test barrel length: 30 inch
Pellets will pierce skin up to 144 yards.

NO. 6 LEAD PELLETS—1¼ OUNCES—281 PELLETS

Mfg: Estate Cartridge **Manufacturer's code:** HV20HMAG
Recoil energy in 8-lb. shotgun: 31.1 ft./lbs. **Recoil velocity in 8-lb. shotgun:** 15.8 ft./sec.

Distance in yards:	Muzzle	20	30	40	50	60	70
Velocity in fps:	1,403	945	810	705	620	548	487
Average pellet energy in ft-lbs:	8.55	3.88	2.85	2.16	1.67	1.31	1.03
Time of flight in seconds:	0	.0531	.0875	.1272	.1727	.2242	.2723

Type of load: Field
Three-foot velocity: 1,300 ft./sec.
Hull: 3-inch plastic
Wad: Plastic
Shot: Hard lead
Buffered: Yes
Test barrel length: 30 inch
Pellets will pierce skin up to 146 yards.

NO. 6 LEAD PELLETS—1¼ OUNCES—281 PELLETS

Mfg: Kent Cartridge America/Canada **Manufacturer's code:** K203TK36
Recoil energy in 8-lb. shotgun: 31.1 ft./lbs. **Recoil velocity in 8-lb. shotgun:** 15.8 ft./sec.

Distance in yards:	Muzzle	20	30	40	50	60	70
Velocity in fps:	1,403	945	810	705	620	548	487
Average pellet energy in ft-lbs:	8.55	3.88	2.85	2.16	1.67	1.31	1.03
Time of flight in seconds:	0	.0531	.0875	.1272	.1727	.2242	.2723

Type of load: Turkey
Three-foot velocity: 1,300 ft./sec.
Hull: 3-inch plastic
Wad: Plastic
Shot: Lead
Buffered: No
Test barrel length: 30 inch
Pellets will pierce skin up to 146 yards.

NO. 7½ LEAD PELLETS—1¼ OUNCES—437 PELLETS

Mfg: Federal Cartridge Co. **Manufacturer's code:** F207
Recoil energy in 8-lb. shotgun: 23.8 ft./lbs. **Recoil velocity in 8-lb. shotgun:** 13.8 ft./sec.

Distance in yards:	Muzzle	20	30	40	50	60	70
Velocity in fps:	1,274	841	714	615	535	466	407
Average pellet energy in ft-lbs:	4.54	1.98	1.43	1.06	.80	.61	.46
Time of flight in seconds:	0	.0592	.0980	.1433	.1957	.2558	.3246

Type of load: Field
Three-foot velocity: 1,175 ft./sec.
Hull: 3-inch plastic
Wad: Plastic
Shot: Lead
Buffered: Yes
Test barrel length: 30 inch
Pellets will pierce skin up to 122 yards.

Hunting ducks in flooded timber is perhaps one of the most enjoyable types of waterfowl hunting. Here the author calls to circling mallards as colleague Nick Sisley prepares to shoot as the greenheads twist through the oaks into the decoys.

NO. 2 STEEL PELLETS—¾ OUNCE—94 PELLETS
Mfg: Estate Cartridge **Manufacturer's code:** HVST20SM
Recoil energy in 8-lb. shotgun: 13.7 ft./lbs. **Recoil velocity in 8-lb. shotgun:** 10.5 ft./sec.

Distance in yards:	Muzzle	20	30	40	50	60	70
Velocity in fps:	1,488	974	827	715	625	551	487
Average pellet energy in ft-lbs:	17.29	7.40	5.34	3.99	3.05	2.37	1.85
Time of flight in seconds:	0	.0509	.0844	.1234	.1684	.2195	.2775

Type of load: Nontoxic
Three-foot velocity: 1,400 ft./sec.
Hull: 2¾-inch plastic
Wad: Plastic
Shot: Steel
Buffered: No
Test barrel length: 26 inch
Pellets will pierce skin up to 144 yards.

NO. 2 STEEL PELLETS—¾ OUNCE—94 PELLETS
Mfg: Remington Arms Co. **Manufacturer's code:** SSP20
Recoil energy in 8-lb. shotgun: 14.3 ft./lbs. **Recoil velocity in 8-lb. shotgun:** 10.7 ft./sec.

Distance in yards:	Muzzle	20	30	40	50	60	70
Velocity in fps:	1,516	987	837	723	631	556	492
Average pellet energy in ft-lbs:	17.93	7.60	5.46	4.07	3.11	2.41	1.89
Time of flight in seconds:	0	.0501	.0832	.1218	.1663	.2170	.2744

Type of load: Nontoxic
Three-foot velocity: 1,425 ft./sec.
Hull: 2¾-inch plastic
Wad: Plastic
Shot: Zinc-galvanized steel
Buffered: No
Test barrel length: 26 inch
Pellets will pierce skin up to 144 yards.

NO. 3 STEEL PELLETS—¾ OUNCE—118 PELLETS
Mfg: Estate Cartridge **Manufacturer's code:** HVST20SM
Recoil energy in 8-lb. shotgun: 13.7 ft./lbs. **Recoil velocity in 8-lb. shotgun:** 10.5 ft./sec.

Distance in yards:	Muzzle	20	30	40	50	60	70
Velocity in fps:	1,494	953	803	689	598	524	460
Average pellet energy in ft-lbs:	14.16	5.76	4.09	3.01	2.27	1.74	1.34
Time of flight in seconds:	0	.0515	.0859	.1263	.1731	.2267	.2879

Type of load: Nontoxic
Three-foot velocity: 1,400 ft./sec.
Hull: 2¾-inch plastic
Wad: Plastic
Shot: Steel
Buffered: No
Test barrel length: 26 inch
Pellets will pierce skin up to 134 yards.

NO. 3 STEEL PELLETS—¾ OUNCE—118 PELLETS
Mfg: Fiocchi **Manufacturer's code:** 20S
Recoil energy in 8-lb. shotgun: 15.7 ft./lbs. **Recoil velocity in 8-lb. shotgun:** 11.2 ft./sec.

Distance in yards:	Muzzle	20	30	40	50	60	70
Velocity in fps:	1,576	1,093	829	710	615	538	472
Average pellet energy in ft-lbs:	15.77	6.21	4.36	3.20	2.40	1.83	1.41
Time of flight in seconds:	0	.0492	.0824	.1216	.1671	.2193	.2789

Type of load: Nontoxic
Three-foot velocity: 1,475 ft./sec.
Hull: 2¾-inch plastic
Wad: Plastic
Shot: Steel
Buffered: No
Test barrel length: 26 inch
Pellets will pierce skin up to 136 yards.

NO. 4 STEEL PELLETS—¾ OUNCE—144 PELLETS
Mfg: Estate Cartridge **Manufacturer's code:** STL20H
Recoil energy in 8-lb. shotgun: 9.5 ft./lbs. **Recoil velocity in 8-lb. shotgun:** 8.7 ft./sec.

Distance in yards:	Muzzle	20	30	40	50	60	70
Velocity in fps:	1,302	844	713	611	529	460	400
Average pellet energy in ft-lbs:	8.61	3.62	2.58	1.90	1.42	1.07	.81
Time of flight in seconds:	0	.0585	.0973	.1428	.1956	.2565	.3265

Type of load: Nontoxic
Three-foot velocity: 1,220 ft./sec.
Hull: 2¾-inch plastic
Wad: Plastic
Shot: Steel
Buffered: No
Test barrel length: 26 inch
Pellets will pierce skin up to 120 yards.

NO. 4 STEEL PELLETS—¾ OUNCE—144 PELLETS
Mfg: Estate Cartridge **Manufacturer's code:** HVST20SM
Recoil energy in 8-lb. shotgun: 13.7 ft./lbs. **Recoil velocity in 8-lb. shotgun:** 10.5 ft./sec.

Distance in yards:	Muzzle	20	30	40	50	60	70
Velocity in fps:	1,500	929	776	660	569	494	429
Average pellet energy in ft-lbs:	11.42	4.38	3.06	2.22	1.65	1.24	.94
Time of flight in seconds:	0	.0522	.0876	.1297	.1787	.2353	.3005

Type of load: Nontoxic
Three-foot velocity: 1,400 ft./sec.
Hull: 2¾-inch plastic
Wad: Plastic
Shot: Steel
Buffered: No
Test barrel length: 26 inch
Pellets will pierce skin up to 125 yards.

NO. 4 STEEL PELLETS—¾ OUNCE—144 PELLETS
Mfg: Federal Cartridge Co. **Manufacturer's code:** W208
Recoil energy in 8-lb. shotgun: 14.3 ft./lbs. **Recoil velocity in 8-lb. shotgun:** 10.7 ft./sec.

Distance in yards:	Muzzle	20	30	40	50	60	70
Velocity in fps:	1,527	940	784	667	574	498	433
Average pellet energy in ft-lbs:	11.85	4.49	3.12	2.26	1.68	1.26	.95
Time of flight in seconds:	0	.0514	.0865	.1280	.1766	.2327	.2973

Type of load: Nontoxic
Three-foot velocity: 1,425 ft./sec.
Hull: 2¾-inch plastic
Wad: Plastic
Shot: Steel
Buffered: No
Test barrel length: 26 inch
Pellets will pierce skin up to 125 yards.

NO. 4 STEEL PELLETS—¾ OUNCE—144 PELLETS

Mfg: Remington Arms Co. **Manufacturer's code:** SSP20
Recoil energy in 8-lb. shotgun: 14.3 ft./lbs. **Recoil velocity in 8-lb. shotgun:** 10.7 ft./sec.

Distance in yards:	Muzzle	20	30	40	50	60	70
Velocity in fps:	1,527	940	784	667	574	498	433
Average pellet energy in ft-lbs:	11.85	4.49	3.12	2.26	1.68	1.26	.95
Time of flight in seconds:	0	.0514	.0865	.1280	.1766	.2327	.2973

Type of load: Nontoxic
Three-foot velocity: 1,425 ft./sec.
Hull: 2¾-inch plastic
Wad: Plastic
Shot: Zinc-galvanized steel
Buffered: No
Test barrel length: 26 inch
Pellets will pierce skin up to 125 yards.

NO. 4 STEEL PELLETS—¾ OUNCE—144 PELLETS

Mfg: Winchester **Manufacturer's code:** XS20
Recoil energy in 8-lb. shotgun: 14.3 ft./lbs. **Recoil velocity in 8-lb. shotgun:** 10.7 ft./sec.

Distance in yards:	Muzzle	20	30	40	50	60	70
Velocity in fps:	1,527	940	784	667	574	498	433
Average pellet energy in ft-lbs:	11.85	4.49	3.12	2.26	1.68	1.26	.95
Time of flight in seconds:	0	.0514	.0865	.1280	.1766	.2327	.2973

Type of load: Nontoxic
Three-foot velocity: 1,425 ft./sec.
Hull: 2¾-inch plastic
Wad: Two-piece plastic
Shot: Steel
Buffered: No
Test barrel length: 26 inch
Pellets will pierce skin up to 125 yards.

NO. 4 STEEL PELLETS—¾ OUNCE—144 PELLETS

Mfg: Fiocchi **Manufacturer's code:** 20S
Recoil energy in 8-lb. shotgun: 15.7 ft./lbs. **Recoil velocity in 8-lb. shotgun:** 11.2 ft./sec.

Distance in yards:	Muzzle	20	30	40	50	60	70
Velocity in fps:	1,583	1,204	801	680	585	507	441
Average pellet energy in ft-lbs:	12.72	4.72	3.26	2.35	1.74	1.31	.99
Time of flight in seconds:	0	.0499	.0842	.1249	.1726	.2277	.2912

Type of load: Nontoxic
Three-foot velocity: 1,475 ft./sec.
Hull: 2¾-inch plastic
Wad: Plastic
Shot: Steel
Buffered: No
Test barrel length: 26 inch
Pellets will pierce skin up to 127 yards.

NO. 6 STEEL PELLETS—¾ OUNCE—236 PELLETS

Mfg: Estate Cartridge **Manufacturer's code:** STL20H
Recoil energy in 8-lb. shotgun: 9.5 ft./lbs. **Recoil velocity in 8-lb. shotgun:** 8.7 ft./sec.

Distance in yards:	Muzzle	20	30	40	50	60	70
Velocity in fps:	1,312	796	658	552	467	396	336
Average pellet energy in ft-lbs:	5.30	1.95	1.33	.94	.67	.48	.35
Time of flight in seconds:	0	.0604	.1020	.1519	.2110	.2808	.3631

Type of load: Nontoxic
Three-foot velocity: 1,220 ft./sec.
Hull: 2¾-inch plastic
Wad: Plastic
Shot: Steel
Buffered: No
Test barrel length: 26 inch
Pellets will pierce skin up to 101 yards.

NO. 6 STEEL PELLETS—¾ OUNCE—236 PELLETS

Mfg: Estate Cartridge **Manufacturer's code:** HVST20SM
Recoil energy in 8-lb. shotgun: 13.7 ft./lbs. **Recoil velocity in 8-lb. shotgun:** 10.5 ft./sec.

Distance in yards:	Muzzle	20	30	40	50	60	70
Velocity in fps:	1,512	872	713	595	502	426	361
Average pellet energy in ft-lbs:	7.04	2.34	1.56	1.09	.78	.56	.40
Time of flight in seconds:	0	.0541	.0923	.1385	.1935	.2584	.3351

Type of load: Nontoxic
Three-foot velocity: 1,400 ft./sec.
Hull: 2¾-inch plastic
Wad: Plastic
Shot: Steel
Buffered: No
Test barrel length: 26 inch
Pellets will pierce skin up to 106 yards.

NO. 6 STEEL PELLETS—¾ OUNCE—236 PELLETS

Mfg: Federal Cartridge Co. **Manufacturer's code:** W208
Recoil energy in 8-lb. shotgun: 14.3 ft./lbs. **Recoil velocity in 8-lb. shotgun:** 10.7 ft./sec.

Distance in yards:	Muzzle	20	30	40	50	60	70
Velocity in fps:	1,540	882	720	600	507	429	364
Average pellet energy in ft-lbs:	7.30	2.40	1.59	1.11	.79	.57	.41
Time of flight in seconds:	0	.0533	.0911	.1369	.1913	.2557	.3317

Type of load: Nontoxic
Three-foot velocity: 1,425 ft./sec.
Hull: 2¾-inch plastic
Wad: Plastic
Shot: Steel
Buffered: No
Test barrel length: 26 inch
Pellets will pierce skin up to 106 yards.

NO. 6 STEEL PELLETS—¾ OUNCE—236 PELLETS

Mfg: Remington Arms Co. **Manufacturer's code:** SSP20
Recoil energy in 8-lb. shotgun: 14.3 ft./lbs. **Recoil velocity in 8-lb. shotgun:** 10.7 ft./sec.

Distance in yards:	Muzzle	20	30	40	50	60	70
Velocity in fps:	1,540	882	720	600	507	429	364
Average pellet energy in ft-lbs:	7.30	2.40	1.59	1.11	.79	.57	.41
Time of flight in seconds:	0	.0533	.0911	.1369	.1913	.2557	.3317

Type of load: Nontoxic
Three-foot velocity: 1,425 ft./sec.
Hull: 2¾-inch plastic
Wad: Plastic
Shot: Zinc-galvanized steel
Buffered: No
Test barrel length: 26 inch
Pellets will pierce skin up to 106 yards.

NO. 6 STEEL PELLETS—¾ OUNCE—236 PELLETS
Mfg: Winchester **Manufacturer's code:** XS20
Recoil energy in 8-lb. shotgun: 14.3 ft./lbs. **Recoil velocity in 8-lb. shotgun:** 10.7 ft./sec.

Distance in yards:	Muzzle	20	30	40	50	60	70
Velocity in fps:	1,540	882	720	600	507	429	364
Average pellet energy in ft-lbs:	7.30	2.40	1.59	1.11	.79	.57	.41
Time of flight in seconds:	0	.0533	.0911	.1369	.1913	.2557	.3317

Type of load: Nontoxic
Three-foot velocity: 1,425 ft./sec.
Hull: 2¾-inch plastic
Wad: Two-piece plastic
Shot: Steel
Buffered: No
Test barrel length: 26 inch
Pellets will pierce skin up to 106 yards.

NO. 6 STEEL PELLETS—¾ OUNCE—236 PELLETS
Mfg: Fiocchi **Manufacturer's code:** 20S
Recoil energy in 8-lb. shotgun: 15.7 ft./lbs. **Recoil velocity in 8-lb. shotgun:** 11.2 ft./sec.

Distance in yards:	Muzzle	20	30	40	50	60	70
Velocity in fps:	1,596	903	734	611	516	437	370
Average pellet energy in ft-lbs:	7.84	2.51	1.66	1.15	.82	.59	.42
Time of flight in seconds:	0	.0518	.0888	.1337	.1872	.2504	.3251

Type of load: Nontoxic
Three-foot velocity: 1,475 ft./sec.
Hull: 2¾-inch plastic
Wad: Plastic
Shot: Steel
Buffered: No
Test barrel length: 26 inch
Pellets will pierce skin up to 107 yards.

NO. 7 STEEL PELLETS—¾ OUNCE—316 PELLETS
Mfg: Remington Arms Co. **Manufacturer's code:** GSTL20
Recoil energy in 8-lb. shotgun: 9.1 ft./lbs. **Recoil velocity in 8-lb. shotgun:** 8.5 ft./sec.

Distance in yards:	Muzzle	20	30	40	50	60	70
Velocity in fps:	1,295	759	619	513	428	356	297
Average pellet energy in ft-lbs:	3.88	1.33	.88	.61	.42	.29	.20
Time of flight in seconds:	0	.0625	.1065	.1599	.2240	.3009	.3932

Type of load: Field
Three-foot velocity: 1,200 ft./sec.
Hull: 2¾-inch plastic
Wad: Plastic
Shot: Steel
Buffered: No
Test barrel length: 26 inch
Pellets will pierce skin up to 92 yards.

NO. 7 STEEL PELLETS—¾ OUNCE—316 PELLETS
Mfg: Estate Cartridge **Manufacturer's code:** STL20H
Recoil energy in 8-lb. shotgun: 9.5 ft./lbs. **Recoil velocity in 8-lb. shotgun:** 8.7 ft./sec.

Distance in yards:	Muzzle	20	30	40	50	60	70
Velocity in fps:	1,317	767	625	518	431	360	300
Average pellet energy in ft-lbs:	4.01	1.36	.90	.62	.43	.30	.21
Time of flight in seconds:	0	.0617	.1052	.1581	.2217	.2980	.3895

Type of load: Nontoxic
Three-foot velocity: 1,220 ft./sec.
Hull: 2¾-inch plastic
Wad: Plastic
Shot: Steel
Buffered: No
Test barrel length: 26 inch
Pellets will pierce skin up to 92 yards.

NO. 7 STEEL PELLETS—¾ OUNCE—316 PELLETS
Mfg: Federal Cartridge Co. **Manufacturer's code:** W208
Recoil energy in 8-lb. shotgun: 9.5 ft./lbs. **Recoil velocity in 8-lb. shotgun:** 8.7 ft./sec.

Distance in yards:	Muzzle	20	30	40	50	60	70
Velocity in fps:	1,344	777	632	523	436	363	303
Average pellet energy in ft-lbs:	4.17	1.39	.92	.63	.44	.31	.21
Time of flight in seconds:	0	.0608	.1038	.1561	.2191	.2946	.3851

Type of load: Nontoxic
Three-foot velocity: 1,220 ft./sec.
Hull: 2¾-inch plastic
Wad: Plastic
Shot: Steel
Buffered: No
Test barrel length: 26 inch
Pellets will pierce skin up to 93 yards.

NO. 7 STEEL PELLETS—¾ OUNCE—316 PELLETS
Mfg: Winchester **Manufacturer's code:** WE20
Recoil energy in 8-lb. shotgun: 14.3 ft./lbs. **Recoil velocity in 8-lb. shotgun:** 10.7 ft./sec.

Distance in yards:	Muzzle	20	30	40	50	60	70
Velocity in fps:	1,344	777	632	523	436	363	303
Average pellet energy in ft-lbs:	4.17	1.39	.92	.63	.44	.31	.21
Time of flight in seconds:	0	.0608	.1038	.1561	.2191	.2946	.3851

Type of load: Nontoxic
Three-foot velocity: 1,300 ft./sec.
Hull: 2¾-inch plastic
Wad: Plastic
Shot: Steel
Buffered: No
Test barrel length: 26 inch
Pellets will pierce skin up to 93 yards.

NO. 7 STEEL PELLETS—¾ OUNCE—316 PELLETS
Mfg: Fiocchi **Manufacturer's code:** 20S
Recoil energy in 8-lb. shotgun: 15.7 ft./lbs. **Recoil velocity in 8-lb. shotgun:** 11.2 ft./sec.

Distance in yards:	Muzzle	20	30	40	50	60	70
Velocity in fps:	1,604	867	696	572	476	397	331
Average pellet energy in ft-lbs:	5.95	1.74	1.12	.76	.52	.36	.25
Time of flight in seconds:	0	.0531	.0919	.1396	.1972	.2663	.3493

Type of load: Nontoxic
Three-foot velocity: 1,475 ft./sec.
Hull: 2¾-inch plastic
Wad: Plastic
Shot: Steel
Buffered: No
Test barrel length: 26 inch
Pellets will pierce skin up to 98 yards.

NO. 7 STEEL PELLETS—⅞ OUNCE—369 PELLETS

Mfg: Remington Arms Co. **Manufacturer's code:** STS20LS
Recoil energy in 8-lb. shotgun: 12.3 ft./lbs. **Recoil velocity in 8-lb. shotgun:** 10.0 ft./sec.

Distance in yards:	Muzzle	20	30	40	50	60	70
Velocity in fps:	1,295	759	619	513	428	356	297
Average pellet energy in ft-lbs:	3.88	1.33	.88	.61	.42	.29	.20
Time of flight in seconds:	0	.0625	.1065	.1599	.2240	.3009	.3932

Type of load: Target
Three-foot velocity: 1,200 ft./sec.
Hull: 2¾-inch plastic
Wad: Plastic
Shot: Steel
Buffered: No
Test barrel length: 30 inch
Pellets will pierce skin up to 92 yards.

Large Canada geese such as this northern Illinois honker require heavy loads of large nontoxic shot to successfully bring them to bag.

NO. 2 STEEL PELLETS—⅞ OUNCE—109 PELLETS

Mfg: Fiocchi **Manufacturer's code:** 203ST
Recoil energy in 8-lb. shotgun: 22.4 ft./lbs. **Recoil velocity in 8-lb. shotgun:** 13.4 ft./sec.

Distance in yards:	Muzzle	20	30	40	50	60	70
Velocity in fps:	1,598	1,025	865	745	649	608	505
Average pellet energy in ft-lbs:	19.92	8.20	5.84	4.33	3.29	2.54	1.99
Time of flight in seconds:	0	.0478	.0798	.1173	.1605	.2098	.2658

Type of load: Nontoxic
Three-foot velocity: 1,500 ft./sec.
Hull: 3-inch plastic
Wad: Plastic
Shot: Steel
Buffered: No
Test barrel length: 30 inch
Pellets will pierce skin up to 146 yards.

NO. 2 STEEL PELLETS—⅞ OUNCE—109 PELLETS

Mfg: Kent Cartridge America/Canada **Manufacturer's code:** K203ST24
Recoil energy in 8-lb. shotgun: 24.5 ft./lbs. **Recoil velocity in 8-lb. shotgun:** 14.0 ft./sec.

Distance in yards:	Muzzle	20	30	40	50	60	70
Velocity in fps:	1,653	1,051	884	759	661	581	513
Average pellet energy in ft-lbs:	21.32	8.62	3.09	4.49	3.41	2.63	2.05
Time of flight in seconds:	0	.0465	.0777	.1145	.1569	.2054	.2604

Type of load: Field
Three-foot velocity: 1,550 ft./sec.
Hull: 3-inch plastic
Wad: Plastic
Shot: Steel
Buffered: No
Test barrel length: 30 inch
Pellets will pierce skin up to 148 yards.

NO. 2 STEEL PELLETS—1 OUNCE—125 PELLETS

Mfg: Estate Cartridge **Manufacturer's code:** HVST20MM
Recoil energy in 8-lb. shotgun: 21.2 ft./lbs. **Recoil velocity in 8-lb. shotgun:** 13.0 ft./sec.

Distance in yards:	Muzzle	20	30	40	50	60	70
Velocity in fps:	1,412	939	801	694	608	536	475
Average pellet energy in ft-lbs:	15.56	6.87	5.00	3.76	2.89	2.25	1.76
Time of flight in seconds:	0	.0532	.0878	.1282	.1744	.2270	.2864

Type of load: Nontoxic
Three-foot velocity: 1,330 ft./sec.
Hull: 3-inch plastic
Wad: Plastic
Shot: Steel
Buffered: No
Test barrel length: 30 inch
Pellets will pierce skin up to 145 yards.

NO. 2 STEEL PELLETS—1 OUNCE—125 PELLETS

Mfg: Federal Cartridge Company **Manufacturer's code:** W209
Recoil energy in 8-lb. shotgun: 21.2 ft./lbs. **Recoil velocity in 8-lb. shotgun:** 13.0 ft./sec.

Distance in yards:	Muzzle	20	30	40	50	60	70
Velocity in fps:	1,412	939	801	694	608	536	475
Average pellet energy in ft-lbs:	15.56	6.87	5.00	3.76	2.89	2.25	1.76
Time of flight in seconds:	0	.0532	.0878	.1282	.1744	.2270	.2864

Type of load: Nontoxic
Three-foot velocity: 1,330 ft./sec.
Hull: 3-inch plastic
Wad: Plastic
Shot: Steel
Buffered: No
Test barrel length: 30 inch
Pellets will pierce skin up to 145 yards.

NO. 2 STEEL PELLETS—1 OUNCE—125 PELLETS

Mfg: Remington Arms Co. **Manufacturer's code:** NS20M
Recoil energy in 8-lb. shotgun: 21.2 ft./lbs. **Recoil velocity in 8-lb. shotgun:** 13.0 ft./sec.

Distance in yards:	Muzzle	20	30	40	50	60	70
Velocity in fps:	1,412	939	801	694	608	536	475
Average pellet energy in ft-lbs:	15.56	6.87	5.00	3.76	2.89	2.25	1.76
Time of flight in seconds:	0	.0532	.0878	.1282	.1744	.2270	.2864

Type of load: Nontoxic
Three-foot velocity: 1,330 ft./sec.
Hull: 3-inch plastic
Wad: Plastic
Shot: Zinc-galvanized steel
Buffered: No
Test barrel length: 30 inch
Pellets will pierce skin up to 145 yards.

NO. 2 STEEL PELLETS—1 OUNCE—125 PELLETS

Mfg: Winchester **Manufacturer's code:** XSM203
Recoil energy in 8-lb. shotgun: 21.2 ft./lbs. **Recoil velocity in 8-lb. shotgun:** 13.0 ft./sec.

Distance in yards:	Muzzle	20	30	40	50	60	70
Velocity in fps:	1,412	939	801	694	608	536	475
Average pellet energy in ft-lbs:	15.56	6.87	5.00	3.76	2.89	2.25	1.76
Time of flight in seconds:	0	.0532	.0878	.1282	.1744	.2270	.2864

Type of load: Nontoxic
Three-foot velocity: 1,330 ft./sec.
Hull: 3-inch plastic
Wad: Two-piece plastic
Shot: Steel
Buffered: No
Test barrel length: 30 inch
Pellets will pierce skin up to 145 yards.

NO. 2 STEEL PELLETS—1 OUNCE—125 PELLETS

Mfg: Federal Cartridge Company **Manufacturer's code:** W211
Recoil energy in 8-lb. shotgun: 24.3 ft./lbs. **Recoil velocity in 8-lb. shotgun:** 14.0 ft./sec.

Distance in yards:	Muzzle	20	30	40	50	60	70
Velocity in fps:	1,488	974	827	715	625	551	487
Average pellet energy in ft-lbs:	17.29	7.40	5.34	3.99	3.05	2.37	1.85
Time of flight in seconds:	0	.0509	.0844	.1234	.1684	.2195	.2775

Type of load: Nontoxic
Three-foot velocity: 1,400 ft./sec.
Hull: 3-inch plastic
Wad: Plastic
Shot: Steel
Buffered: No
Test barrel length: 30 inch
Pellets will pierce skin up to 144 yards.

NO. 3 STEEL PELLETS—⅞ OUNCE—138 PELLETS
Mfg: Fiocchi **Manufacturer's code:** 203ST
Recoil energy in 8-lb. shotgun: 22.4 ft./lbs. **Recoil velocity in 8-lb. shotgun:** 13.4 ft./sec.

Distance in yards:	Muzzle	20	30	40	50	60	70
Velocity in fps:	1,604	1002	838	717	621	542	476
Average pellet energy in ft-lbs:	16.32	6.36	4.46	3.26	2.44	1.87	1.44
Time of flight in seconds:	0	.0484	.0813	.1201	.1651	.2169	.2760

Type of load: Nontoxic
Three-foot velocity: 1,500 ft./sec.
Hull: 3-inch plastic
Wad: Plastic
Shot: Steel
Buffered: No
Test barrel length: 30 inch
Pellets will pierce skin up to 137 yards.

NO. 3 STEEL PELLETS—⅞ OUNCE—138 PELLETS
Mfg: Kent Cartridge America/Canada **Manufacturer's code:** K203ST24
Recoil energy in 8-lb. shotgun: 24.5 ft./lbs. **Recoil velocity in 8-lb. shotgun:** 14.0 ft./sec.

Distance in yards:	Muzzle	20	30	40	50	60	70
Velocity in fps:	1,659	1,026	856	730	632	551	484
Average pellet energy in ft-lbs:	17.47	6.68	4.65	3.38	2.53	1.93	1.48
Time of flight in seconds:	0	.0473	.0794	.1174	.1617	.2126	.2707

Type of load: Field
Three-foot velocity: 1,550 ft./sec.
Hull: 3-inch plastic
Wad: Plastic
Shot: Steel
Buffered: No
Test barrel length: 30 inch
Pellets will pierce skin up to 138 yards.

NO. 3 STEEL PELLETS—1 OUNCE—158 PELLETS
Mfg: Estate Cartridge **Manufacturer's code:** HVST20MM
Recoil energy in 8-lb. shotgun: 21.2 ft./lbs. **Recoil velocity in 8-lb. shotgun:** 13.0 ft./sec.

Distance in yards:	Muzzle	20	30	40	50	60	70
Velocity in fps:	1,417	919	778	669	582	510	448
Average pellet energy in ft-lbs:	12.74	5.35	3.84	2.84	2.15	1.65	1.27
Time of flight in seconds:	0	.0538	.0894	.1310	.1792	.2343	.2971

Type of load: Nontoxic
Three-foot velocity: 1,330 ft./sec.
Hull: 3-inch plastic
Wad: Plastic
Shot: Steel
Buffered: No
Test barrel length: 30 inch
Pellets will pierce skin up to 132 yards.

NO. 3 STEEL PELLETS—1 OUNCE—158 PELLETS
Mfg: Federal Cartridge Company **Manufacturer's code:** W209
Recoil energy in 8-lb. shotgun: 21.2 ft./lbs. **Recoil velocity in 8-lb. shotgun:** 13.0 ft./sec.

Distance in yards:	Muzzle	20	30	40	50	60	70
Velocity in fps:	1,417	919	778	669	582	510	448
Average pellet energy in ft-lbs:	12.74	5.35	3.84	2.84	2.15	1.65	1.27
Time of flight in seconds:	0	.0538	.0894	.1310	.1792	.2343	.2971

Type of load: Nontoxic
Three-foot velocity: 1,330 ft./sec.
Hull: 3-inch plastic
Wad: Plastic
Shot: Steel
Buffered: No
Test barrel length: 30 inch
Pellets will pierce skin up to 132 yards.

NO. 3 STEEL PELLETS—1 OUNCE—158 PELLETS
Mfg: Remington Arms Co. **Manufacturer's code:** NS20M
Recoil energy in 8-lb. shotgun: 21.2 ft./lbs. **Recoil velocity in 8-lb. shotgun:** 13.0 ft./sec.

Distance in yards:	Muzzle	20	30	40	50	60	70
Velocity in fps:	1,417	919	778	669	582	510	448
Average pellet energy in ft-lbs:	12.74	5.35	3.84	2.84	2.15	1.65	1.27
Time of flight in seconds:	0	.0538	.0894	.1310	.1792	.2343	.2971

Type of load: Nontoxic
Three-foot velocity: 1,330 ft./sec.
Hull: 3-inch plastic
Wad: Plastic
Shot: Zinc-galvanized steel
Buffered: No
Test barrel length: 30 inch
Pellets will pierce skin up to 132 yards.

NO. 3 STEEL PELLETS—1 OUNCE—158 PELLETS
Mfg: Winchester **Manufacturer's code:** XSM203
Recoil energy in 8-lb. shotgun: 21.2 ft./lbs. **Recoil velocity in 8-lb. shotgun:** 13.0 ft./sec.

Distance in yards:	Muzzle	20	30	40	50	60	70
Velocity in fps:	1,417	919	778	669	582	510	448
Average pellet energy in ft-lbs:	12.74	5.35	3.84	2.84	2.15	1.65	1.27
Time of flight in seconds:	0	.0538	.0894	.1310	.1792	.2343	.2971

Type of load: Nontoxic
Three-foot velocity: 1,330 ft./sec.
Hull: 3-inch plastic
Wad: Two-piece plastic
Shot: Steel
Buffered: No
Test barrel length: 30 inch
Pellets will pierce skin up to 132 yards.

NO. 3 STEEL PELLETS—1 OUNCE—158 PELLETS
Mfg: Federal Cartridge Company **Manufacturer's code:** W211
Recoil energy in 8-lb. shotgun: 24.3 ft./lbs. **Recoil velocity in 8-lb. shotgun:** 14.0 ft./sec.

Distance in yards:	Muzzle	20	30	40	50	60	70
Velocity in fps:	1,494	953	803	689	598	524	460
Average pellet energy in ft-lbs:	14.16	5.76	4.09	3.01	2.27	1.74	1.34
Time of flight in seconds:	0	.0515	.0859	.1263	.1731	.2267	.2879

Type of load: Nontoxic
Three-foot velocity: 1,400 ft./sec.
Hull: 3-inch plastic
Wad: Plastic
Shot: Steel
Buffered: No
Test barrel length: 30 inch
Pellets will pierce skin up to 134 yards.

NO. 4 STEEL PELLETS—⅞ OUNCE—168 PELLETS

Mfg: Fiocchi **Manufacturer's code:** 203ST
Recoil energy in 8-lb. shotgun: 22.4 ft./lbs. **Recoil velocity in 8-lb. shotgun:** 13.4 ft./sec.

Distance in yards:	Muzzle	20	30	40	50	60	70
Velocity in fps:	1,610	975	809	686	590	511	444
Average pellet energy in ft-lbs:	13.17	4.83	3.33	2.39	1.77	1.33	1.00
Time of flight in seconds:	0	.0492	.0831	.1234	.1706	.2253	.2883

Type of load: Nontoxic
Three-foot velocity: 1,500 ft./sec.
Hull: 3-inch plastic
Wad: Plastic
Shot: Steel
Buffered: No
Test barrel length: 30 inch
Pellets will pierce skin up to 127 yards.

NO. 4 STEEL PELLETS—⅞ OUNCE—168 PELLETS

Mfg: Kent Cartridge America/Canada **Manufacturer's code:** K203ST24
Recoil energy in 8-lb. shotgun: 24.5 ft./lbs. **Recoil velocity in 8-lb. shotgun:** 14.0 ft./sec.

Distance in yards:	Muzzle	20	30	40	50	60	70
Velocity in fps:	1,666	999	826	699	600	520	452
Average pellet energy in ft-lbs:	14.10	5.07	3.46	2.48	1.83	1.37	1.04
Time of flight in seconds:	0	.0482	.0813	.1209	.1673	.2211	.2831

Type of load: Field
Three-foot velocity: 1,550 ft./sec.
Hull: 3-inch plastic
Wad: Plastic
Shot: Steel
Buffered: No
Test barrel length: 30 inch
Pellets will pierce skin up to 128 yards.

NO. 4 STEEL PELLETS—1 OUNCE—192 PELLETS

Mfg: Estate Cartridge **Manufacturer's code:** HVST20MM
Recoil energy in 8-lb. shotgun: 21.2 ft./lbs. **Recoil velocity in 8-lb. shotgun:** 13.0 ft./sec.

Distance in yards:	Muzzle	20	30	40	50	60	70
Velocity in fps:	1,422	896	752	642	554	481	418
Average pellet energy in ft-lbs:	10.28	4.08	2.87	2.09	1.56	1.18	.89
Time of flight in seconds:	0	.0545	.0912	.1344	.1848	.2403	.3099

Type of load: Nontoxic
Three-foot velocity: 1,330 ft./sec.
Hull: 3-inch plastic
Wad: Plastic
Shot: Steel
Buffered: No
Test barrel length: 30 inch
Pellets will pierce skin up to 123 yards.

NO. 4 STEEL PELLETS—1 OUNCE—192 PELLETS

Mfg: Federal Cartridge Company **Manufacturer's code:** PW209/W209
Recoil energy in 8-lb. shotgun: 21.2 ft./lbs. **Recoil velocity in 8-lb. shotgun:** 13.0 ft./sec.

Distance in yards:	Muzzle	20	30	40	50	60	70
Velocity in fps:	1,422	896	752	642	554	481	418
Average pellet energy in ft-lbs:	10.28	4.08	2.87	2.09	1.56	1.18	.89
Time of flight in seconds:	0	.0545	.0912	.1344	.1848	.2403	.3099

Type of load: Nontoxic
Three-foot velocity: 1,330 ft./sec.
Hull: 3-inch plastic
Wad: Plastic
Shot: Steel
Buffered: No
Test barrel length: 30 inch
Pellets will pierce skin up to 123 yards.

NO. 4 STEEL PELLETS—1 OUNCE—192 PELLETS

Mfg: Remington Arms Co. **Manufacturer's code:** NS20M
Recoil energy in 8-lb. shotgun: 21.2 ft./lbs. **Recoil velocity in 8-lb. shotgun:** 13.0 ft./sec.

Distance in yards:	Muzzle	20	30	40	50	60	70
Velocity in fps:	1,422	896	752	642	554	481	418
Average pellet energy in ft-lbs:	10.28	4.08	2.87	2.09	1.56	1.18	.89
Time of flight in seconds:	0	.0545	.0912	.1344	.1848	.2403	.3099

Type of load: Nontoxic
Three-foot velocity: 1,330 ft./sec.
Hull: 3-inch plastic
Wad: Plastic
Shot: Zinc-galvanized steel
Buffered: No
Test barrel length: 30 inch
Pellets will pierce skin up to 123 yards.

NO. 4 STEEL PELLETS—1 OUNCE—192 PELLETS

Mfg: Winchester **Manufacturer's code:** XSM203
Recoil energy in 8-lb. shotgun: 21.2 ft./lbs. **Recoil velocity in 8-lb. shotgun:** 13.0 ft./sec.

Distance in yards:	Muzzle	20	30	40	50	60	70
Velocity in fps:	1,422	896	752	642	554	481	418
Average pellet energy in ft-lbs:	10.28	4.08	2.87	2.09	1.56	1.18	.89
Time of flight in seconds:	0	.0545	.0912	.1344	.1848	.2403	.3099

Type of load: Nontoxic
Three-foot velocity: 1,330 ft./sec.
Hull: 3-inch plastic
Wad: Two-piece plastic
Shot: Steel
Buffered: No
Test barrel length: 30 inch
Pellets will pierce skin up to 123 yards.

NO. 4 STEEL PELLETS—1 OUNCE—192 PELLETS

Mfg: Federal Cartridge Company **Manufacturer's code:** W211
Recoil energy in 8-lb. shotgun: 24.3 ft./lbs. **Recoil velocity in 8-lb. shotgun:** 14.0 ft./sec.

Distance in yards:	Muzzle	20	30	40	50	60	70
Velocity in fps:	1,500	929	776	660	569	494	429
Average pellet energy in ft-lbs:	11.42	4.38	3.06	2.22	1.65	1.24	.94
Time of flight in seconds:	0	.0522	.0876	.1297	.1787	.2353	.3005

Type of load: Nontoxic
Three-foot velocity: 1,400 ft./sec.
Hull: 3-inch plastic
Wad: Plastic
Shot: Steel
Buffered: No
Test barrel length: 30 inch
Pellets will pierce skin up to 125 yards.

NO. 6 STEEL PELLETS—1 OUNCE—315 PELLETS

Mfg: Estate Cartridge **Manufacturer's code:** HVST20MM
Recoil energy in 8-lb. shotgun: 21.2 ft./lbs. **Recoil velocity in 8-lb. shotgun:** 13.0 ft./sec.

Distance in yards:	Muzzle	20	30	40	50	60	70
Velocity in fps:	1,434	843	692	579	489	415	351
Average pellet energy in ft-lbs:	6.33	2.19	1.47	1.03	.74	.53	.38
Time of flight in seconds:	0	.0564	.0958	.1434	.1998	.2665	.3451

Type of load: Nontoxic
Three-foot velocity: 1,330 ft./sec.
Hull: 3-inch plastic
Wad: Plastic
Shot: Steel
Buffered: No
Test barrel length: 30 inch
Pellets will pierce skin up to 104 yards.

NO. 6 STEEL PELLETS—1 OUNCE—315 PELLETS

Mfg: Federal Cartridge Company **Manufacturer's code:** PW209
Recoil energy in 8-lb. shotgun: 21.2 ft./lbs. **Recoil velocity in 8-lb. shotgun:** 13.0 ft./sec.

Distance in yards:	Muzzle	20	30	40	50	60	70
Velocity in fps:	1,434	843	692	579	489	415	351
Average pellet energy in ft-lbs:	6.33	2.19	1.47	1.03	.74	.53	.38
Time of flight in seconds:	0	.0564	.0958	.1434	.1998	.2665	.3451

Type of load: Nontoxic
Three-foot velocity: 1,330 ft./sec.
Hull: 3-inch plastic
Wad: Plastic
Shot: Steel
Buffered: No
Test barrel length: 30 inch
Pellets will pierce skin up to 104 yards.

A solid rest and an equally solid and safe backer for a target are the necessities for pattern testing shotshells. An accurate rangefinder and high-performance recoil-absorbing pads help make the session precise and comfortable.

NO. 4 TUNGSTEN-IRON PELLETS—⅞ OUNCE—122 PELLETS

Mfg: Federal Cartridge Company **Manufacturer's code:** PWT 220
Recoil energy in 8-lb. shotgun: 17.7 ft./lbs. **Recoil velocity in 8-lb. shotgun:** 11.9 ft./sec.

Distance in yards:	Muzzle	20	30	40	50	60	70
Velocity in fps:	1,439	994	859	753	667	596	534
Average pellet energy in ft-lbs:	13.90	6.63	4.95	3.81	2.99	2.38	1.91
Time of flight in seconds:	0	.0510	.0835	.1208	.1632	.2108	.2641

Type of load: Nontoxic
Three-foot velocity: 1,375 ft./sec.
Hull: 3-inch plastic
Wad: Plastic
Shot: Tungsten-iron
Buffered: Yes
Test barrel length: 30 inch
Pellets will pierce skin up to 163 yards.

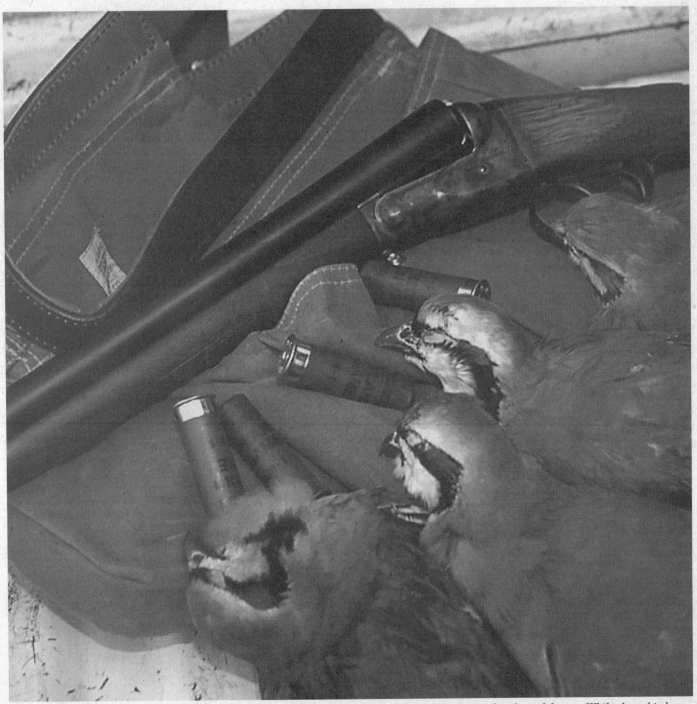

When hunting pen-reared, game-farm birds, lighter loads and small-gauge shotguns can be used with confidence. While these birds can be testing, for the most part they do not fly with the strength of wild birds and often sit tight for a well-trained dog, providing close shots. One-ounce loads in a restored, vintage 16-gauge A. H. Fox Sterlingworth were just the ticket for these red-legged or chukka partridge.

NO. 4 BISMUTH PELLETS—1 OUNCE—181 PELLETS
Mfg: Bismuth Cartridge Co. **Manufacturer's code:** Sporting Game
Recoil energy in 8-lb. shotgun: 16.1 ft./lbs. **Recoil velocity in 8-lb. shotgun:** 11.4 ft./sec.

Distance in yards:	Muzzle	20	30	40	50	60	70
Velocity in fps:	1,284	897	776	680	602	535	477
Average pellet energy in ft-lbs:	10.33	5.03	3.77	2.90	2.27	1.79	1.43
Time of flight in seconds:	0	.0568	.0928	.1342	.1711	.2340	.2934

Type of load: Field
Three-foot velocity: 1,200 ft./sec.
Hull: 2¾-inch plastic
Wad: Plastic
Shot: Bismuth
Buffered: No
Test barrel length: 26 inch
Pellets will pierce skin up to 147 yards.

NO. 4 BISMUTH PELLETS—1 OUNCE—170 PELLETS
Mfg: Eley Hawk **Manufacturer's code:** VIP Bismuth
Recoil energy in 8-lb. shotgun: 19.9 ft./lbs. **Recoil velocity in 8-lb. shotgun:** 12.6 ft./sec.

Distance in yards:	Muzzle	20	30	40	50	60	70
Velocity in fps:	1,394	951	818	714	629	559	498
Average pellet energy in ft-lbs:	12.17	5.66	4.19	3.19	2.48	1.95	1.55
Time of flight in seconds:	0	.0530	.0871	.1265	.1713	.2219	.2788

Type of load: Field
Three-foot velocity: 1,300 ft./sec.
Hull: 2¾-inch plastic
Wad: Photo-degradable plastic
Shot: Bismuth
Buffered: No
Test barrel length: 26 inch
Pellets will pierce skin up to 150 yards.

NO. 5 BISMUTH PELLETS—1 OUNCE—220 PELLETS
Mfg: Eley Hawk **Manufacturer's code:** VIP Bismuth
Recoil energy in 8-lb. shotgun: 19.9 ft./lbs. **Recoil velocity in 8-lb. shotgun:** 12.6 ft./sec.

Distance in yards:	Muzzle	20	30	40	50	60	70
Velocity in fps:	1,401	929	792	686	600	529	467
Average pellet energy in ft-lbs:	9.66	4.25	3.09	2.31	1.77	1.38	1.07
Time of flight in seconds:	0	.0537	.0887	.1295	.1764	.2297	.2901

Type of load: Field
Three-foot velocity: 1,300 ft./sec.
Hull: 2¾-inch plastic
Wad: Photo-degradable plastic
Shot: Bismuth
Buffered: No
Test barrel length: 26 inch
Pellets will pierce skin up to 149 yards.

NO. 7½ BISMUTH PELLETS—1 OUNCE—397 PELLETS
Mfg: Bismuth Cartridge Co. **Manufacturer's code:** Sporting Game
Recoil energy in 8-lb. shotgun: 16.1 ft./lbs. **Recoil velocity in 8-lb. shotgun:** 11.4 ft./sec.

Distance in yards:	Muzzle	20	30	40	50	60	70
Velocity in fps:	1,306	814	678	574	490	420	359
Average pellet energy in ft-lbs:	4.17	1.62	1.12	.81	.59	.43	.32
Time of flight in seconds:	0	.0598	.1003	.1484	.2051	.2713	.3486

Type of load: Field
Three-foot velocity: 1,200 ft./sec.
Hull: 2¾-inch plastic
Wad: Plastic
Shot: Bismuth
Buffered: No
Test barrel length: 26 inch
Pellets will pierce skin up to 108 yards.

NO. 6 BISMUTH PELLETS—1 OUNCE—271 PELLETS
Mfg: Bismuth Cartridge Co. **Manufacturer's code:** Sporting Game
Recoil energy in 8-lb. shotgun: 16.1 ft./lbs. **Recoil velocity in 8-lb. shotgun:** 11.4 ft./sec.

Distance in yards:	Muzzle	20	30	40	50	60	70
Velocity in fps:	1,296	855	726	625	543	475	415
Average pellet energy in ft-lbs:	6.37	2.77	2.00	1.48	1.12	.85	.65
Time of flight in seconds:	0	.0582	.0964	.1410	.1926	.2517	.3193

Type of load: Field
Three-foot velocity: 1,200 ft./sec.
Hull: 2¾-inch plastic
Wad: Plastic
Shot: Bismuth
Buffered: No
Test barrel length: 26 inch
Pellets will pierce skin up to 124 yards.

NO. 6 BISMUTH PELLETS—1 OUNCE—270 PELLETS
Mfg: Eley Hawk **Manufacturer's code:** VIP Bismuth
Recoil energy in 8-lb. shotgun: 19.9 ft./lbs. **Recoil velocity in 8-lb. shotgun:** 12.6 ft./sec.

Distance in yards:	Muzzle	20	30	40	50	60	70
Velocity in fps:	1,408	904	763	654	568	495	433
Average pellet energy in ft-lbs:	7.51	3.10	2.21	1.62	1.22	.93	.71
Time of flight in seconds:	0	.0544	.0907	.1332	.1826	.2392	.3040

Type of load: Field
Three-foot velocity: 1,300 ft./sec.
Hull: 2¾-inch plastic
Wad: Photo-degradable plastic
Shot: Bismuth
Buffered: No
Test barrel length: 26 inch
Pellets will pierce skin up to 128 yards.

NO. 2 BISMUTH PELLETS—1¹/₁₆ OUNCES—128 PELLETS

Mfg: Bismuth Cartridge Co. **Manufacturer's code:** Magnum Buffered Game
Recoil energy in 8-lb. shotgun: 22.7 ft./lbs. **Recoil velocity in 8-lb. shotgun:** 13.5 ft./sec.

Distance in yards:	Muzzle	20	30	40	50	60	70
Velocity in fps:	1,328	958	839	744	665	598	540
Average pellet energy in ft-lbs:	16.95	8082	6.77	5.32	4.25	3.44	2.81
Time of flight in seconds:	0	.0539	.0874	.1255	.1682	.2158	.2686

Type of load: Field
Three-foot velocity: 1,250 ft./sec.
Hull: 3-inch plastic
Wad: Plastic
Shot: Bismuth
Buffered: Yes
Test barrel length: 30 inch
Pellets will pierce skin up to 171 yards.

NO. 4 BISMUTH PELLETS—1¹/₁₆ OUNCES—181 PELLETS

Mfg: Bismuth Cartridge Co. **Manufacturer's code:** Magnum Buffered Game
Recoil energy in 8-lb. shotgun: 22.7 ft./lbs. **Recoil velocity in 8-lb. shotgun:** 13.5 ft./sec.

Distance in yards:	Muzzle	20	30	40	50	60	70
Velocity in fps:	1,339	924	797	697	616	547	488
Average pellet energy in ft-lbs:	11.23	5.34	3.98	3.04	2.37	1.87	1.49
Time of flight in seconds:	0	.0549	.0899	.1302	.1760	.2278	.2859

Type of load: Field
Three-foot velocity: 1,250 ft./sec.
Hull: 3-inch plastic
Wad: Plastic
Shot: Bismuth
Buffered: Yes
Test barrel length: 30 inch
Pellets will pierce skin up to 149 yards.

NO. 5 BISMUTH PELLETS—1¹/₁₆ OUNCES—234 PELLETS

Mfg: Bismuth Cartridge Co. **Manufacturer's code:** Magnum Buffered Game
Recoil energy in 8-lb. shotgun: 22.7 ft./lbs. **Recoil velocity in 8-lb. shotgun:** 13.5 ft./sec.

Distance in yards:	Muzzle	20	30	40	50	60	70
Velocity in fps:	1,345	903	772	670	587	518	458
Average pellet energy in ft-lbs:	8.91	4.02	2.94	2.21	1.70	1.32	1.03
Time of flight in seconds:	0	.0555	.0915	.1333	.1811	.2356	.2972

Type of load: Field
Three-foot velocity: 1,250 ft./sec.
Hull: 3-inch plastic
Wad: Plastic
Shot: Bismuth
Buffered: Yes
Test barrel length: 30 inch
Pellets will pierce skin up to 137 yards.

NO. 6 BISMUTH PELLETS—1¹/₁₆ OUNCES—287 PELLETS

Mfg: Bismuth Cartridge Co. **Manufacturer's code:** Magnum Buffered Game
Recoil energy in 8-lb. shotgun: 22.7 ft./lbs. **Recoil velocity in 8-lb. shotgun:** 13.5 ft./sec.

Distance in yards:	Muzzle	20	30	40	50	60	70
Velocity in fps:	1,352	879	744	640	556	485	424
Average pellet energy in ft-lbs:	6.93	2.93	2.10	1.55	1.17	.89	.68
Time of flight in seconds:	0	.0563	.0934	.1613	.1874	.2452	.3114

Type of load: Field
Three-foot velocity: 1,250 ft./sec.
Hull: 3-inch plastic
Wad: Plastic
Shot: Bismuth
Buffered: Yes
Test barrel length: 30 inch
Pellets will pierce skin up to 126 yards.

Hunting mallards in flooded timber is the crème de la crème of duck hunting. These greenheads were taken with No. 4 tungsten/polymer shot through a classic Winchester Model 21. Because ducks in flooded timber are short-range targets, skeet and improved cylinder chokes are the primary choice.

NO. 5 TUNGSTEN-POLYMER PELLETS—1 OUNCE—182 PELLETS

Mfg: Kent Cartridge America/Canada **Manufacturer's code:** K202NT28
Recoil energy in 8-lb. shotgun: 22.5 ft./lbs. **Recoil velocity in 8-lb. shotgun:** 13.4 ft./sec.

Distance in yards:	Muzzle	20	30	40	50	60	70
Velocity in fps:	1,451	978	839	730	643	570	508
Average pellet energy in ft-lbs:	11.23	5.10	3.75	2.84	2.20	1.73	1.38
Time of flight in seconds:	0	.0513	.0845	.1229	.1667	.2163	.2721

Type of load: Nontoxic
Three-foot velocity: 1,350 ft./sec.
Hull: 2¾-inch plastic
Wad: Plastic
Shot: Tungsten-polymer
Buffered: No
Test barrel length: 26 inch
Pellets will pierce skin up to 152 yards.

NO. 6 TUNGSTEN-POLYMER PELLETS—1 OUNCE—225 PELLETS

Mfg: Kent Cartridge America/Canada **Manufacturer's code:** K202UGNT28
Recoil energy in 8-lb. shotgun: 22.0 ft./lbs. **Recoil velocity in 8-lb. shotgun:** 13.3 ft./sec.

Distance in yards:	Muzzle	20	30	40	50	60	70
Velocity in fps:	1,458	953	809	699	610	537	474
Average pellet energy in ft-lbs:	8.73	2.73	2.69	2.00	1.53	1.18	.92
Time of flight in seconds:	0	.0520	.0862	.1262	.1723	.2247	.2843

Type of load: Nontoxic
Three-foot velocity: 1,350 ft./sec.
Hull: 2¾-inch plastic
Wad: Plastic
Shot: Tungsten-polymer
Buffered: No
Test barrel length: 26 inch
Pellets will pierce skin up to 140 yards.

20 Gauge—Tungsten-Polymer 3 inch

NO. 3 TUNGSTEN-POLYMER PELLETS—1⅛ OUNCES—129 PELLETS

Mfg: Kent Cartridge America/Canada **Manufacturer's code:** K203NT32
Recoil energy in 8-lb. shotgun: 27.9 ft./lbs. **Recoil velocity in 8-lb. shotgun:** 15.0 ft./sec.

Distance in yards:	Muzzle	20	30	40	50	60	70
Velocity in fps:	1,449	1,025	893	789	703	631	570
Average pellet energy in ft-lbs:	17.79	8.90	6.75	5.26	4.19	3.38	2.75
Time of flight in seconds:	0	.0499	.0813	.1171	.1574	.2025	.2526

Type of load: Nontoxic
Three-foot velocity: 1,360 ft./sec.
Hull: 3-inch plastic
Wad: Plastic
Shot: Tungsten-polymer
Buffered: No
Test barrel length: 30 inch
Pellets will pierce skin up to 177 yards.

NO. 5 TUNGSTEN-POLYMER PELLETS—1⅛ OUNCES—205 PELLETS

Mfg: Kent Cartridge America/Canada **Manufacturer's code:** K203NT32
Recoil energy in 8-lb. shotgun: 27.9 ft./lbs. **Recoil velocity in 8-lb. shotgun:** 15.0 ft./sec.

Distance in yards:	Muzzle	20	30	40	50	60	70
Velocity in fps:	1,462	984	843	734	646	573	510
Average pellet energy in ft-lbs:	11.40	5.16	3.79	2.87	2.22	1.75	1.39
Time of flight in seconds:	0	.0509	.0840	.1222	.1658	.2152	.2708

Type of load: Nontoxic
Three-foot velocity: 1,360 ft./sec.
Hull: 3-inch plastic
Wad: Plastic
Shot: Tungsten-polymer
Buffered: No
Test barrel length: 30 inch
Pellets will pierce skin up to 152 yards.

NO. 6 LEAD PELLETS—⁹⁄₁₆ OUNCE—127 PELLETS

Mfg: Eley Hawk **Manufacturer's code:** Grand Prix
Recoil energy in 8-lb. shotgun: 7.0 ft./lbs. **Recoil velocity in 8-lb. shotgun:** 7.5 ft./sec.

Distance in yards:	Muzzle	20	30	40	50	60	70
Velocity in fps:	1,314	903	778	679	598	530	471
Average pellet energy in ft-lbs:	7.51	3.54	2.63	2.00	1.55	1.22	.97
Time of flight in seconds:	0	.0560	.0919	.1333	.1804	.2337	.2938

Type of load: Field
Three-foot velocity: 1,220 ft./sec.
Hull: 2½-inch plastic
Wad: Fiber
Shot: Lead
Buffered: No
Test barrel length: 26 inch
Pellets will pierce skin up to 143 yards.

Tim Dople calls to circling Arkansas mallards as Federal Cartridge's Bill Stevens waits for a shot. Although federal law dictates that ducks and geese can be hunted only with nontoxic shot, ducks require smaller (No. 2 or 3 steel, and No. 4 bismuth and tungsten/polymer) shot and more open chokes.

NO. 2 LEAD PELLETS—1 OUNCE—87 PELLETS
Mfg: ARMUSA **Manufacturer's code:** PLA-1
Recoil energy in 8-lb. shotgun: 19.9 ft./lbs. **Recoil velocity in 8-lb. shotgun:** 12.6 ft./sec.

Distance in yards:	Muzzle	20	30	40	50	60	70
Velocity in fps:	1,378	1,022	904	809	730	662	604
Average pellet energy in ft-lbs:	20.93	11.50	9.00	7.21	5.87	4.83	4.01
Time of flight in seconds:	0	.0511	.0824	.1175	.1566	.1988	.2473

Type of load: Field
Three-foot velocity: 1,300 ft./sec.
Hull: 2¾-inch plastic
Wad: Plastic
Shot: Lead
Buffered: No
Test barrel length: 26 inch
Pellets will pierce skin up to 198 yards.

NO. 4 LEAD PELLETS—1 OUNCE—135 PELLETS
Mfg: ARMUSA **Manufacturer's code:** PLA-1
Recoil energy in 8-lb. shotgun: 19.9 ft./lbs. **Recoil velocity in 8-lb. shotgun:** 12.6 ft./sec.

Distance in yards:	Muzzle	20	30	40	50	60	70
Velocity in fps:	1,390	989	863	762	680	611	551
Average pellet energy in ft-lbs:	13.86	7.01	5.34	4.17	3.32	2.67	2.18
Time of flight in seconds:	0	.0519	.0844	.1215	.1632	.2098	.2615

Type of load: Field
Three-foot velocity: 1,300 ft./sec.
Hull: 2¾-inch plastic
Wad: Plastic
Shot: Lead
Buffered: No
Test barrel length: 26 inch
Pellets will pierce skin up to 172 yards.

NO. 6 LEAD PELLETS—¾ OUNCE—169 PELLETS
Mfg: Fiocchi **Manufacturer's code:** 28HV
Recoil energy in 8-lb. shotgun: 10.6 ft./lbs. **Recoil velocity in 8-lb. shotgun:** 9.2 ft./sec.

Distance in yards:	Muzzle	20	30	40	50	60	70
Velocity in fps:	1,375	932	800	697	613	543	482
Average pellet energy in ft-lbs:	8.22	3.77	2.78	2.11	1.63	1.28	1.01
Time of flight in seconds:	0	.0540	.0888	.1290	.1750	.2271	.2858

Type of load: Field
Three-foot velocity: 1,275 ft./sec.
Hull: 2¾-inch plastic
Wad: Plastic
Shot: Lead
Buffered: No
Test barrel length: 26 inch
Pellets will pierce skin up to 145 yards.

NO. 6 LEAD PELLETS—¾ OUNCE—169 PELLETS
Mfg: Estate Cartridge **Manufacturer's code:** HV28
Recoil energy in 8-lb. shotgun: 11.2 ft./lbs. **Recoil velocity in 8-lb. shotgun:** 9.5 ft./sec.

Distance in yards:	Muzzle	20	30	40	50	60	70
Velocity in fps:	1,403	945	810	705	620	548	487
Average pellet energy in ft-lbs:	8.55	3.88	2.85	2.16	1.67	1.31	1.03
Time of flight in seconds:	0	.0531	.0875	.1272	.1727	.2242	.2723

Type of load: Field
Three-foot velocity: 1,300 ft./sec.
Hull: 2¾-inch plastic
Wad: Plastic
Shot: Hard lead
Buffered: No
Test barrel length: 26 inch
Pellets will pierce skin up to 146 yards.

NO. 6 LEAD PELLETS—¾ OUNCE—169 PELLETS
Mfg: Federal Cartridge Co. **Manufacturer's code:** P283
Recoil energy in 8-lb. shotgun: 11.2 ft./lbs. **Recoil velocity in 8-lb. shotgun:** 9.5 ft./sec.

Distance in yards:	Muzzle	20	30	40	50	60	70
Velocity in fps:	1,403	945	810	705	620	548	487
Average pellet energy in ft-lbs:	8.55	3.88	2.85	2.16	1.67	1.31	1.03
Time of flight in seconds:	0	.0531	.0875	.1272	.1727	.2242	.2723

Type of load: Field
Three-foot velocity: 1,300 ft./sec.
Hull: 2¾-inch plastic
Wad: Plastic
Shot: Lead
Buffered: No
Test barrel length: 26 inch
Pellets will pierce skin up to 146 yards.

NO. 6 LEAD PELLETS—¾ OUNCE—169 PELLETS
Mfg: PMC (Eldorado Cartridge Corp.) **Manufacturer's code:** HF28
Recoil energy in 8-lb. shotgun: 11.2 ft./lbs. **Recoil velocity in 8-lb. shotgun:** 9.5 ft./sec.

Distance in yards:	Muzzle	20	30	40	50	60	70
Velocity in fps:	1,403	945	810	705	620	548	487
Average pellet energy in ft-lbs:	8.55	3.88	2.85	2.16	1.67	1.31	1.03
Time of flight in seconds:	0	.0531	.0875	.1272	.1727	.2242	.2723

Type of load: Field
Three-foot velocity: 1,300 ft./sec.
Hull: 2¾-inch plastic
Wad: Plastic
Shot: Lead
Buffered: No
Test barrel length: 26 inch
Pellets will pierce skin up to 146 yards.

NO. 6 LEAD PELLETS—¾ OUNCE—169 PELLETS
Mfg: Remington Arms Co. **Manufacturer's code:** SP28
Recoil energy in 8-lb. shotgun: 11.2 ft./lbs. **Recoil velocity in 8-lb. shotgun:** 9.5 ft./sec.

Distance in yards:	Muzzle	20	30	40	50	60	70
Velocity in fps:	1,403	945	810	705	620	548	487
Average pellet energy in ft-lbs:	8.55	3.88	2.85	2.16	1.67	1.31	1.03
Time of flight in seconds:	0	.0531	.0875	.1272	.1727	.2242	.2723

Type of load: Field
Three-foot velocity: 1,300 ft./sec.
Hull: 2¾-inch plastic
Wad: Plastic
Shot: Lead
Buffered: No
Test barrel length: 26 inch
Pellets will pierce skin up to 146 yards.

NO. 6 LEAD PELLETS—1 OUNCE—225 PELLETS
Mfg: Winchester **Manufacturer's code:** X28H
Recoil energy in 8-lb. shotgun: 16.1 ft./lbs. **Recoil velocity in 8-lb. shotgun:** 11.4 ft./sec.

Distance in yards:	Muzzle	20	30	40	50	60	70
Velocity in fps:	1,292	892	769	672	593	525	467
Average pellet energy in ft-lbs:	7.26	3.46	2.57	1.96	1.53	1.20	.095
Time of flight in seconds:	0	.0568	.0931	.01349	.1825	.2363	.2969

Type of load: Field
Three-foot velocity: 1,200 ft./sec.
Hull: 2¾-inch plastic
Wad: Plastic
Shot: Lead
Buffered: No
Test barrel length: 26 inch
Pellets will pierce skin up to 157 yards.

NO. 6 LEAD PELLETS—1 OUNCE—225 PELLETS
Mfg: ARMUSA **Manufacturer's code:** PLA-1
Recoil energy in 8-lb. shotgun: 19.9 ft./lbs. **Recoil velocity in 8-lb. shotgun:** 12.6 ft./sec.

Distance in yards:	Muzzle	20	30	40	50	60	70
Velocity in fps:	1,403	945	810	705	620	548	487
Average pellet energy in ft-lbs:	8.55	3.88	2.85	2.16	1.67	1.31	1.03
Time of flight in seconds:	0	.0531	.0875	.1272	.1727	.2242	.2723

Type of load: Field
Three-foot velocity: 1,300 ft./sec.
Hull: 2¾-inch plastic
Wad: Plastic
Shot: Lead
Buffered: No
Test barrel length: 26 inch
Pellets will pierce skin up to 146 yards.

NO. 7½ LEAD PELLETS—¾ OUNCE—262 PELLETS
Mfg: Estate Cartridge **Manufacturer's code:** CT28
Recoil energy in 8-lb. shotgun: 9.1 ft./lbs. **Recoil velocity in 8-lb. shotgun:** 8.5 ft./sec.

Distance in yards:	Muzzle	20	30	40	50	60	70
Velocity in fps:	1,302	854	724	623	541	472	412
Average pellet energy in ft-lbs:	4.74	2.04	1.47	1.09	.82	.62	.47
Time of flight in seconds:	0	.0581	.0964	.1412	.1930	.2524	.3204

Type of load: Target
Three-foot velocity: 1,200 ft./sec.
Hull: 2¾-inch plastic
Wad: Plastic
Shot: Hard lead
Buffered: No
Test barrel length: 26 inch
Pellets will pierce skin up to 136 yards.

NO. 7½ LEAD PELLETS—¾ OUNCE—262 PELLETS
Mfg: Sellier & Bellot **Manufacturer's code:** SBA02805
Recoil energy in 8-lb. shotgun: 9.1 ft./lbs. **Recoil velocity in 8-lb. shotgun:** 8.5 ft./sec.

Distance in yards:	Muzzle	20	30	40	50	60	70
Velocity in fps:	1,302	854	724	623	541	472	412
Average pellet energy in ft-lbs:	4.74	2.04	1.47	1.09	.82	.62	.47
Time of flight in seconds:	0	.0581	.0964	.1412	.1930	.2524	.3204

Type of load: Target
Three-foot velocity: 1,200 ft./sec.
Hull: 2¾-inch plastic
Wad: Plastic
Shot: Hard lead
Buffered: No
Test barrel length: 26 inch
Pellets will pierce skin up to 136 yards.

NO. 7½ LEAD PELLETS—¾ OUNCE—262 PELLETS
Mfg: Baschieri & Pellagri **Manufacturer's code:** Extra Rossa
Recoil energy in 8-lb. shotgun: 11.2 ft./lbs. **Recoil velocity in 8-lb. shotgun:** 10.1 ft./sec.

Distance in yards:	Muzzle	20	30	40	50	60	70
Velocity in fps:	1,341	871	737	633	549	479	418
Average pellet energy in ft-lbs:	5.03	2.12	1.52	1.12	.84	.64	.49
Time of flight in seconds:	0	.0568	.0943	.1383	.1893	.2478	.3149

Type of load: Target
Three-foot velocity: 1,235 ft./sec.
Hull: 2¾-inch plastic
Wad: Plastic
Shot: Hard lead
Buffered: No
Test barrel length: 26 inch
Pellets will pierce skin up to 124 yards.

NO. 7½ LEAD PELLETS—¾ OUNCE—262 PELLETS
Mfg: Fiocchi **Manufacturer's code:** 28HV
Recoil energy in 8-lb. shotgun: 10.6 ft./lbs. **Recoil velocity in 8-lb. shotgun:** 9.2 ft./sec.

Distance in yards:	Muzzle	20	30	40	50	60	70
Velocity in fps:	1,385	891	752	645	559	487	425
Average pellet energy in ft-lbs:	5.37	2.22	1.58	1.16	.87	.66	.51
Time of flight in seconds:	0	.0553	.0921	.1652	.1853	.2429	.3088

Type of load: Field
Three-foot velocity: 1,275 ft./sec.
Hull: 2¾-inch plastic
Wad: Plastic
Shot: Lead
Buffered: No
Test barrel length: 26 inch
Pellets will pierce skin up to 126 yards.

NO. 7½ LEAD PELLETS—¾ OUNCE—262 PELLETS
Mfg: Estate Cartridge **Manufacturer's code:** HV28
Recoil energy in 8-lb. shotgun: 11.2 ft./lbs. **Recoil velocity in 8-lb. shotgun:** 9.5 ft./sec.

Distance in yards:	Muzzle	20	30	40	50	60	70
Velocity in fps:	1,413	903	761	652	565	492	430
Average pellet energy in ft-lbs:	5.59	2.28	1.62	1.19	.89	.68	.52
Time of flight in seconds:	0	.0544	.0907	.1334	.1829	.2399	.3052

Type of load: Field
Three-foot velocity: 1,300 ft./sec.
Hull: 2¾-inch plastic
Wad: Plastic
Shot: Hard lead
Buffered: No
Test barrel length: 26 inch
Pellets will pierce skin up to 126 yards.

NO. 7½ LEAD PELLETS—¾ OUNCE—262 PELLETS
Mfg: Federal Cartridge Co. **Manufacturer's code:** P283
Recoil energy in 8-lb. shotgun: 11.2 ft./lbs. **Recoil velocity in 8-lb. shotgun:** 9.5 ft./sec.

Distance in yards:	Muzzle	20	30	40	50	60	70
Velocity in fps:	1,413	903	761	652	565	492	430
Average pellet energy in ft-lbs:	5.59	2.28	1.62	1.19	.89	.68	.52
Time of flight in seconds:	0	.0544	.0907	.1334	.1829	.2399	.3052

Type of load: Field
Three-foot velocity: 1,300 ft./sec.
Hull: 2¾-inch plastic
Wad: Plastic
Shot: Lead
Buffered: No
Test barrel length: 26 inch
Pellets will pierce skin up to 126 yards.

NO. 7½ LEAD PELLETS—¾ OUNCE—262 PELLETS
Mfg: PMC (Eldorado Cartridge Corp.) **Manufacturer's code:** HF28
Recoil energy in 8-lb. shotgun: 11.2 ft./lbs. **Recoil velocity in 8-lb. shotgun:** 9.5 ft./sec.

Distance in yards:	Muzzle	20	30	40	50	60	70
Velocity in fps:	1,413	903	761	652	565	492	430
Average pellet energy in ft-lbs:	5.59	2.28	1.62	1.19	.89	.68	.52
Time of flight in seconds:	0	.0544	.0907	.1334	.1829	.2399	.3052

Type of load: Field
Three-foot velocity: 1,300 ft./sec.
Hull: 2¾-inch plastic
Wad: Plastic
Shot: Lead
Buffered: No
Test barrel length: 26 inch
Pellets will pierce skin up to 126 yards.

NO. 7½ LEAD PELLETS—¾ OUNCE—262 PELLETS
Mfg: Remington Arms Co. **Manufacturer's code:** SP28
Recoil energy in 8-lb. shotgun: 11.2 ft./lbs. **Recoil velocity in 8-lb. shotgun:** 9.5 ft./sec.

Distance in yards:	Muzzle	20	30	40	50	60	70
Velocity in fps:	1,413	903	761	652	565	492	430
Average pellet energy in ft-lbs:	5.59	2.28	1.62	1.19	.89	.68	.52
Time of flight in seconds:	0	.0544	.0907	.1334	.1829	.2399	.3052

Type of load: Field
Three-foot velocity: 1,300 ft./sec.
Hull: 2¾-inch plastic
Wad: Plastic
Shot: Lead
Buffered: No
Test barrel length: 26 inch
Pellets will pierce skin up to 126 yards.

NO. 7½ LEAD PELLETS—1 OUNCE—350 PELLETS
Mfg: Winchester **Manufacturer's code:** X28H
Recoil energy in 8-lb. shotgun: 16.1 ft./lbs. **Recoil velocity in 8-lb. shotgun:** 11.4 ft./sec.

Distance in yards:	Muzzle	20	30	40	50	60	70
Velocity in fps:	1,302	854	724	623	541	472	412
Average pellet energy in ft-lbs:	4.74	2.04	1.47	1.09	.82	.62	.47
Time of flight in seconds:	0	.0581	.0964	.1412	.1930	.2524	.3204

Type of load: Field
Three-foot velocity: 1,200 ft./sec.
Hull: 2¾-inch plastic
Wad: Plastic
Shot: Lead
Buffered: No
Test barrel length: 26 inch
Pellets will pierce skin up to 136 yards.

NO. 7½ LEAD PELLETS—1 OUNCE—350 PELLETS
Mfg: ARMUSA **Manufacturer's code:** PLA-1
Recoil energy in 8-lb. shotgun: 19.9 ft./lbs. **Recoil velocity in 8-lb. shotgun:** 12.6 ft./sec.

Distance in yards:	Muzzle	20	30	40	50	60	70
Velocity in fps:	1,413	903	761	652	565	492	430
Average pellet energy in ft-lbs:	5.59	2.28	1.62	1.19	.89	.68	.52
Time of flight in seconds:	0	.0544	.0907	.1334	.1829	.2399	.3052

Type of load: Field
Three-foot velocity: 1,300 ft./sec.
Hull: 2¾-inch plastic
Wad: Plastic
Shot: Lead
Buffered: No
Test barrel length: 26 inch
Pellets will pierce skin up to 126 yards.

NO. 8 LEAD PELLETS—¾ OUNCE—307 PELLETS
Mfg: Dionisi **Manufacturer's code:** D 28 GT
Recoil energy in 8-lb. shotgun: 9.1 ft./lbs. **Recoil velocity in 8-lb. shotgun:** 8.5 ft./sec.

Distance in yards:	Muzzle	20	30	40	50	60	70
Velocity in fps:	1,305	839	706	604	521	452	391
Average pellet energy in ft-lbs:	4.05	1.67	1.19	.87	.65	.49	.36
Time of flight in seconds:	0	.0587	.0978	.1438	.1973	.2593	.3307

Type of load: Game & Target
Three-foot velocity: 1,200 ft./sec.
Hull: 2¾-inch plastic
Wad: Plastic
Shot: Lead
Buffered: No
Test barrel length: 26 inch
Pellets will pierce skin up to 129 yards.

NO. 8 LEAD PELLETS—¾ OUNCE—307 PELLETS
Mfg: Estate Cartridge **Manufacturer's code:** CT28
Recoil energy in 8-lb. shotgun: 9.1 ft./lbs. **Recoil velocity in 8-lb. shotgun:** 8.5 ft./sec.

Distance in yards:	Muzzle	20	30	40	50	60	70
Velocity in fps:	1,305	839	706	604	521	452	391
Average pellet energy in ft-lbs:	4.05	1.67	1.19	.87	.65	.49	.36
Time of flight in seconds:	0	.0587	.0978	.1438	.1973	.2593	.3307

Type of load: Target
Three-foot velocity: 1,200 ft./sec.
Hull: 2¾-inch plastic
Wad: Plastic
Shot: Hard lead
Buffered: No
Test barrel length: 26 inch
Pellets will pierce skin up to 129 yards.

NO. 8 LEAD PELLETS—¾ OUNCE—307 PELLETS
Mfg: Fiocchi **Manufacturer's code:** 28GT
Recoil energy in 8-lb. shotgun: 9.1 ft./lbs. **Recoil velocity in 8-lb. shotgun:** 8.5 ft./sec.

Distance in yards:	Muzzle	20	30	40	50	60	70
Velocity in fps:	1,305	839	706	604	521	452	391
Average pellet energy in ft-lbs:	4.05	1.67	1.19	.87	.65	.49	.36
Time of flight in seconds:	0	.0587	.0978	.1438	.1973	.2593	.3307

Type of load: Game & Target
Three-foot velocity: 1,200 ft./sec.
Hull: 2¾-inch plastic
Wad: Plastic
Shot: Lead
Buffered: No
Test barrel length: 26 inch
Pellets will pierce skin up to 129 yards.

NO. 8 LEAD PELLETS—¾ OUNCE—307 PELLETS
Mfg: PMC (Eldorado Cartridge Corp.) **Manufacturer's code:** CT28
Recoil energy in 8-lb. shotgun: 9.1 ft./lbs. **Recoil velocity in 8-lb. shotgun:** 8.5 ft./sec.

Distance in yards:	Muzzle	20	30	40	50	60	70
Velocity in fps:	1,305	839	706	604	521	452	391
Average pellet energy in ft-lbs:	4.05	1.67	1.19	.87	.65	.49	.36
Time of flight in seconds:	0	.0587	.0978	.1438	.1973	.2593	.3307

Type of load: Target
Three-foot velocity: 1,200 ft./sec.
Hull: 2¾-inch plastic
Wad: Plastic
Shot: Hard lead
Buffered: No
Test barrel length: 26 inch
Pellets will pierce skin up to 129 yards.

NO. 8 LEAD PELLETS—¾ OUNCE—307 PELLETS
Mfg: Remington Arms Co. **Manufacturer's code:** STS28SC
Recoil energy in 8-lb. shotgun: 9.1 ft./lbs. **Recoil velocity in 8-lb. shotgun:** 8.5 ft./sec.

Distance in yards:	Muzzle	20	30	40	50	60	70
Velocity in fps:	1,305	839	706	604	521	452	391
Average pellet energy in ft-lbs:	4.05	1.67	1.19	.87	.65	.49	.36
Time of flight in seconds:	0	.0587	.0978	.1438	.1973	.2593	.3307

Type of load: Target
Three-foot velocity: 1,200 ft./sec.
Hull: 2¾-inch plastic
Wad: Plastic
Shot: Hard lead
Buffered: No
Test barrel length: 26 inch
Pellets will pierce skin up to 129 yards.

NO. 8 LEAD PELLETS—¾ OUNCE—307 PELLETS
Mfg: Sellier & Bellot **Manufacturer's code:** SBA02804
Recoil energy in 8-lb. shotgun: 9.1 ft./lbs. **Recoil velocity in 8-lb. shotgun:** 8.5 ft./sec.

Distance in yards:	Muzzle	20	30	40	50	60	70
Velocity in fps:	1,305	839	706	604	521	452	391
Average pellet energy in ft-lbs:	4.05	1.67	1.19	.87	.65	.49	.36
Time of flight in seconds:	0	.0587	.0978	.1438	.1973	.2593	.3307

Type of load: Target
Three-foot velocity: 1,200 ft./sec.
Hull: 2¾-inch plastic
Wad: Plastic
Shot: Lead
Buffered: No
Test barrel length: 26 inch
Pellets will pierce skin up to 129 yards.

NO. 8 LEAD PELLETS—¾ OUNCE—307 PELLETS
Mfg: Baschieri & Pellagri **Manufacturer's code:** Extra Rossa
Recoil energy in 8-lb. shotgun: 11.2 ft./lbs. **Recoil velocity in 8-lb. shotgun:** 10.1 ft./sec.

Distance in yards:	Muzzle	20	30	40	50	60	70
Velocity in fps:	1,344	856	719	614	529	459	397
Average pellet energy in ft-lbs:	4.30	1.74	1.23	.90	.67	.50	.38
Time of flight in seconds:	0	.0573	.0957	.1409	.1936	.2546	.3249

Type of load: Target
Three-foot velocity: 1,235 ft./sec.
Hull: 2¾-inch plastic
Wad: Plastic
Shot: Hard lead
Buffered: No
Test barrel length: 26 inch
Pellets will pierce skin up to 118 yards.

NO. 8 LEAD PELLETS—¾ OUNCE—307 PELLETS
Mfg: Fiocchi **Manufacturer's code:** 28HV
Recoil energy in 8-lb. shotgun: 10.6 ft./lbs. **Recoil velocity in 8-lb. shotgun:** 9.2 ft./sec.

Distance in yards:	Muzzle	20	30	40	50	60	70
Velocity in fps:	1,389	875	733	625	538	466	404
Average pellet energy in ft-lbs:	4.59	1.82	1.28	.93	.69	.52	.39
Time of flight in seconds:	0	.0558	.0934	.1378	.1897	.2496	.3187

Type of load: Field
Three-foot velocity: 1,275 ft./sec.
Hull: 2¾-inch plastic
Wad: Plastic
Shot: Lead
Buffered: No
Test barrel length: 26 inch
Pellets will pierce skin up to 119 yards.

NO. 8 LEAD PELLETS—¾ OUNCE—307 PELLETS
Mfg: Estate Cartridge **Manufacturer's code:** HV28
Recoil energy in 8-lb. shotgun: 11.2 ft./lbs. **Recoil velocity in 8-lb. shotgun:** 9.5 ft./sec.

Distance in yards:	Muzzle	20	30	40	50	60	70
Velocity in fps:	1,417	886	742	632	544	471	408
Average pellet energy in ft-lbs:	4.78	1.87	1.31	.95	.70	.53	.40
Time of flight in seconds:	0	.0549	.0921	.1360	.1873	.2466	.3150

Type of load: Field
Three-foot velocity: 1,300 ft./sec.
Hull: 2¾-inch plastic
Wad: Plastic
Shot: Hard lead
Buffered: No
Test barrel length: 26 inch
Pellets will pierce skin up to 132 yards.

NO. 8 LEAD PELLETS—¾ OUNCE—307 PELLETS
Mfg: Federal Cartridge Co. **Manufacturer's code:** P283
Recoil energy in 8-lb. shotgun: 11.2 ft./lbs. **Recoil velocity in 8-lb. shotgun:** 9.5 ft./sec.

Distance in yards:	Muzzle	20	30	40	50	60	70
Velocity in fps:	1,417	886	742	632	544	471	408
Average pellet energy in ft-lbs:	4.78	1.87	1.31	.95	.70	.53	.40
Time of flight in seconds:	0	.0549	.0921	.1360	.1873	.2466	.3150

Type of load: Field
Three-foot velocity: 1,300 ft./sec.
Hull: 2¾-inch plastic
Wad: Plastic
Shot: Lead
Buffered: No
Test barrel length: 26 inch
Pellets will pierce skin up to 132 yards.

NO. 8 LEAD PELLETS—1 OUNCE—410 PELLETS
Mfg: Winchester **Manufacturer's code:** X28H
Recoil energy in 8-lb. shotgun: 16.1 ft./lbs. **Recoil velocity in 8-lb. shotgun:** 11.4 ft./sec.

Distance in yards:	Muzzle	20	30	40	50	60	70
Velocity in fps:	1,305	839	706	604	521	452	391
Average pellet energy in ft-lbs:	4.05	1.67	1.19	.87	.65	.49	.36
Time of flight in seconds:	0	.0587	.0978	.1438	.1973	.2593	.3307

Type of load: Field
Three-foot velocity: 1,200 ft./sec.
Hull: 2¾-inch plastic
Wad: Plastic
Shot: Lead
Buffered: No
Test barrel length: 26 inch
Pellets will pierce skin up to 129 yards.

NO. 8½ LEAD PELLETS—¾ OUNCE—373 PELLETS
Mfg: Estate Cartridge **Manufacturer's code:** CT28
Recoil energy in 8-lb. shotgun: 9.1 ft./lbs. **Recoil velocity in 8-lb. shotgun:** 8.5 ft./sec.

Distance in yards:	Muzzle	20	30	40	50	60	70
Velocity in fps:	1,308	823	687	584	500	430	369
Average pellet energy in ft-lbs:	1.36	1.13	.95	.68	.50	.37	.325
Time of flight in seconds:	0	.0593	.0993	.1468	.2024	.2671	.3423

Type of load: Target
Three-foot velocity: 1,200 ft./sec.
Hull: 2¾-inch plastic
Wad: Plastic
Shot: Hard lead
Buffered: No
Test barrel length: 26 inch
Pellets will pierce skin up to 111 yards.

NO. 8½ LEAD PELLETS—¾ OUNCE—373 PELLETS
Mfg: Federal Cartridge Co. **Manufacturer's code:** T280
Recoil energy in 8-lb. shotgun: 9.1 ft./lbs. **Recoil velocity in 8-lb. shotgun:** 8.5 ft./sec.

Distance in yards:	Muzzle	20	30	40	50	60	70
Velocity in fps:	1,308	823	687	584	500	430	369
Average pellet energy in ft-lbs:	1.36	1.13	.95	.68	.50	.37	.325
Time of flight in seconds:	0	.0593	.0993	.1468	.2024	.2671	.3423

Type of load: Target
Three-foot velocity: 1,200 ft./sec.
Hull: 2¾-inch plastic
Wad: Plastic
Shot: Hard lead
Buffered: No
Test barrel length: 26 inch
Pellets will pierce skin up to 111 yards.

NO. 9 LEAD PELLETS—¾ OUNCE—439 PELLETS
Mfg: Dionisi **Manufacturer's code:** D 28 GT
Recoil energy in 8-lb. shotgun: 9.1 ft./lbs. **Recoil velocity in 8-lb. shotgun:** 8.5 ft./sec.

Distance in yards:	Muzzle	20	30	40	50	60	70
Velocity in fps:	1,312	805	667	562	478	407	346
Average pellet energy in ft-lbs:	2.88	1.08	.74	.53	.38	.28	.20
Time of flight in seconds:	0	.0601	.1011	.1502	.2082	.2763	.3562

Type of load: Game & Target
Three-foot velocity: 1,200 ft./sec.
Hull: 2¾-inch plastic
Wad: Plastic
Shot: Lead
Buffered: No
Test barrel length: 26 inch
Pellets will pierce skin up to 115 yards.

NO. 9 LEAD PELLETS—¾ OUNCE—439 PELLETS
Mfg: Estate Cartridge **Manufacturer's code:** CT28
Recoil energy in 8-lb. shotgun: 9.1 ft./lbs. **Recoil velocity in 8-lb. shotgun:** 8.5 ft./sec.

Distance in yards:	Muzzle	20	30	40	50	60	70
Velocity in fps:	1,312	805	667	562	478	407	346
Average pellet energy in ft-lbs:	2.88	1.08	.74	.53	.38	.28	.20
Time of flight in seconds:	0	.0601	.1011	.1502	.2082	.2763	.3562

Type of load: Target
Three-foot velocity: 1,200 ft./sec.
Hull: 2¾-inch plastic
Wad: Plastic
Shot: Hard lead
Buffered: No
Test barrel length: 26 inch
Pellets will pierce skin up to 115 yards.

NO. 9 LEAD PELLETS—¾ OUNCE—439 PELLETS
Mfg: Federal Cartridge Co. **Manufacturer's code:** T280
Recoil energy in 8-lb. shotgun: 9.1 ft./lbs. **Recoil velocity in 8-lb. shotgun:** 8.5 ft./sec.

Distance in yards:	Muzzle	20	30	40	50	60	70
Velocity in fps:	1,312	805	667	562	478	407	346
Average pellet energy in ft-lbs:	2.88	1.08	.74	.53	.38	.28	.20
Time of flight in seconds:	0	.0601	.1011	.1502	.2082	.2763	.3562

Type of load: Target
Three-foot velocity: 1,200 ft./sec.
Hull: 2¾-inch plastic
Wad: Plastic
Shot: Hard lead
Buffered: No
Test barrel length: 26 inch
Pellets will pierce skin up to 115 yards.

NO. 9 LEAD PELLETS—¾ OUNCE—439 PELLETS
Mfg: Fiocchi **Manufacturer's code:** 28GT
Recoil energy in 8-lb. shotgun: 9.1 ft./lbs. **Recoil velocity in 8-lb. shotgun:** 8.5 ft./sec.

Distance in yards:	Muzzle	20	30	40	50	60	70
Velocity in fps:	1,312	805	667	562	478	407	346
Average pellet energy in ft-lbs:	2.88	1.08	.74	.53	.38	.28	.20
Time of flight in seconds:	0	.0601	.1011	.1502	.2082	.2763	.3562

Type of load: Game & Target
Three-foot velocity: 1,200 ft./sec.
Hull: 2¾-inch plastic
Wad: Plastic
Shot: Lead
Buffered: No
Test barrel length: 26 inch
Pellets will pierce skin up to 115 yards.

NO. 9 LEAD PELLETS—¾ OUNCE—439 PELLETS
Mfg: PMC (Eldorado Cartridge Corp.) **Manufacturer's code:** CT28
Recoil energy in 8-lb. shotgun: 9.1 ft./lbs. **Recoil velocity in 8-lb. shotgun:** 8.5 ft./sec.

Distance in yards:	Muzzle	20	30	40	50	60	70
Velocity in fps:	1,312	805	667	562	478	407	346
Average pellet energy in ft-lbs:	2.88	1.08	.74	.53	.38	.28	.20
Time of flight in seconds:	0	.0601	.1011	.1502	.2082	.2763	.3562

Type of load: Target
Three-foot velocity: 1,200 ft./sec.
Hull: 2¾-inch plastic
Wad: Plastic
Shot: Lead
Buffered: No
Test barrel length: 26 inch
Pellets will pierce skin up to 115 yards.

NO. 9 LEAD PELLETS—¾ OUNCE—439 PELLETS
Mfg: Remington Arms Co. **Manufacturer's code:** STS28
Recoil energy in 8-lb. shotgun: 9.1 ft./lbs. **Recoil velocity in 8-lb. shotgun:** 8.5 ft./sec.

Distance in yards:	Muzzle	20	30	40	50	60	70
Velocity in fps:	1,312	805	667	562	478	407	346
Average pellet energy in ft-lbs:	2.88	1.08	.74	.53	.38	.28	.20
Time of flight in seconds:	0	.0601	.1011	.1502	.2082	.2763	.3562

Type of load: Target
Three-foot velocity: 1,200 ft./sec.
Hull: 2¾-inch plastic
Wad: Plastic
Shot: Hard lead
Buffered: No
Test barrel length: 26 inch
Pellets will pierce skin up to 115 yards.

NO. 9 LEAD PELLETS—¾ OUNCE—439 PELLETS
Mfg: Sellier & Bellot **Manufacturer's code:** SBA02806
Recoil energy in 8-lb. shotgun: 9.1 ft./lbs. **Recoil velocity in 8-lb. shotgun:** 8.5 ft./sec.

Distance in yards:	Muzzle	20	30	40	50	60	70
Velocity in fps:	1,312	805	667	562	478	407	346
Average pellet energy in ft-lbs:	2.88	1.08	.74	.53	.38	.28	.20
Time of flight in seconds:	0	.0601	.1011	.1502	.2082	.2763	.3562

Type of load: Target
Three-foot velocity: 1,200 ft./sec.
Hull: 2¾-inch plastic
Wad: Plastic
Shot: Lead
Buffered: No
Test barrel length: 26 inch
Pellets will pierce skin up to 115 yards.

NO. 9 LEAD PELLETS—¾ OUNCE—439 PELLETS
Mfg: Winchester **Manufacturer's code:** AA28
Recoil energy in 8-lb. shotgun: 9.1 ft./lbs. **Recoil velocity in 8-lb. shotgun:** 8.5 ft./sec.

Distance in yards:	Muzzle	20	30	40	50	60	70
Velocity in fps:	1,312	805	667	562	478	407	346
Average pellet energy in ft-lbs:	2.88	1.08	.74	.53	.38	.28	.20
Time of flight in seconds:	0	.0601	.1011	.1502	.2082	.2763	.3562

Type of load: Target
Three-foot velocity: 1,200 ft./sec.
Hull: 2¾-inch plastic
Wad: Plastic
Shot: Hard lead
Buffered: No
Test barrel length: 26 inch
Pellets will pierce skin up to 115 yards.

NO. 9 LEAD PELLETS—¾ OUNCE—439 PELLETS
Mfg: Fiocchi **Manufacturer's code:** 28HV
Recoil energy in 8-lb. shotgun: 10.6 ft./lbs. **Recoil velocity in 8-lb. shotgun:** 9.2 ft./sec.

Distance in yards:	Muzzle	20	30	40	50	60	70
Velocity in fps:	1,396	838	691	581	493	420	358
Average pellet energy in ft-lbs:	3.26	1.17	.80	.56	.41	.29	.21
Time of flight in seconds:	0	.0572	.0967	.1442	.2003	.2663	.3438

Type of load: Field
Three-foot velocity: 1,275 ft./sec.
Hull: 2¾-inch plastic
Wad: Plastic
Shot: Lead
Buffered: No
Test barrel length: 26 inch
Pellets will pierce skin up to 106 yards.

NO. 9 LEAD PELLETS—¾ OUNCE—439 PELLETS
Mfg: Estate Cartridge **Manufacturer's code:** HV28
Recoil energy in 8-lb. shotgun: 11.2 ft./lbs. **Recoil velocity in 8-lb. shotgun:** 9.5 ft./sec.

Distance in yards:	Muzzle	20	30	40	50	60	70
Velocity in fps:	1,426	849	699	587	498	424	361
Average pellet energy in ft-lbs:	3.39	1.20	.82	.58	.42	.30	.22
Time of flight in seconds:	0	.0563	.0954	.1423	.1978	.2632	.3399

Type of load: Field
Three-foot velocity: 1,300 ft./sec.
Hull: 2¾-inch plastic
Wad: Plastic
Shot: Hard lead
Buffered: No
Test barrel length: 26 inch
Pellets will pierce skin up to 117 yards.

NO. 6 BISMUTH PELLETS—9/16 OUNCE—152 PELLETS

Mfg: Eley Hawk **Manufacturer's code:** Grand Prix Bismuth
Recoil energy in 8-lb. shotgun: 17.9 ft./lbs. **Recoil velocity in 8-lb. shotgun:** 12.0 ft./sec.

Distance in yards:	Muzzle	20	30	40	50	60	70
Velocity in fps:	1,352	879	744	640	556	485	424
Average pellet energy in ft-lbs:	6.93	2.93	2.10	1.55	1.17	.89	.68
Time of flight in seconds:	0	.0563	.0934	.1370	.1874	.2452	.3114

Type of load: Nontoxic
Three-foot velocity: 1,250 ft./sec.
Hull: 2½-inch plastic
Wad: Fiber
Shot: Bismuth
Buffered: No
Test barrel length: 26 inch
Pellets will pierce skin up to 127 yards.

NO. 4 BISMUTH PELLETS—5/8 OUNCE—106 PELLETS

Mfg: Bismuth Cartridge Co. **Manufacturer's code:** Sporting Game
Recoil energy in 8-lb. shotgun: 7.0 ft./lbs. **Recoil velocity in 8-lb. shotgun:** 7.5 ft./sec.

Distance in yards:	Muzzle	20	30	40	50	60	70
Velocity in fps:	1,339	924	797	697	616	547	488
Average pellet energy in ft-lbs:	11.23	5.34	3.98	3.04	2.37	1.87	1.49
Time of flight in seconds:	0	.0549	.0899	.1302	.1760	.2278	.2859

Type of load: Nontoxic
Three-foot velocity: 1,250 ft./sec.
Hull: 2¾-inch plastic
Wad: Plastic
Shot: Bismuth
Buffered: No
Test barrel length: 26 inch
Pellets will pierce skin up to 149 yards.

NO. 6 BISMUTH PELLETS—5/8 OUNCE—169 PELLETS

Mfg: Bismuth Cartridge Co. **Manufacturer's code:** Sporting Game
Recoil energy in 8-lb. shotgun: 7.0 ft./lbs. **Recoil velocity in 8-lb. shotgun:** 7.5 ft./sec.

Distance in yards:	Muzzle	20	30	40	50	60	70
Velocity in fps:	1,352	879	744	640	556	485	424
Average pellet energy in ft-lbs:	6.93	2.93	2.10	1.55	1.17	.89	.68
Time of flight in seconds:	0	.0563	.0934	.1613	.1874	.2452	.3114

Type of load: Nontoxic
Three-foot velocity: 1,250 ft./sec.
Hull: 2¾-inch plastic
Wad: Plastic
Shot: Bismuth
Buffered: No
Test barrel length: 26 inch
Pellets will pierce skin up to 126 yards.

Shooting ducks from a pit sunk into a levee bordering an Arkansas rice field, these hunters are well equipped with modern repeaters and a skilled caller, Tom Mathews of Avery Outdoors, to bring the ducks close.

NO. 6 LEAD PELLETS—⁵⁄₁₆ OUNCE—70 PELLETS

Mfg: Eley Hawk **Manufacturer's code:** Fourten
Recoil energy in 8-lb. shotgun: 4.0 ft./lbs. **Recoil velocity in 8-lb. shotgun:** 5.7 ft./sec.

Distance in yards:	Muzzle	20	30	40	50	60	70
Velocity in fps:	1,292	892	769	672	593	525	467
Average pellet energy in ft-lbs:	7.26	3.46	2.57	1.96	1.53	1.20	.095
Time of flight in seconds:	0	.0568	.0931	.01349	.1825	.2363	.2969

Type of load: Field
Three-foot velocity: 1,200 ft./sec.
Hull: 2-inch plastic
Wad: Fiber
Shot: Lead
Buffered: No
Test barrel length: 26 inch
Pellets will pierce skin up to 157 yards.

Two great German shorthair pointers, plentiful Hungarian partridge, and a fine double in the hand of a skilled shot paint a true picture of upland hunting at its best.

NO. 4 LEAD PELLETS—½ OUNCE—67 PELLETS
Mfg: Aguila **Manufacturer's code:** N/A
Recoil energy in 8-lb. shotgun: 4.0 ft./lbs. **Recoil velocity in 8-lb. shotgun:** 5.7 ft./sec.

Distance in yards:	Muzzle	20	30	40	50	60	70
Velocity in fps:	1,281	931	817	725	649	584	528
Average pellet energy in ft-lbs:	11.77	6.21	4.79	3.77	3.02	2.45	2.00
Time of flight in seconds:	0	.0556	.0901	.01291	.1729	.2216	.2757

Type of load: Field
Three-foot velocity: 1,200 ft./sec.
Hull: 2½-inch plastic
Wad: Plastic
Shot: Lead
Buffered: No
Test barrel length: 26 inch
Pellets will pierce skin up to 168 yards.

NO. 4 LEAD PELLETS—½ OUNCE—67 PELLETS
Mfg: Estate Cartridge **Manufacturer's code:** HV410
Recoil energy in 8-lb. shotgun: 4.0 ft./lbs. **Recoil velocity in 8-lb. shotgun:** 5.7 ft./sec.

Distance in yards:	Muzzle	20	30	40	50	60	70
Velocity in fps:	1,281	931	817	725	649	584	528
Average pellet energy in ft-lbs:	11.77	6.21	4.79	3.77	3.02	2.45	2.00
Time of flight in seconds:	0	.0556	.0901	.01291	.1729	.2216	.2757

Type of load: Field
Three-foot velocity: 1,200 ft./sec.
Hull: 2½-inch plastic
Wad: Plastic
Shot: Hard lead
Buffered: No
Test barrel length: 26 inch
Pellets will pierce skin up to 168 yards.

NO. 4 LEAD PELLETS—½ OUNCE—67 PELLETS
Mfg: Remington Arms Co. **Manufacturer's code:** SP410
Recoil energy in 8-lb. shotgun: 4.0 ft./lbs. **Recoil velocity in 8-lb. shotgun:** 5.7 ft./sec.

Distance in yards:	Muzzle	20	30	40	50	60	70
Velocity in fps:	1,281	931	817	725	649	584	528
Average pellet energy in ft-lbs:	11.77	6.21	4.79	3.77	3.02	2.45	2.00
Time of flight in seconds:	0	.0556	.0901	.01291	.1729	.2216	.2757

Type of load: Field
Three-foot velocity: 1,200 ft./sec.
Hull: 2½-inch plastic
Wad: Plastic
Shot: Lead
Buffered: No
Test barrel length: 26 inch
Pellets will pierce skin up to 168 yards.

NO. 5 LEAD PELLETS—7/16 OUNCE—74 PELLETS
Mfg: Eley Hawk **Manufacturer's code:** Fourlong
Recoil energy in 8-lb. shotgun: 6.3 ft./lbs. **Recoil velocity in 8-lb. shotgun:** 7.1 ft./sec.

Distance in yards:	Muzzle	20	30	40	50	60	70
Velocity in fps:	1,287	913	795	700	622	556	499
Average pellet energy in ft-lbs:	9.34	4.70	3.56	2.77	2.18	1.75	1.40
Time of flight in seconds:	0	.0562	.0915	.1317	.1772	.2282	.2852

Type of load: Field
Three-foot velocity: 1,200 ft./sec.
Hull: 2½-inch plastic
Wad: Fiber
Shot: Lead
Buffered: No
Test barrel length: 26 inch
Pellets will pierce skin up to 155 yards.

NO. 6 LEAD PELLETS—7/16 OUNCE—98 PELLETS
Mfg: Eley Hawk **Manufacturer's code:** Fourlong
Recoil energy in 8-lb. shotgun: 6.3 ft./lbs. **Recoil velocity in 8-lb. shotgun:** 7.1 ft./sec.

Distance in yards:	Muzzle	20	30	40	50	60	70
Velocity in fps:	1,292	892	769	672	593	525	467
Average pellet energy in ft-lbs:	7.26	3.46	2.57	1.96	1.53	1.20	.095
Time of flight in seconds:	0	.0568	.0931	.01349	.1825	.2363	.2969

Type of load: Field
Three-foot velocity: 1,200 ft./sec.
Hull: 2½-inch plastic
Wad: Fiber
Shot: Lead
Buffered: No
Test barrel length: 26 inch
Pellets will pierce skin up to 157 yards.

NO. 6 LEAD PELLETS—½ OUNCE—112 PELLETS
Mfg: Aguila **Manufacturer's code:** N/A
Recoil energy in 8-lb. shotgun: 4.0 ft./lbs. **Recoil velocity in 8-lb. shotgun:** 5.7 ft./sec.

Distance in yards:	Muzzle	20	30	40	50	60	70
Velocity in fps:	1,292	892	769	672	593	525	467
Average pellet energy in ft-lbs:	7.26	3.46	2.57	1.96	1.53	1.20	.095
Time of flight in seconds:	0	.0568	.0931	.01349	.1825	.2363	.2969

Type of load: Field
Three-foot velocity: 1,200 ft./sec.
Hull: 2½-inch plastic
Wad: Plastic
Shot: Lead
Buffered: No
Test barrel length: 26 inch
Pellets will pierce skin up to 157 yards.

NO. 6 LEAD PELLETS—½ OUNCE—112 PELLETS
Mfg: Estate Cartridge **Manufacturer's code:** HV410
Recoil energy in 8-lb. shotgun: 4.0 ft./lbs. **Recoil velocity in 8-lb. shotgun:** 5.7 ft./sec.

Distance in yards:	Muzzle	20	30	40	50	60	70
Velocity in fps:	1,292	892	769	672	593	525	467
Average pellet energy in ft-lbs:	7.26	3.46	2.57	1.96	1.53	1.20	.095
Time of flight in seconds:	0	.0568	.0931	.01349	.1825	.2363	.2969

Type of load: Field
Three-foot velocity: 1,200 ft./sec.
Hull: 2½-inch plastic
Wad: Plastic
Shot: Hard lead
Buffered: No
Test barrel length: 26 inch
Pellets will pierce skin up to 157 yards.

NO. 6 LEAD PELLETS—½ OUNCE—112 PELLETS
Mfg: Federal Cartridge Co. **Manufacturer's code:** H412
Recoil energy in 8-lb. shotgun: 4.0 ft./lbs. **Recoil velocity in 8-lb. shotgun:** 5.7 ft./sec.

Distance in yards:	Muzzle	20	30	40	50	60	70
Velocity in fps:	1,292	892	769	672	593	525	467
Average pellet energy in ft-lbs:	7.26	3.46	2.57	1.96	1.53	1.20	.095
Time of flight in seconds:	0	.0568	.0931	.01349	.1825	.2363	.2969

Type of load: Field
Three-foot velocity: 1,200 ft./sec.
Hull: 2½-inch plastic
Wad: Plastic
Shot: Lead
Buffered: No
Test barrel length: 26 inch
Pellets will pierce skin up to 157 yards.

NO. 6 LEAD PELLETS—½ OUNCE—112 PELLETS
Mfg: Remington Arms Co. **Manufacturer's code:** SP410/GL410
Recoil energy in 8-lb. shotgun: 4.0 ft./lbs. **Recoil velocity in 8-lb. shotgun:** 5.7 ft./sec.

Distance in yards:	Muzzle	20	30	40	50	60	70
Velocity in fps:	1,292	892	769	672	593	525	467
Average pellet energy in ft-lbs:	7.26	3.46	2.57	1.96	1.53	1.20	.095
Time of flight in seconds:	0	.0568	.0931	.01349	.1825	.2363	.2969

Type of load: Field
Three-foot velocity: 1,200 ft./sec.
Hull: 2½-inch plastic
Wad: Plastic
Shot: Lead
Buffered: No
Test barrel length: 26 inch
Pellets will pierce skin up to 157 yards.

NO. 7½ LEAD PELLETS—⁷/₁₆ OUNCE—153 PELLETS
Mfg: Eley Hawk **Manufacturer's code:** Fourlong
Recoil energy in 8-lb. shotgun: 6.3 ft./lbs. **Recoil velocity in 8-lb. shotgun:** 7.1 ft./sec.

Distance in yards:	Muzzle	20	30	40	50	60	70
Velocity in fps:	1,302	854	724	623	541	472	412
Average pellet energy in ft-lbs:	4.74	2.04	1.47	1.09	.82	.62	.47
Time of flight in seconds:	0	.0581	.0964	.1412	.1930	.2524	.3204

Type of load: Field
Three-foot velocity: 1,200 ft./sec.
Hull: 2½-inch plastic
Wad: Fiber
Shot: Lead
Buffered: No
Test barrel length: 26 inch
Pellets will pierce skin up to 136 yards.

NO. 7½ LEAD PELLETS—½ OUNCE—173 PELLETS
Mfg: Aguila **Manufacturer's code:** N/A
Recoil energy in 8-lb. shotgun: 4.0 ft./lbs. **Recoil velocity in 8-lb. shotgun:** 5.7 ft./sec.

Distance in yards:	Muzzle	20	30	40	50	60	70
Velocity in fps:	1,302	854	724	623	541	472	412
Average pellet energy in ft-lbs:	4.74	2.04	1.47	1.09	.82	.62	.47
Time of flight in seconds:	0	.0581	.0964	.1412	.1930	.2524	.3204

Type of load: Field
Three-foot velocity: 1,200 ft./sec.
Hull: 2½-inch plastic
Wad: Plastic
Shot: Lead
Buffered: No
Test barrel length: 26 inch
Pellets will pierce skin up to 136 yards.

NO. 7½ LEAD PELLETS—½ OUNCE—175 PELLETS
Mfg: Estate Cartridge **Manufacturer's code:** HV410
Recoil energy in 8-lb. shotgun: 4.0 ft./lbs. **Recoil velocity in 8-lb. shotgun:** 5.7 ft./sec.

Distance in yards:	Muzzle	20	30	40	50	60	70
Velocity in fps:	1,302	854	724	623	541	472	412
Average pellet energy in ft-lbs:	4.74	2.04	1.47	1.09	.82	.62	.47
Time of flight in seconds:	0	.0581	.0964	.1412	.1930	.2524	.3204

Type of load: Field
Three-foot velocity: 1,200 ft./sec.
Hull: 2½-inch plastic
Wad: Plastic
Shot: Hard lead
Buffered: No
Test barrel length: 26 inch
Pellets will pierce skin up to 136 yards.

NO. 7½ LEAD PELLETS—½ OUNCE—175 PELLETS
Mfg: Estate Cartridge **Manufacturer's code:** CT410
Recoil energy in 8-lb. shotgun: 4.0 ft./lbs. **Recoil velocity in 8-lb. shotgun:** 5.7 ft./sec.

Distance in yards:	Muzzle	20	30	40	50	60	70
Velocity in fps:	1,302	854	724	623	541	472	412
Average pellet energy in ft-lbs:	4.74	2.04	1.47	1.09	.82	.62	.47
Time of flight in seconds:	0	.0581	.0964	.1412	.1930	.2524	.3204

Type of load: Target
Three-foot velocity: 1,200 ft./sec.
Hull: 2½-inch plastic
Wad: Plastic
Shot: Hard lead
Buffered: No
Test barrel length: 26 inch
Pellets will pierce skin up to 136 yards.

NO. 7½ LEAD PELLETS—½ OUNCE—175 PELLETS
Mfg: Federal Cartridge Co. **Manufacturer's code:** H412
Recoil energy in 8-lb. shotgun: 4.0 ft./lbs. **Recoil velocity in 8-lb. shotgun:** 5.7 ft./sec.

Distance in yards:	Muzzle	20	30	40	50	60	70
Velocity in fps:	1,302	854	724	623	541	472	412
Average pellet energy in ft-lbs:	4.74	2.04	1.47	1.09	.82	.62	.47
Time of flight in seconds:	0	.0581	.0964	.1412	.1930	.2524	.3204

Type of load: Field
Three-foot velocity: 1,200 ft./sec.
Hull: 2½-inch plastic
Wad: Plastic
Shot: Lead
Buffered: No
Test barrel length: 26 inch
Pellets will pierce skin up to 136 yards.

NO. 7½ LEAD PELLETS—½ OUNCE—175 PELLETS
Mfg: Remington Arms Co. **Manufacturer's code:** SP410
Recoil energy in 8-lb. shotgun: 4.0 ft./lbs. **Recoil velocity in 8-lb. shotgun:** 5.7 ft./sec.

Distance in yards:	Muzzle	20	30	40	50	60	70
Velocity in fps:	1,302	854	724	623	541	472	412
Average pellet energy in ft-lbs:	4.74	2.04	1.47	1.09	.82	.62	.47
Time of flight in seconds:	0	.0581	.0964	.1412	.1930	.2524	.3204

Type of load: Field
Three-foot velocity: 1,200 ft./sec.
Hull: 2½-inch plastic
Wad: Plastic
Shot: Lead
Buffered: No
Test barrel length: 26 inch
Pellets will pierce skin up to 136 yards.

NO. 8 LEAD PELLETS—½ OUNCE—205 PELLETS
Mfg: Dionisi **Manufacturer's code:** D 410 GT
Recoil energy in 8-lb. shotgun: 4.0 ft./lbs. **Recoil velocity in 8-lb. shotgun:** 5.7 ft./sec.

Distance in yards:	Muzzle	20	30	40	50	60	70
Velocity in fps:	1,305	839	706	604	521	452	391
Average pellet energy in ft-lbs:	4.05	1.67	1.19	.87	.65	.49	.36
Time of flight in seconds:	0	.0587	.0978	.1438	.1973	.2593	.3307

Type of load: Game & Target
Three-foot velocity: 1,200 ft./sec.
Hull: 2½-inch plastic
Wad: Plastic
Shot: Lead
Buffered: No
Test barrel length: 26 inch
Pellets will pierce skin up to 129 yards.

NO. 8 LEAD PELLETS—½ OUNCE—205 PELLETS
Mfg: Estate Cartridge **Manufacturer's code:** HV410
Recoil energy in 8-lb. shotgun: 4.0 ft./lbs. **Recoil velocity in 8-lb. shotgun:** 5.7 ft./sec.

Distance in yards:	Muzzle	20	30	40	50	60	70
Velocity in fps:	1,305	839	706	604	521	452	391
Average pellet energy in ft-lbs:	4.05	1.67	1.19	.87	.65	.49	.36
Time of flight in seconds:	0	.0587	.0978	.1438	.1973	.2593	.3307

Type of load: Field
Three-foot velocity: 1,200 ft./sec.
Hull: 2½-inch plastic
Wad: Plastic
Shot: Hard lead
Buffered: No
Test barrel length: 26 inch
Pellets will pierce skin up to 129 yards.

NO. 8 LEAD PELLETS—½ OUNCE—205 PELLETS
Mfg: Estate Cartridge **Manufacturer's code:** CT410
Recoil energy in 8-lb. shotgun: 4.0 ft./lbs. **Recoil velocity in 8-lb. shotgun:** 5.7 ft./sec.

Distance in yards:	Muzzle	20	30	40	50	60	70
Velocity in fps:	1,305	839	706	604	521	452	391
Average pellet energy in ft-lbs:	4.05	1.67	1.19	.87	.65	.49	.36
Time of flight in seconds:	0	.0587	.0978	.1438	.1973	.2593	.3307

Type of load: Target
Three-foot velocity: 1,200 ft./sec.
Hull: 2½-inch plastic
Wad: Plastic
Shot: Hard lead
Buffered: No
Test barrel length: 26 inch
Pellets will pierce skin up to 129 yards.

NO. 8 LEAD PELLETS—½ OUNCE—205 PELLETS
Mfg: Fiocchi **Manufacturer's code:** 410GT
Recoil energy in 8-lb. shotgun: 4.0 ft./lbs. **Recoil velocity in 8-lb. shotgun:** 5.7 ft./sec.

Distance in yards:	Muzzle	20	30	40	50	60	70
Velocity in fps:	1,305	839	706	604	521	452	391
Average pellet energy in ft-lbs:	4.05	1.67	1.19	.87	.65	.49	.36
Time of flight in seconds:	0	.0587	.0978	.1438	.1973	.2593	.3307

Type of load: Game & Target
Three-foot velocity: 1,200 ft./sec.
Hull: 2½-inch plastic
Wad: Plastic
Shot: Lead
Buffered: No
Test barrel length: 26 inch
Pellets will pierce skin up to 129 yards.

NO. 8 LEAD PELLETS—½ OUNCE—205 PELLETS
Mfg: PMC (Eldorado Cartridge Corp.) **Manufacturer's code:** CT418/419
Recoil energy in 8-lb. shotgun: 4.0 ft./lbs. **Recoil velocity in 8-lb. shotgun:** 5.7 ft./sec.

Distance in yards:	Muzzle	20	30	40	50	60	70
Velocity in fps:	1,305	839	706	604	521	452	391
Average pellet energy in ft-lbs:	4.05	1.67	1.19	.87	.65	.49	.36
Time of flight in seconds:	0	.0587	.0978	.1438	.1973	.2593	.3307

Type of load: Target
Three-foot velocity: 1,200 ft./sec.
Hull: 2½-inch plastic
Wad: Plastic
Shot: Lead
Buffered: No
Test barrel length: 26 inch
Pellets will pierce skin up to 129 yards.

NO. 8½ LEAD PELLETS—½ OUNCE—249 PELLETS
Mfg: Estate Cartridge **Manufacturer's code:** CT410
Recoil energy in 8-lb. shotgun: 4.0 ft./lbs. **Recoil velocity in 8-lb. shotgun:** 5.7 ft./sec.

Distance in yards:	Muzzle	20	30	40	50	60	70
Velocity in fps:	1,308	823	687	584	500	430	369
Average pellet energy in ft-lbs:	1.36	1.13	.95	.68	.50	.37	.325
Time of flight in seconds:	0	.0593	.0993	.1468	.2024	.2671	.3423

Type of load: Target
Three-foot velocity: 1,200 ft./sec.
Hull: 2½-inch plastic
Wad: Plastic
Shot: Hard lead
Buffered: No
Test barrel length: 26 inch
Pellets will pierce skin up to 111 yards.

NO. 8½ LEAD PELLETS—½ OUNCE—249 PELLETS
Mfg: Federal Cartridge Co. **Manufacturer's code:** T412
Recoil energy in 8-lb. shotgun: 4.0 ft./lbs. **Recoil velocity in 8-lb. shotgun:** 5.7 ft./sec.

Distance in yards:	Muzzle	20	30	40	50	60	70
Velocity in fps:	1,308	823	687	584	500	430	369
Average pellet energy in ft-lbs:	1.36	1.13	.95	.68	.50	.37	.325
Time of flight in seconds:	0	.0593	.0993	.1468	.2024	.2671	.3423

Type of load: Target
Three-foot velocity: 1,200 ft./sec.
Hull: 2½-inch plastic
Wad: Plastic
Shot: Lead
Buffered: No
Test barrel length: 26 inch
Pellets will pierce skin up to 111 yards.

NO. 8½ LEAD PELLETS—½ OUNCE—249 PELLETS
Mfg: Remington Arms Co. **Manufacturer's code:** STS410SC
Recoil energy in 8-lb. shotgun: 4.0 ft./lbs. **Recoil velocity in 8-lb. shotgun:** 5.7 ft./sec.

Distance in yards:	Muzzle	20	30	40	50	60	70
Velocity in fps:	1,308	823	687	584	500	430	369
Average pellet energy in ft-lbs:	1.36	1.13	.95	.68	.50	.37	.325
Time of flight in seconds:	0	.0593	.0993	.1468	.2024	.2671	.3423

Type of load: Target
Three-foot velocity: 1,200 ft./sec.
Hull: 2½-inch plastic
Wad: Plastic
Shot: Hard lead
Buffered: No
Test barrel length: 26 inch
Pellets will pierce skin up to 111 yards.

NO. 9 LEAD PELLETS—½ OUNCE—292 PELLETS
Mfg: Dionisi **Manufacturer's code:** D 410 GT
Recoil energy in 8-lb. shotgun: 4.0 ft./lbs. **Recoil velocity in 8-lb. shotgun:** 5.7 ft./sec.

Distance in yards:	Muzzle	20	30	40	50	60	70
Velocity in fps:	1,312	805	667	562	478	407	346
Average pellet energy in ft-lbs:	2.88	1.08	.74	.53	.38	.28	.20
Time of flight in seconds:	0	.0601	.1011	.1502	.2082	.2763	.3562

Type of load: Game & Target
Three-foot velocity: 1,200 ft./sec.
Hull: 2½-inch plastic
Wad: Plastic
Shot: Lead
Buffered: No
Test barrel length: 26 inch
Pellets will pierce skin up to 115 yards.

NO. 9 LEAD PELLETS—½ OUNCE—292 PELLETS
Mfg: Estate Cartridge **Manufacturer's code:** HV410
Recoil energy in 8-lb. shotgun: 4.0 ft./lbs. **Recoil velocity in 8-lb. shotgun:** 5.7 ft./sec.

Distance in yards:	Muzzle	20	30	40	50	60	70
Velocity in fps:	1,312	805	667	562	478	407	346
Average pellet energy in ft-lbs:	2.88	1.08	.74	.53	.38	.28	.20
Time of flight in seconds:	0	.0601	.1011	.1502	.2082	.2763	.3562

Type of load: Field
Three-foot velocity: 1,200 ft./sec.
Hull: 2½-inch plastic
Wad: Plastic
Shot: Hard lead
Buffered: No
Test barrel length: 26 inch
Pellets will pierce skin up to 115 yards.

NO. 9 LEAD PELLETS—½ OUNCE—292 PELLETS
Mfg: Estate Cartridge **Manufacturer's code:** CT410
Recoil energy in 8-lb. shotgun: 4.0 ft./lbs. **Recoil velocity in 8-lb. shotgun:** 5.7 ft./sec.

Distance in yards:	Muzzle	20	30	40	50	60	70
Velocity in fps:	1,312	805	667	562	478	407	346
Average pellet energy in ft-lbs:	2.88	1.08	.74	.53	.38	.28	.20
Time of flight in seconds:	0	.0601	.1011	.1502	.2082	.2763	.3562

Type of load: Target
Three-foot velocity: 1,200 ft./sec.
Hull: 2½-inch plastic
Wad: Plastic
Shot: Hard lead
Buffered: No
Test barrel length: 26 inch
Pellets will pierce skin up to 115 yards.

NO. 9 LEAD PELLETS—½ OUNCE—292 PELLETS
Mfg: Federal Cartridge Co. **Manufacturer's code:** T412
Recoil energy in 8-lb. shotgun: 4.0 ft./lbs. **Recoil velocity in 8-lb. shotgun:** 5.7 ft./sec.

Distance in yards:	Muzzle	20	30	40	50	60	70
Velocity in fps:	1,312	805	667	562	478	407	346
Average pellet energy in ft-lbs:	2.88	1.08	.74	.53	.38	.28	.20
Time of flight in seconds:	0	.0601	.1011	.1502	.2082	.2763	.3562

Type of load: Target
Three-foot velocity: 1,200 ft./sec.
Hull: 2½-inch plastic
Wad: Plastic
Shot: Lead
Buffered: No
Test barrel length: 26 inch
Pellets will pierce skin up to 115 yards.

NO. 9 LEAD PELLETS—½ OUNCE—292 PELLETS
Mfg: Fiocchi **Manufacturer's code:** 410GT
Recoil energy in 8-lb. shotgun: 4.0 ft./lbs. **Recoil velocity in 8-lb. shotgun:** 5.7 ft./sec.

Distance in yards:	Muzzle	20	30	40	50	60	70
Velocity in fps:	1,312	805	667	562	478	407	346
Average pellet energy in ft-lbs:	2.88	1.08	.74	.53	.38	.28	.20
Time of flight in seconds:	0	.0601	.1011	.1502	.2082	.2763	.3562

Type of load: Game & Target
Three-foot velocity: 1,200 ft./sec.
Hull: 2½-inch plastic
Wad: Plastic
Shot: Lead
Buffered: No
Test barrel length: 26 inch
Pellets will pierce skin up to 115 yards.

NO. 9 LEAD PELLETS—½ OUNCE—292 PELLETS

Mfg: PMC (Eldorado Cartridge Corp.) **Manufacturer's code:** CT418/419
Recoil energy in 8-lb. shotgun: 4.0 ft./lbs. **Recoil velocity in 8-lb. shotgun:** 5.7 ft./sec.

Distance in yards:	Muzzle	20	30	40	50	60	70
Velocity in fps:	1,312	805	667	562	478	407	346
Average pellet energy in ft-lbs:	2.88	1.08	.74	.53	.38	.28	.20
Time of flight in seconds:	0	.0601	.1011	.1502	.2082	.2763	.3562

Type of load: Target
Three-foot velocity: 1,200 ft./sec.
Hull: 2½-inch plastic
Wad: Plastic
Shot: Lead
Buffered: No
Test barrel length: 26 inch
Pellets will pierce skin up to 115 yards.

NO. 9 LEAD PELLETS—½ OUNCE—292 PELLETS

Mfg: Winchester **Manufacturer's code:** AA41
Recoil energy in 8-lb. shotgun: 4.0 ft./lbs. **Recoil velocity in 8-lb. shotgun:** 5.7 ft./sec.

Distance in yards:	Muzzle	20	30	40	50	60	70
Velocity in fps:	1,312	805	667	562	478	407	346
Average pellet energy in ft-lbs:	2.88	1.08	.74	.53	.38	.28	.20
Time of flight in seconds:	0	.0601	.1011	.1502	.2082	.2763	.3562

Type of load: Target
Three-foot velocity: 1,200 ft./sec.
Hull: 2½-inch plastic
Wad: Plastic
Shot: Hard lead
Buffered: No
Test barrel length: 26 inch
Pellets will pierce skin up to 115 yards.

NO. 9 LEAD PELLETS—½ OUNCE—292 PELLETS

Mfg: Remington Arms Co. **Manufacturer's code:** STS410
Recoil energy in 8-lb. shotgun: 4.0 ft./lbs. **Recoil velocity in 8-lb. shotgun:** 5.7 ft./sec.

Distance in yards:	Muzzle	20	30	40	50	60	70
Velocity in fps:	1,312	805	667	562	478	407	346
Average pellet energy in ft-lbs:	2.88	1.08	.74	.53	.38	.28	.20
Time of flight in seconds:	0	.0601	.1011	.1502	.2082	.2763	.3562

Type of load: Target
Three-foot velocity: 1,200 ft./sec.
Hull: 2½-inch plastic
Wad: Plastic
Shot: Hard lead
Buffered: No
Test barrel length: 26 inch
Pellets will pierce skin up to 115 yards.

Woodcock call for close-range shots with fine shot. These Michigan woodcock were taken with a light AyA 28-gauge with skeet and improved cylinder chokes and No. 7½ shot.

NO. 4 LEAD PELLETS—11/16 OUNCE—93 PELLETS
Mfg: ARMUSA **Manufacturer's code:** PLA-1
Recoil energy in 8-lb. shotgun: 19.9 ft./lbs. **Recoil velocity in 8-lb. shotgun:** 12.6 ft./sec.

Distance in yards:	Muzzle	20	30	40	50	60	70
Velocity in fps:	1,390	989	863	762	680	611	551
Average pellet energy in ft-lbs:	13.86	7.01	5.34	4.17	3.32	2.67	2.18
Time of flight in seconds:	0	.0519	.0844	.1215	.1632	.2098	.2615

Type of load: Field
Three-foot velocity: 1,300 ft./sec.
Hull: 3-inch plastic
Wad: Plastic
Shot: Lead
Buffered: No
Test barrel length: 26 inch
Pellets will pierce skin up to 172 yards.

NO. 4 LEAD PELLETS—11/16 OUNCE—93 PELLETS
Mfg: Estate Cartridge **Manufacturer's code:** HV4103
Recoil energy in 8-lb. shotgun: 6.6 ft./lbs. **Recoil velocity in 8-lb. shotgun:** 7.3 ft./sec.

Distance in yards:	Muzzle	20	30	40	50	60	70
Velocity in fps:	1,210	893	787	700	628	566	511
Average pellet energy in ft-lbs:	10.50	5.71	4.44	6.52	2.83	2.30	1.88
Time of flight in seconds:	0	.0270	.0943	.1347	.1800	.2304	.2862

Type of load: Field
Three-foot velocity: 1,135 ft./sec.
Hull: 3-inch plastic
Wad: Plastic
Shot: Hard Lead
Buffered: No
Test barrel length: 26 inch
Pellets will pierce skin up to 165 yards.

NO. 4 LEAD PELLETS—11/16 OUNCE—93 PELLETS
Mfg: Federal Cartridge **Manufacturer's code:** H413/H415
Recoil energy in 8-lb. shotgun: 8.8 ft./lbs. **Recoil velocity in 8-lb. shotgun:** 9.7 ft./sec.

Distance in yards:	Muzzle	20	30	40	50	60	70
Velocity in fps:	1,210	893	787	700	628	566	511
Average pellet energy in ft-lbs:	10.50	5.71	4.44	6.52	2.83	2.30	1.88
Time of flight in seconds:	0	.0270	.0943	.1347	.1800	.2304	.2862

Type of load: Field
Three-foot velocity: 1,135 ft./sec.
Hull: 3-inch plastic
Wad: One-piece plastic
Shot: Lead
Buffered: No
Test barrel length: 26 inch
Pellets will pierce skin up to 165 yards.

NO. 4 LEAD PELLETS—11/16 OUNCE—93 PELLETS
Mfg: Remington **Manufacturer's code:** SP413
Recoil energy in 8-lb. shotgun: 8.8 ft./lbs. **Recoil velocity in 8-lb. shotgun:** 9.7 ft./sec.

Distance in yards:	Muzzle	20	30	40	50	60	70
Velocity in fps:	1,210	893	787	700	628	566	511
Average pellet energy in ft-lbs:	10.50	5.71	4.44	6.52	2.83	2.30	1.88
Time of flight in seconds:	0	.0270	.0943	.1347	.1800	.2304	.2862

Type of load: Field
Three-foot velocity: 1,135 ft./sec.
Hull: 3-inch plastic
Wad: One-piece plastic
Shot: Lead
Buffered: No
Test barrel length: 26 inch
Pellets will pierce skin up to 165 yards.

NO. 4 LEAD PELLETS—11/16 OUNCE—93 PELLETS
Mfg: Sellier & Bellot **Manufacturer's code:** SBA04101
Recoil energy in 8-lb. shotgun: 6.6 ft./lbs. **Recoil velocity in 8-lb. shotgun:** 7.3 ft./sec.

Distance in yards:	Muzzle	20	30	40	50	60	70
Velocity in fps:	1,210	893	787	700	628	566	511
Average pellet energy in ft-lbs:	10.50	5.71	4.44	6.52	2.83	2.30	1.88
Time of flight in seconds:	0	.0270	.0943	.1347	.1800	.2304	.2862

Type of load: Target
Three-foot velocity: 1,135 ft./sec.
Hull: 3-inch plastic
Wad: One-piece plastic
Shot: Lead
Buffered: No
Test barrel length: 26 inch
Pellets will pierce skin up to 165 yards.

NO. 4 LEAD PELLETS—11/16 OUNCE—93 PELLETS
Mfg: Winchester **Manufacturer's code:** X413
Recoil energy in 8-lb. shotgun: 8.8 ft./lbs. **Recoil velocity in 8-lb. shotgun:** 9.7 ft./sec.

Distance in yards:	Muzzle	20	30	40	50	60	70
Velocity in fps:	1,210	893	787	700	628	566	511
Average pellet energy in ft-lbs:	10.50	5.71	4.44	6.52	2.83	2.30	1.88
Time of flight in seconds:	0	.0270	.0943	.1347	.1800	.2304	.2862

Type of load: Field
Three-foot velocity: 1,135 ft./sec.
Hull: 3-inch plastic
Wad: One-piece plastic
Shot: Lead
Buffered: No
Test barrel length: 26 inch
Pellets will pierce skin up to 165 yards.

NO. 5 LEAD PELLETS—11/16 OUNCE—117 PELLETS
Mfg: Federal Cartridge **Manufacturer's code:** H413/H415
Recoil energy in 8-lb. shotgun: 8.8 ft./lbs. **Recoil velocity in 8-lb. shotgun:** 9.7 ft./sec.

Distance in yards:	Muzzle	20	30	40	50	60	70
Velocity in fps:	1,215	876	766	676	602	539	484
Average pellet energy in ft-lbs:	8.33	4.33	3.31	2.58	2.05	1.64	1.32
Time of flight in seconds:	0	.0589	.0956	.1373	.1844	.2371	.2959

Type of load: Field
Three-foot velocity: 1,135 ft./sec.
Hull: 3-inch plastic
Wad: One-piece plastic
Shot: Lead
Buffered: No
Test barrel length: 26 inch
Pellets will pierce skin up to 152 yards.

SHOTSHELLS AND BALLISTICS « 313

NO. 5 LEAD PELLETS—$^{11}/_{16}$ OUNCE—117 PELLETS
Mfg: Clever **Manufacturer's code:** Magnum 410
Recoil energy in 8-lb. shotgun: 8.2 ft./lbs. **Recoil velocity in 8-lb. shotgun:** 8.1 ft./sec.

Distance in yards:	Muzzle	20	30	40	50	60	70
Velocity in fps:	1,325	932	810	713	633	565	507
Average pellet energy in ft-lbs:	9.09	4.90	3.70	2.87	2.26	1.80	1.45
Time of flight in seconds:	0	.0548	.0894	.1289	.1737	.2239	.2800

Type of load: Field
Three-foot velocity: 1,235 ft./sec.
Hull: 3-inch plastic
Wad: Plastic
Shot: Lead
Buffered: No
Test barrel length: 26 inch
Pellets will pierce skin up to 157 yards.

NO. 6 LEAD PELLETS—$^5/_8$ OUNCE—141 PELLETS
Mfg: Eley Hawk **Manufacturer's code:** Magnum
Recoil energy in 8-lb. shotgun: 6.3 ft./lbs. **Recoil velocity in 8-lb. shotgun:** 7.1 ft./sec.

Distance in yards:	Muzzle	20	30	40	50	60	70
Velocity in fps:	1,292	892	769	672	593	525	467
Average pellet energy in ft-lbs:	7.26	3.46	2.57	1.96	1.53	1.20	.095
Time of flight in seconds:	0	.0568	.0931	.01349	.1825	.2363	.2969

Type of load: Field
Three-foot velocity: 1,200 ft./sec.
Hull: 3-inch plastic
Wad: Fiber
Shot: Lead
Buffered: No
Test barrel length: 26 inch
Pellets will pierce skin up to 157 yards.

NO. 6 LEAD PELLETS—$^{11}/_{16}$ OUNCE—155 PELLETS
Mfg: Clever **Manufacturer's code:** Magnum 410
Recoil energy in 8-lb. shotgun: 8.2 ft./lbs. **Recoil velocity in 8-lb. shotgun:** 8.1 ft./sec.

Distance in yards:	Muzzle	20	30	40	50	60	70
Velocity in fps:	1,331	911	784	684	602	534	474
Average pellet energy in ft-lbs:	7.70	3.60	2.67	2.03	1.58	1.24	.98
Time of flight in seconds:	0	.0555	.0911	.1321	.1789	.2319	.2915

Type of load: Field
Three-foot velocity: 1,235 ft./sec.
Hull: 3-inch plastic
Wad: Plastic
Shot: Lead
Buffered: No
Test barrel length: 26 inch
Pellets will pierce skin up to 144 yards.

NO. 6 LEAD PELLETS—$^{11}/_{16}$ OUNCE—155 PELLETS
Mfg: ARMUSA **Manufacturer's code:** PLA-1
Recoil energy in 8-lb. shotgun: 19.9 ft./lbs. **Recoil velocity in 8-lb. shotgun:** 12.6 ft./sec.

Distance in yards:	Muzzle	20	30	40	50	60	70
Velocity in fps:	1,403	945	810	705	620	548	487
Average pellet energy in ft-lbs:	8.55	3.88	2.85	2.16	1.67	1.31	1.03
Time of flight in seconds:	0	.0531	.0875	.1272	.1727	.2242	.2723

Type of load: Field
Three-foot velocity: 1,300 ft./sec.
Hull: 3-inch plastic
Wad: Plastic
Shot: Lead
Buffered: No
Test barrel length: 26 inch
Pellets will pierce skin up to 146 yards.

NO. 6 LEAD PELLETS—$^{11}/_{16}$ OUNCE—155 PELLETS
Mfg: Dionisi Cartridge **Manufacturer's code:** D 410 MG3
Recoil energy in 8-lb. shotgun: 8.8 ft./lbs. **Recoil velocity in 8-lb. shotgun:** 9.7 ft./sec.

Distance in yards:	Muzzle	20	30	40	50	60	70
Velocity in fps:	1,226	859	744	651	575	511	454
Average pellet energy in ft-lbs:	6.53	3.21	2.40	1.84	1.44	1.13	.90
Time of flight in seconds:	0	.0593	.0969	.1401	.1892	.2446	.3069

Type of load: Field
Three-foot velocity: 1,140 ft./sec.
Hull: 3-inch plastic
Wad: One-piece plastic
Shot: Lead
Buffered: No
Test barrel length: 26 inch
Pellets will pierce skin up to 140 yards.

NO. 6 LEAD PELLETS—$^{11}/_{16}$ OUNCE—155 PELLETS
Mfg: Estate Cartridge **Manufacturer's code:** HV4103
Recoil energy in 8-lb. shotgun: 6.6 ft./lbs. **Recoil velocity in 8-lb. shotgun:** 7.3 ft./sec.

Distance in yards:	Muzzle	20	30	40	50	60	70
Velocity in fps:	1,221	857	742	650	574	509	453
Average pellet energy in ft-lbs:	4.41	3.19	2.39	1.83	1.43	1.13	.89
Time of flight in seconds:	0	.0596	.0973	.1406	.1897	.2453	.3078

Type of load: Field
Three-foot velocity: 1,135 ft./sec.
Hull: 3-inch plastic
Wad: Plastic
Shot: Hard Lead
Buffered: No
Test barrel length: 26 inch
Pellets will pierce skin up to 140 yards.

NO. 6 LEAD PELLETS—$^{11}/_{16}$ OUNCE—155 PELLETS
Mfg: Federal Cartridge **Manufacturer's code:** H413/H415
Recoil energy in 8-lb. shotgun: 8.8 ft./lbs. **Recoil velocity in 8-lb. shotgun:** 9.7 ft./sec.

Distance in yards:	Muzzle	20	30	40	50	60	70
Velocity in fps:	1,221	857	742	650	574	509	453
Average pellet energy in ft-lbs:	4.41	3.19	2.39	1.83	1.43	1.13	.89
Time of flight in seconds:	0	.0596	.0973	.1406	.1897	.2453	.3078

Type of load: Field
Three-foot velocity: 1,135 ft./sec.
Hull: 3-inch plastic
Wad: One-piece plastic
Shot: Lead
Buffered: No
Test barrel length: 26 inch
Pellets will pierce skin up to 140 yards.

NO. 6 LEAD PELLETS—¹¹/₁₆ OUNCE—155 PELLETS
Mfg: Fiocchi **Manufacturer's code:** 410HV
Recoil energy in 8-lb. shotgun: 6.6 ft./lbs. **Recoil velocity in 8-lb. shotgun:** 7.3 ft./sec.

Distance in yards:	Muzzle	20	30	40	50	60	70
Velocity in fps:	1,232	862	746	653	577	512	455
Average pellet energy in ft-lbs:	6.59	3.23	2.11	1.85	1.45	1.14	.90
Time of flight in seconds:	0	.0591	.0966	.1396	.1886	.2438	.3060

Type of load: Field
Three-foot velocity: 1,145 ft./sec.
Hull: 3-inch plastic
Wad: Plastic
Shot: Lead
Buffered: No
Test barrel length: 26 inch
Pellets will pierce skin up to 140 yards.

NO. 6 LEAD PELLETS—¹¹/₁₆ OUNCE—155 PELLETS
Mfg: PMC (Eldorado Cartridge Corp.) **Manufacturer's code:** HF41
Recoil energy in 8-lb. shotgun: 6.6 ft./lbs. **Recoil velocity in 8-lb. shotgun:** 7.3 ft./sec.

Distance in yards:	Muzzle	20	30	40	50	60	70
Velocity in fps:	1,221	857	742	650	574	509	453
Average pellet energy in ft-lbs:	4.41	3.19	2.39	1.83	1.43	1.13	.89
Time of flight in seconds:	0	.0596	.0973	.1406	.1897	.2453	.3078

Type of load: Field
Three-foot velocity: 1,145 ft./sec.
Hull: 3-inch plastic
Wad: Plastic
Shot: Lead
Buffered: No
Test barrel length: 26 inch
Pellets will pierce skin up to 140 yards.

NO. 6 LEAD PELLETS—¹¹/₁₆ OUNCE—155 PELLETS
Mfg: Remington **Manufacturer's code:** SP413
Recoil energy in 8-lb. shotgun: 8.8 ft./lbs. **Recoil velocity in 8-lb. shotgun:** 9.7 ft./sec.

Distance in yards:	Muzzle	20	30	40	50	60	70
Velocity in fps:	1,221	857	742	650	574	509	453
Average pellet energy in ft-lbs:	4.41	3.19	2.39	1.83	1.43	1.13	.89
Time of flight in seconds:	0	.0596	.0973	.1406	.1897	.2453	.3078

Type of load: Field
Three-foot velocity: 1,135 ft./sec.
Hull: 3-inch plastic
Wad: One-piece plastic
Shot: Lead
Buffered: No
Test barrel length: 26 inch
Pellets will pierce skin up to 140 yards.

NO. 6 LEAD PELLETS—¹¹/₁₆ OUNCE—155 PELLETS
Mfg: Sellier & Bellot **Manufacturer's code:** SBA04105
Recoil energy in 8-lb. shotgun: 6.6 ft./lbs. **Recoil velocity in 8-lb. shotgun:** 7.3 ft./sec.

Distance in yards:	Muzzle	20	30	40	50	60	70
Velocity in fps:	1,221	857	742	650	574	509	453
Average pellet energy in ft-lbs:	4.41	3.19	2.39	1.83	1.43	1.13	.89
Time of flight in seconds:	0	.0596	.0973	.1406	.1897	.2453	.3078

Type of load: Target
Three-foot velocity: 1,135 ft./sec.
Hull: 3-inch plastic
Wad: One-piece plastic
Shot: Lead
Buffered: No
Test barrel length: 26 inch
Pellets will pierce skin up to 140 yards.

NO. 6 LEAD PELLETS—¹¹/₁₆ OUNCE—155 PELLETS
Mfg: Winchester **Manufacturer's code:** X413
Recoil energy in 8-lb. shotgun: 8.8 ft./lbs. **Recoil velocity in 8-lb. shotgun:** 9.7 ft./sec.

Distance in yards:	Muzzle	20	30	40	50	60	70
Velocity in fps:	1,221	857	742	650	574	509	453
Average pellet energy in ft-lbs:	4.41	3.19	2.39	1.83	1.43	1.13	.89
Time of flight in seconds:	0	.0596	.0973	.1406	.1897	.2453	.3078

Type of load: Field
Three-foot velocity: 1,135 ft./sec.
Hull: 3-inch plastic
Wad: One-piece plastic
Shot: Lead
Buffered: No
Test barrel length: 26 inch
Pellets will pierce skin up to 140 yards.

NO. 7¹/₂ LEAD PELLETS—¹¹/₁₆ OUNCE—241 PELLETS
Mfg: ARMUSA **Manufacturer's code:** PLA-1
Recoil energy in 8-lb. shotgun: 19.9 ft./lbs. **Recoil velocity in 8-lb. shotgun:** 12.6 ft./sec.

Distance in yards:	Muzzle	20	30	40	50	60	70
Velocity in fps:	1,413	903	761	652	565	492	430
Average pellet energy in ft-lbs:	5.59	2.28	1.62	1.19	.89	.68	.52
Time of flight in seconds:	0	.0544	.0907	.1334	.1829	.2399	.3052

Type of load: Field
Three-foot velocity: 1,300 ft./sec.
Hull: 3-inch plastic
Wad: Plastic
Shot: Lead
Buffered: No
Test barrel length: 26 inch
Pellets will pierce skin up to 126 yards.

NO. 7¹/₂ LEAD PELLETS—¹¹/₁₆ OUNCE—241 PELLETS
Mfg: Clever **Manufacturer's code:** Magnum 410
Recoil energy in 8-lb. shotgun: 8.2 ft./lbs. **Recoil velocity in 8-lb. shotgun:** 8.1 ft./sec.

Distance in yards:	Muzzle	20	30	40	50	60	70
Velocity in fps:	1,341	871	737	633	549	479	418
Average pellet energy in ft-lbs:	5.03	2.12	1.52	1.12	.84	.64	.49
Time of flight in seconds:	0	.0568	.0943	.1383	.1893	.2478	.3149

Type of load: Field
Three-foot velocity: 1,235 ft./sec.
Hull: 3-inch plastic
Wad: Plastic
Shot: Lead
Buffered: No
Test barrel length: 26 inch
Pellets will pierce skin up to 124 yards.

NO. 7½ LEAD PELLETS—¹¹/₁₆ OUNCE—241 PELLETS
Mfg: Dionisi Cartridge **Manufacturer's code:** D 410 MG3
Recoil energy in 8-lb. shotgun: 8.8 ft./lbs. **Recoil velocity in 8-lb. shotgun:** 9.7 ft./sec.

Distance in yards:	Muzzle	20	30	40	50	60	70
Velocity in fps:	1,235	824	701	604	526	459	401
Average pellet energy in ft-lbs:	4.27	1.90	1.37	1.02	.077	.59	.45
Time of flight in seconds:	0	.0607	.1002	.1464	.1997	.2609	.3309

Type of load: Field
Three-foot velocity: 1,140 ft./sec.
Hull: 3-inch plastic
Wad: One-piece plastic
Shot: Lead
Buffered: No
Test barrel length: 26 inch
Pellets will pierce skin up to 121 yards.

NO. 7½ LEAD PELLETS—¹¹/₁₆ OUNCE—241 PELLETS
Mfg: Estate Cartridge **Manufacturer's code:** HV28
Recoil energy in 8-lb. shotgun: 6.6 ft./lbs. **Recoil velocity in 8-lb. shotgun:** 7.3 ft./sec.

Distance in yards:	Muzzle	20	30	40	50	60	70
Velocity in fps:	1,229	821	699	603	524	458	400
Average pellet energy in ft-lbs:	4.23	1089	1.37	1.02	.077	.59	.45
Time of flight in seconds:	0	.0609	.1006	.1469	.2003	.2616	.3318

Type of load: Field
Three-foot velocity: 1,135 ft./sec.
Hull: 3-inch plastic
Wad: Plastic
Shot: Hard lead
Buffered: No
Test barrel length: 26 inch
Pellets will pierce skin up to 121 yards.

NO. 7½ LEAD PELLETS—¹¹/₁₆ OUNCE—241 PELLETS
Mfg: Federal Cartridge **Manufacturer's code:** H413/H415
Recoil energy in 8-lb. shotgun: 8.8 ft./lbs. **Recoil velocity in 8-lb. shotgun:** 9.7 ft./sec.

Distance in yards:	Muzzle	20	30	40	50	60	70
Velocity in fps:	1,229	821	699	603	524	458	400
Average pellet energy in ft-lbs:	4.23	1.89	1.37	1.02	.077	.59	.45
Time of flight in seconds:	0	.0609	.1006	.1469	.2003	.2616	.3318

Type of load: Field
Three-foot velocity: 1,135 ft./sec.
Hull: 3-inch plastic
Wad: One-piece plastic
Shot: Lead
Buffered: No
Test barrel length: 26 inch
Pellets will pierce skin up to 121 yards.

NO. 7½ LEAD PELLETS—¹¹/₁₆ OUNCE—241 PELLETS
Mfg: Fiocchi **Manufacturer's code:** 410HV
Recoil energy in 8-lb. shotgun: 6.6 ft./lbs. **Recoil velocity in 8-lb. shotgun:** 7.3 ft./sec.

Distance in yards:	Muzzle	20	30	40	50	60	70
Velocity in fps:	1,241	826	703	606	527	460	401
Average pellet energy in ft-lbs:	4.31	1.91	1.38	1.03	.78	.59	.45
Time of flight in seconds:	0	.0604	.0999	.1460	.1991	.2601	.3300

Type of load: Field
Three-foot velocity: 1,145 ft./sec.
Hull: 3-inch plastic
Wad: Plastic
Shot: Lead
Buffered: No
Test barrel length: 26 inch
Pellets will pierce skin up to 121 yards.

NO. 7½ LEAD PELLETS—¹¹/₁₆ OUNCE—241 PELLETS
Mfg: PMC (Eldorado Cartridge Corp.) **Manufacturer's code:** HF41
Recoil energy in 8-lb. shotgun: 6.6 ft./lbs. **Recoil velocity in 8-lb. shotgun:** 7.3 ft./sec.

Distance in yards:	Muzzle	20	30	40	50	60	70
Velocity in fps:	1,229	821	699	603	524	458	400
Average pellet energy in ft-lbs:	4.23	1089	1.37	1.02	.077	.59	.45
Time of flight in seconds:	0	.0609	.1006	.1469	.2003	.2616	.3318

Type of load: Field
Three-foot velocity: 1,135 ft./sec.
Hull: 3-inch plastic
Wad: Plastic
Shot: Lead
Buffered: No
Test barrel length: 26 inch
Pellets will pierce skin up to 121 yards.

NO. 7½ LEAD PELLETS—¹¹/₁₆ OUNCE—241 PELLETS
Mfg: Remington **Manufacturer's code:** SP413
Recoil energy in 8-lb. shotgun: 8.8 ft./lbs. **Recoil velocity in 8-lb. shotgun:** 9.7 ft./sec.

Distance in yards:	Muzzle	20	30	40	50	60	70
Velocity in fps:	1,229	821	699	603	524	458	400
Average pellet energy in ft-lbs:	4.23	1.89	1.37	1.02	.077	.59	.45
Time of flight in seconds:	0	.0609	.1006	.1469	.2003	.2616	.3318

Type of load: Field
Three-foot velocity: 1,135 ft./sec.
Hull: 3-inch plastic
Wad: One-piece plastic
Shot: Lead
Buffered: No
Test barrel length: 26 inch
Pellets will pierce skin up to 121 yards.

NO. 7½ LEAD PELLETS—¹¹/₁₆ OUNCE—241 PELLETS
Mfg: Sellier & Bellot **Manufacturer's code:** SBA04105
Recoil energy in 8-lb. shotgun: 6.6 ft./lbs. **Recoil velocity in 8-lb. shotgun:** 7.3 ft./sec.

Distance in yards:	Muzzle	20	30	40	50	60	70
Velocity in fps:	1,229	821	699	603	524	458	400
Average pellet energy in ft-lbs:	4.23	1089	1.37	1.02	.077	.59	.45
Time of flight in seconds:	0	.0609	.1006	.1469	.2003	.2616	.3318

Type of load: Target
Three-foot velocity: 1,135 ft./sec.
Hull: 3-inch plastic
Wad: One-piece plastic
Shot: Lead
Buffered: No
Test barrel length: 26 inch
Pellets will pierce skin up to 121 yards.

NO. 7½ LEAD PELLETS—¹¹/₁₆ OUNCE—241 PELLETS

Mfg: Winchester **Manufacturer's code:** X413
Recoil energy in 8-lb. shotgun: 8.8 ft./lbs. **Recoil velocity in 8-lb. shotgun:** 9.7 ft./sec.

Distance in yards:	Muzzle	20	30	40	50	60	70
Velocity in fps:	1,229	821	699	603	524	458	400
Average pellet energy in ft-lbs:	4.23	1089	1.37	1.02	.077	.59	.45
Time of flight in seconds:	0	.0609	.1006	.1469	.2003	.2616	.3318

Type of load: Field
Three-foot velocity: 1,135 ft./sec.
Hull: 3-inch plastic
Wad: One-piece plastic
Shot: Lead
Buffered: No
Test barrel length: 26 inch
Pellets will pierce skin up to 121 yards.

NO. 8 LEAD PELLETS—¹¹/₁₆ OUNCE—282 PELLETS

Mfg: Dionisi Cartridge **Manufacturer's code:** D 410 MG3
Recoil energy in 8-lb. shotgun: 8.8 ft./lbs. **Recoil velocity in 8-lb. shotgun:** 9.7 ft./sec.

Distance in yards:	Muzzle	20	30	40	50	60	70
Velocity in fps:	1,238	810	684	586	507	439	380
Average pellet energy in ft-lbs:	3.65	1.56	1.11	.82	.61	.46	.34
Time of flight in seconds:	0	.0612	.1016	.1491	.2042	.2678	.3413

Type of load: Field
Three-foot velocity: 1,140 ft./sec.
Hull: 3-inch plastic
Wad: One-piece plastic
Shot: Lead
Buffered: No
Test barrel length: 26 inch
Pellets will pierce skin up to 115 yards.

NO. 8 LEAD PELLETS—¹¹/₁₆ OUNCE—282 PELLETS

Mfg: Estate Cartridge **Manufacturer's code:** HV4103
Recoil energy in 8-lb. shotgun: 6.6 ft./lbs. **Recoil velocity in 8-lb. shotgun:** 7.3 ft./sec.

Distance in yards:	Muzzle	20	30	40	50	60	70
Velocity in fps:	1,232	807	682	585	505	438	380
Average pellet energy in ft-lbs:	3.61	1.55	1.11	.81	.61	.46	.34
Time of flight in seconds:	0	.0614	.1020	.1495	.2048	.2686	.3422

Type of load: Field
Three-foot velocity: 1,135 ft./sec.
Hull: 3-inch plastic
Wad: Plastic
Shot: Hard lead
Buffered: No
Test barrel length: 26 inch
Pellets will pierce skin up to 127 yards.

NO. 8 LEAD PELLETS—¹¹/₁₆ OUNCE—282 PELLETS

Mfg: Fiocchi **Manufacturer's code:** 410HV
Recoil energy in 8-lb. shotgun: 6.6 ft./lbs. **Recoil velocity in 8-lb. shotgun:** 7.3 ft./sec.

Distance in yards:	Muzzle	20	30	40	50	60	70
Velocity in fps:	1,244	812	686	588	508	440	381
Average pellet energy in ft-lbs:	3.68	1.57	1.12	.82	.61	.46	.35
Time of flight in seconds:	0	.0616	.1013	.1486	.2036	.2671	.3403

Type of load: Field
Three-foot velocity: 1,145 ft./sec.
Hull: 3-inch plastic
Wad: Plastic
Shot: Lead
Buffered: No
Test barrel length: 26 inch
Pellets will pierce skin up to 115 yards.

NO. 8 LEAD PELLETS—¹¹/₁₆ OUNCE—282 PELLETS

Mfg: Federal Cartridge **Manufacturer's code:** H413/H415
Recoil energy in 8-lb. shotgun: 8.8 ft./lbs. **Recoil velocity in 8-lb. shotgun:** 9.7 ft./sec.

Distance in yards:	Muzzle	20	30	40	50	60	70
Velocity in fps:	1,232	807	682	585	505	438	380
Average pellet energy in ft-lbs:	3.61	1.55	1.11	.81	.61	.46	.34
Time of flight in seconds:	0	.0614	.1020	.1495	.2048	.2686	.3422

Type of load: Field
Three-foot velocity: 1,135 ft./sec.
Hull: 3-inch plastic
Wad: One-piece plastic
Shot: Lead
Buffered: No
Test barrel length: 26 inch
Pellets will pierce skin up to 115 yards.

NO. 9 LEAD PELLETS—¹¹/₁₆ OUNCE—402 PELLETS

Mfg: Dionisi Cartridge **Manufacturer's code:** D 410 MG3
Recoil energy in 8-lb. shotgun: 8.8 ft./lbs. **Recoil velocity in 8-lb. shotgun:** 9.7 ft./sec.

Distance in yards:	Muzzle	20	30	40	50	60	70
Velocity in fps:	1,244	778	647	546	464	395	337
Average pellet energy in ft-lbs:	2.59	1.01	.70	.50	.36	.26	.19
Time of flight in seconds:	0	.0626	.1050	.1556	.2152	.2853	.3675

Type of load: Field
Three-foot velocity: 1,140 ft./sec.
Hull: 3-inch plastic
Wad: One-piece plastic
Shot: Lead
Buffered: No
Test barrel length: 26 inch
Pellets will pierce skin up to 105 yards.

NO. 9 LEAD PELLETS—¹¹/₁₆ OUNCE—402 PELLETS

Mfg: Estate Cartridge **Manufacturer's code:** HV4103
Recoil energy in 8-lb. shotgun: 6.6 ft./lbs. **Recoil velocity in 8-lb. shotgun:** 7.3 ft./sec.

Distance in yards:	Muzzle	20	30	40	50	60	70
Velocity in fps:	1,239	775	645	545	463	394	336
Average pellet energy in ft-lbs:	2.56	1.00	.70	.50	.36	.26	.19
Time of flight in seconds:	0	.0628	.1053	.1561	.2158	.2861	.3685

Type of load: Field
Three-foot velocity: 1,135 ft./sec.
Hull: 3-inch plastic
Wad: Plastic
Shot: Hard lead
Buffered: No
Test barrel length: 26 inch
Pellets will pierce skin up to 102 yards.

NO. 9 LEAD PELLETS—¹¹/₁₆ OUNCE—402 PELLETS
Mfg: Fiocchi **Manufacturer's code:** 410HV
Recoil energy in 8-lb. shotgun: 6.6 ft./lbs. **Recoil velocity in 8-lb. shotgun:** 7.3 ft./sec.

Distance in yards:	Muzzle	20	30	40	50	60	70
Velocity in fps:	1,176	749	625	529	450	383	326
Average pellet energy in ft-lbs:	2.31	.94	.65	.47	.34	.25	.18
Time of flight in seconds:	0	.0654	.1094	.1617	.2233	.2955	.3805

Type of load: Field
Three-foot velocity: 1,145 ft./sec.
Hull: 3-inch plastic
Wad: Plastic
Shot: Lead
Buffered: No
Test barrel length: 26 inch
Pellets will pierce skin up to 100 yards.

Hunting Canada and snow geese requires heavier shot than for ducks. These were taken in Alberta using Kent's Fasteel high-velocity loads and BB shot.

NO. 6 BISMUTH PELLETS—⁷/₁₆ OUNCE—118 PELLETS
Mfg: Eley Hawk **Manufacturer's code:** Fourlong Bismuth
Recoil energy in 8-lb. shotgun: 4.0 ft./lbs. **Recoil velocity in 8-lb. shotgun:** 5.7 ft./sec.

Distance in yards:	Muzzle	20	30	40	50	60	70
Velocity in fps:	1,296	855	726	625	543	475	415
Average pellet energy in ft-lbs:	6.37	2.77	2.00	1.48	1.12	.85	.65
Time of flight in seconds:	0	.0582	.0964	.1410	.1926	.2517	.3193

Type of load: Field
Three-foot velocity: 1,200 ft./sec.
Hull: 2½-inch plastic
Wad: Fiber
Shot: Bismuth
Buffered: No
Test barrel length: 26 inch
Pellets will pierce skin up to 137 yards.

NO. 4 BISMUTH PELLETS—⁹/₁₆ OUNCE—87 PELLETS
Mfg: Bismuth Cartridge **Manufacturer's code:** Sporting Game
Recoil energy in 8-lb. shotgun: 3.8 ft./lbs. **Recoil velocity in 8-lb. shotgun:** 5.5 ft./sec.

Distance in yards:	Muzzle	20	30	40	50	60	70
Velocity in fps:	1,257	883	765	672	594	529	472
Average pellet energy in ft-lbs:	9.89	4.88	3.67	2.82	2.21	1.57	1.39
Time of flight in seconds:	0	.0578	.0944	.1363	.1838	.2373	.2974

Type of load: Field
Three-foot velocity: 1,175 ft./sec.
Hull: 3-inch plastic
Wad: Plastic
Shot: Bismuth
Buffered: No
Test barrel length: 26 inch
Pellets will pierce skin up to 146 yards.

NO. 6 BISMUTH PELLETS—⁹/₁₆ OUNCE—144 PELLETS
Mfg: Bismuth Cartridge **Manufacturer's code:** Sporting Game
Recoil energy in 8-lb. shotgun: 3.8 ft./lbs. **Recoil velocity in 8-lb. shotgun:** 5.5 ft./sec.

Distance in yards:	Muzzle	20	30	40	50	60	70
Velocity in fps:	1,269	842	716	617	537	469	410
Average pellet energy in ft-lbs:	6.10	2.69	1.94	1.45	1.09	.84	.64
Time of flight in seconds:	0	.0592	.0980	.1432	.1953	.2551	.3235

Type of load: Field
Three-foot velocity: 1,175 ft./sec.
Hull: 3-inch plastic
Wad: Plastic
Shot: Bismuth
Buffered: No
Test barrel length: 26 inch
Pellets will pierce skin up to 124 yards.

NO. 7½ BISMUTH PELLETS—⁹/₁₆ OUNCE—233 PELLETS
Mfg: Bismuth Cartridge **Manufacturer's code:** Sporting Game
Recoil energy in 8-lb. shotgun: 3.8 ft./lbs. **Recoil velocity in 8-lb. shotgun:** 5.5 ft./sec.

Distance in yards:	Muzzle	20	30	40	50	60	70
Velocity in fps:	1,278	802	669	567	485	415	355
Average pellet energy in ft-lbs:	3.99	1.57	1.09	.79	.57	.42	.31
Time of flight in seconds:	0	.0608	.0108	.1506	.2079	2748	.3530

Type of load: Field
Three-foot velocity: 1,175 ft./sec.
Hull: 3-inch plastic
Wad: Plastic
Shot: Bismuth
Buffered: No
Test barrel length: 26 inch
Pellets will pierce skin up to 107 yards.

FOSTER-STYLE RIFLED SLUG—1¾ OUNCES

Mfg: Federal Cartridge Co. **Manufacturer's code:** F103RS
Recoil energy in 8-lb. shotgun: 46.8 ft./lbs. **Recoil velocity in 8-lb. shotgun:** 14.7 ft./sec.

Distance in yards:	Muzzle	25	50	75	100	125
Velocity in fps:	1,200	1,160	1,080	1,020	970	
Energy in ft-lbs:	2,785	2,295	1,980	1,775	1,605	
Trajectory in inches:	0	+0.5	0	-2.3	-6.7	

Type of load: Slug
Three-foot velocity: 1,280 ft./sec.
Hull: 3½-inch plastic
Test barrel length: 32 inch

These ruffed grouse were taken in the close, heavy cover in Michigan's northland. Light loads and open chokes are all that are needed for the close shots these wonderful game birds offer.

BARNES EXPANDER SABOT—¾ OUNCE
Mfg: Federal Cartridge Co. **Manufacturer's code:** P152X5
Recoil energy in 8-lb. shotgun: 27.3 ft./lbs. **Recoil velocity in 8-lb. shotgun:** 14.8 ft./sec.

Distance in yards:	Muzzle	25	50	75	100	125
Velocity in fps:	1,900	1,810	1,720	1,640	1,560	1,480
Energy in ft-lbs:	2,605	2,370	2,140	1,940	1,755	1,585
Trajectory in inches:	0	+0.9	+1.2	+1.0	0	-1.9

Type of load: Slug
Three-foot velocity: 1,900 ft./sec.
Hull: 2¾-inch plastic
Test barrel length: 30 inch

PARTITION-STYLE SABOT—⅞ OUNCE
Mfg: Winchester **Manufacturer's code:** SSP12
Recoil energy in 8-lb. shotgun: 37.1 ft./lbs. **Recoil velocity in 8-lb. shotgun:** 17.3 ft./sec.

Distance in yards:	Muzzle	25	50	75	100	125	
Velocity in fps:	1,900	1,743	1,595	1,526			
Energy in ft-lbs:	3,086	2,596	2,176	1,991			
Trajectory in inches:	0	+0.6	+2.0	+2.8	+2.7	+1.8	0

Type of load: Slug
Three-foot velocity: 1,900 ft./sec.
Hull: 2¾-inch plastic
Test barrel length: 30 inch

FOSTER-STYLE—1 OUNCE
Mfg: Remington Arms Co. **Manufacturer's code:** RR12SRS
Recoil energy in 8-lb. shotgun: 16.1 ft./lbs. **Recoil velocity in 8-lb. shotgun:** 11.4 ft./sec.

Distance in yards:	Muzzle	25	50	75	100	125
Velocity in fps:	1,200	1,074	988	926	873	828
Energy in ft-lbs:	1,397	1,118	946	830	739	665
Trajectory in inches:	0	-0.2	0.0	-2.4	-7.4	-15.2

Type of load: Slug
Three-foot velocity: 1,200 ft./sec.
Hull: 2¾-inch plastic
Test barrel length: 30 inch

BRENNEKE-STYLE—1 OUNCE
Mfg: Brenneke **Manufacturer's code:** 211 55 57
Recoil energy in 8-lb. shotgun: 17.9 ft./lbs. **Recoil velocity in 8-lb. shotgun:** 12.0 ft./sec.

Distance in yards:	Muzzle	25	50	75	100	125
Velocity in fps:	1,246	1,104	1,009	941	886	
Energy in ft-lbs:	1,511	1,186	991	862	764	
Trajectory in inches:	0	+3.9	+4.8	+3.6	0	

Type of load: Slug
Three-foot velocity: 1,246 ft./sec.
Hull: 2¾-inch plastic
Test barrel length: 30 inch

HYDRA-SHOK HP—1 OUNCE
Mfg: Federal Cartridge Co. **Manufacturer's code:** P127LRS
Recoil energy in 8-lb. shotgun: 19.9 ft./lbs. **Recoil velocity in 8-lb. shotgun:** 12.6 ft./sec.

Distance in yards:	Muzzle	25	50	75	100	125
Velocity in fps:	1,300	1,200	1,110	1,050	1,000	
Energy in ft-lbs:	1,645	1,390	1,205	1,070	965	
Trajectory in inches:	0	+0.5	0	-2.3	-6.5	

Type of load: Slug
Three-foot velocity: 1,300 ft./sec.
Hull: 2¾-inch plastic
Test barrel length: 30 inch

SABOT—1 OUNCE
Mfg: Winchester **Manufacturer's code:** XRS12
Recoil energy in 8-lb. shotgun: 22.0 ft./lbs. **Recoil velocity in 8-lb. shotgun:** 13.3 ft./sec.

Distance in yards:	Muzzle	25	50	75	100	125
Velocity in fps:	1,350	1,122	988	941		
Energy in ft-lbs:	1,821	1,259	976	885		
Trajectory in inches:	0	+1.2	+2.6	+2.2	0	-4.4

Type of load: Slug
Three-foot velocity: 1,350 ft./sec.
Hull: 2¾-inch plastic
Test barrel length: 30 inch

BRENNEKE-STYLE RIFLED SLUG—1 OUNCE
Mfg: RIO **Manufacturer's code:** Royal Brenneke
Recoil energy in 8-lb. shotgun: 24.3 ft./lbs. **Recoil velocity in 8-lb. shotgun:** 14.0 ft./sec.

Distance in yards:	Muzzle	25	50	75	100	125
Velocity in fps:	1,400	1,282	1,181	1,101	1,039	990
Energy in ft-lbs:	1,902	1,594	1,353	1,176	1,047	950
Trajectory in inches:	0	+1.1	+2.4	+2.1	0	-4.1

Type of load: Slug
Three-foot velocity: 1,400 ft./sec.
Hull: 2¾-inch plastic
Test barrel length: 30 inch

FOSTER-STYLE RIFLED SLUG—1 OUNCE
Mfg: RIO **Manufacturer's code:** Royal Slug
Recoil energy in 8-lb. shotgun: 24.3 ft./lbs. **Recoil velocity in 8-lb. shotgun:** 14.0 ft./sec.

Distance in yards:	Muzzle	25	50	75	100	125
Velocity in fps:	1,400	1,282	1,181	1,101	1,039	990
Energy in ft-lbs:	1,902	1,594	1,353	1,176	1,047	950
Trajectory in inches:	0	+1.1	+2.4	+2.1	0	-4.1

Type of load: Slug
Three-foot velocity: 1,400 ft./sec.
Hull: 2¾-inch plastic
Test barrel length: 30 inch

BARNES EXPANDER SABOT—1 OUNCE
Mfg: Federal Cartridge Co. **Manufacturer's code:** P150XS
Recoil energy in 8-lb. shotgun: 26.7 ft./lbs. **Recoil velocity in 8-lb. shotgun:** 14.6 ft./sec.

Distance in yards:	Muzzle	25	50	75	100	125
Velocity in fps:	1,450	1,380	1,320	1,260	1,210	1,160
Energy in ft-lbs:	2,045	1,860	1,695	1,545	1,420	1,310
Trajectory in inches:	0	+1.4	+2.2	+1.8	0	-3.3

Type of load: Slug
Three-foot velocity: 1,450 ft./sec.
Hull: 2¾-inch plastic
Test barrel length: 30 inch

HYDRA-SHOK SABOT—1 OUNCE
Mfg: Federal Cartridge Co. **Manufacturer's code:** P154SS
Recoil energy in 8-lb. shotgun: 26.7 ft./lbs. **Recoil velocity in 8-lb. shotgun:** 14.6 ft./sec.

Distance in yards:	Muzzle	25	50	75	100	125
Velocity in fps:	1,450	1,380	1,320	1,260	1,210	1,160
Energy in ft-lbs:	2,045	1,860	1,695	1,545	1,420	1,310
Trajectory in inches:	0	+1.4	+2.2	+1.8	0	-3.3

Type of load: Slug
Three-foot velocity: 1,450 ft./sec.
Hull: 2¾-inch plastic
Test barrel length: 30 inch

SOLID COPPER SABOT—1 OUNCE
Mfg: Remington Arms Co. **Manufacturer's code:** PR12CS
Recoil energy in 8-lb. shotgun: 26.7 ft./lbs. **Recoil velocity in 8-lb. shotgun:** 14.6 ft./sec.

Distance in yards:	Muzzle	25	50	75	100	125
Velocity in fps:	1,450	1,382	1,319	1,261	1,208	1,161
Energy in ft-lbs:	2,040	1,854	1,658	1,543	1,416	1,307
Trajectory in inches:	0	-0.2	0.0	-1.1	-3.5	-7.4

Type of load: Slug
Three-foot velocity: 1,450 ft./sec.
Hull: 2¾-inch plastic
Test barrel length: 30 inch

SABOT—1 OUNCE
Mfg: Winchester **Manufacturer's code:** SRSH12
Recoil energy in 8-lb. shotgun: 26.7 ft./lbs. **Recoil velocity in 8-lb. shotgun:** 14.6 ft./sec.

Distance in yards:	Muzzle	25	50	75	100	125
Velocity in fps:	1,450	1,220	1,065	1,012		
Energy in ft-lbs:	2,101	1,488	1,134	1,023		
Trajectory in inches:	0	+0.9	+2.2	+1.9	0	-3.8

Type of load: Slug
Three-foot velocity: 1,450 ft./sec.
Hull: 2¾-inch plastic
Test barrel length: 30 inch

BRENNEKE-STYLE—1 OUNCE
Mfg: Brenneke **Manufacturer's code:** 211 55 22
Recoil energy in 8-lb. shotgun: 28.0 ft./lbs. **Recoil velocity in 8-lb. shotgun:** 15.0 ft./sec.

Distance in yards:	Muzzle	25	50	75	100	125
Velocity in fps:	1,476	1,310	1,174	1,075	1,002	
Energy in ft-lbs:	2,538	2,000	1,606	1,346	1,170	
Trajectory in inches:	0	+1.8	+2.9	+2.4	0	

Type of load: Slug
Three-foot velocity: 1,475 ft./sec.
Hull: 2¾-inch plastic
Test barrel length: 30 inch

SABOT-STYLE—1 OUNCE
Mfg: Brenneke **Manufacturer's code:** 121 18 22
Recoil energy in 8-lb. shotgun: 29.3 ft./lbs. **Recoil velocity in 8-lb. shotgun:** 15.3 ft./sec.

Distance in yards:	Muzzle	25	50	75	100	125
Velocity in fps:	1,500	1,344	1,206	1,101	1,024	
Energy in ft-lbs:	2,184	1,733	1,395	1,162	1,007	
Trajectory in inches:	0	+1.6	+2.6	+2.2	0	

Type of load: Slug
Three-foot velocity: 1,500 ft./sec.
Hull: 2¾-inch plastic
Test barrel length: 30 inch

BRENNEKE-STYLE—1 OUNCE
Mfg: ARMUSA **Manufacturer's code:** BALA
Recoil energy in 8-lb. shotgun: 32.0 ft./lbs. **Recoil velocity in 8-lb. shotgun:** 16.0 ft./sec.

Distance in yards:	Muzzle	25	50	75	100	125
Velocity in fps:	1,550	1,440	1,340	1,250	1,180	1,070
Energy in ft-lbs:	2,335	2,020	1,750	1,530	1,345	1,205
Trajectory in inches:	0	+0.3	0	-1.7	-4.9	

Type of load: Slug
Three-foot velocity: 1,550 ft./sec.
Hull: 2¾-inch plastic
Test barrel length: 30 inch

LEAD RIFLED SLUG—1 OUNCE
Mfg: Fiocchi **Manufacturer's code:** 12TS1
Recoil energy in 8-lb. shotgun: 32.0 ft./lbs. **Recoil velocity in 8-lb. shotgun:** 16.0 ft./sec.

Distance in yards:	Muzzle	25	50	75	100	125
Velocity in fps:	1,550	1,440	1,340	1,250	1,180	1,110
Energy in ft-lbs:	2,335	2,020	1,750	1,530	1,345	1,205
Trajectory in inches:	0	+1.4	+2.2	+1.8	0	-3.3

Type of load: Slug
Three-foot velocity: 1,550 ft./sec.
Hull: 2¾-inch plastic
Test barrel length: 30 inch

BRENNEKE-STYLE—1 OUNCE
Mfg: Brenneke **Manufacturer's code:** 12 09 70
Recoil energy in 8-lb. shotgun: 34.9 ft./lbs. **Recoil velocity in 8-lb. shotgun:** 16.8 ft./sec.

Distance in yards:	Muzzle	25	50	75	100	125
Velocity in fps:	1,600	1,377	1,119	1,072	987	
Energy in ft-lbs:	2,491	1,845	1,399	1,118	948	
Trajectory in inches:	0	+1.3	+2.5	+2.2	0	

Type of load: Slug
Three-foot velocity: 1,600 ft./sec.
Hull: 2¾-inch plastic
Test barrel length: 30 inch

BRENNEKE-STYLE—1 OUNCE
Mfg: PMC **Manufacturer's code:** SL12B1
Recoil energy in 8-lb. shotgun: 28.6 ft./lbs. **Recoil velocity in 8-lb. shotgun:** 15.2 ft./sec.

Distance in yards:	Muzzle	25	50	75	100	125
Velocity in fps:	1,310	1,460	1,330	1,220	1,140	
Energy in ft-lbs:	2,520	2,075	1,725	1,455	1,255	
Trajectory in inches:	0	+0.3	0	-1.5	-4.3	

Type of load: Slug
Three-foot velocity: 1,600 ft./sec.
Hull: 2¾-inch plastic
Test barrel length: 30 inch

FOSTER-STYLE—1 OUNCE
Mfg: Winchester **Manufacturer's code:** X12RS15
Recoil energy in 8-lb. shotgun: 34.9 ft./lbs. **Recoil velocity in 8-lb. shotgun:** 16.8 ft./sec.

Distance in yards:	Muzzle	25	50	75	100	125
Velocity in fps:	1,600	1,161	953	889		
Energy in ft-lbs:	2,488	1,310	882	768		
Trajectory in inches:	0	+0.4	0	-1.9	-5.9	-12.1

Type of load: Slug
Three-foot velocity: 1,600 ft./sec.
Hull: 2¾-inch plastic
Test barrel length: 30 inch

FOSTER-STYLE RIFLED SLUG—1 OUNCE
Mfg: Federal Cartridge Co. **Manufacturer's code:** F127RS
Recoil energy in 8-lb. shotgun: 28.6 ft./lbs. **Recoil velocity in 8-lb. shotgun:** 15.2 ft./sec.

Distance in yards:	Muzzle	25	50	75	100	125
Velocity in fps:	1,610	1,460	1,330	1,220	1,140	
Energy in ft-lbs:	2,520	2,075	1,725	1,455	1,255	
Trajectory in inches:	0	+0.3	0	-1.5	-4.3	

Type of load: Slug
Three-foot velocity: 1,610 ft./sec.
Hull: 2¾-inch plastic
Test barrel length: 30 inch

HYDRA-SHOK HP—1 OUNCE
Mfg: Federal Cartridge Co. **Manufacturer's code:** P127R
Recoil energy in 8-lb. shotgun: 28.6 ft./lbs. **Recoil velocity in 8-lb. shotgun:** 15.2 ft./sec.

Distance in yards:	Muzzle	25	50	75	100	125
Velocity in fps:	1,310	1,460	1,330	1,220	1,140	
Energy in ft-lbs:	2,520	2,075	1,725	1,455	1,255	
Trajectory in inches:	0	+0.3	0	-1.5	-4.3	

Type of load: Slug
Three-foot velocity: 1,610 ft./sec.
Hull: 2¾-inch plastic
Test barrel length: 30 inch

FOSTER-STYLE—1 OUNCE
Mfg: Remington Arms Co. **Manufacturer's code:** SP12SRS
Recoil energy in 8-lb. shotgun: 40.0 ft./lbs. **Recoil velocity in 8-lb. shotgun:** 17.9 ft./sec.

Distance in yards:	Muzzle	25	50	75	100	125
Velocity in fps:	1,680	1,467	1,286	1,144	1,045	974
Energy in ft-lbs:	2,738	2,088	1,604	1,271	1,059	921
Trajectory in inches:	0	-0.2	0.0	-1.1	-3.8	-8.5

Type of load: Slug
Three-foot velocity: 1,680 ft./sec.
Hull: 2¾-inch plastic
Test barrel length: 30 inch

SABOT-STYLE—1⅛ OUNCES
Mfg: Brenneke **Manufacturer's code:** 121 08 22
Recoil energy in 8-lb. shotgun: 30.7 ft./lbs. **Recoil velocity in 8-lb. shotgun:** 15.7 ft./sec.

Distance in yards:	Muzzle	25	50	75	100	125
Velocity in fps:	1,400	1,274	1,165	1,080	1,017	
Energy in ft-lbs:	2,157	1,770	1,478	1.272	1,127	
Trajectory in inches:	0	+1.7	+2.9	+2.4	0	

Type of load: Slug
Three-foot velocity: 1,400 ft./sec.
Hull: 2¾-inch plastic
Test barrel length: 30 inch

FOSTER-STYLE RIFLED SLUG—1¼ OUNCES
Mfg: Federal Cartridge Co. **Manufacturer's code:** F130RS
Recoil energy in 8-lb. shotgun: 38.4 ft./lbs. **Recoil velocity in 8-lb. shotgun:** 17.6 ft./sec.

Distance in yards:	Muzzle	25	50	75	100	125
Velocity in fps:	1,520	1,330	1,260	1,160	1,090	
Energy in ft-lbs:	2,805	2,310	1,930	1,645	1,450	
Trajectory in inches:	0	+0.3	0	-1.7	-4.9	

Type of load: Slug
Three-foot velocity: 1,520 ft./sec.
Hull: 2¾-inch plastic
Test barrel length: 30 inch

HYBRID SABOT—1¼ OUNCES
Mfg: Lightfield **Manufacturer's code:** N/A
Recoil energy in 8-lb. shotgun: 37.9 ft./lbs. **Recoil velocity in 8-lb. shotgun:** 17.5 ft./sec.

Distance in yards:	Muzzle	25	50	75	100	125
Velocity in fps:	1,402	1,282	1,181	1,100	1,038	988
Energy in ft-lbs:	2,387	1,997	1,693	1,470	1,308	1,187
Trajectory in inches:	0	+1.1	+2.4	+2.1	0	-4.1

Type of load: Slug
Three-foot velocity: 1,402 ft./sec.
Hull: 2¾-inch plastic
Test barrel length: 30 inch

These shooters are participating in an Edwardian-era, vintage shoot. Dressed in period clothing, the side-by-sides they are shooting are often true representatives of the golden age of shotgunning.

SABOT—1 OUNCE
Mfg: Winchester **Manufacturer's code:** XRS123
Recoil energy in 8-lb. shotgun: 24.3 ft./lbs. **Recoil velocity in 8-lb. shotgun:** 14.0 ft./sec.

Distance in yards:	Muzzle	25	50	75	100	125
Velocity in fps:	1,400	1,151	1,003	952		
Energy in ft-lbs:	1,958	1,326	1,005	906		
Trajectory in inches:	0	+1.1	+2.4	+2.1	0	-4.2

Type of load: Slug
Three-foot velocity: 1,400 ft./sec.
Hull: 3-inch plastic
Test barrel length: 30 inch

BARNES EXPANDER SABOT—1 OUNCE
Mfg: Federal Cartridge Co. **Manufacturer's code:** P151XS
Recoil energy in 8-lb. shotgun: 30.6 ft./lbs. **Recoil velocity in 8-lb. shotgun:** 15.7 ft./sec.

Distance in yards:	Muzzle	25	50	75	100	125
Velocity in fps:	1,525	1,450	1,390	1,330	1,270	1,210
Energy in ft-lbs:	2,260	2,055	1,870	1,710	1,560	1,325
Trajectory in inches:	0	+1.3	+2.0	+1.6	0	-3.0

Type of load: Slug
Three-foot velocity: 1,525 ft./sec.
Hull: 3-inch plastic
Test barrel length: 30 inch

HYDRA-SHOK SABOT—1 OUNCE
Mfg: Federal Cartridge Co. **Manufacturer's code:** P151SS
Recoil energy in 8-lb. shotgun: 25.8 ft./lbs. **Recoil velocity in 8-lb. shotgun:** 14.4 ft./sec.

Distance in yards:	Muzzle	25	50	75	100	125
Velocity in fps:	1,550	1,440	1,340	1,250	1,180	1,110
Energy in ft-lbs:	2,335	2,020	1,750	1,530	1,345	1,205
Trajectory in inches:	0	+1.4	+2.2	+1.8	0	-3.3

Type of load: Slug
Three-foot velocity: 1,550 ft./sec.
Hull: 3-inch plastic
Test barrel length: 30 inch

SABOT—1 OUNCE
Mfg: Winchester **Manufacturer's code:** SRSH123
Recoil energy in 8-lb. shotgun: 32.0 ft./lbs. **Recoil velocity in 8-lb. shotgun:** 16.0 ft./sec.

Distance in yards:	Muzzle	25	50	75	100	125
Velocity in fps:	1,550	1,323	1,149	1,085		
Energy in ft-lbs:	2,401	1,749	1,319	1,176		
Trajectory in inches:	0	+0.7	+1.7	+1.6	0	-3.2

Type of load: Slug
Three-foot velocity: 1,550 ft./sec.
Hull: 3-inch plastic
Test barrel length: 30 inch

SABOT—1 OUNCE
Mfg: Brenneke **Manufacturer's code:** 121 17 22
Recoil energy in 8-lb. shotgun: 39.7 ft./lbs. **Recoil velocity in 8-lb. shotgun:** 17.9 ft./sec.

Distance in yards:	Muzzle	25	50	75	100	125
Velocity in fps:	1,675	1,478	1,325	1,191	1,090	
Energy in ft-lbs:	2,686	2,122	1,685	1,361	1,139	
Trajectory in inches:	0	+1.1	+2.1	+1.8	0	

Type of load: Slug
Three-foot velocity: 1,675 ft./sec.
Hull: 3-inch plastic
Test barrel length: 30 inch

FOSTER-STYLE—1 OUNCE
Mfg: Winchester **Manufacturer's code:** X123RS15
Recoil energy in 8-lb. shotgun: 45.6 ft./lbs. **Recoil velocity in 8-lb. shotgun:** 19.1 ft./sec.

Distance in yards:	Muzzle	25	50	75	100	125
Velocity in fps:	1,760	1,310	1,040	904		
Energy in ft-lbs:	3,010	1,667	1,052	904		
Trajectory in inches:	0	+0.2	0	-1.5	-4.6	-9.7

Type of load: Slug
Three-foot velocity: 1,760 ft./sec.
Hull: 3-inch plastic
Test barrel length: 30 inch

HYBRID SABOT—1 OUNCE
Mfg: Lightfield **Manufacturer's code:** N/A
Recoil energy in 8-lb. shotgun: 48.5 ft./lbs. **Recoil velocity in 8-lb. shotgun:** 19.8 ft./sec.

Distance in yards:	Muzzle	25	50	75	100	125
Velocity in fps:	1,800	1,638	1,489	1,355	1,239	1,144
Energy in ft-lbs:	3,274	2,712	2,241	1,856	1,552	1,323
Trajectory in inches:	0	+.27	+1.23	+1.21	0	-2.63

Type of load: Slug
Three-foot velocity: 1,800 ft./sec.
Hull: 3-inch plastic
Test barrel length: 30 inch

SABOT—1⅛ OUNCES

Mfg: Brenneke **Manufacturer's code:** 121 07 22
Recoil energy in 8-lb. shotgun: 38.8 ft./lbs. **Recoil velocity in 8-lb. shotgun:** 17.7 ft./sec.

Distance in yards:	Muzzle	25	50	75	100	125
Velocity in fps:	1,525	1,376	1,248	1,144	1,065	
Energy in ft-lbs:	2,536	2,064	1,697	1,426	1,236	
Trajectory in inches:	0	+1.3	+2.3	+2.0	0	

Type of load: Slug
Three-foot velocity: 1,525 ft./sec.
Hull: 3-inch plastic
Test barrel length: 30 inch

FOSTER-STYLE RIFLED SLUG—1¼ OUNCES

Mfg: Federal Cartridge Co. **Manufacturer's code:** F131RS
Recoil energy in 8-lb. shotgun: 43.9 ft./lbs. **Recoil velocity in 8-lb. shotgun:** 18.8 ft./sec.

Distance in yards:	Muzzle	25	50	75	100	125
Velocity in fps:	1,600	1,450	1,320	1,210	1,130	
Energy in ft-lbs:	3,110	2,555	2,120	1,785	1,540	
Trajectory in inches:	0	+0.3	0	-1.5	-4.4	

Type of load: Slug
Three-foot velocity: 1,600 ft./sec.
Hull: 3-inch plastic
Test barrel length: 30 inch

BRENNEKE-STYLE—1⅜ OUNCES

Mfg: Brenneke **Manufacturer's code:** 211 55 65
Recoil energy in 8-lb. shotgun: 55.3 ft./lbs. **Recoil velocity in 8-lb. shotgun:** 21.1 ft./sec.

Distance in yards:	Muzzle	25	50	75	100	125
Velocity in fps:	1,500	1,295	1,136	1,030	995	
Energy in ft-lbs:	3,014	2,241	1,724	1,418	1,219	
Trajectory in inches:	0	+1.9	+3.1	+2.5	0	

Type of load: Slug
Three-foot velocity: 1,500 ft./sec.
Hull: 3-inch plastic
Test barrel length: 30 inch

A variety of loads, from light to heavy magnum loads, are used to bag tough pheasants. Cover and whether or not the birds are wild or planted game-farm birds often determine load selection.

FOSTER-STYLE RIFLED SLUG—⁴/₅ OUNCE
Mfg: Federal Cartridge Co. **Manufacturer's code:** F164RS
Recoil energy in 8-lb. shotgun: 21.5 ft./lbs. **Recoil velocity in 8-lb. shotgun:** 13.2 ft./sec.

Distance in yards:	Muzzle	25	50	75	100	125
Velocity in fps:	1,600	1,360	1,180	1,060	990	
Energy in ft-lbs:	1,990	1,435	1,075	875	755	
Trajectory in inches:	0	+0.3	0	-1.8	-5.4	

Type of load: Slug
Three-foot velocity: 1,600 ft./sec.
Hull: 2¾-inch plastic
Test barrel length: 28 inch

FOSTER-STYLE—⁴/₅ OUNCE
Mfg: Winchester **Manufacturer's code:** X16RS5
Recoil energy in 8-lb. shotgun: 26.8 ft./lbs. **Recoil velocity in 8-lb. shotgun:** 17.4 ft./sec.

Distance in yards:	Muzzle	25	50	75	100	125
Velocity in fps:	1,600	1,158	950	887		
Energy in ft-lbs:	1,962	1,028	692	602		
Trajectory in inches:	0	+0.4	0	-2.0	-5.9	-12.1

Type of load: Slug
Three-foot velocity: 1,600 ft./sec.
Hull: 2¾-inch plastic
Test barrel length: 28 inch

HYBRID SABOT—¹⁵/₁₆ OUNCE
Mfg: Lightfield **Manufacturer's code:** N/A
Recoil energy in 8-lb. shotgun: 35.5 ft./lbs. **Recoil velocity in 8-lb. shotgun:** 16.9 ft./sec.

Distance in yards:	Muzzle	25	50	75	100	125
Velocity in fps:	1,610	1,464	1,333	1,220	1,129	1,059
Energy in ft-lbs:	2,303	1,903	1,578	1,323	1,133	996
Trajectory in inches:	0	+.62	+1.71	+1.59	0	-3.28

Type of load: Slug
Three-foot velocity: 1,610 ft./sec.
Hull: 2¾-inch plastic
Test barrel length: 28 inch

BRENNEKE-STYLE—1 OUNCE
Mfg: Brenneke **Manufacturer's code:** N/A
Recoil energy in 8-lb. shotgun: 29.3 ft./lbs. **Recoil velocity in 8-lb. shotgun:** 15.3 ft./sec.

Distance in yards:	Muzzle	25	50	75	100	125
Velocity in fps:	1,500	1,344	1,206	1,101	1,024	
Energy in ft-lbs:	2,184	1,733	1,395	1,162	1,007	
Trajectory in inches:	0	+1.6	+2.6	+2.2	0	

Type of load: Slug
Three-foot velocity: 1,510 ft./sec.
Hull: 2¾-inch plastic
Test barrel length: 28 inch

Here a shooter is using a 100-year-old Holland & Holland hammer gun that uses 2½-inch shells to participate in an Edwardian-era shoot. Although magnum-loving shotgunners shun light loads, the 2½-inch shells he's using are plenty for all upland game, save for turkey.

HYDRA-SHOK SABOT—⅝ OUNCE
Mfg: Federal Cartridge Co. **Manufacturer's code:** P203SS
Recoil energy in 8-lb. shotgun: 9.5 ft./lbs. **Recoil velocity in 8-lb. shotgun:** 8.7 ft./sec.

Distance in yards:	Muzzle	25	50	75	100	125
Velocity in fps:	1,400	1,290	1,950	1,110	1,050	1,000
Energy in ft-lbs:	1,200	1,010	860	750	670	610
Trajectory in inches:	0	+1.8	+2.8	+2.3	0	-4.3

Type of load: Slug
Three-foot velocity: 1,400 ft./sec.
Hull: 2¾-inch plastic
Test barrel length: 30 inch

SABOT—⅝ OUNCE
Mfg: Winchester **Manufacturer's code:** XRS20
Recoil energy in 8-lb. shotgun: 9.5 ft./lbs. **Recoil velocity in 8-lb. shotgun:** 8.7 ft./sec.

Distance in yards:	Muzzle	25	50	75	100	125
Velocity in fps:	1,400	1,145	998	948		
Energy in ft-lbs:	1,249	836	635	572		
Trajectory in inches:	0	+1.2	+2.5	+2.2	0	-4.4

Type of load: Slug
Three-foot velocity: 1,400 ft./sec.
Hull: 2¾-inch plastic
Test barrel length: 30 inch

FOSTER-STYLE RIFLED SLUG—¾ OUNCE
Mfg: Federal Cartridge Co. **Manufacturer's code:** F203RS
Recoil energy in 8-lb. shotgun: 15.8 ft./lbs. **Recoil velocity in 8-lb. shotgun:** 11.3 ft./sec.

Distance in yards:	Muzzle	25	50	75	100	125
Velocity in fps:	1,600	1,420	1,270	1,150	1,070	
Energy in ft-lbs:	1,865	1,465	1,175	965	835	
Trajectory in inches:	0	+0.3	0	-1.6	-4.8	

Type of load: Slug
Three-foot velocity: 1,600 ft./sec.
Hull: 2¾-inch plastic
Test barrel length: 30 inch

FOSTER-STYLE—¾ OUNCE
Mfg: Winchester **Manufacturer's code:** X20RSM5
Recoil energy in 8-lb. shotgun: 19.7 ft./lbs. **Recoil velocity in 8-lb. shotgun:** 12.6 ft./sec.

Distance in yards:	Muzzle	25	50	75	100	125
Velocity in fps:	1,600	1,160	952	889		
Energy in ft-lbs:	1,865	981	660	575		
Trajectory in inches:	0	+0.3	0	-2.0	-5.9	-12.1

Type of load: Slug
Three-foot velocity: 1,600 ft./sec.
Hull: 2¾-inch plastic
Test barrel length: 30 inch

HYBRID SABOT—⅞ OUNCE
Mfg: Lightfield **Manufacturer's code:** N/A
Recoil energy in 8-lb. shotgun: 17.4 ft./lbs. **Recoil velocity in 8-lb. shotgun:** 11.8 ft./sec.

Distance in yards:	Muzzle	25	50	75	100	125
Velocity in fps:	1,475	1,381	1,295	1,218	1,153	1,097
Energy in ft-lbs:	1,850	1,621	1,426	1,262	1,129	1,024
Trajectory in inches:	0	+0.7	+1.8	+1.7	0	-3.3

Type of load: Slug
Three-foot velocity: 1,475 ft./sec.
Hull: 2¾-inch plastic
Test barrel length: 30 inch

HYDRA-SHOK SABOT—⁵/₈ OUNCE

Mfg: Federal Cartridge Co. **Manufacturer's code:** P207SS
Recoil energy in 8-lb. shotgun: 8.5 ft./lbs. **Recoil velocity in 8-lb. shotgun:** 8.3 ft./sec.

Distance in yards:	Muzzle	25	50	75	100	125
Velocity in fps:	1,450	1,330	1,230	1,140	1,070	1,020
Energy in ft-lbs:	1,285	1,080	820	795	705	630
Trajectory in inches:	0	+1.7	+2.6	+2.2	0	-4.0

Type of load: Slug
Three-foot velocity: 1,450 ft./sec.
Hull: 3-inch plastic
Test barrel length: 30 inch

FOSTER-STYLE RIFLED SLUG—³/₄ OUNCE

Mfg: Federal Cartridge Co. **Manufacturer's code:** F207RS
Recoil energy in 8-lb. shotgun: 18.0 ft./lbs. **Recoil velocity in 8-lb. shotgun:** 12.0 ft./sec.

Distance in yards:	Muzzle	25	50	75	100	125
Velocity in fps:	1,680	1,500	1,340	1,210	1,110	
Energy in ft-lbs:	2,055	1,640	1,310	1,065	890	
Trajectory in inches:	0	+0.2	0	-1.4	-4.4	

Type of load: Slug
Three-foot velocity: 1,680 ft./sec.
Hull: 3-inch plastic
Test barrel length: 30 inch

BARNES EXPANDER SABOT—³/₄ OUNCE

Mfg: Federal Cartridge Co. **Manufacturer's code:** P207XS
Recoil energy in 8-lb. shotgun: 12.2 ft./lbs. **Recoil velocity in 8-lb. shotgun:** 9.9 ft./sec.

Distance in yards:	Muzzle	25	50	75	100	125
Velocity in fps:	1,450	1,380	1,320	1,260	1,200	1,150
Energy in ft-lbs:	1,515	1,375	1,250	1,140	1,040	960
Trajectory in inches:	0	+1.5	+2.3	+1.8	0	-3.3

Type of load: Slug
Three-foot velocity: 1,450 ft./sec.
Hull: 3-inch plastic
Test barrel length: 30 inch

BRENNEKE-STYLE—1 OUNCE

Mfg: Brenneke **Manufacturer's code:** 211 56 11
Recoil energy in 8-lb. shotgun: 28.0 ft./lbs. **Recoil velocity in 8-lb. shotgun:** 15.0 ft./sec.

Distance in yards:	Muzzle	25	50	75	100	125
Velocity in fps:	1,476	1,322	1,193	1,094	1,022	
Energy in ft-lbs:	2,120	1,701	1,385	1,165	1,016	
Trajectory in inches:	0	+1.4	+2.5	+2.2	0	

Type of load: Slug
Three-foot velocity: 1,475 ft./sec.
Hull: 3-inch plastic
Test barrel length: 30 inch

These Hungarian partridge proved to be challenging targets on southwestern Alberta's prairies. Although the two German shorthair pointers were superb, the very dry conditions caused the birds to flush well ahead of the dogs, making for tough shots. Still, 2½-inch loads of No. 6 shot quickly filled limits.

FOSTER-STYLE—⅕ OUNCE

Mfg: Winchester **Manufacturer's code:** X41RS5
Recoil energy in 8-lb. shotgun: 12.1 ft./lbs. **Recoil velocity in 8-lb. shotgun:** 9.9 ft./sec.

Distance in yards:	Muzzle	25	50	75	100	125
Velocity in fps:	1,830	1,318	1,025	946		
Energy in ft-lbs:	651	338	204	174		
Trajectory in inches:	0	+0.3	0	-1.9	-5.8	-12.0

Type of load: Slug
Three-foot velocity: 1,830 ft./sec.
Hull: 2½-inch plastic
Test barrel length: 26 inch

FOSTER-STYLE RIFLED SLUG—¼ OUNCE

Mfg: Federal Cartridge Co. **Manufacturer's code:** F412RS
Recoil energy in 8-lb. shotgun: 9.0 ft./lbs. **Recoil velocity in 8-lb. shotgun:** 8.0 ft./sec.

Distance in yards:	Muzzle	25	50	75	100	125
Velocity in fps:	1,775	1,540	1,340	1,180	1,060	
Energy in ft-lbs:	770	580	435	335	275	
Trajectory in inches:	0	+0.2	0	-1.4	-4.4	

Type of load: Slug
Three-foot velocity: 1,775 ft./sec.
Hull: 2½-inch plastic
Test barrel length: 26 inch

Hunting on southwestern Alberta's prairies can be a great experience. However, because birds can be seen at a long distance, the temptation is to shoot before they are in range. Skilled hunters will carefully place decoys and use good calling to bring the plentiful birds within 25 or 30 yards for clean, killing shots. Even so, large pellets—No. 1 tungsten/polymer, bismuth BBs or BB, BBB, or even T steel for very large Canadas—are used in these situations. Although ducks call for smaller shot, they can be taken just as cleanly with large goose-sized pellets.

BRENNEKE-STYLE—¼ OUNCE

Mfg: Brenneke **Manufacturer's code:** 211 56 38
Recoil energy in 8-lb. shotgun: 11.3 ft./lbs. **Recoil velocity in 8-lb. shotgun:** 9.5 ft./sec.

Distance in yards:	Muzzle	25	50	75	100	125
Velocity in fps:	1,755	1,427	1,179	1,025	930	
Energy in ft-lbs:	781	517	352	266	219	
Trajectory in inches:	0	+1.6	+2.8	+2.4	0	

Type of load: Slug
Three-foot velocity: 1,755 ft./sec.
Hull: 3-inch plastic
Test barrel length: 26 inch

Shooting at a sporting clay target with a side-by-side. Sporting clays offer very challenging targets, but few require heavy loads.

NO. 00 BUCKSHOT PELLETS—18 PELLETS

Mfg: Federal Cartridge Co. **Manufacturer's code:** P108
Recoil energy in 8-lb. shotgun: 52.0 ft./lbs. **Recoil velocity in 8-lb. shotgun:** 18.3 ft./sec.

Distance in yards:	Muzzle	20	30	40	50	60	70
Velocity in fps:	1,109	983	930	882	839	799	762
Average pellet energy in ft-lbs:	144.39	113.45	101.54	91.34	82.52	74.84	68.08
Time of flight in seconds:	0	.0575	.0889	.1220	.1569	.1936	.2320

Type of load: Buckshot
Three-foot velocity: 1,100 ft./sec.
Hull: 3½-inch plastic
Wad: Plastic
Shot: Copper-plated, hard lead
Buffered: No
Test barrel length: 32 inch
Pellets will pierce skin up to 405 yards.

NO. 00 BUCKSHOT PELLETS—9 PELLETS

Mfg: Winchester **Manufacturer's code:** X10C00B
Recoil energy in 8-lb. shotgun: 57.7 ft./lbs. **Recoil velocity in 8-lb. shotgun:** 19.3 ft./sec.

Distance in yards:	Muzzle	20	30	40	50	60	70
Velocity in fps:	1,160	1,023	966	915	868	826	787
Average pellet energy in ft-lbs:	157.94	122.80	109.47	98.14	88.41	79.97	72.60
Time of flight in seconds:	0	.0552	.0854	.1173	.1510	.1864	.2236

Type of load: Buckshot
Three-foot velocity: 1,150 ft./sec.
Hull: 3½-inch plastic
Wad: Plastic
Shot: Copper-plated lead
Buffered: Yes
Test barrel length: 32 inch
Pellets will pierce skin up to 412 yards.

NO. 1 BUCKSHOT PELLETS—24 PELLETS

Mfg: Federal Cartridge Co. **Manufacturer's code:** P108
Recoil energy in 8-lb. shotgun: 52.0 ft./lbs. **Recoil velocity in 8-lb. shotgun:** 18.3 ft./sec.

Distance in yards:	Muzzle	20	30	40	50	60	70
Velocity in fps:	1,110	973	916	865	819	777	738
Average pellet energy in ft-lbs:	108.64	83.44	73.96	65.94	59.08	53.16	48.00
Time of flight in seconds:	0	.0578	.0896	.1234	.1590	.1966	.2363

Type of load: Buckshot
Three-foot velocity: 1,100 ft./sec.
Hull: 3½-inch plastic
Wad: Plastic
Shot: Copper-plated, hard lead
Buffered: No
Test barrel length: 32 inch
Pellets will pierce skin up to 369 yards.

NO. 4 BUCKSHOT PELLETS—54 PELLETS

Mfg: Winchester **Manufacturer's code:** XB104
Recoil energy in 8-lb. shotgun: 46.1 ft./lbs. **Recoil velocity in 8-lb. shotgun:** 17.2 ft./sec.

Distance in yards:	Muzzle	20	30	40	50	60	70
Velocity in fps:	1,176	991	918	855	799	749	704
Average pellet energy in ft-lbs:	62.39	44.29	38.04	32.79	28.80	25.30	22.34
Time of flight in seconds:	0	.0558	.0873	.1212	.1575	.1963	.2376

Type of load: Buckshot
Three-foot velocity: 1,050 ft./sec.
Hull: 3½-inch plastic
Wad: Plastic
Shot: Lead
Buffered: Yes
Test barrel length: 32 inch
Pellets will pierce skin up to 301 yards.

Slugs are the shotgunner's primary choice for big game. White-tailed deer are most commonly hunted with slugs, but author John Barsness used a shotgun and slug to bag this nice black bear. (Photo by John Barsness)

NO. 000 BUCKSHOT PELLETS—8 PELLETS

Mfg: Remington Arms Co. **Manufacturer's code:** 12B
Recoil energy in 8-lb. shotgun: 26.8 ft./lbs. **Recoil velocity in 8-lb. shotgun:** 14.7 ft./sec.

Distance in yards:	Muzzle	20	30	40	50	60	70
Velocity in fps:	1,343	1,176	1,107	1,046	991	941	896
Average pellet energy in ft-lbs:	274.61	210.75	186.71	166.61	149.59	135.00	122.38
Time of flight in seconds:	0	.0478	.0741	.1020	.1315	.1626	.1952

Type of load: Buckshot
Three-foot velocity: 1,330 ft./sec.
Hull: 2¾-inch plastic
Wad: Plastic
Shot: Lead
Buffered: No
Test barrel length: 30 inch
Pellets will pierce skin up to 472 yards.

NO. 000 BUCKSHOT PELLETS—8 PELLETS

Mfg: Winchester **Manufacturer's code:** XB12000
Recoil energy in 8-lb. shotgun: 26.8 ft./lbs. **Recoil velocity in 8-lb. shotgun:** 14.7 ft./sec.

Distance in yards:	Muzzle	20	30	40	50	60	70
Velocity in fps:	1,343	1,176	1,107	1,046	991	941	896
Average pellet energy in ft-lbs:	274.61	210.75	186.71	166.61	149.59	135.00	122.38
Time of flight in seconds:	0	.0478	.0741	.1020	.1315	.1626	.1952

Type of load: Buckshot
Three-foot velocity: 1,330 ft./sec.
Hull: 2¾-inch plastic
Wad: Plastic
Shot: Lead
Buffered: Yes
Test barrel length: 30 inch
Pellets will pierce skin up to 472 yards.

NO. 00 BUCKSHOT PELLETS—9 PELLETS

Mfg: Winchester **Manufacturer's code:** XB1200LR
Recoil energy in 8-lb. shotgun: 17.2 ft./lbs. **Recoil velocity in 8-lb. shotgun:** 11.8 ft./sec.

Distance in yards:	Muzzle	20	30	40	50	60	70
Velocity in fps:	1,135	1,003	948	899	854	812	774
Average pellet energy in ft-lbs:	151.09	118.10	105.49	94.73	85.46	77.41	70.35
Time of flight in seconds:	0	.0563	.0871	.1196	.1539	.1899	.2277

Type of load: Buckshot
Three-foot velocity: 1,125 ft./sec.
Hull: 2¾-inch plastic
Wad: Plastic
Shot: Lead
Buffered: No
Test barrel length: 30 inch
Pellets will pierce skin up to 409 yards.

NO. 00 BUCKSHOT PELLETS—9 PELLETS

Mfg: PMC **Manufacturer's code:** BSL1200
Recoil energy in 8-lb. shotgun: 18.0 ft./lbs. **Recoil velocity in 8-lb. shotgun:** 12.0 ft./sec.

Distance in yards:	Muzzle	20	30	40	50	60	70
Velocity in fps:	1,155	1,019	962	911	865	823	784
Average pellet energy in ft-lbs:	156.55	121.86	108.67	97.45	87.82	79.46	72.15
Time of flight in seconds:	0	.0554	.0857	.1177	.1515	.1871	.2244

Type of load: Buckshot
Three-foot velocity: 1,140 ft./sec.
Hull: 2¾-inch plastic
Wad: Plastic
Shot: Lead
Buffered: No
Test barrel length: 30 inch
Pellets will pierce skin up to 412 yards.

NO. 00 BUCKSHOT PELLETS—9 PELLETS

Mfg: Sellier & Bellot **Manufacturer's code:** SBA01222/36
Recoil energy in 8-lb. shotgun: 18.0 ft./lbs. **Recoil velocity in 8-lb. shotgun:** 12.0 ft./sec.

Distance in yards:	Muzzle	20	30	40	50	60	70
Velocity in fps:	1,160	1,023	966	915	868	826	787
Average pellet energy in ft-lbs:	157.94	122.80	109.47	98.14	88.41	79.97	72.60
Time of flight in seconds:	0	.0552	.0854	.1173	.1510	.1864	.2236

Type of load: Buckshot
Three-foot velocity: 1,145 ft./sec.
Hull: 2¾-inch plastic
Wad: Plastic
Shot: Lead
Buffered: No
Test barrel length: 30 inch
Pellets will pierce skin up to 412 yards.

NO. 00 BUCKSHOT PELLETS—9 PELLETS

Mfg: Armscor **Manufacturer's code:** N/A
Recoil energy in 8-lb. shotgun: 18.0 ft./lbs. **Recoil velocity in 8-lb. shotgun:** 12.0 ft./sec.

Distance in yards:	Muzzle	20	30	40	50	60	70
Velocity in fps:	1,160	1,023	966	915	868	826	787
Average pellet energy in ft-lbs:	157.94	122.80	109.47	98.14	88.41	79.97	72.60
Time of flight in seconds:	0	.0552	.0854	.1173	.1510	.1864	.2236

Type of load: Buckshot
Three-foot velocity: 1,145 ft./sec.
Hull: 2¾-inch plastic
Wad: Plastic
Shot: Lead
Buffered: No
Test barrel length: 30 inch
Pellets will pierce skin up to 412 yards.

NO. 00 BUCKSHOT PELLETS—9 PELLETS

Mfg: Federal Cartridge Co. **Manufacturer's code:** H132
Recoil energy in 8-lb. shotgun: 18.0 ft./lbs. **Recoil velocity in 8-lb. shotgun:** 12.0 ft./sec.

Distance in yards:	Muzzle	20	30	40	50	60	70
Velocity in fps:	1,160	1,023	966	915	868	826	787
Average pellet energy in ft-lbs:	157.94	122.80	109.47	98.14	88.41	79.97	72.60
Time of flight in seconds:	0	.0552	.0854	.1173	.1510	.1864	.2236

Type of load: Buckshot
Three-foot velocity: 1,145 ft./sec.
Hull: 2¾-inch plastic
Wad: Plastic
Shot: Lead
Buffered: No
Test barrel length: 30 inch
Pellets will pierce skin up to 412 yards.

NO. 00 BUCKSHOT PELLETS—9 PELLETS
Mfg: Fiocchi Manufacturer's code: 12LE00BK
Recoil energy in 8-lb. shotgun: 57.7 ft./lbs. Recoil velocity in 8-lb. shotgun: 19.3 ft./sec.

Distance in yards:	Muzzle	20	30	40	50	60	70
Velocity in fps:	1,160	1,023	966	915	868	826	787
Average pellet energy in ft-lbs:	157.94	122.80	109.47	98.14	88.41	79.97	72.60
Time of flight in seconds:	0	.0552	.0854	.1173	.1510	.1864	.2236

Type of load: Buckshot
Three-foot velocity: 1,145 ft./sec.
Hull: 2¾-inch plastic
Wad: Plastic
Shot: Nickel-plated lead
Buffered: No
Test barrel length: 30 inch
Pellets will pierce skin up to 412 yards.

NO. 00 BUCKSHOT PELLETS—9 PELLETS
Mfg: PMC Manufacturer's code: BSL1200
Recoil energy in 8-lb. shotgun: 18.0 ft./lbs. Recoil velocity in 8-lb. shotgun: 12.0 ft./sec.

Distance in yards:	Muzzle	20	30	40	50	60	70
Velocity in fps:	1,160	1,023	966	915	868	826	787
Average pellet energy in ft-lbs:	157.94	122.80	109.47	98.14	88.41	79.97	72.60
Time of flight in seconds:	0	.0552	.0854	.1173	.1510	.1864	.2236

Type of load: Buckshot
Three-foot velocity: 1,145 ft./sec.
Hull: 2¾-inch plastic
Wad: Plastic
Shot: Lead
Buffered: No
Test barrel length: 30 inch
Pellets will pierce skin up to 412 yards.

NO. 00 BUCKSHOT PELLETS—9 PELLETS
Mfg: Sellier & Bellot Manufacturer's code: SBA01222/36
Recoil energy in 8-lb. shotgun: 18.0 ft./lbs. Recoil velocity in 8-lb. shotgun: 12.0 ft./sec.

Distance in yards:	Muzzle	20	30	40	50	60	70
Velocity in fps:	1,155	1,019	962	911	865	823	784
Average pellet energy in ft-lbs:	156.55	121.86	108.67	97.45	87.82	79.46	72.15
Time of flight in seconds:	0	.0554	.0857	.1177	.1515	.1871	.2244

Type of load: Buckshot
Three-foot velocity: 1,140 ft./sec.
Hull: 2¾-inch plastic
Wad: Plastic
Shot: Nickel-plated lead
Buffered: No
Test barrel length: 30 inch
Pellets will pierce skin up to 412 yards.

NO. 00 BUCKSHOT PELLETS—12 PELLETS
Mfg: Dionisi Manufacturer's code: D 12 B S00
Recoil energy in 8-lb. shotgun: 26.8 ft./lbs. Recoil velocity in 8-lb. shotgun: 14.7 ft./sec.

Distance in yards:	Muzzle	20	30	40	50	60	70
Velocity in fps:	1,313	1,104	1,070	1,008	952	902	857
Average pellet energy in ft-lbs:	202.30	152.55	134.27	119.11	106.34	95.46	86.09
Time of flight in seconds:	0	.0491	.0763	.1052	.1359	.1682	.2024

Type of load: Buckshot
Three-foot velocity: 1,300 ft./sec.
Hull: 2¾-inch plastic
Wad: Plastic
Shot: Lead
Buffered: No
Test barrel length: 30 inch
Pellets will pierce skin up to 430 yards.

NO. 00 BUCKSHOT PELLETS—12 PELLETS
Mfg: Federal Cartridge Co. Manufacturer's code: P156/F130
Recoil energy in 8-lb. shotgun: 44.8 ft./lbs. Recoil velocity in 8-lb. shotgun: 19.0 ft./sec.

Distance in yards:	Muzzle	20	30	40	50	60	70
Velocity in fps:	1,313	1,104	1,070	1,008	952	902	857
Average pellet energy in ft-lbs:	202.30	152.55	134.27	119.11	106.34	95.46	86.09
Time of flight in seconds:	0	.0491	.0763	.1052	.1359	.1682	.2024

Type of load: Buckshot
Three-foot velocity: 1,300 ft./sec.
Hull: 2¾-inch plastic
Wad: Plastic
Shot: Lead
Buffered: No
Test barrel length: 30 inch
Pellets will pierce skin up to 430 yards.

NO. 00 BUCKSHOT PELLETS—12 PELLETS
Mfg: Remington Arms Co. Manufacturer's code: 12SB
Recoil energy in 8-lb. shotgun: 44.8 ft./lbs. Recoil velocity in 8-lb. shotgun: 19.0 ft./sec.

Distance in yards:	Muzzle	20	30	40	50	60	70
Velocity in fps:	1,313	1,104	1,070	1,008	952	902	857
Average pellet energy in ft-lbs:	202.30	152.55	134.27	119.11	106.34	95.46	86.09
Time of flight in seconds:	0	.0491	.0763	.1052	.1359	.1682	.2024

Type of load: Buckshot
Three-foot velocity: 1,300 ft./sec.
Hull: 2¾-inch plastic
Wad: Plastic
Shot: Lead
Buffered: No
Test barrel length: 30 inch
Pellets will pierce skin up to 430 yards.

NO. 00 BUCKSHOT PELLETS—12 PELLETS
Mfg: Remington Arms Co. Manufacturer's code: 12SN
Recoil energy in 8-lb. shotgun: 44.8 ft./lbs. Recoil velocity in 8-lb. shotgun: 19.0 ft./sec.

Distance in yards:	Muzzle	20	30	40	50	60	70
Velocity in fps:	1,313	1,104	1,070	1,008	952	902	857
Average pellet energy in ft-lbs:	202.30	152.55	134.27	119.11	106.34	95.46	86.09
Time of flight in seconds:	0	.0491	.0763	.1052	.1359	.1682	.2024

Type of load: Buckshot
Three-foot velocity: 1,300 ft./sec.
Hull: 2¾-inch plastic
Wad: Plastic
Shot: Nickel-plated lead
Buffered: No
Test barrel length: 30 inch
Pellets will pierce skin up to 430 yards.

NO. 00 BUCKSHOT PELLETS—12 PELLETS

Mfg: Winchester **Manufacturer's code:** XB120012
Recoil energy in 8-lb. shotgun: 44.8 ft./lbs. **Recoil velocity in 8-lb. shotgun:** 19.0 ft./sec.

Distance in yards:	Muzzle	20	30	40	50	60	70
Velocity in fps:	1,313	1,104	1,070	1,008	952	902	857
Average pellet energy in ft-lbs:	202.30	152.55	134.27	119.11	106.34	95.46	86.09
Time of flight in seconds:	0	.0491	.0763	.1052	.1359	.1682	.2024

Type of load: Buckshot
Three-foot velocity: 1,300 ft./sec.
Hull: 2¾-inch plastic
Wad: Plastic
Shot: Lead
Buffered: Yes
Test barrel length: 30 inch
Pellets will pierce skin up to 430 yards.

NO. 00 BUCKSHOT PELLETS—12 PELLETS

Mfg: Winchester **Manufacturer's code:** X12XC0B5
Recoil energy in 8-lb. shotgun: 44.8 ft./lbs. **Recoil velocity in 8-lb. shotgun:** 19.0 ft./sec.

Distance in yards:	Muzzle	20	30	40	50	60	70
Velocity in fps:	1,313	1,104	1,070	1,008	952	902	857
Average pellet energy in ft-lbs:	202.30	152.55	134.27	119.11	106.34	95.46	86.09
Time of flight in seconds:	0	.0491	.0763	.1052	.1359	.1682	.2024

Type of load: Buckshot
Three-foot velocity: 1,300 ft./sec.
Hull: 2¾-inch plastic
Wad: Plastic
Shot: Copper-plated lead
Buffered: Yes
Test barrel length: 30 inch
Pellets will pierce skin up to 430 yards.

NO. 00 BUCKSHOT PELLETS—9 PELLETS

Mfg: Clever **Manufacturer's code:** N/A
Recoil energy in 8-lb. shotgun: 26.8 ft./lbs. **Recoil velocity in 8-lb. shotgun:** 14.7 ft./sec.

Distance in yards:	Muzzle	20	30	40	50	60	70
Velocity in fps:	1,344	1,164	1,090	1,026	968	917	870
Average pellet energy in ft-lbs:	211.84	158.92	139.50	123.47	110.03	98.62	88.82
Time of flight in seconds:	0	.0481	.0747	.1031	.1332	.1651	.1987

Type of load: Buckshot
Three-foot velocity: 1,330 ft./sec.
Hull: 2¾-inch plastic
Wad: Plastic
Shot: Lead
Buffered: No
Test barrel length: 30 inch
Pellets will pierce skin up to 433 yards.

NO. 00 BUCKSHOT PELLETS—9 PELLETS

Mfg: Dionisi **Manufacturer's code:** D 12 B S00
Recoil energy in 8-lb. shotgun: 26.8 ft./lbs. **Recoil velocity in 8-lb. shotgun:** 14.7 ft./sec.

Distance in yards:	Muzzle	20	30	40	50	60	70
Velocity in fps:	1,344	1,164	1,090	1,026	968	917	870
Average pellet energy in ft-lbs:	211.84	158.92	139.50	123.47	110.03	98.62	88.82
Time of flight in seconds:	0	.0481	.0747	.1031	.1332	.1651	.1987

Type of load: Buckshot
Three-foot velocity: 1,330 ft./sec.
Hull: 2¾-inch plastic
Wad: Plastic
Shot: Lead
Buffered: No
Test barrel length: 30 inch
Pellets will pierce skin up to 433 yards.

NO. 00 BUCKSHOT PELLETS—9 PELLETS

Mfg: Federal Cartridge Co. **Manufacturer's code:** P154/F127
Recoil energy in 8-lb. shotgun: 26.8 ft./lbs. **Recoil velocity in 8-lb. shotgun:** 14.7 ft./sec.

Distance in yards:	Muzzle	20	30	40	50	60	70
Velocity in fps:	1,344	1,164	1,090	1,026	968	917	870
Average pellet energy in ft-lbs:	211.84	158.92	139.50	123.47	110.03	98.62	88.82
Time of flight in seconds:	0	.0481	.0747	.1031	.1332	.1651	.1987

Type of load: Buckshot
Three-foot velocity: 1,330 ft./sec.
Hull: 2¾-inch plastic
Wad: Plastic
Shot: Lead
Buffered: No
Test barrel length: 30 inch
Pellets will pierce skin up to 433 yards.

NO. 00 BUCKSHOT PELLETS—9 PELLETS

Mfg: Fiocchi **Manufacturer's code:** 12HV4BK
Recoil energy in 8-lb. shotgun: 26.8 ft./lbs. **Recoil velocity in 8-lb. shotgun:** 14.7 ft./sec.

Distance in yards:	Muzzle	20	30	40	50	60	70
Velocity in fps:	1,344	1,164	1,090	1,026	968	917	870
Average pellet energy in ft-lbs:	211.84	158.92	139.50	123.47	110.03	98.62	88.82
Time of flight in seconds:	0	.0481	.0747	.1031	.1332	.1651	.1987

Type of load: Buckshot
Three-foot velocity: 1,330 ft./sec.
Hull: 2¾-inch plastic
Wad: Plastic
Shot: Nickel-plated lead
Buffered: No
Test barrel length: 30 inch
Pellets will pierce skin up to 433 yards.

NO. 00 BUCKSHOT PELLETS—9 PELLETS

Mfg: PMC **Manufacturer's code:** BSH1200
Recoil energy in 8-lb. shotgun: 26.8 ft./lbs. **Recoil velocity in 8-lb. shotgun:** 14.7 ft./sec.

Distance in yards:	Muzzle	20	30	40	50	60	70
Velocity in fps:	1,344	1,164	1,090	1,026	968	917	870
Average pellet energy in ft-lbs:	211.84	158.92	139.50	123.47	110.03	98.62	88.82
Time of flight in seconds:	0	.0481	.0747	.1031	.1332	.1651	.1987

Type of load: Buckshot
Three-foot velocity: 1,330 ft./sec.
Hull: 2¾-inch plastic
Wad: Plastic
Shot: Lead
Buffered: No
Test barrel length: 30 inch
Pellets will pierce skin up to 433 yards.

NO. 00 BUCKSHOTPELLETS—9 PELLETS

Mfg: Remington Arms Co. **Manufacturer's code:** 12B
Recoil energy in 8-lb. shotgun: 26.8 ft./lbs. **Recoil velocity in 8-lb. shotgun:** 14.7 ft./sec.

Distance in yards:	Muzzle	20	30	40	50	60	70
Velocity in fps:	1,344	1,164	1,090	1,026	968	917	870
Average pellet energy in ft-lbs:	211.84	158.92	139.50	123.47	110.03	98.62	88.82
Time of flight in seconds:	0	.0481	.0747	.1031	.1332	.1651	.1987

Type of load: Buckshot
Three-foot velocity: 1,330 ft./sec.
Hull: 2¾-inch plastic
Wad: Plastic
Shot: Lead
Buffered: No
Test barrel length: 30 inch
Pellets will pierce skin up to 433 yards.

NO. 00 BUCKSHOT PELLETS—9 PELLETS

Mfg: Remington Arms Co. **Manufacturer's code:** 12N
Recoil energy in 8-lb. shotgun: 26.8 ft./lbs. **Recoil velocity in 8-lb. shotgun:** 14.7 ft./sec.

Distance in yards:	Muzzle	20	30	40	50	60	70
Velocity in fps:	1,344	1,164	1,090	1,026	968	917	870
Average pellet energy in ft-lbs:	211.84	158.92	139.50	123.47	110.03	98.62	88.82
Time of flight in seconds:	0	.0481	.0747	.1031	.1332	.1651	.1987

Type of load: Buckshot
Three-foot velocity: 1,330 ft./sec.
Hull: 2¾-inch plastic
Wad: Plastic
Shot: Nickel-plated lead
Buffered: No
Test barrel length: 30 inch
Pellets will pierce skin up to 433 yards.

NO. 00 BUCKSHOT PELLETS—9 PELLETS

Mfg: RIO **Manufacturer's code:** N/A
Recoil energy in 8-lb. shotgun: 26.8 ft./lbs. **Recoil velocity in 8-lb. shotgun:** 14.7 ft./sec.

Distance in yards:	Muzzle	20	30	40	50	60	70
Velocity in fps:	1,344	1,164	1,090	1,026	968	917	870
Average pellet energy in ft-lbs:	211.84	158.92	139.50	123.47	110.03	98.62	88.82
Time of flight in seconds:	0	.0481	.0747	.1031	.1332	.1651	.1987

Type of load: Buckshot
Three-foot velocity: 1,330 ft./sec.
Hull: 2¾-inch plastic
Wad: Plastic
Shot: Lead
Buffered: No
Test barrel length: 30 inch
Pellets will pierce skin up to 433 yards.

NO. 00 BUCKSHOT PELLETS—9 PELLETS

Mfg: Winchester **Manufacturer's code:** XB1200
Recoil energy in 8-lb. shotgun: 26.8 ft./lbs. **Recoil velocity in 8-lb. shotgun:** 14.7 ft./sec.

Distance in yards:	Muzzle	20	30	40	50	60	70
Velocity in fps:	1,344	1,164	1,090	1,026	968	917	870
Average pellet energy in ft-lbs:	211.84	158.92	139.50	123.47	110.03	98.62	88.82
Time of flight in seconds:	0	.0481	.0747	.1031	.1332	.1651	.1987

Type of load: Buckshot
Three-foot velocity: 1,330 ft./sec.
Hull: 2¾-inch plastic
Wad: Plastic
Shot: Lead
Buffered: No
Test barrel length: 30 inch
Pellets will pierce skin up to 433 yards.

NO. 0 BUCKSHOT PELLETS—9 PELLETS

Mfg: Aguila **Manufacturer's code:** N/A
Recoil energy in 8-lb. shotgun: 20.4 ft./lbs. **Recoil velocity in 8-lb. shotgun:** 12.8 ft./sec.

Distance in yards:	Muzzle	20	30	40	50	60	70
Velocity in fps:	1,1212	1,058	996	940	890	844	802
Average pellet energy in ft-lbs:	157.01	119.85	106.06	94.48	84.64	76.18	68.85
Time of flight in seconds:	0	.0531	.0823	.1134	.1462	.1808	.2173

Type of load: Buckshot
Three-foot velocity: 1,200 ft./sec.
Hull: 2¾-inch plastic
Wad: Plastic
Shot: Lead
Buffered: No
Test barrel length: 30 inch
Pellets will pierce skin up to 406 yards.

NO. 0 BUCKSHOT PELLETS—12 PELLETS

Mfg: Federal Cartridge Co. **Manufacturer's code:** F127
Recoil energy in 8-lb. shotgun: 35.7 ft./lbs. **Recoil velocity in 8-lb. shotgun:** 16.9 ft./sec.

Distance in yards:	Muzzle	20	30	40	50	60	70
Velocity in fps:	1,288	1,117	1,047	985	931	881	836
Average pellet energy in ft-lbs:	177.46	133.35	117.26	103.88	92.64	83.06	74.82
Time of flight in seconds:	0	.0502	.0779	.1075	.1388	.1719	.2069

Type of load: Buckshot
Three-foot velocity: 1,275 ft./sec.
Hull: 2¾-inch plastic
Wad: Plastic
Shot: Lead
Buffered: No
Test barrel length: 30 inch
Pellets will pierce skin up to 414 yards.

NO. 0 BUCKSHOT PELLETS—12 PELLETS

Mfg: Winchester **Manufacturer's code:** XB120
Recoil energy in 8-lb. shotgun: 35.7 ft./lbs. **Recoil velocity in 8-lb. shotgun:** 16.9 ft./sec.

Distance in yards:	Muzzle	20	30	40	50	60	70
Velocity in fps:	1,288	1,117	1,047	985	931	881	836
Average pellet energy in ft-lbs:	177.46	133.35	117.26	103.88	92.64	83.06	74.82
Time of flight in seconds:	0	.0502	.0779	.1075	.1388	.1719	.2069

Type of load: Buckshot
Three-foot velocity: 1,275 ft./sec.
Hull: 2¾-inch plastic
Wad: Plastic
Shot: Lead
Buffered: Yes
Test barrel length: 30 inch
Pellets will pierce skin up to 414 yards.

NO. 0 BUCKSHOT PELLETS—9 PELLETS
Mfg: Aguila Manufacturer's code: N/A
Recoil energy in 8-lb. shotgun: 26.8 ft./lbs. **Recoil velocity in 8-lb. shotgun:** 14.7 ft./sec.

Distance in yards:	Muzzle	20	30	40	50	60	70
Velocity in fps:	1,212	1,058	996	940	890	844	802
Average pellet energy in ft-lbs:	157.01	119.85	106.06	94.48	84.64	76.18	68.85
Time of flight in seconds:	0	.0531	.0823	.1134	.1462	.1808	.2173

Type of load: Buckshot
Three-foot velocity: 1,330 ft./sec.
Hull: 2¾-inch plastic
Wad: Plastic
Shot: Lead
Buffered: No
Test barrel length: 30 inch
Pellets will pierce skin up to 406 yards.

NO. 0 BUCKSHOT PELLETS—12 PELLETS
Mfg: Remington Arms Co. Manufacturer's code: 12B
Recoil energy in 8-lb. shotgun: 26.8 ft./lbs. **Recoil velocity in 8-lb. shotgun:** 14.7 ft./sec.

Distance in yards:	Muzzle	20	30	40	50	60	70
Velocity in fps:	1,212	1,058	996	940	890	844	802
Average pellet energy in ft-lbs:	157.01	119.85	106.06	94.48	84.64	76.18	68.85
Time of flight in seconds:	0	.0531	.0823	.1134	.1462	.1808	.2173

Type of load: Buckshot
Three-foot velocity: 1,330 ft./sec.
Hull: 2¾-inch plastic
Wad: Plastic
Shot: Lead
Buffered: No
Test barrel length: 30 inch
Pellets will pierce skin up to 406 yards.

NO. 1 BUCKSHOT PELLETS—16 PELLETS
Mfg: Aguila Manufacturer's code: N/A
Recoil energy in 8-lb. shotgun: 26.8 ft./lbs. **Recoil velocity in 8-lb. shotgun:** 14.7 ft./sec.

Distance in yards:	Muzzle	20	30	40	50	60	70
Velocity in fps:	1,345	1,149	1,071	1,003	943	889	840
Average pellet energy in ft-lbs:	159.44	116.42	101.10	88.64	79.31	69.63	62.25
Time of flight in seconds:	0	.0484	.0754	.1044	.1353	.1681	.2028

Type of load: Buckshot
Three-foot velocity: 1,330 ft./sec.
Hull: 2¾-inch plastic
Wad: Plastic
Shot: Lead
Buffered: No
Test barrel length: 30 inch
Pellets will pierce skin up to 393 yards.

NO. 1 BUCKSHOT PELLETS—20 PELLETS
Mfg: Federal Cartridge Co. Manufacturer's code: F130
Recoil energy in 8-lb. shotgun: 53.6 ft./lbs. **Recoil velocity in 8-lb. shotgun:** 20.8 ft./sec.

Distance in yards:	Muzzle	20	30	40	50	60	70
Velocity in fps:	1,085	953	898	849	804	763	726
Average pellet energy in ft-lbs:	103.72	80.10	71.14	63.54	57.02	51.37	64.43
Time of flight in seconds:	0	.0591	.0915	.1259	.1622	.2005	.2408

Type of load: Buckshot
Three-foot velocity: 1,075 ft./sec.
Hull: 2¾-inch plastic
Wad: Plastic
Shot: Lead
Buffered: No
Test barrel length: 30 inch
Pellets will pierce skin up to 365 yards.

NO. 1 BUCKSHOT PELLETS—20 PELLETS
Mfg: Winchester Manufacturer's code: X12C1B
Recoil energy in 8-lb. shotgun: 53.6 ft./lbs. **Recoil velocity in 8-lb. shotgun:** 20.8 ft./sec.

Distance in yards:	Muzzle	20	30	40	50	60	70
Velocity in fps:	1,085	953	898	849	804	763	726
Average pellet energy in ft-lbs:	103.72	80.10	71.14	63.54	57.02	51.37	64.43
Time of flight in seconds:	0	.0591	.0915	.1259	.1622	.2005	.2408

Type of load: Buckshot
Three-foot velocity: 1,075 ft./sec.
Hull: 2¾-inch plastic
Wad: Plastic
Shot: Copper-plated lead
Buffered: Yes
Test barrel length: 30 inch
Pellets will pierce skin up to 365 yards.

NO. 1 BUCKSHOT PELLETS—16 PELLETS
Mfg: Federal Cartridge Co. Manufacturer's code: P156/F130
Recoil energy in 8-lb. shotgun: 40.4 ft./lbs. **Recoil velocity in 8-lb. shotgun:** 18.0 ft./sec.

Distance in yards:	Muzzle	20	30	40	50	60	70
Velocity in fps:	1,263	1,088	1,018	956	901	851	806
Average pellet energy in ft-lbs:	140.65	104.38	91.32	80.55	71.85	63.87	57.30
Time of flight in seconds:	0	.0513	.0798	.1103	.1426	.1769	.2131

Type of load: Buckshot
Three-foot velocity: 1,250 ft./sec.
Hull: 2¾-inch plastic
Wad: Plastic
Shot: Lead
Buffered: No
Test barrel length: 30 inch
Pellets will pierce skin up to 386 yards.

NO. 1 BUCKSHOT PELLETS—16 PELLETS
Mfg: Winchester Manufacturer's code: XB121
Recoil energy in 8-lb. shotgun: 40.4 ft./lbs. **Recoil velocity in 8-lb. shotgun:** 18.0 ft./sec.

Distance in yards:	Muzzle	20	30	40	50	60	70
Velocity in fps:	1,263	1,088	1,018	956	901	851	806
Average pellet energy in ft-lbs:	140.65	104.38	91.32	80.55	71.85	63.87	57.30
Time of flight in seconds:	0	.0513	.0798	.1103	.1426	.1769	.2131

Type of load: Buckshot
Three-foot velocity: 1,250 ft./sec.
Hull: 2¾-inch plastic
Wad: Plastic
Shot: Lead
Buffered: Yes
Test barrel length: 30 inch
Pellets will pierce skin up to 386 yards.

NO. 1 BUCKSHOT PELLETS—16 PELLETS
Mfg: Aguila **Manufacturer's code:** N/A
Recoil energy in 8-lb. shotgun: 20.4 ft./lbs. **Recoil velocity in 8-lb. shotgun:** 12.8 ft./sec.

Distance in yards:	Muzzle	20	30	40	50	60	70
Velocity in fps:	1,212	1,050	985	926	874	827	784
Average pellet energy in ft-lbs:	129.51	97.21	85.43	75.63	67.36	60.30	54.22
Time of flight in seconds:	0	.0533	.0828	.1143	.1476	.1829	.2202

Type of load: Buckshot
Three-foot velocity: 1,200 ft./sec.
Hull: 2¾-inch plastic
Wad: Plastic
Shot: Lead
Buffered: No
Test barrel length: 30 inch
Pellets will pierce skin up to 380 yards.

NO. 1 BUCKSHOT PELLETS—16 PELLETS
Mfg: Remington Arms Co. **Manufacturer's code:** 12B
Recoil energy in 8-lb. shotgun: 26.8 ft./lbs. **Recoil velocity in 8-lb. shotgun:** 14.7 ft./sec.

Distance in yards:	Muzzle	20	30	40	50	60	70
Velocity in fps:	1,345	1,149	1,071	1,003	943	889	840
Average pellet energy in ft-lbs:	159.44	116.42	101.10	88.64	79.31	69.63	62.25
Time of flight in seconds:	0	.0484	.0754	.1044	.1353	.1681	.2028

Type of load: Buckshot
Three-foot velocity: 1,330 ft./sec.
Hull: 2¾-inch plastic
Wad: Plastic
Shot: Lead
Buffered: No
Test barrel length: 30 inch
Pellets will pierce skin up to 393 yards.

NO. 1 BUCKSHOT PELLETS—12 PELLETS
Mfg: RIO **Manufacturer's code:** N/A
Recoil energy in 8-lb. shotgun: 26.8 ft./lbs. **Recoil velocity in 8-lb. shotgun:** 14.7 ft./sec.

Distance in yards:	Muzzle	20	30	40	50	60	70
Velocity in fps:	1,345	1,149	1,071	1,003	943	889	840
Average pellet energy in ft-lbs:	159.44	116.42	101.10	88.64	79.31	69.63	62.25
Time of flight in seconds:	0	.0484	.0754	.1044	.1353	.1681	.2028

Type of load: Buckshot
Three-foot velocity: 1,330 ft./sec.
Hull: 2¾-inch plastic
Wad: Plastic
Shot: Lead
Buffered: No
Test barrel length: 30 inch
Pellets will pierce skin up to 393 yards.

NO. 1 BUCKSHOT PELLETS—16 PELLETS
Mfg: Sellier & Bellot **Manufacturer's code:** SBA01224/38
Recoil energy in 8-lb. shotgun: 26.8 ft./lbs. **Recoil velocity in 8-lb. shotgun:** 14.7 ft./sec.

Distance in yards:	Muzzle	20	30	40	50	60	70
Velocity in fps:	1,345	1,149	1,071	1,003	943	889	840
Average pellet energy in ft-lbs:	159.44	116.42	101.10	88.64	79.31	69.63	62.25
Time of flight in seconds:	0	.0484	.0754	.1044	.1353	.1681	.2028

Type of load: Buckshot
Three-foot velocity: 1,330 ft./sec.
Hull: 2¾-inch plastic
Wad: Plastic
Shot: Lead
Buffered: No
Test barrel length: 30 inch
Pellets will pierce skin up to 393 yards.

NO. 2 BUCKSHOT PELLETS—16 PELLETS
Mfg: RIO **Manufacturer's code:** N/A
Recoil energy in 8-lb. shotgun: 26.8 ft./lbs. **Recoil velocity in 8-lb. shotgun:** 14.7 ft./sec.

Distance in yards:	Muzzle	20	30	40	50	60	70
Velocity in fps:	1,348	1,113	1,049	977	913	857	807
Average pellet energy in ft-lbs:	116.67	82.44	70.69	61.27	53.59	47.20	41.83
Time of flight in seconds:	0	.0487	.0763	.1059	.1377	.1716	.2077

Type of load: Buckshot
Three-foot velocity: 1,330 ft./sec.
Hull: 2¾-inch plastic
Wad: Plastic
Shot: Lead
Buffered: No
Test barrel length: 30 inch
Pellets will pierce skin up to 354 yards.

NO. 3 BUCKSHOT PELLETS—21 PELLETS
Mfg: RIO **Manufacturer's code:** N/A
Recoil energy in 8-lb. shotgun: 26.8 ft./lbs. **Recoil velocity in 8-lb. shotgun:** 14.7 ft./sec.

Distance in yards:	Muzzle	20	30	40	50	60	70
Velocity in fps:	1,357	1,125	1,036	961	894	836	784
Average pellet energy in ft-lbs:	93.98	64.60	54.79	47.06	40.81	35.67	31.38
Time of flight in seconds:	0	.0487	.0765	.1066	.1390	.1737	.2108

Type of load: Buckshot
Three-foot velocity: 1,330 ft./sec.
Hull: 2¾-inch plastic
Wad: Plastic
Shot: Lead
Buffered: No
Test barrel length: 30 inch
Pellets will pierce skin up to 329 yards.

NO. 4 BUCKSHOT PELLETS—27 PELLETS
Mfg: Federal Cartridge Co. **Manufacturer's code:** H132
Recoil energy in 8-lb. shotgun: 18.0 ft./lbs. **Recoil velocity in 8-lb. shotgun:** 12.0 ft./sec.

Distance in yards:	Muzzle	20	30	40	50	60	70
Velocity in fps:	1,171	987	915	852	796	747	702
Average pellet energy in ft-lbs:	61.84	43.62	37.77	32.76	28.62	25.15	22.21
Time of flight in seconds:	0	.0560	.0876	.1216	.1580	.1970	.2384

Type of load: Buckshot
Three-foot velocity: 1,145 ft./sec.
Hull: 2¾-inch plastic
Wad: Plastic
Shot: Lead
Buffered: No
Test barrel length: 30 inch
Pellets will pierce skin up to 301 yards.

NO. 4 BUCKSHOT PELLETS—34 PELLETS
Mfg: Federal Cartridge Co. **Manufacturer's code:** P156/F130
Recoil energy in 8-lb. shotgun: 40.4 ft./lbs. **Recoil velocity in 8-lb. shotgun:** 18.0 ft./sec.

Distance in yards:	Muzzle	20	30	40	50	60	70
Velocity in fps:	1,279	1,063	980	909	847	792	743
Average pellet energy in ft-lbs:	73.86	51.00	43.37	37.30	32.37	28.30	24.88
Time of flight in seconds:	0	.0517	.0811	.1129	.1471	.1837	.2229

Type of load: Buckshot
Three-foot velocity: 1,250 ft./sec.
Hull: 2¾-inch plastic
Wad: Plastic
Shot: Lead
Buffered: No
Test barrel length: 30 inch
Pellets will pierce skin up to 310 yards.

NO. 4 BUCKSHOT PELLETS—27 PELLETS
Mfg: Federal Cartridge Co. **Manufacturer's code:** F127
Recoil energy in 8-lb. shotgun: 26.8 ft./lbs. **Recoil velocity in 8-lb. shotgun:** 14.7 ft./sec.

Distance in yards:	Muzzle	20	30	40	50	60	70
Velocity in fps:	1,362	1,121	1,029	951	884	825	772
Average pellet energy in ft-lbs:	83.76	56.69	47.81	40.85	35.26	30.69	26.89
Time of flight in seconds:	0	.0488	.0767	.1071	.1398	.1749	.2125

Type of load: Buckshot
Three-foot velocity: 1,330 ft./sec.
Hull: 2¾-inch plastic
Wad: Plastic
Shot: Nickel-plated lead
Buffered: No
Test barrel length: 30 inch
Pellets will pierce skin up to 316 yards.

NO. 4 BUCKSHOT PELLETS—27 PELLETS
Mfg: Fiocchi **Manufacturer's code:** 12HV4BK
Recoil energy in 8-lb. shotgun: 26.8 ft./lbs. **Recoil velocity in 8-lb. shotgun:** 14.7 ft./sec.

Distance in yards:	Muzzle	20	30	40	50	60	70
Velocity in fps:	1,362	1,121	1,029	951	884	825	772
Average pellet energy in ft-lbs:	83.76	56.69	47.81	40.85	35.26	30.69	26.89
Time of flight in seconds:	0	.0488	.0767	.1071	.1398	.1749	.2125

Type of load: Buckshot
Three-foot velocity: 1,330 ft./sec.
Hull: 2¾-inch plastic
Wad: Plastic
Shot: Nickel-plated lead
Buffered: No
Test barrel length: 30 inch
Pellets will pierce skin up to 316 yards.

NO. 4 BUCKSHOT PELLETS—27 PELLETS
Mfg: PMC **Manufacturer's code:** BSH124
Recoil energy in 8-lb. shotgun: 26.8 ft./lbs. **Recoil velocity in 8-lb. shotgun:** 14.7 ft./sec.

Distance in yards:	Muzzle	20	30	40	50	60	70
Velocity in fps:	1,362	1,121	1,029	951	884	825	772
Average pellet energy in ft-lbs:	83.76	56.69	47.81	40.85	35.26	30.69	26.89
Time of flight in seconds:	0	.0488	.0767	.1071	.1398	.1749	.2125

Type of load: Buckshot
Three-foot velocity: 1,330 ft./sec.
Hull: 2¾-inch plastic
Wad: Plastic
Shot: Lead
Buffered: No
Test barrel length: 30 inch
Pellets will pierce skin up to 316 yards.

NO. 4 BUCKSHOT PELLETS—27 PELLETS
Mfg: Remington Arms Co. **Manufacturer's code:** 12B
Recoil energy in 8-lb. shotgun: 26.8 ft./lbs. **Recoil velocity in 8-lb. shotgun:** 14.7 ft./sec.

Distance in yards:	Muzzle	20	30	40	50	60	70
Velocity in fps:	1,362	1,121	1,029	951	884	825	772
Average pellet energy in ft-lbs:	83.76	56.69	47.81	40.85	35.26	30.69	26.89
Time of flight in seconds:	0	.0488	.0767	.1071	.1398	.1749	.2125

Type of load: Buckshot
Three-foot velocity: 1,330 ft./sec.
Hull: 2¾-inch plastic
Wad: Plastic
Shot: Lead
Buffered: No
Test barrel length: 30 inch
Pellets will pierce skin up to 316 yards.

NO. 4 BUCKSHOT PELLETS—27 PELLETS
Mfg: Winchester **Manufacturer's code:** XB124
Recoil energy in 8-lb. shotgun: 26.8 ft./lbs. **Recoil velocity in 8-lb. shotgun:** 14.7 ft./sec.

Distance in yards:	Muzzle	20	30	40	50	60	70
Velocity in fps:	1,362	1,121	1,029	951	884	825	772
Average pellet energy in ft-lbs:	83.76	56.69	47.81	40.85	35.26	30.69	26.89
Time of flight in seconds:	0	.0488	.0767	.1071	.1398	.1749	.2125

Type of load: Buckshot
Three-foot velocity: 1,330 ft./sec.
Hull: 2¾-inch plastic
Wad: Plastic
Shot: Lead
Buffered: Yes
Test barrel length: 30 inch
Pellets will pierce skin up to 316 yards.

NO. 000 BUCKSHOT PELLETS—10 PELLETS
Mfg: Federal Cartridge Co. **Manufacturer's code:** P158/F131
Recoil energy in 8-lb. shotgun: 65.0 ft./lbs. **Recoil velocity in 8-lb. shotgun:** 22.9 ft./sec.

Distance in yards:	Muzzle	20	30	40	50	60	70
Velocity in fps:	1,231	1,089	1,029	976	928	884	844
Average pellet energy in ft-lbs:	230.70	180.46	161.35	145.09	131.12	119.00	108.40
Time of flight in seconds:	0	.0519	.0803	.1102	.1418	.1749	.2096

Type of load: Buckshot
Three-foot velocity: 1,220 ft./sec.
Hull: 3-inch plastic
Wad: Plastic
Shot: Copper-plated, hard lead
Buffered: No
Test barrel length: 30 inch
Pellets will pierce skin up to 459 yards.

NO. 000 BUCKSHOT PELLETS—10 PELLETS
Mfg: Remington Arms Co. **Manufacturer's code:** 12HB
Recoil energy in 8-lb. shotgun: 65.0 ft./lbs. **Recoil velocity in 8-lb. shotgun:** 22.9 ft./sec.

Distance in yards:	Muzzle	20	30	40	50	60	70
Velocity in fps:	1,231	1,089	1,029	976	928	884	844
Average pellet energy in ft-lbs:	230.70	180.46	161.35	145.09	131.12	119.00	108.40
Time of flight in seconds:	0	.0519	.0803	.1102	.1418	.1749	.2096

Type of load: Buckshot
Three-foot velocity: 1,220 ft./sec.
Hull: 3-inch plastic
Wad: Plastic
Shot: Lead
Buffered: No
Test barrel length: 30 inch
Pellets will pierce skin up to 459 yards.

NO. 000 BUCKSHOT PELLETS—10 PELLETS
Mfg: Winchester **Manufacturer's code:** X123C00B
Recoil energy in 8-lb. shotgun: 65.0 ft./lbs. **Recoil velocity in 8-lb. shotgun:** 22.9 ft./sec.

Distance in yards:	Muzzle	20	30	40	50	60	70
Velocity in fps:	1,231	1,089	1,029	976	928	884	844
Average pellet energy in ft-lbs:	230.70	180.46	161.35	145.09	131.12	119.00	108.40
Time of flight in seconds:	0	.0519	.0803	.1102	.1418	.1749	.2096

Type of load: Buckshot
Three-foot velocity: 1,220 ft./sec.
Hull: 3-inch plastic
Wad: Plastic
Shot: Copper-plated lead
Buffered: Yes
Test barrel length: 30 inch
Pellets will pierce skin up to 459 yards.

NO. 00 BUCKSHOT PELLETS—15 PELLETS
Mfg: Dionisi **Manufacturer's code:** D 12 B S300
Recoil energy in 8-lb. shotgun: 56.6 ft./lbs. **Recoil velocity in 8-lb. shotgun:** 22.3 ft./sec.

Distance in yards:	Muzzle	20	30	40	50	60	70
Velocity in fps:	1,221	1,070	1,008	952	902	857	815
Average pellet energy in ft-lbs:	175.01	134.34	119.16	106.39	95.51	86.13	77.99
Time of flight in seconds:	0	.0526	.0815	.1121	.1445	.1786	.2145

Type of load: Buckshot
Three-foot velocity: 1,210 ft./sec.
Hull: 3-inch plastic
Wad: Plastic
Shot: Lead
Buffered: No
Test barrel length: 30 inch
Pellets will pierce skin up to 420 yards.

NO. 00 BUCKSHOT PELLETS—15 PELLETS
Mfg: Federal Cartridge Co. **Manufacturer's code:** P158/F131
Recoil energy in 8-lb. shotgun: 57.9 ft./lbs. **Recoil velocity in 8-lb. shotgun:** 21.6 ft./sec.

Distance in yards:	Muzzle	20	30	40	50	60	70
Velocity in fps:	1,221	1,070	1,008	952	902	857	815
Average pellet energy in ft-lbs:	175.01	134.34	119.16	106.39	95.51	86.13	77.99
Time of flight in seconds:	0	.0526	.0815	.1121	.1445	.1786	.2145

Type of load: Buckshot
Three-foot velocity: 1,210 ft./sec.
Hull: 3-inch plastic
Wad: Plastic
Shot: Copper-plated, hard lead
Buffered: No
Test barrel length: 30 inch
Pellets will pierce skin up to 420 yards.

NO. 00 BUCKSHOT PELLETS—15 PELLETS
Mfg: Remington Arms Co. **Manufacturer's code:** 12HN
Recoil energy in 8-lb. shotgun: 57.9 ft./lbs. **Recoil velocity in 8-lb. shotgun:** 21.6 ft./sec.

Distance in yards:	Muzzle	20	30	40	50	60	70
Velocity in fps:	1,221	1,070	1,008	952	902	857	815
Average pellet energy in ft-lbs:	175.01	134.34	119.16	106.39	95.51	86.13	77.99
Time of flight in seconds:	0	.0526	.0815	.1121	.1445	.1786	.2145

Type of load: Buckshot
Three-foot velocity: 1,210 ft./sec.
Hull: 3-inch plastic
Wad: Plastic
Shot: Nickle-plated lead
Buffered: No
Test barrel length: 30 inch
Pellets will pierce skin up to 420 yards.

NO. 00 BUCKSHOT PELLETS—15 PELLETS
Mfg: Winchester **Manufacturer's code:** X12XC3B5
Recoil energy in 8-lb. shotgun: 57.9 ft./lbs. **Recoil velocity in 8-lb. shotgun:** 21.6 ft./sec.

Distance in yards:	Muzzle	20	30	40	50	60	70
Velocity in fps:	1,221	1,070	1,008	952	902	857	815
Average pellet energy in ft-lbs:	175.01	134.34	119.16	106.39	95.51	86.13	77.99
Time of flight in seconds:	0	.0526	.0815	.1121	.1445	.1786	.2145

Type of load: Buckshot
Three-foot velocity: 1,210 ft./sec.
Hull: 3-inch plastic
Wad: Plastic
Shot: Copper-plated lead
Buffered: Yes
Test barrel length: 30 inch
Pellets will pierce skin up to 420 yards.

NO. 00 BUCKSHOT PELLETS—15 PELLETS
Mfg: Remington Arms Co. **Manufacturer's code:** 12HB
Recoil energy in 8-lb. shotgun: 65.0 ft./lbs. **Recoil velocity in 8-lb. shotgun:** 22.9 ft./sec.

Distance in yards:	Muzzle	20	30	40	50	60	70
Velocity in fps:	1,232	1,078	1,015	959	908	862	820
Average pellet energy in ft-lbs:	177.94	136.30	120.81	108.78	96.69	87.16	78.89
Time of flight in seconds:	0	.0522	.0809	.1113	.1435	.1774	.2131

Type of load: Buckshot
Three-foot velocity: 1,220 ft./sec.
Hull: 3-inch plastic
Wad: Plastic
Shot: Lead
Buffered: No
Test barrel length: 30 inch
Pellets will pierce skin up to 421 yards.

NO. 1 BUCKSHOT PELLETS—24 PELLETS
Mfg: Federal Cartridge Co. **Manufacturer's code:** P158
Recoil energy in 8-lb. shotgun: 56.2 ft./lbs. **Recoil velocity in 8-lb. shotgun:** 21.3 ft./sec.

Distance in yards:	Muzzle	20	30	40	50	60	70
Velocity in fps:	1,049	925	873	826	784	744	708
Average pellet energy in ft-lbs:	97.01	75.49	67.24	60.20	54.13	48.85	44.22
Time of flight in seconds:	0	.0610	.0944	.1297	.1670	.2063	.2467

Type of load: Buckshot
Three-foot velocity: 1,040 ft./sec.
Hull: 3-inch plastic
Wad: Plastic
Shot: Copper-plated, hard lead
Buffered: No
Test barrel length: 30 inch
Pellets will pierce skin up to 360 yards.

NO. 1 BUCKSHOT PELLETS—24 PELLETS
Mfg: Winchester **Manufacturer's code:** XB1231
Recoil energy in 8-lb. shotgun: 56.2 ft./lbs. **Recoil velocity in 8-lb. shotgun:** 21.3 ft./sec.

Distance in yards:	Muzzle	20	30	40	50	60	70
Velocity in fps:	1,049	925	873	826	784	744	708
Average pellet energy in ft-lbs:	97.01	75.49	67.24	60.20	54.13	48.85	44.22
Time of flight in seconds:	0	.0610	.0944	.1297	.1670	.2063	.2467

Type of load: Buckshot
Three-foot velocity: 1,040 ft./sec.
Hull: 3-inch plastic
Wad: Plastic
Shot: Lead
Buffered: Yes
Test barrel length: 30 inch
Pellets will pierce skin up to 360 yards.

NO. 4 BUCKSHOT PELLETS—41 PELLETS
Mfg: Federal Cartridge Co. **Manufacturer's code:** P158/F131
Recoil energy in 8-lb. shotgun: 57.9 ft./lbs. **Recoil velocity in 8-lb. shotgun:** 21.6 ft./sec.

Distance in yards:	Muzzle	20	30	40	50	60	70
Velocity in fps:	1,238	1,034	956	888	828	775	727
Average pellet energy in ft-lbs:	69.15	48.27	41.22	35.56	30.94	27.10	23.87
Time of flight in seconds:	0	.0532	.0834	.1160	.1510	.1885	.2285

Type of load: Buckshot
Three-foot velocity: 1,210 ft./sec.
Hull: 3-inch plastic
Wad: Plastic
Shot: Copper-plated, hard lead
Buffered: No
Test barrel length: 30 inch
Pellets will pierce skin up to 307 yards.

NO. 4 BUCKSHOT PELLETS—41 PELLETS
Mfg: Winchester **Manufacturer's code:** X12XCMB5
Recoil energy in 8-lb. shotgun: 57.9 ft./lbs. **Recoil velocity in 8-lb. shotgun:** 21.6 ft./sec.

Distance in yards:	Muzzle	20	30	40	50	60	70
Velocity in fps:	1,238	1,034	956	888	828	775	727
Average pellet energy in ft-lbs:	69.15	48.27	41.22	35.56	30.94	27.10	23.87
Time of flight in seconds:	0	.0532	.0834	.1160	.1510	.1885	.2285

Type of load: Buckshot
Three-foot velocity: 1,210 ft./sec.
Hull: 3-inch plastic
Wad: Plastic
Shot: Copper-plated lead
Buffered: Yes
Test barrel length: 30 inch
Pellets will pierce skin up to 307 yards.

NO. 4 BUCKSHOT PELLETS—41 PELLETS
Mfg: Remington Arms Co. **Manufacturer's code:** 12HB
Recoil energy in 8-lb. shotgun: 65.0 ft./lbs. **Recoil velocity in 8-lb. shotgun:** 22.9 ft./sec.

Distance in yards:	Muzzle	20	30	40	50	60	70
Velocity in fps:	1,248	1,041	962	893	833	779	731
Average pellet energy in ft-lbs:	70.31	48.95	41.75	35.99	31.30	27.40	24.12
Time of flight in seconds:	0	.0528	.0828	.1152	.1500	.1873	.2270

Type of load: Buckshot
Three-foot velocity: 1,220 ft./sec.
Hull: 3-inch plastic
Wad: Plastic
Shot: Lead
Buffered: No
Test barrel length: 30 inch
Pellets will pierce skin up to 307 yards.

NO. 00 BUCKSHOT PELLETS—18 PELLETS
Mfg: Federal Cartridge Co. **Manufacturer's code:** P135
Recoil energy in 8-lb. shotgun: 65.0 ft./lbs. **Recoil velocity in 8-lb. shotgun:** 22.9 ft./sec.

Distance in yards:	Muzzle	20	30	40	50	60	70
Velocity in fps:	1,109	983	930	882	839	799	762
Average pellet energy in ft-lbs:	144.39	113.45	101.54	91.34	82.52	74.84	68.08
Time of flight in seconds:	0	.0575	.0889	.1220	.1569	.1936	.2320

Type of load: Buckshot
Three-foot velocity: 1,100 ft./sec.
Hull: 3½-inch plastic
Wad: Plastic
Shot: Copper-plated, hard lead
Buffered: No
Test barrel length: 30 inch
Pellets will pierce skin up to 405 yards.

NO. 00 BUCKSHOT PELLETS—18 PELLETS
Mfg: Remington Arms Co. **Manufacturer's code:** 1235B
Recoil energy in 8-lb. shotgun: 68.9 ft./lbs. **Recoil velocity in 8-lb. shotgun:** 23.5 ft./sec.

Distance in yards:	Muzzle	20	30	40	50	60	70
Velocity in fps:	1,135	1,003	948	899	854	812	774
Average pellet energy in ft-lbs:	151.09	118.10	105.49	94.73	85.46	77.41	70.35
Time of flight in seconds:	0	.0563	.0871	.1196	.1539	.1899	.2277

Type of load: Buckshot
Three-foot velocity: 1,125 ft./sec.
Hull: 3½-inch plastic
Wad: Plastic
Shot: Lead
Buffered: No
Test barrel length: 30 inch
Pellets will pierce skin up to 409 yards.

NO. 00 BUCKSHOT PELLETS—18 PELLETS
Mfg: Winchester **Manufacturer's code:** XB12L00
Recoil energy in 8-lb. shotgun: 81.5 ft./lbs. **Recoil velocity in 8-lb. shotgun:** 25.6 ft./sec.

Distance in yards:	Muzzle	20	30	40	50	60	70
Velocity in fps:	1,211	1,062	1,001	946	897	852	811
Average pellet energy in ft-lbs:	172.10	132.39	117.53	105.01	94.32	85.10	77.10
Time of flight in seconds:	0	.0530	.0821	.1130	.1455	.1799	.2160

Type of load: Buckshot
Three-foot velocity: 1,200 ft./sec.
Hull: 3½-inch plastic
Wad: Plastic
Shot: Lead
Buffered: Yes
Test barrel length: 30 inch
Pellets will pierce skin up to 418 yards.

NO. 1 BUCKSHOT PELLETS—24 PELLETS
Mfg: Federal Cartridge Co. **Manufacturer's code:** P135
Recoil energy in 8-lb. shotgun: 65.0 ft./lbs. **Recoil velocity in 8-lb. shotgun:** 22.9 ft./sec.

Distance in yards:	Muzzle	20	30	40	50	60	70
Velocity in fps:	1,110	973	916	865	819	777	738
Average pellet energy in ft-lbs:	108.64	83.44	73.96	65.94	59.08	53.16	48.00
Time of flight in seconds:	0	.0578	.0896	.1234	.1590	.1966	.2363

Type of load: Buckshot
Three-foot velocity: 1,100 ft./sec.
Hull: 3½-inch plastic
Wad: Plastic
Shot: Copper-plated, hard lead
Buffered: No
Test barrel length: 30 inch
Pellets will pierce skin up to 369 yards.

NO. 4 BUCKSHOT PELLETS—54 PELLETS
Mfg: Winchester **Manufacturer's code:** XB12L4
Recoil energy in 8-lb. shotgun: 72.9 ft./lbs. **Recoil velocity in 8-lb. shotgun:** 24.2 ft./sec.

Distance in yards:	Muzzle	20	30	40	50	60	70
Velocity in fps:	1,176	991	918	855	799	749	704
Average pellet energy in ft-lbs:	62.39	44.29	38.04	32.79	28.80	25.30	22.34
Time of flight in seconds:	0	.0558	.0873	.1212	.1575	.1963	.2376

Type of load: Buckshot
Three-foot velocity: 1,150 ft./sec.
Hull: 3½-inch plastic
Wad: Plastic
Shot: Lead
Buffered: Yes
Test barrel length: 30 inch
Pellets will pierce skin up to 301 yards.

NO. 1 BUCKSHOT PELLETS—9 PELLETS

Mfg: Aguila **Manufacturer's code:** N/A
Recoil energy in 8-lb. shotgun: 20.4 ft./lbs. **Recoil velocity in 8-lb. shotgun:** 12.8 ft./sec.

Distance in yards:	Muzzle	20	30	40	50	60	70
Velocity in fps:	1,212	1,050	985	926	874	827	784
Average pellet energy in ft-lbs:	129.51	97.21	85.43	75.63	67.36	60.30	54.22
Time of flight in seconds:	0	.0533	.0828	.1143	.1476	.1829	.2202

Type of load: Buckshot
Three-foot velocity: 1,200 ft./sec.
Hull: 2¾-inch plastic
Wad: Plastic
Shot: Lead
Buffered: No
Test barrel length: 28 inch
Pellets will pierce skin up to 380 yards.

NO. 1 BUCKSHOT PELLETS—9 PELLETS

Mfg: RIO **Manufacturer's code:** N/A
Recoil energy in 8-lb. shotgun: 21.2 ft./lbs. **Recoil velocity in 8-lb. shotgun:** 13.0 ft./sec.

Distance in yards:	Muzzle	20	30	40	50	60	70
Velocity in fps:	1,345	1,149	1,071	1,003	943	889	840
Average pellet energy in ft-lbs:	159.44	116.42	101.10	88.64	79.31	69.63	62.25
Time of flight in seconds:	0	.0484	.0754	.1044	.1353	.1681	.2028

Type of load: Buckshot
Three-foot velocity: 1,330 ft./sec.
Hull: 2¾-inch plastic
Wad: Plastic
Shot: Lead
Buffered: No
Test barrel length: 28 inch
Pellets will pierce skin up to 393 yards.

NO. 1 BUCKSHOT PELLETS—12 PELLETS

Mfg: Federal Cartridge Co. **Manufacturer's code:** F164
Recoil energy in 8-lb. shotgun: 21.3 ft./lbs. **Recoil velocity in 8-lb. shotgun:** 13.1 ft./sec.

Distance in yards:	Muzzle	20	30	40	50	60	70
Velocity in fps:	1,233	1,065	998	938	885	837	793
Average pellet energy in ft-lbs:	133.91	100.04	87.77	77.59	69.02	31.72	55.45
Time of flight in seconds:	0	.0525	.0816	.1126	.1456	.1804	.2173

Type of load: Buckshot
Three-foot velocity: 1,220 ft./sec.
Hull: 2¾-inch plastic
Wad: Plastic
Shot: Lead
Buffered: No
Test barrel length: 28 inch
Pellets will pierce skin up to 383 yards.

NO. 1 BUCKSHOT PELLETS—12 PELLETS

Mfg: Winchester **Manufacturer's code:** XB161
Recoil energy in 8-lb. shotgun: 21.3 ft./lbs. **Recoil velocity in 8-lb. shotgun:** 13.1 ft./sec.

Distance in yards:	Muzzle	20	30	40	50	60	70
Velocity in fps:	1,233	1,065	998	938	885	837	793
Average pellet energy in ft-lbs:	133.91	100.04	87.77	77.59	69.02	31.72	55.45
Time of flight in seconds:	0	.0525	.0816	.1126	.1456	.1804	.2173

Type of load: Buckshot
Three-foot velocity: 1,220 ft./sec.
Hull: 2¾-inch plastic
Wad: Plastic
Shot: Lead
Buffered: No
Test barrel length: 28 inch
Pellets will pierce skin up to 383 yards.

NO. 1 BUCKSHOT PELLETS—12 PELLETS

Mfg: Aguila **Manufacturer's code:** N/A
Recoil energy in 8-lb. shotgun: 22.7 ft./lbs. **Recoil velocity in 8-lb. shotgun:** 13.5 ft./sec.

Distance in yards:	Muzzle	20	30	40	50	60	70
Velocity in fps:	1,263	1,088	1,018	956	901	851	806
Average pellet energy in ft-lbs:	140.65	104.38	91.32	80.55	71.85	63.87	57.30
Time of flight in seconds:	0	.0513	.0798	.1103	.1426	.1769	.2131

Type of load: Buckshot
Three-foot velocity: 1,250 ft./sec.
Hull: 2¾-inch plastic
Wad: Plastic
Shot: Lead
Buffered: No
Test barrel length: 28 inch
Pellets will pierce skin up to 386 yards.

NO. 2 BUCKSHOT PELLETS—16 PELLETS

Mfg: Aguila **Manufacturer's code:** N/A
Recoil energy in 8-lb. shotgun: 20.4 ft./lbs. **Recoil velocity in 8-lb. shotgun:** 12.8 ft./sec.

Distance in yards:	Muzzle	20	30	40	50	60	70
Velocity in fps:	1,214	1,036	966	904	849	799	754
Average pellet energy in ft-lbs:	94.75	69.02	59.92	52.47	46.26	41.03	36.56
Time of flight in seconds:	0	.0537	.0837	.1158	.1501	.1865	.2252

Type of load: Buckshot
Three-foot velocity: 1,200 ft./sec.
Hull: 2¾-inch plastic
Wad: Plastic
Shot: Lead
Buffered: No
Test barrel length: 28 inch
Pellets will pierce skin up to 343 yards.

NO. 2 BUCKSHOT PELLETS—12 PELLETS

Mfg: RIO **Manufacturer's code:** N/A
Recoil energy in 8-lb. shotgun: 21.2 ft./lbs. **Recoil velocity in 8-lb. shotgun:** 13.0 ft./sec.

Distance in yards:	Muzzle	20	30	40	50	60	70
Velocity in fps:	1,348	1,113	1,049	977	913	857	807
Average pellet energy in ft-lbs:	116.67	82.44	70.69	61.27	53.59	47.20	41.83
Time of flight in seconds:	0	.0487	.0763	.1059	.1377	.1716	.2077

Type of load: Buckshot
Three-foot velocity: 1,330 ft./sec.
Hull: 2¾-inch plastic
Wad: Plastic
Shot: Lead
Buffered: No
Test barrel length: 28 inch
Pellets will pierce skin up to 354 yards.

NO. 3 BUCKSHOT PELLETS—16 PELLETS

Mfg: RIO **Manufacturer's code:** N/A
Recoil energy in 8-lb. shotgun: 21.2 ft./lbs. **Recoil velocity in 8-lb. shotgun:** 13.0 ft./sec.

Distance in yards:	Muzzle	20	30	40	50	60	70
Velocity in fps:	1,357	1,125	1,036	961	894	836	784
Average pellet energy in ft-lbs:	93.98	64.60	54.79	47.06	40.81	35.67	31.38
Time of flight in seconds:	0	.0487	.0765	.1066	.1390	.1737	.2108

Type of load: Buckshot
Three-foot velocity: 1,330 ft./sec.
Hull: 2¾-inch plastic
Wad: Plastic
Shot: Lead
Buffered: No
Test barrel length: 28 inch
Pellets will pierce skin up to 329 yards.

Although the quarry are clay targets, this lady shooter and her loader, shooting instructor Keith Lupton, are simulating the shooting of driven game using two shotguns.

NO. 1 BUCKSHOT PELLETS—9 PELLETS
Mfg: RIO **Manufacturer's code:** N/A
Recoil energy in 8-lb. shotgun: 21.2 ft./lbs. **Recoil velocity in 8-lb. shotgun:** 13.0 ft./sec.

Distance in yards:	Muzzle	20	30	40	50	60	70
Velocity in fps:	1,345	1,149	1,071	1,003	943	889	840
Average pellet energy in ft-lbs:	159.44	116.42	101.10	88.64	79.31	69.63	62.25
Time of flight in seconds:	0	.0484	.0754	.1044	.1353	.1681	.2028

Type of load: Buckshot
Three-foot velocity: 1,330 ft./sec.
Hull: 2¾-inch plastic
Wad: Plastic
Shot: Lead
Buffered: No
Test barrel length: 26 inch
Pellets will pierce skin up to 393 yards.

NO. 2 BUCKSHOT PELLETS—12 PELLETS
Mfg: Aguila **Manufacturer's code:** N/A
Recoil energy in 8-lb. shotgun: 11.0 ft./lbs. **Recoil velocity in 8-lb. shotgun:** 9.4 ft./sec.

Distance in yards:	Muzzle	20	30	40	50	60	70
Velocity in fps:	1,163	999	933	875	823	776	733
Average pellet energy in ft-lbs:	86.94	64.13	55.94	49.16	43.48	38.66	34.53
Time of flight in seconds:	0	.0558	.0869	.1201	.1555	.1931	.2329

Type of load: Buckshot
Three-foot velocity: 1,150 ft./sec.
Hull: 2¾-inch plastic
Wad: Plastic
Shot: Lead
Buffered: No
Test barrel length: 26 inch
Pellets will pierce skin up to 338 yards.

NO. 2 BUCKSHOT PELLETS—12 PELLETS
Mfg: Aguila **Manufacturer's code:** N/A
Recoil energy in 8-lb. shotgun: 16.8 ft./lbs. **Recoil velocity in 8-lb. shotgun:** 11.6 ft./sec.

Distance in yards:	Muzzle	20	30	40	50	60	70
Velocity in fps:	1,235	1,051	979	915	859	808	763
Average pellet energy in ft-lbs:	97.97	71.01	61.53	53.80	47.38	41.98	37.37
Time of flight in seconds:	0	.0528	.0824	.1141	.1480	.1840	.2222

Type of load: Buckshot
Three-foot velocity: 1,220 ft./sec.
Hull: 2¾-inch plastic
Wad: Plastic
Shot: Lead
Buffered: No
Test barrel length: 26 inch
Pellets will pierce skin up to 345 yards.

NO. 2 BUCKSHOT PELLETS—12 PELLETS
Mfg: RIO **Manufacturer's code:** N/A
Recoil energy in 8-lb. shotgun: 21.2 ft./lbs. **Recoil velocity in 8-lb. shotgun:** 13.0 ft./sec.

Distance in yards:	Muzzle	20	30	40	50	60	70
Velocity in fps:	1,348	1,113	1,049	977	913	857	807
Average pellet energy in ft-lbs:	116.67	82.44	70.69	61.27	53.59	47.20	41.83
Time of flight in seconds:	0	.0487	.0763	.1059	.1377	.1716	.2077

Type of load: Buckshot
Three-foot velocity: 1,330 ft./sec.
Hull: 2¾-inch plastic
Wad: Plastic
Shot: Lead
Buffered: No
Test barrel length: 26 inch
Pellets will pierce skin up to 354 yards.

NO. 3 BUCKSHOT PELLETS—16 PELLETS
Mfg: Aguila **Manufacturer's code:** N/A
Recoil energy in 8-lb. shotgun: 11.0 ft./lbs. **Recoil velocity in 8-lb. shotgun:** 9.4 ft./sec.

Distance in yards:	Muzzle	20	30	40	50	60	70
Velocity in fps:	1,172	994	924	862	807	758	714
Average pellet energy in ft-lbs:	70.01	50.39	43.51	37.90	33.25	29.34	26.01
Time of flight in seconds:	0	.0558	.0871	.1208	.1567	.1951	.2358

Type of load: Buckshot
Three-foot velocity: 1,150 ft./sec.
Hull: 2¾-inch plastic
Wad: Plastic
Shot: Lead
Buffered: No
Test barrel length: 26 inch
Pellets will pierce skin up to 313 yards.

NO. 3 BUCKSHOT PELLETS—20 PELLETS
Mfg: Federal Cartridge Co. **Manufacturer's code:** F203
Recoil energy in 8-lb. shotgun: 20.4 ft./lbs. **Recoil velocity in 8-lb. shotgun:** 12.8 ft./sec.

Distance in yards:	Muzzle	20	30	40	50	60	70
Velocity in fps:	1,223	1,031	955	890	832	781	734
Average pellet energy in ft-lbs:	76.30	54.18	46.56	40.41	35.34	31.10	27.51
Time of flight in seconds:	0	.0536	.0839	.1164	.1513	.1885	.2282

Type of load: Buckshot
Three-foot velocity: 1,200 ft./sec.
Hull: 2¾-inch plastic
Wad: Plastic
Shot: Lead
Buffered: No
Test barrel length: 26 inch
Pellets will pierce skin up to 318 yards.

NO. 3 BUCKSHOT PELLETS—20 PELLETS
Mfg: Remington Arms Co. **Manufacturer's code:** 20B
Recoil energy in 8-lb. shotgun: 20.4 ft./lbs. **Recoil velocity in 8-lb. shotgun:** 12.8 ft./sec.

Distance in yards:	Muzzle	20	30	40	50	60	70
Velocity in fps:	1,223	1,031	955	890	832	781	734
Average pellet energy in ft-lbs:	76.30	54.18	46.56	40.41	35.34	31.10	27.51
Time of flight in seconds:	0	.0536	.0839	.1164	.1513	.1885	.2282

Type of load: Buckshot
Three-foot velocity: 1,200 ft./sec.
Hull: 2¾-inch plastic
Wad: Plastic
Shot: Lead
Buffered: No
Test barrel length: 26 inch
Pellets will pierce skin up to 318 yards.

NO. 3 BUCKSHOT PELLETS—20 PELLETS
Mfg: Remington Arms Co. **Manufacturer's code:** 20N3
Recoil energy in 8-lb. shotgun: 20.4 ft./lbs. **Recoil velocity in 8-lb. shotgun:** 12.8 ft./sec.

Distance in yards:	Muzzle	20	30	40	50	60	70
Velocity in fps:	1,223	1,031	955	890	832	781	734
Average pellet energy in ft-lbs:	76.30	54.18	46.56	40.41	35.34	31.10	27.51
Time of flight in seconds:	0	.0536	.0839	.1164	.1513	.1885	.2282

Type of load: Buckshot
Three-foot velocity: 1,200 ft./sec.
Hull: 2¾-inch plastic
Wad: Plastic
Shot: Nickel-plated lead
Buffered: No
Test barrel length: 26 inch
Pellets will pierce skin up to 318 yards.

NO. 3 BUCKSHOT PELLETS—20 PELLETS
Mfg: Winchester **Manufacturer's code:** XB203
Recoil energy in 8-lb. shotgun: 20.4 ft./lbs. **Recoil velocity in 8-lb. shotgun:** 12.8 ft./sec.

Distance in yards:	Muzzle	20	30	40	50	60	70
Velocity in fps:	1,223	1,031	955	890	832	781	734
Average pellet energy in ft-lbs:	76.30	54.18	46.56	40.41	35.34	31.10	27.51
Time of flight in seconds:	0	.0536	.0839	.1164	.1513	.1885	.2282

Type of load: Buckshot
Three-foot velocity: 1,200 ft./sec.
Hull: 2¾-inch plastic
Wad: Plastic
Shot: Lead
Buffered: Yes
Test barrel length: 26 inch
Pellets will pierce skin up to 318 yards.

20 Gauge Buckshot—3 inch

NO. 2 BUCKSHOT PELLETS—18 PELLETS
Mfg: Federal Cartridge Co. **Manufacturer's code:** F207
Recoil energy in 8-lb. shotgun: 25.2 ft./lbs. **Recoil velocity in 8-lb. shotgun:** 14.2 ft./sec.

Distance in yards:	Muzzle	20	30	40	50	60	70
Velocity in fps:	1,214	1,036	966	904	849	799	754
Average pellet energy in ft-lbs:	94.75	69.02	59.92	52.47	46.26	41.03	36.56
Time of flight in seconds:	0	.0537	.0837	.1158	.1501	.1865	.2252

Type of load: Buckshot
Three-foot velocity: 1,200 ft./sec.
Hull: 3-inch plastic
Wad: Plastic
Shot: Lead
Buffered: No
Test barrel length: 30 inch
Pellets will pierce skin up to 343 yards.

NO. 3 BUCKSHOT PELLETS—24 PELLETS
Mfg: Winchester **Manufacturer's code:** X203C3B
Recoil energy in 8-lb. shotgun: 11.0 ft./lbs. **Recoil velocity in 8-lb. shotgun:** 9.4 ft./sec.

Distance in yards:	Muzzle	20	30	40	50	60	70
Velocity in fps:	1,172	994	924	862	807	758	714
Average pellet energy in ft-lbs:	70.01	50.39	43.51	37.90	33.25	29.34	26.01
Time of flight in seconds:	0	.0558	.0871	.1208	.1567	.1951	.2358

Type of load: Buckshot
Three-foot velocity: 1,150 ft./sec.
Hull: 3-inch plastic
Wad: Plastic
Shot: Copper-plated lead
Buffered: Yes
Test barrel length: 30 inch
Pellets will pierce skin up to 313 yards.

NO. 3 BUCKSHOT PELLETS—9 PELLETS

Mfg: RIO **Manufacturer's code:** N/A
Recoil energy in 8-lb. shotgun: 21.2 ft./lbs. **Recoil velocity in 8-lb. shotgun:** 13.0 ft./sec.

Distance in yards:	Muzzle	20	30	40	50	60	70
Velocity in fps:	1,357	1,125	1,036	961	894	836	784
Average pellet energy in ft-lbs:	93.98	64.60	54.79	47.06	40.81	35.67	31.38
Time of flight in seconds:	0	.0487	.0765	.1066	.1390	.1737	.2108

Type of load: Buckshot
Three-foot velocity: 1,330 ft./sec.
Hull: 2½-inch plastic
Wad: Plastic
Shot: Lead
Buffered: No
Test barrel length: 26 inch
Pellets will pierce skin up to 329 yards.

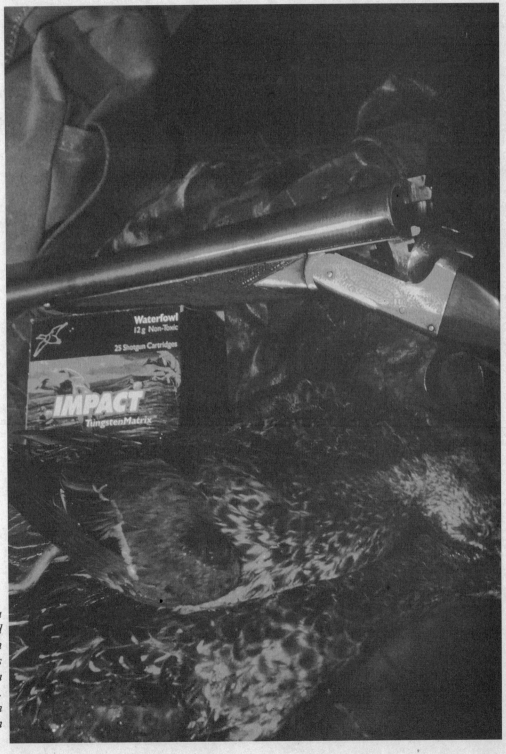

Although generally thought to be a weak load suitable for only clays and quail, these teal were easily taken with one-ounce loads of Kent's Impact tungsten/polymer shot in a 100-year-old William Evans shotgun. All of the ducks were shot at less than 25 yards, making heavy magnum loads unnecessary.

NO. 00 BUCKSHOT PELLETS—4 PELLETS
Mfg: Aguila **Manufacturer's code:** N/A
Recoil energy in 8-lb. shotgun: 4.0 ft./lbs. **Recoil velocity in 8-lb. shotgun:** 5.7 ft./sec.

Distance in yards:	Muzzle	20	30	40	50	60	70
Velocity in fps:	1,211	1,062	1,001	946	897	852	811
Average pellet energy in ft-lbs:	172.10	132.39	117.53	105.01	94.32	85.10	77.10
Time of flight in seconds:	0	.0530	.0821	.1130	.1455	.1799	.2160

Type of load: Buckshot
Three-foot velocity: 1,200 ft./sec.
Hull: 2½-inch plastic
Wad: Plastic
Shot: Lead
Buffered: No
Test barrel length: 16 inch
Pellets will pierce skin up to 418 yards.

Although this speeding teal looks small, it was only 25 yards distant and was folded a moment later with a light load of tungsten/polymer shot.

U.S. STANDARD TO METRIC CONVERSION

yards	x	0.9144	=	meters
grains	x	0.0648	=	grams
feet	x	0.3048	=	meters
ft-lbs	x	1.3558	=	joules
inches	x	25.4	=	mm
inches	x	2.54	=	cm

Yards		Meters	Feet		Meters	Ft-lbs		Joules	Inches		cm	Ft/Sec Recoil Velocity		M/Sec Recoil Velocity
1	=	0.91	950	=	289.6	0.2	=	0.27	20	=	50.8	8	=	2.44
10	=	9.1	975	=	297.2	0.5	=	0.68	21	=	53.34	9	=	2.74
15	=	13.7	1000	=	304.8	1	=	1.36	22	=	55.88	10	=	3.05
20	=	18.3	1025	=	312.4	10	=	13.6	23	=	58.42	11	=	3.35
25	=	22.9	1050	=	320.0	50	=	67.8	24	=	60.96	12	=	3.66
30	=	27.4	1075	=	327.7	75	=	101.7	25	=	63.5	13	=	3.96
35	=	32.0	1100	=	335.3	100	=	136	26	=	66.04	14	=	4.27
40	=	36.6	1125	=	342.9	125	=	169	27	=	68.58	15	=	4.57
50	=	45.7	1150	=	350.5	150	=	203	28	=	71.12	16	=	4.88
60	=	54.9	1175	=	358.1	175	=	237	29	=	73.66	17	=	5.18
70	=	64.0	1200	=	365.8	200	=	271	30	=	76.2	18	=	5.49
100	=	91.4	1225	=	373.4	250	=	339	31	=	78.74	19	=	5.79
125	=	114.3	1250	=	381.0	500	=	678	32	=	81.28	20	=	6.10
150	=	137.2	1275	=	388.6	1000	=	1356				21	=	6.40
200	=	182.9	1300	=	396.2	1250	=	1695				22	=	6.71
225	=	205.7	1325	=	403.9	1500	=	2034				23	=	7.01
250	=	228.6	1350	=	411.5	1750	=	2373				24	=	7.32
275	=	251.5	1375	=	419.1	2000	=	2712						
300	=	274.3	1400	=	426.7	2250	=	3051						
325	=	297.2	1425	=	434.3	2500	=	3389						
350	=	320.0	1450	=	442.0									
400	=	365.8	1475	=	449.6									
425	=	388.6	1500	=	457.2									
450	=	411.5												
475	=	434.3												
500	=	457.2												

WEIGHT, HULL, GAUGE

Shot Weight			Unfired hull length			Gauge	diameter inches	diameter mm
metric	USA/UK		metric	USA/UK		10	0.775	19.7
grams	oz		mm	inch		12	0.729	18.5
14.17	1/2		89	3 1/2		16	0.665	16.9
21.26	3/4		76	3		20	0.615	15.6
24.8	7/8		70	2 3/4		28	0.550	14.0
28.3	1		65	2 1/2		67*	0.410	10.4
31.9	1 1/8		60	2			always referred to as .410 bore	
36.0	1 1/4							
39.0	1 3/8							
42.5	1 1/2							
46.1	1 5/8							
49.6	1 3/4							
53.1	1 7/8							
56.7	2							
63.8	2 1/4							

U.S. COMMON SHOT WEIGHTS, SIZES AND AVERAGE COUNTS FOR LEAD SHOT

ounces	1/2	11/16	3/4	7/8	1	1 1/8	1 1/4	1 3/8	1 1/2	1 5/8	1 3/4	1 7/8	2	2 1/4
grams	14.17	19.49	21.25	24.80	28.35	31.89	35.44	38.98	42.52	46.06	49.61	53.15	56.70	63.78
Shot size	No. pellets	No. pellets	No. pellets	No. pellets	No. pellets	No. pellets	No. pellets	No. pellets	No. pellets	No. pellets	No. pellets	No. pellets	No. pellets	No. pellets
9	292	402	439	512	585	658	731	804	877	951	1024	1097	1170	1316
8.5	249	342	373	435	497	559	621	683	745	808	870	932	994	1118
8	205	282	307	359	410	461	512	564	615	666	716	769	820	922
7.5	175	241	262	306	350	394	437	481	525	569	604	656	700	787
7	150	-	224	262	299	336	374	411	449	486	523	561	598	-
6	112	155	169	197	225	253	281	309	337	366	390	422	450	506
5	85	117	127	149	170	191	212	234	255	276	301	319	340	382
4	67	93	101	118	135	152	169	186	202	219	238	253	270	304
3	55	-	82	96	109	123	136	150	164	177	191	204	218	-
2	43	60	65	76	87	98	109	120	130	141	154	163	174	196
BB	25	34	37	44	50	56	62	69	75	81	128	94	100	112

PATTERN DENSITY

PERCENTAGE OF TOTAL PELLETS IN 30-INCH CIRCLE
RANGE IN YARDS

USA	UK	Constriction	20	25	30	35	40	45	50	55	60 yards
True Cylinder	True Cylinder	.000"	80%	69%	60%	49%	40%	33%	27%	72%	18%
Skeet	Improved Cylinder	.005"	92%	82%	72%	60%	50%	41%	33%	27%	22%
Improved Cylinder	1/4	.011"	100%	87%	77%	65%	55%	46%	38%	30%	25%
Modified	1/2	.020"	100%	94%	83%	71%	60%	50%	41%	33%	27%
Improved Modified	3/4	.027"	100%	100%	91%	77%	65%	55%	46%	37%	30%
Full	Full	.036"	100%	100%	100%	84%	70%	59%	49%	40%	32%

PATTERN SPREAD

Diameter in inches covered by bulk of the charge at various distances for various chokes.
RANGE IN YARDS

USA	UK	Constriction	10	15	20	25	30	35	40 yards
True Cylinder	True Cylinder	.000"	20	26	32	38	44	51	58 inches
Skeet	Improved Cylinder	.005"	15	20	26	32	38	44	51 inches
Improved Cylinder	1/4	.011"	13	18	23	29	35	41	48 inches
Modified	1/2	.020"	12	16	21	26	32	38	45 inches
Improved Modified	3/4	.027"	10	14	18	23	29	35	42 inches
Full	Full	.036"	9	12	16	21	27	35	40 inches

STEEL SHELL STATISTICS

USA Shot size	Diameter Inch	Diameter mm	Ounce 3/4 No Pellets	Ounce 15/16 No Pellets	Ounce 1 No Pellets	Ounce 1 1/8 No Pellets	Ounce 1 1/4 No Pellets	Ounce 1 3/8 No Pellets	Ounce 1 1/2 No Pellets	Ounce 1 9/16 No Pellets	Ounce 1 5/8 No Pellets
F	0.22	5.59	30	37	40	45	50	55	60	62	65
T	0.20	5.08	39	49	52	58	65	71	78	81	84
BBB	0.19	4.83	46	58	62	70	77	85	93	97	101
BB	0.18	4.57	54	67	72	81	90	99	108	112	117
1	0.16	4.06	77	87	103	116	129	142	154	161	167
2	0.15	3.81	94	117	125	141	156	172	187	195	203
3	0.14	3.56	118	143	158	178	197	217	237	247	257
4	0.13	3.30	144	180	192	216	240	164	288	300	312
5	0.12	3.05	182	228	243	273	304	334	364	380	395
6	0.11	2.79	236	295	315	354	394	433	472	492	512
7	0.10	2.54	316	395	422	475	527	580	633	659	685

Shot Sizes

	F	T	BBB	BB	1	2	3	4	5	6	7	7½	8	8½	9
Pellet Diameter	●	●	●	●	●	●	●	●	●	●	●	●	●	●	●
Inches	.22	.20	.19	.18	.16	.15	.14	.13	.12	.11	.10	.095	.09	.085	.08
mm	5.59	5.08	4.83	4.57	4.06	3.81	3.56	3.30	3.05	2.79	2.54	2.41	2.29	2.16	2.03

Buckshot Sizes

	No. 000	No. 00	No. 0	No. 1	No. 2	No. 3	No. 4
Pellet Diameter	●	●	●	●	●	●	●
Inches	.36	.33	.32	.30	.27	.25	.24
mm	9.14	8.38	8.13	7.62	6.86	6.35	6.10

Courtesy of Federal Cartridge Company; used with permission.

SHOT SIZES, CHOKE PATTERNS

Number of Pellets in 30 inch circle at 30 yards from 1 Oz of Shot

Shot Sizes			Diamtr inch	Diamtr mm	Chilled lead Pellets pound	Pellets ounce	Choke true cyl .000"	Choke Skeet- 1 .005"	Choke Imp Cyl .011"	Choke Mod .020"	Choke Imp Mod .027"	Choke Full .036"
USA	British	German										
OOO	LG	Posten II	0.36	9.1	98	6.1	3.7	4.4	4.7	5.1	5.6	6.1
OO	SG	Posten III	0.33	8.4	115	7.2	4.3	5.2	5.5	6.0	6.5	7.2
O	—		0.32	8.1	140	8.8	5.3	6.3	6.7	7.3	8.0	8.8
1 Buck	Spcl LG		0.30	7.6	173	10.8	6.5	7.8	8.3	9.0	9.8	10.8
2 Buck	—	osten I	0.27	6.9	232	14.5	8.7	10.4	11.2	12.0	13.2	14.5
3 Buck	SSG	—	0.25	6.3	284	17.8	10.7	12.8	13.7	14.7	16.2	17.8
4 Buck	—	—	0.24	6.1	344	21.5	13	15	17	18	20	22
FF	—	—	0.23	5.8	400	25.0	15	18	19	21	23	25
F	—	—	0.22	5.6	464	29.0	17	21	22	24	26	29
TT	—	—	0.21	5.3	560	35.0	21	25	27	29	32	35
T	AAA	5/0	0.20	5.1	672	42.0	25	30	32	35	38	42
BBB	—	—	0.19	4.8	800	50	30	36	39	42	46	50
BB	—	—	0.18	4.6	928	58	35	42	45	48	53	58
—	BB	1	0.175	4.4	1040	65	39	47	50	54	59	65
1	—	—	0.16	4.1	1168	73	44	53	56	61	66	73
2	—	—	0.15	3.8	1408	88	53	63	68	73	80	88
3	1	3	0.14	3.6	1744	109	65	78	84	90	99	109
4	3	4	0.13	3.3	2176	136	82	98	105	113	124	136
5	4	5	0.12	3.0	2752	172	103	124	132	143	157	172
6	5	6	0.11	2.8	3568	223	134	161	172	185	203	223
7	6	—	0.10	2.5	4784	299	179	215	230	248	272	299
7.5	7	7	0.095	2.4	5520	345	207	248	266	286	314	345
8	8	8	0.09	2.3	6544	409	245	294	315	339	372	409
8.5	·	·	0.085	2.2	7952	497	298	358	383	413	452	497
9	9	9	0.08	2.0	9360	585	351	421	450	486	532	585
10	—	—	0.07	1.8	13888	868	521	625	668	720	790	868
11	—	—	0.06	1.5	22080	1380	828	994	1063	1145	1256	1380
12	—	—	0.05	1.3	45360	2835	1701	2041	2183	2353	2580	2835
Dust	—	—	0.04	1.0	73040	4565	2739	3287	3515	3789	4154	4565

More and more shooters are attending shooting schools and seeking instruction from individuals such as Bryan Bilinski, whose Michigan-based Fieldsport shooting school teaches numerous students each year.

Hunting geese requires patience and the experience to allow the geese to get well within range before shooting. Although they look farther than they are, these Canada geese are only about 35 yard away and well within shotgun range.

Bryan Bilinski, owner of Fieldsport in Traverse City, Michigan, and a highly experienced gunfitter, checks a shotgun with a sophisticated jig that takes all the vital measurements of a shotgun's stock.